Alan Bullock

Hitler *and* Stalin

Alan Bullock began his academic career in 1945 as a Fellow of New College, Oxford, and in 1960 became Founding Master of St. Catherine's College, Oxford, serving as the first elected vice chancellor of the entire university between 1969 and 1973. He retired in 1980 to write full-time. Lord Bullock—he became a Life Peer in 1976—is a Fellow of the British Academy, a member of the Academia Europaea, and a Corresponding Member of the American Academy of Arts and Sciences. Besides the classic *Hitler, A Study in Tyranny,* he is also the author of *Ernest Bevin: Foreign Secretary, 1945–1951,* and co-editor of the series *Oxford History of Modern Europe.*

Hitler *and* Stalin

P A R A L L E L   L I V E S

Alan Bullock

Vintage Books

A Division of Random House, Inc.

New York

FIRST VINTAGE BOOKS EDITION, OCTOBER 1993

Copyright © 1991, 1993 by Alan Bullock

All rights reserved under International and Pan-American Copyright
Conventions. Published in the United States by Vintage Books,
a division of Random House, Inc., New York.
Originally published in Great Britain by HarperCollins Publishers, Ltd.,
London, in 1991.

First published in the United States by Alfred A. Knopf, Inc.,
New York, in somewhat different form in 1992.

Page 1091 constitutes an extension of this copyright page.

Library of Congress Cataloging-in-Publication Data
Bullock, Alan, 1914–
    Hitler and Stalin: parallel lives / Alan Bullock.
        p.   cm.
    Includes bibliographical references and index.
    ISBN 0-679-72994-1 (pbk.)
        1. Hitler, Adolf, 1889–1945. 2. Stalin, Joseph, 1879–1953.
3. Heads of state — Europe — Biography. 4. Germany —
History — 1933–1945. 5. Soviet Union — History — 1925–1953.
I. Title.
DD247.H5B79   1993
943.086′092— dc20   92-56376
[B]   CIP

Book Design by Robert C. Olsson

Manufactured in the United States of America
10 9 8 7 6 5 4 3 2 1

For my wife, Nibby,

our children and grandchildren

CONTENTS

LIST OF ILLUSTRATIONS

LIST OF MAPS

PREFACE TO THE SECOND REVISED EDITION

THE INTRODUCTION that follows explains how I came to write this book; I should never have brought it to completion if I had not had support and help from a number of people whom this preface gives me the opportunity to thank.

The dedication to my wife, and to the children and grandchildren we have shared, is a testimony to the greatest debt of all, to a lifelong companion from whose trueness of judgment I have derived benefit in so many ways, not least as a perceptive critic both of historical interpretation and literary style.

For many years now I have benefited from the expert advice of my literary agent, Andrew Best, of Curtis Brown, as he has been, since this book was first published, my literary adviser. From our first discussions of my idea for such a study he steadily encouraged me to carry it out in full. When it was only half finished, he put his judgment to the test by securing leading publishing houses in the U.S.A. and Germany, as well as the U.K., to publish it.

I was fortunate that in all three cases the publishers showed as strong an interest in the content of the book as in its financial viability. My good fortune has extended to securing in Jonathan Segal and Stuart Proffitt outstanding editors on both sides of the Atlantic whose enthusiasm has been matched by a readiness to take any amount of trouble to get things right.

There would never have been a book at all if it had not been for the skill and patience of Mrs. Pamela Thomas and Mrs. Patricia Ayling in converting my illegible manuscript into the well ordered printout of the word processor. Mrs. Ayling has put me further in her debt by typing many drafts of this revised edition. I am no less indebted to my two American friends, Joe Slater and the late Shepard Stone, for help in securing support for research and secretarial expenses, including a generous grant from the Deutscher Stifterverband for which I am most grateful.

The Master and Fellows of St. Catherine's College have allowed me the privilege of remaining a member of their community and of carrying on my work in the college. I hope they will look on this and the two other books which I have written since retirement as some return for their continued confidence. I wish also to express my thanks to the staff of the libraries where I have worked in Oxford, the Bodleian Library, the Rhodes House Library, the History Faculty Library, the libraries of St. Catherine's and St. Antony's College, and the library of the House of Lords. Ms. Val Kibble dealt most efficiently with acknowledgments and permissions to quote.

I have received invaluable help in keeping track of new material becoming available in the Soviet Union and in particular must thank my friends Robin Edmonds; Harry Shukman, of St. Antony's College; and Michael Shotton, of St. Catherine's College. Another Fellow of St. Antony's, Anthony Nicholls, performed a similar service for me in commenting on the draft chapters dealing with Hitler, while Richard Ollard read the whole text and gave me the benefit of his experience both as an historian and as an editor. To all four I offer my sincere thanks; needless to say, none of them is to be held responsible for the views I have expressed.

I could not have attempted a panoramic view of two of the most eventful and controversial episodes in European history if I had not been able to draw upon the research and writings of many other scholars. How much I owe to them individually will be obvious from the notes, but I should like to put on record the names of those to whose work I feel I owe the greatest intellectual debt, even when I disagree with them.

They include, for German history, Karl Dietrich Bracher, Martin Broszat, Christopher Browning, Joachim Fest, G. T. Fleming, Eberhard Jäckel, Ian Kershaw, Michael Marrus, T. W. Mason, J. P. Stern, H. R. Trevor-Roper (Lord Dacre); and for Soviet history, in which I can make no claim to be a specialist, Stephen Cohen, Robert Conquest, R. V. Daniels, John Erickson, Merle Fainsod, Leszek Kolakowski, Walter Laqueur, Roy Medvedev, Alec Nove, Leonard Schapiro, Robert Tucker, Adam B. Ulam, D. A. Volkogonov.

In preparing this revised edition I have been able to take advantage of the new material which has become available in the Soviet Union and of a number of new books dealing with German as well as Russian history. The most extensive changes I have made are in Chapter Sixteen, which I have rewritten in order to give it a clearer structure.

Finally, I would like to record my debt to the two masters, now dead, with whom I served my apprenticeship and from whom I first learned what is involved in the study and writing of history: H. T. Wade-Gery, Fellow and Tutor of Wadham College, later Wykeham Professor of Greek History in the University of Oxford; and Sir Ronald Syme, O.M., Fellow and Tutor of Trinity College, later Camden Professor of Roman History in the University of Oxford.

Looking back, I cannot think of a better preparation for writing about

Hitler and Stalin than the familiarity I acquired at Oxford in the 1930s with Thucydides, Tacitus, and those sections of Aristotle's *Politics* that deal with the Greek experience of tyranny.

Alan Bullock
St. Catherine's College
Oxford
January 1993

INTRODUCTION

THE PERIOD OF HISTORY which has interested me most as an historian has been Europe in the first half of the twentieth century. I have been particularly attracted by subjects which allowed me to combine the experience of having lived through the period as a contemporary with later investigation as an historian with access to documentary evidence and witnesses. I had already been able to do this in *Hitler, A Study in Tyranny,* and I was again able to combine the two in my study of British foreign policy in the most critical period of the Cold War, *Ernest Bevin, Foreign Secretary, 1945–1951.*

In the 1970s, I became involved with the international seminar program of the Aspen Institute in Berlin. Every time I flew into the former German capital, then deep in the Soviet occupation zone, I was reminded of the ironical twist to the end of the war in which Hitler's vision of a Nazi empire in Eastern Europe and Russia was turned inside out and replaced by the reality of a Soviet empire in Eastern Europe and Germany.

This led me to start thinking about European history during my lifetime, not along the Berlin-West axis so familiar to British and American historians, but along the much less familiar but, I suspected, more important Berlin-East, or German-Russian, axis.

I started to look for a framework which would enable me to explore this international dimension and combine it with a comparison of the two revolutionary systems of power, the Stalinist and the Nazi, which, looked at from one point of view, were irreconcilably hostile to each other, yet from another had many features in common, and each of which presented a challenge, ideological as well as political, to the existing order in Europe. Their appearance at the same time and the interaction between them seemed to me the most striking and novel feature of European history in the first half of the twentieth century, the consequences of which long continued to dominate it in the second.

I found my framework in a comparative study of the two men, Hitler and Stalin, whose careers alone brought all the different facets together—revolution, dictatorship, ideology, diplomacy, and war. Many historians had pointed to specific similarities or differences between them, but no one, so far as I knew, had attempted to place their lives alongside each other and follow them together from beginning to end.

It is true that in Germany during the 1980s an attempt (the so-called *Historikerstreit*) was made to show that the crimes against humanity committed in the Soviet Union mitigated the offense of those committed in Nazi Germany.* But this use of a highly selective comparison between the two regimes for polemical purposes, strongly criticized by many German historians, seemed to me not to invalidate but to make all the more desirable an overall comparison by an historian who was neither German nor Russian and had no political axe to grind.

It is also true that in the 1950s and 1960s comparison between Nazi Germany, Soviet Russia, and Fascist Italy was used by political scientists as the basis for a general concept of totalitarianism.[1] They were interested, however, in isolating the similarities between them in order to construct a model of a totalitarian state. Leaving aside the criticism which has since led the term to fall out of fashion,[2] my interest has never been in creating a generalized model, but in comparing two particular regimes, limited in time (Stalin's Russia, for example, not Soviet Russia after Stalin, or Communist and Fascist states in general), and in bringing out the differences between them quite as much as the similarities. My purpose is not to show that they were both examples of a general category but to use comparison to illuminate the individual character of each. Hence my subtitle, "Parallel Lives," borrowed from Plutarch: parallel lives, like parallel lines, do not meet or merge.

Having decided on the framework of the book, there still remained the question of its structure. One possible way was to proceed analytically and focus on certain themes—Hitler and Stalin and their parties; Hitler and Stalin and the police state; Hitler and Stalin as warlords—dealing with each separately. This would have the advantage of producing a shorter book, but I felt that analysis would best be pursued in a chronological framework which I believed it was essential to retain.

I was confirmed in this decision, after I had started writing, by the extraordinary events of 1989–91. As I sat in front of the television screen along with millions of others looking in amazement at what was happening in Eastern Europe, Germany, and the Soviet Union, I had the impression of seeing unravelled before my eyes every evening the earlier history of the 1940s and 1930s, back to the Russian Revolution of 1917, which I was writing by day. I found that, not only to young people but to those born in the 1940s and later, the history of those years, once as remote as the French Revolution, had now become alive as something they wished to know about. It is this interplay between present and past which gives

*See below, Chapter Twenty.

history its fascination, and the narrative I was reconstructing suddenly took on a new relevance.

It is the public roles of Hitler and Stalin, not their private lives, for which they are remembered. Although I have discussed their personalities and made use of psychological insights when these seemed helpful in understanding them, this is essentially a political biography, set against the background of the times in which they lived.

How to manage a double narrative, and keep Hitler's and Stalin's careers aligned, set a number of problems. There are parts, such as their origins and early experiences, and, much later, their involvement in foreign policy and the war, where it is possible to write about both in the same chapter. But for much of the time, the very different pattern of their rise to power, and the fact that Stalin was ten years older, make it easier to follow them separately in alternate chapters. To balance this separate treatment I have halted the narrative in the middle of the book, at the end of 1934, and devoted a chapter to a systematic comparison of the two men and their regimes.

There was a further problem at the end. Stalin was not only born ten years before Hitler, but lived on for eight years after him. If I went beyond Hitler's death in 1945, this would mean taking in postwar developments in which Hitler had no part. I was convinced, however, that while Hitler might not have taken a direct part, his ghost (metaphorically speaking) was present at all the postwar discussions as the man who had done most— together with Stalin—to create the agenda that defeated every attempt to reach an agreed settlement.

I decided, therefore, to continue the narrative as far as Stalin's death in March 1953, the real end, as I believe, of the Stalin-Hitler era. This also makes it possible to bring into account the final phase of Stalin's rule over the Soviet Union, which throws further light on the way it developed in the 1930s and during the war. The book concludes with a short chapter which allows me to take advantage of the fact that, having lived through the Hitler-Stalin period, I have now been able to look back on it from the perspective of the twentieth century's closing decade.

EUROPE IN 1914 AND IN 1920

- German Empire 1914
- Austro-Hungarian Empire 1914
- Russian Empire 1914
- Ottoman Empire
- ▬▬ Frontiers in 1914
- ▬·▬· Frontiers in 1920

Atlantic Ocean

North Sea

Baltic

NORWAY

SWEDEN

DENMARK

UNITED KINGDOM

London

Bay of Biscay

Paris
R. Seine
R. Loire

Alsace-Lorraine

FRANCE

SWITZ.

R. Rhône

R. Ebro

PORTUGAL
R. Tagus

SPAIN

GERMANY
Berlin
R. Elbe
R. Oder
R. Rhine

Munich

Braunau

CZECHO

Vienna

AUSTRIA HUN

YUGO

ITALY

Rome

Adriatic Sea

Mediterranean Sea

50

40

0

10

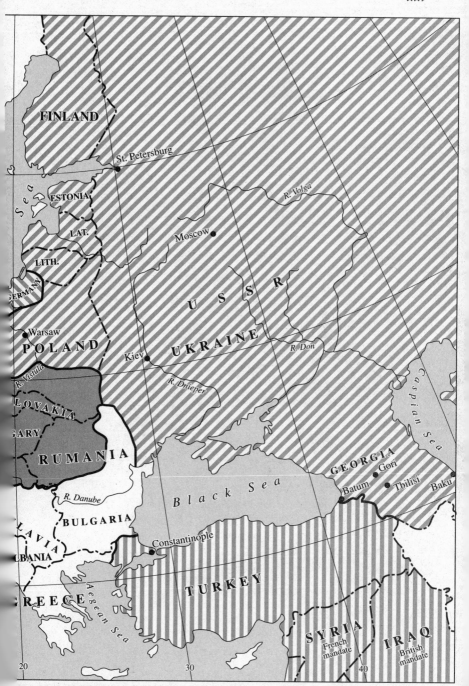

FINLAND

St. Petersburg

Sea

ESTONIA

LAT.

LITH.

GERMANY

Warsaw

POLAND

R. Vistula

SLOVAKIA

GARY

RUMANIA

R. Danube

BULGARIA

LAVIA

LBANIA

GREECE

Moscow

R. Volga

U S S R

UKRAINE

R. Don

Kiev

R. Dnieper

Constantinople

Aegean Sea

Black Sea

TURKEY

GEORGIA

Gori

Batum

Tbilisi

Baku

Caspian Sea

SYRIA

French mandate

IRAQ

British mandate

20

30

40

Hitler *and* Stalin

I

WHO, THEN, were these two men who were to leave such an indelible imprint on European history in the twentieth century?

They were born ten years apart, Stalin on December 21, 1879, at Gori in Georgia, Hitler on April 20, 1889, at Braunau on the River Inn. This gap in age is a fact never to be forgotten in any comparison of the different stages of their careers; it grew even wider at the end, Hitler dying in 1945 at the age of fifty-six, Stalin outliving him to die, in 1953, at the age of seventy-three.

Fifteen-hundred miles separated Georgia, on the borderlands of Europe and Asia, between the Black Sea and the Caucasus, and Upper Austria, in the heart of Central Europe, between the Danube and the Alps. An even greater distance separated their historical and social development. Yet there were features in common in the backgrounds of the two men.

Neither belonged to the traditional ruling class and it is difficult to imagine either coming to power in the world into which they were born. Their careers were possible only in the new world created by the breakdown of the old order in Europe, as a result of the First World War—of the defeat first of tsarist Russia, then of the Central Powers, and of the revolutions that followed. Yet their ideas and beliefs were formed and remained set in the mold of the world in which they grew up. Stalin's Marxism, Hitler's combination of Social Darwinism and racism were nineteenth-century systems that reached the peak of their influence in Europe at the turn of the century, in the last decade of the nineteenth, the first of the twentieth century. The same was true of their tastes in art, architecture, literature, and music, subjects on which they claimed to lay down the law and in which neither showed the least sympathy with the experimental modernism that flowered in Russia and in Central Europe during their lifetimes.

Both were born on the margins of the countries over which they were to rule; like Alexander, a Macedonian, and Napoleon, a Corsican, they were outsiders. Hitler, of course, was a German, but he was born a subject of the

Habsburg Empire, where Germans had played the leading role for centuries. However, with Bismarck's creation in the 1860s of a German Empire based on Prussia, from which the Austrian Germans were excluded, the latter found themselves forced to defend their historic claim to rule against the growing demands for equality of the Czechs and the other "subject peoples." This situation had a profound effect on Hitler's attitudes. He became a rabid German nationalist but, instead of sharing in the vigorous, self-confident expansion of the new German Empire ruled from Berlin, he acquired the anxiety-ridden, pessimistic outlook of a minority group within their "own" state, conscious of a great past but seeing their future increasingly threatened by the growing numbers and influence of other inferior races—Slavs, Polish and Russian Jews—in a "mongrel empire" whose Habsburg rulers had betrayed the sacred cause of *Deutschtum,* the preservation of the character and power of the German nation.

In 1938 Hitler reversed the exclusion of the 1860s and, with the annexation of Austria, "restored my dear homeland to the German Reich." But all the successes of those years in recreating a Greater Germany could not eradicate the legacy of Hitler's Austrian origins, the fundamental feeling that he was fighting to defend a German-Aryan heritage under threat from a rising tide of barbarism and racial pollution.

The effect of Stalin's origins was hardly less important, although it worked in different ways. One was the reappearance in later years of figures from his Georgian past, such as Ordzhonikidze and Beria, his attitude toward whom was affected by the complex relationships and feuds of Georgian politics. But this is superficial by comparison with the key decision in Stalin's life (comparable only with that to become a revolutionary), the repudiation of his Georgian inheritance and—realist that he was—the identification with the Georgians' Russian conquerors instead of the Russians' Georgian victims.

The result, as Lenin belatedly recognized, was to produce a Great Russian chauvinist, who worked to overthrow the tsarist state but not to break up the Russian Empire. Like other neophytes, he could never take his acceptance as a Russian for granted, or forget that his Georgian accent always reminded native-born Russians of his origins. Appointed commissar of nationalities by Lenin because of these factors once the civil war was over, Stalin treated the national aspirations of the non-Russian peoples with the harshness of a renegade. In 1920 and 1921 he ended the brief period of independence enjoyed by Georgia and the Caucasian states, reannexing them to the Soviet Union, and the way he treated the Ukrainians during collectivization remains one of the blackest pages in Soviet history. Stalin's identification with Russia's imperial past was one of the major themes of the Great Patriotic War, and at its end he took pride in recapturing all the territories lost by the Russian Empire in the wars of 1904 through 1905 and 1914–1918, expanding its boundaries to encompass a greater area than under any of his tsarist predecessors.

IN 1 8 7 9, when Stalin was born, all this was an unimaginable world away. Georgia was still imperfectly assimilated to European Russia. Geographically a part of Transcaucasia, it belongs to subtropical Asia, providing one of the historic mainland routes between Central Asia and Europe. Georgia had been a part of the classical world, the legendary land of Colchis and the Golden Fleece, the home of the Prometheus myth, colonized by the Greeks, part of the Roman province of Armenia. Ethnically it has always been mixed: Strabo counted seventy races in the Caucasus, speaking as many languages. The Georgians themselves were divided into a dozen sub-races, yet retained their ethnological identity and purity of language for 2,000 years. As a small but rich and independent kingdom in Byzantine times, Georgian civilization achieved a brilliant peak, never to be repeated, in the twelfth century. Thereafter it was conquered by the Mongols, fought over by the Turks and Persians, and finally, at the beginning of the nineteenth century, annexed by the Russians. Guerrilla resistance continued in the mountains, and not until the 1860s was the Russian military pacification of the country complete.

By then, despite the richness of its natural resources and the antiquity of its civilization, Georgia had been reduced to a miserable level of poverty. Three-quarters of the population were illiterate, there was no industry, and brigandage was rife.

Stalin's internal passport bore a statement that supplies one of the keys to his political career: "Josif Djugashvili, peasant from the Gori District of Tiflis Province." He was, in fact, descended from peasants on both sides. His parents were illiterate, or semiliterate at best, and had been born as serfs. They were emancipated only in 1864. His father subsequently moved to the small town of Gori to practice his inherited trade as a cobbler, and there met and married Ekaterina Geladze.

Two children died at birth before Stalin was born. He himself nearly died at the age of five from smallpox, which left his face pockmarked. His left arm was permanently injured as a result of a childhood accident. Stalin's home until his fourth year was a single-roomed, brick-built house with a lean-to garret above and a well-lit basement below; it was shared with his father's employer or partner. Subsequently the house was turned into a shrine and encased in a neoclassical temple with four marble columns. His father was a rough, violent man who drank heavily, beat his wife and child, and found it hard to make a living. Iremashvili, the friend who knew Stalin best both at school in Gori and at the seminary in Tiflis, wrote in his memoirs:

> Undeserved and severe beatings made the boy as hard and heartless as the father was. Since all people in authority over others seemed to him to be like his father, there soon arose in him a vengeful feeling against all people standing above him. From childhood on, the realization of his

thoughts of revenge became the aim to which everything was subordinated. [1]

Other accounts confirm both the beatings and the boy's reaction to them:
He bitterly resented his father's treatment of him but it did not break his
spirit. Compensation came in the affection and support he received from his
mother, the redheaded Ekaterina, a strong-willed and devout woman who
stood up to her husband, and supported herself and Josif when the father
moved to Tiflis, forty miles away, to take a job in a shoe factory. In 1883,
she moved as housekeeper-servant into the house of an Orthodox priest,
Father Charkviani, taking her son with her. With the priest's help, she
enrolled him in the Orthodox Church school. When he was ten, Josif's
father insisted on taking him away to learn the cobbler's trade in the Tiflis
shoe factory. But his mother was determined he should become a priest and
eventually got him back to complete his schooling.

Ekaterina's ambition for her son meant finding the fees to send him not
only to the Church school, to which peasant children had only recently been
admitted, but also to the Russian Orthodox theological college of Tiflis. By
dint of personal sacrifices, however, and with the help of scholarships, she
achieved her object and kept him at school and seminary until he was
nineteen. Many years later, when he was the most powerful man in the
Soviet Union, she told him to his face that she still wished he had become
a priest, a remark that delighted him.

Stalin served in the church choir, where his voice attracted attention.
Stalin did well enough at school to win a scholarship to the Tiflis seminary,
where he remained as a boarder for the next five years. His mother's
investment of all her hopes and ambitions in his success had an effect on
his personality. He absorbed her confidence that he would prove to be
someone special who would achieve great things; from his relationship with
his father Stalin acquired hardness of heart and a hatred of authority. The
combination was to prove a powerful legacy.

While Stalin was attending Gori Church school, the tsarist government's
policy of Russification meant that Georgian ceased to be the language of
instruction and was abruptly replaced by Russian, which had hitherto been
taught as a foreign language. This led to a series of clashes with the Russian
officials brought in to enforce the change, against which Stalin was one of
the leading rebels. This change accounts for the fact that he required six
years to complete a four-year course. It also led him to take a passionate
interest in Georgian literature, obtained from a lending library run by a local
bookseller. Among the books he seized on were Alexander Kazbegi's romantic tales of heroic resistance by the Caucasian mountain clans to
Georgia's Russian conquerors. One of these, based on a true historical
episode in 1840, made a lasting impression on Stalin. Its title, *The Patricide,*
no doubt caught his eye. It tells the story of Koba, a Caucasian Robin Hood

who defies the Cossacks, defends the rights of the peasants, and avenges his friends, who have been trapped by village traitors. From then on, until he began to use the pseudonym of Stalin twenty years later, the young Djugashvili insisted on being known as Koba. "Koba," Iremashvili records, "had become his god, the sense of his life. He wanted to become another Koba, as famous a fighter and hero: the figure of Koba was to be resurrected to him."²

III

HITLER'S FAMILY also came from the countryside, from the Waldviertel, a district of woods and hills in Lower Austria, lying between the Danube and the Bohemian frontier, where the name Hitler, possibly Czech in origin and spelled in a variety of ways, first appears in the fifteenth century. Hitler's ancestors were peasants, but not serfs, small independent farmers or village craftsmen. The first to break away from the pattern was his father, Alois, who moved up several steps in the social scale by becoming a customs officer in the Habsburg Imperial Customs Service.

Hitler's early life, unlike Stalin's, was not one of hardship and poverty. Contrary to the impression he conveys in *Mein Kampf,* he was neither poor nor harshly treated. His father advanced steadily in the service, and ended with the highest rank open to a civil servant of his education. He had a secure income as well as the social standing of an imperial official, and when he died he left his widow and children well provided for.

Hitler was born while his father was stationed at Braunau on the River Inn, which there forms the frontier between Austria and Bavaria; but his father was moved several times and Adolf attended three different primary schools. Like Stalin, he served as a choirboy, in the Benedictine monastery of Lambach, and was deeply impressed by the solemnity and splendor of the services.

Alois Hitler was not a sympathetic figure. He was authoritarian and selfish, showing little concern for the feelings of his much younger wife and little understanding of his children. But this was no more than could be said of most self-made men of his background and period. He cared more than anything for his bees, looking forward to the day when he could retire with a small property of his own and devote himself to beekeeping, an ambition he finally realized at Leonding on the outskirts of Linz in 1899.

Adolf Hitler's mother was twenty-two years younger than his father, who was her second cousin. She had been his mistress and was pregnant by him at the time his second wife died. Alois was no more successful in making his third wife happy than he had the other two, but Klara Hitler made the best of it and, if in time she grew sad and disappointed, she was proud of her well-kept home and won the affection of both her children and her stepchildren. Until the age of five, when a younger brother was born, all his mother's attention was given to Adolf, but there is no convincing evidence that he suffered particularly from jealousy when this period came to an end; in fact it was followed by the happiest year of his childhood, at Passau.

The boy was bright enough at school, although he already showed signs of being both self-willed and resistant to the discipline of regular work. A move to the secondary school in Linz, however, proved disastrous; the only subject in which he obtained satisfactory marks was drawing. Hitler later tried to explain away his failure as due to his rebellion against his father's wish to see him become a civil servant, while he wanted to become an artist. But his account in *Mein Kampf* has been shown to be a clumsy fabrication, and his father's death in January 1903 made no difference to his behavior. Although now in his teens, he continued to escape from anything resembling work in order to indulge his passion for playing war games out of doors and for reading Karl May's adventure stories about the North American Indians. The latter was a taste that he continued to indulge when he became Reich Chancellor: He reread the whole series and frequently expressed his enthusiasm for Karl May in his table talk.* After he had been asked to leave the Linz Realschule, his mother tried the experiment of sending him to boarding school in Steyr, but this did not alter the pattern: His school reports continued to describe him as idle, willful and disrespectful.

A lung infection from which Hitler suffered in the summer of 1905 helped him to persuade his mother that he should give up school and try to secure admission to the Vienna Academy of Arts. On various pretexts, however, Hitler put off taking the examination at the academy for two years, and between the autumn of 1905 and that of 1907 enjoyed his freedom. Supported by his mother, he occupied himself with sketching and painting, dressing up to look the part of a young man of leisure, hoping to be taken for a university student with his ivory-topped black cane, and indulging in extravagant daydreams of how he would one day overwhelm the world with his deeds.

This was the period, between sixteen and eighteen, when Hitler's image of himself began to take shape. Like Stalin's Koba, it was the image of a heroic rebel, but the special character that it acquired, and in the light of which Hitler continued to see himself throughout his life, was that of an artistic genius, frequently lamenting what the world had lost when, out of a sense of duty, he was forced to turn to politics.

Hitler's only friend, August Kubizek, who was a couple of years younger, provided—in addition to his mother and sister—the necessary audience for the stream of fantasy that he poured out. In what way Hitler was to express his genius remained uncertain—whether as painter, architect (he produced

---

*Shorthand records were made of many of Hitler's informal conversation between 1941 and 1945. These provide invaluable insights into his mind. They have been published in an English translation as *Hitler's Table Talk (1941–44)* (London: 1953) and *The Testament of Adolf Hitler* (London: 1961).

plans for the entire rebuilding of Linz), musician, or writer—but it was always as an artist, a rationalization of his incapacity for any kind of disciplined effort.

The two friends seized every opportunity to attend the Linz opera and the theater. Hitler's great hero was Richard Wagner, whose music dramas held him spellbound. Hitler was later to declare that he had no forerunners, with the single exception of Wagner. Much has been made of the fact that Wagner was anti-Semitic, but what first attracted Hitler to him was the theatricality and epic scale of his operas, which he never tired of seeing, and which were the source of the theatricality and epic scale of his own political style. Even more important was Wagner's personality and the romantic conception of the artist as genius which Wagner had largely created and which he put to the proof by triumphing over every conceivable obstacle to establish the shrine of German art at Bayreuth. Just as Stalin identified himself initially with the hero Koba and later with Lenin, so Hitler identified himself with Wagner. It was an inspiration that never failed him. Whenever his confidence in himself wavered, it was immediately restored by the magical world of Wagner's music and the example of his genius.

In August 1939, shortly before the war, Hitler invited Kubizek to be his guest at Bayreuth. His friend from Linz recalled the occasion when a performance of *Rienzi* had so carried Hitler away that he dragged Kubizek to the top of a local peak, the Freinberg, and there stunned him with a visionary outpouring in which he described how he would one day rescue the German people as Rienzi had the Romans. Delighted with the reminder, Hitler retold the story to Winifred Wagner, the English daughter-in-law of the composer, who was one of his earliest admirers, and solemnly declared: "In that hour it began."[3]

Klara Hitler made various efforts to induce her son to think seriously about his future, including paying for him to spend four weeks in Vienna. At length, she agreed that he could draw the legacy left by his father as well as the pension to which he was entitled as the son of an official, and move to Vienna to study painting at the Academy of Arts. The main reason for her agreement was her discovery that she was suffering from cancer of the breast, and her anxiety to see Adolf settled before she died. He managed to get to Vienna in time to take the entrance examination in October 1907, only to be told that the drawing he had submitted was unsatisfactory, and that he had been rejected. "I was so convinced that I would be successful that, when I received the news, it struck me like a bolt from the blue."[4] His adolescent dreamworld was shattered, and he was so astonished that he requested an interview with the director, who tactfully suggested that his talents lay in architecture, not painting.

Hitler soon convinced himself that the director was right: "In a few days I myself also knew that I ought some day to become an architect."[5] But he lacked the school-leaving certificate necessary to start on a course of professional training. If Hitler had been serious it would not have been difficult for him to secure this. But he did not even bother to find out what would be required. Without telling his mother, he stayed on in Vienna as if nothing had happened, and continued with what he grandly called his "studies," a repetition of the feverish but aimless activity he had pursued in Linz.

He was given a second and still greater jolt by the news that his mother was dying. Like Stalin, Hitler owed his mother a great deal. Freud remarked that "a man who has been the indisputable favorite of his mother keeps for life the feeling of a conqueror, that confidence of success that often induces real success."[6] This may have been true of Stalin; it was certainly true of Hitler. The difference was that Stalin showed little appreciation of the sacrifices his mother had made for him, saw her only a few times after he became involved in revolutionary activity, and shocked Georgian opinion by failing to attend her funeral in 1936. In contrast, Kubizek says that, as soon as Hitler heard of his mother's illness, he at once returned to Linz and devoted himself to nursing and looking after her. Her death, on top of his failure, came as a deep shock to him.

The shock, however, did not bring him to face reality. Refusing to listen to family suggestions that he should get a job, and leading his family to believe that he was a student at the academy, he made off back to Vienna and the shelter of his dreamworld once the formalities about his mother's legacy and his pension were completed. To bolster his illusions, he persuaded Kubizek and his parents that his friend should come to join him.

Sharing a single room into which were crowded a grand piano for Kubizek to practice on, two beds, and a table, they realized their dream of becoming art students in Vienna. Kubizek had no difficulty in securing admission to the Music Academy and set off early every morning to classes, leaving Hitler still in bed. Only gradually did Kubizek become sufficiently curious to ask about his friend's studies, producing a furious outburst from Hitler against the stupid authorities who had denied him admission. Hitler declared, however, that he was determined to triumph over them by becoming a self-taught architect.

His "studying" consisted of walking the streets to look at the nineteenth-century monumental buildings on the Ring, making endless sketches of their facades, and memorizing the details of their dimensions. He spent more than he could afford on tickets for the opera, recouping by cutting back what he spent on food. In Linz he had fallen passionately in love with a young woman named Stephanie, without ever speaking to her. Now in Vienna he talked a great deal to Kubizek about love and women, without ever overcoming his shyness sufficiently to approach one. His imagination, like most young men's, was inflamed by sex, but there is no evidence to show he had sexual relations with anyone. Kubizek was uneasy at his friend's abrupt alternation between moods of exaltation, in which he talked wildly, and periods of despair in which he denounced everything and everybody. Compared with their Linz days, Kubizek describes Hitler in Vienna as "completely out of balance."

In July 1908 Kubizek returned to Linz after completing his first year at the Music Academy. Arrangements were made for him to rejoin Hitler in the same lodgings on his return, and he received a number of postcards from his friend during the summer. But when Kubizek returned in November, he found no trace of him.

Without telling Kubizek or anyone else, Hitler had made a second attempt to enter the Academy of Arts in October, and this time had been turned down without being admitted to the test. This was so bitter a blow, the destruction of his alibi as an "artist," that he could not face anyone who knew him. He cut himself off completely from his family as well as his friend, and disappeared into the anonymity of the big city.

IV

HITLER HAS NATURALLY attracted the interest of psychiatrists, and several studies have been published paying particular attention to his relationship with an overprotective mother and a domineering father, a common enough pattern in the German-speaking world at the turn of the century and one that Freud saw as the origin of an Oedipus complex.[7] Most historians, however, have found difficulty in placing too much reliance on psychological "explanations" of Hitler, for two reasons. The first is the lack of reliable evidence, forcing the psychiatrist into an excessive reliance on speculation and arguments from analogy. The second is that, even if one accepts that it helps to describe Hitler (or Stalin) as a man suffering from the delusions of a psychopathic, a schizophrenic, or a paranoid personality, how does one distinguish between the normally crippling effect of such disorders, as encountered by psychiatrists in their ordinary practice, and the extraordinary measure of success that Hitler (and Stalin) achieved in translating their delusions into a terrifying reality?

In the present state of the art—and of the evidence—it seems best to treat any claim to a comprehensive analysis of Hitler and Stalin with skepticism, but to make use of particular insights that may be brought up in psychological studies. Two examples will make clear what I mean.

The first is Erik Erikson's "identity crisis in adolescence" which he places, in Hitler's case, between his first rejection by the academy in September 1907, when he was eighteen, and his second in October 1908, a period also marked by the shock of his mother's death. According to Erikson, if a young man or woman fails to overcome the crisis of adolescence and establish an identity, serious psychological damage will follow. Erikson argues that this is what happened to Hitler, who remained "the unbroken adolescent who had chosen a career apart from civilian happiness, mercantile tranquility and spiritual peace."[8]

The second is Erich Fromm's argument that the cause of the conflict between Hitler and his father was not, as Hitler claimed, his refusal to accept his father's wish to see him become a civil servant, nor, as the Freudians claim, an Oedipal rivalry for the love of his mother. Instead, Fromm sees Hitler's failure at high school as due to an increasing withdrawal into a world of fantasy, and his quarrel with his father as a rejection of the father's unwelcome attempt to bring him back to a sense of reality and make him face the question of his future. The affection his mother Klara had lavished on him in his first five years was to encourage a sense of his own uniqueness—as in the case of Stalin. Fromm argues that both men, despite the differences between them, were classic cases of the narcissistic personality type.[9]

"Narcissism" is a concept originally formulated by Freud in relation to early infancy, but one that is now accepted more broadly to describe a personality disorder in which the natural development of relationships to the external world has failed to take place. In such a state only the person himself, *his* needs, feelings, and thoughts, everything and everybody as they relate to *him* are experienced as fully real, while everybody and everything otherwise lacks reality or interest.

Fromm argues that some degree of narcissism can be considered an occupational illness among political leaders in proportion to their conviction of a providential mission and their claim to infallibility of judgment and a monopoly of power. When such claims are raised to the level demanded by a Hitler or a Stalin at the height of his power, any challenge will be perceived as a threat to their private image of themselves as much as to their public image, and they will react by going to any lengths to suppress it.[10]

So far psychiatrists have paid much less attention to Stalin than to Hitler. Lack of evidence is part of the reason. There has been no parallel in the case of the Soviet Union to the capture of documents and interrogation of witnesses that followed the defeat of Germany. But more important is the striking contrast in temperament and style between the two men: the flamboyant Hitler, displaying a lack of restraint and extravagance of speech which for long made it difficult for many to take him seriously, in contrast to the reserved Stalin, who owed his rise to power to his success, not in exploiting, but in concealing his personality, and was underestimated for the opposite reason—because many failed to recognize his ambition and ruthlessness. Not surprisingly, it is the first rather than the second who has caught the psychiatrists' attention. All the more interesting then is the suggestion that underlying the contrast there was a common narcissistic obsession with themselves.

There is one other insight, which the American biographer of Stalin, Robert Tucker, has adopted from Karen Horney's work on neurosis. He suggests that his father's brutal treatment of Stalin, particularly the beatings that he inflicted on the boy, and on the boy's mother in his presence, produced the basic anxiety, the sense of being isolated in a hostile world, that can lead a child to develop a neurotic personality. Searching for firm ground on which to build an inner security, someone who in his childhood had experienced such anxiety might naturally search for inner security by forming an idealized image of himself and then adopting this as his true identity. "From then on his energies are invested in the increasing effort to prove the ideal self in action and gain others' affirmation of it." In Stalin's case this fits his identification with the Caucasian outlaw-hero whose name he assumed, and later with Lenin, the revolutionary hero, on whom he fashioned his own "revolutionary persona," with the name of Stalin, "man of steel," which echoed Lenin's own pseudonym. [11]

A D O L E S C E N C E proved a stormy period for Stalin as well as for Hitler. In 1894 he left Gori to become one of the 600 students at the Russian Orthodox theological seminary in Tiflis. The tsarist authorities had refused to allow a university to be opened in the Caucasus, fearing that it would become a center for nationalist and radical agitation. The Tiflis seminary served as a substitute, and was attended by many young men who had no intention of entering the priesthood. Its repressive atmosphere, a cross between those of a monastery and a barracks, proved quite as productive of subversive ideas as the freer atmosphere of a university.

The fourteen-year-old Stalin was mentally tough, rather than physically strong. (He never grew to more than five feet four inches in height.) Nonetheless he was well able to look after himself, and showed no lack of confidence in his relationships with his fellow pupils or teachers.

Stalin continued at the seminary until he was nearly twenty, from 1894 to 1899, but then left abruptly and—like Hitler—without the usual certificate. To begin with, he worked sufficiently hard to learn something from a curriculum that, besides Old Church Slavonic and scholastic theology, included Latin and Greek, Russian literature, and history. One benefit that Stalin derived from his education was the development of a phenomenal memory, an asset that was to prove of no small value in his later career. The fact that it was a church education helped to form the mind of a man who was to become known for his dogmatism and his propensity for seeing issues in absolute terms, in black and white. Anyone reading Stalin's speeches and writings will notice their catechistic structure, the use of question and answer, the reduction of complex questions to a set of simplified formulas, the quoting of texts to support his arguments. The same church influence has been noted by biographers in his style of speaking or writing Russian: "declamatory and repetitive, with liturgical overtones." [12]

Apart from prayers twice a day, on Sundays and religious holidays the boys had to stand through church services that lasted for three or four hours. Not surprisingly, this provoked a strong antireligious reaction. In return the monks spied on their charges, eavesdropping, searching their clothes and lockers, and denouncing them to the principal. Any breach of the rules, such as borrowing books from secular libraries in the town, was punished by confinement in the cells. The official policy of Russification made the seminary a stronghold of Georgian nationalism. A student expelled for his anti-Russian attitude in 1886 had assassinated the principal, and only a few months before Stalin's admission a protest strike of all the Georgian pupils led to the seminary's closure by the police and the expulsion of eighty-seven students.

Those who had known Stalin as a lively and outgoing boy in Gori noticed a marked change after a year or two at the seminary: He became withdrawn and reticent, preferring to go off on his own or with a book, and showing himself quick to take offense even when none was intended.

Stalin learned to conceal his feelings with a skill in dissimulation that became second nature to him. Underneath he nursed his hatred of authority, not so much in principle as in its exercise over him by others. He was equally scornful of those, whether tsarist officials or monks, who upheld it, and of those who were stupid enough to submit to it. For five years he not only learned to survive but observed at firsthand a closed society in which conformity was enforced by a system of spying, denunciation, and fear: The lesson was not lost on him. His daughter Svetlana wrote after his death:

> A church education was the only systematic education my father ever had. I am convinced that the seminary in which he spent more than ten years played an immense role, setting my father's character for the rest of his life, strengthening and intensifying inborn traits.
>
> My father never had any feeling for religion. In a young man who had never for a moment believed in the life of the spirit or in God, endless prayers and enforced religious training could only produce contrary results. . . . From his experiences at the seminary he came to the conclusion that men were intolerant, coarse, deceiving their flocks in order to hold them in obedience; that they intrigued, lied and as a rule possessed numerous faults and very few virtues.[13]

One form that Stalin's rebellion took was spending as much time as possible reading illicit books obtained from a lending library in the town and smuggled into the seminary. Besides Western literature in translation, and the Russian classics—also forbidden—Stalin became acquainted with radical and positivist ideas which he is said to have picked up from reading translations of Darwin, Auguste Comte, and Marx, as well as Georgi Plekhanov, the first Russian Marxist.

Growing discontented with the vague romantic ideals of Georgian nationalism, Stalin organized a socialist study circle with other students, including Iremashvili, and according to the latter soon began to show intolerance towards any member who disagreed with him. He found a natural attraction in the Marxist teaching of the inevitability of class war and the overthrow of an unjust and corrupt social order. The attraction was as much psychological as intellectual, appealing to the powerful but destructive emotions of hatred and resentment that were to prove so strong a force in

Stalin's character, and offering a positive outlet for an ambition and abilities that would otherwise have been frustrated. As Robert Tucker wrote, the gospel of class war legitimized his resentment against authority: "It identified his enemies as history's."[14]

Despite the repressive character of the tsarist regime, a revolutionary tradition had existed in Russia since the army officers' unsuccessful Decembrist revolt of 1825. Lenin himself was very much aware of this tradition and in 1912 described the Bolsheviks as the fourth generation of revolutionaries. But the inspiration of earlier conspirators had been the Populist belief, formulated by Alexander Herzen and N. G. Chernyshevsky during the 1850s and 1860s, in a separate Russian path to socialism, which would avoid the capitalist development of the West and, in a country with an overwhelmingly peasant population, base itself on the traditional Russian village commune with its primitive form of self-government. Not until after the disintegration of *Zemlia i Volya* (Land and Liberty), the first Russian revolutionary party, following the assassination of Tsar Alexander II in 1881, did Marxist ideas begin to penetrate Russian intellectual circles and to find an echo in the growth of industry and an industrial working class. They had been brought back to Georgia by a group, most of them graduates of the Tiflis seminary, who had picked them up while studying in the Warsaw Veterinary Institute. On their return, they committed themselves to the promotion of Marxist social democracy and took the name Messame Dassy (Third Group).[15]

The attraction of Marxism was that it offered what was claimed to be a scientific basis for belief in a future revolution by applying to Russia the model of Western Europe, where the evolution of capitalism was leading (inevitably, as Marx argued) through the bourgeois phase of capitalist democracy and its contradictions to class conflict and a social revolution. *How* the Marxist scheme was to be applied to Russia, with its huge peasant population, was to remain a matter for bitter dispute, but the ground for socialist propaganda was prepared by the rapid development of Russian industry in the twenty-five years before the First World War and by the growth of a working class subject to the same kind of exploitation that had marked the earlier development of capitalism in Western Europe.

One of the centers of this development was in the Caucasus, in the oil fields at Baku on the Caspian, the oil refineries and port at Batum at the other end of the pipeline, and in the building of a Transcaucasian railway. The members of Messame Dassy also made contact with the workers in the railway workshops in Tiflis, who included a number banished to the Caucasus for their socialist sympathies. Meetings had to be conducted secretly, and it was at one of these, held in the house of a Tiflis railway worker, that Stalin and Iremashvili first met an escaped revolutionary and listened, fascinated, to his account of the sufferings of the political prisoners sent to Siberia.

While still at the seminary, Stalin got himself accepted by Messame Dassy and was allowed to try himself out with a study circle of railway workers for whom he acted as a tutor in Marxist ideas. One member of the group, Lado Ketskhoveli, made a great impression on Stalin. Three years older, he had attended the same school at Gori, going on from there to the Tiflis seminary. He had been a ringleader in the revolt that led to the closing down of the seminary; after his expulsion he completed his studies at Kiev and returned to Tiflis illegally to devote himself full time to underground work. Through Lado's younger brother, Vano, who was still at the seminary, Stalin resumed contact with him, coming frequently to the Ketskhoveli apartments to read and often staying to talk with Lado, for whom he developed an admiration close to hero-worship. Stalin was particularly impressed by Lado's practical approach: He had gone to work in a Tiflis printing shop in order to learn the printer's trade, and went on to found the first underground Marxist press in the Transcaucasus, which became famous in Russian revolutionary circles for its mixture of daring and efficiency. Concealed in a house in Baku belonging to a Muslim with the improbable name of Ali-Baba, this press turned out over a million copies of illegal publications (including Lenin's newspaper *Iskra*) before the police discovered it, after a five-year search, in 1906. Three years before, Ketskhoveli had been arrested and shot dead by guards after shouting from his cell window: "Down with the autocracy! Long live freedom! Long live socialism!"

To Stalin he still remained, many years afterwards, the exemplar of a revolutionary fighter and his influence no doubt helped to precipitate Stalin's break with the seminary. By his fifth year the school authorities regarded Stalin as a hardened troublemaker, and he was expelled in May 1899 on the ground that "for unknown reasons" he failed to appear for the end-of-year examinations. Iremashvili, who had accompanied him to the seminary, wrote later that he took with him "a grim and bitter hatred against the school administration, the bourgeoisie and everything in the country that represented Tsarism." [16]

Whatever the occasion, it was the break after which, once made, Stalin never turned back. Marxism provided him with a fixed intellectual framework of ideas, which fitted perfectly his need of a substitute for the system of dogmatic theology in which he had been trained but which he could not accept. The continuity was strengthened by the same requirements of orthodoxy, the exclusion of doubt, the intolerance of dissent, and the persecution of heretics in both systems. Thus, by the time he was twenty, Stalin had settled both his beliefs and his occupation: Henceforward he was committed to the life of a professional agitator, a missionary whose object was the revolutionary overthrow of the existing order. Whatever others may think, in his own mind Stalin never departed from the Marxist ideology, and this conviction was of great importance to him.

V

IT WAS TO TAKE Hitler several years longer than it took Stalin to acquire a comparable sense of direction. Stalin's decision, reached in 1899 when he was in his twentieth year, determined the character of the experience that followed. With Hitler it was the other way around. In his twentieth year, after his second rejection by the academy in the autumn of 1908, he, too, finally abandoned any thought of further education. But in his case it was the experience that followed that determined the decision about what to do with his life, a decision not finally made until the end of the war, in 1918 and 1919, when he was in his thirtieth year.

Between 1899 and 1917, that is between his twentieth and his thirty-eighth year, Stalin lived the life of a revolutionary agitator, always subject to the risk of arrest and frequently in prison or, for long periods, in exile; it was hard, uphill work, but he knew what he wanted to do, was adding to his experience, and could feel that events—Russia's defeat in the war with Japan, the revolution of 1905, the outbreak of war in 1914, the February revolution of 1917—confirmed his belief in the correctness of the Marxist views he had adopted and of Lenin's line as leader of the party. Whatever psychological difficulties he encountered—most of them he created for himself—he was not subject to intellectual doubts. His confidence was justified by the Bolsheviks' seizure of power in the October Revolution and his own emergence as one of the revolutionary government's leaders.

Compare this with Hitler's experience from 1908 to 1919, at roughly the same age, between his twentieth and his thirtieth year. After the first six years spent in Vienna and briefly in Munich, he was no nearer to knowing what he wanted to do, no nearer to doing anything except surviving in a big city. Between 1914 and 1918 he at last found what he wanted in the life of the army, in war and the *Fronterlebnis* (the front-line experience), in emotional identification with German nationalism—only to suffer the profound shock of Germany's defeat and the breakup of the army, followed by a revolution that challenged his most cherished beliefs. Hitler turned to politics out of desperation, an unknown ex-serviceman talking wildly of reversing Germany's defeat and seeking revenge on the "November criminals" who had stabbed the army in the back.

It is evident that these are the years when Hitler's and Stalin's experiences are most widely separated; at the same time they are of great importance for their future. They cannot be compared directly and therefore must be taken in sequence. The two parts of the story come together at the end of the 1914-to-1918 war when Hitler follows Stalin in committing himself to a political career.

TWO Experience

I

WHEN HITLER DISAPPEARED from view in November 1908, he had some of his legacy left and he managed to keep his head above water for a year by taking cheaper lodgings. He had no one to talk to and withdrew more and more into himself, spending much of his time reading in his room or in public libraries.

By the autumn of 1909, however, his funds had run out; he left his room without paying the rent he owed, and took to sleeping out on park benches, even in doorways. When the colder weather came, he stood in line to get a bowl of soup from a convent kitchen and then found a place in the Asyl für Obdachlose, a shelter for the destitute run by a charitable society. The turn of the year 1909–10 saw him touching his lowest point: hungry, homeless, without an overcoat, physically weak, and with no idea what to do. To the defeat of his pretensions to become an artist was now added the social humiliation of the spoiled and snobbish young man from a middle-class home reduced to the status of a tramp.

From this state he was rescued at the beginning of 1910 by Reinhold Hanisch, a fellow tramp who had a far better idea than Hitler of how to survive at the bottom of the heap. Hanisch persuaded him that if, as Hitler said, he knew how to paint, they could go into partnership: Hanisch could peddle what he produced and they could divide the takings equally. There followed three years (1910–13) in the recently built and well-run Home for Men in the Meldemannstrasse, another charitable foundation but one several cuts above the Asyl. He was helped by a legacy from his aunt and learned to support himself by painting Viennese scenes, principally of well-known buildings, which he copied from photographs and turned out with sufficient skill to continue selling to picture framers and other small dealers after he quarreled with Hanisch.

Hitler stayed in the Home for Men not only because it provided him with much better living conditions but also because it gave him much-needed psychological support. He was one of a small group of permanent residents whose position was recognized (for example, in the use of the reading room, where he painted), and who referred to themselves as the "intellectuals," sharply distinguished from the transients, whom they treated as their social inferiors. The reading-room circle gave him that degree of superficial contact that as a "loner" he needed, without compromising the reserve with which he surrounded himself, or involving him in any real human relationship. The circle also provided him with something else he needed, an audience. According to Karl Honisch, who was a member of the circle in 1913, Hitler would go on quietly working until something was said about politics or social questions that irritated him. He would then become transformed, jump to his feet and plunge into a furious harangue. This would end as abruptly as it had begun and, with a gesture of resignation, he would sit down and resume his painting. [1]

Hitler's own account of these years is given in *Mein Kampf,* which he wrote more than ten years after he left Vienna and at a time, after the fiasco of the November 1923 *Putsch,* when he was anxious to impress his readers with the sufferings he had endured and with the unchanging character of the views he had then formed.

If he was poor and hungry, however, it was only, as he himself admits, for a short period before he settled in the Home for Men, and, even before that, his troubles were largely of his own making. He refused to prepare himself seriously for a career or look for a job while he still had sufficient funds to support himself. The worst of his sufferings was the wound to his self-esteem, the shock to his image of himself as a great artist or writer—a great "something," who would leave his mark on history—now that he found himself brought down to the level of the down-and-outs he despised.

Psychologically, this Vienna period is important for two reasons. The first is that, despite the blows he received, Hitler did not abandon, but held on to, his self-image. While outwardly the most he achieved was to rub along on the margin of society, with less idea than ever of how he was to turn his belief in his destiny into reality, the fact that he preserved it over a testing period of six long years shows the latent strength of will that was to prove the foundation of his political success. At the same time and in the same degree as he continued to experience frustration and humiliation, these fed his resentment and his desire for revenge on the world that rejected him, providing additional fuel for his will to succeed when opportunity finally came.

The second important development was Hitler's beginning to reach out from the isolation of his own personal failure to explain this in terms of the social tensions and conflicts he saw around him. Writing in the mid-1920s, Hitler exaggerated the extent to which his ideas were fully formed by the time he left Vienna in 1913, ignoring the impact of his experiences in the 1914–1918 war and his reaction to the German defeat and the unsettled period that followed. Granted that, however, there is no reason to doubt his statement that it was as a result of his experiences in Vienna that his

Weltanschauung "began to take shape." He gives a good example of the impression these experiences made on him when he writes in *Mein Kampf:*

> Those among whom I passed my younger days belonged to the petit bourgeois class, a world that had very little contact with the world of manual laborers. . . . The reason for this division lies in the fear that dominates a social group which has only just risen above the level of the laborer—a fear lest it may fall back into its old condition or at least be classed with the laborers. There is something repulsive in remembering the cultural poverty of that lower class and their rough manners, so that people who are only on the first rung of the social ladder find it intolerable to have any contact with the cultural level and standard of living out of which they have passed. . . .
>
> In the case of such a person the hard struggle through which he passes often destroys his normal human sympathy. His own fight for existence kills his sensibility for the misery of those who have been left behind.[2]

Having suffered this humiliation in Vienna before the war, Hitler was able to use the experience to identify himself with the many Germans who were seized with the same fear of becoming *déclassés* after the war.

Hitler arrived in Vienna already a German nationalist. What he saw there strengthened his defensive-aggressive attitude towards the other nationalities in the Habsburg Empire which now outnumbered the Germans by four to one. After the transformation of the empire in 1867 into the Dual Monarchy of Austria-Hungary, the German-speaking minority in the Austrian half felt their traditional position of superiority under increasing threat from the growing national consciousness and self-confidence of the Slav peoples who made up the majority, especially from the Czechs. Hitler saw the government's attempts to find some form of compromise which would satisfy the Czechs' and other nationalities' claims to equality (for example, in the use of language) not only as doomed to failure but—since it was always the Germans who had to make the concessions—as acts of national betrayal.

The two new threats that Hitler says he discovered for the first time in Vienna were "Marxism and Jewry." The rapid growth of Vienna's population, by 259 percent between 1860 and 1900, an increase far greater than that of London or Paris, and exceeded only by Berlin's, gave anyone living in the Austrian capital unique opportunities to become acquainted with both—especially anyone living at the bottom of the social pyramid.

Bad social conditions—poverty, poor housing, overcrowding, low wages, unemployment—were all made worse by the rapid influx of newcomers. Of the 1,675,000 people living in Vienna in 1900 fewer than half, 46 percent, were natives. The mass of the newcomers, many of them Czechs, came to the city in search of work and packed into the already overcrowded working-class quarters which Hitler knew firsthand. "I do not know which it was that appalled me most at the time: the economic misery of those who were then my companions, their crude customs and morals, or the low level of their intellectual culture."[3] Hitler was appalled, but not out of compassion. He discovered with horror that it was not just Czech, but German laborers as well, who disparaged everything to which he attached importance.

> There was nothing that they did not drag in the mud. . . . the nation, because it was held to be an invention of the capitalist classes; the Fatherland, because it was held to be an instrument in the hands of the bourgeoisie for the exploitation of the working masses; the authority of the law, because that was a means of holding down the proletariat; religion as a means of doping the people, so as to exploit them afterwards; morality, as a badge of stupid and sheepish docility.[4]

Stalin could not have summarized more succinctly the essential tenets of Marxism. For him they had come as a revelation of truth. They produced exactly the opposite effect on Hitler. When he first heard them repeated by German working men, they raised "the profoundly disturbing question: 'Are such men worthy of belonging to a great people?' "[5]

"Days of mental anguish" followed, made worse by encountering a mass demonstration of Viennese working men marching four abreast on such a scale that it took two hours to pass and deeply impressed him. Hitler was finally released from his agony of mind and "brought to think kindly again of my own people" by the explanation that they must be victims of the unscrupulous Social Democratic party's leaders who, by clever manipulation, exploited the sufferings of the masses in order to denationalize them, and alienate them from the other classes in society.

Hitler believed he had found the explanation of why the Social Democrats were hostile to the struggle to preserve German national identity in Austria, where they favored a compromise with their Slav "comrades" and maintained that what united both as common members of an oppressed class was more important than what divided them as members of different peoples. To Hitler's passionate German nationalism was thus added an equally passionate hatred of Marxism.

There remained the third element of his *Weltanschauung,* "the Jewish question." In 1857 there were 6,217 Jews in Vienna, just under 2 percent of the population; by 1910 the number had risen to 175,318, and the percentage to 8.6. In a city population of two million, this still left more than 90 percent who were not Jewish, but there were two factors that drew attention to the Jewish minority. The first was the much higher percentage of Jews, proportionate to their numbers, in secondary and higher education and in the most prominent professions, the law, politics, medicine, journalism, finance, and the performing arts. The second, at the other end of the social scale, was the concentration of the poorer Jews in one or two districts (the Inner City and the old ghetto, the Leopoldstadt, where they made up a third of the population), many of them immigrants from Eastern Europe who attracted attention by their appearance.

According to Hitler's account in *Mein Kampf,* which very much seems

contrived, it was an encounter with one of the latter, dressed in a long kaftan
and wearing black sidelocks, that had the effect of opening his eyes to the
alien character of "the Jew." Hitler goes on to say that he now realized the
Jews were the leaders of social democracy: "In the face of that revelation,
the scales fell from my eyes. My long inner struggle was at an end. . . . Thus
I finally discovered who were the evil spirits leading our people astray."[6]

During his Vienna days Hitler claims to have read "enormously and
thoroughly." Only a few pages further on in *Mein Kampf*, however, he
writes:

> By reading, to be sure, I mean something different than the average
> member of our so-called intelligentsia. . . . I know people who read
> interminably, and yet I should not call them "well-read" people. . . . They
> have not the faculty of distinguishing between what is useful and useless
> in a book; so that they may retain the former in their minds and if
> possible skip over the latter or throw it overboard as useless ballast.
> . . . Each little piece of knowledge thus gained must be treated as if it
> were a little stone to be inserted into a mosaic, so that it finds its proper
> place among all the other pieces that help to form a general *Weltanschau-
> ung* in the brain of the reader.[7]

This accounts for the difficulty in identifying the books Hitler read. He
had no feeling for literature, or interest in books for their own sake, but
regarded them solely as a source from which he could extract material that
fitted in with views he already held. Much of his reading appears to have
been "popularized" editions of books. In these he found many quotations
from original works which he retained and quoted in turn as if it were these
he had read. He had a remarkable memory, particularly for facts and
figures, the dimensions of buildings, the specifications of armaments, which
he used to confound experts and impress the uncritical. As most historians
have come to recognize, it is a mistake to underestimate the power of
Hitler's mind, and of the mental system that he put together from the
material he picked up from his reading and experience.[8] But everything he
ever said or wrote reveals that his mind lacked not only humanity but the
capacity for critical appreciation, for objectivity and reason in the assimilation of knowledge, which have traditionally been seen as the hallmarks of
an educated mind, and which Hitler openly despised.

As in the case of social democracy and Marxism, Hitler claims to have
turned to books for enlightenment about the Jews. In this case we have the
specific statement that the "books" were some anti-Semitic pamphlets that
he bought for a few pennies, and magazines like *Ostara*. This was published
by a defrocked monk calling himself Lanz von Liebenfels, and was dedicated, under the sign of the swastika, "to the practical application of
anthropological research for the purpose of preserving the European master
race from destruction by the maintenance of racial purity." Such publications were a characteristic of Viennese subculture of the time, frequently

pornographic and unrestrained in the violence and obscenity of their language. The passages in which Hitler writes about the Jews in *Mein Kampf* derive from this tradition, for example his preoccupation with sex and the adulteration of German blood: "the nightmare vision of the seduction of hundreds of thousands of girls by repulsive crooked-legged Jew bastards."

As soon as I began to investigate the matter . . . Vienna appeared to me in a new light. . . . Was there any shady undertaking, any form of foulness, especially in cultural life, in which at least one Jew did not participate? On putting the probing knife to that kind of abscess one immediately discovered, like a maggot in a putrescent body, a little Jew who was often blinded by the sudden light. [9]

"The Jew" was everywhere, responsible for everything Hitler detested and feared: modernism in art and music; pornography and prostitution; the organization of the white slave trade (much featured in anti-Semitic literature); the anti-national criticism of the press.

Hitler himself says that it took him considerable time to grasp the meaning of the "Jewish problem." The crucial discovery was that Jews were not, as he had hitherto believed, Germans with a special form of religion, but a separate race. There is no evidence to suggest that, at this early date when he was still in his early twenties, Hitler had any clear view of what should be done to "solve" the Jewish problem, or that he had conceived the possibility of extermination. Nonetheless race was to provide the master key to Hitler's view of history and to his ideology. His emphasis on it fitted well with that other widespread late-nineteenth-century faith that was the foundation of his philosophy: Social Darwinism, the belief that all life was engaged in a struggle for existence in which only the fittest survived. He confronted the socialist belief in equality with "the aristocratic principle of Nature," the natural inequality of individuals and races. The circle was closed with the demonstration that Marxism was a doctrine invented by a Jew, Karl Marx, and used by the Jewish leaders of the Social Democratic party to ensnare the masses and turn them against the state, the German nation, and the Aryan master race.

There were other conclusions Hitler drew from his Viennese days. One was the ease with which the masses could be manipulated by skillful propaganda. Another was the futility of parliamentary institutions (at one time he attended the noisy debates in the Austrian Reichsrat), which he denounced as destructive of leadership, individual initiative, and individual responsibility. He attributed the failure of Georg von Schoenerer's Pan-German Nationalist Movement, whose program attracted him, to its decision to turn itself into a parliamentary party. He contrasted this with the success of those groups who based their power on the organization of mass political parties outside parliament, as illustrated by the Social Democratic party and by the Christian Social party of Vienna's famous mayor, Karl Lueger. Lueger was the leader Hitler most admired, noting in *Mein Kampf* that he had devoted his political activity "to winning over those sections of the population whose existence was in danger," the small shopkeepers and businessmen, the artisans and craftsmen, petty officials and municipal employees who felt their living standards and status threatened by economic and social change.

There was another party in prewar Austria that Hitler does not mention, the strongly nationalistic German Workers' party (DAP), founded in Bohemia in 1904, which attacked the Austrian Social Democrats for trying to bring down the standard of life of the advanced workers, the Germans, to the condition of the backward Slavs. The DAP's contemptuous term for the Czechs was *Halbmenschen,* or half-persons. They campaigned aggressively for an increase in German *Lebensraum* (living space) and when the Habsburg Empire broke up in 1918 called for the German settlements in Bohemia and Moravia to be included in the German Reich. During the early days of the Nazi party in Munich after the war Hitler made contact with the Austrian DAP in Vienna and eventually took it over as the Austrian branch of his own National Socialist German Workers' party. The Nazi program of "race and space" and the German occupation of Bohemia and Moravia in the 1930s both had roots in the politics of prewar Austria. [10]

Before he left Austria Hitler had stored up a number of such observations and insights of which he was to make good use later. His experiences in Vienna had confirmed his fervid German nationalism, and opened his eyes to the three groups that he saw threatening the historic position of the German *Herrenvolk* (the master race) in Central Europe—the racially inferior Slavs, the Marxists, and the Jews. But he still had no notion of how he might contribute to the battle against these when in May 1913, at twenty-four, he left Austria and moved across the border to Germany.

I I

AT THE SAME AGE as Hitler moved from Vienna to Munich, Stalin not only knew what he wanted to do, but had already started his apprenticeship as a revolutionary.

At the beginning of the twentieth century, Russia was the largest and most backward of the Great Powers. With a population of 129 million at the time of the 1897 census, its agriculture (on which a rural population of close to ninety million peasants depended) was inefficient, with crop yields well below those of other European countries. The great mass of the people were poor, unskilled, and uneducated. In European Russia nearly two-thirds of the men and nearly 90 percent of the women could not read; only 104,000 in the whole empire had received a university or equivalent education, and little more than a million had attended secondary school.

The Russian social structure was unbalanced: an upper class of fewer than two million, a still smaller middle class (professional men and merchants), and an alienated intelligentsia, with the rest of the population, whether urban or rural, living either below or close to the poverty line. The government was autocratic, repressive, and without representative institutions, operating an arbitrary censorship over public opinion and pressing a policy of Russification on the large number of Poles, Ukrainians, Jews, Tatars, Armenians, and other peoples under Russian rule.

Industrialization offered the best hope of improvement in the long term, but increased the vulnerability of the tsarist system in the short run. Russian industry—railways and engineering, coal, iron and steel, oil and other minerals (in the Caucasus), textiles—grew rapidly between 1880 and 1914. But this was at the expense of agriculture, which suffered from low investment, rural overpopulation, an antiquated three-field system that was controlled by the *mir* (the village commune), and reliance on indirect taxation which pressed most heavily on the peasantry and the urban poor. The continuing backwardness of Russian agriculture offset the progress of industry, and the simmering discontent of the peasants was a principal cause of the revolutionary explosion that followed Russia's defeat by Japan in 1905.[11]

At the same time, the growth of industry itself produced a second potential breeding ground of revolt in a working class that numbered three million by 1900. Heavily concentrated in a small number of very large plants, and poorly paid, it was forced to live in overcrowded, wretched conditions and forbidden to organize in its own defense. Here was the classic Marxist proletariat, of whom it was no exaggeration to say that "they had nothing to lose but their chains." The revolutions of 1905 and 1917 were to show how effectively they could act when opportunity offered.

During the 1880s and 1890s a number of Russian intellectuals who had been converted to Marxism became involved with workingmen's circles that began to form in St. Petersburg and other industrial centers, and that also called themselves Marxist or social democratic. Besides discussion and propaganda, their main activity was the organization and support of strikes that—although illegal—involved nearly a quarter of a million workers in the last five years of the century and secured a shorter working day. Whether they should go beyond such economic demands ("economism") and engage in political agitation was a subject of impassioned debate in clandestine publications that printed contributions from Russian intellectuals living abroad in Switzerland or exiled in Siberia.

Among the latter was Vladimir Ilyich Ulianov, who became known from the end of 1901 by his pseudonym of Lenin. He was born in 1870 at Simbirsk on the Volga, the son of a provincial inspector of schools and a member of a close and happy family, in which nonetheless both his brothers as well as both his sisters were at one time or another arrested for subversive activity. His elder brother, Alexander, was hanged in 1887 for taking part in a plot to assassinate the tsar, an event that made a deep impression on Lenin, who was seventeen at the time.

Well educated and endowed with an incisive mind, Lenin moved to St.

Petersburg in 1893, where he joined a law firm but spent far more of his time in socialist discussion circles than in the courts. He made his name as a Marxist by his sharp criticisms of populism and "economism" before being imprisoned in 1895, and later exiled, for his part in the wave of strikes. When he returned in 1900 it was with the idea of creating a newspaper that would serve as a center for unifying the underground committees inside Russia. This was *Iskra* (*The Spark*), the first number of which was published abroad in December 1900 and smuggled into Russia.

An attempt to form a Russian Social Democratic Labor party had been made in a small illegal congress that met at Minsk in 1898. Although this is always referred to as the first such congress, it led nowhere. Encouraged by the success of *Iskra* in forming links between the scattered underground groups in Russia, Lenin determined to try again and, as a preliminary, in 1902 published one of the most famous revolutionary pamphlets ever written, *What Is to Be Done?* In this he set out his concept of a centralized, disciplined party, a network of full-time revolutionaries who would act as the "vanguard of the proletariat" and mobilize it to overthrow the tsarist regime. A year later, in the summer of 1903, the *Iskra* group organized another congress (always referred to as the Second) which met in Brussels and, after adjourning to London, founded a Russian Social Democratic party.

As soon as Stalin saw a copy of *Iskra* he became an *Iskrovets*, an "*Iskra*-man" and adopted Lenin's arguments as his own. After leaving the seminary in 1899, he spent the next ten years working in the Caucasus as a local agitator and organizer, with interruptions when he was sent to prison or exiled to Siberia. Living from hand to mouth, he depended on comrades and sympathizers for support, for a place to sleep, and a place to hide. His activities were directed at the workers in the three towns where an industrial working class was beginning to form: the railway center at Tiflis, the oil fields at Baku (in 1904 the most productive oil center in the world), and the oil refineries and port at Batum.

There was a nucleus of Russian factory workers banished to the Caucasus for their socialist sympathies, working for example in the railway shops in Tiflis and in the power station in Baku. The oil fields also attracted Armenians, Turks, Persians, Tatars, as well as Russians, and at Batum a large number of Georgian peasants from the countryside. Stalin had to learn how to explain the Marxist message in very simple terms, to convince the workers that joint action to protest against their conditions was practicable, to help organize strikes and street demonstrations. He also had to learn to draw up proclamations and leaflets and get these printed on underground presses.

Stalin played a part in the May Day demonstrations in Tiflis in 1901, in which 2,000 workers clashed with the police, and in the oil workers' strike at Batum in 1902, in which troops opened fire and killed fifteen. A vivid if hostile picture of him in this period is given by another young party member, F. Khunyanis, who describes her first meeting with him:

> I found Koba in a small room. He was short, thin and somewhat dejected-looking, reminding me of a petty thief awaiting sentence. He wore a dark-blue peasant blouse, tight-fitting jacket and a black Turkish cap.
>
> He treated me suspiciously. After lengthy questioning he handed me a stack of illegal literature. . . . He saw me to the door with the same guarded, mistrustful expression.

She goes on to describe his behavior at local committee meetings.

> It would be time to start, and Koba would not be there. He always arrived late. Not very, but it never failed. . . . When he got there, the atmosphere would change. It was not so much that it became business-like as strained. Koba would arrive with a book under his shortened left arm and sit somewhere to the side or in a corner. He would listen in silence until everyone had spoken. He always spoke last. Taking his time, he would compare the different views, weigh all the arguments . . . and make his own motion with great finality, as though concluding the discussion. Thus there was a sense of special importance to everything he said. [12]

After the strike in Batum, Stalin was picked up by the police and sentenced, for the first time, on July 9, 1903, to three years' exile in Irkutsk province, deep in Siberia. At the second attempt Stalin made good his escape from Vologda and returned to the Caucasus in February 1904 to learn that an All-Russian Social Democratic Labor party had at last been founded at the Brussels-London Congress—and had immediately split into two factions. The split had first appeared at the congress over the issue of party membership. Lenin wanted this confined to those who participated actively in one or another of the party organizations, but L. Martov, one of his closest collaborators on *Iskra,* proposed a looser formula admitting all "who cooperated under the guidance of one of its organizations." The issue did not seem important, particularly as Lenin emphasized that he was not suggesting the party membership should be limited to professional revolutionaries. Nonetheless when the question was put to a vote Lenin was defeated.

The explanation of the split lay in Lenin's efforts behind the scenes not only to ensure that *Iskra* would control the party's activities but also that he would control *Iskra*. This was an issue that divided the *Iskra* group itself, partly because of personal relations and rivalries in the small closed world of émigré politics (the whole congress numbered only fifty or so delegates), and partly because of the suspicion on the part of those whom Lenin labeled "soft" that, if he were allowed to, he would turn the party into the rigidly disciplined, tightly controlled body that he had outlined in *What Is to Be Done?*

In subsequent sessions of the congress, however, the withdrawal of a number of delegates from outside the *Iskra* group who had voted for the alternative proposal turned Martov's majority into a minority. Lenin had no hesitation in using the majority (in Russian, *Bolsheviki*) that he now commanded to secure control of the *Iskra* editorial board and of the party's Central Committee, over the opposition of Martov and the minority (in Russian, *Mensheviki*).

Lenin's victory turned out to be short-lived, and within a year he had lost control of both *Iskra* and the Central Committee. Great efforts were made to patch up the differences between the two factions, especially during the 1905 revolution. Not until 1912 did Lenin force a final break with the Mensheviks. The basic issue, however, on which all attempts at unity broke down remained the same as in 1903.

Both groups accepted Marx's scheme of historical development and believed that Russia must go through the stage of capitalism as a necessary condition for a socialist revolution. But they could not agree on what followed from this. The Mensheviks believed that, in view of Russia's economic backwardness, it would take a long time before such a revolution could take place, and that the immediate task was to work for a middle-class liberal revolution. This would get rid of the autocratic tsarist regime, clear the way for capitalism to fulfill its historic role of industrialization, and at the same time secure constitutional reforms allowing the legal growth of a mass working-class party on the lines of the German Social Democrats.

Lenin was not prepared to wait or leave it to historical processes by themselves to produce the socialist revolution on which all his thoughts were concentrated. To Mensheviks this was an anti-Marxist heresy, a conspiratorial reliance on "subjective factors" such as the revolutionary will, instead of on Marx's "objective factors," the laws of social development that he had worked out and that could not be artificially speeded up.

Lenin's retort was that of course he did not believe that revolutions could be planned or produced at will, but they could—and needed to be—prepared for, so that when the moment came the party could ride the wave of history. He was convinced that the growth of a working-class movement would produce no more than a trade-union consciousness, the need to combine in order to extract concessions; in his view, that amounted to no more or less than accepting the bourgeois system. The task of a Social Democratic party, as Lenin saw it, was to foster the class consciousness of the working class, and so awaken the will to revolution that alone would free it from exploitation and injustice. Such a task could only be undertaken by a quite different sort of party from that envisaged by the Mensheviks. Its core must be full-time revolutionaries working with, but not dependent on, the workers' movement. Thanks to their grasp of Marxist theory these would be able to develop and direct the workers' understanding of their true class interest and historic mission, namely, to act as the agent of the historical process—with the outcome assured.

Lenin remained uncompromising in his opposition to the program that the Mensheviks favored of cooperation with the middle-class constitutionalists in replacing the tsarist autocracy and securing the grant of liberal reforms. Instead he proposed cooperation with the peasantry, in whose unfulfilled demands for the land, and action in seizing it by force during the 1905 rebellion, he saw great revolutionary potential.

Lenin himself compared his dispute with the Mensheviks to the quarrel of the Jacobins and Girondins in the French Revolution. It expressed the fundamental difference of views and temperament that has divided European radical and socialist movements for the past 200 years between "militants" and "revisionists," "revolutionaries" and "reformers," "communists" and "social democrats." The labels change, but not what they represent.

III

STALIN WAS a natural Bolshevik. When he read Lenin's defense of his position at the London Congress, *One Step Forward, Two Steps Back* (1904), he found in the concept of the party developed there the perfect complement to Marx's doctrine of the class war, the means by which economic and sociological analysis could be turned into revolutionary action. His experience of the working class left him with no illusions about the "spontaneity" of socialist development among the proletariat. Lenin's recognition of this and his emphasis on organization immediately appealed to Stalin. In an article published in the underground press (January 1, 1905), "The Class of Proletarians and the Party of Proletarians," Stalin declared:

> The party of the *fighting* proletarians cannot be an accidental agglomeration of individuals—it must be a coherent, centralized organization. . . . Until now our party has been like a hospitable patriarchical family, welcoming any sympathizer in its midst. But now that our party has turned into a centralized *organization,* it has thrown off its patriarchal appearance and come to resemble a *fortress,* the doors of which are open only to the worthy. [13]

Now it had to insist that there must be unity of views not only on the program, but on tactics and organization as well.

Lenin's proposals appealed to Stalin not only by virtue of their militancy—both men belonged by temperament to the "hard" activist left—but because of the central role that they gave to the committed, full-time revolutionary agitators and organizers, living as best they could and hunted by the police, whom Lenin saw as the "vanguard of the proletariat," the real makers of revolutionary history. This recognition was powerful compensation for the disparaging manner in which Stalin and others in the party with a similar background felt they were treated by those who saw themselves as members of the intelligentsia.

The Russian revolutionary tradition, from its beginnings in the nineteenth century, was inextricably linked with the Russian intelligentsia. [14] The word itself is Russian, first coined in the 1850s by a forgotten novelist, Peter Baborykin, and given currency by Ivan Turgenev's novels, particularly by the famous portrait of the nihilist Bazarov in *Fathers and Sons* (1862). The intelligentsia was a mixture of a social group and a state of mind, defined by common hatred of the tsarist regime and commitment to its replacement by a just and equal society. Populism, anarchism, Marxism, each in a variety of forms provided the necessary ideology and rationalization for men and women in whose lives general ideas of a Utopian, universalist character and intellectual debate about them played a far greater part than experience. One of the most famous episodes in nineteenth-century Russian history was the crusade from 1872 to 1874 of hundreds of young educated people, "the going to the people" of the Narodniki (*narod* means "people"), visiting the villages to help awaken the peasant masses, only to return disillusioned when they were driven out by the very people whose wrongs they yearned to right. Yet another was the attempted assassination in 1878 of the police chief, General Fyodor Trepov, by an idealistic young woman, Vera Zasulich (who survived to become a member of the *Iskra* editorial board), and the successful assassination of the tsar in 1881.

A majority of the leaders of both the factions into which the Marxists divided shared the feeling of belonging to this same revolutionary tradition. Stalin did not, a fact that supplies one of the keys to his character and his career. His parents had been born serfs, he had been brought up in poverty, and his apprenticeship in revolutionary politics before 1917 was at the grass roots, inside Russia, not as an émigré intellectual living in Europe. This distinguished him sharply from men like Lenin, Plekhanov, Trotsky, Nikolai Bukharin, coming from a middle-class background, better educated, familiar with other European languages and the world outside Russia, where most of them lived for long periods of exile and where they came into contact with Western socialism.

For such men exploitation and the other social evils against which they rebelled were sociological and economic concepts far more than matters of personal experience. Trotsky, for example, wrote retrospectively:

> The dull empiricism, the unashamed, cringing worship of the fact were odious to me. Beyond the facts I looked for laws. . . . In every sphere I felt that I could move and act only when I held in my hand the thread of the general. The social revolutionary radicalism which has become the permanent pivot for my whole inner life grew out of this intellectual enmity toward the striving for petty ends, toward out-and-out pragmatism, toward all that is ideologically without form and theoretically ungeneralized. [15]

Compare this with Stalin's very different retrospect:

> I became a Marxist because of my social position (my father was a worker in a boot factory and my mother was also a working woman) and also

... because of the harsh intolerance and Jesuitical discipline that crushed me so mercilessly at the seminary. [16]

The personal contact of many leading Social Democrats was with an elite of the working class already attracted to socialism. They knew only from the descriptions they read in books of those backward, inert, and suspicious masses who had broken the hearts of the Narodniki when they "went to the people" in an idealistic spirit in the 1870s and 1880s. In his biography Isaac Deutscher draws the contrast with Stalin:

> He had an exceptional, an almost instinctive, sensitiveness towards that element of backwardness in Russian life. . . . He would treat with skeptical distrust not only the oppressors, the landlords, the capitalists, the monks, and the gendarmes, but also the oppressed, the workers and peasants whose cause he had embraced. There was no sense of guilt in his socialism. No doubt he felt some sympathy with the class into which he had been born; but his hatred of the possessing and ruling classes must have been much stronger. The class hatred preached by the revolutionaries from the upper classes was a kind of secondary emotion that was cultivated from theoretical conviction. In Stalin class hatred was not his second nature, it was his first. Socialist teachings appealed to him because they seemed to give moral sanction to his own emotion. There was no shred of sentimentalism in his outlook. His socialism was cold, sober, and rough. [17]

Stalin's relations with the other Social Democratic leaders (always with the exception of Lenin) show how much he resented the social and intellectual disadvantage that he felt, how rarely he forgot a slight or forgave their condescension. But he also learned how to turn their undervaluation of himself to his advantage. When Trotsky dismissed him as "a gray and colorless mediocrity," it was Stalin who profited from the other's mistake, Trotsky who paid for it—with the loss of the succession to Lenin, and eventually assassination.

The other difference that Stalin was able to turn to his advantage was his experience on the ground in Russia as a local organizer, something that few of the other original Bolshevik or Menshevik leaders could claim, and that recommended him to Lenin. An important part of that experience was the periodic interruption of arrest, imprisonment, exile, and escape. In all he was arrested seven times and five times escaped; of the nine years between March 1908 and March 1917 he spent only a year and a half at liberty. In the Russian revolutionary tradition, prison and exile for many political offenders served as their "universities," where they read widely, got a solid grounding in radical literature and ideas, often from experienced teachers, and took part in frequent debates organized by the prison commune. This was where Stalin did his best to make up the deficiencies in his education, particularly in his knowledge of Marxist writings. Most of those who knew him in prison agree in recollections of a man who subjected himself to discipline, always had a book in his hand, and took a prominent part in debates, in which his manner is described as confident, sharp-tongued, and scornful.

The Caucasus where he served his apprenticeship was a stronghold of the Mensheviks, and this helps to account for the dislike and distrust with which Stalin continued to be regarded by many Social Democrats from that part of the world. But these were due also to his rough tactics and rough language, which made him enemies.

R. Arsenidze, one of the Georgian Mensheviks who lived to publish his memoirs later, claims that when Stalin addressed Georgian workers in Batum in 1905, he declared:

> Lenin is outraged that God sent him such comrades as the Mensheviks! Who are these people anyway! Martov, Dan and Axelrod* are circumcised Yids. And that old woman Vera Zasulich! Try and work with them. You can't go into a fight with them, or have a feast with them. Cowards and peddlers![18]

Discounting the venom with which the Mensheviks, like Trotsky, continued to pursue him long afterwards, there remains a sufficient residue to suggest that Stalin had already by 1905 acquired the reputation of being a difficult man to work with, an ambitious intriguer who set his fellows against one another, who gave no man his confidence, was not to be trusted himself, never forgot a slight, never forgave anyone who put him down in an argument or opposed him.

His ability as an organizer was not in question; he was a man who could get things done, and while Stalin as a Marxist never showed anything like Lenin's originality, he became an effective debater who knew his Marxist texts well enough to be able to support his arguments with quotations from Marx and Engels as well as Plekhanov and Lenin. But even in controversies that were conducted with no regard for civility on either side, he gave offense by his rudeness and sarcasm.

Stalin retained supporters as well as enemies from his Caucasus days, but always on terms that made it clear that they accepted him as leader. Like Hitler he was a "loner," although in a very different way, cold and calculating where the other was excitable and unbalanced; but, like Hitler, he kept people at a distance and left the impression that he was incapable of establishing ordinary human relationships. In June 1906, however, he married Ekaterina, the daughter of a railway employee, Semyon Svanidze, who was involved in underground politics. Her brother, Alexander, had been at school with Stalin, who had him executed in 1938, together with others who had known him in his youth.

Ekaterina herself had no interest in politics, but filled the role of a traditional Georgian wife, praying like his mother that Stalin might give up

*L. Martov, Fyodor Dan, and Pavel Axelrod were the leaders of the Menshevik faction.

his revolutionary ambitions and settle down. To please his wife's mother, Stalin even agreed to a church wedding by a fellow seminarist before they set up house together in Tiflis. There he tried to establish his credentials as a Marxist theoretician by writing a series of articles on "Anarchism or Socialism?" which appeared in installments in illegal Georgian publications in 1906 and 1907. His wife gave birth to a son, Yakov, but six months later, on October 22, 1907, she died from typhus, leaving the boy to be brought up by her sister. [19] Iremashvili was surprised that she was given an Orthodox burial and even more that Stalin, who prided himself on his self-control, showed his grief; he adds that it was only with his wife and child in their impoverished home that Stalin's unquiet spirit ever found love. [20]

IV

WHILE BOLSHEVIKS AND MENSHEVIKS debated how to bring about a revolution in Russia, at the beginning of 1905 a spontaneous wave of strikes, peasant uprisings, and revolts among the non-Russian nationalities spread across the whole vast country and rapidly acquired revolutionary proportions. The loss of the war with Japan in 1904–1905 had weakened the authority of the government in the face of the growing discontent of both workers and peasants at their living conditions and lack of rights. When a huge but peaceful and orderly demonstration led by a priest gathered outside the Winter Palace in St. Petersburg to present a petition to the tsar, the authorities panicked and ordered troops to open fire, killing a hundred and wounding several hundred more. This incident irreparably damaged the traditional image of the tsar as "the father of his people" and sparked the violence that followed.

The industrial working class played a leading part in these events. In St. Petersburg a soviet, or improvised council of workers, was elected; under the defiant chairmanship of the twenty-six-year-old Trotsky, for a short time it rivaled the tsar's government in authority and called upon the people to stop paying their taxes. Similar soviets sprang up in other cities. In the face of the unrest, the government capitulated and promised, for the first time, a constitution and the election of a representative assembly (the Duma). Only after the defeat of the Moscow uprising in December did the revolt pass its climacteric, and even then unrest continued throughout 1906 and part of 1907. Not until June 1907 did a new prime minister, Petr Stolypin, feel strong enough to dissolve the Second Duma and arrest more than fifty of its deputies, all Social Democrats.

Not only did 1905 take the Social Democrats by surprise, but Bolshevik and Menshevik leaders alike failed to get control of the situation and turn it into a revolution. Trotsky alone—at this time maintaining his independence of both factions—put on a bravura performance comparable with his role in 1917. Lenin did not return to Russia until ten months after the trouble began, and left again without ever showing that grasp of the possibilities or the power of decision that made him so remarkable a leader in 1917.

Although the tsarist government reasserted its authority and refused to allow the Duma any real power, it did not feel strong enough to abolish it. A period of semiconstitutional politics followed in which it was possible for political parties to organize—such as the liberal Constitutional Democrats, the leading legal opposition party (known as the Kadets), and a number of nationalist parties, such as the Poles—and even for the socialist parties to exploit the twilight zone between legality and the underground.

While both factions of the Social Democrats were divided about taking part in the Duma, individual deputies of their persuasion (with parliamentary immunity) numbered sixty-five in the Second Duma and, even with a franchise restricted in favor of the right, were represented in the Third and Fourth Dumas (1907–17). So were the rival Socialist Revolutionaries (SRs), a union of populist groups that was formed at the beginning of the century as a revival of *Zemlia i Volya* (Land and Liberty) and that attracted mass support with its program of socializing the land during the peasant revolts of 1905–1906. The SR left wing revived the earlier populist tradition of individual assassination: Among its successes was the assassination of Vyacheslav Plehve, the tsar's minister of the interior, in 1904.

STALIN'S ROLE between 1905 and 1907 was confined to the Caucasus, which saw some of the most violent scenes of the rebellion. He played an active but not at all prominent part in events at a time when the Mensheviks established their ascendancy in the area. The Bolsheviks had the worst of a bitter factional fight and Stalin came in for further criticism for his part in "expropriations." These were armed robberies of banks and mail coaches, carried out by fighting groups of the party. Lenin relied heavily on such actions for funds, but they were loudly condemned by the Mensheviks. The most notorious was a raid on the Tiflis State Bank in June 1907, in which Stalin was accused of being involved behind the scenes. The Georgian Mensheviks, who treated him as an open enemy and accused him of being a police informer as well, demanded his expulsion from the party for his part in the expropriations, and although this was never carried out, Stalin found it expedient to move his activities from Tiflis to Baku.

For the first time, during these years, Stalin managed to get himself elected as a delegate to party congresses. The Stockholm Congress in 1906 was called to reunite the Social Democratic party, but produced more dissension than ever, with the Mensheviks securing seven out of ten seats on the incoming executive.

Stalin spoke several times in defense of Lenin's views, but on an issue that was to prove of great importance in the future he followed a line of his own: what to do with the land when it had been taken away from the landlords. Lenin wanted to nationalize it and hand it over to the central government;

the Mensheviks wanted to put it in the hands of local government. With a first-hand knowledge of the peasants' mentality, which neither Lenin nor the Menshevik leaders could equal, Stalin brushed both proposals aside as unrealistic: "Even in their dreams, the peasants see the landlords' fields as their own property." Stalin felt instinctively that what mattered was not how the solution of the land problem would fit into the theoretical scheme of the revolution, on which there was in any case no agreement, but how to satisfy the peasants. Only the division of the land among them would do that. He succeeded in carrying the majority with him, and although Lenin sharply criticized the narrow-minded realism of Stalin's proposal, he himself was to follow the same course in 1917 as the only way to win the peasants' acquiescence in the Bolsheviks' seizure of power.

The most important outcome of the party meetings for Stalin was that he had met Lenin and seen him in action. Lenin was then in his mid-thirties, not much taller than Stalin, stocky in build, already balding—which added to the impression of a naturally high forehead—with a small, pointed reddish beard. Stalin was at first taken aback by his lack of ceremony; absorbed in what he was doing, Lenin made no attempt to project his personality, employed no rhetoric but relied on argument and his power of persuasion. Although he was at odds with a majority of the Marxist émigrés, this did not affect his self-confidence. Stalin, in search of a master, had found one who spoke with authority.

Addressing the Kremlin military school after Lenin's death in 1924, Stalin recalled his first encounter with Lenin:

> When I compared him with the other leaders of our party it all the time seemed that his comrades-in-arms—Plekhanov, Martov, Axelrod—were a whole head lower. By comparison with them, he was not just one of the leaders but a leader of the highest life, a mountain eagle, knowing no fear in the struggle and boldly leading the party forward along uncharted paths. [21]

This might well seem hyperbole under the influence of Lenin's death, but almost the same phrase—"a real mountain eagle"—and the favorable comparison with Plekhanov, Axelrod, and others occur in a letter Stalin wrote in 1904. The phraseology suggests something else as well. It was not only political arguments and conviction that had drawn Stalin into the revolutionary movement, but also the attraction of joining an enterprise in which he could see himself playing a heroic part. Lenin now took the place of "Koba" as the hero with whom he identified himself, and the Caucasian phraseology—"a mountain eagle"—is carried over directly from the Koba legend. Although Stalin was careful to conceal his ambition, his admiration for Lenin fostered his own self-image, first as Lenin's right-hand man, then as his successor.

It is not difficult to see why Stalin should have been attracted to Lenin, but what did Lenin see in this often rough, often difficult young recruit from the provincial ranks? Lenin had been interested in one or two articles Stalin had written defending the Bolshevik point of view, but Stalin's contribution to the three party meetings he attended had not particularly impressed him. When the Menshevik leader Martov objected to the nomination of Stalin and three others as delegates to the London Congress on the ground that no one knew who they were, Lenin had replied: "Quite true, we don't know either." Yet within less than five years—during more than half of which Stalin was in prison or exile—Lenin co-opted him onto the Central Committee of the Bolshevik party after the final split with the Mensheviks and assigned him a number of important jobs. What accounted for this unexpected promotion?

Although one himself, Lenin had a low opinion of intellectuals. They lacked that combination of views fanatically held with the pragmatic instinct, of consistency of aim with tactical flexibility, that made Lenin a revolutionary leader. They were unstable in their own opinions, and were inclined to question Lenin's. In seeking recruits who could be relied on to accept his direction and get on with the job, Lenin had far more use for a "practical" like Stalin. His judgment was confirmed by Stalin's performance in the five years that followed.

THE 1905 REVOLUTION had been a spontaneous outburst, and, as Lenin had always believed would happen with a spontaneous uprising, it failed. The subsequent years (1907–12) represented a period of counterrevolution in which Lenin and the other leaders of Russian social democracy once again went into exile in the West, and the membership of the party inside Russia fell drastically from its inflated numbers during the 1905 revolution. In St. Petersburg, for instance, it had been reduced from 8,000 in 1907 to 300 when Stalin visited the capital in 1909. Baku, however, where Stalin established himself in the autumn of 1907 as one of the local Bolshevik Committee, was the last place in the whole of Russia where, even in retreat, the undercover movement continued to score successes. The rapidly expanding oil industry and its mass of badly paid workers offered a rich field for agitation, but only if those organizing it could persuade its explosive mixture of races and religions to cooperate in common action.

Election to the Duma—this time the Third Duma, with a much restricted franchise—was in two stages. Each estate, voting separately in constituencies around the country, elected delegates, who in turn chose a deputy for their district. In Baku, the Bolshevik Committee secured the election of workers' delegates who were members of their party, not Mensheviks or Socialist Revolutionaries. Stalin wrote the "Instruction of the Baku Workers to Their Deputy," which was to become a model for Bolshevik parliamentary tactics, adopting Lenin's line that the Duma should be treated as a forum in which no serious reform could be carried out so long as tsarism survived, but which could be used for revolutionary agitation.

After the elections Stalin and the other members of the Baku group moved into labor conflicts, persuading the oil workers to join a single union, and the employers to recognize it as the sole bargaining agent of the "50,000 Baku workers." While the Mensheviks and Socialist Revolutionaries called for a boycott of the negotiations, the Bolshevik group kept them going for several months, debating every point in the collective agreement they finally secured, calling out the workers on strike when necessary and using the meetings as another forum for expounding the party line. Nowhere else in Russia was anything like this happening, and Lenin declared with admiration: "These are the last of our Mohicans of the political mass strike."

Stalin had now adopted Russian in place of Georgian for writing as well as speaking (a further stage in his adoption of a Russian identity) and copies of his articles in the legal news-sheet of the Bolshevik trade unionists as well as the clandestine *Bakinsky Proletarii,* of which he was an editor, were regularly sent to Lenin. If Stalin's pieces contained little that was original, Lenin was impressed by the combination of their down-to-earth tone with unswerving devotion to the Bolshevik line. Even when Stalin and other members of the committee were arrested, the papers continued to print a running commentary as well as instructions to the workers which were smuggled out of prison.

On September 29, 1908, Stalin was sentenced to two years' exile at Solvychegosk in Vologda province, in the middle of what later became one of the largest labor camp areas around Kotlass. A characteristic reminiscence of his stay there is recalled by Khrushchev:

Stalin used to say, "There were some nice fellows among the criminals during my first exile. I hung around mostly with the criminals. I remember we used to stop at the saloons in town. We'd see who among us had a rouble or two, then hold our money up to the window, order something, and drink up every kopek we had. One day I would pay; the next someone else and so on in turn. These criminals were nice, salt-of-the-earth fellows. But there were lots of rats among the political convicts. They once organized a comrades' court and put me on trial for drinking with the criminal convicts, which they charged was an offense. [22]

Stalin escaped in the summer of 1909 and turned up again undercover in Baku in July of that year. By now, even in "Fortress Baku," the revolutionary tide had ebbed, party funds were exhausted, and *Bakinsky Proletarii* had not been published for a year. The first number Stalin succeeded in getting out after his return carried an article in which he analyzed the crisis in the party in unvarnished language:

The party has no roots in the mass of the workers. Petersburg does not know what is going on in the Caucasus, the Caucasus does not know what is happening in the Urals. . . . That party of which we were so proud in 1905, 1906 and 1907 exists no longer. [23]

The émigré centers abroad, both Bolshevik and Menshevik, were equally ineffective, because they were out of touch, and "aloof from Russian reality." He did not argue for the transfer of the leadership to Russia, but he called on the Central Committee to set up a national newspaper published in Russia that would serve as a focus to pull together the scattered elements of the party.

In the same number he published a resolution of the Baku Committee rebuking Lenin for wasting his time and splitting the Bolshevik faction in a philosophical controversy over the revision of dialectical materialism. [24] Stalin was critical of Lenin in this case, but his "Letters from the Caucasus," which he wrote in late 1909 for the Social Democrat (published in Paris and Geneva by a joint Bolshevik-Menshevik editorial board), show that he remained a solid supporter of Lenin's views on policy and tactics. All he wanted to do was to recall Lenin to the real task of preparing for the next phase of the revolutionary struggle which he believed was about to open.

While Stalin was preparing to launch a general strike in the oil industry, he was again arrested, in March 1910, and eventually returned to Vologda. He was then over thirty. When he reemerged in the summer of 1911, it was not to return to Baku and the Caucasus, which he only saw in future on brief visits. Nonetheless, the time he spent there between 1907 and 1910, even with interruptions, laid the foundation from which he was then able to move up to the central organization of the party.

v

TOWARDS THE END OF 1911, Lenin decided to abandon the search for unity with the other elements in the Social Democratic party, to make a clean break with the Mensheviks and those Bolsheviks who questioned his leadership, and to claim the name and authority of the party for his group alone. He summoned those he believed he could trust to a meeting in Prague in January 1912 and submitted to the conference a list of names for a new Central Committee. Stalin was not present—he had just begun a new three-year term of exile in Vologda—and although his name appeared on Lenin's list he was not elected. Lenin, however, persisted and persuaded the other members of the committee, once elected, to co-opt Stalin.

Lenin broke off relations with the émigré intellectuals—among them several such as Trotsky, Lev Kamenev, and Bukharin, who were later to play a major role with him in founding the Soviet Union, as well as the Menshevik leaders Martov and Dan. The only one he retained was Grigori Zinoviev, the son of a Jewish dairy farmer in his late twenties, who had worked as a clerk and teacher before emigrating to join Lenin in exile. There he made himself so useful that he became Lenin's principal collaborator. For other members of the Central Committee Lenin turned to the practical workers of the underground. Two of them had been members of the Baku Committee, Stalin and G. K. (Sergo) Ordzhonikidze, a Georgian like Stalin, who had been picked out by Lenin for training in a party school at Longjumeau, near Paris, in 1911 and sent back to set up an organizing committee inside Russia. He too was to play an important role subsequently, becoming commissar for heavy industry during Stalin's industrialization of Russia, before falling out with Stalin and shooting himself in 1937.

In 1912 Ordzhonikidze, together with Stalin and yet another member of the Baku Committee, made up three of the four-man bureau that was to direct the party's activities inside Russia. Stalin had already suggested the creation of such a bureau in a letter written from exile in December 1910, which he knew would be shown to Lenin. He took care to avoid any suggestion of criticism that might spoil his chances of being considered for membership, and went out of his way to express his support for Lenin in language very different from that of the intellectuals: "Lenin is a sensible *muzhik* [peasant] knowing well where the crayfish hides in the winter."[25]

Later, the Soviet panegyrists of Stalin built up his promotion to make him appear as Lenin's chief lieutenant after the break with the Mensheviks. This is far from true. The party leadership was now much reduced in numbers, and there was a continual turnover in its membership. Stalin was active for only one out of the five years between 1912 and the October Revolution, spending the other four years, out of touch, in Siberia.

Stalin's promotion did not represent a radical alteration in his standing in the party, but it was a first brief opportunity to show what he was capable of and to become known to the rest of the leadership group. Once he heard the news, he wasted no time in escaping from exile. If he was to keep his position, he had to make good Lenin's expectations quickly. He achieved two things, separated by another five months in prison. One was to produce the first number of *Pravda,* the party newspaper published in Russia which he had proposed earlier; the other was to organize the election of Bolshevik deputies to the Fourth Duma.

Of the thirteen Social Democrats elected, six were Bolsheviks and seven Mensheviks. Lenin called a joint conference in January 1913 of the Bolshevik deputies and the Central Committee at Cracow in Austrian Poland, close to the Russian frontier. He wanted to end the close cooperation that had existed between the deputies of the two parties in the Third Duma. There was strong feeling, however, among the working-class electors in favor of unity, and Lenin to his disgust had to agree to postpone confrontation with the Mensheviks. If he was critical of Stalin's reluctance to follow him on this matter, Lenin was impressed by his conversations with him, particularly by the grasp the Georgian showed of the complex relationships of the Caucasian nationalities. Here was the practical experience that might enable Stalin—under Lenin's direction—to write an essay on the important question of the Social Democrats' policy toward the nationalities' problem in Russia, taking account not only of the Caucasian peoples, but also of the aspirations of the Poles, the Ukrainians, the Jews, the Letts, and so on. Lenin suggested that Stalin should visit Vienna and acquaint himself with the program that the Austrian socialists had worked out to deal with the national conflicts of the Habsburg Empire—the feature of Austrian social democracy that had done more than anything else to turn Hitler against its leaders.

Lenin's suggestion was flattering; it offered Stalin the opportunity, for the first time, to make a contribution on the theoretical side of social democracy, the acknowledged preserve of the intellectuals of the party—and to do this under the guidance of Lenin himself.

So Stalin went to Vienna and spent a month there in January–February 1913. This was his longest stay outside Russia during his life; his next visit abroad was to Teheran to meet Churchill and Roosevelt in 1943. Hitler was still in the Austrian capital, and Stalin may even have rubbed shoulders with him in the crowd. The two men he certainly met and was eventually to destroy were Bukharin and Trotsky, the first helpful in assisting the newcomer, who spoke only rudimentary German, to find his way around, the second engaged in a furious controversy with Lenin and barely deigning to notice this uncouth protégé, of whom he later remembered only "the glint of animosity" in his "yellow eyes."

Lenin was delighted with the material Stalin collected, and particularly with his dismissal of the Austro-Marxist concept of "national-cultural autonomy." The chief authority on the national question among the Austrian Social Democratic leaders was Otto Bauer (1881–1938). Faced with the mixture of nationalities in the Habsburg Empire, complicated by areas of mixed language and by constant migration to the towns, Bauer abandoned the territorial basis of nationality for the "personal" principle, namely, that every citizen, *wherever he lived,* should choose his own national status. Each nation would set up its own organization to develop its national culture and institutions. National, self-governing bodies would be the foundation of the state and its authority.

Stalin saw any such proposal setting impossible problems for a revolutionary government if it was adopted in Russia. It was not the business of Social Democrats, he wrote, to "preserve and develop the national attributes of peoples" (one of the objectives of the Austrian party's program); their job was to organize the proletariat for class struggle. The correct solution for the national question in Russia was to grant national minorities in every region the right to use their own language and send children to their own schools, but to organize the workers of all nationalities within a single integrated party, as members not of separate nations but of a single class. Lenin wrote to Kamenev, "The article is *very good,*" and described its author enthusiastically to Maxim Gorki as "a wonderful Georgian."

Whatever help Lenin may have given, the essay, which was published in three numbers of *Prosveshchenie* (*Enlightenment*) with the title "The National Question and Social Democracy," appeared under the name of K. (that is, Koba) Stalin, "man of steel," a new pseudonym that stuck. The essay not only enhanced Stalin's standing in the party (and his self-esteem) by being published in the party's leading theoretical journal, but also won him a reputation as the party's specialist on the subject, the basis for his appointment as commissar of nationalities in the Bolshevik government five years later.

A week after returning to St. Petersburg, Stalin was again arrested. He was betrayed by a fellow member of the Central Committee and the Bolshevik deputy for Moscow in the Duma, Roman Malinovsky, for long an agent of the tsarist secret police (the Okhrana) who reported in secret on the work of the party, but was still high in Lenin's confidence. Stalin was sentenced to four years' exile in one of the most remote penal settlements of northern Siberia, the Yenisei-Turukhansk region, an area the size of Scotland with a population of 12,000, scattered in tiny settlements hundreds of miles apart. North of the Arctic Circle, the temperature in winter fell to below $-40°C$, and the long Arctic winter nights lasted for eight or nine months. The summer, with its "white nights" and plague of mosquitoes, was almost as unpleasant. The frozen soil produced no food and the natives lived by hunting and fishing. Escape was virtually impossible: even by sled it was six weeks' journey to the Trans-Siberian Railway at Krasnoyarsk. Not surprisingly the monotony, solitude, and hardship broke down the physical and mental health of many exiles.

Stalin was tough enough to survive. He took little part in the social life of the other exiles (350 in all). Jacob Sverdlov, a fellow Bolshevik with whom he shared a hut for a short time, moved out, writing to his wife that his companion "turned out to be impossible in personal relations. We had to stop seeing and speaking to each other." [26] Stalin did not encourage casual acquaintances, and kept aloof, preferring to spend his time fishing, trapping, reading, and smoking his pipe. The Alliluyev family, whom he had known in the Caucasus and one of whose daughters he was to marry, sent him an occasional parcel: A letter of thanks in return is one of the few touches of human feeling in those dark and silent years. He asked them to send him some postcards with views of nature.

> In this accursed region, nature is stark and ugly: the river in summer, the snow in winter. . . . That's all the scenery there is around here. So I have an idiotic longing to see some landscape, if only on paper. [27]

He must have felt acutely his removal from political activity, just when he was beginning to work closely with Lenin. Shut away in the Arctic wilderness, with such letters or newspapers as he received taking weeks or months to arrive, he had the greatest difficulty in following what was happening in the outside world.

The outbreak of the First World War threw European socialism into confusion and destroyed the Second International, the federation of socialist parties founded in 1889. Lenin had no patience with socialists who supported the war or with those who declared themselves pacifists. His call was to answer war with revolution and "turn the imperialist war into a civil war," frankly accepting the charge of defeatism. The defeat of tsarism would be the prelude to revolution—as indeed it proved to be.

Stalin is said to have gotten hold of a copy of Lenin's "War Theses" and read these out to a gathering of exiles. In July 1915 he made a long journey to join other exiled Bolshevik leaders in discussing Lenin's line on the war and the conduct of the Bolshevik Duma deputies in supporting it. But he wrote nothing himself for four years and seems to have taken little if any interest in discussing issues in principle, so long as he was remote from the scene of the action. In 1916 he was summoned to Krasnoyarsk for a medical examination, and was turned down for military service because of the defect in his left arm which he had had since childhood. This was a stroke of good fortune. Instead of being sent back to the frozen north, he was allowed to serve the rest of his sentence in nearby Achinsk which was on the Trans-Siberian Railway and only four days away by express train from Petrograd. When the February Revolution of 1917 broke out, the tsar abdicated and a provisional government was formed.* Stalin joined with other political prisoners in sending a cable of "fraternal greetings" to Lenin, and set off for the capital, which they reached on March 12. Back at the center of events he and Kamenev, who had also been exiled, asserted their right to take over *Pravda* and the leadership of the Bolshevik party until Lenin arrived from Switzerland three weeks later.

V I

FOR BOTH STALIN AND HITLER, the war was decisive in opening up political opportunities neither might otherwise have found; but its impact on the personal life of the two men was very different. Outwardly, Stalin's four years in the wilderness were a blank. Their significance lies in the effect they must have had on his inner development. Another exile, B. I. Ivanov, who was shocked by Stalin's refusal to be reconciled with Sverdlov, wrote: "Djugashvili remained as proud as ever, as locked up in himself, in his own thoughts and plans."[28] The result was to deepen the harshness, the lack of human feeling, and the suspicion already ingrained in his character at the same time as it demonstrated his remarkable self-sufficiency and ability to suspend, yet at the same time sustain, his ambition. For Hitler, however, the war, as he said later, was "the greatest of all experiences."[29]

In June 1913, while Stalin was making his way to the Arctic, Hitler left Vienna and moved to Munich. There does not appear to be any substance in the story that he did so to avoid military service, for which he had failed to register. He made no secret of his plans and told his friends in the Home for Men that he would apply for admission to the Munich Art Academy. "Almost from the first moment . . . ," he wrote in *Mein Kampf*, "I came to

*For three changes in Russia between 1914 and 1924 liable to cause confusion (the change in dating from Old Style to New Style (NS), the changes in the name of St. Petersburg, and the change of the capital city) see the note at the end of the glossary, on pp. 1029–30.

love that city more than any other place. 'A German city!' I said to myself. How different from Vienna . . . that Babylon of races."[30]

Hitler duly registered with the Munich police as "a painter and writer," but did nothing about securing admission to the academy. Nor did he take advantage of the fact that at this time Munich was the liveliest city in Germany, attracting a large number of artists, intellectuals, writers, and other "free spirits," who rebelled against the stuffy conventions of bourgeois and official Germany. The city, and especially its northern district, Schwabing, was one of the original centers of the modern movement in the arts, a magnet for every form of experiment and radicalism, not only intellectual and artistic, but political as well, right wing as well as left. Yet Hitler, the frustrated artist, kept well away from all this ferment in which anyone was welcome to take part. He lived an even more isolated life than in Vienna, hardly speaking to anyone beyond the family with whom he lodged, continuing to paint architectural scenes in his stiff academic style and peddling them for a living, spending the rest of his time reading in libraries or his room, getting drawn into angry arguments in cafés.

According to his own account, Hitler plunged deeper into the study of Marxism, "that destructive teaching," and its relations with Jewry. He became more and more critical of the complacency with which the danger they represented was treated in Germany. He was equally critical of Germany's alliance with the Habsburg Empire, and the failure to realize that it had ceased to be a German state and had become a liability that could drag Germany down if war broke out. From these lofty speculations, he was brought down to earth when he was arrested for evading military service in Austria and ordered to report for duty at Linz immediately. A frightened young man drew up a plea for clemency on the grounds of poverty and ignorance of the law, and made so pitiable an impression on the Austrian consul-general that he was finally allowed to report at Salzburg instead of Linz, and was then found "unfit for combatant and auxiliary duties on grounds of physical weakness. Unable to bear arms."

Six months later, however, after the assassination of the Archduke Ferdinand at Sarajevo, he greeted the news that Germany and Austria had joined in declaring war on Serbia and Russia with enthusiasm. A famous photograph (taken by Heinrich Hoffmann, who later became his official photographer) shows Hitler standing in the crowd that had gathered on the Odeonsplatz to cheer the proclamation of war. The outbreak of war came to Hitler, as it did to millions of others, as a liberation from the monotony of their everyday—and in Hitler's case aimless—existence. The early days of August 1914 brought an unparalleled sense of national unity that those who experienced it never forgot, an exalted sense of patriotism, which the kaiser expressed when he told the crowd on the palace square in Berlin that he no longer recognized parties or denominations, but "only German brothers."

Hitler not only shared in this general mood, but felt a personal sense of liberation after so long an experience of failure.

> For me these hours came as a deliverance from the distress that had weighed upon me during the days of my youth. . . . I sank down on my knees to thank Heaven for the favor of having been permitted to live in such a time.[31]

Hitler at once volunteered for service and was beside himself with joy when he learned that the German army would take him. After a couple of months' training, the Sixteenth Bavarian Reserve Infantry Regiment to which he had been posted was sent to the Western Front. It arrived in time for heavy fighting in the First Battle of Ypres. That was in October 1914 and Hitler remained at the front or close to it for two years. He did not return to Germany until he was wounded in October 1916, and could not be persuaded to apply for home leave until October 1917.

There is no doubt that Hitler was a good soldier and saw a lot of fighting, taking part in some three dozen engagements on the Western Front between 1914 and 1918. He served as a regimental runner, carrying messages when other means of communication broke down, as they frequently did. This was a dangerous job, but it suited him because he could work on his own. He was wounded and had many narrow escapes, but his courage and coolness under fire were described as exemplary in the citation that won him the Iron Cross, First Class.

For the majority the actual experience of the horrors of war destroyed their initial enthusiasm, but not in Hitler's case. He remained a super-patriot, never complaining of the hardships and dangers, with an excessive sense of duty, infuriating his fellow soldiers by continuing to "spout" like a recruiting poster. "There was this white crow among us who wouldn't go along with us when we damned the war."[32] He was not unpopular, and was accepted as a good comrade, but he still kept himself apart, refusing leave, showing no interest in women, and neither smoking nor drinking. Every one of the reminiscences of Hitler as a soldier contains a reference to there being something odd about him. This no doubt was the reason why he was never promoted beyond the rank of corporal. His officers were prepared to recommend him for a decoration but believed that he lacked the qualities of leadership, even for an NCO.

It may seem paradoxical, in view of this, that Hitler should have prized so highly the comradeship of life at the front. But, as his German biographer, Joachim Fest, points out, Hitler found in it "the kind of human relationship that suited his nature." Throughout his life he showed himself incapable of forming close personal friendships. The wartime billets and dugouts provided "the social framework that corresponded both to his misanthropic withdrawnness and his longing for contact. In its impersonality it was the lifestyle of the Home for Men,"[33] combined with the sense of being part of a much greater purpose—the army, the nation—that dwarfed and at the same time gave meaning to the individual existences it absorbed.

Vienna had given him an insight into the anxieties of those threatened with the fate of becoming *déclassé*. The war provided another revelation: the identification, where necessary the sacrifice, of the individual to the *Volk*** which Hitler was to make a central part of his political appeal. No longer condemned to the aimless, lonely life he had been living in Vienna and Munich, he responded eagerly to the discipline of the army, enjoying the security of being absorbed into an organization that embraced his whole existence and was dedicated wholly to the task of destroying Germany's enemies. The war turned the fantasy world of adolescence into reality, and he felt pride and exhilaration in the role of a hero "prepared to die for the Fatherland":

> As a boy and a young man I often longed for the occasion to prove that my national enthusiasm was not mere talk. . . . Just as millions of others, I felt a proud joy in being permitted to go through this inexorable test. . . . For me, as for every German, there now began the greatest and most unforgettable time of my life. [34]

This was the *Fronterlebnis,* the unique experience that Hitler shared with other front-line fighters, the *Frontkämpfer,* who played so large a role in the creation of the Nazi party.

The war provided something else, the experience in practice of that belief in struggle, force, and violence that Hitler had already begun to exalt as the supreme law of human life. Far from repelling, the daily contact with death and destruction in their most hideous forms not only reinforced Hitler's beliefs but afforded him a deep psychological satisfaction. In all that he said and wrote about war, in *Mein Kampf,* in his speeches, and in his table talk, he never expressed the revulsion that the majority of those who served in the trenches felt at the sickening waste of millions of human lives, the destruction of every form of civilized existence—towns, villages, houses— and every vestige of organic life. Hitler's reaction was pride that the experience not only toughened his body but hardened his will,† that he did not flinch, that the callow young man had become a veteran whom nothing could shock, impervious to any appeal to pity or compassion. "War," he declared, "is for a man what childbirth is for a woman"—in effect, a declaration of his inability to distinguish between death and life, but one that, as the endless repetition of images of violence, hatred, and destruction in his speeches shows, had a greater appeal than most people were for a long time willing to admit. In Hitler's refusal to take leave, in his frequent

---

*To translate *Volk* as "folk" or "people" does not do it justice. For a discussion of its meaning see p. 68.

†One of the few books that Hitler mentioned specifically and claimed to have carried in his soldier's knapsack was Schopenhauer's *The World as Will and Idea,* which had a great influence on Wagner too.

references to the First World War as the happiest years and the greatest experience of his life, there is the first clear evidence of that fascination with destruction that became his ruling passion in the Second World War, without restraint after the attack on Russia.

What Hitler could not stand was life away from the front. As the war dragged on into a second and third year, the patriotic unity and enthusiasm that had marked the early stages of the war gave way to disillusionment, complaints about shortages, the black market, and the revival of social and political divisions. Sent back to recover from his wound in the winter of 1916–17, he denounced the shirkers he encountered, the profiteers, and draft-dodgers, as traitors. He could no longer recognize Munich and found the mood in the replacement battalion despicable. He begged to be allowed to return to the front: His regiment, he declared, was his home. He got his wish and in the same month that Stalin made his return to Petrograd, March 1917, Hitler was back in Flanders, overjoyed to be in time for the spring offensive. The fighting that followed around Arras in the spring of 1917 and the Third Battle of Ypres in the summer took a heavy toll on Hitler's regiment. In August those who survived were sent to Alsace to recover, and they saw little action for the rest of the year.

Nineteen seventeen produced two great fillips for the German forces: the collapse of Russia and the Austrian breakthrough on the Italian front. The winter of 1917–18, however, tried the morale of all the combatant forces: In Germany it produced severe food shortages and a call for a general strike which brought out 400,000 workers in Berlin in January. Hitler was furious at this "stab in the back," but his hopes revived in March 1918 when the revolutionary government in Russia finally accepted the terms dictated by the Germans. With the war in the East ended, the German High Command concentrated its forces to impose a military resolution in the West. Less than three weeks after the Treaty of Brest-Litovsk was signed, on March 21, 1918, General Erich Ludendorff launched a series of attacks in France that drove the British and French armies back and brought German troops within forty miles of Paris.

Hitler's regiment took part in all the phases of the German four-month offensive: on the Somme, on the Aisne, and on the Marne. His fighting spirit had never been higher. By the summer he was convinced that they were within sight of victory, and on August 4 he was awarded the Iron Cross, First Class "for personal bravery and general merit." This was a rare decoration for a corporal, and Hitler wore it with pride for the rest of his life.

The strength of the German army, however, was exhausted. Ludendorff was later to describe the British counterattack that broke through the German lines at Amiens on August 8 as "the black day of the German army." But the reversal that followed in August and September, and the fact that the High Command had asked for terms of peace, were concealed from the German people. They were also concealed from the German army itself, which, although falling back, did so in good order and still stood outside Germany's frontiers when the war ended. Not until October 2 were the leaders of the Reichstag parties informed that they were in sight not of victory, but of defeat.

For the majority of the German people the shock was too sudden for them to grasp what had happened. For Hitler it was doubly so because of the excitement, the satisfaction, the deliverance that the war had brought him. After the long record of failure and disappointment he had at last discovered a sense of purpose and identity as a soldier in the German army. Now, overnight it seemed, he saw his whole world disintegrating and everything he believed in thrown down.

In mid-October, he was caught in a British gas attack. He was lying in a hospital at Pasewalk, temporarily blinded, as the news came in, first of a German naval mutiny, then of the setting up of Soviets of workers and soldiers, and open insurrection. Finally, on November 10, Hitler learned that the kaiser had abdicated, that a republic had been declared, and that the following day the new government would accept the Allies' armistice terms.

Describing later the emotions that overwhelmed him, Hitler claimed that it was then and there, in the hospital at Pasewalk, that he decided to take up politics and devote himself to reversing Germany's defeat. In fact, it took the best part of another year, during which he drifted from day to day, with no clear ideas about his future, before he turned to politics and found an outlet for the energy that had been latent for so long. But it is true enough that it was the shock of defeat followed by the experience of revolution that finally crystallized his decision and provided the permanent background to his career.

THREE

October Revolution,
November Putsch

I

THE OUTBREAK of the revolution of February 1917, like that of
1905, took the Russian revolutionaries by surprise. Some weeks before,
Trotsky, despairing of developments in Europe, had moved to the United
States, and in January Lenin told a group of young socialists in Zurich: "We
of the older generation may not live to see the decisive battles of the coming
revolution." February 1917 was no more a spontaneous revolt of the masses
than October was to be. October was a coup d'etat, its predecessor in
February the sudden collapse of a tsarist regime which had lasted for three
hundred years but proved incapable of coping with long-standing economic
and social problems made intolerable by the strains of an unsuccessful war.
As the regime's authority crumbled it left a vacuum which was filled by
mutinous soldiers demanding an end to the war, by factory workers demanding food and labor reforms, and by peasants demanding land. As in
1905, what released these pent-up forces was not a revolutionary conspiracy
but the order given to troops to fire on demonstrators in Petrograd which
this time led to a mutiny among the soldiers. The mutiny rapidly spread to
the rest of the capital's garrison, and the government was unable to regain
control.

In the confusion that followed two self-appointed centers tentatively
assumed responsibility. One was the Petrograd Soviet, formed on the 1905
model, but this time with Soldiers' as well as Workers' Deputies, the
executive committee of which took steps to organize food supplies and
recruit a workers' militia to replace the police. The other was a provisional
committee of the Duma. When the tsar abdicated and no successor could
be found, the Russian people for the first time in its history enjoyed a
political freedom only marginally contained by the shaky and divided authority of the provisional committee and the Petrograd Soviet.

Agreement was hurriedly reached between the two bodies on setting up
a provisional government with a program promising to grant an immediate
amnesty along with freedom of speech, of association, and the other demo-

cratic freedoms, and to organize an election by universal, direct franchise of a constituent assembly which would draw up a democratic constitution for Russia. The socialist parties, the Socialist Revolutionaries (SRs), as well as the two Marxist Social Democratic parties, Mensheviks and Bolsheviks, refused to participate in the government, believing that they must retain their freedom of action and keep up the pressure on it to fulfill the democratic program and start peace negotiations.

In effect this meant that the provisional government could get its orders carried out only insofar as the Soviets permitted, since it was the Workers' and Soldiers' Deputies who controlled the actual instruments of power, such as troops, railways, and telegraphs. The Petrograd Soviet, on the other hand, had no inhibitions about issuing orders on its own. On the very day it agreed to set up the provisional government, it issued, without consultation, Order No. 1, establishing elected committees in the Petrograd barracks with the authority to distribute weapons and abolishing traditional forms of military discipline. Whether intended or not, this was rapidly extended to the whole army and was a major factor in the decomposition of the Russian forces facing the Germans.

The revolutionary parties were as divided as they were surprised— divided about their attitude to the provisional government; to the Soviets, which sprang up all over the country; to peace negotiations; to a unification of radical forces. This confusion at the top, the lack of authority in the face of anarchical conditions in the country, and the continuation of the war persisted until the autumn.

Contrary to later legends, the Bolsheviks played only a marginal role in the development of the revolution before August 1917. On the eve of the February events, their membership was fewer than 25,000 and, although this was soon expanded, they continued to have much less support than either of their rivals, the Mensheviks and the Socialist Revolutionaries, the two parties that dominated the Soviets. Nonetheless, there was a difference between the Bolsheviks' position in 1905, when they had played a similar marginal role, and 1917. The difference was Lenin's conviction that this time he could see how to harness the revolutionary flood and prevent it running into the sand.

Neither Lenin and the Bolsheviks nor the other socialist parties "made" the revolution; they did not create the grievances of the peasants about the land, the more recent anger of the workers against their exploitation, or the war-weariness of the army and the nation. But, where the other parties failed to respond decisively to these mass discontents, Lenin showed a genius for finding the slogans—peace, land, bread, workers' control—"to catalyze grievances into revolutionary energy."[1]

Lenin, however, was still abroad, fuming at his enforced inactivity and separated from Russia by the war on the Eastern Front. It was only when the Germans (in the hope of undermining the Russian will to go on fighting) agreed to allow him and other revolutionaries to travel across Germany to neutral Sweden that the Bolshevik leader finally reached the Finland Station in Petrograd on April 3. When he did so, his proposals were as much a shock to his own as to the other parties; but six months later they were to prove the key in turning a revolutionary situation into a revolution.

STALIN HAD REACHED Petrograd from Siberia three weeks before Lenin and had moved in with the Alliluyev family. Sergei Alliluyev had returned from the Caucasus and now lived with his wife and daughter in the Viborg district of the capital. Their home became Stalin's base during the revolution, and for a few days Lenin's hideout as well.

Stalin's part in 1917 was neither as prominent as portrayed by official accounts later, nor as insignificant as Trotsky and his other enemies claimed. Two other leading party members, M. K. Muranov and Lev Kamenev, had returned from Siberia with him, and the three of them at once claimed places on the Russian Bureau of the Bolshevik Party's Central Committee, taking over the editorship of *Pravda* and securing appointment as the Bolshevik representatives on the executive committee of the Petrograd Soviet.

Kamenev, the thirty-four-year-old son of a railway engineer, had studied briefly at Moscow University before moving permanently into revolutionary work. He had spent the last three years in exile in Siberia and shortly after his return to Moscow formed a partnership with Zinoviev which continued until they were expelled from the party by Stalin in the late 1920s and put to death in 1936 during Stalin's purge of the Old Bolsheviks. Kamenev had already taken a different line from Lenin in supporting the defense of Russia during the war, as opposed to Lenin's "revolutionary defeatism," and in the short period before Lenin's return in April 1917 he came out in favor of support for the provisional government and for reunification with the Mensheviks in a single party.

Stalin seems to have had no clear ideas of his own. He followed Kamenev's lead on reunification in articles that he wrote for *Pravda* and in two speeches that he made at the All-Russian Bolshevik Party Conference which met in Petrograd between March 27 and April 4. Lenin's "Letters from Afar" addressed to *Pravda* made it clear that their views clashed sharply with his own. But Stalin, ignoring the contradiction, went on to secure a unanimous vote from the party conference in favor of exploratory talks between the Bolsheviks and the Mensheviks, and was elected one of the four members of the committee to carry out the negotiations.

Lenin wasted no time in making clear his disagreement. He did not wait to disembark from the train arriving at the Finland Station before he started to attack the compromise line that Kamenev and Stalin had been following: "What's this you're writing in *Pravda?* We've seen several issues and really swore at you."[2]

The ten "April Theses" that he presented to the party conference before it broke up ruled out any thought of reunion with the Mensheviks or support for the provisional government. Throwing overboard the conventional Marxist view that a long period of time would have to elapse between the democratic-bourgeois and the socialist-proletarian revolutions, Lenin insisted that there must be an immediate transition to the socialist phase. He rejected support for the war and called, not for a parliamentary republic, but for "a republic of Soviets of Workers', Soldiers' and Peasants' Deputies throughout the land . . . abolition of the police, the Army, the bureaucracy . . . all officials to be elected and subject to recall . . . confiscation of all landlords' lands, nationalization of all land, placing it under the oversight of local Soviets . . . immediate merger of all banks into a single national bank under the oversight of the Soviet . . . changing the party program . . . changing the party name . . . and rebuilding the Socialist International." ³

Lenin's boldness in abandoning any attempt to fit events or plans into a preconceived Marxist schema shocked and further divided his party. To begin with, a majority of the other Bolshevik leaders opposed him, and some, such as Kamenev and Zinoviev, continued to do so up to the eve of the October uprising and even beyond. But his arguments appealed to the rank and file of the party, the factory workers, and the soldiers, who were impatient with the intellectuals' preoccupation with theoretical issues and responded to Lenin's clear sense of direction aimed at the capture of power as soon as possible. Lenin did not believe this could be achieved at once; they would have to work to secure a majority in the Soviets, but it must always be with this single overriding purpose in mind, prepared to take advantage of any opportunity that would advance it.

Stalin was no different from the others in finding the April Theses too radical to assimilate or even grasp at once. At a meeting of the Bolsheviks' Russian Bureau on April 6, he spoke against them, and when they were published in *Pravda* (of which he was still a coeditor), an editorial note added that they represented Lenin's personal views, not those of the party. Nonetheless before the Seventh Bolshevik Party Conference met on April 24, Stalin came around to accepting Lenin's position.* During this period he was sharing an office and working closely with him in editing *Pravda*, and the willingness he showed to understand and absorb the older man's point of view restored the relations of confidence between them which had been established in 1912.

In the course of the conference, where 150 delegates now represented a party with 80,000 members, Lenin demonstrated this by choosing Stalin to undertake the defense of his position on the two issues on which there was the strongest opposition—the April Theses and the nationality question. In

---

*The succession of conferences and congresses of all sorts that met in Petrograd during 1917 reflected—and added to—the confusion of the political situation. The Bolshevik party held a party conference and three party congresses. These should be distinguished from the All-Russian Conference of Soviets and three All-Russian Congresses of Soviets, in which the Mensheviks and SRs were represented as well as the Bolsheviks, and these yet again from the constituent assembly summoned by the provisional government.

return he intervened to recommend Stalin for election to the Central Committee, as one of the four members of its steering committee.

Lenin was building a team and he could see that Stalin had a place on it. The qualities that attracted him were those he had mentioned in recommending him to the conference—"a good worker in all responsible jobs." Not a policymaker, not an intellectual, with Trotsky's gift for moving the masses, or Lenin's own for leading the party, but a man who could be given a job and trusted to get on with it—rough, still inexperienced, but with a willingness to learn (from Lenin at any rate, which was all Lenin cared about) and with an instinct for power.

The jobs Stalin was given to do in May and June bear this out: few speeches or articles in *Pravda,* no part in the prolonged negotiations by which Lenin brought over Trotsky and his group to join the party, but much valuable work behind the scenes in organizing and negotiating between the various opposition groups in a time of continuing tension and confusion. One of his most important jobs was organizing demonstrations of soldiers and workers against continuation of the war.

The war was still a major issue. The Duma liberals who made up the majority of the provisional government sought to reassure Russia's allies that they would continue it. In May 1917 the government was strengthened by the inclusion of several Mensheviks, while the Socialist Revolutionary, Aleksandr Kerensky, became minister of war and toured the front seeking to arouse the same spirit of patriotism that had inspired the armies of the French Revolution. But the demoralization of the army had gone too far to be checked. To the peasants who made up its rank and file, revolution meant land, and few were willing to run the risk of being forestalled by their neighbors in the parceling out. Over a million men were reported to have disappeared from the army already and the numbers steadily rose as it reverted to its peasant origins. The Germans, quick to see their advantage, ordered no attacks on the eastern front and encouraged fraternization.

In contrast to the hesitations and divisions of the other parties, the Bolsheviks, adopting Lenin's line, now urged that the Russian people should put revolution before war. A demonstration organized by Stalin on June 18 brought several hundred thousand onto the streets, with an overwhelming number of banners proclaiming Bolshevik slogans. This represented a triumph for the party against its rivals, who at once accused Lenin of planning a coup.

Stalin had established an influential relationship with the Bolshevik Military Organizations (MOs), whose All-Russian Conference meeting in the capital contributed a great deal, in the shape of more than a hundred experienced and energetic agitators, to the party's capture of the June demonstration. Following that, pressure built up in the MOs to overthrow the provisional government and demand the transfer of power to the Soviets. This made a strong appeal to the soldiers, who saw themselves being ordered to the front if the war continued, and had the backing of an armed contingent of the militant Kronstadt sailors. Lenin, however, after some hesitation, decided that an attempt at a coup would risk defeat, and on July 4 called for a retreat instead of attack, just as the provisional government, with the backing of the Mensheviks and SRs on the Petrograd Soviet's executive committee, mobilized forces to crush the threat of a Bolshevik-led uprising. The Bolsheviks at this stage were almost completely isolated and Lenin was running very substantial risks.

Stalin was in the thick of the action, using his contacts with both the Bolshevik soldiers and sailors on the one hand, and the Soviet's executive on the other, to avoid bloodshed and limit the damage to the party in a trial of strength which they had lost. He was able to render a personal service to Lenin by persuading the Soviet's executive not to back a provisional government press campaign against Lenin which claimed that he had accepted financial support from the German General Staff and was acting as a German agent, an allegation to which Lenin's arrival in Petrograd by arrangement with the German military all too easily lent credence. Stalin again came to Lenin's rescue, when the provisional government issued a warrant for his arrest, by finding a refuge for him in the Alliluyevs' home before smuggling him out to take refuge in Finland. Nothing did more to cement Lenin's trust in Stalin and his practical abilities than the way he stood by him in a crisis that could have destroyed his career.

THE EVENTS of early July were a bad setback to Bolshevik hopes: Very soon Lenin and Zinoviev were in hiding, Kamenev and Trotsky were in prison, and only Stalin and Sverdlov were left to hold the party together. From the very first, however, from July 10, when he published his article on "The Most Recent Political Situation," Lenin insisted that the hostile action taken by the provisional government, and supported by the Soviets, had clarified the situation and made clear the course now to be followed by the Bolsheviks. All hope for a peaceful development had ended; Russia, he claimed, was now ruled by a dictatorship of the counterrevolutionary bourgeoisie supported by the Menshevik and SR majority who had "betrayed the revolution." The Bolsheviks must abandon the slogan "Power to the Soviets" and, instead, prepare for an armed uprising based on the workers and poor peasants. As before, it took time for Stalin to adjust to this new leap in Lenin's thinking. Only at the conclusion of the Sixth Bolshevik Party Congress (July 26 to August 3), in which he presented both the opening and closing reports, did he come out unequivocally in favor of Lenin's revised policy and carry the congress with him. By this time the Bolshevik party had trebled its membership to 240,000.

During August and September, however, Stalin fell into the background. He was again slow to grasp the significance of the quarrel between Kerensky, the young lawyer and minister for war who had become head of the re-formed provisional government in July, and General Lavr Kornilov, whom Kerensky had appointed as commander in chief of the army. Kornilov was persuaded by conservative elements that he should intervene to put an end to the revolution and restore order. His attempt ended in fiasco when the troops he ordered to march on Petrograd deserted before they reached the capital. The affair, however, led to the withdrawal of the Mensheviks from the provisional government and the breakup of the coalition, while the open threat of counterrevolution swung working-class opinion around in favor of a purely socialist government. Lenin at once recognized the change in the political situation as offering to the Bolsheviks the opportunity to seize power, and by October 10 Stalin was ready to vote with the majority of the Central Committee for an armed uprising. To his chagrin, however, he found that his part in the October Days that followed was eclipsed by the meteoric rise of Trotsky.

The son of an independent Russified Jewish farmer, who had settled on the Ukrainian steppe, the young Lev Bronstein, while still at school in Odessa, had already shown signs of intellectual brilliance and literary and linguistic gifts. Like so many Russian revolutionaries, he was drawn into underground activity while still a student and was sentenced to prison and exile before he was twenty. He took the pseudonym Trotsky when escaping with a forged passport and joined Lenin's *Iskra* group abroad. His performance as chairman of the St. Petersburg Soviet in 1905 established his preeminence as a revolutionary orator. After 1905, however, he remained a celebrated but isolated figure among the Russian émigrés, following his own line, as ready to dispute with Lenin as with the Mensheviks, and displaying the same virtuosity in writing as he did in speaking.

In August 1917 Lenin succeeded in persuading Trotsky to join the Bolshevik party, and he soon showed that his intellectual gifts were combined with similar talents as an organizer by making the Military Revolutionary Committee of the Petrograd Soviet, which he dominated, the center of the preparations for the uprising. Stalin had plenty of opportunity to take part in these but failed to grasp the importance of the MRC, did not turn up at the Central Committee for the session on the morning of October 24 when the final assignments for the uprising were made, and was left on the sidelines when the decisive action took place the following day.

Astonishingly, the revolution was over in less than forty-eight hours and with little bloodshed. Of the forces on which the Bolsheviks could rely, the workers' Red Guard, some 20,000 strong, and the sailors from the Kronstadt base and the Baltic Fleet were the most dependable. The Petrograd garrison was the uncertain factor, and it was Trotsky's success in winning them over by direct appeal that destroyed Kerensky's and the provisional government's hopes of suppressing the uprising.

Having set the policy, Lenin took little part in its execution. At the last moment he emerged from hiding and reached Trotsky's headquarters at the Smolny Institute in disguise just before midnight on the twenty-fourth. At 2 a.m. on the twenty-fifth Trotsky pulled out his watch and said, "It's begun," to which Lenin replied: "From being on the run to supreme power, that's too much!" By 3 a.m. on the twenty-sixth Kamenev was able to announce to the newly elected Second All-Russian Congress of Soviets that the Winter Palace had been captured and the members of the provisional government arrested.

As Trotsky himself later remarked: "The final act seems too brief, too dry—somehow out of correspondence with the historic scope of the events." But there was no doubt of the enthusiasm with which Lenin was greeted when he appeared to present the new government to the Congress of Soviets, in which for the first time the Bolsheviks had a majority. The Mensheviks and some of the Socialist Revolutionary delegates withdrew in protest at the Bolsheviks' seizure of power. They were assured by Trotsky as they left: "You have played out your role. Go where you belong: to the garbage heap of history." Those who remained went on, in a single session, to pass decrees pledging the Bolshevik determination to seek an immediate armistice, to conclude peace, and to expropriate all landlords' and Church lands without compensation, handing them over to the peasants for redistribution—the two issues, peace and land, that would attract maximum support for the new government.

II

THERE ARE THREE REASONS why 1917 is a key to the understanding of Stalin's psychological development. The first is that his failure to play the leading role he had dreamed of inflicted a deep and lasting trauma. As soon as he was in a position to do so, from the end of 1929, he took extraordinary steps to heal it. Records were altered or withheld; memoirs suppressed or censored; editors, historians, court painters, and filmmakers pressed into service to create a "revised" version of the most important series of events in the history of the Soviet Union.

One example will suffice. The Bolshevik leaders already in Petrograd went out to join Lenin's train before it reached the Finland Station. Brushing aside their welcome, it was then that Lenin burst out with his criticism of the line they had been taking. Stalin was apparently not among the group; no one noticed whether he was there or not. In Stalin's official biography published in 1940, this became:

> On April 3, Stalin went to Belo Ostrov to meet Lenin. It was with great joy that the two leaders of the revolution, the two leaders of Bolshevism, met after their long separation. They were both about to launch into the struggle for the dictatorship of the working class to lead the struggle of the revolutionary people of Russia. During the journey to Petrograd Stalin informed Lenin of the state of affairs in the party and of the progress of the revolution. [4]

The figure of Trotsky, who had unquestionably played a role second only to that of Lenin—the leading role in the actual seizure of power—was expunged and replaced by that of Stalin. Lenin remained the great leader who returned to Russia from abroad; Stalin was now elevated to the same level with him, as the leader who had never left Russia, and greeted Lenin on his return.

Although Stalin sought to disguise the fact under the appearance of modesty, these changes would never have been made except on his instructions. They were intended to bolster the cult of Stalin, which was as essential to his regime as the "Hitler myth" was to the Third Reich. But this by itself is too simple an explanation, for, while Stalin might disavow the cult, the "evidence" that he had played as commanding a role as Lenin in 1917 was as necessary to his own self-image as to its public presentation, as necessary psychologically as it was politically. Those who worked most closely with him learned that anyone who ventured to query his version, or even omitted to affirm their belief in it, could pay with their lives. Investigation of those who were eliminated in the purges of the 1930s reveals a surprising number who, as participants in 1917, had different recollections and had even, in some cases, published them.

A second consequence of his failure in 1917 was Stalin's psychological need—in addition to reasons of policy, economics, and politics—to match Lenin's revolution with his own. This led to the even more drastic upheaval of 1929 through 1933 in which the industrialization of Russia and the collectivization of her peasantry were carried through by force—the "Second Revolution," without which, Stalin could argue, that of 1917 would have been left incomplete, without a future.

Both these reasons look to the future. The third reason why 1917 was important for Stalin refers immediately to the period 1917–21: not the contribution Stalin made to the revolution, which was not in any way decisive, but the decisive contribution the revolution made to his development. After the four blank years of exile, he was given the opportunity to learn from the concentrated experience of being at the center of one of the great episodes of revolutionary history, and to work closely with one of the outstanding—many would say, the most outstanding—of modern revolutionary leaders.

Stalin's capacity to learn was one of the advantages he had over Trotsky. It appears, for example—after his failure to grasp the boldness of both Lenin's reversals of policy in April and July—in the ability he showed, given time, to absorb and internalize them. These were qualities Lenin could appreciate and use. They were enough to secure Stalin a place in the Council of People's Commissars (abbreviated to Sovnarkom), the name given to the new government's cabinet, and even in the inner cabinet of three Bolsheviks (Lenin, Trotsky, Stalin) and two left Social Revolutionaries. That meant working closely alongside Lenin which, as the earlier period April–July had shown, was the situation in which Stalin learned most readily.

Admiring Lenin, as he undoubtedly did, he must have asked himself what were Lenin's special gifts as a leader. It was not just his intelligence and power of argument, which gave him his unchallenged ascendancy in the party. It was certainly not the gift of foresight or an infallible judgment, since Lenin frequently failed to see correctly what was going to happen. He failed, for example, to foresee the outbreak of revolution in Russia in 1917; he misjudged completely the chances of the European revolution, on which he counted to save the Russian; and he never grasped the consequences for Russia or socialism of the methods he used to carry through his revolution. No, the qualities Lenin possessed that most impressed Stalin were his single-mindedness and power of concentration; his ability to see and seize an opportunity, then bend everything, including his mistakes, to his purpose; his unshakable confidence that he was right, and with this the will to succeed, the determination not to be beaten.

WHEN LENIN reached the Finland Station in April 1917 it was this clarity of mind, driving force, and total commitment, by contrast with the confusion and divided counsels of the others, that had turned the party around and enabled it, against all the odds, to capture power. Lenin, however, had devoted little time in advance to thinking about the transition from capitalism to socialism in a country as backward as Russia. He repeated Napoleon's dictum: *"On s'engage—et puis on voit!"* When he met the Congress of Soviets on the morrow of the insurrection he declared: "We shall now proceed to construct the socialist order," as if it were simply a matter of drawing up plans and issuing decrees.

In practice the seizure of power turned out to be relatively easy: The difficult part began only when the Bolsheviks had taken over the government, with a lost war on their hands, with a social upheaval still in progress, with an economy that had virtually collapsed, and with the prospect of civil war.

Lenin's priority was the same as before the revolution: Then everything had to be subordinated to the seizure of power; now, everything had to be subordinated to retaining it, at any price. "The question of power is the fundamental question of every revolution"—or, in the most famous of all Lenin's remarks: *"Kto kogo?"* or "Who whom?" ("Who masters whom?").

Marx had proposed that the transition from capitalism to socialism should be managed by a dictatorship of the proletariat. But he had visualized this as being established at the end of a long process of industrialization, during which the proletariat would have become the largest element in society. In Russia such a process had only begun at the end of the nineteenth century, and the industrial proletariat was still only a small minority in a country where the overwhelming majority were peasants with very different interests. A dictatorship of the proletariat in Russia meant, therefore, not majority rule, as Marx had seen it, but a minority imposing its will on the majority.

Lenin did not draw back from such a conclusion. As it had done in making the revolution, the party must act *in the name of* the proletariat. A majority of the party leadership, including Stalin and Trotsky, supported him and called for an all-Bolshevik government; when they reluctantly agreed to accept the left Social Revolutionaries as junior partners, it was on the understanding that the Bolsheviks should have a majority of places and be able to enforce their program. A minority, however, including Zinoviev, Kamenev, and Aleksei Rykov, was prepared to resign from the Council of People's Commissars rather than accept Lenin's view, arguing that it was essential to form a government as representative as possible of all the parties in the Soviets. They argued for Mensheviks and right Socialist Revolutionaries to be included as well as Bolsheviks and left SRs, claiming that a purely Bolshevik government would be able to maintain itself only by political terror, leading to the betrayal and ruin of the revolution.

Their objection was overruled, Lenin insisting that such a broad-based coalition would lead only to compromise and the abdication of power. The dissidents were persuaded to rejoin the government, but the same issue resurfaced when the party had to decide whether to allow the elections to a constituent assembly to be held. Generations of Russian revolutionaries had looked forward to the summoning of such an assembly elected by all the people and the constitution it would draw up as the signal for the opening of a new era in Russia; before its fall the provisional government had fixed a date in November for the elections to it to be held.

Lenin had no intention of surrendering the party's newly won power to a hostile assembly, but a majority of the leadership took the view that it was politically inexpedient to cancel or postpone the elections, as Lenin wished. As he had foreseen, however, the Bolsheviks received only a quarter of the votes and, when the assembly met (January 5, 1918), they could not prevent the majority rejecting the decrees passed by the Second Congress of Soviets immediately after the October Revolution, and accepting instead the right Socialist Revolutionaries' proposal to make their program, not the Bolsheviks', the order of the day.

Lenin did not hesitate. The Bolsheviks followed by the left SRs withdrew from the assembly. Red Guards then prevented it from meeting for any further sessions, and it was dissolved by a decree of the Central Executive Committee of the Soviets, which the Bolsheviks dominated.

When some of his own followers questioned Lenin's argument in favor of such action, he warned them:

> Every attempt, direct or indirect, to consider the question of the Constituent Assembly from a formal, legal point of view, within the framework of ordinary bourgeois democracy, ignoring the class struggle and civil war, is a betrayal of the cause of the proletariat, and an adoption of the bourgeois standpoint. [5]

Shortly afterwards the Third Congress of Soviets met the government's need for legitimization by declaring itself the supreme authority and approving the government's action in dispersing the constituent assembly. The task of drafting a constitution was turned over to a committee in which the Bolshevik members numbered twelve out of fifteen. Stalin was included to make sure that its recommendations to place supreme legislative power formally in the Congress of Soviets and its Central Executive Committee should not interfere with the undisputed control of both bodies and of the government, the Council of People's Commissars (Sovnarkom), by the Bolshevik party. "All power to the Soviets" was retained as a constitutional fiction on the understanding that, as Zinoviev made explicit at the Eighth Party Congress in March 1919, "All fundamental questions of policy, international and domestic, must be decided by the Central Committee of our own party."

Well before that, the new regime had taken steps to provide itself with the means to deal with any challenge to its authority. Faced with the threat of a strike by public-service employees, on December 7 Sovnarkom, with Lenin's full approval, authorized the creation of an Extraordinary Commission (known for short as the Cheka), headed by the Pole Felix Dzerzhinsky, to combat counterrevolutionary activities and sabotage. In speaking to his fellow commissars about the internal dangers confronting them, Dzerzhinsky declared:

> We need to send to the front—the most dangerous and cruel of fronts—determined, hard, dedicated comrades ready to do anything in defense of the Revolution. Do not think that I seek forms of revolutionary justice; we are not now in need of justice. It is war now—face to face, a fight to the finish. Life or death![6]

Dzerzhinsky did not exaggerate: the dangers were real enough, and the Cheka, the first political police organization of the Soviet Union (and a model for the police states of the twentieth century), was indispensable. Such was the price to be paid for "giving a push to history," and Lenin did not blanch at it. Shortly before the insurrection, in September 1917, he had written:

> A revolution, a real, profound, "people's" revolution to use Marx's expression, is the incredibly complicated and painful process of the death of the old and birth of the new social order, of the mode of life of tens of millions of people. Revolution is a most intense, furious, desperate class struggle and civil war. Not a single great revolution in history has taken place without civil war.[7]

In Dzerzhinsky, who had already spent eleven of his forty years in prison or exile, Lenin had found the man he was looking for, as deeply committed and incorruptible as himself, prepared to act the part of the Bolshevik Revolution's Fouquier-Tinville, the public prosecutor of Robespierre's Revolutionary Tribunal, who sent thousands to the guillotine in the 1790s. In the five years before Lenin's death at the beginning of 1924, the Cheka is estimated to have carried out at least 200,000 executions, a figure to be compared with the 14,000 executed under the tsars in their last half-century of rule up to 1917.[8]

THE MOST IMMEDIATE THREAT in the winter of 1917–18 came, however, not from the enemy within but from the enemy without, in the form of the German army. All Lenin's calculations had been based on the belief that revolution in Russia would touch off a world, or at least a European, revolution. Without this, he did not believe the Russian Revolution could survive. Peace negotiations with the Germans began at Brest-Litovsk in December 1917 and were turned by Trotsky into a platform from which to appeal to the peoples of the belligerent nations against their governments. But the revolution in Germany and in the rest of Europe failed to materialize, while the peace terms presented by the Germans required the surrender of Russian Poland, the Baltic states, and part of the Ukraine. Refusing to be bound by diplomatic conventions, Trotsky displayed a forensic brilliance that baffled and exasperated the representatives of the Central Powers. But when, after more than two months' delaying tactics, he sought to cap his performance by declaring that Russia was withdrawing from the war, without accepting the German demands, the German army's reply was to resume its advance on Petrograd. Trotsky's attempt to win sufficient time for revolution in Central Europe to remove the German threat had come to nothing.

For two months a bitterly divided Russian leadership had debated what to do. The majority, headed by Bukharin, and supported by the left SRs, called for a "revolutionary war against German imperialism." To accede to the German demands would mean surrendering all the territory Russia had acquired since the sixteenth century. Trotsky urged that they should vote for "neither war nor peace," a policy that Stalin dismissed as no policy at all, belonging to the realm of fiction, not of reality. Only Lenin insisted that they had no option but to sign on the Germans' terms.

Stalin, out of his depth in the discussion, said little and found it hard to make up his mind. "Maybe we don't have to sign the treaty?" he asked, to which Lenin replied: "If you don't, you're signing a death warrant for the Soviet regime within three weeks. I haven't the slightest hesitation. I'm not looking for a 'revolutionary phrase.'" Lenin's firmness convinced him. To those who spoke of betraying the revolution, Stalin retorted: "There is no revolutionary movement in the West; there are no facts of a revolutionary movement, only a potentiality; and we cannot base ourselves on a mere potentiality." On no other issue, however, did Lenin encounter such opposition, which was renewed at the subsequent Party Congress.

The German advance met no resistance from Russian troops, who surrendered in droves. Within days the Germans would be in the capital. Only then, when the continued existence of the Soviet regime was endangered, were six of the fifteen members of the party's Central Committee besides Lenin brought to accept his argument, that they had to buy time with space, and live to fight another day, when all that had been surrendered could be recaptured. Four (including Bukharin) voted against; four (including Trotsky) abstained. Once again, the one consideration to which everything had to be sacrificed was not to risk losing power. Lenin added that, if they would not accept his view, he would resign immediately.

The desperate debate over the treaty, finally signed at Brest-Litovsk on March 3, 1918 (NS), was an experience none of those who went through it ever forgot, least of all Stalin, for whom it was vividly recalled when he faced a second German threat twenty years later. As a result of the territorial losses dictated by the Germans, the population of the tsarist empire would be reduced by no less than a third. In economic terms the loss represented 32 percent of Russia's cultivable land, 27 percent of her railways, 54 percent of her industry, and 89 percent of her coal mines. The terms were much harsher than those imposed on Germany by the Treaty of Versailles, which the Germans denounced as unheard of in their severity.

One immediate consequence was the move of the government to Moscow, out of reach of the German forces, which were now only eighty miles away from Petrograd. Another was a double split in the ruling coalition. A left-wing revolt inside the party (now renamed the Communist party) was led by Bukharin, who was outraged by the betrayal of the ideals of revolutionary socialism in the name of expediency. At the same time the left SRs left the government, denouncing Lenin as a traitor who had sold out Russia to the Germans.

The first split was contained after further debate showed an overwhelming majority in both the Seventh Party Congress and the Fourth Congress of Soviets in favor of Lenin. But the left Socialist Revolutionaries' opposition grew in force, culminating on July 6, 1918, in unsuccessful attempts at uprisings in Moscow and Petrograd and the assassination of the German Ambassador, Count Mirbach. The government had only a handful of troops it could rely on, and so precarious was its position that when their commander, I. I. Vatsetis, was summoned to the Kremlin Lenin's first question was, "Comrade, can we hold out till morning?"

On this occasion, the left Socialist Revolutionaries were treated with relative leniency, but when Moisei Uritsky, a member of the Communist Central Committee, was assassinated and Lenin severely wounded at the end of August, an official campaign of mass terror was launched against all who were suspected of opposition, including the taking of hostages and summary executions as well as mass arrests. By November, the total of executions in the Petrograd region alone was put at 1,300. [10] Even more serious, by then the country had been plunged into a full-scale civil war, with intervention by the Western Allies added to it.

1, 2. *Above*, Stalin's schoolclass *c.* 1889; *opposite*, Hitler's schoolclass *c.* 1899, when both were about ten. By a striking coincidence, each appears in the center of the back row of his class with a touch of defiance in his pose.

3, 4. The most important formative influence in Stalin's life was that of exile; in Hitler's, that of war. The top picture here shows Stalin in exile in Siberia, third from the left in the back row. Others from whom he later broke were removed from subsequent versions of the photograph. *Below,* the photographs from Stalin's pre-war police dossier.

Бакинское Губернское Жандармск

5, 6. *Above,* the famous photograph of Hitler in the Odeonsplatz, Munich, on August 14, 1914, greeting the news of war. Hoffman, the photographer, who later became Hitler's personal photograpHer, picked his face out of the crowd. *Below,* Hitler, seated on the right, recuperating away from the front after being wounded.

7, 8. *Above,* Stalin the general secretary *c.* 1924, the year of Lenin's death.
Below, left to right, with Rykov, Zinoviev, and Bukharin in the same period.

9, 10. *Above,* the defendants at the trial after the unsuccessful putsch of November 1923: *left to right,* Pernet, Weber, Frick, Kriebel, Ludendorff, Hitler, Brückner, Röhm, and Wagner. *Below,* Hitler speaking at a meeting of the leaders of the Nazi Party in 1925. The modest origins of the party are clearly visible.

11, 12. *Above,* the Eighth Bolshevik Party Congress, 1919. Trotsky is away at the front, and Stalin takes the opportunity to seat himself at Lenin's right hand. Kalinin is on Lenin's left. *Below,* the funeral of Felix Dzerzhinsky, the founder of the Cheka, Moscow, July 1926: *left to right,* Rykov, Yagoda (in cap), Kalinin, Trotsky, Kamenev, Stalin, Rakovsky (obscured by Stalin's shoulder), and Bukharin. Rykov, Yagoda, Kamenev, and Bukharin were all shot after the Moscow Trials. Trotsky was assassinated by a Stalinist agent in 1940. Rakovsky was imprisoned and exiled by Stalin during the purges.

13, 14. *Above right,* Hitler rose from street-corner orator in Munich (1923) via the electoral campaigns of the 1930s to his appointment as chancellor; *above left,* leaving a party meeting in 1930.

15, 16. *Left,* greeting President von Hindenburg on Potsdam Day, March 21, 1933. *Below,* joking with Göring and Himmler after consolidating his power by purging Röhm and the SA leadership in 1934.

17, 18. The collectivization of the Russian peasantry: *above,* a typical village commune *c.* 1930; *below,* the organization of labor groups—the second line of the banner reads, "Liquidate the kulaks as a class."

19. One of the very few surviving photographs of the results of the famine in the Ukraine in the 1930s.

III

UNLIKE HITLER, Stalin came to power as the result of a genuine revolution. But Stalin did not make that revolution any more than he created the party that carried it out. The central figure in both cases was Lenin. Stalin suffered from a disadvantage that did not affect Hitler: He had a predecessor whose achievement was bound to overshadow any successor. How Stalin dealt with that problem is one of the most interesting features of his career. In 1918–19, however, the question was how the Bolsheviks, even with Lenin to lead them, could hope to retain the power they had seized.

Lenin's answer was: a German revolution, with which the Bolsheviks could join up and revolutionize the whole of Europe. What Lenin hoped for, the rest of Europe feared. The opening sentence of the *Communist Manifesto*—"A specter is haunting Europe, the specter of Communism"— was exaggerated as a description of Europe in 1848, but not of Europe in the years 1918 to 1923. It is this that provides the link between the events that brought Stalin and the other Bolshevik leaders to power in Russia, and the situation in Germany that gave Hitler the chance to launch himself into politics. Hitler had hoped that the Russian Revolution would open the way to a German victory; instead, it appeared that the German defeat might open the way to a German revolution.

The abrupt collapse of the wartime dictatorship of the German military authorities, the abdication of the kaiser and the proclamation of a German republic strengthened this impression. The *Berliner Tageblatt* declared on November 10 that "the greatest of all revolutions" had triumphed on the streets of Berlin, where enthusiastic crowds cheered the hoisting of the red flag over the royal palace.

Councils (frequently called Soviets) of Soldiers and Workers were set up throughout Germany, and an executive council elected by those in Berlin. This regarded itself as the equivalent of the executive council of the Petrograd Soviet and disputed power with the six-man Council of People's Commissars (another term borrowed from the Russians), the provisional government formed by the two socialist parties, the Majority SPD and the more radical Independent Socialists (USPD), who had split from the Majority SPD in April 1917 on the issue of support for the war, which the USPD regarded as incompatible with the principles of socialism.

It is clear enough now that there was little chance that the fall of the German monarchy could have been turned into a revolution that would have really changed the balance of forces in German society. The German labor movement and the Majority Social Democrats looked to the February, not the October Revolution in Russia for inspiration. Only a minority of the German left was in favor of the radical course pursued by the Bolsheviks and by no means were all of those prepared to adopt Lenin's tactics of subordinating everything to the seizure of power. The objective of the

Majority Social Democrats was to end the war and set up a constitutional democratic republic committed to a program of social reform. The last thing they wanted to see was a replay in Germany of the revolutionary upheaval that had led to civil war in Russia.

Between January 1919 and April 1920, however, there was a whole series of strikes and demonstrations in Berlin and the industrial districts of Germany, which frequently led to fighting. In the Ruhr, in the spring of 1920, this assumed the proportions of civil war when an armed force of 50,000 workers initially drove army and Freikorps units (the irregular volunteer corps formed from officers, NCOs, and soldiers of the old army) out of the Ruhr, and was crushed only after heavy losses. These spontaneous outbursts gave expression to a powerful and widespread wave of social protest, but it never found leaders capable of organizing it into an effective political force. One of the intriguing "might-have-beens" of history is what would have happened if Lenin had been born a German in the most highly industrialized country in Europe, with the largest working-class movement, instead of in Russia, the most backward and so least promising country in which to launch a Marxist revolution.

The Majority Socialist leaders regarded such outbursts as the work of extremists bent on sabotaging the republican regime they were trying to create. Rather than give way, they were prepared to turn for support to the leaders of the Reichswehr (the German army) and to see regular army units as well as Freikorps forces used to suppress them. The Freikorps retained close connections with the regular army and played a leading role in restoring order and breaking the power of the Workers' and Soldiers' Councils, as well as in fighting Poles and Russians in the Baltic states and the German-Polish borderlands. Sharing with Hitler the authoritarian mentality and nationalistic outlook of the *Frontkämpfer* (the "front-line fighters"), they were to prove a fruitful source of recruitment for the Nazis and other extremist organizations.

The rival Independent Socialist and Communist groups lacked leaders capable of harnessing mass support for their program of revolutionary socialism, and the movement remained fragmented with ill-defined objectives. Apart from the Ruhr miners' "wildcat" demand for nationalization of the pits, which was more a syndicalist ("workers' control") answer to their immediate material grievances than the first step toward a socialist economy, those who went on strike and fought were moved by class hostility against the employers, hatred of the military, and bitterness against a government with socialist ministers ready to use troops against workers. With the "pacification" of the Ruhr in April 1920, the wave of strikes and demonstrations was spent, leaving the radical left defeated and the German working class permanently divided.

For those who shared the Marxist view that no revolution was worthy of the name unless, like the 1917 revolution in Russia, it led to a permanent alteration in the relationship between classes, the German revolution of

1918–20 was not a revolution at all. At best, like the German revolution of 1848–49, it was a *revolution manqué*. To borrow a phrase that historian A. J. P. Taylor applied to that earlier revolution: Between 1918 and 1920, too, German history reached a turning point—and failed to turn.

That is how it appears now; but it was not at all how it appeared at the time. With the example of what revolution had led to in Russia (which lost nothing in the telling), fear of its spreading was a prominent feature of European politics after the war even in a country like Britain which had not suffered defeat, and which did not experience anything worse than a series of strikes. It was much more acute in Central Europe, where war and defeat were followed by sweeping changes in frontiers, foreign occupation, inflation, continuing unrest, and fighting. Soviet propaganda pointed to an imminent revolution in Germany as the decisive step toward world revolution, and the news of Soviet republics being established in Hungary and Bavaria in the spring of 1919, and of the Red Army advancing into Poland in the summer of 1920 gave substance to people's fears. Further Communist revolts took place in central Germany in 1921 and 1923, and in Hamburg as well in October 1923.

The fact that all these attempts to seize power failed, and were easily crushed, just as the Poles succeeded in driving the Red Army back out of Poland, did not remove the impression that Germany only narrowly escaped revolution between 1918 and 1923, an impression that the Communists (Kommunistische Partei Deutschlands, KPD for short) did all they could to keep alive with the argument that, if the working-class movement had not been divided and "betrayed" by the Majority SPD, the revolution would have succeeded—and would do so next time, if the workers united behind the KPD.

To keep alive this myth of a Marxist revolution that had narrowly failed and might be repeated was as much to the advantage of the radical right as it was to the radical left and a major factor in the rise of Fascist parties throughout Europe. The advantage they derived from it was increased in Germany by two other developments.

The first was the compulsion that the provisional republican government felt to turn to the German officer corps and to the officials of the former imperial civil service for help in suppressing the threat of revolution and holding the country together after the defeat. This opened the way for the former governing elite—officers, officials, judges, the professional and managerial classes—to retain much of their power under the new dispensation.

The second was that, far from this reconciling them to the republican regime, which did its best to preserve Germany from suffering the same sort of experience as Russia, the former governing classes, still powerfully entrenched, blamed the republic for the German defeat, for acceptance of the "Carthaginian" peace terms imposed by the Allies, and the substitution, in place of the strong authoritarian rule to which Germans were accustomed, of a "weak" democratic government that "encouraged" disorder and rebellion. Such a version of events was a travesty of the truth, but it enabled its authors to push the responsibility for losing the war onto the parliamentary regime and provided an outraged public opinion with a scapegoat for the national humiliations that had followed.

In the elections held in January 1919 to elect a national assembly charged with drawing up a constitution for the new republic, 76 percent of the votes had gone to the three parties that supported a parliamentary democracy,* if only as the best safeguard available against rule by the Workers' and Soldiers' Councils. The assembly drew up a constitution (known as the Weimar constitution after the town in which the national assembly met) which, for the first time in German history, established a genuine democratic parliamentary regime, the Weimar Republic (frequently abbreviated to "Weimar"). A second election, however, held in June 1920, to elect the first Reichstag, or parliament, sharply reduced the 1919 majority of 76 percent to a minority of 47 percent. The parties supporting the new democratic regime polled eleven million votes in 1920 in place of the nineteen million of 1919, and were faced with a double opposition—a right-wing opposition that had nearly doubled its vote since 1919 (from 5.6 to over 9 million), and a radical left that had more than doubled its vote, from just over 2 million to 5.3.

Thus, ten months after the promulgation of the democratic constitution, its founders and supporters found themselves in a minority that they were never again able to convert into a majority. As a result the Weimar Republic was placed on the defensive and never achieved stable democratic government. Between 1920 and 1930, the average life span of its twenty coalition governments was no more than eight and a half months, and the defeat of the one that lasted longest, the Grand Coalition of 1928–30, was followed by the virtual suspension of the constitution in favor of extra-parliamentary presidential cabinets.

The radical left opposition, the Independent Socialists and the Communists, was consistently presented as the main threat to German democracy, but the real danger was from the right. The common ground of all the right-wing groups was nationalism and the desire to wipe out the "shame" of 1918, the wound to pride, particularly pride in the German army, which many Germans refused to accept had ever been defeated.

Before the defeat of 1918, nationalism had played a unifying rather than a divisive role in German society. The term "social imperialism" had been coined to describe its function in diverting social tensions outwards, into an aggressive foreign and military policy. This was a phenomenon to be observed in other countries as well, such as Britain (Jingoism), but it was

---

*These were the Majority Social Democrats, the Catholic Center party, and the liberal German Democratic party (DDP). Appendix I provides a breakdown of votes in all German national elections between January 1919 and January 1933. There is a brief characterization of the parties in the glossary.

particularly marked in Germany, the most popular image of which among its own people was that of a "late arrival" among the Great Powers which had to compensate for this by a vigorous assertion of its "rights." The function of postwar German nationalism was the reverse of this: The aggressiveness of the right-wing nationalist parties was turned inwards, against the republic, the government of the "November criminals," which had betrayed their country and acquiesced in its humiliation. Patriotism was used as a rallying cry to unite in overthrowing the regime, not, as before 1918, to unite in its support.

The pace and scale of economic and social change in Germany between unification in the 1860s and the outbreak of war in 1914 had produced serious conflicts of interest and social tensions. These had been temporarily suspended during the war, but had already reappeared before its end, and were intensified by the defeat of nationalist hopes and the fear of revolution. From 1919 to 1923 Germany was a society shaken to its foundations. This particularly affected the large German *Mittelstand* (middle class).

In the early part of the twentieth century Germans distinguished between an upper middle class (successful professionals, wealthy entrepreneurs and directors of big companies, members of the higher ranks of the civil service), increasingly identified with the historic upper class, and a lower middle class of petit bourgeoisie, the real *Mittelstand*. This in turn was divided between the *Alte Mittelstand,* independent shopkeepers, merchants, and businessmen, operating on a limited scale, often with family businesses, as well as small and medium farmers—essentially the self-employed—and the *Neue Mittelstand,* the army of clerks, petty officials, and white-collar employees in commercial concerns and the civil service (including teachers)—essentially salary dependent and very status conscious.

In the twenty-five years before 1914 the *Mittelstand* (often described as the losers in the process of modernization) had come under the increasing economic pressure of large-scale corporate business from above and the increasing social pressure of organized labor from below. This had already produced a move toward a right-wing radicalism—militant, anti-Semitic, nationalistic—in *Mittelstand* politics. In postwar Germany, with its political instability, scenes of violence, and inflation, the *Mittelstand* felt additionally threatened by the crumbling of familiar landmarks and accepted values and by insecurity about its future.

The social attitudes and nationalism of the older generations were characteristically combined with a desire to see the monarchy restored. But a radicalization of attitudes had also begun to take place before the war among the younger generation as part of a revolt that spread across frontiers and to which French and Italian writers as well as German contributed the general stock of ideas on which postwar Fascist movements were to draw. De Tocqueville had shown his usual perceptiveness when he wrote to the French prophet of racism, the Comte de Gobineau, after the latter's *Essai sur l'inégalité des races humaines* (Essay on the Inequality of the Races of Mankind) was published in 1853–55:

> I think that your book is fated to return to France from abroad, especially from Germany. Alone in Europe, the Germans possess the particular talent of becoming impassioned with what they take as abstract truths, without considering their practical consequences.[11]

Among these "truths" were those of racial superiority, anti-Semitism, and Social Darwinism. The "new wave" of the turn of the century acclaimed the heroic ideal and "living dangerously" against the bourgeois ethos of materialism and conservatism, and pitted feeling and intuition against intellect, the cult of the irrational against the Englightenment belief in rationality, action against reason.

The war brought to a peak the feeling among German intellectuals of separateness from the West and fused German nationalism with the repudiation of Western values: *Kultur* versus civilization, the *völkische* belief in the uniqueness of German culture as opposed to the universalism of the Enlightenment. Both *Kultur* and *Volk* (with its adjective *völkisch*) were key words in German right-wing ideology, the emotional force of which is inadequately conveyed in English as "culture," "folk" or "race." According to Oswald Spengler, whose *Decline of the West* had a tremendous impact when published in German in 1918–22, a *Kultur* has a soul by contrast with a civilization, a French concept representing "the most artificial and external state of which humanity is capable." German use of the word carried with it the conviction of the superiority of German *Kultur,* as expressing an intensity of feeling and idealism not found in other European cultures.

Similarly, *Volk* and *völkisch* expressed what was felt to be a much more comprehensive and emotionally charged German experience, imperfectly understood or shared, if at all, by those content to describe themselves as "peoples" or "nations." They signified the union of a group of people, bound together in a common racial identity that was the source of their individuality and creativity. *Volk* was a word that was never far from Hitler's lips. It was "rooted" in its native soil, and its "organic" community (*Volksgemeinschaft*) protected its members from feelings of alienation. Translated into political terms, the *völkische* ideology glorified war and "renewal by destruction" over internationalism and pacificism, the exaltation of national power and national unity over individual freedom, of the authoritarian state and elitism over parliamentary democracy and egalitarianism.

These feelings were not dispelled but strengthened by the debacle of 1918. For the *Frontkämpfer,* who found it difficult enough to adapt to the banality of a peacetime existence, it was intolerable that the war should have ended in the defeat of Germany and the triumph of the West. They were prepared to listen to anyone who could expose the treachery by which this had been accomplished, providing scapegoats in the form of Jews and Marxists, and offering the hope of revenge.

THE MAN WHO WAS to fill that role was discharged from his hospital at the end of November 1918 and made his way back to Munich through a country he did not recognize. As great a shock as Germany's defeat was the spectacle (as it appeared to him) of those whom he most detested— Social Democrats, Bolsheviks, and Jews (he did not distinguish among them)—as Germany's new masters. In Munich, the Wittelsbach dynasty after a reign of more than seven hundred years had abdicated in the face of a workers' and soldiers' uprising led by an idealistic Jewish left-wing socialist, Kurt Eisner, and a Bavarian republic had been proclaimed. Hitler, with no occupation or home to return to, clung to his uniform and reported to the Munich barracks of his regiment, only to find the buildings filthy, all discipline abandoned, and a Soldiers' Council installed.

He got away by volunteering for guard duty in a prisoner-of-war camp at Traunstein and did not return to Munich until March 1919. By then the situation had been inflamed by the assassination of Eisner, shot by Count Arco-Valley, a right-wing officer. The Founding Congress of the Third (Communist) International, meeting in Moscow, with delegations from nineteen countries, called on the workers of all countries to unite in support of the Soviet Union, the Workers' Fatherland. In Hungary, a Soviet republic was set up by Béla Kun, a Jewish Communist who was reported in the German press to have appointed twenty-five Jewish commissars out of a total of thirty-two. In April, the moderate Social Democratic government of Bavaria, which had taken over after Eisner's murder, was forced to move out of Munich by a left-wing coup proclaiming a Soviet republic, the leadership of which was taken over by three Russian émigrés, two of whom were also Jewish. At the May Day celebration in Red Square, Lenin declared: "The liberated working class is celebrating its anniversary not only in Soviet Russia, but in Soviet Hungary and Soviet Bavaria." He spoke too soon: In Munich and Budapest the Reds were crushed by force.

Hitler was an eyewitness of the Communist seizure of power in Munich, and of the counterattack by the army and Freikorps that ended it, and that was accompanied by a series of massacres, costing hundreds of lives. Only after the episode was over did he come to the surface, giving evidence to an army commission set up to identify those involved in the Soviet regime. He was then sent by the District Army Command to take part in an indoctrination course conducted by "nationally minded professors" at Munich University.

One of the professors, the historian K. A. von Müller, one day found his way out of the lecture hall blocked by a group,

> which stood fascinated around a man in their midst who was addressing them without pause and with growing passion in a strangely guttural

voice. I had the strange feeling that the man was feeding on the excitement which he himself had whipped up. I saw a pale, thin face beneath a drooping, unsoldierly strand of hair, with close-cropped mustache and strikingly large, light blue eyes coldly glistening with fanaticism.[12]

From this, Hitler, who was still on the army payroll, graduated to an "enlightenment squad" attached to the Lechfeld camp for returning soldiers, where he began to develop his gift of persuasion. It was in this capacity that Hitler produced a reply for his superior officer, Captain Karl Mayr, to a request for a position paper on "the danger Jewry constitutes to our people today." It is his first surviving statement (dated September 16, 1919) on a question that he was to make uniquely his own. In it he drew a significant distinction:

> Anti-Semitism on purely emotional grounds will find its ultimate expression in the form of pogroms. The anti-Semitism of reason, however, must lead to the planned legal opposition to and elimination of the privileges of the Jews. Its ultimate goal, however, must absolutely be the removal of the Jews altogether. Only a government of national power and never a government of national impotence will be capable of both.[13]

In his political testament dictated in the underground bunker in Berlin in 1945 immediately before his death, his views had not changed. His final paragraph returned to the earliest of his obsessions:

> Above all, I charge the leaders of the nation and those under them to scrupulous observance of the laws of race, to merciless opposition to the universal poisoner of all peoples, international Jewry.[14]

Hitler was also employed by the Munich District Command in another capacity, as a "liaison man" to investigate the bewildering variety of right-wing radical groups that proliferated in Bavaria. It was in this role that, on September 12, 1919, he visited one such group, the German Workers' party, founded by a locksmith from the Munich railway shops, Anton Drexler, and a sports journalist, Karl Harrer. In the course of the discussion, another visitor proposed the secession of Bavaria from the Reich and its union with Austria. Hitler could not listen to this without bursting in and making a furious attack on the speaker. Drexler was impressed by his fluency and urged him to come again, pressing into his hands a pamphlet he had written, *My Political Awakening*.

Hitler's report was not enthusiastic: The group had no idea of how to recruit a wider following, and not much wish to. But if Hitler meant to enter politics, he had to start somewhere. None of the existing parties satisfied him, or would offer scope to an unknown newcomer. Here, however, was the nucleus of an organization, small and obscure enough to be turned into something different, into a party capable (as none of the existing right-wing parties had shown themselves to be) of attracting the masses in the way both Lueger and his opponents, the Social Democrats, had in Vienna.

So, after a second visit, this time to a committee meeting, and two days' hesitation (always a characteristic of Hitler's decisions), he accepted an invitation to join the German Workers' party as the member responsible for recruitment and propaganda. He immediately set about writing invitations and sending out announcements of a public meeting. When it took place, on October 16, 1919, with just over a hundred people in the audience, he electrified those present by his passionate outpouring and made a collection of 300 marks.

> I talked for thirty minutes, and what I had always felt deep down in my heart, without being able to put it to the test, was here proved to be true: I could make a good speech.[15]

It was to prove a momentous discovery.

The meeting in October 1919 was not large enough for Hitler to show the effect he could achieve, given the chance. That came on February 24, 1920, when an audience of nearly 2,000 filled the Festsaal of the Hofbräuhaus. Hitler was not billed as the principal speaker, and when he did speak he had to face noisy opposition, which led to fighting on the floor of the hall. But he mastered the uproar, secured agreement to changing the name of the party to the National Socialist German Workers' Party (soon shortened to Nazi), and insisted on presenting the twenty-five points of its "unchangeable" program, with the demand for a "yes or no" from the audience.

In retrospect Hitler exaggerated his success into a triumph, which contemporary accounts in the press do not bear out. But it is true that, for him, the experience was decisive. This is the point at which the decision to devote himself to politics became effective. From now on he set to work to develop the gift of arousing the emotions of a mass meeting and made it the foundation of his career. It was not his only gift but it was one in which no other German politician could rival him and one that distinguished him clearly from Stalin, who never possessed it.

IV

SHORTLY AFTER the Hofbräuhaus speech (April 1, 1920), Hitler was discharged from the army, although he retained important links with it. Like Stalin twenty years before, he became a full-time agitator, finding such financial support as he could and living in a single, poorly furnished room. Unlike Stalin he was able to operate openly and with protectors to whom he could turn, but he shared the objective, which Stalin had had in the 1900s, to mobilize the masses—one for revolution, the other for a still vaguely visualized national renewal beginning with the overthrow of the present regime.

"To be a leader," Hitler wrote, "means to be able to move the masses." He was full of scorn for the conservative nationalists who remained cut off from the majority of the nation by the barriers of class prejudice; he was equally contemptuous of right-wing *völkisch* groups who hugged their beliefs to themselves and spoke to—or quarreled with—only the like-minded. His object was to create the nationalist equivalent of the Social Democratic mass party which had made so great an impression on him in Vienna.

It is important to remember that we are talking of a period of history before television, video cassettes, and tape recorders had been invented, and when both radio and motion pictures were in their infancy. If television had been available to him—or radio, either, before he came to power—there is no doubt Hitler would have made the greatest possible use of them. No politician has ever been more enthusiastic or better informed about technology. This is illustrated not only by his record in the Second World War, but also by his passion for automobiles and his use of airplanes to build up the image of himself and his party. But the focus of his activity in these early years was the mass public meeting: one a week to begin with, most of the time in Munich, sometimes in nearby towns, with Hitler himself acting as the organizer as well as the principal speaker. This was the best way in which to attract attention and to win over recruits.

Many descriptions have been given of Hitler as an orator and of the hypnotic effect he produced on an audience. His early efforts were crude by comparison with his speeches of the 1930s, with their elaborate stage-management and the confidence that came from years of experience. But the elements on which he built were there from the beginning.

His aim, repeatedly stated in *Mein Kampf,* was not to persuade an audience by argument, but to appeal to their feelings:

> The psyche of the broad masses is accessible only to what is strong and uncompromising. Like a woman whose inner sensibilities are not so much under the sway of abstract reasoning, but are subject to a vague emotional longing for the strength that completes her being, and who would rather bow to a strong man than dominate a weakling—so the masses prefer a ruler to a suppliant and are filled with a stronger sense of mental security by a doctrine that brooks no rival than by liberal teaching which offers them a choice. They have very little idea of how to make such a choice and are prone to feel they have been abandoned. They feel little shame at being terrorized intellectually. . . . They see only the ruthless force and brutality of its utterances to which they always submit in the end. [16]

To achieve this effect Hitler sought to convince his audience of the sincerity and strength of his own emotions. "Men believe," Nietzsche wrote, "in the truth of all that is seen to be strongly believed in." [17] Hitler frequently gave the impression of being so carried away by what he said as to be out of control, but learned the orator's and actor's art of stopping just short of incoherence, and of varying the effect by dropping his voice, by employing sarcasm, or by switching from bitter denunciation of the "criminals" who had betrayed Germany to a glowing declaration of his faith in her capacity to rise again in renewed strength.

In speeches that often lasted two hours or more he did not make the mistake of haranguing his listeners all the time. He could make them laugh with his mimicry and win their approval by the quick-wittedness with which he answered hecklers. He spent hours practicing his gestures and facial expressions in front of a mirror and studying the shots that the photographer Heinrich Hoffmann took when he was speaking, in order to select those that were most effective, eliminating the rest.

In *Mein Kampf* Hitler insists that to be successful, propaganda must combine simplification with reiteration: "It must confine itself to a few points and repeat them over and over." The surviving notes for his early speeches show the care he took in planning the sequence of his themes and finding the most telling phrases. He paid equal attention to the place and time of meetings:

> There are rooms which refuse steadfastly to allow any favorable atmosphere to be created in them. . . . In all these cases one is dealing with the problem of influencing the freedom of the human will. . . . In the morning and during the day it seems that the power of the human will rebels with its strongest energy against any attempt to impose upon it the will or opinion of another. On the other hand, in the evening it easily succumbs to the domination of a stronger will. [18]

The complement to his preparations, the control by which he constantly revised them, was his sensitivity to the reactions of his audience:

> An orator receives continuous guidance from the people before whom he speaks. . . . He will always be borne along by the great masses in such a way that from the living emotion of his listeners the very words come to his lips that he needs to speak to their hearts. Should he make even a slight mistake, he has the living correction before him. [19]

This is the explanation for the time Hitler often took to warm up, feeling out an audience's mood until he hit upon the best way to reach it. Though he often experienced difficulty in establishing human relationships with individuals, his rapport with a mass audience was exceptional.

But however strong the impression of spontaneity, however unrestrained the torrent of words that poured out, those who knew him well believed that he was never swept away by the enthusiasm he elicited, but knew very well what he was saying and the effect he meant to produce. What made Hitler dangerous was this combination of fanaticism and calculation.

To get Bavarian politicians (in the first place) and the Bavarian public to take him seriously, Hitler had to create a presence, to make a name for himself. "Whether they laughed at us or reviled us; whether they depicted us as fools or criminals," he wrote in *Mein Kampf,* "the main thing was that they took notice of us." [20] He was greatly helped in his search for publicity when (in December 1920) a number of his Munich backers put up the money to buy the nearly bankrupt *Völkischer Beobachter* (*The Racist Observer*), which was then turned into the party's own newspaper.

For Hitler the German defeat represented a betrayal of, and the revolution an attack on, everything he believed in. But they also offered him the chance to generalize and politicize what had been feelings of personal bitterness and hatred, rooted in his own failure before 1914, and strike a response in audiences who shared his feelings. He saw the German people, now more than ever, menaced by enemies within—Socialists, Communists, Jews—working hand in glove with their external enemies, the French and their allies who imposed the Treaty of Versailles and beggared Germany with reparations, the Bolsheviks who threatened them with the Red Terror. In Bavaria it was easy enough to put the blame on the republican government in Berlin, the "November criminals" who should be swept out of office.

This was a time when conspiracy theories found a ready hearing in Europe. Extraordinary attention was paid in Germany in the 1920s to the *Protocols of the Elders of Zion,* purporting to be an account of the "Jewish world conspiracy" to subvert Christian civilization and erect a Jewish world state, planned in a series of meetings in Basel in 1897 at the time of the first Zionist Congress. The *Protocols* were in fact a forgery put together by the tsarist secret police and first published in 1903. [21] Translated into many languages, they became a classic of anti-Semitic propaganda and were eagerly seized on by Hitler, who made anti-Semitism a central feature of his speeches in the earlier 1920s. But he never failed to match denunciation with a moving appeal to national pride and a call for national renewal that gave his listeners the message of hope they were seeking, and left them exalted rather than depressed.

Hitler gradually built up an elaborate ritual around the mass meeting, culminating in the extraordinary spectacle of the party's Nuremberg rallies in the 1930s. Anything on that scale required the resources of the state, and a dictator to command them, but he was already putting the elements together in the early 1920s when they still had great novelty.

Among them were giant posters and party banners, for which he deliberately chose red, to provoke the left; the swastika emblem; the "Heil Hitler!" salute; the mass parades, military style; the solemn dedication of party flags and standards. He spent many hours hunting through old art magazines and the heraldic department of the Munich State Library to find the drawing of the eagle that he wanted for the party's official rubber stamp, and his first circular letter as chairman of the party (September 17, 1921) was largely concerned with party symbols, which he described in detail. Party members were ordered to wear the party emblem at all times. [22] At meetings, tension was built up in advance with martial music and patriotic songs, the entry of picked squads marching in rank and dipping their flags in salute, all leading up to the delayed arrival of "der Führer."

Those who resisted or came to start trouble were beaten up and thrown out by a strong-arm squad whose numbers Hitler recruited from former Freikorps members and *Frontkämpfer,* or who were directed to him by the army's District Command. Hitler welcomed violent scenes, confident that he could master them and that they would attract those who came for excitement. As an East Prussian landowner who later broke with the Nazis and published his reminiscences of Hitler remarked to Hermann Rauschning "Haven't you noticed, after a brawl at a meeting, that the ones who get beaten up are the first to apply for membership of the party?" [23]

Within a year of the Hofbräuhaus meeting, the party had held more than forty more in Munich and almost as many in the surrounding towns. At the majority of these Hitler was the principal speaker. Now that he had found his vocation, his energy was prodigious. The size of audiences frequently reached two or three thousand: On one occasion in February 1921, 6,500 packed into the huge tent of Munich's Krone Circus to cheer wildly when Hitler spoke on "Future or Ruin" and attacked the Allies' claim for reparations.

The forceful way in which Hitler had virtually taken over the leadership of the NSDAP, the radical direction in which he was pushing it, and the notoriety it had acquired were not at all to the taste of the original members of the German Workers' party it had absorbed. Their discontent came to a head in July 1921 when, in Hitler's absence, they started negotiations for linking up with another *völkisch* group, the German Socialist party, and moving their joint headquarters from Munich to Berlin.

Hitler's reply was to resign on the spot, and since it was plain to everyone—even his critics—that, without him, the NSDAP had no future, the opposition collapsed. Hitler seized the opportunity to make his position unassailable. He demanded, and was granted, "the post of first chairman with dictatorial powers." Other changes on which he insisted enabled him to bring in Max Amann, his former sergeant-major, as secretary-general, and his own nominee, Franz Xaver Schwarz, as party treasurer, as well as to increase the size of the secretariat. Munich was to be the seat of the movement in perpetuity, and union with other groups was ruled out. Only unconditional affiliation was acceptable and any negotiations were to be exclusively in his hands.

Hitler's coup secured formal recognition of his dominant position and at the same time established the "leadership principle" (*Führerprinzip*) as the central organizational pattern of the party. The principle, once accepted, not only gave Hitler the right to make arbitrary decisions, but also substituted for the hierarchical structure of the civil service and the army, with its strict regard for rules, precedent, and procedure, the concept of a personal and unconditional loyalty to the Führer. The whole Nazi movement (and eventually the Nazi state as well) followed the same principle. As it expanded, Germany was divided into districts (*Gaue*), the Gauleiters, or leaders, of which enjoyed considerable freedom to make decisions and take the initiative—always provided their loyalty to Hitler was above suspicion, and Hitler himself did not decide otherwise. The result was that the movement came to depend on a network of personal relationships, and this in turn meant that, at every level of power, clienteles were formed, patronage exercised, and rivalries pursued similar to those at the party summit. Far from being accidental or unforeseen, this was Hitler's authoritarian answer to the two political institutions he detested, bureaucracy or government by officials and democracy or government by committees. [24]

The other distinctive Nazi concept, complementary to that of *Führerprinzip*, was *Kampf*, "struggle," the word Hitler used for the title of his book and the term subsequently applied to the whole pre-1933 period: the *Kampfzeit*, "the time of struggle." With the freedom given him by his new position Hitler gave the notion of *Kampf*, as well as that of *Führerprinzip*, institutional form in the summer of 1921 by the creation of the SA. These initials, which had originally stood for Sports Division, now came to mean *Sturmabteilung*, or stormtroops, the Nazi paramilitary arm, later familiarly known as the Brownshirts.

Shortly before, the Bavarian *Einwohnerwehr* ("citizens' militia") and a number of the most notorious Freikorps (the Oberland and Epp Korps as well as the Ehrhardt Brigade) had been dissolved by order of the republican government in Berlin. Many of their members, desperate at the prospect of exchanging a soldier's for civilian life, joined up with the younger members of the Nazi party, who felt they had missed out on the war, to form the "battering ram" of the movement and carry into politics the "spirit of the front." Hitler described its double function in the first issue of the *SA Gazette* as "not only an instrument for the protection of the movement, but also . . . primarily the training school for the coming struggle for freedom on the domestic front."

It was precisely this emphasis on a political rather than a military purpose that distinguished the SA from the other paramilitary associations of the right, which either disbanded after 1923 or became veterans' organizations like the Stahlhelm. The SA was put to the test in the so-called *Saalschlacht* ("Hall battle") in the Hofbräuhaus on November 4, 1921, when Hitler found himself confronted with a large body of socialist workers from nearby factories intent on breaking up the meeting, with only fifty of his SA men to oppose them. In the riot that broke out halfway through his speech SA men took heavy punishment, but they won and thereafter Hitler claimed that the streets of Munich belonged to the Nazis.

A year later, in October 1922 (the month in which Mussolini made his bid for power in Rome), he took a leaf out of the Fascist book by staging a much publicized foray on the lines of the Italian action squads. Accompanied by 800 stormtroops (complete with band) he traveled to Coburg to celebrate "German Day" in an SPD stronghold. They broke up a hostile crowd and paraded twice through the town as victors. A special medal was struck for those who had been present at Coburg, which became a reliable Nazi base. Organized violence was not incidental but central to the Nazi practice of politics. The SA were given many jobs, but most of them revolved around violence or, no less important, the threat of violence. It was a political not a military use of violence. The enemy was the left, to be challenged, beaten, and driven off the streets in their own working-class strongholds.

Yet Hitler was also quite frank in admitting that he had learned a great deal from the left. But, because he refused to distinguish between the Social Democrats and the Communists, whom he lumped together as Marxists, he does not seem to have recognized one very important characteristic that the Nazi party had in common with the second but not the first. Hitler and Lenin shared an insistence on the importance of winning the support of the masses with an equal insistence on the inability of the masses to organize themselves. For both Nazis and Communists they were a resource to be mobilized, not a membership to be represented.

Lenin told the Tenth Congress of the Russian party in 1921:

> Only the Communist party is capable of unifying, educating, and organizing a vanguard of the proletariat and of the whole mass of the working people that alone will be capable of withstanding the inevitable petty-bourgeois vacillations of this mass.

Hitler wrote in *Mein Kampf* in 1924:

> The political understanding of the broad masses is not at all sufficiently developed to enable them to arrive on their own at a definite general political view. [25]

To mobilize them called for a party with a core of committed members organizing mass meetings, taking part in demonstrations, rallies, street battles, and devoting their whole lives to meeting the party's demands. This distinguished both the Nazis and the Communists from other parties.

Hitler was shrewd enough to realize that such demands, far from being resisted, bound those who accepted them more tightly to the party, developing an attachment that was as much religious as political in character, "the faith of a church combined with the discipline of an army." [26] Many of those who joined in the 1920s were attracted by the emotional satisfaction of belonging to a movement (a word often preferred to that of party) of like-minded, equally alienated men who rejected the democratic, pluralist values of the Weimar Republic while taking advantage of them to plot the republic's overthrow. In the meantime they sought to create a microcosm of the very different sort of society, modeled on that of the wartime front, with which they planned to replace it.

To begin with, the local branches enjoyed considerable autonomy, but there was steady pressure to translate into practice the concept of the party, with authority centralized at the top and strict discipline in accepting orders from above. Within this embryonic framework, the position of Hitler was already accepted as unique. From that developed, in the middle and later 1920s, the full-blown Hitler myth ("the Savior sent by Providence, to rescue the German people from its plight, and restore it to greatness"); the role of the charismatic leader answerable only to himself; the identification of the movement with the person of Adolf Hitler, and of its ideology with his *Weltanschauung;* the personalized relations between Hitler and his Gauleiters, frequently described in terms of a neo-feudal relationship of a *dux* and his vassals.

V

UNTIL 1930 the Nazis remained a minor party on the fringe of German politics. Who joined the party in this first phase, and what attracted them to it?

The membership rose from about 1,100 in June 1920 to 6,000 in early 1922, and about 20,000 in early 1923 after the German Socialist party dissolved itself and voted to join the NSDAP (on Hitler's terms), giving it for the first time a membership outside Bavaria. The crisis year 1923 saw a further big increase, reaching 55,000 at the time of Hitler's unsuccessful November putsch, out of a total German electorate of thirty-eight million.

Evidence for the first period, 1919–23, is fragmentary, but careful research has produced a profile that can be compared with the social composition of the German population as a whole. [27] Unlike all other German parties, with the exception of the Catholic Center party, the membership of the Nazi party even at this early date was spread across all classes and subgroups. The working class as a whole was underrepresented, but within it skilled workers, especially craft workers, were overrepresented.

The old *Mittelstand* (or lower middle class)—master craftsmen, shopkeepers and small businessmen—was also overrepresented and was a substantial source of strength, particularly in the south. Farmers, however, did not join in any numbers before 1923. Of the new *Mittelstand,* the white-collar employees were represented in almost equal proportions to their numbers in the Reich, while the lower civil servants (including teachers) were overrepresented.

The elite groups were also overrepresented, although their actual numbers were small (they made up less than 3 percent of the total population). They included managers, entrepreneurs, academics, professional men, and university students (many of them ex-officers from the army and the Freikorps). The one elite group underrepresented was the higher civil servants.

The predominant tone of the party was lower middle class (to which many of the skilled working class aspired): vulgar, heavily male, and beer drinking, chauvinist, xenophobic, authoritarian, anti-Semitic, anti-intellectual, antiemancipatory, antimodernist.

The NSDAP program drawn up by Hitler and Anton Drexler as early as the beginning of 1920, and declared unalterable, reflects their efforts to find something for everyone, except the Jews. For the nationalists there was the promise of a revisionist and expansionist foreign policy; the revocation of the Treaty of Versailles; the union of all Germans in a Greater Reich. For the *völkisch* there was the demand that the Jews be treated as aliens, denied public office, and deported if there was not enough food to go around. For the workers, there was a promise to abolish all unearned income, confiscate war profits, and institute profit sharing in large industrial enterprises. For the middle class, the socialization of the big department stores and their lease to small tradesmen, the abolition of "interest slavery," and generous provision by the state for sickness and old age.

Individual "maverick" workers continued to join the Nazi party but, for all the talk of appealing to the working class, there was little in such a program to attract the class-conscious blue-collar members of the organized labor movement. Hitler never showed much interest in the anti-capitalist clauses and made no effort to implement them when he came to power. But he recognized that their "national" petit bourgeois version of "socialism" had a strong attraction for many middle-class supporters, and for this reason they were never dropped.

Hitler, in fact, never took the party program too seriously and the majority of its clauses were never carried out. He insisted on declaring it unalterable in order to eliminate discussion of the party's objectives, the mistake of the parliamentary parties he despised. His instinct was sound. It was not for the content of his speeches that his audiences came to hear him, but for the gift he had of presenting the commonplaces of nationalist and right-wing propaganda with a force and impact that none of his rivals could equal.

Hitler was already beginning to collect a number of those who stayed with him and some who rose to office in the Third Reich. They came from a variety of backgrounds. Two were former air-force pilots, Rudolf Hess and Hermann Göring. Hess was the son of a German merchant, born in Alexandria and seven years younger than Hitler. Now a student at Munich University, serious, stupid, and completely lacking in humor, he showed a doglike devotion to Hitler and became his secretary. Göring was the last commander of the crack Richthofen Fighter Squadron and holder of Germany's highest decoration for bravery, the Pour le Mérite. A swaggering personality, he was married to a Swedish baroness with means of her own, and lived in some style while dabbling in studies at the university. Hitler made him commander of the SA, the first of many appointments that carried him in the 1930s to the second most powerful position in Germany after Hitler himself.

Gottfried Feder and Dietrich Eckart had joined the German Workers' party before Hitler. Both were educated men, well known in Munich. Feder was a civil engineer with unorthodox ideas about economics and the abolition of "interest slavery" which he preached with the persistence of a crank. For a time he made a great impression on Hitler but, in common with the other radical economists, lost influence as Hitler came close to power and had to be content with the office of under secretary in the Ministry of Economics, from which he was thrown out at the end of 1934.

Eckart was the man from whom Hitler learned most in these early days of the movement. A colorful Bohemian figure, he was nearly twenty years older than Hitler. Widely read and the translator of Ibsen's *Peer Gynt,* he had ended up publishing a scurrilous sheet *Auf Gut' Deutsch (Plain Speaking)* in which he poured out his nationalist, antidemocratic, and anticlerical opinions. A racist with an enthusiasm for Nordic folklore and a taste for Jew baiting, Eckart talked well even when he was drunk, and he knew everyone in Munich. He lent Hitler books, corrected his style in speaking and writing, and at the same time promoted him as the coming savior of Germany, opening many doors for him, helping to raise the money to buy the *Völkischer Beobachter,* and introducing him to the Obersalzberg, a mountainside near Berchtesgaden and close to the Bavarian-Austrian frontier on which Hitler later made his home. Eckart died long before the Nazis came to power, but Hitler paid a tribute to him on the final page of *Mein Kampf.*

The Bechsteins, wealthy and famous piano manufacturers, were one of the families to whom Eckart introduced his protégé. Frau Hélène Bechstein took a great liking to him and gave parties for people to meet the new prophet; so did the Bruckmanns, well-known Munich art publishers, who became friends for life. Hitler, still ill at ease on social occasions, was clever enough to exploit his own awkwardness, deliberately behaving in exaggerated fashion, arriving late and leaving early. He greeted his hostess, Austrian style, by kissing her hand and presenting a bouquet of roses. Having no small talk, he sat in silence until some remark was made that roused him, as it had in the Home for Men, to a furious outburst. He might then go on for half an hour at the top of his voice until he broke off as suddenly as he had begun. He would then turn to his hostess, beg to be excused, and kiss her hand as he left, with no more than a curt bow to the rest of the company.

This is a summary of an account that a fellow guest at a party in 1923 gave to Konrad Heiden*, who remarked that no one at the party ever forgot meeting Adolf Hitler. [28] Another house where he was welcome, holy ground to Hitler, was Wahnfried, the home of the Wagner family in Bayreuth, where the composer's English daughter-in-law, Winifred, became a devoted

---

*Konrad Heiden was one of the earliest observers of the Nazi movements in the 1920s and 1930s. See his three books listed in the bibliography, section 3A.

admirer. Wagner's granddaughter, Friedelind, remembers him as a young man:

> In Bavarian leather breeches, short thick woolen socks, a red-blue-checked shirt and a short blue jacket that bagged about his unpadded skeleton. His sharp cheekbones stuck out over hollow, pasty cheeks, and above them was a pair of unnaturally bright blue eyes. There was a half-starved look about him, but something else, too, a sort of fanatical look. [29]

A member of another art-publishing firm, six-foot-four, of mixed German-American descent, and a graduate of Harvard, Putzi Hanfstaengl endeared himself to Hitler by his ability to help him relax after his speeches by playing Wagner on the piano, and kept him amused with a stream of anecdotes and irreverent comments.

Mysterious but well connected, Max Erwin von Scheubner-Richter was a German refugee from the Baltic provinces of Russia who introduced Hitler to a group of strongly anti-Bolshevik and anti-Semitic White Russian émigrés, the most important of whom was General Skoropadski, the German-appointed governor of the Ukraine in 1918. Scheubner-Richter acted as liaison man with General Ludendorff, the wartime hero of German nationalists, and was shot dead at Hitler's side in the 1923 putsch. Another German refugee from the Baltic, Alfred Rosenberg, belonged to the same group and impressed Hitler because he had been trained as an architect in Moscow. He became editor of the *Völkischer Beobachter* and saw himself as the philosopher of the Nazi movement with his labored and pedantic discussion of race and culture in *The Myth of the Twentieth Century,* which no one read and Goebbels dismissed as "an ideological belch."

Hitler was far more at home "in the servants' quarters," with the rougher elements in the party: Max Amann, his former sergeant-major; Ulrich Graf, his bodyguard, a butcher's apprentice and amateur wrestler with a great taste for brawling, well matched by Christian Weber, a former horse trader of great physical strength who had worked as a bouncer at various beer halls. Hoffmann, the party's official photographer, was another earthy Bavarian with a weakness for drinking parties and hearty jokes. Hitler himself described Hermann Esser as a scoundrel, who sponged off numerous mistresses and made a specialty of digging up Jewish scandals, but remained in favor because of his value as a natural mob orator. Hitler apart, Esser's only rival as that (and also as pornographer) was Julius Streicher, an elementary school teacher in Nuremberg, never seen in public without a whip, who founded *Der Stürmer (The Stormtrooper),* the most notorious of all anti-Semitic publications, in which he published fantastic accounts of Jewish ritual murders and sexual crimes. Hitler was constantly urged to get rid of such unsavory characters but kept both Esser and Streicher on in party jobs in Bavaria throughout the Third Reich, and defended them for their loyalty.

Looking back in the 1940s he showed no illusions about the type of man his movement attracted in the early days but also defended their value:

> Such elements are unusable in time of peace, but in turbulent periods it's quite different. . . . Fifty bourgeois wouldn't have been worth a single one of them. With what blind confidence they followed me! Fundamentally, they were just overgrown children. . . . During the war they'd fought with the bayonet and thrown hand grenades. They were simple creatures, all of a piece. They couldn't let the country be sold out to the scum who were the product of defeat. From the beginning I knew that one could make a party only with elements like that.[30]

A key figure in Hitler's success was Ernest Röhm, a born soldier of fortune and the staff captain through whose hands ran the mysterious links between the District Command of the German army (the Reichswehr), the antirepublican nationalist organizations that proliferated in Bavaria, and the Freikorps groups which had taken cover there when officially disowned. It was Röhm who provided Hitler with undercover subsidies from secret Reichswehr funds; recommended and introduced him to senior officers; made sure it was known that he enjoyed Reichswehr favor; and directed potential recruits to the SA, which he did more to build up than Hitler or anyone else.

It was equally important to Hitler to have friends in the police and the public prosecutor's office who could see that any attempt to charge him for offenses against public order was blocked. Bavaria after 1918 was the most disaffected part of Germany, providing a refuge where right-wing German nationalists and Bavarian particularists could at least agree in their detestation of the republican regime in Berlin. Bavarian officials turned a blind eye to the plotting, demonstrations, and drilling that went on in preparation for "the Day," and with which many of them were in sympathy. The Munich chief of police, Ernst Pöhner, and his political adviser, Wilhelm Frick, as well as the Bavarian minister of justice, Franz Gürtner, were all prepared to give Hitler such protection. At Hitler's trial after the November 1923 putsch, Pöhner and Frick were frank in saying why they had not taken steps to suppress the Nazi party:

> We refrained deliberately because we saw in the party the seeds of Germany's renewal, because we were convinced that this movement was the one most likely to take root among workers infected with the Marxist plague and win them back into the nationalist camp. That is why we held our protective hands over the NSDAP and Herr Hitler.[31]

Both Frick and Gürtner joined the party and were rewarded with ministries when Hitler became chancellor.

In its earliest days the Nazi party was very short of funds. When Hitler obtained an entrée to well-to-do circles in Munich, this brought financial as well as social advantage. Among those who made contributions were Dietrich Eckart, the Bechsteins, the Bruckmanns, and Putzi Hanfstaengl, whose dollar income from the family art gallery in New York proved invaluable during the worst period of inflation. Hitler made several presentations to business circles in Bavaria but with very limited success. More important was an introduction to the influential National Club in Berlin which he owed to a friend of Eckart, Emil Gansser. Twice in 1922 Hitler was invited to address the club, which consisted mainly of army officers and senior civil servants as well as a number of businessmen. He appears to have put his case well, avoiding reference to the anticapitalist clauses of the NSDAP program and laying stress on its anti-Marxism. He at least attracted the enthusiastic interest of one of Germany's best-known industrialists, Ernst von Borsig, head of a famous but no longer leading engineering firm. Borsig certainly provided the NSDAP with funds but failed to raise money from other industrialists to enable Hitler to set up a branch headquarters in Berlin. Other attempts to secure industrial support, this time in the Ruhr, proved equally fruitless, despite persistent rumors, which have proved groundless, that Germany's biggest capitalist, Hugo Stinnes, came to the party's aid.

The one major contributor who can be identified was Fritz Thyssen, the frustrated heir of the octogenarian head of one of Germany's biggest steel firms, who later published a ghostwritten book with the sensational title *I Paid Hitler,* claiming to have given 100,000 gold marks to the NSDAP in October 1923, just before the putsch. But, in another passage, Thyssen explicitly states that the money was given, not to Hitler, but to General Ludendorff, Hindenburg's partner in the wartime High Command who now stood at the head of a coalition of rightist groups and who is thought to have allocated part, but not the whole, of the sum to the Nazis, dividing it between them and other groups. Other help may have come from such right-wing associations as the Pan-German League. But no convincing evidence has been found[32] of the large subsidies that Hitler was reported to have drawn from German big business.

The truth appears to be that, from the beginning, the party made exceptional demands upon its members. Those who held local office were expected to put in many hours of unpaid work (not until 1929 were Gauleiters placed on the party payroll); they received no expenses and were constantly under pressure not only to organize and take part in meetings and demonstrations, but also to raise money. The Nazis followed another Social Democratic practice in enforcing the regular collection of dues from their members. Members and sympathizers were also pestered to provide interest-free loans, pay for admission to meetings and rallies, and contribute to collections after Hitler had spoken. Police agents were quoted as reporting that the sums people of modest means were prepared to give "bordered on the unbelievable."[33]

No other right-wing party in Germany had ever attempted anything like this before. It gave substance to Hitler's claim that the NSDAP was a genuinely populist movement with the potential power to gain a mass following. This was the claim that attracted the interest of those in a position to help—Hitler's ability to use his gifts as an agitator and organizer to act (in the phrase he himself used) as *Trommler zur Deutschheit,* "drummer to Germanism."

But what was the object of all this activity, how was it to produce political results? Hitler hardly ever spoke without expressing his contempt for parliamentary methods and implying his preference for the use of force. But he left vague answers to the question of how the force was to be mobilized and applied. Mussolini's March on Rome at the end of October 1922, which secured him dictatorial powers, suggested a possible answer. For the march had only been threatened. What was carried out was a triumphant parade after Mussolini had arrived in Rome by the regular night train and had been called upon by the king to form a government. If there had been a strong government in power, or if the Italian king had been willing to take the risk, there were sufficient regular army troops in the capital to defeat any attempt at a coup. But the orders were never given. With no one in authority to take responsibility, resistance collapsed and the occupation by the Fascist militia of a number of provincial centers such as Florence and Perugia was sufficient to make the threat of force by itself hoist Mussolini into power legally.

Mussolini's success made a great impression on the nationalist opposition in Germany. In Bavaria, in particular, there was much talk of a March on Berlin, and as the year 1923 began it looked as if the all-important conditions that had made Mussolini's attempt possible, the weakening of the central government's authority and power to resist, might be repeated in Germany.

V I

THE NEW FACTOR that precipitated a return of the insecurity and violence of the years 1918 through 1920 was the Allies' demand for reparations for the war and the Germans' declaration of their inability to pay. Determined to end German prevarication, the French in January 1923 occupied the Ruhr, and the Germans retorted with a call for a national campaign of passive resistance led by the government and supported by all political parties.

In June 1922, the foreign minister, Walther Rathenau, had been assassinated by a right-wing murder gang, and the German government had passed a Law for the Protection of the Republic. This proved ineffective, however, and under cover of the call for resistance to the French, the paramilitary organizations, both nationalist and Communist, which had been banned by the government, were able to come out into the open again and resume the practice of violence with impunity. In Bavaria, the loss of the special state rights and the monarchy that Bavaria had possessed under the empire still rankled, and the government in Munich refused to implement the new law.

Reinforcing the political insecurity produced by the occupation of the Ruhr and the German government's call for resistance was the economic insecurity brought about by the collapse of the mark. The root of the trouble was the wartime government's improvident way of financing the war by loans, which produced a huge increase in the national debt and an excessive volume of currency held by the public. By 1922 the mark had fallen to one-tenth of its 1920 value; during 1923, it ceased to have any value at all. On July 1, a dollar was worth 160,000 marks; on August 1, a million. On November 15, 1923, it took a trillion marks to equal the purchasing power of one 1914 mark.

In November, the stabilization of the currency was carried out without difficulty and substantially without foreign help, but under conditions far worse than would have been the case earlier in the year. Until November, however, the German experts declared stabilization to be impossible and were satisfied to put all the blame on the Allies' demand for reparations. Some Germans made fortunes out of the inflation, especially landowners and industrialists who got rid of their debts and were allowed to repay loans from the Reichsbank in depreciated marks. But the great mass of Germans suffered severely. The majority of the middle classes lost practically all their savings and many were reduced to penury; the purchasing power of working-class wages was wiped out, and many could afford neither adequate food nor shelter. The shock left a permanent mark on German society, producing an immediate political as well as long-term psychological destabilization.

As the weeks passed and the costs of the policy of resistance rose, more and more people throughout Germany declared, "This cannot go on," and blamed the government for allowing it to do so. This was a situation made for Hitler and the Nazis. He could see the opportunity very clearly; his problem was how to turn it to his advantage. He was still the leader of only one among the numerous right-wing groups that proliferated in Bavaria, not yet strong enough to achieve anything on his own and yet in disagreement about objectives with those on whom he would have to depend as allies. This disagreement is the key to the confused maneuvering that followed, ending in the fiasco of the November putsch.

To understand German politics in the 1920s it is necessary to remember that the Weimar Republic, like the German Empire it replaced, had a federal structure. The seventeen states (*Länder*) that made it up ranged in size from Prussia with thirty-eight million inhabitants—two-thirds of the total—to Schaumburg Lippe with 48,000. Besides the central (Reich) government—responsible for taxation, foreign policy, and defense—and the national parliament, the Reichstag, the individual states had their own governments—responsible, for example, for police and education—and their own parliaments (*Landtag*). The most important of these was the Prussian government, the seat of which was in Berlin, and which, with its large population and resources, could easily be seen as a rival to the Reich government, also housed in Berlin.

In 1923, however, it was the conflict between the Reich government in Berlin and the right-wing Bavarian government in Munich (Bavaria was the second-largest state after Prussia) that Hitler was concerned with. There were three issues involved. The first was Bavarian particularism, the dream that captivated right-wing politicians of making Bavaria as autonomous as possible, recovering her prewar status, if not her independence, and restoring the Wittelsbach monarchy. The second was the preoccupation of many Reichswehr officers, including Röhm, with building a secret reserve out of the SA and the former Freikorps units for the hundred thousand men to which the German army was restricted by the Versailles Treaty. The third was the strong pull of nationalist feeling, in the face of French aggression and the occupation of the Ruhr, to unite the German people behind the republican government in Berlin and so strengthen the Weimar regime.

Hitler was opposed to all three. His only interest in Bavaria was as a springboard from which to launch a March on Berlin, which would overthrow the existing federal government and replace it with one that would unite all Germans, including Austrians as well as Bavarians, in a strong national state.

He saw the SA primarily as a paramilitary arm of the party to be used for political purposes rather than as part of a reserve army, believing that the way to rebuild German military power was not by playing at soldiers in the Bavarian woods or carrying on guerrilla operations against the French in the Ruhr, but by the capture of political power and the rearmament to which this would open the door.

As for the call for national unity, he deliberately swam against the tide and insisted that the real enemy of the German people was not the French, but the government of "November criminals" still in power in Berlin, which had accepted the Versailles settlement. Hitler showed the same resolute judgment as Lenin: The one thing that mattered was to capture power; once that had been secured, everything else would follow. But if he had followed so consistent a line openly, he would have been isolated, and this he could not afford. To keep in the political game that was being played in Bavaria, he had to tack and compromise, but he could never overcome the distrust of the other players, who were glad enough of the support he could bring (the party grew by about 35,000, the SA by 15,000, between February and November 1923), but who had no intention of accepting him on equal terms, still less of letting him take control.

A *Kampfbund* (Fighting League) was set up with other militant nationalist groups, and Hitler planned a large-scale demonstration for May Day 1923 aimed at preventing or breaking up the traditional left-wing celebrations. When the Bavarian government agreed to a mass meeting and parade, but forbade any street processions, Hitler ignored the ban and decided to double the stakes. With Röhm's help and in the face of a direct prohibition from the District Reichswehr Commander, General Otto von Lossow, the SA men went to the barracks and secured the weapons, including machine guns, that the "patriotic leagues" kept stored there. The Nazi stormtroops gathered for the parade were convinced that they were at last going to take part in the revolutionary action of which Hitler had so often talked, and when Hitler joined them he was wearing his helmet and his Iron Cross. But von Lossow was not to be hustled: He insisted that Röhm, who was still a regular officer, must secure the return of the stolen weapons, and sent him with an escort of troops and police to see that his orders were carried out. Some of the other Kampfbund leaders were in favor of immediate action, in the belief that they would carry the Reichswehr along with them, but Hitler would not take the risk. He ordered the stormtroops to return the weapons to the barracks and, although he made an effort in his speech at the Krone Circus to explain it away, the outcome was universally taken as a serious reversal for him. Hitler acknowledged as much himself by disappearing from Munich and taking refuge for several weeks at Obersalzberg. His confidence shaken, he was apprehensive (since he was still an Austrian citizen) that he might be deported from Bavaria.

Hitler was encouraged to try his luck again by the intensification of the crisis in Germany during August and September. Wilhelm Cuno's government, which had launched the campaign for passive resistance in the Ruhr, resigned on August 11, in open acknowledgment that it had failed to moderate the French attitude. Both the economic and political unity of the Reich now appeared to be in danger: the former as a result of the final collapse of the currency, the latter in view of French support of Rhenish separatism, Communist-led strikes and riots, and revived talk in Bavaria of a break with Berlin. The only option open to the new government formed by Gustav Stresemann in August was to call off the campaign of resistance to the French, and this could obviously be used as a platform from which to attack them as "traitors to the Fatherland." On the morrow of a huge demonstration at Nuremberg to celebrate the anniversary of the French defeat at Sedan on September 2, 1870, at which Hitler spoke, the Kampfbund was renewed.

Recovering his former energy, Hitler now began to speak five or six times a day.

> The regime of November [1918] nears its end [he told an audience on September 12]. The edifice totters; the framework creaks. There are now only two alternatives before us: the swastika or the Soviet star; the world despotism of the International or the Holy Empire of the Germanic nation. The first act of redress must be a march on Berlin and the installation of a national dictatorship. [34]

The question of who was to be the dictator was left open. General Erich Ludendorff, who had accepted office as president of the revived Kampfbund, assumed that he would be; whether Hitler yet saw himself in this role, as more than the "drummer," is not clear. [35] Hitler's basic problem remained, however. It was not enough to carry the Kampfbund with him: He had to have in addition the support of the Bavarian government, and the support or at least the acquiescence of the Reichswehr. To make clear the limits to the Kampfbund's freedom of action, on September 26, the Bavarian government declared a state of emergency and appointed Gustav Ritter von Kahr, a right-wing politician, as state commissioner with dictatorial powers. He promptly used these to ban the fourteen mass meetings Hitler had called to renew his campaign.

The decisive question, however, was the attitude of the Reichswehr. On the same day as the news of the Bavarian state of emergency reached Berlin, September 26, President Friedrich Ebert and the Reich cabinet met with General Hans von Seeckt, the army commander in chief, and asked him where the Reichswehr stood. The general's reply—"The Reichswehr, Herr Reichspräsident, stands behind me"—amounted to a claim that the army, not the government, was the ultimate guardian of the unity of the Reich and would act as its leadership saw fit in order to preserve it. The cabinet, however, was in no position to argue with von Seeckt; they were glad enough that, on this occasion, the Reichswehr was prepared to support them against the threat of civil war. Relying on this, they were able, in their turn, to declare a national state of emergency, placing their executive functions nominally in the hands of the minister of defense, in fact in the hands of von Seeckt as commander in chief.

For six months, through the commanders of the seven military districts, the army (as it had during the war) controlled everything including prices, currency regulations, and labor conditions. An attempt by the right-wing "Black Reichswehr" to carry out a putsch was immediately disowned, and the threat of the left-wing government in Saxony to stage a revolt with Red militiamen was put down by force. Similar threats in Hamburg and Thuringia were treated in the same way.

Bavaria proved more difficult to deal with, and it was the open split that began to develop between Munich and Berlin that gave Hitler his chance. Not only did von Kahr refuse to recognize the authority of the Reich government, but General von Lossow, the district commander in Bavaria, also refused to obey orders from von Seeckt to suppress the Nazi *Völkischer Beobachter* for its violent campaign against Berlin, or to arrest leading German nationalists in Bavaria. When von Seeckt dismissed von Lossow, von Kahr refused to accept his successor and appointed von Lossow as commander of the Reichswehr troops in Bavaria. Von Seeckt reminded the latter and the troops under his command of their oath of obedience, but von Kahr and von Lossow held their ground, with the support of Colonel Hans Ritter von Seisser, the commandant of the Bavarian State Police.

It is not at all clear what the triumvirate intended to do; most likely, they intended to wait and see how the situation would develop before deciding. Ostensibly von Kahr had committed himself to a march on Berlin, and on October 24 von Lossow summoned a conference to discuss plans for carrying out the operation. But Hitler and the SA were deliberately not invited to be present, and Hitler was suspicious that the triumvirate meant either to act without him or to try to get von Seeckt to set up a national dictatorship, in which case the Bavarians would rally to his support and see that Bavaria's interests were looked after.

Hitler and the Kampfbund had already made their own preparations and were more and more impatient at the delay. Hitler could not afford to repeat the fiasco of May 1; he was aware (as were the triumvirate) that time was running out and that the government in Berlin might soon master the crisis. On November 6, the Kampfbund decided to act on their own, present von Kahr and von Lossow with a fait accompli, and burn their boats for them. Learning that von Kahr had arranged a big meeting for the evening of November 8 at which all the Bavarian notables would be present, Hitler resolved to make this the occasion. It was not so much a "Hitler putsch" as "the last desperate gamble of a man who feared he was being deserted by his fellow-conspirators." [36]

When the meeting took place, 2,000 people packed into the Bürgerbräu Beer Cellar to hear the Bavarian leaders speak. Shortly after it began, Hitler burst in and stormed the platform, gun in hand, shouting that the national revolution had begun. After leading von Kahr, von Lossow, and Seisser into a side room he returned to announce that a provisional national government had been formed, in which he would assume the direction of policy, Ludendorff would become commander in chief of the German army, and the triumvirate would all be given posts. With Ludendorff's help he got all three back on to the platform, where they promised loyalty and shook hands with Hitler in a loudly applauded scene of reconciliation—they then made excuses and disappeared into the night while Hitler was otherwise occupied.

When it came to the decisive action and use of force that Hitler had proclaimed time and again as his objective, he proved singularly ineffective. Nothing had been properly planned, and when Hitler was finally forced to recognize that von Lossow and von Kahr had resumed their freedom of action and were taking measures to suppress the uprising, he suffered a nervous collapse in which he passed through a whole succession of moods—anger, despair, apathy, renewed hope, hesitation. In fact, if he had only roused himself to go out and speak to the crowds—a task he pushed off on Streicher—Hitler would have realized that it was still possible to mobilize popular support for a March on Berlin. Instead he remained shut up in the beer hall, isolated from the crowds from which he had always drawn strength, and unable to make up his mind whether or not to risk a demonstration. It was Ludendorff who decided for him, and at noon the next day led out Hitler and the other Nazi leaders at the head of a column of several thousand men, which crossed the River Isar and marched into the center of the city.

Eyewitness accounts strongly suggest that Hitler had already lost all faith in what they were doing. When a police cordon on the Odeonsplatz opened fire, the ranks broke, fourteen in the procession and three policemen were killed, and many more wounded. While Ludendorff marched on and pushed through the cordon, Hitler, after being pulled to the ground and dislocating his arm, scrambled to his feet and fled, finally taking refuge at Uffing outside Munich. He was arrested two days later and taken to prison in a state of complete despondency, convinced that he would never recover from the disaster he had suffered, and that he would in any case be shot.

Hitler was tried for treason and condemned, but served less than a year in jail. Nonetheless, when he emerged at the end of 1924, he faced the need to build up his position again very nearly from the beginning. The chances of bringing off a coup in 1923 comparable with Mussolini's March on Rome the year before had never been more than marginal. If it had succeeded, it would have left him with everything still to play for, but at least he would have been accepted as a player in the game. Instead, it was to take Hitler five more years to get back into the game at all.

Compared with the historical importance and scale of the events in which Stalin was involved at the same time, the beginning of Hitler's career and the November putsch, which barely rated a paragraph in the world press, must appear insignificant in the extreme. Nonetheless, like Stalin's own years of apprenticeship before 1917, Hitler's experience in 1923, not least the fiasco that cut it short, was to have a formative influence on the way in which he finally achieved power.

FOUR The General Secretary

STALIN 1918–1924 *(Age 38–44)*

I

THE RUSSIAN REVOLUTION of 1917 remains one of the most extraordinary as well as influential events in twentieth-century history. The Bolsheviks were the smallest of the Russian socialist parties, with no more than 25,000 members at the beginning of 1917, in opposition and politically isolated for most of that year. Yet before its end their leaders had emerged, unexpectedly and almost overnight, as the first socialist government in the world, responsible for a huge country with a population of over 170 million. By the autumn of 1918 they had been in office for a year, had ended the war, and had established a single-party dictatorship claiming to represent the workers and peasants of Russia. But their ability to extend their authority to the whole of the country, even to survive as a government, let alone to put into effect their program of economic and social revolution, remained in doubt. The assumption that both Lenin and Trotsky had acknowledged as essential to their hopes of success, the simultaneous outbreak of revolution in Western Europe, particularly in Germany, had proved ill founded. Instead of receiving assistance from friendly socialist governments, they were confronted with Allied intervention in support of the counterrevolutionary forces inside Russia.

The Ukraine, Poland, and the Baltic states, occupied by the Germans during the last year of the First World War, set up independent governments when it ended. White (that is, anti-Red) Russian armies had been formed under former tsarist generals Anton Denikin, Nicholas Yudenich, and Petr Wrangel and Admiral Aleksandr Kolchak. During 1918 White forces joined by the Czechoslovak Legion, which had been formed from prisoners of war, occupied all the key industrial and strategic centers in Siberia, the Urals, and the region of the middle Volga.

In the south, General Petr Krasnov's Cossacks advanced northwards with the aim of joining other White forces at Kazan and cutting the rail connection between Tsaritsyn and Moscow, the link with the capital's last remaining granary in the northern Caucasus. The bread ration for workers

RUSSIA IN THE 1920s

NORWAY

SWEDEN

Murmansk

Kiev
Leningrad
Moscow
Odessa
Gorki
Perm

U   S   S   R

Ufa   Chelyabinsk
Tbilisi
Baku   Omsk   *Trans-Siberian Railway*

Angarsk
MONGOLIA   Harbin
                                              JAPAN
CHINA

FINLAND

L. Onega

L. Ladoga

Baltic Sea

Leningrad
(Petrograd)

ESTONIA

Riga
LATVIA

RUSSIAN   SOVIET   FEDERATED

LITHUANIA

E. PRUSSIA

Moscow

SOCIALIST   REPUBLIC

Minsk

U   S   S   R

BYELO
RUSSIA

POLAND

KHAZAK
SSR

CZECHOSLOVAKIA

HUNG.

Kiev

UKRAINIAN
SSR

Tsaritsin
(Stalingrad)

R. Bug

R. Don   R. Volga

R. Dnieper

RUMANIA

R. Danube

Caucasus   Mts.

YUG

Sochi

BULGARIA

Black
Sea

GEORGIAN
ASSR
TRANSCAUCAUSIAN
FEDERATED
Batum   SOVIET REPUBLIC   Baku
                                                   AZERBAIJAN
GREECE   ARMENIAN   ASSR
                                                ASSR
                                          to Azerb

Aegean
Sea

T   U   R   K   E   Y

L. Van   PERSIA

L. Urmia

in Moscow and Petrograd was reduced to one ounce a day. Caucasia itself was divided between rival local regimes, fighting both Whites and Communists, and intermittently each other as well.

In the west, the Poles were eager to recover the Ukrainian and Byelorussian lands that had once formed part of the Polish-Lithuanian state. In the Far East the Japanese, soon followed by the Americans, landed troops in Siberia. A French force occupied Odessa; the British seized Archangel in the north and Baku in the south. For a time, the area controlled by Lenin's government was reduced to little more than the original fifteenth-century Principality of Moscow.

The party leadership that faced the formidable task of mastering this situation was not short of able men, but none of them had any experience of government or of managing the economy. Not only were they long on theory and short on experience, but they also deeply distrusted the traditional practice of government by both the tsarist autocracy and the bourgeois regimes of Western Europe—and rejected altogether capitalist methods of managing the economy. Lacking experience, they lacked also a model or blueprint of an alternative system; everything had to be improvised.

Neither Lenin nor Trotsky however—one still under fifty, the other like Stalin still under forty—was daunted by what faced them. Lenin had achieved the objective to which he had devoted his life, to secure power, and this reinforced not only his self-confidence but also his authority. Until the Tenth Party Congress in 1921 policy was still hotly debated in the party, differences and criticism tolerated. But after the stand Lenin had taken against a majority in the party in the April Theses, the October Revolution, and the Brest-Litovsk negotiations—in each case justified by the outcome—his leadership was never in question.

Trotsky was always regarded by the Old Bolsheviks as an outsider who had joined the party only in August 1917, and his commanding manner was resented as arrogance by others besides Stalin. But after his performance in the Petrograd Soviet, in 1905 as well as 1917, and his masterminding of the seizure of power, his stature as a revolutionary leader was hardly in doubt.

The same could not be said of the forty-year-old Zinoviev, for whom few of the other party leaders had a good word to say. He had opposed Lenin over the decision to make a bid for power in 1917 and had resigned from the Central Committee in the face of Lenin's rejection of a coalition government. Despite these disagreements, Lenin had forgiven him and Zinoviev became a candidate (that is, probationary) member of the Politburo in 1919 and a full member in 1921, as well as chairman of the Communist International from its foundation and of the important Petrograd Party Organization. He was universally regarded, however, as owing his position to the fact that Lenin had become used to relying on him during the years of exile between 1908 and 1917 and continued to do so afterwards—although as Lenin himself said, "He copies my faults." Zinoviev was a fluent speaker and gifted as a popularizer, but his pretensions to be an intellectual were not taken seriously. Lenin was also on record as saying that he was bold only when danger was past. "Panic personified" was Sverdlov's verdict, and his vanity was a byword. But, having got to the top, Zinoviev was determined to stay there, and at least (unlike Trotsky, whom he hated) he made a fight of it.

A factor in Zinoviev's favor was his alliance with Lev Kamenev, born in the same year, 1883, and also of Jewish parents. After underground work Kamenev had lived abroad between 1908 and 1914, becoming Lenin's closest collaborator after Zinoviev. Exiled in Siberia at the same time as Stalin, he returned with him in 1917 and resumed his partnership with Zinoviev, which lasted until Stalin had them tried and executed in 1936. A man with little personal ambition, taking his lead from his friend Zinoviev, Kamenev incurred Lenin's wrath for his conciliatory attitude in 1917–18. He, too, however, was forgiven and readmitted to the Central Committee and the Politburo as another familiar figure Lenin felt he could rely on and whom he had appointed chairman of the other big city organization, Moscow. A more solid figure than Zinoviev, despite his disposition to follow the other's line, Kamenev was better liked and respected for his talents as a clear-headed writer and speaker, especially as a chairman.

Two others shared Stalin's experience of having spent most of their prerevolutionary careers inside Russia rather than abroad. Both had been on the right wing of the party, but both had the practical experience that Lenin so much valued. Mikhail Tomsky was the only leading Bolshevik who had been an industrial worker; he was a lithographer by trade and had not joined the party until he was twenty-four. His great virtue was that he could take over the chairmanship of the trade unions. Aleksei Rykov was recommended by the fact that he came of a peasant family and was an ethnic Russian. This was an advantage when the three most important positions after Lenin's were held by Jews—Trotsky, Zinoviev, and Kamenev—and a fourth by a Georgian. Anti-Semitism was still a force in Russia and Hitler later never tired of identifying "Moscow" with the "Zionist world conspiracy." Rykov took over the job as top industrial administrator and in February 1918 was made chairman of the Supreme Economic Council, becoming a member of the Organizational Bureau of the Party's Central Committee (the Orgburo), along with Tomsky, in 1921, and of the Politburo in 1922.

The only member of the leadership besides Lenin and Trotsky who could be unquestionably described as an intellectual was Nikolai Bukharin. Another ethnic Russian, born in 1888 with a schoolteacher father, he spent a brief period like Kamenev as a student at Moscow University before graduating into full-time revolutionary activity and emigrating in 1911. Bukharin was fascinated by economic theory and his book *Imperialism and the World Economy* preceded and influenced Lenin's work on the same subject. When Bukharin returned to Russia in 1917, he became a leader of the party's left wing, opposing Brest-Litovsk in favor of a revolutionary war and providing theoretical justification for the compulsory methods of War Communism in *The Economics of the Transition Period,* a bold attempt to estimate and defend "the costs of revolution" as inevitable. He had the same touch of brilliance as Trotsky, although unlike Trotsky he was personally popular, especially among the younger members of the party, gifted with charm as well as talent—the "Benjamin" of the party, as Lenin called him. But Lenin also thought him unstable in his opinions and "soft as wax," perhaps the reason why after being elected a candidate member of the Politburo in 1919 he did not move up to full membership until 1924, after Lenin's death. Bukharin never held any major administrative post in either the party or the government, and he was to prove no match for the others as a politician; but he showed greater intellectual independence, frequently opposing Lenin on theoretical issues. Bukharin became a convert to the New Economic Policy and the principal advocate of it as a permanent change of course. He gathered a group of younger economists around him at the Institute of Red Professors. These acted as propagandists for his ideas, which he was also able to promote in his position as chief editor of *Pravda* and of the Central Committee's new journal, *Bolshevik.*

Such was the group of men who, together with Stalin, shared the top leadership of the Soviet Union in the early 1920s and were his principal opponents in the struggle for the succession after Lenin's death.

Fortunately for them, quarrels among the White Russians, and the lack of any agreed plan for intervention among the foreign powers, made the situation less hopeless for the Communists than appeared at the time, but this was only on condition that they could take advantage of their central position by establishing a unified command and creating an effective fighting force. Considering the state of the defeated Russian army, the morale of which the Communists had done their best to subvert, this was a formidable undertaking. In Trotsky, however, appointed commissar for war in March 1918, they discovered unsuspected talents as a military organizer. Conscription was introduced and 800,000 were enrolled in the Red Army by the end of 1918; at its peak in 1920 it is said to have numbered two and a half million. The failure of its attempt to invade Poland put an abrupt end to Lenin's revived hopes of using the Red Army to spread revolution to the rest of Europe. But it defeated the White Guards, ended the interventionist powers' hopes of reversing the revolutionary seizure of power in Russia itself, and by 1922 had extended the Soviet state's authority to the greater part of Russia's prewar territory, except in the west, where Bessarabia, Russian Poland, the Baltic states, and Finland had been lost.

T HIS WAS the background to Stalin's personal fortunes from 1918 to 1921. Hitler's problem during those years was to create a movement and build it up to the point where it would be taken seriously. If he could do that, he was confident he could maintain his position as its leader. Stalin's problem was the opposite. The Communist party had been created and had already formed a government. Stalin had played a part in both cases, but not such as to justify the later description of him as Lenin's chief lieutenant. At this stage, none of the other Bolshevik leaders saw him as a possible successor to Lenin, and we have no way of knowing how early Stalin himself formed such an ambition. Lenin (age fifty in 1920) was only nine years older than Stalin, who could hardly have foreseen that his leader would suffer the first of a series of strokes in May 1922 and be dead before the end of January 1924, when he was not yet fifty-four. But Stalin was certainly a candidate for the succession in his own mind from the summer of 1922, and possibly earlier. The question was how he was to build up his position in the leadership to the point where his ambitions would be taken seriously.

In the Council of People's Commissars Stalin held the office of commissar of nationalities. His opportunities to make much of this were limited. Three weeks after the Bolshevik coup in 1917, Stalin attended the Congress of the Finnish Social Democratic party and proclaimed the right of the Finns to national independence. The decree granting it was signed by Lenin and Stalin and was in accord with the principle of self-determination stated in Stalin's 1913 treatise on *Marxism and the Nationalities*. Not only Mensheviks such as Martov, but Bolsheviks such as Bukharin and Dzerzhinsky criticized that policy as a "sellout" to the bourgeois nationalism of smaller nations at the expense of Russia and of the Russian Revolution. In the general disintegration that followed the overthrow of the tsarist government, nationalist movements in all the borderlands created new governments that were anti-Bolshevik and bent on complete separation from Russia. This happened not only in Poland and the Baltic states, but also in the Caucasus, Central Asia, and even in the Ukraine.

On the other hand, to repudiate the principle of national self-determination outright would put an end to any hopes of keeping these peoples within the Soviet Union and drive them to look to the anti-Bolshevik forces for support. Stalin squared the circle by interpreting the right of self-determination "as a means in the struggle for socialism, subordinated to the principles of socialism." National autonomy, in other words, was acceptable only when implemented under Communist control.

Opening a preparatory conference on the creation of the Tatar-Bashkir Autonomous Soviet Republic in May 1918, Stalin made clear what he meant:

> Autonomy is a form. The whole question is what class control is contained in that form. The Soviet Government is for autonomy, but only for an autonomy where all power rests in the hands of workers and peasants, where the bourgeoisie of all nationalities is not only deprived of power, but also of participation in the elections of the governing organs. [1]

A further change from the views that Stalin had expressed in his original thesis made it easier to accommodate the new concept of autonomy. In the commission set up to draft the Soviet constitution of 1918, Stalin dropped his earlier advocacy of a centralized structure for the state in favor of a form of federalism, based on national-territorial units. Mikhail Reisner, opposing Stalin's recommendation, argued that it represented "hidden centralism under cover of a federal structure." He was quite right; but Stalin (with Lenin's support) carried the day. [2]

These changes were to prove important for the future, but they remained no more than gestures until the question of the regime's survival was settled. While Lenin remained in Moscow to hold all the strings in his hand, and Trotsky rose to new heights as commissar of war, the other Soviet leaders were sent on special missions to one crisis spot after another as need arose. Lenin showed the same confidence in Stalin as a troubleshooter as he had in 1917, choosing him to deal with some of the most critical situations. Nor was his confidence misplaced. In the chaotic conditions that were general in 1918–19, Stalin did not lose his nerve but showed he could exercise leadership and get things done, however rough his methods, including summary execution without trial. Unlike Hitler's experience as a *Frontkämpfer* in the First World War, Stalin's in the civil war was as a political commissar or special representative at the command level, not at the front. But their earlier experience of war was to influence both men in their role as supreme commanders in the Second World War.

Stalin's first assignment was to the key position of Tsaritsyn, on the Volga (later renamed Stalingrad, and now Volgograd), with the responsibility of making sure that the food supplies to Moscow and Petrograd were not cut off. Twenty-four hours after his arrival on June 6, he reported that he had dealt with a "bacchanalia of profiteering" by fixing food prices and introducing rationing. On July 7, the day after the attempted Socialist Revolutionary coup (see page 61), he reassured Lenin:

> Everything will be done to prevent possible surprises here. Rest assured that our hand will not tremble. I'm chasing up and bawling out whoever requires it. We shall spare no one, neither ourselves nor others. But we'll send you the food. [3]

It was while Stalin was at Tsaritsyn that he first came into open conflict with Trotsky. The issue was Trotsky's decision, as commissar for war, to use former tsarist officers to build up the Red Army, while attaching Communists to them as political commissars to guarantee their reliability. Many Communists questioned the wisdom of such a policy, including Lenin, who dropped his opposition only when he learned from Trotsky that there were over 40,000 such "military specialists" (as they were known) employed in the Red Army, and that without these, and the more than 200,000 former tsarist NCOs, it would be in danger of breaking down. However indispensable, it was not a device that worked smoothly. There were frequent cases of treason during the civil war, and strong opposition continued to be shown by many leaders of Red guerrilla bands, who objected to being subordinated to conservative tsarist ex-officers, as well as by left-wing Communists, who reminded Lenin and Trotsky of their earlier promises to replace the standing army (as well as the political police) with a people's militia.

The North Caucasus Military District soon became a center of opposition to Trotsky's policy and one of the sources, like the earlier Bolshevik Committee in Baku, from which Stalin recruited the men he would rely on later. Closely associated with Stalin was Kliment Voroshilov, an old Bolshevik who had shared a room with him at the first party congress Stalin had attended at Stockholm in 1906. An organizer of the oil workers' union and a member of the Baku committee, Voroshilov had served as a NCO in the tsarist army during the war and thanks to Stalin was appointed as commander of the Tenth Army. Another ally from Baku days and political commissar of the Tenth Army was Sergo Ordzhonikidze, who had persuaded Lenin to co-opt Stalin to the party's Central Committee in 1912. Both men became members of the Stalin mafia together with the colorful Semyon Budenny, a former regular cavalry sergeant who had become a successful guerilla leader and was appointed head of the First Cavalry Army, with Timoshenko as one of his commanders. Trotsky dismissed them contemptuously as "the NCO's association," but all three rose to power in Stalin's train. Voroshilov succeeded Trotsky as Commissar for War; Ordzhonikidze played a key role in Stalin's industrialization program and became a member of the Politburo; Budenny, Voroshilov, and Timoshenko were to be appointed Marshals of the Soviet Union. On the North Caucasus Front in 1918 the Tsaritsyn group ignored orders from the center, refused to work with specialist officers from the former regular army, and were repeatedly accused of insubordination by Trotsky and the Supreme War Council.

In the message to Lenin of July 7 already quoted, Stalin had pressed to be given military as well as civilian authority. Three days later, Stalin sent a further message:

> For the good of the cause, I must have military powers . . . but I have received no reply. Very well. In that event I myself, without formalities, will remove the army commanders and commissars who are ruining things. That's what the interests of the cause bid me do, and naturally the absence of a piece of paper from Trotsky won't stop me.[4]

With Trotsky's agreement, Stalin was granted the powers he asked for, and made chairman of the North Caucasus Military Council, but he was left in no doubt that Lenin supported the authority of the Supreme War Council. This did nothing to restrain Stalin, who encouraged local commanders to pay no attention to orders from above, and in defiance of instructions from Moscow countermanded the orders of the former tsarist General Sytin, whom Trotsky appointed commander of the southern front, and refused to recognize his authority.

This time Trotsky insisted categorically on Stalin's recall, and threatened to court-martial Voroshilov if he did not carry out orders. Lenin gave way, but to soften the blow sent one of his closest collaborators, Jacob Sverdlov, secretary of the party's Central Committee, in a special train to bring Stalin back with honor and appointed him a member of the (renamed) Revolutionary War Council as well as of the new Council of Workers' and Peasants' Defense set up at the end of November 1918 to mobilize the country's resources for war.

Lenin appealed to both Trotsky and Stalin to set aside the friction between them and work together. Stalin made an effort and in a number of speeches spoke highly of Trotsky's role; but Trotsky could not hide his sense of superiority.

> Only much later [he wrote in his autobiography] did I realize that Stalin had been trying to establish some sort of familiar relations. But I was repelled by the very qualities that would strengthen him . . . the narrowness of his interests, his psychological coarseness, and the special cynicism of the provincial who had been liberated from his prejudices by Marxism but who has not replaced them with a philosophical outlook that has been thoroughly thought out and mentally absorbed.[5]

On Stalin's side too there was more than issues of policy or tactics involved in his clash with Trotsky. Before the breakup of the coalition with the left SRs, the Bolsheviks had been represented in the inner cabinet by three men, Lenin, Trotsky, and himself. Subsequently he had been dropped, and while he retired into obscurity the Soviet government became known to everyone as that of Lenin and Trotsky, just as the party was. Stalin had always accepted Lenin's leadership, the more easily since Lenin was older by nine years. But Trotsky was his contemporary, born in the same year. To his intellectual gifts and reputation as an orator Trotsky was now adding fame as the creator of the Red Army and eventually as the "organizer of victory" in the civil war. For a man as ambitious as Stalin, and as burdened by a nagging sense of inferiority, Trotsky's ascendancy was unbearable, and made more so by the fact that Trotsky scorned to take him seriously as a rival.

Lenin did his best to contain the conflict between the two men, both of whom he valued, even if he judged them by different standards. That Stalin had not lost Lenin's confidence is shown by the further missions to the front on which he was employed during the remainder of the civil war. In January 1919 he was dispatched to the eastern front to report on the disastrous fall of Perm; in May he stiffened the defenses of Petrograd against the Whites and had sixty-seven naval officers at Kronstadt executed for disloyalty; later in the year he was switched back to the southern front to block an advance on Moscow by the Whites after Denikin's capture of Orel.

Stalin emerged from the year 1919 with a mixed reputation: able, yes, a man to be relied on, but also a difficult man to work with, who personalized every situation. Loud in his claims of what he had accomplished, he was harsh in his criticisms of everyone else, seeing treachery and conspiracy where others saw inefficiency and muddle, consumed with jealousy and expending as much energy in feuding with colleagues whom he took to be rivals as in defeating the enemy. According to Trotsky, when the Politburo decided to confer the Order of the Red Banner on him for his part in saving Petrograd in the autumn of 1919, Kamenev with some embarrassment proposed that the same decoration be conferred on Stalin. "For what?" Kalinin inquired, and was then taken into a corner by Bukharin, who told him: "Can't you understand? This is Lenin's idea. Stalin can't live unless he has what someone else has. He will never forgive it."[6]

The final episode in which Stalin was involved during the civil war provided further evidence of the faults for which he was criticized. In May 1920 the Polish army invaded the Ukraine and captured Kiev. The Poles were repelled by a Soviet counteroffensive that took the Red Army to the River Bug. Should Soviet troops cross and carry their advance into purely Polish lands, with the aim of capturing Warsaw? Both Stalin and Trotsky opposed such an adventure. Lenin, however, took a different view. He was still hopeful of revolution abroad coming to the aid of Russia. In 1919 delegations from nineteen countries had come to Moscow for the inaugural meeting of the Communist International (usually shortened to Comintern). Marx had been the leader of the First International of Working Men's Associations between 1864 and 1876; the Second International of Socialist Parties and Trade Unions, founded in 1889, was committed to parliamentary democracy and had broken up when its members found themselves on opposite sides in 1914. Lenin had seized the opportunity to set up a Third International committed to world revolution, under Russian leadership, with its headquarters in Moscow. A second Comintern Congress in 1920 brought delegates from thirty-seven countries and accepted the Twenty-one Points that Lenin laid down for admission. The idea of invading Poland attracted him because, as Clara Zetkin, one of the German Communist party's delegates to the Comintern, said, he was eager "to probe Europe with the bayonets of the Red Army," and try to link up with a Germany still in an unsettled state. Trotsky and the two Poles, Dzerzhinsky and Radek, continued to oppose him, but Stalin came around to Lenin's side and voted with the majority of the Politburo for driving on to Warsaw.

Stalin was not involved in the main attack, which was in the hands of the twenty-seven-year-old Mikhail Tukhachevsky, a former tsarist lieutenant who had distinguished himself in the civil war. Stalin was the Politburo representative with the South-Western Army Group, with responsibility for watching Wrangel's forces in the Crimea, and possible intervention by Rumania, as well as for the southern part of the front against Poland. He engaged in acrimonious exchanges with Lenin and the Politburo about a rearrangement of the fronts. "I have your note about the splitting of the fronts," he telegraphed Lenin. "The Politburo should not occupy itself with such nonsensical trifles." Stalin and the military commander of the South-West Front, A. I. Yegorov, were nonetheless ordered to detach substantial forces northwards to support the left flank of Tukhachevsky's advance on Warsaw. This Stalin first delayed, then refused to do, continuing an independent operation with the First Cavalry Army, commanded by Budenny, which was intended to capture the southern Polish city of Lvov. When the Poles launched a counterattack against Tukhachevsky on August 16, the Red Army suffered a decisive defeat, in which the Poles' ability to take advantage of the failure to cover the Russians' exposed left flank played an important part. Bitter controversy continued for years about who was responsible and had its effect on the relations between Stalin and Tukhachevsky in the 1930s.

Stalin was recalled to Moscow, was censured by Lenin at the Ninth Party Conference, and took no part in the final campaign of the civil war against Wrangel's forces in the south. But his position in the leadership was not impaired. At the Eighth Party Congress, held in March 1919, his had been one of six names found on every delegate's list of candidates for the party's Central Committee: He had been made a member of both the Central Committee's subcommittees created by the Congress, the five-man Politburo and the Orgburo, and he had added to the Commissariat of Nationalities a second, the Workers' and Peasants' Inspectorate, shortened in Russian to Rabkrin, charged with exercising control over government departments. None of this impressive accumulation of offices was affected by his share of the responsibility for the debacle in Poland and his withdrawal from military affairs.

The principal reason, no doubt, was that Stalin had proved himself too useful and hardworking a member of the inner group to be dispensed with. Trotsky recalled asking Leonid Serebryakov, a member of the Central Committee serving with Stalin on the Military Council of the Southern Front, whether two committee members were really necessary, whether Serebryakov couldn't manage without Stalin. "After thinking for a moment, Serebryakov answered: 'No, I don't know how to exert pressure the way Stalin does.' The ability to exert pressure was what Lenin valued most highly in Stalin."[7] Lenin's attitude was decisive, and he appears to have appreciated Stalin not only for his readiness to take on any task, but also for precisely that quality of roughness that in the Postscript to his so-called Testament (January 4, 1923) he condemned as *grubost* (rudeness in speech and behavior) and made grounds for urging Stalin's removal from the office of general secretary. In the earlier 1920s Lenin still regarded this as the proletarian forthrightness of a "practical," which had first attracted his attention to Stalin, and which he saw as a valuable element in a party leadership largely made up of intellectuals of bourgeois origins, like himself. Stalin was not slow to realize that this gave him a privileged position with Lenin, and to take full advantage of it.

I I

WHILE VICTORY in the civil war settled the question of the Soviet regime's survival, the cost of it continued to have a powerful influence on its future development. The most obvious effect was the staggering human losses, the first of many such barely credible, yet well authenticated, figures to appear in the first half of the twentieth century: an estimated fifteen million men, women, and children who perished in the civil war itself and the subsequent famine—sixteen or seventeen million in all for the years 1914 to 1922, if one adds those soldiers and civilians killed during the First World War. Russia's population in 1923 was about thirty million less than would have been expected from projections of the earlier figures. The material losses and devastation were hardly less severe. Industrial production in 1920 reached no more than one-seventh of the 1913 level; the currency had collapsed; workers had to be paid in kind, and barter became the only means of exchange.

Such a setback, which came close to wiping out the social and economic gains Russia had made since the emancipation of the serfs in 1861, would have confronted any government with immense difficulties in stimulating a recovery to prewar levels. This was particularly so for a government that depended on the industrialized and urbanized sector for carrying out its program of radical change. Before 1914, the whole urban sector had comprised under 10 percent of the population (most of these in small provincial towns), and only 2 percent had been employed in manufacturing and mechanical industries, compared with more than 11 percent in the U.S.A. It was this sector, far more than the much larger rural sector, that suffered most severely from the civil war, especially the cities: The urban population fell from under 19 percent to 15 percent of the whole; Moscow lost half its population, Petrograd two-thirds. Death and emigration decimated the middle-class administrative, managerial, and intellectual talent in the country, and halved the industrial working class on which the Soviet system depended, many of them killed fighting in the Red Army, many more (an estimated eight million) returning to their native villages.

It was the rural sector and the peasantry that survived best. As a proportion of the population they increased, at the expense of the urban sector, to more than four-fifths of the total, and over 86 percent of the employed population. The peasantry had also consolidated its social strength as a class. Between 1917 and 1921 a rural revolution had taken place in Russia. As Stalin had foretold, to win and keep peasant support, the Communist party had to abandon any idea of nationalizing the land or collectivizing agriculture and allow the peasants (they could hardly have stopped them) to drive out the landlords and divide the land among themselves. The outcome was a leveling out in the size of holdings and a corresponding increase in the number of "middle" peasants (*serednyaki),* reducing the number of poorer and landless peasants on the one hand, and of the richer peasants on the other. This had important economic effects, cutting the amount of surplus produce that the latter supplied to the market, with serious consequences for the food supplies of the towns and the Red Army.

The social consequences were even more important. For, while the urban-industrial sector, to which the Communists looked for support in the process of modernization, emerged weakened, the rural-agrarian sector, rooted in an older, deeply conservative culture of its own, emerged strengthened, reversing prewar trends. In the peasants' eyes, the division of the land, which they had always believed belonged to them and had been stolen from them by the landowners, righted an ancient wrong and completed the emancipation of 1861—which had abolished serfdom but had cheated them of the land. Any government that tried to take the land back from them in order to collectivize agriculture would meet determined resistance.

The other major effect of the civil war, besides this shift in the balance of social forces, was on the character of the Communist party. "War Communism," the phrase used to describe this phase in the party's history, refers not just to its involvement in military operations but to the "militarization" of the other sides of the party's activities as well. It would need the genius of Goya in a Russian version of *The Disasters of War* to convey the horrors of the civil war, and the casual attitude it bred on both sides toward the everyday occurrence of torture, atrocities, the burning down of villages, and the shooting of prisoners. Habituated to giving commands and employing force as well as terror, the Communist leadership came to see compulsion as a way of solving intractable economic and social problems as well. Karl Radek* characterized it as a period in which "they hoped to force their way by a short cut, rifle in hand, into a classless society." In the decree of September 2, 1918, which declared a state of emergency, the government proclaimed the Soviet republic "an armed camp," and similar military metaphors became commonplace in describing its policies to deal with industrial, labor, and supply problems.

The most acute of these, in a devastated and disorganized country, was the supply of food. If Lenin reluctantly accepted the postponement of the collectivization of agriculture, he was determined not to allow free trade in grain to continue, declaring it to be tantamount to the restoration of capitalism. A central feature of War Communism was the organization of armed "food detachments" to requisition surplus grain supplies (or what they declared to be surplus) from the peasants. Resistance was widespread. The peasants hid their stocks and cut production, so that less food than ever became available. As Lenin himself later admitted, it was a disastrous policy[8] and had to be abandoned. But in 1918 through 1920 he described it as "a truly fundamental battle between capitalism and socialism" and

---

*Polish-born Karl Radek was a brilliant political journalist who played a leading role in the Communist International in the early 1920s. Expelled from the party as a Trotskyite, he recanted and sought to ingratiate himself with Stalin. This did not save him from being arrested and perishing during the purges of 1936–38.

insisted that it should be ruthlessly pursued without regard to the consequences in terms of alienating the peasantry.

There was a parallel case in the treatment of industrial labor. In the first flush of enthusiasm, the workers' control of industry was decreed in November 1917. The results, however, were disastrous. Industrial production came close to collapse and Lenin was forced to turn to bourgeois specialists to provide the necessary technical and managerial advice, and put pressure on the trade unions to raise productivity. The government had already started to militarize labor. First, the armies were employed on such tasks as felling timber and transporting food and fuel. Then, on Trotsky's initiative, they were reorganized into "Labor Armies." The third stage, instead of using conscripted soldiers for industrial work, was to conscript industrial workers for labor like soldiers, a measure that Trotsky, newly appointed commissar of transportation, advocated as a way of reintroducing labor discipline.

In 1920 Trotsky published *The Defense of Terrorism,* the most forthright statement of the principles of War Communism. Brushing aside parliamentary democracy, equality before the law, and civil rights as bourgeois frauds, he argued that the class war could be fought and won only by force, not by votes. To reject terror was to reject socialism. He who willed the end must will the means as well: *À la guerre comme à la guerre,* a favorite remark of Lenin's. The state was organized in the interest of the working masses, but

> this does not exclude the element of compulsion in all its force. The principle of compulsory labor service has just as radically and permanently replaced the principle of free hiring as the socialization of the means of production has replaced capitalist property. [9]

Once the end of the civil war was in sight, however, the militarization of labor and requisitioning had to be abandoned, as part of Lenin's abrupt change of policy in the spring of 1921. The period of War Communism was no more than a temporary phase that ended with the exceptional circumstances of the civil war, but a substantial number of members of the party, as we shall see, while accepting Lenin's arguments in 1921 for a change of course, did so with reluctance, and continued to look back with pride to the civil war and War Communism as the heroic period of the party's history, when the revolutionary will to break with the past and impose a new order on society, at whatever price, was untrammeled by compromise and accomplished the seemingly impossible by turning defeat into victory. As a result, when Stalin, who had shared this experience, decided at the end of the 1920s to renew the attempt to complete the revolution by storm, it was of great advantage to him, in seeking to generate a further release of revolutionary energy, to be able to appeal to the tradition of War Communism as a precedent.

. . .

A T T H E B E G I N N I N G of the 1920s, however, the current began to flow in the opposite direction, and Stalin, taking his cue from Lenin, went with it.

Throughout the civil war, fear that a defeat for the Reds would be followed by a restoration of the old order and a demand by the former landowners for a return of their estates had acted as a restraint on carrying resistance to the Communists too far. With victory for the Reds now certain, this was removed. Returning soldiers and deserters stiffened the villages' resistance, and peasant risings, in which bands of several thousand men were involved, reached the proportions of a guerrilla war in Tambov and other provinces in the winter of 1920–21. At the same time the growing unrest among the workers in Moscow and Petrograd and other industrial centers found expression in strikes and demonstrations, particularly after the government announced that the bread ration would be cut by a third.

As the Communists' military fortunes improved, so opposition to Lenin's and the leadership's policies began to appear inside the party as well. At the Ninth Party Congress in March 1920, a group calling itself the Democratic Centralists protested against the growing centralization of power and the authoritarian tone the leadership had adopted. Its leader, T. V. Sapronov, described the Central Committee as "a small handful of party oligarchs." During the summer and autumn of 1920, it was the issue of democracy in the industrial sector that became the focus of criticism. There was a substantial body of opinion in the party, in the trade unions, and the working class, which found it hard to give up the belief in the workers' control of the factories, which Lenin had discarded as a utopian illusion when he brought back professional management and pressed the unions to give priority to industrial discipline and raising productivity. The Workers' Opposition, led by Alexandra Kollontai and Alexander Shliapnikov (a former metalworker and the first people's commissar for labor) with strong support from the rank and file, called for increased reliance on the proletariat in decision making, for autonomy for the trade unions, and for a dominant union role in managing industry.

In the six months leading up to the Tenth Party Congress in March 1921, an open debate developed within the higher echelons of the party in protest against the growing centralization and militarization of power and the gap opening up between its leaders and the proletariat they claimed to represent. Lenin was more prepared than Trotsky to make practical concessions to the trade unions, but he was determined to make none at all on his fundamental principle, the role of the party as the vanguard, the authoritative leader, of the proletariat. In 1902, he had written in *What Is to Be Done?*: "There can be no talk of an independent ideology being developed by the working masses on their own." [10] Experience had only confirmed that view: Without the party to exercise it, the dictatorship of the proletariat was nonsense. He had no intention now of allowing the party's unity to be destroyed by left-wing calls for workers' democracy. Throwing his unique authority into the scale and using all the leadership's resources to mobilize support in the elections, he succeeded in securing an overwhelming majority among the delegates to the Party Congress due to meet on March 8, 1921.

Six days before it met, however, the party was shaken to its foundations by the armed revolt of the sailors and garrison at the Kronstadt naval base, which had been a Bolshevik stronghold in 1917, but which now called, in the name of October, for a third revolution to overthrow the oppressive regime of the Communists, the "Commissarocracy." "This was the flash," Lenin later admitted, "which lit up reality better than anything else," and revealed how serious was the crisis confronting the party.

Lenin's response was unhesitating. First, the uprising must be suppressed. The fact that the Kronstadt Provisional Revolutionary Committee justified its action by quoting, against the Communist leadership, demands and slogans borrowed from the Bolsheviks in the early days of the revolution was irrelevant. In Lenin's eyes this was counterrevolution, and the only consideration was, "Who whom?" The Red Army soldiers' reluctance to fire on sailors and workers was overcome by a combination of promises, threats, and lies, and in an offensive directed from Moscow by Trotsky and led by Tukhachevsky, the fortress was stormed and several hundred, possibly thousands, of its defenders shot without trial.

Lenin seized on the opportunity to identify his left-wing critics with the "counterrevolutionary forces" at work in Kronstadt. In his opening speech to the Party Congress he denounced the Workers' Opposition as a threat to the security of the revolution. It represented an "anarcho-syndicalist deviation" and, "hiding behind the back of the revolution, a petit-bourgeois anarchist element."

Lenin, however, was not content with repressing the revolt and turning the table on the Workers' Opposition. He proceeded to attack the root of the trouble, showing again his remarkable ability to draw unpalatable conclusions and act upon them decisively. As he later admitted:

> We had advanced too far . . . we had not secured a sufficient base. . . . The masses had sensed what we ourselves could not as yet consciously formulate . . . namely, that the direct transition to purely socialist forms was beyond our strength and that unless we proved able to retreat and to confine ourselves to easier tasks, we would be threatened with disaster.[11]

Following the same principle that had led him to accept the Brest-Litovsk Treaty, Lenin showed his readiness to sacrifice everything else to the retention of power, not from personal ambition but for the ultimate achievement of his objectives. The decisive concession ("the peasant Brest-Litovsk," the independent-minded Ryazanov called it) was the immediate abolition of the forced requisitioning of grain and food, to be replaced by ordinary taxation, first in kind, then in money, leaving the peasants free to sell any surplus. No sooner was this passed by the congress than over two hundred delegates set off to harangue the reluctant Red Army soldiers, who were being driven across the ice, at pistol point, to attack the Kronstadt garrison. According to one experienced political commissar, the announcement that the requisitioning was to be abolished produced "a radical change of mood among the peasant soldiers." [12]

The measures Lenin persuaded the party to adopt were intended as more than temporary expedients. Subsequent changes allowed private enterprise to be reintroduced in small- and medium-sized industry and trade; foreign capital was invited to restart investment in Russia, even in large-scale industry, and the ruble was stabilized. In effect, a mixed economy and a large measure of free trade were restored in Russia in place of War Communism, a major change in strategy.

With this New Economic Policy (NEP), Lenin hoped to break through the shortages that were crippling the country and reestablish an economy that worked:

> We have gone too far [he told the Party Congress] on the road of nationalizing trade and industry. . . . We know that only an agreement with the peasantry can save the socialist revolution in Russia, until the revolution breaks out in other countries. [13]

Meanwhile, for the long term, the state reserved to itself the ownership of large-scale industry, foreign trade, and transport, as well as overall economic control, allowing the nationalized and private sectors to compete on a commercial basis, in the confidence that socialism would prove its superiority and gradually expand while the private sector contracted.

Under the impact of the Kronstadt uprising, Lenin's proposals were carried almost without debate. The question whether it was a tactical retreat or an "evolution" remained unanswered. But there was an obvious danger that so radical and sudden a reversal of policy might deepen the divisions within the party once the crisis was over. Lenin sought to guard against this by matching greater freedom in the economic sphere with a tightening of central control in the political. It is here that the importance of the 1921 crisis for Stalin's career begins to emerge.

During the congress debates Lenin had endorsed Bukharin's promise that with the end of the civil war the military style of centralization would be dropped and inner-party democracy restored. But this was only preliminary to Lenin's real purpose. "The time has come," he declared, "to put an end to opposition, to put a lid on it; we have had enough of opposition now!"

On the last day of the congress he suddenly produced two new resolutions, on "The Syndicalist and Anarchist Deviation in Our Party" and on "Party Unity." The first formally condemned the Workers' Opposition's demand for the trade unions to manage the economy as "inconsistent with membership of the party," a revival of syndicalist heresies. Such views, it was said, offended against Marxism; but the language used made clear that what they really offended against was Lenin's own insistence that:

> Only the political party of the working class, i.e., the Communist party, is capable of uniting, educating, and organizing such a vanguard of the proletariat and the working masses as is capable of resisting the inevitable petit-bourgeois waverings of these masses . . . and their relapse into trade union narrowness and prejudices. [14]

The second resolution dissolved all groups with a separate platform, such as the Workers' Opposition and the Democratic Centralist group, on pain of their members' immediate expulsion from the party. A further clause (section 7), not made public until January 1924, authorized the Central Committee, "in case of breach of discipline or a revival or tolerance of factionalism, to apply all party penalties, including expulsion," even to members of the Central Committee itself.

Both resolutions were carried by overwhelming majorities, and Karl Radek summed up the mood of the congress in words that were prophetic of his own and many others' fate:

> In voting for this resolution I feel that it can well be turned against us, and nevertheless I support it. . . . Let the Central Committee in the moment of danger take the severest measures against the best party comrades if it finds this necessary. . . . Let the Central Committee even be mistaken! That is less dangerous than the wavering which is now observable. [15]

Once the Tenth Congress had dispersed, Lenin soon showed how little importance he attached to the resolutions on trade-union and party democracy with which he had found it expedient to meet his critics. He was determined to enforce the ban on "factionalism" within the party with the same conviction as he had shown in using force to suppress the Kronstadt uprising. As many as a third of the party's members were either expelled or left in the purge that followed during 1921–22. When the leaders of the Workers' Opposition refused to abandon their right to maintain their views, even appealing (in vain) to the Communist International, they were again condemned by Lenin and the Eleventh Party Congress in March 1922, and two of the "faction's" leaders were then expelled.

III

STALIN DID NOT FIGURE at all prominently in the controversies that divided the party in 1921–22. He had followed Lenin's line during the period of War Communism, and when Lenin swung around to promote the NEP, turned with him. No one, however, benefited more from their outcome, for two reasons. In the long run, Lenin's proscription of "factionalism" legitimized Stalin's later efforts to go a stage further and turn the party into a monolithic structure, just as Lenin's approval of the use of terror by the Cheka legitimized Stalin's later erection of it into a system of government.

The second reason produced a more immediate effect than anyone could have foreseen at the time. If Lenin really meant to root out dissent and protect the party against the disruptive effects of factionalism, it required more than winning debates and passing resolutions at party congresses; it required the systematic day-to-day management of the party. This was not a job for which Lenin, the recognized leader of both government and party, could possibly find time; it was not a job for which any of the three other members of the Politburo, Trotsky, Kamenev, Zinoviev, had either the taste or the gifts. For the fifth member, however, Stalin, it was a natural extension of a role that he had been playing since 1917 and in which he enjoyed Lenin's confidence: that of maintaining contact between the center and the party officials and members from outside the two capitals, who found it easier to come and talk to a man like Stalin, with the same provincial background as themselves, than to former émigrés and intellectuals like Trotsky, Zinoviev, or Bukharin.

The ministerial offices Stalin already filled fit the same pattern. As commissar of nationalities, a position that acquired renewed importance now that the civil war had been won, he was the representative of the Politburo and the Central Committee with whom the local bosses in the Ukraine, the Caucasus, and Central Asia had to deal, in what amounted to the reconstitution of the Russian Empire. His second governmental post resulted from a visit to the Urals in the beginning of 1919 when he found that virtually all the 4,766 Soviet civil servants in the province of Vyatka were holdovers from the tsarist bureaucracy, that the administration was riddled with corruption and inefficiency, and that there was no effective means of communication by which the central government could make sure its instructions were carried out. Stalin proposed that a "control-auditing commission," acting through mixed teams of workers and peasants, should be set up. Lenin liked the idea, and this was how Stalin came to be appointed as commissar of Rabkrin, the Workers' and Peasants' Inspectorate.

Stalin's proposal and Lenin's acceptance of it showed, however, how inexperienced they were in dealing with the problems of bureaucracy. Although a start was made on training a new generation of government officials, Rabkrin failed to provide an answer in the meantime. The real problem went much deeper. Only after the October Revolution did Lenin begin to think seriously about the role of the party once it was in power. In 1920 when he wrote *Left-Wing Communism—An Infantile Disorder,* he described the dictatorship of the proletariat as:

> A persistent struggle against the power and traditions of the old society . . . the force of habit of millions and tens of millions.

Without an iron party tempered in the struggle, without a party

enjoying the confidence of all that is honest in the given class, without a
party capable of watching and influencing the mood of the masses, it is
impossible to conduct such a struggle successfully. [16]

Lenin was clear enough about the principle, but far less so about the ways
in which the party was to carry out this role and the changes that would be
necessary now that it had ceased to be a conspiracy and become a government.

The answer lay in the relationship between the formal and the real
distribution of power in the Soviet Union. The new Russian state was
constitutionally proclaimed a Republic of Soviets. Its government, the
Council of People's Commissars (Sovnarkom—often translated as cabinet
or council of ministers) was formally the executive arm of the All-Russian
Congress of Soviets, each commissar responsible for one or more government departments. But real power continued to reside in the Communist
party, a body not mentioned in either the 1918 or the 1924 constitution.
Policy was decided not in the Congress of Soviets or in the Council of
People's Commissars. The latter was the executive arm, not, as the constitution said, of the Congress of Soviets, but of the Central Committee of the
Communist party and its Politburo. That was where policy was decided—
by members of the Council of People's Commissars meeting in a different
capacity as leaders of the Communist party, then putting on their other hats
as People's Commissars and giving orders through the state machinery, the
different government departments for which they were responsible, for the
policy to be implemented.

But who was actually to carry it out? Five years after the revolution, Lenin
told the Fourth Congress of the Communist International:

> There are hundreds of thousands of old officials who came over to us
> from the tsar and from bourgeois society and who, sometimes consciously
> and sometimes unconsciously, work against us. Many years of hard work
> will be required to improve the machine, to reform it and to enlist new
> forces. [17]

There was no question of the party taking over the administration of the
state or the management of the industries which had now been nationalized.
Its members lacked the necessary expertise for that; until a new generation
could be trained—up to 1928—the new regime had to continue to rely (as
in the case of the Red Army) on administrators and managers who had
survived from the prerevolutionary period. The party's job during this
period was to act in a supervisory, energizing role, to animate the formal
machinery of the state. It had already been called upon to stiffen the army
through the network of political commissars, and to guide the elections and
debates of the Soviets, from the village assembly to the Supreme Soviet.
During the 1920s it extended its penetration of the governmental apparatus
at all levels, including the administration of the union republics (such as the

Ukraine), of the big cities such as Petrograd and Moscow, of the nationalized industries, and of the trade unions.

To carry out such a policy required systematic and detailed work by the
party Secretariat, and first of all a radical restructuring of the party's own
organization. A first attempt at this had been made in March 1919, following the death of Jacob Sverdlov, the party manager who had required a
staff of only fifteen and carried the details in his head. It was then that
the Politburo, concerned with policy, was given formal recognition, and the
Orgburo established to see to its execution and the organization of the
party. The arrangements made after Sverdlov's death, however, proved
unsatisfactory; at the same time, the need to organize the work of the central
bodies so that they were not overwhelmed with business became more and
more apparent. After the Tenth Party Congress (March 1921) it was natural
for Stalin to take over responsibility for directing the work of the secretari-
ats, as a man on whom Lenin knew he could rely and as the only Central
Committee man who was a member of the Orgburo, responsible for distributing the forces of the party, as well as of the Politburo, its policy-
making body. His formal appointment on April 4, 1922, after the Eleventh
Congress, registered a de facto authority that Stalin was already exercising
and received no more than a routine notice in the press. In retrospect this
is a remarkable fact, considering that it was as general secretary of the
party—he assumed no other office until May 1941*—that he built up a
position of arbitrary personal power that has scarcely been equaled in a
modern state. But at the time he almost certainly did not himself see how
far he might develop his new post.

W H A T U S E did Stalin make of the opportunities this gave him?

Robert Tucker has argued that, contrary to the stereotype, Stalin was not
an "organization man," and that, with his instinctive personalization of
every issue, he was not well suited temperamentally to the role of administrator. This is true, but he was no ordinary administrator, interested in
administration for its own sake. What distinguished Stalin (as surely as his
gifts as a charismatic speaker distinguished Hitler) was his instinctive grasp
of how administrative could be transmuted into political power. Both men's
originality lay in seeing how their gifts, as a speaker in Hitler's case, as an organizer and committee man in Stalin's, could be used to secure control of
the party, and how this in turn could be made the means to create a
personal form of power that no one could challenge.

Lenin and the other members of the Politburo allowed so much power
to be concentrated in the hands of one man because no one at the time
grasped the extent of Stalin's ambition, or thought of his accumulation of

---

*Stalin then appointed himself chairman of Sovnarkom, the Council of Ministers, six weeks
before the German invasion.

assignments in those terms; there were jobs to be done that none of the
other leaders particularly wanted, which Stalin was willing to take on, and
for which Lenin, Kamenev, Zinoviev, and even Trotsky on occasion were
glad to propose him. The one man who might have been expected to see
the danger in advance was Lenin, but his normally acute political sensitivity
was blunted by his need for someone to carry out tasks that he saw urgently
needed attention, and his feeling that Stalin was the only one among the
party leaders on whom he could rely to tackle them.

When a former member of the party Secretariat, Evgeni Preobrazhensky,
spoke up at the Eleventh Party Congress (March 1922) and asked how
Stalin or anyone else could combine his party responsibilities as general
secretary with directing the work of two commissariats, Lenin replied:

> Who among us has not sinned in this way? Which of us has not taken
> on several responsibilities at once? And how could we do otherwise?
>
> What can we do now to maintain the present situation in the Commis-
> sariat of Nationalities and get to the bottom of all those Turkestan,
> Caucasian, and other questions? . . . We have to have a man to whom
> any national representative can go and explain in detail what the problem
> is. Where can we find him? I don't believe that Preobrazhensky could
> name any candidate other than Comrade Stalin. The same applies to the
> Rabkrin. A gigantic job. But in order to cope with the inspection work,
> you have to have at the head of it a man with authority, otherwise we'll
> bog down and drown in petty intrigues. [18]

Lenin was not blind to Stalin's shortcomings; according to Trotsky, when
Stalin's name was first proposed for general secretary, Lenin remarked:
"That cook will concoct nothing but peppery dishes." But he suggested no
other name. [19] He had always been impressed by Stalin's "practical" abilities and he was confident that he could manage him. He certainly did not
feel his own position threatened—until he was incapacitated by his first
stroke in May 1922, the month after Stalin's appointment as general secretary.

In the three years between Sverdlov's death and Stalin's succession, a
good deal had already been done. The Secretariat staff had grown from 30
to 600 a year before he took over, and its functions had been divided among
a number of separate departments and bureaus. As general secretary Stalin
gathered around him, as he had at Tsaritsyn, a number of lieutenants who
identified their own careers with his and rose with him. Chief among them
was V. M. Molotov, Stalin's shadow and the quintessential Soviet bureaucrat. Born Scriabin and a cousin of the composer, he joined the party as a
student in 1906 and adopted the name Molotov (which in Russian means
"Hammer") as a pseudonym. At the time of the February Revolution, he
was twenty-seven years old with a bad stammer, a pince-nez, and an
impenetrable "poker-faced" manner which he never dropped. He became
a full member of the Central Committee and its "responsible secretary" in

1921, and remained the executive head of the secretariat when Stalin became General Secretary of the party a year later. Hard working and absolutely dependable in carrying out Stalin's wishes, he was elected a full member of the Politburo in 1925 and went on to serve as Chairman of the Council of Ministers (Sovnarkom) and to achieve fame as the Foreign Minister who signed the Nazi-Soviet Pact.

Lazar Kaganovich, a renegade Jew, was a hard, untiring and ruthless apparatchik who acquired a reputation as the best administrator in the USSR. With no more than a minimal education, but determined to rise from the poverty in which he had been brought up in a Ukrainian village, he decided at an early stage, like Molotov, to pin all his hopes on total identification with Stalin. Like Molotov, Kaganovich laid the foundation of his career in the party's Central Committee secretariat. He was deeply involved in Stalin's program of industrialization and achieved fame as the man who got the Moscow Metro built. Kaganovich passed the test of loyalty during the purges when Stalin unexpectedly asked him: "Lazar, do you know that your brother Mikhail (the commissar for the aircraft industry) is hob-nobbing with the Rightists? There is solid evidence against him." Kaganovich swallowed hard, but replied: "Then he must be dealt with according to the law." The one thing he did was to telephone his brother, who decided not to wait for arrest and shot himself the same day. Molotov was called upon only to submit to his wife's being sent to a labor camp.

After Stalin's death Molotov and Kaganovich were expelled from the Central Committee when the so-called "antiparty group" was defeated by Khrushchev in 1957. Both, however, lived on until their mid-nineties, drawing their pensions and avoiding publicity. Molotov, born in 1890, died in November 1986 and Kaganovich, born in 1893, in July 1991.

The arch-survivor, politically, was the Armenian Anastas Mikoyan, a member of the Central Committee and a candidate member of the Politburo in the 1920s. He became the Soviet Union's permanent commissar for trade, and proved quick enough on his feet to outdo all other survivors of the Stalin era by remaining a member of the Politburo, later Presidium, until 1966, and then retiring with honor.

Within the Secretariat of the Central Committee, which occupied a large building on Staraya Ploshchad, (Old Square), Stalin created his own personal office, the so-called Secret Department. The senior of his personal assistants was Ivan Tovstukha, a tall, thin intellectual who had been an exile in Siberia and had lived as an émigré in France. (According to Boris Bazhanov, another member of the Secret Department, Stalin once remarked to Tovstukha, "My mother kept a billy-goat who looked exactly like you, only he didn't wear a pince-nez.") One of his tasks was to organize the "Special Section," which maintained a liaison with and kept a watch on the OGPU,* providing Stalin

---

*The Cheka, the political police, became known as the GPU after February 1922, and became in turn the OGPU in July 1923 to mark the creation of the USSR. See the glossary under OGPU.

with a private intelligence service of his own, a unique advantage in the struggle for power which followed Lenin's death. Stalin also used Tovstukha to secure control, as an assistant director, of the Lenin Institute and later of the Marx-Engels-Lenin Institute, the Soviet equivalent of the Vatican's Holy Office, for maintaining the "purity" of the Leninist-Marxist ideology.

Boris Bazhanov was Stalin's secretary for Politburo matters from 1923 to 1925. Defecting to the West in 1928, he is a valuable source for the inner workings of the Secret Department. Lev Mekhlis acted as Stalin's personal secretary and later played a sinister role in purging the Red Army. Grisha Kanner was responsible for security, transport, and clandestine operations; in this capacity he supervised the installation of an automatic telephone system, including a "control post" placed in Stalin's desk which enabled the latter to listen in secretly to the conversations of all the others on the circuit, a valuable instrument in the struggle for power which brought Stalin to the top. The Czech technician who carried out the work was shot on Stalin's orders as a spy.

Among others who served for a time as personal assistants of Stalin in the Secret Department and later rose to prominence were Georgi Malenkov and Nikolai Yezhov. The longest-serving was the most surprising appointment. Alexander Poskrebyshev was recruited while working in the packing department of the Central Committee, because Stalin's secretariat included no manual worker. He is described as accustomed to speaking quietly in the coarsest possible language and giving the impression of being almost totally uneducated. Nonetheless he rose to become one of Stalin's assistants, replacing Tovstukha in the early 1930s as Stalin's principal secretary and head of the Special Section. With a phenomenal memory, he served Stalin like a slave, working sixteen hours a day without questioning whatever he was told to do. No one knew more of Stalin's secrets or knew better how to keep them. He came to control access to Stalin as Bormann did to Hitler. This made him one of the most powerful men in the Kremlin, but, unlike Bormann, he made no use of his position for his own benefit. Poskrebyshev survived all the changes and purges only to fall a victim, in the last year of Stalin's life, to the dictator's all-consuming suspicion, and to suffer abrupt dismissal.

The Central Committee Secretariat developed a number of departments, including one for Agitation and Propaganda (Agitprop) which concerned itself with ideology and culture as well as propaganda and the press. But the Secretariat's most important function was to get a grip on, reorganize, and where necessary reallocate or purge the full-time officials of the party throughout the length and breadth of the vast hinterland which lay beyond the two capitals of Moscow and Petrograd.

After the civil war there were large areas where regional and district party committees and bosses had become accustomed to acting on their own, maintaining only the most tenuous links with Moscow. The Secretariat had already set to work on the Augean task of restoring the authority and lines of communication of the party. On the basis of the up-to-date information it had collected, in Stalin's first year in office he was able to report that more than 10,000 assignments of party officials had been made in the previous twelve months. Another 1,000 appointments were approved in the following year, including 42 party secretaries at regional level. It was to direct these operations that Stalin brought Lazar Kaganovich into the Secretariat, which by 1925 employed a full-time staff of 767.

Stalin did not create the party machine, but he completed the work of organizing it. By 1923 the Orgburo and Secretariat had details of the 485,000 members of the party and were able to place nominees they could trust at every level of the party structure. Quite as much as Hitler, not only Stalin but Lenin and the rest of the Communist leaders believed that authority and leadership had to be exercised from above, and that those at the lower levels must be answerable to seeing that the "correct line" was carried out. Stalin could claim that he had provided them with the means to make the model work. "Cadres determine everything" became one of his favorite watchwords. "After the correct line has been decided, success depends on organizational work . . . and the correct choice of people."[20]

But it was also true that Stalin was to prove the main beneficiary. In practice, the thousands of party officials were no longer elected locally, or made responsible to local organizations, even in Moscow and Petrograd; their appointments were "recommended" from the center, and they became part of a unified bureaucracy in which appointment and promotion were in the hands of the General Secretary of the party. The *apparatchiki,* many of them belonging to a tough new generation hardened by the civil war and intent (like Khrushchev, for example) on making their way up the ladder, formed a distinctive group with vested interests in defending their power and prerogatives. It did not take them long to realize that, for both, they depended not only on the favor of Stalin, but also on the increased power he could exercise at the top—no longer than it took Stalin himself to recognize that there was a mutual dependency and that the reliability of the *apparatchiki* was his own greatest asset in any struggle for power that might develop.

No one else in the Politburo had so extensive a knowledge of the party, not only in Moscow and Petrograd but in Siberia, the Ukraine, and the Caucasus; no one else knew so many of the rising generation of officials whose "election" he could secure to party congresses and conferences, or put forward as candidates for the Central Committee; no one, to borrow a term from Roman history, had so large a following of clients. Thanks to his gift of memory, Stalin rarely forgot a face or a name. He was also, far more than any of his rivals among the leadership, the one with whom the party secretaries could most naturally identify, a man whose whole experience had been in Russia, not in exile, a "practical" like themselves who understood their problems and outlook, not an intellectual who patronized them *de haut en bas.* A difficult man with his colleagues, Stalin was always accessible to someone who had come up from the provinces with a problem, ready to listen patiently and give advice, in the process enrolling another client.

By the time Lenin was recovering from his first stroke, in 1922, Stalin had created his power base. There had been nothing spectacular about it; to Trotsky, with his fondness for grand gestures (which aroused fears of Bonapartism), it was typical of the drab mediocrity that was all he could see in Stalin. But it was effective. In the new perspective opened up by Lenin's illness Stalin was in a position to bring to bear the influence he had built up in the party's country-wide structure on the policy-making bodies at the center—the Party Congress, the Central Committee, and the Politburo—where the fight for the succession would be decided.

I V

STALIN'S ADVANCEMENT, so far, had depended upon Lenin's continued confidence and support. In 1922–23 this was withdrawn and Stalin faced the most dangerous crisis in his career. The unforeseen event that changed the whole picture was Lenin's stroke in May 1922. Lenin was only fifty-two at the time, and recovered sufficiently to return for a few months in the second half of 1922. But the question of the succession was immediately opened. Inevitably, his authority was impaired; and he himself began to look on Stalin and his other colleagues in quite a different light. Stalin as a right-hand man whom he could control was one thing. Stalin as his successor, already beginning before the end of 1923 to stake out his claim to an independent position, was quite another.

What precipitated the change in Lenin's attitude was not Stalin's accumulation of power in the party but his handling of the question that had first attracted Lenin's interest to him before 1914, the nationalities question. With the end of the civil war and the Communist recovery of the greater part of the tsarist empire, this became a matter of the first importance, involving close to half the total population, 65 out of 140 million, who were either not Slavs or, if they were, were not Great Russians but Ukrainians. Now that they were in office, how far were the Communists prepared to go in implementing their earlier promises of national self-determination?

No one in the Communist leadership, certainly not Lenin, questioned the centralization of power under the control of a single party. But Lenin distinguished this from that "Great Russian chauvinism" which treated all non-Russians as inferiors, and which he attacked as a vestige of the tsarist regime and the arrogant mentality of its officials. He criticized Communists who wanted a unified school system, in which only the Russian language would be taught, with the comment: "In my view such a Communist is a Great Russian chauvinist. He exists in many of us and we have to fight him." For Stalin, however, who had repudiated his Georgian origins and assumed a Russian identity, this was an unreal distinction: He saw the Bolshevik revolution and Leninism as "the highest achievement of Russian culture," and had less and less patience with the "bourgeois nationalism" of Ukrainians and Caucasians who threatened it by their demands for national-cultural autonomy.

Until his illness Lenin seems to have treated any differences between himself and Stalin as a question of emphasis, or tactics. It was over Stalin's treatment of Georgia that Lenin—who may have been no longer so confident, after his first stroke, of his ability to control Stalin—became convinced of the seriousness of their disagreement. The background was the need to redefine the relations between the huge Russian Republic (itself a federation in which a number of smaller nationalities such as the Bashkirs were given an "autonomous" status) and the so-called "union republics," the historic nationalities—the Ukraine, Byelorussia, and the three Caucasian republics, Georgia, Azerbaijan, and Armenia. As Commissar for Nationalities, Stalin was appointed in 1922 to head a commission and come up with an answer. Stalin's solution was for the latter to enter the Russian Federal Republic on the same basis as the existing "autonomous" republics and for the supreme governmental organs of the Russian Federated Republic in Moscow to become the central authority for all. Georgia and the two other Caucasian republics were not to enter the Russian Federation separately, but as members of the newly formed Caucasian Federation.

Home affairs, justice, education, and agriculture would, at least nominally, be administered by the republican governments; finance, economy, food, and labor were to be "coordinated" from Moscow; foreign policy, military affairs, security, foreign trade, transport, and communications were to be the exclusive responsibility of the central government. When circulated to the borderland republics, Stalin's scheme met with little enthusiasm; only the Central Committee of Georgia's Communist Party, however, openly opposed it.

An independent Georgia under a Menshevik government had been established during the Civil War. It was the last of the Caucasian republics to be occupied by the Red Army in February 1921, after a brief but bloody campaign. The local Bolsheviks, aware of the strength of outraged national feeling, were in favor of a policy of conciliation. Stalin, particularly after a rough reception when he visited his homeland, had no patience with such pleas; he instructed his fellow Georgian Ordzhonikidze, who acted as the Central Committee's proconsul in Transcaucasia, to purge the Georgian party of opponents of his federation scheme. At the same time, without waiting for Lenin's comments on his draft, he went ahead with securing Central Committee approval after his commission accepted it with only one abstention, that of the Georgian representative, Budu Mdivani.

Lenin was still convalescing at Gorki, but his reaction was immediate. Declaring the issue to be one of supreme importance, he asked the Politburo to await his return, adding that "Stalin has a little tendency to be in a hurry." [21] Instead of Stalin's scheme, which he criticized for its overcentralization, he proposed the creation of a new state, a Union of Soviet

Socialist Republics (the USSR), in which the Russian Republic would be on the same level as the other national republics, with equal rights for all. Instead of making the Central Executive Committee of the Russian Federation the supreme organ of the new Union, Lenin argued that a new *federal* Executive Committee must be created, so giving substance to the concept of "a new level, a federation of equal republics." In his response, Stalin made no attempt to disguise his irritation. Of Lenin's five suggested changes, he described one as acceptable, the second "absolutely not," the third of editorial significance only, the fifth as superfluous. Of the fourth, Stalin wrote that it was Comrade Lenin who had "hurried a little." Turning Lenin's own criticisms back on him, he added sarcastically: "There is hardly a doubt that his hastiness will 'supply fuel to the advocates of independence,' to the detriment of Comrade Lenin's reputation for liberalism on nationality questions." [22]

Nonetheless, after a three-hour talk with Lenin at Gorki, Stalin reworked the scheme to meet Lenin's objections along the lines of the Union of Soviet Socialist Republics eventually proclaimed in 1924. The Central Committee, however, added a proviso that the Transcaucasian republics must enter the union not individually but as part of Stalin's Caucasian Federation. The Georgian Central Committee petitioned for Georgia's direct entry into the new union. This went too far for Lenin. He upheld the decision of the Central Committee and rebuked the Georgians for their bitter complaints against Ordzhonikidze's treatment of them. Ordzhonikidze, egged on by Stalin, replied by carrying out a purge of the Georgian party and removing the chief oppositionists from their governmental posts.

The continuing protests from the Georgian party, however, had convinced members of the Politburo, as well as Lenin, that an inquiry needed to be made. Lenin was by now back at work and sensed that a change had taken place since his illness, the most obvious sign of which was the number of issues on which it was necessary to refer to Stalin to learn what was going on. A curiously trivial incident acted as a catalyst to his accumulating doubts about the general secretary. Rykov reported that, when he was talking with one of the Georgian opposition leaders in Ordzhonikidze's apartment in Tiflis, an altercation broke out between the two Georgians in which Ordzhonikidze had slapped the other's face. Lenin found Ordzhonikidze's behavior intolerable. Not even in tsarist Russia would a high official lay hands on a subordinate: In becoming assimilated, Ordzhonikidze and Stalin had acquired the worst habits of Russian officialdom—*khamstvo,* a mixture of brutality and boorishness.

He refused to accept a report exonerating them and directed Dzerzhinsky, the head of the GPU, who had made it, to go back to Georgia and find out more about the quarrel in Ordzhonikidze's apartment. Four days later Lenin was taken ill again, and on the night of December 22–23 suffered a second stroke.

What followed has only become known over a long period of time, much of it after Stalin's death; it leaves no doubt that Lenin's attitude to his former protégé had now changed to outright distrust. This was increased by the steps that the Politburo took to control the situation. After a conference among Stalin, Kamenev, Bukharin, and the doctors on December 24, it was decided:

> Vladimir Ilyich has the right to dictate every day for 5 or 10 minutes, but this cannot have the character of correspondence and Vladimir Ilyich may not expect to receive any answers. He is forbidden visitors. Friends or those around him may not inform him about political affairs. [23]

The justification for such measures was the prospect that Lenin, although almost certainly never able to resume office again, might live on half paralyzed for years and still be able to intervene in politics. Lenin's reaction was to do his damnedest to evade these instructions, a determination increased by the Politburo's choice of Stalin to see that they were carried out.

Searching for an ally, Lenin turned to Trotsky. Twice in the course of 1922 he had urged Trotsky to accept the post of a deputy chairman of the Council of People's Commissars, and twice Trotsky had refused, failing to see the opportunity Lenin was offering him to establish his political position as first among his deputies. In December, however, when Lenin opposed a move by Stalin to relax the government's monopoly of foreign trade, he was delighted to find that Trotsky was willing to put his views to the Central Committee, and even more delighted when the committee was persuaded to reverse its original decision. "We have captured the position without a fight," he wrote. "I propose that we do not stop but press on with the attack." In a private talk with Trotsky Lenin renewed his offer of the post of deputy chairman and declared he was ready to form a bloc to fight bureaucratism in both the state and the party. A few days later, however, Lenin suffered his second stroke and nothing more came of a proposal that could have had far-reaching consequences for Stalin. [24]

Confined to his apartment in the Kremlin, Lenin's only channel of communication now was through his wife Nadezhda Krupskaya, his sister Mariya, and his secretaries. But the former conspirator (the status to which he was now effectively reduced) had not lost his fighting spirit. By threatening to go on strike and refuse to cooperate with the doctors' treatment, he secured the right to work for more than a few minutes a day on what he called his "diary." It was no diary but the last message to the Party Congress, which Lenin, in the face of death, secretly dictated at intervals between December 23 and January 4, 1923, and which has become known as his "Testament." [25]

Alarmed that the increasing bureaucratization of party and state was leading to the alienation of both from the workers and peasants whose interests they should serve, Lenin urged an expansion in the numbers of the Central Committee. At the time this had thirty-seven full members and nineteen candidate members, including Lenin and the other members of the

Politburo. Lenin called for the committee to be increased to 50, or even 100. An expanded Central Control Commission, again with as many as 100 members, would assume responsibility for the control of both government and party, and join the Central Committee in a plenum which would become the party's supreme political authority. In both cases Lenin insisted that the new members should be workers and peasants, chosen:

> Preferably not from among those who have had long service in Soviet bodies, because those have already acquired the very traditions and prejudices which it is desirable to combat. . . . They must be closer to being rank-and-file workers and peasants.

Lenin hoped that these new members, by attending all the sittings of the Central Committee and the Politburo and reading all the documents, "would be able, first to give stability to the committee itself and second to work effectively on the renewal and improvement of the state apparatus."

By stability, Lenin said, he meant the avoidance of a split, the chief danger of which arose from the relations between Stalin and Trotsky.

> Comrade Stalin, having become general secretary, has concentrated limitless power in his hands, and I am not sure that he will always manage to use this power with sufficient caution. Comrade Trotsky on the other hand is distinguished not only by his exceptional capabilities (perhaps the most able man in the present Central Committee) but also by his excessive self-assurance and excessive absorption in administration.

Lenin did not speak of either man as a successor; what preoccupied him was the danger that the qualities of "the two outstanding members of the Central Committee" could lead inadvertently to a split in the party. He believed that the best way of averting this was by increasing the size of the committee.

Lenin referred in passing to Zinoviev and Kamenev, but did not include either in the same class as Stalin and Trotsky, any more than he did two younger members of the Central Committee, Bukharin and Grigori Pyatakov, whom he described as possessing exceptional talents but needing more time to develop.

Nine days later, Lenin added a postscript:

> Stalin is too rude, a fault tolerable in the relations among us Communists, which becomes intolerable in the office of general secretary. Therefore I propose to the comrades to find a way to transfer Stalin from that office and appoint another man more tolerant, more loyal, more polite and more considerate of comrades, less capricious, etc. This circumstance may appear an insignificant trifle, but in view of what I have written above about the relations between Stalin and Trotsky, it is not a trifle, or it is such a trifle as may acquire a decisive significance. January 4, 1923 [26]

Once the letter was completed, several copies were made and placed in a sealed envelope marked "Secret, not to be opened except by V. I. Lenin and after his death by Nadezhda Krupskaya."

The letter was addressed to the Twelfth Party Congress (to be held in the spring of 1923), which Lenin still hoped he might attend. It has hitherto been assumed that the letter remained unknown to the other Russian leaders until May 1924 when Krupskaya, following Lenin's death in January, placed it before a plenum of the Central Committee discussing the arrangements for the Thirteenth Congress. However, a carefully documented article published in *Pravda* in February 1988 suggests that Lydia Fotieva, Lenin's secretary, gave Stalin and several other Politburo members an account at the time (December 1922) of the evaluation Lenin had made of six of them, although not of what was said in the postscript.[27] No mention of the letter, however, was made at the 1923 congress.

Trotsky later claimed that it had been Lenin's intention to create a position that would allow him to succeed as chairman of the Council of People's Commissars. This may indeed have been what Lenin had in mind in urging Trotsky to accept appointment as a deputy chairman, the opportunity that—unlike Stalin and the general secretaryship—Trotsky failed to seize. But in his letter (the so-called "Testament") to the congress Lenin deliberately avoided naming anyone as his successor; this suggests that he thought in terms of a collective leadership, with all six of those he mentioned working together under strict supervision by the Central Committee and the Central Control Commission.

At the same time that he dictated his letter to congress, in notes dated December 30–31, 1922, Lenin returned to the nationalities question. Angered by reports of Stalin and Ordzhonikidze speaking of burning out nationalist sentiments with a red-hot iron, Lenin described the episode of the slap on the face as symptomatic of "the swamp in which we have landed." It was essential to avoid such rudeness (the word he had applied to Stalin, *grubost*) in Great Russian dealings with the minority nations. Ordzhonikidze deserved exemplary punishment; but the real blame rested with Stalin and his precipitate haste, his rancor against Georgian nationalist feeling, his excess of administrative zeal, and his dictatorial methods. Stalin's constitution was a sham. It would not protect the non-Russian peoples "from invasion of their rights by this typical Russian man, the chauvinist, whose basic nature is that of a scoundrel and repressor, the classical type of Russian bureaucrat." The fact that neither Stalin nor Dzerzhinsky (who had carried out the inquiry) could claim to be Russians only made the offense greater: "It is well known that Russified aliens always overdo things when they try to show themselves authentic Russians by adoption."[28]

While the notes on the Georgian issue were set aside for use in the Twelfth Party Congress, Lenin dictated two articles in January and February 1923 that were intended for publication in *Pravda*. Their subject was the need to make better arrangements for controlling the growth of bureaucratism in the Soviet (that is, governmental) and party administrations. A particular object of Lenin's criticism in the second article was Rabkrin, over which Stalin had presided until he became general secretary, and which

Lenin now castigated for the bureaucratic vices it had been set up to eradicate. Stalin was not mentioned by name, but Lenin's scathing attack on bureaucracy left no doubt that he was the target. "Everyone knows that a worse-organized institution does not exist and that under present conditions nothing can be expected from this commissariat." Lenin added, with a glance at the parallel Central Control Commission of the party which Stalin also headed: "Let it be said parenthetically that we have bureaucracy not only in Soviet institutions but in party institutions as well." Lack of civilized manners (the same complaint) was at the root of the trouble.

> People dilate at too great length . . . on proletarian culture. We would be satisfied with real bourgeois culture for a start and we would be glad, for a start, to dispense with the cruder types of prebourgeois culture, i.e., bureaucratic and serf culture. In matters of culture, haste and sweeping measures are the worst possible things.

The first article appeared in *Pravda* on January 25, 1923, but Bukharin, the editor, hesitated to publish the much more critical second one, with its specific proposals for reform. At a special meeting of the Politburo, called at Trotsky's request after Krupskaya had asked for his assistance, a majority was against; Valerian Kuibyshev even suggested printing a single number of the paper containing the article in order to satisfy Lenin. But the view that an article by Lenin could not be concealed from the party prevailed, and under the title "Better Less, But Better," it appeared on March 4.[29]

By then Lenin, perhaps acting from a premonition, summoned up his failing strength to make his final move against Stalin. On March 5 he dictated a letter to Trotsky asking him to take up the defense of the Georgians in the Central Committee. With the letter he sent the December notes he had made on the nationalities question. The next day he sent a telegram to the Georgian leader Budu Mdivani and his supporters saying that he was "following your case with all my heart" and preparing to support them.[30] But Trotsky declined to act, on the grounds of ill health, and Stalin was able to overwhelm the Mdivani ruling group in Georgia by packing their party conference and sweeping them out of office.

At the same time that he wrote to Trotsky, Lenin also wrote to Stalin, taking up an episode that had occurred in late December. Angered at Lenin's intervention in the dispute about the foreign-trade monopoly, and taking advantage of the responsibility he had been given to supervise Lenin's medical regimen, Stalin had telephoned Krupskaya, upbraiding her violently for allowing the doctors' orders to be violated, and threatening to bring her before the Central Committee. Krupskaya said nothing to Lenin at the time, contenting herself with a dignified letter to Kamenev asking for his and Zinoviev's protection. But at the beginning of March Lenin came to hear of what had happened and wrote to Stalin:

Respected Comrade Stalin,

You had the rudeness [the same word, *grubost*] to call my wife to the telephone to abuse her. Although she expressed her willingness to forget what was said, the fact became known, through her, to Zinoviev and Kamenev.

I do not wish to forget so easily what was done against me, and there is no need to point out that what is done against my wife I consider to be against me also. Therefore I ask you to consider whether you agree to take back what you said and apologize, or whether you prefer to break relations between us.

With respect,
Lenin[31]

A recent discovery has produced a note from Stalin to Lenin in which he wrote: "If you consider that I must take back my words, I can take them back, but I fail to understand what the issue is, where my guilt is."[32] Lenin is reported to have been too ill to read Stalin's letter. An apology of some sort is also said to have been sent to Krupskaya, but Lenin's breach with Stalin was never healed. On March 6 his health took a turn for the worse and on March 10 he suffered a further stroke which deprived him of the power of speech and paralyzed his right side, preventing him from taking any further part in affairs. In the summer and autumn of 1923 he improved sufficiently to walk a little, even to pay a secret farewell visit to Moscow. A number of party and government officials paid him visits, but Stalin was not among them; the two men never met again.

v

FOR STALIN it must have come as a shock to realize that the man whom he had admired more than anyone else, and to whose confidence he owed his rise, had now become an enemy. He kept Lenin's last letter for the rest of his life; when he died it was found in a drawer of his writing desk and was read out for the first time by Khrushchev in his secret speech to the Party Congress of 1956. In 1923, Stalin still did not know how far Lenin was prepared to go, or of his intention to propose that he should be removed from office as general secretary; but he was well aware that something was being planned for the next (the Twelfth) Party Congress, and the knowledge that he would no longer have to face Lenin in person was a great relief.

In Lenin's absence, party policy and the day-to-day conduct of affairs was decided by a troika of Zinoviev, Kamenev, and Stalin. There was no love lost among them, but they were united by their even greater distrust of Trotsky. On paper their position appeared strong. Kamenev, who acted as chairman of the Politburo in Lenin's absence, was one of his two deputies as chairman of the Council of People's Commissars and also in his own right chairman of the Moscow Soviet; Zinoviev was chairman of the other big city organization, the Leningrad Soviet, and also of the Comintern, the Third

(Communist) International; Stalin, besides being commissar for nationalities, held the key position of general secretary of the party. What Trotsky had, however, was something quite different, not an accumulation of offices, but stature and charisma, the aura of the revolutionary leader which he shared with Lenin and which drew a tumultuous ovation when he appeared at the congress. For most members of the party—and for Trotsky himself— he was still the obvious successor to Lenin, if the need arose.

If Trotsky should make a bid for the succession, there were three issues on which there was already a groundswell of criticism against the party leadership and which he could turn to his advantage. One was bureaucracy and the threat to inner-party democracy; the second was economic policy; the third was the problem of the nationalities and the new constitution. On all three Lenin, as he turned away from Stalin, had shown a disposition to turn to Trotsky.

Enough has been said about the growth of bureaucracy and the reaction to it. Economic policy reappeared as an issue only when the NEP had achieved its immediate objectives. By the spring of 1923, the economy had recovered sufficiently from the setbacks of the civil war to open the way to debate and disagreement about options for the future. The underlying issue was how to deal with the so-called "scissors crisis," falling agricultural prices and rising industrial prices. The cautious right-wing answer adopted by the majority of the leadership, led by the troika of Zinoviev, Kamenev, and Stalin, gave priority to the recovery of the peasant sector of the economy, financing the growth of industry from the peasants' growing prosperity and purchases. These, it was argued, would produce a market-led expansion of small-scale and consumer-goods industries, and that in turn would stimulate the expansion of the heavy, capital-goods industry. As part of the extension of the NEP, a more lenient tax system was designed to conciliate the peasantry, while a tight control of credit would stabilize the currency and force industry to concentrate production in the most efficient enterprises even if this meant a rise in unemployment.

The left opposition, led by Trotsky, sought to give priority to the development of industry and the interests of the industrial workers which, it was argued, must be the heart of any socialist program. Trotsky's "Theses on Industry," prepared for the Twelfth Party Congress, declared: "Only the development of industry creates an unshakable foundation for the proletarian dictatorship." With Lenin's support, Trotsky called for expansion of the authority of Gosplan, the State Planning Commission, and a comprehensive economic plan, with the subsidization of industry, particularly heavy industry, using the state's allocation of capital to achieve the plan's long-term objectives.

At the Politburo meeting to settle arrangements for the congress, Stalin proposed that Trotsky should make the principal speech in Lenin's place. Trotsky declined, fearing that he would be thought to be bidding for the leadership even before Lenin was dead; he proposed Stalin instead, but the latter also refused, leaving it to the vain Zinoviev to accept. Trotsky suffered further embarrassment when Kamenev revealed to the Central Committee that Lenin had asked Trotsky to take up the cause of the Georgians and had sent him a copy of his explosive "Notes on the Nationality Question" with their criticisms of Stalin, which Trotsky had kept to himself for over a month without saying anything about them to his colleagues. Stalin coolly reproached Trotsky with acting deviously and deceiving the party. The Central Committee, impressed by Stalin's candor, decided not to publish the notes but to make them known to delegates in confidence.

When the congress opened on April 17, 1923, Trotsky made another mistake by staying away from the debate on policy toward the nationalities, so allowing Stalin to divert the force of Lenin's criticisms by identifying himself with them, reiterating the principle of self-determination, and denouncing Great Russian chauvinism in forthright language. The disease was not limited to the center, he added, in answer to his Georgian critics: It reappeared in local Georgian chauvinism, directed by the ruling Communist group against other minorities in Georgia such as the Armenians. One reason for stamping out Great Russian chauvinism was because this would mean "overthrowing nine-tenths of that nationalism which has survived or is developing in the individual republics."

In preparation for the congress, Stalin had succeeded in using the resources of his party machine to make sure that a majority of the delegates would support him. Fifty-five percent of the voting delegates were full-time party officials, more than double the number at the Tenth Congress only two years earlier. Ignoring the tension that had developed between the party's absent leader and himself, Stalin referred to Lenin as his "teacher," the leader who always showed them where they had gone wrong, adding with a characteristic touch, "It is long since I have seen a congress as united and inspired as this one. I am sorry that Comrade Lenin is not here." [33]

If Lenin had been, it is unlikely that Comrade Stalin would have continued as general secretary; as it was, Stalin was free to make a virtue of adopting Lenin's own words from his article "Better Less, But Better" in order in his turn to denounce the growth of Soviet and party bureaucracy. He was now prepared to accept Lenin's plan to merge Rabkrin with an enlarged Central Control Commission and make this responsible for checking the degeneration of both. He accompanied this by offering his own version of Lenin's other proposal, to expand the Central Committee and subordinate the Politburo to it. It had not taken long for Stalin to see that such a shift in the balance of power at the center could be made to work to his advantage. While he could not be sure—yet—of a majority on the Politburo, he was already in a position to control the elections to the other two bodies.

Stalin's proposals did not go unchallenged by former members of the Workers' Opposition, but they were adopted by comfortable majorities and even attracted support from former oppositionists, who responded to his call to bring new blood into the leadership. While ostensibly accepting

Lenin's criticism of the party's increasing bureaucratization and his call for reform of its structure, Stalin had in effect turned his proposals inside out. The Central Committee and the Central Control Commission were enlarged, as Lenin had urged, and the latter's powers increased, but no more was heard of Lenin's demand that those to be recruited should be not party officials but rank-and-file workers and peasants. Thanks to Stalin's sleight-of-hand the result of the changes was to increase not reduce centralized control, the opposite of what Lenin had intended.

The elections that followed showed the soundness of Stalin's calculations. While members of the Politburo remained virtually unchanged (one new candidate member, Yan Rudzutak, who was a Stalinist), all the fourteen new candidate members of the Central Committee (including Lazar Kaganovich) proved to be dependable followers of Stalin throughout the 1920s. The Central Control Commission, enlarged from five to fifty, and with greatly increased powers, was controlled by a presidium of nine members who were given the right to attend Central Committee meetings. The attitude that the new commission adopted in protecting party and state against the evils of bureaucracy was made clear by one of the presidium members, S.I. Gusev, in an article on its tasks published in January 1924:

> The Central Committee establishes the party line, while the Central Control Commission sees that no one deviates from it. . . . Authority is acquired not only by work but by fear. And now the Central Control Commission and the Workers' and Peasants' Inspectorate [the former Rabkrin] have already succeeded in imposing this fear. In this respect, their authority is growing.[34]

As chairman of the new Control Commission, Stalin appointed another of his own men, Valerian Kuibyshev, first tried out in the Secretariat, then serving as chairman of the Control Commission until 1926 when he moved on to be Stalin's nominee as chairman of the Supreme Economic Council. His place was taken by Ordzhonikidze. Like Kaganovich, both Kuibyshev and Ordzhonikidze (more briefly) were members of the Politburo, and both played leading roles in driving through Stalin's industrial program in the early 1930s. Unlike Kaganovich, however, they still retained sufficient independence to oppose Stalin; as a result neither survived the purges.

With his hold on the party machine strengthened, Stalin could afford to see the congress adopt a resolution on economic policy that closely followed Trotsky's theses, with their emphasis on the planned development of industry as the essential priority. Following the congress, it was sufficient for the majority on the Politburo to see that no steps were taken to implement the resolution for it to become a dead letter. Only five years later, when not only the left but the right opposition as well had been destroyed, was Stalin ready to put Trotsky's and the left's program into effect.

Trotsky himself was later to recognize the opportunity he had lost. In his autobiography he wrote:

I have no doubt that if I had come forward on the eve of the 12th Congress in the spirit of a bloc of Lenin and Trotsky against the Stalin bureaucracy, I should have been victorious. . . . In 1922–23 it was still possible to capture the commanding position by an open attack on the faction . . . of the epigones of Bolshevism.

It was a failure in political willpower: "Independent action on my part would have been . . . represented as my personal fight for Lenin's place in the party and the state. The very thought of this made me shudder." [35]

Such scruples did not trouble Stalin, but, recognizing the potential strength of Trotsky's position, he was careful as yet not to challenge him outright, being content to draw advantage from the fear that the possibility of a coup by Trotsky still aroused among the other leaders and in the party. Stalin's own manipulation of elections before and during the Twelfth Congress had not passed unnoticed. Zinoviev called an informal meeting of a number of colleagues on holiday, in the conspiratorial setting of a cave near the Caucasian spa of Kislovodsk, and secured agreement to a plan to curb Stalin's powers.

When the letter setting out their proposals reached Stalin, he reacted by going to Kislovodsk in person and proposing that Zinoviev, Trotsky, and Bukharin as members of the Politburo should be given seats on the Orgburo and see the "Stalin machine" from the inside. At the same time, he offered to resign: "If the comrades were to persist in their plan, I was prepared to clear out without a fuss and without any discussion, be it open or secret." [36] Zinoviev, however, took advantage of Stalin's offer to attend Orgburo meetings only once or twice, while Trotsky and Bukharin failed to put in an appearance at all. As to his offer of resignation, Stalin well knew that, if he did resign, it would leave the way clear for Trotsky to claim the succession to Lenin, a prospect that was quite enough to stop Zinoviev and company from pressing their differences with him further.

The Soviet economy ran into a fresh crisis in the summer of 1923, which the government met with orders to industry to put its house in order by cutting back and concentrating production in the most efficient factories. Rising unemployment and wage cuts brought a wave of strikes which underground opposition groups sought to exploit; arrests by the GPU were followed by expulsions from the party. At this point a recommendation of a Central Committee subcommittee, headed by Dzerzhinsky (the head of the GPU), that every party member be compelled to denounce to the GPU anyone involved with underground factional activity, at last led Trotsky to end his vacillations and come out of his tent to fight.

Trotsky's decision was influenced by two other factors. The first was a move by the troika to maneuver him out of his stronghold in the Commissariat of War by expanding the Revolutionary Military Council and adding to it two of his old enemies from civil war days, Voroshilov and M. M. Lashevich. When Trotsky asked for an explanation, Kuibyshev, the chairman of the Central Control Commission, told him: "We consider it necessary to undertake a struggle against you but we cannot declare you an enemy; therefore we must have recourse to such methods."[37]

The second was the developing crisis in Germany, brought on by the occupation of the Ruhr and the runaway inflation, which faced the Russian leadership (through its dominant position in the Comintern) with a decision whether or not to encourage the KPD (the German Communist Party) to attempt to seize power. The Russians were sharply divided: Trotsky, this time allied with Zinoviev and Bukharin, was strongly in favor; Stalin and Karl Radek (the Comintern expert on Germany) were equally strongly against. These divided counsels contributed to the disastrous muddle that followed. The Hamburg Communists, who launched a revolt in the belief that a general uprising had started, were bloodily suppressed; in Saxony and Thuringia, where action was called off at the last moment, the Reichswehr turned out the Communist-socialist coalition governments. A fortnight before Hitler's unsuccessful putsch in Bavaria, the revived Russian hopes of a Communist revolution in Germany were finally shattered amid bitter recriminations over who was to blame.

Against this background, Trotsky published an open letter to the Central Committee on October 8, 1923, in which he denounced the leadership's "flagrant radical errors of economic policy" which had produced the crisis of the summer and put the blame for the deteriorating situation inside the party on the stifling of freedom of discussion by the methods Stalin's Secretariat used to control elections:

> There has been created a broad stratum of party workers who completely renounce their own opinion, at least the open expression of it, as though assuming that the secretarial hierarchy is the apparatus which creates party opinion and party decisions. Beneath this stratum . . . there lies the broad mass of the party, before whom every decision stands in the form of a summons or command. In this foundation mass of the party there is unusual dissatisfaction . . . which cannot express itself by way of the influence of the mass upon the party organization (election of party committees and secretaries) but accumulates in secret and leads to internal strains.[38]

The Politburo retorted that Trotsky's criticisms were motivated by personal ambition to be given unlimited power in the spheres of industry and military affairs. On October 15, however, a secret statement, which could not be dismissed so easily, was submitted to the Politburo, signed by forty-six party figures who had been prominent in the opposition to the leadership since the end of the civil war. This "Declaration of the Forty-six," which soon became known, repeated the same double criticism against "the casual, unconsidered, and unsystematic decisions of the Central Committee" which threatened to produce a serious general economic crisis, and against "the absolutely intolerable regime within the party."[39]

The Central Committee (Trotsky again absent through illness) met these attacks, which it linked together, by formally condemning Trotsky and the forty-six for factionalism and splitting the party on the one hand, while reaffirming, on the other, the principle of democracy and, as proof of its sincerity, throwing open the columns of *Pravda* for a party-wide discussion of issues with a view to working out a program of reform.

Zinoviev opened the debate on November 7 with refreshing candor in an article in *Pravda:* "Our chief trouble consists often in the fact that almost all very important questions go predecided from above downwards." A lively discussion followed in the local party organizations, reflected in the pages of *Pravda,* and lasting for the rest of the month. Toward the end the exchanges grew sharper: Stalin insisted that it was necessary "to preserve the party, which is the fighting unit of the proletariat, from degenerating into a discussion club," while Zinoviev declared: "The good of the revolution—this is the highest law. Every revolutionary says: To the devil with the 'sacred' principles of 'pure democracy.' "[40]

In an effort to preserve the appearance of unity, the Politburo held lengthy sessions in Trotsky's apartment, where he was recovering, in the hope of drawing up a resolution that would end the debate. When Trotsky rejected the first draft, Stalin and Kamenev sat down with him to produce a revised version that would satisfy him. A long list of reforms was drawn up, including genuine elections of party officials, the promotion of new party workers, and renewed efforts by the Control Commission to check "bureaucratic perversion." In return Trotsky accepted a reference to the Tenth Congress ban on factionalism. The Politburo published the resolution, on December 5, loudly proclaiming agreement at last on real reform.

Neither side, however, trusted the other. While enthusiastically endorsing the resolution, Trotsky insisted, in an open letter of December 8, that it would be effective only if the 400,000 members of the party made it so. It was not enough to leave it to the bureaucrats "to take note of the New Course, that is, to nullify it bureaucratically."

> Before anything else, the leading posts must be cleared of those who, at the first word of criticism, of objection or protest, brandish the thunderbolts of penalties. The "New Course" must begin by making everyone feel that from now on nobody will dare to terrorize the party.[41]

Trotsky's letter, and a mass meeting of the Moscow Party Organization at which representatives of the leadership were shouted down, brought a renewal of the original controversy with redoubled fury. When Trotsky called on younger members of the party to save the Bolshevik Old Guard from the degeneration that threatened it, Stalin retorted that no one would make the mistake of thinking that Trotsky, a late arrival in the party, was a member of the Bolshevik Old Guard. He followed up with a question that put Trotsky and the opposition on the defensive. Were they demanding that Lenin's own rules, which Trotsky had endorsed at the Tenth Party

Congress in 1921 and which banned factions and groupings inside the party, be put aside? Yes or no?

At this critical moment, after engaging the Establishment in open conflict, Trotsky abruptly withdrew, ostensibly because of a renewal of his illness, in effect from what appeared to be political paralysis, leaving the opposition without a leader and retreating from Moscow to the Black Sea coast to recuperate. The other members of the Politburo, led by Stalin, Zinoviev, and Bukharin, set to work to smother the opposition by their control of the press and the application of party discipline, cutting off its communication with the party rank and file.

To bring the issue to a head, the Central Committee decided to call, not an elected party congress, but a party conference at which the local branches would be represented by their secretaries and officials, not elected but appointed by the Secretariat. So successfully did Stalin organize the elections that of 128 voting delegates, only 3 belonged to the opposition.

The Thirteenth Party Conference met in January 1924, and this time, in Trotsky's absence, Stalin attacked him directly, listing six principal errors.[42] Who was to guide the party, he asked—its Central Committee, or some individual who thought himself a superman, agreeing with the Central Committee one day, attacking it the next?

> This is an attempt to legalize factions [he declared], above all, Trotsky's faction. . . . The opposition in its unrestrained agitation for democracy . . . is setting loose the petit-bourgeois element. . . . The factional work of the opposition is water in the mill of our party's enemies.

When Preobrazhensky, one of the forty-six, recalled Lenin's criticisms of Stalin in his notes on national questions, Stalin turned on him. They were now praising Lenin as a genius, but:

> Permit me to ask, Comrade Preobrazhensky, why did you disagree with this "genius" about the Brest-Litovsk treaty, why did you abandon this "genius" at such a desperate moment, and disobey him? Where and in whose camp were you then?

"You are terrorizing the party!" Preobrazhensky shouted back. No, Stalin retorted, only issuing a warning to those who bring discord into its ranks. He went on to make public for the first time the secret clause of Lenin's 1921 resolution which prescribed expulsion from the party as the penalty for factionalism. He also threatened severe measures against anyone circulating confidential documents, a possible reference to Lenin's Testament and the postscript proposing Stalin's removal as general secretary. Taking its cue from Stalin, the conference, with only three votes against, censured Trotsky and the forty-six dissidents not only for "factional activity, a direct departure from Leninism, but also for a clearly expressed petit-bourgeois deviation."

VI

THE THIRTEENTH PARTY CONFERENCE of January 1924 represents an important milestone in the development of the Russian Communist party. Up to that point national party conferences and congresses had been real events at which opposition views were not only heard but also listened to, often attracting support that delegates were not afraid to express. If the leadership normally had its way, it was only after it had defended its case and won its majority in open debate. The 1924 conference was the first at which the proceedings were stage-managed and the decisions made in advance, a precedent followed on every succeeding occasion. Stalin had not acted on his own but as a member of the Politburo majority, and he could claim to have tried to reach a compromise with Trotsky. But he was the one who, thanks to the political machine he had created in the secretarial apparatus, had the power to act, to translate resolutions and threats into reality. The Thirteenth Party Conference was the first occasion on which that power was displayed with irresistible effect, and the change it made in the character of the party was recognized as a threat no longer but as a fact.

At this moment, however, when Stalin may have hoped that he had succeeded in suppressing opposition in the party for good, the situation was transformed by Lenin's death. For the last nine months of his life Lenin was in the tragic position of a leader who was aware of the crisis within the party he had created, yet, totally paralyzed and unable to move or speak, could do nothing about it. *Pravda* published a report of the Thirteenth Party Conference and Krupskaya read it to him. He showed agitation at what he heard but could not communicate what he felt. The next morning, January 21, 1924, he suffered yet another stroke and died before evening.

The question of the succession, although never openly admitted, now provided a new focus for opposition and faction fights which henceforward found leaders not on the floor of congress but in a permanently divided Politburo. Far from being put down by the prospect, however, Stalin (according to Bazhanov, his secretary for Politburo affairs at the time) "was jubilant. I never saw him in a happier mood than during the days following Lenin's death. He was pacing up and down the office with satisfaction written all over his face."[43]

This was not surprising. As long as Lenin was alive and might still recover, Stalin was at risk. During the past year he had put on a bold face to cover his uneasiness, and had shown toughness of nerve and skill in maneuvering, thanks to which he came out of a testing time with greater credit than any of the other leaders. Stalin had still to face the further test of Lenin's condemnation in his Testament. But he had not only demonstrated his ability to survive: The moment Lenin was dead he gave the first indication of how he would turn the tables on the man who might have destroyed him by appropriating Lenin's legend.

Once again, Trotsky failed to put in an appearance, this time at Lenin's funeral, a great and emotional occasion. "It was like long, long ago," Nadezhda Mandelstam, the poet's wife, wrote:

Mandelstam marveled at the spectacle: this was the Moscow of ancient days burying one of her tsars. . . . This was the only occasion in my lifetime on which the population of Moscow came out into the streets and formed queues of its own free will. [44]

Another who was present, a French newspaper correspondent Rollin, wrote: "*Mon Dieu,* what an opportunity to miss! Achilles sulking in his tent. . . . If Trotsky had come to Moscow, he would have stolen the whole show." [45]

Trotsky himself later claimed that he was tricked by the Politburo, which gave him the wrong date for the funeral. But the paralysis of his will continued. In his autobiography he wrote: "I knew only one urgent desire, to be left alone. I could not stretch out my hand to lift my pen."

Stalin did not make the same mistake. He was "discreetly prominent" [46] among the leaders bearing Lenin's coffin and lowering it into the vault by the Kremlin wall as a temporary resting place, until the embalmed corpse could be placed in a specially erected mausoleum in Red Square—a suggestion that Stalin is said to have made and that Krupskaya opposed. The evening before, a memorial ceremony had been held in the Bolshoi Theater, which was draped in black. Soviet accounts later contrived to make it appear that Stalin was the only speaker. In fact he was only one of more than a dozen. But the style of his tribute in the catechistic form of a vow, recalling his seminary upbringing, was so unlike that of any of the other speakers that it immediately attracted attention.

Beginning with the declaration, "Comrades, we Communists are people of a special cut," Stalin then went on to repeat, six times in all, a series of liturgical statements and responses:

In leaving us, Comrade Lenin ordained us to hold high and keep pure the great title of member of the party. We vow to thee, Comrade Lenin, that we shall honorably fulfill this thy commandment.

In leaving us, Comrade Lenin ordained us to guard the unity of our party like the apple of our eye. We vow to thee, Comrade Lenin, that we shall honorably fulfill this thy commandment, too. . . . [47]

Krupskaya and the Old Guard Bolsheviks were outraged by what they saw as a display of the worst possible taste, which Lenin himself would have repudiated with scorn. Bazhanov could see only the hypocrisy of Stalin publicly vowing loyalty to a leader over whose death he had privately rejoiced.

Both comments are just, but besides the calculation and sanctimonious playacting, it may well have been that Stalin was relieved, not only to see Lenin dead, but also to be able to reestablish the close relationship with him that had been interrupted by Lenin's illness and hostility in the past eighteen months, a relationship that was necessary to Stalin emotionally as well as politically—his identification with the leader, the *vozhd'*, whose successor he believed himself destined to become.[48] Conviction as well as ambition lay behind that belief. Stalin was beginning to see himself as the one man who had the strength of will and the determination to take the steps necessary to realize Lenin's ideas in practice, ideas from which even Lenin himself had drawn back once he fell ill, and which such prima donnas as Zinoviev and Trotsky lacked the application to carry through.

Was he right? Was "Stalinism," if not the inevitable, at least the logical, outcome of the Russian Revolution, if the Communists were not to abandon their attempt to create a socialist society? Or was there an alternative? These are questions to return to. For the moment it is sufficient to note the part played by chance in the unforeseen illness that first incapacitated, then at the early age of fifty-three killed, the one man who had always had the authority, and eventually had the will, to check Stalin's rise to power at a time when this was still possible.

FIVE

The Creation of the Nazi Party

I

EXACTLY A MONTH after Stalin's "oath" speech in the Bolshoi Theater, on February 26, 1924, the trial for treason of Hitler and the other members of the unsuccessful putsch opened in Munich. The news that he would be given a public trial had rescued Hitler from his mood of despair at the time of his arrest. Confident in his powers as a speaker, he saw the opportunity to remove the sorry impression left by his failure as a man of action and turn the November fiasco into a retrospective triumph.

The device he used was simple, but highly effective. In form, the trial was one in which Hitler, Ludendorff, and the other leaders of the Kampfbund were the defendants, and the triumvirate of von Kahr, von Lossow, and von Seisser the chief witnesses for the prosecution. Hitler, however, reversed the position by not denying, but embracing the charge of high treason, and in effect putting the prosecution witnesses in the dock, with the countercharge that they had been as deeply involved as the defendants but had not the courage and honesty to admit it. "If our enterprise was high treason," Hitler declared in his opening speech, "then Lossow, Kahr, and Seisser must have been committing high treason along with us, for during all these weeks we talked of nothing but the aims of which we now stand accused. . . ." Since everyone in the Munich courtroom knew this was true, Hitler at once succeeded in regaining the initiative. He went on: "I alone bear the responsibility, but I am not a criminal because of that. If today I stand here as a revolutionary, it is as a revolutionary against the revolution. There is no such thing as high treason against the traitors of 1918. . . ."[1] His conclusion, "I consider myself not a traitor, but a German who wanted the best for the German people," was greeted with loud applause in the crowded courtroom.

Von Kahr and Seisser were no match for so skillful an opponent; but von Lossow, who had seen his career terminated after the events of November and now heard himself taunted publicly as a coward, was not to be put down. His speech expressed all the contempt of the officer corps for the

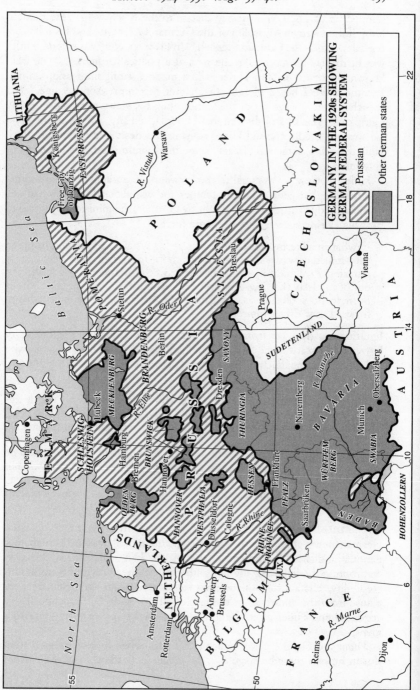

GERMANY IN THE 1920s SHOWING
GERMAN FEDERAL SYSTEM

Prussian

Other German states

jumped-up corporal who tried to dictate to the Reichswehr: "He thought himself the German Mussolini or the German Gambetta, and his followers regarded him as the German Messiah." In his view, von Lossow said, Hitler was fit to play no more than the part of a political drummer. "The well-known eloquence of Herr Hitler at first made a strong impression on me. But the more I heard of him, the fainter the impression became." His speeches were always about the same thing; his views were those of any German nationalist and showed that Hitler lacked any sense of reality. Von Lossow repeatedly accused Hitler of lying and described him as "tactless, limited, boring, sometimes brutal, sometimes sentimental, and unquestionably inferior."

Hitler, however, was equal to the occasion. In an angry cross-examination he made the general lose his temper and was allowed by a sympathetic presiding judge (prompted no doubt by Gürtner, the minister of justice) to turn his closing speech into a tour de force.

> In what small terms small minds think. . . . What I had in mind from the very first day was a thousand times more important than becoming a minister. I wanted to become the destroyer of Marxism. . . . It was not out of modesty that I wanted to be a "drummer." . . . The man who is born to be a dictator is not compelled; he wills it. He is not driven forward, but drives himself.

Ignoring his own far from heroic part, he declared that the failure of November 1923 was the failure of individuals, of a von Lossow and a von Kahr, and that the Reichswehr, the most permanent of German institutions, was not involved.

> When I learned that it was the police who fired, I was happy that it was not the Reichswehr: The Reichswehr stands as untarnished as before. One day the hour will come when the Reichswehr will stand at our side, officers and men. . . .
> It is not you, gentlemen, who will deliver judgment on us; that will be pronounced by the eternal court of history. . . . That other court will not ask us: Did you or did you not commit high treason? That court will judge us . . . as Germans who wanted the best for their people and their Fatherland, who were willing to fight and to die.

The trial lasted for twenty-four days and was front-page news in every German newspaper. For the first time, Hitler had broken through to a national audience. By the end of the trial he had achieved his objective, confronting the failure of the November putsch head-on and restoring his credibility. His appeal to nationalist feeling had again and again won applause from the audience. In the face of all the evidence, Ludendorff was acquitted and Hitler given the minimum sentence of five years' imprisonment.

Thanks to Hitler's performance at his trial, when he was released from prison he had the advantage over his rivals for leadership of the *völkisch* groups of being able to point to himself as the one man who had dared to attempt a putsch and when "betrayed" had refused to repudiate responsibility but had declared he would continue the fight against the hated republic. Nothing shows Hitler's flair for propaganda better than the fact that instead of trying to forget the unsuccessful putsch he built it up into one of the enduring legends of the Nazi movement. Every year on the anniversary he returned to the Bürgerbräukeller and the Odeonsplatz to renew the memory of what had happened there in November 1923, and to salute the courage of those who had died.

Historians have been inclined to accept Hitler's view of November 1923 as a turning point, after which he abandoned any thought of overthrowing the regime by force and decided to work within the constitution, concealing his revolutionary intentions under a guise of respect for "legality," and working to secure power by political means. No doubt the defeat of November 1923, which he was later to describe as "the greatest stroke of luck in his life," forced Hitler to clarify his own mind and clear up the ambiguity that he had exploited by constant references to the "seizure of power" and a "March on Berlin." Henceforward, like Mussolini and his so-called "March on Rome," he would make sure of his reception in advance and arrive by sleeping car on the night train in advance of his followers. But when Hitler spoke of "a new decision," he was exaggerating. Scheubner-Richter, who was close to him, wrote in a memorandum of September 24, 1923: "The nationalist revolution must not precede the acquisition of political power; rather, control over the nation's police constitutes the prerequisite for the nationalist revolution."[2]

Scheubner-Richter paid with his life for the neglect of this advice, shot dead by the police while marching arm in arm with Hitler in the front row on November 9. But Hitler had always premised any attempt to overthrow the government on the willingness of the Bavarian authorities and the Reichswehr to go along with it or at least connive at it—"a revolution by permission of the Herr Präsident," his opponents mocked. Driven by frustration and fear of seeing the opportunity lost, he gambled on bluffing von Kahr and von Lossow into compliance; but once he realized that they had deceived him, and that his plan had failed, he despaired. It was not from lack of courage, for which his war record is sufficient warrant, but from the conviction that the Kampfbund could not succeed on its own, and that the cause was now lost. The reason why the failure of November 1923 marked a turning point was that it strengthened Hitler's hand in his argument with his critics who still dreamed of storming their way into power:

That evening and that day [November 8-9] made it possible for us afterwards to fight a battle for ten years by legal means; for, make no mistake, if we had not acted then I should never have been able to found a revolutionary movement and yet all the time maintain legality. One could have said to me with justice: "You talk like all the others and you will act just as little as the others." [3]

After the putsch I could say to all those in the party what otherwise it would never have been possible for me to say. My answer to my critics was: Now the battle will be waged as I want it, and not otherwise. [4]

Hitler's closing speech at his trial makes a striking contrast with Stalin's celebration of Lenin only two months before. The contrast is more than one of temperament and style. Hitler's shrill insistence on his role as a man of destiny expressed not only his egotism but also a desperate need to reassert his claim to be taken seriously in German politics. Stalin was just as much an egotist as Hitler and no less bent on playing a role as man of destiny, but the outcome of a crisis, which could have brought him as close to a disastrous setback as Hitler, left him with his position strengthened, with no need to reestablish his reputation, and with every reason not to draw attention to his ambitions, but to conceal them under cover of a cult of Lenin with whom neither he (nor, by implication, any other member of the Politburo) was fit to be compared.

One element remains in common, despite the disparity in the positions of Hitler and Stalin in the 1920s: Neither thought of seizing power by force. In Russia the revolution had already been made by Lenin; Stalin wanted the succession to Lenin, but not by a coup—that was the damaging ambition he fastened on Trotsky—but legitimately, with the consent of the party. Everything depended not only on getting rid of his rivals, but also on his persuading the majority of the party *apparatchiki* that the revolution—and they as its beneficiaries—had a better chance of overcoming the contradictions with him in command than with any of the other leaders.

In Germany the revolution still had to be made, but only (as Scheubner-Richter had argued) after the Nazis had come to power. In this case, while maintaining the enthusiasm of his supporters, Hitler had to persuade those whom he hoped would help him into power—the conservative Establishment, the other nationalist parties, above all the Reichswehr—that he was an ally who could be relied on, who might talk in extreme terms, thus mobilizing the mass support that was his great asset in their eyes, but who once accepted as a partner would prove sensible and manageable in office.

In each case, it was only after they had come to power with at least the appearance of legality preserved that Stalin at the beginning of 1930, and Hitler three years later, embarked on their "revolution from above" (Stalin's phrase) represented in his case by the forced collectivization of the Russian peasantry and the crash program of industrialization, and in Hitler's case by the "coordination" (*Gleichschaltung*) of German institutions.

To most of Hitler's supporters such a prospect must have seemed remote when the furor created by the Munich trial died down and he was shut up in Landsberg jail to serve his sentence. Yet, despite the fact that the Nazi party was banned, that its leaders were scattered, and that Hitler, even when released, would have to start again, he himself showed no signs of doubt that he would eventually come to power.

Some forty other National Socialists were in prison with him, and they had an easy and comfortable life. They ate well, had as many visitors as they wished, and spent much of their time out of doors in the garden. Emil Maurice acted partly as Hitler's orderly, partly as his secretary, a job that he later relinquished to Rudolf Hess, who returned voluntarily from Austria to share his leader's imprisonment.

The prison staff treated Hitler with respect as no ordinary prisoner. On his thirty-fifth birthday, which fell shortly after the trial, the parcels and flowers he received filled several rooms. He had a large correspondence in addition to his visitors, and as many newspapers and books as he wished. Hitler presided at the midday meal, claiming and receiving the regard due to him as leader of the party. Much of the time, however, from July onwards, he shut himself up in his room to dictate *Mein Kampf,* which was begun in prison and taken down by Emil Maurice and Hess.

In fact he wrote three books between 1924 and 1928: volume I of *Mein Kampf,* dictated in prison in 1924 and published in 1925; volume II of *Mein Kampf,* dictated at his villa in Obersalzberg and published at the end of 1926; and his so-called *Zweites Buch (Second Book),* dictated to his publisher Max Amann in 1928, but not published until 1961 or even known to exist until the typescript was exhumed in 1958.

Given his indolent habits and his contempt for the written word when compared with the spoken, it is possible that Hitler would never have begun at all if he had not been confined to prison and then banned from public speaking after his release. But there were at least three good reasons why it was worthwhile for him to make the effort. The first was the help it could give him in making good his claim to re-create and lead the National Socialist movement after he left prison. This is not incompatible with the fact that *Mein Kampf* did not sell widely, even among party members, before the party's breakthrough in 1930 (23,000 copies of volume I were sold and 13,000 of volume II by 1929), and that many of those who bought it found it heavy going and never finished it. The British historian Donald Watt has pointed out that movements that make political loyalty a matter of faith seem to have found it essential to have an equivalent to the Bible: Stalin's *Foundations of Leninism* and the works of Karl Marx, Mao's *Red Book,* Louis Napoleon's *Idées napoléoniennes.* Like the Bible, which languishes unread on the shelves of many Christians, such a text need not be read or comprehended. "Its message must of course be capable of reduction to simplicity. . . . But its own complexity and obscurity are an advantage, since they demonstrate the profundity of the leader's vision . . . his ability to grapple with the problems which his followers have admitted their inability to handle. . . . It was enough for them that it existed."[5]

The second reason was the opportunity that it gave him to begin laying the foundations of the Hitler myth, that image of the Führer that was to prove one of the most powerful forces—perhaps the single most powerful one—in attracting the support and devotion of millions of Germans. The third was the chance to sort out his ideas and develop his *Weltanschauung,* the underpinning of ideas that he saw as essential to effective political action.

Like Stalin, Hitler was scornful of intellectuals, yet at the same time eager to establish his own intellectual authority. Stalin sought to do this in the *Foundations of Leninism* (published in the year Hitler was writing *Mein Kampf*), with the claim not to be an original thinker himself, but the authoritative interpreter and heir of the Marxist-Leninist tradition. By preserving the outward appearance of conformity and repeating the ritual phrases, he was able to conceal the extent to which in practice he was deviating from the tradition and acting as an innovator. Hitler, by contrast, never acknowledging the sources on which he drew for his ideas ("the intellectual detritus of centuries" is Hugh Trevor-Roper's description), constantly exaggerating his own originality. Every one of the elements in his worldview is easily identified in nineteenth-century and turn-of-the-century writers, but no one had previously put them together in quite the same way. More important is the fact that, having created his own version, the essential elements of which were set out in *Mein Kampf* and completed by the time he wrote his *Zweites Buch* in 1928, Hitler never altered it. There is a recognizable continuity between the ideas he expressed in the 1920s, his table talk in the 1940s, and the political testament that he dictated in the bunker just before he committed suicide in April 1945.

This is a statement easily misunderstood, since Hitler combined unusual consistency in his governing ideas with an equally striking flexibility in regard to program, tactics, and methods. He drew a clear distinction between the political thinker and the politician, and accorded the latter greater significance. But in a well-known passage of *Mein Kampf,* he wrote: "It may happen occasionally within long periods of human life that the political thinker and the politician become one."[6] Hitler clearly believed that he was an example of such a combination and there is this much truth in his belief: If he was not unique, he was rare among political leaders in the extent to which he sought to put his worldview into literal effect.

II

THE VALUE of *Mein Kampf,* a book that has few rivals in the repulsiveness of its language, its tone, and above all its contents, is that it provides insights into Hitler in both roles—into his mind and his views of the world on the one hand, into the way in which he set about organizing a political movement on the other, with the creation of the Hitler myth as the link between the two.

The basis of Hitler's beliefs was a crude Social Darwinism: "Man has become great through struggle. . . . Whatever goal man has reached is due to his originality plus his brutality. . . . All life is bound up in three theses: struggle is the father of all things, virtue lies in blood, leadership is primary and decisive." [7] In *Mein Kampf* he wrote: "He who wants to live must fight, and he who does not want to fight in this world where eternal struggle is the law of life has no right to exist." [8]

Hitler was fascinated by history, and like Oswald Spengler saw it as a succession of human ages each expressing itself in a distinctive culture of interrelated ideas and institutions: the Greco-Roman culture of the ancient world, which he professed to admire without showing much knowledge of it; the Middle Ages, the culture of which he saw as "Germanic," eclipsed at the Renaissance by the modern capitalist society of the West which, again like Spengler, he believed to be sick and in decline. The capacity to create such cultures was confined to the "Aryan" race, a concept Hitler never defined. "If we divide mankind into three categories—founders of culture, bearers of culture, destroyers of culture—the Aryan alone can be considered as representing the first category.* It was he who laid the groundwork and erected the walls of every great structure in human culture." [9]

Each culture or empire had declined for the same reason: miscegenation, which weakened, then destroyed, the power to continue the struggle that is the law of life. "All the great civilizations of the past became decadent because the originally creative race died out, as a result of contamination of the blood." [10] Hitler believed that Western civilization was decadent and that the future destiny of the German people was to replace it, just as the Germanic tribes had replaced a Roman empire no longer able to defend itself and gone on to create a vigorous new culture.

To achieve this, the Germans must conquer a new German empire which would dominate the European continent. This pointed to a foreign policy that went far beyond the demands for the revision of the Treaty of Versailles with which Hitler began his career as an agitator. No more than sketched in volume I of *Mein Kampf,* this became in volume II a full-blooded policy of acquiring *Lebensraum* ("living space") in Eastern Europe at the expense of Russia. To wage another war for the reestablishment of Germany's 1914 frontiers would be criminal; the only purpose that would justify such action was "to secure for the German people the soil and territory to which it is entitled on this earth."

And so we National Socialists consciously draw a line beneath the foreign policy of our prewar period. We take up where we broke off six hundred years ago. We stop the endless German movement to the south and west and turn our gaze toward the land in the east. At long last we break off the colonial and commercial policy of the prewar period and shift to the territorial policy of the future.

And if we speak of territory in Europe, we can have in mind only Russia and her vassal border states. [11]

*Hitler mentions the Japanese as an example of the second; the third was represented by the Jews.

In his *Zweites Buch* Hitler explains that, thanks to the Bolshevik revolution, this would be a comparatively simple undertaking: "The gigantic empire in the East is ready to collapse." The Slav masses were incapable of creating a state for themselves, and the Germanic ruling group that had dominated them hitherto had now been replaced by a Jewish Bolshevik leadership which, for reasons to be explained shortly, could neither organize nor maintain a state. The war with France, which Hitler had earlier seen as necessary to secure the revision of frontiers, now became (as it proved to be in 1940–41) the preliminary to the primary objective of a successful attack on Russia. The other prerequisites were an alliance with Mussolini's Italy (to which Germany should be ready to surrender the South Tyrol), and with England, with which Germany should at all costs avoid the rivalry overseas that had proved fatal to the kaiser.

The gaps in such a conception are obvious—for example, the fact that, far from suffering from overpopulation, Germany did not have the numbers needed to take over and develop the territory in the East that her armies occupied. But they are less important than the correspondence between the objectives Hitler set out in the 1920s and those he sought to accomplish in the 1940s.

Hitler fully shared that belief in the primacy of foreign over domestic policy which was the traditional view of German history. He had no interest in constitutional and legal or economic and social policies in themselves, looking upon them, in this period of the 1920s, as primarily a means of attracting support and securing a place in the political game. He extended this view to the state itself: "The state is only a means to an end. Its end and its purpose is to preserve the existence of the race. . . . The state is only the vessel and the race is what it contains." [12] So far as the form of the state went, Hitler based everything on the *Führerprinzip,* the principle of leadership. This visualized the concentration of power in the hands of a leader, unlimited by any kind of constitutional or parliamentary control, and with the authority to direct the state to give priority to foreign policy and rearmament, including the conquest of new living space in the East.

Drawing on the experience he had gained since leaving Vienna and the period for reflection in Landsberg jail, Hitler summed up the art of politics in 1928 as "carrying out a people's struggle for existence," subordinating both foreign and domestic policy to that end.

> Foreign policy is the art of safeguarding the momentary, necessary living space, in quantity and quality for a people. Domestic policy is the art of preserving the necessary employment of force for this in the form of race value [*Volkswert*] and numbers. [13]

"Race value" needs explanation. "The source of a people's whole power," Hitler says, "does not lie in its possession of weapons or in the organization of its army but in its inner value, that is, its racial value." [14] To preserve that, it was important for the state to defend its people against contamination by three poisons, each of which he identified with the Jews. These are: internationalism, a predilection for things foreign which springs from an underestimation of one's own cultural values and leads to miscegenation; egalitarianism, democracy, and majority rule, which are hostile to individual creativity and leadership, the origin of all human progress; and pacifism, which destroys a people's healthy natural instincts for self-preservation. In a speech at Nuremberg on July 21, 1927, Hitler declared:

> A people has lost its inner value as soon as it has incorporated into itself these three vices, as it has eliminated its racial value, preached internationalism, given up its self-direction, and put in its place majority rule, i.e., incompetence, and has begun to indulge in the brotherhood of mankind. [15]

I have left to the end the most distinctive feature of Hitler's system, his anti-Semitism, in order to place it in the more general framework of his *Rassenpolitik* (race policy). This extended, on the one hand, to the extermination of the unfit, under the 1933 program for the prevention of hereditarily diseased offspring, even when born to non-Jewish Germans, and thus to the racial basis of Nazi agrarian policy; and on the other to the exploitation and extermination of non-Jewish Poles and Russians as *Untermenschen* (subhumans). There is no question, however, that the Jews occupied a unique place in his *Weltanschauung*. No personal experience has come to light that could help to explain the intensity of Hitler's hatred of the Jews, although some biographers have pointed to the obscene language in which he habitually wrote and spoke of this as pointing to a sexual origin. It is disturbing to consider when exactly was the last occasion on which this man, who was responsible for the death of six million Jews, actually spoke to or met a Jew in person. But "the Jew" as one encounters him in the pages of *Mein Kampf* and Hitler's ravings bears no resemblance to flesh-and-blood human beings of Jewish descent: He is an invention of Hitler's obsessional fantasy, a Satanic creation, expressing his need to create an object on which he could concentrate his feelings of aggression and hatred.

Hitler rationalized these feelings by declaring that what distinguished the Jews from other races was the fact that they possessed no territory of their own, and so could not participate in that struggle for living space that he saw as the basic pattern of history. Lacking territory, the Jews could not carry out the construction of a state but had to become parasites (an obsessive metaphor of Hitler's) battening on the creative activities and work of other nations.

> The ultimate goal of the Jewish struggle for existence is the enslavement of productively active people . . . by the denationalization, the promiscuous bastardization of other peoples, the lowering of the racial level of the highest peoples as well as the domination of this racial mishmash through the extirpation of the *völkisch* intelligentsia and its replacement by members of its own people. [16]

In international affairs Jewish capitalists sought to divert nations from their true interests and plunge them into wars, gradually establishing their mastery over them with the help of the power of money and propaganda. At the same time, the Jewish leaders of the international Communist revolution had provided themselves with a world headquarters in Moscow from which to spread subversion internally through the propagation by the Marxist parties of internationalism, egalitarianism, and pacifism, all of which Hitler identified with the Jews and saw as a threat to Aryan racial values.

Turning the argument the other way, anti-Semitism provided Hitler with further justification for Germany to follow a policy of conquering additional living space in the East at the expense of Bolshevik Russia, which Hitler constantly identified with the "Jewish world conspiracy." Not only would this strengthen the racial character of the German people, but it would also destroy the base of international Jewry, and cut off the poisonous plant of Marxism at the root.

In Hitler's twisted cosmological vision, the eternal enemy of the Aryans, the race that possessed the power to create, was the Jew, the embodiment of evil, the agent of the racial pollution that had undermined and destroyed one civilization after another.

> Should the Jew, with the help of his Marxist creed, conquer the nations of this world, his crown will become the funeral wreath of mankind, and once again this planet, empty of mankind, will follow its orbit through the ether as it did millions of years ago . . .[17]

What Hitler meant by the "elimination" of the Jewish danger remained undefined, but to a German National Socialist from Bohemia who visited him in prison and asked if he had changed his position about the Jews, he replied:

> Yes, yes, it is quite right that I have changed my opinion about the methods to fight Jewry. I have realized that up to now I have been much too soft. While working out my book I have come to the realization that in the future the most severe methods of fighting will have to be used to let us come through successfully. I am convinced that this is a vital question not just for our people, but for all peoples. For Judaism is the plague of the world.[18]

The twin tenets of Hitler's worldview, his determination to "root out" the Jews (whatever he meant to suggest by that) and to conquer *Lebensraum* in Eastern Europe, not only remained unchanged but were repeatedly stated, years before he came to power, in *Mein Kampf* and in many speeches and interviews.

It is misleading, however, to see in his personal ideology the key to Hitler's power to attract supporters to join the Nazi party in thousands in the 1920s and later, in the early 1930s, to vote for it in millions. On the contrary, the evidence suggests that, while anti-Semitism was part of the common currency of the German right and was taken for granted as part of the Nazi package, the prominence Hitler gave to it—and this was much less in the second half of the 1920s than in the first—did not prove a particular attraction except for a minority of initiates in the party (Himmler, for example) who took it with the same seriousness as Hitler did himself. This corresponds with Hitler's own distinction in *Mein Kampf* between the followers of a movement, the majority for whom "the simple effort of believing the political doctrine is enough," and the minority "who represent the idea and fight for it." [19] The same appears to have been true of *Lebensraum,* the dream of German expansion to the east. The staple of his foreign-policy speeches in the 1920s was very different: revisionism, the abolition of the Treaty of Versailles, and the recovery of Germany's 1914 frontiers, if necessary by war with France, not with Russia.

In this formative period before the party came to power, many other sources besides Hitler contributed to National Socialism: for example, such neoconservative thinkers as Moeller van der Bruck and other Nazi leaders such as Gottfried Feder, the Strasser brothers, Gregor and Otto, and Walther Darré. Hitler had not yet imposed his own personal vision on the party; there continued to be competing tendencies (for example, in economic policy) into the mid-1930s, and Hitler himself showed a striking flexibility in varying his appeal to different audiences and in different circumstances.

But he was able to do this because, as he claimed in *Mein Kampf:* "In this period there took shape within me a world picture and a philosophy which became the granite foundation of all my acts. In addition to what I then created, I have had to learn little since, and have had to alter nothing." [20] Hitler wrongly dates this to his years in Vienna before 1914; it was a process that began then but was not complete until he committed it to paper in the mid-1920s. After that, however, he was quite right in saying that his *Weltanschauung* provided a granite foundation to which he added nothing. His was a closed mind impervious to argument or doubt. It was thanks to this, the assurance that he possessed the key to history, and with it could unlock the future as well, that he felt able to exploit tactical opportunities, without any risk of losing sight of his objectives, awaiting his time, believing that it would arrive and that he would then be able to commit the German people to a program that remained as primitive and brutal as when he spelled it out in *Mein Kampf.* The advantage this gave was already evident in the years up to 1930, when circumstances did not favor him and few outside the party took him seriously, but he nonetheless prepared for a change in his favor which he could not foresee but was confident would come.

Throughout the whole period of the *Kampfzeit* (the "time of struggle" before he came to power), however, audiences came to listen to Hitler, less for the contents of his speeches, which for the most part were the commonplaces of nationalist and right-wing propaganda, than for the gift he had of presenting these with an effect that none of his rivals could equal. As Otto Strasser, no admirer, said of him:

> If he tries to bolster up his argument with theories or quotations from books he has only imperfectly understood, he scarcely rises above mediocrity. But let him throw away his crutches, speaking as the spirit moves him, and he is promptly transformed into one of the greatest speakers of the century. . . . Adolf Hitler enters a hall. He sniffs the air, feels his way, senses the atmosphere. Suddenly, he bursts forth. His words go like an arrow to their target, he touches each private wound on the raw, liberating the unconscious, exposing its innermost aspirations and telling it what it most wants to hear.[21]

Hitler himself was well aware of this power. In *Mein Kampf* he writes of the way to overcome emotional resistance: "Nothing but an appeal to these hidden forces will be effective here. Only the orator can hope to make it."[22] No less important was the gift he possessed of concealing his exploitation of this power and convincing his audience that the fanaticism he conveyed was the proof of his sincerity.

This was the heart of Hitler's appeal, his ability to use these gifts to create belief, not so much in arguments, a program, or an ideology, as in himself as a charismatic leader uniquely endowed with superhuman powers enabling him to achieve the impossible. This was what rank-and-file Nazis meant when they declared, "Our program can be expressed in two words— 'Adolf Hitler.' "

III

LATER RESEARCH has shown the autobiographical framework of *Mein Kampf* to be very unreliable. As a necessary first step in mythologizing himself Hitler had to dramatize his feckless and self-indulgent early years into a period of poverty, suffering, and loneliness, out of which were forged the determination and self-confidence of a future leader. He avoided the political revelations about the failure of the 1923 putsch for which his publisher had hoped and filled his pages with frequent digressions on any subject that occurred to him, displaying the same cocksure ignorance of the half-educated as in his later table talk. The exception is when he speaks about the way in which to create a mass movement, the use of propaganda, the attraction of violence—in short, the political skills needed to implement the convictions of the ideologue.

The surprising thing is the frankness with which Hitler wrote about the manipulation of audiences, the stupidity of the masses, the exploitation of emotion, the use of slogans and posters to hammer home the basic points. Clichés now, his attention to such matters showed his originality in the 1920s.

The very first condition which has to be fulfilled in every kind of propaganda [is] a systematically one-sided attitude. . . . Propaganda must not investigate the truth objectively . . . it must present only that aspect of the truth which is favorable to one's own side. [23]

And again:

For the great majority of a nation . . . thought and conduct are ruled by sentiment rather than by sober reasoning. This sentiment, however, is . . . not highly differentiated, but has only the negative and positive notions of love and hatred, right and wrong, truth and falsehood. Its notions are never partly this and partly that. [24]

Hitler was equally convincing when he turned to the subject of political organization. Analyzing the failure to check the growth of Marxism and Marxist parties after the defeat of 1918, he wrote:

The so-called national parties were without influence, because they had no force which could effectively demonstrate in the streets. . . . The Combat Leagues had all the power, they were the masters of the street but they had no political idea, and above all no definite political aim in view.

The success which Marxism attained was due to perfect cooperation between political purposes and ruthless force. What deprived national Germany of all practical hopes shaping German development was the lack of a determined cooperation between brute force and political aims wisely chosen. [25]

Hitler insisted that the two had to go together, and that the success of the French Revolution, the Russian Revolution, and the Fascist movement in Italy showed this.

The lack of a great idea which would reshape things anew has always meant a limitation in fighting power. The conviction of the right to employ even the most brutal weapons is always associated with an ardent faith in the necessity for a new and revolutionary transformation of the world. [26]

The bourgeois parties were incapable of this, and thought only of restoring the past. For that reason, Hitler would make no alliances with them, but preferred to see the Nazi party stand on its own. On the other hand, he continued to insist that the SA should not be turned into a combat league with a concealed military rather than a political purpose; its job was to provide protection for the party and secure for it the freedom of the streets, as it had at Coburg.

BY THE TIME he was dictating the second volume of *Mein Kampf,* in which many of these passages occur, Hitler's friends in office had secured his release from prison, and he was free to set about refounding the Nazi party. The tide of right-wing extremism that had carried him along in the postwar years had subsided. In the Reichstag elections of May 1924 the radical right had still been able to attract 6.5 percent of the national vote and win thirty-two seats; in the December elections of the same year its vote was more than halved and the number of seats reduced to fourteen. Left-wing extremism suffered a similar setback, the KPD losing a third of its seats. The years 1924 through 1928 saw the nearest approach to normalcy under the Weimar Republic: the stabilization of the currency, economic recovery, a reparations settlement (the Dawes Plan), large U.S. loans, Stresemann's success in negotiating the Treaty of Locarno, and Germany's admission to the League of Nations.

This was the only period of his political career when Hitler found the tide flowing against him, and at the same time lost the political protection that he had received from the Bavarian authorities. After only one meeting at the beginning of 1925 he was prohibited from speaking in public in Bavaria, a ban soon extended to Prussia and other German states, lasting until May 1927 in Bavaria and September 1928 in Prussia. This struck at Hitler's greatest asset; he was confined to speaking to closed meetings of party members. For some time after leaving prison he remained on parole and, lacking German citizenship (until 1932), was still exposed to the threat of deportation to Austria.

The Nazi party had been banned and the Nazi newspaper, the *Völkischer Beobachter,* suppressed immediately after the 1923 putsch. Rosenberg, whom Hitler had named to lead the movement while he was in jail, proved a hopeless choice. There was a strong suspicion that he had been chosen by Hitler for precisely that reason: He was the least likely to prove a rival when Hitler returned to the scene. Hitler was not at all pleased when— despite his known opposition to parliamentary politics—Rosenberg agreed to an electoral alliance with a *völkisch* group, the Deutschvölkische Freiheit-spartei (DVFP, the German Racist Freedom Party). He was even less pleased when this alliance—without him—unexpectedly won almost two million votes in the Reichstag elections of May 1924.

This show of *völkisch* unity, however, proved short-lived and soon broke up into feuding groups. The most important division within the Nazi movement was between the Bavarian group, whose leaders had been born before 1890, and a younger group, stronger in northern Germany, who formed the NS Freiheitspartei (NSFP, the National Socialist Freedom party). The first could claim several leading Nazi officials—Esser, Streicher, Schwarz, and Max Amann—but had little strength outside the three cities of Munich, Nuremberg, and Bamberg. Scornfully labeled the "pioneers" by Goebbels, their outlook is characterized by Dietrich Orlow in his *History of the Nazi Party* as formed by the experience of the lower middle class who had seen their status as shopkeepers and petty officials endangered even before the war, who were opposed to industrialization, and who blamed the

Jews for everything they disliked. The formative experience of the second group was that of the "Front generation," who saw the *völkisch* program in terms of "front-line socialism" (hostility to the power of large corporations and finance capital), revolution not social reaction, and an appeal to the working masses rather than the middle class. Both groups rejected parliamentary democracy in favor of dictatorship, were anti-Semitic, and still looked to Hitler as their leader.

Hitler, while still in prison, listened to the rival appeals and accusations, but refused to arbitrate between them or commit himself to either group. In July 1924 he resigned his position as leader, unmoved by the criticism that he preferred such a state of affairs to seeing any group secure a dominant position. One of his close associates, Kurt Lüdecke, wrote, "He was the one man with the power to set things straight; yet he never so much as lifted his little finger or spoke one word." 27 His tactics worked. The result of the second Reichstag election, held in the more stable conditions of December 1924 and cutting the *völkisch* vote by half, meant returning to a marginal position in German politics. When Hitler came out of prison two weeks later, the Nazi movement was hopelessly divided and nobody else appeared capable of reuniting it.

Thanks to the influence of sympathizers, Hitler served less than nine months of his five-year sentence and was home for Christmas. Far from going out of his way to be accommodating, now that he was free again, he made no concessions at all to those who urged him to form another coalition with the other nationalist groups. He alienated the *völkisch* deputies in the Bavarian Landtag (state parliament) by his arrogance; picked a quarrel with Ludendorff, who had overshadowed him in 1923; and slighted the leaders of the NSFP in north Germany. It was only with difficulty and after the intervention of his old patron Gürtner that he got the ban on the party and the *Völkischer Beobachter* lifted in Bavaria. After keeping both supporters and critics waiting for two months by refusing to commit himself, he then suddenly announced, the day before, that he would speak at the Bürgerbräukeller, the scene of the putsch that had failed, on February 27.

The doors had to be closed after 3,000 of the faithful had packed in, and another 2,000 had to be turned away. From the moment he appeared he was greeted with a wild enthusiasm that no other right-wing leader could arouse. He spoke for two hours, and at the end there were emotional scenes of reconciliation in the middle of which Amann called out: "The quarreling must stop. Everyone for Hitler!" This was after Hitler had left no doubt of where he stood:

> If anyone comes and wants to set me conditions, I tell him: "My friend, wait until you hear the conditions I am setting you. I'm not wooing the masses, you know." After a year has passed you be the judges, my party comrades. If I have not acted rightly, then I shall return my office to your

hands. But until then, this is the rule: I, and I alone, shall lead the movement, and no one sets me conditions as long as I personally bear the responsibility. And I on the other hand bear all the responsibility for everything that happens in the movement.[28]

The demonstration that he had not lost his power as a spellbinder led to a renewal of the ban on his addressing further public meetings. Hitler, however, who would have been thrown into despair by such a setback in 1923, was unaffected even by the personal loss of fees that it meant. This confirmed the impression, on which witnesses agree, that after his defeat and year in prison Hitler emerged not only hardened, but with a confidence in his role as a man with a mission that was unshakable, even in these years when he was no more than the leader of an insignificant and unsuccessful party.

Before he left prison he told Rudolf Hess, "I shall need five years before the movement is on top again"—a remarkably accurate forecast as it turned out. But he meant to do it his own way. In April 1925 he was prepared to part with Röhm, to whom he owed so much in earlier days, rather than compromise over the role of the new SA. Röhm wanted to keep it out of politics and make it part of the underground force, the Frontbann, which would enable the German army to evade the restriction on numbers imposed by the Versailles Treaty; Hitler was adamant that it must be subordinate to his political leadership and serve the party as its defense arm. When Röhm resigned, Hitler did not reply to his letter or respond to his appeal not to sever their personal friendship.

With the help of Esser and Streicher, Hitler regained his old hold over the Nazi movement in south Germany. But Bavaria was no longer an adequate base for a national movement without the north, with its much larger potential membership. The interim NSFP in the north dissolved itself, but the hostility of its younger and more radical leadership to the "pioneers" in the south remained and found expression in resistance to the attempts of the Nazis' Munich headquarters to bring local groups outside Bavaria under their control.

The most energetic figure in the north was Gregor Strasser, a *Frontkämpfer* from Landshut in Bavaria who had already built up a 900-strong SA regiment in Lower Bavaria in 1923. He had been a prime mover in setting up the NSFP while Hitler was in prison and had won a seat in the Reichstag as a deputy for Westphalia. When the NSFP was dissolved, and the Nazi party refounded, Hitler gave Strasser carte blanche to build up the party in the north, where his drive and organizing ability had already made considerable impact. At the same time Strasser was appointed Gauleiter of Lower Bavaria, his native territory, where his former secretary, Heinrich Himmler, became his deputy.

During the next twelve months, while Hitler spent much of his time at Obersalzberg working on the second volume of *Mein Kampf,* Strasser spoke at nearly a hundred meetings, mostly in the industrial areas of north and central Germany. The young activists whom he gathered around him included his brother Otto, the twenty-seven-year-old Joseph Goebbels, and the later Gauleiters Karl Kaufmann, Erich Koch, and Josef Terboven. They developed a more radical form of National Socialism than the Munich version of Esser and Streicher, appealing to a younger generation and picking up the anticapitalist points from the party program: the abolition of unearned income, ground rent, and land speculation; the attack on "interest slavery," finance capital, and big department stores; the call for the nationalization of heavy industry, profit sharing, and land reform. These demands were presented as a national "German," idealist form of socialism, an alternative to the international, materialistic, leveling class war preached by the Marxists. The activists' hope was to use such a program to make "an opening to the left" in such industrialized strongholds of the SPD and KPD as the Ruhr and to create a *völkisch* trade-union movement. Strasser was also attracted by National Bolshevism, the proposal for an alliance between Germany and Russia, the two nations that had lost out in the 1914–1918 war, against the capitalist, imperialist, Jew-ridden West.

Hitler's response was enigmatic. His temperament was radical and he, too, could use anticapitalist language when it suited him. He had no intention of tying his hands with such a program, but since he could not afford to lose the north he temporized and avoided committing himself. Disappointed, the northern leaders went ahead on their own in August–September 1925, organizing a Working Party Northwest (*Arbeitsgemeinschaft*, AG for short) to counteract the influence of the Munich group, in the hope that they could liberate Hitler from its influence and win him over to their ideas.

Strasser's attempt, however, to produce a revised form of the party program, with more emphasis on the anticapitalist parts than the 1920 version, broke down in the face of rivalries among the northern leaders, and its own contradictions. Whether Strasser went further and thought of challenging Hitler's position as leader is uncertain. More than any of the other Nazi leaders, he had the personality and the ability to become a leader, but of a very different kind. A much more straightforward character than Hitler, a gifted organizer, and a good speaker, he lacked Hitler's charismatic power. Strasser was not the stuff of which myths are made, and it was his recognition of Hitler's superiority in this respect that held him back again and again. But the possibility that he could prove a rival must have occurred to both men, certainly to Hitler.

So far Hitler had not intervened, but he was provoked to do so by a combination of developments in the winter of 1925–26. A left-wing proposal to expropriate the property of the former princely houses raised a storm of controversy in Germany over rights of property. Hitler was against expropriation, the Strasser group came out in favor. The draft program prepared by Strasser was a direct challenge to Hitler's own declaration that the original twenty-five points were immutable; so was the decision to set up an independent publishing house, the Kampfverlag, and start a newspaper, *Der Nationale Sozialist,* without authorization. Finally, a call by Strasser for the party to abandon its timid policy of legality and follow a "politics of catastrophe" ran counter to Hitler's refusal to countenance another attempt at the seizure of power by force.

Having made up his mind to act, Hitler did so decisively, and with skill. At short notice he called a meeting of all the party leaders at Bamberg, in Streicher's territory, where he could be sure of putting on a show of strength and resources that would impress the north Germans—not least the column of cars in which he arrived.

In a speech that lasted for four hours in all, he took the Strasser platform apart, point by point. "The program of 1920," he declared, "is the foundation of our religion, our ideology. To tamper with it would be an act of treason to those who died [in the November putsch] believing in our Idea." [29] In effect Hitler was avoiding a choice between rival interpretations of the party program and instead "mythologizing his own person into a program." [30] Strasser attempted to reply but without success and without support. Hitler had played his trump card: Without him as leader, there was no movement, and his audience knew it. Having won, however, Hitler went out of his way to avoid humiliating Strasser by demonstratively going over to him and putting his arm around his shoulders in a gesture of comradeship, which impressed the rest of the audience, if not Strasser himself.

Hitler did not let it rest as a gesture. He offered Gregor Strasser the post of chief of the party's propaganda office [31] and invited Strasser's most gifted lieutenant, Goebbels, to pay a visit to Munich, where he won him over completely and in November 1926 appointed him as Gauleiter of Berlin. This twenty-seven-year-old, slightly built, clubfooted, failed intellectual, a mixture of vanity and insecurity, showed unsuspected talents as a tough, aggressive leader in a Communist/SPD stronghold; and developed gifts as a provocative speaker and writer hitherto with little scope, which made him second only to Hitler in his flair for propaganda.

These were two of the best appointments Hitler ever made, diverting both men from what he saw as the futile and divisive occupation of arguing about the party program to the real tasks of propaganda and organization. At Bamberg he repeated what he had been writing in the second volume of *Mein Kampf*: The National Socialists were not a debating club or a party of intellectuals—the same view that Lenin had expressed at the Tenth Congress of the Russian Communist party in 1921. The Nazis' job was to build up the strength of the party and harden its will to secure power, the same objective Lenin had proclaimed. "Such a struggle," Hitler declared, "is not waged with 'intellectual' weapons, but with fanaticism." [32]

Now that he had avoided a split in the party, Hitler called a general membership meeting at Munich in May 1926 and changed the rules of association. The National Socialist German Workers' Association in Munich was made the sole "bearer" of the movement. The directors chosen by the members of the Munich local group would automatically become the leadership of the whole party. German law required that they should also choose the first chairman; but, once chosen, he would have the right to appoint or dismiss Gauleiters, chairmen of committees, and other local officers. He also had the authority to lead the party independently of majority decisions of the managing board and of committees. In practice, no board of directors ever came into existence. Apart from the secretary, responsible for the membership rolls, and the treasurer, specific tasks were given to central departmental chiefs (*Amtsleiter,* such as Strasser for propaganda), appointed by Hitler and responsible to him.

Early in July 1926 he felt ready to hold the first party rally since the putsch, at Weimar, in Thuringia, one of the few states where he was still free to speak. Only those motions were admitted that had received his approval as first chairman, henceforward standard practice. Strict limits were set to speeches (except Hitler's); no votes were taken, and Hitler made it clear that he wanted "endless discussions smothered." After the plenary meeting in the National Theater (where in 1919 the constitution of the Weimar Republic had been adopted), Hitler reviewed a parade of 5,000 party and SA members, and for the first time, copying the Italian Fascist practice, saluted them with outstretched arm.

IV

HITLER HAD SUCCEEDED in reasserting his own position within the Nazi party. But the party was no nearer to finding a way to break out of its marginal position in national politics. Its 1926 membership figure of 35,000, compared with the 15.6 million Germans who had taken the trouble to vote in a referendum on the expropriation of the princes, gives the measure of how far it still had to go.

So long as the regime's policy of stabilization continued to produce results, it was very unlikely that the party could make further progress. These results were visible not only in Germany's improved international position, but also in the economic sphere as well. Thanks to American loans, German industry was modernized, and productivity in almost every sector of the economy showed greater increases between 1923 and 1928 than in any other European country. In 1928 national income was 12 percent higher than in 1913, despite the loss of territory following the war, and the registered unemployed had been reduced to under half a million. Lacking the disaster from which he claimed he alone could rescue Germany, Hitler was a self-proclaimed messiah whom few Germans took seriously.

The weakness of the party's position appeared at every level: policy, organization, recruitment, finance. If a putsch was ruled out, how was Hitler planning to secure power? Was it by winning elections or (on the pattern of the March on Rome, which he much preferred) by the *threat* of revolution? In either case it was essential to mobilize mass support. But where was this to come from? The workers? The farmers? The middle classes? And in support of what policies?

Most parties would have sought to answer such questions with a set of policies embodied in a party program. But the Nazi party was unlike any other; whatever policies it might adopt were not the result of committee meetings or majority decisions, not even of a consensus among its leaders. As the Bamberg meeting had made clear, it was a movement held together by the loyalty of its members, whatever their views on particular issues, to a single leader, Adolf Hitler. And Hitler understood that, to succeed in such a role, he had as far as possible to distance himself from controversy about specific policies and avoid deciding in favor of one faction rather than another.

Hitler's ideology, however crude and unconvincing to those who did not share it, provided him with a view of the historical process that gave him the same assurance as Marxism gave to the Communist leaders. Like Lenin and Stalin, he treated policies and tactics as matters, not of principle, but of expediency, the object of which was to gain support and win power. The difference was that the Communists were prepared to change the party line overnight and justify the switch as due to a change in "objective circumstances," while Hitler preferred to keep his options open and talk in large terms of the evils of the "System," national renewal, and *Volksgemeinschaft* (the strengthening of the German sense of racial community), committing himself as little as possible on current issues of economic and social policy, which he regarded in any case as of secondary importance.

Such a stance laid him open to the criticism that the Nazis, as a party without policies, were not to be taken seriously. But he saw greater advantage in allowing people with very different views, both within the party and as yet outside it, to identify themselves with him at a time when he could not know from which sections of the German people he had the best chance of winning large-scale support. This view of Hitler's attitude in the years 1926 through 1930 is borne out by the contrast, to which we shall come shortly, between his attitude on questions of policy on the one hand and questions of organization on the other.

DESPITE THE DIFFERENCES that had led him to call the Bamberg meeting, for the rest of 1926 and 1927 Hitler allowed Strasser and his group to follow the so-called "urban plan" aimed at winning support for an anticapitalist, "national" socialism and concentrating the party's efforts on the big industrial centers in the Ruhr, Hamburg, Saxony-Thuringia, and Berlin. In 1927, Gregor Strasser declared in a party periodical: "We National Socialists are enemies, deadly enemies, of the present capitalist system with its exploitation of the economically weak . . . and we are resolved under all circumstances to destroy this system."[33] Goebbels followed the same line as Gauleiter of Berlin, challenging the Communists in one of their strongholds and at the same time using his gifts as a propagandist to attack "the money pigs of capitalist democracy." [34]

This bid for working-class support brought the Nazis some gains in membership in 1926–27, although it appears to have been mainly among workers living in small towns and villages (for example, in the Ruhr), from which they commuted to the big cities for work. The industrial cities remained the preserve of the KPD and SPD, and at its peak in 1927 the blue-collar workers' share in the membership of the Nazi party—estimated at between 21 and 26 percent—still remained well below their proportion in the gainfully employed population. [35] Those Nazis who were keenest on this approach believed it could have produced bigger results if the Nazis had been allowed to create their own *völkisch* trade unions and to come out unequivocally in support of strikes.

Hitler banned both as going too far in copying Marxist tactics. On the other hand, when priority shifted from the urban plan to mobilizing other sectors of the population, such as the middle class and the farmers, the earlier campaign was not repudiated and the radical wing of the party was not prevented from going on trying to win working-class support. In the period 1927–30 for example, the small Nazi delegation in the Reichstag not only introduced (with no hope of passing them) bills calling for the confiscation of stock-market fortunes and wartime profits, but was the only party to support the openly anticapitalist line of the Communists on a significant number of occasions. [36] Hitler even acquiesced in the device by which leftist activists in the party got around his ban on trade unions by founding cells in the factories, which challenged the SPD and KPD monopoly by conducting Nazi propaganda and running candidates in the elections to the factory councils. In January 1931, the NS Factory Cell Organization (NSBO) was accepted as a full-fledged organ of the party.

This did not inhibit Hitler from making a series of attempts to win support from business circles. In doing so he not only said nothing about the radical economic clauses still in the NSDAP's official program, or the anticapitalist campaign of the party's radical wing, but also played down themes so central to his own view of politics as anti-Semitism, *Lebensraum* in the east, and the state's unlimited right of intervention in the economy, all of which he recognized might alienate his listeners. [37] His party's aim, he told business audiences, was to purge Germany of Marxism and restore her greatness in the world. He had some success with the heads of smaller businesses and middle management, but none with big business, either in the Ruhr or elsewhere. The exception was Emil Kirdorf, an eighty-year-old maverick, once known as the "Bismarck of coal," who was impressed by Hitler, made a single donation of 100,000 marks, and undertook to try to influence industrial circles in his favor. After little more than a year, however, in August 1928, he resigned from the party in disgust at a Nazi attack on the coal cartel which he had taken a leading part in founding.

Hitler tried another line of approach when he went to Weimar in October 1926 and argued the case for a union between the Nazis and the right-wing veterans' associations, in particular the Stahlhelm. Had he succeeded, this would have given him access to over a million voters and a much-needed pool of potential leaders, many of them with Freikorps experience. His failure this time arose not from differences over policy, but from the unwillingness of the veterans' leaders to accept his claim to a unique status as Führer. The breakdown of talks led to recriminations and a ban on fraternization with other nationalist groups, which only isolated the Nazis from their natural allies.

An alternative course was to build up the SA to a membership target of 100,000. As part of the 1926 reorganization, Hitler found a successor to Röhm as OSAF (Oberst SA-Führer) in Captain Franz von Pfeffer, a former Freikorps leader. In a letter to von Pfeffer, Hitler insisted that "the training of the SA must be guided by party needs rather than by military points of view." Most of the younger, active members of the party were members of the SA as well, but the old jealousies and rivalries between the command of the SA as the fighting arm of the party, mostly consisting of former army officers, and the Party's *Reichsleitung,* its national political leadership based in Munich, as well as the local Gauleiters, was not ended with von Pfeffer's appointment. In 1927, the Munich SA, frustrated at the refusal to "unleash" them in preparation for another putsch, rebelled against the OSAF's authority and were quieted only by Hitler's personal intervention. In Berlin the violence of the SA's street battles with the Communists alienated public opinion and led the police to secure a ban on the Nazi organization in the capital. The difficulties with the SA continued even when Hitler replaced von Pfeffer and made himself its supreme commander in 1930.

THESE VARIOUS EFFORTS by Hitler and the Nazis to attract support between 1924 and 1928 present an unimpressive and incoherent picture. Nothing brings out more clearly that, until circumstances changed in their favor and large numbers of people began to be receptive to their message, there was nothing even such talented propagandists as Hitler and Goebbels could do to secure a hearing.

Hitler's efforts to build up the party organization, however, bring out a different point: his confidence that such a change would take place and his preparation for it. The first steps in creating a national headquarters in Munich had been taken before the Bamberg meeting, with the appointment of two colorless but efficient administrators, Philipp Bouhler as executive secretary and Franz Xavier Schwarz, a former accountant in the Munich City Hall, as treasurer. Bamberg opened the way to the second stage, replacing the loose association of local organizations accustomed to following their own course, without too much regard to instructions from Munich, with a central bureaucracy. Gauleiters and local organizations alike had to be brought to see that loyalty to Hitler personally was not enough; they had also to accept that they were part of a national organization and accountable to its headquarters and the Reichsleitung that Hitler had appointed. This encountered resistance and took time, but insistence on central control of finance and of admission to membership of the party imposed discipline.

Hitler grasped clearly that, if the party was ever to attract a mass membership, it must have an administrative apparatus capable of handling large numbers. As early as 1926 he insisted on the need to expand the headquarters staff and accommodations, to acquire up-to-date office equipment, and to develop an elaborate system for registering members well in advance of the numbers that would justify such expenditure. The contrast between this and his own irregular habits of work, frequently disappearing to Obersalzberg or some other retreat for days, even weeks on end, reflected more than a temperamental dislike of office work. It was essential to his concept of leadership that he should not become involved in such activities himself, but should devolve the detailed work of administration to an impersonal bureaucratic machine. Those who ran the machine—Bouhler, Schwarz, later Hess—understood very well that Hitler alone would make the decisions but that it was important to give the implementation of them institutional force and preserve the distance that separated the Führer-figure from his followers.

In the same way, Hitler revived the national investigating committee, the USCHLA,[38] to exercise day-to-day control over any disposition on the part of local leaders to question decisions or depart from the party line, but took care to put someone else whom he could trust in the chair. "The Committee effectively protected Hitler's standing as living myth by drawing any possible dissatisfaction with its decisions to itself, not to the leader-figure whose creature and instrument it was."[39]

After the Party Congress at Nuremberg in 1927, Hitler felt sufficiently confident that reorganization had been accepted to carry it a stage further. The need to do so was driven home by the failure of the "urban plan." It was underlined by the party's proscription in Berlin, and the recognition that if they were to achieve a breakthrough to a higher level of recruitment the party would have to find a new strategy. This required the tacit acceptance of two things.

The first was that there was no more hope of Hitler becoming a German Mussolini by the threat of a putsch than there was of overthrowing the regime by a real one. However much it went against the grain, this left taking part in elections and winning an increasing share of the votes as the only way to get within reach of power. The second was that the best chance of doing so was by directing their appeal to the middle classes who, though they would seldom take part in a demonstration or a street fight, might be persuaded to vote for the Nazis.

New appointments were made in the Reichsleitung—Gregor Strasser, for example, as Reich organization leader—and among the Gauleiters, who were increasingly expected to have the education and ability to fill their new role of regional party managers running election campaigns, and had the chance of figuring on the party's list of candidates. The SA might grumble that the party was being choked with bureaucratic red tape—there was a second revolt in the Munich SA, which again required Hitler to pacify it—but the Reichsleitung devoted all its energies to preparing for the elections to a new Reichstag in May 1928, with candidates in all thirty-five election districts and 10,000 electoral rallies.

The result was a totally unexpected defeat, 100,000 fewer votes than in December 1924, no more than 800,000 out of the 30,750,000 who went to the polls. Once they got over the shock, however, the Nazi leadership was quick to learn from the experience. While the party had done badly in the cities, it had done unexpectedly well in a number of rural areas—both in the north (Schleswig-Holstein and Hannover) and in the south (Franconia). This was the feature on which Hitler fastened.

Instead of a national congress (which the party, heavily in debt after the elections, could not afford), he summoned a conference of the whole leadership in Munich in August 1928. Hitler called for a switch in priorities from the cities to the countryside and a redrawing of the boundaries of the districts (*Gaue*) into which the party was divided. The rural electorate was spread out, not concentrated as in the cities, requiring much more effort to reach, in effect a year-round electioneering campaign.

Having laid down the new line, Hitler left Schwarz and Strasser to work it out, going off to spend several weeks with his wealthy friends the Bruckmanns in Berchtesgaden. A second conference in January 1929 saw the completion of the reorganization that had been put into effect after the Bamberg meeting two years earlier. The two most important features were the redefinition of the Gauleiters' role and the firm establishment of a vertical structure, in which each level was clearly subordinate to the one above.

In practice, of course, the party was a good deal less streamlined than it appeared on the organization charts. The weakness of the system was its dependence on one man for all decisions not of a routine character, including the decision as to which was and which was not a matter of routine. Since Hitler refused to attend "to" the office, settle disputes, or answer letters at all regularly, this meant congestion at the top, eased only when Hitler found in his personal secretary, Rudolf Hess, an informal deputy who could be trusted to exercise power in his name without any danger that he would abuse his position or detract from the Hitler myth, to which he showed a religious devotion.

Hitler always thought organization important, but only as a means to an end. The party's efficiency would be judged by one test—whether it could win votes.

V

HITLER TOOK CARE not to repudiate publicly the radical socialist elements in the party, but their hankering after a social revolutionary strategy, which they never succeeded in defining, was henceforward subordinated to winning support in both the rural and urban middle classes. Hitler saw an opportunity in responding to the growing discontent over falling prices, rising taxation, and bankruptcies, a forerunner of the 1929 depression, among the once-prosperous livestock farmers in Schleswig-Holstein. There were angry protests when increases in the salaries of civil servants were announced in December 1927, and these spread rapidly in the Protestant agrarian districts of Oldenburg, Lower Saxony, Pomerania, and East Prussia. A worldwide fall in agricultural prices began at the end of 1927 and was made worse by trade treaties with countries such as Poland, from which Germany agreed to increase imports of agricultural produce in return for German manufactured goods. The rural depression that resulted affected not only farmers but also artisans and small traders in rural areas who were dependent on agriculture.

Hitler had gone to Schleswig-Holstein to speak to the protesters in December 1927 and had been sufficiently persuaded of the possibility of capturing rural votes to introduce a change in the "unalterable" party program. In April 1928 he announced that point 17 of the program, advocating the expropriation of private property, was directed solely against Jewish property. This came too late to affect the overall result of the 1928 election, but in some northwest rural districts, where the protest movement had been strongest, the Nazis polled over 10 percent of the votes, compared with their average vote of 2 percent. This was the beginning of a very successful Nazi campaign, skillfully adapted to the political circumstances of a scattered small-town and village electorate.

The artisans and small retailers of the *Mittelstand* in the industrial as well as the rural areas were also among the first to feel the onset of the Depression, as a result of a shift in the economic balance of power toward big business and organized labor on the one hand, and against agriculture and the old middle class on the other. This was a consequence of the rationalization of German industry in the 1920s, accelerating the historical trend toward the concentration of big trusts and cartels against which small businesses found it hard to compete. At the same time, the trade unions and the SPD were successful in pressing for higher wages and improved welfare measures. An example was the major new unemployment insurance introduced—along with the rise in the salaries of civil servants—at the end of 1927. That meant higher contributions from employers in addition to higher taxes.

The immediate result of this economic deterioration was a fragmentation of the old middle-class electorate and the multiplication of special-interest groups. But these did not last, and increasing their attacks on the department stores and consumer cooperatives so much resented by small business paid big dividends to the Nazis from 1929 to 1933.

At the same time the party leadership bent its energies to organizing, or reorganizing, affiliated groups, such as the League of Nazi Lawyers, or Nazi Doctors, or Nazi Teachers, as well as the Nazi Student League, all of which were designed to attract middle-class support.

Foreign policy was not neglected. Hitler redoubled the Nazi appeal to the "nationally minded" in all classes by launching a strident campaign against Foreign Minister Stresemann's *Erfüllungspolitik* (the policy of compliance with the terms of the Versailles Treaty), which he denounced as a betrayal of Germany's national interests. In the summer of 1929 an international committee of experts under the chairmanship of an American banker, Owen D. Young, proposed to settle the reparations issue by requiring Germany to make a series of annual payments extending until 1988, nearly sixty years into the future. The Young Plan gave Hitler the chance to revive all the anger felt by Germans at the defeat of 1918, the loss of territory imposed by the Treaty of Versailles, and the notorious Article 231 asserting Germany's sole responsibility for the 1914–1918 war, on which the claim for reparations was based. Not only did this allow him to whip up feeling against the Allies and the Weimar regime which acted as their tool, but it also gave added impetus to the rapprochement already under way with other right-wing nationalist groups, such as the Stahlhelm, from which the Nazis had been estranged since 1926.

It opened the way to more than that. In the autumn of 1928, the leadership of the principal conservative party, the Nationalists (Deutschnationale Volkspartei or DNVP), had fallen into the hands of Alfred Hugenberg, a bigoted, ambitious, and domineering press baron who had made a fortune out of the inflation and had built up a media empire with a whole group of newspapers, a news agency, and Germany's leading film company, UFA. Hugenberg was more interested in using these to press his reactionary views than in making money. He had committed himself to destroying the "Socialist Republic," breaking the power of the trade unions and matching class war from below with class war from above. For this purpose he was able to draw on large sums from big business. A substantial part of the conservative membership of the DNVP left the party in protest against Hugenberg's policy, but he was far more interested in attracting mass support and believed that in Hitler he had found the man to win it for him.

Hitler handled his opportunity with skill. When he met Hugenberg he showed no eagerness to accept his proposal of a joint campaign against the Young Plan. He knew that, quite apart from the certain opposition of the radical groups in his party, many loyal Nazis would be troubled at the thought of his supping with the Devil in the form of so rabid an opponent, not only of organized labor, but of any measure of state intervention or reform. If he was to agree to Hugenberg's proposal, it could only be on his own terms: complete independence for the Nazis in their conduct of the campaign, and a sizable share of the available funds to finance it. When this was conceded, Hitler added as a finishing touch the appointment of Gregor Strasser, the Nazi leader most prominently identified with anticapitalism, as his representative on the joint finance committee. Few in the Nazi leadership liked the deal Hitler had made, but he succeeded in convincing them that they should wait and see what came of it: No one resigned or protested openly.

On August 3–4, 1929, Hitler staged the most impressive Party Congress yet, at Nuremberg, with thirty special trains bringing 200,000 members and sympathizers from all over Germany, and a grand parade in which 60,000 SA men in uniform paraded before the Führer for three and a half hours. The new tone of Nazi self-assurance was expressed even more strongly in the propaganda campaign against the Young Plan that followed. For years Hitler had poured scorn on the conservative right for their failure to go to the masses: Now he was able to demonstrate, on a scale beyond the party resources before, how this could be done. For six months, every speech that he and the other Nazi leaders made was carried with great prominence by the Hugenberg press. To millions of Germans who had scarcely heard of him before, Hitler became a familiar figure, thanks to a publicity campaign paid for with funds raised by Hugenberg.

The campaign failed in its ostensible object, to secure a majority in a plebiscite calling on the Reichstag to pass "a law against enslavement of the German people," which would reject the Young Plan. Hugenberg and Hitler came nowhere near a majority, winning less than six of the minimum of twenty-one million votes needed for the referendum to succeed. But defeat for Hugenberg's campaign and his "Freedom Law" was no defeat for Hitler. He at once broke with Hugenberg and the Nationalists, placing the entire blame for the failure on their halfhearted support. The fact that the DNVP had split over Hugenberg's tactics added weight to his criticism. But what mattered most to Hitler was that at long last he and his party had broken into national politics. In the following June, they took almost 15 percent of the vote in the state (*Land*) elections in the traditional left-wing stronghold of Saxony, where two years before they had attracted less than 3 percent. Party membership rose as well as votes: between October 1928 and September 1929 from 100,000 to 150,000 and by the middle of 1930, allowing for lapses, reaching 200,000.

During the state and local elections of 1929 Gregor Strasser acted as national campaign director, working through the Gauleiters. The Barlow Palace in Munich, renamed the Brown House, was bought in the spring of 1930 to provide impressive new headquarters and to house the rapidly growing staff. Among other centralized functions was the preparation of guidelines, posters, and leaflets on which great care was lavished before being submitted for Hitler's and Hess's approval.

The key to success, however, was the Nazis' realization that central organization and planning could be effective only if they were matched by and linked to organization on the ground. This called for party activists at the village and small-town level, aware of the individual characteristics of their own locality and with the power of initiative and the resources to exploit them. Their success in recruiting such a network of local insiders and notables right across Germany enabled the Nazis to penetrate a majority of the several thousand communities that made up the nation..

The best-known example of this linkup between center and localities is the plan developed by the Argentinian-born Walther Darré, who took up the ideas of A. G. Kenstler, the founder and publisher of the periodical *Blut und Boden* (*Blood and Soil*), for "the advancement and extension of the active, national revolutionary agrarian movement of Schleswig-Holstein throughout the Reich."⁴⁰ Darré was appointed as the party's adviser on agrarian affairs and presented the Reichsleitung with two memoranda in August 1930, the first of which expounded the importance of agriculture in the coming struggle for power in Germany, and the second of which set out an "Outline of a Plan to Develop an Agrarian Organizational Network throughout the Reich."

A particular target of the NS Agrarpolitische Apparat (aA) that Darré created was the farmers' associations. In the guidelines he drew up in November 1930 he demanded:

> Let there be no farm, no estate, no village, no cooperative, no agricultural industry, no local organization of the Reichslandbund etc. etc. where we have not—at the least—placed our agents [*Vertrauensleute*] in such numbers that we could paralyze at one blow the whole political life of these structures.⁴¹

In the early 1930s this aim was largely achieved, and one after the other the farmers' associations were captured. Darré's network, however, did not limit its propaganda activities to agrarian issues, but made the three most successful themes of its rural campaign: anti-Semitism, the fight against liberalism and the Weimar Republic, and fear of Bolshevism.

To overcome the shortage of speakers to address local rallies and meetings, especially in the countryside, a school started by one of the Gauleiters, Fritz Reinhardt, was turned into a party institute providing rudimentary instruction in public speaking, a stock of set speeches, and ready-made answers to questions from the audience. This was an effective means of taking the message to the villages instead of expecting the farmers to make the journey to the local town. A Nazi Film Service proved so successful, especially in the countryside where movies were a novelty, that all local branches were ordered to equip themselves with projectors.

Following a suggestion first made by Goebbels two years earlier, the Propaganda Division of the Reichsleitung drew up a plan in December 1928 to carry out concentrated "propaganda actions" which would saturate one district after another, not just during election campaigns but year-round. Between 70 and 200 rallies were to be held in a single *Gau* over a period of seven to ten days. Motorized SA parades were to be organized and public meetings addressed by party leaders, including Hitler, if possible; these were to be followed up by a systematic program of *Sprechabende* ("talk evenings") at which locally prominent speakers would hammer home the themes of the big rallies. Selection of the areas, based on local reports, and planning the timetable for such "actions" were carefully worked out under the supervision of Himmler (still head of the Propaganda Division), Hitler, and Hess. An example is the "saturation" of Saxony before the state election of June 1929. Working from two Nazi strongholds, Hof and Plauen, party agitators fanned out over the whole of Saxony, organizing a total of 1,300 rallies during the election campaign, more than half of which were held in the Erzgebirge with its large number of marginal farmers and homeworkers.

How was all this activity paid for? The belief that the Nazis were heavily subsidized by German big business before Hitler came to power has not stood up to historical research. The funds made available by the major corporations for political purposes from 1930 through 1932 continued to go to their right-wing rivals, the more conservative DVP, DNVP, and, after the latter split, to the Konservative Volkspartei, than to the Nazis. This confirms the view of the Prussian political police at the time that the Nazis raised most of the money themselves, a great deal by countless small donations, many of these in kind, or volunteer services by devoted party members. The Nazis made substantial admission charges of one or two marks for their numerous rallies: A big one, addressed by Hitler, could yield a profit of several thousand marks. The police report from which this is taken adds that the traditional parties in the same region spent no more than 22,000 to 30,000 marks on an entire election campaign.[42]

The local network that the party had established was in fact responsible not only for organizing the campaign but to a surprising extent for financing it as well. In addition to members' dues, which were systematically collected and recorded, and special levies (for example, two marks from each member to help pay for the purchase of the Brown House in Munich), the party was ingenious in the number of other ways it devised to raise money. Among them were a compulsory insurance scheme and a "Sympathizer" file containing the names of well-to-do individuals and firms who fought shy of joining the party but could be counted on to make occasional undercover contributions.

The enthusiasm that sustained this sort of effort was remarkable. At the beginning of 1930, many of the leadership group had been with Hitler for between seven and ten years; their faith in him had survived not only the failure of the 1923 putsch but also the long years of waiting since, during which the prospect of overthrowing the Weimar regime grew steadily more remote. The reorganization of 1926 through 1928 had been followed by a serious defeat in the election of May 1928, and, although the campaign against the Young Plan had allowed the party to play a role in national politics for the first time, the fact was it had failed and any hope of coming to power once again had to be postponed. At times even Hitler himself spoke of twenty or more years that might have to pass "before our idea is victorious." And yet despite the turnover among the newcomers, the core of the movement remained loyal, still prepared to meet greater demands on their time and pockets than any other German party.

This was part of Hitler's achievement in the 1920s when his leadership and the myth of Hitler as the man chosen by Providence to save Germany had none of the glamour of success to support them. The other part was the reorganization of the party, which between 1929 and 1930 had reached the point where it was capable of taking advantage of the dramatic change in the political climate at the beginning of the 1930s, and could cope with a sudden influx of members and voters which exceeded the most optimistic forecasts. To have created such an instrument in advance of the circumstances that would favor its successful employment—and so justify its cost—was far more important than the zigzags and inconsistencies of party policy.

The Nazi success in the nationwide state and local elections that followed suggested that the change of circumstances had already begun in the breakup of the Weimar party system and the impact of the world Depression.

V I

THE SO-CALLED Weimar coalition, which had drawn up the republican constitution, consisted of three parties, the Social Democrats (SPD), the liberal German Democratic party (DDP), and the Catholic Center. These lost their majority at the 1920 election, and the Reich government was reduced to a succession of unstable coalitions, twelve in the eight years 1920 to 1928, for the last four of which Germany was ruled by a coalition of the right and center and the Social Democrats were excluded from office.

German society had found it hard to come to terms with the growth of the socialist and trade-union movement, which had been a European phenomenon even before 1914. Bismarck had tried to suppress it with his ban on all social democratic activity between 1878 and 1890, to no avail. By 1912 the SPD had become the largest party in the Reichstag, and easily the leading socialist party in the Second (Socialist) International. Its rise was resented by the ruling class and employers, who regarded the workers' organized power as a threat to the established order, and by the middle class who looked down on them as their social inferiors.

Such feelings were exacerbated by the events of 1918 through 1923, beginning with the impact on Germany of the Russian Revolution in 1917, the big strikes of January 1918, and the revolutionary outbreaks of 1918 through 1920. These were blamed for the loss of the war and the replacement of the monarchy by a republic that never lost the taint of being "socialist." Even when excluded from the Reich government, the SPD remained the leading party in the coalition government of Prussia, the largest of the German states. The trade unions were strong enough to secure some of the most advanced social and industrial legislation in Europe, while the combined vote of the "Marxist" parties, the Social Democrats (29.8 percent) and the Communists (10.6 percent), added together, passed 40 percent (12.4 million) in the 1928 national elections.

Their success in those elections brought the SPD back into the Reich government, with one of their leaders, Hermann Müller, as chancellor. But the attempt to revive the original Weimar coalition* soon ran into difficulties. The SPD's partners had all lost seats and were alarmed by the growth of the left-wing vote. As a result they began to move toward the right, just as the Social Democrats themselves, feeling the pressure of increased rivalry from the Communists, began to move toward the left, making it more and more difficult for the Müller government to hold together and reach agreement, especially after the death of the foreign minister, Stresemann, in October 1929, the one major figure produced by the republic.

This was not the end of the SPD's troubles. Nineteen twenty-eight was the year in which the Third (Communist) International, based in Moscow and under pressure from Stalin, directed that the main thrust of Communist activity in Germany (where the KPD's share of the vote was over three million) should henceforward be directed against the Social Democrats, now to be labeled "Social Fascists." This directive, imposed solely in the interests of Stalin's faction in the Russian Communist party, without regard for those of the German working class or the KPD itself, both of which were weakened by it, was enforced right through the onset of the Depression, the rise of the Nazi party, and even after the Nazi takeover of power, and the destruction of the German Communist party that followed. How much the Nazis benefited from it is impossible to calculate; but there can be no doubt that the split between the two working-class parties, with the Communists attacking the Social Democrats and raising their own vote to five million in the 1932 elections, must have been a major factor in reducing resistance to the rise of Nazism and in undermining the morale of the SPD and trade-union leadership. Stalin was impervious to every attempt to persuade him to change his policy. If it led to the defeat of German democracy and of the cause of moderate socialism, so much the better; the official Comintern line remained that a Nazi victory would be followed by a working-class revolt and the creation of a Soviet Germany.

Hitler was quick to see that the destabilization and increased polarization of German politics between 1928 and 1930 offered him new opportunities.

*Müller's "Great Coalition" differed from the original Weimar coalition—SPD, DDP (German Democratic Party, progressive liberals), and the Catholic Center party—by the addition of Stresemann's party, the DVP (German People's Party, right-wing liberals). It was this addition that gave it a majority in the Reichstag. For details of the German parties and their electoral support during the Weimar period, see Appendix One.

The Nazis could step up their attacks on the SPD, lumping them together with the Communists as Reds who threatened revolution, at the same time that the Communists themselves were attacking the SPD as traitors to the working class. As for the nonsocialist parties, their loss of votes was an unmistakable sign that many middle-class voters who had voted for the conservative Nationalists (whose share of the poll had been cut from 20 to 14 percent) or for one or another of the two liberal parties (DDP or DVP), even for the Catholic Center, were breaking or drifting away from their traditional party allegiances without yet having found a satisfactory new one. If the reason, as everyone assumed, was a shift to the right in German politics, the Nazis were better placed to outbid any of the other antisocialist parties in taking advantage of it and appealing to their disillusioned supporters.

The much discussed "crisis of the bourgeois parties" was intensified by a second new factor, the impact of the Depression. This had already affected farming and the other occupations dependent on agriculture. In the course of 1929 its effects spread to the rest of the economy: The number of registered unemployed, which had fallen as low as 400,000, passed the three million mark for the first time. Germany was particularly vulnerable because so much of its economic revival had been financed by foreign loans, mostly short-term, which were now called in. The downturn in world trade and the collapse of share prices on the New York Stock Exchange in October 1929 were followed by a similar collapse of prices in Germany, by foreclosure on debts, restriction of credit, a wave of bankruptcies, forced sales of property and farms, the closure of factories. Those who had so far escaped were oppressed by the fear that they too would fall victims in the future.

For the German population was not only economically but psychologically vulnerable. The slump was the latest in a series of traumatic shocks beginning with the losses in the war, the defeat of 1918, the overthrow of the old regime, the threat of revolution and civil war, inflation, and the hardly less painful experience of stabilization. The few years of prosperity in the mid-1920s only heightened the sense of insecurity when they ended abruptly in yet another crisis. A feeling of despair began to affect people in all classes. The working classes feared the loss of jobs and the privations of unemployment. Many in the middle class feared the loss of their social status as well as their standards of living and economic survival. The young rebelled against the closing down of opportunities and expectations. All turned against the regime and the members of the coalition government, whom they blamed for allowing Germany to suffer a repetition of disaster and for being unable to agree on what steps should be taken to relieve it.

Where other politicians were dismayed, Hitler was excited. Nothing could better suit his apocalyptic style of politics than the prospect of disaster, in which exaggerated fears and irrational beliefs easily gained ground. He grasped instinctively that, as the crisis deepened, an increasing number of people would be willing to listen to a leader who promised not a program of economic and social reform, but a spiritual transformation, a national renewal, drawing on Germans' pride in their nation's historic destiny, and his own passionate conviction that will and faith could overcome all difficulties.

The Communists were as unrestrained as the Nazis in their condemnation of the present "System" and as dogmatic in their claim that history was on their side. But their insistence on the class war as its instrument limited their appeal and repelled more than it attracted, even among the working classes. In contrast, Hitler did not address himself to any particular class. He appealed to the German longing for national unity, a *Volksgemeinschaft,* a people's community, which would embrace Germans of all classes, at the same time leaving it open for anyone to believe that this was entirely compatible with the safeguarding of their own sectional interests. Traditional themes were embodied in the figure of an authoritarian leader—no more government by committees or coalitions—and combined with a novel, radical style of propaganda and presentation which attracted the young and anyone tired of the shabby, unexciting compromises of Weimar democracy.

The round of state and local elections in the autumn of 1929 and spring of 1930 showed a rising curve of support for the Nazis, but not yet enough to produce the breakthrough for which Hitler had waited so long. He was convinced that, as in 1923, the crisis created by the Depression would work in his favor, and that he now had a party organized to exploit it. But how far and how fast the radicalization of the electorate, particularly of the middle class, was proceeding, only a national Reichstag election would show.

There seemed no reason, however, why there should be an election. In March 1930 the Müller cabinet broke up after prolonged argument about the budget. Rather than share responsibility for financial reforms that they believed would threaten the unemployment-insurance scheme, and vulnerable to Communist attacks for failing to defend working-class interests, the Social Democratic party insisted on withdrawing its members from the coalition.

No alternative group could be put together capable of assembling a majority in the Reichstag, and the stalemate this produced gave the president, Paul von Hindenburg, the opportunity to make use of his emergency powers under Article 48 of the Weimar constitution. These allowed him to appoint a chancellor who could govern by presidential decree, if necessary. But the emergency powers were not unrestricted. A chancellor appointed by the president did not have to put together a majority to support him in the Reichstag, but his use of the president's powers to issue emergency decrees was open to challenge by a vote of no confidence in the Reichstag, if a majority could be found to carry it. If that happened, the president could dissolve the Reichstag but a new election would have to be held within sixty days. There were some among the president's advisers who were already looking for a way out of this, by creating a truly "presidential" form of government above parties and independent of the Reichstag. In due course this is what happened, but, until the Enabling Act was passed in March 1933, the Reichstag, even if it could not produce a working majority to form a government, could not be left out of account, because of its ability to force an election by a vote of no confidence.

The man von Hindenburg chose, Heinrich Brüning, leader of the Center party's parliamentary delegation, hoped that he would be able to persuade enough members of the Reichstag with the argument that, faced with a parliamentary stalemate, government still had to be carried on, and so avoid a vote of no confidence. At the time, in March 1930, it certainly looked as if the president had given the Weimar regime a new lease on life, an impression increased by the tougher line that the authorities in the largest German states started to take in dealing with the violence of both the Communists and the Nazis. Bavaria and Prussia banned demonstrations in uniform, such as the SA's Brownshirts; Prussia prohibited any of its civil servants from joining either extremist party, and the number of prosecutions for offenses against public order went up sharply. Hitler was consumed with anxiety that, as in 1923, the party would become frustrated with the long-delayed moment for action and lose the driving force and élan that accounted for so much of the attention it attracted.

The unresolved contradictions that could still compromise the party's chances of success are illustrated by the confrontation between Hitler and Gregor Strasser's younger brother, Otto. While Gregor Strasser moved to Munich, Otto remained in Berlin and through his paper *Arbeitsblatt* (which was actually still the official Nazi journal in the north) and his publishing house, the Kampfverlag, maintained an independent radical line which irritated and embarrassed Hitler. In April 1930 the trade unions in Saxony declared a strike, and Otto Strasser came out in full support of their action in the papers that he controlled, notably the *Sächsischer Beobachter,* the Nazi paper in Saxony. Hitler enforced an order that no member of the party was to take part in the strike, but he was unable to silence Strasser's papers. On May 21 he invited Otto Strasser to meet him for a discussion at his Berlin hotel. [43]

Hitler's tactics were a characteristic mixture of bribery, appeals, and threats. He offered to take over the Kampfverlag on generous terms and make Otto Strasser his press chief for the entire Reich; he appealed with him, with tears in his eyes and in the name of his brother Gregor, as an ex-soldier and a veteran National Socialist; he threatened that, if Strasser would not submit to his orders, he would drive him and his supporters out of the party and forbid any party members to have anything to do with him or his publications.

The discussion began with an argument about race and art, but soon shifted to political topics. Hitler attacked an article Strasser had published on "Loyalty and Disloyalty," which had distinguished between the Idea, which is eternal, and the Leader, who is only its servant.

This is all bombastic nonsense [Hitler declared], it boils down to this, that you would give every party member the right to decide on the Idea—even to decide whether the Leader is true to the so-called Idea or not. This is democracy at its worst, and there is no place for such a view with us. With us the Leader and the Idea are one, and every party member has to do what the Leader orders. You were a soldier yourself. . . . I ask you: Are you prepared to submit to this discipline or not?

After further discussion, Otto Strasser came to what he regarded as the heart of the matter. "You want to strangle the social revolution," he told Hitler, "for the sake of legality and your new collaboration with the bourgeois parties of the right."

Hitler, who was rattled by this suggestion, retorted angrily:

I am a Socialist, and a very different kind of Socialist from your rich friend, Count Reventlow. I was once an ordinary workingman. I would not allow my chauffeur to eat worse than I eat myself. What you understand by Socialism is nothing but Marxism. Now look: The great mass of workingmen want only bread and circuses. They have no understanding for ideals of any sort whatever, and we can never hope to win the workers to any large extent by an appeal to ideals. . . .

There are no revolutions except racial revolutions: There cannot be a political, economic, or social revolution—always and only it is the struggle of the lower stratum of inferior race against the dominant higher race, and if this higher race has forgotten the law of its existence, then it loses the day.

The conversation was continued the following day in the presence of Gregor Strasser, Max Amann, and Hess. When Otto Strasser demanded the nationalization of industry, Hitler retorted with scorn:

Democracy has laid the world in ruins, and nevertheless you want to extend it to the economic sphere. It would be the end of the German economy. . . . The capitalists have worked their way to the top through their capacity, and on the basis of this selection, which again only proves their higher race, they have a right to lead.

When Strasser asked him what he would do with the Krupps company if he came to power, Hitler at once replied:

Of course I should leave it alone. Do you think that I would be so mad as to destroy Germany's economy? Only if people failed to act in the interests of the nation, then—and only then—would the state intervene. But for that you do not need an expropriation . . . you need only a strong state.

For the moment the argument was left without a sequel. But at the end of June, Hitler instructed Goebbels, as Gauleiter of Berlin, to turn Otto

Strasser and his supporters out of the party. Very few followed them. His brother Gregor resigned from editorship of the Kampfverlag newspapers, and dissociated himself from his brother's views. Otto himself, after publishing his talks with Hitler, set up a Union of Revolutionary National Socialists known as the Black Front. Later, he emigrated and continued his opposition as a refugee, but without effect.

Shortly after Otto Strasser's expulsion, on July 16, 1930, the new chancellor solved Hitler's problem of timing for him. The opposition parties challenged the constitutionality of Brüning's action in making use of the president's emergency powers to put his fiscal program into effect by decree. Brüning's answer, much criticized subsequently, was to accept the challenge by dissolving the Reichstag and fixing new elections for September 14.

This proved to be a fateful decision, for it opened the way for Hitler at last to get into the political game. Hitler could hardly believe his luck. His party was far better prepared for an election than any of its rivals, and the political climate was more favorable to the Nazis than at any time since 1923. In the spring of 1930 he had appointed Goebbels as head of the Propaganda Division of the Reichsleitung and in the six weeks that followed the Nazi party, for the first time, let loose on a nationwide scale the sort of campaign they had been trying out in state and local elections. Everything was concentrated on producing the overriding impression of an energetic, confident, brash, youthful, dynamic party, bent upon "action—no more talk," and pointing out, in every way, how different they were from their rivals, whom they derided as out of date, elderly, discredited, divided, and defective.

The tone Goebbels set in his opening call was more reminiscent of a circus barker summoning the crowds outside the big top than the dull, wordy party manifestos to which German voters were accustomed:

> Throw the scum out! Tear the masks off their mugs! Take them by the scruff of their necks; kick them in their fat bellies on September 14 and sweep them out of the temple with trumpets and drums!

The satirist Kurt Tucholsky dismissed Hitler with the crack: "The man doesn't exist. He is only the noise he makes." But it was the noise that counted. The operation, centralized in the Brown House down to the design of posters and the wording of slogans, was seriously planned and left nothing to chance. The *Völkischer Beobachter* announced that 34,000 rallies were planned for the last four weeks of the campaign. A police report to the Prussian minister of the interior noted:

> Meetings attended by between a thousand and five hundred persons are a daily occurrence in the larger cities. Often, in fact, one or several parallel meetings have to be held because the previously selected halls cannot hold the number of persons wishing to attend. [44]

Hitler himself delivered at least twenty major speeches between August 3 and September 13. He was supported by a corps of a hundred speakers, all of them, like Goebbels and Strasser, experienced mob orators, and by the two to three thousand "graduates" of Reinhardt's school. These last were used to blanket the country districts as well as the cities with a nonstop series of rallies which attracted the crowds, if only for their entertainment value.

It was Germany's first encounter with a political circus with which they were to become only too familiar in the next few years. Most commentators dismissed it as ballyhoo designed to conceal the Nazis' lack of a program and did not take them seriously. Party enthusiasts expected fifty, perhaps hoped for seventy seats in the new Reichstag. The result was to show how much both critics and enthusiasts underestimated the polarization of German politics, to the advantage of both the extremist parties: The Communists jumped to four and a half million votes and 77 seats, and the Nazis to six and a half million of one and 107 of the other.

SIX Lenin's Successor

I

DURING THE PERIOD 1924 to 1929 Stalin was as intent as Hitler on securing power and, like Hitler, saw the party as the means of achieving it. The circumstances, however, were very different. In Russia the Communist party was already in power, had eliminated all its competitors, and accepted no limits in principle, however far it fell short in practice, to its right to control the economy and the whole life of society as well as the machinery of state. In a few years' time Hitler and the Nazi party would be able to make a similar claim, but in the 1920s Stalin was obviously an actor on a much bigger stage than Hitler. The advantages, however, were not all on Stalin's side.

Unlike Hitler, whose unique position as Führer was openly accepted by all the members of the Nazi party as the linchpin that held them together, Stalin had both to conceal his ambition and at the same time find means of defeating any rivals in an unremitting but covert struggle for power, from which, until his fiftieth birthday in December 1929, he could never be sure he would emerge the victor.

The fact that the struggle was not open but took the form of a series of debates on party policy favored Stalin in one respect: He showed himself to be a master of dissimulation with a gift for political intrigue and maneuvering that none of the other members of the Politburo could equal. He never made the mistake, which the others were inclined to, of allowing himself to be distracted by the questions under discussion from the real issue of power, and as general secretary he was better placed than anyone else to continue building up a power base inside the party. On the other hand, it was essential to a Marxist party to relate every decision about policy to its ideological framework, and this put Stalin at a disadvantage since he was not the equal of the others in his understanding of Marxist theory or, to begin with, in his facility in employing it.

Both men attached great importance to the organization of the party. Hitler, however, although he never let go of his power to decide on appointments and the allocation of responsibilities, preferred to exercise his behind the screen of an impersonal party bureaucracy, so protecting the "Führer myth" from compromise. In the same way he kept aloof from disputes over policy, refusing to take sides and engaging his authority only when it became necessary to silence controversy.

Once he had secured the same unique position in relation to the party as Hitler, Stalin carried the "cult of personality"—the equivalent of the "Führer myth"—close to deification; but any suggestion of this in the 1920s would have been fatal. The role he adopted then was that of the plain man who spoke the same practical language as the party workers from the provinces and was accessible to them. Instead of disguising his exercise of power, he personalized it, leaving no doubt as to whose door to knock on. In the same role he represented the voice of common sense and moderation, opposing the exaggeration of the extremists on either side, stressing the need for unity.

The arena in which Stalin conducted his six-year-long campaign to become Lenin's successor was the closed world of the upper echelons of the Communist party and the Communist International. At no point were the contestants—either Stalin or his opponents—willing to take the issues between them to the Russian people or even to such representative bodies as the Soviets.

The largest bodies involved, their membership increasingly controlled by Stalin, were the Party Congress and the specially summoned Party Conference, each of which met three times between Lenin's death in 1924 and Stalin's victory at the end of 1929. At the Fourteenth Congress in December 1925 there were over 600 delegates with votes, and this particular congress was repeatedly postponed until Stalin could be sure of carrying the majority, a necessary precaution in going to the body that had the final voice. But the two main bodies in which the more open running battles over policy and power were fought out were the Politburo (seven rising to nine full members with four to eight candidates), where the confrontation was face-to-face across the table, and the Central Committee Plenum. At the same time that Lenin had recommended increasing the size of the Central Committee and the Central Control Commission, he had urged that the two should meet together to form a plenum which would meet several times a year and become a superior party conference. With a Central Committee that (counting candidates as well as full members) grew from 85 in 1924 to 121 in 1928, Lenin's proposal produced a plenum of between 250 and 300, which brought together the whole of the top leadership of the Communist party.

In such a setting, where the proceedings took the form of debates subject to interruption and ending in votes, there was no place for Hitlerian histrionics. What Stalin had to develop was something of which Hitler was temperamentally incapable: the ability to meet reasoned argument and show himself sufficiently master of the background to maneuver in debate and to cap his case with a telling quotation from Lenin, or from his opponents' earlier writings, so justifying the accusation of deviation or opportunism. Aware of his limitations, he adopted a plain style of speaking, making full use of his position as general secretary to prepare the ground and manipulate membership, procedure, and timing so as to place his opponents at a disadvantage.

By comparison with Hitler's exaggerated statements and highly charged appeal to the emotions of his audience, a characteristic Stalin speech from this period—even to the larger Party Congress—follows a logical line of argument within a conventional Marxist framework and is dull to read, unless one has the key, as his listeners would have had, to the "coded" references with which he scored his points. Nothing shows his astuteness more than his disclaimer of any originality as a Marxist theoretician and the use he made of his claim to be no more than an interpreter of Lenin. As time passed and he became more sure of speaking before a "packed" audience, his confidence grew and his manner became more menacing.

THE POINT has often been made that, in appointing Stalin as general secretary, the other members of the Politburo failed to recognize the power they were placing in his hands to use for his own aggrandizement. They also failed to recognize the necessary changes in the role and the character of the party from the one they had known in prerevolutionary days.

One was in size. Lenin had insisted on purging the party of many who had joined it during the civil war. This reduced it from 567,000 to 350,000 members at the end of 1923, a number that was inadequate to carry out the tasks now envisaged in a country as large and backward as Russia. Beginning with the "Lenin enrollment," which the party proclaimed in 1924 as a memorial to its dead leader, the number of members (including candidates) more than doubled from under half a million to over a million in two years, and continued to rise until it reached three and a half million by the beginning of 1933.

Judged by social origins, the peasantry, which made up the overwhelming majority of the population, was seriously underrepresented in the party: an average of 27 percent from 1924 to 1926, falling to an average of 21 percent from 1927 to 1929. Comparable percentages for those of worker origin were: 52 percent from 1924 to 1926, rising to 58 percent from 1927 to 1929. Judged by actual occupation, not just origins, the figures look even less impressive. On January 1, 1928, for example, the breakdown of party membership was as follows:

Serving in the Red Army	6.3%
Wage earners in industry	35.2%
Agricultural laborers	1.2%
Better-off farmers, often employing hired labor	9.2%

Party officials (including part-time)   38.3%
Others employed in nonmanual occupations   9.8%

In 1927, the number of village Communists was just over 300,000 in a rural population of more than 120 million, and most of these were party functionaries, not farmers. From first to last, unlike the Nazis, the Russian Communist party's greatest problem was to establish effective links with the peasantry.

The other characteristics of the new intake were youth, inexperience, and a low educational standard. In 1927 fewer than 1 percent had completed higher education, fewer than 8 percent had received even secondary education. As the British historian Leonard Schapiro says, the Lenin enrollment provided the Secretariat with "a mass of malleable recruits to counterbalance the more intractable older Communists."[1] It was not that the leaders themselves were so old. Taking the 121 members of the Central Committee elected in December 1927, which included most of the men who were to govern Russia under Stalin, nearly half were under forty, three-quarters under forty-five. The "undergrounds," as those were known who had joined the party before 1917, numbered no more than 8,500; they and the civil war veterans still dominated the higher party echelons in 1927, but at the lower end of the party over 60 percent of the secretaries of primary cells had joined after 1921.

More important than the gap of age was the gap of experience. The tradition of intraparty democracy, the ideological and theoretical issues that had so preoccupied the older generation, especially those who had lived abroad as émigrés and acquired a European outlook, meant little to the newcomers, many of whom had served a rough apprenticeship as youngsters in the civil war. They were ready enough to accept what they were told by their instructors: that the duty of the rank-and-file party member was to support the leaders in getting on with the formidable job of turning Russia into a modern socialist state, and that in return they would enjoy certain privileges—and the prospect of further advancement. All they asked was to be told what to do, and in Stalin (whom Lenin had criticized for his rudeness and lack of culture) they saw the man who was prepared to tell them in the sort of language they could understand. Molotov spoke the truth when he told the 1924 Party Congress, "the development of the party in the future will undoubtedly be based on this Lenin enrollment."

The strength of Stalin's position was that the concentration of power that followed "objectively" from the party's need to strengthen its organization coincided with his personal interest. To those who claimed, justifiably, that the general secretary was using the party to build up his own power, Stalin could reply—with equal justification—that he was providing what Lenin had called for. What alternative was there, if the decisions made by the leadership were to be carried out on the ground?

In addition to moving officeholders up, or down, the levels of the hierarchy, Stalin was also able to remove those who opposed him by proposing transfer—either to diplomatic posts abroad or to official duties in the remoter parts of Siberia or Soviet Central Asia. By 1926 these combined powers covered the 5,500 top party officials whose appointments were reserved to the central bodies, the group to which the term *nomenklatura* was originally restricted. The most important of these were the party secretaries, especially at the regional (*obkom* and *kraikom*) level, powerful figures with their own clienteles, the *apparat,* the vital network on which the center had to rely for putting its policies into effect. Since the careers of the remainder, numbering some 20,000 in 1925, depended on those appointed by the center, Stalin had no difficulty in making his influence felt at the middle and lower levels as well.

It was in these provincial levels of the party that the selection of delegates to the Party Congress was made, and it is hardly surprising that the percentage of full-time officials among their number rose from 25 percent at the Tenth Congress in 1921 to 55 percent at the Twelfth in 1923, 65 percent at the Thirteenth in 1924, and 70 percent at the Fourteenth in 1925.

Far from reducing the power of the general secretary and the bureaucracy, the proposals that Lenin had made for strengthening the Central Committee and the Central Commission served only to increase it. As Stalin had been shrewd enough to realize when he supported them at the congress, the inclusion of more "local party workers," from which Lenin had hoped so much, turned out in practice to mean the appointment of more party officials.

Henceforward, the key promotion for the ambitious was candidate-membership of the Central Committee, on which they served alongside the senior figures in the party, including the members of the Politburo. Those who were advanced to such a place were left in no doubt of whom they had to thank, or of what was expected of them, if they hoped to proceed further. In the later stages of the struggle for power, veterans of the revolution attempting to maintain the right to question and debate party policy in the Central Committee or the Party Congress found themselves interrupted, and shouted down, by an audience increasingly made up of full-time party officials well briefed on what the general secretary wanted.

I I

IF THE SIX OTHER MEMBERS of the Politburo, or even a majority of them, had united to prevent Stalin from building up too powerful a position, there is good reason to suppose they would have succeeded, at least in the first year after Lenin's death. An obvious opportunity was at the meeting of the Central Committee on May 22, 1924, just before the Thirteenth Party Congress was due to open. Krupskaya, Lenin's widow, pressed for the text of Lenin's Testament, including the postscript, which called for

Stalin's removal from the post of general secretary, to be laid before the congress, and insisted that this had been Lenin's express wish. If such a course had been followed, it is impossible to say for certain what would have happened; Lenin had been dead only four months, and his authority was still great. Stalin at least seems to have felt that his future was in the balance. Boris Bazhanov, who was present at the Central Committee meeting, later recalled that, while the Testament was being read to the committee,

> Stalin, who was sitting on the edge of the low dais on which the conference was mounted, was staring out of the window with the ostentatious composure of a man who was inwardly anxious. He displayed every sign of realizing that his fate was being decided—which was unusual for Stalin, for normally he knew how to hide his feelings. And he had reason enough to fear for his future, because in the atmosphere of worship surrounding everything Lenin had said and done, could it be supposed that the Central Committee would dare to challenge Lenin's solemn warning, and leave the general secretary in his post?[2]

Stalin was saved by the intervention of Zinoviev and Kamenev, who believed that the only one to benefit from making Lenin's views known would be Trotsky. Stalin had agreed that Zinoviev should deliver the main report to the Party Congress; in return, Zinoviev declared that, happily, Lenin's fears about Stalin had proved unfounded, and Kamenev urged the committee to keep Stalin on as general secretary. Trotsky expressed his contempt for this charade by grimaces and gestures, but said nothing. The committee then decided that the contents of Lenin's Testament should be communicated confidentially to the heads of delegations in closed session, but not read out to the congress. No further action was taken and neither Lenin's letter nor the closed sessions were included in the record of the congress.

Not only Zinoviev and Kamenev, but also the other members of the Politburo in turn, fell into the same trap of taking others more seriously as rivals in the contest for power than they did Stalin. So Trotsky refused to combine with Zinoviev and Kamenev when they fell victims of Stalin's maneuvering. Not until the spring of 1926 were the three of them prepared to form a united opposition to Stalin, only to find that Bukharin, Rykov, and Tomsky by then thought it more important to join Stalin in defeating them than to guard against themselves becoming his next victims. At no point in the six years separating Lenin's call in his Testament for the general secretary's removal from office and his final triumph was Stalin ever met by a common front.

Stalin was able to benefit from his rivals' underestimation of him because of his success in concealing for a long time the extent of his own ambitions. Bazhanov wrote in his memoirs:

> Stalin did not confide his innermost thoughts to anybody. Only very rarely did he share his ideas and impressions with his closest associates.

He possessed in a high degree the gift of silence, and in this respect he was unique in a country where everybody talked far too much.

Bazhanov goes on to describe Stalin's behavior at meetings of the Politburo and the Central Committee. Stalin never presided at these:

> He smoked his pipe and spoke very little. Every now and then he would start walking up and down the conference room regardless of the fact that we were in session. Sometimes he would stop right in front of a speaker, watching his expression and listening to his argument while still puffing away at his pipe. . . .
>
> He had the good sense never to say anything before everyone else had his argument fully developed. He would sit there, watching the way the discussion was going. When everyone had spoken, he would say: "Well, comrades, I think the solution to this problem is such and such"—and he would then repeat the conclusions toward which the majority had been drifting. [3]

This strengthened the impression of moderation, a man of the middle course, belonging to neither the left nor the right, which he took care to cultivate. As an illustration Bazhanov cites the difference between the ways the members of the triumvirate treated Trotsky at sessions of the Politburo. They were the last to arrive, after the preliminary meeting at which they had decided how to handle the agenda: Zinoviev ignored Trotsky, Kamenev gave him a slight nod, Stalin alone leaned across the table to shake hands and greet him.

In the years following Lenin's death, Stalin played a waiting game, leaving it to the other side to move first, and then exploiting its mistakes. Even when the split between them was open, and despite many early threats and warnings, it was not until the end of 1927 that he moved to expel Trotsky and Zinoviev from the party. In the final phase, when he had destroyed the left opposition and turned against Bukharin and the right, he took great care to keep the quarrel confined within the inner circle until he was sure, after more than a year, that he had isolated Bukharin and only then moved against him in public. Stalin's persistence was phenomenal; so, in this period, were his patience and caution.

Another contemporary view of Stalin is provided by Ruth Fischer, a member of the German Communist Party (KPD), who was summoned to Moscow in January 1924 for a discussion between the German and Russian Communist leaders about the lessons to be drawn from the unsuccessful attempt at a German revolution in the previous autumn. Unexpectedly, since Stalin was not a member of the Comintern Presidium, or involved in the formal discussions, Fischer and Arkadi Maslow, the leaders of the left-wing faction of the KPD, were invited to several private interviews with him, at his request. The Germans were surprised at the "amazing capacity" Stalin showed in his grasp of every detail of the German party organization and the divisions within it. He showed much less interest in the policy issues, and Fischer was shocked by the emphasis he put on how to acquire power within the party: "His discussion of organization and groupings was not haphazard but directly related to a concept of how to arrange them best for power."[4]

He had tried, so he maintained, to overcome the dissension in the Russian party resulting from the Trotsky crisis, and to recreate an iron guard of leaders who would cooperate without words or theses and be bound together by the necessity of unalterable self-defense. We would soon return to Germany, and he wanted to find out whether we would be reliable enough to be accepted into the inner group.[5]

On one occasion, Stalin asked the two Germans to come unobtrusively to his apartment in the Kremlin. What impressed his visitors was the modest style in which Stalin lived: He occupied a single-story, two-room house in the former servants' quarters of the Kremlin, shabbily furnished, despite the fact that he was the organizer of

tens of thousands of salaried employees, including the state police . . . and could offer party jobs and state jobs, give influential assignments in Russia and abroad, and very often "responsible party tasks" combined with substantial material advantages—apartments, automobiles, country residences, special medical care, jobs for members of the family.[6]

The simplicity of Stalin's life-style was not a pose. He was interested in the substance not the trappings of power. Bazhanov and other witnesses confirm this: "This passionate politician has no other vices. He loves neither money nor pleasure, neither sport nor women. Women, apart from his own wife, do not exist for him."[7]

In 1919, during the civil war, Stalin had married a second time. His wife, Nadezhda Alliluyeva, twenty-two years younger, was the daughter of the railwayman, Sergei Alliluyev, who had known Stalin since his days in Tiflis and had provided a home for him when he returned to St. Petersburg in 1917. Nadezhda had been brought up in a family passionately committed to the revolution; she became one of Lenin's secretaries and kept a job of her own after marriage. But she also proved to be a good homemaker, bearing two children, Vasily and Svetlana, and presiding over the country house, twenty miles from Moscow, Zubalovo, which had belonged to an oil magnate of that name before the revolution and now became Stalin's home. Stalin improved and kept up the estate, and in her memoirs Svetlana writes nostalgically of the happy days she spent there, in a house that was always full, for it was her father's habit to invite his closest colleagues and their families to stay, among them the Ordzhonikidzes, the Bukharins, and Sergei Kirov. Others, including the Molotovs, the Voroshilovs, and the Mikoyans joined them for summer trips to the Black Sea coast. This was not the way the proletariat lived, but it was a solid bourgeois existence, private, informal, and domestic, not ostentatious or extravagant, and untouched by scandal.

· · ·

A MAJOR DIFFICULTY in writing about the Stalin of the 1920s is to know how far he is to be viewed in the light of the characteristics he was to reveal in the later 1930s, at the height of his power. Contemporaries already saw him as a rough, cunning, sly, and unscrupulous politician, and those who worked closely with him were aware of a violent and suspicious temper, which they took care not to arouse. But revolutionary politics are a rough trade, and the same could be said of many other historical figures who have not gone on to inflict suffering and death on their own people on a scale for which there is literally no parallel. In retrospect, of course, the continuity is clear, but if the potentiality was already there, it was not yet recognized, and Stalin himself showed no sign of having a presentiment of what might lie ahead.

This cannot be more than speculation; but there are several reasons for regarding it as a more plausible hypothesis than the opposite, that of the "monster in embryo." One is the fact that, furious though the factional fights became, they were still contained within limits. Until the end of 1927, they were still fought out openly before the Central Committee Plenum, the Party Congress or Conference, where the opposition was free to challenge the leadership, issues were settled by votes, and the debates reported. The opposition spokesmen were more and more subject to heckling and interruption, but that is true even of parliamentary assemblies; they had increasing difficulty in rallying support inside the party, but even when in 1928–29 the clash between Stalin and the right opposition took place behind closed doors, the opposition could not be suppressed, it had to be defeated. The leaders were not arrested or shot; even Trotsky was banished, not imprisoned or executed, and most of the others, like Zinoviev and Kamenev, were allowed back into the party—even, like Bukharin, to hold official posts.

There is no doubt that Stalin's confidence and stature grew during the 1920s. The Stalin of the earlier 1920s whom Bazhanov describes as taking care not to express an opinion of his own in Politburo meetings was not the same as the man who hammered the opposition for their defeatism, and who roused the Party Conference of 1926 to enthusiasm with his call to create socialism in one country, or who confronted Trotsky and faced him down in the Central Committee Plenum in October 1927. As his confidence grew, so did his ambition. It is not only the appetite for power that grows with its exercise, but also the conception of how much further it can be pushed. Stalin in the era of the First Five-Year Plan (1928–33) could conceive of an historical role for himself, something more than that of Lenin's successor, which was beyond his imaginative as well as political reach in the mid-1920s.

To begin with, Stalin was preoccupied with building an instrument in the party organization that would enforce unity, and defeat the opposition to this of other groups in the party. A first step to grasping what could be done with it was the adoption of the slogan "socialism in one country." Once

Trotsky and the left opposition were defeated he was free to develop the idea of breaking with the New Economic Policy, and carrying through the collectivization of agriculture and the modernization of industry not gradually, but by storm, in the shortest possible time. From this emerged the resort to the methods of War Communism, coercion backed by terror, and the justification that the nearer one comes to the achievement of socialism, the more intense becomes the class struggle. Out of this grandiose conception, far different from the moderate middle-of-the-road course that he had adopted in the mid-1920s, emerged the figure of the "Great Leader of the Soviet People," the architect of the Second Revolution, completing the task that Lenin had begun but left unfinished.

That was five or six years away in 1924. When, at the Fourteenth Party Congress, Kamenev accused Stalin to his face of trying to set up one-man rule, Stalin blandly replied:

> To lead the party otherwise than collectively is impossible. Now that Ilyich is not with us, it is silly to dream of such a thing [applause]. It is silly to talk about it. Collective work, collective leadership, unity in the party, unity in the organs of the Central Committee, with the minority submitting to the majority—that is what we need now. [8]

The second part of Stalin's reply is as revealing as the first. In all the debates of these years, two standard charges constantly reappear. Each opposition group in turn, as it felt itself forced on to the defensive and sensed defeat, renewed the charges of bureaucratization and the suppression of inner-party democracy. The countercharge was factionalism, the blackest crime in the Communist book.

When Lenin called an informal meeting at the Tenth Party Congress (1921) to organize support for his resolution banning factions, Stalin expressed anxiety that the Lenin group might be accused of "factionalism" themselves. Lenin laughed and replied:

> What's this I hear from a zealous old factionalist? . . . You must know that Trotsky has long been at work gathering the supporters of his platform and has probably called his faction together at this very moment while we sit here talking. Shliapnikov and Sapronov are doing the same. Why close our eyes to the clear fact, unpleasant as it is, that factions exist in the party? It is just the calling of this conference of adherents of "the platform of the ten" that will bring about conditions excluding all factionalism in our party in the future. [9]

Stalin learned his lesson well. He was helped in doing so by one of the most distinctive characteristics of Communist politics, which followed logically from the belief that Marxism provided a unique, incontrovertible and unambiguous guide both to the historical development of society and to the correct policy to be followed by the party in the future. If this were so, then there was clearly no room for alternative views or alternative policies within the party. The trick was to capture the higher ground before anyone else could do so, establish the claim to represent the "correct" view according to Marxist doctrine, and proceed to denounce those who opposed it as guilty of "factionalism" and endangering the unity of the party. Faction, like treason, was by definition unsuccessful. As Lenin as well as Stalin clearly recognized, when successful—like treason that prospers—it was legitimized and went by a different name. A threat to party unity was something that affected all members of the party, and hence was a more damaging charge than the countercharge of suppressing inner-party democracy, which only appealed to a minority of intellectuals—and to most of them, as the examples of Trotsky, Zinoviev, and Bukharin show, only when they were out of office and in opposition.

None of the contestants attempted to appeal to the nation at large, the masses that they claimed to represent. All accepted that, however bitter their disputes, they had to be confined to the party's upper echelons.

Nothing could have been more to Stalin's advantage. That men like Trotsky, Zinoviev, and Bukharin, fighting for their political lives and with much greater gifts of communication, in both speaking and writing, should have voluntarily accepted such a prohibition, shows how strong was the hold exercised by the Bolshevik dogma. Even to carry the debate to the rank-and-file party members immediately invited the accusation of splitting the party, and was deliberately ruled out by Bukharin, to his great disadvantage. Even more powerful, shared by all though rarely acknowledged, was the underlying feeling that the party was a beleaguered garrison in an occupied country, and the fear that to appeal to the masses might reopen the question of a revolutionary settlement imposed on them by force and lead to the party's, and their own, destruction.

THE ANXIETY to avoid a charge of factionalism was closely related to a second characteristic of Communist politics that Stalin had to master if he was to defeat his rivals—Communism's ideological dimension. For a party that elevated unity, in both theory and practice, to an absolute value, the Communist party was remarkably contentious, and had been since Marxism first made its appearance in Russia in the 1890s. Marx might have provided his disciples with the immutable laws of social development, but there was endless argument about their interpretation and application. Since there was no room, in principle, for such disagreement, difference of opinion became error which it was a duty to excoriate. Almost all Lenin's writings are polemical in character; denunciation and a ban of factionalism could not quell the scholastic passion for controversy.

This continued as strongly as ever after Lenin's death, and the struggle for power among his heirs was fought out in a series of arguments about the problems with which the regime was confronted and the general line that the party ought to take in seeking to solve them. The distinctive feature of these debates was that, while both sides sought to justify their positions as the most effective way of dealing with the problems pragmatically, they regarded it as even more important to show that it was the correct way in terms of Marxist ideology. As the Stalinist Lazar Kaganovich said in 1929: "Treachery in politics always begins with the revision of theory."

This posed a special challenge for Stalin, who was once told by the veteran Marxist scholar, David Ryazanov, the director of the Marx-Engels Institute: "Stop it, Koba, don't make a fool of yourself. Everybody knows that theory is not exactly your field."[10] Stalin's strength lay in his gifts as a pragmatic politician, a master of intrigue, above all in the singlemindedness that drove him to devote all his waking hours to thinking how best to manipulate situations and people in the course of building up a formidable political machine. As Robert Tucker says, this would enable him to become the party's boss (its *khozyain*, as he came to be known during these years) but would not secure him acceptance as the party's new leader or *vozhd'* in succession to Lenin. "To win the Lenin succession as distinguished from the contest for power, Stalin had to legitimize himself in the supreme-leader role by acquiring special political authority in Bolshevik eyes—would have to prove himself in Lenin's role as chief ideological spokesman of the party and as a Marxist thinker."[11]

Stalin's way of dealing with the challenge was shrewd. Although like all Bolsheviks he quoted from Marx and Engels, he made no pretense of being a Marxist scholar; nor did he attempt to make an original contribution to Marxist theory such as Bukharin had already proved himself capable of doing. Instead, he concentrated on mastery of Lenin's writings and speeches, so that he could hold his own in debates which frequently resembled theological controversies with a running exchange of scriptural texts.

Immediately after Lenin's death, among the spate of commemorative articles, Stalin produced something different—a course of lectures on the "Foundations of Leninism," which he delivered at Sverdlov University, a college for party officials, and then turned into a book of the same title. The presentation was often clumsy and the writing wooden. It could be justly criticized for concentrating on the dogmatic at the expense of the more lively and flexible elements in Lenin's thinking; it suffered, to borrow a phrase of Trotsky's, from "a certain ideological petrification." Nonetheless, it provided, for the first time, something that more sophisticated thinkers in the party would have considered beneath them to supply: the first short, comprehensive, and systematic account of Lenin's ideas, in less than a hundred pages, copiously illustrated by quotations—for which Stalin owed a considerable debt (unacknowledged) to a research assistant, F. A. Ksenofontov.[12] The shrewdness is shown by the timing and by the dedication to the "Lenin enrollment," the new generation of party workers with little education, who found Lenin's own writings heavy going and confusing, and who seized eagerly on this work of popularization, the authority of which was vouched for by no less a person than the general secretary himself.

The Foundations of Leninism was not only a popular success but also

strengthened that identification with Lenin that had already begun with
Stalin's part in inaugurating the cult of Lenin. Not surprisingly, it was a
version of Lenin cast in Stalin's own image. The link between them was the
fact that, without either admitting or perhaps even realizing it, both men
saw the party, rather than social forces, or Marx's changes in the mode of
production, as the driving force of history. It was the party that had to
create the proletarian class-consciousness the workers lacked.

> The Party [Stalin wrote] has to guide the proletariat in its struggle
> . . . it has to instill in the millions of the mass of unorganized nonparty
> workers a spirit of discipline . . . of organization and steadfastness.
> . . . The party is the highest form of the class organization of the
> proletariat. [13]

In another passage Stalin defined Leninism as Marxism brought up to
date:

> the Marxism of the epoch of imperialism and of the proletarian revolu-
> tion . . . Leninism is the theory and tactic of the proletarian revolution
> in general, and the theory and tactic of the dictatorship of the proletariat
> in particular.

There was nothing in this with which Lenin would have disagreed, nor in
Stalin's conclusions: "The proletariat needs the party for the establishment
of the dictatorship. It needs it even more to maintain the dictatorship."
Hence the need for "iron discipline" and "unity of will," and the condemnation of factions as destructive of both.

Stalin's use in debate of quotations from Lenin to bolster his own
position did not pass unchallenged. More than once he got the worst of a
clash with Trotsky, Zinoviev, or Kamenev, who showed him to be standing
Lenin's argument on its head or quoting him out of context. But Stalin
persisted in his bid to capture the ideological succession to Lenin by
presenting himself as the defender of Lenin's heritage against an opposition
which was seeking to revise or abandon it. When he wanted to find
justification for the doctrine of socialism in one country, he insisted that it
had first been formulated by Lenin, and maintained this in spite of the
conclusive proof to the contrary by Trotsky and Zinoviev. Undeterred, he
relied on a packed congress to vote them down; thereafter, as one after
the other of his critics was silenced, his claim to be the authoritative
interpreter of Marxism-Leninism could no longer be questioned. The
Marxist-Leninist ideology, combined with the defense of party unity against
the factionalism of the opposition, had become an instrument of power in
Stalin's hands.

Stalin's victory over his rivals was neither inevitable nor planned in detail
in advance. There were setbacks, retreats, constant improvisation. Luck and
the mistakes of his opponents played a major part. More than seven years
were needed from his appointment as general secretary in April 1922 before
he could be sure that he had won.

The power that he built up through control of the Secretariat and the party machine was indispensable: Thanks to this, he was able increasingly to promote his own candidates, demote or expel opponents. Through his power to pack committees and secure a majority vote, Stalin was able to fasten on any who attempted to organize opposition the charge of factionalism, of splitting the party, indulging in counterrevolutionary activity, and betraying the revolution—in short, treason. To this he was able to add the charge of heresy, of petit-bourgeois deviation from the canon of Marxism-Leninism, which he alone had the authority to declare and, when necessary, to extend. In short, borrowing a term from earlier European history, it was Stalin's combination of the spiritual with the secular arm that made him invincible.

But invincibility, disarming and defeating the opposition, was not enough for the authority Stalin sought; he had to win the argument as well as winning the vote with a packed jury. In the end, as we shall see, he achieved this too by convincing those who shared the leadership with him that he offered a better chance than anyone else available of overcoming the problems Russia was faced with and preserving the regime.

I I I

THERE WERE FOUR PHASES in the confrontation of Lenin's heirs. The first began in 1923 while Lenin was still alive but incapacitated and ended in 1925: In this, the troika of Zinoviev, Kamenev, and Stalin was ranged against Trotsky. The second, Stalin and Bukharin against Zinoviev and Kamenev, in 1925–26, runs into the third, Stalin and Bukharin against the United Opposition of Zinoviev, Kamenev, and Trotsky in 1926–27. The final act of the drama, 1928–29, with the United Opposition defeated, sees Stalin turn against Bukharin, Rykov, and Tomsky. By his fiftieth birthday in 1929, Stalin had driven out of the Politburo five of the six other members with whom the period began; the sixth, Rykov, remained only on sufferance.

This series of maneuvers, by which Stalin secured a conclusive victory over the other three factions in the Politburo, has often been cited as a classic example of the art of power politics. There is no doubt about Stalin's remarkable gifts as a politician, but it is a mistake to suppose that he (any more than Hitler) was following a carefully worked-out plan, as is often suggested by the statement in summary accounts that he first allied with the right in order to defeat the left, and then took over the program of the left in order to defeat the right. Like Hitler, he was unswerving in his single-minded purpose of attaining a dominant position, but he was as flexible as he was unscrupulous in the means by which he secured it, ready to reverse his position, make and break tactical alliances, and to take full advantage of any opportunities unexpectedly offered by his rivals' mistakes.

With far greater perception than the other Soviet leaders, Lenin had grasped that, once he was removed from the scene, the fight for the succession would be between Trotsky and Stalin. Stalin had reached the same conclusion, and acted accordingly; Trotsky failed to and, largely for that reason, lost. It was only belatedly, in 1926, that he took the full measure of Stalin and at last showed himself ready to join with others to try and check the general secretary's growing power.

It is still hard to explain why Trotsky should have misjudged the situation so badly, how far he was affected by illness, why he should have proved so inept in tactics and timing (including being absent on crucial occasions), why he should have failed, to the despair of his followers, to rally the support that he could still have won in the party. Trotsky, however, could play only commanding roles. He was ill at ease with those who regarded themselves as his equals, and lacked the political instinct which prompted Stalin to concentrate on building up a power base in the party. Instead, as Walter Laqueur says, "he involved himself in constant ideological and political controversies, more befitting a pre-revolutionary litterateur than a post-revolutionary statesman." [14] But Stalin was right: with all his faults and mistakes Trotsky was the man he had to fear most; a born leader, however flawed; second only to Lenin in the part he had played in the October Revolution and the Civil War, with natural powers as an intellectual and speaker which Stalin could never match.

His record does not suggest that Trotsky would have been any less of an autocrat than Stalin, equally ready to adopt coercive methods, or any less ruthless in enforcing his will. In Stalin's eyes this made him all the more dangerous a rival, in a different class from any of the other members of the Politburo. Whatever moves Stalin made, whatever other opponents he had to deal with, he never for a moment lost sight of Trotsky. It was this unrelenting concentration of attention, fueled by hatred and matched by a far greater understanding of Trotsky's weaknesses than the latter had of Stalin's, as well as by patience, persistence, and a flair for tactics and timing that Trotsky lacked, that enabled Stalin to win a duel in which the natural advantages appeared to be all on Trotsky's side.

In 1923, while Lenin was still alive, although incapacitated, Trotsky had made two powerful attacks on Stalin but had failed to follow up on them. The Thirteenth Party Conference, meeting less than a week before Lenin died, in January 1924, after listening to a threatening speech by Stalin, censured Trotsky and the "forty-six" for factionalism. Stalin had perfected his stage management: Of 128 voting delegates, only 3 belonged to the opposition.

Trotsky came in for still further reprimand at the Thirteenth Party Congress in May 1924, but he retained his seat on the Politburo, and there were signs in the summer that the troika might soon break up. Instead of allowing the rift to develop, however, Trotsky opened what became known as the "Literary Controversy," with a lengthy essay, *The Lessons of October,* published for the seventh anniversary of the revolution. This was intended as a reply to the reproach always made against Trotsky, that he had joined Lenin only in the summer of 1917 and before that had been closer to the Mensheviks than the Bolsheviks.

Naming Zinoviev and Kamenev, whom he still regarded as his real enemies rather than Stalin, Trotsky countercharged that it was they who had been tainted with the Menshevik heresy, who had attacked Lenin's plans for an insurrection in 1917 as "adventurist," and had followed the Menshevik line that the bourgeois democratic revolution must be completed first and an interval elapse before the proletarian revolution. He added that the same temporizing attitude accounted for the failure of the Comintern (chairman, Zinoviev) to exploit with sufficient boldness the revolutionary situation in Germany and Bulgaria in 1923. Of all the present Soviet leaders, according to Trotsky, it was only he who had worked in complete agreement with Lenin, from the first day of his arrival in Petrograd.

Later, Zinoviev was to admit to Trotsky that *The Lessons of October* served only as a pretext for the furious attack on him that followed. "Failing that, a different motive would have been found." [15] But the particular line Trotsky chose to take had the effect of uniting the rest of the Politburo against him—Bukharin, Rykov, and Stalin as well as Zinoviev and Kamenev—all of whom had a vested interest in overthrowing Trotsky's version of 1917 precisely because it was uncomfortably close to the truth.

The most effective answer was to divert attention from 1917 by concentrating on Trotsky's own record before that year. Following the 1903 split in the Russian Social Democratic party, he had pursued a highly individual course and engaged in a whole series of polemical exchanges, some of the sharpest of which had been with Lenin. These were now exhumed and plundered for quotations which, often taken out of context, could be used to make it appear that Lenin, whose authority was now above challenge, had rejected Trotsky as the leading representative of a political tendency different from and opposed to his own.

No one set to this task with greater zeal than Stalin. In a speech of November 19, 1924, "Trotskyism or Leninism?" he not only began rewriting the history of the 1917 revolution but also accused Trotsky of seeking to discredit Lenin as the inspirer of it and the party as the force that carried it through—all for the purpose of substituting "Trotskyism" for "Leninism." "The task of the party," Stalin declared, "is to bury Trotskyism as an ideology."

Their invention of "Trotskyism" enabled Trotsky's opponents, above all Stalin, to identify him with a permanent heresy, anti-Leninist and anti-Bolshevik by definition, yet capable of being extended to cover any other issue that Trotsky might take up, or that it was convenient to attribute to him. Trotsky reports Zinoviev telling the members of his Leningrad faction:

"You must understand that it was a struggle for power. The trick was to string together old disagreements with new issues. For this purpose 'Trotskyism' was invented." [16]

The other charge against Trotsky was that he was the author of the doctrine of "permanent revolution." First developed at the time of the 1905 revolution, this postulated the need for the revolution to be permanent in two senses. The first was in continuing without a break from its antifeudal (democratic) to its anticapitalist (socialist) phase. The second was in passing from a national to an international phase, starting in Russia, but not stopping at her frontiers. Only when the revolution spread from Russia to Western Europe would socialism be securely established even in Russia.

Lenin, while certainly an internationalist, rejected Trotsky's formulation—until 1917. He then, without admitting it, adopted Trotsky's theory as his own, putting the first part into practice and accepting the second, international part as the necessary premise for the success of the revolution in Russia. If anyone doubted this, they had only to look at the authoritative summary of Lenin's view in Stalin's *Foundations of Leninism:*

> For the final victory of socialism . . . the efforts of one country, particularly of a peasant country like Russia, are insufficient; for that, the efforts of the proletarians of several advanced countries are required.

Ignoring the historical context in which the thesis of "permanent revolution" had been formulated, however, and the fact that it was largely identical with Lenin's own revolutionary strategy in 1917, Stalin made it appear as Trotsky's view of the present situation of the Soviet Union and twisted it into a doctrine of "permanent hopelessness": "Lack of faith in the strength and capacities of our revolution, lack of faith in the strength and capacity of the Russian proletariat—that is what lies at the root of the theory of 'permanent revolution.' " [17]

To such lack of faith Stalin opposed his own belief in "the possibility of the victory of socialism in one country," namely Russia. [18] This was in fact Stalin's most original and powerful contribution to the debate on the future of the Soviet Union. But he was at pains to deny this, claiming on the basis of a short statement by Lenin in 1915, in a quite different context, that "it was Lenin, and no one else, who discovered the truth that the victory of socialism in one country is possible." [19] In fact Lenin had never ceased to think of socialism in international terms, but by this double falsification of what both Trotsky and Lenin had said and meant, Stalin was able to draw a damaging contrast between "Leninism," now identified with a belief in the possibility of socialism in one country, and "Trotskyism," depicted as a defeatist, semi-Menshevik, anti-Leninist tendency particularly associated with the "adventurist" theory of "permanent revolution." The American scholar Robert Daniels has described this as inaugurating "the practice of proof by textual manipulation, with no questioning of the correctness of the authority, but similarly with no regard for what the authority really meant." [20]

For the present Stalin was content to have shown, as he claimed, that "Trotsky's 'permanent revolution' is the negation of Lenin's theory of 'proletarian revolution'." At the sessions of the Central Committee in January 1925 that condemned Trotsky, socialism in one country was not even mentioned. But, however dubious its origin, it was a thesis with a future, reversing the accepted view of the dependence of socialism in Russia on socialist revolution in other countries, and making the victory of the revolution in Russia, as Stalin was to boast, "the beginning and the premise of world revolution." Such a claim made a strong appeal to Russian nationalism, indisputably putting Russia first, and branding those who doubted or opposed it as fainthearted, mistrustful of the Russian people, and skeptical of their ability and resolution to complete what they had started.

Trotsky made no effort to reply to the storm he had raised with his *Lessons of October.* Summoned to appear before the Central Committee in January 1925, he apologized for being unable to attend because of illness and resigned as commissar for war. Zinoviev and Kamenev were all for expelling him from the party altogether, but Stalin counseled restraint. In a passage that few biographers of Stalin have been able to resist quoting, he told the Party Congress at the end of the year:

> We, the majority of the Council Committee, did not agree with Comrades Zinoviev and Kamenev because we realized that the policy of cutting off heads is fraught with major dangers for the party. . . . It is a method of bloodletting—and they *did* want blood—dangerous and contagious; today you cut off one, tomorrow a second, and then a third. Who would remain in the party? [21]

This quotation illustrates very well the difficulty of seeing Stalin in the 1920s except in the light of later events. When he made this remark, was he—consciously or unconsciously—looking forward to a time when it would become possible to remove opponents in this way, or is it we who, knowing what followed, read an ironical significance into the words? Who can say?

After his condemnation by the Central Committee, Trotsky remained a member of it and of the Politburo but refrained from any further opposition during 1925, not only taking no part in controversy, but also in September publishing an article that repudiated an American book by Max Eastman accurately reproducing long extracts from Lenin's Testament. Trotsky denied that such a document existed and declared that talk of concealing it was "a malicious invention." It may well be true, as Trotsky later claimed, that he did this under pressure from Stalin, as did Krupskaya; what mattered, however, was the effect on those who still looked to him to lead the opposition to Stalin.

With Trotsky again withdrawing, at least for the present, Stalin was free to move against the two other members of the troika. He did so by undermining the foundations of Zinoviev's independent position in his control of the Comintern, and of the Leningrad Party Organization. In both cases he used the same method: carefully studying the personalities of those involved in order to find who could be suborned by a mixture of threats and bribery.

His agent in the Comintern was a Ukrainian member of the party Secretariat, Dmitri Manuilsky, who later achieved minor prominence as the Ukrainian delegate to postwar UN conferences. Stalin got the Politburo to appoint Manuilsky to the Comintern, ostensibly to help Zinoviev, but in fact to build up a Stalinist network in the German Communist Party (KPD), which was only second in importance to the Russian in the Third International. In the German elections of May 1924 the KPD had polled 3.7 million votes and raised its representation in the Reichstag from fifteen to sixty-two seats: No other Communist party came near such electoral success. This explains why a Comintern mission was sent to Germany, headed by Manuilsky, with headquarters in Berlin and reporting directly to Stalin.

In 1924 Stalin began to take an interest himself in the proceedings of the Comintern, attending for the first time the Fifth World Congress of Communist Parties held in Moscow in June of that year. He did not speak but introduced himself to the delegates inconspicuously. Ruth Fischer, who was present, describes him moving about the salons and corridors around the historic St. Andrew's Hall in the Kremlin.

> Smoking his pipe, wearing the characteristic tunic and Wellington boots, he spoke softly and politely with small groups, presenting himself as the new type of Russian leader. The younger delegates were impressed by this revolutionary who despised revolutionary rhetoric, the down-to-earth organizer whose quick decisions and modernized methods would solve the problems in a changed world. The men around Zinoviev were old, fussy, outmoded. [22]

Stalin's long-term objective was to secure a German Communist party submissive to Russian control of the Communist International. With the help of Walther Ulbricht and Wilhelm Pieck (later to become founders of the postwar German Democratic Republic) he divided the KPD and played off the different factions against each other. The process has been described in detail by Ruth Fischer, whom Stalin repeatedly tried to win over. By 1927 he had succeeded in purging the KPD of any power of independent action that might conflict with Russian objectives.

The consequences of this for German politics and the Communists' attitude to Hitler's rise to power have already been mentioned. But Stalin's success also had consequences in the struggle for power in Russia. The Comintern, dominated from the first by the Russians, had become an extension of the interplay of factions and policies in the Soviet party. No other Communist party suffered or resented this subordination more than the German; and no one insisted on it more vigorously than Zinoviev. Stalin's intervention in the international field put an end not only to the KPD's efforts to maintain its independence (denounced by Stalin as the attempt to create a Fourth International) but ironically also to Zinoviev's authority over the Comintern apparatus. By the beginning of 1926, Zinoviev's position as chairman of the International was purely formal; before the end of 1926 he had lost even that.

At the same time Stalin moved to deprive Zinoviev of control over his other stronghold, the Leningrad Party Organization. To begin with, Zinoviev and his ally Kamenev had been chairmen of the Soviets and controlled the party organizations in Moscow as well as Leningrad. Kamenev was the first to feel the effect of Stalin's intrigues. In 1924 he lost the position of chairman of the Council of People's Commissars, which he had filled de facto during Lenin's illness, and then control of the Moscow party machine when his man, the secretary of the Moscow Party Committee, I. A. Zelensky, was packed off to Central Asia and replaced by N. A. Uglanov, a defector from the Zinoviev-Kamenev camp. Leningrad proved a tougher nut to crack. After getting rid of two of Zinoviev's supporters, Stalin ran into unexpected resistance when he placed one of his own men, Nikolai Komarov, in the key post of Leningrad party secretary. Zinoviev rallied his forces, curbed Komarov, and protested at the interference of the Central Committee and its general secretary. For the moment Stalin found it politic not to press, but he had every intention of returning to the charge when he had prepared the ground better.

I V

IN THE SUMMER OF 1925 Zinoviev mounted a counterattack, intervening in the debate on economic policy that had begun in 1924. The fundamental issue was how to solve the problem created by Lenin's seizure of power in a country not yet ready, according to the Marxist scheme, for a socialist revolution because it had not yet been industrialized and modernized by capitalism.

The first answer, during the period of War Communism, had been by using the power of the state to reorganize the economy and society on socialist lines, that is, an economic as well as a political dictatorship of the proletariat, employing coercion vis-à-vis the peasants (compulsory requisitioning) and the workers (militarization of labor). The chief theoretical advocate of such a left-wing policy had been Bukharin, who had published *The Economics of the Transition Period* (1920) and had earlier collaborated with E. A. Preobrazhensky in producing the authoritative *ABC of Communism* (1919).

When the attempt to build socialism by the methods of War Communism had to be abandoned, Lenin had fallen back on the gradualist approach of his New Economic Policy. Bukharin, like the rest of the leadership, followed Lenin's reversal of policy, and after his death became the chief spokesman for regarding the NEP, not as a retreat, or temporary phase, but as the pattern for a long-term period of coexistence with a peasant economy, free trade in farm products, and the toleration of small-scale private industry. This meant focusing on agriculture, the twenty-five million peasant farms, and encouraging the more enterprising peasants to prosper. *"Enrichissez-vous"* was the phrase of Guizot's that Bukharin used: "Enrich yourself, develop your farms, do not fear that you will be subjected to restrictions." [23] The way to draw them into building socialism, he declared, was not through collectivization but, as Lenin had urged in his final phase, through the development of rural cooperatives.

Before his death, Lenin had spoken of a whole historical epoch, a decade or two as a minimum, being needed to persuade the peasants to adopt cooperatives, and Bukharin thought it might take longer still, given Russia's backwardness. It could succeed only if the peasants were provided with material incentives, an adequate supply of consumer goods, and high enough prices for their crops to be able to buy them.

The left opposition and those who had always been reluctant to accept the NEP as more than a tactical retreat saw its prolongation as leading to the restoration of capitalism, and attacked Bukharin's appeasement of the peasants as the abandonment of socialism and the betrayal of the dictatorship of the proletariat. Their alternative was formulated by Preobrazhensky, Bukharin's coauthor when they had both been advocates of methods of War Communism, who now criticized Bukharin for his change of attitude. Preobrazhensky argued that the key to the building of socialism in Russia was industrialization, and the key to that was the accumulation of capital for accelerated investment in nationalized industry at the expense of the predominantly agrarian private sector.

Marx had declared the historic mission of the bourgeoisie to be the accumulation of wealth—"Accumulate, accumulate! That is Moses and the prophets!"—thereby providing the capital with which to launch the industrial revolution. Marx believed this had been secured by colonial plunder and the dispossession of peasants through enclosures. Marx called the process "primitive capitalist accumulation." Preobrazhensky argued that Soviet industrialization required a form of "primitive socialist accumulation," to be secured by such fiscal devices as the manipulation of prices (low prices for agricultural, high prices for industrial products), high taxation, quotas for grain delivery, and so on. These would transfer resources from the private sector (in effect, from the peasants) to investment in state-owned industry. The key was to take production rather than consumption as the starting point.

Bukharin responded by attacking Preobrazhensky's model as a proposal to replace the exploitation of the peasantry by capitalists with their exploitation by the industrial working class. This would represent "a proletarian dictatorship in a state of war with the peasantry," instead of the alliance (*smychka*) between workers and peasants, which Lenin had seen as the axis of the Soviet system. Bukharin argued that a prosperous peasantry would not only guarantee the country's food supplies but would also provide the effective demand for industrial growth, as well as investment funds through a progressive income tax and voluntary saving.[24]

When the poor 1924 harvest prompted concern, Bukharin argued that the way to raise production was to remove the peasants' fears that they would be penalized for success. His advice was followed after the Fourteenth Party Conference in April 1925, when the leadership took action to lower agricultural taxes and (within limits) to legalize the hiring of labor and the leasing of land. Zinoviev in particular called for more concessions to the peasants, urging the party "to turn its face to the countryside." This was the high point of the New Economic Policy.

It came as a surprise, therefore, when in the summer of 1925 Zinoviev and Kamenev reversed their position and attacked the agricultural policy, which they had supported earlier, as a dangerous concession to the better-off peasants, the kulaks. Zinoviev now argued, with copious references to Lenin, that the NEP had never been intended as a way forward, but as a "strategic retreat"; the main reliance should continue to be on the industrial proletariat and the poor, not the more prosperous peasants.

The evidence strongly suggests that Zinoviev's concern was not so much with economic policy as with the need to find a way of recovering the political initiative. In June 1925 Krupskaya had written a letter denouncing the favoritism shown to the kulaks and Bukharin's defense of it. This was a view shared by many on the left of the party, and Zinoviev and Kamenev evidently saw it as an issue on which they could mobilize opposition to the leadership for deviating from the true Leninist faith.

Stalin himself had not played a particular part in the economic debate so far. Like the other members of the Politburo, he supported the NEP and the 1925 agricultural policy but dissociated himself from Bukharin's unguarded language, particularly his slogan *"Enrichissez-vous."* If they were to raise the slogan of "Strike the kulak," he said in 1925, ninety-nine out of a hundred Communists would be in favor. But that made it all the more important not to let emotions cloud their judgment. Such a slogan, if put into practice, would lead to civil war, since the mass of the "middle peasants" would look on the blow at the kulak as directed at themselves as well. Stalin was in fact responsible, with Rykov, for a sharp increase in industrial investment which helped to maintain a balance. But he was ready to accept Zinoviev's challenge, and formed an alliance with Bukharin to do so. Since Rykov, Lenin's successor as chairman of the Council of People's Commissars and a peasant by origin, as well as Tomsky, the leader of the trade unions, were in general agreement with Bukharin's policies, this gave Stalin a majority in a Politburo of seven, especially as Trotsky gave no support to Zinoviev and Kamenev.

. . .

WHEN THE CENTRAL COMMITTEE met in October 1925, the
opposition was found to include Grigori Sokolnikov, the commissar for
finance, as well as Zinoviev and Kamenev. They complained about policy
toward the peasants and called for an open debate. This was refused, and
the Fourteenth Party Congress, which had been due in the spring, was again
postponed, allowing Stalin to tighten his hold on the party organization.
Zinoviev responded in kind by beating off Stalin's attempts to penetrate the
Leningrad organization, removing every known supporter of the national
leadership from it and from the Leningrad delegation to the congress. A
vigorous exchange of accusations and insults followed between Moscow and
Leningrad, where the opposition controlled its own daily, *Leningradskaya
Pravda*. The atmosphere of tension was heightened by widely circulated
rumors that Stalin was responsible for the death of Mikhail Frunze, who
had succeeded Trotsky as commissar for war and had been ordered to
undergo surgery by the Politburo against his own better judgment—a
question that still remains open.[25] Frunze's successor was Stalin's candidate, Voroshilov.

Just before the Fourteenth Party Congress finally met in December 1925,
Stalin offered "a compromise" to avoid an open conflict. Zinoviev dismissed it as tantamount to capitulation. Stalin's offer, however, had the
effect (as it was no doubt meant to) of placing the responsibility for forcing
a split on Zinoviev, whose claim to deliver a minority report to the congress,
for the first time since 1918, at once exposed him to the charge of factionalism. The opposition accused the leadership of favoring the kulaks at the
expense of the proletariat, pursuing a policy of state capitalism, not socialism; abandoning Lenin's internationalism for Stalin's heresy of socialism in
one country; undermining intraparty democracy; and turning the dictatorship of the proletariat into a dictatorship over the proletariat.

Stalin and Bukharin indignantly denied the charges. They retorted that
the attack on socialism in one country revealed the opposition's lack of faith
in the Russian people's ability to create a socialist society. Zinoviev and
Kamenev, they declared, were now challenging the slogans of party unity
and suppression of factionalism which they had defended against Trotsky
at the last Party Congress. "When there is a majority for Zinoviev,"
Mikoyan remarked, "he is for iron discipline, for subordination. When he
has no majority, he is against it."

The climax of the congress was Kamenev's demand for the freedom of
minorities to state their views: "Back to Lenin," he urged. "We are against
making a leader [*vozhd'*]. We are against the secretariat, which has in
practice combined both policy and organization, standing over the political
organ." Calling for the Politburo to subordinate the Secretariat to itself,
Kamenev declared amid an uproar:

> I have come to the conviction that Comrade Stalin cannot fulfill the role
> of unifier of the Bolshevik staff.

Stalin's supporters shouted "Stalin! Stalin!" and were answered by the Leningraders' cry of "The party above all!" Over the din, Kamenev reiterated: "We are against the theory of one-man rule; we are against creating a *vozhd'*."

Stalin was quick to endorse the cry for collective leadership: Anything else, he declared, was impossible. Turning the tables on the Opposition, he claimed that it was they who wanted to lead the party "without Rykov, without Kalinin, without Tomsky, without Molotov, without Bukharin."

It is impossible to lead the party without the comrades I have mentioned. Why does all this unwarranted slander of Bukharin continue? You demand Bukharin's blood? We won't give you his blood.

After 1938, by which time he himself had taken the blood of Bukharin, Rykov, and Tomsky, any mention of them was expurgated from this passage in the later editions of Stalin's speeches.

In Stalin's concluding remarks there was some evidence of the way in which his mind was already working.

Perhaps it is not known to the comrades of the opposition that for us, for Bolsheviks, formal democracy is a cipher, while the real interests of the party are everything. . . .

We must not be distracted by discussion. We are a party which is ruling a country—do not forget that. Do not forget that any exchange of words at the top is a minus for us in the country; our differences may reduce our influence. [26]

The debate had been uninhibited, but the conclusion was never in doubt. When the congress voted on the Central Committee reports delivered by Stalin and Molotov, the figures were 559 in favor, 65 against. A few concessions were made in the resolution passed by the congress, including recognition of the kulak problem and of the need to boost the socialized sector of the economy. But the main lines of policy remained unchanged.

Trotsky, who had been present as a nonvoting delegate, but took no part in the controversies, observed with gloomy satisfaction the defeat of those who had been his principal assailants less than a year before. It was now their turn to pay the penalty for challenging Stalin, although still in the style of the 1920s, not the 1930s. On January 5, 1926, a team led by Molotov, and including Kirov, Voroshilov, and Kalinin, arrived in Leningrad. Ignoring the local party hierarchy, they went directly to the party organizations in the factories, explaining the decisions of the Fourteenth Congress and mobilizing support for them against the local bureaucracy. These tactics enabled them to sweep the board, including a majority at the famous Putilov machine factory, to which special attention was devoted. The Leningrad Organization was purged, and the *Leningradskaya Pravda* taken over. Kamenev paid for his boldness in attacking Stalin directly by losing his governmental posts and being reduced from full Politburo member to candidate. Zinoviev kept his place for the present, but the Politburo was enlarged from seven to nine, three of Stalin's henchmen, Molotov, Kalinin, and Voroshilov, filling the vacancies. Similar changes strengthened Stalin's position in the Central Committee, further enlarged to sixty-three members and forty-three candidates. Among the younger generation making a first appearance in the list of candidates was Andrei Zhdanov, first secretary of the important Nizhni-Novgorod (later Gorki) province, who was to rise to the heights of power at the end of the Second World War.

The same month Stalin brought theory into line in a characteristic way. He had been angered by Zinoviev's use of a quotation from his *Foundations of Leninism* to show that in 1924 he had held the opposite view of the possibility of socialism in one country from that which he preached in 1925. He acknowledged that he had "modified" the earlier statement, but solely in the interests of clarity: "This formulation may give grounds for thinking that the organization of socialist society by the efforts of a single country is impossible—which, of course, is wrong."[27] To quote Robert Daniels again, this was a perfect example of the type of reasoning he was soon to make standard for the whole country: "Changes of doctrine are never to be recognized; people who advance the old interpretation are attacked for committing a new misinterpretation of what was previously supposed to have been said."[28]

STALIN'S VICTORY at the end of 1925 appeared to be complete enough; yet the years 1926 and 1927 saw the opposition to his leadership openly renewed and reaching fever pitch in the bitterness of the conflict both in the Soviet Union and in the Communist International. After three years of quarreling, Trotsky, Zinoviev, and Kamenev at last recognized their common interest in challenging Stalin, and succeeded in creating a united opposition. Steps to recruit support, necessarily taken under cover, began in the spring of 1926. On one occasion, which Stalin and the Politburo seized on as proof of conspiracy, a meeting was held in the woods outside Moscow and addressed by the deputy commissar for war, Lashevich. In preparation for the battle, which was joined at the Central Committee Plenum with the Control Commission in July 1926, the opposition drew up the "Declaration of the Thirteen," setting out the essential points of their case against the party leadership.

To meet the inevitable charge of factionalism and counterrevolution, Trotsky developed a parallel with the French Revolution and Thermidor, the name of the month in 1794 when Robespierre and the Jacobin regime had been overthrown. In the revolutionary tradition, the downfall of Robespierre was always presented as the victory of bourgeois counterrevolutionary forces over the true representatives of revolution and social reform. Trotsky argued that there was a real danger that this could happen in Russia, and that the forces of "Thermidor," represented by the party bureaucracy, would defeat the revolutionary tradition represented by the masses—of which the opposition now claimed to be the authentic spokesmen.

All the faults of the existing regime, the argument continued, stemmed from the gap that had opened between the bureaucracy and the proletariat. The repressive measures taken against any expression of dissent and the suppression of party democracy followed from "the divergence between the direction of economic policy and the direction of the feelings and thoughts of the proletarian vanguard."

In saying this, the opposition leaders were appealing to those members of the party, especially those who had joined it before 1917, who were asking— nine, soon to be ten, years after the revolution—what had become of the hopes and promises with which it had been launched? The NEP had returned the economy almost to the previous level, and by 1930 it would be back to where it was in 1913; but at that time Russia had been denounced as a poverty-stricken, backward, and barbarous society. Was this all that the revolution had accomplished? If the present line of policy was continued, it could lead only to further degeneration. What was needed, they argued, was to implement the demands repeatedly made by the opposition: priority for the development of industry, improvements in the impoverished condition of the industrial workers, and a curb on the menace to socialism represented by the growing wealth and power of the middle peasants and kulaks.

In the international sphere, the opposition blamed the failures of the Comintern (for example, the failure to support the British General Strike in May 1926) on the lack of revolutionary enthusiasm, which sprang from the concentration on a policy of socialism in one country, and the abandonment of the link between the building of socialism in Russia and the spread of the revolution in Europe and Asia. The two were indissolubly linked: a genuinely Bolshevik policy in the interests of the proletariat inside Russia with a genuinely revolutionary policy in the Comintern. Under the existing leadership both had been abandoned.

The meeting of the Central Committee Plenum, at which the first open confrontation took place, lasted from July 14 to 23, 1926, with the small band of oppositionists led by Trotsky, Zinoviev and Kamenev using all their powers of persuasion to try to shake the hold that the leadership had over the majority of its members. The issues of industrialization and policy toward the peasants were fiercely debated, but the most damning charge made by Stalin, Bukharin, and Rykov, and repeated in the committee's conclusion, was that of conspiracy against the party.

> All these disorganizing steps of the opposition testify that they have already decided to go over from the legal defense of their views to the creation of a nationwide illegal organization opposing itself to the party and thus preparing a split in its ranks. [29]

The blame for the conspiracy was placed, not on Trotsky, but on Zinoviev (no doubt with a view to splitting them), and the latter was thrown out of the Politburo. His place was taken by the Latvian Yan Rudzutak, at that time a follower of Stalin, and five new candidate members were appointed: Ordzhonikidze, Andreyev, Kirov, Mikoyan, Kaganovich—all stalwart *apparatchiki*.

At the end of September, the opposition decided to appeal to the rank and file at party cell meetings throughout the provinces. In Moscow, a demonstration was staged in an aircraft factory, with Trotsky and Zinoviev among the speakers; the latter made another attempt at the Putilov works in Leningrad. This was striking at the grass roots of the party organization, and the *apparat* was mobilized to deny the opposition a hearing by heckling and intimidation. Under increasing pressure, the opposition leaders signed a capitulation, abjuring future factional activity and repudiating their left-wing supporters in the Comintern and the Workers' Opposition. The effect of this sudden *volte face* was disastrous for many of their followers, who were already being harassed by the OGPU and now lost all faith in those who had abandoned them without warning.

The surrender was in any case futile, encouraging Stalin to press a disintegrating opposition still harder. In October the world press published the full text of Lenin's Testament, supplied by the opposition. The Central Committee Plenum therefore decided to end the truce, and Stalin brought to a meeting of the Politburo on the twenty-fifth the "theses" on the opposition he was going to present to a specially summoned party conference. The meeting was a tense one. Trotsky denounced the breach of the new truce, attacked Stalin for bad faith, and warned the majority that they were embarking on a course that would lead to fratricidal strife and destroy the party.

Confronting Stalin face to face, Trotsky declared: "The first secretary poses his candidature for the post of grave digger of the revolution!"—the phrase Marx had applied to both Napoleon and Louis Napoleon. Rising to his feet, Stalin struggled unsuccessfully to contain himself, then rushed out of the hall, slamming the door behind him. Pyatakov, describing the scene to Trotsky's wife, declared: "You know, I have smelt gunpowder, but I have never seen anything like this. Why, why did Lev Davidovich say this? Stalin will never forgive him to the third and fourth generation." [30]

Next morning the Central Committee Plenum deprived Trotsky and Kamenev of their seats in the Politburo and removed Zinoviev from the Comintern Executive, where he was replaced by Bukharin. When the Party Conference met, it lasted no less than nine days (October 26 to November 3, 1926). The opposition leaders were not allowed to present their case but had to listen while Stalin, describing them as "a combination of castrated forces," gave his version of the issue at stake:

> Is the victory of socialism possible in our country, bearing in mind that it is so far the only country of the dictatorship of the proletariat . . . and that the tempo of the world revolution has slowed down? [31]

In the debate that followed, the handful of opposition representatives had great difficulty in making themselves heard in the face of jeering and interruptions. Yet the more the leadership used its power to stifle the opposition, the more it showed how much it felt itself threatened by criticism from a Communist standpoint from within the party. This accounts for the fury with which they were attacked, not only by Stalin, but by moderates like Bukharin and Rykov, when Bukharin for one had earlier repeatedly opposed moves to expel Trotsky from the party. Bukharin now demanded not just that the opposition should abandon their activities, but also that they should admit publicly they had been wrong:

> Come before the party with head bowed and say: "Forgive us for we have sinned against the spirit and against the letter and against the essence of Leninism." Say it, say it honestly: Trotsky was wrong . . . Why do you not have the courage to come and say that it was a mistake?[32]

Even Stalin was impressed, calling out: "Well done, Bukharin, well done. He does not speak, he slashes with a knife."

Everybody present knew that the opposition leaders could not possibly win the vote, but the more obvious it became that the meeting had been packed to prevent this, the more it pointed to the leaders' lack of confidence in their own arguments, the greater the danger of conceding a moral victory to the opposition.

Stalin had done his best to legitimize his argument by invoking the authority of Lenin; but he got the worst of the battle of quotations. When Trotsky cited Lenin's unambiguous declaration that "the complete victory of the socialist revolution in one country is unthinkable," Stalin could only fall back on an unconvincing attempt to distinguish the "victory" from the "complete victory" of socialism. Yet there appears to be no doubt that, in his concluding speech, Stalin scored a forensic triumph and turned the tables on his opponents. For the longer Trotsky and his allies prolonged their opposition and focused it on Stalin, the more they strengthened his claim to be defending the unity of the party against factionalists who were prepared to sacrifice it to their own ambitions. What appealed to the rising generation moving into the party, and well represented at the conference, was Stalin's robust confidence in Russia and the future. After arguing with Zinoviev about the meaning of a quotation from Engels, he added, to loud applause, that if Engels were living now, he would say, "To hell with all the old formulas, long live the victorious revolution in the USSR!"

Stalin hammered relentlessly on the opposition's lack of faith in "the internal forces of our revolution"; on their defeatism; their disparagement of everything that had been achieved in Russia; their insistence that the future of the revolution would be decided abroad. By contrast, he opened up the prospect of what might be accomplished on the huge stage of Russia, regardless of what happened elsewhere. In 1917, against all odds, they had startled the world by accomplishing a political miracle; why should they not now, against all the odds, startle the world again by accomplishing an economic miracle?

WHEN THE COMINTERN EXECUTIVE met in December 1927, Stalin showed himself in confident form and obtained the total exclusion of the opposition from the International. Bukharin had already visited Berlin and secured the expulsion of five leading left-wingers from the KPD; Maurice Thorez, a staunch Stalinist, had become the new leader of the French party. The Communist International had been brought into line with the balance of power in Russian politics.

Yet it was a major defeat for the Politburo's international policy, in China, that roused the opposition to renew their campaign of criticism. Since 1923, as a result of an agreement between the Soviet government and the Kuomintang (the National People's party of Sun Yat-sen), the Chinese Communists had been committed to working with the Kuomintang. Part of Trotsky's and Zinoviev's case had been that the policy of the "United Front" and reliance on non-Communist allies, pressed on the Comintern by Stalin and Bukharin, led to the sacrifice of revolutionary opportunities. In May 1926, the hopes placed in the Anglo-Russian Trade Union Unity Committee had been dashed by the failure of the British General Strike. The opposition warned that there could be a similar disappointment in China, where there was a strong feeling that the Russian leadership was more interested in acquiring influence with Sun Yat-sen's successor, Chiang Kai-shek, and the Kuomintang as the prospective government of China than in the revolutionary fortunes of the local Communists.

In April 1927, Chiang Kai-shek turned on his Communist allies in Shanghai and massacred a large number of them. The opposition's "Declaration of the Eighty-four," put before the Politburo on May 25, not only criticized its "opportunist" policy in international affairs but also linked the series of setbacks to which this had led with the mistakes of the Politburo in domestic policy, particularly with the adoption of the "untrue, petit-bourgeois theory of socialism in one country which has nothing in common with Marxism or Leninism." The cry for party unity was raised only in order to suppress real proletarian criticism: "The incorrect line is mechanically imposed from above."

A raid by the London police on the Soviet trade offices and the subsequent breaking off of diplomatic relations by the British government (May 1927) led both the opposition and the Soviet government to believe that war with Britain was imminent. The first called for the abandonment of the "United Front" policy and the replacement of the present "fumbling and repressive" Soviet leadership; the second called for party unity in the face of "a united front from Chamberlain to Trotsky" and the threat of war, attacking the dissenters as defeatist. When the Trotskyist Ivan Smilga was "transferred" to the Far East, there was a public demonstration at the railway station and Trotsky made a speech. The OGPU pressed for the right to arrest the opposition leaders, and Stalin for their expulsion from the party.

When the Politburo still hesitated, Stalin turned to the joint Plenum of the Central Committee and the Control Commission. There Trotsky declared that the opposition alone was competent to guide the country through its difficulties and drew a parallel with wartime France, where Georges Clemenceau in the face of disaster had pursued his opposition to the ministry until the opportunity came for him to provide the necessary leadership. This led to another furious uproar, the organization of strong-arm squads to break up opposition attempts to hold meetings, and elaborate preparations for the Fifteenth Party Congress, already several times postponed, at which Stalin was determined to silence his critics for good.

With the tenth anniversary of the October Revolution approaching on November 7 (NS), the confrontation between Stalin and Trotsky dominated Soviet politics. In September the opposition produced its third and longest statement of policy and, when the Politburo refused to let it be printed, defied the ban and used an underground printing plant, which in turn was raided by the OGPU. In the last speech he was to make as a leader of the Soviet Communist party, Trotsky delivered a slashing attack on the Politburo members for their betrayal of the revolution and forced an open discussion, at another joint Plenum (October 21–23), of Lenin's Testament and its criticisms of Stalin:

> The rudeness and disloyalty of which Lenin wrote [Trotsky declared] are no longer mere personal characteristics. They have become the fundamental character of our present leadership [with] its belief in the omnipotence of methods of violence—even in dealing with its own party. [33]

Stalin met the challenge head-on. He began by quoting Trotsky's denial of the existence of such a document two years earlier (made under pressure from Stalin); then acknowledged that of course there was such a document, and that it was quite true that in it Lenin suggested replacing Stalin as general secretary in view of his roughness. He read out the passage himself, agreeing, "Yes, I am rough, comrades, in regard to those who are roughly and disloyally ruining and splitting the party. I have never concealed this and do not conceal it now." Lenin's Testament also criticized Trotsky, Kamenev, and Zinoviev, all of whom Lenin had characterized as not to be trusted politically.

> But not a single allusion in the Testament [Stalin continued] touches on Stalin's mistakes. Only his roughness is mentioned. Lack of civility, however, is not a shortcoming in Stalin's political attitude or political position, and cannot be so.

Was it true that dissident Bolsheviks were being arrested in great numbers? "Yes," Stalin said, "we *are* arresting them. And we mean to go on doing so unless they stop undermining the party and the Soviet government." [34]

On the day of the anniversary of the Bolshevik seizure of power, the opposition staged street demonstrations in Moscow and Leningrad, only to see them dispersed by the police and their banners torn down by organized gangs. A week later both Trotsky and Zinoviev were at last expelled from the party, and at the Fifteenth Congress in December 1927 another seventy-five members of their faction and eighteen Democratic Centralists suffered the same fate. Zinoviev and Kamenev petitioned for readmission, were required to renounce their views as anti-Leninist—and then had their petition rejected. They were told that they could apply again in six months' time, which they did. The congress itself was turned into a demonstration of loyalty to the leadership. A Stalin who had never appeared surer of himself poured scorn on the practices of petit-bourgeois intellectuals cut off from life, from the revolution, from the party, and from the workers.

The thirty-four-year-old Khrushchev, who was present as a member of the Ukrainian delegation, enjoyed it all hugely. They had been carefully briefed in advance on what was required of them and cheered loudly when Rykov presented Stalin with a steel broom "so that he may sweep away our enemies."

> At the time [Khrushchev writes in his memoirs] we had no doubt that Stalin and his supporters were right. . . . We realized that a merciless struggle against the opposition was inevitable. We justified what was happening in a lumberjack's terms: when you chop down a forest the chips fly. After all, it was no accident that Stalin held the leading position . . . he had come a long way in a short time. He had brought our Party and our people with him. [35]

At the first Central Committee Plenum after the Fifteenth Congress Stalin offered to resign as general secretary. Addressing the joint meeting, he said:

> I think that until recently there were circumstances that put the party in the position of needing me in this post as a person who was fairly rough in his dealings, to constitute a certain antidote to the opposition. . . . Now the opposition has not only been smashed, it has been expelled from the party. And still we have the recommendation of Lenin, which in my opinion ought to be put into effect. Therefore I ask the Plenum to relieve me of the post of general secretary. I assure you, comrades, that from this the party only stands to gain. [36]

Stalin insisted that his proposal should be put to the Plenum. As he well knew it would be, his resignation was rejected by a vote that was unanimous except for one abstention. At a single blow, Stalin had buried Lenin's Testament and secured an overwhelming vote of confidence to justify any measures he might now take.

Another 1,500 expulsions followed among the party rank and file. Trotsky refused to recant, and in January 1928 was hauled out of his Kremlin apartment by the OGPU, put on a train at a suburban station to avoid any demonstration, and exiled to Alma Ata, 2,500 miles away on the farthest frontier of Soviet Central Asia. He never returned.

v

THE EXPULSION of Trotsky and Zinoviev marked the end of open legal opposition in the party. In the final phase of Stalin's rise to power that followed, the word "opposition" was no longer used: Bukharin and his associates were found guilty, not of "opposition"—this could no longer be admitted—but of "deviation." In keeping with this change, no mention of the clash between Stalin and Bukharin, Rykov, and Tomsky was made in public for over a year, both sides denying rumors of a split in the Politburo. Opposition now had to be covert, no longer overt, and Stalin first defeated his opponents in private, only attacking them in public afterwards.

Until the United Opposition was crushed, Stalin had taken care to keep the moderate group in the Politburo—Bukharin, Rykov, Tomsky—on his side. With Bukharin in particular Stalin had been on friendly terms for a long time. They always addressed each other as "Nikolai" and "Koba," employing the familiar "ty" form, and up to 1928 Stalin had relied heavily on Bukharin in economic matters. Unlike his relations with Zinoviev and Kamenev, Stalin's alliance with Bukharin had been a close one, and Bukharin had been as sharp in his attacks as Stalin. The breach which now developed between them was not of Bukharin's making; the cause was a reversal of policy on Stalin's part, not his. The efforts of Bukharin and his associates to resist this were branded as deviation, and they were called upon to recant the views which they had hitherto shared with Stalin, and accept the new orthodoxy.

Stalin's final confrontation with Trotsky, the boldness with which he took up the opposition's reference to Lenin's Testament and turned it against them, showed how much confidence he had gained. Trotsky's and Zinoviev's open defeat and removal from the scene gave him greater room to maneuver. With no one else likely to challenge his position, he was free to take the initiative himself, and free to look at questions of policy without the restrictions imposed by tactics in a struggle for power.

With hindsight it is possible to see earlier differences of emphasis in the way he and Bukharin spoke about economic policy, but no great importance was attached to these at the time. Despite a bumper crop, there was certainly alarm over the fall in grain procurements in the summer of 1927, as a result of the peasants' withholding a large part of the harvest from the market in response to low grain prices, which Stalin is alleged to have intervened to hold down.[37] The Trotsky-Zinoviev opposition proposed to take what was needed from the peasants by force; but this was rejected by the Central Committee (in August) as "absurd and demagogical."

Nor was there any evidence of dissension in the resolutions adopted by the Central Committee meeting in October and confirmed by the Fifteenth

Party Congress. Cautious in tone, these sought to strike a balance between industry and agriculture. "It is essential to proceed from the optimal combination of both factors," was the recurrent note of Rykov's speech on the economic plan; while Molotov, introducing the resolution on agriculture, spoke confidently of the victory of socialist elements and the middle peasantry over the kulaks, endorsed collectivization so long as it was gradual and voluntary, and pointed to cooperatives as the way forward to socialism.

Stalin himself said at the congress:

> Those comrades are wrong who think that we can and should do away with the kulaks by administrative fiat, by the OGPU: write the decree, seal it, period. That's an easy method, but it won't work. The kulak must be taken by economic measures. . . . This does not rule out the application of some administrative measures, but these must not replace economic ones. [38]

Only at the last minute, without discussion, as the resolution on agricultural policy was being voted, was an amendment hurriedly added declaring: "At the present time the task of transformation and amalgamation of small individual farms with large-scale collective farms must be set as the party's fundamental task in the countryside." [39] Nothing was said about the scale of the transformation or the period of time required to carry it through.

No sooner had the delegates returned home, however, than Stalin persuaded the Central Committee (with the agreement of Bukharin, Rykov, and Tomsky) to send out not one, but three directives ordering "extraordinary measures" to secure the forced requisitioning of grain which he and the congress had just rejected. The last ended with threats against local party leaders if they did not achieve a breakthrough in grain procurements in the shortest possible time.

The energy with which Stalin enforced his orders started a process that acquired its own momentum. Thousands of party members were drafted to help the rural party organizations. Accompanied by Molotov, Stalin himself took the unprecedented step of visiting western Siberia in person (January 1928) and, for the only time in his life, spent three weeks touring a major agricultural area. He berated the local officials, accusing them of failing, for the sake of a quiet life, to use force and make the kulaks surrender the grain with which, he insisted, their barns were overflowing. In order to persuade the poorer peasants to inform against their better-off neighbors a quarter of the grain confiscated was to be sold to them at low prices. Those who resisted should be prosecuted as "speculators" under Article 107 of the Criminal Code. When objection was raised that this would be an emergency measure for which the courts were not prepared, Stalin retorted: "Let's allow that it will be an emergency measure. So what?" Judges and prosecutors who were "unprepared" should be dismissed. The Soviet government was not going to stand by and let the kulaks hold the country to ransom:

"There will be sabotage of grain procurements as long as the kulak exists."[40]

The emergency measures worked: The shortfall in grain supplies was made up. But the methods of forcible search and requisitioning employed, even if intended to deal with an immediate crisis, had far-reaching consequences. To the kulaks and to the middle peasants they appeared to be a return to the period of War Communism, and produced a chain reaction. They countered by sowing less; many sold their farms.

The events in the early months of 1928 marked the opening of one of the most tragic chapters in the history of Russia: the collectivization of Soviet agriculture, the disastrous effects of which continue to be felt in the 1990s. Here, as it begins, it is important to make clear the way in which Stalin exploited the ambiguity of the word "kulak" (the Russian word for "fist") which was always on his tongue when talking about collectivization.

In a pamphlet published in 1926, A. P. Smirnov, the commissar of agriculture in the Russian Soviet Republic, distinguished between two kinds of better-off peasants. One was the kulak, "the devourer of the commune . . . a skinner alive" who hired laborers, traded, and lent money. This was the traditional use of the word, but Smirnov went on to say that this type had almost disappeared from the countryside since the revolution and the redistribution of land. The second kind was that of the strong and capable farmer who might hire some laborers in order to increase his output, but was not a usurer or a capitalist and was not to be confused with the kulak of prerevolutionary days.[41] Bukharin made the same distinction between "the well-off innkeeper, the village usurer and the kulak," and the "strong farmer."[42] Stalin, however, ignored this distinction, maintaining that the NEP had produced a new "kulak class" which was waxing fat and deliberately pursuing an anti-Soviet policy by withholding large supplies of grain. It followed that the correct tactic was for the party to support the poor peasantry and expropriate the exploiters.

Figures subsequently published by Soviet economists show that, despite some growth during the NEP, in 1927 there were no more than one million kulaks in all, or 3.9 percent compared with 15 percent of the total peasantry before the 1917 revolution. A commonly used criterion for defining the kulak was the possession of twenty-five to forty sown acres. Subject to a discriminatory tax, "these more energetic and more prosperous farmers bore no resemblance whatever to the prewar kulak who was a man of substance and much the social superior of the average peasant smallholder. The prewar kulak if not physically eliminated [during the civil war] had been reduced to the ranks."[43]

Stalin's attempt, which he openly acknowledged, to stir up class hatred in the countryside ignored another major change in the rural population, the growth of the middle peasantry. These *serednyaki,* farming between five and twenty-five acres, had numbered only 20 percent before the revolution, but in 1927 represented 62.7 percent of the total. As a result of the refusal to distinguish between the kulaks and the much more numerous middle peasants, much of the deliberate persecution intended to wipe out the kulaks fell on the *serednyaki*—thereby alienating the more energetic and able section of the rural population on whose cooperation the success of any attempt to reorganize Russian agriculture was bound to depend.

S TA L I N   WA S   AWA R E of the opposition in the Politburo to any suggestion of a revival of War Communism and the abolition of the NEP. After his return from Siberia, in April 1928, he found it necessary to declare that such talk was "counterrevolutionary gossip." "The NEP is the basis of our economic policy and will remain such for a long historical period."[44] Nonetheless, that same month, as the flow of grain again fell off, the emergency measures were renewed with greater intensity.

The kulaks' reserves had already been taken; now the search was for the stores of grain still held by the middle peasants. In June there were reports of peasant riots, particularly in the rich grainlands of the North Caucasus. Even Stalin's own supporters in the Politburo and Central Committee were confused and alarmed. To provide reassurance, grain prices were raised and between June and August 1928 a quarter of a million tons of grain were imported.

In anticipation of the July 1928 Plenum, Bukharin, Rykov, and Tomsky mobilized support among the Central Committee members, many of whom had not yet taken a firm stand on agricultural policy. But the paper majority that they believed they could count on crumbled under the pressure Stalin exerted through his control of the party organization. Bukharin argued that no sustained growth in the industrialization could take place without a prosperous agriculture, and that the latter was now in decline as a result of the requisitioning. Answering him, Stalin dismissed Bukharin's fears as "capitulationism" and revived Preobrazhensky's argument (which he had denounced at the time) that, as Russia had no colonies, the peasantry would have to pay "something in the nature of a tribute" to fund increased investment in industry.

Stalin executed a characteristic sleight-of-hand and, with a selection of quotations from Lenin, gave the NEP a new meaning: It was not a retreat, but "a victorious and systematic offensive against capitalist elements of our economy," in which vigorous measures against the kulaks and collectivization of the rest of the peasantry had a natural place. Concealing his own move to the left under the cloak of orthodoxy, he maneuvered, as Bukharin complained, "in such a way as to make us appear the schismatics." Stalin declared that the source of all the difficulties was kulak sabotage and antagonism to the Soviet regime. But, he added, such resistance was natural, going on to propound the thesis that the class struggle would inevitably grow sharper as the country drew nearer to socialism. The very antithesis of everything Bukharin believed in, this was henceforward to be the central tenet of Stalin's version of Marxism-Leninism. [45]

In the face of heckling and interruptions, Bukharin argued that they were risking the alienation of the middle peasants and endangering the *smychka,* the union of proletariat and peasantry that Lenin had seen as essential to overcoming Russian backwardness. Whether this had ever been more than a slogan concealing another illusion was a question no one asked.

Stalin did not win a decisive victory at the July Plenum, nor did he seek to. He needed more time in which to develop his plans and isolate those who opposed him, postponing an open confrontation until he was ready for it, which proved to be not until the next summer. Bukharin, Rykov, and Tomsky were equally anxious to avoid any disagreement becoming public. They had seen what had happened to Trotsky and Zinoviev, had taken part in the maneuvers that destroyed them politically, and knew what use Stalin would make of a charge of factionalism if they gave him a chance. They continued to hope that, if they limited themselves to stating their case in the Politburo, they might be able to persuade Stalin, or at least restrain him and prevent too abrupt a break with the NEP.

To begin with, it appeared that these tactics were succeeding. The resolution published after the July 1928 meeting suggested that a compromise had been reached; Rykov speaking to the Moscow Party Organization reported (whether he believed it or not) that the left turn of the winter had been reversed, and Trotsky (still in touch with his supporters) prophesied a right-wing victory, believing that Stalin had overplayed his waiting game.

Immediately after the July debate, however, Bukharin took the risk of paying a secret visit to Kamenev, whom he had helped to drive out of the party. Apparently fearing that Stalin would make a rapprochement with the Kamenev-Zinoviev group, he had come to warn the former of the dangers of the situation. Bukharin spoke in desperation (Kamenev noted that he "gave the impression of a man who knows he is doomed"); he described Stalin, his ally until a few months before, as "a Genghis Khan" whose "line is ruinous for the whole revolution. I have not spoken with Stalin for several weeks. . . . Our arguing with him reached the point of saying 'You lie!' He has made concessions only so that he can cut our throats later." Kamenev was noncommittal but added to his note of the talk (which the Trotskyists published clandestinely six months later): "Stalin knows only one method . . . to plant a knife in the back." [46]

Bukharin was convinced that Stalin's real aim was not to reform the NEP but to throw overboard its reformist, gradualist policies in favor of "a second revolution," a return to the methods of War Communism's "orders and command." Beginning with the forcible requisitioning of grain, and civil war in the countryside, this would be extended to the elimination of private trading, a drastic speeding up of industrialization, and a reversal of the right-wing policies Stalin himself had imposed on the International—in short, a takeover of the program for which the left opposition had been destroyed the previous year.

There were several pointers to such a conclusion. The first of the big show trials, with Andrei Vyshinsky making his debut as prosecutor, was held in Moscow following the announcement in March 1928 of a counter-revolutionary plot, involving technical specialists and foreign powers, to sabotage the Shakhty mines in the Donets Basin. Foreign correspondents were invited to attend, and the fullest publicity was given to the proceedings. Fifty-five persons were charged with sabotage, many of whom "confessed," eleven of whom were condemned to death, and five actually executed. Stalin blew the affair up into a national scandal, declaring: "We have internal enemies. We have external enemies. This, comrades, must not be forgotten for a single moment."[47] Thereafter, the theme of conspiracy, like that of the sharpening of the class struggle, became a constant feature of Stalin's speeches, of the Soviet press, and of the party's "agitprop" work. An atmosphere of tension and fear was being created.

In May 1928 the State Planning Commission (Gosplan), which had worked on the assumption that the growth of industry must be limited by the speed with which capital could be accumulated by the expanding prosperity of agriculture, was confronted with a report from the Supreme Economic Council, headed by Stalin's nominee Kuibyshev, proposing a sensational expansion of 130 percent in industry in five years. At the end of May, Stalin issued a new call to party members declaring that the only solution to the country's problems was the collectivization of agriculture and the rapid development of heavy industry. The usual qualifications, that collectivization would be gradual and voluntary, were omitted.

Further evidence was provided by the proceedings of the Sixth World Congress of the Comintern, which met in the same Hall of Columns in Moscow where the Shakhty trial had ended five days before and lasted from mid-July until September 1928. To all outward appearances Bukharin, as secretary and titular head of the Comintern, was the central figure, delivering the opening and closing speeches and presenting all three of the main reports. But Stalin's majority in the Russian delegation challenged Bukharin's keynote theses and pressed for a radically new course, in which foreign Communist parties would move to the left and concentrate their attack on the Social Democrats as "Social Fascists," split the trade unions, and purge their own ranks of right-wing deviationists. This was as complete a break with Bukharin's Comintern policies as the proposed new course in economic policy was with his view of the NEP.

The issue was not pressed to a conclusion in the summer of 1928: that came a year later. In 1928 there was still strong opposition, and the resolution, as in the case of the July Plenum, represented a series of ambiguous compromises. But again the balance had shifted in Stalin's favor. His agents conducted a "corridor campaign" against Bukharin, who was represented as the epitome of right deviation, suffering from "political syphilis" and destined to join Trotsky in Alma Ata. So effective was the campaign that the Politburo issued a collective denial of any split among its members—which no one believed. At the end of the congress a majority of the foreign delegates accepted Stalin's axiom that "the right deviation now represents the central danger," and Bukharin himself publicly endorsed it. Once established in the International, the category of "right deviationism" and "right opportunism" could, when the time came, be easily transferred to Russia to brand Bukharin and his associates as the deviationists who were splitting the party, while Stalin defended the continuity of the correct line.

At the end of September 1928, Bukharin published an article, "Notes of an Economist,"[48] which, without naming anyone, was a direct reply to the manifesto from Kuibyshev and the Supreme Economic Council demanding a radical acceleration of investment in heavy industry at any price—including economic imbalances and "discontent and active resistance" among the population. The new slogan of the Stalinist planners was the economist S. G. Strumilin's paraphrase of Marx: "Our task is not to study economics but to change it. We are bound by no laws. There are no fortresses that Bolsheviks cannot storm. The question of tempo is subject to decision by human beings."[49] Bukharin retorted that economic planning meant paying attention to the conditions of equilibrium, not defying them, and that Kuibyshev's policy would produce chaos throughout the economy. "You can beat your breast, swear allegiance, and take an oath to industrialization, and damn all enemies and apostates, but this will not improve matters one bit."[50] The Politburo, by a majority, reprimanded Bukharin for "unauthorized" publication.

In the autumn of 1928, Stalin moved to destroy the independent bastions of the right by the same means as he had used to undermine Zinoviev's position in Leningrad and Bukharin's in the Comintern. Uglanov, who had been Stalin's nominee as boss of the Moscow Party Organization but had now deserted to the right, knew that he was on the way out when his regular report to the Moscow committee was received in silence, without the customary applause.

In protest at the hounding of their sympathizers, Bukharin, Rykov, and Tomsky had an angry scene with Stalin and confronted him with a threat of resignation. Stalin was still not ready for an open breach, offered concessions (which were never actually implemented), and persuaded the trio to agree to a compromise at the Central Committee's November (1928) Plenum. With Rykov's endorsement, Stalin blandly reported to the Central Committee that there were no differences in the Politburo.

The new economic course was now married to the nationalist theme of socialism in one country. Stalin set up the goal of overtaking the capitalist nations and putting an end to "the age-long backwardness of our country." Socialism was no longer the product of capitalism, as Marx had thought, but an alternative designed to accelerate the development of those parts of the world left behind by the industrial progress of the West.

The Central Committee condemned not only the rightists and the conciliatory tendency toward them, but also any inclination to conciliate the conciliators. The Bukharinists, in their anxiety to avoid being named as a faction, gave their full endorsement to this condemnation. The futility of such gestures was shown by what followed. The "resignations" of Uglanov and three other members of the Moscow committee were accepted. Stalin's jackal, Kaganovich, took Uglanov's place. After delays to give time for a similar campaign of subversion, the Trade Union Congress met in December 1928. Tomsky knew that his days as the trade-union boss were over when five heavyweight Stalinist leaders, including Kaganovich, were elected to the Trade Union Council. Stalin himself appeared at the Comintern Executive to demand the expulsion of right-wing opportunists and "conciliators"; a wave of expulsions followed in the KPD and other foreign Communist parties.

Stalin seized on Bukharin's article, along with the publication by the Trotskyists of his talk with Kamenev the previous July, as grounds for bringing Bukharin before a joint meeting of the Politburo and the Presidium of the Control Commission, twenty-two members in all, and charging him with opposition to the party line, "a right-opportunist, capitulatory platform" and forming "an antiparty bloc with the Trotskyists."

Bukharin was no match for Stalin in political maneuvering, but he did not lack courage. He defended himself with a thirty-page counterattack on Stalin, refused to consider a compromise resolution, and repeated his attack at a further session on February 9, 1929, this time with the support of Rykov and Tomsky. Stalin, he declared, was usurping power, organizing the "political slaughter" of those who disagreed with him, and following a policy of "splits, splinters, and groups," which was leading to the "decomposition of the International." He characterized Stalin's economic policy as "going over to the Trotskyist position," and charged him with basing industrialization on "the military-feudal exploitation of the peasantry," a phrase taken by all who read it as equating Stalin's treatment of the peasantry with that which they had suffered under the despotic tsarist state, a charge that Stalin never forgave. [51] The Politburo censured Bukharin for "factionalism" and "intolerable slanders," but it did not go as far as Stalin wanted. "We are treating the Bukharinists too liberally and tolerantly," he declared: "Has not the time come to stop this liberalism?" But none of the three dissenters lost his place in the Politburo, one of whose members, Kalinin, is reported to have said privately: "Yesterday Stalin liquidated Trotsky and Zinoviev. Today he wants to liquidate Bukharin and Rykov. Tomorrow it will be my turn."

Stalin renewed his attack at the Central Committee Plenum in April 1929 when the Bukharinists numbered a mere thirteen in a meeting of over three hundred. Stalin began his speech by dismissing his personal friendship with Bukharin:

> Comrades, I will not dwell on personal matters because the personal element is trivial. Bukharin read several letters from which it was plain

that yesterday we were personal friends, and now we are parting company politically. I don't think all these complaints and wailings are worth a brass farthing. We are not a family circle or a coterie of personal friends; we are the political party of the working class.

Stalin accused Bukharin and his followers of opposition to the party's policy all along the line, "a betrayal of the working class, a betrayal of the revolution." Recalling his exile in Siberia, he asked:

Have you ever seen fishermen before the storm on a great river like the Yenisei? I have, more than once. It happens that one group of fishermen mobilizes all its forces in the face of the oncoming storm, inspires its people, and boldly heads the boat into the storm, saying "Hold fast, boys, tighten the rudder and cut through the waves. We'll win."

But there is another kind of fishermen who lose heart when they see the storm coming, start to whine, and demoralize their own ranks: "Oh, woe, the storm is breaking. Lie down, boys, on the bottom of the boat, close your eyes, maybe we'll somehow be borne on to the shore." [General laughter.]

Need it be demonstrated that the Bukharin group's outlook and behavior are as similar as two drops of water to the outlook and behavior of the second group of fishermen, those who retreat in panic in the face of difficulties?

In the English translation, Stalin's speech "On the Right Deviation in the CPSU" fills fifty-three closely printed pages.[52] Sure of himself, and of his audience, Stalin was determined to beat Bukharin to the ground. Long jealous of the high regard Lenin had for Bukharin's intellectual abilities, Stalin took particular pleasure in quoting passages from an exchange between the two men in 1916 in which Lenin criticized Bukharin for his failure to understand Marxist dialectics, and then read out another passage from an article in which the latter had appeared to criticize Lenin after his death, and (so Stalin claimed) had demonstrated how completely he misunderstood him. "Here you have a pretty example of the hypertrophied pretentiousness of a half-educated theoretician."

Bukharin himself sat silent, but two or three of his supporters had the temerity to interrupt Stalin and claim he was misrepresenting Bukharin. Stalin riposted:

I see that [D. P.] Rozit has sworn to do Bukharin a good turn. But his service is really like that of the bear in the fable; for in his eagerness to save Bukharin he is hugging him to death. It is not for nothing that the proverb says "An obliging bear is more dangerous than an enemy." [Loud laughter.]

The Plenum endorsed the censure on Bukharin and Tomsky and relieved them of their offices at *Pravda,* in the Comintern, and the trade unions. It also endorsed Stalin's Five-Year Plan for the modernization of Soviet industry, with its escalation of targets, tripling or quadrupling investment in the state sector, and setting an increase of 230 percent in five years for the production of capital goods. Yet the Bukharinists were still not deprived of their Politburo membership, and the public show of unanimity was preserved at the Sixteenth Party Conference that followed.

In July 1929, however, Stalin held back no longer. The Comintern Executive, now presided over by Molotov in place of Bukharin, carried through the radical change of course prefigured the year before. Having gotten rid of the left-wing leaders in the KPD and other Communist parties in 1927, the right wing was now eliminated, in both cases in line with the changing balance between the different factions in the Soviet Union. The new directives required Communists throughout Europe, in the face of the rise of Nazism and Fascism, to make the Social Democrats their principal enemy as "social Fascists," to promote rival trade unions, and deliberately split the European labor movement.

In 1929 Bukharin's life was not in danger, but the onslaught that was launched against him in August, and that consisted of literally hundreds of articles, many written in advance, some the previous year, amounted to a campaign of political assassination. Not a single episode or scrap of writing was left out in the effort to characterize him as "un-Marxist, anti-Leninist, anti-Bolshevik, anti-party, petit-bourgeois, and pro-kulak." The object was to eradicate irrevocably the influence of the man Lenin had saluted as the leading theoretician of the party and provide a warning of what might happen to anyone else who questioned the new orthodoxy.

When the Central Committee Plenum met in November 1929, the first attempt by the three defeated leaders to produce the confession of political error demanded of them incensed Stalin and led to Bukharin's immediate expulsion from the Politburo. Only then were the three brought to admit that they had been wrong and to undertake that they would wage "a decisive struggle against all deviations from the party's general line and above all against the right deviation."

The long battle for the succession was over. Both the left and right oppositions had been defeated. By the time the Central Committee Plenum met again, in April 1930, there would be no doubt either about the use Stalin intended to make of his victory or about the justification of the warnings Bukharin had been forced to repudiate.

SEVEN

Hitler Within Sight of Power

HITLER 1930–1933 *(Age 41–43)*

I

THE EQUIVALENT PHASE in Hitler's career to Stalin's rise to power (1924–29), which we have just traced, was September 1930 to January 30, 1933. In Stalin's case the phase began with Lenin's illness and death, which precipitated a struggle for the succession; in Hitler's it began with the election of September 1930 which created the breakthrough for which he had been looking for ten years. Then the Nazi party captured 18.6 percent of the national vote, raising its total from 800,000 in 1928 to no less than 6.4 million, an eightfold increase, for which it is hard to think of a parallel in European history. With 107 deputies in the Reichstag, Hitler stood at the head of the second strongest party in Germany (after the SPD) and could no longer be left out of the political game.

Not surprisingly, the 1930 election and the succeeding election in July 1932, when the Nazis more than doubled their vote again, from 6.4 to 13.75 million, have attracted more interest than any others in German history. Since the ballot was secret the question of who voted for the Nazis is one that cannot be answered with certainty; but great ingenuity has been shown in studying the evidence even if there is still controversy about the results. [1]

Part of the explanation for the change in the Nazis' fortunes was a dramatic increase in the turnout: 82 percent of those eligible to vote, approximately 35 million against the 31 million of 1928, 4 million new voters who had either not bothered to vote before or had come on to the register for the first time.

The other main source of the increased Nazi vote was among former voters from the "bourgeois" parties: the Nationalists (DNVP), the right-wing liberals (DVP), and the progressive liberals (the DDP, known after July 1930 as the DSP, the Deutsche Staatspartei).* In summary terms, the "bourgeois" parties' share of the vote came close to being halved in 1930 and halved again in July 1932. By contrast, as the table shows, the Catholic

---

*The scale of their losses is shown in the table in Appendix One.

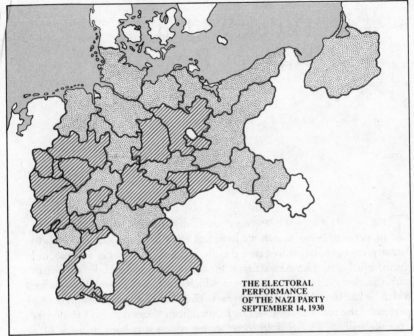

THE ELECTORAL
PERFORMANCE
OF THE NAZI PARTY
SEPTEMBER 14, 1930

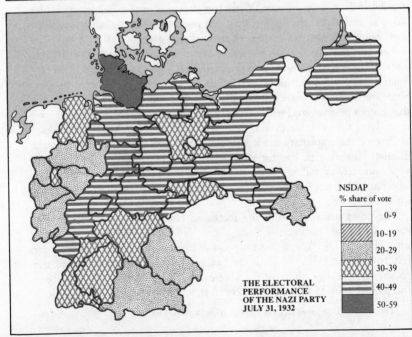

NSDAP
% share of vote

	0-9
	10-19
	20-29
	30-39
	40-49
	50-59

THE ELECTORAL
PERFORMANCE
OF THE NAZI PARTY
JULY 31, 1932

Center party held its own, and while the SPD's (Socialist) share of the vote was eroded, the KPD (Communist) was the only other party besides the Nazis to raise its percentage, strongly suggesting that the majority of the SPD's losses were to the Communists. If the vote for the two working-class parties is combined, it holds remarkably steady during these Depression years when the working class suffered an unprecedented level of unemployment.

The denominational division of Germany was as important as social stratification. The Nazis attracted a large part of the churchgoing population in the Protestant parts of the country; much less in the Catholic areas (including Bavaria) until after Hitler came to power and signed the Concordat with the Vatican in the summer of 1933. It was also in the Protestant rather than the Catholic parts of Germany that the Nazis—with their emphasis on traditional family life, *Kinder, Kirche, Küche* ("Children, church, and kitchen")—in 1930 expanded their vote among women, for the first time.

The different regions of Germany showed wide variations in September 1930. The highest percentage of Nazi voters was to be found in the Protestant and agricultural districts of north and east Germany, such as Schleswig-Holstein, Pomerania, and East Prussia. They also did very well in districts with a mixed economy of agriculture and small-scale industry, such as Lower Silesia-Breslau and Chemnitz-Zwickau.

The Nazis did much less well in urban, heavy-industrial, or Catholic areas, such as Berlin, North Westphalia, and Lower Bavaria. The two regions that proved the most resistant to their appeal were Upper Silesia and Württemberg, both with a predominantly industrial economy and strong religious ties. Within this broad general picture, much research has been done on the electoral sociology of particular districts, producing at least a provisional answer to the question: Who voted for the Nazis?

The most important point brought out by the research is the extent to which the Nazis, unlike all other German parties, with the exception of the Catholic-based Center party, refused to be confined within the traditional lines of division—economic, social, religious, regional—on which the party system had been based since its formation in the nineteenth century. The Nazi ambition was to mobilize support across those lines. Even after the switch in its strategy after 1928, from the so-called "urban plan" to concentrate more on the middle-class electorate, particularly in the smaller towns and the countryside, it refused to let itself be shut out of industrial districts like the Ruhr and the working-class quarters of the cities, to abandon its effort to reach Catholic as well as Protestant voters, or to write off any region or occupational group as beyond its reach. The gibe that it was a catch-all party, offering something to everybody, was justified, but it only pointed to the Nazis' claim—unlike the others—to be a people's party capable of rising above class and religious divisions and representing the whole nation.

There is no doubt that the Nazis failed to achieve this. The effort to overcome divisions that were intensified by the Depression involved them in a maze of contradictions and, at their peak in free elections in July 1932, they never persuaded more than 37 percent of the voters to accept their claim. But the fact that they should have been the only party besides the Center to make the attempt was an attraction to many of those who voted for them and meant that they drew on support, even in 1930, more so in 1932, from across a wider spectrum of the electorate than any of the other parties.

In 1930, in the hope of attracting working-class votes, the Nazis made the most of the rising tide of unemployment, arguing that the SPD had done nothing to prevent it. But where the SPD lost votes among the blue-collar workers in mining and heavy industry whose jobs were most at risk, these went to the KPD, not the Nazis. An exception was the SA (the Nazi Brownshirts), which had some success in recruiting among the unemployed in Berlin and Hamburg. Where the Nazis made more of a breakthrough, however, was in their appeal to the large body of workers still engaged in handicrafts and small-scale manufacturing, who remained outside the unions and were frequently hostile to the collectivism of the organized labor movement.

Nineteen thirty also marks the beginning of the Nazis' success in attracting support from the professions, to which such organizations as the NS League of German Lawyers, founded in 1928, and the NS League of German Doctors, founded in 1929, were directed. The Nazis' expansion among the academically trained professions was guaranteed by the success of the NS German Student Union in recruiting up to an estimated half of the German university student body to join the party by 1930 and capturing control of ASTA, the self-governing student organization.

Much was made by the Nazis of their appeal to youth. "Make Way, You Old Ones" was the title of an article by Gregor Strasser which was turned into another slogan. No less than 43 percent of the 720,000 new members who entered the party between 1930 and 1933 were under thirty years of age.[2] Many contemporary accounts note that it was particularly young people of traditional liberal or conservative backgrounds who rebelled against their parents' political attitudes and joined the Nazis. There were many for whom the Depression sharply reduced their job expectations, and among whom, as the leading Social Democrat, Carlo Mierendorff, wrote at the time, "social despair, nationalistic romanticism, and intergenerational hostility form a positively classic compound."[3]

However, with a population in which well over half of the total belonged to the working class, and with the Nazis unable seriously to challenge the SPD and the KPD on their own ground, it was still the case that the only other source from which mass support could be mobilized was the middle classes, which made up more than 40 percent of the total population. This corresponds with the fact that as the Nazi vote shot up in 1930 and July 1932, it was the traditional middle-class parties that lost most heavily.

The most stable element in the Nazi vote was the steadily growing support provided by the *Alte Mittelstand* (the old middle class), both in the town and the countryside.* In 1930 the Nazis made a great effort to penetrate a second conservative stronghold, the rentiers, pensioners and disabled veterans, the *Rentnermittelstand* (the pensioner middle class) which had suffered most from the inflation and the inadequate revaluation of debts and mortgages that followed stabilization. Their success here balances any tendency in earlier accounts to lay too much emphasis on the youth of Nazi voters. More than half the *Rentnermittelstand* were over sixty, just as less than 10 percent of the shopkeepers and self-employed in the *Alte Mittelstand* were under thirty.

Where the traditional view appears to need revision is in relation to the third group, the *Neue Mittelstand* (the new middle class). Their support for the Nazis in 1930, although important, now appears to have been less than that of the *Alte Mittelstand*. The white-collar workers in the private sector were slower than the civil servants and officials, especially in the lower and middle grades, in voting for the Nazis. The overall conclusion, however, is not changed and is summed up by the American historian Thomas Childers:

> By 1930 the NSDAP had begun to transcend its lower-middle-class origins, establishing itself on an electoral terrain traditionally occupied by the conservative Right. . . . In 1930 [they] achieved a breakthrough into each of the major components of the middle-class electorate. As the liberals and conservatives disintegrated, the NSDAP was well on its way to becoming the long-sought-after party of middle-class integration—a *Sammelbewegung* (united front).[4]

A second way of breaking down the results explored in recent research is by the size of the community. The Canadian historian Richard Hamilton brings out the importance of this with two striking generalizations. The first is that in the late Weimar period over half of the valid votes in German elections were cast in rural and urban communities of less than 25,000. Despite all that has been written about the impact of urbanization and industrialization (alienation and anomie), more voters "lived in the Diederfelds and Schifferstadts of Germany than in the Düsseldorfs and Stuttgarts"—let alone in Berlin which, with its four million inhabitants, was by far the largest city in the country, but contained less than 6 percent of the total population.

This leads to Hamilton's second observation:

> The vote for the National Socialists varied inversely with the size of the community. Prior to 1930, National Socialism was an urban phenomenon. It began in cities and was carried out, with great success, to the small towns and countryside.[5]

*For the definition of the middle class, see p. 67.

Even in the Nazis' peak election before Hitler came to power (July 1932) when they polled nearly fourteen million votes, it was still true that their percentage of the vote reached its peak of 41 percent in communities (rural as well as urban) of under 25,000 and fell to 32 percent in those of over 100,000.[6]

An important feature of the differences between the villages and the smaller towns with populations of less than 100,000 was the existence in many of the latter of a working class with trade unions and SPD and/or KPD party organizations. In towns situated in Protestant areas, this had a decisive effect. The American historian W. S. Allen in his classic study of such a town, which he calls Thalburg, with a population of 10,000, writes: "It was hatred for the SPD which drove the Thalburgers into the arms of the Nazis."[7] In Catholic towns, on the other hand, the existence of a strong Center party prevented such polarization. Even where the workers registered a substantial SPD or Communist vote, the Center provided an anti-Marxist alternative to the NSDAP, with strong traditional claims on middle-class voters.

It is more difficult to generalize about the big cities (ten with a population of over half a million). Berlin remained a stronghold of the left with more than 55 percent voting either for the Socialists or the Communists in September 1930, 54.6 percent in July 1932, and 54.3 percent in November 1932. The only change was that the Communist vote, which had been equal with the SPD in 1930 and July 1932, gained a clear lead over the Socialists in November 1932, with 31 percent against the SPD's 23 percent. The Center's vote, although much smaller than that for the left, actually rose in September 1930 and again in July 1932. The Nazis' gains were entirely at the expense of the liberal and conservative parties.

The only other city with a population of more than a million was Hamburg. There was more support for the Nazis there than in Berlin, rising to a third of the total vote in July 1932 compared with 19 percent in September 1930. But the left in Hamburg, although losing more ground than in Berlin, still kept a combined vote of half in 1930 and 1932, and the Center, although insignificant, held steady. As in Berlin, the Nazis' gains were at the expense of the traditional middle-class parties.

THE QUESTION of why people voted for the Nazis is more difficult to answer. With the highly individual mixture of motives that entered into the electoral choice of six million voters in 1930, thirteen million in 1932, this is not surprising. The class analysis that figures so prominently in the sociological approach to the question, *Who* voted for Hitler? is of much less value in asking *why* they did—if only because it cannot explain why people in identical social circumstances cast their votes for opposing parties. If we take the *Alte Mittelstand,* from which the Nazis drew substantial support, it is clear that they had different and often conflicting material interests. This was one of the principal reasons why the traditional bourgeois parties had lost more and more of their votes to the special-interest groups and why the latter in their turn could never combine to form a united middle-class party. The Nazis came nearer to filling that role than any other party, precisely because, while they showed no inhibitions in promising satisfaction for the economic and other material interests of different sections of the middle class, and indeed of the other classes as well, they never made these the central issue of their campaign. Confronted with the conflicting interests, for example of farmers, who wanted higher prices for food, and the urban population, which wanted lower, they did not attempt to explain how they would reconcile them; instead, they rode off on rousing talk of "national renewal," and *Volksgemeinschaft,* national unity in place of class war, which would enable them to look after the interests of each sectional group by looking after the interests of all. It is the psychological dimension rather than the sociological to which we have to pay attention. [8]

It was no accident that Hitler began to attract mass support only with the onset of the Depression. He had always believed that it would be catastrophe in some form or other that would give him his chance. For many this was represented by the rise in the number of registered unemployed to three million for the first time at the beginning of 1929, and further still in the month of the election, September 1930. The figure rose to six million in the winters of 1931–32 and 1932–33. But just because catastrophe took an economic form—producing not only mass unemployment, but also cuts in salaries and wages, and a dramatic rise in the number of bankruptcies, with farms as well as businesses being sold at rock-bottom prices—Hitler never made the mistake of supposing that the best way to exploit its impact for electoral purposes was by making economic policy and promises the centerpiece of the party's appeal. He grasped, as no other German politician did, that the effect of such economic factors on people's lives was one of psychological shock and that it was the emotions this created—fear, resentment, despair, the longing for reassurance and a renewal of hope—to which a political leader should address himself.

There was a particular reason why this should have been the case in Germany, and why the impact of the Depression there produced a more severe crisis than anywhere else. Between 1918 and 1923 the German people had already suffered a cumulative series of such shocks: defeat after the heavy losses of the war, Versailles, reparations, the collapse of the monarchy, revolution, near–civil war, and inflation. All the fears and insecurity of that postwar period were revived and made the harder to bear by the brief interlude of recovery, now seen to be a treacherous illusion. In the early 1930s, millions of German men and women felt like the survivors of an earthquake starting to put their homes together again, only to see the fragile framework of their lives cracking and crumbling around them a second time. In such circumstances human beings lose their bearings and entertain extravagant fears and fantastic hopes. This situation did not create Hitler, but it represented what a German biographer of Hitler, Ernst

Deuerlein, has called his *Ermöglichung* ("possibility"): "It made Hitler possible," by giving him the opportunity for the exercise of talents uniquely suited for its exploitation. [9] Hitler offered to millions of Germans a combination of the two things they most wanted to hear: total rejection of everything that had happened in Germany since the war, plus an equally unconditional promise to restore to a divided nation the lost sense of its own greatness and power. He swept together in a comprehensive condemnation the November criminals who had stabbed the German army in the back and had accepted the vindictive demands of the Allies; the Marxists who preached class war, internationalism, and pacifism; the permissive pluralist society epitomized by godless Berlin and the *Kulturbolshewismus*, which mocked traditional values and treated nothing as sacred; and the Jews whom he portrayed as battening on corruption and profiting from Germany's weakness.

In place of this democratic *Schweinerei* ("swinishness"), Hitler proclaimed his faith in a renewal of Germany's moral and political strength; in the restoration of the Prussian virtues—order, authority, sacrifice, service, discipline, hierarchy—on which she had risen to greatness; in the rebirth of a sense of community *(Volksgemeinschaft);* and in the creation of a strong authoritarian government, speaking with a single voice at home and enforcing respect abroad for a Germany rearmed and restored to her natural position as a Great Power.

Columbia historian Fritz Stern has suggested that the special attraction that Hitler had for German Protestants, not least Protestant pastors, owed much to the "silent secularization" of Protestantism during the previous century in which the Church became identified with the fate of the nation and the monarchy. Defeat leading to the overthrow of the monarchy and the existing order left the Protestant churches feeling lost and bewildered in an alien world. For many Protestants, Hitler's promise of a structural regeneration of the nation, his call for sacrifice and unity, met the need of a revitalized faith that the churches could no longer satisfy from their own enfeebled resources. [10]

At the same time Hitler was able to attract neoconservative intellectuals who rejected the rationalism and flabby liberalism of the modern world in favor of a Nietzschean irrationalism, heroic man in place of economic man. He made an equally strong appeal to members of the former governing elites, bitter at their loss of position and influence; to the *Alte Mittelstand* menaced by the process of modernization, including the rise of the working class, which threatened their livelihood and social status; and to many of a younger generation, frustrated by lack of opportunities and the longing for a passionate commitment to the future. This heterogeneity, inadequately reflected by any class-centered analysis, is the most distinctive feature of the support Hitler drew on, already apparent in 1930 and even more so in subsequent elections. It takes us to the heart of the Nazi phenomenon. For the Nazis differed from all the other parties in making the *style* of their campaigning more important than the content: To borrow a later phrase, in their case it was literally true that "the medium was the message." Not only Hitler's speeches but everything about a movement that dramatized politics as a mixture of theater and religion was aimed to appeal not to the rational but to the emotional faculties, those "affective interests," against which (as Freud pointed out) students of human nature and philosophers had long recognized that logical arguments were impotent.

> Our intellect can function reliably only when it is removed from the influence of strong emotional impulses: otherwise it behaves merely as an instrument of the will and delivers the inference that the will requires. [11]

Hitler was well aware from the beginning, as *Mein Kampf* shows, of the truth of this. His most original achievement was to create a movement that was deliberately designed to highlight by every manipulative device—symbols, language, ritual, hierarchy, parades, rallies, culminating in the Führer myth—the supremacy of the dynamic, irrational factors in politics: struggle, will, force, the sinking of individual identity in the collective emotions of the group, sacrifice, discipline.

It was entirely consistent with the character of such a movement for Hitler to refuse to be pinned down to specific policies and a program, leaving these to be decided when he had achieved power, the single overriding objective of the party, as it had been for Lenin. This had the advantage not only of increasing his freedom to maneuver as opportunity offered, but also of making it possible for groups with very different and sometimes conflicting interests and views to project these on to the Nazi movement, convincing themselves in each case that Hitler sought the same things that they did.

Many of those among the conservative older generation who voted for the Nazis did so because they believed Hitler would restore the traditional values of the German past. Others, especially among the younger generation, voted for the Nazis because they saw them as free of the class-ridden image of *Reaktion* which stuck to other right-wing parties, and because they believed Hitler would sweep away these relics of the past as well as the present, and carry through a radical right-wing revolution.

Both could be described as "the moral and spiritual renewal of the nation," and far from trying to resolve the contradiction, Hitler did his best to keep alive the expectations of both conservative and radical supporters. This was essential if he was to persuade enough Germans that here was a man and a movement capable of uniting the nation, relieving its fears, and pointing a way out of the mess in which it was stagnating. In 1930, eight times as many voters as in 1928 were persuaded to take his claim seriously; in July 1932 it was to be twice again as many.

IN 1930, Hitler had achieved his first objective and broken through into national politics. The question he now had to answer was how he was going to convert his six and a half million votes into a National Socialist government with himself as its head.

There were two obvious ways in which he might do this. The first was the parliamentary way, by piling up more and more votes until the Nazis could command a majority in the Reichstag, either alone over all the other parties or as part of a right-wing coalition. The second was by a coup d'état. Hitler saw objections to both. It was not in his power to decide when further national elections would be held, and in any case he scorned becoming a parliamentary chancellor dependent on votes in the Reichstag. The Nazi campaign had been based, from the beginning, on the claim to be a movement that would sweep away the swamp of parliamentary politics, in which great issues were decided—or, more likely, left undecided—by majority votes put together by coalition compromises. But to take the other way, and try to seize power by force, was to challenge the superior forces of the state and risk defeat on the streets, as he had in 1923. What Hitler wanted was a revolution with the power of the state on his side. But revolution was not to be the means of securing power; that had to be obtained with at least the appearance of legality.

It suited Hitler throughout 1930 and 1932, whatever he might find it politic to say in public, to leave both options open. But he hoped to combine them into a third way, a possibility created by the peculiar system of government by which, since March 1930, Germany was governed by a chancellor and ministers, not at the head of a majority in the Reichstag, but appointed by the president, von Hindenburg, and making use of the president's emergency powers to issue decrees under Article 48 of the Weimar constitution. The power to choose the chancellor and in effect give him the means of governing had been transferred to the little group of men around the president. But such a system of government was unsatisfactory for more than a limited period since it was open to challenge by a majority in the Reichstag. In the long run the chancellor either had to put together a majority in the Reichstag, so restoring parliamentary government, or if the president and his advisers wanted to get rid of dependence on the Reichstag altogether, to secure sufficient backing in the country to amend the constitution.

It was the latter course that President von Hindenburg and his advisers wished to follow, but neither Heinrich Brüning nor his two successors as chancellor, Franz von Papen and Kurt von Schleicher, was able to find the electoral support it required. At the same time the need to produce a solution to the political impasse impressed itself on the president's advisers, as the Depression deepened and the threat of a breakdown of civil order, as in the early years of the republic, grew stronger. The last thing the army wanted was a repetition of 1923 and simultaneous uprisings by left and right extremists.

In such a situation, Hitler had two assets. The Nazi success in the elections of September 1930, maintained by regional elections during 1931, was a promise of the support he could provide, if he was made a player in the political game. The organized violence of the SA was a threat of the revolution he might make if he were left out. Hitler's tactics, therefore, were to use the revolution he was unwilling to make and the mass support he was never able to turn into a majority—the first as a threat, the second as a promise—to persuade the president and his advisers to make him a partner in government. Thanks to the move from parliamentary to presidential government Hitler was offered an alternative route to power which would enable him to dispense both with the electoral majority that eluded him and with the risk of attempting a second putsch.

This is the key to the long-drawn-out and tortuous series of political moves from the end of 1930 to the end of January 1933, when Hitler at last achieved his objective and became chancellor. But it is a key to be used with care, for, unlike the historian, Hitler had no way of knowing whether his tactics were going to work. When negotiations broke down or led nowhere, as they frequently did, he had to fall back on the possibility of a coalition with the Nationalists, even at one time with the Center, or on winning an outright majority at the next elections, of which there were no fewer than five, of one sort or another, in 1932. Yet each time he gave the impression of having his eye on a resumption of negotiations, using the alternatives he turned to as a way of increasing his leverage and putting pressure on the other side to begin talks again.

As in Stalin's case, the steadiness with which he pursued his goal through a maze of twists and turns was remarkable. Even more so was his ability to retain the confidence of his followers and inspire their level of activity over the twenty-eight months of frustration that separated the expectations roused by the September 1930 election from the moment of their realization—twenty-eight months punctuated by numerous setbacks and, in the final stages, by the loss of two million votes and the prospect of failure. Neither man was swept to power. In Stalin's case it took nearly twice as long as in Hitler's: over five years from the death of Lenin to the moment of triumph on his fiftieth birthday.

AFTER A BRIEF meeting between Brüning and Hitler shortly after the 1930 election, which led nowhere, it was another twelve months before negotiations started, in the autumn of 1931. Brüning told the Nazi leader that the economic crisis would last a long time. This was encouraging news for Hitler. But how was he to maintain the morale and impetus of the party and the SA during this long period of waiting?

Ten days after the 1930 election he told a Munich audience:

We are not in principle a parliamentary party, that would be a contradiction of our whole outlook. We are a parliamentary party by compulsion, under constraint, and that constraint is the constitution. The constitution compels us to use this means. . . . It is not for seats in the Reichstag that we fight, but we win seats in parliament in order that one day we may be able to liberate the German people.[12]

Although now the second largest party in the Reichstag, the 107 Nazi deputies (Hitler himself, still without German citizenship, was not one of them) made it clear from the first day that they were not going to engage in parliamentary politics, but would simply use the Reichstag as a platform from which to attack the "System" and hold up its institutions to contempt. The main energies of the party continued to be directed at keeping up the strategy of "perpetual campaigning" outside parliament, in the country at large.

In the aftermath of the 1930 election, there was a big jump in applications for membership, almost 100,000 being added to the rolls between September 1930 and the end of the year. Thanks to Hitler's preparation of an organizational framework in advance, these were absorbed "into the great pot of the National Socialist idea"[13] without too much trouble, although there was jealousy among the *Alte Kämpfer* (veteran fighters) at the rapid advance of the often better-educated and better-qualified *Septemberlinge,** who joined only after the September success at the polls.

Two affiliated organizations that showed a similar growth in members were Darré's AA, the Agrarpolitischer Apparat, and the Hitlerjugend, appealing to middle-class parents as well as their children, which Baldur von Schirach took over and combined with the Nazi Student Association. Much less successful was the NSBO (the Nazi Factory Cell Organization). Given national status under Reinhold Muchow after the September elections, and backed by Gregor Strasser and Goebbels, it reached a peak membership of no more than 300,000 in 1932 (still mainly in Berlin) by comparison with the millions of the blue-collar unions, but this was not for lack of resources or effort.

The increased membership helped to maintain the impression of incessant activity which was the party's most important means of building up its power. The now well-developed "saturation campaigns" enabled it to win an average vote of over 40 percent in the 1931 regional elections. Between April and August another vehement campaign was waged, along with the Stahlhelm, the Nationalists, and the Communists—curious bedfellows—all demanding the dissolution of the Prussian parliament. The referendum failed, but the campaign allowed the party to maintain its high visibility. In December 1931 over 13,000 rallies and public meetings were reported to have been held throughout the Reich compared with a total of fewer than 500 organized by its rivals.[14]

Septemberlinge is a play on the word *Pfefferlinge,* a popular kind of mushroom.

After the election results, Hitler's domination of the party was complete, symbolized by the large office in the Brown House, with its three paintings of Frederick the Great and the official photograph of Hitler seated at his desk with the caption: "Nothing happens in this movement, except that which I wish." His myth image as "the unchallenged, sole leader of the NSDAP" (Gregor Strasser's description in the *Völkischer Beobachter*) was more than ever what held the party together and served as a substitute for a program.

In fact, Hitler spent little time in his office, far more touring the country winning support at mass rallies, which were an important source of revenue as well. But he strengthened the institutionalization of his Führer image by new appointments to the party's Reichsleitung, which carried out the organization and made the day-to-day decisions, without ever being left in doubt that Hitler's right to intervene was absolute. The most important of these was that of Goebbels, formally made early in 1931, to head the Reich Propaganda Leadership (RPL), with exclusive control over organization of the various propaganda campaigns, the selection of speakers, and the line to be followed by the party on every issue. Goebbels had already proved his remarkable gifts as a propagandist in the election campaign. Characteristic of his approach was the system of monthly reports on grass-roots sentiment that he demanded from the Gauleiters, urging them to send agents into "the bakeries, butchers' shops, grocery stores, and taverns," to find out what people were saying—material that the RPL then used in developing its campaign literature.

The sudden influx of new members; the increase in business advertising in the *Völkischer Beobachter* and the increased number of party papers; and the bigger audiences at party rallies and other events for which admission was charged all helped the party to wipe out the heavy debts it had incurred in the election campaign, and to face the permanent expansion in its activities. It was still true in 1931, and largely so in 1932 as well, that the Nazi party was self-financing. The major industrialists and bankers continued to show mistrust of a party that was unable or unwilling to produce an unambiguous or even coherent statement of its economic policy and intentions toward the capitalist enterprises that they directed. But the Nazis began to derive some benefit in 1930–31 not from corporate funds but from the individual contributions of a number of fellow travelers—among them the former president of the Reichsbank, Hjalmar Schacht, the Ruhr industrialist Fritz Thyssen, and Ludwig Grauert, director of the employers' association of the iron and steel industry. The sums involved, however, ranged from tens of thousands up to one or two hundred thousand marks, and were often paid not to the party but to individual Nazis—not Hitler, but Göring, Gregor Strasser, and Walther Funk, journalist and Nazi contact man with industry.

The commitment on the part of the rank and file was the movement's greatest asset; but there was always the danger that the increased activity that sustained it would slip over the ill-defined line between legal and illegal. Hitler had to hold the balance between "illegality"—which, if allowed to get out of hand, put at risk his credibility as a possible partner in the eyes of the army leaders, and the group around the president—and "legality," which, if pressed too hard, could disillusion the large number who had joined the party and the SA in the belief that force, not majority votes, should settle national issues, and who still hankered for a March on Berlin and the seizure of power. Hitler's skill lay in deliberately leaving an aura of uncertainty around his assurances of "legality," so as to keep alive, on the one hand, the belief of the conservative elements with whom he hoped to negotiate that he exercised a restraining influence on the party; and on the other, the belief of the radicals in the party that his talk of "legality" was so much clever camouflage concealing the intention to launch a putsch when the moment came. As Göring put it:

> We are fighting against the state and the present system because we wish to destroy it utterly, but in a legal manner—for the long-eared plain-clothes man. Before we had the Law for the Protection of the Republic, we said we hated this state; under this law we say we love it—and still everyone knows what we mean.[15]

Hitler's ability to play this double game was put to the test immediately after the 1930 election. He had started a campaign aimed at influencing opinion in the army with a speech at Munich in 1929 attacking the attitude that von Seeckt, now retired as chief of the army command, had consistently maintained, that the Reichswehr must stand apart from politics. Hitler's arguments had an effect among the younger officers, who saw little prospect for advancement in an army limited by the Versailles Treaty to a hundred thousand men, and who were attracted by Hitler's promises that, if he came to power, he would expand the army and restore Germany to its rightful position in Europe. Three lieutenants, Richard Scheringer, Hans Ludin, and Hans Friedrich Wentz, were sufficiently impressed to get in touch with the Nazis and undertake to bring other officers around to their point of view. Arrested on a charge of spreading Nazi propaganda in the army, they came up for trial before the Supreme Court in Leipzig a few days after the 1930 election. Hitler immediately asked to be heard and, deliberately aiming his remarks at the leaders of the Reichswehr, declared categorically that the SA had been set up solely for a political purpose; that any idea of their using force and involving the army in a civil war, or of seeking to replace it (particularly the traditional officer corps) with a Nazi-style New Model Army was out of the question. "We will see to it that when we have come to power, out of the present Reichswehr a great German People's Army will arise. There are thousands of young men in the army of the same opinion." When the president of the court interrupted to say that the Nazis could hardly hope to achieve their aims legally, Hitler indignantly denied this. His orders alone were valid, "and my basic principle is that if a party regulation conflicts with the law, it is not to be carried out." Those who did not comply had been expelled, "among them Otto Strasser, who toyed with the idea of revolution."

Then, with that calculated ambiguity that he maintained on legality as much as on the issues of the party's anticapitalism, Hitler added:

> I stand here under oath to God Almighty. I tell you that if I come to power legally, then there will be a Nazi Court of Justice too, the November 1918 revolution will be avenged, and quite a few heads will roll, legally.

At this there was loud applause from the gallery, but when the president asked what Hitler meant by the expression "German National Revolution," he blandly replied that it had nothing to do with domestic politics but meant simply "a German patriotic uprising" against the provisions of the peace treaties, "which we regard not as binding law, but as something imposed upon us."

> Our propaganda is the spiritual revolutionizing of the German people. Our movement has no need of force. . . . We will enter the legal organizations and make our party a decisive factor in this way. But when we do possess constitutional rights, then we will form the state in the manner we consider to be the right one.
> *The President:* "This too by constitutional means?"
> *Hitler:* "Yes." [16]

When General Alfred Jodl, Hitler's chief of staff during the war, was interrogated at the Nuremberg Trials after the war, he told the tribunal that he had not been reassured until Hitler swore under oath in the court that he opposed any interference with the army. This explicit statement was designed to open the way to the subsequent negotiations with the Reichswehr leaders. But the dangers inherent in such tactics were illustrated by the subsequent history of Lieutenant Scheringer. Condemned to eighteen months' imprisonment, he went over to the Communists while still in prison. When Goebbels telegraphed to ask if Scheringer's letter announcing his switch of allegiance was genuine, Scheringer wired back: "Declaration authentic. Hitler revolution betrayed."

The dangers were most acute in the SA. The Brownshirts were essential to the Nazis' campaign: They acted as guards at the unending series of rallies; they challenged the Communists in the street; and with their parades they put on the display of force that was central to the Nazi image. It was propaganda, however, the image of the party, that Hitler had in mind: The SA were to be the shock troops of a revolution that was never to be made. But to let this belief gain ground would weaken their fighting spirit, which had to be kept alive—without ever allowing it to get out of control.

That Hitler was aware of the problem was shown by the swiftness of his reaction when the Berlin SA, notorious for its violent clashes with the KPD, mutinied just before the September election and refused to protect the party's rallies. Their principal grievance was over pay, but the separate structure of the SA meant constant friction with the party's political organization, and there was a strong feeling that they were undervalued by the Reichsleitung in Munich: As far as they are concerned, one SA Oberführer wrote, "the SA is here just to die." Hitler rushed to Berlin and went from one beer hall and club room to the next, pleading with the rank and file and promising them better pay and treatment as "the soldiers of the revolution." To provide the funds he ordered a special levy on every party member and capped the effect of his personal appearance face-to-face by announcing that he himself would become the SA supreme commander in place of von Pfeffer.

As soon as he could after the election, Hitler persuaded Ernst Röhm to come back as chief of staff of the SA and gave him a free hand to reorganize a force whose strength at the beginning of 1931 fluctuated between 60,000 and 100,000 men, including large numbers of the unemployed, attracted by the promise of pay, food, and adventure. At the same time Hitler allowed Himmler to expand his elite SS Order (which originally numbered 280 and was much disliked by the more proletarian SA) into an inner-party police, to which he gave the motto: *"SS-Mann, deine Ehre heisst Treue"* ("SS man, thy loyalty is thine honor").

The grumbling at Hitler's policy of "legality," however, continued. At the end of March 1931, when the government issued a decree requiring political rallies to be approved by the police twenty-four hours in advance, Hitler ordered all party agencies to obey the letter of the law. This was too much for Walther Stennes, the SA leader in Berlin, who denounced Hitler's compliance with the decree, drove out the party's political leadership in Berlin, and placed both party and SA under his command. SA officers in Pomerania, coming out in support of Walther Stennes, declared "that the NSDAP had departed from the revolutionary course of true National Socialism . . . and relinquished the pure ideal for which we are fighting."[17]

Hitler again placed his personal prestige on the line, dismissed Stennes, and required all SA leaders to submit unconditional declarations of loyalty to himself personally. Although Stennes joined Otto Strasser in open opposition to Hitler, his revolt failed and only a handful followed him. The power of the Führer myth held the majority firm, even in Berlin. Göring carried out a purge of the SA; a number of reforms were introduced to deal with rank-and-file grievances; and Hitler and Röhm put a lot of effort into indoctrination courses for the SA leaders in a Reich Leadership School. But the problem remained inherent in a policy that could resolve the tension created by its contradictions only if it led to success.

III

HITLER NEEDED not only confidence but patience. He could build up the pressure from outside, but as long as he held to his tactics of legality, he had to wait for those on the inside to take the initiative in bringing him into negotiations. This waiting game was a severe test of the party's and of Hitler's own faith in his predestined success, the core of the Führer myth. But there were four objective factors outside his control that were yet capable of being turned to his advantage.

The first was the intensification of the Depression during 1931–32, during which registered unemployment passed the six-million figure, a higher percentage than in any of the other industrialized countries.

The second was the intensification of the political crisis that accompanied the Depression. The increased vote for the radical right (the Nazis) and the radical left (the KPD), and the rise in political violence that went along with it, represented one form of this. Another was the end of the temporary stabilization of the republic that had followed the election as president of the republic in 1925 of Field Marshal von Hindenburg, a symbolic substitute for the monarchy. For a brief period, the traditional German elites became, if not reconciled, at least less aggressive toward the republic. The Depression put an end to this. The economic crisis became a political crisis as well.

All the ills from which Germany was suffering were blamed on the "system," showing how shallow were the roots of parliamentary democracy in Germany, and how deeply alienated from the republic were those groups whose privileges and position in society should have made them the strongest supporters of the state. This can be seen clearly in the case of the leading conservative party, the Nationalists (DNVP). They not only started to lose more and more votes to the Nazis in the rural areas, but also saw their party captured by the reactionary and autocratic Pan-German Alfred Hugenberg, who tried, without much success, to rival the Nazis in raucous, unremitting opposition to the republic, and at times to form an alliance with them.

Hugenberg's invitation to Hitler to join in the referendum campaign against the Young Plan (see pp. 160–61) was an important stage in Hitler's progress toward political respectability and possible access to the influence and financial resources of upper-class, right-wing circles. The more conservative members of the DNVP were repelled by Hugenberg's political style and broke away to form a splinter group, the Volkskonservativen. But Hugenberg, pigheaded and undismayed, continued on his course, learning nothing from his earlier experience with Hitler and bringing him into the "National Opposition," the so-called Harzburg Front, which briefly assembled all the right-wing enemies of the Weimar Republic in October 1931. This was the same coalition that was revived in January 1933 to make Hitler

chancellor, in the mistaken belief that he had been pinned down to following where his partners led.

The third factor that worked in Hitler's favor was a change in the policy
of the Reichswehr. One of the most striking and dangerous anomalies of the
Weimar Republic was the success of the army's leaders in surviving defeat
and the fall of the monarchy to emerge as a state within the state, loyal not
to the government of the day or the republic but to what the officer corps
conceived to be the interests and values of the "eternal Germany."

The architect of the unique position enjoyed by the Reichswehr was
General Hans von Seeckt, its commander in chief (*Chef der Heeresleitung*)
from 1920 to 1926. Not only was he successful in defending the autonomy
of the army leadership against the politicians on the grounds that politics
must have no place in the army, but also as the representative of the army
he played a major role in politics himself with the claim that the army was
the ultimate arbiter of the national interest. In the domestic crisis of 1923,
the German government had entrusted von Seeckt with full executive
powers to preserve the state, and he was responsible for the secret policy
of close relations with the Soviet Union on which the German army relied
to evade the military clauses of the Treaty of Versailles.

The election in 1925 of Field Marshal von Hindenburg, the last commander of the old Imperial Army, as president of Germany, followed by the
retirement of von Seeckt in 1926, opened the way to a rapprochement
between the army and the republican authorities. The lead was taken by an
influential group of younger officers serving in the Ministry of Defense and
in the Truppenamt, the disguised successor to the former General Staff,
forbidden by the peace settlement. They were motivated not by republican
sympathies, but by recognition that their professional objectives could be
achieved only by close cooperation with both the Reich and the Prussian
governments. Their plans envisaged the creation of a new model army of
twenty-one infantry and five cavalry divisions (the peace treaty allowed
seven and three); the equipping of these forces (and an air force) with the
most modern weapons, almost all forbidden by the treaty, and a secret
rearmament and training program in the Soviet Union.

The architects of this new relationship were Wilhelm Groener, the first
general to become minister of defense, and Kurt von Schleicher, who was
head of the Ministeramt, a new office to handle all political questions on
behalf of the army and navy. Groener had succeeded Ludendorff as second-
in-command in the final days of the First World War and had shown his
realistic grasp by telling the kaiser (when von Hindenburg remained silent)
that the army was no longer behind him. He then went on to conclude an
agreement with the new socialist chancellor, Ebert, and took the responsibility for advising the republican government that Germany was unable to
continue the war and must sign the Treaty of Versailles. The idea of
recalling him at the age of sixty to serve as minister was promoted by von

Schleicher, who had been closely associated with him as a staff major in 1918 and 1920, and who persuaded von Hindenburg to nominate him.

Von Schleicher, clever, self-confident, endowed with both charm and a passion for political intrigue (he became known as "the field-gray eminence"), won the confidence not only of Groener, but also—through his friendship with Oskar von Hindenburg (with whom he saw service in the Third Foot Guards, von Hindenburg's old regiment)—that of Oskar's father, the president, as well. Very soon, hardly a day passed without a request from the presidential palace for von Schleicher's advice. Despite Groener's efforts, however, the distrust on both sides (particularly among the Social Democrats) was too deep-rooted for the cooperation to succeed. Groener was disillusioned with the weakness of coalition government, in which the participating parties maneuvered against one another, and by December 1929 he and von Schleicher were looking for some other way of finding the political stability and support that the Reichswehr required to carry out its rearmament program.

The army's search for this was to become a major factor in making possible Hitler's admission to office. That was still a long way off, but well before 1933 the army's change of attitude had a powerful effect in contributing to the substitution of presidential for parliamentary government, the fourth factor that worked to Hitler's advantage. Von Schleicher was one of those most active among the president's advisers in working out the plan to appoint a chancellor who, relying on the president's emergency powers, would be able to provide what both the state and the Reichswehr needed: a strong government capable of conducting long-range policies without being at the mercy of party leaders.

BRÜNING WAS duly appointed, with the sequel already described: his decision to dissolve the Reichstag, only to lose the election that followed in September 1930.

It is important, however, not to jump from Hitler's unexpected gains in the 1930 elections to the conclusion that this made his ultimate success inevitable. There were alternative scenarios.

After the election, the 107 Nazi deputies at once joined forces with Hugenberg's 41 Nationalists and the 77 Communists in turning the Reichstag into a free-for-all and making it impossible to conduct serious business. But the opposition overreached itself. A change of heart on the part of the SPD made it possible to put together the majority needed to change the Reichstag rules and restore order to its proceedings (February 1931). This same combination, stretching from the moderate left (SPD) to the moderate right (the Volkskonservativen, who had broken away from Hugenberg and the DNVP), could have been used to defeat any vote of no confidence and provide the majority in the Reichstag needed to restore parliamentary government. But Brüning and the group around the president were not interested in that; the only use they made of the majority was to secure agreement to a suspension of the Reichstag, a further step toward replacing parliamentary by presidential government.

Another alternative that might have been explored was the proposal of Otto Braun, the SPD prime minister of Prussia, to merge the Prussian and federal governments, and defeat the threat of political extremism not only to democracy in Germany but to the idea of stable, constitutional government. It was one of the paradoxes of the Weimar period that, unlike the federal government, which was plagued with coalition crises, the Prussian government was remarkable for its stability and progressive policies, based on cooperation between the Social Democrats and the Center party. Braun, a former agricultural worker from East Prussia, held office as prime minister, with two short breaks of a few months, from 1920 to 1932.

The Prussian government had already taken the lead in seeking to curb Nazi extremes. This included a ban on outdoor meetings and parades, a ban on the SA wearing uniforms, and a law making membership of the NSDAP and KPD incompatible with being a civil servant or holding public office in Prussia. The Prussian minister of the interior, Albert Grzesinski, who controlled a police force of 180,000 men, 80,000 of whom were kept in barracks, motorized and armed, refused to be intimidated by furious Nazi demands for his dismissal. Following an attack on Jewish shops the day the new Reichstag met, Otto Braun appointed Grzesinski to the job of Berlin police president. The *Frankfurter Zeitung* commented: "Herr Braun knows how to govern in Prussia." Grzesinski's own comment to Braun was: "It is necessary to be tough, as tough as iron." He soon proved that he meant what he said.

Braun repeated the proposal of a merger in November 1931, offering to step down and let Brüning combine the office of Reich chancellor with that of Prussian prime minister. In his postwar memoirs, Brüning described this suggestion as "of the greatest importance . . . All the events of 1932 [including his own dismissal] could have been prevented."[18] But at the time he did nothing to pursue either this or Braun's earlier approach. If he had, such a move would almost certainly have been vetoed by von Hindenburg, Groener, and von Schleicher. A merger with the Prussian government, a reform long discussed in Germany, or an attempt to build on the majority in the Reichstag, would have meant cooperation with the SPD, still the largest party, but the one that the right saw as epitomizing everything it most detested about the republic. When Groener and von Schleicher had tried to effect a rapprochement with the republic, it was this hostility of the right, combined with the Social Democrats' skepticism about any real change in the attitude of the German officer corps and the landowning Junker class with which it was identified, that defeated them. That was the end of any "opening to the left" as far as the army was concerned.

In the autumn of 1930, however, neither Groener nor von Schleicher was yet ready to draw the conclusion that the only direction in which to look was the Nazis. Groener was responsible for the arrest and trial for treason of the three lieutenants who had sought to win support for National Socialism in the army, and at a conference of divisional commanders in October 1930 both he and von Schleicher defended themselves vigorously against the criticism the trial had aroused in the army. Yet the Nazi electoral success and nationalist propaganda had made a great impression, and the opinion of the officers who talked to the British military attaché at the autumn maneuvers has often been quoted: "It is the *Jugendbewegung* [Youth Movement]," they said; "it can't be stopped."

In the course of 1931 von Schleicher changed his mind, more quickly than Groener. Once Röhm returned to take over the SA, he got in touch with von Schleicher and underlined the fact that Hitler had acted to get rid of Stennes and the more revolutionary-minded elements from the SA. Hitler as well as Röhm visited von Schleicher, Groener, and General Kurt von Hammerstein-Equord, the chief of the army command, and von Schleicher began to develop the idea of "taming" the National Socialists by admitting them to a share of responsibility for unpopular measures, part of a scheme, this time, for an "opening to the radical right."

The need to find greater support was made more pressing by Brüning's lack of success in dealing with the economic problems created by the Depression. His priority was to end reparations. He believed that the prerequisite for this was to impress the former Allies with Germany's efforts to put her economic situation in order by cutting expenditures and increasing taxes so as to secure a balanced budget. Convinced that this was the right policy to pursue, Brüning accepted the fact that it would be unpopular; but the German public did not and dubbed him the "hunger chancellor."

Eighteen months after he had first taken office, in the autumn of 1931, Brüning had no more to offer than before, and in the meantime had run into heavy trouble in his foreign policy. A proposal by his foreign minister, Julius Curtius, to create an Austro-German customs union produced an angry reaction in Paris, and French financial strength was mobilized to force abandonment of the scheme. The leading Austrian bank, the Creditanstalt, was forced to close, and a flight of foreign capital began from Germany as well, leading to a financial panic and the closure of the principal German banks for three weeks in the summer of 1931. On September 3, 1931, a humiliated German government had to announce withdrawal of the plan. A further program of cuts in wages and salaries united right- and left-wing radicals in a furious attack on the chancellor's policies.

Von Schleicher had for some time foreseen the need to strengthen Brüning's government. He took advantage of the foreign minister's resignation in October to get rid at the same time of the minister of the interior, Christian Wirth, particularly hated by the radical right, and to secure the appointment of Groener, already minister of defense, in his place. He was less successful in rallying the active support of the Nazis and Hugenberg's Nationalists.

When Hitler received a telegram from Brüning inviting him to a meeting, he waved it in front of his companions, exclaiming: "Now I have them in my pocket! They have recognized me as an equal partner in negotiations." His exaltation was premature. The autumn of 1931 was a bad time for Hitler. In September, his niece Geli Raubal, with whom he was in love, had committed suicide in protest against his possessiveness.* In his meeting with Brüning and subsequently with Hindenburg (October 10), he was nervous and overplayed his hand by launching into a monologue which made a poor impression on both chancellor and president. A deliberate leak from the presidential palace let it be known that von Hindenburg thought "the Bohemian corporal a queer fellow who might make a postmaster general, but certainly not chancellor."

The next day Hitler had to appear at Bad Harzburg, where Hugenberg had assembled all the leading conservative personalities (including Schacht, General von Seeckt, all the right-wing politicians, and two Hohenzollern princes) as well as the forces of the Stahlhelm and the SA. The purpose was to show the strength of a united "national opposition" and demand the resignation of Brüning's and Otto Braun's governments, followed by new elections in both the Reich and Prussia.

Hitler was in the worst of tempers. He felt oppressed by all the frock coats, top hats, officers' uniforms, and formal titles—the *Reaktion* on parade—among which the great popular tribune was out of place. When the Stahlhelm turned up in much bigger numbers than the SA, he had to share the platform with their leader, Franz Seldte, and Hugenberg. Hitler read his own speech in perfunctory fashion and left before the Stahlhelm marched past. The united "national opposition" collapsed before it was formed, and bitter recriminations continued for the rest of the year.

In contrast, when Brüning defended his policies before the Reichstag on October 13, he did better than most people had expected. With the support of the SPD and the Center he won the vote of confidence by twenty-five votes. Hitler vented his frustration by writing an angry letter to Brüning attacking his record and, the day after the Reichstag vote, held a giant torchlight parade in Brunswick, to which thirty-eight special trains and 5,000 trucks brought over 100,000 SA and SS men to march before him. This was a show the like of which no one else in Germany could put on: While the others talked of the need for popular support, Hitler could claim he already had it. But he was no nearer to power than a year before.

I V

IT TOOK HITLER fifteen more months to get there, from October 1931 to the end of January 1933. Those fifteen months were filled with two things: elections and negotiations. There were five elections in 1932: two for the presidency; two for the Reichstag; and a series of elections in April 1932 for the state legislatures, the most important of which were the Prussian and the Bavarian. The negotiations were intermittent, tortuous, and inconclusive up to the very last day.

On Hitler's side, elections and negotiations represented two alternative tactics. These were never wholly separated, since the results of elections, even when they were not decisive, altered the balance of the negotiations. Nonetheless they represented two different ways of seeking to come to power. The first was by becoming a partner in a right-wing alliance, expanding Nazi influence in every possible interest group (as they had in the farmers' associations) and taking every opportunity to increase Nazi participation in government, in the states (*Länder*) as well as the Reich, so as to capture power from within. The second option meant going it alone and trying to achieve a breakthrough by winning an outright majority in elections.

On the other side, the situation was more complicated, since there were more actors with different, and in some cases conflicting, interests. None of those who took part in the negotiations, however—von Hindenburg, von Schleicher, Groener, von Papen, Hugenberg, even Brüning—saw Hitler and the Nazi movement as the threat that it now appears obvious they ought to have recognized. They agreed with much of what Hitler said: his attacks on the "system," his denunciation of democratic politics and the Marxist parties, his call for national unity, the abolition of the peace settlement including reparations, and the restoration of Germany's greatness, including her military power. As the chief of the army command, General von Hammerstein, said after a four-hour talk with Hitler: "Apart from the speed," Hitler really wanted the same things as the Reichswehr.

Neither the president, cabinet, nor generals saw themselves committed to the defense of the Weimar political system which, in their view, had proved incapable of producing the stable government necessary to end the crisis and start Germany on the path to recovery. They were moving from the use of the president's powers for a limited period of emergency—during which the parliamentary constitution was suspended, with the understanding that it would eventually be restored—toward a permanent form of presidential government, not so far from that of the former monarchy, with the president taking the place of the kaiser. Viewed in that light, the National Socialists appeared not as a threat to be crushed—even if they could be—but as a valuable source of strength, if they could only be persuaded to join the other forces of the right in supporting a common program.

There were sides of the Nazi movement that the Establishment did not like: the violence of the SA, the vulgarity of the party's propaganda, its overt anti-Semitism, the persistence of anticapitalist ideas. But they found a number of ways of reassuring themselves that the crudity and violence had to be accepted as part of the Nazis' ability to appeal to the masses and mobilize the popular support that, in their eyes, was the great asset Hitler could contribute to an authoritarian regime. Had they not gotten Hitler's promise on oath, which he was always glad to repeat, that he would respect "legality," as well as his assurance that any idea of the SA replacing or interfering with the army was absolutely ruled out, just as surely as that he would never countenance interference with the rights of property and management?

After a talk with Hitler in January 1932, the experienced Groener agreed with von Schleicher that Hitler was "determined to eradicate the revolutionary ideas." The official note records Groener's view of Hitler as:

> Sympathetic impression, modest, decent fellow who wants the best. In his demeanor, type of the earnest autodidact . . . The minister has clearly stated that he will support the legal effort of Hitler by all means, but that Nazi fomenters of unrest will be opposed as before. . . .
> Hitler's intentions and aims are good, but he is an enthusiast, fiery, many-sided. The minister fully agreed with him to further his intentions for the good of the Reich. The minister also instructs the [governments of the] states, in the sharpest form, to be fair toward the Nazis: Any excesses should be opposed, not the movement as such.[19]

From time to time Groener's doubts about the reliability of the Nazis recurred. But then he would let himself be persuaded by von Schleicher that there was no question of letting Hitler become chancellor or president; that, like all other opposition leaders, once in office, Hitler would prove amenable to "management," would be "tamed" and held back from radical courses by his coalition partners.

Groener subsequently admitted to his friend, the historian Friedrich Meinecke, "We ought to have suppressed them by force."[20] But when he finally moved to ban the SA in April 1932—initially with von Schleicher's strong support—it was to find himself stabbed in the back and driven out of office by von Schleicher, in the name of the army. Groener's treatment showed Hitler how easily the unity of the other side fell apart under pressure. After Groener, it was Brüning's turn to be discarded, then von Papen's, finally von Schleicher's. Each time Hitler was the gainer.

The mistake made by the groups who controlled access to power was in underestimating not Hitler's hostility to the democratic Weimar Republic, for that was what recommended him to them, but the danger that he represented to the conservative, authoritarian Prussian tradition they sought to restore. In the face of all the evidence supplied by the Nazi election campaigns and the organized violence, they failed to grasp the dynamic character of the movement Hitler had created, the lengths to which the man they looked down on as an upstart demagogue was prepared to go to secure his objectives, and the destructive forces he would let loose before he finished. Besides the dissimulation that both Hitler and Stalin learned to practice, this underestimation of them by the other players in the political game was another important common factor in their success.

The first choice between elections and negotiations presented itself at the beginning of 1932. Von Hindenburg was due to retire in May. The last thing the group around the president wanted to see was someone else replacing him. At eighty-four, the old man was reluctant to go on, particularly if it meant facing another election. Brüning therefore sought agreement to an extension of the president's term of office, for one or two years, by a simple vote of confidence in the Reichstag.

Although Hitler continued to attack Brüning fiercely for the disastrous consequences of his policies, the chancellor believed he might be willing to agree to such a proposal rather than put his own myth to the test against that of the field marshal, whom millions of Germans saw as the one symbol of stability in a chaotic world. There was no doubt about Hitler's interest, and talks followed with Groener, von Schleicher, and Brüning himself.

There was only one question Hitler wanted an answer to: What was in it for him? The answer appeared to be: nothing. The question then became: Was Hitler prepared to risk an open contest with the president?

Opinions in the Nazi camp were sharply divided. Gregor Strasser's view was that von Hindenburg would be unbeatable and that Hitler should not challenge him. This was in keeping with Strasser's preference throughout 1932 for negotiating rather than fighting elections; for making deals by entering coalitions with other parties (the center, for instance), locally as well as nationally; for penetrating and taking over interest groups, so expanding and accumulating power by stages rather than trying to capture it outright and risking failure.

Strasser's chief opponent was Goebbels, who urged Hitler to run, well aware (as his diary shows) that an electoral contest would make him, as head of the propaganda directorate, the most important of Hitler's lieutenants—just as the tactics of negotiation and coalition would magnify Strasser's role as head of the party organization. Göring and Röhm were Goebbels's strongest supporters—Göring because he had no power base in the party and could establish himself only if Hitler came to power and made him a minister, Röhm because he needed the excitement and activity of an election campaign to give the SA an outlet for their energies.

Hitler hesitated for a month, the characteristic display of uncertainty that preceded so many of his big decisions. Not until February 22, with the election no more than three weeks away, was he ready to say yes, and then hurriedly had himself made a German citizen through temporary appointment as a minor official by the Nazi minister of the interior in the insignificant state of Brunswick.

Already engaged in planning the campaign, Goebbels's worry was money. "Money is wanting everywhere," he wrote in his diary. "Nobody will give us credit. Once you get the power, you can get the cash galore, but then you need it no longer. Without the power you need the money, but then you can't get it."[21]

Goebbels finally succeeded in finding the money needed to plan a campaign the like of which Germany, or for that matter any other European country, had never seen before. By February 4, 1932, he wrote in his diary: "The lines of the election campaign are all laid down. We now need only to press the button to set the machine going." He had the success of the 1930 election to build on, and since then the party membership had increased more than threefold to around 450,000.[22] The party organization—no Gau had a staff of fewer than a thousand—could now reach into every German village, and the scale of the Brunswick demonstration showed what it was capable of. No radio or television was available, but the walls of every town in Germany were plastered with Nazi posters, and films of Hitler and Goebbels were made and shown everywhere (an innovation in 1932). As in 1930, but with much bigger and better-organized forces, the Hitler-Goebbels strategy was to cover every district in Germany in a saturation campaign, with propaganda targeted at each separate social and economic group. It was now that the strength of the Nazis' local organization on the ground proved its value.

The Nazi press and millions of leaflets carried the written message, but true to Hitler's belief in the superiority of the spoken word, the main effort went into organizing several thousand rallies, complete with SA parades, at the biggest of which the principal party speakers worked their audiences up with mob oratory of the most unrestrained kind. The president himself was not spared, nor anyone else, in the sweeping attack on the "system." Between February 22 and March 12 Goebbels made nineteen speeches in Berlin (including four in the huge Sportpalast) and addressed mass meetings in nine other cities, dashing back to Berlin by night train to supervise the work of his party propaganda organization.

But the central figure, even more than in 1930, was Hitler himself. This time it was not a question of a mass of candidates, many of them little known, standing for election to the Reichstag or one of the state parliaments, but of a single candidate, the Führer in person, the embodiment of the movement, calling on his supporters to elect him to the highest office in the state. His appearances aroused hysterical enthusiasm. At Breslau, he spoke to 60,000 people; in other places to crowds estimated at still larger numbers. By the time the vote was taken on March 13, the party, members and leaders alike, had convinced themselves that they were on the threshold of power, with Hitler about to become the German president, able to use the president's emergency powers to carry out a "legal" revolution.

The result stunned them. The Nazi campaign had pushed up their vote from the six and a half million of September 1930 to eleven and a half, 30 percent of the total in a record turnout. But this was still seven million behind von Hindenburg's figure of 46.6 percent. The decisive factor was the recognition by the Social Democrats, the trade unions, and the Catholic Center party that it was better not to put up candidates of their own but to vote, as the lesser evil, for a president who was Protestant, Prussian, and a monarchist who detested social democracy and the republic. However it was to be explained, the result was defeat, and Goebbels was in despair.

Von Hindenburg's vote, however, was still 200,000 votes short of the absolute majority required. A second election therefore had to be held. This time Hitler did not hesitate. As the result was declared, he announced that he would run, and before morning on the day after the poll, special editions of the *Völkischer Beobachter* were on the streets carrying a new election manifesto:

> The first election campaign is over, the second has begun today. I shall lead it.

In the hope of preventing the violence from getting out of hand over Easter, the government limited the second campaign to a single week. To make the maximum use of it, Hitler chartered a plane and visited twenty-one cities with as many as four or five demonstrations organized to greet him. Apart from its practical advantages, this unprecedented use of air travel, with its futuristic touch, made an extraordinary psychological impression, especially when a violent storm grounded all other air traffic and Hitler insisted on flying to Düsseldorf to keep his engagement. Here was the man Germany needed, with the courage to act, the Nazi press blared, the savior who arrived from the skies. "Hitler over Germany" was the slogan, all the more effective for its double meaning. Carried away by the power of his own myth, Hitler declared that he felt himself to be the instrument of God, chosen to liberate Germany.

There was never any doubt that he would be beaten, but unlike the Nationalist candidates who dropped out, and the Communists whose vote fell by a million, Hitler's determination turned defeat into a triumph, pushing up the Nazi vote by more than two million. Von Hindenburg was safely home with a comfortable majority, but the Nazi success in more than doubling their 1930 election vote (13.4 compared with 6.5 million) was what made the news. Hitler at once ordered preparations for the state elections two weeks later. These would involve four-fifths of the entire population and offer the chance of unseating the Social Democratic–Center coalition in Prussia, the last stronghold of the republic. "We go on without a breathing spell," Goebbels gasped.

At this point, however, the rules of the game were altered. The winter of 1931–32 was marked by an upsurge in violence, much of it, especially in the big cities like Berlin and Hamburg, taking the form of gang warfare between Nazis and Communists. Evidence of Nazi plans to seize power had been accumulating since the Frankfurt police came into possession of secret draft documents (known as the Boxheim Papers) drawn up by local Nazi leaders in Hesse. These represented preparations for a Nazi coup following a Communist uprising and included decrees for the immediate execution of anyone resisting, refusing to cooperate, or found in the possession of arms. The discovery was made in November 1931, causing a sensation that obliged Hitler to disclaim any knowledge of the plans (probably justly so), but not leading to any action by the government against those incriminated. The Prussian police then found copies of orders from Röhm and marked maps confirming the report that the SA and SS had been ordered to stand by in readiness for a coup if Hitler won the presidential election. Other orders were captured instructing the local SA in Pomerania not to take part in the defense of the frontiers in the event of a surprise Polish action.

As a result the state governments, led by Prussia and Bavaria, delivered an ultimatum: If the Reich government would not take action to dissolve the SA and the SS, they would.

Believing that he had the support of von Schleicher and the army, Groener, minister of the interior as well as defense, issued a decree to this effect immediately after the second presidential election. Röhm, who claimed four times as many men in the SA as the Treaty of Versailles allowed the army, for a moment thought of resistance; but Hitler insisted on obedience to the order, foreseeing that if the SA complied and removed their brown shirts, they could reappear as ordinary party members and their organization would be preserved intact. Brüning and Groener, he declared, would get their answer at the Prussian elections.

This time he was wrong. Taking to the air once again, Hitler spoke in twenty-five cities in eight days. "Our whole life," Goebbels wrote, "is now a frantic chase after success and after power." But still it eluded them. In Prussia the Nazis won the same 36 percent of the votes they had secured in the second presidential election, enough to deprive the long-established SPD-Center coalition of its majority, but not enough to give the Nazis, even with the support of Hugenberg's Nationalists, sufficient votes to form a Prussian administration. In Bavaria and Württemburg, they were still further short of a majority. After three exhausting campaigns, even Goebbels had had enough and complained wryly, "We are winning ourselves to death in these elections."

Hitler, however, was far from despairing; he had received a tip-off that may have made it easier for him to comply with Groener's order. With von Hindenburg confirmed in office, von Schleicher now felt free to pursue his plan of getting rid of Brüning and moving a step further toward a form of presidential government independent of a Reichstag majority. It was an essential part of his program to secure Hitler's and the Nazis' support, and he used all his talents as an intriguer to undermine Groener's ban on the SA and organize a whispering campaign against him.

This was an act of personal treachery on the part of von Schleicher, whom Groener had treated as a son and trusted implicitly; it was also a reversal of his own earlier advice to Groener in favor of the ban. When Hitler met von Schleicher in secret, however (twice, on April 26 and May 17), he learned that the removal of Groener was intended to open the way to getting rid of Brüning as well. Both men, whom von Schleicher had promoted in the first place, had served their purpose and become liabilities. "Everything is going well . . . " Goebbels noted. "Delicious feeling that nobody suspects anything. Brüning himself least of all." [23]

After a humiliating scene in the Reichstag, in which Groener was jeered at and shouted down by the Nazis, and a vain appeal to von Hindenburg to intervene, the general resigned on May 12. Brüning was subjected to the same treatment. His policies had made him other enemies on the right besides Hitler. A draft decree to take over insolvent properties in eastern Germany and use them for land colonization aroused passionate protest from the powerful Junker class, to whom von Hindenburg owed the gift of his estate at Neudeck, and who denounced Brüning's proposal as "agrarian Bolshevism." Returning from a conveniently arranged visit to his estate after Groener's resignation, von Hindenburg refused to sign the decree and told Brüning that, if he wished to see him again, he should bring his letter of resignation with him. When he did, it was at once accepted. "We have news from General von Schleicher," Goebbels recorded in his diary. "Everything is progressing according to plan."

Brüning's fall marks a further stage in the breakdown of the Weimar Republic. However ill judged the policies he pursued, and however much he lacked the appeal of a popular leader, or the skills of a politician, he had made an honest attempt to deal with Germany's problems. As long as the Brüning cabinet was in office, with the tacit support of the Social Democratic and Center parties in the Reichstag, the tradition of responsible government had not finally been abandoned in Germany. With the appointment of von Papen as his successor, it had, and von Hindenburg expressed his relief that the "time of republican ministers" was over.

Von Schleicher's purpose appears to have been to remove the last traces of the democratic regime and replace it with an upper-class authoritarian government, the majority of whom would be drawn from the old nobility. The choice of von Papen, of whom the French ambassador reported that he was "taken seriously by neither his friends nor his enemies," was greeted with incredulity. A former cavalry officer, he was plausible enough to keep himself from being murdered by Hitler in 1934 and survived to talk himself out of a prison sentence at the Nuremberg Trials in 1946. With all the charm of a born courtier, he quickly endeared himself to the president, but he was angrily repudiated by his own Center party as well as Hugenberg's Nationalists and had no political base. Von Schleicher saw him in the role of a front man, who would do what he was told. When von Schleicher's friends protested that von Papen was a man without a head, the general replied: "I don't need a head. I need a hat." Von Schleicher himself, taking Groener's place as minister of defense, would supply the head.

Hitler had no intention of becoming involved with so anachronistic a setup. All he had agreed to was to tolerate the new government in return for the lifting of the ban on the SA and the calling of new elections. Even after the disappointing result of three elections in less than three months, the only purpose Hitler saw in negotiations was not a share in power, but yet another electoral contest, which alone could provide him with what he wanted: all the power on his own terms.

The Reichstag was dissolved on June 4; the SA ban was lifted on June 16, and the elections set for July 30. However, von Papen and von Schleicher failed to secure in return any binding promise of support from Hitler once the election was over. What they got instead was a demonstration of what the SA could do when it was unleashed. Ernst Thälmann, the Communist leader, described the lifting of the ban as an open invitation to murder. The violence of the street battles created the atmosphere of a civil war: In the five weeks up to July 20 there were nearly 500 such clashes in Prussia, leaving 99 dead and 1,125 seriously injured. The response of the new minister of the interior, Freiherr von Gayl, was to condemn the Prussian police for one-sided intervention, taking insufficient measures against the Communists, and being too strict with the Nazis. His reply was intended to pave the way for von Papen's greatest coup, the proclamation of a state of emergency in Prussia and the appointment of a Reich commissioner to replace the SPD-Center government.

A particularly bitter battle in Hamburg-Altona provided the excuse. Seven thousand Nazis paraded through a working-class quarter and engaged the Communists in street fighting across barricades, leaving seventeen dead and many more wounded. Three days later, on July 20, von Papen acted to remove the Prussian government from office. The legality of von Papen's action, based on the president's emergency powers under Article 48 of the constitution, was open to challenge, but the SPD and the trade unions, which had defeated the Kapp putsch by a general strike in 1920 and discussed the possibility of similar action again, did so only to reject it. Nothing so much impressed German opinion as the fact that Prussia, the stronghold of social democracy throughout the Weimar period and with the most powerful police force in Germany, surrendered without resistance, its leaders exhausted and their self-confidence sapped by the long-drawn-out struggle on two fronts, against the extremists of both left and right, the Communists and the Nazis.

The overthrow of "Red Prussia," long a Nazi objective, was heralded as an omen of triumph in the Reichstag election that followed ten days later on July 31, 1932. Thanks to an administrative reorganization of the party by Gregor Strasser during the summer, it was better prepared than ever and was now uninhibited by any restrictions on its activities. Once selected as a candidate, each party member was required to take a personal oath of obedience to Hitler, since "it is necessary that they obey blindly."[24] For the fourth time in five months the whole familiar apparatus of Nazi ballyhoo was brought into play. Hitler again took to the skies and on his third "Flight over Germany" visited and spoke in close to fifty towns in the second half of July; and once again he roused—and shared—the emotions of a revivalist campaign. When he was held up by bad weather and could not reach Stralsund before 2:30 in the morning, a crowd of thousands waited for him in the pouring rain. When he finished his speech, they saluted the dawn with the singing of "Deutschland über Alles." His message hammered home, over and over again, that after more than two years of economic depression and mass unemployment which the government had completely failed to relieve, there had to be a drastic change—and that only one party had the drive and total commitment to bring it about.

When the results were announced, the Nazis had more than doubled the figures for 1930, and had become the largest party in Germany, with 13,745,000 votes and 230 seats in the Reichstag: a gain of close to thirteen million votes in four years. The runners up, the Social Democrats, were far behind with under eight million votes, the Communists with five and a quarter, the Center with four and a half.*

V

YET, ONCE AGAIN, the Nazis had won a resounding success without gaining the outright majority that Hitler sought. A closer look at the figures showed hardly any advance for the Nazis in terms of the percentage of the votes cast in April—36.7 percent in the second presidential election; 36.3 percent in the Prussian elections; 37.3 percent in the Reichstag. The highest percentages had again been returned by the rural districts of the north and east—Schleswig-Holstein 51 percent, East Prussia 47.1 percent. But those for the industrialized and the southern parts of Germany were between 20 and 30 percent, substantially below the average. The British ambassador, summing up the general view, reported from Berlin:

> Hitler seems now to have exhausted his reserves. He has swallowed up the small bourgeois parties of the middle and the right and there is no indication that he will be able to effect a break in the Center, Communist, and Socialist parties. . . . All the other parties are naturally gratified by Hitler's failure to reach anything like a majority, especially as they are convinced that he has now reached his zenith. [25]

If Hitler was prepared to negotiate, however, he was in a strong position, as the head of by far the strongest political party in Germany. The question was, how much should he ask for? At a conference with the party leadership, a coalition with the Center party (which Strasser consistently favored) was discussed, but Hitler favored going for "all or nothing," all the power, not a share in it.

At Fürstenberg, on the fifth, he put his demands before von Schleicher:

*See Appendix One for the detailed results, and the maps on p. 214.

Together with the chancellorship for himself in any right-wing coalition, he asked for other Nazis to be appointed as minister president of Prussia, the Reich, and Prussian ministers of the interior (with control of the police), the Reich minister of justice, and the new office of minister of popular enlightenment and propaganda, reserved for Goebbels. To end dependency on either the president or the Reichstag, Hitler also asked for an enabling bill giving the chancellor full power to govern by decree; if the Reichstag refused to pass the bill, it would be dissolved. Whatever von Schleicher may have said, Hitler came away convinced that the general would use all his influence to get him the chancellorship. He was so pleased that he suggested a tablet should be put up on a wall of the house to commemorate their historic meeting.

On the eighth, Goebbels noted in his diary:

> The air is full of presage. . . . The whole party is ready to take over power. The SA own everyday tools to prepare for this. If things go well, everything is all right. If they do not, it will be a terrible setback. [26]

To quiet the SA and at the same time lend weight to his demands, Hitler had them parade through Berlin. Elsewhere the tension produced an increase in violent clashes and led to a decree threatening the death penalty for anyone who killed an opponent. The next night five SA men in uniform broke into the home of a Communist worker in Potempa, a village in Upper Silesia, pulled him out of bed, and kicked him to death in front of his horrified mother.

With no word from Berlin, Hitler asked for a meeting with the chancellor, von Papen, and the president on the thirteenth. The night before, he learned from Röhm that there was considerable doubt about von Papen's resigning the chancellorship in his favor, and he spent hours pacing up and down in Goebbels's house debating how high he should pitch his demands—and how low he could afford to go, if his control over the SA and the party was not to be shaken.

Von Papen, indeed, saw no reason at all why he should now resign. The results of the election, which had produced no clear majority, justified the continuation of a presidential cabinet; no one had ever enjoyed better relations with von Hindenburg, and the president himself had no wish to exchange the aristocratic von Papen for the uncouth Hitler, whom he disliked. The continued violence had produced a reaction against the Nazis among the propertied classes, and the possible repercussions abroad of Hitler coming to power had impressed both cabinet and army. Like everyone else, von Papen believed that the Nazis had reached their peak and would begin to lose votes. By the time he and von Schleicher met Hitler, the most they were prepared to offer him was the vice-chancellorship in the existing von Papen government and the Prussian ministry of the interior for one of his followers.

Hitler rejected their offer out of hand and worked himself up into a rage, talking wildly of three days' freedom of the streets for the SA and wiping out the "Marxists." After a further argument, in which he declared that he wanted only as much power as Mussolini had claimed in 1922, he refused to continue the discussion. He was persuaded to answer a summons to the president only when he was told that nothing had yet been settled. But the president received him standing up and spoke sharply of the wild elements in his party being out of control. He was ready to accept Hitler and the Nazis in a coalition, but not to give him exclusive power. To complete Hitler's humiliation, the official account of the interview, with the president rebuking him for the Nazis' excesses and rebuffing his overambitious demands, was published to the world—and to the party—before Hitler could get out his own version.

The manner in which he had been turned down rankled as much as the refusal. This was 1923 all over again, the corporal who was welcome to play the part of a *Trommler,* a drummer in the nationalist cause, but whom one could scarcely make chancellor. All the scorn and hatred he felt for the "respectable" bourgeois world, the officer caste, and the smug politicians in their frock coats and top hats boiled over:

> I know what those gentlemen have in mind. They would like to provide us with a few posts now and silence us. No, gentlemen, I did not form the party to haggle, to sell it, to barter it away. This isn't a lion's skin that any old sheep can slip into. . . . Do you really think you can bait me with a couple of ministerial posts? Those gentlemen have no idea how little I give a damn about all that. If God had wanted things to be the way they are, we would have come into the world wearing a monocle. Not on your life! They can keep those posts because they don't belong to them at all. [27]

The temptation was stronger than ever to let the SA loose and show them whether he was just talking for effect when he spoke of giving them the "freedom of the streets." When the five SA men responsible for the murder of the Potempa worker were sentenced to death, he sent them a telegram:

> My comrades: In the face of this most monstrous and bloody sentence, I feel myself bound to you in limitless loyalty. From this moment, your liberation is a question of our honor. [28]

Yet Hitler could still keep his emotions and his calculation separate. On the very day of his humiliating interview with von Hindenburg, he summoned Röhm and the other SA leaders to insist that there must be no thought of a putsch. He still held to his tactics of "legality," and the demonstration in favor of the Potempa murderers was designed to help Röhm hold his men in check, not to whip them up.

Von Papen and von Schleicher understood well enough the game Hitler was playing and continued the process of wearing him down to the point where he would accept their terms. On his side, Hitler agreed to Strasser's resuming his talks with the Center party: A combination of NSDAP and

Center would represent a majority in the Reichstag and was actually used to elect Göring as its president at the end of August. Strasser believed that the party had reached the limits of its own electoral appeal and that a coalition with the left and moderate elements of the Center was the best way for it to reach the nonsocialist voters, and to come into power with a parliamentary majority. Goebbels remained as opposed to this as ever but saw the value of putting out feelers to the Center as a way of bringing pressure to bear on von Papen.

The climax of these maneuvers came with the first full session of the Reichstag since the election, on September 12, 1932. Von Papen, who was now firmly established in von Hindenburg's favor, had secretly provided himself in advance with a decree dissolving the Reichstag as a trump card to be played if necessary. But the course of events took both sides by surprise. At the end of a confused and angry session the Nazis voted in support of a Communist vote of censure, inflicting an overwhelming defeat on von Papen by 512 to 42 votes; and von Papen retaliated by producing the decree dissolving the Reichstag after it had sat for less than a day, leaving the Nazis to face the fifth election of the year.

Hitler, as always attracted to the gambler's throw of an election, was unrepentant and full of confidence. But even Goebbels blanched at the thought of going through yet another repeat of the earlier campaigns. Morale in the party was low and many of the *Gaue* still had debts from the July elections. There had been a strong public reaction to the Potempa affair, and there was a widespread belief, shared by many in the party, that the Nazis were bound to lose votes. Only Hitler's determination and unshakable conviction in his destiny kept them going. When the party leadership assembled at Munich early in October, the power of the Führer myth still worked: "He is great and surpasses us all," Goebbels wrote. "He raises the party's spirits out of the blackest depression. With him as leader the movement must succeed."[29] Not long afterwards, however, Goebbels noted in his diary: "Money is extraordinarily difficult to obtain. All gentlemen of 'Property and Education' are standing by the government."[30] This was certainly true of German big business, alarmed by the increasing radicalism of Hitler's appeal. For the first time a representative group of politically active industrialists and officials of the major industrial associations met in Berlin on October 19, 1932, and undertook to raise the political fund of two million marks asked for by the von Papen cabinet.[31]

Hitler, however, made no concessions and drove himself to the limit. In his fourth airplane campaign he visited even more towns and spoke at even more meetings than in the summer. "Against Reaction!" was the undisguised radical slogan he adopted, and the full blast of the Nazi propaganda machine was directed at von Papen and "the corrupt Junker regime." In a desperate move to avoid losing ground in his own headquarters of Berlin, Goebbels ordered the party and the SA to cooperate openly with the

Communists in a five-day transport strike which the SPD and the trade unions had disavowed. Goebbels's final diary entry reads:

> Last attack. Desperate drive of the party against defeat. We succeed in obtaining 10,000 marks at the very last moment. These are to be thrown into the campaign on Saturday. We have done all possible. Now let Fate decide.[32]

For the first time since 1928 there was a drop in turn-out. Wearied by the political turmoil and alarmed by the violence, two million fewer voters went to the polls than in July, and the Nazi vote fell by the same figure. This was no gain for moderation, however: The Communists passed the Center to become the third party (16.9 percent), the SPD fell to just over 20 percent, and while the Nazis remained by far the largest party, Hugenberg's Nationalists staged a modest revival. Extremism was still in the ascendancy. Von Papen, although (as Hitler pointed out) 90 percent of the voters were ranged against him, was delighted with the result and more convinced than ever that the Nazis would have to come to terms.

Von Papen's position, however, was not so strong as he believed. Von Schleicher was angered by his independence and the close relationship he had established with the president and was disturbed when he heard von Papen talking of calling another election to force the Nazis to come to terms, or of governing the country by a dictatorship if they did not. According to Brüning, von Schleicher had always been worried by the possibility of the army having to deal with a simultaneous uprising by the Nazis and the Communists. Their actual cooperation in the Berlin strike and the increase in the Communist vote had made a great impression on him, and as minister of defense he began to impress on the other members of the cabinet that von Papen's continuation in office brought with it the danger of civil war. He urged that von Papen should resign and allow the president to consult the party leaders—in the first place Hitler—and try to find a way out of the deadlock.

Von Papen took the gamble (November 17), confident that von Hindenburg's talks with Hitler, which followed on the eighteenth and twenty-first, would lead nowhere, and that he would return to office with his hand strengthened. His skepticism was justified. Hitler demanded the office of chancellor with the same sweeping powers that the president had given to von Papen. Von Hindenburg (prompted by von Papen in the background) would agree to Hitler as chancellor only if he could assemble a majority in the Reichstag; if Germany had to go on being governed by the emergency powers of a presidential cabinet, there was no point in replacing von Papen.

Discussions between the president and the other party leaders produced no better result, nor did an approach by von Schleicher (through Gregor Strasser), in which he sounded out the possibility of the Nazis joining a cabinet in which he himself, not von Papen, would be the chancellor. Hitler was not to be drawn, and von Papen proposed that he should now resume office as chancellor, suspend the sittings of the Reichstag indefinitely, and prepare a reform of the constitution. Until that could be carried out, he would proclaim a state of emergency, govern by decree, and use force to smash any attempt at a coup. Overriding von Schleicher's objections, von Hindenburg agreed and commissioned von Papen to form a new government.

At this point von Schleicher played his trump card. At the first cabinet held after von Papen resumed office (on December 2), von Schleicher as minister of defense announced that the army no longer had confidence in the chancellor and was not prepared to take the risk of civil war.

The final act in this extraordinary story of political intrigue opened with von Hindenburg's bowing to the army's ultimatum, as conveyed by von Schleicher, and inviting him instead of von Papen to become chancellor, on the assumption that he could succeed in creating that national front, including the Nazis, that von Papen had failed to produce. Von Schleicher's hopes of doing this depended on the ability of Gregor Strasser, with whom he had been in touch, to persuade Hitler that it was in the Nazis' interest to enter von Schleicher's government.

For over a year Strasser had been pessimistic about the chance of Hitler's ever securing the unfettered powers as chancellor that he demanded. The setback suffered by the party in the November election, the heavy debts, and the mood of disappointment it had left behind led him to believe that Hitler's policy of no concessions, no compromise, the full power and nothing less, would destroy the party if it was persisted in. Von Schleicher's concept was a broad front extending from the moderate Nazis to the moderate socialists, with an energetic program to reduce unemployment. By making his offer through Strasser, he obviously hoped that, if Hitler would not agree, Strasser might accept the post of vice-chancellor and split the party.

There is no evidence that this was Strasser's intention, but the fact that he supported von Schleicher's offer, when it was debated by the Nazi leadership, soon led to accusations of treachery and trying to oust Hitler from the leadership. After a further angry meeting with Hitler on December 7, Strasser wrote a long letter defending himself against charges of bad faith and resigned all his posts. He made no effort, however, to rally support in the party, disappearing instead to Italy on a family holiday.

The resignation of Hitler's second-in-command and head of the party organization created a profound shock at a time when morale was at its lowest point. No one was more shocked than Hitler himself. But within twenty-four hours he had convinced himself that Strasser was a Judas who had "stabbed him in the back five minutes before the final victory." Summoning all the party leaders to meet him in Göring's official residence as president of the Reichstag, he denounced the absent Strasser in an emotional scene and cast him into outer darkness. All his old adherents were required to shake hands with the Führer and promise never to desert the cause. Goebbels, who was Strasser's bitterest enemy, wrote at the end of the evening that it had been "an enormous success for the unity of the movement. . . . Strasser is now completely isolated. A dead man." [33] Less than two years later, this was to become the literal truth.

Strasser made no attempt to fight back, and Hitler proceeded to visit all the cities in which the Gauleiters had been known to sympathize with Strasser, breaking up the centralized party organization that Strasser had created. As in the case of the SA, he named himself as the head of the organizational structure and placed men on whom he could rely—Hess, Robert Ley, Darré, Goebbels—in charge of the different parts. But his efforts to reassert his hold over the party did not produce an answer to the party's financial or political problems. Salaries of party officials had to be cut; Goebbels described the situation of *Gau* Berlin as hopeless, and SA men were sent into the streets with collecting boxes to ask passers-by to spare something "for the wicked Nazis." As to politics, Hitler had successfully killed Strasser's proposal for a way out of the dead end in which the party found itself, without being able to suggest an alternative. On the eve of Christmas 1932, Goebbels wrote in his diary:

> This year has brought us everlasting bad luck. . . . The past was sad; and the future looks dark and gloomy; all chances and hope have quite disappeared. [34]

This time it was not von Schleicher, but von Papen seeking his revenge on von Schleicher, who unexpectedly offered an opening. As chancellor, von Schleicher showed much more recognition than either von Papen or Brüning of the positive steps needed to break out of the Depression which still gripped the German economy. In a broadcast to the nation on December 15 he made the provision of work his overriding priority. On paper his program was impressive, but it aroused strong opposition among the industrialists and landowners whose vested interests he proposed to attack, without overcoming the distrust of the trade unions and Social Democrats, or even of the Center. After the intrigues with which von Schleicher had forced Groener, Brüning, and von Papen out of office, none of the political parties was willing to join him in a coalition. Sensing his opportunity, the last named, von Papen, who had stayed on the best of terms with the president, set about putting together his own alternative.

On January 4, von Papen met Hitler secretly in the house of a Cologne banker, Baron Kurt von Schroeder. There was no love lost between them, but both showed themselves willing to put aside their differences if they could get the better of von Schleicher. Hitler still insisted that he must become chancellor, but he was now prepared to enter a coalition with von Papen and Hugenberg's Nationalists, in effect the Harzburg Front resurrected. The exact terms of such a coalition were the subject of feverish discussions throughout January and were still being disputed when the members of the new government were formally presented to the president on January 30, 1933.

There is no need to follow the course of the negotiations, during the course of which every conceivable option was canvassed. [35]

By January 23 von Schleicher had to admit defeat: He was unable to put together a parliamentary majority and was reduced to asking von Hindenburg for the power to govern by emergency decree, which he had vetoed when proposed to von Papen at the beginning of December. Von Hindenburg was unwilling to grant to von Schleicher what the latter had insisted he should deny to von Papen. Whether von Papen could do better, however, depended on his ability to overcome three obstacles. The first was von Hindenburg's strong objection to making Hitler chancellor. The second was the large demands made by Hugenberg for dictatorial powers over the economy if he was to join the government. The third was to find a minister of defense who could command the support of the army, for which von Schleicher had so long claimed to speak.

A meeting between Hugenberg and Hitler on January 27 broke up in acrimony, and Göring had great difficulty persuading Hitler not to leave for Munich and withdraw from the negotiations. Hitler's threat to do so was sufficient. Up to that point von Papen had not abandoned the notion that he might become chancellor again himself; but he now became convinced of the danger that all his scheming might come to nothing and, the next day, told the president plainly that a solution could be found only if Hitler was made chancellor. He reassured von Hindenburg with the promise that he himself would become vice-chancellor and that only two other Nazis would be members of the cabinet, in which they would be outnumbered more than three to one by conservatives. The two proposed were Göring, who had been highly decorated for his war record as a fighter pilot, and Frick, a lawyer and former civil servant who was the least colorful and could pass for the most respectable of the Nazi leadership. The president's resistance was gradually worn down, and all Hitler's demands were eventually conceded, apart from the post of Reich commissioner for Prussia, which von Papen reserved for himself as well as the vice-chancellorship. In return, Hitler, equally reluctantly, agreed to Hugenberg's demand for control of the economic ministries.

The third problem, finding a minister of defense who could replace von Schleicher, was crucial to the president's agreement. Von Papen and Hitler found him in General Werner von Blomberg, an enemy of von Schleicher's since the latter in 1929 had removed him from the key post in the ministry of defense, the head of the Truppenamt, the disguised general staff, and had him posted to command the First Division in East Prussia. There he had been converted to a favorable view of the Nazis by his chief of staff, General Walther von Reichenau, and his divisional chaplain, Joseph Müller, later the Nazi Reich bishop. An ambitious man who had by now a better claim than von Schleicher to represent opinion in the army, von Blomberg had already been sounded out and summoned to Berlin in the early morning of January 30. He reached agreement with Hitler at eight o'clock and was sworn in as minister of defense before Hitler and the rest of the cabinet, thereby assuring von Hindenburg that the Reichswehr was in safe hands.

Hugenberg was still holding out against Hitler's insistence that the Reichstag should be dissolved and the new government seek a majority in what he promised would be the last elections to be held. They were still arguing when summoned to take the oath and be admitted to office. In addition to the chancellorship for Hitler, only two of the eleven posts were held by Nazis, and both were in the second rank: the Reich ministry of the interior for Frick,* and a ministry without portfolio for Göring. The foreign minister (Freiherr Konstantin von Neurath) and the minister of defense were career appointments from the Foreign Service and the army, of which von Hindenburg approved. The economics ministry and the ministry of food and agriculture (both in the Reich and Prussia) were in the hands of Hugenberg; the ministry of labor in those of Franz Seldte, the leader of the Stahlhelm, satisfactory to both the landed interest and industry. Göring was made Prussian minister of the interior, with control of the police force, but was responsible to von Papen as head of the Prussian state government. As well as being vice-chancellor of the Reich, von Papen also enjoyed the newly established right to be present whenever the chancellor made a report to the president.

To his friends, von Papen boasted that he had succeeded where von Schleicher and Brüning had failed, in securing the leader of the largest party in Germany to provide the mass support that the conservatives and Nationalists could never win for themselves. And he had done this, von Papen added, without giving away anything that mattered: Hitler might be chancellor, but it was he as vice-chancellor who had the confidence of the president and the conservatives and Nationalists who had the majority in the cabinet. To those who questioned whether there were not dangers ahead, he replied: "No danger at all. We've hired him for our act."

Von Papen had only himself to blame for one of the most egregious mistakes in twentieth-century history. Although Hitler constantly repeated his intention to observe "legality," he had never made a secret of what he meant by it. In his testimony at the Leipzig trial of 1930, he explained:

> The constitution only marks out the arena of battle, not the goal. We enter the legal agencies and in that way will make our party the determining factor. However, once we possess the constitutional power, we will mold the state into the shape we hold to be suitable.[36]

Even clearer was the reply Hitler gave to Brüning, when the chancellor, as he still was, challenged him directly in a public exchange of letters in

---

*Control of the police force was in the hands not of the Reich minister of the interior but of the individual states, of which much the most important was Prussia with Berlin as its capital.

December 1931. Brüning wrote: "When a man declares that once he has achieved power by legal means he will break through the barriers, he is not really adhering to legality."

Hitler at once replied:

Herr Chancellor, the fundamental thesis of democracy runs "All power issues from the people." The constitution lays down the way by which a conception, an idea, and therefore an organization, must gain from the people the legitimation for the realization of its aims. But in the last resort it is the people itself that determines its constitution.

Herr Chancellor, if the German nation once empowers the National Socialist Movement to introduce a constitution other than that which we have today, you cannot stop it. . . . When a constitution proves itself to be useless for its life, the nation does not die—the constitution is altered. [37]

This was clear enough, and it was for this reason that those who sought to bring Hitler into government always thought in terms of "taming" him, and resisted—as Groener, as von Schleicher and, up to the very last days, as von Hindenburg too had—allowing him to become chancellor.

Hitler was equally insistent that he would never join a government except as chancellor and equally sure that, when he did, none of the checks with which von Papen sought to tie him down would prevent him from "molding the state into the shape we hold to be suitable." It took Hitler less than two months to show who had been right; within six he had completed the revolution, with the power of the state on his side, which had always been his aim.

EIGHT

Stalin's Revolution

STALIN 1928–1934 *(Age 48–55)*

I

WHILE HITLER was still trying to secure power, Stalin was demonstrating how power could be used on a scale and with a ruthlessness that gave the years 1928 through 1933 the character of a second revolution as convulsive as that of 1917 through 1921 and even more decisive in breaking the mold of Russian history.

Ten years after the October Revolution, despite the economic recovery from the civil war produced by the NEP, Russia had caught up only with the level of industrialization achieved by 1913 and had been left still further behind by the advanced industrial countries. In 1927 the number of industrial workers was still no more than two and a half million. The party, ten years after seizing power, had yet to make good the gamble of 1917, when Lenin had seized power before the country had acquired the economic and social basis that Marxism made the prerequisite of a socialist revolution. Lenin had been confident that, once they controlled the state, the Bolsheviks would be able to provide the prerequisite—after the event. Ten years later, however, this still remained to be done: The power structure of party and state still lacked the necessary economic base.

There was no disagreement within the party that a socialist economy and society could be created only by the modernization and expansion of Russian industry, which was also needed to provide the Soviet Union with the means to defend itself in a hostile capitalist world. Nor was there any disagreement that industrialization could not proceed without the modernization of agriculture. Without a sustained rise in agricultural productivity it would be impossible to provide the food needed to support an increase in the numbers and standard of living of the industrial work force and to build up reserve stocks in case of war and famine. Restoring grain exports to prewar levels was equally necessary to pay for the import of tractors and of agricultural as well as industrial machinery.

The differences centered on how the increased surpluses were to be secured, how far the peasants could be *induced* to provide them by economic measures (for example by higher prices for the goods they produced, increased supplies of the goods they needed, and the development of cooperatives), how far they must be *forced* to do so by "administrative action"—and how long it would take to produce results. Hitherto Stalin had been content, in public at least, to accept Bukharin's argument that the process of consolidating the peasants' small, scattered strips of land and converting them to the benefits of modern methods of cultivation and cooperative action must be carried out "gradually, steadily eschewing forcible methods, through demonstration and persuasion"—Stalin's own words, as late as December 1927.[1]

Both Bukharin and Lenin (in his later days) recognized that such a policy meant taking time, one or two decades, even longer, to carry through the modernization of the Russian economy. At some stage—the lack of evidence precludes any attempt to say when—Stalin must have recognized the attraction of adopting an alternative course and by reviving the coercive methods of War Communism to make another attempt to find a short cut (comparable with Lenin's original short cut in 1917) to the creation of a modernized, socialist Russia. So long as Stalin was engaged in the struggle for power with Trotsky and the left, whose program ran along similar lines, he could not afford to develop his ideas and risk losing the support of Bukharin, Rykov, and the right, who had become wedded to maintaining the NEP and not risking the alienation of the peasantry. No sooner, however, had the Fifteenth Party Congress in December 1927 finalized the defeat of Trotsky and the United Opposition than Stalin secured the agreement of the Central Committee to order "administrative measures" (the code phrase for coercion) to requisition grain by force.

This was a first step. The historical pattern of the two years that followed, culminating in the celebration of Stalin's fiftieth birthday in December 1929, is made up of three interwoven themes.

One (already described in Chapter Six) was the final stage in Stalin's rise to power with the suppression of the right opposition. In the earlier stages, the initiative had been taken by Trotsky, then by the United Opposition of Trotsky, Zinoviev, and Kamenev in an open challenge to Stalin's growing control over the party. For the final stage the initiative came from Stalin. Unlike Trotsky, neither Bukharin nor Rykov represented a serious challenge to his position in the party; what led them into opposition was an attempt to restrain their former ally from making a radical new departure in policy.

Stalin did not yet exercise the autocratic power that he enjoyed in the late 1930s, nor did he possess Lenin's authority in matters of policy. He had therefore to win support in the party. How he did this constitutes the second theme. Bukharin was later to describe Stalin as "a master of dosage," knowing how to administer poison by degrees. There is no better example of this than the skill with which he habituated the Communist party to the use of "administrative measures" to enforce requisitioning, while presenting these as a response to a temporary emergency, never revealing until the winter of 1929–30 how far he meant to go in making them permanent.

It is likely that Stalin's control of the party machine would in any case have given him the support he needed. As one disillusioned Stalinist remarked: "We have defeated Bukharin not with argument but with party cards." Most historians, however, accept the view that the votes of the delegates who had risen through Stalin's patronage ratified an outcome that had already been decided by a smaller informal group of twenty to thirty "influentials," the party leaders of the most important Central Committee delegations, notably those representing Moscow, Leningrad, Siberia, the North Caucasus, and the Ukraine. [2]

These were men closely associated with Stalin, but not his creatures. Enjoying a certain independence in their own right, they were tough, pragmatic, and above all concerned with the transformation of Soviet Russia into a modern industrial country. Stalin could not ignore their opinion, and their influence is the most plausible explanation of his delay in adopting drastic measures against the right-wing leaders as he would have liked to do in the spring of 1929.

In the end they came down in favor of Stalin rather than Bukharin because they preferred Stalin's optimism and promise of resolute leadership to the pessimism and policy of concessions and compromises offered by the right. Three quotations from leading members of the Central Committee illustrate their disenchantment with the Bukharin group:

Kuibyshev: "History will not allow us to proceed quietly . . . by tired steps."

Kirov: "In a word, don't be in a hurry. . . . In a word, the right are for socialism, but without particular fuss, without struggle, without difficulties."

Ordzhonikidze [conceding Bukharin's good intentions]: "It is not a question of wishing but of policies, and Comrade Bukharin's policies will drag us backward, not forward." [3]

What the practical politicians failed to foresee was how much further and how much faster Stalin would carry them than anything they contemplated when voting for him. Bukharin had been a close ally and at one time as close a friend of Stalin's as anyone could be. He foresaw more clearly than anyone else the consequences for Russia and the party of Stalin's radical change of course, and Stalin was aware of this. In June 1928, after the breach had opened between them, Stalin said to Bukharin: "You and I are the Himalayas; the others are nobodies." If he could not win Bukharin over, he had to discredit him. In this he succeeded: Bukharin's warnings against "policies of adventurism" were disregarded and Bukharin himself forced to recant.

This leads to the third theme, the one that links 1928–29 to the 1930s. The economic and political arguments were sufficient to persuade a majority of the party leadership that a return to the original Bolshevik concept of a "revolution from above" imposed by Soviet power was the best way out of the impasse in which they found themselves. But what gave Stalin the psychological strength to override all obstacles was something else—his realization that another "October," identified with him personally as the earlier one was with Lenin, offered him, as nothing else could, the chance to justify his claim to fill the place left empty by Lenin's death.

II

MUCH MORE THAN ECONOMICS was involved in the campaign against the peasantry that lay at the heart of Stalin's revolution. The unique feature of Russian society was the size of its peasant population, 80 percent of the whole, the muzhiks of Russian literature and folklore, the "dark people," surrounding and outnumbering the inhabitants of the towns, living in a dense, impenetrable world and time of their own, with their own institutions and customs, their own language and beliefs, richly expressed in their store of proverbs. The Bolsheviks/Communists had never been able to come to terms with this phenomenon, which had no place in the Marxist schema. They resented their dependence on this huge rural sector, which they had been unable to bring within the framework of the socialist society that they were trying to create and which was left in a position to hold for ransom the builders of the new order. Not without justification, they saw it as the source of Russian backwardness, "A vast, inert and yet somehow threatening mass of people, barring Russia's path to industrialization, modernity, socialism; a kingdom of darkness that must be conquered before the Soviet Union could become the Promised Land."[4]

The party's hostility toward the peasantry was increased and their view of it skewed by the habit that Stalin encouraged of looking at rural society through Marxist spectacles and importing the notion of class stratification and class warfare. Central to this was Stalin's identification of the kulak as a rural capitalist, the exploiter who must be expropriated. It is not surprising that no clear or convincing definition of the kulak of the 1920s was ever produced. As the British historian Robert Conquest says: "However defined, the kulak, as an economic class, was no more than a party construct."[5] Such a construct was necessary to mobilize the party against "the class enemy" in the countryside for the task of extirpating him with the same ruthlessness as every other capitalist. Or as E. H. Carr put it: "It was no longer true that class analysis determined policy. Policy determined what form of class analysis was appropriate to the given situation."[6]

The policy as it finally emerged in 1929–30 amounted to nothing less than the attempt to find a permanent solution to the social as well as economic problems posed by the Soviet rural sector in a single operation. It was designed to produce three results. The first was the elimination of the kulaks, the most energetic and experienced farmers, who were to be ex-

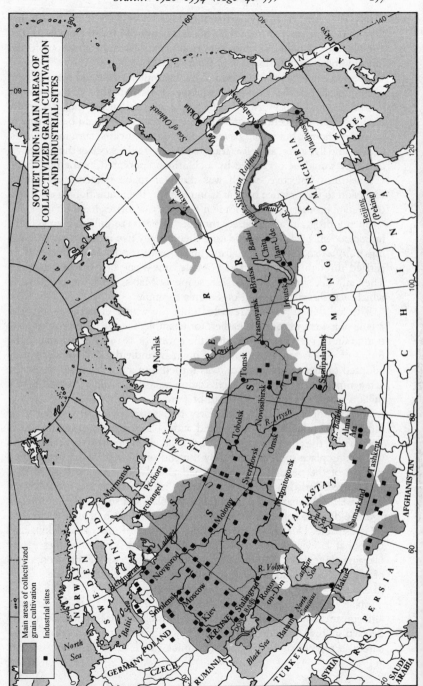

SOVIET UNION: MAIN AREAS OF
COLLECTIVIZED GRAIN CULTIVATION
AND INDUSTRIAL SITES

Main areas of collectivized
grain cultivation

■ Industrial sites

cluded altogether from any part in Soviet life. "Dekulakization" meant that they were to be evicted from their homes, deprived of all their possessions, and together with their families deported as outlaws to the most remote and inhospitable parts of Siberia and Central Asia.

The second was the conversion of the individual farms and strips of land owned by all the other peasants into large collective farms, often combining several villages. Henceforward, they would work as landless laborers on the land they had so recently acquired as their own. They would be allowed to keep their homes but would have to surrender their carts, farm implements, horses, and livestock, as well as their land, to form the stock of the collective, and they would be organized by a chairman appointed by the party.

The third objective, which was the first to be implemented, was a reversion to the practice of War Communism: the requisitioning of quotas of grain and other crops, by force if necessary, at prices fixed by the state.

Such a program would affect the lives of over 120 million people living in 600,000 villages, by consolidating their twenty-five million peasant holdings into 240,000 collective farms under state control, and it was to be carried through in the shortest possible time—one or two years at most. The only decision of comparable scope is Mao's Great Leap Forward, which was directly modeled on Stalin's example.

The full design was not revealed until the winter of 1929–30, but elements of it were introduced earlier; for example, the use of force to requisition grain in 1928 was repeated in the spring of 1929. In the summer the fixing of quotas for the delivery of grain by individual villages, originally adopted to meet an emergency, was turned into a regular practice. At the same time the target for collectivization was drastically increased to 7.8 million family holdings by the end of 1930.

Secret orders issued by the Party Secretariat put pressure on party officials down the line to push ahead with collectivization, using threats to "persuade" the peasants so that Stalin could claim publicly that the process was taking place spontaneously. By the end of the year Stalin declared 20 percent of the peasant population had already joined their local *kolkhoz* (collective farm). No one asked what this meant in practice, or whether it was true. What mattered was to fulfill the plan and so give the impression that the drive to collectivization was gathering momentum and would soon be irresistible. During the same period, the parallel process of dekulakization, that is eviction and deportation, forced out 33,000 families in the Ukraine alone, over 200,000 souls, to use the old Russian expression, many of whom died of cold, hunger, or exhaustion during the week-long journey to the east in cattle trucks.[7]

Stalin continued to insist that any "local difficulties" were due to kulak antagonism to the Soviet regime. The formula of class war that he had devised in 1928 provided an automatic justification for "retaliatory" measures: "Progress toward socialism cannot but lead to resistance to that progress by exploiter elements [that is, the kulaks] and the exploiters' resistance cannot but lead to an inexorable aggravation of the class struggle." [8]

In an article "Year of the Great Breakthrough," published in *Pravda* on November 7, the twelfth anniversary (NS) of the October Revolution, Stalin at last spoke without equivocation. Freed from any need for further restraint by the defeat and humiliation of the right opposition, he announced as already a fact

> the radical change that has taken place in the development of our agriculture from small, backward individual farming to large-scale, advanced, *collective* farming.
>
> The new and decisive feature of the peasant collective farm movement is that the peasants are joining the collective farms not in separate groups, but in whole villages, whole regions, whole districts, and even whole provinces.

With an eye to the meeting of the Central Committee Plenum about to take place, Stalin boasted:

> We are advancing full steam ahead along the path of industrialization—to socialism, leaving behind the age-long "Russian" backwardness. We are becoming a country of metal, a country of automobiles, a country of tractors. And when we have put the USSR on an automobile, and the muzhik on a tractor, let the worthy capitalists, who boast so loudly of their "civilization," try to overtake us. We shall see which countries may then be "classified" as backward and which as advanced. [9]

There was now no hesitation in openly intensifying pressure from the center to speed up the process of collectivization. Molotov urged the members of the Central Committee to seize an opportunity not to be missed to solve the agrarian problem once and for all in a matter of weeks or months, speaking of "a decisive advance" over the next four and a half months.

A new All-Union Commissariat for Agriculture and a new Commission for Collectivization were set up to carry it out, but their plans did not satisfy Stalin. His fiftieth birthday fell in December and was made the occasion for a fulsome celebration of his emergence as Lenin's successor, the party's new *vozhd',* committed to a "rural October" which would open the way to the construction of socialism. In the exuberance of victory Stalin demanded new deadlines for completing the collectivization of the grain-producing areas—one year or at the very most two, for the Ukraine, the North Caucasus, and the Middle Volga.

Since the middle peasants, according to the official view, had already turned to the collectives, the time had come to deal finally with the kulaks, "the accursed enemy of the collective farm movement." On December 27 Stalin, in an address to Marxist students on the agrarian problem, in effect condemned to deportation and death several million men, women, and children, with the dread formula:

> We have gone over from a policy of limiting the exploiting tendencies of the kulak to a policy of liquidating the kulak as a class.
>
> To take the offensive against the kulaks means to deal the kulak class such a blow that it will no longer rise to its feet. That's what we Bolsheviks call an offensive. [10]

The majority of the peasant households collectivized so far came from the 30 percent of the rural population in the poor peasant and landless laborer categories who had least to lose by the change. But the middle peasantry who made up two-thirds, and had much more to lose, were still hesitating, despite Stalin's confident declarations. The brutal treatment of the kulaks was meant as an object lesson of what would happen to the middle peasants if they continued to hold back. A decree issued by the Central Committee on January 5, 1930, after drastic revision by Stalin, doubled, even trebled the pace of collectivization in some regions. Even that was not enough for Stalin, who insisted on weekly reports: The target was to finish the business by the autumn of 1930. The new slogan for the harassed party and Soviet officials was "Who will collectivize fastest?" For the rural population it was, "He who does not join the kolkhoz is an enemy of Soviet power." The campaign for procuring grain and that for getting the peasants into the kolkhozes were merged.

Despite repeated efforts to stir up class hatred and set the poorer against the more prosperous peasants, the results fell short of what was hoped. Of course there were some in most locations willing to take part in attacking and plundering their neighbors, especially when this was encouraged by the authorities. But the mass of the peasantry was deeply shocked by the methods used, and there was none of the spontaneity shown when they had seized the big estates of the landowners in 1917–18.

"Collectivization was in essence a gigantic party-and-police operation." [11] At the regional and lower levels it was in the hands of a troika, composed of the secretary of the party committee, the chairman of the regional or local Soviet, and the local OGPU chief. To overcome the inhibitions of local party members, 25,000 party activists from the cities, usually entirely ignorant of rural life, were sent to act as shock brigades, often as chairmen of the newly organized collectives. They were given a two-week course in January 1930 and then sent off to their assignments. Their job, which many tackled with enthusiasm, was to drag the peasants out of their backward condition and force them into the enlightened world of socialism. If no one else would do it, *they* would decide who was a kulak, and how to collectivize. Another 72,000 workers were made available in the spring of 1930 on temporary assignment and 50,000 troops and junior army officers were given special training for the campaign.

Beyond the bare statement of intent and the need to speed up the process, no guidance was available on the structure and organization of the collectives, the size of which Stalin constantly insisted should be increased—or on how decisions were to be taken, not even how payment should be made to the members. There was no time to wait for the planners to work out the answers to such questions: What mattered was to drive the peasants into accepting that this was their only future.

The attack on the peasant economy was accompanied by a fierce campaign against the Orthodox Church, the center of traditional peasant culture, which was seen by the Stalinist leadership as one of the main obstacles to collectivization. In village after village, not only was the church closed, but the cross was knocked from the cupola, the bells removed, and icons burned. Historic Russian churches were the object of destruction or wrecking and many priests were arrested. The monasteries were closed, although many of them operated as model agricultural cooperatives, and thousands of monks and nuns were deported to Siberia. By the end of 1930, roughly 80 percent of village churches are said to have been closed.

On March 1 it was announced that in less than two months the number of collectivized households had more than trebled—from 4,393,100 in January 1930 to 14,264,300. The confusion and misery caused by this rape of a traditional society in which the lives of 120 million who lived on the land were wrenched out of their accustomed ways beggar description. It was more than flesh and blood could stand. Resistance, at first sporadic and hesitant, spread rapidly; a particular feature in the Ukraine and North Caucasus was the part played by women. OGPU and Red Army units had to be called in and in a number of areas were hard pressed to put down what amounted to peasant uprisings. Mass arrests, shootings, and deportation followed.

The peasants' most effective resistance was to slaughter their cattle. In two months at the beginning of 1930 alone they killed 14 million out of the country's 1928 total of 70.5 million as well as a third of all pigs, and a quarter of all sheep and goats, rather than see them driven into the kolkhozes. Stalin was impervious to human suffering; but the loss of so valuable an asset as farm animals was a different matter, an economic disaster from which Soviet agriculture did not recover for twenty-five years.

Various Politburo members, including Ordzhonikidze and Kalinin, had become aware of conditions in the countryside during visits in February, and on the twenty-fourth of that month a special Central Committee meeting was held to discuss the situation. It was agreed that a public statement was needed and the Politburo commissioned Stalin to draft it. It was assumed that he would clear it with the other members of the Politburo before publication. But Stalin had other ideas and produced an article that took them completely by surprise.

On March 2, five months after it had published "Year of the Great Breakthrough," *Pravda* carried another signed article, headlined "Dizzy with Success," in which the man who had first conceived of and then been

the driving force behind the whole operation blandly reproved party activists for allowing themselves to become intoxicated with the belief "We can
do anything."

They become dizzy with success, lose all sense of proportion, lose the
faculty of understanding realities, reveal a tendency to overestimate their
own strength and to underestimate the struggle of the enemy; reckless
attempts are made to settle all the problems of socialist construction in
"two ticks." . . .
    Who benefits by these distortions, this bureaucratic decreeing of a
collective farm movement, these unseemly threats against the peasants?
Nobody but our enemies!
    And what about those "revolutionaries" if one may call them that, who
begin the job of organizing collective farms by taking the bells from the
churches. To take a bell—just think!—how r-r-revolutionary!

Stalin solemnly reminded his readers that the success of the collective
farm policy—which he declared was already assured—rested on its *voluntary* character:

Collective farms cannot be set up by force. To do so would be stupid and
reactionary. The collective farm movement must rely on the active support of the great bulk of the peasantry. . . .
    Can it be said that the voluntary principle and that of allowing for local
peculiarities are not violated in a number of districts? No, unfortunately
that cannot be said. . . .

Calling upon the party to put an end to these "distortions" and the frame
of mind that produced them, Stalin ended:

The art of leadership is a serious matter. One must not lag behind the
movement, because to do so is to become isolated from the masses. But
neither must one rush ahead, for to rush ahead is to lose contact with the
masses. He who wants to lead a movement, and at the same time keep
in touch with the masses, must wage a war on two fronts—against those
who lag behind and against those who rush on ahead. [12]

Stalin's article had the effect of a bombshell. Thousands of party officials
and activists who had been sweating their guts out and driving themselves
to the limit to carry out what they believed to be the orders of the general
secretary were taken aback to find it was they, not Stalin, who were out of
touch with the masses. Measures were taken, with great publicity, to punish
those local officials who had "violated revolutionary legality" in the countryside; few of those who had issued the orders were brought to justice. Even
his enemies could not fail to be impressed by the adroitness with which
Stalin had diverted criticism by making himself the spokesman of the critics
and recapturing the initiative, while still claiming that collectivization had
been a great success.
    The peasants did not wait to take advantage of this abrupt disavowal of

forced measures. In all, nine million families left the collectives. By August 1, 1930, the March 1 figure of 50 percent of households collectivized had fallen to 21 percent. A new model statute for the kolkhoz allowed its members to keep a cow, sheep, and pigs, and the implements to work private plots of their own, a victory that was some compensation for the slaughter of their livestock.

But the government retreat was only temporary. Those who left the collectives found every difficulty placed in their way. The allocation of land and seed was delayed. When it was made, they were given the worst land, half of what they had had before, marsh, scrubland, wasteland several miles away. They lost their vegetable gardens and could not recover their implements, horses, or cows. With the harvest, they had to meet heavier grain quotas and fines for failure to fulfill them. Those who made trouble suffered the fate of the kulaks in a second wave of arrests and deportation.

At the Sixteenth Party Congress in the summer of 1930, Stalin boasted of the achievement of collectivization and the liquidation of the kulaks. He called for recognition of his "rural October" and recorded it in the congress resolution:

> If the confiscation of the land from the landowners was the first step of the October Revolution in the countryside, the changeover to collective farms is the second and the decisive step which marks a most important stage in building the foundation of a socialist society in the USSR.[13]

Not one of the 2,100 delegates questioned Stalin's claim, or so much as referred to the crisis that had convulsed rural Russia in the previous twelve months. Even the elements worked in his favor, producing a bumper crop, the biggest since 1913, which made it easy to brush aside reports of difficulties as exaggerated and justify resuming pressure on the peasants to return to the collectives.

Many fled to the towns looking for work in the new construction and industrial projects of the Five-Year Plan. Although this was discouraged, according to Soviet sources no fewer than 4.1 million peasants moved from the villages to the towns in 1931 and a total of 17.7 million during the years 1929 through 1935.[14] Tougher measures in 1932–33 included the reintroduction of the hated "internal passports," the abolition of which had been one of the main demands of the radical-revolutionary movement in tsarist Russia, and one of the first reforms after the October Revolution. Now office and industrial workers were tied to their work by their passports, peasants to the land by the denial of one.

By then the back of peasant resistance had been broken. The number of peasant households collectivized rose to a total of over fifteen million by the end of 1933; by the end of 1934, nine-tenths of the sown acreage of the USSR was under collective cultivation. However, this only shifted the battle between the state and the peasants to different ground, to the issue that had started the whole process of procurement: how to secure the delivery of sufficient grain to meet the needs of a rapidly growing population. Kaganovich declared that it was not collectivization but procurement that was "the touchstone by which our strength and weakness, and the strength and weakness of the enemy are measured."

The majority of the peasants might now be collectivized, but every twist and turn of peasant cunning was employed to stop the state from taking everything it wanted, and leaving them with nothing. Nature might produce a bumper crop in 1930, but it took a special mobilization of workers and party officials, heavy fines, mass searches, and arrests to get possession of little more than a quarter of it (22 out of 77 million tons). And the bumper crop was not repeated. The disorganization, destruction, and waste that had accompanied the upheaval and the gross incompetence with which many of the kolkhozes were managed meant a succession of much reduced harvests and much heavier pressure in the form of forced requisitioning. While harvests (except in the very good weather of 1937) remained below even the inadequate levels of 1928 through 1932, state procurements rose from an average of 18.2 million tons from 1928 to 1932 to an average of 27.5 million from 1933 to 1937.[15] After the demands of the state had been met (and the kolkhozes that produced the most were squeezed the hardest, with the authorities coming back three or four times), little enough was left for fodder and seed, even less for distribution among the work force, which was officially stated to have the lowest priority.

A huge bureaucratic network was built up to supervise and manage this crucial operation, adding a further stratum to be supported by the peasants, which became a byword for corruption and inefficiency: "The chairman of our kolkhoz would not know one end of a pig from another, and spends all his time drinking with his cronies."

Another stratum was added with the Machine Tractor Stations (MTS), which had a monopoly of agricultural machinery, and after June 1931 were charged with organizing the work on the farms and the delivery of their produce. The tractor was the much-lauded symbol of the progressive character of the Soviet agrarian revolution, the "industrialization" of the countryside. Payment in kind (20 percent of the grain harvest) for the MTS's service came second only to fulfilling the state's needs. After January 1933 a deputy chief, always an OGPU agent, was appointed to head a political department in each MTS, and these departments soon became a decisive factor in the countryside, with overriding powers.

The root of the trouble, to which Stalin's revolution from above failed to address itself, was that the whole system remained dependent on the labor of the peasants but offered them less than ever before as an incentive to work harder. If they did, twice as much was taken from them. Tied once again to the soil, with party and state officials taking the place of the landlords, they regarded themselves with justice as twentieth-century serfs, no better off—if anything, worse off—than they had been before the emancipation of 1861.

The Central Committee decree of January 11, 1933, however, giving new powers to the MTS, recognized only sabotage and conspiracy as explanations of the poor performance of collectivized agriculture.

> Anti-Soviet elements, penetrating the kolkhozes in the capacity of accountants, managers, storekeepers, brigade leaders, and so on, are trying to organize wrecking, putting machines out of order, sowing badly, squandering kolkhoz property, undermining labor discipline, organizing the theft of seeds, secret granaries, and the sabotage of the grain harvest. Sometimes they succeed in breaking up the kolkhozes. [16]

An average of a third of the agrarian bureaucracy was charged with wrecking. "Kulaks," needless to say, had penetrated it right to the top. Earlier trials of the most prominent, charged with being "organizers of famine and agents of imperialism," were given prominence in September 1930. N. A. Kondratiev, a former minister of food, and a number of economic specialists were indicted as leaders of a "Toiling Peasant Party," which was alleged by the OGPU to include nine underground groups in Moscow alone, in ministries and research institutes, and a membership of between one and two hundred thousand in the countryside. Over a thousand "members" of the "party" were arrested. The truth had to wait until 1987 when the Soviet Supreme Court declared that the "Toiling Peasant Party" had never existed and then went on to annul the trials and rehabilitate the fifteen leading defendants. [17]

III

THERE WAS NO PART of Russia where dekulakization and collectivization bore more harshly on the peasantry than the Ukraine, where the social and economic problems they created were complicated by a Ukrainian nationalism that Stalin was determined to crush.

The Ukrainians were (and are) the second-largest nationality in the Soviet Union, with a population in 1930 of twenty-five million, more numerous than the Poles. Their country is as large as France and hardly less rich in natural resources, both in minerals and in its famous black earth. Kiev, which grew up on the ninth-century trade route from the Baltic to the Black Sea via the Dnieper, became Eastern Europe's earliest political and cultural center, and the Ukrainians' identity as a nation has survived as many terrible calamities as the Poles'.

Freeing itself from Polish overlordship in the seventeenth century, the Ukraine was conquered by the Russians in the eighteenth. The Ukrainian peasantry were enslaved and their institutions, including the Ukrainian Church, treated to the same harsh Russification as other subject peoples under Russian rule. In 1740, in left-bank Ukraine lying to the east of the River Dnieper, which divides the country, there had been 866 schools; in 1800 there were none. In 1863 an edict declared that there was no Ukrainian language, merely a dialect of Russian, and banned Ukrainian schools, newspapers, and books.

The West was inclined to accept the Russian claim, ignoring the fact that elsewhere in Europe although two languages may belong to the same linguistic family (in the case of Ukrainian and Russian, to the East Slavic) that is no guide to a shared national or cultural identity, as the examples of Portugal and Spain, Norway and Sweden, Holland and Germany show. As in other Slav countries, the national idea and the use of the Ukrainian language survived, not among the professional classes, who were either Russian or accepted assimilation, but among poets and intellectuals, and above all among the peasantry. An active national movement was reborn in the early years of the twentieth century, and a Ukrainian Central Council (Rada), proclaiming a short-lived Ukrainian People's Republic, was formed when tsarist rule collapsed in 1917.

The Ukraine, however, was the first East European country to experience, from 1918 to 1920, the forcible suppression of its independence by Russia, an experience extended to the Baltic states, Poland, Hungary, and the rest of Eastern Europe between 1939 and 1945. The Ukrainians, the largest national group in Europe without independence, only achieved it with the breakup of the Soviet Union in 1991.

During the 1920s the Ukraine still enjoyed a considerable measure of cultural and linguistic freedom. But the former commissar of nationalities had not changed his mind about the divisive nature of national feeling, whether Ukrainian or Georgian and, when the opportunity offered, its elimination would still be on his agenda.

By 1929-30 the time had come, and Stalin was ready to attack "the nationalist deviation in the Ukraine," linking it with collectivization, which would accomplish "the destruction of Ukrainian nationalism's social base— the individual landholdings." "The kulak was blamed as a bearer of nationalist ideas, the nationalist as a sponsor of kulak attitudes."[18]

In July 1929, some 5,000 members of an alleged underground organization, the Union for the Liberation of the Ukraine, were arrested and the forty-five most prominent scholars and intellectuals among them arraigned in a set piece public trial, staged in the Kharkov Opera House. Among the charges, in addition to conspiring to seize power, was one of working to make the Ukrainian language as distinct as possible from Russian. After confessions had been obtained by the usual methods, they were sentenced to long terms of imprisonment. In February 1931 further arrests took place, this time of leading Ukrainians who had returned from exile in the mid-1920s and were now accused of forming a "Ukrainian National Center." Their leaders were said to be the doyen of Ukrainian intellectuals, Mykhailo Hrushevsky, and Vsevolod Holubovych, the former premier of the Ukrainian Republic during its brief period of independence.

At the peasant level, which Stalin declared "the very essence of the nationality problem,"[19] collectivization was pressed more strongly and met with more militant resistance in the Ukraine than in the rest of Russia. By mid-1932, 70 percent of Ukrainian peasants were in kolkhozes, compared with the figure of 59 percent for Russia overall. But this only meant that the class war now had to be pursued within the kolkhozes, where (so Stalin declared) many kulaks and other anti-Soviet elements had sought to take refuge—and where they were responsible for the resistance to meeting the procurement quotas.

Stalin was incensed with the efforts of the Ukrainian party leadership to get the targets set by Moscow reduced. Stanislav Kossior, the Ukrainian first secretary, passed the message on. Addressing a meeting of activists in the summer of 1930 he told them:

> The peasant is adopting a new tactic. He refuses to reap the harvest. He wants the bread grain to die in order to choke the Soviet government with the bony hand of famine. But the enemy miscalculates. We will show him what famine is. Your task is to stop the kulak sabotage of the harvest; you must bring it in to the last grain and immediately send it off to the delivery point. The peasants are not working. They are counting on previously harvested grain they have hidden in pits. We must force them to open their pits. [20]

In normal times the Ukraine and the North Caucasus provided half the Soviet Union's total marketable grain. In the good harvest of 1930, the Ukraine alone accounted for 27 percent of the total Soviet grain harvest but had to supply 38 percent of the grain deliveries, 7.7 million tons. In 1931, when the harvest everywhere was much poorer (in the Ukraine 18.3 million tons as against 23.9 million in 1930), the same quota of 7.7 million tons was demanded, now 42 percent of the total grain deliveries.

Protests to Moscow met with no response, and 7 million tons was actually collected but only at the cost of leaving so little for the peasants themselves that they were reduced to a near-starvation level by the spring of 1932. Stalin was convinced that the root of the trouble was the Ukrainians' anti-Soviet attitude. Party purges were ordered, and delivery of the same quota of 7.7 million tons for 1932 although the new harvest in the Ukraine produced only 14.7 million tons. At a meeting with Molotov and Kaganovich in July, the Ukrainian party and government leaders spoke forcefully of the "unrealistic plans" that had been accepted by the kolkhozes and the impossibility of fulfilling them. Molotov dismissed such talk as "anti-Bolshevik." "There will be no concessions or vacillations in the fulfillment of the task set by the party and the Soviet government." [21]

The Ukrainian Central Committee was under no illusions about what awaited them if they failed, but despite great efforts the target (finally reduced to 6.6 million) could not be met. Stalin was unrelenting: These peasants, these *Ukrainian* peasants, must be made to produce the grain he was convinced they had hidden away. Two senior *apparatchiki* were sent from Moscow to stiffen the resolve of the local party and a second procurement was announced. A new decree declared all collective-farm property such as cattle and grain to be state property and threatened the death penalty for offenses against it such as theft. A decree of August 7, 1932, set down on paper in Stalin's handwriting, prescribed death by shooting or (in mitigating circumstances) ten years' imprisonment for stealing collective-farm property and prohibited amnesty in all such cases. Since any amount, however small, could and often was made the basis of conviction, the law became known among the peasants as the "five stalks law." This was not a bluff: 55,000 people were convicted under it in less than six months, and 1,500 death sentences were reported in one month from the Kharkov court alone. Thousands more activists were mobilized from outside the Ukraine, to search and browbeat people into saying where they had hidden their reserves.

By now people were dying of starvation, not only in the Ukraine. One of the activists, Lev Kopelev, later to become one of the best-known Russian writers in exile, describes his experiences in *The Education of a True Believer*:

> I heard the children . . . choking, coughing with screams. And I saw the looks of the men: frightened, pleading, hateful, dully impassive, extinguished with despair or flaring up with half-mad, daring ferocity. "Take it. Take everything away. There's still a pot of borscht on the stove. It's plain, got no meat. But still it's got beets, taters, and cabbage. And it's salted! Better take it, comrade citizens! Here, hang on. I'll take off my shoes. They're patched and repatched, but maybe they'll have some use for the proletariat, for our dear Soviet power."
>
> It was excruciating to see and hear all this. And even worse to take part in it. . . . I persuaded myself, explained to myself, I mustn't give in to debilitating pity. We were realizing historical necessity. We were performing our revolutionary duty. We were obtaining grain for the socialist fatherland. . . .
>
> I saw what "total collectivization" meant—how they kulakized and dekulakized, how they mercilessly stripped the peasants in the winter of 1932–33. I took part in this myself, scouring the countryside, searching for hidden grain, testing the earth with a rod for buried grain. With the others I emptied out the old folks' storage chests, stopping my ears to the children's crying. . . .
>
> In the terrible spring of 1933, I saw people dying from hunger. I saw women and children with distended bellies, turning blue, still breathing but with vacant lifeless eyes. And corpses—corpses in ragged sheepskin coats and cheap felt boots; corpses in peasant huts, in the melting snow in old Vologda, under the bridges of Kharkov. . . . I saw all this and did not go out of my mind. Nor did I curse those who had sent me to take away the peasants' grain in the winter, or the spring; to persuade the barely walking, skeleton thin or sickly swollen people to go into the fields in order "to fulfill the Bolshevik sowing plan in shock-worker style." Nor did I lose my faith. As before, I believed because I wanted to believe. [22]

In spite of all the party's efforts, at the end of 1932 only 4.7 million instead of 6.6 million tons had been delivered. Stalin's response was to blame sabotage by kulak elements and a lack of vigilance on the part of local officials, tainted with Ukrainian nationalism. He called for renewed war on the "class enemy." When R. Terekhov, the Kharkov first secretary, told him that famine was raging in the Ukraine, Stalin sneered at him:

> We have been told you are a good storyteller, Comrade Terekhov. You made up a story about hunger, you meant to frighten us; but nothing doing. Why don't you leave your post as regional secretary and the Central Committee and go to work for the Writers' Union? You could write your fables and folk would read them. [23]

Stalin, who took over personal command of what he regarded as a military operation, called for "a smashing blow" at the *kolkhozniki,* because "whole squads of them had turned against the Soviet state." [24]

A third procurement levy was announced, and Pavel Postyshev, the secretary of the Central Committee, was sent to reorganize the Ukrainian party, carry out a thorough purge, and put new steel into it. Two hundred and thirty-seven secretaries of party district committees and 249 chairmen of district executive committees were replaced. In the North Caucasus, where there was a Ukrainian population of three million, Kaganovich threw out half the party officials, many of whom were arrested for sabotage and exiled to "distant locations." Ten thousand fresh activists were transferred to the Ukraine, 3,000 of them to act as chairmen of kolkhozes, party secretaries, and organizers. With fresh vigor they renewed the struggle for grain against a starving peasantry.

PEOPLE HAD BEEN DYING all through the winter of 1932–33, but death on a mass scale began early in March 1933. In other parts of Russia, outside the areas with large Ukrainian populations, shortage of food was much less, or, as in the rich Russian "Central Agricultural Region," there was no famine at all. The total Soviet grain crop was no worse than that of 1931, only 12 percent below the 1926–1930 average, and well above famine level. It was not a crop failure but the excessive demands of the state, ruthlessly enforced, that cost the lives of as many as five million Ukrainian peasants, out of a farm population of twenty to twenty-five million.

There were large reserves of grain that Stalin could have ordered made available, as the tsarist government always had, and the Soviet government too in the famine of 1918 through 1921. But in 1932–33 it was strictly forbidden to organize relief. There would have been even larger reserves if the government had not insisted on exporting abroad a massive 4.8 million tons of grain in 1930 and the even larger amount of 5.2 million tons in 1931. In 1932 and 1933 these exports were cut to under 2 million tons. In fact, there were stores of grain in the Ukraine itself, some of it in local granaries under armed guard—much of it in large heaps piled high in the open (for example at Kiev-Petrovka station), where it was left to rot, still under guard.

Hordes of the starving wandered across the countryside, gathering at the stations, only to be chased away by the guards. Corpses were piled by the sides of the roads, even in the towns: Only in the larger cities were the dead collected each morning and thrown into pits. Troops were stationed along the borders of the Ukraine with the rest of Russia to prevent anyone from leaving. Those who attempted to get onto trains without special permits were turned away and sent back. Any who tried to make their way over the frontier from Russia with supplies of bread were liable to be arrested and have their packs confiscated.

Victor Kravchenko, an activist at the time who later escaped abroad, was told by M. M. Khatayevich, one of Stalin's agents:

> A ruthless struggle is going on between the peasantry and our regime. It's a struggle to the death. This year was a test of our strength and their endurance. It took a famine to show them who is master here. It has cost millions of lives, but the collective farm system is here to stay. [25]

An important part of Stalin's policy was what Boris Pasternak has called "the inhuman power of the lie." No word about the famine was allowed to appear in the press, and anyone referring to it was subject to arrest for anti-Soviet propaganda and five years in a labor camp. Reports began to appear in the foreign press and efforts were made to mount an international relief operation from abroad, such as had operated in 1921, but these were rebuffed as based on lies, and the Soviet press printed resolutions by collective farmers rejecting such impertinent offers of help. Kalinin, the only member of the ruling group from a peasant background, was instructed to tell a congress of collective-farm workers in June 1933: "Every farmer knows that people who are in trouble because of lack of bread are in that trouble not as the result of a poor harvest, but because they were lazy and refused to do an honest day's work." [26]

Deaths from the famine reached their peak in March through May 1933. Although the mortality rate remained abnormally high, the number of deaths began to fall after the end of May. Reports from the Ukraine may at last have produced recognition of the scale of the disaster, and of the consequences. Eyewitnesses who managed to travel through the countryside, including a small number of foreigners, such as the British journalist Malcolm Muggeridge, reported that "some of the most fertile land in the world has been reduced to a melancholy desert." Another British eyewitness described "Field after field covered with ungarnered grain that had been allowed to rot . . . and districts where it was possible to travel for a whole day between fields of blackening wheat." [27] If the peasants no longer had the strength to keep the fields free of weeds and bring in the crop, what prospect was there of their being able to carry out the sowings for the next harvest?

This was a practical argument that could make an impression on Stalin and the Politburo, when humanitarian pleas left them cold. On February 25, 1933, a seed subsidy for the next harvest was authorized, with 325,000 tons to go to the Ukraine. The last grain requisition was not called off until the middle of March, but by April Mikoyan was reported in Kiev ordering the release of some army grain reserves to the peasants. In May efforts were at last made to save the survivors' lives, among them opening clinics and making food available to the starving, as well as fodder for the emaciated horses.

From May onwards, a depleted and exhausted work force was pressed into starting on the sowing. Once again students and party workers from the towns, backed up by army squads, were mobilized to help. The purge of local party cadres continued, and Stalin warned Kossior, the Ukrainian first secretary, in a personal letter with copies sent to the secretaries of all provincial, district, and city party committees:

> For the last time you are reminded that any repetition of the mistakes of last year will compel the Central Committee to take even more drastic measures. And then, if you will pardon my saying so, even their old party beards will not save these comrades. [28]

The same letter laid down that only 10 percent of the total threshed grain could remain in the kolkhozes "for subsistence, after the fulfillment of deliveries, payment to the Machine Tractor Stations, seed and forage." After these and all the other claims on the harvest, including exports, reserve stocks for the army, and increased rations for party officials and activists, the last on the list were the peasants, who were expected to do all the work for a subsistence standard of living at the best.

Although hard to document and quantify, there is sufficient evidence to show that Russian peasants from outside the Ukraine were moved in to take over deserted villages, "meeting the wishes" of inhabitants of the central districts of the USSR to settle in "the free parts of the Ukraine and North Caucasus." [29] Such moves were meant to be permanent, and special rations were provided as an inducement.

Having dealt his "smashing blow" to the peasantry, Stalin continued his campaign against the national identity of the Ukrainians. One way in which this had been sustained in the countryside since time immemorial had been by the *kobzars,* peasant bards, often blind, who wandered from village to village singing songs and reciting ballads, which reminded the Ukrainian peasantry of their independent and heroic past. Such a survival was an anachronism in the brave new world of Soviet Communism. The bards were invited to their first All-Ukrainian Congress, several hundred of them, only to be arrested and for the most part shot. Reporting this, the Russian composer Dmitri Shostakovich says in his *Testimony* that the *kobzars* were "a living museum, the country's living history: all its songs, all its music and poetry. And they were almost all shot, almost all these pathetic blind men killed. . . . Hurting a blind man—what could be lower?" [30]

Stalin's henchman Dmitri Manuilsky (described by Trotsky as "the most repulsive renegade of Ukrainian Communism") was appointed to help Postyshev root out the "petit-bourgeois, nationalist deviationists" by a purge of every conceivable cultural and scientific organization in the Ukraine. Kossior reported: "Whole counterrevolutionary nests were formed in the People's Commissariats of Education, of Agriculture, of Justice, in the Ukrainian Institute of Marxism-Leninism, the Agricultural Academy, the Sherchenko Institute, etc." All of these "enemy agents," Postyshev declared, had been "hiding behind the broad back of the Bolshevik Skrypnyk," the Ukrainian commissar of education. After three times defending himself before the Ukrainian Central Committee, Mykola Skrypnyk shot himself (July 7, 1933), only to be condemned for "an act of faintheartedness particularly unworthy of a member of the Central Committee of the All-Union Communist Party."

With "Skrypnyk's nationalist deviation unmasked," Postyshev was able to claim the successful purge of over "2,000 nationalists and White-guardists to my personal knowledge." In February 1934 he boasted to the Seventeenth Party Congress that "we have annihilated the nationalist counterrevolution during the past year; exposed and destroyed the nationalist deviation."[31]

MANY ATTEMPTS have been made by demographers to work out the human losses due to dekulakization and collectivization as well as famine in the USSR as a whole. While the overall figures for the loss of livestock are reasonably complete, more than fifty years later the Soviet government has still not made available the figures that would establish the true scale of the catastrophe. All Khrushchev says in his memoirs is: "I can't give an exact figure because no one was keeping it. All we knew was that people were dying in enormous numbers."[32]

It is necessary first to look at the estimates of those who suffered dekulakization and deportation. According to later Soviet studies, the original figure of those to be evicted was fixed by the Politburo at 1,065,000 families, that is between five and six million persons. In practice the total is recognized to have been much higher, including many middle peasants, and to have extended until May 1933 when a decree signed by Stalin and Molotov ended mass deportations and fixed future movements at the rate of 12,000 individual families a year. The Soviet agricultural economist, V. A. Tikhonov, estimates that about three million peasant households were liquidated between 1929 and the end of 1933, leaving not fewer than fifteen million people without shelter or any place in the future rural society.[33]

What happened to them? All of them lost their farms, their homes, and their possessions. Some were shot. Some were sent to labor camps such as those on the White Sea Canal or the gold mines at Magadan, the coldest area of the northern hemisphere, where whole camps, including the guards and guard dogs, are known to have perished from the terrible winters.

Some escaped to the cities and got jobs, at least for a time, in industrial plants short of labor. The majority, including the women and children in kulak families, were deported in cattle trucks to the harsh conditions of the Northern Territory and Siberia. A great many children died on the way. Frequently the kulaks were put down in unsettled country, without any shelter or food, and left to fend for themselves. To take a specific example: The former German Communist Wolfgang Leonhard has described how kulaks from the Ukraine and Central Russia were marched into empty country between Petropavlovsk and Lake Balkash in Kazakhstan. A survivor whom he met in Karaganda told him:

> There were just some pegs stuck in the ground with little notices saying: Settlement No. 5, No. 6, and so on. The peasants were brought here and told that now they had to look after themselves. So there they dug themselves holes in the ground. A great many died of cold and hunger in the early years. [34]

Attempts to calculate the total number of kulaks deported produce a rough figure of ten to twelve million, of which a third were dead by 1935; a third in labor camps; a third in special settlements. Like the Jews under the Nazis, the kulaks (or anyone whom a local official or a neighbor with a grudge declared to be one) were pushed out of human society and declared to be subhuman. In both cases what counted was not what a kulak or a Jew had done, but the simple fact of what they were, which condemned them, members of an outlawed class or race denied all human rights.

In the absence of reliable official figures, Soviet statistics have long been a subject of continuing controversy. One of the first to attempt to bring together and compare the different estimates for deaths was Robert Conquest in *The Great Terror,* published in 1968. His most recent estimate, published in 1991, puts the number of those who died prematurely between the beginning of 1930 and the beginning of 1937 at around 11 million.

Of this total, Conquest concludes that around 7 million died in the famine of 1932–33, around five million of them in the Ukraine. The remaining figure of around four million is made up of around 1.5 million believed to have perished in the Central Asian republic of Kazakhstan, [35] and around 2.5 million as a result of collectivization and dekulakization. In addition to the 11 million who died before 1937, another 2.5 million peasants arrested before 1937 died in the camps or exile in 1937–38.[*] For comparison, Conquest adds: "Though confined to a single state, the number dying in Stalin's war against the peasants was higher than the total deaths for all countries in World War One." [36]

*See p. 501.

IV

WHILE STALIN and the Soviet leadership were waging war on the Russian rural population—for it was hardly less than that—the parallel process of industrialization was being carried out under the Five-Year Plan.

Collectivization in Stalin's eyes was directed to breaking up the alien world of peasant Russia and forcing its inhabitants into the framework of a socialist society. But industry was the matrix within which socialism itself had developed; and the industrial working class was its natural constituency. Once freed from the dead hand of capitalism, industrialization was seen as the key to the new socialist society, into which a mechanized agriculture with its Machine Tractor Stations, its giant "grain factories" and industrial farming would be assimilated.

The question was how fast the Soviet Union could proceed to build up new investment in heavy industry. In 1926 Stalin had poured scorn on Trotsky and the left as "super-industrializers," opposing their project for a great hydroelectrical power station on the Dnieper, which he said made as much sense as a muzhik buying a gramophone instead of a cow. Stalin's conversion to the virtues of industrialization, however, made the Five-Year Plan one of the great myths of the first half of the century, not only in the Soviet Union but in the rest of the world, a symbol of the superiority of Communist planning over the failure of capitalism in the face of the Depression.

It was characteristic of the mythlike character of the "Plan" that it was formally adopted in mid-1929; simultaneously backdated to the previous October, in which month it was retrospectively deemed to have begun; and finally declared in January 1933 to have been fulfilled, not in five, but in four and a quarter years. It would be difficult to improve on the Oxford scholar Ronald Hingley's description:

> Forever publicizing percentages and tonnages relating to what allegedly had been, was being, should be, would be, could be, might have been produced in the way of coal, oil, pig iron, steel, tractors, combine harvesters, factories, hydroelectric stations and the like, Stalin invested with an air of spurious exactitude pronouncements essentially magical and liturgical.[37]

Under the slogan "There are no fortresses which cannot be conquered by the Bolsheviks," Stalin systematically demanded the impossible. Russia produced 3.3 million tons of pig iron in 1928; Stalin set an annual target of 10 million tons by the end of 1933, then raised it to 17 million by the end of 1932. In fact, Russian output of pig iron was only just approaching the final figure in 1941. Steel production at 4 million tons per annum in 1928 was given a target of 10.4 million and achieved less than 6 million. The electricity industry, producing just over 5 million kilowatt hours, was ordered to reach a target of 22 million kilowatt hours, and achieved 13.4

million. Economists and managers who questioned such targets as unrealistic were denounced as wreckers.

But the magic worked. After the gray compromises of the NEP, the Plan revived the flagging faith of the party. Here at last was the chance to pour their enthusiasm into building the New Jerusalem they had been promised. The boldness of the targets, the sacrifices demanded, and the vision of what "backward" Russia might achieve provided an inspiring contrast with an "advanced" West with millions unemployed and resources left to waste because of the Depression. None of Stalin's targets might be achieved, but in every case output was raised: 6 million tons of steel was little more than half the 10 million allowed for, but 50 percent more than the starting figure.

Waste and inefficiency were often as great as on the collective farms: There were constant breakdowns, and valuable machinery was left to rust or was ruined by unskilled operators, many of them peasants who had hardly seen a machine before. Many thousands lost their lives because of lack of safety precautions, or froze to death in the cold. Food was short, conditions primitive, lives cheap. But the difference from the collectivization of agriculture is clear: With all its shortcomings and failures, Soviet industry under the Five-Year Plans achieved the quantum leap that made good Stalin's premature boast of June 1930 that the USSR was on the eve of changing from an agrarian into an industrial society. If it had not, Russia could not have recovered sufficiently from the German attack of 1941 to continue the war and eventually carry it back to the Elbe.

It was only during the second Five-Year Plan that the worst mistakes began to be corrected and the cost in privation and the workers' reduced standard of living to be relieved. But it was during the first that the foundations were laid. Roy Medvedev[38] the first Soviet historian who, twenty years ago, had the courage to break the conspiracy of silence about the Stalin period, gives a figure of approximately 1,500 big enterprises built, the largest power station in Europe, on the Dnieper; the Magnitogorsk and Kuznetsk metallurgical complexes; the Ural machine factory and chemical works; the Rostov agricultural machinery plant; tractor factories at Cheliabinsk, Stalingrad, and Kharkov; automobile factories in Moscow and Sormovo; the Kramator heavy machinery plant, and so on.

New sectors of industry were established that had not existed in tsarist Russia: machine tools, automobile and tractor manufacture, airplane factories, the production of high-grade steel, ferrous alloys, synthetic rubber. The construction was begun of thousands of kilometers of new railways and canals, and of many new cities and workers' settlements. New centers of heavy industry were sited in the territories of the non-Russian peoples, the former borderlands of tsarist Russia—in Byelorussia, the Ukraine, Transcaucasia, Central Asia, Kazakhstan, the North Caucasus, Siberia, and Buriat-Mongolia. This wider dispersal of industry created a second center of the metallurgical and oil industries in the eastern part of the country.

John Scott, one of the many American engineers who were left unemployed in the U.S.A. and took jobs in the Soviet Union, wrote a famous account of his experiences in *Behind the Urals.*

> In Magnitogorsk I was precipitated into a battle. I was deployed on the iron and steel front. Tens of thousands of people were enduring the most intense hardships in order to build blast furnaces, and many of them did it willingly, with boundless enthusiasm, which infected me from the day of my arrival.
> I would wager that Russia's battle of ferrous metallurgy alone involved more casualties than the battle of the Marne. [39]

As the strain mounted, Stalin more and more openly appealed to Russian nationalism. In an often quoted speech to industrial managers in February 1931, he declared:

> No, comrades, the pace must not be slackened. On the contrary, we must quicken it. . . .
> To slow down the tempo [of industrialization] means to lag behind. And those who lag behind are beaten. The history of Old Russia shows that, because of her backwardness, she was constantly being defeated. By the Mongol Khans, by the Turkish beys, by the Swedish feudal lords, by the Polish-Lithuanian gentry, by the British and French capitalists. Beaten because of backwardness—military, cultural, political, industrial, and agricultural backwardness. . . . You remember the words of the poet: "Thou art poor and thou art plentiful, thou art mighty and thou art helpless, Mother Russia."
> . . . We are fifty or a hundred years behind the advanced countries. We must make good this lag in ten years. Either we do it or they crush us. [40]

As the American historian of Soviet Russia Adam Ulam points out, Stalin's version of Russian history was highly misleading. Old Russia, "constantly being defeated," had nonetheless pushed out her frontiers to incorporate one-sixth of the world's landmass and swallow up not a few of her conquerors.

> The true sense of Russia's history was different: "The State became swollen while the people shrank," as a great Russian historian wrote. Her own rulers had "beaten" her people and always on the same pretense: The greatness of the state required it. [41]

But Stalin was not mistaken in his intuitive grasp of the force to be tapped in the Russian people's national pride. First exploited effectively in his proclamation of "Socialism in one country," and later in the wartime resistance to the German invaders, Stalin harnessed it in the 1930s to the economic and social transformation that he sought to impose on the country. As early as the Fifteenth Party Congress in December 1927, he compared the revolution they were about to embark on to the achievement of the greatest of his tsarist predecessors:

> When Peter the Great, competing with the more developed Western countries, feverishly constructed industrial works and factories to provide

supplies for the army and to strengthen the country's defense, this too was an attempt to liquidate backwardness. [42]

Stalin's new course had to appeal to and motivate the middle and lower levels of the party as well as the leadership. This process of winning support and stimulating pressure from below was a necessary complement to the "revolution from above." It began at the same time as the "extraordinary measures" of early 1928, and continued throughout 1928 and 1929, building up a mood of militancy in important sections of the party on which Stalin was able to draw when he launched his all-out "socialist offensive" at the beginning of 1930. [43]

There are three themes that establish a pattern in a diffuse mass of evidence from different parts of the country. The first was discontent with the compromises of the NEP and a return to the tradition of War Communism as the "heroic period" of the revolution. The second was the presentation of collectivization, industrialization, and the so-called "cultural revolution" of the late 1920s, as *class war*, rooting out and destroying the "class enemies" of the revolution. The third marked the recruitment of a new vanguard of the proletariat, largely drawn from a younger, upwardly mobile generation of workers, prepared to act as "shock troops."

The first made a strong appeal to the Komsomol, the party's youth movement. Their mood is well described by a young Leningrader:

> The Komsomols of my generation—those who met the October Revolution at the age of ten or younger—took offense at our fate. When our consciousness was formed, we joined the Komsomol. When we went to work in the factories, we lamented that nothing would be left for us to do, because the revolution was over, because the severe [but] romantic years of civil war would not come back, and because the older generation had left to our lot a boring, prosaic life that was devoid of struggle and excitement. [44]

He leaped at the opportunity to organize a shock brigade in 1929.

The second, Stalin's ideological justification of his "socialist offensive" in terms of class war, enabled the militants to see those whom they hounded out of jobs and homes, informed against, and condemned to death, not as fellow human beings but as "class enemies," guilty of an irredeemable crime simply by virtue of having been born into a bourgeois or kulak family. Stalin's thesis that the nearer Soviet society approached to the final achievement of socialism, the more class hatred and warfare would be intensified, provided the sanction of an "objective" and ineluctable law of history for brutalities carried out in the name of a future reign of virtue.

The third theme was the product of the demands made by the drive for industrialization and rationalization, the doubling and redoubling of production targets, the call for stricter labor discipline, and sacrifices in the form of higher quotas, lower real wages, and falling living standards. These bore most heavily upon the industrial workers who had been the party's core of support in 1917 and the civil war. The effect was compounded by the fact that the expansion of industry required an expansion of the labor force as well, which in turn led to an influx, much resented by the older skilled workers, of a mass of unskilled labor from the villages, without experience of factory life.

Stalin and the other leaders had to recognize that the process of dilution meant that the smaller, more homogeneous working class of Leningrad and Moscow, with its strong class consciousness, on which they had relied from 1917 through 1921, no longer existed. They found a replacement as the "vanguard of the proletariat" in the activist members of the younger generation of workers. These had experienced the revolution and civil war as children or in their teens, and were critical alike of the resistance of the older workers to change, and of the ignorance and lack of discipline among the new arrivals from the villages. Taking the initiative in forming shock brigades, they were responsible for starting up a campaign of "socialist competition" to raise levels of productivity, which swept through Soviet factories and workplaces late in 1928. Stalin and his group were not slow to latch on to the possibilities of such a movement, and in early 1929 ordered party, Komsomol, and management to give it all possible assistance, as the radical catalyst for which they had been looking to break down the obstacles to the acceleration of Russia's industrial development.

The impact of the shock movement extended far beyond the factories. It was from 70,000 industrial workers who volunteered that the 25,000 "Best Sons of the Fatherland" were selected as "shock troops" to lead the collectivization drive in the countryside. It was the same young organizers of "socialist competition" who provided the new cadres to replace those purged as "unfit" in the state, the party, and trade-union bureaucracies. Ambitious as well as energetic, hard-liners whose radical slogans were untempered by experience, they represented the spearhead of the large-scale upward mobility of the sons and daughters of the working class moving into higher education, administrative, and managerial jobs in the years 1928 to 1931.

This was "the substance behind the rhetoric of class war,"[45] the Russian "cultural revolution" (the term, *Pravda* declared, "is now really in the air"), which created "the new class," the future Communist elite of postpurge and postwar Russia, the Brezhnev generation.

Although the process of upward mobility continued, the "cultural revolution" as such did not last more than three to four years. It belonged to a particular period in the history of Soviet Russia, beginning with the breakup of the NEP in 1928–29, when radical support against the right opposition had political value, and tailing off in 1931–32. The signal for both the beginning and the end of official encouragement for it was given by Stalin himself. He took advantage of the Shakhty affair in 1928, as he had of the grain crisis earlier, to sound a clear call for the renewal of class militancy in place of the class conciliation of the NEP.

The trial of fifty engineers for sabotage of the Shakhty mines was clumsily conducted but was the first big occasion on which the Soviet judicial process was used by the OGPU to drive home a political message to the population at large. The primary target was the "bourgeois specialists," the equivalent of the kulaks in agriculture. They were denounced for conspiring with foreign powers (memories of the war scare of 1927 were still fresh) and with former mine owners living abroad, to undermine the industrialization that would "strengthen the proletarian dictatorship" and so make a return to capitalism impossible. Apart from its value in providing a scapegoat for the shortcomings of the Soviet economy, the breakdowns and shortages with which ordinary life was plagued, the trial was a dramatized signal that henceforward the bourgeois intelligentsia and nonparty specialists, survivors from prerevolutionary days, who had been given special privileges under the NEP to the anger of the workers, were to be treated as politically suspect and dispensed with.

V

THE SHAKHTY TRIAL and the purges that followed made clear that Stalin did not intend, any more than Peter the Great, to rely upon enthusiasm alone. If there was no equivalent of dekulakization or peasant resistance, then industrialization as much as collectivization, once it had been taken over, was a revolution imposed from above, and its feverish pace was maintained by whatever degree of force was found necessary.

Central to the Stalinist system of government was the secret or security police, the OGPU,* whose operations came to overshadow the whole of Soviet life during the 1930s. Already leading the campaign against the peasantry, the OGPU was also employed, more selectively, to strike fear into the managers, engineers, and officials from whom Stalin demanded the fulfillment of impossible targets in the Plan. To begin with, their activities were principally directed against the "bourgeois specialists" who were not members of the party; the turn of the party elite was to come later.

The Shakhty trial of 1928 set a precedent, and was clearly intended by Stalin to do so. In April 1929 he told the Central Committee:

> Shakhtyites are now ensconced in every branch of our industry . . . By no means have all been caught. Wrecking by the bourgeois intelligentsia is one of the most dangerous forces of opposition to developing socialism, all the more dangerous in that it is connected with international capitalism. The capitalists have by no means laid down their arms; they are massing their forces for new attacks on the Soviet government. [46]

In November–December 1930, members of a so-called "Industrial Party" led by a Professor Leonid Ramzin were systematically charged with wrecking Soviet industry on the improbable instructions of the former French president Raymond Poincaré, Sir Henry Deterding (of Royal Dutch

*See glossary.

Shell), Lawrence of Arabia, and other "enemies of the Soviet people." The charges were grotesque, but the guilt of the accused was loudly proclaimed before their trial. Among the bodies demanding the death penalty was the Soviet Academy of Sciences, while half a million workers dutifully trudged past the courtroom shouting "Death! Death! Death!" Once the public trial began, with Vyshinsky again as president of the court, the defendants repeated the ritual confessions that had been beaten into them by the OGPU, and five of the eight were condemned to death. The fact that the sentences were subsequently commuted, and Ramzin himself pardoned, later freed, and even decorated, did not detract from the propaganda effect of the trial, which was given intensive publicity throughout the USSR.

Three months later, in March 1931, a group of former Mensheviks who held senior posts in economic and planning agencies were tried on charges of forming a "Union Bureau" to organize the sabotage of plans for economic development, and of forming a secret bloc with the "Industrial Party," and the "Toiling Peasants Party," to prepare for armed intervention from abroad and insurrection at home. The majority of those arrested never appeared in public but were dealt with out of hand, either being shot or sent to labor camps.

Stalin, however, was more successful at understanding the problems of industry than he ever was of agriculture. In the interests of efficiency, he recognized the need to free managers from the constant interference in the workplace of party officials and trade-union representatives, the so-called "troika" that had been characteristic of Soviet industry in the 1920s. In its place he called for concentration of responsibility for output under "one-man management," a call repeated by the reformers in post-Mao China in the 1980s.

Another proof of Stalin's willingness to learn in industrial matters, as he never was in agricultural ones, was his recognition that, at least for the time being, Russian industry was dependent on the "bourgeois specialists" he had denounced, even if they had acquired their expertise in prerevolutionary days or were hired from abroad. Reversing the policy he had proclaimed in March 1928, three years later, in June 1931, he announced to a conference of industrial managers:

> We must change our policy toward the old technical intelligentsia . . . Whereas during the height of the wrecking activities our attitude toward them was mainly expressed by the policy of routing them, now our attitude must be expressed mainly in the policy of enlisting them and solicitude for them. . . . It would be wrong and unwise to regard practically every expert and engineer of the old school as an undetected criminal and wrecker. We have always regarded and still regard "expert-baiting" as a harmful and disgraceful phenomenon. [47]

There is a touch of the effrontery that marked his "Dizzy with Success" article in Stalin's last remark, as if it were others, not he, who had taken the lead in "expert-baiting" at the time of the Shakhty trial. His speech did not prevent a revival of persecution when living conditions hit their lowest point in the winter of 1932–33. In January 1933, for example, six British Metro-Vickers engineers and ten Russian technicians were put on trial for the sabotage of power stations.

Nonetheless, Stalin's announcement to the industrial managers in June 1931 was as clear a signal for the end of the "cultural revolution" as the Shakhty affair had been for its beginning. Relieved of the danger of harassment, many nonparty specialists, including a substantial number who returned from prison or labor camps, were allowed to resume responsible jobs. Stalin not only needed, but could afford, this relaxation, because the foundation for a Russian alternative had been created in the opportunities opened up for the talented and the ambitious in the younger generation of workers.

An indication of the scale of this upward mobility is given by the fact that 43 percent of the three and a half million party members in 1933 were working in white-collar occupations, while only 8 percent of the membership had been in such occupations when they were admitted to the party. Between January 1930 and October 1933, 660,000 worker-Communists moved into administrative or political work, or returned to an educational institution to qualify them for such work. Most of the future engineers, managers, and political leaders who crowded into the new technical institutes had not completed secondary education but came straight from minor jobs in the party or from industry. They included Nikita Khrushchev (entered the Moscow Industrial Academy in 1929, age thirty-three), Leonid Brezhnev (entered the Dneprodzerzhinsk Metallurgical Institute in 1931, age twenty-five), Aleksei Kosygin (entered the Leningrad Textile Institute in 1930, age twenty-six).

As they rose, they became bound to the system of unequal privileges and rewards that Stalin established for those upon whom the regime depended, party and ministry officials, OGPU agents, and now the new managerial elite. These included bonuses, access to scarce goods and special closed shops, better housing, schools, and private transportation. These privileges and rewards were not guaranteed; they could be, and often were, withdrawn without notice, if a manager or official failed to achieve what was expected of him or, worse still, showed signs of deviating from the "correct" line, very soon leading to charges of "wrecking" and treason. Such insecurity created a powerful bond of self-preservation among those who became part of the new Soviet elite, "a new species of moral unity" (Leszek Kolakowski's phrase) in which all Communists became accomplices in Stalin's policies of coercion and ruthlessness and embarked upon a course from which there was no turning back.

THE CRUCIAL PROBLEM was how to find the additional labor to carry out the huge construction and industrial program of the Five-Year

Plan. In the chaotic conditions of the earlier years of the Plan, managers grabbed labor as they could and asked no questions. In this way millions of dekulakized peasants or runaways from the collective farms (estimated at over sixteen million from 1929 through 1935) were absorbed into the labor force. But they were neither trained nor used to labor discipline, and labor turnover and absenteeism were rampant, as workers deserted their jobs in search of better conditions. The system of internal passports introduced in 1932 to check this was stiffened by depriving "deserters" and absentees of their ration cards and living quarters. Thus the more organized Soviet industry became, the more the ordinary worker was tied to his job, unless required to move in accordance with the needs of the Plan.

In his June 1931 speech Stalin outlined a new approach, which was to have major consequences for Soviet society. Denouncing egalitarianism in wages as a leftist deviation, he called for a clear distinction between the rewards of skilled and unskilled work: "Marx and Lenin said that only under Communism would this difference disappear; under socialism, even after classes have been abolished, wages must be paid according to work performed, and not according to needs."[48] With this sanction, higher wages began to be offered to attract workers to the Urals and the east; piece rates were rapidly extended to match wage rates to productivity, while the performance of those willing to work harder and longer, soon to be known as Stakhanovites, not only earned them large bonuses and other advantages but raised the norms for the rest of the work force.

For the great mass of workers, however, it was a long time before increased productivity began to raise their general standard of living. Throughout the first Five-Year Plan, overriding priority was given to construction projects, the production of capital goods, and armaments. The urban population, unlike the peasants in the Ukraine, did not starve to death, but they suffered not only from rationing but also from constant food shortages, interminable lines, sharp rises in prices, a desperate lack of housing, and overcrowding.

At the lowest point, in the grim winter of 1932–33, Stalin declared: "It is clear that the workers' living standards are rising all the time. Anyone who denies this is an enemy of Soviet power."[49] This was an extraordinary statement to make, in plain contradiction of the majority of workers' own daily experience. Stalin, however, understood as well as Hitler that, if you tell a big enough lie, people are more likely to believe that there must be some truth in it.

This became easier now that (after three decades of argument and factionalism in the party) all opposition was silenced. Former leaders of the opposition, like Kamenev, Zinoviev, and Bukharin, were obliged to confess in public how wrong they had been, and the Stalinist leadership exercised a monopoly control over the press and radio. From the end of 1929 there was no voice raised in public to question or criticize anything the leaders said. Stalin made a series of statements about the success of the collectivization campaign and the Five-Year Plan that the members of the Central Committee and the Party Congress who heard them must have known were untrue. Far from challenging, they applauded them, and every newspaper in the country carried prominently both the statements and the confirmation conveyed by the applause. If one asks who believed them, one should remember how many people in the West, including such visitors to the USSR as Sidney and Beatrice Webb, Bernard Shaw, and H. G. Wells, were impressed by the achievements that Stalin claimed for Soviet planning and dismissed as anti-Soviet propaganda the reports of famine in the Ukraine or of mass deportations to the camps. Stalin made it easier for people to believe, or half-believe, what he told them by his skill at "double-talk." His use of the term "kulak" for a long time helped many in the party to deceive themselves about what was happening in the countryside. "Dekulakization," "the expropriation of agriculture" were Marxist-sounding terms that disguised the ugly realities of mass eviction, transportation, starvation, and the deaths of millions.

Stalin was as much aware as Hitler of the importance, and possibilities, of manipulating public opinion, and his regime employed many of the same techniques as well as some of his own. The unmasking of traitors and wreckers provided the urban population, ill-fed, ill-housed, and short of everything, with a focus for the hatred and anger that might otherwise have been directed against the party leadership. Failures to achieve economic targets, shortages of every kind were due, not to human error or mistakes in planning, but to sabotage designed to undermine the socialist regime. All Russians, especially party members and Komsomols, were exhorted to be on their guard against the "enemies within," to watch neighbors and workmates and report anything suspicious.

Stalin, who had none of Hitler's personal gifts as a performer, faced a greater problem than Hitler in the difficulty of communicating with a population spread out over a huge country, with much lower standards of living and education. One way of doing this was the series of public trials, propaganda in the form of political theater, built around the confessions of the accused. Extracted beforehand—with the aid of psychological and physical torture—these were the only evidence heard by the court and were given maximum coverage by press and radio, including the international press, which was then quoted back, selectively, by *Pravda* and other Soviet papers.

One lesson well understood in both Stalin's Russia and Nazi Germany was that propaganda is most effective when it is backed by terror. Russia was not yet the full-blown police state that it became in the later 1930s, and there were still limits to Stalin's arbitrary exercise of power. But the period

1930 through 1934 was the decisive stage in the expansion of both. The OGPU, like the Gestapo and the SS in Germany, was the instrument that Stalin used whenever he wanted to secure the execution of orders outside the normal administrative and legal procedures, from the forced eviction of the kulaks, the fabrication of false evidence and confessions, the arrest and "disappearance" of individuals, to the management of the punishment and labor camps.

The relationship between Stalin and the OGPU was a close one; its head (Genrikh Yagoda from 1934 to 1937) reported directly to him and was also responsible for his personal security. Its officers were among the most highly paid and privileged of Soviet officials, but no more exempt than the rest from the insecurity that was the hallmark of the regime. Both Yagoda and his successor Nikolai Yezhov eventually aroused Stalin's suspicion and were executed.

The secrecy that surrounded the activities of the OGPU—arbitrary arrest, the use of torture, the existence of the camps—was a powerful additional form of control through the pervasive atmosphere of fear that it created. To mention any of these activities publicly was to invite denunciation and arrest; there was a conspiracy of silence about them, in which millions of people were participants, uneasily aware of what had happened to others and might happen to themselves if they aroused suspicion.

Those who came into conflict with the system and were condemned to a term of years in one of the labor camps were not lost to the economy. The Soviet state had made use of forced labor from the start, and its administration occupied the largest division of the OGPU, known from its acronym as the Gulag, the Chief Administration of Corrective Labor Camps. It was an entire subcontinent or, as Solzhenitsyn described it, an archipelago, the Gulag Archipelago, an enormous network of penal institutions, inhabited by a population of slaves, who made up some 10 percent of the total Soviet work force and who could be worked literally to death, at the cost of a third of an average worker's wages. The archipelago absorbed the millions deported under dekulakization and collectivization and put them to "socially useful work." Forced labor was used successfully in the mining industry (including gold mining) and forestry and in any particularly harsh or hazardous area such as the Northern Territories and Siberia. By the end of the 1930s the Gulag had also become the main construction agency of the USSR.*

Because the death rate in the camps was high and fresh batches of prisoners were always arriving, estimates of the numbers held in them at any one time vary widely. Recent Soviet analysis suggests that the numbers fluctuated between two and four million.

*For the Gulag camps, see the map on pp. 750–51.

VI

NEVER BEFORE HAD a population of 150 million been subjected by its government to so great a convulsion or series of changes in the space of four years. But there is a danger that the sheer scale of the upheaval may so impress the imagination as to lend support, unconsciously, to Stalin's claim[50] that it amounted to an unparalleled success which anywhere else would have been regarded as a miracle—without first asking what sort of success, and how measured.

To begin with, how far was it an *economic* success, as Stalin asserted at every stage with a shower of glittering and often incompatible statistics?

So far as agriculture was concerned, it would be hard to devise a more disastrous policy than Stalin's forced collectivization, which began by driving the most energetic and experienced farmers off the land in pursuit of the chimera of rural capitalism and soon developed into an all-out war of the state against the peasants who made up four-fifths of the population. Stalin himself later told Churchill that it had been as hard a war as that against the Nazis and cost ten million lives.[51]

The farming work force was not only permanently weakened but permanently alienated. Once more tied to the soil, their revenge was to reduce cooperation with the regime to a bare minimum, forcing the state and the party, which knew nothing about agriculture—and even less about Stalin's pet idea of large-scale mechanized production—to intervene more and more frequently, with the result that could be expected. The authority on Soviet social and economic development, Moshe Lewin, quotes the French historian Marc Bloch's description of the situation in medieval Europe: "The lords' abuse of force had no longer any counterweight except the amazing capacity for inertia of the rural masses—often, to be sure, very effective—and the disorder of the lords' own administration."[52] Nothing, he adds, could better describe the twentieth-century situation in Russia. The peasants' real efforts were reserved for the small private plots that largely supported them and their families. Ironically, in 1937, these plots were also responsible for supplying more than half the nation's potatoes, vegetables, and fruit, and more than 70 percent of its milk and meat, a relic of private enterprise serving as an indispensable mainstay of the Soviet Union's food supplies.

Leaving aside, for the moment, the human costs of collectivization, and considering it solely from an economic point of view, the results were unimpressive. The level of grain production, which had been rising during the 1920s, began to fall after 1928. The average crop for 1928 through 1930 was 74 million tons; this fell to 67 million for the five years 1931 through 1935; recovered with an exceptional crop of 87 million tons in 1937, and fell back again to just over 67 million in 1938 and 1939. Only the fact that the state succeeded in doubling the percentage of the crop taken (from an average of 18 million tons from 1928 through 1932 to 32.1 million from 1938 through 1940) avoided a recurrence of famine with a growing population.

The figures for the loss of livestock speak for themselves:

	Million Head	
	1928	1933
Cattle	70.5	38.4
Pigs	26.0	12.1
Sheep and goats	146.7	50.2[53]

It was not until after Stalin's death in 1953 that these losses were made good. At meetings of the Central Committee in 1953–54 Khrushchev reported that grain production was still less, per capita, and cattle figures less absolutely than in tsarist times. Agriculture, which had recovered to 1913 levels in the 1920s, remained, after Stalin's collectivization in the 1930s, the weakest sector of the Soviet economy for the rest of the twentieth century.

If the appalling human suffering that it cost is taken into account, then the policy of collectivization must be described as a spectacular failure. The only justification could be that Stalin had no alternative, that (as he constantly claimed) the peasants were the aggressors, seeking to blockade and subvert the state. On the contrary, however, it was Stalin's unilateral action in ordering the "extraordinary measures" of December 1927–January 1928, so reversing the outcome of the discussions at the Fifteenth Party Congress earlier in December (with which he had concurred), that convinced the peasants there was going to be a return to the forced requisitioning of War Communism. There was undoubtedly a procurement crisis in grain in the winter of 1927–28, but it was argued at the time, and has been since,[54] that this was due to mistakes in government economic policy, which had neglected the rural sector, and could still have been overcome by economic measures (such as an alteration in price policies), without resorting to Stalin's "Ural-Siberian" methods.

Although Stalin's "left turn" in late 1927–early 1928 has been seen as the starting point of the "leap forward," no serious preparations for a program of mass collectivization had been made when it was launched in late 1929 and early 1930. The pattern that emerges characterizes the whole of the so-called "second October": A succession of crises as a result of hasty and ill-considered decisions, for which further makeshift solutions and desperate expedients had then to be found, thus creating not only self-perpetuating chaos, but also a self-justifying policy of coercion and emergency measures to deal with it.

Stalin had surely not foreseen the extent of the upheaval that collectivization would cause or of the resistance it would arouse. Where his leadership was decisive was in his refusal to compromise. Shutting his ears and eyes to what he was told and to the reports he received, he insisted on pressing forward after the momentary halt in the spring of 1930. He saw no victims, only enemies to be beaten down, by whatever degree of force was necessary.

The industrialization of Russia was clearly more of an economic success than the collectivization of agriculture. How much, if anything, it owed to the latter is a matter of debate. Preobrazhensky's original argument in favor of "squeezing" the peasants had been the need of "primitive socialist accumulation" to provide the funds for financing industrialization. But how much in practice could a crippled agriculture and starving villages provide? The most that can be claimed is that under half the surplus product derived from agriculture was used for industrial development at the beginning of the Five-Year Plan; by 1932, 18 percent; by the end, virtually nothing.

Wherever the funds came from, the foundations of a major industrial power were laid during the first Five-Year Plan and completed during the second. By 1937, it is estimated that total production was nearly four times higher than in 1928.[55] This was a remarkable and lasting achievement. But that is not the same thing as accepting the argument that, if it had not been for Stalin's leadership and his constant interventions, it would never have been accomplished.

Unlike the problems presented by the backwardness of Russian agriculture, which the Bolsheviks neither understood nor could fit into their Marxist scheme, the industrialization of Russia had always been seen as the key to their success in creating a socialist society. The Bolsheviks started with the advantage that here was a world with which, unlike that of the muzhik, they were familiar, and in which their plans for expansion aroused the enthusiasm of the party and never encountered the open resistance that the peasants put up to the "second revolution" in the countryside.

That said, however, the view that Stalin was the only man with the determination to master the chaos and drive the Plan through to completion has been challenged with the question whether Stalin's style of leadership and intervention did not contribute as much or more to creating the chaos as to clearing it up. A strong case can be made for the view that "at least the same degree of industrial development could have been achieved with less drastic methods."[56]

While they did not have the same disastrous consequences in the case of industry as in that of agriculture, the same faults of judgment reappear.

First, without any attempt to present a reasoned case, Stalin made a surprise appearance at the Council of Commissars and insisted that the figures that Gosplan (the State Planning Commission) proposed for the Five-Year Plan should be increased by up to—and in some cases over—100 percent.

Medvedev illustrates the consequences of the "willful" method of planning, which Stalin introduced, from the development of synthetic rubber. The first batch of the material produced by a new experimental method became available in January 1931. Against the advice of all the engineers, including the inventor of the process, academician A. S. Lebedev, it was decided to go ahead at once with the construction of one or two factories. Stalin, however, insisted on *ten* factories being built before the end of the first Five-Year Plan. Quite apart from the many unsolved technical problems, this meant that limited construction resources were spread out over ten sites. The upshot was that starts were made on only three factories during 1932–33; the rest were not built either in the first or second Five-Year Plan. [57]

Second, as in the case of the collective farms, Stalin was obsessed with "gigantomania." He demanded that industrial complexes be built, like the kolkhozes, on a scale beyond Russia's resources to construct or operate. The result was that they either took far longer to complete than was economical, and then were constantly subject to breakdowns, or were left unfinished. Similar emphasis on the spectacular, from the "heroic," but often contrived, deeds of Stakhanovites to crash programs, showed how little Stalin understood the steady, systematic rhythm of work needed to make a modern industrial plant produce efficiently.

Third, Stalin's obsession with size was matched by his unrelenting insistence on haste. Not only did he throw the balance of the Five-Year Plan into chaos by doubling the target figures, regardless of what was practicable, but he then also demanded that it should be carried out in four, not five, years. The result was counterproductive: constant disruption of production schedules, maximization of waste, and the encouragement of an unplanned scramble for scarce resources of raw materials and labor.

Finally, confronted with the failure to meet impossible dates and targets, Stalin denounced those responsible as guilty of sabotage, wrecking, and conspiracy, attacking in particular the former bourgeois and foreign specialists who provided him with convenient scapegoats, but on whom Soviet industry was heavily dependent for technical and managerial expertise. In this case Stalin was forced to recognize that the cost of losing their services could be fatal to the success of the Plan, but he never abandoned his suspicions or his belief that the way to get the most out of anyone in a responsible position was to keep them in a permanent state of insecurity.

There are always alternatives in history, and it has been argued that there was an alternative to the excesses of Stalinism in the moderate policy represented by Bukharin. That policy rested on a continuation and modification of the NEP, retaining the confidence of the peasantry—the *smychka,* the bond between town and countryside—developing rural cooperatives, and giving time for the peasant majority and private sector to "grow into socialism" through interaction with the socialist sector of the economy. Bukharin's proposals, it has been claimed, developed the themes of Lenin's later writings with their elaboration of the NEP as a road to socialism and at the same time anticipated the Czech reformers' search in 1967–68 for "a socialism with a human face." [58]

But it was an alternative in principle, not a *practical* alternative in the actual situation in Russia in 1928–29. After Stalin's break with him, there was no one on the political scene at the time—certainly not Bukharin—capable of getting such a policy adopted. It was this that convinced the other leading figures on the Central Committee that backing Stalin and his policy, not Bukharin and the right, was the only realistic course to follow if they wanted to see Russia transformed into a modern industrial state.

WHAT HAS SO FAR been left out in this attempt at evaluation is the political factor. One of the characteristics Stalin and Hitler shared was the belief that it was politics, not economics, that decided the development of nations: Given the will and the power to enforce it, anything was possible. How incomplete a view of history *and* politics this provides is shown in the examples, cited above, of political decisions in Russia between 1928 and 1933 frustrated and distorted by social and economic factors. But it is equally clear that without the political dimension it is impossible to understand the character of Stalin's revolution, and the system he created.

Stalin's boldest claim, dutifully repeated by the Communist International, was to equate what took place in Russia between 1928 and 1934 with "building socialism," a claim constantly reiterated by every Soviet organ. At the specially summoned "Congress of Victors," the Seventeenth Party Congress held in January 1934, Stalin proclaimed success in the struggle to overcome Russian backwardness, proved by the doubling of industrial output and the collectivization of 85 percent of agriculture. "How was it possible," he asked the congress, "for the colossal changes to take place in a matter of three or four years in the territory of a vast state with a backward technique and a backward culture? Was it not a miracle?" It would be indeed, he answered, if all this had taken place on the basis of capitalism and individual small farming; but the first had been eliminated, the second pushed into a secondary position. It could not be described as a miracle, however, because it had taken place on the basis of socialism. Socialism now held unchallenged sway in the national economy.

Marxism has achieved complete victory on one-sixth of the globe. And it cannot be regarded as an accident that the country in which Marxism has triumphed is now the only country in the world which knows no crises and no unemployment, whereas in all other countries, including the fascist countries, crisis and unemployment have been reigning for four years now. No, comrades, this is not an accident.[59]

Stalin's claim for many years confused and divided left-wing opinion outside Russia. It took a long time for the left to recognize that, however remarkable the transformation Stalin had effected, his revolution from above was not the replacement of a capitalist by a socialist economy, but something which has become much more familiar since in underdeveloped countries: using the power of the state to launch an assault on a backward society, employing methods and at a cost that were a perversion of socialist ideals.

It is clear that one of the motives behind Stalin's offensive against the peasantry was his determination to end the state's dependence on an external force outside his control—and therefore to be considered hostile. When he encountered peasant resistance to his grain procurement and dekulakization, he did not draw back but widened the conflict in order, once and for all, to destroy the potential power of the largest and most conservative class in Russian society. Economically it might be rated a disaster, or at most a mistake, but politically he saw it as representing a major victory.

Although the industrialization program was much more of a success, there was a balance of loss and gain there too. The size of Russia and the lack of the large numbers of administrators, economists, technicians, and managers its industrialization required meant that such a system of centralized planning and decision making was bound to be inefficient and cumbersome, at least to begin with. It was one thing to sit in Moscow and give orders, quite another to make sure that they were carried out, or that there was anyone there competent to carry them out on the spot.

Yet, with all its shortcomings, centralization had the same decisive advantage for Stalin of allowing him to keep control, to intervene—arbitrarily, when it might be least expected—by sending Molotov or Kaganovich or Postyshev to investigate and get a grip on situations that were out of control. As they did in the Ukraine, and as he himself had done during the civil war, they were empowered to break down obstruction, purge those responsible—if necessary, shoot them—and strike fear into the rest.

In this way the revolution of 1928 through 1934 acquired a third and overriding characteristic besides industrialization and the collectivization of agriculture: the building of a powerful state confronting a weak society.

VII

IN THE SOVIET UNION the place of the old governing class had been taken by the party; it was the party leadership that animated and directed the state. Stalin himself was neither head of state nor prime minister—that is, chairman of the Council of People's Commissars—but general secretary of the party. His power over the state and its bureaucracy, therefore, derived from his ability to control the party.

Stalin did not take this for granted. When former members of the left opposition were readmitted to the party and given jobs again, he did not forget their past record. Although a number, like Pyatakov, for instance, who became president of the State Bank and deputy commissar for heavy industry, played an important role in pushing through the Five-Year Plan, all were arrested before the end of the 1930s and either shot or dispatched (like Radek) to the camps. But Stalin insisted: "It is the right opposition that is most dangerous: greater fire to the right!"[60] The reason is clear enough: Now that he himself had taken over the policies of the left, it was to the right, and the position most clearly enunciated by Bukharin, that those members of the party could be expected to gravitate who became disillusioned with, even protested against, Stalin's policies and the brutal methods used to drive them through.

At the Sixteenth Party Congress, in the summer of 1930, the right-wing "opportunists" were charged with a new crime: In place of open opposition, they were accused of acknowledging their past errors in order to conceal their secret opposition to the party line. The attack on "right opportunism" was the main feature of the congress. One of Stalin's own henchmen summed up dissident party opinion in the provinces in these terms: "Stalin's policy is leading to ruin and misery . . . the proposals of Bukharin, Rykov, and Uglanov are the only correct, Leninist ones; only they are capable of leading the country out of the dead end."[61] To eradicate these attitudes, purges continued throughout 1930, and the trial of former Mensheviks in March 1931 was used to smoke out economists and planners who had expressed skepticism about the targets of the Five-Year Plan and to eliminate the last independent Marxist scholar, Ryazanov, a veteran Bolshevik and director of the Marx-Lenin Institute.

As the disorder and suffering in the country rose to its peak in the autumn and winter of 1932–33, they were matched by growing doubts and anxieties among the members of the party, reflected in growing tension among its leaders. Three further expressions of dissent criticizing Stalin were uncovered, one at the end of 1930, the other two in 1932–33. The first involved two highly placed party officials who had been protégés of Stalin. Sergei Syrtsov had been a member of the Central Committee in the 1920s, before replacing Rykov as chairman of the Council of Commissars of the Russian Federation and becoming in 1930 a candidate member of the Politburo. V. V. Lominadze, promoted to the Central Committee at the same Sixteenth Congress, had been prominent in Comintern affairs, had organized the Canton uprising of December 1927 on Stalin's orders, and was party secretary in the important Transcaucasian Federation. These two men were now accused of forming a counterrevolutionary faction, with a platform expressing the "panic-stricken" views of the right. They did not constitute an organized opposition group but gave vent to a dissatisfaction that was widespread among many of Stalin's supporters who had backed him against Bukharin, but now echoed the latter's earlier criticisms. Syrtsov was critical of the consequences of "extraordinary centralization" and "rampant bureaucracy," speaking of such industrial projects as the Stalingrad Tractor Project as "eyewash." Lominadze denounced the regime's "feudal lord attitude toward the needs and interests of workers and peasants." Both men lost their jobs and were demoted to minor posts.[62]

The years 1931 and 1932 saw no improvement in conditions. Alexander Barmine, a Soviet diplomat who later emigrated, wrote:

> Loyalty to Stalin at the time of which I am writing [1932] was based principally on the conviction that there was no one to take his place, that any change of leadership would be extremely dangerous, and that the country must continue on its present course, since to stop now or attempt a retreat would mean the loss of everything.[63]

In 1932 came the famine and the circulation of the "Ryutin platform." M. N. Ryutin, who worked in the Central Committee Secretariat and for several years headed the party committee of one of Moscow's districts, had supported the right in 1928 and in 1930 criticized Stalin's policies in a stormy interview with him. He was arrested and accused of organizing a counterrevolutionary group but released for lack of evidence. In 1932, angered by the deteriorating conditions in the country, Ryutin drew up a document of 200 pages addressed "To All Members of the CPSU," criticizing Stalin's policies in the most forthright terms. On August 21, ten or twelve party members met to discuss and revise his indictment, which was later passed on to others (including Zinoviev and Kamenev) but not widely circulated. A month later Ryutin and the other conspirators were arrested, along with anyone known to have read his document.

In the trials and purges that followed later in the 1930s, the "Ryutin plot" was built up and referred to again and again as the original conspiracy, in which all the main oppositionists were accused of participating. The platform was notable for two reasons. It endorsed the positions that had been taken up by both the right- and left-wing oppositions: the former for its criticism of economic policy; the latter for Trotsky's criticism of the party regime. Among the reforms called for were an economic retreat, the reduction of investment in industry, freedom for the peasants to leave the collectives, and the readmission of all those expelled from the party including Trotsky. The second reason is even more striking. In a fifty-page section it described Stalin as "the evil genius of the Russian Revolution, who, motivated by a personal desire for power and revenge, has brought the revolution to the verge of ruin" and demanded that he should be removed from office.

In the Bukharin-Rykov trial of 1938 the platform was spoken of as "registering the transition to the tactics of overthrowing the Soviet power by force." In 1988 this was rejected by the Soviet Supreme Court, and Ryutin and his associates were cleared of committing any criminal act. In 1932, however, Stalin regarded Ryutin's platform as a call for his assassination and wanted Ryutin shot; the OGPU referred his case to the Central Control Commission and they in turn to the Politburo. Although the latter body by now consisted solely of men who had supported Stalin against the opposition in 1929–30, Kirov, Ordzhonikidze, Kuibyshev, and others opposed what would have been the first execution from within the ranks of the old party. Instead, at a Plenum of the Central Committee (September 28–October 2), Ryutin was sentenced to ten years' imprisonment and, along with other members of the group, expelled from the party as:

> Degenerates, enemies of Communism and the Soviet regime, traitors to the party and the working class who, under the flag of a spurious "Marxism-Leninism," have attempted to create a bourgeois-kulak organization for the restoration of capitalism and particularly the kulaks in the USSR. [64]

At the same time further measures were taken against many of the old oppositionists, including Zinoviev, Kamenev, and Uglanov.

Stalin's failure to get his own way rankled. Four years later, in September 1936, he sent a telegram calling for the replacement of the OGPU chief Yagoda and angrily declaring that "the OGPU is four years behind in unmasking the Trotskyite-Zinovievite" bloc—a charge taken by most scholars to refer to the refusal of the Politburo to agree to his wishes four years before, in September 1932. This is supported by the fact that in each of the show trials of 1936, 1937, and 1938 the accused were called upon to confess to complicity in the Ryutin plot, which was described as the first coming together of the oppositions on a basis of terrorism. On January 1, 1937, Stalin had his revenge. After a forty-minute trial, Ryutin was summarily executed, followed by two of his sons and many of his associates. [65]

In January 1933 a third center of opposition was uncovered, organized by the former commissar of agriculture, A. P. Smirnov. He and his associates, two other Old Bolsheviks, N. B. Eismont and V. N. Tolmachev (party members since 1907 and 1904), had circulated a manifesto similar to Ruytin's platform and discussed Stalin's replacement as general secretary. "Only enemies," Stalin told the Central Committee, "can say that you can remove Stalin and nothing will happen." [66] But any suggestion of shooting Smirnov and the others was again blocked in the Politburo: They were expelled from the party and later given prison sentences.

At the same meeting of the Central Committee Plenum at which the Smirnov group was charged, a general purge of the party was agreed, which led to the expulsion of 800,000 (out of 3.5 million) during 1933, and another 340,000 in 1934. The purge was particularly directed against those who had been newly recruited to the rural organizations, leaving many collective farms and rural areas without party organizations at all, or only a single Communist. As late as the Eighteenth Party Congress in 1939, it was reported that there were only 12,000 party primary organizations for 243,000 collective farms, with a total membership, including candidates, of 153,000—an indication of how complete remained the alienation of the peasantry from the party. Further measures to put renewed pressure on the peasants to raise productivity in the collectivized sector to somewhere near the level they achieved on their private plots were announced in the summer of 1940, but the campaign was interrupted before it got going properly by the German invasion in June 1941. The peasants, however, did not forget that it was only because of the German attack that they were spared another assault by the party. [67]

The opposition within the Politburo to more severe punishment was quite different from that of the Ryutin and Smirnov groups, in two ways. Its members had been among Stalin's chief supporters, had helped him to defeat Bukharin and the right and to put into effect the policies of the first Five-Year Plan period. Ordzhonikidze, the head of the Supreme Economic Council and of the important Commissariat for Heavy Industry, and Kirov, the head of the Leningrad Party Organization, were men whose views Stalin could not lightly disregard. The names most commonly associated with theirs were those of Kuibyshev, Kossior (First Secretary of the Ukraine party), and Rudzutak, who had given up membership of the Politburo to head the Central Control Commission and returned to the Politburo as a candidate member in January 1934. All of them had been born between 1886 and 1889, and so belonged to a younger age group than Stalin (born 1879), and all had joined the party between 1903 and 1907. Two at least were sufficiently independent-minded to give employment to former oppositionists, Ordzhonikidze to Bukharin and Pyatakov in his Commissariat, Kirov to one of the leading members of Bukharin's circle, Petr Petrovsky, whom he appointed in 1934 as head of the Leningrad party's ideological department and editor of the Leningrad *Pravda,* despite his involvement in the Ryutin affair. All, it may be added, met their deaths during the purges that followed: two shot after arrest, one assassinated (Kirov), and two (Ordzhonikidze and Kuibyshev) dying in mysterious circumstances with at least a suspicion that they were murdered.

None of them sought to go back on the policies of industrialization and collectivization or to challenge Stalin's leading position. But they took the view that a breakthrough had been achieved and argued that the time had come to recognize that the worst was over, to put an end to the use of terror and coercion, and to meet the widespread desire in both the population at large and the party for a relaxation of pressure and the chance to enjoy more normal lives. Disillusionment and protest over the situation in the country and Stalin's policies affected not only some of the Old Bolsheviks, but also some of the more active Komsomol members. Informal discussion groups were formed; at times there were demonstrations and distribution of leaflets, which led to the OGPU arresting several groups of young people in the summer of 1933. Stalin called for extreme measures against them but was once again blocked by the Politburo. The leaders of the opposition urged a policy of reconciliation with former oppositionists and supported their argument with the need to unite the nation in the face of the increased danger from abroad after the Japanese occupation of Manchuria and Hitler's accession to power in Germany.

From the sequel it is clear that Stalin was not persuaded by such arguments, saw them as a threat to his own position, and moved to destroy those who put them forward. But it is not known how long it took him to reach this conclusion, and then to prepare the ground for putting it into effect. In 1933 it evidently suited him to make some concessions.

In January the procurement system for grain had been changed, replacing arbitrary requisitioning by a fixed obligation based upon the acreage of collective farms. In May a secret circular ordered the number of peasant deportations to be limited to 12,000 householders a year. The same month, Zinoviev and Kamenev, who had been expelled from the party a second time and deported to Siberia after the Ryutin affair, were allowed to return and purge their guilt by a further confession, calling upon former oppositionists to end their resistance. Rakovsky, the Bulgarian veteran revolutionary, the last of the leading Trotskyites to make his peace, and Sosnovsky, another exile, were welcomed back into the fold.

Boris Nicolaevsky, an émigré Menshevik, whose "Letter of an Old Bolshevik" was based on talks with Bukharin in Paris in 1936, underlines the care the moderate group in the leadership took to avoid antagonizing Stalin:

> Whereas formerly all forms of opposition had been opposition *against* Stalin and for his removal from the post of chief, there was no longer any question of such removal. . . . Everyone emphasized tirelessly his devotion to Stalin. It was rather *a fight for influence over Stalin,* a fight for his soul, so to speak.[68]

These pointers were confirmed by the Seventeenth Party Congress, held in January–February 1934 and felicitously named the "Congress of Victors." The date deliberately chosen for the opening session, January 26, was the tenth anniversary of Stalin's "oath speech" after Lenin's death, and *Pravda's* commemorative article declared:

> Looking back on the ten-year path traversed, the party is entitled to declare that the Stalin oath has been fulfilled with honor. *The decade following Lenin's death has been the decade of a great work—the historic victory of Leninism.* Under Stalin's leadership the Bolsheviks have brought it about that
>
> **SOCIALISM IN OUR COUNTRY HAS WON**[69]

Stalin himself was in a confident mood. In a lengthy report to the congress he claimed the complete success of the Five-Year Plan and compared it with the plight of the capitalist countries devastated by the Depression:

> The abolition of exploitation, the abolition of unemployment in the towns, and the abolition of poverty in the countryside are such historic achievements in the material standards of the working people of the Soviet Union as are beyond even the dreams of the workers and peasants in bourgeois countries, even in the most "democratic" ones.

His audience did not deny Stalin his triumph: They cheered him wildly. He responded with a declaration that produced, according to the official report, "thunderous, prolonged applause":

> At the Fifteenth Party Congress [1927] it was still necessary to prove that the party line was correct and to wage a struggle against certain anti-Leninist groups; and at the Sixteenth [1930], we had to deal the final blow to the last adherents of these groups. At this congress, however, there is nothing more to prove, and it seems no one to fight. . . . It must be admitted that the party today is united as it has never been before. [70]

It was a different story, however, behind the scenes. The congress in fact was the last gathering of the Old Bolsheviks of Lenin's party. By now those who had joined the party before the revolution or during the civil war represented only 10 percent of the total membership, but 80 percent of the delegates to the congress came from this group, which was still strongly entrenched in the party leadership. The official party history was revised in Khrushchev's time to include this paragraph:

> The abnormal situation which the personality cult was creating in the party caused deep concern to some Communists, above all, to the old Leninist cadres. Many congress delegates, particularly those who were familiar with Lenin's Testament, held that it was time to transfer Stalin from the office of general secretary to some other post. [71]

This refers to an informal bloc that came together at the congress consisting mainly of party regional secretaries and secretaries of the non-Russian republics' Central Committees who knew at first hand of the disastrous results of Stalin's policies. Talks were held in the Moscow apartments of leading party figures, among them Ordzhonikidze, Mikoyan, and Petrovsky. The suggestion was made that Stalin should be made chairman of the Council of People's Commissars or chairman of the Central Committee and Kirov should be elected general secretary in his place. Accounts vary as to whether Kirov refused and told Stalin or, when summoned by Stalin, did not deny that the offer had been made. [72]

Whichever account is true, there is no doubt about Stalin's reaction. According to an extract from Mikoyan's diary published in 1987, Kirov met "only with hostility and vengefulness toward the whole congress and of course toward Kirov himself." [73] The fact that the congress was also "the scene of the most excessive praise of Stalin," recorded by the same official history, has led Adam Ulam to suggest that there may have been a "plot-by-adulation," designed to play on Stalin's megalomania and persuade him not to step down, but to step up, and devote himself to foreign, military, and state affairs. The Chinese Communist leadership unsuccessfully tried to persuade Mao to do the same in the early 1960s. [74]

Stalin had evidently agreed that the congress should be made the occasion for an ostentatious display of reconciliation. Among figures from the past allowed to speak and express their complete conversion to Stalinist orthodoxy were Zinoviev, Kamenev, Bukharin, Rykov, Tomsky, Preobraz-hensky, Pyatakov, Radek, and Lominadze. Some were even allowed to become members (Pyatakov) or alternates (Bukharin, Rykov, Tomsky) of the Central Committee. Kamenev's recantation set the tone for all:

> I want to say from this tribune that I consider the Kamenev who fought the party between 1925 and 1933 to be dead and I don't want to go on dragging that old corpse after me. . . . This era in which we live . . . will be known as the era of Stalin, just as the preceding era entered history as the time of Lenin.

Bukharin saluted Stalin "as the field marshal of the proletarian forces, the best of the best." He quoted a Nazi philosopher who wrote: "The nation needs priest kings who spill blood, blood . . . who strike and slaughter" and contrasted this barbarism with the humane philosophy that prevailed in the Soviet Union.[75]

Kirov, whom some saw—and Stalin knew they saw—as a possible successor, played his part with the enthusiastic reply he made to Stalin's report:

> It seems to me, comrades, that as a result of the detailed consideration . . . which has taken place in this congress, it would be useless to think what kind of resolution to adopt on the report of Comrade Stalin. It will be more correct, and more useful for the work at hand, to accept as party law all the proposals and considerations of Comrade Stalin. . . . Our successes are really huge, colossal, the devil knows: to put it frankly, you must want to live and live. Just take a look at what's actually happening. It's true all right.[76]

According to the transcript, Kirov's speech was constantly interrupted by "stormy applause." The congress did as he suggested and took the unprecedented step of voting that all the party organizations should "be guided in their work by the proposals and tasks presented by Comrade Stalin in his speech."

In his peroration, Kirov referred to Stalin's "oath speech," declaring: "We are fulfilling that vow and will go on fulfilling it, because the vow was given by the great strategist of the liberation of the working people of our country and the whole world—Comrade Stalin!"[77] This speech was ostensibly a tribute to Stalin, but as the delegates streamed out of the hall, most took the prolonged standing ovation that had followed to be intended for Kirov.

Stalin was not taken in, and during his report he had given a signal that those who knew him well understood—and were intended to. Immediately after saying the party was united as never before, he went on to discuss at length the ideological confusion that led "certain members" to suppose that the classless society would come by a spontaneous process, that they could relax the class struggle, moderate the dictatorship of the proletariat, and get rid of the state altogether. He added:

> If this confusion of mind and these anti-Bolshevik sentiments gained a hold over the majority of the party, the party would find itself demobilized and disarmed. . . . That is why we cannot say that the fight is ended and that there is no longer any need for the policy of the socialist offensive.[78]

This suggestion of the need for continuing vigilance was supported by Stalin's proposal that the existing arrangements for political control of the party should be changed. He had already placed the 1933 purge in the hands of a special commission rather than the Central Control Commission. In his view the latter's members were too much inclined to respond sympathetically to appeals, and to take advantage of their presence at the combined meetings of the Plenum with the Central Committee to criticize shortcomings in the administration of the economy. The old commission was to be replaced by a new Party Control Commission whose job would be to check up on the execution of the Central Committee decisions; there was no mention of its being given a right to hear appeals.

Stalin's dissatisfaction with the party was turned to fury when he received the results of the vote for election to the Central Committee. It was found that in the secret ballot, while only three votes were cast against Kirov, 270 delegates (almost a quarter of those voting) had voted against Stalin, who was elected only because there were exactly as many candidates as there were members to be elected. When this was reported to Stalin, he insisted that only three votes should be recorded against him as well, the same number as against Kirov. A special commission of the Central Committee, which examined the records of the Seventeenth Congress in 1957, after Stalin's death, found that 267 votes were missing.[79]

The congress of reconciliation, as Robert Tucker puts it, had turned into the congress of "Stalin's final estrangement from the Bolshevik party."[80] Over the next few years, Stalin took his revenge in the same way that Mao did in the 1960s, and with the same thoroughness. According to the figures Khrushchev gave to the Twentieth Congress in 1956, no fewer than 1,108 of the 1,966 delegates who attended the "Victors' Congress" in 1934 were arrested on charges of counterrevolutionary crimes, and 98 out of the 139 members and candidate members of the Central Committee elected at the congress were arrested and shot.

HOWEVER DECEPTIVE, the newly found atmosphere of unity at the top of the party was maintained in public for the rest of 1934 until December 1. Many of the former members of the opposition were allowed to take up useful employment. Bukharin, for example, was appointed chief editor of *Izvestia*, second only to *Pravda* as the voice of official policy, and was now able to write regular signed and unsigned articles.

A series of decrees making the OGPU part of a reorganized People's Commissariat of Internal Affairs (NKVD) raised hopes that its judicial powers, which had been arbitrarily used, including condemnation to death, would now be restricted. In the same month of July, local procurators were ordered to halt the indiscriminate prosecution of engineers and managers. Such measures were not much more than gestures, but they encouraged the hope that the rigors and horrors of the first Five-Year Plan and the collectivization drive were past and could be forgotten. The fact that the targets of the second Five-Year Plan, thanks in no small part to the efforts of Ordzhonikidze, were much more realistic than those of the first suggested that the future would be better. There was even hope that this might be true of the collective farms as well. The grain procurement from the 1933 harvest had been up 27 percent compared with the previous year, up again the following year, leading the Central Committee in November 1934 to agree that bread rationing should be abolished in 1935; that the special political departments in the Machine Tractor Stations should be dismantled, and the rights of the peasants to cultivate their private plots should be substantially increased.

A very different denouement, however, continued to be prepared behind the scenes. What mattered was not whether there was a plot, but that Stalin convinced himself that there was. Once again, Stalin showed his mastery of political intrigue. He had two great advantages. Thanks to the OGPU/NKVD, which reported directly to him, he was far better informed of any suspicious moves or contacts they might make than those he meant to eliminate. At the same time, by concealing his own intentions, he confused his victims as he had in the 1920s, playing one off against another, and taking care never to unite them against him until he was ready to act. At all times, the initiative and the timing remained in his hands.

A series of changes in 1933–34 can be seen, in retrospect, as placing men on whom Stalin believed he could rely in key positions. The most important were the appointment of Yagoda, with Agranov as his deputy, to head the reorganized NKVD; Kaganovich's appointment to head the new Party Control Commission and the creation (in June 1933) of an All-Union Prosecutor General's department in which Andrei Vyshinsky, who had already gained experience and attracted Stalin's attention as a compliant judge in the Shakhty trial, and was to achieve infamy in the Moscow trials of the later 1930s, rapidly became the leading figure. From this period also dates the first public mention of the "Special Sector" of Stalin's personal secretariat, which acted as the link with the NKVD, with Poskrebyshev and Agranov, the deputy commissar of the NKVD, as its two most important members.

A second list of those promoted later in 1934 contains the names of Nikolai Yezhov, Lavrenti Beria (each of whom in turn was to head the NKVD), Georgi Malenkov, Andrei Zhdanov, and Khrushchev, all of whom were to fulfill his expectations. Among those whose places they took and who had offended him by showing too great independence and who were now reduced to candidates were Bukharin, Rykov, and Tomsky, former members not only of the Central Committee but of the Politburo. In the meantime Stalin showed the same patience as in the 1920s and allowed the situation to develop.

At the Seventeenth Congress the secretariat of the Central Committee had been reorganized to bring in two newcomers besides Stalin and Kaganovich. The better known was Sergei Kirov, a candidate member of the Politburo since 1926, and a full member since 1930; the other was Zhdanov, ten years younger, hitherto secretary of the Gorki Party Organization. Zhdanov's appointment was certainly a promotion—he was not yet a member of the Politburo—but Kirov's was more equivocal. A popular figure in the party, a pure-bred Great Russian (unlike the Georgian Stalin), and said to be the best speaker since Trotsky, he had made a success of rebuilding the party organization in Leningrad after Zinoviev's removal (1926) and had built up a power base of his own. Stalin always viewed anyone who controlled Leningrad with suspicion and three times in his career broke up and decimated its party organization—in 1926 after the removal of Zinoviev, in 1934–35 after the assassination of Kirov, and in 1950, following Zhdanov's death.

It is uncertain whether Kirov was elected a secretary of the Central Committee on Stalin's initiative or as a move against him. Stalin had known Kirov from the revolutionary days of October 1917. His harsh, cold, introverted nature was drawn to the cheerful, warm, and open character of the other who attracted a crowd wherever he went. With the possible exception of Bukharin, there appears to have been no other party figure toward whom Stalin showed such feeling. Their families were friends, they had often gone on vacations together, and in 1924 Stalin sent him one of the rare autographed copies of his book, *On Lenin and Leninism,* with the inscription: "To S. M. Kirov, my friend and beloved brother, from the author, Stalin." [81] Ten years later when the chairman announced "Comrade Kirov has the floor," the whole of the Seventeenth Congress had risen to give him a standing ovation—in which Stalin too joined. But Stalin had also not forgotten that when he pressed for Ryutin to be executed, it was Kirov who opposed this without consulting him first: "We mustn't do this. Ryutin is not a hopeless case, he's merely gone astray. . . . Who the hell knows how many hands wrote that 'Platform.' . . . We'll be misunderstood." [82]

While Zhdanov was relieved of his post in Gorki in order to allow him to take up his new job in Moscow, Kirov was allowed to remain in Leningrad, an unprecedented arrangement. Although not certain, it appears likely that Stalin wanted to bring Kirov more directly under his supervision and that Kirov resisted it. It may also be relevant that, at the beginning of July 1934, Stalin is reported to have been deeply impressed with the news that Hitler had stamped out potential trouble in his party by the ruthless purge of Röhm, the SA leadership, and other former opposition leaders.* Alone among the Soviet leadership Stalin is said to have insisted that Hitler's action would strengthen, not weaken, the Nazi regime.[83]

In the late summer Stalin invited both Kirov and Zhdanov to stay with him on vacation at Sochi on the Black Sea. At the end of an uncomfortable stay, Stalin is said to have pressed Kirov again to move full-time to Moscow, and Kirov to have held out for staying in Leningrad until the end of the second Five-Year Plan, that is until 1937. Whatever the relations between the two men, after attending a meeting of the Central Committee in Moscow at the end of November, Kirov returned to Leningrad and was shot dead in party headquarters by a thirty-year-old party member with a grievance, Leonid Nikolayev.

There is no doubt that Nikolayev did not act on his own. The question debated ever since is how far Stalin knew in advance what Nikolayev planned to do. Khrushchev in his 1956 speech to the Twentieth Party Congress hinted that Stalin was involved, without saying so outright. What is not in dispute is the use Stalin made of the opportunity to issue an immediate directive that, according to Khrushchev, was used to deprive those accused of terrorist attacks of virtually any rights of defense. A call for vigilance which was circulated to all party committees—"Lessons of the Events Connected with the Evil Murder of Comrade Kirov"—put an abrupt end to any thoughts of relaxation. Whatever the truth about Stalin's involvement,† the murder was subsequently seen by those who survived the terror of the later 1930s as the event that marked its beginning.

*See pp. 333–41.
†See pp. 461–65, for further discussion of Kirov's murder.

NINE

Hitler's Revolution

I

NEITHER STALIN NOR HITLER came to power in the traditional revolutionary manner that many of the Nazi SA still dreamed of, by using force to overthrow the existing regime from the outside. Both secured power from the inside, Stalin by exploiting the position of general secretary of the CPSU, Hitler by exploiting the position of chancellor in a right-wing coalition government. The advantage of this was that it enabled each of them to establish himself with the power of government on his side, Stalin claiming continuity with the unassailable authority of Lenin, the founder figure of the Bolshevik Revolution, and Hitler with the authoritarian tradition in German history.

It was the general view in Germany, on the left as much as on the right, that Hitler would be the prisoner of a cabinet in which the real power lay with von Papen, Hugenberg, and their friends. Within no more than seven weeks, however, the Enabling Act passed by the Reichstag on March 23 transferred overriding powers to the cabinet and ended the government's dependence on both parliament and the president's emergency powers. At a single blow, Hitler had turned the tables and established an ascendancy that was obvious to everyone, freeing himself from the constitutional and political limits on his power as head of government but preserving the constitutional facade in doing so, a continuation of the tactics of "legality" to which he had adhered since the failure of the 1923 putsch.

Without waiting for the Enabling Act, Hitler had no sooner sworn to uphold the constitution on taking office than he immediately set about destroying it by the use of the president's emergency powers, *provided by the constitution,* so reconciling the contradictory faces of National Socialism as a revolutionary movement committed to observing "legality."

Von Papen and his conservative allies were not blind to what Hitler was doing. They had themselves provided clear precedents by using the same emergency powers, not to protect the republic's democratic institutions as the framers of the Weimar constitution had intended, but to erode and subvert them. Like Hitler, they too aimed to free government from dependence on the Reichstag, and to do so with the approval of the Reichstag, so preserving the appearance of constitutional legitimacy which was so important in reassuring and securing the continued cooperation of the army, the civil service, the courts, the whole structure of German officialdom. What they failed to grasp was that Hitler meant to carry the same process to its logical conclusion, by using the same emergency powers to free himself from dependence not only on the Reichstag, but on the president, the cabinet, his coalition partners, and their parties. It was the same mistake as that made by the Old Bolsheviks in Stalin's case: failure to realize how far the man they had to deal with was prepared to go in making himself independent of them.

So little did von Papen and Hugenberg understand what Hitler had in mind that at the very first cabinet meeting they agreed to dissolve the Reichstag and hold new elections. Von Papen declared, without any prompting from Hitler, that this had to be the last election. In preparation for it the Nazis mobilized all their resources, now including access to the radio, of which Hitler and Goebbels made masterly use, demonstrating its political possibilities for the first time in history.

For the first month, however, Hitler was careful to avoid disturbing his Nationalist partners. In his "Appeal to the German People," broadcast on February 1, he presented himself not as a party leader but as the head of a national coalition, the "Government of the National Revolution," called upon to reunite a divided nation and restore its "unity of mind and will." The Nazi party was not once mentioned, and the whole address was framed in conservative, not radical, terms:

> The national government will preserve and defend the foundations on which the strength of our nation rests. It will take under its firm protection Christianity as the basis of our morality, and the family as the nucleus of our nation. Standing above estates and classes, it will bring back to our people the consciousness of its racial and political unity, and the obligations arising therefrom. It wishes to base the education of German youth on respect for our great past and pride in our traditions. It will therefore declare merciless war on spiritual, political, and cultural nihilism. Germany must not and will not sink into Communist anarchy. [1]

Hitler concentrated his attack, as both Nazis and Nationalists did throughout the campaign, on "the Marxists," lumping together the Social Democrats and the trade unions with their bitterest enemies, the Communists.

> Fourteen years of Marxism have undermined Germany. One year of Bolshevism would destroy her. If Germany is to experience political and economic revival, a decisive act is required: We must overcome the demoralization of Germany by the Communists. [2]

Hitler had resisted Hugenberg's suggestion of an immediate ban on the KPD, preferring to take advantage of their call for a general strike and their election campaign to whip up fears of a Communist uprising. Another emergency decree, "For the Protection of the German People," signed by the president (on February 4) gave the government wide power to ban newspapers and public meetings. The administration of this was in the hands of the *Länder* (the German states), and the government reaped the benefit of von Papen's coup d'état of July 1932 which had placed Prussia under the provisional control of a Reich commissioner. Von Papen still held that office, but effective control of the Prussian police, the largest force in Germany, and of the Prussian civil service was in the hands of Göring, who had been appointed Reich commissioner for the Prussian ministry of the interior and simply ignored the fact that he was nominally responsible to von Papen.

Göring's control of Prussia played a key role, opening the way to actions of which Hitler as Reich chancellor could affect to have no official knowledge. Göring was in his element. Within a week he had provided himself with a list of police officers and government officials to be purged. Raids were carried out on Communist offices and Göring's order to the police throughout Prussia, issued on February 17, left no doubt as to what was required of them:

> I assume that it is unnecessary to point out that the police must avoid giving even the appearance of a hostile attitude, still less the impression of persecuting the patriotic associations [SA, SS, Stahlhelm].
> The activities of subversive organizations are on the contrary to be combatted with the most drastic methods. Communist terrorist acts are to be proceeded against with all severity, and weapons must be used ruthlessly when necessary. Police officers who in the execution of their duty use their firearms will be supported by us without regard for the effect of their shots; on the other hand, officers who fail from a false sense of consideration may expect disciplinary proceedings. [3]

On February 22 Göring issued another order which had far-reaching consequences. The Prussian police force was to be reinforced by enlisting voluntary auxiliaries to combat "the growing excesses of the radical left, especially in the Communist camp." Recruitment was in practice limited to the "National Associations," the SA, the SS, and the Stahlhelm (some 50,000 in all), who continued to wear their uniforms with the addition of a white armband, and were virtually given the freedom of the streets, without interference from the regular police. Hitler's observance of "legality" had always been combined with the threat of violence, personified in the brown-shirted SA; now that he had assumed the authority of the head of government, far from being dropped, the threat was realized in that "symbiosis of legality and terror" [4] that was to become the hallmark of the Third Reich.

The reign of terror that followed in the months after January 30 had a different character from the systematic acts of violence carried out by the

SS later. Carried on for the most part by the SA, it was more in the nature of an elemental outbreak of hatred and revenge, the "Day" long promised to the rank and file, continually deferred, but now at last conceded as their reward for loyal service. While Hitler in a broadcast of March 10 officially urged restraint as a gesture to conservative opinion at home and abroad, on the same day Göring declared in a speech at Essen: "For years past we have told the people 'You can settle accounts with the traitors.' We stand by our word. Accounts are being settled." [5] Rudolf Diels, the head of the Prussian Gestapo, wrote later:

> The uprising of the Berlin SA electrified the remotest parts of the country. Around many big cities in which the authority of the police had been transferred to the local SA leaders, revolutionary activities took place throughout the whole area. . . .
>
> In Silesia, the Rhineland, Westphalia and the Ruhr unauthorized arrests, insubordination to the police, forcible entry into public buildings, smashing up of homes, and nightly raids had begun before the Reichstag fire at the end of February.
>
> No order was issued for the establishment of concentration camps; one day they were simply there. The SA leaders put up "their" camps because they did not trust the police with their prisoners. No information about many of these ad hoc camps ever got as far as Berlin. [6]

As a result there is no proper record of the numbers arrested, tortured, and killed, and such figures as are given seriously underestimate the extent of the violence and the terror it created. Old scores to be settled from the street battles of the previous two or three years were largely directed against Communists and socialists. Jews, Catholic priests, politicians, and journalists were other obvious targets. The SA soon extended their activities to anyone whose car or property they fancied or against whom they felt resentment for being better off or better educated and who were now, as if in fulfillment of the Brownshirts' secret dreams, within their power.

Less than a week after Göring's order, on the night of February 27, the Reichstag building in the center of Berlin mysteriously burst into flames, thereby providing him with the pretext he had been looking for to expand the scope of official action and match the "national uprising" from below. Rudolf Diels, who was present at the scene and interrogated Marinus van der Lubbe, the young Dutch ex-Communist caught in the act of starting the fires, was convinced he had acted on his own. [7] But neither Göring nor Hitler was prepared to listen. "This is the beginning of the Communist revolt," Göring declared. Hitler, standing in the chamber, which was lit by the burning paneling, was in a state of great excitement: "This is something really cunning, prepared a long time ago." Diels continues:

> Hitler shouted uncontrollably, as I had never seen him do before: "There will be no mercy now. Anyone who stands in our way will be cut down. The German people will not tolerate leniency. The Communist deputies

must be hanged this very night. Everybody in league with them must be arrested. There will no longer be any leniency for Social Democrats either."[8]

Losing no time, Göring ordered the arrest of all Communist deputies and leading officials, the closing of the party's offices, and a ban on all their publications, as well as a fourteen-day ban on the SPD press. As many as 4,000 arrests were made. But the opportunity was too good to let the matter rest there. The next day Hitler secured another emergency decree signed by the president, "For the Protection of People and State: to guard against Communist acts of violence endangering the state," Article 1 of which suspended until further notice the seven sections of the constitution guaranteeing the fundamental rights of the citizen.

Thus restrictions on personal liberty, on the right of free expression of opinion, including freedom of the press, on the right of association and assembly, and violations of the privacy of postal, telegraphic, and telephonic communications, and warrants for house searches, orders for confiscations as well as restrictions on property rights are permissible beyond the legal limits otherwise prescribed.[9]

This provided the "legal" warrant for the device of "protective custody" used by the Gestapo to imprison without trial.

Article 2 gave the Reich government the right to take over, if necessary, the powers of the *Länder* governments and use them to restore security and order, while further articles authorized the death penalty for any violations of the decree, attempted assassination of members of the government, or arson. Contrary to the usual practice, no guidelines for the interpretation of the decree were issued. In Prussia Göring's directive laid down that, in addition to the basic constitutional rights, "all other restraints on police action imposed by Reich and *Land* law are abolished insofar as this is necessary and appropriate to achieve the purpose of the decree." On the basis of incomplete police reports, it is estimated that the number of arrests made by the regular police in Prussia during March and April came to around 25,000.

Seeing it as a temporary measure directed against the left, and blind to its long-term implications, Hitler's conservative partners in the coalition offered no objection, and Hitler himself, when asked by Sefton Delmer, of the London *Daily Express,* whether the suspension of personal freedom was to be permanent, replied: "No! When the Communist danger is eliminated things will get back to normal." But the suspension of constitutional rights was never repealed. Hitler never abrogated or replaced the Weimar constitution. Instead this emergency decree hastily improvised on the night of the Reichstag fire served to provide the legal basis for the Nazi police state for the twelve years of the Third Reich.

The threat of a Communist uprising was taken seriously by ordinary Germans, and the confidential reports by police and other official agencies on the state of public opinion confirm that the drastic measures taken by the government encountered little criticism, were widely welcomed, and gave Hitler's popularity a new boost on the eve of the election. [10] Seizing upon the "evidence" now provided of Communist subversion and the ruthlessness with which Hitler was prepared to defend the German people, the Nazi propaganda machine achieved new levels of mass suggestion and intimidation before election day, which Goebbels declared "The Day of National Awakening." Casualties among the Nazis' opponents amounted to fifty-one dead and several hundred injured, almost certainly an underestimate; the Nazis themselves lost eighteen dead. As the climax, all German radio stations carried Hitler's final speech to a giant demonstration in East Prussia, the province separated by the Versailles Treaty's Polish Corridor which was to return the highest Nazi vote of the election. "Now hold your heads high and proud once again," Hitler ended. "Now you are no longer enslaved and in bondage; now you are free again . . . by God's gracious act." [11] His messianic note was answered by a hymn sung by thousands of voices, over the last verse of which the bells rang out from Königsberg Cathedral. After the broadcast, "freedom fires" were lighted on the mountains and along the frontiers of the Reich, while SA columns started marching in every city.

Despite all the Nazi efforts, however, the election results were tantalizing.* With a record turnout of 88 percent, they added 5.5 million votes to their November 1932 figure, giving them over seventeen million by comparison with their partners', the Nationalists', three million. But, even with all the resources of the government at their command, the Nazi vote of 43.9 percent still fell short of a majority, and only with the addition of the Nationalists' vote were they able to claim 51.8 percent for the coalition government. The Center party gained nearly 200,000, the SPD, despite the harassment to which they had been subject, held steady with a loss of only 60,000 votes, and even the Communists polled 4.8 million, not much more than the loss of a million compared with November 1932.

It was still in the agrarian provinces of north and east Germany (East Prussia, Pomerania, Schleswig-Holstein) that the Nazis secured the biggest share of the vote; they improved in Württemberg and Bavaria, where they had been underrepresented, but still fell below the average, into the 30–40 percent bracket, in Berlin (31.3 percent) and the urban-industrial centers of the Catholic west (Cologne-Aachen, Düsseldorf, Westphalia South). Protestant rural areas and small towns continued to furnish the NSDAP's strongest support.

Hitler did not hesitate to claim the results as a victory for the Nazis alone and told the cabinet it amounted to a revolution. He spoke no longer as the head of a national government but as a triumphant party leader who now felt no necessity to pay more than cursory regard to his coalition partners.

*For the full results see Appendix One.

By arresting the KPD deputies but not formally banning the party, and even allowing a KPD ticket in the elections, Hitler had secured the best of both worlds. The nearly five million KPD votes might otherwise have gone to other parties, but as all the Communist seats in the Reichstag and in the Prussian Landtag remained vacant following the earlier arrests, the Nazis had an absolute majority in both parliaments without the Nationalists.

Whatever restraints still remained on the pent-up Nazi aggression and rapacity were now removed by the characteristic interplay of "legal" authorization from the highest level of government with the mixture of threats, blackmail, and terrorism at the local level. At the latter, throughout the country, the object was to secure official posts—everything from state governors and city mayors to postmasters and municipal caretakers—together with directorships and jobs in private companies (there were still six million registered unemployed). These were the "perks" of revolution. Making use of their auxiliary police powers, SA and SS detachments occupied town halls and government offices, newspaper and trade-union offices as well as businesses, department stores, banks, and courts, enforcing the dismissal of "unreliable" officials, demanding the appointment of *Alte Kämpfer* (veteran fighters), and even removing fixtures and fittings.

During the period when Hitler was concerned not to arouse opposition abroad or disturb the image of a "legal" takeover of power, there was no *official* persecution of the Jews. A party-directed boycott against Jewish businesses, doctors, and lawyers took place for four days in April 1933 but was abandoned when it proved unpopular at home and roused opposition abroad. In fact, one of the reasons why Hitler had agreed to it was to channel demands from the party radicals and the SA for action against the Jews into an organized boycott, which could be controlled.

The attacks continued, however, without any central direction. Members of the party and the SA had long been looking forward to the day when they could vent their malice against the Jews. Jewish officials in public employment were a prime target for purges, just as Jewish doctors and lawyers, academics, artists, and writers were for harassment and exclusion, Jewish businesses and shops for boycotts and looting. The regular police were by now well enough instructed to know they should not interfere: If anybody made trouble, they were beaten up or taken off to improvised SA houses or camps.

At the top, the priority was to use the pressure from below to provide the Reich minister of the interior, Wilhelm Frick, with an excuse under the Reichstag fire decree to appoint Reich commissioners in the nine *Länder* that did not already have Nazi governments, including Bavaria, Hesse, Saxony, and Württemberg. The "threat of disorder," which Frick gave as the pretext for his intervention, had nothing to do with "defense against Communist acts of violence injurious to the state," but arose from the Nazis' own provocative tactics. However, the confusion these produced, the hesitations and, in the case of Bavaria, the resistance of the existing authorities (who aimed to restore a constitutional monarch in Munich under the Wittelsbach Crown Prince Rupprecht) gave sufficient coloring to Frick's action in installing local Nazi or SA leaders as Reich commissioners with overriding police powers. By the middle of March the takeover was complete and all the German *Länder* had Nazi administrators.

When his Nationalist allies continued to protest against SA terrorism, they got short shrift. Hitler's response was to send a sharp reply to the vice-chancellor, von Papen, with a copy to the president. Rejecting the "systematic barrage aimed at stopping the National Socialist uprising," he declared that he "marveled at the tremendous discipline" of the SA and the SS: "History will never forgive us if in this historic hour we allow ourselves to be infected by the weakness and cowardice of our bourgeois world and use the kid glove instead of the iron fist." Hitler told von Papen he would permit nobody "to deflect him from his mission of destroying and exterminating Marxism" and urgently requested him "not to make these complaints any more in future. You are not entitled to." [12]

II

THE "DESTRUCTION OF MARXISM," the corollary of the "national revolution," provided Hitler's justification for his "toleration" of terrorism at the same time that he preserved the appearance of legality. But Hitler took the same care that Stalin did to see that terrorism was combined with propaganda, each intensifying the effect of the other. At the first meeting of the cabinet after the election he announced his intention to set up a Reich Ministry of Information and Propaganda, and on March 11 he appointed Goebbels as minister with a seat in the cabinet. Goebbels, who was Hitler's chief lieutenant along with Göring during this critical first year of the Third Reich, soon showed what he could do with the resources of the state at his disposal.

Hitler had insisted on holding new elections with one objective in mind, to use a majority in the Reichstag to pass a single law, which would give the cabinet the power to enact laws on its own authority. The election results had been disappointing, failing to provide him with anything like the two-thirds majority the constitution required for the passage of such an Enabling Act. But Hitler did not for a moment alter his course. Thanks to the Reichstag fire decree, all the eighty-one Communist and another six SPD deputies elected on March 5 had either been arrested or gone underground. Hitler, however, with an eye always to the value of a formal constitutional basis for his exercise of power, wanted a genuine two-thirds majority of the 647 seats (432) and believed he could get this if the Catholic Center and the fragmented middle-class parties as well as his Nationalist allies voted with the Nazis' 288 deputies.

He had two advantages. The first was the enthusiasm and relief that many unpolitical Germans of all classes, including intellectuals, felt at seeing a government that, for the first time for years, acted with decision and confidence in the future, and did so not by repudiating but by reasserting faith in the traditional German virtues of strong authoritarian rule, regard for order and security, respect for morality and religion. Many compared the first days of the Third Reich with the feelings of national unity and exaltation at the beginning of the First World War, the so-called *Burgfrieden* (party truce). How they could deceive themselves into believing this remains a matter of debate. The other advantage, not inconsistent with the first, but affecting many who were more skeptical about the character of the Nazi movement, was the impression of its irresistibility. As the Austrian novelist Robert Musil noted (without enthusiasm), "What this feeling probably signifies is that National Socialism has a mission and that its hour has come, that it is no puff of smoke, but a stage of history."[13]

The desire to be "on the side of history" to which the Marxists were so often to appeal, both before and after the Second World War, worked this time to the advantage of the Nazis and was exploited to the full by propaganda that used every device—including the propaganda effect of terrorism—to magnify the dynamism of the "Wave of the Future." Opportunism and idealism, fear and fatalism, all contributed to the flood of applicants to join the ranks of the victors, no fewer than 1,600,000 new members* (twice the previous total) between January 30 and May 1, 1933, when a ban was placed on further enrollments.

These powerful tides of feeling account for the fact that although the Nazis, even in March 1933, could not secure a majority vote in the biggest turnout of any election, Hitler and Goebbels themselves were surprised by the lack of anything more than token resistance to their proposals and the speed with which the Nazi takeover was accomplished. Experienced politicians in the Nationalist (DNVP) and the Center parties ought to have seen what would be the result of passing the Enabling Law, yet they still clung to the belief that Hitler was directing his attacks solely against the left, failing to realize that once the act was passed, they too would be vulnerable and Hitler free to dispense with them.

Two state occasions, separated by only forty-eight hours, showed the mask and the real face of Nazism. The first, the formal opening of the Reichstag, was named by Goebbels "The Day of the National Uprising," another magic formula like "legality." It was staged in the Potsdam Garrison Church, above the tomb of Frederick the Great, on the anniversary of Bismarck's opening of the first Reichstag after the unification of Germany on March 21, 1871. The choir and gallery of the church were filled with generals of the Imperial Army and the new Reichswehr, all in full-dress uniform, diplomats, judges, and senior civil servants, the representatives of the old Establishment, making, as it turned out, their last appearance. The

---

*The party's *Alte Kämpfer* referred to those who waited for the party's success before joining by the scornful term *Märzgefallene,* the "heroes who fell in March."

government, sitting in the nave, was supported by the solid mass of brown-shirted Nazi deputies making their first.

The central figure was the aged president, dressed in his field marshal's uniform, who saluted the empty throne of the kaiser as he moved slowly to his seat. President and chancellor had met on the steps of the church and there shaken hands, a gesture of acceptance and reconciliation between the old and the new Germany, which was reproduced a million-fold in post-cards and posters. In a performance no actor could have bettered, Hitler, dressed in a formal black cutaway coat, and deliberately, as it seemed, stressing his awkwardness in this self-effacing role, bowed deferentially to the president as the representative of national tradition, then followed behind, as the whole congregation rose to sing the chorale, *"Nun danket alle Gott"* ("Now Thank We All Our God"), which the victorious army of Frederick the Great had sung after recapturing Silesia for Prussia at the battle of Leuthen in 1757.

In his address von Hindenburg appealed for national unity and called upon the nation to support the government in its difficult task, invoking "the old spirit of this shrine . . . and a blessing upon a free, proud Germany united within herself." Hitler's response struck the same solemn and re-spectful note, paying tribute to the president whose "great-hearted deci-sion" had made possible this union "between the symbols of old greatness and youthful strength." In his turn he asked Providence to give them "that courage and their perseverance which we feel all around us in this shrine, sacred to every German, as men struggling for our nation's freedom and greatness at the tomb of the country's greatest king."[14] This invocation of nationalist feeling, after so many humiliations since the defeat of 1918, left an indelible impression on all who were present and was shared by the millions who crowded the streets outside, listened to its broadcast, or watched it in the movie theaters. Nothing could have done more to reassure the conservative elements in the nation and reconcile them to the new regime.

Two days later, on March 23, when the newly elected Reichstag met for its first and only business session, in the improvised setting of the Kroll Opera House, Hitler appeared in a very different role, one much more congenial to the party faithful who had little patience with the ceremonial mummery of Potsdam. The setting was dominated by a mass of swastika flags and banners; the corridors and aisles were lined with brown-shirted SA men.

Hitler too had discarded the chancellor's formal clothes for the brown shirt of the party leader. His first and only parliamentary speech began with assurances that the existence of the Reichstag, the rights of the president, and the position of the *Länder* would not be affected by the Enabling Act.

But it would be against the meaning of the national uprising and would hamper its intended purpose if the government were to negotiate with and petition for the Reichstag's approval of its measures from case to case.

With a clear majority behind it, the number of times the government would have to resort to such an act would be limited.

> But the government of the national uprising insists all the more on the passing of this bill. It offers the parties of the Reichstag the chance for peaceful development in Germany and reconciliation. . . . But it is resolute and equally prepared to meet refusal and will take it as a statement of opposition. You, the deputies, must decide for yourselves what it is to be, peace or war.[15]

In five short clauses the act gave the government power to alter the constitution; authorized the cabinet to enact laws; transferred the right to draft legislation to the chancellor; gave the cabinet the power to implement treaties with foreign states; and limited the validity of the act to four years, making it also dependent on the continued existence of the present government.

While the parties discussed among themselves how to vote, the massed detachments of SA men kept up a menacing chant of "We want the Enabling Act—or there'll be hell to pay." Hitler had given reassurances to the Center party and promised to put them in writing. Despite repeated inquiries, no letter was received, but the majority (against Brüning's opposition) decided to vote in favor. Only the Social Democrats, who had had to endure harassment and taunting from the SA, opposed it. The speech of their chairman, Otto Wels, rejecting the bill roused Hitler to fury. Brushing aside von Papen, who tried to restrain him, he launched into an abusive tirade, shouting that it was only on account of justice and for psychological reasons that he was appealing to the Reichstag "to grant us what in any case we could have taken." As for the Social Democrats: "I can only tell you: I do not want you to vote for it. Germany shall be free, but not through you!"[16] A prolonged ovation and loud shouts of "Heil!" greeted Hitler's outburst, to be repeated when the result—441 to 94 in favor—was announced.

IT WAS CHARACTERISTIC of Hitler's tactics that he did not abolish the Reichstag overnight, and even from time to time made use of it as a lawmaking body when it suited him—for example, to pass the anti-Jewish Nuremberg Laws of 1935. Already bypassed, however, by the use of the president's emergency powers, the Reichstag finally lost any power to resist the government and served only as a platform for Hitler to make speeches and major statements on foreign policy.

In line with the same policy of preserving the constitutional facade, the Enabling Law guaranteed the continued existence of the Reichsrat, the federal body representing the *Länder* as well as the Reichstag. The first steps had already been taken to prevent this concession from affecting the Nazi monopoly of power that Hitler was bent on creating. All the *Länder* were now under Nazi administration, and the Reichsrat, representing them, duly passed the Enabling Act unanimously the same evening as the Reichstag. On March 31 the Law for the Coordination (*Gleichschaltung*) of the *Länder* empowered the *Land* governments to make laws and reorganize their administrations independently of the *Land* assemblies. A week later, a second law with the same title set up Reich governors (*Reichsstatthalter*) to ensure "compliance in the *Länder* with the policies set out by the Reich chancellor," a hasty measure that appears to have been principally designed to curb independent action by party Gauleiters, as well as the SA and SS leaders (Röhm and Himmler), a political rather than a constitutional problem which was to lead to the Röhm purge of June 1934.

By then the constitutional process had been carried to its logical conclusion by yet another Law for the Reconstruction of the Reich (on January 30, 1934), which ended the Bismarckian federal settlement by abolishing the *Land* assemblies, transferring the sovereign rights of the *Länder* to the Reich, and making the *Land* governments, as well as the Reich governors, subordinate to the central government. Since this went beyond the terms of the original Enabling Law, Hitler preserved appearances by resorting to the Reichstag, which obligingly passed an "improved Enabling Law" allowing the abolition of the Reichsrat to take place "legally." At the same time, the government was given the power to introduce new constitutional laws at will, and, six months later, invoked it to abolish the office of Reich president.

All this elaborate constitutional scene-shifting was designed not only to remove obstacles to the political will of the new leadership, but to secure the cooperation of the civil service and the smooth working of the government machine.

Most German civil servants were willing to accept and work with the new regime, which made a strong appeal to the nationalist, antidemocratic, authoritarian traditions of the service. Its initial purge was directed against those with political affiliations (for example, with the SPD) or of Jewish descent; such action was now regularized retrospectively by the euphemistically named Law for the Restoration of the Professional Civil Service (April 7). Civil servants were prominent among those seeking to insure their positions and pensions by joining the Nazi party. All Hitler had to do was to preserve legal forms, to make clear that the national revolution would be implemented by due administrative process, and to reassure them (as he reassured the army) that the party would not take over the state, but that the two would coexist as the twin pillars of the Third Reich.

The civil service was to discover—as the army was, too, in the end—that Hitler's assurances were of more value to him in winning their cooperation than to them in providing guarantees against arbitrary intervention in their sphere of activity. But Hitler could not have managed without them in the first few years, and the process of encroachment in their case was gradual.

In the case of the political parties, however, their raison d'être was removed with the end of parliamentary government in both Reich and *Länder,* and the dissolution of all but the Nazi party followed within four months of the Enabling Act.

The KPD, although never formally banned, had already been effectively suppressed. Its leaders were in prison, concentration camps, or exile; its papers had been closed down, its offices occupied and assets seized. Henceforth it could function only from abroad or underground. The SPD was able to operate legally a little longer, but the move of part of its leadership to a base abroad in Prague provided the excuse to prohibit its activities in Germany and seize its assets as "an organization hostile to the German state and people" (June 22).

The other parties came under pressure to dissolve themselves. The efforts of the Nationalists and the Stahlhelm to maintain their equality as partners with the Nazis were not only forcefully opposed by the latter, but undercut by the growing number of defections to the Nazis. Hugenberg, who held no fewer than four Reich and Prussian ministries, resigned them all in protest, only to find that this led not to the collapse of the government, but to that of his own party, the active members of which were absorbed by the Nazis. The Center party was weakened by a similar flow of members and accommodations with the new regime, but the decisive blow to its position was the Vatican's eagerness, and Hitler's willingness, to conclude a Concordat which promised the continuation of parochial schools in exchange for a ban on the political activities of priests and Catholic organizations. The Center party dissolved itself on July 5, and the Concordat was signed in Rome three days later.

The National Socialists completed their capture of a monopoly of political power, less than six months after Hitler's appointment as chancellor, with the Law against the New Formation of Parties, enacted on July 14, 1933. This declared the Nazis to be the only legal party in Germany and threatened severe penalties for any other form of political activity. The number of Nazi ministers in the cabinet was raised from three to eight, and the other ministers who survived did so no longer as representatives of other parties but because Hitler wished it so. Finally, on November 12 elections took place to a new Reichstag, elections in which the German people were invited to vote for only one prearranged list of candidates, the "Führer's list." This was the first of a series of "yes" plebiscites, neatly defined by the German historian K. D. Bracher as "the preferred means of pseudo-legal, pseudo-democratic self-approbation" in dictatorships. On this occasion, helped by threats of what would happen to those who said no or failed to vote, the referendum was officially declared to have provided 95 percent support.

A year before, with the loss of two million votes in the Reichstag elections of November 1932, and with the blow of Strasser's resignation, many believed the Nazis had passed their peak. If they were given a second chance in January 1933, it was thanks to von Papen and the group around the president, but in the use they made of it they owed nothing to anyone but themselves.

It was an astonishing performance by any standards. Hitler had able lieutenants in Göring and Goebbels, but it was he who made the original discovery of how to combine the revolutionary threat from below with the tactics of "legality" and exploited this with such virtuosity as to disarm opposition and eliminate one after the other of the safeguards against the concentration of power in the hands of a single party and of himself as its unchallenged leader.

It is perfectly true that in doing so Hitler solved none of Germany's underlying economic, social, and structural problems and gave only the vaguest indications of how he thought of doing so. But the same could be said of Lenin in 1917. Lenin had to fight a civil war to make good his seizure of power; Hitler's *Machtübernahme* ("takeover of power") was completed within less than half a year, without civil war, while preserving the forms of the constitution and with every indication that he had reversed the mood of pessimism that had gripped the nation since the beginning of the crisis in 1929. Whatever they might think of his followers—and they clearly distinguished between Hitler and his party—the evidence points to a majority of Germans believing that, for the first time since Bismarck, they had found a leader capable of reversing the national decline and disunity that they dated from the humiliation of 1918.

III

THE QUESTION NOW BECAME what use Hitler proposed to make of the power he had accumulated. It was the question to which the Communist party in Russia had found no agreed answer more than ten years after their own seizure of power, and which Stalin then undertook to settle. The Nazi party was no different. Contemporary sources show how much argument there was about the answers. The controversy was revived in the 1960s and 1970s by a younger generation of historians coming of age after the war who reacted sharply against

> the persistent popular image of the Third Reich as a monolithic society subject to the personal rule and will of one man. In this view Hitler operated at the pinnacle of a tightly organized society which he manipulated in all respects. His regime was seen as centralized and highly efficient, and often contrasted with the more protracted decision-making process characteristic of parliamentary democracy. [17]

The value of the historical controversy has been not to substitute a different stereotype for the one now brought under attack, but to open up the subject in the same way that all major historical episodes—for example, the French Revolution—remain open to continuing debate. It can be assumed that, if the process of opening up continues in the former Soviet Union, it will submit both Lenin's and Stalin's revolutions to the same process of critical discussion.

Putting aside for the moment the question of Hitler's personal role, some of the most important points raised in the principal areas of revisionist controversy are worth summarizing—without necessarily accepting them.

Hitler, it has been argued, had no economic or social policy, and the Third Reich produced no restructuring of the German economy or revolutionary transformation of German society, both of which maintained a basic continuity with earlier periods. The anticapitalist elements in the Nazi program were ignored: The big corporations and banks were not nationalized, the department stores were not closed, the big estates were not broken up. The corporatist ideas that had attracted a great deal of support among the middle classes while the Nazis were still a movement were discarded once they formed a government. The trade unions were suppressed, collective bargaining banned, wages held down. In contrast, the capitalists were left to run the economy, and they made large profits out of rearmament, the war, and German conquests. The Nazi movement represented not a revolution but a counterrevolution, the German form of Fascism. The real revolutionary development was the loss of the war and the occupation and partitioning of Germany that followed.

Once he had removed the checks that the Weimar constitution provided against the arbitrary use of power, Hitler made no attempt to replace it with a new constitutional settlement. The cabinet, like the Reichstag, was not abolished, but met less and less frequently, finally not at all, thus abandoning any pretense of collective responsibility.

There was no more a Code Hitler to rival the Code Napoléon than a Hitler Constitution. He preferred to subvert, ignore, or bypass the legal and judicial system rather than reconstitute it on National Socialist principles. Nor did he show any interest in reorganizing the state administration to produce a more coherent division of responsibilities. When he wanted something done to which he attached great importance, he created special agencies outside the framework of the Reich government: Göring's organization for the Four-Year Plan, for example, which cut across the jurisdiction of at least four ministries.

Relations between the state and the party remained equally ill defined. The party was disappointed in its hopes of taking over the state, as the Communist party had effectively done in the Soviet Union, but the civil service had to accept Hitler's and other Nazi leaders' constant interference with due process. The most powerful of the Nazi leaders built up rival empires—Göring (the Four-Year Plan and the air force), Goebbels (propaganda and culture), Himmler (police and SS), Robert Ley (labor)—feuding with each other in a continuing fight to take over parts of each other's territory.

Historians continue to debate whether Hitler allowed this state of affairs to continue because he was unable to master it;* because by practicing "divide and rule" he protected his own position and obliged everyone to turn to him for decisions; or because it suited his personal style of leadership, and his disorderly, unsystematic habits of work. Whatever the reasons, this "polycratic" state, with competing centers of power, is very different from the earlier model of a monolithic, totalitarian dictatorship.

Even in the area in which Hitler showed the greatest personal interest, foreign policy, there is disagreement whether he pursued consistent ideological objectives or was an opportunist who relied upon bluff and improvisation without any clear aims to guide him. Some historians have stressed the continuity with the expansionist aims of German foreign policy in the First World War and earlier, from Bismarck's time. Others have argued that his success was primarily due to the weakness, divisions, and illusions of the other powers, which he was able to exploit in the same way that he owed his success in gaining power to exploiting the blindness and misjudgment of the right-wing and nationalist parties in Germany. Yet others have seen his gambles in foreign policy, and in risking war in 1939, as a way of diverting attention from and relieving domestic social tensions and economic problems for which he could find no solution, a revived form of late-nineteenth-century social imperialism.

This is the historiographical background against which any subsequent attempt to understand the first two years of the Nazi regime has to be set, with the reminder that Hitler's was a "revolution by installments," the character of which (like Stalin's "dosage") only became clear as the different stages succeeded each other, a warning that particularly applies to the earlier period when Hitler was at pains to conceal his real thoughts and objectives.

ON FEBRUARY 8, just over a week after coming to power, Hitler laid down his secret priority when he told the cabinet: "The next five years have to be devoted to rendering the German people again capable of bearing arms." When the minister of labor (Seldte) agreed but added that, besides the purely military tasks, there was also other economically important work that ought not to be neglected, Hitler reiterated:

Every publicly sponsored measure to create employment has to be considered from the point of view of whether it is necessary to render the German people again capable of bearing arms for military service. This has to be the dominant thought, always and everywhere. [18]

Summing up at the end he repeated: "For the next four–five years the main principle must be: everything for the armed forces."

Hitler's concept of *Wiederwehrhaftmachung* ("making the German people again capable of bearing arms") embraced much more than rearmament.

*One German historian, Hans Mommsen, has described him as "a weak dictator."

That was essential, but the fundamental task, without which material preparations for war would be wasted, was the psychological mobilization of the German people, the restoration of a sense of national unity and national pride, the undermining of which, Hitler believed, had produced the collapse of 1918 and the divided nation of the Weimar interlude.

Goebbels, whose Ministry of Popular Enlightenment and Propaganda was the first ministry Hitler created, understood very well what his directive was. At his first press conference he told his audience:

> I see the setting up of the new ministry as a revolutionary act, insofar as the new government no longer intends to leave the people to their own devices. . . .
> It is not enough for people to be more or less reconciled to our regime, to be persuaded to adopt a neutral attitude toward us; rather we want to work on people until they have capitulated to us, until they grasp ideologically that what is happening in Germany today not only *must* be accepted, but also *can* be accepted. [19]

Defeating his rivals in the party, Goebbels persuaded Hitler to give him control not only over the press, radio, films, and theaters, but also over the arts as well, including books, music and the visual arts, all brought under the Reich Chamber of Culture. It was Goebbels who greeted the "Burning of the Books" organized by the German student body on May 10, 1933: "It was a great and symbolic act, bearing witness to the world that the spiritual foundation of the November Republic has disappeared. From these ashes will arise the phoenix of a new spirit." [20]

The word "propaganda" is inadequate to convey the revolutionary character of Hitler's objective: nothing less than the transformation of people's consciousness, corresponding to his constantly repeated belief that it was politics, faith, and will, not economics and material circumstances, that were the deciding forces in history, corresponding also to his own unique ability to move the masses.

This was the main role, of ideological education and mobilization, that Hitler saw the party continuing to play. "For the *Weltanschauung,*" as Hitler wrote in *Mein Kampf,* "is intolerant . . . and peremptorily demands its own exclusive and complete recognition as well as the complete adaptation of public life to its ideas." [21] Like "propaganda," the colorless word *Gleichschaltung,* usually translated as "coordination," disguises rather than expresses the aggressive spirit in which the Nazis set about "politicizing" German life. Expanding a process already begun before 1933, the Nazis honeycombed society with party associations and institutions, infiltrating, and either taking over or displacing the existing professional organizations and the hundreds of voluntary bodies involved in sports, charitable activities, education, the arts, veterans', women's, farmers', and youth movements. As Joachim Fest says:

> One of Hitler's fundamental insights, acquired in the loneliness of his youth, was that people wanted to belong. . . . It would be a mistake to

see nothing but coercion in the practice of taking every individual into the fold according to his age, his function, and even his preferences in sport or entertainment, of leaving people nothing but sleep as their private domain, as Robert Ley remarked. [22]

Hitler and Goebbels did not rely on the spoken and written word alone to convey their message. Myth, ritual, and ceremony had an equally important part to play. Contemporary observers were impressed not only by the stage management of such spectacles as the annual harvest festival held on the Bückeberg near Hameln, or the Nuremberg rally of 1934 in which Hitler's architect, Albert Speer, and his favorite film producer, Leni Riefenstahl, cooperated to celebrate *The Triumph of the Will,* but also by the exhilaration those taking part experienced in submerging their personal identities in the reborn *Volksgemeinschaft,* the all-embracing "togetherness" of the ethnic community, personified in the myth figure of Adolf Hitler. This was something more than manipulation; it was the sharing of a common experience deeply felt by leaders as well as followers.

NATIONALIST FEELINGS APART, which were shared by the majority of Germans, the Nazi claims of success in converting the nation to their set of values, even in the euphoric early period, were exaggerated. The clearest expression of this was the split in the Protestant churches. In the spring of 1933 the Nazi Movement of German Christians (who called themselves "the SA of Jesus Christ") sought to carry out the *Gleichschaltung* of the Protestant churches under a single Reich bishop, the army chaplain Ludwig Müller; to abolish all elected church bodies in favor of the *Führerprinzip*; to implement a program of "racial purification," and to end the separation of church and state.

Resistance took the form of a call for a Confessional Church "independent of the state and the pressure of political power," led by two Berlin pastors, Martin Niemöller, a former U-boat captain, and the young Dietrich Bonhoeffer, with the backing of the leading Lutheran theologian Karl Barth. It reached a high point in the Barmen Declaration of May 1934 (Article 5: "We reject the false teaching by which the state is equated with the sole and total order of human life . . ."), and again in a June 1936 memorandum which attacked the Nazi ideology, the persecution of the Jews, the actions of the Gestapo outside the law, and the Führer cult.

Out-and-out resistance was continued by only a minority of brave men; the majority accepted an uneasy compromise, but the Nazis had to modify their tactics as well, and the attempt at *Gleichschaltung* was abandoned.

Hitler recognized in the cabinet discussions at the beginning of his government that it would take thirty or forty years to complete the conversion of the German people to the Nazi ideology; and he dismissed the older age groups who had acquired their values in a different world as "a lost generation." All the more reason, then, to concentrate their efforts on the young.

Characteristically, there was more rivalry than coordination among the different agencies concerned with indoctrinating the younger generations with Nazi beliefs. The federal structure of German education was replaced by a national Ministry of Education, but the minister's (Bernhard Rust's) attempts to lay down guidelines for the schools were held up by a running fight over jurisdiction with Hess and Bormann in party headquarters, as well as with Ley and Goebbels.

"The principal task of the school," according to Rust's directive of December 18, 1934, "is the education of youth in the service of nationhood and state in the National Socialist spirit." Equally clear was the definition of the role of the NS Teachers' League (NSLB) to which very soon a majority, and, by 1937, 97 percent, of teachers (always overrepresented in the party) belonged:

> National Socialism is a Weltanschauung whose claim to validity is total and does not wish to be subject to the random formation of opinion . . . German youth must no longer—as in the liberal era in the case of so-called objectivity—be confronted with the choice of whether it wishes to grow up in a spirit of materialism or idealism, or racism or internationalism, of religion or godlessness, but it must be consciously shaped according to . . . the principles of NS ideology.
>
> It is being carried out with the same methods with which the movement has conquered the whole nation: indoctrination and propaganda. [23]

The influence of Nazi ideology was particularly evident in the teaching of history, biology (the "theory of race"), German language and literature, and the marked increase in the time devoted to sports and physical education. Outside the school, Baldur von Schirach, appointed Reich youth leader in July 1933, built up the Hitler Youth to a monopoly position, finally recognized by the Law of March 1939, making membership in it compulsory between the ages of ten and eighteen for all boys and girls.

The party had been strongly represented in higher education before 1933, and membership of the Deutsche Studentenschaft (which organized the Burning of the Books) was made compulsory in April 1933. Students were required to do four months of labor service and two months in an SA camp as part of the twin cults of community (*Volksgemeinschaft*) and experience (*Erlebnis*, as distinct from the academic stress on knowledge, *Erkenntnis*), which the Nazis had taken over from the earlier independent Youth Movement, and now manipulated for their own ideological purposes.

Nazi penetration of the universities was not confined to the students. The years 1933 and 1934 saw a purge that led to the dismissal or resignation of 15 percent of the 7,700 tenured university teachers, 18 percent in the natural sciences. The majority of German professors, however, gave their support to the regime: 700 signed a declaration to this effect in November 1933, and Martin Heidegger, one of the most influential philosophers of the century, declared in his rector's inaugural address to Freiburg University: "No dogmas and ideas will any longer be the laws of your being. The Führer himself, and he alone, is the present and future reality for Germany and its law." [24]

In March 1935 Hitler reintroduced universal military service and made clear his expectation that the armed forces would not only, as a matter of course, remain loyal to the National Socialist view of the state, but would also select their officers "according to the strictest racial criteria, going beyond the legal regulations" (which already required proof of Aryan descent), [25] and appoint as reserve officers only those with a positive attitude to National Socialism "who do not behave indifferently, let alone hostilely towards it." [26]

The Wehrmacht was thus required to become, in Hitler's words, "educators in the military school of the nation." [27] Even more was expected of the SS, the most rapidly growing of all the Nazi fiefdoms, whose head, Heinrich Himmler, was fanatically committed to a biologically oriented racism and to the creation of a new Nazi elite based on racial criteria, an explicitly anti-Christian ideology, and unconditional obedience to whatever was asked of its members.

I V

ALTHOUGH HITLER constantly asserted the primacy of politics, he was too astute a politician not to recognize that just as the Depression, and the Nazi claim that they could find a way out, had been a powerful factor in winning them votes, so nothing would do more to promote the national revival he called for than economic success.

While he had been willing to listen to such economic radicals as Otto Wagener with their hostility to big business, he had always refused to do more than listen and came into office free of commitments. If he wanted to end unemployment—in four years, as he proclaimed publicly—and rearm Germany as quickly as possible—the secret priority he stated to the cabinet—there were strong practical reasons for working as closely as possible with the existing economic system and not throwing the economy into turmoil by untried radical schemes. There was more than expediency, however, in Hitler's attitude. The Princeton historian Harold James puts the point succinctly when he writes:

> There was nothing socialist about Hitler's economics. . . . Nazi collectivism was political, not economic, and left individuals as economic agents. The repeated declarations of the Nazi intention to socialize people rather than factories meant that far-reaching programs of state control over the economy were unnecessary. [28]

As James goes on to point out, Hitler's emphasis on will led to an insistence, unusual at the time, on the importance of innovators and designers such as Porsche, and the Junkers family of airplane manufacturers whom he greatly admired. He saw such individual entrepreneurs, threatened by the bureaucratized trusts, as the key to innovation, and innovation as the key to the future. Unlike the romantic agrarians among the Nazis, who looked on industrialization as an evil, Hitler was an enthusiast for technological progress and had no fear that it would increase unemployment: "I will simply build twice the length of Autobahn if it requires half the amount of labor."

Hitler also believed that economic success would help him to achieve his ideological objective of recapturing the German working class for "the national idea." The alienation of the German workers he had encountered in Vienna and their adoption of the Marxist ideology of class war in place of national solidarity had made a deep impression on him. Even in the March 1933 elections he had failed to shake the loyalty of the Social Democrat and Communist voters, who still represented more than 30 percent of the total. He was all the more determined to break the hold of the "Jewish-Marxist lies" and win the industrial working class back for the German *Volksgemeinschaft*.

Parallel with the prohibition of the two working-class political parties, Hitler moved against the trade unions. The Christian trade unions were spared for a few weeks longer, until after the conclusion of the Concordat with the Vatican; Hitler's target was the much larger socialist federation with a membership of four and a half million. Its leaders, dismayed by loss of membership in face of the Nazi tide of success and by the collapse of political resistance, offered to end their ties with the SPD and cooperate loyally with the Hitler government. But any hope that this would enable them to preserve their organization was soon dashed. While an Action Committee for the Protection of German Labor, led by Robert Ley, secretly drew up plans for the future German Labor Front (DAF), Goebbels prepared the way with another spectacular propaganda coup comparable to Potsdam Day.

The first of May, the day of the international workers' movement, was redesignated the Day of National Labor and made an official holiday. A giant meeting at the Tempelhof Airfield in Berlin brought together up to a million workers and their families, honored the "production workers of all classes," and celebrated National Socialism as a movement that would level outdated social distinctions, end snobbery and the class war, and establish mutual respect among the different groups that made up the nation. In his address Hitler reproved those who looked down on and underestimated manual labor, praised the industry of its people as the nation's greatest asset, and declared measures to end unemployment as the regime's highest priority.

The following morning the regime showed its other face: At 10 a.m. the SA and auxiliary police occupied all the premises of the trade unions and seized their property and assets. A week later, the first Congress of the German Labor Front inaugurated a new organization that soon included all German workers and employees.

The NSBO (the NS Factory Cell Organization), which Gregor Strasser had built up to develop a radical anticapitalist policy in industrial relations, and which had a million members by August 1933, saw this as its opportunity to take over the trade unions' functions and capture the German Labor Front for the representation of the workers' interests vis-à-vis the employers. But Hitler had not closed down the trade unions to see collective bargaining continue in another guise. The NSBO was brought under the control of the party's Political Organization in Munich and the leading radicals in it purged.

By a law of May 19, 1933, the state removed the responsibility for regulating wages from both workers and employers by appointing Reich Trustees of Labor, twelve in all, each covering a separate district, and in practice consisting of a mixture of officials with lawyers from employers' organizations.

Whatever the workers' opinion of it, Nazi labor policy was reassuring to the employers. The relationship of German big business to the new political masters had started awkwardly. Summoned by Göring on February 20 to meet Hitler before what he promised them would be "the last election," twenty-five leading industrialists found themselves required to put up an electoral fund of three million marks. Their hopes that their principal association, the Reichsverband der Deutschen Industrie (RDI, chairman: Gustav Krupp von Bohlen), might be allowed to retain its independence were roughly shattered when a Nazi vigilante squad led by Otto Wagener invaded its Berlin headquarters on April 1 and staged a forcible takeover. Protests produced no effect; in May the Reichsverband "voluntarily" dissolved itself and merged with other industrial associations in a new Nazi-sponsored organization.

But fears that radicals like Wagener or the activists of the NSBO would dictate economic policy were soon proved groundless. With the dissolution of the trade unions and the works councils, the industrialists were once again, to their great satisfaction, masters in their own house. Even more important, for the attitude of both employers and workers, was the dramatic upturn in economic activity that between 1933 and 1936, turned unemployment figures of six million into a labor shortage.

HOSTILITY TO big business in the Nazi party was to be found not only in the NSBO, but also among the members of the middle-class interest groups representing small businessmen, craftsmen, and retail traders. These had been absorbed into the party and expected its coming into power to be followed by the realization of their demands, such as the closing down of the big department stores and consumer cooperatives. These had been major themes in the party's electoral campaigns as well as in its original program, and it was not easy for Hitler to ignore them.

This accounts for the appointment, as Reich commissioner for the economy, of Otto Wagener, with his radical plans for breaking up large, imper-

sonal concentrations of ownership and his attempt to take over the citadel
of big business, the RDI. Without waiting for decisions at the top, many
local actions were launched by the party and SA in the early days of the new
regime, culminating in a national boycott of Jewish firms, launched on April
1, the same day Wagener stormed the RDI headquarters in Berlin.

These aggressive tactics, however, met strong resistance from big business and from those Nazi leaders who took their side, particularly Göring.
To block Wagener from becoming economics minister, Göring persuaded
Hitler to appoint in his place Kurt Schmitt, the managing director of the
Munich Allianz insurance group, and to create an additional state secretary—Hans Posse, a former Weimar civil servant—to work in the economics ministry alongside Gottfried Feder, that figure from the Nazi past who
had once impressed Hitler so much and committed the party in the 1920
program to "breaking the servitude of interest." The test case was the
appeal of a Jewish business, the big Hermann Tietz department-store chain,
for help in rescheduling its debts. Hitler himself was strongly opposed but
had to yield to the argument that, if help was not given, the bankruptcy of
Tietz and other department stores would lead to the loss of tens of thousands of jobs as well as a wave of price rises.

In the summer of 1933 the Nazi Combat League of Middle-Class Tradespeople was dissolved, and Otto Wagener finally disappeared into obscurity.
A new body for small businessmen, the Nazi HAGO, was created under much
tighter control by Hess and the party bureaucracy. In his important speech to
the Reich governors on July 6, Hitler made it clear that the revolution had
ended and could not be allowed to extend into the economic field: "More
revolutions have succeeded in their first assault than, once successful, have
been stabilized and held there. Revolution is not a permanent state." [29]

There was one economic sector, however, where ideology was allowed to
override both economic and social considerations. This was agriculture. "It
is necessary from now on to separate the peasant economy from the capitalist market economy." [30]

Tax cuts and debt reduction gave immediate relief to farming districts,
which had been among the hardest hit during the Depression and had
returned the highest vote for the Nazis. There was a strong element of
agrarian romanticism in National Socialism, which expressed a deep-rooted
distrust of urban and industrial civilization, called for the protection of the
peasantry as "the biological blood-renewal source of the body politic," and
was linked in Himmler's SS fantasies with the settlement policy based on
race in the *Lebensraum* to be conquered in the east.

The party's agricultural leader, Walter Darré, was well placed to give
practical expression to these ideas. Under his leadership the Nazis had
already secured a firm foothold in the agrarian interest associations (such
as the Reich Land League) and the chambers of agriculture, even before
1933. When Hugenberg resigned all his economic ministries, Hitler made
Darré minister for agriculture and the fourth Nazi member of the cabinet.

He was thus able to combine control of the party's Agrarian Policy Apparatus (AA) with that of the self-governing agricultural organizations *and* the appropriate ministry. Largely as a result of this, he was able to initiate a program aimed at the stabilization of land ownership, total control of markets and prices, and a land-settlement scheme.

Where Stalin saw the kulak as the greatest obstacle to his policy of modernization, Hitler hailed the peasants as "the enduring foundation of German nationality." To mark the importance the Nazi government attached to them as "the future of the nation," an *Ehrentag* (memorial day) for the German peasantry was instituted on October 1, 1933, to match May 1 as the festival of labor. This became the occasion of an annual demonstration on the Bückeberg, at which half a million farmers in 1933, a million in 1935, were mobilized to hear Hitler speak.

FÜHRERPRINZIP and the Hitler myth notwithstanding, in the early period of office, certainly up to June 30, 1934, Hitler was no more exempt than any other politician from the need to tack, give contradictory promises, and accept compromises he disliked. Its critics had always believed that a party that had made so many promises to so many different groups in order to come to power would fall apart when it got there. With the expectations of millions of supporters raised to fever pitch, Hitler did well to ride the tide and not be submerged. In many areas, local Nazi and SA leaders did not wait for leave from Berlin to start taking action on their own initiative, and Hitler's speech to the Reichsstatthalter in July 1933 shows the difficulty he and Göring still had in keeping control.

When allowance is made, however, for the confusion and tactical switches characteristic of any revolutionary episode, it is not difficult to follow a consistent line in Hitler's handling of economic issues to which he reverted after temporary diversions. There were undoubtedly a substantial number in the Nazi movement who looked for the takeover of power in the first six months of 1933 to be followed by a radical restructuring of the economy. Hitler was not among them: To say that he "failed" to carry out such a fundamental reform ignores the evidence that he never meant to do so. For Hitler the revolution remained a political one, a decisive change in the internal balance of power, the centerpiece of which was the elimination of the "Marxist" parties of the left, including the trade union movement. Having accomplished that, the uses to which he meant to put the position he had established had to remain concealed, until he had prepared the way by the material and psychological mobilization of the German people, their *Wiederwehrhaftmachung*, which he told the cabinet would take five years.

Hitler did not underestimate the importance of economics, but he took an instrumental view of it. He told building workers on his Berchtesgaden estate:

A lot is said about the question of a private-enterprise economy or a cooperative economy, a socialized economy or a private-property economy. Believe me, the decisive factor is not the theory but the performance of the economy. [31]

If the economy under the existing system could produce the results Hitler wanted—economic recovery and the elimination of unemployment in the short run, German rearmament in the longer run, but still as quickly as possible—he saw no reason why he should jeopardize its performance by a series of radical changes that, from his point of view, were irrelevant. The future of the German nation would be assured not by economic and social reforms but by the conquest of additional *Lebensraum* once the power to acquire it had been created.

V

MUCH THE SAME can be said about rearmament and foreign policy: continuity with policies and plans of earlier governments; cooperation with the existing Establishment in industry, the army, and the Foreign Office. In each case, the same misleading impression is given, if the perspective is limited to 1933 to 1935.

The efforts of Hitler's predecessors, Brüning, von Papen, and von Schleicher, secured the cancellation of reparations at the 1932 Lausanne conference and the concession of parity by the General Disarmament Conference. Production of forbidden weapons (for example, airplanes and poison gas) had begun in Soviet Russia in 1922, and secret planning for German rearmament in 1926. In 1928 the Defense Ministry had sanctioned a program for sixteen divisions by 1932; when that year came, the program was again expanded to produce an army of twenty-one divisions (300,000 men) by 1938. Even Hitler's plans for expansion in the east (carefully concealed in this period) took up the theme of a German Mitteleuropa, familiar from Pan-German propaganda of the 1890s, and aimed to restore a German hegemony in Eastern Europe, which had been achieved in 1917 and lost after Brest-Litovsk.

What Hitler offered the German generals when he met them on February 3, 1933, four days after becoming chancellor, was not a new policy but enhanced prospects of achieving the common nationalist aim of "throwing off the shackles of Versailles" and recreating German military power. To the question of how that power should be used when it had been gained, Hitler's answer was deliberately vague. General Liebmann's notes of his talk read: "That is impossible to say yet. Perhaps fighting for new export possibilities, perhaps—and probably better—the conquest of new living space in the East and its ruthless Germanization." [32]

Hitler promised the German army that they would not be called upon to intervene in domestic politics; but there remained the anxiety that the army's position might be undercut by the SA, whose two and a half million members were the principal source of reserves in an emergency, and whose chief of staff, Röhm, was quite open about his ambition to replace the traditionalist Reichswehr with a People's Militia. This anxiety appears to have been the impetus behind the new program that the Defense Ministry produced in December 1933 for expanding the proposed peacetime army of twenty-one divisions to sixty-three in wartime. Such a program could be carried out only if conscription were introduced, so ending the army's dependence on Röhm's SA militia for reserves.

Hitler's chief concern, to begin with, was to provide the necessary camouflage during the period of rearmament. It was then, as he reminded the generals on February 3, that Germany would be most vulnerable. "That will show whether or not France has *statesmen*: If so, she will not leave us time but will attack us, presumably with eastern satellites." He made use of a series of press interviews with foreign correspondents to allay French and British fears, and in his first speech on foreign policy (May 17) skillfully combined assurances of peaceful intentions with a measured statement of Germany's "just claims" to the revision of Versailles.

> The present generation of this new Germany [he declared], which so far has experienced the poverty, misery, and distress of its own people, has suffered too deeply from the madness of our time to contemplate treating others in the same way. Our love for and loyalty to our own national traditions makes us respect the national claims of others and makes us desire from the bottom of our hearts to live with them in peace and friendship. . . . The French, the Poles are our neighbors and we know that through no possible development of history can this reality be altered.
>
> It would have been better for the world if in Germany's case these realities had been appreciated in the Treaty of Versailles. For the object of a really lasting treaty should be not to cause new wounds and keep old ones open, but to close wounds and heal them. . . . Nevertheless no German government will of its own accord break an agreement unless its removal could lead to its replacement by a better one.
>
> But the legal character of such a treaty must be acknowledged by *all*. Not only the conqueror but also the conquered party can claim the rights accorded in the treaty. [33]

At the Geneva Disarmament Conference, which continued in session throughout 1933, it was the German Defense and Foreign Ministries that instructed their representatives to take a hard line and threaten withdrawal, bypassing Hitler, who was more inclined to be cautious. Only in October 1933 was von Blomberg able to persuade Hitler to put the threat into effect; but, once convinced, Hitler brought off the first of his foreign-policy coups, by combining withdrawal from the Disarmament Conference (October 14) with withdrawal from the League of Nations, a course for which Japan had set a useful precedent in May. Hitler made the most of the argument that, if the other powers were serious in proclaiming the principle of equality, they either had to disarm themselves or accept the rearmament of Germany. Following a technique that was to become all too familiar, Hitler accompanied his announcement with an emotional broadcast in which he disclaimed any intention of aggression, calling France "our ancient but glorious opponent," and declaring that "anyone who can conceive of a war between our two countries is mad."

Convinced that the German people would rise to his declaration of independence, after all the humiliations they felt they had suffered at the hands of the victorious powers and the double-talk of the League, Hitler called for a plebiscite on November 12, one day after the fifteenth anniversary of the 1918 armistice and launched another giant propaganda campaign: "We want honor and equality!" His political instinct was sure. Even though the figures of 95 percent approval for his action in the plebiscite and thirty-nine million votes for the Nazi "unity" candidates in the simultaneous Reichstag elections bore evidence of the manipulation and intimidation that were part of Nazi propaganda technique, no one seriously questioned that the results reflected the overwhelming mood of the nation.

His success in confusing and dividing opinion in the Western democracies confirmed Hitler's contempt for their leaders. His assurances of peace had the same success in foreign affairs as his promise to respect legality had in domestic. Anxious to be reassured, the British and French deluded themselves with the same disastrous belief as the German right, that it would be possible to contain the National Socialist dynamic. As a result, they allowed themselves to be drawn into policies of appeasement that undermined the system of European security built up against a revival of German power, and gave Hitler the freedom to carry out Germany's rearmament and remove the restrictions of Versailles, as the preliminary to a resumption of German expansion. These were aims that had the additional advantage for Hitler of coming closer than anything else to uniting the German people. Rearmament was the best answer to Germany's political as well as economic problems, equally acceptable to industry, the army, the nationally minded members of the civil service, Foreign Office, and diplomatic corps as well as the party and the man in the street.

Ironically, the first two powers to grant international recognition to the new regime in Germany were the Kremlin, which secured the extension in May 1933 of the Treaty of Berlin, a treaty of friendship and neutrality negotiated with Weimar in 1926, and the Vatican, which signed the Concordat in July. Simultaneous efforts by Mussolini to promote a four-power treaty between Italy, Britain, France, and Germany, although it was never signed, meant the tacit acceptance of Nazi Germany into their ranks.

While Hitler continued to provide diplomatic camouflage, he gave Göring as Reich commissioner for civil aviation the green light to go ahead secretly with creating the military air force that was forbidden by Versailles. Göring insisted, over the opposition of the army, in making the Luftwaffe an independent service, with a separate ministry of which the able Erhard Milch, head of Lufthansa, and an enthusiastic Nazi, was made state secretary.

The essential function of the new air arm was to fulfill the same purpose as Admiral Alfred von Tirpitz's famous "risk theory," which justified the expansion of the German navy before 1914: It was the quickest way of increasing the risks of war for any potential enemy and so reducing the danger of a preventive strike while Germany was rearming. Although Hitler did not admit the existence of a German air force publicly until March 1935, the anxiety aroused in Britain by unofficial reports as early as the summer of 1933 gave substance to the risk theory and created opportunities for Hitler to drive a wedge between Britain and France. In November 1933 Hitler sent his "representative for disarmament questions," Joachim von Ribbentrop, as a personal emissary to London, where he broached the idea of an agreement between Britain and Germany, in which the latter would "guarantee the British Empire" in return for a free hand in Eastern Europe. A naval agreement was proposed as the basis for a nonaggression pact, a suggestion repeated by the commander in chief of the German navy, Admiral Erich Raeder, to the British naval attaché at the end of November, and by Hitler himself to the British ambassador in December.

The use of Ribbentrop for this purpose was a pointer. During his first year in office Hitler had given another apparent proof of continuity by leaving von Neurath undisturbed in the Foreign Office, listening to the permanent officials' advice, replacing none of Germany's representatives abroad, except in Washington, where the ambassador resigned. But during 1934 Hitler began to show greater independence, and the Foreign Office to discover that it had rivals in the party with large ambitions in foreign policy. Among them were Goebbels, Göring, Ribbentrop, Gauleiter Bohle, head of the party's Foreign Countries Organization (Auslandsorganisation, AO), which organized German ethnic groups abroad, and Rosenberg, head of the party's Foreign Affairs Department (Aussenpolitisches Amt, APA).

Ribbentrop, a former champagne salesman of whom Goebbels said, "He bought his name, he married his money, and he swindled his way into office," was the most persistent, persuading Hitler (who was impressed by his salesman's knowledge of foreign countries and languages) to send him on occasional missions abroad. Setting up his own Ribbentrop Büro, he concentrated on Hitler's favorite idea of an alliance with Britain, flattering him and building up his hopes against the skepticism of professionals. So successful was Ribbentrop in winning Hitler's confidence that he was able to supplant von Neurath as foreign minister in 1938 and reduce the once-confident Foreign Office to the role of a "technical apparatus"—the phrase used by Ernst von Weizsäcker, its state secretary, to describe its humiliation.

Hitler's second coup, which stood traditional German foreign policy on its head, was his Non-Aggression Pact of January 1934 with Poland. If there was one country whose very existence was an offense in German nationalist eyes it was Poland, to which Germany had lost Posen, West Prussia, and Upper Silesia after the First World War, and whose Polish Corridor separated Danzig and East Prussia from the Reich. Poland was the key to the *cordon sanitaire* that the French had built up against Germany in Eastern Europe.

When Hitler came into office, Marshal Joseph Pilsudski had proposed to the French a preemptive attack on Germany. French unwillingness to support him made Pilsudski receptive to the alternative course, which Hitler suggested, of safeguarding Poland by a guarantee from Germany. Hitler could see great advantage in such a move, at one and the same time ending the threat of a Polish attack which the German army had long regarded with anxiety; devaluing the French alliance system; and presenting a German-Polish agreement as the foundation for the defense of Europe against Bolshevism. The move was not popular in Germany; the recovery of the territories lost to Poland at the end of the war was at the top of the revisionist program. But Hitler's interest in Eastern Europe was directed at something more than frontier revision, at the much bigger objective of the conquest of *Lebensraum*. The time for that had not yet come; in the meantime, as Hitler foresaw, his willingness to sign a pact with Poland made a deep impression abroad and provided a precedent for the series of bilateral pacts with which Hitler was able to destroy every attempt to organize collective security.

The fact that relations with Russia had by this time deteriorated into a propaganda war (another break with the Weimar tradition of German-Soviet friendship which went back to the Rapallo Treaty of 1922) did Hitler no harm. There was considerable profit to be derived in conservative European circles as well as in Germany from transforming the anti-Marxist campaign that had been the staple of Nazi electoral propaganda into an anti-Bolshevik crusade. The possibility that Poland might become a partner in such a crusade remained open until 1939.

Hitler's third initiative in foreign affairs was as inept as his pact with Poland was astute. Pilsudski is reported to have been influenced in favor of Hitler's offer by the fact that he was an Austrian who would not share the traditional Prussian hostility toward the Poles. It was even more natural for Hitler, the Austrian who had become German chancellor, to think of carrying out the oldest of all his political dreams and bringing the Germans of Austria into a Greater Germany. The Austrian Nazis already recognized him as their leader, and a massive program of support for them was launched, reinforced by an economic boycott and aimed at overthrowing the government of Engelbert Dollfuss in Vienna by an internal coup.

The Polish pact was a matter of calculation; in Austria, Hitler's judgment was clouded by emotion. He was badly informed about the strength of the Austrian Nazis and maladroit in his failure to realize the effect his threats and boycott of Austria were having on France, which had vetoed an Anschluss—a union of Germany and Austria—in 1931, as well as on his relations with Italy, the other country besides Britain that he had always regarded as an essential ally if he was to isolate France. Mussolini, with

Central European ambitions of his own, appointed himself the Austrian chancellor Dollfuss's protector, and in February 1934 joined France and Britain in publishing a declaration on the need to maintain Austria's independence. Dollfuss's wife and family were actually staying with Mussolini when the Austrian Nazis attempted their coup (July 25, 1934), breaking into the chancellery and fatally wounding Dollfuss. This was another putsch that failed: The Nazis were overpowered, and thousands fled across the German frontier. Mussolini ordered Italian troops to the Brenner Pass and sent the Austrian government promises of aid in the defense of their country's independence.

Hitler had no option but to repudiate all connection with the conspiracy and order the surrender of Dollfuss's murderers. The German minister in Vienna was recalled, and von Papen, a Catholic and still vice-chancellor in Hitler's cabinet, was sent to Vienna to repair the damage.

Nineteen thirty-four ended badly for Hitler's diplomacy, with the French foreign minister, Louis Barthou, putting new life into the French alliances in Eastern Europe and Russia accepting election to a permanent seat on the Council of the League of Nations. Hitler responded with more foreign press interviews in which the word "peace" was never out of his mouth. "If it rests with Germany," he told Ward Price of the London *Daily Mail,* "war will not come again. This country has a more profound impression than any other of the evil that war causes." [34]

The Austrian fiasco illustrates clearly the limited room for maneuvering that Hitler had in international relations in the first half of the 1930s, just as the revisionist program that he took over underlines the continuity with the foreign policy of earlier governments. But it would be misleading to take this as incompatible with Hitler's having long-term plans of the kind discussed in *Mein Kampf,* as misleading as it would be to take Hitler's eloquent declarations of his devotion to peace as incompatible with accepting and preparing for the risk of war. Like his threats against the Jews, these long-term plans were not in the nature of a "blueprint for aggression" or a timetable: Hitler was a thorough opportunist in both tactics and timing, as his fluctuating attitude to Great Britain, the ally he was never able to win over, demonstrates. They were rather in the nature of a magnetic pole to which his compass needle and course reverted after every tactical diversion or change of program. The first marker that he laid down as early as his first years in power was the German-Polish pact, and it was characteristic of his flexibility that this left open the question of whether Poland was to become a partner in an anti-Bolshevik crusade, or to be destroyed—even, as it turned out, partitioned with the Russians—as a preliminary to the invasion of the Soviet Union.

THE FIRST STAGE of Hitler's revolution opened with the dramatic sequence of events that followed his appointment as chancellor in January 1933 and culminated in the recognition in July of the Nazis as the only party in a single-party state. It ended with the even more dramatic events of June 30, 1934, justified by Hitler's claim to be the "supreme judge of the German people" and culminated in his merger of the offices of president, chancellor, and Führer on the death of von Hindenburg. The politics of this initial period "oscillated between making revolution and halting the revolution,"[35] focusing on the role the party was to play in the one-party state, now that the movement phase in its history was over. Hitler sought to settle the matter in July 1933 with the slogan "Unity of Party and State." "The party has now become the state. All power rests with the Reich government." This, however, was to state the issue, not to settle it.

In the Soviet Union the meaning of a one-party state was clear enough: The party decided policy and issued orders to the state. Many in the Nazi party assumed that, once in power, they too would take over the state and issue the orders. By the summer of 1934, it was settled that they would not. The alternative model developed in Germany, a triad of party-state-Führer with the last at the apex of the triangle, was not at all clear-cut, however, and was constantly subject to fluctuation.

The "revolution from below," the spontaneous action of party and SA leaders as Reich commissioners and special commissioners at the *Land* and local level was the motive power that supplied the pressure and the threat with which Hitler was able to push through the "revolution from above." But once this was completed it was essential, as K. D. Bracher puts it, "to protect the power won against unchecked inroads by the Party."[36]

There was strong opposition to the extension of the revolution not only from business but from senior civil servants, who feared that, if the purge was allowed to continue, the service would collapse. This was a risk that the new government could not afford to take. Frick, the Reich minister of the interior, and Göring, minister of the interior for Prussia (with much the larger civil service), combined with conservative ministers to back the Law for the Restoration of the Professional Civil Service (April 7, 1933), and before the end of the month Göring acted in Prussia to abolish the "army of commissioners" who threatened to undermine and shatter the authority of the state.[37] Hitler's move at the same time to keep the headquarters of the Party Organization in Munich, and make Hess his deputy with power to settle all questions concerning the party leadership on his behalf, was aimed to prevent the party from exercising direct influence over the government. An insignificant personality, but tenacious in his loyalty to Hitler, Hess could be relied on (with the help of his own deputy, Martin Bormann) to act as a screen between the individual party bosses and Hitler, now that the latter had become chancellor.

The increased size of the party made it much more suited to the role Hitler foresaw of a broad-based organization with the tasks of mobilizing and controlling the nation rather than of a hand-picked elite to provide its leadership. Although the party had set up in advance shadow departments for all the main functions of government, there had been no merger of party and state bureaucracies, and only four party leaders—Göring, Goebbels, Frick, and Darré—succeeded in becoming heads of government departments. As late as 1937, seven out of the twelve departmental ministries were headed by nonparty ministers, still only five by real party members. [38]

Much more of a problem than the party was the SA, also increased in size by the transfer to it of the nationalist Stahlhelm in June. Unlike the other Nazi leaders who, whether at the Reich or *Land* level, sought to secure a foothold in state as well as party offices, Röhm deliberately kept his mass army of Brownshirts separate from the state. This gave him an independent power base, for which he openly proclaimed the role of "completing the National Socialist revolution," and submerging the "gray rock" of the Reichswehr, the regular army, "in the brown flood" of the SA. In June 1933, he published an article in the *NS Monatshefte* in which he spoke of the SA and the SS standing beside the army and the police "as the third power factor of the new state with special tasks":

> The course of events between January 30 and March 21, 1933 does not represent the sense and meaning of the German National Socialist revolution. . . .
> The SA and the SS will not tolerate the German revolution going to sleep or being betrayed at the halfway stage by noncombatants. . . . The Brown Army is the last levy of the nation, the last bastion against Communism.
> If those bourgeois simpletons think it is enough that the state apparatus has received a new sign, that the National Revolution has already lasted too long, for once we agree with them. It is in fact high time the National Revolution stopped and became the National Socialist one. Whether it suits them or not, we shall continue with our struggle. If they finally grasp what it's all about: with them! If they don't want to: without them! And if need be: against them! [39]

The SA came increasingly to represent the army of the dissatisfied who wanted the revolution to continue until they, too, were provided for.

It was against this attitude that Hitler had directed his remarks on July 6 at the Reich governors' conference on the need to bring the revolution to an end. [40] Frick and Goebbels spoke out to the same effect, the latter proclaiming "the winding up of the Nazi revolution" in a warning against "camouflaged Bolshevik elements who talk about a second revolution." In Prussia, on Göring's orders, the auxiliary police were disbanded, and efforts were made to bring the SA and SS concentration camps under police control and to suppress terrorist acts.

These measures did not impress Röhm, and Hitler allowed him to install

SA special deputies in Prussia, despite Göring's earlier ban, while still telling the Reich governors at their September conference that the advocates of a second revolution were his enemies "whose hash we would yet unexpectedly settle." But not yet: Several remarks by Hitler that autumn show him without a clear idea of how to proceed, and the Law for Ensuring the Unity of Party and State, drafted by Frick, did nothing to remove the confusion. The statement that "after the victory of the Nazi revolution," the party was "the bearer of the concept of the German state and is inseparably tied to the state" meant no more than the proclamation of "the unity of party and state" six months before. Hess and Röhm were appointed ministers, but insofar as this created an "indissoluble" link between party and state, it worked in favor of the state whose directing organ, the cabinet, Hess and Röhm now joined without portfolios or executive powers.

The regular reports on public opinion from all parts of the Reich, of which Hitler was well aware, showed a significant deterioration in the popular mood during the first half of 1934. [41] The enthusiasm of the summer of 1933, briefly revived by the withdrawal from the Disarmament Conference and the League in the autumn, had faded. The new regime had not added to its credit with the trial of the Communist leaders accused of planning the Reichstag fire, which ended in a fiasco and the release of all the defendants except the young Dutchman van der Lubbe. [42] The promised economic benefits had not yet materialized, and, while Hitler himself remained popular, there was increasing resentment at the corruption and insolent behavior of the local party bosses. In his study *The Hitler Myth* the British historian Ian Kershaw sums up the reports:

> Most of all the "unacceptable face of the Third Reich" was mirrored in the bullying arrogance and rowdy disturbances of the power-crazed SA, whose unsavory behavior—once the "troublemakers" of the left and other "antisocial elements" had been cleared away—was deeply offensive to the sense of public order and morality of middle-class Germans. [43]

RÖHM AND THE SA posed a special problem for Hitler, for two very different reasons. The SA, the armed force of the party, and the army, the armed force of the state, represented the party-state relationship in its most dangerous form, which could lead to more than a clash of jurisdictions, to actual hostilities. And his own relationship with Röhm was the most difficult one for Hitler to manage. Röhm had been his original patron in the earliest days of the movement, when he was on the staff of the Army District Command in Munich. The clash between them over the function of the SA—Hitler's political versus Röhm's paramilitary conception—had already led to a quarrel and Röhm's dismissal in 1925. Faced with a rebellious SA, chafing at the restraints of "legality," Hitler had called him back in 1931, only to see the same issue surface again, the incompatibility between the politician's and the Freikorps mentality.

Now that Hitler had become chancellor, Röhm took no more trouble than he had in the 1920s to guard his mouth or disguise his scorn for Hitler's compromises with the established order. His appointment to the cabinet, and Hitler's particularly cordial letter of thanks at the end of the year only strengthened his belief that "Adolf" secretly agreed with him. He not only continued to be free in his criticisms of the regime and its policies, but also carried out an ostentatious series of SA parades, inspections, and demonstrations throughout Germany and began to secure additional supplies of arms, partly from abroad.

The intensified SA activities, even if without a definite aim as yet, represented a challenge to Hitler's authority that he could not ignore and that could not have come at a worse time. If he did not meet the challenge and persuade Röhm to drop his talk of a second revolution—worse still, if the SA leaders with their two and a half million men began to take their talk of "action" seriously and threaten a confrontation with the army, the whole basis of the regime could be called into question. The army's new plan for conscription, aimed to cut out the SA, showed that it would not sit by and let this happen—and they would have strong support from the conservative forces in the state, and from a public opinion that was more and more fed up with SA behavior. Hitler had not forgotten the lesson he drew from the earlier putsch of 1923: never to come into open conflict with the army, least of all at a time when he was dependent on its leaders for carrying out the priority task of rearmament and while Germany was still vulnerable to intervention from abroad. Finally, the failing health of the aged president made it very likely that the question of his successor would have to be resolved in the near future. Hitler was determined that no one else should become head of state, but a mutiny by the SA, or even the threat of one, could compromise his chances, especially with the army, which was certain to claim a major voice in deciding who was to become von Hindenburg's successor as commander in chief as well as president.

At the beginning of January 1934 Hitler called in Rudolf Diels, the head of the Prussian Gestapo (*Ge*heime *Sta*atspolizei, Secret State Police), and ordered him to collect any incriminating evidence about "Röhm and his friendships" (Röhm and some other SA leaders were homosexuals) and the SA's involvement in terrorist actions. "This is the most important assignment you have ever received," he told Diels. [44] He still hoped to head off a confrontation, but there was no doubt which side he would come down on if he had to choose. When he received Anthony Eden, already a minister in the British government, in Berlin on February 21, he confided to him that he meant to reduce the SA by two-thirds and make sure that the remaining formations received neither arms nor military training. [45] A week later, he called the army commanders and the SA and SS leaders to a meeting in the Ministry of Defense and set out the basis of an agreement between them, limiting the SA to minor military functions and making their chief assignment the same as that of the party: the political education of the nation. He urged the SA leaders not to obstruct him at such a critical time, adding that he would crush anyone who did.

The generals were delighted. Röhm kept his self-control in public, but in private he swore he would never accept such an agreement—a remark duly reported to Hitler by one of Röhm's own senior SA officers, Viktor Lutze. Another report, this time from General von Blomberg, the minister of defense, informed Hitler that the SA had set up armed guards around its various headquarters: In one military district alone these amounted to 6,000 to 8,000 men armed with machine guns as well as rifles.

A systematic isolation of the recalcitrant SA began in March. The overbearing attitude of Röhm and his chief lieutenants had created dangerous enemies: the Reichswehr, the Gauleiters and the Party Organization, and Göring and Himmler, whose SS increasingly distanced itself from the SA. Himmler had already secured control of the political police in Bavaria and had soon extended this to the other *Länder* as well, including Prussia, from which the term Gestapo was borrowed. While the Gestapo kept up a close surveillance of the SA and its leaders, preparations for any action that might be necessary were made jointly by the SS and the Reichswehr.

By June an uneasy atmosphere of crisis had built up in Germany. As von Hindenburg left for his summer vacation, he said to the vice-chancellor, "Things are going badly, Papen. Try to straighten them out." Aware that the president, who was eighty-seven and fading, might never return to Berlin, Hitler saw Röhm on June 4 and in a lengthy discussion made a final attempt to persuade him to accept a settlement and so avoid conflict. Röhm agreed to go ahead with his plan to send the SA on leave during July, promising his staff that he would meet with them at Bad Wiessee before the leave began, to discuss the future of the movement. But the language of Röhm's Order of the Day, announcing the month's leave, did not give Hitler much grounds for hope that he had convinced him:

> If the enemies of the SA think that it will not return from leave, let them enjoy their illusions while they can. When the day comes, these people will receive an adequate reply, in whatever form necessity dictates. The SA is, and will remain, the destiny of Germany.[46]

VII

DURING THE REMAINDER of June, Göring and Himmler put together "evidence" of an SA conspiracy aimed at overthrowing the present regime by force and merging the army, the SA, and the SS under a single command to be held by Röhm. Hitler himself was to remain as chancellor, with von Schleicher (who was alleged to be a central figure in the conspiracy) as vice-chancellor. The evidence remains unconvincing, but it served its purpose, justifying Göring and Himmler in making preparations to preempt such a move by seizing and shooting those alleged to be involved, a list of whom was steadily added to as the opportunity arose to settle old scores.

How far Hitler believed what he was told and shown is impossible to say. In the end, when he had decided to act, he may have convinced himself. But the decisive consideration for Hitler was not the question of whether Röhm was actually planning a putsch, but the fact that as long as Röhm remained wedded to his plans for the SA to replace the army, he represented, as Joachim Fest puts it, "the permanent threat of a potential putsch" which could bring him into conflict with the army and destroy the regime.

Once Hitler had reached such a conclusion, he had to decide whether he could allow such a threat to continue hanging over him, especially with the succession to von Hindenburg in the balance. If he could not, then the options were limited. Röhm was too powerful simply to remove from office; that could well start the uprising Hitler wanted to avoid. On the other hand, Röhm knew too much to risk the scandal of another Reichstag fire trial. The only way out was to force the issue and, in appropriate gangster language, to frame Röhm.

Hitler was not in a hurry to reach such a conclusion, however, and for good reason. To strike at the SA meant striking at the movement by which he had risen to power, breaking with his oldest comrade and giving comfort to all those conservative elements in Germany whom (as Röhm rightly guessed) Hitler secretly hated. An unexpected intervention by von Papen as their spokesman, warning the government in a speech at Marburg that the revolution must come to an end, roused all Hitler's radical fury; but a visit to the ailing president on his estate, and three days' reflection on his own at Obersalzberg, convinced him that the situation could not continue.

It is probable that on his return to Berlin on June 26 Hitler agreed to the plans Göring and Himmler had drawn up: These had gone so far that it would have been hard for him to turn back. The date was fixed for Saturday, June 30. On that day Hitler arrived unexpectedly early at the hotel in Bad Wiessee, where he had summoned all the SA leaders to meet him, burst into the rooms where they were still asleep, and had them all, including Röhm, arrested and taken under guard to Munich. There and in Berlin, where Göring and Himmler directed operations, executions without any pretense of trial went on throughout the weekend. Not until Sunday evening did Hitler finally give the order for Röhm to be shot, allowing him the option of suicide, which he refused to take.

The number of those killed remains unknown: eighty-seven for certain, but generally assumed to be in the hundreds, when the many personal accounts settled by local leaders are included. At the same time as Röhm and the SA commanders were liquidated, a number of figures from the past were also murdered. Among them were Gregor Strasser, Hitler's other principal collaborator besides Röhm; the former chancellor, General von

Schleicher, and his associate General von Bredow; von Kahr (from the days of the 1923 putsch), and Edgar Jung, who had written von Papen's Marburg speech. Brüning, who listened to a warning von Schleicher ignored, left the country in time to save his life.

Although Hitler acted with decision, and confronted Röhm personally, the strain on his nerves showed in the agitation that struck everyone who met him on the thirtieth. His first instinct was to play down the importance of what had happened. Göring ordered the police to destroy "all documents concerning the action of the past two days"; the press was forbidden to publish obituary notices, and a two-line decree—"The measures taken on June 30, July 1 and 2, to suppress treasonous attacks are legal as acts of self-defense by the state"—was slipped in among twenty others authorized by the cabinet on July 3.

The following day, at a ceremony in Berlin, all those involved, from Himmler down to the SS executioners, were honored by the presentation of an honorary dagger. But Hitler, uncharacteristically, remained silent for another ten days, a silence that may have been due to revulsion and shock after so violent a break with his own past, and to uncertainty how best to present what amounted to mass murder—"by order of the Führer," the actual phrase used when the execution squads were ordered to fire.

The reports from all over Germany, confirmed by those reaching the exiled Social Democratic leadership in Prague (Sopade), showed not only an almost total absence of criticism of the Führer, but also admiration for the forcefulness with which he had acted. There seems to have been little doubt that there had actually been a plot, and the detestation of the SA was reflected in the general satisfaction that the Führer had put them down so decisively. Goebbels's propaganda machine built on this favorable reaction, but there was also a growing desire for Hitler himself to speak to the people and explain more clearly what had happened.

Hitler's speech to the Reichstag (July 13) was not one of his best performances, rambling and verbose. But he still showed his ability to respond to the popular mood, by the emphasis that he put upon the immoral life-style, especially the homosexuality, of Röhm and the other SA leaders, by his repudiation of revolution as a permanent condition, and by his justification of his action as necessary to guarantee order and security. Toward the end, he stated boldly and without equivocation, his claim to stand above the law:

> If anyone reproaches me and asks why I did not turn to the regular courts for conviction of the offenders, then all I can say to him is this: in this hour I was responsible for the fate of the German people, and thereby I became the supreme judge of the German people. . . .
> I gave the order to shoot the ringleaders in this treason, and I further gave the order to cauterize down to the raw flesh the ulcers of this poisoning of the wells in our domestic life. . . . Let the nation know that

its existence—which depends on its internal order and security—cannot be threatened with impunity by anyone! And let it be known for all time to come that if anyone raises his hand to strike the state, then certain death is his lot. [47]

Political opinion in the West was as much shocked by Hitler's claim to stand above the law as by the official sanction of murder as a means of removing potential opponents. In Germany, however, the evidence points to widespread approval not only of Hitler's action, which was seen as forestalling greater bloodshed, but also of his refusal to be bound by legal conventions and his courage in acting in accord with natural justice. "People said approvingly that no previous Reich chancellor would have dared act as he had done." [48]

This view was not confined to the man in the street. Carl Schmitt, the country's leading professor of public law at Berlin University, published an article in the *German Law Journal* of August 1, 1934, under the title "The Führer Protects the Law," in which he praised the mass executions as "the justice of the Führer" meting out "direct justice," and the "highest law" of the New Order. [49] Nine years later, in his speech to the SS commanders at Posen (October 4, 1943), in which he justified the policy of exterminating racially inferior peoples and political enemies, Himmler specifically looked back to the murders of June 30, 1934, as establishing ruthlessness, unimpeded by respect for the law, as a principle of the regime. [50]

In the course of his speech Hitler renewed his pledge to the army that it would remain the sole bearer of arms in the state and that he would preserve it as "an unpolitical instrument." The generals were well satisfied, their rivals had been eliminated. The inclusion of two of their number, von Schleicher and von Bredow, among those murdered was not allowed to cloud the congratulations that von Blomberg offered on behalf of the officer corps.

For the present Hitler was content that the army and the other conservative forces in the state should feel reassured that he had broken decisively with the radical elements in the party. In return he was happy to accept their support and that of the army when, three weeks after his Reichstag speech, von Hindenburg died. The president's office and with it that of the commander in chief were transferred to Hitler smoothly, without delay or demur.

This gave Hitler, already leader of the only party and head of the government, a unique position. He underlined it by abolishing the office of Reich president, and with it the link with the past that von Hindenburg represented. In its place he created his own title. Instead of the oath to the constitution, all officers, soldiers, and civil servants, including the Reich ministers, were required to swear "before God" a personal oath to "Adolf Hitler, the Führer of the German Reich and German People." "With the revival of the personal oath of allegiance," as the German historian Martin Broszat points out, "a part of the monarchy was restored at the same time." But as Broszat goes on to say:

> In reality Hitler's power as Führer exceeded that of any monarch. The notion of a "divine right" was replaced by the claim that the Führer was the savior appointed by Providence and at the same time the embodiment and medium of the unarticulated will of the people. [51]

To celebrate the peaceful succession, gloss over the events of June 30, and mark the end of the revolution, Hitler and Goebbels put on a "rerun" of Potsdam Day in the form of a grandiose Act of Veneration for the deceased president. Hitler spoke at a memorial session of the Reichstag, followed by the funeral march from Wagner's *Götterdämmerung,* and a parade of the army before its new commander in chief. The celebration ended with von Hindenburg's interment in the Tannenberg memorial, commemorating his victory over the Russians in 1914, and with Hitler's Wagnerian farewell: "And now enter thou upon Valhalla."

A plebiscite, to legitimize the constitutional changes, produced the usual approval but with a drop in the *"Ja"* vote by comparison with November 1933. This may have been because the preceding campaign had been low-key and Hitler himself had taken no part. If this was the reason, the party congress in Nuremberg the following month more than made up for the mistake on both counts. No display of Nazi virtuosity in propaganda has left a deeper impression than *Triumph of the Will,* the film that Leni Riefenstahl made of the 1934 congress, with Albert Speer's architectural masterpiece, the "Cathedral of Light" provided by 130 searchlights. The first version of the film had been made at the Victory Rally a year earlier and was called *Sieg des Glaubens (Triumph of Faith)*; it had to be replaced because Röhm figured so prominently in it. It was Hitler who chose the new title and set the double theme of will overcoming all obstacles and the unity of Führer, party, and people. The Hitler image overshadowed everything and everybody else, beginning with his airplane in its descent casting a cruciform shape over the marching storm troopers and the ecstatic crowds in the streets below, and ending with Hess's mystical incantation: "The party is Hitler. But Hitler is Germany, just as Germany is Hitler. *Hitler! Sieg Heil!*"

Hitler performed his role as a ritual figure in the service of a myth, the myth of the leader risen from obscurity to guide the destinies of a nation. Part of the message was clear enough: "The National Socialist revolution as a revolutionary power process is closed." The relationship of party and state had been resolved by confirming Hitler as the head of both, of the party by his purge of the SA, of the state by the succession to von Hindenburg. At the Party Congress in September 1934, he reassured the party: "It is not the state which commands us, but rather we who command the state. It was not the state that created us, but rather we who created the state." [52]

Frick as minister of the interior hurriedly issued a statement to make clear that Hitler did not mean by this that the party was thereby made superior to the state, merely "that the leaders of the party fill the top posts in the state and govern it." [53] But Frick did not say what Hitler had meant when, after declaring that the leadership "in Germany today has the power to do anything," he went on to add that "the final consolidation of National Socialist power" would be followed by "the realization of a National Socialist program directed from above."

The crisis of 1934, however, suggests a way of reconciling the view of those who see Hitler as essentially an opportunist with the conviction of those who believe that, in speaking of a "program directed from above," Hitler had certain clear objectives in mind. For if Hitler's handling of the crisis of 1934, the course of which he can hardly have foreseen, was essentially opportunist, the outcome can hardly be regarded as fortuitous and shows how firm a grasp he had of the way in which opportunities could be fitted to the end he had in view, turning what could have been a self-inflicted disaster for him and the Nazi party into a personal triumph that placed him above both party and state.

In the same way, no one suggests that Hitler foresaw the difficulties that were to beset his rearmament program or the expediency of a pact with the Soviet Union, but it is straining coincidence too far to suppose that he was not looking ahead when, three weeks after he had crushed the SA, he raised the SS, hitherto subordinate to the SA, to the rank of an independent organization, built up on the principle of blind obedience to the Führer's will. Thereby he replaced the ill-disciplined and therefore unreliable SA with a far better instrument, capable of performing all the functions of the SA and many more besides, particularly in the creation of that racist empire in the East that was his ultimate objective. This view is strengthened by the fact that, within a week of solemnly promising the army that it would remain the sole bearer of arms in the state, Hitler accorded the same privilege to the SS, limited initially to a single division, but capable, as events were to show, of providing that revolutionary alternative to the regular army that Röhm had conceived of prematurely and did not live to see.

TEN

Stalin and Hitler Compared

STALIN   LATE 1934   (*Age 54–55*)
HITLER   LATE 1934   (*Age 45*)

I

IN A FAMOUS series of lectures on the philosophy of history at Berlin University, more than a hundred years before Hitler became chancellor, Georg Wilhelm Friedrich Hegel pointed to the role of "world-historical individuals" as the agents by which "the will of the world spirit," the plan of Providence, is carried out.

> They may all be called heroes, inasmuch as they have derived their purposes and their vocation, not from the calm regular course of things, sanctioned by the existing order; but from a concealed fount, from that inner spirit, still hidden beneath the surface, which impinges on the outer world as on a shell and bursts it into pieces. (Such were Alexander, Caesar, Napoleon.) They were practical, political men. But at the same time they were thinking men, who had an insight into the requirements of the time—what was ripe for development. This was the very truth for their age, for their world. . . . It was theirs to know this nascent principle, the necessary, directly sequent step in progress, which their world was to take; to make this their aim, and to expend their energy in promoting it. World-historical men—the heroes of an epoch—must therefore be recognized as its clear-sighted ones: *their* deeds, *their* words are the best of their time. [1]

To the objection that the activity of such individuals frequently flies in the face of morality, and involves great suffering for others, Hegel replied:

> World history occupies a higher ground than that on which morality has properly its position, which is personal character and the conscience of individuals. . . . Moral claims which are irrelevant must not be brought into collision with world-historical deeds and their accomplishment. The litany of private virtues—modesty, humility, philanthropy, and forbearance—must not be raised against them. [2]
>
> So mighty a form [he adds elsewhere] must trample down many an innocent flower—crush to pieces many an object in its path. [3]

Whether either Hitler or Stalin ever read these passages or not, they describe very well the belief that the two men shared, that they were chosen to play such a role, and therefore exempt from the ordinary canons of human conduct. And this belief, in turn, provides the basis for a direct comparison between them.

The end of 1934 is a good time at which to pause and make such a comparison, for two reasons. With the tension between the SA and the army settled, and the succession to von Hindenburg secured, Hitler had consolidated his hold on power, and from then on any comparison between him and Stalin can be made on more equal terms. The other reason is that 1934 was a watershed for both men, and this makes it possible not only to look back and compare their careers up to the end of that year, but also to look forward and establish pointers for the future.

Hitler saw himself as called on by Providence to rescue the German people from the humiliation of defeat and the decadence of Weimar; to restore them to their rightful historic position as a master race, and to guarantee it for the future by creating a new Germanic empire in Eastern Europe. Stalin saw his mission as ending the centuries-old backwardness of Russia, turning a peasant society into a modern industrialized country and at the same time creating the first socialist state in the world. Neither task could be carried out without countless material and human sacrifices, but on the stage of world history on which they were actors the cost had never counted. History would justify and forgive them, as it had forgiven their predecessors—provided they were successful.

The process by which these convictions took possession of their minds remains a mystery. In the copy of Napoleon's *Thoughts* found in his library, Stalin had marked the passage: "It was precisely that evening in Lodi that I came to believe in myself as an unusual person and became consumed with the ambition to do the great things that until then had been but a fantasy."[4] Neither Stalin, however, nor Hitler, ever pinpointed a similar moment of revelation.

In an earlier chapter* I explored the connection between such beliefs and narcissism, the term used to describe a psychological state in which the subject becomes so absorbed in himself that nobody and nothing else in the world is real by comparison. Narcissistic personalities are convinced of their special qualities and their superiority over others, and any threat to this self-image—such as being criticized, shown up, or defeated—produces a violent reaction and often a desire for revenge.

Even if such a connection is accepted, it still leaves unexplained why, out of the multitude of cases where narcissism has been a factor, in these two alone it should have produced so exceptional a psychological drive, giving each a sense of a historic mission, proof against disappointments and

*See pp. 11–13.

failures, guilt and remorse, skepticism and opposition, lasting a lifetime, carrying both to extraordinary peaks of success and even, in Hitler's case, surviving defeat.

Inability to do more than speculate about the origins of this conviction, however, does not invalidate the hypothesis, for which there is a mass of supporting evidence, that this was the cardinal fact in the careers of both men, unaffected by the great differences in temperament and circumstances, or by their identification with irreconcilable ideologies.

IN STALIN'S CASE the conviction encountered two obstacles—one of which, but not the other, affected Hitler, too. What the two men had in common was the fact that both began from the bottom, with no natural or inherited advantages. Stalin had a start over Hitler in knowing what he wanted to do before he was twenty. Even so, for the next eighteen years he spent more than half his time in prison or in exile. Hitler was thirty before he found his vocation, not in art, but in politics, and discovered that he had a gift for speaking in public. To anyone who came across either of them before the age of thirty a suggestion that he would play a major role in twentieth-century history would have appeared incredible.

The material obstacles to a political career for Stalin were more than compensated for by the stroke of luck that brought him from exile in Siberia to a place in the revolutionary government before the end of 1917. But the experience of the first half of his life, living on the margins of society, often in the company of thieves and other low-lifes—becoming, to use a Georgian word, a *kinto*, "street-wise"—left psychological handicaps from which he was never to free himself. He emerged as a rough, coarse, difficult man, whose original motivation as a revolutionary was colored far more by hatred and resentment than by idealism, who neither gave nor inspired trust, believing (as Trotsky put it) "that well-organized violence was the shortest route between two points." Another inheritance, perhaps from his Caucasian background, was his vindictiveness, his unfailing memory for an insult or injury, with an implacable determination to be revenged, however many years might pass. One of the best-known stories about Stalin is told by Serebryakov, a party member who had known him since the time of the civil war. When a group of comrades was discussing everyone's idea of a perfect day, Stalin said, "Mine is to plan an artistic revenge upon an enemy, carry it out to perfection, and then go home and go peacefully to bed."[5]

This *grubost*—rudeness, lack of cultivation—which Lenin described as "a trifle that may take on decisive significance," was often submerged, but remained part of Stalin's character all his life. Long after he had become the effective ruler of Russia, he could still lose his temper and turn angrily on anyone who crossed or even irritated him—an abrupt withdrawal of confidence that was all too often followed by arrest and disappearance.

These primitive characteristics ("Asiatic" was the term Trotsky and other members of the Politburo applied to him) stood out more clearly in a group most of whose other members had spent years abroad in exile in Europe and, whatever their other shortcomings, had acquired at least a patina of sophistication. This compounded Stalin's difficulty, for he harbored a resentment against the others' better education, their familiarity with foreign countries and foreign languages, the ease with which they handled theoretical issues in writing or debate. He learned to turn the difference to his advantage in dealing with the next generation of party members, whose experience was much closer to his own, but for a long time he could not rid himself of an inferiority complex that threatened the image he had formed of himself as Lenin's natural successor.

The other handicap Stalin had to contend with was the ingrained hostility of the Communist party to anything like a cult of personality, the pride that its leading members took—as good Marxists—in excluding personal considerations, claiming to make decisions on the basis of a scientific analysis of objective factors. Practice fell a good deal short of theory, but Stalin was well aware that to allow any hint to appear of his conviction that he was a man with a historic mission would be fatal to his advancement.

Stalin learned early to keep his secrets to himself, and those who saw him frequently in the mid-1920s were astonished to discover later the image of himself that he had already been nourishing. A master both of dissimulation and of acting a part, he took Lenin's criticism of his rough manner to heart, curbed his tongue, and for the next few years assumed the role of a moderate, the spokesman of common sense, advocating a middle-of-the-road course. Always preferring to make a hostile move through others, he let Zinoviev and Kamenev take the initiative in attacking Trotsky, while he played down the extent of the disagreement and counseled restraint when they pressed for Trotsky's expulsion from the party. Only later did Trotsky realize that his most dangerous enemy was neither Zinoviev nor Kamenev, but the third member of the troika. When Kamenev, now thoroughly aware of the danger from Stalin, denounced "the theory of one-man rule" at the Fourteenth Party Congress in 1925, Stalin coolly replied that, of course, anything other than collective leadership was impossible. It was the opposition, he claimed, who were trying to drive out the other members of the leadership, mentioning five by name who were indispensable, three of whom he later condemned to death.

The maneuvering by which over a period of six years Stalin eliminated both rivals and opposition was a model of Machiavellian politics, in which every device and ruse recommended by the Florentine master found a place. Like Hitler, he paid great attention to timing and showed the same intuitive skill in probing an opponent's mentality and weaknesses. There is no doubt that he had great abilities as an organizer and leader, flawed by faults of character and temper. He combined, for example, a remarkable capacity for detail with an instinctive suspicion, especially of allies and those who protested their loyalty. Deceit and treachery were second nature to him. Wherever he could, he preferred stealth and manipulation behind the scenes to open confrontation, leaving it to an opponent to make the first move and then taking him by surprise, finding someone else to plant the dagger in an unsuspecting back.

Plotted on paper, his campaign shows a bewildering pattern of indirect approaches, tactical retreats, knight's moves, changes of direction—all the elements of opportunism combined with a singleness of purpose that never for a moment lost sight of the objective: the aggrandizement of Stalin's personal position. His progress was reflected in the growing confidence with which the general secretary—no Führer—denounced faction and deviation, concealing his own intrigues with the claim to be acting only in the name of the party and under the authority of Lenin. Not until the celebration of his fiftieth birthday, in December 1929, was Stalin's own share of responsibility, first tentatively, and then at the Congress of Victors in January 1934, fulsomely acknowledged by a grateful party—never claimed by Stalin himself. The climax as well as the process bears the authentic stamp of Stalin as a politician in the 1920s, the covert exercise of power, by comparison with Hitler's open claim to a unique position in his party from its earliest days.

THE QUOTATION from Hegel at the beginning of the chapter points to the advantage Hitler had in the existence of a deep-rooted belief in "heroic leadership" reflected in nineteenth-century German thought and literature and characterized by J. P. Stern, the Czech-born British historian of ideas, as "the powerful, embattled personality which imposes its demands upon the world and attempts to fashion it in its own image."[6]

Friedrich Nietzsche sums up this tradition in inimitable fashion. The future, he declared, belonged to the artist-politician, the political leader who was the artist in another medium.

> Such beings are incalculable, they come like fate without cause or reason, inconsiderately and without pretext. Suddenly they are here like lightning: too terrible, too sudden, too compelling and too "different" even to be hated. . . . What moves them is the terrible egotism of the artist of the brazen glance, who knows himself to be justified for all eternity in his "work" as the mother is justified in her child.[7]

Stern completes his quotation from Nietzsche with a double quotation from Mussolini, another "artist of the brazen glance": "When the masses are wax in my hands, when I stir their faith, or when I mingle with them and am almost crushed by them, I feel myself to be a part of them," and "Lenin is an artist who has worked in men as others have worked in marble or metal."[8]

The experience of defeat, the fragmentation of postwar German society, and the rejection of the values of Weimar democracy by the "nationally minded" sections of the population gave new strength to these ideas.

Mussolini showed how they could be translated into action in Italy, an example that made a profound impression on Hitler. Once Hitler had made up his mind to look to politics rather than art as the field in which to realize his sense of vocation, there was a tradition and an audience in Germany to which he could naturally appeal. Where Stalin was inhibited by the Marxist tradition of hostility to personalized politics, and had therefore to conceal both his ambition and his personality, Hitler was free to exploit his to the fullest.

An early illustration of the success with which Hitler could appeal to the "nationally minded" was his recovery from the humiliating failure of the 1923 putsch as a result of his performance at the subsequent trial. Nonetheless, when he came out of prison at the end of 1924, he had to start to rebuild the Nazi party from scratch in the very much less favorable environment of the brief period of prosperity and stability enjoyed by Germany in the late 1920s. Hitler could not know that it would be brief, and these years provided a test of his belief in his "world-historical role" and of his willpower.

For his faith in the decisive power of the human will, Hitler could again draw on the teaching of German nineteenth-century thinkers, two in particular. The first was Arthur Schopenhauer, the author of *The World as Will and Idea,* from which his secretary says he could quote whole passages. The second was Friedrich Nietzsche: He presented his collected works to Mussolini, "that unparalleled statesman" whose March on Rome proved to Hitler that it was possible to reverse a historic decline. Hitler refused to recognize any difficulties as inherent in a problem. He saw only human incompetence and human ill will. This corresponded to Stalin's belief that the difficulties encountered in collectivization were due to the failure of the local party officials to push the program through with sufficient determination, and to the malevolent resistance of the kulaks and the other ever-present enemies and wreckers with whom he saw himself surrounded.

But willpower, the singleness of aim, was in both cases combined with flexibility of tactics. Stalin's reiteration of his attachment to the principle of "collective leadership," while working all the time to replace it by his own, was matched by Hitler's proclamation of the principle of "legality" as the facade behind which to carry out a political revolution and overturn the rule of law.

Stalin had the advantage of being a leading member of a party already in office, exercising a monopoly of power. At no time in his career was he called upon to fight an election or appeal to a popular electorate. Unlike Hitler, he never went to the masses; "the people," from whose sufferings and needs Communism derived its legitimation, remained an abstraction. He worked his way up as an organizer and committee man, taking over the party machine from the inside. Almost all his speeches were addressed to party meetings of one sort or another, where he might well encounter criticism and opposition but always within a Marxist framework, and increasingly with a packed audience ready to heckle and vote down his opponents.

Hitler had no more use for democratic politics than Stalin, but he accepted, however reluctantly, that in order to get into a position to abolish them the only alternatives were another attempt at a putsch, which he ruled out except as a threat, or taking part in the democratic system he blamed for everything, and winning votes.

Part of Hitler's originality as a politician consisted in his grasp of the weakness of the traditional right-wing parties. From the Austrian and German Marxists he learned the need to go to the people, and so built up for the first time a mass following for an antidemocratic, anti-Marxist, nationalist platform. Between them, he and Goebbels devised a political style that held up to ridicule the very institutions that gave them the freedom to work for their overthrow. The Nazis made no secret of what they were doing. When Goebbels ran for election to the Reichstag in 1928 and won one of the Nazis' twelve seats, he wrote in an eve-of-the-election article for *Der Angriff*:

> We go into the Reichstag in order to acquire the weapons of democracy from its arsenal. We become Reichstag deputies in order to paralyze the Weimar democracy with its own assistance. If democracy is stupid enough to give us free travel privileges and per diem allowances for this service, that is its affair. . . . We'll take any legal means to revolutionize the existing situation. If we succeed in putting sixty to seventy agitators of our party into the various parliaments in these elections, then in future the state itself will supply and finance our fighting machinery. . . . Mussolini also went into parliament, yet soon thereafter he marched into Rome with his Blackshirts. . . . One should not believe that parliamentarism is our Damascus. . . . We come as enemies! Like the wolf tearing into the flock of sheep, that is how we come. Now you are no longer among yourselves![9]

No one paid attention in 1928, but when the Nazis captured seven million votes and 107 seats two years later, becoming the second largest party in the Reichstag, Goebbels's forecast was fulfilled to the letter.

IN CREATING his own party, Hitler was spared the contortions to which Stalin had to resort in order to cloak his ambitions. There was no need to disguise Hitler's unique position as the Führer, who alone had the authority to decide on policy and issue orders. Whoever joined the NSDAP, even in the mid-1920s, knew and accepted this. Unlike Stalin's Old Bolsheviks, who looked back with regret to the days of Lenin's leadership, when the party line was freely debated, and who could never in their hearts recognize Stalin as his equal or successor, the Nazi *Alte Kämpfer* might grumble but never questioned Hitler's position as Führer.

As a result, Hitler was never troubled by the need for recognition that haunted Stalin, and the Nazi party experienced none of the convulsive series of purges that Stalin imposed on the Communist party leadership. Hitler had no need to pursue a policy of divide and rule; he had no rivals to fear. Both Gregor Strasser and Röhm, although they disagreed with him on policy, recognized they could never replace him. The Röhm purge of 1934 does not contradict this. For the grievances of Röhm and the SA sprang not from their rejection of Hitler, but from their fear that Hitler was rejecting them; while Hitler himself agreed reluctantly to the purge for political reasons, in order to keep the support of the army in securing the succession to von Hindenburg.

Hitler was as full of resentments as Stalin—against the "November criminals" who had betrayed Germany, against the Marxists who had seduced the honest German worker, against the Jews who conspired to undermine the supremacy of the Aryan race, against the bourgeois world that had rejected him in Vienna, against the top-hatted, frock-coated conservative nationalists who looked down their noses at the Nazis as too raucous and vulgar to be accepted as allies. He swore he would be revenged on them all—and he was. But, however socially awkward he might be, however many the scores he meant to pay off, Hitler did not suffer from an inferiority complex; he despised and scorned all of them as effete, incapable of greatness. "Hatred is like wine to him," Rauschning wrote. "It intoxicates him. One must have heard his tirades of denunciation to realize how he can revel in hate." [10]

Stalin originally derived his sense of mission from his identification with a creed, Marxism-Leninism, which he believed had uncovered the laws of historical development, and with a party that was the instrument for their realization. Hitler, too, saw his destiny as part of history. "A man who has no sense of history," he declared, "is like a man who has no ears or eyes." But he read it very differently from Stalin, his mind ranging over centuries and forming the bits and pieces he snatched from his reading into a preconceived framework. "I often wonder why the ancient world collapsed," he speculated in his table talk. His favored explanation was that Christianity—the invention of the Jew, Saul of Tarsus, better known as St. Paul—had played the same disintegrative role as Bolshevism—the invention of the Jew, Karl Marx—in the Europe of his own time. [11]

Seeing himself in this perspective of world history, Hitler believed he had been born at a similarly critical time, when the liberal bourgeois world of the nineteenth century was disintegrating. The future would lie with the "Jewish-Bolshevik" ideology of the Marxist-led masses unless Europe could be saved by the Nazi racist ideology of the new elite which it was his mission to create. The German tribes who had conquered the Roman Empire had been barbarians, but they had replaced a decaying order by laying the foundations of a vigorous new civilization. The Nazis had the comparable task of replacing the dying civilization of the West.

· · ·

BOTH MEN shared the passion to dominate, were dogmatic in their assertions, angered by argument or criticism. In temperament, however, they were poles apart.

Hitler constantly spoke of willpower as the decisive factor in politics, but the impression of strength that he sought to convey, far from being natural, as in Stalin's case, appeared to require an effort to achieve. His manner was artificial and overemphatic rather than spontaneous; his gestures were theatrical, his movements jerky and awkward.

Faced with the need to make a decision, Hitler would often procrastinate and hesitate. He not only found it difficult to make up his mind but, once he had, frequently changed it, a process that could sometimes go on for weeks, driving his staff to despair. He needed to convince himself that the time was ripe to act, and he was always sensitive to the effect of any decision on public opinion and the image of the Führer. Examples are his refusal to consider devaluation, any kind of inflation, or the wartime conscription of women. Even when he had made a decision, he often showed anxiety about the outcome, working himself up into a nervous state that found expression in outbursts of rage, recrimination, even despair. In a crisis, whereas Stalin's nerves were steady, Hitler was at the mercy of his.

This temperamental display, however, which could easily be taken for instability of purpose, actually concealed, as the record over any extended period of time shows, great determination, a boldness that constantly took opponents (and allies) by surprise, a refusal to accept defeat, and a ruthlessness that took no more account of the cost in human lives and suffering than did Stalin.

It was no less easy to be deceived by the volatility of his moods. Whereas Stalin left an impression of self-control and self-assurance, Hitler was easily excited. Stalin concealed his emotions and did not talk more than was necessary. Hitler exploited his and never stopped talking. What he concealed was the element of calculation. When Hitler worked himself up into one of his rages, he appeared to lose all control of himself. His face became mottled and swollen with fury, he screamed at the top of his voice, spitting out abuse, waving his arms wildly, and drumming on the table with his fists. Those who knew him well, however, were sure that Hitler remained—in a phrase he often used of himself—"ice-cold underneath."

Stalin was playing a role as much as Hitler, but he did not let it show. Stalin's passions were concealed, but they were all the stronger for that. The first public hint of his later paranoia was his declaration at the time of the Shakhty trial: "There are internal enemies, comrades. There are external enemies. This is never to be forgotten." Only with the declaration of war on the kulaks as class enemies was it given full rein.

In Hitler's case, it was paranoia that aroused his national consciousness in the first place and took him into politics: the defense of the beleaguered Germans against their enemies in the Habsburg Empire, Slavs, Marxists, Jews; the betrayal of the German Empire by its internal enemies, who stabbed it in the back in 1918; the imposition of the Versailles settlement and the exaction of reparations by Germany's external enemies. His open appeal, from the beginning of his political career, was to the large number of Germans who shared the same paranoid emotions, seeing themselves as victims of a conspiracy by unseen enemies—capitalists, social democrats and trade unions, Bolsheviks, Jews, the Allied Powers. They were ready to respond to a politician who not only shared but powerfully confirmed their suspicions, a mass of potential converts waiting for a messiah to liberate and focus their energies.

Their response is summed up in a simple sentiment, constantly repeated in the remarkable collection organized by the sociologist Theodore Abel of autobiographies written in 1934 by 581 Nazis who had joined the movement before 1933: "My belief is that our leader, Adolf Hitler, was given by fate to the German nation as our savior, bringing light into darkness."[12]

The effectiveness of Hitler's appeal was greatly increased when, as happened in his case but not in Stalin's, paranoia was combined with charisma. Originally a "gift of grace" from God with which religious leaders and prophets were endowed, even its secularized version (first identified by the German sociologist Max Weber) can be put to beneficent as well as destructive use. Examples of the first, in the twentieth century, were Gandhi and Franklin Roosevelt; Hitler is the classic example of the second.[13]

Hitler always had the personal conviction of being chosen and endowed with powers out of the ordinary; what charisma added was the ability to recruit a group of followers bonded to him by their recognition of these superhuman gifts and calling. The mark of this was their willingness to accept whatever he said, because he said it, just as they were prepared to carry out his orders without question simply because he gave them.

The vehicle of this relationship and of his gift of self-dramatization was Hitler's remarkable powers as a speaker, different in kind from political speeches of the traditional sort, even when made by accomplished speakers. Indeed, judged by the standards they set, Hitler had obvious faults as an orator. He spoke at too great length, was often repetitive and verbose, began awkwardly and ended too abruptly. But these shortcomings mattered little beside the force and immediacy of the passions, the intensity of the hatred, fury, and menace conveyed by the sound of his voice alone. The sentence from Nietzsche already quoted explains the effect he produced: "Men believe in the truth of all that is seen to be strongly believed in."

Hitler had a flair for divining what was hidden in the minds of his audiences, and for this reason often showed uncertainty at the start of a speech as he sensed and probed their mood. Years after he had broken with Hitler, Otto Strasser, Gregor's brother, wrote:

Hitler responds to the vibration of the human heart with the delicacy of a seismograph, or perhaps of a wireless receiving set, enabling him, with a certainty with which no conscious gift could endow him, to act as a loudspeaker proclaiming the most secret desires, the least admissible instincts, the sufferings, and personal revolts of a whole nation.[14]

But Hitler did more than exploit the emotions of his audience. In another passage published in 1878, but which might have been intended as a description of Hitler, Nietzsche wrote:

In all great deceivers a remarkable process is at work to which they owe their power. In the very act of deception with all its preparations, the dreadful voice, expression and gestures, they are overcome *by their belief in themselves*; it is this belief which then speaks, so persuasively, so miracle-like, to the audience.[15]

It was a two-way relationship. Hitler not only gave his audience reassurance and hope, but also received back renewal of his confidence and confirmation of his own self-image. In this sense the Hitler myth was as much the creation of his followers—the embodiment of their unconscious needs—as imposed on them by the Führer.

THIS WAS A GIFT that Stalin did not possess. It would have been out of place and counterproductive with the audience he had to convince: not the crowded mass meetings of an electoral campaign, but the closed world of the central bodies of the Russian Communist party. How much resistance anyone would encounter who was suspected of setting up to play the role of Napoleon Bonaparte in a Thermidorian reaction is shown by the example of Trotsky, the only one of Lenin's successors who possessed a charismatic personality, and paid dearly for it.

The tradition on which Hitler drew allowed him openly to declare and prove his claim. Stalin on the other hand was denied this intense reciprocal relationship, not only because he did not possess Hitler's special gifts as a speaker (who did?), but because it had no place in the tradition to which he belonged.

Paranoid beliefs in conspiracy and persecution found a fruitful soil in the history of Russian Marxism as an underground movement, as well as in Russian history in general, which from the Decembrist revolt in 1825 displayed a passion for secret societies. But anything that smacked of a charismatic claim was suspect, if only because of its associations with religion and with the powerful irrational forces in Russian life depicted, for example, by Fyodor Dostoevsky, which the older Russian Marxist intellectuals had rejected. It was only Lenin dead who could be made the object of a cult; alive, he vehemently opposed any move toward apotheosis.

By identifying himself with Lenin, Stalin was able in time to claim a share in the magic of his name and to find a precedent for his own "cult of personality." But it is inconceivable that Stalin in 1934 would ever have received the sort of spontaneous welcome that Albert Speer describes when driving with Hitler in the Thuringian countryside. Greeted by a crowd of thousands and showered with flowers as he came out of the inn where they had made an unexpected stop, Hitler turned to Speer and said: "Hitherto only one German has been hailed like this: Luther. When he rode through the country, people gathered from far and wide to cheer him. As they do for me today!" [16]

Stalin made a show of being bored or irritated by praise and flattery, but his need for a recognition that Hitler could take for granted remained unsatisfied, and the sort of device to which he resorted is described by Khrushchev in his memoirs: "He cautiously but deliberately sprinkled into the consciousness of those around him the idea that privately he wasn't of the same opinion about Lenin that he professed publicly." Lazar Kaganovich, as always, was quick to take his cue:

> Kaganovich used to throw himself back in his chair, bring himself up to his full height and bellow: "Comrades, it's time for us to tell the people the truth. Everyone in the party keeps talking about Lenin and Leninism. We've got to be honest with ourselves. Lenin died in 1924. How many years did he work in the party? What was accomplished under him? Compare it with what has been accomplished under Stalin! The time has come to replace the slogan 'Long Live Leninism' with the slogan 'Long Live Stalinism.' "
>
> While he would rant on like this, we would all keep absolutely silent and lower our eyes. Stalin was always the first and only one to dispute Kaganovich.
>
> "What are you talking about?" he would say. "How dare you say that?" But you could tell from the tone in Stalin's voice that he was hoping someone would contradict him. This device is well known among village folk. . . .
>
> Stalin liked to rebuke Kaganovich: "What is Lenin? Lenin is a tall tower! And what is Stalin? Stalin is a little finger!" Kaganovich was encouraged all the more. . . . This dispute between Kaganovich and Stalin became more and more frequent, right up until Stalin's death. No one ever interfered and Stalin always had the last word. [17]

II

STALIN WAS UNABLE to overcome his suspicion that the rest of the party leadership, even when they supported his policies and applauded him, would never accept him as the equal of Lenin, still less see him in the light in which he saw himself. His distrust of them strengthened one of his characteristics, recognized by those who came across him even in his early days: his self-sufficiency and reliance on himself alone. Few of those he met impressed him (Lenin is perhaps the only certain exception), and he cared little for what they thought of him. Those who came up against him soon recognized the strength of will, coupled with a noticeable lack of human sympathies, which enabled him to survive three years in the frozen wastes of Siberia with little apparent need for human company. Long frustrated, his sense of being marked out for some special destiny made him morose and difficult; but when it crystalized around the ambition to become Lenin's successor, his willpower provided a formidable inner drive.

Ruthlessness in Stalin's eyes, as in Hitler's, was a sovereign virtue, to be curbed only for the sake of expediency. The Russian revolutionary tradition made a virtue of a complete indifference toward human life in the pursuit of a more just and equal society. The Socialist Revolutionaries found in this a justification for individual terrorism, the Bolsheviks for a collective terrorism, directed against whole classes such as the bourgeoisie and the kulaks. Terrorism had been openly endorsed by Lenin and Trotsky and put into practice in a fanatical spirit of self-sacrifice by the first head of the Cheka, the incorruptible Dzerzhinsky. If any lingering inhibitions were left in Stalin's mind they would have been exorcised by that sense of mission that provided an automatic justification, and armored him against any feelings of compassion or guilt for the millions of lives he destroyed as the agent of historical necessity.

Difficult though it may be to accept, the key to understanding both Stalin and Hitler is the recognition that they were entirely serious about their historic roles; it was certainly as much as anyone's life was worth to question or mock them. Skeptical about the motives and claims of others, their cynicism stopped short of their own. They saw themselves not as tyrants or evil men, but as leaders prepared to devote their entire lives to a higher cause, and entitled to call on others to do the same, so releasing in themselves and in those who accepted their claim a perverted moral energy and self-confidence.

If Stalin's pursuit and exercise of power had been motivated solely by the enjoyment of power for its own sake, he would never have launched out, immediately after he had eliminated the right as well as the left opposition, on an undertaking so full of risks as his Second Revolution. If he had been a mere hardheaded realist his success in defeating his rivals for the leadership would have been enough, and he would at least have paused to enjoy his victory. But that view of him fails to understand his need to prove to himself, and to win the recognition of those he had defeated, that he was the successor and equal of Lenin.

This is not to revive the "great man" theory of history or to suggest that Stalin alone could have carried through so profound a change in Russian life without the enthusiastic—or at least the willing—cooperation of many thousands of party members. Frustrated by the shabby compromises of the NEP, they were convinced that Stalin's plan would revive the party's militancy and effect the breakthrough to a socialist society. To maintain the momentum called for a prodigious effort of will on Stalin's part: He was able to sustain it by more than personal qualities of leadership, by his conviction and power of self-dramatization in acting out the role that he believed the dynamics of history had created for the Russian Communist party and for himself as its leader.

THE EXPERIENCE of the "revolution imposed from above" left a permanent mark on Stalin. The result was not to create doubt or remorse, rather to strengthen the paranoid tendencies already apparent and contribute to the extraordinary episode of the trials and purges later in the 1930s, a classic example of the phenomenon described by the American political scientist Harold Lasswell as "the displacement of private affects upon public objects."[18]

The earliest recorded diagnosis of Stalin as paranoid appears to have been made in December 1927, when an international scientific conference met in Moscow. A leading Russian neuropathologist, Professor Vladimir Bekhterev from Leningrad, made a great impression on the foreign delegates and attracted the attention of Stalin, who asked Bekhterev to pay him a visit. After the interview (December 22, 1927) Bekhterev told his assistant Mnukhin that Stalin was a typical case of severe paranoia and that a dangerous man was now at the head of the Soviet Union. The fact that Bekhterev was suddenly taken ill and died while still in his hotel has inevitably led to the suspicion that Stalin had him poisoned. Whether this is true or not, when the report of Bekhterev's diagnosis was repeated in *Literaturnaya Gazeta* in September 1988, it was accepted as correct by a leading Soviet psychiatrist, Professor E. A. Lichko. He added that experience showed paranoid attacks were provoked by external circumstances and difficult situations, and they normally followed a wave pattern, flaring up and then falling away again. Professor Lichko suggested that such psychotic attacks had occurred in Stalin's case in 1929–30, followed by the campaign against the kulaks, and then in 1936–37, followed by the purges of the party and army leadership. "Perhaps there was an attack right at the beginning of the war, in the first few days, when he in effect abandoned the leadership of the state. Finally, the period at the end of his life, the period of the 'Doctors' Case.' "[19]

Without entering into a controversy about the validity of psychohistory, two points can be made with little risk of contradiction. The first is that it is important to distinguish between a mental illness that incapacitates the person suffering from it and various abnormal states of personality in which a person who displays psychopathic traits remains perfectly competent, knows what he is doing, and can be held responsible for his actions.

There is no question that it is this second state, not a mental illness, that is referred to when speaking of Stalin's—and Hitler's—paranoid tendencies. Two of the standard textbooks of psychiatry, *The Harvard Guide to Modern Psychiatry* and *The Oxford Textbook of Psychiatry,* describe the essential features of such a paranoid personality as a well-systematized and unshakable delusional system, developing in middle life, which is encapsulated so that there is no impairment of other mental functions and the personality remains essentially intact and can function well in relation to the environment.

The other point is that whether or not we employ psychiatric terms and Greek words like *paranoia* or stick to everyday language, the symptoms associated with paranoid states—chronic suspicion, self-absorption, jealousy, hypersensitivity, megalomania—are those that recur most often in descriptions of Stalin by those who were in close contact with him.

Stalin reacted sharply to anything—criticism, opposition, or unwelcome news—that might disturb his image of himself and arouse painful emotions of self-questioning or self-reproach. To guard against such threats he developed a variety of psychological strategies, which Robert Tucker summarizes under the headings of repression, rationalization, and projection. [20]

The first was the simplest. Stalin would blankly deny the truth of awkward or alarming facts with which he was confronted and accuse those who presented them of sabotage, malicious exaggeration, and other threatening charges which had a powerful effect in discouraging others from running the same risks.

The best-known example of rationalization is his initiative in admitting Lenin's criticism of his rudeness, at the same time as he turned it to his advantage as a proof of his zeal: "Yes, I am rude, comrades—toward those who rudely and treacherously smash and split the party." [21]

The third device, projection, enabled him to attribute to others motives and attitudes that he refused to admit in himself. Many examples can be quoted of Stalin moving to betray a friend or ally and justifying this to himself and others by accusing the victim of the treachery he was himself intending.

There is no need to spend time proving that Stalin could play the hypocrite and liar with the same degree of accomplishment as he showed in all the other political arts. But a good many of the claims he made about the success of collectivization, the progress of the Five-Year Plan, and the conditions of the Russian people were so blatantly untrue—and known to those who heard them to be so—that they may well have been due to unconscious self-deception, what he wanted, and needed, to believe was true.

The commonest symptom of a paranoid state, however, is the combination of delusions of grandeur with the conviction that one is the victim of persecution and conspiracy, producing an excessive suspiciousness and distrust of others, and an eagerness to strike at enemies before they can injure oneself. Equally characteristic is the systematic nature of the delusions: the seizing on significant details, working them into a logical pattern capable of ingenious adjustment to protect its credibility. In the paranoid's world nothing happens by chance.

Two other characteristics have a particular relevance to the sort of politics in which Stalin and Hitler were engaged. First, the strength of such delusions is increased the more they have a nucleus of fact. This was provided in Stalin's case by the tradition of conspiracy in Russian revolutionary politics, with the constant formation of factions and the bitterness of the disputes. It was all too easy for Stalin to detect, then exaggerate—and eventually act to forestall—potential threats to his position.

Second, the development of a paranoid personality is not necessarily disabling. It is compatible with the exercise of political abilities of a high order: as speaker, organizer, leader. In situations of crisis it can give positive advantages, providing a powerful source of energy and self-confidence, the conviction of being right, and a spur to the relentless pursuit of enemies.

Stalin had always been suspicious, but during the experience of collectivization his suspicions became obsessional. He projected the blame for everything that went wrong onto the victims. It was the resistance of the kulaks that was responsible, the cunning of the peasants who hid their grain and refused to hand it over, the treachery of Ukrainian nationalists who conspired against the Soviet state. He could trust no one but himself; even his own wife had betrayed him by committing suicide. He saw enemies everywhere and suspected his closest collaborators. Stalin's daughter, Svetlana, writes:

> When the "facts" convinced my father that someone he knew well had turned out "badly" after all, a psychological metamorphosis came over him. . . . At this point, and this was where his cruel, implacable nature showed itself, the past ceased to exist for him. Years of friendship and fighting side by side in a common cause might as well never have been. He could wipe it all out at a stroke—and X would be doomed. "So, you've betrayed me," some inner demon would whisper. "I don't even know you any more."[22]

Lacking Hitler's charismatic power to attract and hold the loyalty of his followers, Stalin built up his position on the power to inspire fear. He believed that he was the only one of the Communist leaders capable of carrying through the revolution to completion because, as a man of the people himself, not an intellectual or former émigré, he alone understood that the Russian people had always been ruled, and could only be ruled, by fear, by suffering. And the key to that, as Peter the Great and Ivan the Terrible had understood before him, was to keep the *apparat* itself in a state of fear which it would in turn pass on to the people. Convictions might change, but fear lasted.

After Yagoda had completed two years as head of the secret police, Stalin decided that the time had come to liquidate him. He was succeeded by Yezhov, after whom the worst period of the terror is known in Russian as the *Yezhovschina*; Yezhov also lived in fear, and, when Stalin decided that the time had come, he, too, was liquidated.

One of Stalin's maxims was that in politics there is no room for trust. Here again there is a striking contrast with Hitler. Hitler trusted his closest collaborators to the point where he allowed Göring and Himmler, for

example, to take over large areas of power, and his trust was not betrayed.*
But it was the party leadership that Stalin regarded with the greatest
suspicion, even after he had purged it of his rivals. Too many of those who
had rallied to him in 1929–30 and helped him to carry through the "Second
Revolution" regarded themselves as partners in the victory, retained ties
with one another, presumed to hold independent opinions, and did not
realize, as Molotov and Kaganovich did, that without Stalin they would be
nothing. Once this attitude aroused his suspicion, it took no time at all for
Stalin to convince himself that they were enemies, conspiring against him,
and that he must forestall them, replacing them with a Politburo and
Central Committee all of whose members would understand that they were
simply instruments of his will.

The correlative of Stalin's suspicion was his need for reassurance, as an
answer to the doubts and the sense of inferiority that, however much
suppressed, lived on at the subconscious level and disturbed his inner
security. Outwardly, Stalin gave an impression of being completely in command of himself, of an unshakable self-confidence; but beneath the surface
passions ran deep—the passion for autocratic power that would relieve him
of the need to consult or listen to anyone, the passion for revenge, the
intolerance of opposition, and, as we have already seen, the thirst for
recognition.

Once he was in the saddle and controlled party, bureaucracy, and the
security forces, Stalin had little to fear in the way of a direct challenge, and
work could begin on rewriting the history of the revolution so as to present
him as Lenin's chief collaborator. The cult of Stalin was designed to project
his view of himself as Lenin's successor to the mass of the Russian people
remote from party politics. But he also wanted recognition from the men
he had defeated, from the survivors of the original Leninist party, the inner
group who made up the membership of the central bodies and had watched
his rise to power at close quarters—recognition not just that he had won,
but that his victory was deserved and that they accepted him, as they had
accepted Lenin, of their own volition, as the *vozhd'*. This explains his
insistence over and over again during the period of the trials that the
accused, the generation of the Old Bolsheviks, should confess in humiliating
terms that they had been wrong, and Stalin always right.

Just before the first of the trials, early in 1936, Nikolai Bukharin, no
longer a member of the Politburo, but editor of *Izvestia,* visited Paris to
purchase the archives of the former German Social Democratic party (including Marx's manuscripts). He spoke at length with two Menshevik
émigrés, Boris Nicolaevsky and Fyodor Dan, who were involved in the
transaction. Bukharin made no pretense to be unprejudiced and indeed told
André Malraux as well as the others that Stalin was going to kill him. But

---

*Hess's flight to Scotland is not an exception to this; his motive was to regain Hitler's
confidence, not to betray him. See pp. 413–14.

what he said in Paris and when he was arrested and put on trial two years later shows that he understood, as none of the other victims did, what motivated Stalin and why he and others not only had to die, but also to confess.*

What he had to say about Stalin was published in 1964 by Dan's widow:

> You say you don't know him well, but we do. He is unhappy at not being able to convince everyone, himself included, that he is greater than everyone, and this unhappiness of his may be his most human trait, perhaps the only human trait in him. But what is not human, but rather devilish, is that because of this unhappiness, he cannot help taking revenge on people, on all people, but especially those who are in any way higher or better than he. If someone speaks better than he does, that man is doomed! Stalin will not let him live, because that man is a perpetual reminder that he, Stalin, is not the first and the best.[23]

Hitler's paranoid tendencies are obvious enough in his earlier days and in *Mein Kampf.* But the enemies against whom he saw himself battling remained impersonal and collective (the Jews and the Marxists), not personalized and individual as in Stalin's case. By comparison with Stalin's innate suspicion of his own party and those who worked with him, Hitler showed a surprising degree of trust and loyalty. As the curve of his success mounted from the early 1930s he also became more and more confident and aggressive. The paranoid symptoms only reappeared when success turned to the struggle to avoid defeat after Stalingrad (January 1943) and when he came to see the German generals and the officer corps as traitors. By 1944–45 he had convinced himself that every setback was further proof of betrayal, and that there was no one he could any longer trust, in the end not even his closest associates.

While paying attention to the psychopathological elements in both men's behavior, however, it is important to recognize—as so many failed to do at the time—Hitler's as well as Stalin's outstanding ability as politicians. They were both secretive: "I have an old principle," Hitler told Kurt Lüdecke, who was close to him in the 1920s, "only to say what must be said to him who must know it, and only when he must know it." Schacht, who quarreled bitterly with him, wrote: "He never let slip an unconsidered word. He never said what he did not intend to say, and he never blurted out a secret. Everything was the result of cold calculation."[24] Both leaders practiced the art of playing off people against one another, of telling one man one thing and another the opposite. Both employed unpredictability as an instrument of power, making it difficult even for those close to them to be certain what they would do. No one, summoned to see Stalin, knew what to be prepared for. He would begin a conversation with an unexpected question, or talk about some unimportant matter, then suddenly confront his visitor with the real issue in a wholly changed and menacing manner. He pounced on trivial

*See Chapter Twelve.

or casual remarks let slip in nervousness and built them up into evidence of deviation, hostility, or treachery.

Hitler showed the same inveterate distrust of experts, particularly economists, as Stalin did; in wartime this was extended to the German generals. Refusing to be impressed by the complexity of problems, he insisted that, if the will was there, any problem could be solved. Both Stalin and Hitler were masters of simplification. It was this, combined with their dogmatism, that made so strong an appeal to those who wanted the assurance of black and white pronouncements that admitted no qualifications or doubts. Schacht, whose advice he refused to listen to, reluctantly admitted: "Hitler often did find astonishingly simple solutions for problems that had seemed to others insoluble. . . . His solutions were often brutal, but almost always effective." [25] The crudest of Hitler's simplifications was also the most effective: In almost any situation, force or the threat of force would settle matters. Stalin would not have disagreed.

The comparison with Stalin is valuable because he, too, like Hitler, owed his initial success to historical circumstances, to the help of others, and to luck. Thus, without the historical circumstances of war and defeat, he would have had no more chance than Hitler of making a start. He did not have to create his own party as Hitler did, and he found himself in office as a result of a revolution to which he was originally opposed and in which his own part, compared with that of Lenin and Trotsky, was a modest one. It was again thanks to Lenin's favor that he kept his place in a government where he was the odd man out and was given the job that proved to be the foundation of his later career.

Finally, thanks to the same element of luck that produced von Papen's renewed offer of negotiations to Hitler just when the loss of two million votes and Gregor Strasser's resignation marked a downturn in the Nazis' fortunes, so Stalin was rescued by Lenin's early death in 1924, just when Lenin had turned against him and was preparing to propose his removal from the post of general secretary. Yet no one would claim that these essential but extraneous factors detract from the importance of the role Stalin himself played. The same is true of Hitler.

It is quite true that from 1929 to 1933 Hitler was as much dependent on the goodwill of the "National Opposition" and its willingness to consider him as a partner as he had been earlier in Bavaria. But—again without exculpating von Papen, von Schleicher, and the group around von Hindenburg from responsibility for the mistake they made—what is striking is Hitler's skill in grasping the situation and seeing how to exploit it by the cleverly devised tactic of "legality," while all the time allowing his own party followers to believe that, when the time came, legality would go by the board. This is the equivalent of Stalin's masterly playing off of the other members of the Politburo against one another, while all the time building up his own following in the party. This was a period when both learned to conceal their real aims and to wait for their opponents to give them opportunities.

The reason why politicians like Hugenberg and von Papen, while holding their noses, sought an alliance with the Nazis was not because they felt attracted to them, but because Hitler could offer them something that they wanted, namely mass support. This was Hitler's own creation: both the idea of a radical right-wing party appealing to the masses—which he had first picked up from the Social Democrats in prewar Vienna—and the actual organization of it. So was the originality that he brought to the use of propaganda and novel methods of electioneering. Well before the electoral successes of the 1930s (for which he built up the organization in advance), Strasser, Goebbels, and the other leaders had recognized that without Hitler there would be no Nazi party.

After the unparalleled electoral success of September 1930, it is natural for attention to be focused on Hitler's radical campaigning to capture a majority—and on his failure. But what showed his powers of judgment, in the midst of all the ballyhoo and propaganda stunts, was his recognition that he might not succeed, that the way to secure office was by negotiation—and his persistent refusal to lower his demands by accepting anything less than the chancellorship. If he could get that, he was confident the rest would follow, as it did—another example of his ability to calculate in advance.

On the day he became chancellor, he seized the initiative and never let it go until six months later his political revolution, characteristically disguised under the word *Gleichschaltung* (coordination), was complete. His tactics were a mixture of effrontery, terror, and reassurance, balancing between the pressures of the "revolution from below"—the SA and the local party bosses let off the leash—and Göring's takeover of Prussia, while all the time continuing to deceive his conservative partners, the president, the Reichswehr, and civil service, with the ritual incantations of "legality," "continuity," "national unity," "respect for the constitution."

Like all revolutions, it was a period of great confusion, improvisation, unauthorized initiatives. Hitler could not have carried it out without powerful help from others, notably Göring, Goebbels, and Frick. But, amid the confusion and his own temperamental oscillations, he never lost his sense of direction and his sense of limits. In the summer of 1933, he announced the end of the revolution, and, a year later, acted to put down those who would not accept this. The hesitations, rumors, compromises, changes of course, the normal disorder of revolutionary politics, should no more prevent one from seeing Hitler's underlying consistency of purpose and timing—with an eye always to the succession—than in the case of Lenin's revolutionary leadership in 1917–18 or of Stalin's elimination of his rivals (over a six-year period) and his Second Revolution of 1929 through 1933.

Forget the image immortalized by Charlie Chaplin in *The Great Dictator* and look at the record instead. Taking the development of German politics between September 1930 and the point we have now reached, four years later, who showed the better political judgment and foresight: Hugenberg, von Papen, and von Schleicher; Brüning and Monsignor Kaas, leader of the Center party; the Social Democrats and trade-union leaders; the Communists; von Blomberg and the Reichswehr; Gregor Strasser and Röhm—or Hitler, the man whom all the others underestimated?

Every other party, as well as the trade unions, had been dissolved. Hugenberg and Kaas had been pushed out of politics; von Schleicher, Strasser, and Röhm were dead. The best that can be said for Brüning is that he had the sense to get out of Germany in time and remain abroad until after the war; von Papen, who had assured everybody that Hitler and the Nazis were pinned down, thought himself lucky to have escaped with his life and had been sent to Vienna after his speechwriter, Edgar Jung, had been shot. The Social Democrats and Communists had seen their impressive organizations destroyed and were either in prison or in exile, the Communists still keeping up their feud with the Social Democrats and comforting themselves with the "correct" party line, which foretold that a Nazi victory would be no more than the prelude to their own triumph. Only Blomberg and the Reichswehr, and the leaders of big business, had cause to congratulate themselves that the radical threats of the SA and of the anticapitalist factions in the Nazi party had been removed. But Hitler was satisfied to see them content: He could continue to count on them as willing collaborators in his priorities to rebuild Germany's military strength and end unemployment.

Surprisingly, nothing brings out so clearly as the Hitler myth the relationship between the two sides of Hitler's political personality: his appeal to the emotional, nonrational forces in men and women on the one side, and the time he spent in mulling over and weighing possible courses of action on the other.

"Heroic" leadership was one of the characteristic elements in the nineteenth-century romantic-*völkisch* "cult of the German nation." The anger and bewilderment felt by so many Germans after 1918 revived the yearning for a leader, now in radical form and often expressed in language close to that of charisma, "the bearer of godly power of destiny and grace." This is well illustrated by two quotations from a collection of antidemocratic tracts published in the Weimar years:

> In our misery we long for the leader. He should show us the way and the deed that could make our people honest again.

> The leader cannot be made, can in this sense also not be selected. The leader makes himself in that he comprehends the history of his people. [26]

The beginnings of a spontaneous "Führer cult" in the Nazi party have been traced to the year before the 1923 putsch, the year of Mussolini's March on Rome. Hitler himself appears only to have become finally convinced of the

role of Führer in place of that of *Trommler* (drummer) during his imprisonment, in response to calls from those who admired his performance in the
1924 trial and saw no hope for a demoralized party, other than in him. His
leadership was, in fact, the one point of unity around which the NSDAP
was rebuilt after 1925. With the appointment of Goebbels as propaganda
chief and the Nazi triumph in the 1930 election, the Hitler myth was well
launched.

There is convincing evidence to show that, in the absence of a consistent
program, Hitler's personality was the biggest draw in attracting both voters
and new party members, greatly underestimated though it was by opponents of Nazism at the time. Goebbels was later to claim, with some
justification, that the creation of the Hitler myth was his greatest propaganda achievement. But Goebbels, in many ways the most cynical of the
Nazi leaders, was also—like Hitler himself—a believer in the cult he promoted. The last bizarre scene of the Third Reich, in the underground
bunker in Berlin, saw Goebbels, alone among the Nazi bosses, joining
Hitler in a final gesture of faith sealed by the murder of his family and his
own suicide.

The power of the myth derived precisely from the fact that it was a
combination of genuine popular belief and sophisticated manipulation.
After the Nazi takeover Hitler was both presented and seen by the party
and by millions of Germans outside it as the embodiment of *Volksgemeinschaft,* of "national unity" standing above all sectional interests; the architect
of Germany's recovery, personally incorruptible; a fanatical defender of
German honor and Germany's just rights against both internal and external
enemies—yet a man of the people, a corporal who had won the Iron Cross,
First Class, and shared the experience of the common soldier at the front.
His popularity fluctuated but was always well ahead of that of the Nazi
party, reaching high points, for example, after the suppression of the SA in
1934, the remilitarization of the Rhineland in 1936, and the occupation of
Prague followed by his fiftieth birthday in April 1939. His appeal cut across
class, regional, and religious boundaries, affecting both young and old, men
and women, an appeal that combined strength and vulnerability, the former
evoking fanaticism and aggression, the latter arousing strong emotions of
devotion and protection.

No one took the Hitler myth more seriously than Hitler himself, both the
manipulation and the response. Before any decision, he took care to weigh
the likely effect on public opinion and his image. So long as his sense of
mission, which was the heart of the Hitler myth ("I go the way that
Providence dictates with the assurance of a sleepwalker"), [27] was balanced
by the "ice-cold" calculations of the Realpolitiker, it represented a great
source of strength. But success was fatal. When half of Europe lay at his feet,
Hitler abandoned himself to megalomania and became convinced of his
own infallibility. But when he began to look to the image he had created
to work miracles of its own accord—instead of exploiting it—his gifts

deteriorated and his intuition betrayed him. His belief in the special powers with which he had been endowed by Providence kept him going, when the more skeptical Mussolini faltered. Hitler played out his "world-historical" role to the bitter end. But it was this same belief that curtained him in illusion and blinded him to what was actually happening, leading him to commit the sin that the Greeks called *hybris,* of believing himself to be more than man. No man was ever more surely destroyed by the image he created than Adolf Hitler.

In the mid-1930s, the end was ten years away. In those days, Hitler recognized that people's capacity for enthusiasm and willingness to make sacrifices were bound to flag unless revived by recurrent and spectacular successes. He was able to provide these, with hardly a setback, until the end of 1941. No effort was spared to secure a massive turnout in the plebiscites that acclaimed them; but they also reflected genuine approval of the achievements for which he claimed credit in foreign policy and the successful campaigns of the earlier part of the war.

The popular support Hitler could count on had its effect on those who viewed the Nazi regime with critical eyes, both abroad (including Stalin) and at home. Foreign powers that had counted on the regime lasting for only a brief period had to revise their estimates. The conservative-nationalist elite, who had been so confident they could contain Nazi radicalism when they took Hitler into partnership in January 1933, congratulated themselves that the threat of a "Second Revolution" had been removed when he suppressed the SA leadership in 1934; but then they had to recognize that the Hitler myth gave him an independent position that made him no longer dependent on their support or susceptible to pressure.

The striking thing, as Ian Kershaw points out, is that, despite the "institutionalization of Hitler's charismatic leadership" after he became head of government and then head of state as well, the Hitler myth still kept its hold on his "paladins," the second-rank Nazi leaders and Gauleiters, many of them *Alte Kämpfer* from before 1933, who now saw much less of him. With his absorption into public life, the compromises of office, the repudiation of the SA and the Second Revolution, the disappointment of their hopes of taking over the state, they might have been expected to become disillusioned and cynical about the Führer myth as anything more than a propaganda device for the masses. On the contrary, for them as for many of the younger activist elements in the party and the SS, it was the figure of Hitler, as they perceived him in the light of the myth, that not only retained their loyalty but also continued to represent for them the "idea" of Nazism, so holding the party together and guaranteeing that Hitler's ideological program of a confrontation with Bolshevism, the conquest of *Lebensraum,* and the elimination of the Jews still remained the ultimate aim.

IN CONTRAST TO HITLER, Stalin deliberately avoided direct contact with the Russian people. He was haunted by the fear of an attempt on his life, was ill at ease in a crowd and, lacking Hitler's rapport with a mass audience, recognized that the less he was seen by those over whom he ruled the easier it would be to create the image of himself, remote and all-seeing, which he wanted to project. The cult of Stalin, therefore, the counterpart to the Hitler myth, while fulfilling some of the same functions, was very different in character.

One difference, for example, was the stage at which it emerged—briefly on Stalin's fiftieth birthday, in 1929, but only as a permanent feature in the latter part of 1933. The Hitler myth dated from the early days of Hitler's career, when he was in his thirties—not, like Stalin, in his fifties—and had a spontaneous origin in the party before being taken over by Hitler himself well before he came to power. There was nothing spontaneous about the Stalin cult. From its first appearance in October 1929, it bore all the marks of official inspiration. Articles appeared with such titles as "Under the Wise Direction of our Great Genius Leader and Teacher, Stalin," and an official biography underlined the identification with Lenin by the use of the title hitherto reserved for Lenin alone.

> In the years since Lenin's death, Stalin, the most outstanding continuator of Lenin's cause and his most orthodox disciple, the inspirer of all the most important party measures in the struggle to build socialism, has become the generally acknowledged *vozhd'* of the party and the Comintern.*

A second difference was the association with Lenin, a retrospective laying on of hands to establish the apostolic succession, going back through Lenin to Marx and Engels, which Hitler did not need.

From the latter part of 1933—perhaps influenced by Hitler's success in Germany—an established ritual was developed. Painters, sculptors, musicians, as well as poets and journalists, were pressed into service, medals were struck and portraits painted, just as busts of Augustus had been distributed to every city in the Roman Empire. Soon there was no school, office, factory, mine, or collective farm in the USSR that did not have its picture of Stalin on the wall or that failed to send effusive greetings to "Our Beloved Leader" on important anniversaries.

The party leadership collaborated. At the Leningrad Party Conference that preceded the Congress of Victors in January 1934, none other than Kirov declared: "It is hard to conceive such a grand figure as Stalin. For years past, we have not known one turning in our work, not one great initiative, slogan, directive in our policy, the author of which was not

---

*In another officially inspired piece, printed in *Pravda*, the poet-publicist Demyan Bedny claimed: "We therefore have the right to look on the Stalin portrait of Lenin [the childhood image of the eagle flying still higher than the majestic Caucasian peaks] as a subconsciously executed self-portrait." This can only have come from Stalin himself. Both quotations are taken from Robert Tucker, *Stalin as Revolutionary* (New York: 1973), pp. 470–73.

Stalin."[28] The same month *Pravda* carried a poetic tribute with the significant couplet

> *Now when we speak of Lenin*
> *It means we are speaking of Stalin.*

But it is very doubtful if Kirov and the other members of the Politburo believed in the same sense as Gregor Strasser (none other) when, as early as 1927, he described the relationship of party members to Hitler, in Germanic neo-feudal terms, as that of duke and vassal:

> Dux and vassal! In this ancient Germany, both aristocratic and democratic, relationship of leader and follower, fully comprehensible only to the Germanic mentality and spirit, lies the essence of the structure of the NSDAP. . . . Friends, raise your right arm and cry out with me proudly, eager for the struggle, and loyal unto death, "Heil Hitler!"[29]

Such a personal relationship to the man, not the office, was hard to reconcile with socialist tradition and the ethos of a Marxist-Leninist party, in which authority was vested in the party itself, not in a leader. But the Stalin cult, which acquired much more of a Russian nationalist, quasi-religious character, enabled Stalin to draw on the powerful, age-old emotions driven underground with the abolition of the tsardom and the suppression of the Orthodox Church, but now given a new object to identify with: not the party but the state and its autocratic ruler, the successor of the tsars as well as the heir of Lenin and the revolution. The identification with such Russian rulers as Peter the Great and Ivan the Terrible made as strong an appeal to Stalin as it did to the Russian workers and peasants. It helped to fill the yawning gap between government and people, and with the Great Patriotic War Stalin, familiar only from photographs and as a name, became the focus for a swelling of Russian patriotism and pride, a wonder-working icon in whose name millions advanced to battle and death.

This later development led to a convergence between the Stalin cult and the Hitler myth, in both of which there was present the same yearning for a substitute religion, for a messiah in the guise of a leader, salvation rather than solutions. Ian Kershaw notes evidence as early as 1932–34 of a growing disposition to distinguish between the Führer and his party henchmen. "The myth of 'if only the Führer knew' was already at work."[30] The Röhm purge was seen by many as proof of how decisively Hitler was prepared to act when those who surrounded him were no longer able to cover up how badly the SA leaders had abused his confidence. Exactly the same phenomenon of a desire to excuse Stalin from any share of the blame for the misdeeds of his subordinates appears in the Soviet Union, and not just among the peasant masses, but among intellectuals as well. Ilya Ehrenburg, a Soviet writer who enjoyed official favor, confesses in his memoirs that he thought of Stalin as a kind of Old Testament God, and quotes Boris Pasternak meeting him during the purges and using the very same phrase: "If only *he* knew."

Who can tell how many of the ordinary Russian people, reading of the purges and trials with which Stalin harried the party and the intelligentsia, may not have concluded that, like Hitler with the SA, he was getting rid of evil advisers and those responsible for their sufferings—and applauded him?

III

THANKS TO MODERN TECHNOLOGY Hitler and Stalin were able, as no political leaders had been before them, to make their public images omnipresent: the faces staring from every billboard, every office wall and newsreel, the voices over the radio which whole populations were required to listen to. But few historical figures are more difficult to grasp as individual human beings, and this was true even for those who saw them frequently at close quarters and worked with them. Hitler's closest military collaborator, General Alfred Jodl, wrote to his wife while awaiting trial at Nuremberg in 1946:

> I ask myself: "Do I then know this person at all, at whose side for so many years I led so thorny an existence?" . . . Even today I do not know what *he* thought, knew and wanted to do, but only what *I* thought and suspected about it. [31]

Stalin's collaborators—those who survived like Khrushchev—found him equally impenetrable, equally unpredictable in his reactions, equally impossible to "read."

Both men took special pains to conceal, as well as to exploit, their personalities. Both owed a great deal of their success as politicians to their ability to disguise, from allies as well as opponents, their thoughts and their intentions. This applied not only to what they intended to do in the present or the future, but also to the past. Anyone who tried to explore or get witnesses to talk about the earlier years of either man was likely to run into obstacles and, once they had come to power, into danger as well. The Hitler myth and the Stalin cult of personality played a central part in their exercise of power, and anything that might disturb the official, carefully constructed version was liable to suppression.

While they promoted the public images of themselves, the two men sought at the same time to protect their private lives—such as they were. The qualification is important, for the strongest impression left, even when it is possible to penetrate the protective screen—for example in Speer's memoirs or Svetlana Alliluyeva's *Twenty Letters*—is that in neither case do their private lives make it easier to understand their public careers. If anything, the banality and lack of human feeling that they show make it harder.

IN THE 1920S when Stalin, as general secretary of the party and a member of the Politburo, was enjoying his growing influence but was not yet freed from the restraints of collective leadership, he came as near as he ever did to a normal family life. These were the years to which his daughter, Svetlana, looked back as her happiest, when the family home that her mother, Nadezhda Alliluyeva, had created at Zubalovo was filled with relatives and friends (including Kirov, Ordzhonikidze, and Bukharin—all three, friends of her mother), when they spent their time in picnics and parties, and when her father took pleasure in developing the estate.

By 1934 those days were long since over. The destructive pressures created by the campaign Stalin let loose on the peasantry found a victim in his own home. Some of the horror of it reached Stalin's wife. Twenty years younger (she was only thirty-one when she died) and a committed party activist, she idealized her husband in the earliest years of their marriage. But she became troubled by the power and privileges that went with his position and the change that came over him in the late 1920s and early 1930s. Attempting to make a life of her own, she enrolled as a chemistry student, studying synthetic fibers at the Industrial Academy, to which she insisted on traveling by public transportation.

From fellow students who had been called up to help with the collectivization campaign she is reported to have learned what was happening in the Ukraine and to have reproached her husband with it. Personal relations between them were already strained and on at least one occasion she had taken her two children and left him. The idea of suicide had evidently occurred to her already, for she had asked her brother when he was on official business in Berlin to bring her back a revolver, without telling him why she wanted such a present.

On the evening of November 8, 1932, at a party in the Kremlin given by the Voroshilovs, a quarrel broke out between Nadezhda and her husband. When Stalin insulted her in front of the others, she walked out of the room. After walking round the Kremlin courtyard with her friend, Pauline Molotov, Nadezhda went to her own room. She telephoned the dacha to see if Stalin was there. According to Khrushchev, who got the story from Stalin's majordomo, Vlasik, the guard on duty said that he was, and, when asked by Nadezhda if he was alone, added, "No, he has a woman with him." (Khrushchev says that she was later identified as the wife of a party member by the name of Gusev.) How far this discovery influenced her is not known; later, however, during the course of the night, Nadezhda shot herself. [32]

Svetlana felt that her father was both deeply affected and incensed by her mother's death. "He was shaken because he couldn't understand why it had happened. What did it mean?" Her death was announced without any mention of suicide, and the note she left was destroyed. Stalin, along with other relatives and friends, came to view the open coffin. After standing for a moment in silence, he suddenly made a gesture as if to push the coffin away, saying as he turned to go, "She left me as an enemy!" Far from feeling any sense of guilt or responsibility for his wife's death, he saw it only as an act of treachery. He did not attend her funeral or her memorial service, nor did he ever afterwards visit her grave. [33]

Stalin did not allow his loss to weaken his resolve: On November 27, he delivered a speech before the Central Committee that was so intemperate in its tone and threats against the peasantry that it was never published. But he could never reconcile himself to Nadezhda's action, and her suicide put an end to his family life. He exchanged the Kremlin flat in which she had died for another one, and gave up using Zubalovo for a new dacha at Kuntsevo, which he built on the outskirts of Moscow.

There was no abrupt break with his wife's relatives. Her father and mother, whom he had known since his Tiflis days, were allowed to go on living at Zubalovo. But Stalin gradually became more and more isolated from ordinary human relationships. His children no longer lived with him, staying in the new apartment in the Kremlin, where he himself never slept. The arrangements for his own and his children's lives were taken over by the security police. To Svetlana it was like living in a prison. The whole establishment was under the control of Nikolai Vlasik, a former bodyguard of Stalin's from civil war days, now a major (eventually lieutenant general) in the NKVD, who arrogated increasing power and built up an empire of his own in Stalin's name, including several other residences, fully staffed, which Stalin hardly ever visited.

Stalin was not interested in possessions, but in power. In his last years, he moved into a small wooden house built next to his dacha and, according to Volkogonov, the inventory made at his death showed that he possessed no valuables of any kind.[34] The furniture was cheap; the pictures on the walls were printed reproductions. He slept under an army blanket and, apart from his marshal's uniform, he had no more than a couple of ordinary suits (one of them in canvas), a pair of embroidered felt boots, and a peasant's sheepskin.

There was nothing sexually abnormal about Stalin, as there may well have been about Hitler. He had never shown much interest in women, however, and no appreciation of them as persons in their own right. A waitress from Zubalovo, Valechka (described by his daughter, Svetlana, as "a young one with a snub nose and a gay, ringing laugh"), became his housekeeper at Kuntsevo. She was "plump, neat, served softly at table and never joined in any conversation," much more to Stalin's taste than the first wife his son Vasily chose and whom Stalin contemptuously described as "a woman with ideas . . . a herring with ideas—skin and bones." Valechka stayed with him until his death and remained fiercely loyal to his memory.[35]

By 1934 Stalin's life was settling into a regular pattern. In the early 1930s he had moved his office into the Kremlin. He did not get up much before noon, would then drive from Kuntsevo to his office and work there until evening. He frequently dined with other party leaders in a room adjoining his office, occasionally with his son and daughter in the flat below, where they lived, but where he never slept. One of Stalin's habits was to ring up heads of government departments or party officials late at night and ply them with questions, a possibility which kept many of them anxiously at their desks until the small hours. Stalin had a bedroom in his office where he sometimes slept; more often, however late the hour, he would drive back to his dacha.

As an alternative, once or twice a week Stalin would take his companions to see new Soviet or foreign films, followed by a late night supper. For both dictators films were virtually the only opportunity they had to see life in other countries. For Stalin, living in his secluded official world, they provided the only window on his own, although the Soviet films he saw presented a highly unrepresentative picture of the Soviet reality. Stalin made few journeys outside Moscow except for his summer vacation, usually at Sochi on the Black Sea. After January 1928 he never, according to Khrushchev, visited the rural Russia that he devastated. Nor did he ever visit Leningrad again after Kirov's murder at the beginning of December 1934, not even after the city's epic resistance to a siege of 900 days during the war. Most of what he saw of Moscow was from behind the curtains of his armored American Packard, as he swept by at high speed with a phalanx of security guards down the specially cleared highway between Kuntsevo and his office. Almost all the meetings he attended were held in the Kremlin, the most important in his own office (complete with Lenin's death mask), where he followed his old habit of appointing someone else, usually Molotov, to act as chairman while he walked up and down or perched briefly on the arm of a chair.

The historic role Stalin cast for himself, the tensions and obsessions to which it led, not only ended such personal life as he had ever had but destroyed the lives of his family as well. Both his sons came to unhappy ends. He treated the elder, Yakov, the child of his first marriage, with contempt, largely it appears because he reminded Stalin of his own Georgian origins. When Yakov was captured by the Germans at the beginning of the war, his father repudiated him as a traitor, because "no true Russian would ever surrender" and later refused a German offer to exchange him. The younger son, Vasily, after a disastrous career as an air-force officer, died an alcoholic wreck at the age of forty-one. Stalin's relations by both his marriages suffered as well. On the side of his first wife, Ekaterina Svanidze, her brother Alexander, once one of Stalin's closest friends, was shot as a spy; at the same time his wife was arrested and died in camp, while their son was exiled to Siberia as "a son of an enemy of the people." Ekaterina's sister, Maria, was also arrested and died in prison. On the side of his second wife, Nadezhda Alliluyeva, her sister Anna was arrested in 1948 and sentenced to ten years for espionage; Anna's husband, Stanislav Redens, had already been arrested in 1938 as "an enemy of the people" and later shot. Ksenia, the widow of Nadezhda's brother Pavel, and Yevgenia, the wife of Nadezhda's uncle, were both arrested after the war and not released until after Stalin's death.

The one human being whose affection Stalin seems to have made an effort, however clumsy, to retain was his daughter, Svetlana. After her mother's suicide she grew from a child into a teenager in the gloomy, impersonal, and confined environment of the Kremlin. Stalin tried to follow her progress at school, called her his "housekeeper," and insisted she sit on his right at his working dinners. After dinner if they went off to see films in the special theater at the other end of the Kremlin,

> He'd push me in front and say with a laugh: "You show us how to get there, Housekeeper. Without you to guide us, we'd never find it." I'd lead a whole long procession to the other end of the deserted Kremlin. Behind me came the many members of the bodyguard and the heavy armored cars crawling at a snail's pace. We generally saw two films, maybe more, and stayed till two in the morning. [36]

From time to time Stalin would take Svetlana to the opera or the theater for a change. On vacation in Sochi, he would send her fruit and a brief note addressed to "My little sparrow" or "My little housekeeper." But any sign of independence on Svetlana's part roused his anger, for example when she tried to wear short skirts. After reducing her to tears by shouting at her, he insisted on her dressing in the way girls had dressed when he was younger. As she grew up and tried to live her own life, particularly when she formed a friendship with a man of whom he disapproved, he interfered brutally. His intolerance led in 1942–43 to a lasting estrangement between them. Nonetheless, she adds: "I shall never forget his affection, his love and tenderness to me as a child. I loved him tenderly, as he loved me." [37] Her letters are a pathetic commentary on her defeated attempts to reach out to a man who had become walled up in himself, possessed by the role he had assumed, and incapable of responding to human affection.

HITLER, an archetypal "loner," had never had any family life since he left home and went to Vienna. The one episode that could be counted as such was the period when his half-sister Angela came to keep house for him in the villa he first rented at Obersalzberg in 1928, bringing her two daughters with her. He had little to do with his other relations, although in a will made in 1938 he left bequests to Angela, his sister Paula, his half-brother Alois, and a few others in the village of Spital, his mother's family home, where he had spent several summer holidays.

Superficially Hitler was much more attractive to, and more attracted by, women than Stalin. He owed much at the start of his career to the encouragement of married women of good social position such as Hélène Bechstein and Winifred Wagner. Many were fascinated by his hypnotic power, and there are well-attested accounts of the hysteria that affected women at his big meetings. Hitler himself attached great importance to the women's vote, and this was one of the reasons that he gave for not marrying. He liked to have beautiful women in his company. On such occasions, Speer remarks in his memoirs:

> Hitler behaved rather like the graduate of a dancing class at the final session. He displayed a shy eagerness to do nothing wrong, to offer a

sufficient number of compliments, and to welcome them and bid them good-bye with the Austrian kissing of the hand. [38]

The one thing that was fatal was for a woman to have intellectual pretensions, or try to argue with him: He had the same scornful view as Stalin of women with opinions of their own, and they were not invited again.

There were only two women in whom he took more than a passing interest, both twenty years younger. Geli Raubal, whom he described as the one great love of his life, was Angela's daughter. Geli was seventeen in 1928, and over the next three years Hitler became infatuated with her, making her his constant companion in Munich. Geli enjoyed going about with her uncle, especially as his political rise from 1929 to 1931 began to bring him fame. But she suffered from his possessiveness and jealousy of her having a life of her own. There was a furious row when he discovered that she had let Emil Maurice, his chauffeur, make love to her; he forbade her to have anything to do with other men and refused to let her go to Vienna to have her voice trained.

In September 1931 Geli shot herself, a suicide that had as great an effect on Hitler as Nadezhda's had on Stalin. For days he was inconsolable, and it appears to have been as a result of the shock that he refused to touch meat or alcohol for the rest of his life. Her room in the villa at Obersalzberg was kept exactly as she had left it, when it was rebuilt as the Berghof; her photograph hung in his rooms in Munich and Berlin, and flowers were always placed before it on the anniversaries of her birth and death, which Hitler never failed to remember.

Of Eva Braun, Speer wrote: "For all writers of history she is going to be a disappointment." A pretty, empty-headed blonde, with a round face and blue eyes, she worked as a receptionist in the photographer Hoffmann's shop, where Hitler met her. He paid her a few compliments, gave her flowers, and occasionally invited her to join his party on an outing. The initiative, however, was all on Eva's side; she set her cap for him, telling her friends that Hitler was in love with her and that she would make him marry her. Failing to attract his attention in any other way, in the autumn of 1932 she attempted to commit suicide. This was a critical year for Hitler, when he was particularly vulnerable to the threat of a scandal little more than a year after Geli had taken her life. According to Hoffmann, who had seen what was happening from the beginning, "It was in this manner that Eva Braun got her way and became Hitler's *chère amie*." [39]

It brought her little joy. Her diary, which survived her death, is full of complaints about Hitler's neglect and humiliation of her, leading her to a second suicide attempt in 1935, again in order to attract his attention. Hitler went to great lengths to conceal their relationship, and she was denied recognition even as Hitler's mistress outside the close circle of his entourage. In 1936 she succeeded in taking Frau Raubal's place as *Hausfrau* at the Berghof and sat on Hitler's left when he presided at lunch. But Hitler rarely allowed her to come to Berlin, or to appear in public beside him; and at big receptions or dinners, when she longed to be present, she was confined to her room upstairs. She suffered from the same petty tyranny Hitler had sought to establish over Geli. She was forbidden to smoke or dance or enjoy the company of other men, tastes that she could indulge only in secret for fear that she would be found out.

Hitler's contemptuous attitude toward women as well as his egotism and vanity appear in a passage from Speer's memoirs in which he reports Hitler declaring, in front of Eva Braun:

> A highly intelligent man should take a primitive and stupid woman. Imagine if, on top of everything else, I had a woman who interfered with my work. . . . I could never marry. Think of the problems if I had children! In the end they would try to make my son my successor. The chances are slim for someone like me to have a capable son. Consider Goethe's son—a completely worthless person!
>
> Lots of women are attracted to me because I am unmarried. That was especially so during our days of struggle. It's the same as with a movie actor; when he marries, he loses a certain something for the women who adore him. Then he is no longer the idol as he was before. [40]

Only with the war, when social life virtually ceased, did Eva's position become more secure, although she then saw Hitler even less. At least he came as near as he ever did to being human in her company, no longer acting a part but sprawling in his chair beside her at the tea table, often falling asleep, or playing with the dogs on the terrace at the Berghof. Eva's greatest virtue in Hitler's eyes was her loyalty, and this finally brought its reward. Her dearest wish was the respectability of marriage, to become Frau Hitler, and on the next-to-last day of their lives Hitler granted it in the Berlin bunker. Less than forty-eight hours later, this time at Hitler's wish, they committed suicide together.

Without any conclusive evidence to go on, there is a strong presumption that Hitler was incapable of normal sexual relations, whether for physical or psychological reasons, or both. Soviet doctors who carried out an autopsy on Hitler's corpse in 1945 confirmed that he had only one testicle, a condition, usually congenital, known as monorchism (see p. 888). This does not necessarily exclude sexual intercourse; Putzi Hanfstaengl, however, who was one of Hitler's closest companions until the mid-1930s, maintained that he was impotent and that his "abounding nervous energy" found no normal release.*

In the sexual no-man's land in which he lived, he only once nearly found the woman [Geli] and never even the man who might have given him

---

*In a broadcast interview I had with Hanfstaengl after the war, while he was sitting at the piano and recalling some of the Wagner transcriptions he used to play for Hitler, he illustrated the latter's sexual condition with inimitable vulgarity: "You see, all he could do was to play on the black notes, never the white."

relief. . . . My wife summed him up very quickly. "Putzi," she said, "I tell you, he is a neuter."[41]

After reviewing such evidence as there is, psychoanalyst Erich Fromm concluded: "The most one can guess, I believe, is that his sexual desires were largely voyeuristic, anal-sadistic with the inferior type of women, and masochistic with admired women."[42]

UNTIL he became chancellor, Hitler had never lived in Berlin. When he visited the capital he took a suite in the Kaiserhof Hotel. In Munich, at the time that the Nazi party took over the Barlow Palace as its headquarters (1929), he moved from his bed-sitting room to one of the fashionable quarters across the Isar and rented a nine-room apartment occupying the whole of the second floor of No. 16 Prinzregentenstrasse. But his real home remained the Berghof at Obersalzberg, close to the German-Austrian frontier near Berchtesgaden, to which he had been introduced by Dietrich Eckart in the early 1920s.

At first he stayed there in a pension; then, in 1928, he rented an unpretentious villa of his own on the mountainside, Haus Wachenfeld. In the later 1930s a much larger and more luxurious house, the Berghof, was built around the original, and Bormann went on to surround it with a whole complex of roads, barbed-wire fences, barracks, garages, a guest hotel, and other buildings wholly out of keeping with the character of the place. But nothing could alter Hitler's affection for it. For the rest of his life the Berghof remained home. "Here and here alone," he told a journalist who interviewed him in 1936, he could "breathe and think—and live. . . . I remember what I was, and what I have yet to do."[43]

When Hitler became chancellor, Speer created a new and more impressive office for him in his official residence (once Bismarck's) and then in January 1938 was given the commission to build a new chancellery, which 4,500 workers, working in double shifts, were mobilized to complete in twelve months.

As party leader, Hitler had already distanced himself from administration, leaving all but the key decisions to Hess; the party treasurer, Schwarz; and the other headquarters staff in Munich. For the first year or so after taking office—so long as von Hindenburg was alive—Hitler made a show of attending to business in the Chancellery and keeping regular hours. But this went against the grain of his temperament. He detested committees, and soon the intervals between cabinet meetings grew longer and longer. He preferred to do business with one man at a time, and even that as infrequently as possible. He had no interest in administration, which did not correspond with his image of himself as Nietzsche's artist-politician or the irregular habits that went with it.

After von Hindenburg's death, Hitler reverted to his former way of life, absenting himself more and more, and leaving matters to be dealt with through one or other of the two Chancellery offices, with their civil-servant heads, the Reich Chancellery under Lammers, the Presidential under Meissner, to which was eventually added the Party or Führer Chancellery under Bormann. Ministers and party leaders found him hard to reach; he refused to read documents of more than a page, but still insisted that he alone would make important decisions. Instead of involving asking for appointments or taking part in formal discussions, the art of politics in the Third Reich reduced itself to being the last man to catch Hitler's attention, informally, anywhere, at any time, and hoping (often with good reason) that Hitler would say "agreed," leaving it to ministers, civil servants, and party bosses to fight over exactly what he had agreed to.

Like Stalin, Hitler was a night bird. He rarely appeared much before noon, having read the newspapers, and did not go to bed until the early hours of the morning. Lunch in the chancellery did not begin until some time between two and three o'clock and went on till half-past four. According to Speer, between forty and fifty persons had easy access to the table, and the company usually included one or two Gauleiters or other party leaders who happened to be in the capital, a few cabinet ministers, and the members of his entourage, but no army officers or people from other professions.

Goebbels and Göring came only when they wanted something. "To tell the truth," the latter told Speer, "the food there is too rotten for my taste. And then, those party dullards from Munich! Unbearable." [44] Both comments were just. Hitler, who was an aggressive vegetarian and teetotaller, forbade smoking and kept a simple table. As for the company, it was notable for its total lack of distinction or liveliness of mind. Hitler was wary of admitting anyone who might disturb the ascendancy that he exercised over his familiar circle. The conversation was trivial, only occasionally enlivened by the appearance of Goebbels, who made Hitler laugh with malicious gossip, usually directed—with a purpose—against other leading party members. "I frequently reflected," Speer adds, "that this mediocre group was assembling at the same spot where Bismarck used to talk brilliantly with friends and political associates." [45]

Life at Obersalzberg was even more tedious, there being nowhere to escape for relief: the same routine, the same repetitive repertoire of anecdotes and comments. In between lunch and supper, Hitler would lead a little procession to the teahouse. "The company always marveled at the panorama in the same phrases," according to Speer, "Hitler always agreed in much the same language." Here Hitler would frequently launch into one of his endless monologues, while the company struggled to keep awake; occasionally he himself would fall asleep while he was talking. Two hours later the same group would reappear for supper, followed by a late-night film show, often films that had been shown before. [46] "When, I would ask myself," Speer wrote, "did Hitler really work?" [47] The long periods of inactivity, however, especially at Obsersalzberg, were not wasted: Hitler used them to mature a decision or to let his thoughts ripen or to recharge his energies before a big speech. When the period of gestation was over, he would burst into sudden activity, with apparently inexhaustible energy.

Hitler was not a man with whom anyone could have a normal conversation. Either the Führer talked and everyone else present listened, or the others talked and he sat lost in thought, taking no notice of what was being said. His inability to listen, his unwillingness to engage in discussion, meant that he became intellectually isolated, locked into the convictions he had formed in his earlier life, instinctively resisting any exposure of them to criticism. Thus he spoke constantly of his interest in history but showed no appreciation at all of the fact that historians' conclusions are constantly subject to revision in the light of fresh evidence or further debate. No historian, no expert of any kind other than in technical matters, was ever admitted to his company; they might have disturbed the "granite foundation" of his *Weltanschauung,* which in fact was derived from popularized racist and pseudoscientific views circulating in Germany and Austria at the turn of the century.

But Hitler was convinced—or determined to convince himself—that originality was an essential part of the role he was called on to play. Rauschning describes the sort of Hitlerian monologue in which this resulted:

> He tried to acquire the semblance of creativeness by endless talk. . . . His views were a mixture of misunderstood Nietzsche and popularized ideas in current philosophy. All this stuff he poured forth with the air of a prophet and a creative genius. He seemed to take it for granted that the ideas were his own. He had no notion of their actual origin and considered that he worked them out for himself, and that they were inspirations, the product of his solitude in the mountains. [48]

Delivered with every appearance of self-confidence, this was enough to impress the many Nazi party members and voters who did not pretend to understand what he was saying or pay much attention to it, but accepted the Führer's claim to be an original thinker who had unlocked the secret of history and could match the Marxists by providing an ideological backing for the party's policies.

IN MOST OF these respects Stalin presents a sharp contrast. The man who had built up his position, not by his ability as a speaker, but by the mastery he established over the party machine, was the last person to underestimate the importance of administration, not for its own sake like the stereotype of a petty bureaucrat, but for the power of control that it gave him. This is the contrast, remarked on at the beginning of this chapter, between Hitler's greater security and Stalin's greater control, between the Führer and the general secretary. Unlike Hitler, Stalin lived for his work, spending long hours every day at his desk, reading a constant flow of reports and drafts which he annotated with the briefest of instructions. To the end of his life he enjoyed intervening unexpectedly in trivial issues, especially if they had to do with appointments or misbehavior by local officials; this gave him the opportunity to fire off a personal telegram, giving the impression that nothing happened in the Soviet Union which escaped the eye of the ever-watchful General Secretary.

The size of Russia and the inadequacies of communication must always have meant that there were large areas over which Stalin's control was much less than he believed or would have liked. But this was not for lack of interest or trying on his part, and no regional secretary, however powerful he might be in his own satrapy, or however remote from Moscow, could ever be sure that one of Stalin's right-hand men—Molotov, Kaganovich, or Voroshilov—would not descend on him unexpectedly and sweep the whole setup away, some into exile or prison, some to face a firing squad.

Such purges were virtually unknown in Germany after the removal of Röhm and the SA leadership. The Third Reich would have been very much better administered if further purges had cleared out the networks of patronage and corruption established by many of the Gauleiters or had attacked the duplication, conflicts of authority, and inefficiency in ministries—not least the empires built up by such figures as Göring or Ley, the boss of the Labor Front. But Hitler, although prepared to dismiss generals, or ministers who were only nominally party members (for example, Schacht), was always reluctant to take action against any of the Nazi Old Guard—even against Röhm. Whatever their shortcomings, to which he was indifferent, he prized their loyalty and reliability, and (one of his more human characteristics) repaid them with a surprising degree of loyalty and tolerance on his part.

Loyalty and trust were not qualities in which Stalin put much stock, any more than gratitude. His suspicion never slept: It was precisely the Bolshevik Old Guard whom he distrusted most. Even men who had been closely associated with him in carrying out the Second Revolution as members of the Politburo or the Central Committee were executed, committed suicide, or died in the camps.* There was nothing comparable with this in the history of the Third Reich, where the original group of Nazi leaders largely survived unchanged until the end.

Stalin appears to have had no personal friends or familiars, and almost always his companions at dinner were the same inner group with whom he ran the country, plus the occasional visitor—usually a party chairman or secretary from the Ukraine or the Caucasus who happened to be in Moscow. Much of their talk was shop, but there was a good deal of drinking and, if they did not go on to see a film, Stalin, who had a sardonic sense of humor, enjoyed baiting his comrades and making them drunk.

These dinner parties seem to have been his only regular form of relaxa-

*See Chapter Twelve.

tion. "I don't think," Khrushchev wrote, "there has ever been a leader of comparable responsibilities who wasted more time than Stalin did just sitting around the dinner table eating and drinking." [49]

Stalin did not need to indulge in Hitler's displays of temper and exaggerated behavior in order to impress others with his strength of personality. Although he could lose his temper when angered, he did not do so for effect, any more than he felt it necessary to talk all the time or raise his voice; he habitually spoke quietly. Physically unimpressive (he was no more than five feet four inches tall and every photographer had to take account of his touchiness on this point), he dominated any group simply by virtue of being "the boss" and by the proven ruthlessness with which he could act.

Priding himself on his shrewdness—"It is not so easy to take Stalin in"—he would have had nothing but scorn for Hitler's flights of fantasy about race and the rise and decline of nations. If ghosts and Goyaesque apparitions began to haunt him as he grew older, he kept them to himself and took great care not to reveal his thoughts.

BOTH STALIN AND HITLER were alive to the importance of the arts and of control over them if they were to change the way people thought and felt. By 1934, however, their total absorption in politics did not leave much room for them to enjoy the arts for their own sake, any more than it did for personal relationships.

In addition to films, one of Stalin's few pleasures was the theater. He owed this interest to his wife, and they were often to be seen together at performances of plays, opera, and ballet. He continued to visit the theater after her death, particularly the Bolshoi, usually alone and taking his seat at the back of his box after the lights had gone down. He took a close (often critical) interest in what was staged, as he did in what was published.

To the end of his life Stalin retained a certain respect for artists and writers as such, even when he persecuted particular individuals. His library has been examined and shows more evidence, both in the number of books and passages underlined, of the habit of reading than appears in Hitler's case. [50] The majority of Stalin's books were concerned with politics, with Marxism and with history. His familiarity with the classics of Russian literature, however, was evident from his conversation—far more than Hitler's with German. Among authors he is reported to have referred to were Chekhov, Gogol, Gorki, and the satirist Saltykov-Shchedrin, Tolstoy, even Dostoevsky and Pushkin.

Hitler remained devoted to Wagner and in the 1930s never missed putting in an appearance at the Bayreuth Festival. Other music appears to have had little attraction for him apart from operetta—*Die Fledermaus* and Franz Lehár's *Merry Widow*. His taste in films was for undemanding light entertainment. It was the fine arts in which he believed he might have succeeded—painting and sketching—and the art in which he believed he might have achieved greatness—architecture—in which he still took an impassioned interest. On these he permitted no one to question his judgment.

In painting, his interest was shown by the drastic purges he imposed on German galleries,* and by his activity as a collector. His taste in art remained as set as his historical and racist *Weltanschauung*; the foundations for both had been laid in prewar Vienna. Although he admired classical and Italian Renaissance art, Hitler's real enthusiasm was for nineteenth-century German romantic painting, from "schmaltzy" genre pictures—drinking scenes by Eduard Grützner—to heroic, idyllic, allegorical, historical-patriotic themes, the visual equivalent of Wagner without the genius. Among the artists of whom he thought most highly were Hans Makart, Carl Spitzweg, and Adolf Menzel. As early as 1925 he sketched a plan for a German national gallery, and in the 1930s he started to make a collection of nineteenth-century German works for the museum he wanted to create in Linz, the Austrian town where he had first become aware of the fascination of Wagner and of architecture.

Hitler returned from his visit to Italy in 1938 so impressed by what he saw that he decided he must match Rome and Florence by turning his Linz project into "the greatest museum in the world." The war and the occupation of half the continent offered the opportunity to carry out a redistribution of the treasures of European art. Guided by Hans Posse, director-general of the Dresden Gallery, and a staff of assistants, Hitler gathered together—partly by compulsory purchase, partly by confiscation—a collection that by the end of the war included 10,000 paintings in addition to drawings, prints, tapestries, sculpture, and furniture. Thanks to Posse's influence, Hitler had been persuaded to widen his choice to include earlier centuries besides his favorite nineteenth. Among the 6,755 paintings stored in a salt mine at Alt-Aussee were the Ghent altarpiece by the brothers Van Eyck, and works by Rubens, Rembrandt, Vermeer, Leonardo da Vinci, and Michelangelo.[51] An order received from Hitler's headquarters in the final weeks of the war to blow up the repository and destroy its contents, on pain of death if not obeyed, was fortunately not carried out.

But it was in architecture that Hitler came closest to realizing the artistic genius he believed himself to possess. With the help of Speer and other architects he saw his ideas and sketches for buildings turned into working drawings and then large-scale models on which he never tired of feasting his eyes. These were his creations, with which he was determined to outshine the buildings he most admired: the nineteenth-century Paris and Vienna Operas, the Palace of Justice in Brussels, the Vienna Ringstrasse, the same "inflated baroque" that had attracted Kaiser Wilhelm II, "the style [as Speer noted] that accompanied the decline of the Roman Empire."[52]

Hitler knew by heart the detailed measurements of all the buildings he regarded most highly. His megalomania drove him to demand that *his*

*See p. 404.

buildings should be two, three, four times as big, a demand that sacrificed any sense of style to size. Like so many tyrants from the pharaohs onward, he saw his equivalent of the pyramids as providing the "imperishable confirmation" of his power.

In Albert Speer, Hitler believed he had found the gifted young architect he imagined he might have become himself. "I was wild to accomplish things at twenty-eight years old," Speer wrote in his memoirs. "I would have sold my soul like Faust. Now I had found my Mephistopheles."[53] The bond between them became as close as Hitler formed with any other human being. With Speer he relaxed and talked as he had with Kubizek, the only friend of his youth. "Ultimately," Speer wrote later, "he would philosophize that all that remained to remind men of the great epochs of history was their monumental architecture. What had remained of the emperors of Rome? What would still bear witness to them today, if their buildings had not survived?"[54] Taking Hitler's vision literally, Speer even prepared plans for using special materials and construction methods that would enable them "to build structures that even in a state of decay, after hundreds or (such were our reckonings) thousands of years, would more or less resemble Roman models."[55]

Among the commissions Hitler gave Speer was a grandiose plan for a stadium and group of buildings to house the annual Party Congress at Nuremberg: The colonnade alone was to be twice the length of the Baths of Caracalla in Rome. But this was eclipsed by the plan Hitler conceived in 1936 for rebuilding the whole of the center of Berlin on a scale that would outdo what Georges Haussmann had done for Paris—"comparable only to ancient Egypt, Babylon, and Rome." A grand avenue three miles long was to link a triumphal arch, 240 feet high, to a domed assembly hall, with a capacity for 180,000 people. The dome itself was to rise to nearly 900 feet and be modeled on the Pantheon in Rome, with this difference—that the round opening at the top, 152 feet in diameter, was to be larger than the entire dome of the Pantheon or of St. Peter's. His own Führer Building was to cover six million square feet. The cost of such buildings was brushed aside as irrelevant. Hitler had a model made of the new Berlin a hundred feet long, which he delighted in showing off to favored visitors while reeling off the statistics. At any hour of the day or night whenever he was in Berlin—during the war as well—Hitler would bear Speer off for yet one more inspection of his masterpiece, as he regarded it.

Only one thing spoiled Hitler's enjoyment: the discovery that the Russians were planning an even taller assembly building in Moscow in honor of Lenin. Stalin did not regard himself as an artistic genius or an architect manqué, but like Hitler he grasped clearly the unique capacity architecture had to express political power, to impress upon subjects and visitors alike the strength and values of a regime. Like Hitler, again, his taste was provincial and petty bourgeois, rejecting Modernism in favor of monumental buildings, the essential characteristic of which was their size.

Stalin, too, was bent upon rebuilding his capital, and in 1934 established the Russian Academy of Architecture to produce architects who would carry out his wishes. The reward for those who turned their faces to the sun was admission to a privileged elite enjoying "huge fees and luxurious apartments and studios"; the construction work was frequently provided by forced labor equipped with little more than picks and shovels, another reminder of the pyramids.

Stalin personally attended all the meetings of the building committee for the Palace of Soviets, which was to be the largest building in the world, topped by a statue of Lenin a hundred feet high. In order to make room for it facing the Kremlin, he ordered the demolition of the largest cathedral in Moscow. Stalin turned down the suggestions for a new metropolis offered by Le Corbusier and other leading radical architects in favor of a more conventional plan which was approved in 1936 with ten years allowed for its realization. In the meantime the stations of the Moscow Metro, the job of building which was given to Kaganovich and Khrushchev, provided a foretaste (its first line was opened in 1935) of what the new capital might look like.

The war supervened ("Now this will be the end of their building for good and all," Hitler remarked with satisfaction), and the Palace of Soviets, like Hitler's domed hall, was never built. But unlike Hitler, who took his life in the ruins of Berlin, Stalin lived to see the rest of his plan for rebuilding Moscow carried out, with six skyscrapers taking the place of the palace, and the wedding cake-style buildings of Moscow University completed on the Lenin Hills the year he died. [56]

A MARXIST REGIME was "godless" by definition, and Stalin had mocked religious belief since his days in the Tiflis seminary. Hitler had been brought up as a Catholic and was impressed by the organization and power of the Church, claiming to have learned much from its skill in dealing with human nature. He had no use for the Protestant clergy: "They are insignificant little people, submissive as dogs, and they sweat with embarrassment when you talk to them. They have neither a religion they can take seriously nor a great position to defend like Rome." [57] It was the "great position" of the Church that Hitler respected, the fact that it had lasted for centuries. He had no time at all for its teaching, regarding it as a religion fit only for slaves and detesting its ethics. "Taken to its logical extreme, Christianity would mean the systematic cultivation of human failure." [58]

Hitler declared conscience to be "a Jewish invention, a blemish like circumcision," and (except when it suited his political purpose, as in the denunciation of the SA leaders' homosexuality) would brush aside complaints about the obscenities of a Julius Streicher or the corruption and abuse of power by other party bosses as unimportant in comparison with their loyalty and services to the movement. Stalin simply added such information to the files that were kept on all party members against the day when it might be necessary to hand them over to the NKVD.

Hitler poured scorn on the earnest efforts of those among his followers, like Himmler, who tried to reestablish pagan mythology and rites or, like Hess, who resorted to astrology and reading the stars. In such matters he shared with Stalin the same materialist outlook, based on the nineteenth-century rationalists' certainty that the progress of science would destroy all myths and had already proved Christian doctrine to be an absurdity. On the other hand Hitler's own myth at least had to be protected, and this led him, like Napoleon, to speak frequently of Providence, as a necessary if uncon-scious projection of his sense of destiny which provided him with both justification and absolution. "The Russians," he remarked on one occasion, "were entitled to attack their priests, but they had no right to assail the idea of a supreme force. It's a fact that we're feeble creatures and that a creative force exists." [59]

Stalin's assault on the Russian peasantry had been as much an attack on their traditional religion as on their individual holdings, and the defense of it had played a major part in arousing peasant resistance, especially among the women. Only when Stalin began to cultivate Russian nationalism did he begin to moderate his hostility to the Orthodox Church. Political reasons led Hitler to restrain his anticlericalism and refuse to let himself be drawn into attacking the Church publicly, as Bormann and other Nazis would have liked him to do. But he promised himself that, when the time came, he would settle his account with the priests of both creeds. When he did, he would not be restrained by any judicial scruples.

Stalin and Hitler were materialists not only in their dismissal of religion but also in their insensitivity to humanity as well. The only human beings who existed for them were themselves. The rest of the human race was seen either as instruments with which to accomplish their purposes or as obsta-cles to be eliminated. They regarded life solely in terms of politics and power: Everything else—human relationships and emotions, knowledge, beliefs, the arts, history, science—was of value only insofar as it could be exploited for political purposes.

Both men were remarkable only for the roles they assumed. Outside of those, their private lives were insignificant and impoverished. And each of the roles was consecrated to a vision of a world that, however great the differences between them, was equally inhuman—a world in which whole populations could be uprooted and moved about; whole classes could be eliminated, races enslaved or exterminated; millions of lives sacrificed in war and even in time of peace; individual men and women dwarfed by the scale of the monolithic structures—state, Volk, party, army, giant industrial com-plexes, collective farms, labor and concentration camps—into which they were organized.

THE INSTRUMENT by means of which the two men came to power was the party: the Communist party of the Soviet Union (CPSU) in the one case; the National Socialist German Workers' party (NSDAP) in the other. In their ideologies and stated aims, the parties were in open and irreconcilable conflict with each other, but in structure and function they had much in common. Both for example differed radically from democratic parties, which exist to organize an open, constitutional competition for political power; the purpose of both the CPSU and the Nazi party was to abolish such competition and secure a permanent monopoly of power. They both claimed with justification to be a new type of party, making heavy demands on their members and requiring them to accept strict discipline in carrying out the orders of the leadership.

The most important differences between them were due to their different historical experiences. Unlike the Nazis, the Bolsheviks, until just before they came to power in 1917, were not only in opposition but were also an illegal organization. Lenin's concept of a revolutionary vanguard party, with its cells penetrating the society it sought to replace, derived from the nineteenth-century Russian Populists. It was adapted to the Bolsheviks' situation as an underground party, as well as to Lenin's conviction that the revolution had to be organized by committed full-time revolutionaries and could not be left to the development of historical forces or the spontaneous action of the working class.

This Leninist tradition of a vanguard party seeking to mobilize the support of the masses, but always maintaining its distance from them and never allowing its leadership and policies to be dependent on their consent, remained characteristic of the CPSU long after it had formed the government of the country and had eliminated its rivals.

In contrast, the Nazis had never been an underground party and following Hitler's policy of "legality" were able to operate in the open. In the early 1930s they became a mass party (800,000 at the end of 1932) which, far from being isolated from the population, attracted a bigger percentage of votes than any other party in German history.

The difference in historical experience also affected Stalin's and Hitler's own positions. The tradition of collective leadership in the CPSU was still too strong at the end of 1934 for Stalin to dispense with it at least in appearance. One reason for retaining it was the accusation of abandoning the European tradition of social democracy. This had already begun under Lenin's leadership, as the Menshevik exiles and Western socialist leaders never ceased to point out.

The more the Russian course diverged from that of socialist parties in the West, with the forced collectivization of the early 1930s—and the more bitter the attacks of the Russian-dominated Comintern against the "social Fascists"—the more advantage there was to Stalin in maintaining the facade of continuity and holding on to the talismanic phrases that buttressed his claim to be the true heir of the Marxist tradition. Stalin's relationship to the party was to change radically after 1934, but in the early 1930s the "cult of the party," of which he was the guardian, was the best answer to charges of a cult of personality.

Owing nothing to any predecessor, Hitler demanded and secured acceptance of his unique position as Führer by the Nazi party even in the 1920s. There was no provision for discussion of policy or tactics; decisions on such matters were not made by votes but reserved to the Führer. Hitler had as little use for the election of officers as for committees: It was for the Führer to appoint or dismiss them as he saw fit. As for opposition within the party, that was ended with the elimination of Strasser and Röhm. The party, as its members proudly claimed, was for action, not talk.

Hitler and the Nazis continued to look on themselves as a revolutionary party. The policy of legality implied no conversion to constitutionalism, only the exploitation of the democratic freedoms promised by the Weimar constitution to work for its overthrow. Now that that had been achieved, the question Hitler had to answer was what role the party had to play after its leaders had come to power.

In the case of the Soviet Union the answer was easy enough: The Communist party had taken over the government. After seventeen years in office, not only the state administration but also the economy, the nationalized industries, the collectivized agriculture, and the armed forces all operated under the direct leadership of the party. The center of power was not the Council of People's Commissars (eventually renamed the Council of Ministers) but the party's Politburo, whose members reappeared in the council as chairman, deputy chairman, and leading commissars to ensure that the policies decided on by the Politburo were carried out by the administration. Nothing made this clearer than the fact that the most powerful man in Russia was neither head of state, head of government, nor even a member of the Council of Commissars, but was content to exercise his power in the party post of general secretary and as a member of the Politburo.

The biggest problem in Russia was the shortage of trained and experienced people to run the country. For years the Communists had to rely on "bourgeois specialists" remaining from tsarist times or recruited from abroad and always suspected of being hostile to the new regime. In 1928 Stalin launched a campaign to get rid of these, only to have to retract it three years later and call for the recognition of their services as indispensable. The party had able men in its ranks but never enough of them. The purges it carried out—four between 1921 and 1934—were aimed at the corrupt, the incapable, and the opportunists as well as "deviationists" and "oppositionists." The size of the party's membership reflected the problem. In March 1921 it numbered 730,000 (including candidate members) in a country with a population of around 120 million. The figure rose to over 3.5 million by the beginning of 1933, but the purges reduced it to 2.35 million by the end of 1934 and just over 2 million by 1937, far more of an elite than a mass party. Stalin's watchword "Cadres are everything" summed up the overriding priority to recruit and train a younger generation of party members in sufficient numbers to fill the gaps.

Hitler, too, declared that "the conquest of power is a never-ending process," and once the Nazi party had secured a monopoly of power, its members, especially the *Alte Kämpfer* who had made sacrifices for it and suffered in the *Kampfzeit*, expected to take over the government—and all the jobs and perks that went with it in a highly organized country—in the same way as the Communist party had in the Soviet Union. The more radical members looked for more than that: Röhm and the SA to replace the army; the enthusiasts for the corporate state to break the hold of big business and the banks on the economy (as promised in the original party program); the NSBO (the Nazi Factory Organization) to redress the balance between labor and capital.

For a brief period in the chaotic spring of 1933, it looked as if they were going to; by July 1934, it was clear they were not. It was a difficult decision for Hitler to make, but, once he made up his mind, he acted in so brutal and unambiguous a way in eliminating the SA as an independent force as to leave no doubt that the revolution—or this phase of it—was at an end.

The political arguments for such action were pressing enough: the succession to von Hindenburg and the attitude of the army. But so far as the party was concerned, the most important reason was Hitler's realization that it did not contain enough men with the ability to take on the job of running the country. This was the same lesson as had had to be learned in Russia, with this important difference: that Germany still had in place a professional civil service, business management, and armed forces with standards few other states could equal. Taking the long view, Hitler recognized that, to attempt to replace these, or put them under the control of party comrades whose education, expertise, and experience were plainly inferior, would seriously set back his immediate objective of economic recovery and the restoration of German power.

Characteristically, however, Hitler gave nothing like so clear an indication of what role he saw the party playing in the future. He preferred, as always, to keep his options open and avoid a decision, refusing (for example) to define the future relationship between the civil service and the party in regard to jobs and jurisdiction in a way satisfactory to either side.

The party members could share vicariously in the successes of the new regime, they could still be reunited with their Führer and uplifted by his words at the annual party rallies. The Hitler myth was still potent, and many still clung to hopes kept alive by the hints Hitler dropped of great tasks ahead. The local Gauleiters enjoyed a good deal of local power and, no less important, of local patronage. Most party members found employment, but except for a minority of the party leadership it was at the lower levels of the much swollen official and party local staffs. Those who made it to higher posts (Göring is an obvious example) took on the color and habits of ministerial or official authority. The remainder could no longer enjoy the illusion that they were an elite body from which a new governing class would be recruited. After July 1934, there were no more purges, and the party's numbers continued to rise. By the end of 1934 it had grown to two and a half million in a country considerably less than half that of the USSR, and was far more a mass than an elite party. Their role after power had been won was essentially the same as before, to mobilize and educate the masses in support of the objectives proclaimed by Hitler.

Hitler would never repudiate the party, which was his creation and the means by which he had come to power; but he was no longer dependent on it. Besides being head of the only party, he was now head of state, head of government, and, most important of all, "Führer of the German Reich and German people." This was the beginning of a process by which Germany started to move from a single-party state to an autocracy.

Despite the much more powerful position of the Communist party in the Soviet Union, it was the signs that Stalin was beginning to move in the same direction, from oligarchy to autocratic rule, that in 1933–34 alarmed those members of the Politburo and Central Committee who have been loosely called the "opposition." The difference was that in Germany, even if there were disappointed party members who grumbled that Hitler had betrayed the original ideals of the movement, there was no longer resistance from the party or the SA. In Russia, however, whether there was real opposition or not, Stalin became convinced that there was and acted to suppress it, by the same means Hitler had used to suppress Röhm and the SA, only on a far greater scale.

TO CREATE and maintain autocratic rule required a special instrument responsible to one man alone and organized to carry out his orders arbitrarily without questioning them, without regard to the law, and without any form of restraint. The party was no longer adequate for either man's purpose, which in Russia was to include the destruction of what was left of the party Lenin had known. Its place was taken by the secret police, the NKVD in Stalin's case, the SS in Hitler's.

The Soviet secret police was founded by decision of the Council of People's Commissars, on December 20, 1917, as the Cheka (Extraordinary Commission for Combating Counter-Revolution and Sabotage) and took over the Lubyanka, a former insurance-company building in Moscow. This was less than a year after the provisional government had abolished the hated tsarist Okhrana, well known to the leaders of the Bolshevik party, whose organization it had successfully penetrated.* Lenin had no scruples

---

*One of the most celebrated Okhrana agents, Roman Malinovsky, became Lenin's trusted chief agent in Russia and led the Bolshevik deputies in the Fourth Duma. In 1908–09, four out of five members of the Bolsheviks' St. Petersburg Committee were Okhrana agents. Persistent rumors that Stalin was one as well have never been confirmed.

about setting up a Bolshevik counterpart. He greatly admired the Jacobin terror during the French Revolution and as early as 1905 foresaw the need for its repetition in Russia. Both he and Trotsky defended terror as an essential element of revolution. The Cheka carried out its first reported execution without trial on February 24, 1918, and its record under Dzerzhinsky has been described earlier.

The Cheka was nominally abolished in February 1922 but only underwent a series of transformations (GPU—NKVD—KGB)* without changing its essential character. The turning point in its history was the collectivization-kulak campaign. Arbitrary arrest and execution without trial became commonplace and there was an enormous increase in the number of prisoners sent to the so-called labor camps, established as early as 1918–19. The statute that governed their great expansion in the 1930s was passed on April 7, 1930, establishing GULAG, the Main Administration of Labor Camps. Its first head was Yagoda, the deputy chairman of OGPU, later its chairman, who had joined the Cheka during the civil war and became known to Stalin in Tsaritsyn. In that year, 1930, the number of inmates is estimated at 600,000. Estimates for 1931–32 put the number of prisoners in "places of detention" at nearly two million, the majority of them in camps. That was before the purges and trials of the 1930s, when these figures were trebled or quadrupled.

In Germany, the use that could be made of violence and terror had been well understood by Hitler and the other Nazi leaders from the beginning, long before they came to power. Once in power, and particularly after the Reichstag fire, a campaign of terror was let loose against the Communists and Social Democrats. The SA took full advantage of their opportunity to arrest, beat up, and often torture thousands with whom they had old scores to settle from the street battles of the last two years. By the summer of 1933, their excesses had become an embarrassment to Hitler, and the employment of the SA as auxiliary police was ended. The basic rights, however, abolished in 1933, including freedom from arbitrary arrest, were not restored.

The confrontation with Röhm and the SA in the summer of 1934 brought home to Hitler the need for a much more disciplined and better trained elite force, like the NKVD, responsible to him alone and absolutely responsive to his orders. Neither the SA nor the party, as mass organizations, could meet this need. Hitler found what he wanted in the SS (*Schutzstaffeln*, Guard Battalions), which originated in Munich in 1925, taking over the duties and insignia of the former "Hitler Assault Squad," and charged with the protection of Hitler and the other Nazi leaders. It formed part of the SA empire but under the ambitious Himmler, appointed Reichsführer SS in January 1929, it began to expand its limited numbers (to 10,000 by the end of 1929, to 50,000 by spring 1933) and change its character. Himmler

*See glossary.

set about distinguishing it from the rest of the SA, which was also expanding in 1929–30 by taking in young unemployed and working-class recruits. Himmler looked in the opposite direction and by strict control of enlistment and service started to build up an SS *corps d'élite*.

In April 1934 Himmler and Heydrich completed the takeover of the political police, the Gestapo, and in the summer it was SS armed squads that carried out the executions of the SA leaders. Himmler's rewards were recognition of the SS as an independent organization; the right to form armed SS units (*Verfügungstruppe*, the origin of the wartime Waffen SS); and responsibility for the concentration camps (the origin of the SS *Totenkopfverbände*, the SS Death's Head camp guards).

July 1934 therefore has a double importance: the reduction of the SA to a veterans' organization which, once the political revolution was complete, was left with no further role; and, in the SS, the creation of the executive organ of the alternative Führer state, which Hitler was to develop, independent of both party and state, responsible to himself alone and outside the framework of the constitution and the law.

It is unlikely that Hitler foresaw in 1934 the full development of his conception. But the compass bearing, the instinct for personal power as a function of his Providential mission, not of his office, was there from the beginning of his career, as he had already shown in the party. If he did not know how far it would take him, he knew instinctively the direction in which to move. Development slowed down in the mid-1930s—in 1937 there were not more than 10,000 prisoners and 4,000 guards in the three main concentration camps—but took off with the outbreak of war. At its peak (1944) the SS rival to the Reichswehr, the Waffen SS, consisted of thirty-eight divisions, mostly motorized or armored, with a total of 910,000 men, while the three concentration camps of 1937 had grown to the Nazi slave empire in the east under SS control, rivaling in size and horror the other that Stalin and the NKVD had created in Russia.*

V

BESIDES INTELLIGENCE AND SECURITY, there were a number of other key areas in which Stalin and Hitler sought to exercise a monopoly of control. Most of them were common to both regimes. Control of the economy, however, was one in which there was a major difference between them.

As a Marxist, Stalin naturally considered the answer to the question of who controlled the economy to be the key to all other social and political questions. As a candidate for the succession to Lenin, he had made a break with the compromises of the New Economic Policy the issue on which to defeat his rivals. As Lenin's successor, he threw himself into completing the

---

*See the map on pp. 750–51.

nationalization of the means of production, distribution, and exchange—in agriculture no less than in industry and trade—as the missing element needed to consolidate Lenin's unfinished capture of power in 1917. As the leader of a huge, underdeveloped country, he seized on planned economic development from above as the only way in which to create the industrial base that would enable the Russian people to rid themselves of their backwardness.

Once Stalin had made his bid to do this by the Five-Year Plan, everything had to be subordinated to making a success of it, at whatever cost. Concentrating investment in heavy industry producing capital, not consumer goods; creating the managerial cadres and the skilled work force needed to carry the initial breakthrough forward; raising productivity—these became Stalin's priorities.

What Stalin was seeking to do in Russia, however, had already been accomplished in Germany in the previous century, and had been the basis of German economic and military power in the First World War. Hitler's aim was to re-create that power and secure Germany's future by expansion in the east, a return to the classic formula of imperialism. The prerequisite was to get rid of the limits imposed by the Treaty of Versailles; the priority, to rearm.

Hitler was shrewd enough to see that nothing would do more to win acclaim for the new regime than restoring the economy and reducing unemployment. But he insisted at one of the first cabinet meetings after becoming chancellor that recovery was not an end in itself but a means to an end—"rendering the German people again capable of bearing arms"— the criterion by which every measure for creating employment had to be judged.

Hitler's belief that rearmament and recovery could be pursued at the same time was justified by the outcome: The German economy recovered and Germany was rearmed. The relationship between the two—exactly what contribution rearmament made to recovery—can be left to the economic historians. What is clear is the instrumental view Hitler took of economics. It was this, and not a preference for capitalism, that led him to suppress the anticapitalist campaign in the Nazi party. His decision was a pragmatic one: The quickest way to achieve both rearmament and recovery was to work with the existing economic arrangements instead of throwing them into turmoil by radical and untried experiments which would arouse strong opposition. But no more than in the case of the generals did Hitler's readiness to work with them in the initial phase mean that he was willing to let either industrialists or bankers (like Schacht) determine longer-term policy. The relationship, in both cases, changed in the course of the 1930s, and the question of the Hitler state's control over the economy received a different answer when Hitler launched Germany's own Four-Year Plan in 1936.

IN A SECOND AREA, foreign and defense policy, 1934 marked a watershed, with Stalin recognizing the reality of the Nazi threat to the Soviet Union. This was the opening phase in a relationship between the two regimes that came to dominate the 1940s, with an aftermath in the Cold War after Hitler's death.

Preoccupied with the revolution he had launched at home, Stalin showed no great interest in foreign policy before 1934. At the Sixth Comintern Congress of 1928 he had established his position as the leader of the world Communist movement, but he viewed it solely from the point of view of Russia. The Congress resolved: "International Communism must be expressed in the subordination of the local and particular interests of the movement, and in the execution without reservation of all decisions made by the leading bodies of the Communist International." [60] In practice this meant the Comintern Executive in Moscow, was presided over initially by Molotov, and then by one of Stalin's second-rank henchmen, Manuilsky. Since its only function was to convey orders to the German, French, Italian, and other parties, there was no need of discussion, and there were no more congresses of the Communist International until the Seventh in 1935—which proved to be its last.

It was at Stalin's urging that the Sixth Congress adopted the resolution that Communists everywhere should concentrate on attacking socialist parties, denounced as "a particularly dangerous enemy of the proletariat, more dangerous than the avowed adherents of predatory imperialism."

This was of particular importance in Germany where the KPD, second only to the Russian Communist party in size, polled over five million votes in 1932. If they had cooperated, the KPD and the SPD would have represented a solid bloc of 13.2 million voters to the Nazis' 13.7 million in July 1932, and 13.2 million to the Nazis' 11.7 million—a majority of a million and a half—in November 1932. Instead, following the policy that Stalin had forced on them, the German Communists concentrated their attack on the SPD as "social Fascists," even going so far as to cooperate with the Nazis against them in the Berlin transport strike of 1932.

What attracted Stalin and clouded his judgment was the prospect of how much a friendly Communist Germany, with its industrial resources and skilled manpower, could contribute to the modernization of Russia—the same illusion that Lenin had nursed from 1917 through 1919. This led Stalin to persist in the wishful belief that the Nazis' mounting success would radicalize the German masses, unite them behind the KPD, and lead to a Communist victory.

The great success of Soviet diplomacy had been the special relationship with Weimar Germany established by the Treaty of Rapallo (1922) and based on a common opposition of the two pariah powers to the European system established by the victorious powers after 1918. Politically, Rapallo ended Russian isolation and reduced the threat of an anti-Bolshevik capitalist coalition. In 1926 the two countries signed the Berlin treaty of neutrality, renewed in 1931. Economically, Germany became Russia's most important trading partner, accounting for a quarter of all Soviet imports and exports. Militarily, it produced a clandestine military collaboration that allowed Germany to build and test weapons forbidden by the peace treaty, including planes and tanks, and to carry out training exercises in Soviet territory, while making available to the Russians the benefit of German military expertise and technology.

Trade and military cooperation between the two countries reached a peak in the early 1930s, and Stalin was anxious to see the special relationship continued. He neither objected nor attempted to intervene when the KPD was liquidated, and Soviet representatives (Litvinov, Krestinsky, Molotov) went out of their way, in the early months of the Nazi regime, to assure the Germans that there would be no change in Soviet policy and to welcome renewal of the 1926 Berlin treaty between the two countries.

As late as January 1934, while recognizing the increased dangers of war, Stalin told the Seventeenth Party Congress:

> Of course we are far from being enthusiastic about the fascist regime in Germany. But fascism is not the issue, if only for the reason that fascism in Italy, for example, has not prevented the Soviet Union from establishing the best relations with that country. [61]

The very same day that Stalin said this, Hitler concluded a nonaggression pact with Poland which was not only a reversal of traditional Prussian policy but also widely taken to be directed against the USSR. Although Stalin never admitted the mistake he had made, he was forced, however reluctantly, to change his policy in the face of the undeniable threat to Russia from a hostile Nazi Germany on one front, coupled with that from an aggressive Japan, which since 1931 had been occupying Manchuria, on the other. The overriding motive was his concern with the protection of domestic Russian interests, in particular her economic development, not the Comintern and world revolution or a taste for dangerous adventures like Hitler's Austrian fiasco. He was sincere when he said in the same report in January 1934, "He who wants peace and seeks businesslike relations with us will always be welcome," although he now felt it necessary to add: "and those who would dare attack our country will receive a crushing blow, so that they will not be tempted to stick their piglike snouts into our Soviet garden." [62]

HITLER'S ATTITUDE, when it was a question of foreign policy and defense, was as different from Stalin's as in economics. This was where his priority lay, and his view of economics was governed by the contribution economic recovery could make to the restoration of German power. Stalin's was the other way around: His priority was the modernization of Russia's economic and social structure, and his view of foreign and defense policy was governed by the need to provide the protection necessary for completing his Second Revolution.

Hitler was also anxious about external security in 1933–34. The witchhunt against Jews, socialists, and Communists; the mass arrests, the concentration camps and reports of torture; the boycott of Jewish businesses; the suppression of the trade unions and the burning of the books—all these, widely reported abroad and reinforced by the arrival of 50,000 refugees, had produced both a profound shock in the Western democracies and alarm at the strident tone of Nazi fanaticism and nationalism. The possibility that the French and their Polish allies might intervene by force was taken seriously by the German army as well as by Hitler. It was only ten years since the French had occupied the Ruhr, only three since they had evacuated the Rhineland. Intervention in 1933–34 to enforce the Versailles Treaty, before German rearmament could begin to produce results, could have been disastrous to Hitler's plans.

In foreign policy as in economics, there were elements in the Nazi party eager to supplant the conservative German Foreign Office and replace a foreign minister, von Neurath, who was not a Nazi. Hitler allowed Alfred Rosenberg and Ribbentrop to set up rival party organizations of their own, but it was Göring, another interloper in foreign policy, who negotiated the Nonaggression Pact with Poland, Hitler's biggest diplomatic success in his first two years of office.

The dangers that more radical initiatives could produce in this critical early stage were made very clear by the ill-judged attempt to topple the Dolfuss government in Austria. Germany's diplomatic isolation in late 1934 was complete. The successful coup of the Polish pact was offset by France's success in reviving her links with her allies in Eastern Europe (the Little Entente),* while the gesture of withdrawing from the Disarmament Conference and the League of Nations, which had so delighted German nationalist feeling, was matched by the Russian reversal of policy in joining the League (September 1934).

If Stalin learned his lesson, so did Hitler. Nineteen thirty-five saw the Franco-Soviet alliance and the Comintern's adoption of a Popular Front policy aimed at creating the broad anti-Fascist coalition that, following Stalin's lead, the Communists had done their best to prevent. But it also registered the successful repudiation of the Versailles restrictions on German rearmament and the Anglo-German Naval Treaty, first fruits of Hitler's skillful exploitation of the Western democracies' fear of war and anti-Communism.

Hitler saw advantages for the present in leaving von Neurath and the traditional German diplomatic service in place, while he was free to use Ribbentrop and Göring on special missions and the party's Foreign Countries Organization (*Auslandsorganisation*—AO) under Gauleiter Bohle to

*See p. 528.

organize ethnic German groups abroad, the twenty-seven million world-wide of the German diaspora—a parallel to Stalin's use of the Comintern to organize other Communist parties. At some stage he would no longer need the facade of respectability that von Neurath provided to reassure conservative opinion at home and abroad; by then Germany would be strong enough for Hitler to appear in his true colors.

MUCH MORE IMPORTANT was Hitler's relationship with the generals. At the end of 1934, the historic claim of the army to be a law unto itself appeared to be intact. The army's agreement had been crucial to Hitler's appointment as von Hindenburg's successor, and Hitler himself admitted: "We all know well that if, in the days of the revolution, the army had not stood at our side, then we would not be standing here today." [63] Hitler later claimed that he had avoided conflict with the army in the first years of office only because he knew he could rely on the effect of introducing conscription:

> Once that was accomplished, the influx into the Wehrmacht of the masses of the people, together with the spirit of National Socialism and with the ever-growing power of the National Socialist movement, would, I was sure, allow me to overcome all opposition among the armed forces and in particular in the corps of officers. [64]

If true, it is a good example of Hitler's astuteness, for the German officer corps, numbering 4,000 in 1933, provided a totally inadequate basis for an army that increased fourfold in four years. With 25,000 new officers added to the rolls, many from a younger generation more in sympathy than the generals with the Nazi movement, the cohesion of the officer corps and its traditional conservatism were diluted beyond the point where it could hope to retain its autonomous position, if the time came when Hitler should decide to challenge it. It was significant that when he made the dramatic announcement on March 16, 1935 that Germany would rearm and introduce compulsory military service, he did not consult the High Command or the army General Staff in advance, and the target of a peacetime army of twelve army corps and thirty-six divisions came as a surprise to them.

Hitler had hitherto assumed that, once he gave them the chance to rearm, the German army would carry it through with enthusiasm. But at a staff conference in the summer of 1941 he spoke bitterly of the disillusionment he had suffered during the course of his first five years of office.

> Before I became chancellor, I thought the General Staff was like a mastiff that had to be held tight by the collar because it threatened all and sundry. Since then I have had to recognize that the General Staff is anything but that. It has consistently tried to impede every action that I have thought necessary. . . . It is I who have always had to goad the mastiff. [65]

At the end of 1934 the time had not yet come to apply the goad, but the generals who believed that the deal that they had made with Hitler in the summer would last were deceiving themselves. Two developments should have put them on their guard. One was Hitler's directive to Göring to go ahead with the creation of a military air force, and his agreement, over the opposition of the army, to Göring's demand that it should be an independent service with a separate ministry of its own. The other was the advancement of Himmler and the SS in Hitler's favor, the portent of a much more effective threat to the army's independence than had been posed by Röhm and his SA.

THE RED ARMY had changed since Stalin first knew it during the civil war. The tsarist officers who had numbered 48,000 then, three-quarters of the total, had been reduced to 4,500, 10 percent, in 1930. In 1934, 68 percent of all officers, including all the senior commanders, were members of the Communist party. The size of the standing army was 562,000; its strength lay in its cadre troops, which made up between a tenth and a sixth of the total, the highest proportion in the technical branches. The rest were the pick of the conscripts, serving for two years, after two years' preservice training. The territorial army to which the remainder were allotted, mostly as infantry, served on a part-time basis.

While no longer a peasant army, there was still a large component recruited from the villages, and political education and indoctrination (at least two hours a day) had equal priority with training as soldiers. The army's political reliability was put to the test during the years of collectivization. Stalin and the party leadership could not have survived if they had not been able to call on the army to suppress the peasant revolts and blockade the Ukraine. So far as is known, discipline held and there were no serious problems. The figures for the purges bear this out: 3.5 percent of party members in the army were purged in 1929 compared with 11.7 percent in the civil organizations. The comparable figures for 1933 were 4.3 and 17 percent.

At no time, however, was the Red Army allowed to assume the independent position enjoyed by the German army. "To prevent any institutions from becoming nests of conspiracy," as Trotsky's original decree of 1918 put it, and to organize the work of political education, a system of political commissars was established. This constituted an independent network of agents in army bases and units, who were directly responsible to the military department of the party's Central Committee.

During the 1920s the original form of dual command was modified to give the commander sole responsibility and make the commissar his political assistant, but the latter maintained independent relations with his political superiors outside the military hierarchy, and friction continued, particularly at the higher levels where the commanders were mostly veterans of the civil war. There was no question, however, of Stalin agreeing to abandon the commissar system, and it was duplicated by the separate form of control maintained by the OGPU. The secret police was responsible for security in the army and maintained its own network of agents at all levels, operating independently of the military command as well as the political commissars and keeping a sharp watch on the loyalty of both.

The greatest weakness of the Red Army was its lack of modern mechanized equipment and its soldiers' lack of technical training. One of the principal arguments for Stalin's crash program of industrialization was the need to create a technically advanced armaments industry. The first Five-Year Plan succeeded in laying the foundation for this and, as Stalin came to recognize the external danger from a hostile Germany and Japan, the Red Army's needs were given the highest priority. During the Second Five-Year Plan (1933–38) Russia's defense industries expanded two and a half times as rapidly as Russian industry as a whole.

Stalin was anxious to continue the close cooperation between the Russian and German military, which had made possible the secret rearmament of the Wehrmacht and produced benefits for the Red Army as well. Forced, however reluctantly, to accept the withdrawal on which Hitler insisted, Stalin turned to matching Hitler's expansion of the German armed forces with his own: In 1934 the Russian army's strength was increased from 562,000 to 940,000, and in 1935 to 1,300,000, with plans to produce an all-cadre force by 1939. The military and naval budget rose from 1.42 billion rubles in 1933 to 23.2 billion in 1938, and was more than doubled again by 1940. Great emphasis was placed on the development of artillery, tanks, and planes, and on industrial self-sufficiency, with new arms factories sited beyond the Urals.

Like the NKVD, the Red Army and Navy benefited substantially from Stalin's policies. This extended to improvements in their pay and in the status of the officers, which brought a rush of students to the military academies. At the same time the system of political commissars, as well as the NKVD's supervision, appeared to provide adequate safeguards against the development of that corporate spirit of military professionalism with which Hitler had to contend. At the end of 1934, any observer able to compare the position in the two countries would have concluded that Stalin was closer than Hitler to establishing secure control over the armed forces. Yet it was Stalin who moved suddenly, in 1937, to execute the Red Army's leading commanders for treason, as the prelude to a drastic purge of the entire high command and the Russian officer corps.* Hitler strengthened his own position vis-à-vis the German army in 1938, but without anything approaching the scale of Stalin's action; only years later after the July 1944 attempt on his life did he express regret that he had not followed Stalin's example earlier and carried out an equally thorough purge of the German army's leadership.

*See pp. 485–89.

VI

THE TWO OTHER KEY AREAS, control over mass communications and over all groups and organizations, were closely linked and were central features of both regimes.

By the end of 1934 both Hitler and Stalin claimed to stand at the head of a united people. Opposition was neither tolerated nor admitted. In Russia as well as Germany the government could count, as it can in any society, on political indifference, the wish to believe, the habits of obedience and conformity as well as on ambition, careerism, and vested interests, to secure a minimal degree of compliance. Neither regime, however, left anything to chance—or spontaneity. They shared a common and fundamental distrust of any individual or group acting on his or her own initiative and placed the perpetual mobilization of mass support as one of their highest priorities. In no other respect did the two regimes come closer to each other.

There were, of course, great differences between the conditions in which the two operated. The Nazis had to deal with a highly literate and educated nation which they could reach easily by radio and press, the movies and theater. The Communist party under Stalin's leadership faced a nation in which there was still a high level of illiteracy and ignorance, combined with a low level of accessibility through the media—newspapers, radio, or films. The forced march by which Stalin was driving the Russian people from their state of economic and cultural backwardness into the modern age required a campaign against mass illiteracy and the primitive living habits of the millions of peasants who had poured into the cities before the crudest propaganda message could begin to have an impact. The basic education, which was the first task of the Communist party, in addition to inculcating labor discipline and raising productivity had, as part of industrialization, been accomplished in Germany in the previous century. With German education and social and industrial discipline to build on, Hitler and Goebbels were able to employ technically advanced means to reach the mass of the German people.

A further obstacle for Stalin was the bitterness left by the brutal policies he had enforced on the largest class in the country, the peasantry, whom the Soviet agitators and propagandists now had to try to convince of their benefits. Hitler by comparison was able to follow policies leading to the economic recovery and the overthrow of the Versailles settlement for which it was easy to arouse enthusiasm.

The Communists had some advantages. Russia was a huge country, much more remote than Germany from the rest of Europe. It was a country whose links with the mainstream of European political and cultural tradition had always been more tenuous than Germany's and whose educated class, many of them ambiguous in their attitudes to the West, had been much smaller and was greatly reduced in numbers by the revolution and civil war. These geographical and historical facts made it much easier to isolate Russia from the outside world, something that Soviet propaganda was able to exploit.

Against this had to be set Russia's poverty, its lack of resources, and technical backwardness, as well as the much smaller proportion of trained people available, not only for propaganda but also to meet the other pressing demands made on the party. Unable to reach the Russian populace through the poorly developed media of mass communication, the leadership had to rely on oral agitation and propaganda by the individual member. It had to employ a direct approach, by exhortation and by personal example on the spot, in the factory, mine, and collective farm. In Germany, where the economic development was much more advanced and the cultural level higher, the Nazis were able to make greater use of indirect methods, which allowed the propaganda message to be concealed and conveyed through a variety of other activities. It is all the more striking that, despite these differences, there should have been so clear a parallel between the priority the two regimes gave to social control and to the means by which to secure it.

IN BOTH RUSSIA AND GERMANY the huge apparatus of the police and security forces played a major role in the practice of "coercive persuasion." Its impact upon those *not* arrested or sent to concentration or labor camps was as important as the removal of those who were. In her unequaled account of life in Russia during the purges of the 1930s, Nadezhda Mandelstam has described how no one referred to those who suddenly disappeared, or dared to admit even to friends knowledge of the existence of the camps. This conspiracy of silence, in which everyone was involved, produced a pervasive fear that not only destroyed trust between people but created a feeling of inevitability against which it was useless to struggle.[66]

In Germany, there was more support and fewer arrests, but the principle was the same—no one was free to opt out, and those who did knew the risk they ran. As early as March 21, 1933 (Potsdam Day), a decree against malicious gossip provided imprisonment—in severe cases, penal servitude—for spoken criticism of the government.

No society, however, certainly no modern industrialized society, can function with a cowed and fearful population. Even a passive support is not enough. Once the background of "coercion, if . . ." had been established, all available resources were called into play to win a willing compliance,* to persuade people that, if they cooperated, anything was possible, and to offer them opportunities and rewards, not only in their careers, but also in educational, social, and cultural activities as well. The one condition was that all such activities must either be provided by the state or the party, or be controlled by them and have official approval. A reciprocal interaction

---

*In Russia this is known as the principle of *dobrovol'no—obyazatel'no,* "voluntarily—obligatorily." See A. L. Unger, *The Totalitarian Party* (Cambridge, Eng. 1974), p. 31.

was thus established among terror, propaganda, and organization, with Stalin in the 1930s relying more on the first, Hitler on the second, and both putting equal stress on the third.

No political movement in history has ever paid more attention to psychological factors than the Nazis. This was where Hitler had shown his own special gifts in the 1920s; it accounted for much of the Nazi success in the early 1930s, and was a hallmark of the regime when it came to power. Formulating the concept of "total propaganda" at the 1934 Party Congress, Goebbels declared:

> Among the arts with which one reaches a people, it ranks in first place . . . Without it, the implementation of great things has become well nigh impossible in the century of the masses. . . . There exists no sector of public life that can escape its influence. [67]

Hitler and Goebbels had already shown the unprecedented use they could make of radio in the March 1933 election. By coordinating the news services, holding daily press conferences at the ministry, issuing a stream of directives, and laying down the terminology that was to be used, Goebbels effectively extended control from the radio to the press. Non-Nazi papers—the *Frankfurter Zeitung,* for example—were tolerated in order to preserve some variety of style and so avoid a dull uniformity which would lose readers and so reduce the impact of the propaganda message. Goebbels's instructions to all the media were "to be monoform in will, polyform in the expression of it."

The comparable functions in the USSR, where the party dominated the state, were performed not by a ministry, but by two of the six main sections of the party's Central Committee Secretariat, under Stalin's supervision as general secretary. These were the Agitation and Mass Campaigns and the Culture and Propaganda sections. Following Georgi Plekhanov, the father of Marxism in Russia (1856–1918), Soviet usage distinguished between *propaganda*—"presenting many ideas to a few persons," and being concerned with a more intellectual elucidation of Marxism-Leninism—and *agitation*—"presenting one or a few ideas to a mass of people," putting across a few simple arguments and slogans. In the course of reorganization in 1934 and 1935, the two sections were first combined into one (Kul'tprop) and then broken up into five: Party Propaganda and Agitation; Press and Publishing; Schools; Cultural Instruction Work; and Science.

IT WAS ONE THING to draw up plans, issue directives, and prepare material, but who put these into operation? The answer was provided by the third element in the triad of terror-propaganda-organization. In both countries it was the party that provided the driving force of organization, indirectly through its control of various associated groups—trade unions, professional groups, youth organizations (such as the Hitler Jugend and the

Komsomol), cultural and sports associations—and directly through its own network of primary organization.

This was Hitler's answer to the question of the role the Nazi party should play after it had become the sole party in the state. While discouraging its ambition to govern, he insisted that the new Reich could not exist without it. "The conquest of power," he declared at the 1935 Party Congress, "is a never-ending process." Revolutions in the past had failed because they had not realized that "the essential thing is not the assumption of power but the education of men." [68] "Education" meant stamping the new ideology on Germany as the bond that bound the German people together. In keeping with this role, Hitler envisaged a mass party numbering 10 percent of the population, a percentage that the NSDAP had almost reached in 1939 when it passed the five-million mark.

In the later 1920s the Nazis had set to work to infiltrate or create professional groups; and the Soviet Communist party had long since taken over in one way or another, or suppressed, every autonomous body—the exception was the Orthodox Church, which it persecuted instead. The most important of the auxiliary or associated organizations were those responsible for youth and labor.

The Hitler Youth (HJ) first appeared as a party organization in 1926; under its leader, Baldur von Schirach, it took over all the other youth movements in 1933. By the end of 1934, it had 3.5 million members. At the end of 1936, membership was made compulsory for all young men and women from ten to eighteen, and the HJ became part of the Hitler state, with its leader responsible directly to the Führer, although financially still dependent on the party.

The Communist League of Youth (Komsomol) originated in Petrograd in 1917 and held its first congress in 1918. It had played a leading role in the collectivization campaign and the Five-Year Plan, supplying many of the leaders of shock brigades. Its membership grew from three million in 1931 to four million in 1936. Its main task was then broadened from emergency economic activity to the Communist indoctrination of youth, including many cultural, social, and sporting activities. By 1939 it had expanded to nine million. The organization of the Komsomol, and its junior section, the Pioneers (nine to fifteen), was modeled on that of the party, with the same regional and district network. Although it was formally autonomous, it was tightly controlled by the party as the training ground of the next generation of cadres.

The work of the youth organizations has to be seen in the context of a Communist and Nazi takeover of the system of education: the reorganization of the school system and teacher training; the reworking of textbooks; and the purging of the curriculum in order to make room for the Marxist-Leninist—or in Germany the racist—interpretation of history, for Marxist economics and racist biology. The Nazi penetration of the student movement before 1933 and the readiness of many academics to accept the New Order meant the end of the critical tradition of thought in the German universities, while in the Soviet Union the existing system of higher education was replaced in a conscious decision to break with the traditions of both Russian and European education.

To the effect of these changes must be added that of compulsory labor service and conscription for military service, both with an element of political education. Only when all these are put together is it possible to realize the effort each regime put into capturing the minds and allegiance of the younger generation, creating the Soviet or the Nazi "New Man" (a phrase in use in both countries) with a set of values and beliefs in each case hostile to and intolerant of all others.

In Communist Russia as well as Germany, the trade unions were deprived of their original function of representing the workers in bargaining over wages and conditions of work. In Russia the unions survived in name but were given the task of organizing the working class (especially the new recruits from the villages) to meet the objectives of management, educating them in workshop discipline, administering welfare, and above all raising productivity. In Germany the trade unions, which had been one of the main targets of Nazi and right-wing hostility, were dissolved and their assets taken over by the German Labor Front, which by 1934 had been finally purged of its ambitions to shape economic, labor, and social policies. In Germany, as in Soviet Russia, the reintroduction of the "work book" represented a reversion to the control of the movement of labor, matching the abandonment of free collective bargaining. In compensation the Labor Front was given the job of elevating the status of manual labor ("Work Ennobles") and winning back the working class from its former Marxist allegiance to an equal place in the *Volksgemeinschaft,* based not upon class solidarity but upon national unity.

Employers as well as employees were obliged to join this giant organization of "soldiers of labor," which eventually embraced twenty-five million members, almost half the German population—far bigger and disposing of larger resources than the party of which it was an auxiliary organization. In its program for the elimination of class distinctions, it extended its reach into the organization of the workers' leisure (not yet a problem in the USSR in the 1930s), offering fringe benefits such as model housing and subsidized vacations (in 1938 ten million, three-fifths of the workers, participated in "Strength through Joy" vacation trips) and a massive program of cultural and sporting activities.

STALIN AND HITLER saw the advantage of harnessing literature and the arts to the support of their regimes. They also saw the advantage of doing this through organizations that gave the appearance of being self-regulatory. In May 1933 Goebbels told a meeting of theater directors that the new regime "would link up all of cultural life with conscious political-ideological propaganda" and wrench it out of the "Jewish-liberalistic" course it had followed in the Weimar period. The Reich Cultural Chamber, set up under his presidency, created separate Reich chambers for literature, theater, music, the fine arts, and films as well as press and broadcasting.

The ambitious, the opportunists, and the second-rate competed to offer their services in bringing their profession or branch of the arts into line with the wishes of the new masters. Everyone involved in any of these activities, including publishers, technicians, and technical suppliers, was required to belong by law to his or her appropriate Reich chamber. Refusal of admission or expulsion meant being banned altogether from publishing or practicing one's art. Richard Strauss accepted the presidency of the Reich Chamber of Music; but the work of the majority of those German (and German-Jewish) artists, musicians, writers, and scientists whose names had given Germany a leading place in twentieth-century culture was banned and they themselves preferred to go into exile, a loss from which Germany has hardly yet recovered.

In the early years of the century, including the first ten years after the revolution, Russians, too, had made a striking contribution in literature and the arts.* By the mid-1930s most of them were either dead (one or two, like the poet Vladimir Mayakovsky, committing suicide), had gone into exile, or had been silenced. For a short time in the later 1920s, at the beginning of his Second Revolution, Stalin found it expedient to encourage and allow scope to the so-called cultural revolution led by the younger generation in the Komsomol and RAPP (the Association for the Advancement of Proletarian Literature), whom Bukharin described as suffering from "revolutionary avant-gardism." This enabled Stalin to claim that his "revolution from above" was responding to a surge of militancy from below. In the early 1930s, however, he intervened directly to bring intellectual and cultural activity into line with a party policy that he increasingly dominated.

In December 1930, Stalin appeared in person at the Institute of Red Professors and told them, "We have to turn upside down and turn over the whole pile of manure that has accumulated in questions of philosophy and natural science," in particular the heresy of "Menshevizing idealism." Taken up by the Central Committee's organ, *Bolshevik,* in 1931, Soviet philosophy was directed into its new course, "the elaboration of materialist dialectics on the basis of the works of Marx, Engels, Lenin, and Stalin"— recognition at last of Stalin's claim to be taken seriously as a theoretician.

It is a fascinating sidelight on how seriously Stalin himself took this claim that between 1925 and 1928, at the height of the fight with the Left Opposition, he asked a philosopher, Jan Sten, deputy-head of the Marx-Engels Institute, to visit him twice a week to give him tutorials on the dialectic and the philosophical background of Marxism, including Hegel

---

*Among them, Alexander Blok, Chagall, Diaghilev, Naum Gabo, Kandinsky, Kasimir Malevich, Vladimir Mayakovsky, Vsevolod Meyerhold, Pasternak, Prokofiev, Scriabin, Stanislavsky, Stravinsky.

and Kant. Sten became depressed not only by Stalin's scorn for philosophers' concern with abstract ideas, but by their conversations on politics
and the insight these gave into Stalin's ambitions.

It was against the school of Abram Deborin (1881–1963), to which Sten
belonged, that his pupil's accusation of "Menshevizing idealism" was directed in his speech of December 1930:

> Everything written by the Deborin group has to be smashed. Sten and
> Kayev can be chucked out. Sten boasts a lot, but he is a desperate
> sluggard. All he can do is talk.

When asked what the Institute should concentrate on in philosophy, Stalin
replied:

> To beat, that is the issue. To beat on all sides and where there hasn't been
> any beating before. The Deborinites regard Hegel as an icon. Plekhanov
> has to be unmasked. Even Engels was not right about everything. It
> wouldn't be a bad thing if we could implicate Engels somewhere in
> Bukharin's writing.[69]

Stalin's speech is a good example of how he could deliberately use rough
language to create an atmosphere of menace. The menace was not imaginary: In 1937 Sten was arrested on the personal order of Stalin and shot in
Lefortovo prison on June 19 of that year.[70]

In October 1931, it was the turn of Soviet historians to be rebuked by
Stalin, this time in a signed article printed in *Bolshevik* and in the historians'
journal, *Proletarian Revolution*. They were accused of a false objectivity and
"rotten liberalism." "Who but archive rats would fail to realize that parties
and leaders must be tested by their deeds primarily and not simply by their
declarations?" The historians were summoned "to put the study of party
history on to a scientific Bolshevik basis and to sharpen vigilance against
Trotskyist and all other falsifiers of the history of our party, systematically
ripping off their masks."[71] Stalin's letter caused consternation in the Communist Academy, which called upon its institutes and journals, ranging from
economics and law to technology, as well as the historians, to purge their
subject of "Menshevik-Trotskyite contraband" and intensify the hunt for
heresy. An address by Kaganovich to the Institute of Red Professors made
clear in peremptory style that Stalin's article was intended as a directive to
the whole Soviet intelligentsia to devote their energies to the Marxist-
Leninist indoctrination of the new generation of party and Komsomol
members, and to recognize that the party was no meeting place of many
currents, as Radek had falsely claimed, but "a monolithic stream" capable
of destroying all obstacles in its path.

To begin with, the historians were told to remove the "foul slanders" in
the party history, which turned out to be paying too little attention to
Stalin's role and "grossly exaggerating" Trotsky's, in 1917 and later. The

majority, dependent on the party for jobs, accommodation, and privileges, fell over one another in their haste to comply, as they have done in other countries, such as China, where similar regimes have been established.

Another characteristic that Hitler and Stalin shared was their hostility to experimentation, in particular to the modernist movement in the arts and to "progressive" ideas in education, the family, and the treatment of crime, all of which had flourished in Soviet Russia in the 1920s as well as in Weimar Germany. Where Hitler condemned *"Kultur-Bolshewismus,"* Stalin attacked "formalism" and "bourgeois individualism." Where Hitler put the blame on the "Jewish inspiration" of modernism, Stalin denounced the spread of contamination from the corrupt capitalist world. By 1934 each had moved to establish an intellectual and artistic as well as political censorship. Bormann spoke for both men when he wrote: "Cultural work is political work . . . not a deviation from it, but the fulfillment of the task of practical leadership in that sphere that speaks most directly and profoundly to the people."[72]

Stalin attached importance to influencing the work of contemporary writers in favor of the regime, making much of his success in persuading the novelist Maxim Gorki, Russia's greatest living writer, with strong socialist sympathies, to return to the Soviet Union from Italy. In 1932 Stalin took part in the meetings of the commission set up by the Central Committee to carry out the decree "On the Reconstruction of Literary-Artistic Organizations," approving the slogan of "socialist realism," which was proclaimed by Gorki in 1934. This had been summed up as "harnessing the nineteenth-century techniques of art, fiction, and the theater to the portrayal of exemplary Soviet characters ('the positive hero') and a rosy future ('the positive conclusion')."[73] The Union of Soviet Writers and the Composers' Union, which it set up, could be relied upon to police the work of their contemporaries to the party's satisfaction.

But Stalin was not satisfied with that and continued to make arbitrary personal interventions in praise or condemnation of individual books, plays, operas, even scientific theories. A famous example is his angry reaction to the twenty-nine-year-old Shostakovich's powerful opera *Lady Macbeth of Mtensk.* An unsigned editorial in *Pravda,* "Muddle Instead of Music," denounced it as cacophonous, perverted, and suffering from the same "leftish deformity" that marked so much modern music and art. The opera was at once taken off the stage (Shostakovich never wrote another), and the party organized meetings at which his faults were condemned and held up as a warning to others.

Stalin wanted an art that depicted Soviet life not as it was but as he wished—and needed—to believe it was. It was an expression not only of policy, but also of the inner compulsion he felt to close the gap between reality and his vision. Those writers and artists who sought to follow the "general line" in praise of Soviet life and achievement soon discovered that they were most likely to win favor if they also contributed to the cult of Stalin by giving prominence to the role of the great leader of a grateful Soviet people in guiding them to the promised land.

Hitler was content to delegate responsibility for control of literature and the arts to Goebbels and the Reich Chamber of Culture. His personal interventions were limited to those fields in which he regarded himself as an authority—the visual arts and architecture. His taste, like Stalin's, did not move beyond the conventional styles of 1880–1924; he hated all forms of modern art, which, again like Stalin, he saw as clear proof of the spiritual sickness and decadence of the Western world. The selection of paintings for the exhibition in the Munich House of German Art, of which he laid the foundation stone in 1933 and was to open in 1937, so infuriated him that he first threatened to cancel it, then turned over the job of making a fresh choice to his photographer Hoffmann. Even Hoffmann could not persuade him to accept a single room for more modern works. Instead Hitler organized a concurrent exhibition of modern art under the title "Degenerate Art" with 730 examples from the work of George Grosz, Paul Klee, Kandinsky, Picasso, Matisse, Van Gogh and Cézanne. In Munich and other cities which it visited, it attracted two million people between July and November 1937, the most successful art exhibition in history up to that time. Some may have come because it was their last chance to see art which they admired; it seems likely, however, that many came to stare and mock, sharing Hitler's and the Nazis' opinion of modern art as distorted, ugly, and threatening. When Hitler went on to sweep out of German galleries all the pictures and sculpture of the modern movement, today seen as one of the great periods of European art (Law for the Withdrawal of Decadent Art, May 1938), he could claim with some justice that he was allowing the people, as he had promised, to be the judges of what was art.

THE PARTY in both countries maintained direct contact with the masses through its own primary organizations. The CPSU organized its members according to their place of work (factory, office, collective farm, army unit), the NSDAP according to their place of residence. The first continued a tradition from prerevolutionary days when the Bolsheviks found that maintaining contact through the workplace was the best way of reducing the risk of illegal activity. In the 1930s it reflected the preoccupation with raising productivity, and the number of these primary organizations rose from 39,000 in 1927 to 102,500 ten years later. In a big industrial enterprise or government office, these would form numerous subdivisions, so as to break down the mass of employees into small groups.

"Every Bolshevik an agitator!" was an early slogan and one on which the party continued to lay great stress. An army of agitators was recruited from the ranks of the party, the Komsomol, and the nonparty activists to serve in the primary organizations. They were chosen for their ability to convince not only by argument, but even more importantly by personal example:

Hence the need to be "well versed in production"—meeting the requirements of the plan as well as the party line, were the sort of qualifications to be looked for in a leading hand or foreman. The agitator was expected to know well all the members of his group, working alongside them and concerning himself with their personal problems, as well as their performance at work in the factory or collective farm. This long remained the most effective way in which the Communist party sought to achieve its objective of reaching everyone.

The Nazi party, with a mass membership of millions, was equally aware of the value of personal propaganda, and party members were frequently reminded that it was their duty "always and everywhere to regard themselves as carriers of the Führer's word." Person-to-person propaganda could reach people in a way that the mass media could not, and was doubly effective when it was presented as a personal opinion rather than the repetition of an official slogan. When party members heard subversive views or malicious talk, they were told they should not remain silent but speak out—and report what they had heard. Informing had a corrosive effect in destroying trust between individuals: an effect well understood by the secret police, who recruited informers with this in mind as well as for the information they could bring in. In the Soviet Union informing is described by many witnesses as a national vice, the way to pay off a grudge or secure someone else's job or apartment.

Not being obsessed with productivity as the Russians were, the Nazis made their primary unit the residential "block" of forty or fifty families with which the "block leader" was expected to be in constant personal contact. He was required to visit each family regularly, to see that they were kept informed of the slogans and demands of the regime, attended party meetings, contributed to party campaigns, and so on. He was not only the party whip but also its watchdog, keeping a careful check on everyone's activities and reporting what he saw or suspected was amiss. Next to the Gestapo they were the most unpopular members of the community, and for the same reason no one felt safe with them—or was meant to.

VII

IDEOLOGY IN THE GENERAL SENSE of a coherent body of beliefs is something that most political parties would claim—or admit to having, even if they dislike the word. The regimes created by Stalin and Hitler, however, were ideological in a more specific sense: a set of beliefs, acceptance of which by everyone was obligatory, and deviation from which could be a capital crime.

To the believer in either the Nazi or the Communist ideology, the opposition between them was absolute: If one was a Nazi, by definition one was anti-Marxist; if a Communist, anti-Fascist. No compromise was possible. But to the observer, even at the time and certainly now, the similarity of function between their ideologies appears as important as the conflict of beliefs.

This was a view developed by Georges Sorel, whose influential *Réflexions sur la violence* of 1908 (read by Lenin as well as by Mussolini, both of whom Sorel admired) developed the concept of the "social myth." Sorel saw this neither as a calculated plan of action, nor as a scientific prediction, nor as a Utopian blueprint, in none of which he believed, but as a vision that could inspire and galvanize the masses into action. His best-known example was the general strike, which he thought unlikely ever to take place, but the idea of which could have a powerful influence in persuading the working classes of their capacity for collective action: "The goal is nothing; the movement everything."

Looked at from the point of view of function rather than content, there are clear parallels between the Communist and Nazi ideologies. "Race," "class," "the bourgeoisie," "the Jew" play the role of mythical symbols rather than sociological categories—symbols with which the masses can identify positively, as with *"Volk"* or "proletariat," or that they can reject, as with "capitalists" or "kulaks." In a time of upheaval (collectivization in Russia) or anxiety (the renewal of crisis in Germany with the Depression) these were symbols of great potency, particularly in providing a focus for fears and hatreds. Hitler and Stalin alike depicted history as struggle, the first as a struggle between races, with "the Jew" doubling in the roles of both capitalist and Communist, the second as a struggle between classes, or between "the Revolution" and the "enemies of Soviet power," "agents of foreign powers," "imperialists" who sought to overthrow its achievements and restore the old order.

All revolutionary movements stand in need of justification to support their challenge to the status quo. If successful, they then stand in need of legitimization as a substitute for the prescriptive authority of traditional forms of government. These are the two primary functions of every revolutionary ideology. They were not affected by the fact that, in one case, Hitler found it natural to present them in the personal terms of the Führer and his mission to defend the Aryan race against racial pollution, and European civilization against Bolshevism, while, in the other, Stalin exalted "the party" and "the revolution" (with both of which he identified himself) and called for their defense against class enemies at home, Fascist and capitalist aggressors abroad.

The other main purpose served by ideology is mobilization, the mobilization of the party to turn out the Nazi voters in 1932, the year of five elections, or of the Communist party to push through collectivization and the Five-Year Plan in four. Both leaders appealed to nationalist feeling, Hitler by whipping up anger against the unjust verdict of the lost war and the humiliations of Versailles; Stalin by proclaiming the goal of "socialism in one country," the backward country that would overtake the capitalist powers, and whose people would rise (as they did, in spite of all) to defend it against invasion and another war of intervention.

THERE WERE two distinct elements in the ideologies of Nazi Germany and the Soviet Union. In Nazism, the first, official and openly avowed, was nationalist and conservative in character. The other was racist and radical, and while not secret was in practice largely restricted to the party leadership and its original members. In the Soviet case, the ideological front presented to the world, and indeed to the Communist party, was Marxist-Leninist; the second, never openly acknowledged, was Stalinist. The relationship between the two elements is different in each case, and important in comparing the two regimes.

There is no doubt that the reason why Hitler was able to build up a mass vote and to secure access to office as a member of a right-wing coalition was that he could be seen as belonging to, and was able to draw support from, the broad conservative-nationalist tradition that rejected both Weimar and Versailles. This responded to Hitler's exaltation of *Volksgemeinschaft* and national unity over class-based politics; his anti-Marxism; his hatred of modernism and his evocation of the authoritarian values of will, discipline, order, hierarchy, which had made Germany great in the past.

Two unusual features distinguished the Nazis from other right-wing parties. The first was their combination of political and cultural reaction with enthusiasm for technological modernization. The experience of war, the *Fronterlebnis,* was said to have revealed to a generation of young Germans that technology need not be "soulless and impersonal" but could be reconciled with the other romantic, antirationalist values that they held dear. Hitler himself was fascinated by technological advance, which he saw as the expression of the "Aryan will." The *Autobahn* became the cultural symbol of the new regime, and Goebbels in opening the Berlin Auto Show in 1939 summed up this aspect of Nazi ideology with the declaration:

> We live in an age that is both romantic and steel-like. While bourgeois reaction was alien and hostile to technology and modern skeptics believed the deepest roots of the collapse of European culture lay in it, National Socialism has understood how to take the soulless framework of technology and fill it with the rhythm and hot impulses of our time. [74]

The other feature that particularly caught the eye of the German man in the street was not the Nazis' ideology but their political style: their freedom from the stuffiness and snobberies of prewar Germany; their readiness to go out and court the masses; and their brash adoption of every modern trick and technique for doing so.

The older generation of *Bildung und Besitz* (the educated and propertied) swallowed this side of the Nazis with distaste as the price to be paid for their drumming up of votes. Even after the shock of *Gleichschaltung,* they reassured themselves that Hitler's suppression of the SA and his refusal to support the economic radicals in the Nazi party meant that he was sincere in saying that the revolutionary phase of National Socialism was over. In this, they were mistaken. The Nazi style of politics was more than a vote-catching device; it expressed a radical mood and purpose that, if frustrated in the social and economic sphere, would seek outlet in another direction.

Those who had voted for Hitler on national-conservative grounds were not, however, disappointed. In April 1939 he reviewed the achievements for which he claimed the credit: the restoration of authoritarian in place of democratic rule; economic recovery and the end of unemployment; German rearmament; the recovery of "the provinces stolen from us in 1919"; and the "re-creation of the 1,000-year historic unity of German living space" by the annexation of Austria and the breakup of Czechoslovakia. This came nearer than anyone could have believed possible in 1933–34 to realizing a "national" program that united the great majority of the German people in support.

Although the German people went to war, later in 1939, with little of the enthusiasm that had so moved Hitler in 1914, the astonishing series of rapid victories from 1939 through 1940, at a minimal cost, concluded a period of national renewal and triumph without an equal in German history. The nationalists' dream of Greater Germany was realized, and a German hegemony established over Europe, with France defeated, Britain humiliated and isolated, and Russia neutralized. The question why, having reached this peak of success, Hitler was unwilling or unable to call a halt needs a provisional answer in order to throw light on the development of Nazi ideology in the 1930s.

In *Mein Kampf*, written in the 1920s, Hitler set out the racist *Weltanschauung*, which was his special contribution to Nazism and the distinctive feature that marked the Nazi ideology from the mainstream German nationalist tradition and from other Fascist movements.

In the 1940s, following the attack on Russia, a major effort was made to establish a slave empire in Eastern Europe which in conception appears to correspond with Hitler's earlier ideas.

Many of those who flocked to join the party when it proved successful did not take Hitler's racist ideas or his anti-Semitism too seriously. Many who have written about Hitler since have taken the same view, finding it easier and more acceptable to explain the phenomenon of Nazism in terms of such familiar rationalizations as class interest, capitalism, nationalism, militarism, or the pursuit of power for its own sake, rather than to treat as politically important, or more than a personal idiosyncrasy, the bizarre racist myths that inflamed his imagination. On such a view the attack on Russia and the attempt to found a new German empire in the east are to be seen as a product of the unsolved contradictions in German society and the German economy that it was unable to master and that drove or tempted the regime to seek relief in war and ever greater expansion, finally leading to its collapse.

But to present an "intentionalist" *or* a "structuralist" view as alternatives between which one must choose seems to me an unnecessary polarization not required by the evidence. Far from feeling that his hand was being forced, or looking for a way out of the impasse, Hitler was ready to welcome any sociopolitical argument or perceived economic benefit that would rein-force objectives that he had had in mind from the beginning. One can argue about the relative importance of Hitler's vision and the social and economic forces that could be harnessed to it, but it is still, I believe, a case of both/and, not of either/or.

Hitler's "racist ideology" remained the lodestar of his imagination and his long-term goal for the remaining twenty years of his life. Even after he came to power, Hitler had no idea when, how, or even whether he would have the chance to realize his goals in practice. There was nothing in the way of a blueprint or a timetable until the plans for Barbarossa, the invasion of Russia, were drawn up in the winter of 1940–41, and in the 1930s he had already begun to worry about his health and whether he would live to "complete my task."

Hitler himself frequently said that, unless the time was ripe for an idea, it was useless to try to realize it in practice. In the election campaigns of the early 1930s he recognized that the racist elements, which for him were the heart of Nazi ideology, were not vote winners and dropped the prominence that he had given to anti-Semitism in the early 1920s in favor of the threat from Marxism. He insisted to Otto Wagener and others with whom he talked privately before coming to power: "We alone can and must think clearly about racial questions. For us these questions are a key and a signpost. But for the public at large they are poison."[75]

Hitler's racist ideology helps to explain another contradiction that many have found puzzling: the paradox of a political leader who appeared tem-peramentally to be the epitome of a revolutionary, a man who preached fanaticism, called for and in the end adopted extreme measures, yet, when he came to power in the 1930s, refused to allow the political revolution to be carried over into the social and economic sphere.

Tactics, of course, made caution necessary at the beginning, in 1933–34, when he still had to consolidate his position and needed the support, or at least the continued tolerance, of the conservative-nationalist forces in Ger-many. But later, when he felt strong enough to dismiss Schacht, set up the Four-Year Plan, and at the beginning of 1938 replace the conservative heads of the Foreign Office and the army, it was not in order to launch into sweeping domestic reforms, to revive earlier Nazi proposals for a corporate state, breaking up the big corporations, re-creating the guilds or workers' control.

As he told Otto Strasser, such ideas were no better than Marxism. They shared the same characteristic of turning aggression inwards and dividing the nation, instead of uniting it and directing aggression outwards. His alternative answer was equally if not more revolutionary: to direct the energies and tensions of German society into creating a new empire in the Slav east, a German equivalent of the Roman Empire of antiquity or of the British Empire in India—much more ruthlessly exploited—so providing the German people, far better than any internal revolution could, with the psychological satisfaction as well as the material advantages of becoming a master race.

During the 1930s he was fully preoccupied with restoring German power, drawing upon the ideology of national renewal, a nationalist, not a racist program. But he never saw the successes he won in foreign policy and war between 1933 and 1940 as ends in themselves. He continued to nurse the further ambition that they would open the way to a realization of his radical solution for the problem of Germany's future. Nothing of this sort was said in public. Until the end of 1939, German policy was presented within the framework of reversing the Versailles settlement and realizing the historic dream of Greater Germany. Nor was the nationalist ideology ever superseded by the racist, although it was the latter that more and more inspired German policy in the east, especially after the decision had been made to attack Russia. Even after the successes that carried German troops within sight of Moscow and Leningrad and later as far east as the Caucasus, the enormous effort that was put into reorganizing the occupied territories on racist principles was concealed.

But everyone in the inner circle of Nazi leaders was well aware of the fascination that *Lebensraum* in the east and racist ideas exercised over Hitler's imagination. Many other Nazis—for example, Darré, Himmler, Rosenberg, Garbeiter of East Prussia Erich Koch—saw the new German empire in the east as the final goal of the Nazi revolution, and were deeply involved in organizing it in the 1940s.

In the summer of 1932, the summer before they came to power, Darré is said to have reported to a small circle of party leaders including Hitler on the commission he had been given by Himmler to create a detailed register of the biological heritage of the Nazi elite, especially the SS, with a view to the planned breeding of a new aristocracy of race. After outlining the "eastern space policy" extending from the Baltic states in the north to the Black Sea and the Caucasus in the south, Darré argued that it could be properly organized only if Germany followed a policy of depopulation and colonization.[76] This was an initiative, unlike those for social and economic reform, that Hitler did not discourage.

Two years later, in the very same week of July 1934 that Hitler put an end to the SA's hopes of a Second Revolution, he conferred on the SS the status of an independent organization, on the basis of which Himmler and Heydrich were to set about making the SS the instrument of racist ideology. At the Council of Ministers on September 4, 1934, Göring explained that

German rearmament "started from the basic thought that a showdown with Russia is inevitable."[77]

This interpretation is supported by the fact that, while Hitler made no serious attempt to bring order into the conflict between rival interests and power blocs in the constitutional, administrative, and economic fields, he asserted himself forcefully in those that interested him and were related to his racist ideology—in foreign policy, rearmament, and strategy. It also fits well with the corresponding fact that, while there was endless bickering and intrigue among the Nazi bosses over questions of competence and power right up to the end, there was a complete absence of ideological conflict within the leadership. The authority of the Führer and his ideology remained unchallenged.

The two were in fact the same—an identification that Hitler had made the basis of his leadership from the re-creation of the party in the 1920s, when rank-and-file Nazis were accustomed to say, "Adolf Hitler is our ideology." As the American social scientist Arthur Schweitzer has pointed out, by fusing his personal charisma with his ideology, Hitler succeeded in overcoming the greatest drawback that Max Weber saw in charismatic authority: its instability.[78] Even more important, he provided the movement with a vision that found expression in its millenarian overtones: the "Thousand-Year Reich"—literally the millennium—the "Third Reich," echoing the twelfth-century Italian visionary Joachim da Fiore's "Third Age," and the Jewish conspiracies that were a staple of medieval millennia. That vision provided a moral imperative, enabling the SS man to feel that, if he was called upon to kill, he was obeying and acting as the agent of a "higher law" (just as Dzerzhinsky and, for that matter, Lenin and Trotsky, believed in their justification of terrorism). Far from rejecting such "inner values" as loyalty, obedience, honesty, self-discipline, comradeship, and bravery, which Himmler never ceased to inculcate in his SS recruits, Hitler's revolutionary vision enabled them to be appropriated and perverted in the service of an inhuman ideal.

Hitler's racist ideology was not a contradiction, but an extension, a more extreme version of German nationalism. For the majority of the German army and the German nation it was still the appeal of that traditional nationalism that counted even after the opening of the Eastern Front. But for the SS and the Nazi party officials serving in the occupied territories in the east, it was the racist elements that bound them in a special relationship to Hitler, providing them with the legitimization for the terrible crimes against humanity for which they were responsible, involving the forced deportation, and often the massacre, of millions of the indigenous peoples (Poles, Russians, Ukrainians) and culminating in the Holocaust, the deliberate, planned extermination of Europe's Jewish population. Other Germans, other Europeans, had talked and written in racist terms before Hitler; but he alone set about translating ideology into action, beginning with the development and indoctrination of the SS in the 1930s and eventually staking the whole future of Germany, at the height of his success, on the fatal attempt to make his fantasies come true. Hitler's originality lay not in his ideas but in his literal application of them.

VIII

JUST AS HITLER laid claim to the nationalist-authoritarian tradition in Germany, so Stalin laid claim to the Marxist-Leninist inheritance in Soviet Russia. From the time when he joined the Russian Social Democratic party, Marxism provided him with a distinctive set of concepts and a language in which he thought and expressed himself for the rest of his life. Along with the rest of the Bolshevik party, he adopted the additions that Lenin made to the Marxist canon, such as the role of the party and his theory of imperialism, and one of the most important reasons for Stalin's success in defeating his rivals was the position he established of being the authoritative interpreter of Lenin's thought.

Unlike Hitler, Stalin made no claim, even in private, to ideological originality. When asked for his ideas by interviewers, he invariably replied that these had been laid down once and for all by Marx and Lenin, and that he had nothing to add. Considering how much Stalin was prepared to claim for himself, this unexpected modesty requires explanation.

There were difficulties for Stalin that did not affect Hitler. One was the criticism that first Lenin, then Stalin, had to meet from Mensheviks and socialist leaders in the West, that they were not the inheritors but the betrayers of Marxism and socialism, to which Trotsky later added the claim that Stalin had betrayed Leninism as well. This was a charge that haunted Stalin throughout the 1930s. It points to the contradiction, first between an official ideology couched in the traditional socialist language of democracy, social justice, freedom, and equality, and the conditions of Soviet life; and, second, between the Communist ideology in its Marxist, or even Marxist-Leninist form, and the distorted counterversion developed by Stalin under the same name. The double talk and systematic falsification in which this involved the Communist party led to an intellectual and moral corruption from which it never succeeded in freeing itself.

Nazism bred its own forms of corruption, but not this particular one. On his way to the top, Hitler had been prepared to adopt any slogan or clause that would serve his purpose—"legality," "continuity," "anticapitalism," respect for traditional and Christian values, and, in his early days in power, love of peace and respect for other nations' rights. But Hitler's opportunist tactics never affected his ideological consistency. If, for tactical reasons, it was desirable to emphasize in public the nationalist and play down the movement's racist objectives, there was no secret about the latter; they were there for anyone to read in *Mein Kampf*. In marked contrast with Stalin and the Communist party, in the case of Hitler and the Nazis there was no conflict between their objectives and the means that were used when the time came from 1941 to 1945 to secure them. The corruption at the heart of Nazi ideology lay in its ends. Domination, enslavement, extermination are evil in themselves and will corrupt any movement that pursues them.

The corruption at the heart of Communist ideology lay in the means. Social justice, greater freedom and equality, an end to exploitation and alienation are noble, humane ends. What compromised them fatally was the inhumane methods employed to achieve them. This was as true of Lenin and Trotsky as of Stalin. Leszek Kolakowski, himself a former Polish Communist and Marxist philosopher, has put it well:

> If you build equality by increasing *in*equality, you'll be left with *in*equality; if you want to attain freedom by applying mass terror, the result will be mass terror; if you want to work for a just society through fear and repression, you will get fear and repression rather than universal fraternity. . . .
> Suppression of the "class enemy," the abolition of civil liberties and indeed terror were accepted as the necessary evil that precedes the new society. Today we can see clearly enough that means define ends, but Communist thinking has always held the reverse to be true. [79]

Lenin had based the seizure of power in 1917 on the gamble that the social and economic development of Russia would catch up with the Bolsheviks' political preemptive strike. It could be seen to have failed once it became clear that the revolution was not going to spread, that the Bolsheviks were isolated, and that no help was going to arrive from abroad. The civil war delayed recognition of this fact, but once that was over the Communist leadership had to face the fact that, far from inheriting an economy and society already transformed by capitalism—Marx's prerequisite for the success of a socialist revolution—they faced an economy and a society too impoverished, backward, and exhausted to generate, from within itself, the forces to carry through such a transformation.

During the short time left to him Lenin found no solution to the problem, but he left pointers in two opposite directions. One was reformist, on the basis of the New Economic Policy, a gradual, long-term "cultural revolution" remaking the popular mentality by education—beginning with the conquest of illiteracy—and winning the population's voluntary acceptance of the development of cooperative socialism, a task that would occupy "a whole historical epoch," one or two decades as a minimum. This was "Lenin's Political Testament" (as Bukharin described it) from his final years. The other was revolutionary, described by Lenin in November 1920 as "a change that breaks the old order to its very foundations, and not one that cautiously, slowly, and gradually remodels it, taking care to break as little as possible." This was the course Lenin had originally favored, a radical and violent break with Russia's past. It had been followed during the period of War Communism and then abruptly abandoned in favor of the NEP, to the regret of many Communists.

Stalin built his power on convincing the majority of the Communist leadership that, if they were not to abandon any thought of completing the revolution in three or four years—as they, and Lenin, had originally hoped ten years before—their only chance was by resuming the earlier, revolutionary course. He carried them with him in giving up the idea that limited intervention by the state could produce the changes needed. Instead the full power of the state must be used, as massively and brutally as was necessary, to break down the existing mold and force society—that is to say tens of millions of human beings—into new ways of life, not over twenty or thirty years, but in four or five. Compressing the state's assault upon society into the briefest possible time and attacking on the industrial, at the same time as the agricultural front, were deliberate tactics; they heightened the effect of destabilization, of a total crisis from which no aspect of life was exempt. The result was the obliteration of all familiar landmarks, producing disorientation and undermining resistance.

Kolakowski is not exaggerating when he calls this assault "probably the most massive warlike operation ever conducted by a state against its own citizens."[80] The consequence for Soviet ideology was the emergence—never acknowledged—of a distinctive Stalinist version, the greatest deviation of all.

The process had begun earlier with Stalin's adoption of the slogan "Socialism in one country," an abandonment of the international perspective that both Marx and Lenin had seen as an essential part of Marxist ideology, but that Stalin sought to present, by selective quotation, as Lenin's.[81] He used the same device to justify two other central theses of Stalinist ideology. The first was his belief, presented as an ineluctable law of historical development, that, as society approached closer to the final breakthrough to socialism, the fiercer would become the class war and the resistance of the exploiters, and the harsher would have to be the measures needed to achieve victory. "There have been no cases in history," Stalin declared in April 1929, "where dying classes have departed from the scene voluntarily."[82] Bukharin's failure to understand this, he added, was due to the fact that he approached the class struggle in a philistine, not a Marxist way.

The possibilities of Stalin's thesis were shown in the coercive measures taken to enforce collectivization, the class struggle in the countryside as Stalin described it. Hitler had said in *Mein Kampf,* "The art of leadership consists in concentrating the attention of the people on a single adversary, making different opponents appear as if they belonged to the same category."[83] Hitler found his "single adversary" in "the Jew"; Stalin found his in the kulak, later in "the enemies of the people"—the personification of the "evil forces" each had to subdue.

Stalin and Hitler shared the same capacity for applying literally such slogans as "racial pollution" (in Hitler's case) and "class warfare" (in

Stalin's), as grounds for extermination. For the next twenty-five years the concept of class enemies could be invoked, "objectively," whenever the Soviet Union—or, after the Second World War, governments in other Communist countries—wanted to launch campaigns of repression or destroy resistance. Anyone resisting, or accused of resisting, collectivization could be classed as a "kulak." Stalin himself did not put the proportion of kulaks at more than 5 percent of the Russian population; but all the violence involved in forcing the peasants into the collective farms was brought under the rubric of "the liquidation of the kulaks as a class," the last opponents to be destroyed before agriculture could be socialized.

The second thesis was Stalin's announcement in June 1931 that, in order to stop the heavy turnover in labor, it was necessary to do away with the equalization of wages. To those managers and trade unionists who thought that the principle of equality ought to prevail under the Soviet system, he declared that it was they who were "breaking with Marxism, breaking with Leninism." Marx and Lenin had always understood that:

> The difference between skilled and unskilled labor would exist even under socialism, even after classes had been abolished, and that only under Communism would this difference disappear. . . . Under socialism wages must be paid according to work performance and not according to needs. Who is right, Marx and Lenin, or the egalitarians? [84]

Once the principle of inequality was admitted, the way was open to make productivity the overriding priority; to keep on raising labor norms and, finally, to introduce labor passports, which tied workers to their jobs—the abandonment of principles for which trade unions in the West continued to fight under capitalism. When Marx came across similar ideas in the nineteenth-century Russian revolutionary Sergei Nechaev's *Basis of the Future Socialist Structure,* in which "people must produce as much as possible and use as little as possible," and where all personal relations were to be strictly regimented, he exclaimed in indignation, "What a splendid model of barrack Communism!" [85] There could not be a better short description of Stalinism in the 1930s; but, Stalin constantly repeated, exploitation and alienation had "ceased to exist" under the Soviet socialist regime.

The most important development was the adjustment of Soviet ideology to accommodate the principal feature of Stalin's revolution, the use of the power of the state, the substitution for the building of a socialist society of a state-building process, the construction not of a welfare state, but as Robert Tucker puts it, "of a powerful, highly centralized, bureaucratic, military-industrial Soviet Russian state." [86]

It was increasingly to the OGPU, the state's security services, and even to the army, that Stalin turned to enforce the collectivization program, and to manage the enormous expansion of the labor camps. The twin hallmarks of the full-blown Stalinist state as it developed in the 1930s became the coercive power of the secret police, the camps and the fear they inspired, and the growth in the power and privileges of the party-state bureaucracy at the expense of the emasculated civil society which it dominated.

How was this to be reconciled with the familiar Marxist doctrine of the "withering away of the state"? Stalin again proved equal to the occasion. At the Sixteenth Party Congress in 1930 he declared:

> We are for the withering away of the state. But at the same time we stand for the strengthening of the proletarian dictatorship, which constitutes the most powerful, the mightiest of all governing powers that have ever existed. The highest development of governmental power for the purpose of preparing the conditions for the withering away of governmental power, this is the Marxist formula. Is this "contradictory"? Yes, it is "contradictory." But this contradiction is life, and it reflects completely the Marxist dialectic. [87]

Just as the class struggle would be intensified, the nearer one approached the abolition of classes, so the state must first be built up to its maximum strength, in order to prepare for its withering away, both in keeping with the Marxist dialectic.*

There must have been other Old Bolsheviks besides Bukharin among the party members gathered to praise Stalin in the Congress of Victors (January 1934) who recognized, as scholars have since, that Stalin had gone a long way toward substituting a new and harsher creed of his own for the original ideology that had attracted them into the party. He could have made a good case for doing so. Marx's own vision of how a socialist, and eventually a Communist, society was to be constructed had been vague. In particular neither he nor Engels offered guidance on how to transform a backward agricultural country like Russia, in which capitalism was still embryonic, into an industrialized socialist society. Nor had Lenin, for all his boldness as a revolutionary leader, succeeded in finding an answer either. Stalin believed that he had, and that there was no alternative way; it is still a matter of debate whether in practice there was.

He could have argued that, under his leadership, Russia was the first country in the world to have carried out the two most important items in Marx's program: the abolition of private property, in land and agriculture as well as industry and commerce, and the abolition of the traditional classes, with the elimination of the bourgeoisie, the capitalists, and landowners, including the rural capitalists, the kulaks. He could have gone on to argue that, if the methods used and the consequences of them were very different from what many Marxists had foreseen, no Communist had ever supposed, certainly not Lenin, that a revolution could be made without much suffering and the loss of many lives. The difference, this time, was that his revolution, unlike 1905 and even 1917, had made a decisive, irreversible

*See pp. 625–28.

break with the past and opened the way to a wholly new prospect for the Russian people.

But that was not what Stalin claimed in January 1934. It was Marxism, he declared, that "has achieved complete victory over one-sixth" of the globe—in the very country in which Marxism was considered to have been utterly destroyed.

> To what does our party owe its superiority? To the fact that it is a Marxist party, a Leninist party. It owes it to the fact that it is guided in its work by the tenets of Marx, Engels, and Lenin. . . . Yes, comrades, our successes are due to the fact that we have worked and fought under the banner of Marx, Engels, and Lenin. [88]

It was clearly of great importance to Stalin to have the party—including the former oppositionists now allowed back—acknowledge not only what he had achieved, as they did, but publicly accept that this was the realization of the original Marxist vision of a socialist society.

There were of course obvious political advantages. During Stalin's lifetime, Marxism was more successful than any other millenarian movement in attracting converts, and Marxism-Leninism in providing the most widely adopted model for revolutionary movements. Stalin himself had drawn upon the enthusiasm that the certainties of Marxist-Leninist ideology could create to carry out his Second Revolution. This enthusiasm extended far beyond Russia. The image of the Soviet Union as the socialist fatherland, to which the working class and intellectuals throughout the world owed allegiance, enabled Stalin to maintain Soviet domination of the international Communist movement and to retain the active support of left-wing sympathizers in the West who were eager to preserve the belief, at almost any cost, that Stalin's Russia represented the best hope for the future.

But, important though these considerations were, they do not go to the heart of the matter. That lay in the nature of the Communist party, the essence of which was a common ideology based upon what was believed to be a scientifically proven set of propositions about history and society, with the same degree of certainty for the converted as the doctrines of the Catholic Church.

Ideology mattered to Hitler, but it was not an issue in the Nazi party; the majority were content to say "Adolf Hitler is our ideology" and to leave it to him, as Führer, to proclaim what it was. The equivalent of the "Führer myth" for a Communist was the "cult of the party," the party as the guardian of the original unalterable doctrine, not open to dispute, and the embodiment of authority on its interpretation and application, the party line. It was through the party and the "mystery" of the doctrine, the Marxist ideology that it embodied and protected, that legitimacy was conferred. Instead, therefore, of challenging its authority or weakening the power of its mystery by setting himself up to produce a revised ideology in his own name—the crime of deviationism which he had fastened on his opponents—Stalin could never admit to himself or the party that, while retaining the original facade, he was changing the substance. Remembering how much damage he and the other members of the troika had done to Trotsky's standing in the party by inventing and foisting Trotskyism on him, he had no intention of letting anyone do the same with Stalinism, a usage that he absolutely forbade. In the case of Hitler, ideology was what the Führer said it was; in the case of Stalin it was what the general secretary said Marx and Lenin had said it was.

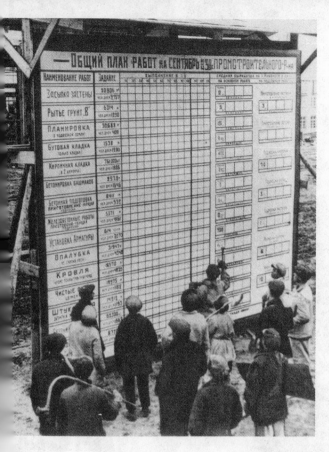

20, 21. The Five-Year Plan: *above,* workers surveying a "chart of socialist competition" *c.* 1930; *below,* a photograph described as "at the front of socialist construction."

ИЛЕТКА В ДЕЙСТВИИ. НА ФРОНТЕ СОЦИАЛИСТИЧЕСКОГО СТРОИТЕЛЬСТВА

22–25. Stalin and Hitler on the brink of power: Stalin in 1927 and (inset, in the 1930s with Yezhov, "the malignant dwarf," who headed the NKVD during the purges of the 1930s; *facing page,* Hitler in the Brown Hous in Munich in 1931 and (inset) with Röhm.

26, 27. *Above,* the Congress of Victors, 1934: *left to right,* Yenukidze, Voroshilov, Kaganovich, and Kuibyshev; *front,* Ordzhonikidze, Stalin, Molotov, and Kirov. *Below,* by the end of the same year, Kirov was dead. Stalin, strongly suspected of being responsible for his death, appears as the principal mourner at his funeral.

28–30. Stalin in private life: *above left,* with his son, Vasily, and daughter, Svetlana, at Kuntsevo; *above right,* Stalin's second wife, Nadezhda, who killed herself; *below,* Stalin working on his papers at Kuntsevo while Svetlana plays on Beria's knee.

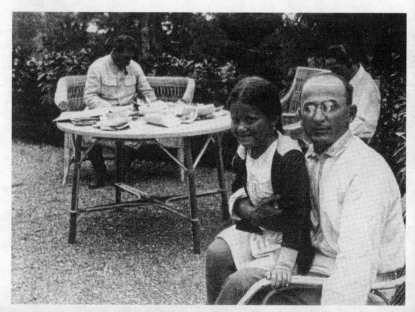

31, 32. The carefully orchestrated, but genuine, mass enthusiasm generated by and around Hitler: *above,* September 1933 in Nuremberg; *below,* at the Bückeberg rally in 1934.

33, 34. Hitler in private life: *above right,* snoozing with Geli Raubal; *above left,* with Eva Braun and his Alsatian dog Blondi.

35, 36. *Left,* Hitler examining plans with Speer; *below,* the Berghof.

37. Hitler speaking. "Men believe in the truth of all that is seen to be strongly believed in."
—*Nietzsche*

ELEVEN

The Führer State

I

IN BOTH GERMANY and the Soviet Union there were hopes in the autumn of 1934 that, with Hitler's suppression of the SA, and with the signs of relaxation following the Communist party's Congress of Victors, the revolutionary period was over, and life might settle down to a more normal level of activity.

These hopes were to be disappointed, although for different reasons and over different time-scales. Neither Hitler nor Stalin could be satisfied with a perpetuation of the status quo. Hitler had acquired a personal position without precedent in modern German history, but he had still to make use of it to achieve his real aims. Stalin had completed his Second Revolution, but the methods by which it had been carried out and the upheaval to which it led left him with an obsessional suspicion of enemies within the party, a determination to destroy them, and the ambition to be recognized, like Hitler, as without equals and responsible only to "history."

Hitler had accepted that he could not hope to bring about economic recovery and rearm Germany without the cooperation of the traditional elites in the army, civil service, and business, but he had no intention of allowing this "temporary accommodation," as he saw it, to become permanent, as so many conservatives hoped and assumed it would. The interest of the period 1934 through 1938, therefore, lies in the way in which Hitler managed to make the most of the advantages that cooperation brought, without letting himself and the Nazi movement be absorbed by it—on the contrary, strengthening his position by 1938–39 to the point where he could end his dependence on anybody but himself, free to embark on his program of revolutionary imperialism.

Stalin moved to the same end the other way around, disrupting the cooperation with the leading cadres of the Communist party on whom he had relied to push through the revolution from above and substituting instead of cooperation a demand for unconditional personal loyalty to himself. This he enforced by a purge on an unprecedented scale, which effectively destroyed what remained of Lenin's original Bolshevik party. The interest of this same period in Russia, therefore, lies in the way in which Stalin carried out this extraordinary assault on the party with which he had built up his power, without sacrificing the changes made by the Second Revolution or undermining his own position. On the contrary, he strengthened it to the point where he, too, successor to the Autocrat of All the Russias, ceased to be dependent on anybody but himself, and yet avoided weakening his claim to be at the same time the leader of the only successful Marxist-socialist state in the world.

IN HITLER'S CASE, foreign policy—which for him always meant a combination of diplomacy and military policy—came to absorb all his attention from the beginning of 1938. But to get to that point there had to be a period of preparation, best considered in relation to three areas: the state, the economy, and society.

Surprisingly, considering the powers he had now concentrated in his hands, Hitler was least active in the first. The point at which he had intervened in the summer of 1934 to put an end to hopes of a Second Revolution had left unresolved most of the conflicts and contradictions involved in the redistribution of functions, both between state and party, and within the state. In the period that followed, however, he resisted rather than supported attempts to clear up the confusion. Two examples will illustrate how he added to it by his own actions.

The first was the attempt to implement the Law for the Reconstruction of the Reich (January 30, 1934), which, in half a dozen lines, swept away the federal structure of German government and transferred the sovereign rights of the *Länder* to the Reich, subordinating both the minister-presidents and their *Land* governments, as well as the Reich governors, to the central government. This law, drawn up by Frick, the one-time civil servant who had become Reich minister of the interior, was intended to create a uniform, centralized structure of government for the whole of Germany—"a centuries-old dream fulfilled," Frick called it. It got as far as merging most of the Reich and Prussian ministries, and then got stuck. The reason was the resistance of the Reich governors in the other states. All but one were Gauleiters appointed as Hitler's personal representatives in the *Länder,* and they were determined to defend their privileged positions. Frick insisted, and both sides appealed to Hitler.

Hitler would never go against the Gauleiters. He ruled that, "generally speaking," if there was a difference of opinion between the central government and the Reich governor in one of the states, this would have to be settled as the new law required. But he added "that an exception must be made in matters of special political importance," an invitation that the Reich governors, as old party fighters, were not slow to exploit.

Frick's attempts to subordinate the minister-presidents in the *Länder* (another office often held by Gauleiters) and to subdivide the Reich into regions and *Gaue* of uniform size met with similar resistance from old party hands who saw themselves threatened with the loss of their jobs or sovereign territory. His patience exhausted by the dissension, Hitler ordered, "All written and spoken public discussion of the reform of the Reich, particularly of questions concerning territorial reorganization must cease" (March 1935). This did not prevent Fritz Sauckel, Reich governor and Gauleiter of Thuringia, from presenting a thirty-six-page memorandum to Hitler in January 1936 claiming that:

> The party men, whether Reich governors, minister-presidents, or state ministers, are being more and more excluded from the administration. The whole process shows the infinitely subtle, secret, and persistent endeavors of civil service cliques to acquire sole authority and to neutralize the influence of the party representatives. . . .[1]

In effect, the reform of the Reich was halted and the relationship between the central government and such offices as those of the Reich governors, the Prussian Oberpräsidenten (their equivalent in the Prussian provinces), and the minister-presidents, all of them party monopolies, remained unresolved, with the in-fighting continuing as opportunity offered and as the balance in the endemic struggle for power shifted.

The second example is Frick's attempt as Reich minister of the interior to secure the passage of a new Law on the German Civil Service, introducing a code of conduct and uniform system of rights for Reich and *Land* civil servants. A draft had already been agreed with the minister of finance in 1934 but was delayed for over two years by objections from Hitler and Hess (the latter representing the views of the party as the Führer's deputy). The argument moved from one clause to another, but the underlying issue remained the clash between the principle of an impartial civil service whose members' rights—including tenure, promotion, and pension—should be defended against outside interference and the party's insistence (and Hitler's) that the civil service should be no more exempt than any other organization from intervention to see that Nazi views prevailed, and that those who showed themselves "politically unreliable" should not be protected.

Hitler finally agreed, with ill grace, to publication of the law at the end of January 1937. But party attacks on the "reactionary" civil service continued, and Hitler showed his sympathy with them. He still continued to make use of the civil service and to benefit from its professionalism. But Frick—an *Alter Kämpfer* as well as the minister responsible for the civil service—finally despaired of his efforts to bridge the gap, "and develop in the service the old Prussian conception of duty as well as the National Socialist character." In a letter to Hitler in the early part of the war, he wrote:

> The course of the last years makes me doubt whether my efforts can in any way be regarded as successful. To an ever-growing degree, bitter

feelings are spreading in the civil service about the lack of appreciation of their abilities and services as well as of unjustified neglect. [2]

Hitler further undermined the principle of a unified structure of government by ignoring existing departments and creating special organizations, which became Supreme Reich Authorities, charged with carrying out tasks to which Hitler gave priority. By 1942 there were eleven such, of varying size and importance. The earliest was the Organization Todt (1933); the most spectacular was the Four-Year Plan (September 1936); and the most fateful, the merging of the police and the SS under Himmler, already Reichsführer SS, and from June 1936 chief of the German police as well.

Without consulting the minister of transport, Hitler handed over the responsibility for the *Autobahn* program to Fritz Todt, whom he made general inspector for German roads outside the ministry and directly responsible to himself as chancellor. From this base Todt went on to create a huge empire, taking over all construction work for the state (including the frontier defenses in the west, the West Wall) and in 1940 becoming, in addition, Reich minister for armaments and munitions. The special character of the Organization Todt was its combination of many firms from the private construction industry with the powers of a state building authority, including state control of labor service and conscription in the building sector. Thanks to its direct relationship to the Führer, it was freed from the control of the regular state administration, and like the SS and the police became part of the alternative executive that came into existence alongside the inherited governmental structure.

The second example, the Four-Year Plan, provided a personal power base for Göring. His original position as minister-president and minister of the interior in Prussia had been eroded by the amalgamation of the Reich and Prussian Ministries of the Interior under Frick, and by the monopoly of control over the police being built up by Himmler and Heydrich. The one real asset he preserved from his Prussian episode was his personal intelligence and research agency, the *Forschungsamt,* based on telephone tapping and monitoring radio and telegraph communications, which gave him an important advantage over rival Nazi bosses. But he failed to secure the leading place he hoped for in foreign policy and military affairs, and he held no party office that would enable him to compete with Himmler, Goebbels, and Ley, all three of whom combined power in the party with governmental office.

Göring rebuilt his position by extending the scope of the Reich Aviation Ministry, which Hitler had set up as a Supreme Reich Authority under his direction in May 1933. He defeated the attempt of the army and Ministry of Defense to keep the new Luftwaffe and its massive armaments program under their control, and he used the latter to break through into the economic field, not only capturing the leading position in it but also reestablishing himself in Hitler's confidence to the point where he was seen as the Führer's second in command.

Yet a third variation in the pattern of centers of power outside the established framework of government was the fusion of SS and police, the core of an SS "empire" that eventually eclipsed all the others. The removal of the police from the control of the Reich minister of the interior was strongly contested by Frick. When finally conceded in June 1936, Frick still insisted that Himmler's title should read "Reichsführer SS and Chief of German Police within the Reich Ministry of the Interior." But the proviso that Himmler in his second capacity, as chief of German police, was "personally and directly subordinate to the Reich and Prussian minister of the interior" was rendered ineffective by the fact that, in his first capacity as Reichsführer SS, Himmler was directly responsible to Hitler. Frick's identification with the civil service put him at a disadvantage, and, as his standing declined, Himmler succeeded in reversing the relationship, finally (in August 1943) taking over the Ministry of the Interior itself, as well as the police.

"Police state" can be a misleading description. It fails to bring out the point that, with the decree of June 1936, what Hitler and Himmler set about achieving was the withdrawal of the police—traditionally the instrument for enforcement of the law—from control by the state, and its merger with the SS, the organization that more than any other was identified as the instrument of the Führer's arbitrary authority to act outside the law. It was significant that Himmler did not set up a separate office as chief of the German police, indicating his intention of incorporating the police into the SS, which saw itself as a *corps d'élite* committed unconditionally to carrying out the Führer's will. Dividing the police into two sections—*Ordnungspolizei,* the regular, uniformed police, and *Sicherheitspolizei,* the security police—Himmler placed both the political police (the Gestapo) and the criminal police in the second, under Reinhard Heydrich, who held the rank of SS Obergruppenführer, the equivalent of a lieutenant general in the army.

Although set up in a traditional form with a minister who was a member of the cabinet, the Ministry of Popular Enlightenment and Propaganda displayed the same aggressive characteristics and disregard for established procedures and interests as any of the special organizations already described. This was largely due to the character of the minister himself. Unlike most of the Nazi leaders, Goebbels displayed outstanding ability and self-confidence in his ministry's central activity, coupled with a naturally radical, aggressive attitude and vaulting ambition. He had the great advantage of having built up the Propaganda Directorate of the party since 1930 as the successful model for a future Propaganda Ministry.

Goebbels's personal standing and influence were strengthened by the fact that he combined office as a minister with a leading position in the party, not only as a member of its Reich directorate, but also as Gauleiter of Berlin and one of Hitler's closest associates during the struggle to achieve power. With Hitler's support Goebbels succeeded not only in establishing a centralized direction of the German radio and press but also in securing control of the entire range of cultural activities by the establishment of the Reich Chamber of Culture, with separate divisions for literature, the theater, films, music, and the creative arts. Under Goebbels's direction, the Propaganda Ministry and the Reich Chamber of Culture were as much a part of the alternative executive as Göring's Four-Year Plan and Himmler's SS.

HITLER'S PERSONAL WITHDRAWAL from the day-to-day business of government after he succeeded von Hindenburg has already been mentioned. Coupled with his resistance to comprehensive reforms designed to clear up the confusion and contradictions in administration, this left the more powerful of the Nazi leaders free not only to build up rival empires but also to feud with one another and with the established ministries in a continuing fight to take over parts of one another's territory. The result, made worse by Hitler's own unpredictable interventions, has been variously described as "authoritarian anarchy," "permanent improvisation," "administrative chaos." However described, this polycratic state, with competing centers of power, was very different from the outside world's picture of a monolithic, totalitarian state run with typical German efficiency.

This state of affairs extended to the policy-making and legislative functions of government as well as the administration. The Weimar constitution was never formally replaced. Instead under the "temporary" provisions of the Enabling Act of March 1933 the Reich cabinet was authorized to enact laws. These were to be prepared by the chancellor and, once passed by the cabinet (without any requirement for a collective decision), were simply published in the *Official Gazette*. In effect this abolished the distinction between laws and decrees. Characteristically, the Reichstag was not abolished, nor its powers removed: But it was called on to pass only seven more laws. Similarly, the president did not lose his right to sign decrees, but this too was no longer needed, and von Hindenburg signed only three more. Henceforward decrees and laws alike were issued on the authority of the chancellor.

Hitler detested discussion and never called for a formal vote in the cabinet, which continued to have non-Nazi ministers among its members. He reduced the number of cabinet meetings: In the whole of 1935, there were twelve; in 1936, four; in 1937, six. The last meeting of all took place on February 5, 1938. Hitler's authority was unquestioned and, whenever he chose to intervene, was decisive. But he more and more avoided discussion with ministers, making the Reich Chancellery an independent Supreme Reich Authority and leaving its head, the career State Secretary Lammers (with the rank of Reich minister from November 1937), to manage the business of government. The right to legislate and issue decrees was increasingly delegated to departmental ministers, and the numbers of those with ministerial rank increased. Hitler directed that drafts were only to be submitted to him for signature when agreement had been reached between the departments concerned. Since the cabinet ceased to meet, this meant that, instead of being discussed orally, drafts were circulated to and fro until any disputed issues had been resolved.

To avoid this laborious process, laws *(Gesetze)* came to be replaced by edicts *(Erlasse)* to which Hitler's signature could be secured quickly. For the majority of ministers, who rarely if ever saw Hitler personally, this meant an approach through Lammers; but Göring, Goebbels, and Himmler had direct access to the Führer and could secure his agreement to decrees without consultation or coordination with other ministers. The same lack of consultation marked Hitler's own initiatives. As the German authority on the Nazi state Martin Broszat sums up:

> The authoritative Führer's will was expressed only irregularly, unsystematically and incoherently. . . .
> . . . The end of regular political discussions in the cabinet, the absence of regular and reliable information on the Führer's will for cabinet members, and the sporadic and abrupt transmission of directives from the Führer, which were often obscure in their meaning and effects, and arrived through different and often unreliable middlemen, generated a crippling uncertainty even over politically unimportant legislative projects. . . .
> As a result the disintegration of the government into a polycracy of separate departments was accelerated. . . . And the spread of departmental decree-making . . . became still more significant through the growing number of central authorities directly subordinate to the Führer. [3]

II

THE PATTERN of Hitler's behavior as head of government and head of state had been set by the way he had run the Nazi party. Hans Frank, the leading Nazi jurist, who had as good reason as Frick to know how much Hitler scorned legal rules and bureaucratic procedures, wrote in his memoirs:

> Hitler had been a party man. . . . His will was party law. He was the absolute autocrat of the NSDAP. The Reich, however, especially the state apparatus bound by formal lines of jurisdiction and a hierarchy of command, was unfamiliar and strange to him. . . . Instead of transferring to the party the traditional form of a legally ordered, expertly supervised, formally independent, juridically controlled state executive, his whole aim was to transfer the independent position he had in the NSDAP and its inner structure to the state. On January 30, 1933, he brought this aim with him. [4]

Führerprinzip, the principle that Hitler made the basis of the party, placed all authority in the hands of its leader, untrammeled by any committee or need for consultation. It was as much opposed to the hierarchical—bureaucratic as to the democratic concept of authority. Hitler's authority derived not from his *office,* nor from any form of election, but from his exceptional, charismatic gifts as a *person,* recognized and accepted by all members of the party.

The same concept governed the relations between the leader and his chief associates. They were appointed by Hitler, and their position depended not upon whatever office they held but upon their continuing personal relationship with and access to the Führer. "Duty," which in a bureaucracy as much as in an army means accepting the impersonal rules and regulations binding on all ranks in the hierarchy, including the highest, was replaced by "loyalty," the personal fealty owed by all followers to their chief. This meant that the "inner structure" of the party, as Frank called it, did not correspond to the clear-cut divisions and subdivisions of an organization chart, but to a constantly shifting network of interpersonal relationships between individuals and the development of personal patronage, clienteles, rivalries, and feuds at all levels.

Having created this unique position of authority for himself, Hitler was determined not to see it institutionalized. He delegated the routine business of party administration, and as far as possible disputes over jurisdiction—who had the right to do what—to Hess and the other members of the secretariat in Munich. This suited not only his irregular habits of work, his dislike of reading documents and spending time in committees or keeping appointments, but also his political style as the intuitive, inspired leader who kept himself aloof from faction fights, refusing to commit himself to one side or another in disputes over policy.

Hitler recognized that organization was necessary and prepared for it in advance of the party's growth in numbers; but beyond the minimum necessary to keep track of membership and control finances, he resisted attempts to turn the leadership of a fighting movement into a party bureaucracy to settle the division of responsibilities and coordinate the activities of the different departments.

The relationship between the Gauleiters and the various parts of the central organization was a perpetual subject of dispute. Even Schwarz, the party treasurer to whom Hitler gave legal authority to establish centralized financial control, was in constant battle with the Gauleiters and *Gau* treasurers over their high-handed misappropriation of party funds and membership dues, for which they frequently claimed to have Hitler's personal authorization. Hitler himself remained outside the hierarchy, free to deal directly with the Gauleiters, to make new appointments and to intervene when and where he chose. His concept of power was not only personal, but also arbitrary and unpredictable.

I F F R A N K was right, however, in saying that Hitler's aim on becoming chancellor was to transfer "his independent position in the party and its inner structure to the state," Hitler soon learned that this was impracticable. However reluctantly, he had to accept that there was not enough talent or experience in the party to take over and run the state, any more than there was in the SA to take over and run the army. Although in a different form, the alliance with the conservative forces in the state had to continue, and the pact with them was renewed with their acceptance of Hitler as von Hindenburg's successor.

It was his own position, not that of the party, that Hitler transferred to the state. The traditional concept of the supreme office in the state, whether held by a president or kaiser, was replaced by his own concept of personal leadership. On the death of von Hindenburg, the Law Concerning the Head of State of the German Reich (August 1, 1934) merged the offices of Reich President and Reich Chancellor to create the new office of Führer of the German Reich and People, soon shortened to "Der Führer."

Constitutional theory duly conformed. In his authoritative *Verfassungsrecht (Constitutional Law)* of 1939, the leading constitutional lawyer E. R. Huber, wrote:

> The office of Führer emanates from the National Socialist movement. In origin, it is not a governmental office. This fact must not be overlooked if the present position is to be understood.
>
> All public authority both in the state and in the movement stems from that of the Führer. The correct term for political authority in the People's Reich is therefore not "the authority of the state" but "the authority of the Führer." This is so because political authority is wielded not by an impersonal entity, the state, but by the Führer as executor of the united will of the people. [5]

The Führer state consisted of two different types of authority in parallel: the traditional state bureaucracy and an alternative executive, extra-constitutional and extra-legal, to the second of which in the event of conflict between the two Hitler almost invariably gave precedence. This diagnosis was first made fifty years ago by Ernst Fränkel, in *The Dual State,* a study written in exile and published in New York in 1941. Fränkel described the Führer state as a fusion between the "normative state" with its established norms and rules, and the "prerogative state," which expressed Hitler's claim to an overriding authority for which he was responsible only to history. "Fusion" was hardly the right word, since Hitler made no attempt to reconcile their conflicting activities, or clash of jurisdictions. In practice he made use of either as he wished.

Neither sector was complete in itself: The state bureaucracy had no coercive power at its disposal, having lost control of the police to the SS; while the alternative executive, which began as an ad hoc collection of separate functions, had no separate budget or finance office of its own, but drew on the Ministry of Finance, whose head, Schwerin von Krosigk, a non-Nazi member of the original coalition, remained in office from 1933 to 1945. Nor was the relationship between the two sectors ever stabilized, allowing the second to gain steadily at the expense of the first, which it was no doubt ultimately intended to supplant.

HITLER'S HOSTILITY to the idea of law and due process and his scorn for lawyers were more of a break with German tradition than his attack on democracy. While democratic ideas had failed to take firm root in Germany, the concept of a *Rechtsstaat,* a constitutional state, guaranteeing the rule of law and judicial independence, was accepted in principle in Prussia and other German states from the end of the eighteenth century and had been consolidated in practice during the nineteenth.

It is often forgotten that Point 19 of the original Nazi program of 1920 demanded that "Roman Law, which serves a materialistic world order, be replaced by a German Common Law." Nazi lawyers such as Frank hoped to restore what they regarded as Germanic principles of law in a *völkisch-Führer* state with an independent German judiciary. This proved as vain a hope as Frick's of creating a *völkisch*-authoritarian constitution. Hitler regarded any system of law and any constitution with suspicion as restrictions on his arbitrary authority as Führer, a role that he claimed Destiny had conferred on him to express the will of the German people. He instinctively preferred to retain the existing legal system formally, as he did the existing constitution, while overriding and eroding both by the exercise of emergency powers, and by developing alternative instruments ad hoc as these were needed.

The civil law (and the principle of private property) was the area least affected by this attitude; in such matters, the Nazi party and its offshoots hardly enjoyed any special status in the courts after 1933. But in the area of public law and criminal law, Hitler's intentions were made clear in the very first weeks after achieving power by the decree For the Protection of People and State suspending all guarantees of individual freedom and establishing what became a permanent state of emergency on the morrow of the Reichstag fire. This gave the Gestapo the right, which they continued to exercise throughout the regime, to take any person into "protective custody" and hold him or her indefinitely without any right to a trial or form of appeal. A second decree, Against Treason to the German Nation and Against Treasonable Activities, issued the same day (February 28, 1933), enlarged the concept of treason beyond the provisions of the penal code.

Three other decrees, issued over President von Hindenburg's signature on March 21, 1933 (Potsdam Day),* gave an amnesty for all offenses committed (by the Nazis) "in the struggle for the national renewal of the

*See p. 311.

German people" (including the Potempa murder)*; made malicious gossip a punishable offense (an opening much employed by informers against neighbors), and set up special courts, with "simplified" procedures to deal with this and other offenses under the Reichstag fire decree. A further decree stiffening the provisions for "malicious attacks on state and party" was issued in December 1934.

After the Reichstag fire, the Nazi members of the cabinet, Hitler, Göring, and Frick, were infuriated by the fact that the law did not provide the death penalty for arson, and that the Communists accused of complicity with van der Lubbe in setting fire to the Reichstag were acquitted by the Supreme Court for lack of evidence. They demanded a law introducing death by hanging for arson which was applied retrospectively to van der Lubbe, so breaking the natural-law principle of *nulla poena sine lege* ("no crime without law"). They followed this by removing trials for treason from the Supreme Court to a new People's Court, consisting of two judges, carefully selected for their loyalty to the regime, and five party officials as lay judges.

The effect of these various measures to deal with political crises is shown by a comparison of the number (268) of those people accused of such offenses in the already troubled year of 1932 with the 11,156 accused in the revolutionary year of 1933, of whom over 9,500 were found guilty. These figures, of course, take no account of those who were arrested, imprisoned, and often tortured by the Gestapo and the SA auxiliary police without any form of trial. [6]

The essence of the Nazi view of law was the distinction between friends and enemies of the national community as defined by the Nazis. Hitler spelled it out when he spoke to the Reichstag on the Enabling Law (March 23, 1933):

> The government of the national revolution regards it as its duty . . . to keep those elements from influencing the nation which consciously and intentionally act against its interests. The theory of equality before the law cannot be allowed to lead to the granting of equality to those who treat the law with contempt. . . . But the government will grant equality before the law to all who, by taking part in the formation of a national front against this danger, back the national interest and do not fail to support the government.
>
> Our legal system must serve to maintain this national community. The irremovability of the judges must, in the interests of society, be paralleled by an elasticity in sentencing. The nation rather than the individual must be regarded as the center of legal concern. [7]

As usual, Hitler did not clarify the implications of what he said. No Nazi code of law was ever developed, and the existing codes continued to be used, modified by decrees and laws on special issues, placing a heavy

*See p. 244.

burden on the judges who were required to interpret the law. Although they were appointed for life, and could not be dismissed, judges were career civil servants and many of them were sympathetic to the "national revolution." Those who were not were subject to a continuing pressure to conform to the new orthodoxy. In particular, they were repeatedly told by the authorities, and by their own NS League of German Lawyers, that the basis for their interpretations must not be legal precedents but Nazi ideology, the speeches and decisions of the Führer, and "the sound feelings of the people."

Where the courts dealt too leniently with a case in the view of the Gestapo, the latter could always take anyone who was acquitted or had served his or her sentence into preventive custody and send him or her off to a concentration camp. Attempts to limit or regulate such actions only led to compromises that failed to stop the Gestapo while drawing the courts more deeply into complicity with an organization consciously operating outside the law.

THE QUESTION LEFT to be answered is why Hitler made no serious attempt to clear up the uncertainty and conflicts of authority that persisted throughout so many areas of government.

Three combined elements provide the answer.

The first already suggested was Hitler's attitude toward "accommodation" with the established elites, which he was determined not to see made permanent. To prevent that happening, he refused to agree to the replacement of the Enabling Law by a new constitutional settlement or of the emergency decrees by a new code of law, preferring to keep everything fluid. That allowed him to make random interventions, and so keep the existing bureaucracy unsure of what he intended, and at the same time left him free to outflank it by setting up special agencies ad hoc for tasks he regarded as urgent.

The second element was Hitler's view of his own position and his interest in protecting it. He saw himself, in the phrase of Nietzsche's already quoted, as an artist-politician, the inspired leader who molded the thoughts and feelings of the nation and uplifted them into a vision of unity and greatness. This image, to which he attached overriding importance, must not be compromised by involvement in the administrative problems, the arguments, clashes of interests, and controversial decisions that are the day-to-day business of government.

This separation of roles corresponded to Hitler's strengths and weaknesses as a politician: on the one hand, his gifts as a speaker and virtuoso performer who must always maintain a distance between himself and his audience; on the other, his instinctive recognition that he would always be at a disadvantage in any situation that required discussion and a patient search for solutions rather than self-dramatization and reliance on willpower.

If he was not going to play the role of chief executive, others had to undertake such work in his place. Hitler accepted this and, to a degree unthinkable in the case of Stalin, was prepared to allow other Nazi leaders—Göring and Himmler, for example, Goebbels and Ley—to build up their own jealously guarded empires. He protected his own position by dividing responsibilities, taking care not to define them at all precisely or give up his right to revoke them and make other appointments in the same field without consultation. His habit of leaving decisions open to different interpretations, or deferring a decision altogether, encouraged rivalry and distrust, making it easy to play off one Nazi boss against another and keep them all dependent on him.

The third element was Hitler's narrow view of power and of the state. He had few equals as a politician but little understanding or gift for government. He thought of power purely in personal terms. He was opposed not just to the bureaucracy and the particular code of laws he had inherited from the German past, but to any form of bureaucracy and law as such, rejecting them as limitations on his right to account to no one but himself for the use he made of power. He had no concept of the need for power in a complex modern state to be articulated and given institutional form if it is to be effectively exercised.

This was of a piece with his equally rudimentary view of the state, which he valued primarily as an instrument of coercion against enemies within and rival powers without. He said repeatedly that the state was only a means to an end, and the end was defined as the conquest of additional *Lebensraum* in the east and the protection of racial purity, including the elimination of the Jews: "The state is only a vessel, and the race is what it contains. . . . The vessel can have a meaning only if it preserves and safeguards the contents. Otherwise it is worthless."[8] All the other purposes of the state, just as all the other needs to be supplied by the economy, were subordinate in Hitler's mind to the preservation of the Nazi regime (first and foremost his own position) and to preparation for a war of conquest—no more, no less than the classic program of ambitious rulers throughout the greater part of earlier history.

In the 1930s he could convince himself and the other Nazi leaders that such a program would provide answers to all Germany's problems. In fact, however, all it did was to postpone them into the indefinite future. And nothing in the vague statements he made about the Greater Germanic Reich suggests that he ever understood the problems involved in creating it, or, even if he had won the war, that he was capable of finding answers to them other than further improvisation backed by force.

III

THE ECONOMY PROVIDES a variation on the pattern already described in the field of government administration and law.[9]

The Nazis had come to power with high expectations among those groups in the party with radical programs for economic reform. The dissolution of the NSBO (Factory Cell Organization) and the Combat League of Middle-Class Tradespeople effectively put an end to these. Some concessions were later made to middle-class interest groups by curbing the share of consumer cooperatives and department stores in retail trade, and by allowing the craftsmen to create a modern version of the medieval guilds with compulsory membership—and control over admission—for anyone practicing a craft. But these were no more than marginal to an industrialized economy and did not disturb the new regime's cooperation with big business.

Hitler had never shown real interest in any of these initiatives. Agriculture was a different matter. Because of its links with the race and settlement program envisaged for the future *Lebensraum* in the east—and the high level of voting for the Nazis in farming districts—it was initially favored above any other sector of the economy. This makes it all the more striking that, when ideology came into conflict with economic facts, it was ideology that had to give way.

To give the peasant security and check the flight from the land, the *Erbhofgesetz* (Entailed Farm Law) of May 15, 1933, created family farm units normally of between eighteen and twenty-five acres, which were protected against foreclosure and could not be sold, mortgaged, or divided among heirs. Although made much of in Nazi propaganda, this law applied to not more than 35 percent of the units in production in 1933. Provision was made for more to be created, but few were, and for good reason. The honorific term of peasant *(Bauer)* was limited to those who owned entailed farms, but status and security, except for the well-to-do, did little to compensate for the fact that the farmer was tied to his land, with which he was not free to do what he wanted.

A second innovation was the creation, in September 1933, of the *Reichsnährstand* (Reich Food Estate), employing the same corporatist language as the organization of craftsmen, but in practice introducing state control of production, marketing, and prices as well as of the importing of agricultural products. To begin with, this worked to keep prices up, but in 1935, when cheap food became essential to sustain the industrial expansion required for rearmament, it started to work the other way around, keeping prices down, transferring real resources from a less efficient agricultural sector to a more efficient industrial one.

The result was that profit margins fell and farm debt rose, particularly on small and middle-sized farms. To stay on the farm meant working ever-longer hours for ever-less return. One contemporary survey of 1940 reported 65 percent of all farms without running water. Not surprisingly, the flight from the land accelerated and farm labor became more and more difficult to get.[10] Mechanization, the alternative to human labor, was increasingly beyond the means of the small farmer.

In these circumstances the number of new homesteads created by the Third Reich, the third element in Darré's program, was little more than half that created by the Weimar Republic.[11] Ironically it was the traditional East Elbian Junker estates that survived best, primarily because they were big enough to take advantage of the subsidies and rationalize their farming operations. The net result was to show that a regime ideologically committed to giving the farmers a preferential treatment they had never enjoyed before was nonetheless unable to insulate them from the pressures generated in the rest of the economy.[12]

THE NAZIS were as far removed from the world of corporate business and banking as they were from the other established German elites. If Hitler showed himself ready and eager to cooperate with its leaders when he became chancellor, it was for the same pragmatic reasons as led him to seek the support of the army leadership: This was the only way he could see of achieving his immediate objectives, rearmament and, in the case of the industrialists and financiers, Germany's economic recovery as well. Just as he was able to remove whatever doubts existed among the officer corps by the priority he gave to re-creating Germany's military power, so he was able to overcome the reserve of the industrialists by the suppression of the trade unions and collective bargaining, and of the bankers by his willingness to follow a conservative fiscal policy. At least until 1936, the German economy continued to function within the same institutional framework of industrial capitalism as it had before 1933.

There is no doubt about the economic recovery that took place in the early years of the new regime. To take the figure that made the greatest impression on public opinion: Between January 1933 and July 1935, the number of employed persons rose from 11.7 to 16.9 million (over 5 million new jobs), and the number of unemployed fell from 6 million to 1.8 million. By 1936 the worst unemployment figures in Europe had been turned into a labor shortage.

All sorts of reservations can be made about Hitler's claim that this was an economic miracle and that the credit for it was due to the Nazis. The other industrialized countries shared in it, suggesting that it was in part due to the working of the normal business cycle. Signs of an end to the Depression had already appeared before Hitler became chancellor. The credit for negotiating a settlement of Germany's international debt problems belongs to the Brüning government, and for ending reparations to von Papen, while many of the economic policies adopted were the product of the Weimar period, not uniquely Nazi policies at all. It is also true that throughout the interwar years the German economy failed to match the growth rates of the period before 1913 or after 1950. The German recovery outstripped that of other European economies because the Depression had hit it harder, and the climb back started from a lower point. If Germany's economic performance is compared with other industrialized countries, over the longer period 1913 to 1937–38, it is less impressive not only than that of the U.S.A. but also than those of Sweden, the U.K., and Mussolini's Italy. [13]

But these are sophisticated arguments ex post facto. At the time, seeing was believing, and what people saw (powerfully aided by the Nazi propaganda machine) was that, since Hitler had taken over, the economy had been turned around.

There is still disagreement among economic historians about the relative importance of the different factors that contributed to the recovery. Apart from the unquantifiable general revival of confidence produced by the impression that Germany had once again found a government prepared to act with decision, three other specific factors are seen as the most important: work-creation schemes, such as the construction of houses and *Autobahnen*; rearmament; and measures to control inflation and hold down wages and prices.

The importance of the first has probably been exaggerated. The plans had been drawn up before Hitler came to power. Although a total of 5.2 billion marks was spent by the central government on construction and road building between 1932 and 1935, this was balanced by cuts in expenditure by communes that had spent heavily in the 1920s. Roads, for example, received less total investment in 1934 than in 1927, and the level of investment in housing also remained below Weimar levels. Only after 1935 were really large sums put into the *Autobahnen*.

Where the Third Reich undoubtedly spent much more than the Weimar Republic was on rearmament. The Wehrmacht had already begun planning for a sixteen-division army in 1928, and between then and 1933 over 5,000 firms were visited and listed as suitable for employment. Under Hitler the plans were put into operation on a much bigger scale (to equip an army of twenty-one divisions as well as an air force and enlarged navy), although the need for concealment makes it difficult to distinguish between arms expenditure and public works, particularly in the early period. Harold James gives 10.4 billion marks as the *minimum* spent on rearmament up to March 1936, representing 5.2 percent of GNP over the period 1933–35 or more than twice as much as was spent on work creation. [14] The fact that such expenditure, unlike road-building and construction programs, meant orders for engineering works with their skilled work force provided a particularly important stimulus for the economy.

After all the Nazi propaganda attacking the Weimar regime for providing "jobs for the boys," the largest increase in investment in Nazi Germany turns out to have been in public administration, reflecting the number of jobs created in the state and party bureaucracies. Compared with 19.3 percent of total German investment in 1928 and 25.9 in 1932, this rose to 35.7 in 1934. But there was a difference: While the size of the civil service had not grown much in the later Weimar years, thanks to the unions, its pay did; under National Socialism, the size of the bureaucracy grew fast but salaries were maintained at the low levels of the Brüning era.

This was true of wages right across the board. As a result of the replacement of collective bargaining by state control, wage rates hardly moved after 1932, and wages as a proportion of the national income fell from 56 percent in 1933 to 53.3 percent in 1936 and 51.8 percent in 1939. If there was trouble over wages, as there was on some construction sites, the Gestapo was called in. "The first cause of the stability of our currency," Hitler told the banker Hjalmar Schacht, "is the concentration camp." The same applied to prices. "I will ensure that prices remain stable," Hitler assured Rauschning. "For that I have the SA. Woe to the man who puts up prices! We don't need any legal measures, we can do this through the party alone." [15]

Hitler regarded the control of inflation as vital after the Weimar experience and refused to consider devaluation. In 1933 he appointed Schacht, whom he disliked, as president of the Reichsbank and, in 1934, as minister of economics as well because he believed he was the best safeguard against inflation. Fiscal policy remained stable: Tax reforms were put off and tax rates hardly changed from the Brüning period, with no real attempt to apply an economic stimulus by tax reduction. Government deficits rose but were funded by conservative measures: 56 percent from taxes and public revenue between 1933 and 1939, only 12 percent by short-term loans.

Following an example set in von Papen's and von Schleicher's time, a major part of the work-creation programs was financed by certificates that could be used in the future to pay taxes and in the meantime were discountable by the banks. A similar concealment device was employed in financing rearmament, the so-called MEFO bill. The acronym stands for Metallurgische Forschungsgesellschaft, the Metal Research Corporation, an innocuously named institution set up to issue the bills to contractors. MEFO bills were introduced by Schacht in 1934, this time following a precedent from Brüning's years. It was a way of financing public expenditure that was bound eventually to produce inflationary pressures, but these did not appear before 1935, by which time Hitler could boast that he had carried out his promise and ended the Depression. The economic problems of the second half of the 1930s were due no longer to underused but to insufficient resources.

Besides controls over wages and prices, recovery also required controls over foreign exchange and foreign trade. These had been introduced in 1931 as a necessary defense of the German economy against the effects of the world Depression. But they still remained necessary as the revival of the economy in 1933–34 threatened to suck in more imported goods, especially imported raw materials, on which German industry was heavily dependent. Exporting remained difficult in the face of the collapse of world trade, of protectionism abroad, the refusal to follow the pound sterling in devaluation (which left the Reichsmark overvalued), and the growing attraction of the domestic market. The result was an imbalance in foreign trade that reached crisis level when the Reichsbank's reserves of gold and foreign currency were reduced below the figure of 100 million marks in June 1934.

Schacht's response on becoming minister of economics as well as president of the Reichsbank was the comprehensive system of controls contained in his New Plan of 1934. Its most publicized feature was the system of bilateral trade agreements, covering trade with twenty-five countries by 1938 and regulating more than half Germany's foreign trade. Different rates of exchange for the mark were set for each country, and "free" foreign exchange was strictly limited to the most urgent imports.

Schacht was a master of the financial and fiscal manipulation required to make such a system of controls work—and for this reason regarded himself as indispensable. But the system depended on the different interests inside Germany being prepared to exercise restraint in order to keep it in balance. Industrialists were irritated by the complicated regulations that the system required, although the big companies at least could appreciate the economic arguments behind it. Hitler and the Nazi leaders thought in political-ideological, not economic, terms.

The disputes of 1936, which led to Schacht's defeat and the establishment of the Four-Year Plan, began with a shortage of fats and meat at the end of 1935. Any shortage of food was taken seriously by the regime, especially by Hitler, because of its effect on public morale. Schacht put the blame for the crisis on poor planning by Darré's Agriculture Ministry, arguing that agricultural policy should be brought back under the control of the Ministry of Economics. Darré retorted by demanding more foreign currency to pay for food imports. Hitler's response was to appoint Göring to act as arbitrator. To general surprise, Göring found in favor of Darré and against Schacht.

Behind the immediate issue of foreign exchange for food lay the bigger question of how to provide raw materials and finance for the rearmament program. With the economic recovery providing a solution to unemployment, rearmament was left without a rival at the top of Hitler's agenda, the indispensable prerequisite for all the rest, and one that must take priority over all other considerations. By 1936 it had become clear that this was not a view shared by Schacht and the Ministry of Economics or the major industrial companies. Now that Germany was approaching full employment, they looked forward to a return to more normal economic conditions. For them this meant the pursuit of economic growth and profitability, which in turn meant a reduction in government spending and investment and the expansion of exports. The latter would make it possible to earn more foreign currency and so dismantle the New Plan's controls, now viewed as a temporary response to an emergency that was coming to an end.

In place of these economic objectives, which would mean a curb on the rearmament program, Hitler gave priority to the expansion of government expenditure. This was needed for the purpose of investment in the industrial infrastructure required to maintain rearmament, at the expense of curbing consumer demand and foreign trade. Exports were only important insofar as they earned the foreign currency needed to import such strategic raw materials as oil, iron ore, and rubber in which Germany was deficient. Controls would be maintained on all foreign trade and foreign exchange and would be backed up by a program of import substitution, which meant the expansion of domestic production and the development of synthetic substitutes, even where these were uneconomical. With the lessons of 1914–18 in mind, Hitler wanted an economy freed from dependence on foreign supplies and insulated against a repetition of the blockade and economic warfare that had hit Germany so hard then.

The chief enthusiast in Hitler's circle for autarkic ideas and economic self-sufficiency was Wilhelm Keppler. He had joined the Nazis in the late 1920s, coming from the characteristic background of small business, a family chemical firm in the southwest. Appointed as an economic adviser by Hitler in early 1932, he had no more success in getting Hitler to accept his advice or in establishing links with big business than any of the others who had been recruited or recruited themselves in that capacity. But, unlike most of the others, he survived, and although poor health denied him the succession to Kurt Schmitt as economics minister, a position that went to Schacht, his persistent advocacy of a German economy oriented toward self-sufficiency rather than foreign trade helped to convert Göring and Himmler as well as Hitler to a policy of autarky.

Such a policy appealed to the residual hostility in the Nazi party to large-scale corporate business, and to the links with international finance and world trade that were Schacht's stock-in-trade. While Schacht poured scorn on the "primitive" notion of autarky, which he dismissed as impracticable, Hitler committed himself to it at the Nuremberg Party Congress in September 1935.

In the early months of 1936 a fresh series of rows blew up, in which Schacht blamed increasing difficulties over foreign currency on Nazi leaders who ignored the regulations. The idea of appointing someone with a special commission to investigate the foreign-currency and raw-material problems had already been floated. Hitler's choice of Göring for the job was made easier by the fact that both Schacht and the minister of defense, General von Blomberg, recommended him, but it came as a surprise since Göring frankly admitted that he had no understanding of economics. This was precisely why Schacht and von Blomberg had recommended him, believing that, as a man with a wide circle of acquaintances in business and politics but no knowledge of the technical problems involved, his appointment would satisfy the party but leave them and their experts free to make the decisions while Göring acted as a figurehead.

Thanks to his upbringing as an officer cadet, his outstanding war record as a fighter pilot, and his social assurance, Göring was one of the few leading Nazis who could move in the upper reaches of German society without feeling or causing embarrassment. He had never held any post of importance in the Nazi party, and his value to Hitler had always been his sociability and commanding personality, which gave him obvious advantages as a contact man with the conservative Establishment. As a result he had acquired in such circles—and did nothing to dispel—the reputation of being a moderate, the sort of man with whom army officers and business-men, including Schacht, felt more at ease than with Hitler, and whom they saw as likely to use his influence with Hitler in favor of maintaining the "accommodation" with the traditional ruling class which had been con-firmed in 1934.

They could not have been more mistaken. Göring was not only deeply loyal to Hitler but also dependent on him, accepted his leadership as inspired, and had adopted as his own Hitler's radical racist *Weltanschauung*. He was also, underneath his flamboyant, extrovert exterior, an unscrupu-lous intriguer, who might boast of his ignorance of economics but concealed a natural political cunning, unlimited ambition, and ruthlessness toward anyone who stood in his way.

Göring had not yet found a substitute for the powerful position that he had lost in Prussia and was now given an opening into the key area of economic control which no leading Nazi had yet succeeded in penetrating. He had exactly the combination of qualities needed to enlarge his opening into a breakthrough: He showed his intention at his first conference when he announced that he was not "heading some kind of investigation commit-tee but would take over the responsibility for the necessary control." When Schacht, realizing the mistake he and von Blomberg had made, called at the Council of Ministers for a continuation of a moderate policy, pursuing "a steady, prosperous economy . . . and renouncing the execution of other irrational ideas and aims of the party," Göring rejected his appeal. His own version of the objective that should govern economic policy echoed Hitler's: "The primary political necessity is to maintain the same tempo of rearma-ment."[16]

Göring had another compelling motive in his personal ambition to create the world's most powerful air force. From the day Hitler took office and brought him into the cabinet as Reich air commissioner as well as minister without portfolio, Göring had pushed and intrigued, first to take over the Air Office set up in the Ministry of Defense to manage Germany's secret rearmament in the air; then, when this was conceded, to set up an indepen-dent organization for procuring aircraft and weapons outside the control of the Ministry of Defense and the Wehrmacht. In April 1936, the month Göring was appointed to "investigate" the raw-materials position, he de-feated a last attempt by von Blomberg to defend the unity of the armed forces and a balanced rearmament program.

Creating an air force virtually from scratch—with heavy expenditure on airfields as well as on a high-cost technology—was bound to be particularly expensive. Göring had already persuaded Hitler in 1935 to agree to a doubling of its strength. This had been in the face of the efforts of Schacht, von Blomberg, and the finance minister to restrain him. If he could succeed in turning his entry into the economic field into a commanding position, there would be no limit on what he could demand and get, not only for rearmament over all, but for the particular service with which he was identified. His hopes were not disappointed. Total German military expenditure rose from 1.953 trillion marks in 1934–35 to 8.273 trillion in 1937–38, and the Luftwaffe's share of that fourfold increase rose from 32.9 percent to 39.4 percent.

All this was yet to be fought for, but the double prospect of breaking the economic experts' hold over the economy and the Wehrmacht's monopoly of control over rearmament and the armed forces explains the drive Göring put into expanding his initial bridgehead and the support he could count on from Hitler. Hitler's own self-confidence and impatience with the conservative leadership of the army and the economy had been strengthened by his coup in reoccupying the Rhineland (March 1936) against the advice of the generals.

In the long run Göring's appointment proved a disaster, both for the economy and for the Luftwaffe; but in the short run it promised Hitler three of his major objectives: the politicization of economic decision-making, the preparation for the transition to a war economy, and a start on the Nazification of the armed forces. The air force was the youngest and most glamorous of the three services. Always fascinated by military technology and ready to believe Göring's forecast that air power would be a decisive weapon in the next war, Hitler was delighted with the possibility of breaking the mold of Prussian military tradition and creating an ethos for the Luftwaffe (as later in the parallel case of the Waffen [Armed] SS) much closer to that of National Socialism.

Both Schacht and the army leaders opposed any further growth in Göring's power, but on different grounds. Schacht painted a black picture of the dangers of inflation and the difficulties Germany would encounter in increasing exports and securing food and strategic raw materials, if Göring continued to insist on a high level of rearmament. The army, on the other hand, supported rearmament but wanted to restrict Göring's role and keep preparations for war under the unified military control of the Ministry of Defense.

Thanks to the wiretapping activities of his Forschungsamt, Göring was able to keep Hitler well informed of the opposition's moves. The two spent much time together during the summer, and in August, while staying at Obersalzberg, Hitler drew up the memorandum that served as a basis for the Four-Year Plan. With the outbreak of the Spanish Civil War, he had already commissioned Göring to set up a raw-materials and trade commission in Seville, known as Hisma-Rowak, to manage Germany's economic relations with Franco's Nationalist Spain and safeguard Germany's access to Spanish iron-ore supplies. He now decided to put Göring in charge of his new plan, characteristically leaving him to fight out the division of responsibilities with Schacht and von Blomberg, a challenge that Göring was happy to accept.

On September 4, Göring informed the cabinet of the new task with which he had been charged and read them Hitler's memorandum, which assigned an absolute priority to rearmament and the achievement of self-sufficiency. Göring added: "All measures have to be taken as if we were actually at the stage of imminent mobilization." [17]

A decree giving Göring power to promulgate decrees himself and "to issue instructions to all authorities" was published on October 18, and ten days later Göring told a cheering crowd of Nazis in the Berlin Sportpalast:

> The Führer has given me a heavy office. . . . I come to it not as an expert. The Führer chose me only, simply and only, as a National Socialist. I stand before you and will complete this task as a National Socialist fighter, as his plenipotentiary, as the plenipotentiary of the Nazi party. [18]

IV

THE ESTABLISHMENT of the Four-Year Plan marked more than a change in economic policy: It marked also a shift in the balance of power in Germany. The fact that a self-proclaimed *Alter Kämpfer* was put in control of the German economy and German rearmament instead of a banker, a businessman, or a representative of the army was evidence that the terms of the alliance between the Nazi leadership and the traditional German elites, reaffirmed in 1934, had been changed, not by agreement, but by unilateral action on Hitler's part, and without consultation. Nothing makes this clearer than Hitler's treatment of the memorandum giving the army's view of the Four-Year Plan which von Blomberg sent to him in February 1937.

The army called for three conditions to be accepted. As minister of defense, von Blomberg should have the responsibility for war preparations and for running the war economy; Schacht, not Göring, should be responsible for the preparation of the economy in peacetime; Göring's office should be abolished if war broke out, and in peacetime should be restricted to a limited range of raw materials under the supervision of the minister of defense. If these conditions were not met, the army was not prepared to work with Göring. [19]

Hitler did not reply, ignoring the protest and leaving Göring to get on with the job. For the first time in modern German history, the army's veto had failed to produce an effect.

Hitler's own memorandum, of which, according to Speer, only three copies were made and the text remained secret,* provides confirmation of something else as well: the continuity of his ideas about the inevitability of war. It is true that, on this occasion, Hitler chose to emphasize the threat to Germany rather than the opportunity to safeguard her future, but the basic assumption was still the same as in *Mein Kampf* ("the historical

---

*Schacht claimed not to have seen it until he was put on trial at Nuremberg after the war; Speer then showed his copy to Schacht.

struggle of the nations for survival"), and both threat and opportunity (two sides of the same coin) were, as before, located in the East.

> Since the French Revolution, the world has been moving toward a new conflict, the most extreme solution of which is Bolshevism; and the essence and goal of Bolshevism is the elimination of those strata of mankind that have hitherto provided the leadership and their replacement by worldwide Jewry.
> No nation will be able to avoid or abstain from this historical conflict. Since Marxism, through its victory in Russia, has established one of the greatest empires as a forward base for its future operations, this question has become a menacing one.

Only Germany was capable of defending herself and the rest of Europe against the disaster of a victory for Bolshevism.

> The extent of the military development of our resources cannot be too large, nor its pace too swift. All other desires without exception must come second to this task. . . .
> The Economics Ministry has only set the national economic tasks, and private industry has to fulfill them. If, however, private industry believes itself incapable of doing so, then the National Socialist state will know how to solve the problem itself. . . . German business will grasp the new economic tasks or it will show itself unfit for survival in this modern age, when the Soviet state is establishing a giant plan. Then, however, Germany will not go under, but at most a few businessmen.

Hitler reiterated that the final solution of Germany's economic problems lay in extending her people's *Lebensraum,* but in the transitional period everything must be subordinated to preparations for war.

> I therefore set the following tasks:
> 1. The German armed forces must be operational within four years.
> 2. The German economy must be fit for war within four years. [20]

In presenting it to the cabinet, Göring repeated what he had said in 1934: "The memorandum starts from the basic premise that the showdown with Russia is inevitable. What Russia has done in the field of reconstruction, we also can do." [21]

Plainly, Stalin's Five-Year Plan, carried out in four, had made a great impression on both Hitler and Göring. What followed in Germany, however, was nothing like as clear-cut as the expropriation of capitalist industry by the state that had taken place earlier in Russia. It has been described as "disorganized capitalism," a parallel in the economic sphere to "administrative chaos" in the civil service—and for the same reason: Hitler's refusal to define jurisdictions. This left the way open to the tactics of penetration and annexation practiced by Göring and Himmler in implementing the Nazi "revolution by installments," Hitler's version of Stalin's "dosage."

In Göring's case, these tactics brought him into conflict with ministries,

industry, the army, and the party. His trump card was his knowledge—
which he did not disguise—that Hitler would back him. When he could not
count on that, he could overreach himself—as in his bid to replace von
Blomberg as the minister of defense. But Göring had a flair for spotting the
most promising areas in which to press and, as he had shown in Prussia
earlier, for disconcerting opponents by his refusal to be bound by rules,
conventions, and the other props of authority. The initiative always lay with
him, and the first a minister or industrialist might know of his intentions was
the news that a decree had already been published, without notice, removing some well-established part of his jurisdiction or rights.

During 1937 the Four-Year Plan's operations were extended into trade,
manufacturing, and transport as well as investment. When the army wanted
an increase in funds, von Blomberg applied to Göring, not Schacht. Controls over the capital market and share issues were tightened, and Göring
took powers to sequester the foreign assets of German nationals in exchange
for marks. To expedite his ambitious program of synthetic and raw-material
production, he assumed further powers to direct labor and allocate national
resources. Schacht protested but failed to get the measures reversed. Once
it became obvious that Göring, not Schacht, was Hitler's choice to put his
policy into effect, power produced its own attractive effect, and an increasing number of offices and businesses that had hitherto taken their lead from
Schacht and his ministry turned to Göring's organization instead. As a
result, it has been calculated that nearly two-thirds of the total German
fixed-capital investment in 1937 and 1938 was made through the Four-Year
Plan, the Air Ministry, or other offices under Göring's control. [22]

In July 1937, Hitler was persuaded by the army to propose a settlement
of the dispute between the two men over jurisdiction but Göring ignored
it, and Schacht thereupon suspended his own activities first as plenipotentiary for the war economy, and then as minister of economics. This had no
more effect than the attempted reconciliation. According to Schacht, Göring told him in front of Hitler, "But I must be able to give you instructions,"
to which Schacht replied: "Not me—my successor, perhaps." [23] In November 1937, Hitler finally accepted Schacht's resignation as part of the general
replacement of the conservative leadership in the army and Foreign Office
at the same time. According to Schacht, Göring's first act on moving into
the former minister's room was to pick up the telephone and announce
triumphantly, "I am now sitting in your chair." [24]

Göring had by that time turned the Four-Year Plan into an alternative
center of economic authority, not by sweeping away the existing structure
(as in Russia) but by a continuing transfer of activities and initiative to the
new one. Schacht was not only defeated politically but also discredited as
an economic prophet as well when the predictions he had made of disaster
as a result of the policy of all-out rearmament proved ill founded. Government expenditure, government investment, public debt, all rose in every
year 1935 through 1938. By contrast, in 1938, exports were no higher than

in 1932, while gold and foreign-currency reserves had fallen to a seventh of Germany's holdings in 1933. Yet Göring's remark to the Council of Ministers in May 1936 proved nearer the mark than Schacht's predictions: "Measures that in a state with a parliamentary government would probably bring about inflation do not have the same results in a totalitarian state."[25] There was no inflation, and, with the government in control of the flow of investment, there proved to be no difficulty in raising loans of 3.1 billion marks in 1937 and 7.7 billion in 1938.

Göring's success at the political level made it easier for him to attract the administrative staff without which the Four-Year Plan would have remained a facade. But at the administrative level, too, Göring was interested in making appointments that would extend his outreach and draw ministries as well as the most important sectors of the economy into his network. One way of doing this was by giving the state secretaries in the economic ministries important positions in the Four-Year Plan as well. In this way, Darré, the minister of agriculture, rapidly found himself losing influence to his ambitious state secretary, Herbert Backe, who was appointed director of farm production, one of the seven divisions of the Four-Year Plan, reporting directly to Göring and running the Ministry of Agriculture and Food virtually as Göring's agent. Göring took care to keep on good terms with Himmler and Goebbels, but other party leaders (Hess and Ribbentrop in particular) were jealous of his close relationship with Hitler and of his personal popularity, which he took much trouble to cultivate. He had good reason, therefore, to appoint a number of veteran party members, enthusiastic for autarky and for Nazi economic ideals, "the creation of an empire built around the small producer and the barracks."[26] All came from the same background of provincial small-business companies, often family firms, and were committed Nazis.

A very different appointment was that of Carl Krauch, one of the ablest chemists in the giant German chemical corporation I. G. Farben, to head the plan's research and development section, with responsibility for developing the maximum degree of self-sufficiency for the Reich in twenty-five to thirty major products, including textiles, rubber, oil, copper, fats, fodder, and phosphates. This led to a connection between the plan and Europe's largest industrial corporation, which kept I.G. Farben from being a leading target for Nazi attacks as a citadel of "Jewish international capitalism" (it had ten Jews on its various governing boards), into so close an identification with the Nazi regime (including building and operating a factory at Auschwitz) that after the war the surviving members of its main board were placed on trial as war criminals.

BETWEEN 1936 and 1939 the controls to which German business was subject were extended to include imports and foreign exchange, allocation of raw materials, allocation of labor, prices, wages, profits, and investment. Their impact varied between one sector and another but extended to agriculture as well as industry, the plan being responsible for producing and distributing the tractors and fertilizers. Business still remained in private or corporate hands, but to a large extent the government through the Four-Year Plan dictated what companies should produce, how much new investment they should be allowed to make, where any new plants should be sited, what raw materials they could obtain, what prices to charge, what wages to pay, how much profit they could make—and how they should use it (after paying increased taxes) for compulsory reinvestment in their business or the purchase of government bonds.

Besides formal controls, Göring appointed plenipotentiaries for the industries that were essential to rearmament: iron and steel, oil, machine tools, construction (Fritz Todt), textiles, automobiles. Their job was to see that policies were carried out and targets met, and to pressure manufacturers to rationalize and standardize their methods of purchase—"greatest output with least resources." Behind the bluster and the propaganda, the results were patchy. If I. G. Farben and the chemical industry are the obvious example of successful cooperation between industry and the plan at one end of the spectrum, the Ruhr and the coal, iron, and steel industries are the obvious examples of reluctance to cooperate at the other.

It was the great English economist John Maynard Keynes who first remarked that "the German Empire was built more truly on coal and iron than on blood and iron." "The Ruhr" organized in such bodies as the Rhenish-Westphalian Coal Syndicate, founded in 1893 and often regarded as the first modern industrial cartel, had long been a potent force in German politics as well as the economy. "Without coal nothing ran, and when it became too expensive, nothing could be sold."[27] Both imperial and republican governments had learned to treat the syndicate's power with respect, and the French had to abandon their occupation of the Ruhr in 1923 when the withholding of coal deliveries threatened to destroy the value of the franc.

To begin with, the Ruhr industrialists were well disposed toward the Nazi government. The differences that arose between them were economic, not political, in origin. Coal production everywhere had entered a prolonged period of crisis in the 1920s, due to high costs and excess capacity, above all to competition from new forms of energy. This experience made the Ruhr coal operators obstinately conservative: They resisted all attempts to push them into expanding the mines' capacity for production or to involve them in the synthetic-fuels program, and they opposed the uneconomical exploitation of Germany's native resources of low-grade iron ore. In the initial period of recovery from the Depression, Ruhr coal production (which made up three-quarters of total German production) rose again to the level of 1929, and, in 1937, boosted by the recovery of the Saar, marginally surpassed it. It rose to a peak of 130 million tons in 1939, a figure that was never equaled again during the war. This was well short of what was required by the rearmaments program.[28] Mining experts put the annual shortfall at anywhere between 7.5 and 11.5 million tons; Hitler in an exasperated guess (in January 1937) at 20 to 30 million.[29] But the shortages continued from 1937 to 1945.

As long as Schacht was in charge of the economy, he defended the Ruhr industrialists' right to make decisions according to their own view of their interests: "The state should not run business itself, and take the responsibility away from private enterprise."[30] Göring insisted that the Ruhr, like the rest of German business, must subordinate its private interests to the national need, pointing to the fact that Germany was heavily dependent on foreign sources of iron ore (Sweden, France, Spain, in that order), and so more vulnerable than in 1914, a comparison to which Hitler constantly returned.[31] Out of 21 million tons of iron ore smelted in 1935, only a quarter could be provided from domestic sources, and Göring demanded that the Ruhr industrialists should undertake the development of the low-grade ores in central and southern Germany. When they refused, he declared that "the State must take over when private industry has proved itself no longer able to carry on."[32]

In the summer of 1937 Göring announced plans approved by Hitler for an industrial complex (to be named the Hermann Göring Reichswerke) for extracting and smelting iron from the low-grade Salzgitter ore fields in Brunswick. When the iron and steel industrialists produced a paper rejecting Göring's autarkic policy, he threatened them with arrest as saboteurs and compelled the private firms to invest some of their own funds in the state-owned competitor with which he now confronted them. Krupp was offered a large arms contract at the same time in order to split any attempt at a united front in opposition. It was this clash and the Ruhr's defeat that finally destroyed Schacht's position and led to his resignation.

The foundation of the Hermann Göring Reichswerke marked a further shift in the balance of economic power, already tilted by the Four-Year Plan. For not only did it carry the Führer state from control of the economy into state ownership and management of industry, but Göring also rapidly decided to expand the operations of this sector, again with Hitler's agreement, and make the Reichswerke "the core of the whole of German rearmament, of supplies for the arms industry in peace and war."[33] Early in 1938 he authorized an increase in state funds for the new enterprise, raising its capital from 5 to 400 million marks. He described it as an economic and political instrument that would not only speed up rearmament by providing more steel from domestic ores, but also bypass the conflict of interests between the Führer state and corporate business by creating an alternative economy, the equivalent of the prerogative sector of Ernst Fränkel's dual state. The second purpose was reflected in the important part assigned in the operation of the Reichswerke to men long identified with the party and Nazi populist economics. Its managing director, Paul Pleiger, had been a small steel producer and was hostile to large-scale capitalism; one of his closest associates, Wilhelm Meinberg, had been a Nazi peasant leader in the 1920s; and another director, Dietrich Klagges, a former elementary schoolteacher and old party member.

Göring maintained the expansion of the Reichswerke, which he regarded as a personal memorial to himself and the Nazi movement, by assigning to it all the industrial assets he could lay his hands on. These included Jewish firms compulsorily "Aryanized"; the Thyssen coal holdings in the Ruhr, confiscated in December 1939; armament works like Rheinmetall Borsig, and the greater part of the industry taken over in Austria and Czechoslovakia. By the time war broke out the Reichswerke had replaced I. G. Farben as the largest industrial enterprise in Europe and was on the way to becoming the economic instrument of Nazi imperialist expansion.

Peter Hayes, the historian of I. G. Farben, describes Göring's economic operations as "strip-mining the German economy" for the sake of rearmament, pointing out that by aiming for the highest degree of self-sufficiency, regardless of cost, Hitler "hardened German economic policy into a self-fulfilling prophecy":

> Hitler could increasingly justify a militant drive to the East as the solution to the economic problems he had largely imposed. [34]

One can argue about the balance between the positive and negative aspects of the policy in economic terms, but in the end the test was that of war, the end toward which Hitler had directed it. The questions that need to be answered are how far the timetable Hitler laid down in 1936 was realized; what kind of war he envisaged; what kind of armaments program was adopted; and, above all, how far it achieved its object of making Germany powerful enough to carry out his long-term aims. An answer to these will emerge in a later discussion of foreign policy (Chapter Thirteen).

V

STATE, ECONOMY—SOCIETY. With the first Hitler never advanced beyond improvisation. The second he treated as instrumental and left, first to Schacht, then to Göring, to organize. It was the third, society, in which he was most involved personally. It was there that he sought to prove the advantage of "socializing people" over the Marxist method of socializing production; to unite the German people in a *Volksgemeinschaft* in place of liberal individualism and the Marxists' class war; and to revive their readiness to bear arms in the war to capture *Lebensraum* for the German *Herrenvolk* in the east. Standing Marx on his head, Hitler set out to change the German people's consciousness as the preliminary to changing their material conditions.

Apart from these central beliefs of Nazism and its racist and eugenic principles, all of which were systematically inculcated and enforced, there was a whole litany of secondary values that mixed up archaic and modern features frequently in contradiction with one another. *"Blut und Boden"*

(Blood and Soil), for example, was an old dream of the German right, which expressed a longing to escape from the corruption and complexity of city life and turn back to a preindustrial age of peasant agriculture and rural simplicity.

Another example was the abolition of the structure of industrial relations established in 1918–19. The character of the new structure was indicated by the quasi-feudal language of the Law for the Ordering of National Labor of January 1934. The employer was described as "Leader of the Plant" and the work force as his "retinue," who owed him loyalty according to the principles of the "plant community" *(Betriebsgemeinschaft)*. In place of collective bargaining, wages were henceforward to be fixed by Reich Trustees of Labor appointed by the state. [35]

It was hard to reconcile such nostalgia for the past with the contempt that Hitler and many other Nazis felt for the stiff, class-ridden, hierarchical society of pre-1914 Germany, reflected in the passion for status and titles and epitomized in the snobbery of the officer corps (including the reserve officers). It was equally difficult to combine the campaign to break up the big industrial corporations and department stores, or to revive the guild structure of handicrafts, with the demand to provide Germany's army and air force with the most up-to-date technology.

The Nazi movement, however, had always thrived on its ability to appeal to incompatible interests and aims, and its dynamic, aggressive propaganda, making use of the most modern techniques of publicity, swept them all along on the broad tide of enthusiasm for national unity, national renewal, and national power.

Propaganda continued to be combined with organization. There were few additions to the scope of the themes already established in 1933–34, and in many cases before. The new factor reinforcing both propaganda and organization was success—success in ending the Depression, getting rid of reparations, restoring German power and prestige abroad. Not only was the message of success drummed home by every means, day in and day out, but its effect was doubled by the fact that any note of skepticism or criticism was suppressed. Success thus exercised a coercive as well as an attractive force, making it appear impossible to resist.

These were the years in which the Nazis, with the resources of the state at their command, perfected the art of visual propaganda with the displays and parades that they organized, and that even now have hardly been equaled by any other regime.

The calendar of celebrations was now well established:

January 30	Hitler's appointment as Reich chancellor
February 24	Refounding of the party in 1925
March 24	National Day of Mourning for Germany's war dead, converted into "Heroes' Remembrance Day"

April 20	Hitler's birthday
May 1	National Day of Labor
2nd Sunday in May	Mothering Sunday
June	Summer Solstice
September	Nuremberg Party Rally
October 1	Harvest Thanksgiving (*"Blut und Boden"*) held at Bückeberg, near Hameln
November 9	Anniversary of the 1923 putsch in Munich

The scale of these commemorations was extraordinary, involving hundreds of thousands of participants directly, and then being repeated ad nauseam (especially any speech by Hitler) on radio and film. The peak was reached with the Olympic Games of 1936 when Berlin *en fête* acted as host to the world.

Failure to attend or at least to hang out a flag on either the annual or special occasions was duly noted by the local party block warden, and might well lead to being identified as "politically unreliable," with consequences that could range from failure to secure promotion at work—or dismissal— to arrest and appearance in court. The same consequence could result from failure to contribute to the continual collections for the Winter Relief Program and Days of National Solidarity. This was equally true of the professional or "voluntary" associations that people were badgered into joining.

The objective was, literally, to leave no one alone, to allow no one to contract out or escape being involved, in their leisure activities as well as at work and at home. Of course the objective was never achieved. The "inner emigration" was more than a phrase and many people became adept at insulating themselves against the continual blare of propaganda and working out the minimum of conformity necessary to survive—exactly as they did in Stalin's Russia. Nonetheless, the overriding effect on most people, even if they grumbled, was to produce acceptance of National Socialism as something inevitable; and the rest could only retire into isolation. As one socialist observer reported to Sopade (the exiled SPD in Prague) in November 1935:

> The purpose of all Nazi mass organizations is the same. Whatever one thinks of the Labor Front, or Strength through Joy, or the Hitler Youth, everywhere they serve the same purpose: to involve or to look after the "national comrades," not to leave them to themselves, and if possible not to let them think at all . . . to prevent any real common ground, any voluntary combination from coming about. . . . The essence of Nazi control of the masses is compulsory organization on the one hand and domination on the other.[36]

The enmity between the Communist and Socialist parties, which had destroyed any possibility of a united front against the Nazis, did not alter the fact that there were thirteen million working-class voters hostile to the Nazis and still over twelve million of them prepared to defy Nazi threats after the takeover of power, and to vote against them in March 1933. Hitler's priority had long been to destroy the organizations of the KPD and SPD, arrest and beat up their leaders, close down their papers, and seize their assets. That done, however, a major objective became to win back their supporters for the "national community." The idea of national unity could be relied on to attract massive support from the middle classes. The crucial test was how far it could extend its reach beyond the middle classes into that sector of German society where for more than half a century the German working-class movement had been built up on belief in the inevitability of class conflict.

One of the achievements of the regime, but one that the workers could hardly be expected to appreciate, was its success in holding wage rates down. The average real value of weekly wages rose from a base of 100 in 1932 (the bottom of the Depression) to 123 in 1939, no more than 5 points above the figure for 1929 when the Depression had still to strike home. Prices were also controlled, with particular attention to food prices: These rose above the average figure for 1933–34, but remained, up to the final year of the war, below that for 1928–29. Levels of food consumption, however, increased only marginally between the crisis year of 1932 and 1938, with constant complaints about the shortage of fats. There were constant complaints, also, about the quality of textiles and other goods in which a high percentage of *Ersatz* (substitute) materials were used. Finally, as the labor shortage became more severe, limits were placed on freedom to change jobs, beginning with specific industries and agriculture, culminating in 1938 in a general power to conscript labor for work on the construction of the West Wall and in the munitions industries. [37]

But these facts give an incomplete picture. For example, out of a total labor force of twenty-three million, only a million were conscripted for work in 1938–39, fewer than 300,000 of these on a regular basis, the rest for limited periods. Similarly, the low figure overall for an increase in average wage rates conceals the fact that workers in industries involved in the rearmament boom were much better off. Above all, Hitler had ended unemployment. This was far and away the most important fact for the millions of working-class families who had known what it meant to be out of work, and without hope of it, only a few years before. Here was the great difference between the early 1930s and the middle and later years of the decade.

Excluded from trade-union activities and collective bargaining, Ley's Labor Front (DAF) built up the largest of the Nazi empires before the end of the decade, overshadowing the party itself. It operated on a scale that far eclipsed its original inspiration, the *Dopo il lavoro* of Fascist Italy, and Ley was not exaggerating when he claimed that no other country in the contemporary world, capitalist or socialist, offered its workers such facilities.

One reason for the DAF's success was the resources it could command. It started with the assets confiscated from the trade unions and built up an income more than three times that of the party from the dues of the theoretically voluntary but virtually compulsory membership of the industrial workers and their employers. By 1939 it was employing 44,500 paid functionaries and owned banks, insurance companies, housing associations, travel agencies, even the Volkswagen car plant destined to provide—some-day—the People's Car.

The link between the DAF's multifarious activities was the attempt to provide psychological in addition to—or as the skeptical said, in place of—material satisfaction. Like the Hitler Youth and the Reich Labor Service (with its compulsory period of physical labor for all young men, beginning with all students), the DAF set out to raise the status of manual work and the manual worker. Hitler repeatedly laid stress on the greater equality of status and the increased equality of opportunity and social mobility (for example, in the armed forces) offering, as the sociologist David Schoenbaum puts it, a labor ideology in place of a labor policy. The last thing he thought of doing was carrying out a social revolution on Stalin's model: "Beneath the cover of Nazi ideology, the historic social groups continued their conflicts like men wrestling under a blanket."[38]

WITH A WORK FORCE of twenty-three million, it is impossible to say how much the workers were convinced. From the many reports, however, both from the Gestapo and other Nazi agencies, and from those sent to the exiled SPD headquarters abroad, it appears possible to distinguish between three broad tendencies.[39] One reflected the attitudes of those who had been closely involved with the KPD, the SPD, and the trade unions, and who continued to see the Nazis as the enemy. Many of them had been arrested and roughly handled in 1933–34; some took part in active opposition, such as distributing pamphlets, at least until the big Gestapo crackdown on "Marxist" underground organizations in 1935; all of them tried in some way to keep in touch and help one another to survive and not abandon their beliefs. At the other extreme was another grouping, for the most part younger than the first, who either swallowed uncritically what they were told or were ambitious and realized that the way to advance themselves was to get on board the Nazi bandwagon.

The evidence suggests that the largest group belonged neither to the irreconcilable nor to the converted. They accepted what was offered by the DAF and gave the regime some credit for it, as for full employment; they grumbled about shortages and restrictions, but in a nonpolitical way, absorbed with their own affairs and accepting the regime passively without enthusiasm as something you put up with, like the weather.

Their attitude is well described in a report to the SPD in June 1936, shortly after one of the big successes of the regime, the remilitarization of the Rhineland:

Wherever one goes one can see that people accept National Socialism as something inevitable. The new state with all its institutions is there, one cannot get rid of it. The great mass has come to terms with this situation to such an extent that it no longer thinks about how the situation could be changed. . . .

The Nazis have succeeded in achieving one thing: the de-politicization of the German people . . . in persuading the masses to leave politics to the people at the top. . . . The Nazis try to turn everybody into committed National Socialists. They will never succeed in that. People tend rather to turn away inwardly from Nazism. But the Nazis are ensuring that people are no longer interested in anything. And that is at least as bad from our point of view.[40]

Looking at the broader spectrum of popular opinion, including, but not limiting it to, working-class opinion, most observers agreed that during the mid-1930s there were certain features of the regime that were viewed positively. High among them was the image of Hitler as a man of the people, above politics, clearly distinguished from the Nazi party, which by no means shared his popularity. Hitler was seen as providing Germany, for the first time since Bismarck, with the authoritarian leadership that many Germans in all classes regarded as the authentic German political tradition. The contrast with Weimar was underlined by his success, not yet offset by fear of involvement in a second war, of which there was no suggestion until the Czech crisis of 1938. On the contrary, Hitler, the ex-combatant, presented himself and the Germans as peace-loving people who had seen too much of war ever to contemplate another. Still less was anything said of Hitler's secret agenda: a war of conquest and the foundation of a racist empire in the east.

How far all the Nazis' efforts succeeded in producing an ideologically committed nation, particularly in the age groups under forty, is one of the questions about the Third Reich that most likely will never be settled. Even if one could begin to quantify individual attitudes and improbably produce, let us say for the sake of argument, convincing statements that 50 percent of the age group were more than 50 percent converted to the Nazi value system, the result would look significantly different according to whether one used the figures to show that "the glass was half full" or "half empty." Expert opinion is as much divided about the answer as it is about the question of whether the Nazis represented more of a break with, or a logical continuation of, attitudes already developed in earlier, pre-1914 Germany. Of course, there was some continuity; the question to which there is no agreed answer is how important or representative it was.

So, if we press the question of how far the Nazis succeeded in indoctrinating the younger half of the German population, who bore the brunt of the Second World War, we can choose between two answers. The first is Hitler's own confession of failure given in the privacy of the bunker in the last days of the Third Reich (February 25, 1945) and recorded by Martin Bormann:

From my own point of view, the ideal thing would have been . . . to form a youth imbued deeply with the National Socialist doctrine—and then to have left it to future generations to wage the inevitable war. . . .

The task I have undertaken is unfortunately not a task that can be accomplished by a single man or in a single generation.[41]

The second is the fact, for which Hitler showed not the slightest trace of gratitude, that after six years of war, during the last two and a half of which the German armies were forced to retreat step by step and German cities were blasted first by bombs, then by artillery and tanks, the German people, without hope and in the face of overwhelming Allied superiority, did not break until Hitler himself released them by committing suicide.

Half empty, or half full?

VI

BEHIND PROPAGANDA and organization stood the third and ultimate resource of terror. During the mid-1930s the implicit threat of it was more important than its use. Not only were Hitler's success and popularity on the rise, but also with rearmament still at risk he was concerned to avoid hostile reaction abroad—such as a boycott of German goods or a move to prevent the Olympic Games from being held in Berlin—which could disturb cooperation with his conservative allies.

The wave of Gestapo arrests in 1935 had broken up the Communist, socialist, and trade-union underground organizations, and the numbers in the three concentration camps still in use fell to their lowest point, 7,500, in the winter of 1936–37. Even for the Jews, the essential ideological enemy for the Nazis, 1936–37 was, relatively speaking, the quietest time during the Third Reich, and a number of Jews who had emigrated ventured to return.

This did not mean, however, any slackening in the insidious campaign, in schools as well as in films and other media, designed to "fix" the image of the Jews as pariahs and "vermin," not part of the human race. By 1939 this conditioning process had produced a significant change in psychological and social attitudes, especially among the younger generation. Subject to local attacks on their families and businesses, Jews were increasingly excluded from the economic recovery, from social welfare, from education and the professions, and so, effectively, "ghetto-ized." The Nuremberg Laws of 1935 forbade marriage or sexual relations outside marriage between "Germans" and Jews, and forbade Jews to employ "German" women as domestic servants or display the German national flag. The Reich Citizenship Law passed at the same time deprived Jews of German citizenship, redefining their status as "subjects." It is now known, however, that these were hurriedly introduced at the Party Congress in September 1935 as a sop to impatient Nazi veterans rather than to encourage further outrages. Hitler's obsession with the Jews remained as strong as ever but the lengths to which he was prepared to go in giving expression to it in action were governed by expediency and grew by stages, the last of which was only reached with the invasion of Russia in the summer of 1941.*

The years 1936 to 1938, however, saw the preparation of the SS for the role it was to play later in the countries occupied by Germany, especially in Eastern Europe. After the initial period of terrorism in 1933–34, the ministries of the Interior and Justice made strenuous efforts to bring the Gestapo's operations within the limits of the law. The merger of the police with the SS in June 1936 signaled their defeat. Himmler made clear the scope that he claimed for his combined force when he addressed the police law panel of the German Law Academy on October 11 of the same year. He told his audience that from the time he became police president of Munich in March 1933:

> I worked on the assumption that it did not matter in the least if our actions were contrary to some paragraph in the law; in working for the Führer and the German people, I basically did that which my conscience and common sense told me was right. The fact that others were bemoaning "violations of the law" was completely immaterial when the life and death of the German people were at stake. . . . They called it lawlessness because it did not correspond to their conception of law. In fact by what we did we laid the foundations for a new code of law, the law of destiny of the German people. [42]

The major expansion of the SS took place with the beginning of the war and the appointment of Himmler to carry out the policy of racial "resettlement" in occupied Poland. But Himmler continued to build up its strength during the 1930s, deliberately giving it an elitist character, and attracting recruits whenever he could from the aristocracy and upper-middle class as well as from among university graduates. At the same time, Heydrich worked to raise the standards of the Gestapo and integrate it with the SS, while Theodor Eicke, who had laid down the basic regulations when commandant of Dachau and combined brutality with efficiency, took over the training of the SS guard battalions as inspector of concentration camps.

Among Heydrich's protégés was Adolf Eichmann, appointed deputy head of the section that in December 1937 was given responsibility for "the centralization of the entire work on the Jewish question in the hands of the SD and Gestapo." Among Eicke's protégés was Rudolf Höss, the future commandant of Auschwitz. By March 1938, the first SS detachments to serve outside the Reich were ready to move into Austria immediately behind the army and carry out a trial run in the activities that were to make their name feared and hated throughout Europe.

THERE WERE several reasons for Hitler's decision in the autumn of 1937 to adopt a more radical and aggressive policy.

*See below, pp. 583–89 and pp. 747–57. In 1933, there were 503,000 Jews in Germany according to the Reich Statistical Office, less than 1 percent of the population.

The first was the growing impatience he felt with the restraints imposed by the alliance with the conservative elements in the armed forces, government, and business. This was illustrated by the long-drawn-out wrangle with Schacht over economic policy. At the Nuremberg Trials after the war, Speer recalled a visit to the Berghof in the summer of 1937:

> While I was waiting on the terrace I heard a loud discussion between Schacht and Hitler coming from Hitler's room. Hitler's voice rose to a very high pitch. When the discussion was over Hitler came out onto the terrace in an obviously excited mood and declared to those around him that he could not work with Schacht. He had just had a serious argument with him. Schacht with his finance methods would disturb his plans. [43]

Hitler always found it hard to stomach argument or disagreement, but hitherto he had put up with Schacht's criticisms of Göring and the Four-Year Plan because he thought that Schacht's continued presence at the Ministry of Economics was essential if the regime was to retain the confidence of the business community at home and abroad. Schacht naturally agreed. But Hitler now began to ask himself if it any longer mattered whether Schacht stayed or went.

A second reason was his awareness of disillusionment among the *Alte Kämpfer* in the party that the revolution they had looked forward to had, like so many revolutions in the past, ended in compromise with the existing order and the repudiation of the SA and the other elements that made up the radical wing of the party. The Nuremberg Laws had been a gesture toward them, a token that their confidence in the Führer had not been misplaced. But they needed more than gestures to keep their support. It was also a year and a half since the last great success, the Rhineland, and the Hitler myth needed reinforcement by further proof of his inspired leadership.

Martin Broszat points to a third factor when he writes of Hitler's own "panic-ridden anxiety in 1937/8 that—after the preceding period of relative moderation—it might not be possible to take off for the great final aims." [44] Later, looking back after the change had been made, Hitler told a private meeting of newspaper editors on November 10, 1938, after Munich:

> Circumstances forced me to talk almost exclusively of peace. Only by constantly laying stress on Germany's desire for peace was it possible for me to win freedom for the German people bit by bit and to provide the nation with the arms that were necessary as the prerequisite to the next step.
>   It is obvious that such peace propaganda also has its dubious aspects; for it can easily lead to fixing in many people's minds the idea that the present regime is identical with the decisions and the desire to preserve peace in all circumstances.
>   That, however, would lead to a false view of the aims of this system. Above all, it would lead to the German people's . . . becoming imbued

with a spirit that in the long run would amount to defeatism and would undo the achievements of the present regime.

I spoke only of peace for so many years because I had to. It has now become necessary to bring about a gradual psychological change in the German people's course and make it realize, slowly, that there are things that must, if they cannot be carried through by peaceful means, be carried through by force and violence. . . .

This work has required months; it has begun systematically; it is being continued and reinforced.[45]

The conviction that he must act quickly to recover the initiative was reinforced by anxiety about his own health. In an address to the leading propagandists in October 1937, he said, according to the notes of one of the participants:

As far as man's knowledge could go, he did not have long to live. People did not grow old in his family. . . .

It was therefore necessary to solve the problems that had to be solved [*Lebensraum*] as quickly as possible. . . . Later generations would no longer be able to do it. Only he himself was still in a position to. . . . After grave inner struggles he had freed himself from what remained of his childhood religious notions. "I now feel as fresh as a colt in a pasture."[46]

It was not, however, religious or moral scruples that had held Hitler back but uncertainty about the risks he could afford to take. Would the army and industry withdraw their cooperation in rearming Germany if he let Schacht go and got rid of the conservative leadership with which he had renewed the tacit compact in the summer of 1934? If they did, would this endanger his own position?

Hitler gave his answer in the New Year of 1938. All he would say in public in November 1937 was:

I am convinced that the most difficult part of the preparatory work has already been achieved. . . . Today we are faced with new tasks, for the *Lebensraum* of our people is too narrow.[47]

TWELVE

The Revolution,
Like Saturn,
Devours Its Children

"There is reason to fear that, like Saturn, the revolution
may devour each of its children in turn."
                                    —Pierre Vergniaud, Paris 1793[1]

STALIN   1934–1939   *(Age 54–59)*

I

WHILE HITLER between 1934 and 1938 accepted the need to curb
radical excesses and allow a period of accommodation and restraint,
Stalin in the same years moved in the opposite direction. The rigors of the
campaign for collectivization and the first Five-Year Plan were followed, not
by a period of relaxation, which many in the Communist party believed
necessary, but by a renewal of the "revolution from above," culminating in
a reign of terror, directed this time not against the peasantry and the
survivors of capitalism, but in successive waves of arrests, trials, and purges
against the party itself.

In the 1950s, when political scientists were attempting to create a model
of the totalitarian state, these Russian purges were seen as a response to the
functional needs of the single-party state, an "instrument of permanent
instability" which was a necessary requisite of totalitarianism *as a system.*[2]
This, however, is one of those reassuringly impersonal generalizations that
explain nothing. For the key questions are *"Whose* needs was it a response
to?" and *"Whose* hand guided the instrument?"

Far from meeting the needs of the Soviet regime *as a system,* Khrushchev
was surely right when he told the Twentieth Party Congress that the purges
and trials of the 1930s came close to wrecking it.

> Only because our party has such great moral-political strength was it
> possible to survive the difficult events in 1937–38 and to educate new
> cadres. There is, however, no doubt that our march forward toward
> socialism and toward the preparation of the country's defense would
> have been much more successful if it had not suffered so tremendous a
> loss of cadres as a result of the baseless and false mass repressions in
> 1937–38.[3]

Once the process was set in motion, of course, it acquired a momentum
and a multiplier effect of its own, if only as a result of the method of forced

denunciation practiced by the NKVD, the successor to the OGPU. But who, within the system, set the process in motion, continued to direct it, and decided when it was in danger of going too far? It was not the political leadership of the party as a whole, the Politburo and the Central Committee; not the governmental bureaucracy or the High Command of the armed forces who provided the driving force: It was against them that it was directed, and it was they who supplied the most prominent of its victims. Nor was it the Party Secretariat or the NKVD; they were the instruments of the process, not its originators.

In Russia the climax of the purges became known as the *Yezhovschina,* or the "time of Yezhov," after the head of the NKVD in 1937–38; but as Khrushchev made clear, Yezhov was only Stalin's creature and was himself eliminated when Stalin found it convenient to make him a scapegoat for "excesses." It was not the *Yezhovschina* but the *Stalinschina,* the "time of Stalin." For it was Stalin who grasped the value of terror, not simply as a response to an emergency—as in the collectivization campaign—but as a permanent "formula of rule."⁴ It was Stalin who initiated the purges of the mid-1930s and renewed the process after the war, not only repeating it in Russia but exporting the formula to purge the satellite regimes of Eastern Europe.

BY ANY ordinary human standards, both Stalin and Hitler were abnormal. For laymen to debate, however, whether this means they were either clinically or legally insane is an unprofitable exercise. For whatever their psychological condition, in neither case did it disable them from functioning as masterly politicians, at least until the final period of their lives. Among the many people who had to deal with Stalin at close quarters, and who survived to give their impressions, it is hard to find one prepared to say that he was mad. On the contrary, he left the impression of a man in full possession of his faculties who knew what he was doing, retained control of the situation, and maintained his normal routine, even when the fear and tension in Moscow became almost unbearable. At every stage Stalin remained several moves ahead of the other players in the grim political game that was played out in Russia between 1934 and 1939, constantly surprising them by the subtlety of his calculation, the depth of his duplicity, and above all by the lengths to which he was prepared to go in ruthlessness. In fact the paranoid tendencies that were his most distinctive psychological characteristic were highly functional in such a situation, making it easier for him to satisfy both his political and his psychological needs at the same time, each reinforcing the other.

His *political* needs in the mid-1930s were threefold. The first was to overcome the opposition to and criticism of his policies within the party. This had existed, although muted, during the crisis of collectivization. It surfaced in 1933–34 as pressure for relaxing the drive to secure better economic results by coercion, for making concessions to the working population, and for reconciliation with former oppositionists. Although for tactical reasons Stalin gave the impression that he was ready to go at least partway with such a program, even at the Congress of Victors (January 1934), where he had declared "there is nothing more to prove and, it seems, no one to fight," he had gone on immediately to warn against the "ideological confusion" that led some members of the party to suppose that the class struggle was over and the dictatorship of the proletariat could therefore be moderated. In fact there is no reason to suppose that Stalin ever changed his view that relaxation would risk losing all that had been gained so far, that the pressure had to be kept up, not reduced—and that in any alternative scenario there would be no place for him or the emergency powers he exercised.

Stalin saw his second need as not only to defeat the opposition on this particular issue, but also to attack and root out the source of opposition and criticism in the collegial structure of the party leadership and the tradition of intraparty democracy. Stalin found it more and more irksome to have to listen to the opinions of colleagues like Kirov and Ordzhonikidze, who presumed to hold independent views and on occasion to disagree with him. Only those like Molotov and Kaganovich who saw their role as carrying out, not questioning, his wishes were acceptable to him, not as colleagues, but as agents.

Even less did he trust such former oppositionists as Zinoviev and Kamenev, Bukharin and Rykov, who had made their submission and been readmitted to the party, but whose earlier record he had neither forgotten nor forgiven. Sooner or later they would have to be eliminated for good, along with all those other Old Bolsheviks who still thought of themselves as members of Lenin's party and did not realize that this was now Stalin's party, and that Stalin, unlike Lenin, did not regard himself as first among equals, did not admit there were equals, and already saw himself as an autocrat whose nod was final.

The logical conclusion of this was a move from a single-party to a single-ruler state. This was a conclusion from which Stalin did not draw back. Believing that he was the only man who understood how to govern Russia and complete the revolution, he was also convinced that he was the only man with the strength of will to carry through the necessary measures—provided he was not hampered by the need to pay attention to any other person or institution (such as the party). The third and ultimate stage of Stalin's program, therefore, was to get rid of all such hindrances and govern alone.

No more than Hitler did Stalin foresee how he would carry out such a program. But there were signs already in 1932 of the direction in which it was likely to point, in the anger he showed when opposition in the Politburo and the Central Committee prevented him from having Ryutin and his associates shot for circulating a 200-page "platform" that called for Stalin's replacement as the "evil genius of the Revolution." Stalin's ability to dissemble and conceal his thoughts, however, stood him in good stead at the Congress of Victors and afterwards. While apparently agreeing to the relaxation that Kirov, Ordzhonikidze, and other "moderates" pressed for, he was already quietly making preparations for a counterattack and moving subordinates he could rely on into key positions from which he could exploit a suitable opportunity. We do not know at what stage these preparations crystallized into a plan of action, or how far he foresaw in 1934–35 the lengths to which he would ultimately pursue it—any more than he had when launching collectivization. Like Hitler, Stalin could afford to be an opportunist because, unlike his opponents, he was clear about his aims.

The other great advantage Stalin shared with Hitler was that his political aims corresponded with his psychological nature and needs. As has been said earlier, two features of Stalin's psychology were most important. The first was his narcissistic personality, characterized by his total self-absorption, his inability to see other people as real in the same sense that he saw himself, and his conviction that he was a genius marked out to play a unique historical role. The second was the paranoid tendency that led him to picture himself as a great man facing a hostile world peopled with jealous and treacherous enemies engaged in a conspiracy to pull him down, if he did not strike and destroy them first. Typical of the paranoid's mental world was the systematic nature of the delusions that obsessed him: He was ceaselessly occupied in collecting evidence from which to erect and then buttress the logical structure that sustained it.

Throughout his life Stalin had a psychological need to confirm and reassure himself about both these beliefs. There is an obvious convergence between the first of these and Stalin's ultimate political aim. The same obsession that had provided the drive to defeat his rivals and match Lenin's revolution with his own now drove him to outdo his predecessor by freeing himself from the constraints of the party and becoming the sole ruler of the Soviet state.

Even more striking is the coincidence between Stalin's second psychological need—that is, to reassure and confirm his belief about himself by fitting events in the external world into his own mental framework—and his political aim, in the years 1934–39, to destroy the original Bolshevik party created by Lenin and replace it with a new one, maintaining a facade of continuity but in fact remaking it in his own image.

In this new version, a central role was found for Trotsky as the chief "enemy of the Soviet people." Not content with exiling Trotsky to Alma-Alta, where he remained a potential rallying point for opposition, in 1929 Stalin ordered him to be deported to Turkey, from which Trotsky moved on to France, then to Norway, before finding asylum in Mexico in 1936. Instead of silencing Trotsky, this had the effect of giving him greater freedom. In 1933 he set up a Fourth International of socialist groups which accepted his leadership. These never attracted much support, but Trotsky's polemical power as a writer found a worldwide audience for his denunciation of the Soviet regime's "degeneration" in a stream of articles, pamphlets and books, amongst the latter, *My Life, The History of the Russian Revolution, The Stalin School of Falsification,* and *The Revolution Betrayed.*

Trotsky's writings were banned in the Soviet Union, but his attacks infuriated Stalin. Every one of Trotsky's articles and books was collected and where necessary translated especially for him. Trotsky's opposition activities, blown up into a full-scale conspiracy, provided the perfect focus for Stalin's paranoia. Whatever else was alleged, a standard accusation in the trials that followed was "belonging to and acting under the instruction of the Trotskyist center." To take only one example, in the summing up of the second Moscow trial of Pyatakov and the sixteen other defendants, Trotsky's name occurred no less than fifty-one times.

The scenario of conspiracy and treachery that hundreds of NKVD investigators were employed in fabricating as the basis of the indictments in the purges and trials was a remodeling of history to match Stalin's personal myth and suit his political needs. The millions who were arrested, shot, or dispatched to the camps—like the kulaks before them—were acting out in real life a morality play which Stalin directed and in which Trotsky was cast as Satan. What more compelling assurance could there be of its objective truth than the three great show trials in which no evidence was presented, but one after another of the surviving members of Lenin's original party stood up and repeated the confessions written for them by the NKVD, accusing themselves in public of the most improbable crimes which, but for the vigilance of Stalin, would have betrayed the revolution and destroyed the Soviet Union?

Successive versions refined the details and enlarged the scope of the indictment. The final trial in 1938 brought together, in a consolidated script, all the charges—against left oppositionists, right oppositionists, Trotskyites; acts of wrecking and sabotage in industry and agriculture, attempts at assassination and espionage on behalf of foreign intelligence agencies. The principal target was none other than Bukharin, the man Lenin had described as "the favorite of the whole party," now, like Lucifer, another "favorite son" cast out of heaven on a charge of rebellion and plotting to murder his beloved master, Lenin. Lenin's entire original leadership group—Trotsky, Zinoviev and Kamenev, Bukharin, Rykov and Tomsky— were implicated and condemned; all, with the exception of Stalin.

Viewing the bizarre events of 1934–39 in Russia from the outside, it is hard not to regard them as an expression of madness, but not if one puts oneself in the context within which Stalin was operating. Within that context Stalin pursued his objectives not only ruthlessly but rationally, with a logic that was consistent both politically and psychologically.

I I

EVGENIA GINZBURG opened her book *Into the Whirlwind,* in which she described her own arrest in 1937, with the words: "That year, 1937, really began on December 1, 1934"—the day Kirov was assassinated. At first sight, this is surprising. After an initial burst of activity during December and the first six months of 1935, the crisis appeared to subside, and the period from July 1935 to August 1936 was to outward appearances one of relaxation. Ginzburg was right, however. The Kirov case gave Stalin the opportunity he needed. It reappeared in all three of the Moscow show trials and provided him with the Archimedean point from which to move the Soviet world.

There are two possible explanations of what happened, and why Kirov's murder should have immediately assumed so much importance.[5]

The first and official explanation was that it showed Stalin and the other members of the Politburo the danger in which the regime and they themselves stood, the necessity not to relax but to redouble their efforts to stamp out those elements who would never rest content until the revolution had been overthrown. The honors paid to the murdered man, including a state funeral in which Stalin was one of the guards of honor, lent support to the official version. Kirov was presented as a victim of counterrevolutionary violence, a view confirmed by the investigations and trials, which continued for another four years, revealing, in the confessions of the accused, how widespread and threatening a conspiracy lay behind the attack.

The other and more likely explanation is that Stalin planned or at least authorized the murder himself, and that it was intended to strike down the man whom he saw as the potential leader of any move to replace him and turn the country toward more moderate policies. Having gotten rid of him and thereby having delivered a severe blow—as well as a powerful warning—to any opposition group that might be forming in the party, Stalin doubled the advantage this brought him by treating Kirov dead, when he could no longer answer back, as a loyal supporter: "Stalin's best friend and comrade-in-arms," a revolutionary hero who had died at the post of duty. This allowed him to denounce the critical tendency, with which Kirov alive had identified himself, as counterrevolutionary terrorism responsible for his death. "The enemy," *Pravda* declared, "did not fire at Kirov personally. No! He fired at the proletarian revolution."[6]

The full truth about Kirov's murder may never be known. But as in the case of another mystery—who started the Reichstag fire?—what mattered most was not who was responsible for his death, but the use that was made of it. As soon as he received the news of Kirov's death, Stalin issued an emergency decree, without waiting for the Politburo's approval. In three short sections this directed investigating agencies to speed up the cases of those accused of preparing acts of terror, instructed judicial organs not to hold up the execution of death sentences in such cases (since the possibility of pardon could not be considered), and ordered the NKVD to carry out death sentences immediately after they had been passed.

That done, Stalin left at once for Leningrad, traveling overnight by special train and taking with him his closest associates, Molotov, Voroshilov, and Zhdanov, as well as a powerful NKVD team. Upon his arrival he took over the investigation personally, so capturing the initiative and with it a perfect justification for any measures he might take to liquidate those who were implicated by the NKVD's investigations.

There is no doubt that the assassin, Nikolayev, acted out of personal rather than political motives. He was a misfit who had failed to keep an official post to which he believed he was entitled and had been expelled from the party for refusing to take one involving manual labor. As a result, he had conceived a deep hatred of the bureaucracy and planned Kirov's murder as a protest against the injustice of which he believed he was the victim.

However, Nikolayev could never have obtained admission to the Smolny Institute, the party's Leningrad headquarters, if the usual guards on each floor had not been withdrawn. At the same time, Kirov's personal bodyguard was detained and prevented from accompanying his boss into the building. In the course of the investigation, it emerged that the NKVD was responsible for removing the guards, knew all about Nikolayev and his grudge, had twice arrested him on earlier occasions when he was found in the vicinity of Kirov with a revolver—and had twice released him despite the protests of those on guard duty. It was later revealed that the NKVD was responsible for a faked "accident" in which Borisov, Kirov's bodyguard, was killed while being driven to the Smolny to give evidence to Stalin and the other investigators. Those who were involved in the "accident" were subsequently liquidated. [7]

After his arrest Nikolayev evidently realized that he had been used by the NKVD and, when asked by Stalin why he had shot Kirov, replied by pointing to the NKVD officers present and shouting that Stalin should ask *them*. Stalin, however, was not interested in Nikolayev's personal motives or in the complicity of the NKVD. As a first step, under the new decree of December 1, 102 White Guards, who had recently been arrested on charges of terrorism (including a substantial number of Ukrainian intellectuals), were summarily tried and executed. They were not charged with Kirov's murder, but the announcement of their execution was the signal for an intensified press campaign against "enemies of the people." This was Stalin's real interest, to show that the assassination of Kirov was part of a far-reaching conspiracy. That was the directive he gave to Yezhov, a key figure in the Central Committee Secretariat, whom he put in political control of the case, and to Ya. D. Agranov, who was now appointed to conduct the investigation.

The fact that the murder had taken place in Leningrad, Zinoviev's onetime fiefdom, suggested that Zinoviev's former associates in the Leningrad Party Organization and Komsomol should be among the first to be arrested and investigated. Yezhov, visiting Moscow for further instructions, returned with a list in Stalin's own handwriting of the members of what came to be known as the Leningrad Terrorist Center as well as of a Moscow Center. The indictment, when published, charged that Nikolayev had killed Kirov on the order of the Center as part of a long-range plan for the assassination of Stalin and other party leaders. In return for the promise of his life, Nikolayev "confessed" that his original claim to have acted from personal motives had been invented, in agreement with the Zinovievite group, in order to conceal their participation and to represent Kirov's murder as an act of individual terrorism.

At the end of December, the trial of the Leningrad Center was held in camera before three judges, led by the unspeakable V. V. Ulrikh, who, together with Andrei Vyshinsky as prosecutor, was to perform the same parody of justice in one trial after another during the 1930s. The preparation of this particular case had been rushed and could not be held in public, because the majority of the accused would admit only to membership of the group and denied involvement in the murder. They were all condemned to death, including Nikolayev, despite the promise he had received, and were shot the same night in the cellars of the Liteini prison.

In the middle of December, Zinoviev and Kamenev, twice before arrested and expelled from the party and twice rehabilitated, had been arrested again in Moscow, together with five other former members of the Central Committee. By the time the indictment against them was drawn up in mid-January 1935, they had been joined by nine more former leading members of the party expelled in 1927 and then reinstated, making nineteen in all who were said to have formed an "underground counterrevolutionary Moscow Center" which "for a number of years had systematically guided the counterrevolutionary activities of both the Moscow and the Leningrad centers." At this stage, however, the charges against them were limited to the moral and political responsibility for the Leningrad group's resort to terrorism without evidence of their direct involvement in the Kirov murder. They were sentenced to five to ten years in prison.

At the same time the members of the Leningrad NKVD responsible for the failure to protect Kirov were charged with criminal negligence leading to his assassination. All pleaded guilty, but instead of the summary execution that would normally have followed, all, with one exception, received the mild sentence of two or three years' imprisonment. Only one, who was found guilty, in addition, of "illegal actions during the investigation"—possibly the "accident" to Kirov's bodyguard, Borisov—was given ten years. Contrary to all precedents, they were treated with "exceptional and unusual solicitude" by Yagoda, the head of the NKVD, and, when they ended up in Kolyma, the most isolated of the islands of the Gulag Archipelago, were rapidly given responsible posts, with every privilege, in the camp administration. This happy state of affairs continued until late 1937 when they were taken back to Moscow and shot.

More came to light at the trial of Yagoda himself in March 1938. At the time of Kirov's murder Yagoda was directly responsible to Stalin for all the operations of the Security Police. At his trial Yagoda confessed that he had then ordered the assistant chief of the Leningrad NKVD, Ivan Zaporozhets, "not to place any obstacles in the way of the terrorist act against Kirov," including the order to release Nikolayev after he had been arrested with a revolver, cartridges, and a chart of the route Kirov usually took, two months before the assassination. Subsequently Yagoda admitted that he had taken care to see that Zaporozhets and the other NKVD men were well looked after.

Yagoda told the court he acted this way because he had received orders to this effect from Abel Yenukidze, the secretary of the Central Executive Committee of the Congress of Soviets since 1918 and also, it was alleged, a member of the terrorist group—who had conveniently been shot six months before, in October 1937. When he had objected, Yagoda declared, Yenukidze had overruled him and insisted that he must obey the orders of the group. This was implausible since Yenukidze was in no position to insist that the much more powerful Yagoda should do anything. So the question remained, who else could have given Yagoda such orders?

In his "Secret Speech" to the Twentieth Party Congress in 1956, Khrushchev told the delegates:

> It must be asserted that to this day the circumstances that surrounded Kirov's murder hide many things that are inexplicable and demand a most careful examination. . . . After the murder, top functionaries of the Leningrad NKVD were given very light sentences but in 1937 were shot. We can assume that they were shot in order to cover the traces of the organizers of Kirov's killing. [8]

The careful examination proposed by Khrushchev was carried out in 1956 or 1957 by a Commission of Inquiry which had access to all the archives and interviewed hundreds of witnesses. But the commission's report has never been made public. At the Twenty-second Congress in 1961, Khrushchev repeated that the NKVD men "were killed in order to cover up all traces" and added: "The more deeply we study the materials relating to Kirov's death, the more questions arise." He was still not prepared, however, to mention the name that was on everyone's lips. In an extract from his memoirs finally published in 1989, Khrushchev left no doubt of his real opinion: "I believe that the murder was organized by Yagoda, who could have taken this action only on secret instructions from Stalin, received face-to-face." [9]

The trials and the accusations against Zinoviev and Kamenev, Bukharin and Rykov have been dropped from Soviet official publications, such as the party history, and Yenukidze, named in 1938 as the man who gave Yagoda his orders, was fully rehabilitated in 1962. So far, however, no other name has been substituted in his place.

THE POLITICAL SITUATION at the end of January 1935 was very different from that a year before, when the Congress of Victors had been meeting. Then, underneath the praise lavished on him, Stalin had been well aware of the support in the party for a policy of relaxation and had gone some way to meet it. Now the man he evidently saw as a potential rival was dead, and overnight he had recaptured the initiative with the cry of "the revolution is in danger." The party and the propaganda machine launched a campaign for unmasking "enemies of the people," and everyone who could be associated with the former Zinoviev-Kamenev opposition, however remotely, now felt themselves to be in danger of denunciation and arrest. As an example to the rest of the country, the purge in Leningrad—including supporters of Kirov as well as of Zinoviev—led to mass arrests and deportations, including whole families, in many cases of workers as well as former aristocrats, civil servants, and officers, and reaching a total by the end of March estimated at close to 100,000.

A general party purge ordered in January 1933 had already expelled as unsatisfactory 800,000 of the three and a half million members to which the party had grown during the first Five-Year Plan. Following Kirov's assassination the pressure was stepped up and given a much more political direction. A secret letter from the Central Committee in December 1934, "Lessons of the Events Connected with the Evil Murder of Comrade Kirov," the first of a series of such circulars, was sent to all party organizations, urging them to hunt down, expel, and arrest all suspected—or accused in mutual denunciation sessions—of oppositionist tendencies.

The members of the Leningrad Komsomol group whom the NKVD investigators had "associated" with Nikolayev in plotting to kill Kirov, although subjected to "severe interrogation" and eventually shot, refused to confess to the end and provided no evidence implicating Zinoviev or Kamenev. As a result the case against the two former opposition leaders was dropped on December 20 for lack of evidence. Further pressure on them allowed a trial to be mounted in January, but the most that could be established, or that they would admit, was links with the Leningrad Center, and a general moral and political responsibility for the spread of counterrevolutionary ideas, not direct involvement in Kirov's murder. This trial, too, was held in camera and not fully reported in the press.

Moderate opinion in the political leadership still resisted treating former members of the Politburo and the Central Committee too harshly, a fact that Stalin found it politic to recognize by himself proposing in the Politburo that the death penalty should not be considered for Zinoviev and Kamenev.

Stalin did not abandon his objectives, but evidently more time and preparation were needed. Hence the impression, which many shared both in Russia and abroad, that the crisis following Kirov's murder was over and the return to normalcy was resuming. The new slogan launched by Stalin was "Life has become better, comrades; life has become more joyous." [10] Material conditions began to show signs of improvement: Fine weather produced a bumper harvest in 1935, and it was possible to abolish rationing. More goods appeared in the shops, and prices fell. The second Five-Year Plan began to bear fruit: There was a steady rise in production of iron, steel, coal, and cement, at least by comparison with the very low figures for 1932 and 1933. The Stakhanovite movement took off in the latter part of 1935, leading to a much-publicized increase in productivity. At the same time, ranks were reintroduced into the Red Army, the pay and privileges of the officer corps increased, with a sharp rise in morale, and the first five marshals of the Soviet Union appointed—changes that Trotsky, the creator of the Red Army, described as a revolution.

The hopes of a new era dawning appeared to be confirmed by the decision to adopt a new constitution. Stalin appointed himself chairman of the constitutional commission and as an apparent gesture of reconciliation included Bukharin and Radek among its thirty members. In June 1936, the draft was published and the whole population invited to engage in a nationwide discussion of its contents. It was reported to have been "greeted with enormous enthusiasm and approved with one accord." Bukharin played a central role in drafting the charter, particularly the provision for universal suffrage, direct election by secret ballot, and the guarantees of civil rights for the citizen, including freedom of speech, freedom of the press, freedom of assembly, freedom of street demonstrations, and the right to personal property protected by law.

The text made clear that only one party would be permitted to exist and that all the rights granted were to be exercised "in conformity with the interests of the working class and in order to strengthen the socialist system." Despite the fatalism that led him to tell friends in Paris this same summer of 1936—correctly—that Stalin meant to kill him, Bukharin could not suppress the hope that the new constitution might mean that "people will have more room. They can no longer be pushed aside." [11] Stalin, in presenting the final draft to the Extraordinary All-Union Congress of Soviets, did not deny this. On the contrary, he boldly declared that the new constitution, which he took care should bear his name, "proceeds from the fact that there are no longer any antagonistic classes in our society; that it consists of two friendly classes, of workers and peasants; that it is these classes, the laboring classes, that are in power." [12] It was because of this absence of social conflict that it was possible to grant universal suffrage, secret ballots, and all the other rights of the citizen.

The exceptional prominence given to the constitution (which remained "in force" until 1989) and to the process of "discussion" by which it had been produced was aimed as much at impressing the Western world as the

Russian people. Soviet foreign policy, after Russia's entry into the League of Nations in 1934, was directed at building up collective security to restrain Hitler, and the Stalin Constitution was meant to impress Western opinion—as it undoubtedly did—with the acceptability of the Soviet Union as a society moving in a democratic direction with the full support of the Soviet peoples. Stalin concluded his speech to the Congress of Soviets with the declaration:

> The constitution of the USSR is the only thoroughly democratic constitution in the world. What millions of honest people in capitalist countries have dreamed of, and still dream of, has already been realized in the USSR . . . the victory of full and thoroughly consistent democracy. Its international significance . . . can hardly be exaggerated. Today, when the turbulent wave of fascism is bespattering the socialist movement of the working class and besmirching the democratic strivings of the best peoples in the civilized world, the new constitution of the USSR will be an indictment against fascism, declaring that socialism and democracy are invincible. It will give moral assistance and real support to all those who are today fighting fascist barbarism. [13]

Stalin was proved right in his belief that the 1936 constitution would make an extraordinary impression abroad; but by the time he made his speech (November 25, 1936) the Russian people—and the Communist party in particular—had begun to learn that its provisions were in practice compatible with a reign of terror.

Stalin himself had never had any doubt that they were compatible. While he allowed others to form hopes of a relaxation of pressure, with occasional gestures of encouragement, he continued to make preparations to renew his attack on the former opposition by discrediting them in a carefully staged public trial and establishing that no one, even if he had been a member of the Politburo, was immune from the death penalty.

The death of Valerian Kuibyshev, head of Gosplan, the State Planning Commission, left another vacancy in the Politburo, besides Kirov's place. Kuibyshev, like Kirov, is reported to have been a member of the group favoring a more moderate policy, and to have opposed the trial of Zinoviev and Kamenev. At the time, January 26, 1935, his death was said to be due to heart disease, but at the trial of Yagoda in 1938 it was attributed to deliberate medical mistreatment carried out on Yagoda's orders. No attempt was made to identify the person from whom Yagoda himself received such orders, and unless further evidence comes to light, the case remains open.

Stalin was able to secure Mikoyan, a man he could rely on, to fill one of the places (the other went to Vlas Chubar, who was subsequently executed), and another, Andrei Zhdanov, who had succeeded Kirov as the first secretary for Leningrad, as one of the two new candidate members. The other key post, that of first secretary for Moscow, went to Khrushchev, who was then, like Zhdanov, coming into prominence. Yezhov, a rising favorite of Stalin's, was promoted to be head of the party's Central Control Commission, with Malenkov, already in charge of the Cadres Department of the Secretariat, as his deputy, both positions from which continuing pressure could be kept on the regional party organizations to step up the purge.[14] Yagoda, as head of the NKVD, already reported directly and in secret to Stalin, and in June 1935 Vyshinsky, who was to be the chief prosecutor in the Moscow trials, was promoted to be procurator-general.

It is very unlikely that any of the group was taken into Stalin's confidence. He worked on the principle that each should know no more than was required to carry out orders: Those who looked doubtful or asked questions did not survive. Even some who did neither, but knew too much, were expendable, as Yagoda and Yezhov were to discover.

Two changes in Soviet law during the spring of 1935 provided Stalin with threats that could be used with great effect in securing evidence as confession. One extended all penalties, including the death penalty, down to twelve-year-old children (decree of April 7, 1935). The other (decree of June 9) provided the death penalty for flight abroad and made members of the "traitor's family," if he was serving in the armed forces, subject to up to twenty years' imprisonment if aware in advance of the offense, and to five years' exile if knowing nothing but either living with him or dependent on him. This was the introduction of the hostage system, soon extended to put families, including young children, automatically at risk if any of their number was suspected or denounced for any hint of dissent. The reform of the legal system also provided for treason cases to be tried by a specially created military collegium of the Supreme Court presided over by V. V. Ulrikh, who could be relied upon to conduct such trials in close cooperation with the NKVD.

The close personal relationship Stalin had established with the OGPU during the collectivization now proved its value. The reorganized People's Commissariat of Internal Affairs (NKVD) was responsible for the administration of labor camps (GULAG), of border and internal troops, and of militia. A special board of the NKVD was given the right of administrative (that is, nonjudicial) sentencing to terms of up to five years' exile, deportation, or imprisonment in camps.

The central core, however, remained the Chief Administration of State Security (GUGB), a group of Old Bolsheviks who had had long experience of security and terrorist operations, in many cases reaching back to the days of Dzerzhinsky's Cheka. While the party continued its purge operations at the middle and lower levels under constant prodding from the reorganized Party Control Commission and Poskrebyshev's Special Sector, the GUGB became the instrument of Stalin's assault on the upper echelons of the party and state bureaucracies, the Soviet leadership itself.

The NKVD officers were treated as a *corps d'élite,* with their own special uniform, quarters, and privileges. Yagoda, appointed commissar-general in

1935, ranked with the newly created marshals of the Soviet Union; his first deputy, Agranov, responsible for GUGB, the security side of the NKVD, and often referred to as a crony of Stalin's, ranked with the other five commissars of state security, Grade 1, as equivalent to full generals of the Red Army. The thirteen commissars in Grade 2, who were in their posts by November 1935, including the heads of the six principal departments of GUGB,[15] were equivalent in rank to colonel-generals in the army. This made them no more indispensable, however, in Stalin's eyes, than the officer corps of the Red Army: Of the twenty NKVD commissars listed in November 1935, including the commissar-general and his successor, every single man was sooner or later shot as an enemy of the people, with the exception of one murdered more informally. The NKVD was the last of the Soviet elites Stalin liquidated.

III

IN THE SPRING of 1935 some forty people were arrested in connection with an alleged plot to kill Stalin in the Kremlin. Stalin again attempted to involve the opposition. Kamenev had a brother, the painter Nikolai Rosenfeld, who was married to a doctor working in the Kremlin. With no more than this tenuous link to build on, Yezhov, as chairman of the Control Commission, demanded the death penalty for Kamenev. The resistance however remained strong enough to defeat him. Instead, at the end of July 1935, Kamenev was sentenced to ten years' further imprisonment; his brother appeared as a witness against him. Two other prominent Old Bolsheviks lost their jobs: Abel Yenukidze, responsible for general supervision of the Kremlin, and the Latvian A. A. Peterson, the Kremlin commandant, who had commanded Trotsky's mobile headquarters train in the civil war. This was followed by the dissolution of the Society of Old Bolsheviks and of the Society of Former Political Prisoners, carried out by special commissions, headed in the first case by Shkiryatov, and in the second by Yezhov, two of Stalin's most aggressive hatchet men.

The petty spite with which Stalin pursued personal grudges is illustrated by the case of Yenukidze. Yenukidze had enjoyed a close relationship with Stalin going back thirty-five years to the time when they were both young activists in Georgia. He had served as secretary of the Central Executive of the Congress of Soviets and had no connection with any of the opposition groups. He had, however, published memoirs of the early revolutionary movement in Transcaucasia. These were brought to Stalin's notice by Beria, another aspirant to Stalin's favor, and Yenukidze was obliged to write a signed article in *Pravda* (January 16, 1935) confessing that he had committed grave errors in exaggerating his own role and failing to do justice to Stalin's stature already at that early date. (One of the criticisms of the Society of Old Bolsheviks was that it had its own publishing house which printed members' memoirs. This was now closed down.) An intimate friend of the Alliluyev family, Yenukidze had been the godfather of Stalin's wife Nadezhda Alliluyeva, had made the funeral arrangements after her suicide, and was regarded by Stalin's daughter Svetlana as an uncle. This may have been an additional offense in Stalin's eyes.

Shortly after Yenukidze's expulsion from the party, Zhdanov and Khrushchev sought to please their patron by parallel attacks on Yenukidze in Leningrad and Moscow. The former accused him, "in the course of his infamous subversive work against the party and the Soviet state, of getting together the contemptible remnants of Fascist-Zinovievite-Kamenevite-Trotskyite groups and the chaff of bourgeois-landlord counterrevolutionaries." Arrested in 1937 and shot as a spy and traitor, Yenukidze was posthumously made responsible for Kirov's assassination by being named in the 1938 Moscow trial as the man who ordered Yagoda to organize his murder. He has since been completely rehabilitated.

Not only the veterans but also the Komsomol attracted Stalin's attention. The NKVD reported that, following the murder of Kirov, various younger groups had begun to talk of getting rid of Stalin. The NKVD had no difficulty in identifying and arresting these, but Stalin decided that the Komsomol as a whole needed purging. Its reorganization to eliminate "enemies of the people" was announced at the end of June 1935.

One of the Komsomol groups uncovered by the NKVD was in the Pedagogical Institute in the town of Gorki. Its members were about to be tried when the case was held back after instructions from above. One of the NKVD agents involved, Valentin Olberg, had worked earlier as an undercover informer in a Trotskyite group in Berlin and had tried to get a job as Trotsky's secretary. This offered an opportunity to establish a link between the Gorki group and Trotsky, and Olberg was ordered to "confess" that he had been sent by Trotsky to recruit professors and students willing to join a conspiracy to kill Stalin at the 1936 May Day Parade in Moscow. After further work to improve Olberg's story, a decision was made early in 1936 to make this the basis of the operation against the former opposition leaders for which Stalin had been pressing.

The head of the NKVD Secret Political Department, G. A. Molchanov, then held a conference of some forty NKVD executive officers who were told that a vast conspiracy had been uncovered and that they would all be released from their ordinary duties in order to investigate it. The Politburo regarded the "evidence" as settling the matter of the accused persons' guilt; all they had to do was to discover the details. It was not evidence that was required (none was ever presented) but confessions and denunciations. According to Alexander Orlov, an NKVD officer who defected and published an account in 1954,[16] the officers, who had been responsible for supervising the oppositionists for years, realized that the whole affair was a frame-up. But the tradition of public trials based upon fabricated plots had been established in the Shakhty affair in 1928, followed by a whole series of similar trials, the majority in camera, but some in public, such as that of the Ramzin Industrial party in 1930, the Menshevik trial in 1931, and the Metro-Vickers trial of 1933. The officers therefore understood what was expected of them and how to set about it.

In his secret speech of 1956 to the Twentieth Party Congress Khrushchev provided the two essential clues as to what Stalin was trying to do:

> Stalin originated the concept "enemy of the people." This term automatically rendered it unnecessary that the ideological errors of a man or men engaged in a controversy be proven; this term made possible the most cruel repression, violating all norms of revolutionary legality, against anyone who in any way disagreed with Stalin, against those who were only suspected of hostile intent. . . .
> This concept "enemy of the people" actually eliminated the possibility of any kind of ideological fight or the making of one's views known on this or that issue, even those of a practical character. [17]

In effect, disagreement with Stalin on any issue became not a matter of political opposition, but a capital crime, proof, ipso facto, of participation in a criminal conspiracy involving treason and the intention to overthrow the Soviet regime.

Stalin knew perfectly well that the conspiracy was a fiction, the scenario for which had been prepared on his orders and was constantly revised to meet his criticisms. Yet at another level of his consciousness he found no difficulty in believing that it was essentially true. His whole life had been spent in a conspiratorial atmosphere, a point well put by the former Yugoslav Communist leader, Milovan Djilas, when he was asked by G. R. Urban in a radio interview: "Was it the tradition of the conspiratorial party in which Stalin and his lieutenants had their roots, that lived on long after the need for conspiracy had ended?" Djilas replied:

> Ah, but this is the whole point—*had* the need for conspiracy ended? What my visit to Stalin taught me was that these men regarded themselves as appointed to rule over and against the will of the people. They acted like a group of conspirators . . . [in] a conquered land, not their own. Power for Stalin was a plot with himself as chief plotter as well as the one cast to be plotted against. [18]

If that was true in the 1940s, when Stalin was far more secure, it was much more likely to have been true from 1935 to 1938 when he was still engaged in establishing his supremacy. If it had been he and not his rivals who had been defeated, Stalin had no doubt that he would be looking for every opportunity to seek revenge and overthrow those in power. In fact, although there must have been individuals and groups among those accused who had talked about the possibility of getting rid of Stalin, no evidence has come to light to confirm the actual charges against them. They were fabrications put together by the NKVD on Stalin's direction.

As Robert Tucker says: "It need not be supposed that Stalin believed them literally. But they must have appeared to him as being true in principle, and false, if at all, in being embellishments on reality itself."[19] This is where Khrushchev's second clue comes in: "In actuality, the only proof of guilt used was the 'confession' of the accused himself; and, as subsequent probing proved, 'confessions' were acquired through physical pressures against the accused."[20]

Dzerzhinsky had always stressed the importance of confessions, and no other evidence was presented in the Shakhty trial of 1928. The same practice was followed in the Ramzin Industrial party trial, and again, with less success, in the Metro-Vickers case. To satisfy Stalin, those accused had to condemn themselves out of their own mouths. The method (including the use of prisoners as witnesses to incriminate one another) had been tried out and accepted before the Moscow trials, and the NKVD had this experience to draw on. The advantage from Stalin's point of view is obvious. By producing leading figures in Soviet history accusing themselves publicly of high treason, he supplied convincing proof of the political charges, and at the same time satisfied his own psychopathological needs.

In the course of the preparations for the trial Stalin is said to have had as many as 300 former members of the opposition already in prison or exile examined by the NKVD for their suitability to provide the eight political figures and eight accomplices, mainly *agents provocateurs,* who were to appear in court.

A "Trotskyite-Zinovievite Center" was now to be made directly responsible for the Kirov murder, as part of a terrorist campaign to wipe out Stalin and the rest of the top Soviet leadership. Zinoviev, Kamenev, and two more of their principal associates, G. E. Evdokimov and Ivan Bakayev, had been under arrest since December 1934 and had been put through a lengthy course of interrogation and negotiation for confession. With Trotsky himself out of reach, it was harder to provide a convincing representative of the Trotskyite side of the center. The choice eventually fell on Ivan Smirnov, a former factory worker who had been an active revolutionary since the age of seventeen and had fought in the 1905–1906 revolution and the civil war, during which he had led the Fifth Red Army to victory over Kolchak in Siberia. He had actually been proposed as general secretary of the party before the job went to Stalin—a fascinating might-have-been. Exiled with other Trotskyites in 1927, he had been in trouble again in the early 1930s when he had expressed support for Ryutin's proposal to remove Stalin and had been in jail since January 1933. Faced with Smirnov's objection that since he was in prison he could hardly have played a leading part in any conspiracy, Vyshinsky brushed it aside at the trial as "a naive assertion." A secret code had been discovered, he declared, which enabled Smirnov to maintain contact with the other members: This "proved" that he had been able to communicate with them, although no copy of the code—still less of any communication—was ever produced.

In mid-May Stalin held a conference with the NKVD officials and ordered them to produce further links between the conspiracy and Trotsky.

Two other NKVD agents besides Olberg were selected to do this, Fritz David and Berman-Yurin, who had been working in the German Communist party and the Comintern. They were arrested at the end of May and instructed to confess that they had each visited Trotsky and received orders from him to kill Stalin.

However, both Smirnov and Sergei Mrachkovsky, another Trotskyite who had fought in Siberia and run Trotsky's underground press in 1927, denied everything and refused to confess, although Mrachkovsky's interrogation is reported to have been maintained by relays of investigators for ninety hours on end, with Stalin telephoning periodically to find out whether he had yet been broken. Zinoviev, Kamenev, and Evdokimov proved equally obdurate, despite particular brutality in the treatment of the last named. When Mironov, the NKVD commissar in charge of the interrogation, reported this to Stalin, Orlov reports that the following exchange took place:

"You think that Kamenev may not confess?" Stalin asked. "I don't know," Mironov answered. "He doesn't yield to persuasion."

"You don't know?" Stalin inquired, staring at Mironov. "Do you know how much our state weighs, with all the factories, machines, the army, with all the armaments and the navy?"

Mironov and all those present looked at Stalin in surprise. "Think it over and tell me," demanded Stalin. Mironov smiled, believing Stalin was getting ready to make a joke.

"I am asking you, how much does all that weigh?" he insisted. Mironov was confused. But Stalin kept staring at him and waited for an answer. Mironov shrugged his shoulders and, like a schoolboy undergoing an examination, said in an irresolute voice, "Nobody can know that, Yosif Vissarionovich. It is in the realm of astronomical figures."

"Well, and can one man withstand the pressure of that astronomical weight?" asked Stalin sternly.

"No," answered Mironov.

"Now then, don't tell me that Kamenev, or this or that prisoner, is able to withstand that pressure. Don't come to report to me," Stalin said to Mironov, "until you have Kamenev's confession in this briefcase."[21]

While these preparations were taking place behind closed doors, another death occurred. Maxim Gorki, Russia's greatest living writer, whom Stalin had persuaded to return and lend his support to the regime, had fallen out of favor because he disapproved of the harassment of the opposition. He fell ill at the end of May and died on June 18. At the 1938 trial, the same doctors who were accused of murdering Kuibyshev were found guilty of poisoning Gorki as well, again acting on Yagoda's orders. The deaths of both men fell conveniently for Stalin: Whether he was responsible for them remains another open question.

During July and early August 1936 pressure was stepped up to secure the necessary confessions in time for the trial to be held in the vacation period when many members of the Central Committee including Stalin himself and the members of the Politburo would be away from Moscow. The pressure took a variety of forms: repeated beatings, torture, making prisoners stand or go without sleep for days on end, all-night interrogations, threats to the prisoners' families, confrontations with one another. Yezhov is reported to have told Zinoviev that Soviet intelligence was sure that Germany and Japan would attack the USSR in 1937. It was necessary to destroy Trotskyism in advance, and Zinoviev must help by publicly implicating Trotsky in the plot. If the defendants refused, the alternative was a closed trial and the execution of the entire opposition, including thousands in the camps. [22]

On the other hand, promises were held out that their own and their families' lives would be spared if they cooperated. Zinoviev and Kamenev finally accepted these promises, including guarantees for their supporters' lives and their families' liberty as well as lives. They asked for a meeting with the Politburo to confirm the terms, but had to be content with assurances given in a face-to-face interview with Stalin, Voroshilov, and Yezhov, acting (so they said) on behalf of the Politburo.

The confessions were not completed until the last few days before the trial began. Signatures were made easier to obtain by the publication on August 11 of a decree reestablishing public hearings and allowing the use of defense lawyers as well as appeals from the accused for three days after sentencing. Yezhov held a final conference with Zinoviev, Kamenev, and the other principal defendants in which he repeated Stalin's assurance that their lives would be spared but warned them that an attempt by any one of them at "treachery"—repudiating a confession—would implicate the whole group.

The indictment was published on August 15, only four days before the trial began. A violent press campaign, demanding "death to the traitors," was launched to coincide with it. Resolutions calling for them to be shot were passed by the workers in hundreds of factories, kolkhozes, and party organizations and reproduced in the press. Amid the pages crowded with these there also appeared "manifestos" from three prominent party leaders, Rakovsky, Rykov, and Pyatakov, also demanding the death penalty. Pyatakov wrote:

> One cannot find words fully to express one's indignation and disgust. These people have lost the last semblance of humanity. They must be destroyed like carrion that is polluting the pure, bracing air of the land of Soviets, dangerous carrion that may cause the death of our leaders. [23]

This gesture of submission did not prevent all three from being arraigned at subsequent trials, and Pyatakov and Rykov from suffering the death penalty they had demanded for their predecessors in the dock.

The trial was held in open court, with thirty-odd foreign journalists and diplomats present as well as an audience of 150 Soviet citizens, the majority selected by the NKVD from its own staff in case it was necessary to raise an uproar. The interrogators who had extorted the confessions from the prisoners sat facing them in the courtroom. No places were available for members of the Central Committee or relatives of the accused. The official line represented the charges as a matter for the judiciary,* not the political leadership, and Stalin himself took care to keep out of the way in his Black Sea retreat.

The proceedings, which lasted two days, consisted of Vyshinsky taking the accused through their "confessions" in which they fully admitted their part in setting up a terrorist center inspired by Trotsky. Two of Trotsky's supporters, Ivan Smirnov and E. S. Holtzmann, admitted belonging to the center but denied any part in terrorist acts such as the murder of Kirov and the various unsuccessful attempts that the center was alleged to have organized to kill Stalin and others. As the others, however, insisted that they had taken part, this made little difference.

Vyshinsky began his final speech by referring to Stalin's wisdom in forecasting, three years before: "the inevitable resistance of elements hostile to the cause of socialism . . . and the possibility of the revival of Trotskyite counterrevolutionary groups."[24] He ended with "the demand that these dogs gone mad should be shot—every one of them."

The last pleas of the accused continued their self-condemnation. Zinoviev, whose first expulsion and recantation had taken place in 1927, summed up his progressive decline into error: "My defective Bolshevism became transformed into anti-Bolshevism, and through Trotskyism I arrived at Fascism. Trotskyism is a variety of Fascism and Zinovievism is a variety of Trotskyism."[25] Khrushchev told the Twentieth Party Congress that sentences in cases tried by the Military Collegium of the Supreme Court were prepared in advance, before the trials, and submitted to Stalin for his personal approval. However, to preserve appearances, an interval of several hours was allowed to pass while the court "considered its verdict," and then characteristically reassembled at two-thirty in the morning to announce it. With total disregard of the promises made beforehand, all were sentenced to death, removed to the Lubyanka prison, taken down to the cellars, and shot. The announcement of their execution, made twenty-four hours later, added that the condemned men had appealed but that their appeals had been dismissed. Those few relatives who could be traced were either sent to the camps or, in the case of Evdokimov's son, shot.

IV

NOW THAT THE CHARGES have long since been admitted to be false, the methods by which the "confessions" were obtained exposed, and the condemned men rehabilitated, it is hard to recapture the shock that the trial

---

*The three judges included I. I. Nikitchenko, treated with great respect by his British, American, and French colleagues when he joined them ten years later in presiding over the trial of the major war criminals at Nuremberg.

and the sentences produced. Just as Zinoviev and Kamenev themselves believed that their lives would be spared, so it seems clear that the majority of the party, possibly including some of the NKVD officers, did not expect Stalin actually to put the opposition leaders to death, once he had got their admissions of guilt. Once again he showed his capacity to take opponents by surprise by going further than they had ever believed possible.

However bitter the factional quarrels in the past, the penalty of defeat had been expulsion from the party, exile, or confinement in the camps for politicals. Not only was it the first time members of the party leadership had been put to death, but the prospect had also been opened up of further arrests and trials. During the hearings, Zinoviev and Kamenev had named others—Tomsky, Bukharin, Rykov, Uglanov, Radek, Pyatakov, Serebryakov, and Sokolnikov—all of whom Vyshinsky undertook to investigate and bring to trial if the evidence justified it. Vyshinsky's announcement was printed along with a resolution promptly passed by the workers of the Dynamo Factory calling for the charges to be "pitilessly investigated." One at least of those implicated—Mikhail Tomsky—did not wait, but committed suicide in his dacha as soon as he read Vyshinsky's speech. Henceforward, it could be assumed, the penalty for having opposed Stalin was death.

The threat was not limited to the party notables. At the end of 1935 the Central Committee had declared the general mass purge at an end. But the very next month, January 1936, the same body launched a fresh one in the guise of an order for all party cards to be exchanged for new ones. This went on until May, leading to many more expulsions. No sooner was the exchange completed than on July 29, 1936, a secret letter was sent to all party committees down to the lowest level with the title "On the Terrorist Activity of the Trotskyite, Zinovievite Counterrevolutionary Bloc." It called for "revolutionary vigilance against hidden enemies." The announcement of the trials and death sentences stimulated feverish efforts to send in lists of those denounced, expelled, or arrested on suspicion of anti-Soviet activities, or harboring dangerous ideas. While many of these were sent to the camps, Orlov reports that a week after the Zinoviev executions, Stalin ordered Yagoda to select and shoot 5,000 of the oppositionists already in the camps.

There is a mass of evidence from those who lived through these years in Russia that the great majority of Soviet citizens, not only the industrial and office workers but intellectuals as well, believed that those who were arrested and tried were real enemies of the people engaged in a genuine conspiracy. It could hardly have been otherwise. The violent and bitter experiences of the civil war were still fresh in everyone's memory; it was not difficult to imagine the defeated still conspiring to overthrow the regime. Hitler's rise to power in Germany and the Spanish Civil War gave substance to the prediction of an inevitable war with Fascism, preceded by espionage and subversive activities.

People had no access to information other than the Soviet press and radio, which day in and day out reiterated the official version; those accused did not contest but reinforced it by confessing their guilt. What alternative explanation could there be? The cult of Stalin and the image of him assiduously propagated through every medium—wise, benevolent, watchful, the protector of the nation against its foes, "the Great Helmsman," as *Pravda* described him—made it virtually impossible to conceive of him as the very opposite, the chief conspirator himself. This would have been to turn the world upside down in the most alarming way and undermine all sense of security. Even those arrested and convinced of their innocence did not blame Stalin for their misfortune but clung to the belief that if only they could reach him and tell him what was happening, he would intervene and order their release. To think otherwise would have been to feel the solid ground giving way beneath one's feet.

The reaction to the trial abroad lends support to this view. After the change in Soviet policy toward the West, and the announcement of the constitution that Stalin claimed was "the only thoroughly democratic constitution in the world," the news was greeted with astonishment. Opinion tended to divide along preconceived lines. Apart from the Communist faithful who duly echoed what Moscow said, several of the foreign observers at the trial and those commenting on it were impressed by the combination of the actual murder of Kirov, the possibility that Trotsky and others must have thought of, and might have conspired to effect, the overthrow of Stalin, the public confessions of the accused, and the absence of any hesitation in executing them by comparison with their treatment on earlier occasions. All these factors suggested that the charges might be true. For those who were already looking to the Soviet Union as the best hope of resisting Fascism—especially after the outbreak of the Spanish Civil War in mid-July—it was less disturbing to believe that former revolutionaries might plot assassination (especially when they admitted it) than to believe that the only socialist state in the world would tell lies and extort confessions.

In short, Stalin had succeeded in reading a sharp lesson to anyone in Russia tempted to criticize or question his policy and his position, without destroying his credibility among the Russian people or in the outside world. But it was not in Stalin's nature to rest content with a warning, and his determination was strengthened by what appears to have been a revival of opposition in the Politburo. Stalin remained in the south, at Sochi, but all the other full members, apart from Mikoyan, were in Moscow at the end of August, within a week of the executions and Tomsky's suicide. According to Boris Nicolaevsky,[26] it was in the face of pressure from some of their number that the investigation into the charges against Bukharin and Rykov was dropped, and an inconspicuous announcement to this effect was printed on an inside page of *Pravda*.[27]

Stalin chose to vent his anger not on the Politburo, but on Yagoda. A sharply worded telegram from Sochi, signed by Stalin and Zhdanov, demanded his replacement by Yezhov as "absolutely necessary and urgent." Yagoda, Stalin declared, had proved himself incapable of unmasking the

Trotskyite-Zinovievite bloc. Yezhov must move from the Control Commission and put new life into the NKVD's investigations, which Stalin declared were four years behind time.

WORK HAD already begun on building up a case for a second trial and it was to this that Yezhov now devoted his energies. More time was needed to prepare indictments against Bukharin and Rykov, and Grigori Pyatakov was chosen instead as the central figure. Neither he nor any of the other sixteen defendants finally chosen had ever been members of the Politburo, but Pyatakov had so impressed Lenin with his abilities as an organizer and his potential for leadership that the latter had included him with the four other party members besides Stalin and Trotsky whom he had discussed in his Political Testament. Expelled from the party with other Trotskyites in 1927, Pyatakov had discovered that there could be no life for him without it and told a former colleague in 1928 that in order to become one with it he would abandon his own personality and be ready to declare black white, and white black, if the party required it.²⁸ Breaking with Trotsky and returning to Russia, he had become deputy commissar for heavy industry. According to Ordzhonikidze, the commissar, no one contributed more to the creation of Russia's industrial base as the brains and driving force behind the Five-Year plans. A major critic of Stalin in the 1920s, Pyatakov had since abandoned all opposition and accepted Stalin's leadership without reservations. But his loyalty was to the party, not to Stalin as a person; this was no longer enough. Moreover, the fact that he had made so great a contribution to the industrialization of Russia made him, in Stalin's eyes, the obvious choice for a scapegoat for the economic failures and sabotage that were made the centerpiece of the second Moscow trial.

Ordzhonikidze, who knew and acknowledged how much the regime owed to Pyatakov, was determined to do all he could to save him. He is reported to have visited him in jail, to have protested to Stalin and to have secured a promise that his life and those of his wife and ten-year-old child would be spared. The same source, Orlov, adds that, in view of this, Ordzhonikidze visited Pyatakov a second time and persuaded him that nothing more could be done.²⁹ Pyatakov then agreed, in December 1936, to make the required confession, and the others followed suit.

As the case was built up by the NKVD, it rested on charges against Pyatakov, Serebryakov, and a group of Trotsky's former supporters, since rehabilitated, of organizing three sabotage groups. The target of the first was said to be wrecking the railways. The second, the "West Siberian Anti-Soviet Trotskyite Center" at Novosibirsk, was held responsible for serious accidents in the mines and factories of the new "Kuzbas" industrial region, which had already been the subject of a preliminary trial on the spot in November 1936. The third group was responsible for sabotage in the chemical industry. Espionage on behalf of the Germans and Japanese and the preparation of terrorist attacks were thrown in for good measure. At least fourteen separate groups of industrialists were named who had been given the task of assassinating Stalin and other members of the Politburo, but who nonetheless proved unable to carry out a single overt act, apart from a highly unconvincing accident to Molotov's car in which no one was hurt.

The trial began in public on January 23 and, on the first day, the whole Bukharin-Rykov-Tomsky group was again incriminated. For no obvious reason, Karl Radek, a brilliant journalist, never taken seriously as a politician, who had betrayed the opposition on every possible occasion and fawned on Stalin, had been arrested and added to the defendants in the Pyatakov trial. Once persuaded to cooperate—after a long meeting with Stalin and Yezhov³⁰—he collaborated wholeheartedly with the NKVD in rewriting the scenario of the plot and put on a spectacular performance in court. Only when Vyshinsky pressed him too hard did he retort: "You are a profound reader of human hearts, but I must nevertheless comment on my own thoughts in my own words." And again, when Vyshinsky suggested that his long silence before confession cast doubts on his reliability, Radek's answer threatened to give the game away: "Yes, if you ignore the fact that it was only from me that you learned about the [center's] program and about Trotsky's instructions—yes, it does cast doubt on what I have said."³¹

One important service that Radek performed was to mention casually that in 1935 Red Army Corps Commander Vitort Putna, already mentioned in the earlier trial as a Trotskyite, had brought him a request—which he could not recall—from Marshal Tukhachevsky. This unexpected mention of the leading figure in the Red Army was deliberate, a repetition of the use of Kamenev in the earlier trial to mention names of others under investigation (including Radek himself as well as Pyatakov and Bukharin). The reference was at once taken in Moscow—and meant to be taken—as a threat to the marshal. In a characteristic touch, a further exchange took place in the evening, when Radek was recalled by Vyshinsky to repeat that he had not intended to incriminate the marshal in any way—"I know Tukhachevsky's attitude to the party and to the government to be that of an absolutely devoted man." The renewed mention, however, of the marshal's name ten times in the course of the exchange made sure that the threat was understood. It was, no doubt, in return for these services that Radek was sentenced not to death but to imprisonment.

In his closing speech Vyshinsky excelled himself: "This is the abyss of degradation! This is the limit, the last boundary of moral and political decay!" Answering criticisms from abroad, he declared: "A conspiracy, you say, but where are the documents? I am bold enough to assert, in keeping with the fundamental requirements of the science of criminal procedure, that in cases of conspiracy, such demands cannot be met." He listed the hundreds of workers, "the best sons of our country," who had been killed as a result of the accused's criminal activities.

I do not stand here alone! I feel the victims are standing here beside me, pointing at the dock, at you, accused, with their mutilated arms! . . .

I am joined in my accusation by the whole of our people! I accuse these heinous criminals who deserve only one punishment—death by shooting![32]

After all the lies that had been told in court, Pyatakov ended his final plea with a *double entendre* that conveyed the truth:

In a few hours you will pass your sentences. And here I stand before you in filth, crushed by my own crimes, bereft of everything, through my own fault, a man who has lost his party, who has no friends, who has lost his family, who has lost his very self.[33]

The court took twenty-four hours to "consider the evidence," and then, reassembling at three o'clock in the morning, met Vyshinsky's request with the death sentence for all but four of the accused. Radek, along with three others, was sent to the camps, where he is reported to have been killed in a brawl in 1939. All other promises made beforehand were ignored and the executions carried out forthwith.

As the press reports of the trial appeared, they were seized on by other members of the party elite, anxiously trying to find clues with which to read Stalin's mind and discover who might be the next to disappear into the Lubyanka. At least in the previous trial, Zinoviev and Kamenev had had a record of open opposition to Stalin, could be plausibly represented as irreconcilable enemies, and were accused of Kirov's murder, which had actually taken place. None of this was true of Pyatakov and his fellow defendants. They were administrators and engineers, not political figures; and the acts of sabotage of which they were accused, mine accidents and derailments, even if true, were hardly a way of seeking to overthrow a regime or to destroy the achievements of industrialization and collectivization.

As Yakov Livshits, the deputy commissar of railways, was being led off to execution, his last word was "*Zachto?*" ("Why? What for?") This was the story circulating in the party that prompted Army Commander Ion Yakir, a member of the Central Committee, to remark that the question was a good one, as the accused were obviously innocent of the charges brought against them.[34] What, then, were they guilty of? The only answer appeared to be, that in Stalin's eyes, a past history of opposition, whatever had been a man's record since, was sufficient to brand him as capable of that critical, independent attitude that he was determined to root out—even if it meant sacrificing someone as valuable to the regime as Pyatakov. As the events of 1937–38 were to show, Stalin's sole criterion had become total and unquestioning obedience to his will.

One man who understood perfectly what was going on was Ordzhonikidze. One of the more humane and popular among the Soviet leadership, he had known Stalin intimately from their early days together in

Georgia, more than thirty years before. He had been a member of Stalin's Tsaritsyn group in the civil war and had carried out with him the forced federation of Transcaucasia, which had aroused Lenin's anger in 1922–23. In 1926 he had been brought in as a staunch *apparatchik* to serve as a candidate member of the Politburo, along with Kirov, Mikoyan, and Kaganovich, had then chaired the Central Control Commission and helped to destroy the opposition in the late 1920s. In 1929, again with Kirov and Kuibyshev, he had belonged to the small group of party notables whose support played a decisive role in Stalin's successful bid for the leadership; in the Stalin revolution he had held the key post of commissar of heavy industry—but in the move for relaxation that followed in 1933–34 he is always spoken of, again with his close friend Kirov and with Kuibyshev, as a leading member of the moderate group that opposed Stalin.

He was now the last of the three left alive. His fiftieth birthday on October 28, 1936, had been celebrated with lavish praise in the press and at meetings. But the arrest of Pyatakov, his deputy commissar, was evidently a move directed at him as well. Ordzhonikidze had intervened, secured a promise from Stalin of exemption from the death penalty for Pyatakov and his family, and relying on this had advised the latter to cooperate and "confess." The double cross that followed led to an open quarrel with Stalin and the reported threat: "I am still a member of the Politburo, and I am going to raise hell, Koba, if it is the last thing I do before I die!"[35] NKVD operatives were already collecting "evidence" against Ordzhonikidze, and almost every day brought news of the execution of a close friend or associate. Stalin sent him the depositions extracted from prisoners by torture, with the comment: "Comrade Sergo, look what they're writing about you." The Politburo, on Stalin's motion, directed Ordzhonikidze to give the report on "wrecking" industry at the approaching Central Committee Plenum. He was increasingly harassed personally and suffered a nighttime search of his apartment by the security police. When he complained to Stalin, the latter replied that the police were liable to do this to him, too; there was nothing extraordinary about it.

On February 17, Ordzhonikidze had a long talk with Stalin in which he tried to persuade him that "dark forces" were exploiting his lifelong suspiciousness and that the party was losing its best cadres. A second conversation between them on the telephone turned into an angry exchange of insults and curses in Russian and Georgian. The following day, February 18, Ordzhonikidze stayed in bed and spent the time working. Shortly after five o'clock his wife heard a shot and ran in to find him dead. After summoning Stalin, who waited for other Politburo members before he came, she picked up the sheets on which Ordzhonikidze had been writing, but had them taken out of her hands by Stalin. Over her protests Stalin ordered Ordzhonikidze's death to be described as due to a heart attack: "Heavens, what a tricky illness! The man lay down to have a rest and the result was a fit and a heart attack."[36] The death certificate, signed by the people's commissar for health and three other doctors, confirmed Stalin's diagnosis.

As Kirov, Kuibyshev, and Gorki had been before him, Ordzhonikidze was honored in his death and incorporated into the Stalin cult. The authoritative *Soviet Encyclopaedia* described him as "the favorite comrade in arms of the great Stalin . . . who died at his post as a warrior of the Lenin-Stalin Party." [37] Three of the four doctors who signed the death certificate were subsequently liquidated, but no charge of murder was brought against them or anyone else. Not until Khrushchev's secret speech of 1956 was it revealed that "Stalin permitted the liquidation of Ordzhonikidze's brother and brought Ordzhonikidze himself to such a state that he was forced to shoot himself." [38] However Ordzhonikidze was "persuaded" to remove himself from the scene, his death, like that of Kirov, Kuibyshev, and Gorki before him, turned out to be very conveniently timed for Stalin's purposes. For a crucial session of the Central Committee, of which Ordzhonikidze had been a leading member, began four days after his death.

V

DESPITE THE ANNOUNCEMENT that it had been dropped, the investigation into the charges against Bukharin and Rykov continued. As the depositions and denunciations were extracted by the NKVD, Stalin circulated them to all the 139 members of the Central Committee, including the two most heavily implicated in the scenario on which the interrogators were working. Bukharin wrote letter after letter to Stalin rejecting the charges but received no reply.

At the 1936 anniversary celebrations of the revolution, Stalin noticed Bukharin sitting with his wife in one of the stands on Red Square and sent a guard to tell him he should take his rightful place with the other party leaders on the top of Lenin's mausoleum. This was part of the psychological pressure to which Stalin was subjecting his one-time friend and ally. Another was requiring Bukharin to attend personal confrontations with "witnesses" who testified against him.

In early December, NKVD agents invaded Bukharin's apartment in the Kremlin with an order for his eviction. As he was arguing with them, the internal phone rang. It was Stalin. "How are things with you, Nikolai?" he asked. When Bukharin told him he was being evicted, Stalin roared into the phone: "Chase them the hell out of there!" Shortly afterwards Stalin summoned a secret meeting of the Central Committee at which Yezhov was put up to accuse Bukharin and Rykov of being the ringleaders in the most serious conspiracy of all.

This was a dress rehearsal for the regular session of the Plenum in February–March 1937. It was held under the shadow of the condemnation and execution of the defendants in the Pyatakov trial at the end of January and of Ordzhonikidze's unexpected death. When Bukharin received the agenda for the Plenum and saw that the main item was the decision to be made about himself and Rykov, he went on a hunger strike in protest.

As he arrived for the meeting of the Central Committee, Stalin came up and asked him:

> "Who is your hunger strike directed against? The party's Central Committee? Take a look at yourself, Nikolai; you look completely emaciated. Ask the Plenum's pardon for your hunger strike."
>
> "Why should I?" Bukharin replied. "You're getting ready to expel me from the party in any case."
>
> "No one will expel you from the party," Stalin answered. [39]

Bukharin made the appropriate apology at the opening of the session only to find himself violently attacked by Yezhov, Molotov, and Kaganovich. When he declared: "I am not Zinoviev or Kamenev, and I will not tell lies against myself," Molotov told him: "If you don't confess, that will prove you're a fascist hireling. Their press is saying that our trials are provocations. We'll arrest you, and you'll confess." [40]

When a motion to arrest Bukharin and Rykov was proposed, there was another stormy scene. Radek and Sokolnikov, brought in under guard, gave evidence of their involvement in the conspiracy; but Bukharin and Rykov rejected every charge. Constantly interrupted and baited by Molotov, Voroshilov, and other leading members of the party, Bukharin read out a joint statement, which declared that there *was* a conspiracy, but that its leaders were Stalin and Yezhov, who were plotting to set up an NKVD state and give Stalin unlimited power. Bukharin appealed to the committee to make the right decision and appoint a commission to investigate the activities of the NKVD. "Well, we'll send you there and you can take a look for yourself," Stalin exclaimed.

After the session Bukharin returned home and dictated a last letter "To a Future Generation of Party Leaders," which he asked his wife to memorize:

> I feel my helplessness [it began] before a hellish machine, which has acquired gigantic power . . . and which uses the Cheka's bygone authority to cater to Stalin's morbid suspiciousness. . . . Any member of the Central Committee, any member of the party can be rubbed out, turned into a traitor or terrorist. [41]

Larina, Bukharin's young wife, was eventually able to publish the letter after her return from prison and was still alive when "the future generation of party leaders" to whom Bukharin appealed finally allowed his rehabilitation in 1988.

A commission was appointed, but it was to decide Bukharin's and Rykov's fate. No one opposed their expulsion and trial; not all, however, were prepared to accept Yezhov's proposal of execution, trial, and death by shooting. Foreseeing the division of opinion, Stalin was ready with the suggestion of expelling them from the party, but instead of putting them on trial, letting the NKVD handle the case. This received a unanimous vote. When the two deposed leaders returned to hear the verdict, they were arrested as they left and removed to the Lubyanka, to reappear for the last of the Moscow trials thirteen months later.

The Plenum continued for another six days, dominated by Stalin and his group. Stalin himself made two speeches, both of which were reproduced in full in *Pravda* and set the line for the campaign that was to follow.

In the first he described the situation as he saw it, or certainly as he wanted the party and the Russian people to see it. The Soviet Union was encircled by hostile powers whose agents, recruited from Trotskyites with party cards and hiding behind Bolshevik masks, had penetrated all party, governmental, and economic organizations and were engaged in wrecking and espionage, not stopping short of murder. They had been able to do this because "our comrades" at all levels were blind to what was happening and had allowed the economic successes of the Five-Year Plan to dull them into complacency. The party at all levels must wake up to the need for vigilance as never before, must "liquidate our political trustfulness," must abandon the old "methods of discussion" and replace them with the new methods needed to fight present-day Trotskyism, recognizing that, as socialism got stronger, the class struggle would not weaken but grow stronger too.

To orient themselves to the dangers of the situation, the party's leadership, from republic and regional party secretaries to the secretaries of local party cells, must undergo ideological reeducation. New cadres, in line for advancement, must be brought in. Stalin gave an indication of the radical extent of the purge he had in mind with his requirement that all secretaries, from top to bottom of the party, "should select two party workers, in each case capable of being their real substitutes."[42]

The Plenum did not pass without doubts being expressed about the way in which the purge was being carried out in particular cases; but the majority of those present were either cowed by the example of what had happened to Bukharin and Rykov or only too anxious to show their fervor in supporting the Stalinist line. Stalin was not so easily satisfied. Having rebuked party officials earlier for their "blindness," he now criticized them for being overzealous and failing to discriminate between "real Trotskyists" and those who had repented of their error and reformed. With an eye to its reception in the country at large, he devoted his concluding speech to criticism not of oppositionists, but of those party bosses who acted as if they were all-powerful in their regions, surrounded themselves with a "tail" of clients, and lost touch with "the simple people down below" with whom the general secretary now identified himself.

We the leaders should not be conceited and should understand that if we are members of the Central Committee or people's commissars, this does not yet mean that we possess all the knowledge required to give correct leadership. The rank in itself gives neither knowledge nor experience. Still less does the title. [43]

With this ominous warning to speed them on their way, the members of the Central Committee were allowed to disperse.

THE FEBRUARY–MARCH PLENUM is a landmark in Soviet history for two reasons. The first is because the expulsion and arrest of Bukharin and Rykov marked not only the final defeat of the opposition in the party, but also the emasculation of the Central Committee. Henceforward Stalin felt strong enough to order the arrest of any of his colleagues without consultation or appeal to the Central Committee or anyone else—the classic definition of a tyrant's power. The second is because it opened the way to the tenfold increase in the number of arrests between 1936 and 1937 of which Khrushchev spoke in his secret speech to the Party Congress twenty years later.

Stalin's objective was no longer limited to destroying the relics of the former opposition but reached beyond that, as his remarks at the Plenum foreshadowed, to a purge deliberately aimed at destabilizing the party by removing the security of tenure which might allow a future growth of opposition to take place. Nor was terror any longer to be restricted to the party. The purges of the NKVD and of the officer corps of the armed forces that now followed show that he was concerned to destroy potential opposition (described as "enemies of the people" or "enemies of Soviet power") wherever it might appear. Stalin's choice of these for his next move, once any veto by the party had been removed, shows how logically he proceeded. Like every other tyrant in history he saw the army as potentially the most dangerous threat to his power. The Red Army High Command had only to decide to seal off the Kremlin with picked troops and arrest the members of the Politburo for the regime to be decapitated. On the other hand, it was essential before moving against the armed forces to make sure of the NKVD, on which he would have to rely.

He had already prepared for this necessary preliminary by building up an alternative instrument of terror inside the Party Secretariat in which the key role was played by Yezhov. No other figure in Soviet history has inspired a greater mixture of hatred and contempt than this malignant dwarf, no more than five feet tall, whom Stalin had found as a party secretary in Kazakhstan, transferred to work in the Central Committee's Department of Cadres and Assignments (with Malenkov as his deputy), then made head of the Party Control Commission. The only matter in dispute is whether Yezhov was malicious and cruel by nature or acquired these characteristics when he assumed the role of Stalin's creature, totally committed to his master and prepared to carry out any task, however repellent—his supreme recommendation in Stalin's eyes. With the experience Yezhov had gained in carrying out the party purges and keeping a check on the security police for the Central Committee, Stalin had a replacement from outside the NKVD when he decided to get rid of Yagoda as commissar-general for internal affairs.

Yezhov brought with him a substantial number of his own men from the Party Secretariat and after six months in office started on a thorough purge of the NKVD organization, in which as many as 3,000 of Yagoda's officers are reported to have been executed during 1937. One of the devices used was to order the heads and deputy heads of the NKVD departments to proceed to different parts of the country on a major inspection. The different trains that they boarded were stopped at the first stations out of Moscow, and the NKVD chiefs were then arrested and brought back to prison. Yagoda himself was arrested in April 1937 and tried with Bukharin in 1938; his dacha was taken over by Molotov. At the same time Vyshinsky carried out a mass purge in the central and provincial offices of the procurator-general's organization, the other element in the purge machinery. Both were now ready for the next task.

On June 11, without previous warning, it was announced that nine of the leading figures in the Red Army High Command had been arrested on charges of conspiracy and treason and the next day that they had been tried and executed. The accused, all except one in their forties, were the pick of the group that had pioneered the reorganization of the Red Army in the 1930s. They included Marshal Tukhachevsky, the leader of the group; the Army Commanders Ion Yakir and I. P. Uborevich, commanding the two largest and most important military districts, Kiev and Byelorussia; Army Commander A. I. Kork, the head of the Frunze Military Academy; and Yan Gamarnik, the first deputy commissar of defense and head of the political administration of the Red Army since 1923, who committed suicide.

The so-called plot was based on Tukhachevsky's "favorite plan," to seize the Kremlin and kill the political leadership. At the time, however, no evidence was published and no statement issued other than the bare announcement. Stalin's own plot in fact had begun to take shape eleven months earlier, in July 1936, when Dmitri Shmidt, commanding a tank unit in the Kiev Military District, had been arrested. As so often with Stalin, revenge for a personal affront affected his choice of who should be selected for investigation. The son of a poor Jewish shoemaker, a party member since 1915 and a bold cavalry commander in the civil war, Shmidt had become involved with the Trotskyites. At the time of the 1927 Party Congress, at which the Trotskyites were expelled from the party, Shmidt, in his black Caucasian cloak with his fur cap cocked over his ear, had met Stalin coming out of the Kremlin and had started to curse him, threatening to draw his curved saber and telling the general secretary that one day he would lop his ears off. [44] The incident was soon forgotten, but not by Stalin. This was the officer about whom the NKVD was told to start collecting evidence in the form of "confessions" for a Trotskyite conspiracy in the party. After months of interrogation, beatings, and torture, Shmidt broke down and agreed to sign; he was described as a changed man: gray, thin, and listless. In the end his evidence was not needed, and he was shot out of hand on May 20, 1937.

By then a number of other officers had been arrested and Tukhachevsky was well aware that a move against the army leadership was planned—and that meant against him. Born into an impoverished but aristocratic family in 1893, Tukhachevsky was commissioned a second lieutenant in the Semeonovsky Guards in 1914. In 1918 he joined the Communists as the party most likely to revive Russia's fortunes and was appointed by Trotsky to command the First Red Army in the civil war. His military talents and success were such that he was made commander of all Soviet forces in the war of 1920 against Poland, so accomplishing his objective of fame or death before the age of thirty.

This same campaign and the dispute over the responsibility for the failure to capture Warsaw sealed the feud between Tukhachevsky and "that scheming triumvirate of war and politics—Stalin, Voroshilov, and Budenny," all three associated with the former First Cavalry Army at Tsaritsyn (Stalingrad) during the civil war.

An unexpected portrait of Tukhachevsky appears in the memoirs of Shostakovich. [45] Tukhachevsky's hobby was making violins, and the two men became close friends when the composer was a student. Shostakovich describes him as "a very ambitious and imperious person" who seemed to be "Fortune's favorite," the outstanding personality in the Red Army—impetuous, generous, with a streak of arrogance—a man who provoked Stalin's jealousy as well as his desire for revenge.

Early in May 1937, Tukhachevsky's nomination to represent the USSR at the coronation of George VI in London was canceled at the last moment, and Voroshilov, Stalin's commissar of defense, removed him from his post as a deputy commissar, sending him to a minor command at Kuibyshev on the Volga. A series of such transfers were made, so removing those to be arrested from their power bases. At the same time the old system of "dual command" was restored by a large increase in the powers of the political commissars vis-à-vis the fighting officers.

The timing may have been due to an extraordinary subplot which placed in Stalin's hands by mid-May a dossier containing letters secretly exchanged between Tukhachevsky and members of the German High Command. The accusation that Tukhachevsky and the Soviet High Command were engaged in a conspiracy with the German General Staff—with whose members they had had close contacts before 1934—originated with the NKVD, which "planted" the evidence, most likely with Stalin's knowledge. It had been picked up by Heydrich's SD (Security Service) for possible use against the German army. In 1936, however, it was decided by Hitler and Himmler to feed it back to Stalin as a "plant" with the purpose of compromising

Tukhachevsky and the Red Army leadership. It took time for the documentary evidence to be forged, but after the story of the contacts had been leaked to Stalin (and to the Russians' French allies) through the Czech president, Edvard Beneš, the material was smuggled to Moscow through underground contacts between the SS and the NKVD. [46]

As it turned out, Stalin did not make use of the forged letters, possibly suspecting a double cross, and preferring to rely on the well-tried system of confessions extracted from arrested officers. At a meeting of the Military Revolutionary Soviet with members of the Politburo on June 1 through 4, attended by over a hundred army officers, he made a personal report on the exposure of "a military-Fascist" conspiracy against the Soviet government, the leaders of which were Trotsky, Rykov, Bukharin, Yenukidze, and Yagoda, as well as the generals under arrest.

> These men [Stalin declared] are puppets in the hands of the *Reichswehr*. The *Reichswehr* wants the government here to be overthrown and they undertook to accomplish that but didn't succeed. The *Reichswehr* wanted the army to be disrupted so that it would not be ready to defend the country. . . . They wanted to make a second Spain out of the USSR. [47]

On the basis of this oral statement of Stalin's, supported only by "confessions" obtained by torture and blackmail, a summary trial was held in camera before a court presided over by the inevitable Ulrikh. He was assisted by two of the five marshals of the USSR (Vasily Blyukher and Semyon Budenny), five army commanders, and a corps commander, five of whom were themselves subsequently shot. Execution of the accused took place at once and was followed by the arrest, execution, or deportation to the camps of their wives, relatives, and children. Every stage in the operation was closely directed by Stalin, who subsequently ordered the execution of Tukhachevsky's wife, two brothers, and one of his sisters, the deportation to camps of three other sisters, and the internment of his young daughter, Svetlana, when she reached the age of seventeen, as "socially dangerous."

While the trial was still in session, Stalin sent out orders over his own signature to the authorities in the republics and regions, ordering them to organize meetings of workers, peasants, and soldiers to demand capital sentences. The NKVD at the same time began a series of arrests and executions, on an unprecedented scale, throughout the officer corps and the political commissars of the Red Army, Navy, and Air Force. A second wave followed in the spring of 1938, reaching a climax on July 27 through 29 when the naval commander in chief, Admiral Orlov, and no less than six army commanders were shot, along with eighteen political figures, including the former Politburo member Rudzutak and nine members of the Central Committee. The Far Eastern Command was savaged at the same time. Marshal Blyukher, a former factory worker who had built up Russia's defenses against Japan with great success, was recalled to Moscow and arrested in October 1938 on a charge of having been a Japanese spy since

1921. He died from injuries received while being beaten until he was "unrecognizable"—without signing the confession presented to him.

As now given in the Soviet press, [48] the military purge accounted for:

3 of the 5 Soviet marshals
13 of the 15 army commanders
8 of the 9 fleet admirals and admirals grade I
50 of the 57 corps commanders
154 of the 186 divisional commanders

16 of the 16 army political commissars
25 of the 28 corps commissars
58 of the 64 divisional commissars

11 of the 11 vice-commissars of defense
98 of the 108 members of the Supreme Military Soviet

The effect was not confined to the upper echelons. Between May 1937 and September 1938, 36,761 army officers and over 3,000 navy officers were dismissed. Allowing for 13,000 reenrolled and adding the numbers "repressed" after September 1938, this gives a total for 1937–41 of 43,000 officers at battalion and company-commander level arrested and either shot or sent to the camps (the great majority) or permanently dismissed. Roy Medvedev sums up an operation without parallel in the striking sentence: "Never has the officer corps of any army suffered such great losses in any war as the Soviet Army suffered in this time of peace." [49]

Numbers alone do not provide an adequate criterion of the damage inflicted. Since the revolution and the civil war great efforts had been made to create a modern army and a professional command capable of meeting the demands of mechanized warfare. It was precisely the men who had contributed most to that process and shown a capacity for independent thought who were eliminated. All their experience and ability were now lost. At a time when the threat of war, with either or both Germany and Japan, was greater than ever, virtually a new command of all three of the armed forces—at least a thousand senior officers—had to be created, in circumstances that hardly encouraged the development of self-confidence. At the very least this would take years. The weakness that an enemy could take advantage of in the meantime was used as a major argument by Hitler in overcoming any doubts among the German generals about attacking Russia in 1941. As it turned out, the Russians proved able to produce as talented a group of military leaders as any shot in 1937 through 1939. But neither Stalin nor anyone else could be sure of this at the time of the purge, and it was only at the cost of appalling losses in the early years of the war, while the Red Army and Stalin learned from bitter experience and the victorious commanders of the Second World War rose to the top.

VI

STALIN CANNOT of course have been responsible for all the individual decisions involved. This no doubt was what he meant when he later found it convenient to refer to "excesses." But he was the only man who could have allowed the purges to assume such proportions or who could have taken the risk this involved. Most army officers, virtually all those of high rank, were members of the party and subject to its supervision. From its earliest days the Red Army had been unique in having not one but two additional structures of control built into it: the political commissars, who operated in all units and formations, and the OGPU-NKVD, which maintained special branches at all levels above the battalion, both with independent hierarchies of their own. There was little chance that any conspiracy could have developed unnoticed in so suspicion-laden an atmosphere. Nor has any evidence of one come to light subsequently, after an official Soviet inquiry which rehabilitated Tukhachevsky and his brother officers. The only secret contacts with the Nazi regime were those that Stalin himself attempted to open up through the Soviet commercial attaché in Berlin, David Kandelaki, whom he had sent to Berlin for this purpose.

The explanation can only be that Stalin was prepared to run the risk of drastically weakening the Soviet Union's capacity to defend itself in order to make sure that there would be no command group which, in the event of war and serious initial reverses, might seize the opportunity to carry out a coup d'état against him. It was not the actions of the Soviet generals—any more than those of Old Bolsheviks like Kirov and Ordzhonikidze—that aroused his suspicion but that same attitude of mind that led him to judge them capable of acting independently, and therefore potentially unreliable. If the suspicions can be justified on such rational political grounds, the scale of the action that he took to guard against the danger—literally "overkill"—suggests reinforcement by the psychopathic elements in his character.

IN PARALLEL with the attack on the officer corps, the Yezhovschina also saw an intensification of the purge of the party, governmental, and industrial elites throughout the country. As an index of its severity, Roy Medvedev gives a figure of 90 percent of the members of regional and city committees and of the central committees of the republics expelled from office in 1937–38.

Nowhere was the purge more thorough than in Leningrad, always a focus for Stalin's suspicion, and already hard hit after Kirov's murder. Zhdanov launched the new assault in May 1937 at a conference of the regional organization, which, repeating the ritual formula, "uncovered and expelled from its ranks the anti-Soviet rightist–Trotskyite double-dealers, the Japanese-German diversionists and spies." One of the men Zhdanov relied on most was Leonid Zakovsky, a veteran of the original Cheka-OGPU-NKVD. Zakovsky's methods were described by Khrushchev in his secret speech of 1956, when he cited the experience of Rozenblum, a party member since 1906, who was arrested in 1937. After being beaten and tortured, he was taken before Zakovsky, who offered him his freedom if he would testify in court about the operations of a terrorist center in Leningrad.

> Zakovsky told me, "The case has to be built solidly and for this reason witnesses are needed. Social origin (in the past, of course) and the party standing of the witness will play more than a small role. You yourself will not need to invent anything. The NKVD will prepare for you a ready outline for every branch of the center, you will have to study it carefully, and to remember well all questions and answers that the court might ask. This case will be ready in four to five months, perhaps half a year. During all this time you will be preparing yourself so that you will not compromise the investigation and yourself. Your future will depend on how the trial goes and on the results. If you begin to lie and testify falsely, blame yourself. If you manage to endure it, you will save your head and we will feed and clothe you at the government's cost until your death." [50]

Khrushchev spoke from firsthand knowledge. At the same time that Zhdanov was hounding the Leningraders, he himself was in charge of the purge in Moscow. No mention of this, or examples from Moscow, was included in his 1956 speech.

At the same time as hundreds of the most active party workers were rounded up and either sent to the camps or shot, the heads of the leading Leningrad industrial enterprises were removed. As the old cadres were eliminated, Zhdanov filled their places with his own protégés—among them N. A. Voznesensky, A. A. Kuznetzov, and P. S. Popkov, who were to perish in a later "Leningrad case" after the war.

What happened in Leningrad was repeated in every center in the country. Elsewhere, however—apart from Beria, in Georgia and Transcaucasia—the regional and republican first secretaries could not be trusted, as Zhdanov and Khrushchev could, to destroy their own existing *apparats* and replace them with new ones. Stalin sent his own men out from Moscow to see that the purge was carried out with sufficient rigor. Kaganovich, for example, was sent to Ivanovo, the Kuban, and Smolensk; Malenkov to Byelorussia and (with Mikoyan) Armenia; Andreyev to Tashkent.

Quotas were fixed for the number of Trotskyites, spies, and saboteurs that each district was required to produce and either shoot or deport to the camps. Kaganovich, visiting Ivanovo, reported several times to Stalin by telephone, and as a result the quota was fixed initially at 1,500. A local troika was set up, consisting of the regional head of the NKVD, first secretary of the party, and the chairman of the Soviet Executive Committee. Stalin's advice that each party secretary at every level should select two replacements left them in no doubt that if they failed to deliver the required numbers, they themselves would be liquidated. After shooting most party and government officials in Ivanovo, the troika rounded up all the political prisoners already in the local prisons and any one else they could lay hands on (for example, former employees of the Chinese Eastern Railway who had returned home after it was closed) in order to meet the quota—only to see this raised under further pressure from Moscow.[51]

The Ukraine had already suffered more than any other part of Russia during the collectivization campaign; it attracted Stalin's concentrated and malevolent determination to break its independent stand again in 1937–38. A Politburo commission consisting of Molotov, Khrushchev, and Yezhov arrived in Kiev in August 1937 with a large force of NKVD troops and orders to carry out 30,000 more executions, the victims to be selected by the local NKVD. During the next year virtually a clean sweep was made of those in charge of every institution in the republic, from the Ukrainian government (all seventeen members were arrested, soon followed by their successors) and the Ukrainian Central Committee (only 3 of its 102 members survived), to the educational system, scientific bodies, and Ukrainian Union of Writers. The Ukrainian party was effectively destroyed and the republic became "little more than an NKVD fief where even the formalities of party and Soviet activity were barely gone through,"[52] until it could be reconstructed from the ground up. This was the job left to Khrushchev, who was appointed first secretary and in 1938 raised 1,600 party members—among them the young Leonid Brezhnev—to be secretaries of district and city committees. This was the new guard which everywhere throughout the USSR moved into the vacant positions.

The greater number of those who suffered in the Yezhovschina came from the provinces. No part of the Soviet Union escaped, even the most remote, such as the Far East.

As general secretary, however, Stalin knew better than anyone that if he meant to make as thorough a purge of the rest of the Soviet Establishment as of the armed forces, the crucial operation had to be carried out in Moscow. It was there that the main concentration of power at the top was situated—in the Politburo, the Central Committee, and the Central Committee's Secretariat; in the people's commissars and their ministries, including those responsible for Soviet industry; in the headquarters of the NKVD, the Komsomol, the trade unions; in the intellectual, cultural, and scientific institutions of the capital.

Stalin trusted no one but himself to direct such an operation, with Yezhov to carry it out. In preparation, simplified trial procedures were introduced by a decree of September 14, 1937, forbidding appeals and petitions for clemency as well as publicity in open-court trials.

According to Khrushchev, who was also involved as first secretary of the Moscow Party Organization, Yezhov sent in to Stalin during the period 1937–38 383 lists containing the names of those important enough to require his personal approval for their execution. The form that the lists took was as follows:

Comrade Stalin,

I am sending for your approval four lists of people to be tried by the Military Collegium:

List No. 1 (General)
List No. 2 (Former military personnel)
List No. 3 (Former personnel of the NKVD)
List No. 4 (Wives of enemies of the people)

I request sanction to convict all in the first degree.

Yezhov [53]

"First degree" conviction meant death by shooting, and the lists, after being examined, apparently as part of the normal routine of Stalin's office, were sent back with the note:

Approved—J. Stalin
                    V. Molotov

On a single day, December 12, 1937, Stalin and Molotov confirmed the death sentence for no fewer than 3,167 prisoners. [54] In all, Yezhov's death lists presented for Stalin's personal decision are calculated to have contained some 40,000 names. Appeals were met with abuse. At the June 1957 Plenum of the Central Committee, Marshal Zhukov read out the comments attached to a letter from a general pleading his innocence on the eve of his execution. It was annotated by the members of the Politburo who rejected it:

"A pack of lies! Shoot him. J. Stalin."
"Agreed. Blackguard! A dog's death for a dog. Beria."
"Maniac. Voroshilov."
"Swine! Kaganovich." [55]

It is a remarkable fact that, throughout the period of the purges and trials, as an endless flow of reports on conspiracy, sabotage, and plots to murder him—involving leading figures in the party, state, and armed forces—poured onto his desk, Stalin betrayed no sign of his morale or nerve being affected. Pity was unknown to him. He continued with his routine as before, dictating letters, receiving officials, holding meetings, and attending the theater. He showed the same total lack of compassion when men with whom he had worked closely for years were executed. His occasional comments express only satisfaction at stamping out treachery, never regret.

In some cases, those whose arrests were authorized were allowed to remain in office for weeks and months; in others, while removed from office, they were not arrested immediately but were left waiting, a procedure deliberately designed to soften up the victims—and their wives—by prolonging the destructive uncertainty under which they lived.

It was no longer former oppositionists, few of whom remained at liberty, who were at risk. Many who had been active in enforcing collectivization and carrying out the Five-Year Plans had incurred Stalin's wrath by resisting the arrest and execution of party members, or at least expressing doubts or showing too little zeal.

Of the Council of People's Commissars, for example (responsible for the most important government departments), the two deputy chairmen of the council, Arkady Rosengolts (Foreign Trade) and Andrey Bubnov (Education), G. M. Kaminsky (Health), V. I. Mezhlauk (Gosplan and Heavy Industry), M. Rukhimovich (Defense Industry), G. F. Grinko (Finance), and M. A. Chernov (Agriculture), together with another ten, can be identified as victims of the purges. In most cases their removal also meant the decimation of their staffs. These included not only the central administration but also directors of enterprises, chief engineers, and plant managers.

To take another example from a quite different sector: Not only the officials of the Comintern but several thousand foreign Communists who had taken refuge in the Soviet Union—refugees from Nazi Germany, Austria, Italy, Poland, Spain, and other countries where the party was banned—were arrested and either shot or sent to camps.

VII

THE LAST BIG PUBLIC TRIAL took place in Moscow in March 1938. Its function was different from that of the first two, which had been to publicize and justify the message that anyone, even members of the Central Committee and Politburo, who expressed opposition to or even had reservations about Stalin's policy put themselves and their families in danger of death. The last was designed to draw together publicly all the different types of opposition, terror, counterrevolution, sabotage, espionage, and treason, and present them as branches of a single conspiracy. The right opposition, represented by Bukharin and Rykov, was linked to Trotsky, to the earlier Zinovievite and Trotskyite conspirators, to other Trotskyites not yet tried, to Tukhachevsky and the army, to the different terrorist centers' action groups that had been identified, and to at least four foreign intelligence services. The twenty-one defendants represented the different sectors of the Soviet Establishment involved in the "conspiracy": three members of Lenin's Politburo (Bukharin, Rykov, Krestinsky); Yagoda, the former head of the NKVD; four people's commissars, heads of government economic departments who confessed to promoting large-scale sabotage; four diplomats who confirmed the collusion with Nazi Germany and the links with Trotsky; four leaders from the federated republics—Uzbekistan, the Ukraine, and Byelorussia—pleading guilty to encouraging bourgeois nationalism. The secretaries of Kuibyshev, Gorki, and Yagoda gave evidence that the first two had been murdered on the orders of the third; and three doctors, including the leader of the Soviet medical profession, Professor Dmitri Pletnev, confessed that they had carried out the murders, adding to them the deaths of Gorki's son and Menzhinsky, Yagoda's predecessor as head of the NKVD.

The indictment included every crime in the counter-revolutionary lexicon from espionage for foreign powers and assassination to plotting the dismemberment of the USSR and the overthrow of the social system in favor of a return to capitalism. A brand-new charge, against Bukharin alone, accused him of having plotted to seize power in 1918 by murdering Stalin and Lenin at the same time. The evidence—as always in the form of interlocking confessions—had taken a year's preparation by Yezhov and his team, all of whom were to be liquidated themselves in the next year.

Even so, there were surprises, the first as soon as the trial opened and the accused were asked for their pleas. While all the others pleaded guilty, one replied firmly: "I plead not guilty. I am not a Trotskyite. I was never a member of the bloc of Rightists and Trotskyites, of whose existence I was not aware. Nor have I committed any of the crimes with which I personally am accused."[56] The speaker, described by Fitzroy Maclean of the British embassy, who was present, as "a pale, seedy, dim little figure, his steel-rimmed spectacles perched on his beaky nose,"[57] was Nikolai Krestinsky, with Stalin one of the five members of Lenin's original Politburo, and once senior secretary of the Central Committee, who had been expelled from the party with Trotsky but had been readmitted in 1929, becoming deputy commissar for foreign affairs.

When Vyshinsky asked why he had misled the prosecution by making false statements in his confession under interrogation and then repudiating them only when he came into court, Krestinsky replied: "I simply considered that if I were to say what I am saying today—that it was not in accordance with the facts—my declaration would not reach the leaders of the party and the government."[58] Maclean reports that this bold statement was greeted with a "shocked hush" in the court.[59]

Vyshinsky did not pursue the matter further until the evening of the following day. By then Krestinsky had spent more than twenty-four hours in the hands of the NKVD. When he returned his tone and appearance were altogether different. When Vyshinsky demanded: "What then is the meaning of the statement you made yesterday?" Krestinsky replied, as if repeating a lesson he had learned:

> Yesterday, under the influence of a momentary keen feeling of false shame, evoked by the atmosphere of the dock and the impression created by the public reading of the indictment, which was aggravated by my poor health, I could not bring myself to tell the truth. . . .
> In the face of world opinion, I had not the strength to admit the truth that I had been conducting a Trotskyite struggle all along. I request the court to register my statement that I fully admit that I am guilty of all the gravest charges brought against me personally, and that I admit

my complete responsibility for the treason and treachery I have committed.[60]

The highlight of the trial was the cross-examination of Bukharin and Rykov. Bukharin had been selected by Stalin to epitomize in his own person the degeneration and criminality of the entire Old Bolshevik leadership. As Maclean recognized: "To Bukharin belonged the role of archfiend. He had been behind every villainy, had had a hand in every plot. Each prisoner, as he blackened himself, was careful at the same time to blacken Bukharin."[61]

For three months after his arrest Bukharin held out against the demand that he should cooperate in "this symbolic role of representative Bolshevik,"[62] by incriminating himself. He is reported not to have been tortured but finally to have agreed under the threat to kill his young wife and newborn son. He continued to battle with his interrogators and Stalin's emissaries, Voroshilov and Yezhov, over the text of his "confession" until the eve of the trial. His plan, which Rykov also followed, was to accept a general responsibility for all the crimes of the "bloc," but to reduce this to a formality by disclaiming it in every specific case. His reply to the indictment was:

> I plead guilty to being one of the outstanding leaders of this "bloc of Rightists and Trotskyites." Consequently, I plead guilty to what directly follows from this, the sum total of crimes committed by this counter-revolutionary organization, irrespective of whether I knew of, whether or not I took part in, any particular act.[63]

Far from being intimidated by Vyshinsky's attempts to bully him, Bukharin, supported by Rykov, got the better of a whole series of exchanges and provoked the chief prosecutor into losing his temper.

Vyshinsky: "Accused Bukharin, do you plead guilty to espionage?"
Bukharin: "I do not."
Vyshinsky: "After what Rykov says, after what Sharangovich says?"
Bukharin: "I do not plead guilty."
Vyshinsky: "When the organization of Rightists was set up in Byelorussia, you were at the heart of it; do you admit that?"
Bukharin: "I have told you."
Vyshinsky: "I am asking you, do you admit it or not?"
Bukharin: "I took no interest in Byelorussian affairs."
Vyshinsky: "Did you take any interest in espionage affairs?"
Bukharin: "No."
Vyshinsky: "And who did take an interest?"
Bukharin: "I received no information with regard to activities of this kind."
Vyshinsky: "Accused Rykov, was Bukharin receiving any information with regard to activities of this kind?"
Rykov: "I never spoke to him about it."
Vyshinsky, turning to Bukharin: "I am asking you again, on the basis of testimony here given against you: do you choose to admit before the

Soviet Court by which intelligence service you were enlisted—the British, German or Japanese?"
Bukharin: "None." [64]

In view of Bukharin's close association with Lenin, Stalin had inserted a charge against him, alone, of planning to kill the Bolshevik leader in 1918—along with Sverdlov and Stalin himself. Bukharin strongly denied it and, when confronted with witnesses, rejected their testimony as false:

Vyshinsky: "How do you explain the fact that they are not telling the truth?"
Bukharin: "You had better ask them about it." [65]

Stalin was not present in the court but, as had been arranged in the earlier trial, the courtroom was wired so that he could listen to the proceedings in private. Maclean reported:

At one moment during the trial a clumsily directed arc lamp clearly revealed to attentive members of the audience a drooping moustache and yellowish face peering out from behind the black glass of one of the private boxes that commanded a view of the courtroom. [66]

In his final speech Vyshinsky declared:

The historical significance of this trial consists before all in the fact that it has been shown, proved, and established with exceptional scrupulousness and exactitude that the Right, Trotskyites, Mensheviks, Socialist Revolutionaries, and bourgeois nationalists are nothing other than a gang of murderers, spies, and wreckers without any principles or ideals . . . not a political party, a political tendency, but a band of felonious criminals who have sold themselves to enemy intelligence services. [67]

Vyshinsky was particularly incensed with the tactics of Bukharin—"that damnable cross between a fox and a swine"—and Rykov in refusing to plead guilty to the Kirov murder or any of the other specific charges made against them, while accepting a general political responsibility for all the activities of the "bloc."

In this way, while admitting the case against him, Bukharin "proceeded," the *New York Times* correspondent wrote, "uninterrupted this time, to tear it to bits, while Vyshinsky, powerless to intervene, sat uneasily in his place, looking embarrassed and yawning ostentatiously." [68]

In the closing section of his speech, however, Bukharin submitted and accepted the justice of the sentence that awaited him, declaring that he deserved death several times over because he had degenerated into an enemy of socialism.

While in prison [he said], I made a revaluation of my own past. For when you ask, "If you must die, what are you dying for?" an absolutely black vacuity suddenly rises before you. There was nothing to die for if one wanted to die unrepentant. And on the contrary everything that glistens in the Soviet Union acquires new dimensions in a man's mind. This in the end disarmed me completely and led me to bend my knees before the party and the country. . . . The result is a complete internal moral victory of the USSR over its kneeling opponents.[69]

There is nothing to show how far Bukharin's act of submission was due to the realization that, if he did not in the end keep his bargain with Stalin, his wife and child would suffer; how far to a feeling that, only if he sacrificed himself as an individual to the party, could he make sense of his life and die with something better to hope for in the future.

Stalin was not interested in motives; as long as Bukharin and the others confessed, death could be left to settle the rest. The accused were found guilty on all charges and all except three were sentenced to death. Bukharin asked for a pencil and a sheet of paper on which he wrote a short note to Stalin. "Koba," it began, "why do you need me to die?" There was no answer, but the note was found among documents in Stalin's desk drawer after he died, fifteen years later.[70]

The sentences were carried out without delay, and, to make sure, the history of the Soviet Union was rewritten to blot Bukharin out and give only Stalin's version. But in the long run Bukharin had the better of the argument. The appeal to the future generation that he had addressed in the letter he dictated to his wife was not in vain. In the 1980s his ideas began to attract increasing attention among those in search of a "socialism with a human face," from Czechoslovakia and Hungary to China, and in 1988, fifty years precisely after his trial, a "future generation of party leaders" in the USSR rehabilitated his name and condemned Stalin.

NO FURTHER PUBLIC TRIALS were held after March 1938, although it was not until the summer of 1938 that the terror reached its climax with the executions of leading military and political figures at the end of July already referred to. After that, the purge still continued: The Soviet Foreign Service and the central administration of the Komsomol, as well as the Far Eastern Army Command, were all subjected to the process of arrest-execution-deportation in 1938–39. Not until February 1939 were Stanislav Kossior and Vlas Chubar, the former Politburo members from the Ukraine, executed after prolonged torture; others not until 1940–41.

Nonetheless, the intensity of the terror slackened after the summer of 1938. The NKVD itself, at the operative level, could no longer keep up with the numbers that their own system of mutual denunciation drew into the machine. Three thousand investigators are reported to have been at work in Moscow alone, but if every victim who was battered into confessing named five or ten more, the numbers soon threatened to become unmanageable. Even Stalin was forced to recognize that the purge had now extended so far that there was not an institution in the Soviet Union the efficiency of which was not affected by the loss of its most experienced staff.

Although Stalin without doubt was the driving force behind the terror, seeing Yezhov every day and giving him detailed instructions, he succeeded in avoiding the responsibility and the blame for it. One way of doing this was by rarely appearing in public and giving no major speech for two years after the March Plenum in 1937. He also moved his own office and personal secretariat from the Central Committee offices in Stavaya Square into the Kremlin, putting its thick walls between himself and the people. This helped to encourage the belief to which so many clung, including many who suffered from it, that the NKVD concealed the terror from him.

In 1938 he moved to provide a scapegoat, who could be blamed for "excesses," in the form of Yezhov. This was a repetition of the same maneuver that had diverted blame for the excesses of collectivization with the article "Dizzy with Success" in 1930.

In July 1938, Stalin appointed Beria as deputy head of the NKVD; in August Yezhov was named as people's commissar for water transport, while retaining his position as commissar for internal security. A commission appointed on the motion of Kaganovich, with Beria as a member, carried out an investigation of the work of the NKVD, finding many irregularities and excesses. As a result two resolutions were approved by the Central Committee: "On arrests, supervision by the procuracy, and the conduct of investigations," and "On the recruitment of honest people for work in the security organs." Within two weeks (December 1938) Beria replaced Yezhov as head of the NKVD, leaving the latter in the limbo of uncertainty. He was still commissar for water transport and occasionally attended meetings there, without ever intervening. Sometimes he made little paper airplanes or birds, sent them flying, and then retrieved them, crawling under a chair if need be, but always in silence.

When the Eighteenth Party Congress met in March 1939, Yezhov, who had become an "un-person" but was still a member of the Central Committee, attended a meeting of the *Senioren Konvent* (the Committee of Elders). E. G. Feldman, the first secretary of the Odessa Region Party Committee, who was present, gave this description to Medvedev:

> As the congress was drawing to a close, the *Senioren Konvent* gathered in one of the halls of the Kremlin. Sitting in front at a long table, as if on stage, were Andreyev, Molotov, and Malenkov. Behind them, far to the back in a corner on the left . . . Stalin took a seat, puffing away at his pipe. Andreyev spoke. He said that, as the congress was finishing up its work, it was time to propose candidates for election to the Central Committee. The first to be named were people from the outgoing Central Committee, excluding of course those who had already become casualties. Then it was Yezhov's turn.
>
> "Any opinions?" asked Andreyev. After a brief silence, someone remarked that Yezhov was a good Stalinist commissar, known to them all, and should be kept.

"Any objections?" There was silence. Then Stalin asked for the floor. He got up, walked to the table, and, still puffing at his pipe, called out: "Yezhov! Where are you? Come on up here!" Yezhov appeared from a row at the back and came to the table.

"Well, what do you think of yourself?" Stalin asked. "Are you fit to be a member of the Central Committee?"

Yezhov turned pale and in a cracked voice replied that he didn't understand the question, that his whole life had been devoted to the party and to Stalin, that he loved Stalin more than his own life and had no idea what could have prompted such a question.

"Really?" asked Stalin ironically. "And who was Frinovsky? Did you know him?"

"Yes, of course I did," answered Yezhov. "Frinovsky was my deputy. He . . ."

Stalin interrupted Yezhov and began to ask about others: Who was Shapiro? Did he know Ryzhov [Yezhov's secretary]? and What about Fedorov, and so on [all these people had been arrested] . . .

"Josif Vissarionovich! But you know that it was I—I myself—who exposed their plot. I came to you and reported that . . ."

Stalin didn't let him continue. "Yes, of course! When you felt the game was up you came in a hurry. And what about before that? There was a plot, a plot to kill Stalin. Do you mean to tell me that top people in the NKVD were organizing a plot and you weren't in on it? Do you think I'm blind?" Stalin went on: "Well, come on! Think about it! Who did you send to guard Stalin? With revolvers! Why revolvers near Stalin? Why? Was it to kill Stalin? And if I hadn't noticed? Then what?"

Stalin accused Yezhov of running the NKVD at a feverish pitch, arresting innocent people while covering up for others.

"Well? Clear off! I don't know, comrades, can this man be a member of the Central Committee? I have my doubts. Of course, think it over . . . it's up to you . . . but I have my doubts."

Yezhov of course was crossed off the list by unanimous vote; he did not return to the hall after the break and was not seen again at the congress. [71]

Yezhov was not arrested until a few days later in the middle of a meeting at his commissariat. When the NKVD agents finally appeared, he stood up saying, "How long have I been waiting for this!" He put his gun on the table and was led away. [72]

FOR STALIN the Eighteenth Party Congress in 1939, far more than the Seventeenth in 1934, was the real Congress of Victors—or survivors. The roll call of the delegates showed how successfully he had created an entirely new party in the five intervening years. Of the 1,966 Congress delegates in 1934, 1,108 (Khrushchev's figure) had been arrested for counterrevolutionary crimes. Of those who were fortunate enough to have survived, only 59 appeared again as delegates in 1939. The turnover in the membership of the Central Committee was equally dramatic. Of the 139 full and candidate members elected in 1934, 115 no longer appeared in 1939. Khrushchev reported that 98 of them had been shot, but Medvedev puts the true figure at 110.[73]

Beria made almost as clean a sweep of the top posts in the NKVD as Yezhov had before him. The few who had survived from Yagoda's time, like Frinovsky and Zakovsky, who had prepared the Bukharin trial, followed their colleagues to execution. So did the Yezhov generation. All told, more than 23,000 members of the NKVD are estimated to have perished at the end of the 1930s. By March 1939 Beria's men were finally in control, with the Georgian following that he had brought to Moscow well represented among them. After the report of the investigating commission, charges against some 50,000 people were dropped, a gesture that signaled not so much a change of policy as a modification in its application. Under Beria, the purge that Yezhov had operated as an emergency measure to deal with a crisis was institutionalized as a permanent instrument of rule.

Now that Yezhov had been identified as the scapegoat, Stalin was ready to concede that there had been mistakes. In his report to the congress, he told delegates: "It cannot be said that the purges were conducted without serious mistakes. Unfortunately there were more mistakes than might have been expected." However, he reassured delegates: "Undoubtedly we shall have no further need of resorting to the method of mass purges. Nevertheless, the purge of 1933 to 1936 was inevitable and its results, on the whole, were beneficial."

The delegates, whose sense of hearing was no doubt sharpened by their feeling of insecurity, did not miss the fact that Stalin referred only to the years 1933 to 1936 when expulsions from the party had been constitutionally authorized by the Central Committee. Those for the years 1937 to 1938, when the numbers expelled and executed had been ten times greater, and when the authority for all but the handful tried was Stalin and one or two of the members of the Politburo acting in secret, were passed over without comment. Only at the end of his report, referring to the rapid promotion of the younger generation, did he add with a characteristic touch of black humor, "But . . . there are always fewer old cadres than are needed, and their ranks are already beginning to thin out by force of nature's laws."[74]

How many in all were arrested, shot, or sent to the camps remains a question that may never be satisfactorily answered. A revised estimate by Robert Conquest published in 1991 suggests a total of eighteen million deaths in the period from the beginning of 1930 to the beginning of 1939. Volkogonov suggests ca. sixteen million, other Soviet estimates ca. twenty million.

Allowing up to eleven million deaths before 1937, Conquest estimates numbers in jail or camps at the beginning of that year as ca. seven million. Another seven million were arrested in 1937–38.

Of this combined total of ca. fourteen million, up to eight million were executed or died in 1937–38, leaving ca. six million still in jail or camps at the beginning of 1939. These figures do not include those executed, dying in camps, or imprisoned during the years 1939–53.[75]

VIII

ARGUING ABOUT the total number of those who suffered, plus or minus one or two million—the quantitative question—obscures the qualitative fact that, for every one of the millions, however many they were, what happened to each of them was in every case a unique individual experience. It was his grasp of this that led Aleksandr Solzhenitsyn, having spent eleven years in a labor camp himself, to write his classic story *One Day in the Life of Ivan Denisovich* and then go on, at great risk, to collect secretly the individual experiences of several hundred former prisoners, out of which he created—without access to official documents—his memorial to the victims of Stalin's terror, *The Gulag Archipelago*. The "archipelago" consisted of "islands" inhabited by millions of the Zek people;* some of its islands were as big as a large European country, others as small as a detention cell in a railway station. The archipelago was scattered geographically but fused psychologically into an almost invisible continent located within another continent, that of the Soviet Union.

At the beginning of Chapter 1, Solzhenitsyn writes:

> The universe has as many different centers as there are living human beings in it. Each of us is a center of the universe, and that universe is shattered when they hiss at you: "You are under arrest." . . .
>
> We have been happily borne, or perhaps have unhappily dragged our weary way—down the long and crooked streets of our lives, past all kinds of walls and fences made of rotting wood, rammed earth, bricks, concrete, iron railings. We have never given a thought to what lies behind them. . . . But there is where the Gulag country begins, right next to us, two yards away. In addition we have failed to notice a number of closely fitted, well-disguised doors and gates in these fences. All those gates swing quickly open and four hands grab us by the leg, arm, collar . . . and drag us in like a sack,·and the gate behind us, the gate to our past life, is slammed shut once and for all. That's all there is to it! You are arrested! And you'll find nothing better to respond with than a lamblike bleat: "Me? What for?" That's what arrest is: it's a blinding flash and a blow that shifts the present into the past, and the impossible into omnipotent actuality.[76]

Unlike collectivization, which was publicly proclaimed and affected whole villages, the terror was always an individual experience, which struck silently and unpredictably, like lightning out of a clear sky, and this difference explains why, in the latter case, there was no organized resistance. For anyone living in such a situation will convince themselves that the best way

---

Gulag was the Russian acronym for Chief Administration of Corrective Labor Camps, part of the NKVD. *Zek* is prison slang for "prisoner."

to avoid trouble is to know nothing about what happens next door, to hear none of the cries in the middle of the night, to avert one's eyes at the railway station, not to ask why a colleague suddenly fails to appear at work. As Solzhenitsyn writes:

> Maybe they *won't take* you? Maybe it will all blow over? . . . The majority sit quietly and dare to hope. Since you aren't guilty, then how can they arrest you? *It's a mistake.* They are already dragging you along by the collar, and you still keep on exclaiming to yourself: "It's a mistake. They'll set things straight and let me out!" Others are being arrested en masse, but "maybe *he* was guilty . . .?" But as for you, you are obviously innocent!
>
> Why then should you run away . . . or resist right there? After all, you'll only make your situation worse; you'll make it more difficult for them to sort out the mistake.[77]

The instinct to turn away in the hope of escaping notice was reinforced by the fear of informers, which made everyone afraid to speak, producing that atomization of society that Aristotle long ago saw as one of the safeguards of tyranny—"the creation of mistrust, for a tyrant is not overthrown until men begin to have confidence in one another."[78]

This sense of individual helplessness was kept alive after arrest by the prisoner's inability to discover why he or she had been arrested, the bewilderment that sprang from being unable to understand what was happening, to read the intentions of those now in total control of his or her fate. On the other side, what was experienced by the prisoner as an inexplicable nightmare was the product of careful calculation. Behind the apparently casual brutality and indifference there was a body of knowledge built up over centuries of experience in breaking down the resistance and identity of human beings, passed on from one generation of interrogators and torturers to another. As Solzhenitsyn came to realize, there was a "scientific theory." This classified arrests according to a variety of criteria: nighttime, daytime, at home, at work, during a journey; first time or repeat; the thoroughness of the search required; what should be done with the wife—arrest, deportation with or without children. The operations of the NKVD, as of the Gestapo, were scientific in being firmly based upon, and kept up to date by, constant observation and experimentation, while drawing upon the whole range of medical and psychological research into the behavior of human beings under stress.

The secrecy in which the existence of the camps and all their operations were wrapped made them much more frightening. No lists of arrests were published; the labor camps were never mentioned in the newspapers, yet everyone knew that such things were part of Soviet life, while never speaking of them to one another. This created, as Kolakowski says, "a dual consciousness . . . and made people accomplices in the campaign of lies inculcated by the party and the state."[79]

Those who held or had held a job at the top must have had a better idea of what would happen to them, if arrested. But what they did not know was whether they would be, and the long periods of uncertainty in which they were deliberately held, sometimes for weeks, sometimes for months, had the same crippling effect. Once arrested, they were stripped of all privileges and left as naked and vulnerable as anyone else. Thus, in his secret speech, Khrushchev chose not former oppositionists as examples of those who suffered severe torture, but Stalinist members of the Politburo, Rudzutak, Eikhe, Chubar, and Kossior, all of whom were cleared of the charges against them after Stalin's death. Bukharin appears to have been the only one who was not tortured and was allowed so much scope to defend himself in open court.

All Bolsheviks were further disarmed by the fact that they themselves, from the civil war on, had taken part in mass acts of violence, for example in the collectivization campaign. None of them had objected to fake trials and executions when the victims were not party members, nor had they questioned the right of the party leaders to decide who was a class enemy, a kulak, or an imperialist agent. When the rules of the game they had accepted were turned against them, they had no independent moral principles to turn to.

The effect of this was reinforced by the mystique of the party as the sole source of truth and all other values. Trotsky expressed the feelings of many when he said:

> The English have a saying, "My country, right or wrong." . . . We have much better justification in saying, whether it is right or wrong in certain individual cases, it is my party. . . . And if the party adopts a decision that one or other of us thinks unjust, it is my party, and I shall support the consequences of the decision to the end. [80]

Pyatakov declared in a conversation of 1928 already quoted,

> According to Lenin the party is based on the principle of coercion which doesn't recognize any limitations or inhibitions. . . . This principle of boundless coercion is the absence of any limitation whatsoever—moral, political, even physical. . . .
>
> A true Bolshevik has submerged his personality in the collectivity of the party. . . . In order to become one with this great party, he would fuse himself with it, abandon his own personality, so that there was no particle left inside him which did not belong to the party. [81]

In 1936, Bukharin denounced Stalin's insane ambition in his talk with Nicolaevsky in Paris; but when the latter asked why, then, the opposition had surrendered to him, Bukharin replied: "You don't understand, it is not like that at all. It is not him we trust, but the man in whom the party has reposed its confidence. It just so happens that he has become a sort of symbol of the party." [82] Pyatakov had said to himself in 1928 that there could be no life for him outside the party. Ten years later Bukharin, who had no illusions about the extent to which Stalin had perverted the party, still ended his final speech with the same confession:

> There was nothing to die for, if one wanted to die unrepentant. . . . And when you ask yourself: "Very well, suppose you do not die; suppose by some miracle you remain alive, again what for?" Isolated from everybody, an enemy of the people, an inhuman position, completely isolated from everything that constitutes the essence of life. [83]

THE SYSTEM on which the NKVD worked was that of securing confessions, in which prisoners admitted their own guilt and accused others. Stalin insisted on confessions even in the much greater numbers of cases that were only tried in secret. Since the cases were based upon imaginary, not real, crimes, it was more convenient and effective to establish guilt in this way than by fabricating independent evidence which could then be denied. There is no doubt that it was the fact that the accused were seen and heard standing up in court, incriminating themselves and accusing one another, that made so great an impression on Western observers and on the Soviet people. The building up of this huge body of detailed falsehood occupied the time of many thousands of NKVD agents and interrogators. It would have been possible, and have saved a great deal of time and trouble, if arrests had been followed by executions and deportation simply by administrative order. But confessing, like the formal procedure of trials before a court, helped to maintain the appearance of legality to cloak terrorism and murder. Even if disbelieved, defendants who admitted their guilt were discredited politically—and in their own eyes morally as well. Their self-condemnation and self-humiliation were part of the penalty which Stalin exacted for arousing his suspicion.

What was little understood at the time, but has since been conclusively established, were the methods by which the NKVD secured the confessions. The basic one was known as the "conveyor"—continuous interrogation by relays of interrogators for hours and days on end, frequently without allowing the prisoner either sleep or food. One week was reported as enough to break almost anybody. An alternative was the long interrogation at intervals over several months, even one or two years. A Polish witness who experienced this speaks of the effect of cold, hunger, bright lights shining in the eyes, and especially sleeplessness: "After fifty or sixty interrogations with cold and hunger and almost no sleep, a man becomes like an automaton—his eyes are bright, his legs swollen, his hands trembling. In this state he is often convinced he is guilty." [84] He added that most of his fellow accused reached this condition between their fortieth and seventieth interrogation.

Beating and torture were commonplace, a fact frankly admitted by Khrushchev in his secret speech, when he went on to quote a circular from Stalin to the secretaries of regional and republican parties in 1939, confirming that this had been authorized by the Central Committee in 1937. Stalin defended the use of "methods of physical influence" on the grounds that this was the practice of bourgeois intelligence agencies "in their most scandalous forms." The Central Committee considered that it was "both justifiable and appropriate" when applied to "known and obstinate enemies of the people."[85]

The most effective methods were a combination of physical and psychological torture—the threat to arrest and torture a prisoner's wife—with sound effects of a woman screaming and weeping in the next room; the threat to shoot a man's children while forcing him to stand without food, drink, or sleep for three, four, five days.

Informing and denunciation were an essential part of the system. Spite and envy were powerful motives that could be mobilized against those who belonged to the privileged class of officeholders. "Tale bearing was the chief method of getting on in life." The NKVD employed blackmail and threats to recruit large numbers forced to "cooperate" by reporting on neighbors and fellow workers; others saw denunciation as a way to divert attention from themselves and win the favor of those in power. The corrosive effect of this was to destroy that minimum of mutual trust on which human relations depend and leave individual human beings isolated from one another. Many accounts speak of the atmosphere of fear and silence that pervaded Moscow, Leningrad, and the other big Russian cities from 1936 through 1938.

Only a minority of those arrested between 1936 and 1939 were executed. The great majority were deported to one of the Corrective Labor Camps that made up the larger islands in the Gulag archipelago. A detailed list of camps was published as early as 1937, detailing thirty-five clusters, each with about 200 camps. Between 1935 and 1937, their total population is estimated to have been at the level of five to six million men and women. Many did not survive the horrors of the railway journey which might last months, in overcrowded trucks, unheated in winter, unbearably hot in summer with inadequate food, water, and sanitation. Those who did might die from the cold—many camps were in the Soviet Arctic—from epidemics or untreated diseases, from exhaustion as a result of heavy manual labor, from brutal treatment by guards, who terrorized the political prisoners, or on orders from Moscow for the mass execution of a further quota. The latter was usually carried out in the Central Isolation Prisons. Some 50,000 prisoners are reported to have been transferred for execution to one of those in Bamlag (the Baikal-Amur camp complex in eastern Siberia) in the two years 1937 and 1938. They were tied up with wire like logs, stacked in trucks, driven outside the camp, and shot.

The two biggest settlements of the NKVD empire were in northwest Russia, in the Komi Autonomous Republic, and in the Far East, between the River Lena and the Kolymskoye (Gydan) range of mountains north of the Bay of Shelikhova. In the first of these, the basin of the Pechora River contained the largest single concentration of forced labor in Russia, with more than a million prisoners. In the Vorkuta coal-mine district, the temperature was below freezing for two-thirds of the year and few survived for more than a year or two. In the second, an area four times the size of France, the camps came under Dalstroy, the Far Eastern Construction Trust, and contained around half a million. The main concentration was in the Kolyma River gold (and later uranium) mines, where the temperature can sink to −70°C. Outside work for prisoners was compulsory until it reached −50°C. Described by Solzhenitsyn as the "pole of ferocity" of the Gulag Archipelago, the death rate at Kolyma was so high that more individual prisoners inhabited its camps at one time or another than those in any other location.

Although rarely economic, slave labor in the camps was an accepted part of the Soviet economy: A million were occupied in mining, three and a half million in general construction, such as railways and factories. Incentives were provided by matching the inadequate rations to the achievement of norms. The mortality rate in the camps in 1938 has been estimated at 20 percent yearly. Of those sent to the camps only a small proportion ever came out again; even if they survived, they were given a fresh sentence when their first expired. Solzhenitsyn believed that the longest a man could last was ten years, and this was at a much better period in camp history. Of those arrested in the period from 1936 to 1938, the survival rate is put at 10 percent, and Andrei Sakharov calculated that of more than 600,000 party members sent to the camps, only 50,000 survived.

Any organization charged with carrying out so large an operation develops a momentum of its own and is difficult to control. Effective control becomes impossible when, as in the case of the NKVD, the operation is carried out in secret, often at great distances from the center, and provides constant opportunities for the abuse of power and the indulgence of criminal and psychopathic characteristics. No more than Hitler with the concentration camps did Stalin visit any of the NKVD prisons or camps. He was dependent on what he was told and may well not have known of many excesses which he later found it politic to disavow; whether he would have intervened if he had known is another matter.

But even if we accept that much of the responsibility for the brutal way in which the NKVD carried out its tasks rests with its senior officers and the commandants of the camps, and that these were allowed to get out of hand, the responsibility for the policy and the authority for carrying it out rest with Stalin. Above all, he was responsible for the scale of the terror and the purges. This is no longer disputed in the former Soviet Union. After the agitated discussion in the late 1980s that followed the extension of *glasnost* to Soviet history, particularly to the period of the purges, *Pravda* declared flatly in April 1988: "Stalin did not simply know, he organized them, directed them. Today this is a fact, already proved." [86]

But this still leaves unanswered the question What conceivable objective could Stalin have had that was important enough to pay the price of killing and imprisoning millions of men and women for the second time within a decade? The first time, during the period of collectivization and industrialization, it could at least be argued that the suffering and loss of life were the price paid for the modernization of a backward country—even if most historians now question whether this was a necessary price. But by 1936 collectivization had been accomplished and the foundations of an industrial economy laid. Far from consolidating, the terror of the later 1930s threatened to undermine what had been achieved, by liquidating a great number of those who had contributed most to it, at all levels. The only reason Stalin advanced for his actions was a huge conspiracy to overthrow the regime, involving not only the party organization throughout the country, but also all the other elites and networks—including the NKVD itself as well as the armed forces—which had come to the top in postrevolutionary Russia.

The threatening international situation and the danger of war were pressed into service to add substance to the threat; yet there is not so much as one authenticated case of a real traitor or spy among the thousands of victims listed by name, and there was no sector whose efficiency suffered more from the Yezhovschina than the armed forces on which the regime would have to depend if war came.

The psychological characteristics and the conspiratorial experience that made it easy for Stalin to persuade himself that there was a potential threat to the regime have already been mentioned, and the light this throws on the importance he attached to confession and the admission of guilt. But the element of calculation is never to be left out of any explanation of Stalin's attitudes; it was the combination and convergence of the two, his psychological and his political needs, that made him so formidable.

The political element in this case can easily be identified if we turn the original question around and no longer ask what objective was important enough to pay the price of liquidating so many able, experienced people but recognize that, for Stalin, this was not the price but the objective itself. The reason becomes clear if we place the period of 1936 to 1939 in the context of Soviet history after 1917.

Stalin's revolution of 1929 to 1933 was an economic and social revolution, underpinning and completing Lenin's political revolution, the seizure of power, from 1917 to 1921. But as the Soviet Union moved forward into the mid-1930s, Stalin came to see his own revolution as incomplete without a further political phase, a radical purge also imposed from above. It did not follow immediately: There was a period of relaxation in 1933–34, then a period of preparation in 1934–35 before the full force of it was felt between 1936 and 1939. It began with the elimination of the former oppositionists; widened to include the Stalinists who had pushed through the revolutionary changes of 1929 through 1933, but then sought a policy of relaxation and reconciliation; and went on to the liquidation of virtually the whole of Lenin's original party, not only in the party organization, but also of the same generation, both party and nonparty, in the other sectors of the Soviet elite, the military, the managerial, the cultural, and finally the NKVD itself. The test was no longer opposition, or even doubt, but extended to those Stalin called the "silent ones," any who had built up a power base or "family circle" of their own or in whom there were still traces of an independent attitude. Many, if not actually suspected by those conducting the purges, fell victim to denunciation.

Psychologically, the purge reduced Stalin's ever-present fear of conspiracy, overthrow, and assassination and satisfied that desire for revenge in which there was not a trace of magnanimity or human feeling and in which calculation was reinforced by an instinctive cruelty. Politically, it silenced dissent for good and cleared the way to an autocratic form of rule. It did this by wiping out what was left of the original Bolshevik party, in which memories were still alive of the 1917 revolution and civil war, no more than twenty years earlier, of Lenin's style of leadership and inner-party democracy, and of Marxism-Leninism as the ideology that gave the party its identity and bound its members together in a common faith.

There is no need to idealize that original party or to forget the sufferings that it had imposed on the Russian people without any mandate other than the conviction of its own infallibility. Continuity with it was maintained by the rhetoric, the claim to the revolutionary tradition, and to Stalin's inheritance of Lenin's authority. This was of great importance in concealing the radical changes Stalin was making, thereby preserving the loyalty of Communist parties and left-wing sympathizers abroad. But behind the facade Stalin created a very different party from the one in which he had risen to power.

S T A L I N H A D A L R E A D Y taken steps to provide his own version of the way in which this development had taken place. On his direction work began in 1935 on a *History of the All-Union Communist Party,* known for convenience as the *Short Course.* Dissatisfied with the result, in 1937 he provided guidelines for the book he wanted, giving a breakdown into twelve chapters and pointing to his own writings and speeches as the obvious source. Once a draft was produced, Stalin took an active part in editing and rewriting it, adding a whole new ideological chapter of his own on "Dialectical and Historical Materialism."

The account that emerged presented Stalin as the party's co-leader with Lenin from the 1912 Prague Conference, replacing Trotsky as the organizer who directed the seizure of power in 1917 and the strategy of the civil war. Together Stalin and Lenin had foiled the disruptive efforts of Trotsky, Zinoviev, Bukharin, and Rykov, revealed in the trials of the later 1930s as having been "two-faced enemies of the revolution" from the beginning. No mention was made of any disagreement between Lenin and Stalin, and as a precaution a Politburo decision (which only became known in 1957) banned publication of any further studies or memoirs of Lenin.

According to the *Short Course,* when Lenin died Stalin took his place as the unquestioned leader who carried out the industrialization of Russia and collectivization with strong popular support (no mention of the human cost), in the face of collaboration between hostile foreign powers and spies and saboteurs within. The victory of socialism in the USSR was confirmed by the democratic constitution of 1936 and sealed by the extermination of the enemies of Soviet power, the "Bukharin-Trotsky gang," with the approval of the Soviet people.

Stalin took care not to appear as author or editor of the *Short Course*; its title page described it as edited by a commission of the Central Committee. But he made sure by a Central Committee decree of November 1938 that it should become the basis of all Soviet political education, the central text to be mastered by everyone ambitious to secure a place in the leading cadres of party, government, and economic management. By the time he died it had been reprinted 300 times, a total in print of over forty-two million copies in sixty-seven languages. Here was the sole source from which the rising generation who were now called upon to take over the running of the Soviet Union would derive knowledge of its origins and history.

Between 1934 and 1939 about a million administrators, engineers, managers, economists, and other professionals had graduated from the high schools and colleges and were eager to step into the places left vacant. Their strength lay in their youth and its response to the upward mobility in Soviet society; their corresponding weakness lay in their inexperience. At the Eighteenth Congress Stalin announced that half a million party members, largely drawn from this new intelligentsia, had been promoted to leading positions in the party and state during the same period. (Brezhnev and Kosygin both graduated in 1935; by 1939, the former was people's commissar for textiles, the latter a regional first secretary.) The process continued: More than 70 percent of the recruits to the party in the years following came from the same background.

The delegates to the Eighteenth Congress already represented this new Soviet-trained elite: There were scarcely any over fifty; well over three-quarters were under forty, and half under thirty-five. They had known no other leader than Stalin, no other world as adults than the Soviet regime, and their knowledge of its earlier history and its Marxist-Leninist ideology would be derived entirely from Stalin's version of both. They had no loyalty to the party or to an ideology independent of its leaders. They were unlikely to cause any trouble. The future was theirs, but they knew that if they did cause trouble or failed to meet the targets set, they were as vulnerable to denunciation, dismissal, or arrest as their predecessors. The mechanism of the purge had been brought under control and regularized; it had not been abolished.

THIRTEEN　1918 Revoked

HITLER　1934–1938　(*Age 44–49*)
STALIN　1934–1938　(*Age 54–59*)

I

THE YEARS 1933 AND 1934 represented a transitional phase in the foreign policy of both Nazi Germany and the Soviet Union, although for very different reasons. Hitler's basic presupposition was that Germany must avoid the risk of war—until she had restored her military power. He spoke movingly, as an ex-combatant, of the horrors of war, and the new regime's desire for peace became a main theme of German propaganda aimed to impress public opinion in Britain, France, and the smaller European countries, while he pressed ahead with his rearmament plans.

For the present, Hitler discouraged the Nazis in Austria and Danzig, and the German minorities in Czechoslovakia and Poland, from arousing alarm by demanding to be incorporated in the Reich. Instead he presented a strong Germany as the defender of European civilization against the threat of Bolshevism. When pressed, however, to take part in a common effort to work out and guarantee a European settlement, he avoided any commitment that might tie his hands. The only agreements he was prepared to make were bilateral—the 1934 pact with Poland, or the Anglo-German Naval Agreement of 1935—leaving him free to disavow them when they would no longer serve his purpose.

Stalin, too, was feeling his way in 1933–34 toward a reappraisal of the international situation and of Soviet foreign policy. Although it had long been an article of faith for Communists to represent Russia as encircled by hostile capitalist powers, in fact, after the civil war and the Allies' intervention, the Soviet Union had not been under any threat and had been left free to pursue her own development up to the early 1930s. With the establishment of diplomatic relations with the U.S.A. in November 1933, all the Great Powers and most of the other states recognized the Soviet government as the legitimate government of Russia and entered into trade relations with it. The Communist government, however, did not abandon its role as the base of the Comintern, an organization committed to world revolution, and this continued to prove a stumbling block to the normalization of

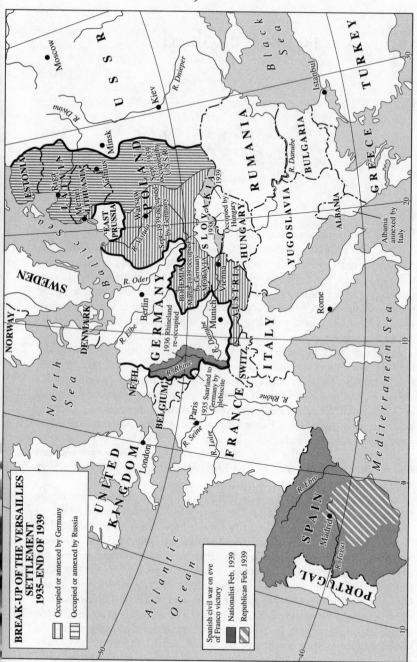

BREAK-UP OF THE VERSAILLES
SETTLEMENT
1935–END OF 1939

Occupied or annexed by Germany

Occupied or annexed by Russia

Spanish civil war on eve
of Franco victory

Nationalist Feb. 1939

Republican Feb. 1939

relations. But the Sixth Comintern Congress in 1928 saw the final reduction of the organization to a dependency of Soviet power, well illustrated by its acceptance of Stalin's call to make socialist parties everywhere the main target for attack.

Stalin's preoccupation throughout was with carrying through his own revolution in Russia. The Soviet Union must be prepared to defend herself, and the creation of a strong arms industry was a priority in the program of industrialization. But his overriding objective was to avoid war, and not until 1931–32 did this present serious problems.

The relatively low priority assigned to foreign policy was shown by the fact that neither George Chicherin nor Maxim Litvinov, who replaced him in 1930 as commissar for foreign affairs, was a member of the Politburo, only of the Central Committee. The reputation Litvinov established abroad as Russia's foreign minister during the 1930s was an asset that Stalin recognized, but Litvinov did not make Soviet policy, remaining the official spokesman for views and decisions that he might hope to influence but that were taken by the Politburo. When it met to discuss foreign affairs, Litvinov would be present. But Stalin had other sources of information than those available to the Foreign Ministry—for example, the NKVD—and might choose to intervene at any point. When he did, his views were decisive.

The Soviet reaction to the rise of an aggressive Japan displayed the same mixture of tactics later employed in Europe. The first, following the Japanese occupation of Manchuria in 1931, was to offer the Japanese a non-aggression treaty, a policy of appeasement (including the sale of the Chinese Eastern Railway), which the Russians were to continue to follow until 1941. The second was to strengthen the Soviet Far Eastern army under Marshal Blyukher and in a series of frontier incidents during the 1930s, often involving large numbers of troops, to impress on the Japanese that the conquest of the Soviet Far East would be a more costly option than further expansion at the expense of China.

A third line of approach in 1932 was to use the Chinese Communists to put pressure on the Chinese Nationalist leader, Chiang Kai-shek, to take up the Japanese challenge and accept a renewal of relations with Russia after the breach of 1928, so preventing any deal between China and the Japanese directed against the USSR.

The Russian leadership found greater difficulty in deciding how serious the danger of war in Europe was, and how to meet it. Neither Britain nor France, although assumed to be hostile as capitalist powers, appeared to present any immediate threat. Nor did Germany, worse hit than any other country by the economic crisis. The huge extent of Russian territory occupied by the Germans in the First World War and the humiliation of Brest-Litovsk had certainly not been forgotten but were offset by the fact that Germany had been disarmed and by the close cooperation between the two countries in the military and economic fields throughout the 1920s.

The rise of National Socialism, matched by a steady increase in the

Communist vote, was taken as providing evidence that Germany's capitalist democracy was about to collapse. Hitler, seen from a Marxist point of view as a front man for bankers and industrialists, was not at first taken seriously; the official Soviet line was that any government he formed would represent merely a temporary interlude, offering the German working class, united under Communist leadership, a unique opportunity to capture power. Even when this was proved to be an illusion, the Russians calculated that it would take years before German rearmament reached the point where the German army would be strong enough to attack them.

In the meantime, despite the virulence with which Hitler continued to attack Communism, and despite incidents in which Soviet citizens were roughly handled in Germany, Stalin did not despair of maintaining friendly relations and cooperation between the two states, a hope reciprocated by the German military and Foreign Office. In May 1933, while Hitler was still anxious about German isolation and vulnerability, the Russians secured his agreement to ratify the 1931 extension of the Berlin Treaty of Friendship and Neutrality, originally signed in 1926. Even after the long-standing cooperation between the Reichswehr and the Red Army was closed down during 1933—with expressions of mutual esteem—Stalin went on record with his statement that there was no reason why the fact that Germany had a Fascist government should prevent the two countries remaining on friendly terms and trading with each other, any more than it did in the case of Italy.

There had always been a sharp division of opinion in Berlin, especially in the Foreign Ministry, between the Ostlers, who agreed with the army leaders in seeing the Russian connection as a major asset in promoting Germany's revisionist aims, and the Westlers, who felt that Germany's interests were best served by cooperation with the West. Germany's ambassadors in Moscow during the Weimar period, Ulrich von Brockdorff-Rantzau and his successor, Herbert von Dirksen, had been ardent Ostlers, and this tradition did not end with Hitler's accession to the chancellorship. Rudolf Nadolny, who was appointed ambassador to Moscow in November 1933, was a disciple of von Brockdorff-Rantzau, and his successor from 1934 to 1941, Friedrich Werner von der Schulenburg, was eventually to take part in negotiating the Nazi-Soviet Pact of 1939.

But Hitler's attitude, although not unfriendly, was noncommittal. Until German military power had been restored, he had no reason or wish to bring about an open rupture with Russia—or, on the other hand, to let relations become too close. They remained correct, but efforts by German diplomats to improve them, or the feelers that Stalin put out from Moscow, led nowhere. Trade between the two countries continued in a desultory way, but at a very much lower level than in the Weimar period.

Stalin never lost sight of the desirability of reaching an agreement with Germany if he could, especially if it would encourage Hitler to become embroiled with the Western powers. Soviet approaches continued to be made in Berlin and through the German embassy in Moscow. But Stalin, although both patient and persistent, did not stake too much on his hopes in that direction. Major measures were taken to expand and rearm the Soviet armed forces. In 1933, expenditure on the Red Army and Navy had reached over 1.4 billion rubles; in 1934 the Defense Commissariat was given 5 billion. The years 1934–35 were the brief halcyon period of Red Army modernization and reorganization under the leadership of Tukhachevsky. Among the decisions finally adopted was to separate the Far Eastern and Western fronts by building up separate forces which could act independently of each other.

At the same time the search continued for an alternative diplomatic approach to the problem of avoiding war. The first clear sign of this was in a speech that Litvinov made to the Central Executive of the Congress of Soviets at the end of 1933. "If it is possible to speak of diplomatic eras," he said, "then we are now without doubt standing at the junction of two eras. . . ." A new period of imperialist wars was just beginning, and Litvinov pointed to Hitler's intention, proclaimed in *Mein Kampf,* "to cut a road for expansion to the East by fire and sword . . . and enslave the Soviet peoples." He still held out hope that Soviet-German relations could improve, but the Soviet Union would give special attention to closer relations "with those states that, like us, give proof of their sincere desire to maintain peace, and are ready to resist those who break the peace." [1]

Litvinov's speech gave notice of a radical change of course leading to Soviet entry into the League of Nations (September 1934), hitherto referred to in the Soviet press as the "robbers' league," where for the next four years Russia pursued a policy of collective security. The leading advocate and symbol of this alternative approach was Litvinov himself, an Old Bolshevik with an English wife, whose Jewish descent left no doubt of his anti-Nazi feelings and whose usefulness to Stalin at Geneva enabled him to survive the purges, to make a comeback after Hitler attacked Russia, and to die in his bed.

The obvious choice of partner for the Soviet Union was France, which had provided Russia with an ally before the First World War. Following Germany's withdrawal from the League (October 1933) and Hitler's non-aggression pact with Poland, Louis Barthou, the French foreign minister (who had read *Mein Kampf*), began a vigorous attempt to revive the French alliance system. In talks at Geneva during the summer of 1934, he and Litvinov agreed on plans for two new treaties.

By the Locarno Pact of 1925, negotiated by Stresemann in pursuance of the policy of "fulfillment" which Hitler denounced, Germany had agreed with France and Belgium to maintain her western frontiers as established by the Treaty of Versailles, including the demilitarized zone of the Rhineland. The agreement was guaranteed by Britain and Italy. The Germans, however, had refused to agree to a similar pact which would mean their accepting the postwar frontiers in the east. The first of the two Barthou-

Litvinov plans revived the idea of such an eastern Locarno proposing a mutual-assistance pact to include the USSR, Germany, the Baltic states, Poland, and Czechoslovakia. Russia would join the League of Nations, and Germany as well as the USSR would be protected against attack by any neighbor, perhaps rejoining the League as well as having her rearmament recognized by France. In return, each would have to renounce any aggressive moves in Eastern Europe unless prepared to face a coalition of powers pledged to assist one another. The second treaty was a separate Franco-Soviet pact, under which France undertook to assist the Soviet Union against aggression by a signatory of the suggested Eastern Pact and the Russians assumed the obligations of a signatory of the original Locarno Treaty toward France.

From Stalin's point of view, the two together would have given him everything he wanted: a Russian return to European politics, ending any danger of isolation; guarantees against German or Polish aggression, with a corresponding guarantee to both those countries against any Soviet attack. From Hitler's point of view, it was the last thing he wanted: giving up his long-term plans for the conquest of *Lebensraum* at Russia's expense and tying his hands in advance by the sort of multilateral pact to which he was totally opposed. Both Germany and Poland rejected it in the same month that the Soviet Union joined the League of Nations (September 1934).

Barthou had evidently expected Germany to do so, for he told the French cabinet that he would go ahead with both treaties even if Hitler refused to join. However, when King Alexander of Yugoslavia on a visit to France in October 1934 was assassinated by a Croat terrorist, Barthou, sitting in the same carriage, was killed as well. His place as foreign minister was taken by Pierre Laval, the only member of the French cabinet who had opposed his plans.

Laval did not openly discard Barthou's Eastern Pact, but he turned it inside out. Instead of seeking to contain Germany as Barthou had intended, Laval set out to reach a lasting Franco-German settlement. The Germans gave him every encouragement, without committing themselves to anything, and they watched with satisfaction as Barthou's proposal dissolved into inconclusive discussion of a general European settlement while they pressed ahead with rearmament. The fallacy of appeasement was illustrated in the period just preceding the Saar plebiscite due in January 1935, in which the Saarlanders had a choice between union with Germany, union with France, or remaining under League administration. While Hitler concentrated on winning a resounding success, as a way of recovering the Saar for Germany, Laval did everything he could to avoid any incidents in the hope that a heavy vote for Germany would remove an obstacle to better Franco-German relations afterwards.

THE MORE Hitler learned of the French and British governments' attitudes, the more he became convinced that, while they would undoubtedly protest, he ran very little risk of their opposing him if he were now to take a bolder line. Even before the Saar plebiscite, he told a meeting of ministers: "The French have definitely missed the opportunity for a preventive war. This also explains France's effort for rapprochement."² The German strategy in the face of British and French approaches was reconfirmed in January 1935; there might be negotiations, but there would be no agreement in any way limiting German rearmament or committing Germany to a comprehensive settlement. Negotiations would simply be used to cover the time during which Germany rearmed. The real question for Hitler was whether he should not go further and take the initiative himself.

A 90 percent vote in the Saar for reunion with Germany was hailed by the Nazis as the first of the Versailles fetters to be struck off. Hitler now followed it with the unilateral abolition of a much more important prohibition imposed on a defeated Germany. On March 9, 1935, Berlin announced that a German air force was already in existence, and then a week later—after a pause to see what reaction this aroused—that the German government proposed to reintroduce conscription and create a peacetime army of thirty-six divisions, with a strength of 550,000 men.

Timed to coincide with Heroes' Memorial Day the same weekend, this repudiation of the hated Versailles Treaty and the rebirth of the German army was greeted with an outburst of patriotic enthusiasm. That could be taken for granted: But how would the British and French react? The British issued a solemn protest—and then asked if Hitler was still willing to receive the British foreign minister, Sir John Simon. The French appealed to the League and called a conference of the signatories of the Locarno Pact—Britain, Italy, and France—at Stresa but spoke of searching for means of conciliation and the need to dispel tension. This was not the language of men who intended to back up their protests with action.

When the British foreign secretary, accompanied by Anthony Eden, arrived in Berlin—in itself a triumph for Hitler's diplomacy—they were politely received but found Hitler adamant that he would never sign a pact of mutual assistance that included the Soviet Union, a skillful use of the anti-Communist card to avoid the main issue. Germany, he declared, was rendering a great service by rearming in order to protect Europe against the Communist menace.

In April, the three Locarno signatories duly met at Stresa, condemned Germany's action, reaffirmed their commitment to the Locarno Treaty, and repeated their support for Austrian independence. They followed this by a meeting of the League Council (on which the USSR now had a seat), which in turn appointed a committee to consider what steps should be taken *the next time* any state endangered peace by repudiating its obligations. Finally, as all that was left of Barthou's Grand Design, Laval reluctantly agreed to the signing of the Franco-Soviet Treaty of mutual assistance on May 2, the day he succeeded to the French premiership.

Although it was soon to become clear that the so-called Stresa Front was a cardboard structure, Hitler had to take account of the possibility that the League's unanimous condemnation might leave Germany isolated. On May 21, the day that he signed the second Reich Defense Law, which conferred upon him as supreme commander the power to declare war and order mobilization, Hitler delivered a speech to the Reichstag that showed at its most convincing his ability to combine arbitrary unilateral action with an intuitive understanding of the longing for peace in the Western democracies—the same skill he had shown in playing on German illusions.

> The blood shed on the European continent in the course of the last 300 years bears no proportion to the national result of the event. In the end France has remained France, Germany Germany, Poland Poland, and Italy Italy. What dynastic egoism, political passion, and patriotic blindness have attained in the way of apparently far-reaching political changes by shedding rivers of blood has, as regards national feeling, done no more than touched the skin of the nations . . . The principal effect of every war is to destroy the flower of the nation. . . . Germany needs peace and desires peace. And when I hear from the lips of a British statesman that such assurances are nothing, and that the only proof of sincerity is the signature to collective pacts, I must ask Mr. Eden to remember . . . that it is sometimes much easier to sign treaties with the mental reservation that one will reconsider one's attitude at the decisive hour than to declare, before an entire nation and with full publicity, one's adherence to a policy that serves the cause of peace because it rejects anything that may lead to war. [3]

Collective security, Hitler pointed out, was a Wilsonian idea, but Germany's faith in Wilsonian ideas had been destroyed by her treatment after the war. Germany had been denied equality, treated as a nation with second-class rights, and driven to rearm by the failure of the other powers to carry out their promise to disarm. Despite this experience, Germany was still prepared to cooperate in the search for security. But she had no use for multilateral pacts: That was the way to spread, not localize, war. And in Bolshevik Russia there was a state pledged to destroy the independence of Europe, with which a National Socialist Germany would never come to terms. Instead of multilateral treaties, Germany offered nonaggression pacts with all her neighbors. Her improved relations with Poland as the result of such a pact showed how much they could contribute to the cause of peace.

Hitler supported his offer with a most convincing display of goodwill. Because Germany had repudiated the disarmament clauses of the Treaty of Versailles, that did not mean that she had anything but the strictest regard for the other clauses of the treaty—including the demilitarization of the Rhineland—or for her other obligations under Locarno. She had no intention of annexing Austria and was ready to strengthen the Locarno Pact by an agreement on air attack, as the British and French had suggested. Hitler laid particular stress on his willingness to limit Germany's naval power to 35 percent of the strength of the British navy. Germany was ready to agree to the abolition of heavy arms—such as the heaviest tanks and artillery—and to limit the use of bombers and poison gas by international convention. She was also ready to accept an overall limitation of armaments, provided it was to apply to all the other powers.

This was what Hitler had meant when he told Rauschning after leaving the League that he would now more than ever speak the language of Geneva, adding: "And my party comrades will not fail to understand me when they hear me speak of universal peace, disarmament, and mutual security pacts!"⁴

Even Hitler can hardly have expected a decisive response to his speech within less than three weeks. In *Mein Kampf* he had laid great stress on the importance of an alliance with Britain. Germany's future lay in the east, a continental future, and Britain was a natural ally whose power was colonial, commercial, and naval, with no interest on the European continent. He described the failure to see this and to avoid quarreling with Russia and Britain at the same time as the greatest blunder of the kaiser's government.

Hitler had already agreed with Admiral Raeder in November 1934 that German naval construction would go ahead to the limit of Germany's shipyard capacity and resources of raw materials. But this would take even longer than the expansion of the army, and during that period he saw advantage in securing British goodwill in exchange for setting a limit—arbitrarily fixed at one-third of British naval strength—that the German navy would not in any case reach for several years. This figure and Germany's interest in naval negotiations were communicated to the British in November 1934 and mentioned again in the talks with the British Foreign Secretary, Sir John Simon, and Eden the following March. Hitler claimed the recognition of British naval supremacy as a great concession, and at the end of March 1935 he offered the ambitious Ribbentrop the opportunity to go and negotiate an agreement, if the British took up his offer.

Undeterred by the condemnation of German rearmament in which they had just joined with the French and Italians, and saying nothing to either power of what was now proposed, the British cabinet agreed to a meeting with Ribbentrop on June 4. By the next evening they had accepted not only German naval rearmament in principle but also the German formula of 35 percent of British naval strength which Ribbentrop insisted must be adopted first, before any details were discussed. In fact the British went on to accept a German claim to 45 percent of their strength in submarines—the weapon that had nearly proved fatal to them in 1917—and ultimately 100 percent, at which point (actually reached in 1938) the treaty provided for retrospective legitimation of its violation.

Only when this triumph for Hitler's bilateral diplomacy was a fait accompli did the British consult other interested powers. The French were furious and embittered by what they regarded, justifiably, as an act of bad faith by their wartime ally, after the efforts they had made to keep in step over negotiations with Germany. The Stresa Front was broken, confirming Mussolini's as well as Hitler's estimate of British weakness and leaving the French and British already divided—when they were confronted with a new crisis over Mussolini's plan to conquer Ethiopia.

At the Stresa Conference the British prime minister and foreign secretary had deliberately avoided bringing up the subject of Ethiopia in order to preserve a united front against Germany. Even when Mussolini inserted a restrictive phrase in the formula referring to the maintenance of peace, adding "in Europe," there was no objection, and this appears to have been taken by the Italian leader as tacit acquiescence in his plans. Laval was prepared to acquiesce in Mussolini's African adventure rather than risk losing Italian support in reaching a settlement with Germany and preventing the annexation of Austria, and so far an Ethiopian appeal to the League, made in March 1935, had been handled discreetly. A large section of British public opinion, however, saw resistance to Mussolini as the touchstone of collective security, and when the League met in September the British government infuriated the Duce and astonished the world for the second time in four months by taking the lead in demanding and securing the imposition of sanctions on Italy.

The one assumption on which the British move could be defended was if they were prepared to support sanctions to the point of war, so making collective security credible as a means of putting a check on aggression, whether by Italy or Germany. The outbreak of war between Italy and Ethiopia in October put British intentions to the test and led the government of Stanley Baldwin to make the worst of both worlds. By insisting on the imposition of sanctions in the first place, the British made an enemy of Mussolini and ended any hope of a united front against German aggression. By then failing to make sanctions effective, in the face of Mussolini's bluster, they went on to deal a fatal blow to the hopes placed in collective security and the authority of the League.

Hitler, who followed a policy of strict neutrality throughout the Ethiopian crisis, was quick to see the advantages he could draw from it. The preoccupation of the Western powers and Italy with the Mediterranean diverted attention from German rearmament and put an end to the various proposals for a multilateral pact without further need for action on Germany's part. If Italy lost the trial of strength, that must weaken her ability to organize resistance to German ambitions in Central and Southeastern Europe, including the annexation of Austria. If she won, it would further discredit the League and undermine belief in the ability of France and Britain to check further acts of aggression. Hitler's one fear was that the quarrel might be patched up with some such compromise as the Hoare-Laval Agreement.* The final outcome left Mussolini victorious but isolated,

---

*After a striking call for unity against Italian aggression, the recently appointed British foreign secretary, Sir Samuel Hoare, secretly negotiated with Laval a plan for mediation that would allow Mussolini to keep most of the Ethiopian territory the Italians had occupied. When this was leaked to the press, the outcry forced both men to resign in December 1935.

furious with the Western powers and for the first time prepared to listen to German suggestions of an alliance.

In *Mein Kampf* Hitler bracketed Italy with Britain as the two countries Germany should seek as allies in her drive to secure *Lebensraum*. Hitherto Mussolini's guarantee of Austrian independence, and his ambition to create an Italian sphere of influence in Southeastern Europe, had stood in the way. As he was later to acknowledge, it was in the autumn of 1935, during the Ethiopian crisis, that the idea of the Rome-Berlin axis was born.

I I

THE ENTRY OF the USSR into the League of Nations meant the end of her isolation, which had lasted since the Bolsheviks seized power in 1917 and published the tsarist government's secret treaties with the Allies. The Russian leaders, however, required time to adjust to the changes in the world since they had first formed their stereotype of Britain and France as the two imperialist powers from which the Soviet Union had most to fear, as the two most powerful states in the postwar world. It needed the failure of the League in the Ethiopian crisis and the divided and weak leadership of Britain and France that it revealed to bring home finally to the Russians that it was no longer the two Western democracies but the "aggressive powers," Germany, Japan, and Italy, that represented more serious potential problems. The consolation was that it showed the capitalist powers so divided that it relieved the Communists' ingrained fear (briefly renewed by the formation of the Stresa Front) of their uniting in an attack on the Soviet Union.

The Franco-Soviet Pact of mutual assistance, finally and reluctantly signed by a right-wing French government under Laval in May 1935, had little value in itself as a guarantee of Soviet security. Unlike its famous predecessor, the Franco-Russian alliance of the 1890s, it included no specific military agreements, no arrangements for collaboration between the general staffs, no provision for automatic activation. The fact of aggression first had to be established by the League of Nations before the pact became operative. The pact did not provide for French assistance to Russia in the event of a Japanese attack and, in the absence of a common frontier such as Russia and Germany had shared before 1914, it failed to say how Russia would come to the assistance of France in the event of a German attack. In a telegram to Moscow (April 22, 1935), Litvinov admitted this frankly:

> One should not place any serious hopes on the pact in the sense of military aid in the event of war. Our security will still remain exclusively in the hands of the Red Army. For us the pact has predominantly a political significance.[5]

Like the similar Czech-Soviet Pact signed the same month, it symbolized the return of Russia to European politics and brought the prime minister of what was still regarded as the greatest military power in Europe to Moscow. Stalin was sufficiently impressed to give Laval, in return, public approval of the French national defense budget, which the French Communist party had hitherto opposed.

Neither side regarded the pact as incompatible with attempts to improve relations with Germany, although each hoped it would prove an obstacle to the other's successfully doing so. After signing it, Laval devoted much effort in the remaining months of 1935 to trying to reach an agreement with Germany. The Soviet leaders did the same. The German ambassador in Moscow had been repeatedly assured that the Russians did not regard their pact with France as ruling out other possibilities. Negotiations for a new trade treaty between Russia and Germany in the summer of 1935 appeared to offer encouragement.

The Soviet negotiator was the Georgian head of the Russian trade mission in Berlin, David Kandelaki, who let it be known that he had a direct line to Stalin and was in his confidence. Schacht, who had at first been uncooperative, came up in June 1935 with the offer of a general credit for 500 million marks, a very much larger sum than had previously been mentioned, over a ten-year period. The Russians tried to extend the trade negotiations to political as well as economic issues, by suggesting in December 1935 that the Berlin Treaty of 1926 could be supplemented by a nonaggression pact. But these hints, although repeated in 1936, elicited no response, and all that came of the negotiations was a routine trade and payments agreement. In both the French and the Russian cases, the opposition came from Hitler himself. Although he was prepared to let discussions drag on, and so gain more time for rearmament, he had no intention of tying his hands by any commitment. Having failed to find a better alternative, in February 1936, the French and Russians proceeded to ratify their pact, an action that Hitler immediately seized upon to justify his next initiative.

A major factor in Hitler's refusal to enter into closer relations with the Russians was the ideological advantage he derived from presenting Nazi Germany as Europe's defense against Communism. Stalin had no intention of abandoning his own counterpart, the Popular Front Against Fascism, the new line in Soviet policy to which individual Communist parties had been struggling to adapt and which received its formal blessing at the first Comintern Congress to be summoned for seven years (Moscow, July–August 1935). Dimitrov, the Bulgarian Communist who had been arrested in connection with the Reichstag fire and then won world fame by taunting Göring into losing his temper at the subsequent trial, was elected as secretary-general.

Stalin showed how little regard he had for the International by staying on the Black Sea and not appearing at the six-week-long congress, content to leave it to Molotov and Manuilsky to secure the predictable assent of the delegates to whatever was asked of them. The Comintern never met again. Nonetheless, the Popular Front Against Fascism, like its counterparts,

Russian support for collective security and for the Republican cause in the
Spanish Civil War, was more successful than earlier calls for world revolu-
tion in winning sympathy and support for the Soviet Union in Europe and
America in the mid-1930s.

LIKE THE COMMUNIST PARTIES *in partibus infidelium* ("among
the infidels") the German-speaking populations outside the Reich were
assets that could be manipulated as Hitler thought best suited the needs of
the Fatherland. Hitler was naturally attracted to the annexation of Austria,
the key to which was Mussolini, whose intervention in 1934 had been
decisive in preventing it. In January 1935 Hitler told a group of leading
Austrian Nazis that action would have to be deferred for three to five years
until Germany had rearmed. In the meantime the Austrian Legion made up
of émigré Nazis was moved away from Bavaria, the German press was
forbidden to report Austrian news, and the Austrian Nazis were told to
make themselves as inconspicuous as possible.

Italy's Ethiopian adventure and Mussolini's quarrel with Britain and
France promised to alter the situation radically. Hitler was not in a hurry;
he waited to see first what would happen in the Mediterranean and East
Africa. He followed the same policy in Vienna, authorizing von Papen to
continue informal talks with the Austrian chancellor, Schuschnigg, about a
possible German-Austrian agreement, even to produce a draft, but then
delaying any further move until the outcome of the Ethiopian war became
clearer.

The wide variation in the tactics Hitler followed in dealing with minority
questions elsewhere in Europe is best illustrated by a comparison of his
handling of the situation in the South Tyrol, in Czechoslovakia, and in
Poland. The South Tyrol had been part of the Habsburg lands from the
fourteenth century to 1918. Its transfer to Italy at the end of the war led to
a continuing struggle by the German-speaking minority which Hitler, as a
nationalist politician, could have been expected to support. As early as
1926, however, he took the opposite and highly unpopular view that
the South Tyrol must be sacrificed to the much greater importance of a
German-Italian alliance. To secure this he was prepared to move the
German minority out and resettle them elsewhere.

Hitler's hostility to the Czechs dated from his Vienna days. He regarded
Czechoslovakia as an artificial creation, a satellite of France, which—after
the signature of the Czech-Soviet treaty—he described as Russia's aircraft
carrier in Central Europe. The three and a half million Germans were the
largest of all German minorities, over 22 percent of Czechoslovakia's total
population in 1930. In elections held in May 1935, Konrad Henlein's
Sudeten German Front, already receiving large subsidies from Berlin, absorbed the majority of German voters and was kept in hand by Hitler as
a weapon for future use against the Czech state from within. Efforts by
Edvard Beneš, the Czech president, to reach agreement directly with Hitler

in 1936–37 got nowhere: When the time was ripe Hitler would show his hand; until then, he had nothing to say to the Czechs.

The German minority in Poland (excluding Danzig) numbered no more than 744,000 in 1931, 2.3 percent of the population. Unlike the Sudeten Germans, however, who had never formed part of the German Empire, the German minority in Poland had done so before 1918. In this case it was Hitler who had taken the initiative in reaching a settlement with the Warsaw government that ran counter to the long-standing German nationalist demand for the return of the lost provinces. The struggle of the German minority to retain its position in Upper Silesia, especially in the economic field, and the constant pressure by the Danzig Nazis under the leadership of the aggressive local Gauleiter Albert Forster for annexation to the Reich continued to trouble Polish-German relations. But Hitler showed himself determined not to let such problems interfere with the policy of cooperation with the Poles that he had initiated. The interests of the Danzigers and the German minority must take second place, at least for a few years, to the importance of neutralizing France's leading ally in Eastern Europe, Poland, and preventing her from becoming part of a coalition, including Russia as well as France, that could block the eventual drive to the east that Hitler always had in mind.

THE FOCUS OF ATTENTION in the autumn and winter of 1935–36 was the effect sanctions would have on Italy, and whether the British and French would call for their extension to oil, so precipitating a final rupture with the Italians. The possibility that Hitler might take advantage of these preoccupations to remilitarize the Rhineland, from which German troops were excluded by the Versailles Treaty, was already being discussed in Paris and London.

The French documents leave no doubt that, despite the warnings they received, neither the French government (which fell in January 1936, Laval being replaced by a stopgap ministry under Albert Sarraut) nor the French officials and general staff were able to draw up a plan to deal with either possibility. The British were no more prepared than the French to face a situation that they continued to hope would not arise. "Each looked to the other for reinforcement of its own weakness rather than confirmation of a strong resolve, and both were well satisfied."[6]

The best time for Hitler to act was while the outcome of Mussolini's challenge was still uncertain, before he either had to admit defeat in the face of oil sanctions—a victory for the League—or himself won an outright victory in Africa, so opening the way to a possible rapprochement with Britain and France. Hitler was well aware that to occupy the demilitarized zone would be a breach of the Locarno Pact as well as of the Treaty of Versailles. He took care to sound out likely reactions in advance, including Mussolini's as a signatory of the Locarno Pact. The Duce was still uncertain about oil sanctions and promised to take no action if Germany broke it.

Hitler began to consider the possible concessions he could offer at the same time and settled on the issue he would use to justify his action, the ratification of the Franco-Soviet Pact by the French Chamber on February 11, an act that he knew would further divide and polarize French opinion. Orders to the German army were issued on March 2, and the date set for Saturday the seventh, in the hope of gaining a weekend's delay before any counteraction could be taken.

Hardly had the news of the reoccupation reached London and Paris than it was overtaken by the report of new and far-reaching German peace proposals. In place of the Locarno Treaty which he had discarded, Hitler offered a twenty-five-year pact of nonaggression to France and Belgium, supplemented by the air pact to which the British attached so much importance. The new agreement would be guaranteed by Britain and Italy, with Holland as well if she so wished. A new demilitarized zone was to be drawn on *both* sides of the frontier, placing France and Germany on an equal footing, while Germany offered nonaggression pacts to her neighbors in the east on the model of that already concluded with Poland. Finally, now that equality of rights had been restored, Germany offered a return to the League to discuss reform of the League Covenant and the possible reinstatement of her former colonies.

Hitler later admitted:

> The forty-eight hours after the march into the Rhineland were the most nerve-racking in my life. If the French had then marched into the Rhineland we would have had to withdraw with our tails between our legs, for the military forces at our disposal would have been wholly inadequate for even a moderate resistance. [7]

According to General Jodl at the Nuremberg Trials the force consisted of a single division, but this was joined by four divisions of armed police already in the demilitarized zone, who had been receiving intensive training and now became four divisions of infantry.

The French still had overall military superiority in numbers, but they lacked the will or even an operational plan for an eventuality clearly foreseen. There were anxious consultations between Paris and London and protests—always accompanied, however, by appeals for reason and calm. After all, people said, the Rhineland was part of Germany; the Germans had not breached the French frontier, and were only "occupying their backyard." "A Chance to Rebuild" was the title of the London *Times'* leading article. There was a brief moment when the other Locarno powers met in London, the weekend after the occupation, when it looked as if their response might stiffen. Reports to this effect reached Berlin, and the German General Staff through von Blomberg urged Hitler to make a conciliatory gesture, such as withdrawing the three battalions that had actually crossed the Rhine and undertaking not to build fortifications on the west side of the river. Hitler after some hesitation refused, and ever afterwards held it against the army leaders that they had wavered while he had held firm. Years later, reminiscing after dinner, he congratulated himself:

> What would have happened on the thirteenth of March, if anybody other than myself had been at the head of the Reich! Anyone you care to mention would have lost his nerve. I was obliged to lie, and what saved us was my unshakable obstinacy and my amazing aplomb. I threatened, unless the situation eased in twenty-four hours, to send six extra divisions into the Rhineland. The fact was, I only had four brigades. [8]

Whether Hitler's figures were accurate or not, there is no doubt that it was his determination, not the generals', that was decisive. He was proven right on the two things that mattered. After all the talk, no one marched— except the Germans. And once his "peace proposals" had served their purpose of confusing public opinion—in Germany as well as elsewhere—he was able to avoid their leading to anything further, indignantly refusing to answer a "questionnaire" about them presented by the British.

Before the month of March ended, Hitler dissolved the Reichstag and went to the people. He again appeared before them as the peacemaker:

> All of us and all peoples [he declared at Breslau] have the feeling that we are at the turning point of an age. . . . Not we alone, the conquered of yesterday, but also the victors have the inner conviction that something was not as it should be, that reason seemed to have deserted men. . . . Peoples must find a new relation to each other, some new form must be created. . . . But over this new order which must be set up stand the words: *reason* and *logic, understanding* and *mutual consideration.* They make a mistake who think that over the entrance to this new order can stand the word *Versailles.* That would be, not the foundation stone of the new order, but its gravestone. [9]

The election figures showed a suspicious unanimity: 99 percent of the forty-five million qualified were officially stated to have voted and 98.8 percent to have voted for the only list of candidates presented to them. No one seriously doubted, however, that, as in the plebiscite that followed withdrawal from the League in 1933, a majority of the German people approved Hitler's action, many because of the display of German power and the defiant repudiation of Versailles, the rest because of relief that their anxiety at the prospect of war had been dispelled by the leader who had again proved to be right.

IN RETROSPECT, the re-militarization of the Rhineland has been seen as a watershed in interwar history marking the collapse of the postwar security system. But the descent into Avernus was not at all dramatic. For two and a half years afterwards, the illusion persisted in the Western democracies that, in some way or other, it should be possible to satisfy Hitler by producing a settlement of his demands that would avoid war. For a moment after Munich (October 1938), the British prime minister, Neville

Chamberlain, believed he had found the key to it in the Anglo-German Declaration; not until the occupation of Prague (March 1939), three years after the Rhineland crisis, was the illusion finally dispelled.

Hitler had scored a great success and he was confident, after testing the determination of the other European leaders three times, that there was no longer danger of a preventive war. But he needed more time for German rearmament before he was ready to raise the stakes: Not until November 1937 did he confront the heads of the armed forces and the Foreign Ministry with his program of expansion by the threat of force, and the timetable he had in mind. Important developments took place between March 1936 and November 1937—the rapprochement with Italy, the outbreak of the Spanish Civil War, the Anti-Comintern Pact—but their denouement did not appear until 1938-39.

The diplomatic history of 1936-37 therefore remains inconclusive, providing indicators for the future, not conclusions. Hitler appointed Ribbentrop as ambassador to London in the summer of 1936. If he could repeat his triumph of the Naval Treaty and return with a British alliance—on German terms—no one would be more pleased than Hitler. Even when Ribbentrop failed, and returned convinced that German and British interests were irreconcilable, Hitler left open the possibility that the British might still come to take a different view of their interests; but for the rest of 1936-37 he was content to let discussions continue intermittently without ever bringing them to a conclusion. Léon Blum's Popular Front government in France, which succeeded Laval's in 1936, also made a number of approaches to Berlin, but without effect. Hitler preferred to make capital out of the fact that France, the Soviet Union's ally, now had a Jew and a socialist as its prime minister as further ammunition for the anti-Communist campaign which he intensified in 1936.

Von Papen was certainly able to bring his negotiations with Schuschnigg to a conclusion with a German-Austrian agreement of July 1936, another success for bilateral over multilateral diplomacy. But the agreement was less important for its recognition of Austrian independence, which Hitler regarded as a temporary expedient, than for what he saw it opening the way to—the removal of an obstacle to a rapprochement with Mussolini, and the Duce's eventual acquiescence in the end of Austrian independence in 1938.

In 1931 France's position in Europe had been strong enough to force the German government to withdraw its proposal for an Austro-German customs union; in 1938 the French, like the Italians, saw no alternative to acquiescing in the Anschluss and reneging on their alliance with the Czechs in the Munich Agreement. The undermining of the French security system in Central and Eastern Europe, already begun in 1934, was the most serious consequence of the remilitarization of the Rhineland—more important than any effect it had on France's own security in the west. Once the Germans had fortified the Rhineland, the French could no longer come to the aid of their Eastern European allies by an immediate invasion of German territory through the demilitarized zone. The fact that France had not responded to the breach of the Versailles and Locarno treaties by sending in its army, when it still had clear military superiority over Germany and the Rhineland was wide open, strengthened doubts about the dependability of France's other commitments in a crisis.

The Popular Front government made two new attempts to restore the confidence of France's allies. One was a loan of two billion francs to Poland, 800 million of them to go to the purchase of French arms. The other was an offer of a full defensive alliance with the Little Entente,* provided its members agreed to assist one another against aggression by any power instead of by Hungary alone. Both came to nothing: the first because the French armaments industry failed to produce the arms; the second because of Yugoslav reluctance to get involved in a conflict with Germany or Italy, and British pressure on France not to assume greater commitments in Eastern Europe—a constant tendency in British relations with France throughout the 1930s.

The result was to leave the way open to the Nazis to exploit the impression of German strength and the Western powers' weakness left by the Rhineland episode.

Hitler, then and later, was willing to use Danzig as a means of testing how far he could go. In June 1936, Gauleiter Albert Forster stepped up the campaign of intimidation to force the surviving independent German parties to accept *Gleichschaltung* and turned this into a German demand for the removal of the League High Commissioner in the Free City of Danzig, Sean Lester. Receiving no support from the League powers, Lester resigned. The Poles, although not interested in the rights of Germans opposed to National Socialism, were very much interested in protecting their own rights. They made it clear that they would not agree to the abolition of Danzig's status as a free city under the auspices of the League of Nations, and a new high commissioner (Carl Burckhardt), acceptable to both Germans and Poles, was appointed. Forster, however, succeeded in getting Hitler's approval for outlawing the Danzig socialists and then, carried away by his success in forcing Lester's resignation, overreached himself. In a speech to his party followers he told them that the new Four-Year Plan meant Germany was preparing for war, that Hitler would be entering Danzig in a few months, and that the Poles as well as the League would be eliminated. In the uproar that followed, the Germans reassured the Poles that they would continue to respect their rights in Danzig, and Forster was told to restrain himself. The moment had not yet come for talking publicly about Germany's further goals; the 1934 treaty had not outlived its usefulness. But Hitler was no doubt content to leave the Poles to ponder whether Forster had done more than blurt out prematurely the truth about his intentions.

*The Little Entente was formed after the 1919 peace settlement by Czechoslovakia, Rumania, and Yugoslavia to resist revisionist claims by Hungary. Its members looked to France for support as the guarantor of the postwar settlement.

Further south, the German Foreign Office and the Economics Ministry had been keen to develop German economic and political relations with the countries of southeast Europe well before Hitler came to power. Hitler was not particularly interested, to begin with. However, trade agreements with them could help to meet domestic shortages in meat and butter, as well as provide raw materials needed for armaments, such as bauxite, copper, and petroleum. Nor was he indifferent to the fact that, if Yugoslavia and Rumania as well as Hungary were drawn into the German orbit, this would weaken the Little Entente and help to isolate the Czechs.*

Schacht's New Plan of 1934 redirected foreign trade through bilateral agreements that aimed at equalizing imports and exports with each individual trading partner, buying only from countries willing to buy German goods in return. By this means a substantial increase was achieved in imports from the three southeastern states, doubling those of meat from Hungary from 1934 to 1936 and increasing those from Yugoslavia fivefold. There were similar increases in the few raw-material imports southeast Europe could provide, notably an increase of 50 percent in oil imports from Rumania.

However, as recovery and rearmament began to absorb an increasing amount of German industrial production, it became more difficult to match the growing demand for imports with German exports that her partners wanted to buy. This was a problem that affected the whole of Germany's foreign trade and became part of the general economic crisis of 1936. The outcome was the Four-Year Plan and Schacht's replacement by Göring. Priority was given to rearmament and to the imports of raw materials and food necessary to sustain it, at whatever price. The Germans solved the problem of paying for these by the export of arms, a boon to a nation that needed to maintain a steady demand for armaments to keep production at near-peak levels of efficiency. In effect they drew economic advantage from the political anxiety they had created.

Significantly, only Poland among the agricultural countries of Eastern Europe refused to be drawn into this pattern of trade, preferring to curtail its exports to Germany and to buy its arms elsewhere for the sake of its political independence.

III

AT THE LONDON MEETING of the League Council to consider the remilitarization of the Rhineland, Litvinov took the line that Germany had violated her obligations and the League would become a laughingstock if it

---

*There were German-speaking minorities in all three countries, but they were descendants of settlers from earlier periods—the Saxons of Transylvania from the thirteenth century, the Swabians in Hungary and Yugoslavia from the eighteenth—and they did not figure in Hitler's long-term plans for expansion, which were directed east and northeast rather than southeast, into the lands briefly secured by the Treaty of Brest-Litovsk in 1918.

did not take some action. When it came to asking What action? he left the Locarno signatories to answer; the USSR would join in whatever course the council might decide to follow. He urged the other powers, however, not to be taken in by Hitler's proposals for new treaties when he had just torn up the old, adding a warning that Ivan Maisky, the Soviet ambassador in London, repeated on March 19:

> I know that there are people who think that war can be localized. These people think that, given definite agreements, war may break out in (shall we say?) the East or Southeast of Europe, but can pass by without affecting the countries of Western Europe. . . . This is the greatest of delusions. . . . Peace is indivisible.[10]

It is easy enough to argue in the light of the subsequent Nazi-Soviet Pact that the Russian advocacy of collective security was not to be taken seriously. But the same could be said of Britain and France in the light of their subsequent behavior over Ethiopia and Czechoslovakia, and their search for a settlement with Germany. All the powers "played on both sides of the street." More realistic than the British or French about the threat posed by Hitler and the danger of war, the Russians saw obvious advantages in not facing it alone. But they were as suspicious of British and French reliability as the British and French were of theirs. They were prepared to go as far as the other powers in committing themselves but were wary of exposing themselves before the others were committed—at which point they would be able to decide whether to join them, or stay out. A gloss provided by Molotov on Soviet policy was evenhanded, keeping all the options open: The USSR would welcome collaboration with Hitler's Germany, provided the latter would abide by international agreements and, for example, rejoin the League; and the USSR would stand by France if attacked, in accordance with the Franco-Soviet Treaty and "with the political situation as a whole." Whether the undertaking of Soviet help to France, *if attacked,* covered French military action against the remilitarization of the Rhineland, and if so how much help was to be given when the USSR had no common frontier with Germany, were questions left unanswered.

Finally, for the benefit of anyone listening in Berlin, Molotov added:

> There is a tendency among certain sections of the Soviet public toward an attitude of thoroughgoing irreconcilability to the present rulers of Germany, particularly because of the over-repeated hostile speeches of German leaders against the Soviet Union. But the chief tendency, and the one determining the Soviet government's policy, thinks an improvement in Soviet-German relations possible.[11]

Nineteen thirty-six saw the beginning of the purges in Russia; the executions that came close to wiping out the Soviet High Command began in June 1937. The effect abroad was greatly to reduce the Soviet Union's impact on the international situation. If the succession of more and more fantastic charges were true, the regime must be honeycombed with treachery and vulnerable to counter-revolution; if they were not true, how was it possible to take seriously a government that published such allegations against its recent political and military leaders, and even took the trouble to have the proceedings translated and published abroad? Russia's reliability as an ally was marked down heavily in Paris, her credibility as an opponent in Berlin.

A WAY OF COMPARING Hitler's and Stalin's foreign policies from 1936 to 1938 is provided by their intervention in the Spanish Civil War. Neither had shown any particular interest in Spain before 1936. Hitler was at Bayreuth for the Wagner festival in July when Hess arranged for him to see two Germans from Morocco, local officers of the Nazi Auslandsorganisation (AO), which had built up an extensive network among the German colony in Spain. One of them, Johannes Bernhardt, was a friend of Franco, then commander of the Spanish Army of Africa, and he brought with him a letter asking urgently for help in moving Franco's troops to the mainland. A right-wing army rebellion against the left-wing Republican government elected in February 1936 was in danger of failing; the one chance of saving it lay with Franco and the troops under his command, but with the Spanish navy and air force declaring for the government, he had no means of crossing the Straits without help from either Germany or Italy in the form of air transportation.

Hitler took no notice of the Foreign Office's advice, which was against becoming involved in Spain. After consulting with Göring, von Blomberg, and Admiral Wilhelm Canaris, the head of the Armed Forces Intelligence Service, who knew Spain well, he decided to send help. Two days later German planes started the ferrying operation, and by the end of the first week in August the advance party of a small German expeditionary force was operating in Spain. A special staff in the Ministry of War in Berlin and a German headquarters in Spain were matched by two disguised trading companies, Hisma, in the peninsula, and its counterpart, Rowak, in Germany. These handled the movement of troops and military supplies, the export of raw materials to Germany in return, and the necessary financial arrangements. But German military aid was never on the scale of the Italian forces, which at their maximum in 1937 numbered 40,000 to 50,000. The strength of the Germans reached around 10,000 in autumn 1936, consisting mostly of the Condor Legion, the best air force in Spain, with eight squadrons and an average strength of 5,600 men (it was the Condor Legion that bombed the Basque town of Guernica). They were accompanied by a force of antiaircraft, antitank, and armored units.

The original assumption was that the war would be quickly over, and Germany and Italy recognized Franco and the Nationalists as the government of Spain in November 1936, only to see Franco's bid to capture Madrid fail. Franco's allies were then faced with the prospect of a prolonged war, from which they could not disengage without loss of prestige. General Wilhelm Faupel, the German representative with Franco, urged that three German army divisions should be made available, but at a conference on December 21 Hitler decided against a force of this size, and in the course of the discussion set out the guidelines that governed German policy for the rest of the war.

The outbreak of the Spanish Civil War so soon after the end of the Ethiopian war was a remarkable piece of luck for Hitler, who could watch the other powers continue their Mediterranean quarrel while Germany concentrated on rearmament. Germany's interest therefore lay in focusing European attention on Spain, especially that of France, Britain, and Italy, for a long time to come, not in securing a quick victory for Franco. Germany had to make sure that Franco was not defeated but leave the major burden of military support for him to Italy. The more deeply the Italians became committed to intervention, the more difficult it would be for them to restore relations with France and Britain, and the more they would be obliged to continue the process, already begun during the Ethiopian war, of drawing closer to Germany.

Stalin had a more difficult decision to make. His first thought was to leave it to France to give aid to the Republican government. Because of the common frontier she shared with Spain, the outcome of the war would affect France more than any other power. But the political and class divisions in France, exacerbated by the advent of the Popular Front government under Blum, made it dangerous for her government to take sides openly. The British, as always, pressed the French to be prudent, and together they set up a Nonintervention Committee.

The Comintern had already been mobilized to organize support and raise funds on an anti-Fascist, nonparty platform from sympathizers around the world; the Soviet trade unions made a large grant to start this off. But to send Soviet arms or troops to intervene directly in a civil war at the other end of Europe was an entirely different matter. Stalin had to balance three considerations: to keep Russia out of war; not to step out of line with France and the other League powers; and to avoid reviving the specter of the Soviet Union as the exporter of revolution. On the other hand it was difficult to withhold support from a cause that made a unique appeal to progressive opinion throughout the world,* and to allow the Republican government to be defeated.

In August Stalin joined the other powers, including Germany and Italy, in accepting the Nonintervention Agreement, but at the same time formally established diplomatic relations with the Spanish Republican government and sent a large Soviet mission to Madrid. Vladimir Antonov-Ovseyenko,

*Hugh Thomas in his study of the Spanish Civil War makes the comment that, "for intensity of emotion, the Second World War seemed less of an event than the Spanish War. The latter appeared a 'just war' as civil wars do to intellectuals, since they lack the apparent vulgarity of national conflicts," *The Spanish Civil War* (London: 1961), p. 616.

who had commanded the Red Guards when they stormed the Winter Palace in 1917, and had later been a member of Lenin's first government, took up the post of consul general in Barcelona, a stronghold of anarchist and "Trotskyite" politics in which Stalin took a special interest. While waiting to see how nonintervention worked, the Comintern was instructed to go further than dispatching nonmilitary aid to the Republic and to set up an organization for the supply of arms.

In September Stalin agreed to two Spanish Communists joining the new government formed by Largo Caballero. The Spanish party had already complained at the failure of Russia to send aid, only to be told by the Italian Palmiro Togliatti, as a representative of the Comintern: "Russia regards her security as the apple of her eye. A false move on her part could upset the balance of power and unleash a war in Eastern Europe."[12] The same month, a number of other Russian and Comintern figures appeared in Spain, among them Alexander Orlov, formerly head of the economic section of the NKVD, who was sent to keep watch on the activities of the Comintern and foreign Communists in Spain. But Stalin still hesitated to go further.

His doubts appear to have been resolved by the French Communist Maurice Thorez, one of the leaders in the Comintern, who visited Moscow on September 22 and suggested a way in which military aid could be sent through the Comintern, without ostensibly involving the Soviet government or Soviet troops. Thorez proposed that the Comintern should raise international brigades of foreign volunteers, including the Communist émigrés who had taken refuge in Russia. These, under Communist leadership, would be the chief recipients of Soviet military aid, and such aid could be channeled by the organization that the NKVD had already set up for the Comintern. This consisted of a chain of import-export firms in eight European capitals, which were well placed (always with an NKVD man as a silent partner controlling payments) to procure arms from a variety of sources, including Germany.

Stalin was still wary, however, and drove a hard bargain. No Soviet weapons were actually used in Spain until the greater part of the Spanish Republic's gold reserve, valued at 500 million dollars, was dispatched from Cartegena to Odessa as payment in advance. In addition to the gold, the Republicans sent raw materials in bulk to Russia as the Nationalists did to Germany. The number of Russians is believed to have been under 2,000 all told, probably not more than 500 most of the time, serving in staff posts or as instructors. The Red Army was as interested as the German in the experience of performance under battle conditions. In the winter of 1936–37 most Russian planes in Spain were flown by Russian pilots, and the attack to drive the Nationalists back from Madrid was opened on October 29 by Russian tanks, driven by Russians, led by the tank specialist General Pavlov and supported by Russian planes. A heavy bombing campaign against the capital was launched by the other side on the same day, partly to satisfy Franco's German advisers, who were curious to see the civilian reaction.

The number of foreigners who fought in the International Brigades was much exaggerated. A realistic figure is about 40,000, although at any one time the number never exceeded 18,000. The largest contingent was French, some 10,000 in all, of whom 3,000 died; the next largest the German and Austrian, 5,000, of whom 2,000 died. They were recruited by the Comintern through its member parties—Josip Broz, the future Marshal Tito, was one of those engaged in organizing their passage to Spain from a small Left Bank hotel in Paris. In the field they came under the command of General Kleber, the *nom de guerre* of Lazar Stern, who had been born in Bukovina and served as a captain in the Austrian army before being captured by the Russians and joining the Bolsheviks.

Soviet aid to the Republic was substantially less than that promised by Germany and Italy to Franco.[13] Nonetheless, Soviet support was decisive in the autumn of 1936, preventing the Nationalists from winning the war in a few months. Russian advisers and the International Brigades brought order and discipline into the Republican army, the latter playing a major part in the Jarama and Guadalajara battles in the spring of 1937. The falling-off in Soviet and Comintern supplies during 1938 sealed the Republic's fate. As the British historian of Spain Raymond Carr points out: "It is misleading to argue in terms of quantity of supply. . . . In the long run it was the *continuity* of German and Italian aid, and the regularity with which the Axis supplies met every crisis of Franco's armies, which decided the war."[14]

The Nonintervention Committee spent a great part of its time listening to charges and countercharges between the supporters of the two sides, in which the three foreign ministers, Ribbentrop, Ciano (Italy), and Maisky (USSR) vied with one another in righteous indignation at the others' bare-faced intervention. Stalin never publicly acknowledged the aid the Russians gave to the Spanish Republic, but as their contribution was reported by every correspondent in the country, he was content to let others describe the Soviet Union as the only country that took the cause of anti-Fascism seriously and came to the aid of Spanish democracy. This provided a valuable counterbalance, among the many sympathizers with the Republican cause, to the disastrous impression left by the Russian purges.

Stalin insisted that Comintern support for the Republican government was always to be justified on nonpartisan, anti-Fascist grounds as "the defense of the democratic, parliamentary republic, the republic of the Popular Front which guarantees the rights and liberties of the Spanish people . . . the cause of peace and the common cause of all advanced and progressive mankind."[15] This is a quotation from a resolution passed by the Comintern Executive in December 1936. A week before, Stalin had sent a letter to the Spanish prime minister, Largo Caballero, signed by Molotov and Voroshilov as well as himself, in which he urged the Republican government to avoid social radicalism, enlist the support of the middle class, and broaden the basis of his government "in order to prevent the enemies of Spain from presenting it as a Communist republic." [16]

The fact that the Soviet Union through the Comintern was the only reliable source of arms and supplies gave Stalin the power to intervene in Spanish politics as well as in the war. It was the use he made of this, more than anything else, that tarnished the Soviet and Communist record in Spain and left bitter memories behind. The Spanish left had long been divided by disagreements over ideology and policy. The Communist party leadership accepted the Moscow line on the need to unite in defense of the democratic republic and postpone talk of revolution. But there were plenty of committed Spaniards who did not and who accused the Republican government and the Communists of betraying the revolution. The Anarchists, with a bigger following in Spain than anywhere else, were old ideological enemies of the Communists, a quarrel that went back to the disputes between Bakunin and Marx in the nineteenth century. The other group against whom Stalin's venom was directed was the POUM (Partido Obrero de Unificación Marxista), a non-Communist Marxist party which Stalin identified with Trotskyism and which had dared to propose that Trotsky should come to Spain. POUM attacked the Moscow trials, and using Trotskyite language spoke of "Stalinist Thermidorians" who had established in Russia "the bureaucratic regime of a poisoned dictator." POUM's largest following was also in Barcelona and Catalonia, and Stalin was determined they should be wiped out. An article in *Pravda* on November 17, 1936, pointed the way: "So far as Catalonia is concerned, the clearing up of Trotskyists and Anarchists has begun, and it will be carried out with the same energy as in the USSR." [17] In May 1937 tension in Barcelona had reached the point where it spilled over into four days of street fighting between the Communists and the police on one side, and the Anarchists and POUM on the other, leaving 400 dead and 1,000 wounded.

This May crisis brought about the fall of Caballero, who refused to follow the Moscow line and dissolve POUM. The NKVD, answerable only to Stalin and acting on its own authority, arrested the forty members of POUM's Central Committee, murdered Andres Nin, the POUM leader who had served as a minister in Caballero's government, and broke the back of the revolutionary opposition by the same methods as in the Soviet Union. Shortly afterwards many of the Russians in Spain, including Antonov-Ovseyenko, General Ion Berzin, the head of the Red Army group, and Marcel Rosenberg, the ambassador and head of the Russian mission, were recalled to Russia and disappeared in the purges.

After Munich, Stalin decided there was no further advantage in continuing Soviet aid to Spain. The last action of the International Brigades was on September 22, 1938, and the war ended with Franco's victory in the spring of 1939. Besides the Russian advisers who perished in the purges, many non-Russian Communists also suffered for their participation in the

Spanish Civil War. In the late 1940s most of those Communists in Eastern
Europe who were veterans of the International Brigades came under Stalin's
suspicion. After the trial and execution of László Rajk, in 1949, nearly all
were arrested and many shot. Rajk himself, at that time Hungarian foreign
secretary, had been commissar of the Rákosi Battalion in the XIII International Brigade. He "confessed" to having gone to Spain to sabotage the
military efficiency of the battalion and carry on Trotskyist propaganda. So
far did the shadow of the purges reach out into the future.

IV

ALTHOUGH HITLER backed the winner in the Spanish war and Stalin
the loser, there are parallels in both their attitudes and their experiences.
In a secret review of the future of German policy in November 1937 Hitler
said that a 100-percent Franco victory was not desirable from the German
point of view: "Our interest lay in a continuation of the war and in keeping
up the tension in the Mediterranean."[18] Both Hitler and Stalin valued the
diversionary effect of the war: Hitler in allowing Germany to continue with
rearmament; Stalin in keeping the other European powers divided and so
allowing him to carry out the purges without anxiety about external threats.
Each was able to make use of his participation for propaganda purposes—
Hitler for his anti-Bolshevik crusade, Stalin for Russia's identification with
the anti-Fascist cause. Both Germans and Russians had an excellent opportunity to try out their weapons and to give their officers and pilots experience of combat conditions—although the Germans made better use of the
lessons they learned than the Russians. Both also benefited from shipments
of Spanish raw materials. Finally, there was, in both cases, the eclipse of the
Foreign Office. The initiative in persuading Hitler to intervene in Spain
came from the party's Auslandsorganisation, and was opposed by the
professional diplomats. The AO continued to be involved on the economic
side, as did Göring as head of the Four-Year Plan and commander in chief
of the Luftwaffe, Canaris, the chief of military intelligence, and Ribbentrop
on the Nonintervention Committee. Stalin chose to use the Comintern, the
NKVD, and the Red Army as his instruments, employing Litvinov and
Maisky mainly in the Nonintervention Committee and the League of Nations.

Hitler's remark about a Franco victory showed prescience. All the benefits accrued from the continuation of the war. Once he had won, Franco
proved to be the most exasperating and evasive of allies. But the greatest
benefit of all for Hitler—and one for which there was no parallel in Stalin's
case—was the working relationship with the Italians, which laid the basis
for their future alliance. As Hitler had foreseen, Mussolini's African and
Mediterranean ambitions, by embroiling him with the British and French,
obliged him to draw nearer to Germany.

Mussolini's appointment of his son-in-law, Galeazzo Ciano, to the Italian

Foreign Office advanced a minister more sympathetic to the idea of cooperation with Germany than his predecessor. Italo-German discussions during the summer of 1936 covered the whole field of common interests—and differences—between the two powers. This was preliminary to a visit Ciano paid to Germany in October, when Hitler was anxious to please, and the two agreed on the establishment of a common front which Mussolini christened the Rome-Berlin Axis. Its basis was common hostility to the British and the exploitation of the anti-Communist campaign. Behind this screen, Germany and Italy could continue their rearmament, and Ciano reported that at Berchtesgaden Hitler had told him: "In three years Germany will be ready, in four years more than ready; if five years are given, better still." [19]

There was a legacy of distrust and jealousy on the Italian side to be overcome, distrust especially of German intentions toward Austria. Nonetheless, Mussolini's Mediterranean ambitions, his anxiety to be on the winning side and share in the plucking of the decadent democracies, his resentment against the British and the French over sanctions, and the bruised vanity of a dictator with a bad inferiority complex in international relations all highlighted the advantages of the partnership that Hitler pressed on him. The seal was set on the alliance when Mussolini, in a new uniform specially designed for the occasion, paid a state visit to Germany in September 1937.

Hitler received the Duce at Munich and, with the showmanship at which the Nazis excelled, put on a display of German power—parades, army maneuvers, a visit to Krupps, culminating in a mass demonstration in his honor in Berlin—which bewitched the Italian, leaving an indelible impression from which he was never able to set himself free. It was a fatal step for the Duce, the beginning of that surrender of independence that led his regime to disaster and himself to the end of a rope in the Piazzale Loreto in Milan. Yet Hitler's feeling of comradeship for Mussolini was unfeigned. Like himself—and like Stalin, for whom Hitler also expressed admiration on occasion—Mussolini was a man of the people, with whom Hitler could feel at ease as he never felt with members of the traditional ruling classes, least of all the Italian royal family. Despite Hitler's later disillusionment with the Italian performance in the war, he never betrayed or abandoned Mussolini even when he had been overthrown—more than could be said of Stalin and any man.

Shortly after the Duce's visit in November 1937, Ribbentrop appeared in Rome to persuade him to put his signature to the Anti-Comintern pact he was promoting.* Ribbentrop pleased and relieved the Duce by declaring that he had failed in his mission to London and that German and British interests were irreconcilable. Hitler was equally delighted with the report Ribbentrop brought back of Mussolini's remarks about Austria. According

*See pp. 539–40.

to Ciano's minutes, Mussolini said he was tired of guarding Austrian independence, especially if the Austrians no longer wanted it:

> Austria is German State No. 2. It will never be able to do anything without Germany, far less against Germany. Italian interest today is no longer as lively as it was some years ago, for one thing because of Italy's development, which is now concentrating her interest on the Mediterranean and the colonies. . . .
>
> The best method is to let events take their natural course. One must not aggravate the situation. . . . On the other hand France knows that if a crisis should arise over Austria, Italy would do nothing. This was said to Schuschnigg too in Venice. We cannot impose independence on Austria.[20]

All Mussolini asked was that nothing should be done without a previous exchange of information: When the time came, even that was lacking.

THE OTHER ALLIANCE on which Hitler had placed his hopes in *Mein Kampf*—with Britain—proved as elusive as ever. It was certainly not for lack of trying on the British side to reach a settlement with Germany. Neville Chamberlain succeeded Baldwin as prime minister at the end of May 1937. "His all-pervading hope," Churchill later wrote, "was to go down in history as the Great Peacemaker; and for this he was prepared to strive continually in the teeth of facts, and face great risks for himself and his country.[21] There is no need to follow the course of the discussions that Chamberlain initiated with Germany, including the visit to Berchtesgaden by the British foreign secretary, Lord Halifax, in November 1937. All that is necessary is to pin down the reason for Chamberlain's failure.

Nineteen thirty-seven brought to the fore the question of the return of the German colonies taken from her by the Allies after the First World War. A colonial agitation had been whipped up in Germany comparable to the propaganda for a bigger navy of the *Flottenverein* (the German Navy League), in the 1900s. Schacht, for example, was one who looked to colonial expansion as a way of relieving Germany's economic problems and providing an alternative to Hitler's plans for eastern conquests. Hitler did not discourage the agitation, which kept up pressure on Britain and France; and he was ready to accept the return of colonies, provided it was a unilateral act without strings. But he refused to be diverted from his continental strategy by the offer of colonial or economic concessions.

The British object, as Hitler well understood, was to make any return of colonies part of a comprehensive settlement, the German contribution to which would be to abandon Hitler's designs in Eastern Europe, return to the League, and agree to settle all problems by peaceful negotiation. The only result of the British approaches, however, was to confirm Hitler in his belief that, while they were opposed to German continental expansion, the

British would never take the risk of war to prevent it. But neither would they give Germany a free hand in Europe, which was the only basis for an agreement that would have interested Hitler.

In a note to Hitler (January 2, 1938) Ribbentrop wrote that Germany should abandon any hope of an understanding with the British and instead concentrate on creating a network of alliances against them, beginning with the agreements she already had with Japan and Italy. An agreement with Japan had first been proposed as a private initiative of Ribbentrop's in the summer of 1935 as a result of talks with the Japanese ambassador, Hiroshi Oshima. It was then conceived of as an anti-Comintern pact directed against the Soviet Union. It ran into strong opposition from the German Foreign Office and the German army, which had built up a long-term connection with China through German military advisers working closely with Chiang Kai-shek as well as through trade. Nonetheless, after a year's delay, Ribbentrop succeeded in getting Hitler's approval.

The pact, which was open to other powers to join, was signed on November 25, 1936 and was regarded with special pride by Ribbentrop as its author. It provided for cooperation between the two powers in opposing the Communist International—a neat reversal of Stalin's use of the Comintern in Spain as a cover for Soviet intervention. Its announcement caused a sensation. Despite denials, everyone was sure there were secret clauses. So there were, each promising not to assist Russia if there was an unprovoked attack or threat of attack by the Soviet Union on the other parties. This commitment, however, was modified by equally secret reservations: "On the basis of the agreement [the partners] could move jointly; on the basis of the reservations, each could go its own way."[22]

A continuing obstacle to developing the pact was the conflict of views in Berlin between those who thought it in Germany's interests to maintain the good relations with China built up over two decades and those who were prepared to sacrifice these for an alliance with the rising power of Japan. Göring, for example, who was strongly attracted to Japan, began to think again when HAPRO, the German agency for trade with Nationalist China, was transferred from the Ministry of War to the Four-Year Plan, and he realized the value of the raw materials (for example, tungsten) and foreign exchange provided by China in return for military and industrial supplies. Ribbentrop, however, was persistent, and in November 1937 persuaded Mussolini to add Italy's signature to the pact, describing it as "the alliance of the aggressive nations against the satisfied countries." The Italians valued it for the pressure a link with Japan could put on British and French interests in the Far East, and Ribbentrop henceforward spoke of his policy of the "World Triangle," writing in an end-of-the-year report to Hitler: "England now sees its East Asian possessions threatened by Japan, its sea route through the Mediterranean to India by Italy, and the mother country, the British Isles, by Germany."[23]

· · ·

HISTORICAL REALITY never lived up to the hopes or fears created by the Anti-Comintern Pact. As was demonstrated by the signature of the Nazi-Soviet Pact in 1939 and the Japanese attack at Pearl Harbor—neither revealed in advance to the other partners—in practice it was the freedom for each to go its own way that counted more than the opportunity for joint action. Knowing this, its importance in the late 1930s and early 1940s can easily be underestimated, when it forced the other powers to take into account the possibility of global cooperation among the three signatories, an alarming possibility for Britain and France with their empires as well as for the USSR.

The pact helped to strengthen the impression that Germany in less than five years had become the most powerful country and Hitler the most successful leader in Europe. The extent of her rearmament may have been exaggerated, but this was a tribute to the impression of confidence and strength that both exuded in a world where everyone else was apprehensive and asked: What will Germany do? When German planes bombed Guernica and German warships shelled Almeria,* people everywhere were shocked, but also impressed.

By contrast, Russia appeared isolated and her leadership riven by accusations of treachery and the operation of the purge. In May 1937 Litvinov paid a visit to Paris and urged the French to establish closer relations with the Red Army and to undertake the necessary technical contacts that had still not taken place two years after the pact had been concluded. Hardly had he left when the French learned that almost the entire command structure of the Red Army had been destroyed on Stalin's orders. In March 1938, the U.S. ambassador in Moscow reported Litvinov's view that "France has no confidence in the Soviet Union and the Soviet Union has no confidence in France."[24]

The Anti-Comintern Pact appeared to underline the extent to which Stalin had lost ground by comparison with Hitler's success. When put to the test, however, it failed to produce the promised alignment of Japanese and German policies, providing instead the first of many disappointments for the pact's architect, Ribbentrop, and a rare success in foreign policy for Stalin.

For nearly ten years, during which the Japanese had conquered Manchuria, relations between the Russians and Chiang Kai-shek had remained soured by the latter's suppression of the Chinese Communists in 1928. In 1936 the Russians became disturbed by reports of negotiations for a truce between Chiang and the Japanese. This would leave the latter free to turn their undivided attention to probing weaknesses in the security of the Soviet Far Eastern territories, while Chiang concentrated on destroying the Com-

*In May 1937, following a Spanish Republican attack on the German battleship *Deutschland* which had killed thirty-one of its crew.

munist stronghold in northwest China created by the "Long March."*
Attempts to persuade Chiang to join the Russians instead in a common
front against the Japanese had been rebuffed, and the Generalissimo had
already earmarked the troops that were to carry out the attack on his
internal enemies.

Their commander, however, a former warlord of Manchuria, Chang
Hsueh-ling, refused to fall in with the plan and, when Chiang flew to his
base in December 1936 to persuade him, Chang imprisoned him—the
so-called Sian incident. In the negotiations that followed, Chou En-lai, the
righthand man of the Communist leader, Mao Tse-tung, played a crucial
role in persuading Chiang to reverse his policy and make common cause
with the Chinese Communists against Japan.

Without waiting for the new alliance to take effect, the Japanese attacked
on July 7, 1937, and, despite German attempts to mediate between Nanking
and Tokyo, in the winter of 1937–38 Japan became more and more committed to Chiang's defeat and overthrow. As the Germans pointed out to their
Japanese partners in the Anti-Comintern Pact, the renewed conflict in
China helped instead of hindering the spread of Communism. In August
the Russians signed a treaty of nonaggression and friendship with Chiang
and began to make Soviet arms, credits, and instructors available, although
never on a large scale. The benefit for Stalin was not only the renewed
foothold that this gave the Russians in China after the disaster of 1928, but
also the diversion of Japanese energies away from the Russians' Far Eastern
territories. The threat of war with Japan was not finally removed until Pearl
Harbor, but the danger of it, which had appeared imminent at times during
the 1930s as a result of frontier incidents, was greatly reduced.

v

HITLER'S OVERRIDING CONSIDERATION in his conduct of
foreign policy during 1936 and 1937 continued to be gaining the time and
freedom for Germany to rearm. By the closing months of 1937, however,
he was beginning to think of reversing the order and using Germany's
growing military strength and the implicit threat of force to reinforce a more
aggressive attitude in international relations. This in turn helped to create
the widespread belief among the other powers, virtually unchallenged until
after the war, that Germany was making much more rapid progress than
any other country toward the mobilization of her economy as well as her
armed forces for war.

In fact, it was not until the beginning of 1942 that the Germans began

---

*In the early 1930s Chiang Kai-shek and the Chinese Nationalists destroyed the Communist
stronghold on the Fukien-Kiangsi border in southeast China. One hundred thousand survivors
broke out and began the Long March of 6,000 miles (1934–35) to Shensi in northwest China
where they created a new revolutionary base. The Long March was a decisive event in the
history of the Chinese Communist party and in the rise of Mao to its leadership.

to put their economy onto a full wartime footing and draw into the production of armaments largely hitherto untapped industrial resources, allowing them to achieve in 1943–44—the years that saw the Anglo-American bombing attacks reach their peak—the greatest increases in productivity. An index for overall arms production from 1942 to 1944, taking the figures for January through February 1942 as the baseline, provides a startling illustration of the results:

January–February 1942	100
July 1942	153
July 1943	229
July 1944	322

These figures took the Americans and British very much by surprise when brought to light after the war. One explanation is that the rest of the world was taken in by German propaganda, which succeeded in the late 1930s in building up the impression of German military power and so gave an edge to Hitler's diplomacy. In the same way, once the fighting began, propaganda was used with similar effectiveness to reinforce the Blitzkrieg and spread panic and defeatism.

But this is too simple an explanation by itself. For, when every allowance is made for the inflated estimates of German strength that Nazi propaganda produced, the fact is that the achievement underlying it was real enough. In six and a half years the German armed forces had been built up from the army of 100,000 (seven divisions) allowed by the Treaty of Versailles—without a military air force—to the 2,750,000 men mobilized in the autumn of 1939, in 103 divisions, no fewer than six of which were armored and four fully motorized. By the same date the air force, created from scratch, had over 4,000 front-line aircraft of modern design, 90 percent immediately operational.

The mistake the other powers made was not so much in exaggerating Germany's readiness for war in 1939 as in misunderstanding its character. They assumed that *military* was matched by a comparable degree of *economic* mobilization; they failed to distinguish between "rearmament in breadth" (which was what the Germans had carried out) and "rearmament in depth" (which was what the British reluctantly embarked on in 1938, wrongly supposing the Germans had done the same). The Germans concentrated on maintaining a relatively high level of armaments to meet the forces' immediate needs—often with dangerously low reserve stocks of weapons, ammunition, and fuel—and had not undertaken, as the British had already begun to, the basic investment in new plant or the reorganization of industry for the sustained mass production that would be required in a long war.

The lesson of the First World War was that Germany must avoid a long war that would expose her lack of strategic raw materials—all except coal—and her inability to feed her own population, so making her vulnerable to a renewal of the Allies' economic blockade. Determined not to see the stalemate of trench warfare repeated, Hitler seized on the concept of the Blitzkrieg, a "lightning war," directed against one opponent at a time, diplomatically isolated and overwhelmed by an initial knockout blow with a concentration of forces, taking the enemy by surprise and leading to a quick victory.

It is not difficult to see the attraction a Blitzkrieg had for Hitler. A short intensive war, even a succession of such campaigns as in 1939 through 1941, could be sustained without converting the whole economy to war production. By not allowing Germany to be drawn into a long war, and so not making too heavy demands on scarce raw materials, or imposing too heavy sacrifices on the civilian population (a key point for a regime that was always sensitive to public opinion), Hitler believed he could avoid the mistakes which had led to defeat in the First World War.

But what happened if the Germans became involved in a long war against their will? One man who asked that question was Colonel (later General) Georg Thomas, who played a leading role in the planning of rearmament and in 1939 became head of the Economic Staff in the War Ministry, finally moving to the OKW, the High Command of the German armed forces, as head of what became, in 1939, the War Economy and Rearmaments Office (*WiRüAmt,* as it was known).

It was Thomas who first made the distinction between "armament in breadth" and "armament in depth" in 1936, arguing that it was the failure to recognize the need for the latter by adequate economic preparations in time that had nullified the victories of the German army in the First World War, despite an exemplary military mobilization and performance in the field. Thomas went on to argue that Hitler was making the same mistake and was dismissed from office in 1943 for being proven right. He wrote immediately after Germany's defeat:

> I can only repeat that in Hitler's so-called Leadership State there existed in economic affairs a complete absence of leadership, and an indescribable duplication of effort and working at cross-purposes. For Hitler shut his eyes to the need for fixed, long-range planning, Göring knew nothing of economics, and the responsible professionals had no executive powers. [25]

Historical research since the war has confirmed Thomas's view and made clear that the military leadership bore as much responsibility for the shortcomings of the program as Hitler and Göring. [26]

The rearmament program for the expansion of the peacetime army was already approved in 1932 before Hitler came to power; but there was no comparable program to provide a much larger field army with supplies and equipment.

The objective finally set by Hitler, a field army substantially larger than that with which Germany had gone to war with France, Russia, and Britain in 1914, was actually achieved by the date set of October 1939, but it was still without an adequate long-term economic program to support and maintain it.

Despite the huge sums of money committed to the rearmament program—by 1938, greater than that of any other power, amounting to 52 percent of government expenditure and 17 percent of the gross national product—no coherent national program was ever drawn up to relate its speed and scale to Germany's economic capacity or to establish priorities among the claims of the different services. Instead, each branch set and pursued its own targets, without regard to those of the other two, lobbying and competing to secure the necessary allocation of capital investment and of the raw materials in which Germany was so deficient. Göring, who as economic supremo might have been expected to press for coordination, was the most determined—in his other capacity as commander in chief of the newly created Luftwaffe—to prevent it.

Coordination between the different services is a problem that has vexed every government and for which few, if any, have ever found a satisfactory solution. It was a commonplace, if naive, comment in the 1930s and 1940s that this was a problem that dictatorships found it easier to overcome than democracies. On the contrary, as far as Hitler was concerned, nothing more clearly shows his inadequacy in discharging the administrative responsibilities of a dictator. Unlike the day-to-day business of government in which Hitler refused to involve himself, the success of rearmament was the heart of his program. He was passionately interested in military technology: He grasped at once General Guderian's concept of a *Panzer* (armored) division acting independently and gave it his full support, and he is reported to have suggested the conversion of the 88mm antiaircraft gun to provide the German tanks and antitank units with one of the most successful weapons of the war. Here, if anywhere, is where he could have been expected to give decisive leadership—where he alone had the power to knock heads together and insist on a coherent overall plan for the allocation of resources and production. Instead, the economy, with every sector, military and civilian, competing for raw materials, skilled manpower, and finance, and no clear definition of responsibilities or enforcement of priorities, remained the most striking example of the "authoritarian anarchy" and "administrative chaos" that in practice characterized the much-lauded dictatorship.

Telling him that he wanted to be bothered with as few decisions as possible, Hitler pushed the responsibility for the war economy onto Göring. But Göring was the last man to make good Hitler's shortcomings. Both he and Hitler regarded his ignorance of economics and lack of industrial experience as assets in undertaking to create an alternative economy. Will, as Hitler never tired of repeating, was what was needed to overcome economic difficulties. If ambition was a measure of will, Göring had plenty of it. Avid to create a political position that would make him second only to Hitler, he accumulated responsibilities far beyond his ability to discharge and then, to defend his position, insisted on monopolizing decision making without the technical competence to form a judgment. In order to preserve his credit with Hitler, he was prepared to suppress information and deliberately misrepresent the comparative levels of German and enemy production, an example that his own subordinates soon learned to copy.

Göring's position as commander in chief of the Luftwaffe, and the disproportionate share of resources he claimed for it, have already been mentioned as major obstacles to coordination, but they could at least have been expected to guarantee the success of Germany's rearmament program in the air. On the contrary, its failure was the most striking example of Göring's ineffectiveness. Jealous of those who had the knowledge and experience he lacked, Göring preferred to appoint deputies he could dominate or who would not show up his ignorance.

But the failure to achieve Hitler's hopes of the Four-Year Plan and its successor was due to deeper causes than Göring's personal shortcomings. The real problem was structural. A considerable part of the different military bureaucracies' time was spent on resisting the claims of the other services to raw materials, manpower, and other economic resources and promoting their own. By 1941, administration took some 60 percent of all expenditure by the army, and only 8 percent of the military budget in 1940 was spent on the procurement of weapons. [27] Hitler was no more prepared to intervene to check this than he was in the case of the polycratic rivalries that divided the civilian administration. Apart from anything else, the ever-growing army of officials, both military and civilian, was heavily recruited from party members.

Both army and air force were opposed to and despised mass production, shift working, and standardization of parts, strongly preferring small workshops with the highly skilled craftsmen who would respond to changes in design. Even when larger numbers of aircraft were produced during the war, the habit of building in single units persisted. One example from many must suffice. The standardization of parts was not achieved until the end of the war: The Junkers 88 medium bomber was designed with 4,000 different types of screw and bolt and had to be riveted by hand instead of with the automatic machine-tools that were available but not used. Such conservative practices were wasteful of raw material as well as skilled labor.

The Nazi party itself was as guilty as the armed services of resisting the steps necessary for rationalization to have been begun earlier. The Gauleiters regarded themselves as the guardians of the economic life of their areas and immediately challenged any move directed toward a greater concentration of war production that might mean that their *Gau* lost out. Following Hitler's own example, the party bosses stubbornly resisted any attempt to cut back on the grandiose construction projects that Thomas criticized for squandering essential resources. They were equally vociferous in protesting against cuts in the production of consumer goods, food rationing, labor conscription, and anything else that threatened the standard of living of the

ordinary population. Whereas Britain began to draw on women for armaments production, and eventually to conscript them for war work, Hitler
himself put a ban on Germany's following the same course, and two and a
half million women who might otherwise have been drafted were still in
domestic service at the end of the war.

The Four-Year Plan and the Hermann Göring Reichswerke had been
seen by Hitler as the Nazis' answer to the businessmen and industrialists
who believed that German rearmament could be carried through only with
their cooperation. In effect it meant the end of the alliance with the business
establishment that had produced Germany's economic recovery in the years
1933 through 1935 and Schacht's New Plan.

With a few notable exceptions such as Carl Krauch and I. G. Farben, the
leading German industrialists and businessmen were excluded from any
role in the planning and execution of German rearmament. Many of the
Nazis whom Göring recruited to carry out the plan and build up the
Reichswerke were drawn from the anticapitalist wing of the party, favored
small businesses, and were hostile to large-scale corporate enterprises. The
big firms, of course, were given contracts, which they duly carried out, but
the managerial experience and technical knowledge of the men responsible
for one of the largest industrial sectors in the world were largely ignored.
Unimpressed by the mixture of ignorance and arrogance displayed by
Göring and the new elite, the majority retreated into their own factories and
offices. They did what they were asked to do, but without any incentive for
innovation or rationalization, looking after the interests of their firms and
making large profits from an inefficient and wasteful administration.

How much the German war effort lost by this was shown when Hitler
at last brought himself in the winter of 1941–42 to bypass Göring and allow
first Todt, then Speer, to take over responsibility for arms development and
production. Reversing the official attitude, they began to establish what
Todt called the "self-responsiblity of the armaments industry," involving
industrialists—frequently as chairmen—in the work of the committees set
up to reorganize and improve production in each sector of industry. It was
with this shift of policy, and the realization by the German people of the
changes that threatened them, that the full mobilization of the economy for
war was at last achieved and production figures began to show a dramatic
rise. That was after the failure of the Blitzkrieg against Russia, too late to
affect the outcome of the war. If the necessary steps had been taken earlier,
Speer later commented, in the middle of 1941, when the Germans first
invaded Russia, "Hitler could easily have led an army equipped twice as
powerfully as it was."[28]

BUT IT IS IMPORTANT to remember the very real achievements of
the German rearmament program as well as its weaknesses. The real test of
every rearmament program is military effectiveness, and few armed forces
have given a clearer demonstration of this than the Germans did in 1939

and 1940. Other things besides Germany's restored military strength helped to account for it, particularly those political and psychological factors in the handling of which Hitler excelled as clearly as he fell short in the handling of economic issues. But the ability to take advantage of the opportunities he created depended on the effectiveness of the instrument the German military had created and their operational skill in handling it. The result was an unbroken record of success between the occupation of Austria in February 1938 and the autumn of 1941, punctuated only by the defeat of the Luftwaffe in the Battle of Britain and halted only by the Russian counterattack before Moscow in December 1941. The map on pages 734–35 shows how much of Europe and North Africa—including the Ukraine and a large part of western Russia, as well as France, Poland, and the Balkans—had by then been brought under the control in one form or another of the Germans and their Italian allies—at a small fraction of the cost in German lives during the First World War.

Comparison with the rearmament of the other European powers in the 1930s confirms that, whatever its shortcomings in the long run, German rearmament had given the Reich an initial advantage, which Hitler recognized would be reduced as the others caught up but which he was prepared to gamble could prove decisive before that happened.

The most interesting comparison is with Russia. The Soviet Union was militarily much weaker at the end of the 1930s than it had been four or five years earlier. At the beginning of the 1930s the Russians were producing more aircraft and tanks than any other power. Although defense expenditure fell off during the first Five-Year Plan, it was sharply increased during the second, rising from 1.42 billion rubles in 1933 to 23.2 billion in 1938. The plan's industrial program put special emphasis on developing a self-sufficient armaments industry and creating new arms factories beyond the Urals, out of reach of both Germans and Japanese.

The years 1934 and 1935 were the halcyon years of the Red Army. Prompted by the Manchurian crisis and Hitler's accession to power, Stalin agreed to increase its numbers from 600,000 to 940,000 in 1934 and 1.3 million in 1935, backed by a reserve in the militia of twice that size, although of much more doubtful efficiency. Its officers, led by the group around Tukhachevsky, studied and vigorously debated the new ideas of Western theorists about the future of warfare, developing their own version of mechanized formations, chemical warfare, air-to-ground cooperation, and the use of paratroops, as well as the creation of an independent bomber force.

Here was a force that in the mid-1930s could match the German Wehrmacht, backed up by Russia's own arms industry, the virtual self-sufficiency of the Soviet Union in raw materials, and the largest reserves of manpower in the world. How seriously Hitler took it is shown by the prominence he gave to Russia in his memorandum of July 1936 on the Four-Year Plan.

Marxism, through its victory in Russia, has established one of the greatest engines as a forward base for its future operations. . . .*

The military resources of this aggressive will are in the meantime rapidly increasing from year to year. One has only to compare the Red Army as it actually exists today with the assumptions of military men ten or fifteen years ago to realize the menacing extent of this development. Only consider the results of a further development over ten, fifteen, or twenty years and think what conditions will be like then. . . .

In the face of the necessity of warding off this danger, all other considerations must recede into the background as completely irrelevant. . . .

The extent of the military development of our resources cannot be too large, or its pace too swift. It is a major error to believe that there can be any comparison with other vital necessities. [29]

In his memorandum, Hitler based his whole case for the rearmament of Germany and the mobilization of the economy on the military strength of the Soviet Union. He chose to present it in the form of a threat to European civilization, which Germany alone could be relied on to resist; but it applied with equal force to the threat that a strong Russia represented to the realization of his own plans for the conquest of *Lebensraum* in the east. Hitler's evaluation of the Red Army in 1936 highlights Stalin's extraordinary decision to wipe out its High Command and half its officer corps in 1937 and 1938, a decision apparently made without regard to its international consequences. These are to be measured not only by the number of experienced officers who were eliminated, running into many thousands, but also by the devastating blow dealt to the quality of the Soviet military leadership. The first victims of the purge were those who had been most active in adopting new ideas—thereby arousing Stalin's suspicions. Their removal left the armed forces in the hands of leaders characterized by the historian Paul Kennedy as "politically safe but intellectually retarded."

Stalin continued to pump resources into expanding and rearming the armed forces, raising expenditure on defense from 16.5 percent of the total budget in 1937 to 32.6 percent in 1940. But the innovative spirit that the Red Army's commanders had encouraged before the purges was killed and replaced by blind obedience. With the exception of Shaposhinikov, who was appointed chief of staff in May 1937, the new command "was stamped either by mediocrity or lack of experience." These were shown up by the incorrect evaluation of the lessons learned in the Spanish Civil War, leading to the disbanding of the seven mechanized corps and a similar abandonment of the Soviet Union's lead in developing the most powerful strategic bomber force in existence.

The consequences of Stalin's downgrading of the Soviet armed forces affected the policies of both dictators. Stalin's recognition—never, of course, admitted—that it would require a longer time, all the time he could win, for the army to recover, and for the increased investment to produce

*Hitler's italics.

results in military effectiveness, was a major factor in his handling of foreign policy in 1938 and 1939 and in opting for the Nazi-Soviet Pact as the best way to secure it. The effect on Hitler was the opposite. When he addressed the German military leaders at the secret meeting in November 1937, the emphasis that he had placed on the development of Soviet military strength in his memorandum of July 1936 was completely missing. The only mention of Russia was in connection with a possible German attack on Czechoslovakia: "Military intervention by Russia must be countered by the swiftness of our operations; but whether such intervention is a practical contingency is more than doubtful in view of the attitude of Japan."[30]

This change in Hitler's appreciation of Russian strength was a direct result of the impression made on him by Stalin's purge of the Red Army leadership. It was confirmed by the poor showing that the Russians made against the Finns in the Winter War of 1939–40 and it played a major part in the miscalculation that led him to base his plans for the 1941 invasion on defeating the Red Army in a single campaign, making no provision for its prolongation into the winter, and rejecting the opportunity for exploiting discontent with Stalin's regime in the Ukraine and other parts of occupied Russia. This was the mistake from which Hitler and the German army never recovered.

VI

THE GERMAN ARMY'S August 1936 program marked the decisive change from a defensive rearmament to one explicitly offensive. But the program had been drawn up and approved without any understanding by the military leaders of when and in what circumstances the forces they were creating were to be used. The final directive did not go beyond the general statement in the opening sentence: "According to the Führer, a powerful army is to be created within the shortest possible time."[31]

By November 1937 Hitler was ready to reveal his thoughts, at least in part. On the fifth of that month he called a closed meeting in the Reich Chancellery to which he summoned the three commanders in chief, of the army (von Fritsch), navy (Raeder), air force (Göring); the minister of defense (von Blomberg), and the foreign minister (von Neurath). The only other person present besides himself was Colonel Frëdrich Hossbach, the adjutant who took the minutes of the discussion.[32]

The ostensible reason for the meeting was the need to make a decision on the allocation of steel in light of the navy's demand for more, if it was to complete its construction program. It was at once clear, however, that much more than that was on Hitler's mind. He went out of his way to stress the importance of the occasion, declaring that:

> His exposition was the fruit of thorough deliberation and the experience of his four and a half years in power. He wished to explain his basic ideas concerning the opportunities for the development of our position in

foreign affairs and its requirements. He asked that it be regarded, in the event of his death, as his last will and testament.

Hitler began by restating his familiar view that increased participation in world trade could not solve Germany's problems. He was equally skeptical—much more definitely than in his memorandum on the Four-Year Plan, eighteen months before—about autarky and also about colonies. He defined the problem as a racial community of eighty-five million Germans suffering from the fact that they were much more tightly packed in their existing territories than any other people ("which implied the right to a greater living space") and that, "as a consequence of centuries of historical development, there existed no political result, territorially speaking, corresponding to this German racial core"—a characteristically involved way of saying that German unification in a Greater German Reich still had to be achieved. "The only remedy, and one that might seem visionary, is the acquisition of greater living space—a quest that has in every age been the origin of the formation of states and of the migration of peoples."

The problem must be confronted immediately and additional *Lebensraum* sought in Europe, not overseas.

There had never been spaces without a master, and there were not today. . . . Germany's problem could only be solved by means of force, and this was never without attendant risks.

If he was still living, it was his unalterable resolve to solve Germany's problem of space at the latest by 1943 through 1945.

The solution thus obtained must suffice for one or two generations. Whatever else might later prove necessary must be left to succeeding generations to deal with.

The date was fixed by the relative progress of Germany's and other nations' rearmament. After the period 1943 to 1945, the relative advantage given by German rearmament would decrease; German equipment would begin to be out of date, and other nations which had begun to rearm later would overtake her.

Hitler defined the first objective as "to overthrow Czechoslovakia and Austria simultaneously in order to remove the threat to our flank in any possible operation against the West." In addition to providing shorter and better frontiers as well as the manpower for twelve new divisions, the incorporation of the two Central European states with Germany would mean "an acquisition of foodstuffs for 5–6 million people, on the assumption that the compulsory emigration of 2 million people from Czechoslovakia and 1 million from Austria was predictable." At no point did Hitler refer to the "liberation of the Sudeten Germans from intolerable persecution by the Czechs" which he made the justification for his actions in the Czech crisis of 1938; he spoke only of the "overthrow" of Czechoslovakia as a state, and "crushing the Czechs."

Hitler, however, did not pursue this glimpse into the future. He hardly referred to Eastern Europe, where the conquest of *Lebensraum* was to take place, or to Russia and Poland, but confined himself to the preliminary phase, "the necessity for action which might arise before 1943–45" and to "the two hate-inspired antagonists, Britain and France . . . who were opposed to any strengthening of Germany's position in Europe or overseas." He saw the opportunity for action arising in two cases: if internal strife in France reached the point of civil war and she became incapable of waging war, or if France became embroiled in war with another country and so became unable to act against Germany. If either contingency occurred, the opportunity must be seized to overthrow Austria and Czechoslovakia. Hitler spoke of the second "coming definitely nearer," possibly emerging from the tensions in the Mediterranean, "even as early as 1938," especially if Mussolini chose to remain in the Balearic Isles and became involved in a war with France and Britain. This would provide a splendid opportunity for Germany to begin "the assault on Czechoslovakia . . . with lightning rapidity." German policy therefore should be to prolong the Spanish war and encourage the Italians to establish a permanent occupation of the Balearics.

None of this came as a surprise to Hitler's listeners. No one disagreed with the annexation of Austria or the destruction of Czechoslovakia as the objectives of German policy. Nor did they question his assessment that, provided the German operations were successful and rapidly concluded, the risk of military intervention by Russia or Poland need not be taken seriously. But Hitler expressed the view that "almost certainly Britain, and probably France as well, had already tacitly written off the Czechs," and went on to say:

> Difficulties connected with the empire, and the prospect of being once more entangled in a protracted European war, were for Britain decisive reasons against taking part in a war against Germany. . . . An attack by France without British support and with the prospect of the offensive being brought to a standstill on our western fortifications was hardly. probable.

Hitler told Göring before the meeting that he meant to "light a fire" under von Blomberg and von Fritsch as he was dissatisfied with the progress in the rearmament of the army. He succeeded. Both generals reacted strongly and argued that it was wrong to assume that Britain and France would stay out of any conflicts Germany might start in Central Europe, and that the Germans might well find themselves faced with a general war that they were not yet prepared to fight. They supported their doubts by pointing to the incomplete state of Germany's western fortifications, France's military power, and the strength of the Czech defenses. Von Neurath added his own doubts about the likelihood of war between the Western powers and Italy in the Mediterranean on which Hitler appeared to be counting. Raeder said nothing. His interest was in the navy's allocation of steel, which came up in the second part of the meeting—and he got what he wanted.

Hitler largely left Göring to conduct the argument about risks, which became heated and ended inconclusively. Four days later von Fritsch requested a further meeting and renewed his objections. Von Neurath, too, asked to see Hitler in an effort to dissuade him from the course he proposed, but Hitler by this time was thoroughly irritated and left Berlin abruptly for Berchtesgaden. It was not until the middle of January that the foreign minister could see him, and by then Hitler's mind was made up.

THE NOVEMBER 5 meeting did not mark a turning point after which there was no turning back. No decisions followed; Hitler retained his flexibility, the action against Austria five months later was hastily improvised, and the Czech crisis did not follow the course Hitler had foreseen. The importance of the meeting lay not in what was decided but in the fact that Hitler called it when he did, what was said at it, and the conclusions he drew from it.

A week after taking office in 1933, Hitler had told the cabinet that priority for the next four or five years must be given to rearming and expanding the armed forces. This was presented, of course, as part of the nationalist program for the reversal of the Versailles settlement; only at his first meeting with the generals had he mentioned, in passing, the possibility—among others—that Germany's military power, once re-created, might be used "for the conquest of *Lebensraum* in the east and its ruthless Germanization." By keeping his objectives undefined, Hitler had secured maximum support for rearmament from the army, the civil service, and big business.

But the time had now come when he was ready to move beyond such generalizations as the restoration of Germany's military position as a great power and adopt a more radical and aggressive policy. The importance Hitler attached to the meeting of November 5 suggests that he saw it as a test of how far the military leaders and the foreign minister were prepared to go with him.

In the first part of his exposition Hitler argued that the long-term goal of "solving the German problem of living space" would have to be launched by the period 1943 to 1945. He made it clear that this was bound to involve the use of force, but did not elaborate on what that would mean—the conquest of *Lebensraum* in Eastern Europe and Russia—confining himself to the preliminary stage of improving Germany's military and economic situation by the annexation of Austria and Czechoslovakia.

Such a possibility had been frequently discussed in the Foreign Ministry and the army for years, and neither the two generals nor von Neurath can have been taken by surprise—any more than they demurred in principle—when he began to talk of incorporating both countries in a Greater German Reich. What they objected to was his dismissal of the risks involved. This was enough for Hitler: If they balked even at this self-evident first step, he needed no further evidence that with such men he could never hope to carry out the much greater gamble he believed necessary to secure Germany's future. Reasoned criticism of any kind always angered him, and in the days that followed he convinced himself that they must go and that he could take the risk of removing them.

The winter of 1937–38 thus marks both a beginning and an end. The beginning was a change not in Hitler's objectives, which remained the same as they had always been, but in his judgment of the risks he could now afford to take. In his first five years of office he had been cautious, relying on his skill as a politician to win a series of diplomatic successes without even a display of force, other than in the remilitarization of the Rhineland. By the autumn of 1937, with German rearmament now out in the open and his confidence fortified by success, Hitler was ready to move to the second stage, from the removal of restrictions imposed by the Treaty of Versailles to the creation of Greater Germany, opening the way ultimately to the east. He was prepared to take the bigger risks involved in the threat and possible use of force, while still hoping to draw the maximum advantage from diplomacy without actual resort to war.

The same winter also marked an end—the end of the alliance with the traditional elites on the terms renewed with the repudiation of the "second revolution" in 1934. The alliance had served its purpose in the economic sphere, and the tacit understanding on which it was based had already been abandoned with the inauguration of the Four-Year Plan and Schacht's eclipse by Göring. Hitler had been reluctant to let Schacht go altogether, but on December 8 he finally accepted his resignation as minister of economics. There was no open breach. Schacht was not dismissed, and Hitler insisted, in order to preserve appearances, that he should remain a Reich minister without portfolio, as well as president of the Reichsbank. He was not arrested and shot, as he would have been in Russia, but allowed to retire undisturbed into private life.

His successor as minister of economics was Walther Funk, an economic journalist, once one of Hitler's "contact men" with business. The casual way in which he was appointed shows how slight was the authority he could expect to enjoy. Meeting him at the opera one night, Hitler took him aside during the intermission, told him he must take Schacht's place, and sent him to Göring for instructions. The ministry was not transferred until February 1938, by which time it had been shorn of its power and made wholly subordinate to Göring as plenipotentiary for the Four-Year Plan.

There were two other leading institutions of the state that still had to be *gleichgeschaltet* (coordinated): the Foreign Service and the army. Both were strongholds of that upper-class conservatism that Hitler so much disliked. At first he had accepted the view that their cooperation was indispensable to him, but he soon came to regard their political as well as social traditions as too limiting and backward-looking for the half-revolutionary, half-gangster tactics with which he meant to conduct foreign policy. Von Neurath, like von Blomberg, was one of von Hindenburg's appointments, put into the Wilhelmstrasse to act as a brake on Nazi impetuosity; he still retained some independence of position, enough to argue with Hitler on November 5.

In Ribbentrop Hitler had a potential foreign minister eager to start on the Nazification of the Foreign Service. Hitler had reassured von Neurath, who reached his sixty-fifth birthday on February 2, 1938, that he would continue in office, but two days later, on February 4, he removed him. Among other diplomatic changes made at the same time was the retirement of von Papen from Vienna. Like Schacht, von Neurath was not dismissed but early in 1938 was appointed president of a newly created cabinet Privy Council which never met. In 1939 he was made the first Protector of Bohemia and Moravia, eventually ending in the dock at Nuremberg.

The critical relationship, however, was that with the army, with its unique tradition of an independent position in the state. Hitler had accepted this in 1933–34, when its tacit support had been a decisive factor in his securing and retaining power. Closer acquaintance, however, had long since reduced the exaggerated respect which he had once felt for the senior generals, whose formative experience had been the defeat of 1918 and the humiliation which followed it. Naturally conservative in outlook, they had become cautious and regarded skeptically such ideas as the use of Blitzkrieg tactics to carry out the conquest of *Lebensraum.* There were able and ambitious officers—Guderian, Manstein, Rommel, Richthofen, Student—who were to prove that such ideas could be given substance with deadly effect, but during the period of German rearmament they were still of middle rank.

Unlike Stalin, Hitler did not attempt to carry out a complete purge of the High Command. He was later to regret that he had not, but he did not share Stalin's paranoid suspicion of the army as a potential center of opposition, and he still saw it as essential to his purpose of conquering territory by force. He was determined, however, to end once and for all the claim of the High Command to express independent views as von Fritsch and von Blomberg had done. An apparently unconnected series of events provided him with the opportunity to do so.

The trap was sprung by Göring and Himmler. Von Blomberg was a widower who was eager to get married a second time, to a lady whose social origins were obscure and who had a "past." He was aware of the shock this would give to the rigid views of the officer corps on the social suitability of the wife of a field marshal who was also minister of war. Unwisely he consulted Göring, who not only encouraged him but helped to ship an inconvenient rival off to South America. When the marriage took place, very quietly, on January 12, 1938, Hitler and Göring were the principal witnesses.

Shortly afterwards, it was disclosed that the wife of the field marshal had a police record as a prostitute and had been convicted of posing for indecent photographs. Von Blomberg was unpopular with his fellow officers, who disliked his compliant attitude toward Hitler. With the support of Göring, who acted as intermediary, von Fritsch requested an interview with Hitler and presented the army's protest: Von Blomberg must go. Hitler appears to have felt that he had been made a fool of and was not unwilling to accept the protest. The question then arose as to who was to succeed von Blomberg as minister of war and commander in chief of the armed forces.

Von Fritsch was the obvious candidate, but there were powerful figures in opposition. One was Göring, who wanted the position for himself and may well have played the double role he did to get it. Himmler saw von Fritsch as the man who had defeated his attempts to extend the power of the SS to the army. Finally, Hitler himself regarded von Fritsch as the epitome of the qualities he disliked in the officer corps and had not forgiven him for his opposition at the Hossbach meeting. To settle the matter, Himmler and Göring, acting in concert as they had in disposing of Röhm, produced another police dossier and a witness to support a charge that the commander in chief of the army had been guilty of homosexual practices. By the time it had been shown that the man in question was not von Fritsch but a retired cavalry officer named Frisch—a fact known to the Gestapo all the time—the trick had served its purpose.

Whatever Hitler's part in the plot, if any, he showed his skill in the way he turned it to his advantage. Von Blomberg was to have no successor who could represent the views of the armed forces in opposition to his own. Already von Hindenburg's successor as supreme commander, Hitler now took over from von Blomberg the immediate command of the Wehrmacht (that is, as commander in chief of all the armed forces: army, navy, and air force) and at the same time abolished the office of minister of war. The former Wehrmacht office in the War Ministry became the High Command of the armed forces (*Oberkommando der Wehrmacht,* the OKW), acting as Hitler's military staff, quite separate from and a rival to the High Command of the army (*Oberkommando des Heeres,* the OKH), which had traditionally advised Prussia's and Germany's rulers.

But this did not mean that Hitler intended to allow the OKW to succeed to the independent position and prestige once enjoyed by the army High Command and its general staff. He made this clear enough by his choice for the head of the OKW of General Wilhelm Keitel, a man who was to prove quite incapable of withstanding him. Asked about the suitability of Keitel for this position, von Blomberg answered: "Oh, Keitel, there's no question of him; he's nothing but the man who runs my office." To which Hitler replied: "That's exactly the man I'm looking for." [33] General Walter Warlimont, who served on the OKW staff from September 1939 to September 1944, wrote in his memoirs that "Hitler by nature worked in a disorderly manner and was averse to anything institutionalized." [34] Nothing like the Chiefs of Staff Committee in Britain or the Joint Chiefs of Staff in the U.S.A. was ever allowed to develop in Hitler's Germany. The heads of the separate services only met when summoned to Führer conferences to receive the Führer's orders. Insofar as there was coordination, it was reserved to Hitler alone. He used his new position, with the OKW as his military secretariat, to extend to the military sphere the division of power and the dispersal of activity at every level below his own, which he had already created in the political and economic.

In General von Brauchitsch, Hitler found someone acceptable to the officer corps for von Fritsch's position as commander in chief of the army, while again showing his flair for picking out men who would not give him trouble by their independence. He took the opportunity to retire sixteen of the senior generals and to transfer forty-four others to different commands. As a gesture to console Göring for his disappointment Hitler promoted him to the rank of field marshal, a step that appealed to Göring's vanity by giving him precedence over the commanders in chief of the army and navy and making him the senior-ranking German officer without adding to his already large accumulation of offices.

Hitler announced these changes to the cabinet on February 4, 1938, at what proved to be its last meeting during the Third Reich. At a single blow he had removed the few remaining checks on his freedom of action by replacing von Blomberg and von Fritsch, von Neurath and Schacht with creatures of his own will, Keitel and von Brauchitsch, Ribbentrop and Göring, while adding to his own concentration of powers by assuming direct control of the armed forces. As a sop to the officer corps, Hitler agreed to let the case against von Fritsch be investigated by a military court. This vindicated von Fritsch's reputation but he was not reinstated in office, retiring into private life like Schacht, with the single distinction of commander in chief of his old regiment.

By the time the court pronounced its verdict Austria had been annexed and the regime was unassailable. Von Fritsch himself acquiesced in the result. Ex-Ambassador Ulrich von Hassell, who lost his post in Rome at the same time, made a note in his diary of the ex-commander in chief's comment: "This man Hitler is Germany's destiny for good and for evil. If he now goes over the abyss (which Fritsch believes he will) he will drag us all down with him. There is nothing we can do." [35] The von Fritsch affair, soon forgotten in the triumph of the Anschluss, marked the end of the first part of Hitler's revolution, the end of the conservatives' hopes of restraining him, and the beginning of a new phase leading to the second part of the Nazi revolution in Hitler's war.

FOURTEEN

The Nazi-Soviet Pact

HITLER   1938–1939   *(Age 48–50)*
STALIN   1938–1939   *(Age 58–59)*

I

THOSE WHO FOLLOWED international affairs had little doubt at the end of 1937 that German action to end Austrian independence was imminent. The only questions were when, and what form it would take.

Nazi attempts to exploit the concessions made by the agreement of July 1936 had ended in frustration. On the other hand, the Austrian Chancellor, Kurt von Schuschnigg, realized that Austria's international position was weak and that, unless he succeeded in normalizing relations with Germany, Austria's future would become increasingly insecure. During 1937 he had made a confidant of Arthur Seyss-Inquart, a right-wing Austrian lawyer without political ties. With his help Schuschnigg worked out in secret a set of concessions, which he hoped would forestall further German pressure by offering an increased role for National Socialists in the Austrian government and Seyss-Inquart's own appointment as minister of the interior. He planned to present these as a fait accompli at a personal meeting that von Papen had arranged with Hitler. What Schuschnigg did not know was that Seyss-Inquart passed on details of the proposals to Hitler in advance, so robbing Schuschnigg of any room for maneuver when he arrived at Berchtesgaden.

This is the key to the meeting in Hitler's villa, the Berghof, at Obersalzberg, on February 12, 1938. Knowing the concessions Schuschnigg was already prepared to make, Hitler could turn these into an ultimatum to be accepted at once under threat of force. Taking the chancellor into his study and brushing aside his remarks about the famous view over the German-Austrian border, he launched into a tirade against Austrian policy. Austria was alone, Hitler declared: Neither France nor Britain nor Italy would lift a finger to save her. And now his patience was exhausted: "Think it over, Herr Schuschnigg. Think it over well. I can only wait until this afternoon. If I tell you that, you will do well to take my words literally, I don't believe in bluffing. All my past is proof of that."

At lunch, Hitler was an attentive host, but the atmosphere of menace was maintained by the presence of the three generals who would be responsible for any operations against Austria. Not until the middle of the afternoon did Ribbentrop and von Papen present Schuschnigg with Hitler's demands. He recognized bitterly that they were an expansion of the changes he had already agreed to with Seyss-Inquart. They included full scope for the activities of the Austrian Nazis, to be guaranteed by the appointment of Seyss-Inquart with control of the police, and an amnesty for all Nazis in prison. The ambitious Seyss-Inquart, it was now clear, had been playing a double game, acting as Schuschnigg's confidant and using this as a way of securing acceptance in Berlin as a possible successor. In addition, a second pro-Nazi, Edmund von Glaise-Horstenau, was to be made minister of war, to assure an exchange of officers and close cooperation between the two armies, and a third German nominee was to be appointed minister of finance in order to assimilate the two economic systems. The Austrians were given three days in which to undertake the whole program.

Hitler refused to allow a word to be changed: "You will sign it as it is and fulfill my demands within three days, or I will order the march into Austria." When Schuschnigg explained that, although willing to sign, he could not guarantee ratification, Hitler told him to leave the room and sent for General Keitel. According to von Papen, who was present, when Keitel came hurrying in, Hitler smiled and said, "There are no orders, I just wanted you here." Having left Schuschnigg for half an hour, during which the Austrian State Secretary Guido Schmidt said he would not be surprised if they were arrested on the spot, Hitler had them brought back and said: "I have decided to change my mind. For the first time in my life. But I warn you—this is your very last chance. I have given you three more days before the agreement goes into effect." [1]

Once Schuschnigg had signed, Hitler calmed down; but when the chancellor asked that the communiqué contain the promised confirmation of the 1936 agreement, with its guarantee of Austrian independence, Hitler refused. "Oh no! First you have to fulfill the conditions of our new agreement."

There seems no doubt from the remarks Hitler made to a group of leading Austrian Nazis on February 26 that he hoped the threat of force would be enough. A show of military preparations was continued to keep up the pressure, but Schuschnigg duly announced a general amnesty for all Nazis (including those convicted of the murder of Dollfuss) and the promised reorganization of the cabinet, with Seyss-Inquart as minister of the interior.

However, when the latter began to act more and more independently, taking his orders from Berlin, and the Nazis began to boast openly of being in power within a matter of weeks, Schuschnigg changed his mind and, rather than see Austrian independence lost by default, resolved to take a stand. He announced a plebiscite in which the Austrian people would be invited to declare whether they were in favor of an Austria that was "free and independent, German and Christian."

When told by the Austrian military attaché of Schuschnigg's plan, Mussolini's comment was, "This piece of ordnance will explode in your hands." Hitler was particularly incensed by Schuschnigg's use of his own favorite device of a plebiscite. At all costs this had to be prevented.

No detailed military plans for the occupation of Austria existed, but they were hastily improvised. On March 10 Hitler gave two orders. The Austrian Nazis were urged to take to the streets, and Seyss-Inquart was instructed to present an ultimatum. When Schuschnigg, rather than risk bloodshed, agreed to call off the plebiscite, his resignation was demanded as was the appointment of Seyss-Inquart as chancellor. Schuschnigg resigned but President Wilhelm Miklas, believing Hitler was bluffing, refused to appoint Seyss-Inquart.

Still anxious to avoid the direct use of force and to retain the veneer of legality for any action, Hitler delayed giving the order to march, hoping in the meantime to have a reply from Mussolini to the urgent personal message he had sent by a special envoy, Prince Philip of Hesse. Göring found a way around the difficulty with the argument that, although Schuschnigg had resigned, Seyss-Inquart still remained in office and had the authority to act in the government's name. After dictating a telegram, which Seyss-Inquart was to send, calling for German military intervention to restore order, Göring added: "Well, he does not even have to send the telegram—all he needs to do is to say, 'Agreed.' "[2] When Seyss-Inquart made difficulties, Wilhelm Keppler, who was acting as Hitler's representative in Vienna, telephoned Berlin and gave the required answer himself. "Tell the general field marshal that Seyss-Inquart agrees."

Because of telephone trouble, the calls to Vienna had to be made from the Reich Chancellery switchboard. An eyewitness, General Grolmann, relates:

> When it was already dark Hitler was called to the telephone booth, and I saw Göring push in with him. When they came out again Göring was talking excitedly to Hitler and while they were on their way back to the sitting room Hitler, who had previously been listening thoughtfully to Göring, suddenly slapped his thigh, threw his head back and said "Now for it." At once Göring rushed off, and from then on the orders followed thick and fast.[3]

Hitler's order, timed 8:45 p.m. on March 11, directed the German armed forces to enter Austria the following morning at daybreak. Just after midnight, with a noisy mob filling the streets and the threat of a Nazi putsch, Miklas capitulated and appointed Seyss-Inquart as chancellor. The latter's first act was to try to get the entry of German troops called off—without success. Hitler was now confident that the army would meet no resistance and had received the message from Mussolini for which he had been waiting. When Prince Philip telephoned from Rome at half-past ten that the Duce had accepted Hitler's action in a very friendly manner, Hitler became almost incoherent with gratitude:

> *Hitler*: "Please tell Mussolini that I will never forget him for this. Never, never, never, whatever happens . . . As soon as the Austrian affair is settled, I shall be ready to go with him, through thick and thin, whatever happens."
>
> *Hesse*: "Yes, my Führer."
>
> *Hitler*: "Listen, I shall make any agreement—I am no longer in fear of the terrible position which would have existed in case we had got into a conflict. You may tell him that I thank him ever so much; never, never shall I forget." [4]

Göring dealt with Hitler's other anxiety by seeing the Czech minister and assuring him that what was happening in Austria would have no effect at all on Germany's relations with Czechoslovakia: "I give you my word of honor that Czechoslovakia has nothing to fear from the Reich." In return he asked for assurances that the Czechs would not mobilize, which the minister, after consulting Prague, was happy to give. Göring then reiterated the assurances he had given, this time in the name of the German government.

The German proclamation, broadcast as the Eighth Army drove into Austria, spoke of the oppressive misgovernment from which its people had been suffering and praised Hitler's decision to liberate his native country and come to the help of Austria's brother Germans in distress. At Linz, where he had once gone to school, he was greeted by cheering crowds and went to lay a wreath on his parents' grave. Much moved by the enthusiastic reception he had met, he decided not to set up a satellite government under Seyss-Inquart but to incorporate Austria directly into the Reich, the objective he had stated on page one of *Mein Kampf* fourteen years before. His decision did not leave any room for debate, and after a hurried cabinet meeting Seyss-Inquart returned to Linz with the text of a law already promulgated, the first article of which read: "Austria is a province of the German Reich."

The same night, the arrests began: 76,000 in Vienna alone. Immediately behind the German army came a large force of 40,000 police and SS Death's Head Formations who began the systematic persecution of Austria's 200,000 Jews. Adolf Eichmann, later to be tried in Israel and condemned to death for his part in the Holocaust, set up operations in an old Rothschild palace, and by the autumn reported the expulsion of 45,000 Jews, who had to pay heavily for the privilege of emigration. The local Nazis of the Austrian Legion, given the freedom of the streets, gave full rein to their pent-up feelings of envy, malice, and lust for revenge.

The treatment of the large Jewish community in Vienna was a foretaste of the uninhibited savagery that was to follow in the Kristallnacht in Berlin and other German cities later in the year. Crowds gathered to enjoy what were known as "rubbing parties" in which Jews, often elderly, were forced to rub out with their bare hands or toothbrushes the slogans left over from the aborted Schuschnigg plebiscite.

An English journalist described one of these *Reibparteien*:

SA men dragged an elderly Jewish worker and his wife through the applauding crowd. Tears rolled down the cheeks of the old woman . . . I could see how the old man, whose arm she held, tried to stroke her hand. "Work for the Jews. At last, work for the Jews," howled the crowd. "We thank our Führer, he has made work for the Jews!"[5]

Carl Zuckmayer, the German playwright, who was in Vienna at the time, wrote:

The underworld had opened its gates and let loose its lowest, most revolting, most impure spirits. The city was transformed into a nightmare painting by Hieronymus Bosch, the air filled with an incessant, savage, hysterical screeching from male and female throats . . . in wild, hate-filled triumph.[6]

Austria was to have its plebiscite after all. Hitler dissolved the Reichstag and fixed new elections for April 10, combined with a plebiscite for the whole of Germany, now including Austria. The Anschluss represented the fulfillment of a German dream of *Grossdeutschland,* older than the Treaty of Versailles, which had forbidden it, or than the unification of Germany, from which Bismarck had deliberately excluded Austria. With the dissolution of the Habsburg Empire at the end of the war, many Austrians saw in such a union the only future for a country that, shorn of the non-German parts of the old empire, appeared to be left hanging in the air. If disillusionment was to follow—Vienna became a provincial backwater and even Austrian Nazis were to complain about the shameless way in which the country was plundered—there was no doubt of the genuine enthusiasm with which the Anschluss was greeted initially on both sides of the border. Hitler's popularity reached a peak of approval never equaled before or after, "above all because our Führer has pulled it off without bloodshed."[7]

For Hitler himself, for whom Vienna was the city in which he had suffered frustration and humiliation, his return as the heir to the Habsburgs was "the proudest hour of my life." During the election campaign he traveled from one end of Germany to the other: Huge rallies acclaimed what was seen as a national triumph. The last ten days were devoted to Austria, with a closing demonstration in Vienna. As he stood before the wildly cheering crowd, the belief in his mission as the man of destiny took possession of him: "I believe it was God's will to send a youth from here into the Reich, to let him grow up, to raise him to be the leader of the nation so as to enable him to lead back his homeland into the Reich."[8]

II

ON MARCH 1 3, the day Hitler was celebrating his triumphal return to Linz and the annexation of Austria, Stalin was celebrating a triumph of a different kind: March 1 3 saw the end of the last Moscow trial and the summary execution of all but one of the remaining members of Lenin's Politburo—Bukharin, Rykov, and Krestinsky.* The difference in the two men's priorities is striking. Even in the middle of the purges, however, Stalin could not ignore the wiping off of one state from the map and the obvious threat to another. If Czechoslovakia, too, was now to be swallowed up, the balance of power in Europe would be radically altered and German forces brought within striking distance of the Soviet frontier.

Litvinov warned the Central Committee: "The annexation of Austria is the greatest event since the World War and is fraught with the greatest dangers, not least to our union." But all that Litvinov could do was to offer to consult with the other powers on the best way to check further acts of aggression: "It may be too late tomorrow but today the time for it is not yet gone if all the states, and the Great Powers in particular, take a firm and unambiguous stand." [9]

Litvinov was referring specifically to Czechoslovakia, which Russia as well as France was bound by treaty to assist, if attacked. When asked how Russia would give support—since she had no common frontier with either Czechoslovakia or Germany—Litvinov replied that a way would be found, some sort of corridor created. In fact, as he told the U.S. ambassador privately, neither the French nor the Russians had any confidence in each other and he thought it likely that the Czechs would cave in. [10] When the British and others declined the invitation to meet, Litvinov expressed no surprise, remarking to the Hungarian minister that he had never had much hope of a favorable response and had no specific plan in mind.

The Russians may well have believed that a firm enough guarantee to Czechoslovakia by the British, French, and themselves would halt Hitler—and been ready to play their part. Stalin had none of the difficulty British and French leaders had in recognizing that Hitler was following a course that would lead to war if he was not stopped, that there was a common interest in preventing war, and that if the powers acted together they could force him to back down. The Western powers' response showed how far they still were from seeing the problem as clearly as Stalin did. The French did not reply at all, the British thought Litvinov's proposal of a conference inappropriate, as it would divide Europe into two camps and appear to be branding Germany as an aggressor. This confirmed Russian skepticism that they were not serious about collective security, in which case Litvinov's proposal absolved the Soviet government from responsibility for its failure. The Russian ambassador was instructed to tell President Beneš of

---

*Trotsky alone survived until his death sentence was carried out informally, by assassination in 1940.

Czechoslovakia that the Soviet Union stood ready to take the necessary steps to guarantee the security of his country, provided the French were prepared to act. Ironically, it had been at Beneš's own suggestion, at the time when the Soviet-Czech treaty was signed, that mutual assistance was made conditional on France fulfilling its obligation to the party under attack. He had pressed for this to make sure that the Czechoslovak government was not drawn into a war on the side of the USSR, unless the French were too. Throughout the six-month-long Czech crisis this now became the touchstone for Russian intervention on the side of Czechoslovakia.

Hitler had hated the Czechs since his days in Vienna, when he had formed his stereotype of them as he had of the Jews—in the Czech case as the type of the Slav *Untermenschen* ("subhumans") who were attacking the supremacy of the Germans in the Habsburg monarchy. The postwar Czechoslovak state, which he referred to with scorn as "an artificial creation" of the peace settlement, was the symbol of Versailles—democratic, a strong supporter of the League of Nations, and the ally of France and Russia. The Bohemian quadrilateral* was a natural defensive position, possession of which Bismarck described as the key to the mastery of Central Europe, within less than an hour's flying time from Berlin and other German industrial areas. The Czech army, a first-class force, equipped by the famous Skoda armament works and with frontier defenses comparable to the French Maginot Line in strength, was a factor that had to be eliminated before Germany could move eastward as Hitler planned. Apart from the strategic gain, the capture of its equipment and the Skoda works would be a valuable reinforcement for German rearmament.

The weakness that Hitler hoped to exploit was the multinational composition of a state in which the ruling Czechs made up only just over half the population, and the rest—particularly the Sudeten Germans (representing over 22 percent) and the Slovaks (representing just under 18 percent)— were discontented with their lot. In 1935 the German government began to subsidize the Sudeten German party of Konrad Henlein with a view to its acquiring a dominant position in the German-speaking community which could be exploited when the time was ripe.

Hitler's advantage throughout the Czech crisis, from March 1938 to March 1939, lay in keeping the initiative, except for a few days in May and again at the end of September 1938, both times rapidly recovering it. He was able to enjoy this advantage for four reasons, which may be summarized as follows.

First, alone among the protagonists he had a clear objective: the destruction of the Czechoslovak state.

Second, he was able to mask this objective by a propaganda campaign focusing attention on the injustices suffered by the Sudeten Germans—real,

---

*The frontiers of Bohemia-Moravia with Germany and Austria form a rough quadrilateral running through mountainous country. It was from the Sudeten range of mountains in northern Bohemia-Moravia that the German-speaking majority in the Sudetenland adjoining the frontier took its name. See the map on p. 512.

exaggerated, or invented—so presenting himself as the defender of the German minority's rights rather than as an aggressor attacking the Czech state. When the Sudeten claims were satisfied he was able to repeat his fifth-column stratagem by answering the "appeal" of Slovak nationalists for protection against their Czech oppressors.

Third, he understood the motives and anxieties of the other governments far better than they succeeded in divining his, an intuitive flair powerfully assisted by the ability of Göring's Forschungsamt (his phone-tapping bureau) to intercept and decode many of the diplomatic communications between the British, French, and Czech governments, and between each of them and their ambassadors in Berlin and Prague.

Fourth, he was convinced that the British and French governments were not prepared to risk a war over the claim of the Sudeten Germans—and subsequently of the Slovaks—to equal rights and national self-determination. The most they would do, he believed, would be to threaten intervention, and he was confident surprise and speed would enable the Germans to produce a fait accompli before the threat could be put into effect.

The basic strategy was worked out with the Sudeten leader, Henlein, in a series of meetings in Berlin on March 28 and 29, just over two weeks after the Anschluss. Henlein's role was to raise demands that the Czechoslovak government could never agree to, a formula that Henlein represented to Hitler in the words, "We must always demand so much that we cannot be satisfied." Henlein announced his eight-point program for Sudeten autonomy in a speech at Karlovy Vary (Karlsbad) on April 24. Backed by a steady build-up of organized violence inside the Sudetenland, and of Nazi propaganda from outside, this would provide the pretext for German intervention.

AN ATTACK ON CZECHOSLOVAKIA had figured in the German army's contingency planning before 1938, but it was not until April 21 of that year that Hitler instructed Keitel as the head of the OKW to prepare an operational directive for a surprise attack, which would break the Czechs' frontier defenses and win a decisive victory within four days, before the other powers could intervene. No date for such an attack was specified, and the draft finally sent to Hitler on May 20 began with a paragraph that repeated Hitler's own words in briefing Keitel:

> It is not our intention to smash Czechoslovakia by a military action in the immediate future without provocation, unless an unavoidable development of political conditions inside Czechoslovakia forces the issue, or political events in Europe create a particularly favorable opportunity that may never recur.
>
> Operations will be launched, either:
>
> (a) After a period of increasing diplomatic controversies and tension linked with military preparations that will be exploited so as to shift the war guilt onto the enemy;

(b) By lightning action as the result of a serious incident, which will subject Germany to unbearable provocation and which, in the eyes of at least a part of world opinion, affords the moral justification for military measures.

Case (b) is more favorable both from a military and political point of view.[11]

The directive makes clear that Hitler counted on action by both the Poles and the Hungarians to take advantage of the breakup of Czechoslovakia by pressing their own territorial claims. The day after talking to Keitel, Hitler sent for the Hungarian envoy in Berlin, Döme Sztójay, and told him that, in the event of the Czech state being divided up, Germany had no interest in the Slovak parts and it would be up to Hungary to recover the territory she had lost after the First World War, including Hungary's old coronation city, Bratislava (Pressburg). The position of the Poles, on bad terms with the Czechs but still allied to France, was more delicate, and Hitler made no attempt to put pressure on them, confident that, when the time came, the Poles would need no urging to seize Teschen and other frontier districts in dispute between them and the Czechs.

There remained the Italians. Although Mussolini had acquiesced in the German occupation of Austria, he was still sensitive to any suggestion that his support could be taken for granted as the junior partner of the Rome-Berlin Axis. An Anglo-Italian agreement signed in April 1938, although of little practical importance, was intended as a gesture of Italian independence, and Hitler understood that this was no time to press for completion of a formal military alliance between their two countries, or to ask the Duce to commit himself to more than a benevolent neutrality toward a German attack on the Czechs.

The opportunity to revive Mussolini's confidence occurred when Hitler arrived in Rome on a return visit for the Duce's 1937 reception in Germany. Four special trains were hardly enough to carry every Gauleiter, party boss, and Nazi hanger-on who wanted to share, at Italian expense, in the galas, receptions, and banquets with which they could expect to be regaled. Nothing appealed to the gutter elite of Nazi Germany more than a free trip south of the Alps, and wagonloads of special uniforms accompanied them. The Italian comment was that nothing had been seen like it since the Barbarian invasion.

The occasion provided some interesting sidelights on Hitler as a human being. The celebration of his forty-ninth birthday had impressed him with his own mortality and the limited number of years left to him, which could at any moment be curtailed by an assassin's bullet—perhaps in Italy. On the journey from Berlin he spent the time drawing up his will and putting his affairs in order. Apart from bequests to his relatives, he left all his personal possessions, the Berghof, his furniture and pictures, to the party.

When the cavalcade set out from the Rome station, a million Italians lined the route to greet him. Among them was Eva Braun, traveling incognito, her fare paid privately by Hitler, but getting no nearer than being hoisted onto the shoulders of a friendly Italian to see her "friend" ride by in the king of Italy's coach. Far from being flattered by being treated as the king's guest and lodged in the royal palace, Hitler was furious, making little effort to conceal his impatience at what he regarded as the out-of-date nonsense of palace protocol and ceremonial, and complaining loudly that he should have been entertained by Mussolini. Nonetheless, the frustrated artist in him was captivated by his first sight of Rome and Florence, and at the state banquet in the Palazzo Venezia he reassured his hosts by making it clear that he had no intention of reclaiming the South Tyrol: "It is my unalterable will and my bequest to the German people that it shall regard the frontier of the Alps, raised by Nature between us, as forever inviolable." [12]

At the end of April, British and French ministers conferred in London: Both sides were at pains to reassure Hitler, separately, that they were putting pressure on the Czechs to reach agreement with Henlein. Hitler was delighted: Czechoslovakia's friends were doing his work for him. The situation was suddenly reversed, however, when the Czech government, alarmed by reports of German troop concentrations on the frontier, ordered partial mobilization. Britain and France at once sent messages to Berlin warning of the danger of a general war if the Germans made any aggressive move against the Czechs.

The effect on Hitler was much the same as that produced by Schuschnigg's proposal to call a plebiscite: He felt the tables were being turned on him at his own game, and that he was the victim of a preemptive strike in the war of nerves. It is more likely that the Czech government's move was made out of genuine alarm than out of calculation, but it caught Hitler unprepared. Although he was working on plans for the elimination of Czechoslovakia, still no date had been fixed and everything was in a preparatory stage. However much it went against the grain, and however infuriated he was when the Western press spoke of his being forced to retreat, Hitler had no option but to agree that the German Foreign Office should deny the reports of troop movements and disclaim any aggressive intention toward Czechoslovakia.

In fact, once the immediate fears of war had been dispersed, the May crisis did not alter the situation. The other powers made no attempt to follow up the warning they had given to Germany but renewed their pressure on the Czechs, and Hitler was able to recapture the initiative. Having mastered his anger, he summoned a meeting of military and political leaders on May 28 and gave them a revised version of what he had said at the Hossbach meeting in November. Making use of handwritten notes and pointing at the map spread out on the table in the winter garden of the Chancellery, he repeated his familiar thesis of the need to secure Germany's future by the capture of *Lebensraum* in the east. Britain and France would oppose Germany, and in the event of war—in which the object would be to extend the German coastline by the conquest of the Low Countries—Czechoslovakia presented a threat to the German rear. This had to be removed first, and there could not be a more propitious moment to act. Britain and France did not want war and were not prepared for it; Russia would not participate; Hungary would join the Germans; Poland would not oppose out of fear of the Russians; and the Italians were not interested.

Hitler gave two reasons for not reacting to the Czechs' "provocation": The German army was not yet prepared to break through the Czech fortifications; and the German fortifications in the West Wall were not sufficiently advanced to hold the French in check. These were the tasks, together with the psychological preparation of the German people for war, to be completed in the next few months; until they were, "no amount of provocation will force me to change this attitude." Hitler repeated the phrase that he was to make the new preamble to Keitel's draft directive, approved on May 30: "It is my unalterable decision to smash Czechoslovakia by military action in the near future. It is the business of the political leadership to await or bring about the suitable moment." In the covering letter, which Keitel circulated to the High Command with the directive, he added that "its execution must be assured by October 1, 1938, at the latest."[13]

Hitler was careful to distance himself from the anxious but inconclusive diplomatic exchanges that filled the three months following the May crisis. The official German line treated the issue as still one between the Sudeten German party and the Czech government, for which the German government took no responsibility. Hitler, reading the intercepted messages, noted with satisfaction that the British and French governments appeared to accept the same view, renewing their pressure on the Czechs to reach agreement, including the dispatch of Lord Runciman as a mediator. German diplomatic activity was limited to keeping a watchful eye on relations with the Italians as well as the Poles—without telling either what Hitler intended to do—and to putting pressure on the Hungarians to take part in the dismemberment of Czechoslovakia. This would enable Hungary to recover the Slovak territory lost in the peace settlement and establish the common frontier with Poland which would be as welcome to Warsaw as to Budapest.

The Hungarians longed to do so, but they feared the outbreak of a general war in which Germany would again be defeated and Hungary crushed beyond any hope of recovery. An invitation to the Hungarian regent, Admiral Horthy, and the prime minister, Béla Imrédy, to visit Germany in August only exposed the dilemma which the Hungarians could not resolve. Explaining his plan for destroying Czechoslovakia, Hitler offered to let the Hungarians annex Slovakia and the easternmost part of the country, Ruthenia,* which they had lost at the peace settlement, provided

---

*Ruthenia, which had belonged to the Hungarian crown for centuries, was also known as Carpatho-Ukraine and the majority of its inhabitants, the Ruthenians, were closely related to the Ukrainians.

they were willing to take part in a joint attack from the beginning. If they missed the opportunity, Poland might well annex the whole of Slovakia: "Those who wanted to share in the meal had to help with the cooking." The Hungarians were not to be moved, or, as Hitler put it, "they failed to pass the test of will."

HITLER'S REAL PROBLEM was where it might least have been expected: with the army leaders, to whom he had given the opportunity to re-create German military power. The removal of von Blomberg and von Fritsch had not solved it, and the creation of the OKW had only made it worse. Keitel was not taken seriously either by Hitler or by his fellow officers: his military bearing was impressive, but nothing else. Alfred Jodl, the chief of the OKW Operations Staff, was a gifted soldier on whom Hitler came to rely for turning his ideas into detailed plans. But Jodl was reserved by nature and had learned not to contradict Hitler directly or question his strategic decisions. He admired Hitler, would not listen to criticism of him, and was isolated from the rest of the officer corps. Members of the OKH, the army's General Staff, hitherto the most prestigious of German institutions, regarded the OKW with scorn, but found themselves excluded from their traditional role of advisers to the country's rulers on strategy and the military implications of policy. Only twice in his five years in office as Chief of the Army General Staff did Ludwig Beck obtain a face-to-face interview with Hitler on official matters.

Beck was cautious by nature, adhering to the dictum of Field Marshal Helmuth von Moltke, the most famous of his predecessors, *"Erst wägen, dann wagen"*—"First consider, then venture." As early as 1935 he had opposed a proposal by von Reichenau, at that time the most pro-Nazi of the generals, to prepare plans for a preemptive attack on Czechoslovakia. He had done so on the grounds that this would bring Britain and France together against Germany, just as the German attack on Belgium had in 1914. Beck tried to get the military operations against Austria canceled, and several times in the summer of 1938 he restated his opposition to Hitler's plans to attack Czechoslovakia, arguing that it would develop into a general war that would end in disaster for Germany. He presented four separate memoranda to von Brauchitsch, the army commander in chief, in May, June, and July and, not content with that, urged von Brauchitsch on at least three occasions in July to organize collective resistance among the generals, urging him to tell Hitler that Germany was unprepared for war and that the military leaders could not accept responsibility for such adventures.

Von Brauchitsch refused to do as Beck wanted, but he agreed to summon a meeting of the senior commanders in August. When the meeting took place, von Brauchitsch read out a version of Beck's argument, with the conclusion that it was not worth risking the existence of the nation in order to acquire the Sudetenland. The commander in chief ended by inviting the generals to exert their influence on Hitler by confronting him with the views that had been expressed. The discussion made it clear that the majority of those present agreed that the mood of the people, and of the soldiers, was against war, and that although the army could probably defeat the Czechs, it was not strong enough to face a general war. When one general, Ernst Busch, suggested that it was not the business of soldiers to interfere in political decisions, Beck argued strongly for the traditional view of the function of the General Staff, that all trained staff officers ought to be capable of making correct judgments in the political-military field.

It was precisely this claim to independence of judgment that Hitler would not tolerate. But, with a military operation on which he had staked his future only a few weeks away, Hitler could not afford to follow Stalin's example and make a clean sweep of the army High Command. He brushed aside whatever von Brauchitsch worked up the courage himself to say; but he did not leave it at that.

His first move was to invite not the senior generals, but the chiefs of staff to dinner at the Berghof. Afterwards he set out the political and military assumptions on which his plans were based. This time, however, the magic did not work; and the rare invitation to discuss his views afterwards proved disastrous. The chief of staff of the Army Group in the west got up and said bluntly that it was the view of General Wilhelm Adam, its commander, as well as his own, that the fortifications against France could be held for only three weeks. A furious scene followed with Hitler cursing such defeatism and shouting: "I assure you, General, that position will be held not just for three weeks, but three years. The man who does not hold these fortifications is a scoundrel." Jodl,* who was present and recognized that the doubts in the minds of Hitler's audience had not been overcome, wrote in his diary: "The vigor of the soul is lacking, because in the end they do not believe in the genius of the Führer."[14]

Five days later, Hitler invited all the senior generals to a demonstration at the Jüterbog artillery school, where exact replicas of the Czech fortifications had been constructed. An infantry attack on an artillery barrage was mounted as well. The actual damage was disappointing, but Hitler—after clambering through the concrete fortifications—proclaimed himself astonished by the devastation. In the mess afterwards he spoke for ninety minutes, presenting his plans as the culmination of the crusade that had begun with the foundation of the Nazi party:

> However the situation may develop, Czechoslovakia has got to be eliminated before anything else. . . . It is my own great fear that something

---

*Field Marshal Keitel was the head of the OKW (Armed Forces High Command), but it was General Alfred Jodl, the gifted soldier who was the chief of the OKW Operations Staff, on whom Hitler relied more than anyone else to turn his ideas and demands into detailed plans and see they were carried out.

may befall me personally before I can put the necessary decisions into effect. . . . In political life you must believe in the Goddess of Fortune. She passes by only once, and that's when to grasp her. She will never come by that way again. [15]

Hitler repeated his performance to the generals again at Döberitz on August 17. The following day, Beck offered his resignation and demanded that von Brauchitsch should do the same. The army commander in chief refused. As von Hassell, the former ambassador to Rome and future conspirator, noted in his diary: "Brauchitsch hitches his collar a notch higher and says: 'I am a soldier; it is my duty to obey.' " [16] After Beck persisted with his resignation, Hitler accepted it but ordered "for reasons of foreign policy" that this should not be communicated to either the army or the public. Out of loyalty to his country at a time of crisis, Beck agreed.

A report by Göring and Todt on a visit to the western fortifications in June had alerted Hitler to the danger that they would not be ready in time for his autumn deadline. Since the remilitarization of the Rhineland in March 1936, the army had succeeded in completing only 640 blockhouses and planned to add 1,360 more during 1938. Hitler demanded 12,000 and drew up a memorandum on the design of fortifications and the infantryman's psychology, based on his experience from 1914 to 1918, in which he ridiculed the army engineers' ignorance of modern technology and what was needed. He ordered work on all other building projects to stop if it was necessary to move men and equipment to finish the western defenses. Not content with redesigning the blockhouses in detail, he decided the position of each one and drove the rate of completion up to seventy sites a day. He also decided the placing of the heaviest weapons. How much difference Hitler's intervention made is impossible to say, but he did highlight and publicize the importance of speeding up the work. General Förster, the army's inspector of fortifications, who got the rough edge of Hitler's tongue, later made the shrewd comment:

> The Führer was interested in the very big issues, and also in the tiniest details. Anything in between did not interest him. What he overlooked was that most decisions fall into this intermediate category. [17]

In the last week of August, Hitler carried out a two-day inspection of the West Wall. General Adam, the commander on the western front, gave his opinion that only a third of the fortifications would be completed by the time the winter frosts set in and that, if fighting began in the east, the Western powers would march. Hitler's claim that Germany would have 2,000 tanks on the western front and an outstanding antitank mine did not impress him. Each division, Adam pointed out, would have to hold a thirteen-mile front and during the initial phase, while the army concentrated on breaking through the Czech fortifications, he would have no reserves to call on.

Hitler's reply was: "I will not call off the attack on Czechoslovakia." At the end of his tour he congratulated everyone concerned on the progress they had made, declared that German troops could never be driven out of the West Wall, and repeated in front of Adam: "Only a scoundrel could not hold this front." The general was later relieved of his command and retired.

III

HITLER'S SELF-CONFIDENCE and determination during the summer impressed all who met him. Yet no one was sure how far he was serious and how far he was bluffing when he said that he meant to destroy Czechoslovakia by force. Nor did he mean them to be. When General Franz Halder was appointed to take Beck's place as the army's chief of staff, Hitler told him: "You will never learn my real intentions. Not even my closest colleagues, who are convinced they know them, will ever find them out." [18] Hitler might well have said the same of himself. He was quite clear that he meant to eliminate Czechoslovakia, but how, when, in one or two stages, by the actual use of force or simply by the threat to use it—all these were matters he would not decide until the very last moment. By keeping his options open in this way he retained maximum flexibility, enabling him to enlarge the risks he could take by always leaving open a way of retreat. To keep people guessing—his own staff, even Göring and the generals, as well as the British, the French, and the Czechs—created uncertainty and so made it more difficult to know what to do to restrain or block him.

This refusal to be bound by the conventional rules, which created so many problems in administration and economics, was an asset in the psychological warfare of which he was a master. Hitler never said anything, even when he appeared to have lost his temper, without calculating the effect both on those present and on those to whom they would recount it.

On one occasion, July 2, when Ribbentrop was lunching with Hitler in Munich, the arrival of a British emissary was announced. Hitler started up and said: "*Gott im Himmel!* Don't let him in yet. I'm still in a good humor." He then proceeded, in front of his staff, to work himself up until his face darkened, he was breathing heavily, and his eyes were glazed. His reception of the Englishman was so stormy that it was clearly audible through the door to those still sitting at the lunch table. When he had finished, Hitler returned, wiping his brow. "Gentlemen," he said with a chuckle, "I need tea. He thinks I'm furious." [19]

A press and radio campaign of propaganda and intimidation was built up and varied according to the reports (including wiretaps) that Hitler received on reactions in Prague, London, and Paris. Most observers believed—and Hitler did nothing to dissuade them—that the Nuremberg Party Rally during the second week of September would see the Sudeten issue and German-Czech relations reach a crisis. There had been little trouble in the Sudetenland during the summer, and the negotiations between the Sudeten

Germans and Prague—especially now that the British mission led by Lord Runciman had arrived to mediate—had roused Sudeten hopes that "self-determination" alone would bring Czechoslovakia under German control without any need for war. Hitler received such talk with a hard stare, and on August 26 ordered Karl Hermann Frank, Henlein's deputy, to prepare to stage incidents that would provide the excuse for German intervention. When Henlein, belatedly realizing that the Sudeten Germans were being used as pawns in a much bigger game, came to repeat the same argument that a political solution would give the Sudeten Germans self-determination, Hitler was adamant that he still planned a military operation. In high spirits he saw Henlein off from the Berghof on September 2 with the parting words: "Long live war—even if it lasts eight years!" Whether this was meant to encourage the Sudeten Germans or impress the Czechs, Hitler himself could hardly have said.

On September 5, Beneš took a step that had long been urged on him by the British and French: He invited the Sudeten German leaders to visit him and write down the full list of their demands, which he promised to grant, whatever they might be. This knocked the bottom out of the argument that the issue was Sudeten grievances. To cover their embarrassment, new incidents were staged in Moravska Ostrava, providing an excuse for breaking off negotiations with Prague. Hitler had now told the army that he would fix the day and hour for the assault on Czechoslovakia by noon on September 27.

There was disagreement, however, between Hitler and the High Command on how the attack should be made. The General Staff wanted to cut Czechoslovakia in two by a joint attack from north and south, separating Bohemia-Moravia from Slovakia. To Hitler this was conventional planning according to the book, exactly what the Czech army would expect. He demanded a political objective, the capture of the Czech capital, Prague, by a surprise attack straight through the Czech fortifications with a massed force of tanks. When he discovered that von Brauchitsch and Halder (Beck's successor as the army's chief of staff) had ignored his wishes and sent out orders in accordance with their original plan, he summoned them and Keitel to Nuremberg.

The argument between them went on into the small hours of the morning, Hitler maintaining that, whatever the strategic merits of the army plan, it ignored the political need for a quick result by a knockout blow. When the generals would not give way, Hitler finally ordered them to do as he said. Halder shrugged; but the army commander in chief, von Brauchitsch, startled those present by an about-face and an effusive declaration of loyalty. Reflecting on the situation, Jodl wrote in his diary:

It is the same problem as in 1914. There is only one undisciplined element in the Army—the generals, and in the last analysis this comes from the fact that they are arrogant. They have neither confidence nor discipline because they cannot recognise the Führer's genius. This is no doubt due to the fact that they still look on him as the Corporal of the World War instead of the greatest statesman since Bismarck. [20]

Hitler's own comment to Keitel was: "It's a pity I can't give my Gauleiters an army each—they've got guts and they've got faith in me." [21]

IN OPPOSING Hitler's plans and calling on the other generals to support him, Beck had taken care to base himself on professional, not political grounds. There were other officers, however, who were prepared to go further and plan a coup d'état if Hitler persisted in giving the order to attack Czechoslovakia. The center of the conspiracy was in the OKW Intelligence Branch (*Abwehrabteilung,* usually shortened to *Abwehr*), where its driving force was Colonel Hans Oster. Among those privy to the plot and ready to play a political role, if it succeeded, were Schacht and Karl Goerdeler, a former Oberbürgermeister of Leipzig and for three years Reich price controller. Halder was actively involved in late August and early September, but as the conspirators came to realize, having taken the first step, he was never able to make up his mind to take the second and proved as great a disappointment as von Brauchitsch.

The conspirators' first need was to find a general with troops under his command who was prepared to act. They found him in General Erwin von Witzleben, commanding the Third Army Corps based in Berlin, who with Graf Erich von Brockdorff-Ahlefeld, commander of the Potsdam Garrison, Graf Helldorf, the Berlin police president, and his deputy, Graf Fritz von der Schulenburg, undertook to seize the government quarter in Berlin and take Hitler prisoner with as many other Nazi leaders as possible. General Erich Hoepner, commanding an armored division in Thuringia, was ready to block any attempt by the SS to mount a rescue operation. Once seized, Hitler was either to be declared insane or brought to trial, and, after a brief period of military rule, a new civil constitution was to be established. However, a younger inner group, led by Major Friedrich Heinz, who was to lead the raiding party of twenty or thirty officers escorting von Witzleben in storming the Reich Chancellery, planned to shoot Hitler in the process.*

The coup was timed to take place between the issue of the final order to invade Czechoslovakia and the first exchange of shots. The conspirators depended on Halder for adequate notice of the order being given. They regarded it as essential to the success of the plot and to securing the support of the army, to get an unequivocal commitment from the British and French governments to go to war if Czechoslovakia were attacked. To put the case for this to the British, Ewald von Kleist-Schmenzin, a gentleman farmer and descendant of the famous poet, Ewald von Kleist, volunteered to go to London in mid-August. He saw and made a deep impression on Sir Robert

---

*Oster, Goerdeler, von Witzleben, von der Schulenburg, Höpner, and Helldorf, as well as Heinz, remained members of the resistance, and were put to death after the July 1944 attempt on Hitler's life. See pp. 831–32.

Vansittart, the permanent under secretary at the Foreign Office, as well as on Lord Lloyd, who was close to Chamberlain, and on Churchill, then in opposition. Reports of what he said were seen and discussed by Chamberlain and Lord Halifax, the foreign secretary. But the prime minister drew a parallel with the Jacobites seeking to persuade Louis XIV that, if only he were sufficiently threatening, they would be able to overthrow William III; he decided that his chance of averting war would be compromised rather than advanced if he repeated the warning given to Hitler in May. His view was confirmed by the British ambassador to Berlin, Sir Nevile Henderson, who urged that nothing should be done to provoke Hitler. Further appeals on behalf of the conspirators in September failed to alter Chamberlain's mind.

TENSION BUILT UP as the Nuremberg rally approached its final night on September 12. Several hundred thousand party members filled the huge stadium to listen to Hitler as he stood, a solitary figure under the searchlights, waiting for the roar of *"Sieg Heil! Sieg Heil!"* to die down. He began by talking of the party's early struggles, then suddenly launched into a tirade against President Beneš and the Czechs. At every taunt the crowd bayed in approval; but Hitler, for all his tone of menace, did not commit himself to precise demands—only "justice" for the Sudeten Germans—or indicate the course of action he would follow if his demands for that were not met.

The speech was taken as a signal for an uprising in the Sudetenland, and several people were killed. But the Czechs did not lose their nerve, proclaimed martial law, and put the uprising down. The Nazi press proclaimed "CZECH MURDER TERROR NEARS ANARCHY," and Henlein fled across the border with several thousand followers. Hitler gave orders that they should be formed into a Freikorps, but he also told the Sudeten leaders that they must hold back: The time was not yet ripe.

Chamberlain had formed the idea of flying to Germany in a bid to avert war by talks with Hitler, a much more striking proposal in 1938 than now. It was one that appealed strongly to Hitler's vanity—*"Ich bin vom Himmel gefallen,"** he declared, agreeing to meet the British prime minister but making no offer to leave the Berghof and meet him halfway. After a journey of several hours on September 15—the prime minister's first flight, at the age of sixty-nine—Chamberlain joined Hitler in the study where Schuschnigg had been received earlier in the year.

Chamberlain's attempt to discuss ways of settling the Sudeten problem— by a transfer of populations as well as a redrawing of frontiers—was met by Hitler's insistence that "All this seems to be academic; the thing has got to be settled at once. . . . I am prepared to risk a world war rather than allow it to drag on." [22] When Chamberlain retorted by asking why then Hitler had let him come to Germany if he had already determined on war, Hitler's reply was that war could be averted if the principle of self-determination

*"I've fallen from heaven."

was accepted. Seeing an opportunity, Chamberlain said he could agree to that personally and would be willing to seek agreement to a transfer of territory if Hitler would take steps to calm the situation. With two weeks before he intended to move in any case, Hitler saw no difficulty in agreeing to let the prime minister try. Chamberlain, on the other hand, unaware of this and under the impression that Hitler was on the verge of making an attack at once, came away believing that, if he could secure agreement, war might be avoided altogether.

After the prime minister had left, Hitler gave an account of their discussion to Ribbentrop and von Weizsäcker. According to the latter's notes, Hitler was full of self-congratulation on having prodded Chamberlain into undertaking to work toward the cession of the Sudetenland to Germany:

> "If the Czechs reject this, the way will be clear for a German invasion; if the Czechs yield, then Czechoslovakia's own turn will come later, for instance next spring. There are advantages in disposing of the first—Sudeten German—stage amicably." The Führer then related . . . the little tricks of bluff and bluster with which he had dueled his conversation partner back into his corner. [23]

Any intervention by the Soviet Union during the long-drawn-out Czech crisis was limited by the fact that it was separated from Czechoslovakia by Poland and Rumania, neither of which was willing to allow Russian troops to cross its territory. But, even if a way had been open, Stalin needed to be convinced first that the French were prepared to stand by their treaty obligations and make more than a gesture of support to the Czechs before he made any overt move himself. It was certainly more to Russia's advantage to see Britain and France stand by the Czechs, and inflict a setback on Hitler, than for them to appease him and encourage him to look to the east for further expansion. But skepticism grew as the summer passed. In an important speech in Leningrad at the end of June, which the German embassy reported to Berlin as an indication of Russian policy, Litvinov expressed renewed Soviet criticism of the Western powers' attitude. Without firing a shot Germany had already come close to nullifying the results for which the Western powers had fought the World War:

> The entire diplomacy of the Western powers in the past five years resolves itself into an avoidance of any resistance to Germany's aggressive actions, to compliance with its demands and even its caprices, fearing to arouse its disapproval in the slightest degree.

But, when he came to what the Soviet Union would do, Litvinov had nothing to say:

> We strictly refrain from giving any unsolicited advice to the Czechoslovak government. . . . The Soviet government at least has relieved itself of responsibility for the further development of events. The Soviet Union asks nothing for itself, does not wish to impose itself on anybody as partner or ally, but merely agrees to collective cooperation. [24]

It was assumed at the time and has been since that a major factor in determining the Russian attitude was the effect of the purges on the Soviet armed forces. It is true that in the summer of 1938 heavy fighting with the Japanese, involving tens of thousands of troops, planes, and guns, ended in a Russian victory. But the same summer saw a second and more severe purge in the Far East. This eliminated the core group of officers with whom Marshal Blyukher had established Soviet ascendancy in the continuing clashes with the Japanese. The Red Banner Front, which Blyukher had made famous, was broken up and the marshal himself removed from his post and sent under arrest to Moscow. As a consequence the victory in the Far East did nothing to alter the impression in Paris and London as well as Berlin that, following the purges, the Russian army could not be considered an effective military power.

According to President Beneš, no serious military conversations took place between the Czechs and the Russians, any more than between the Czechs and the French. However, a book published by Professor Rzheshevsky, of the Institute of World History in Moscow, in 1989, which he claims is based on archival sources, raises doubts about the received version. [25] According to this, despite reluctance on the part of the Czech government, a Soviet invitation to the commander of the Czech air force, General Fajfr, was finally accepted in August 1938. A later account by Fajfr himself is quoted for the statement that an agreement was reached "under which the Soviet Union would promptly help us by sending 700 fighters on condition that we prepared suitable airfields and provided antiaircraft cover." In 1938 the Soviet air force was still the largest in the world, and to reach Czechoslovakia would have required only a brief flight over Rumanian or Polish territory. The head of the French mission in Bucharest is reported to have been told by the Rumanian government that it would shut its eyes to Soviet aircraft flying over Rumania, provided they kept to an altitude of 3,000 meters—which was practically out of range of the Rumanian antiaircraft guns in any case.

It is already a matter of record that in early September, Maisky, the Soviet ambassador in London, told Churchill (who reported it to the foreign secretary) that the Soviet Union would use force if Germany attacked Czechoslovakia. On September 21, Litvinov said in Geneva that three days previously the Czechs had for the first time asked the Soviet government whether it would provide support if France did, and had been given "a clear and positive answer."

But was there any substance to these assurances? Part of the answer, already known, is the warning that the Russians gave to the Poles against occupying Czech territory by force: If they did, the USSR would denounce its Nonaggression Pact with them. The French ambassador in Moscow reported subsequently that the vice-commissar for foreign affairs, Vladimir Potemkin, appeared thoroughly put out when Czechoslovakia accepted the

Polish demands and this particular opportunity for Soviet intervention lapsed.

But if the former chief of staff of the Red Army, Marshal M.V. Zakharov, is to be believed, the Russians were prepared to exert pressure on a much bigger scale than that. In 1938 Zakharov was on the staff of Boris Shaposhnikov, the Russian chief of staff at the time. In a book written in 1969, but not published until twenty years later, Zakharov claims that the reply to Beneš made clear that the Russians would come to the assistance of Czechoslovakia, whether or not the French did so, and he gives in precise detail the military forces mobilized to back up this assurance. The Soviet mobilization began with orders to the Kiev Military District at 6 p.m. on September 21 to set up and deploy close to the Polish border a force equivalent to ten divisions (particulars are given of these) under the command of Marshal S. K. Timoshenko. During the remainder of the month orders were sent to the other military districts west of the Urals which brought to "a state of war-readiness" altogether sixty infantry and sixteen cavalry divisions, three tank corps, twenty-two independent tank and seventeen air brigades, as well as calling up 330,000 reservists and retaining tens of thousands of others due for release. In a cable already published in Moscow in 1958 the French military is already shown to have been informed on September 25 of the progress made in mobilizing these forces, and this was repeated to the French military attaché in Moscow on the twenty-eighth.

What is not known is how far the French military passed on the information they received; or how far the French and British governments were aware of the measures taken by the Russians, and, if they were, whether they did not take the reports seriously or preferred to ignore them.

IV

AFTER HIS RETURN from Berchtesgaden on September 16, Chamberlain had busied himself in drawing up a plan that would meet Hitler's demands by separating from Czechoslovakia all districts with more than 50 percent German population, including those in which the frontier fortifications were situated. These proposals were presented to the Prague government on September 19, with the offer, in return for their acceptance, of an international guarantee for the rest of their country. It was following this that Beneš put his question to Moscow. It is a reasonable guess that it was under the influence of the encouraging reply that he received that he sent the formal refusal of the Anglo-French terms received in London on the evening of the twentieth. But after renewed pressure from the British and French, whose envoys woke Beneš in the middle of the night, the Czech government replied at 5 p.m. on September 21 that "it sadly accepts the British and French proposals."

As a result, when Chamberlain met Hitler for the second time, on the twenty-second, at Bad Godesberg on the Rhine, he was able to report with satisfaction that the Czechs had agreed to the comprehensive Anglo-French plan for the transfer of the Sudetenland to Germany. To the Englishman's astonishment and anger, Hitler replied that such a solution was no longer practicable: The Sudetenland must be occupied by German troops immediately, leaving the frontier to be settled later by a plebiscite. The activities of the Freikorps in the Sudetenland (at Hitler's direction) provided his justification for asserting that conditions inside Czechoslovakia were so bad that the German army had to move in right away. Working himself up into a frenzy, Hitler declared there was no longer time for discussion of commissions, percentages, property rights, refugees, and so on. First, occupation of the Sudetenland, at once; then several additional areas subject to plebiscite as well—the Austrian model provided the pattern—and the satisfaction of Polish and Hungarian demands.

All Chamberlain succeeded in getting after a further day spent in an exchange of notes and acrimonious argument was a map and memorandum setting out Hitler's new demands—without modification. These Chamberlain undertook to forward to Prague without committing himself: The Czechs' evacuation of the territory to be ceded was to begin on September 26 and be completed by the twenty-eighth, in four days' time. At the last moment, with an actor's sense of timing, Hitler kept the game going by declaring: "To please you, Mr. Chamberlain, I will make a concession. You are one of the few men for whom I have ever done such a thing. I will agree to October first as the date for evacuation if that will facilitate your task." [26] Chamberlain reported that "he had a feeling a relationship of confidence had grown up between himself and the Führer"; and he told the cabinet, when he got back, that he was sure "Herr Hitler would not deliberately deceive a man whom he respected and with whom he had been in negotiation."

The British cabinet, however, was no longer prepared to let Hitler string them along. In agreement with the French, they decided not to press the Czechs when they rejected the German demands. Instead they issued a statement that, if Czechoslovakia was attacked, France would be bound to come to her assistance and Britain and Russia would stand by France. A message from Chamberlain conveying this, but still arguing that the issue could be settled by negotiation, roused Hitler to such a display of anger that he was only with difficulty persuaded to stay in the room to hear the message out, continuing to interrupt and shouting that the Germans were being treated like niggers—worse than the Turks: "If France and England decide to strike, let them. He did not care a pfennig." [27]

THE CONSPIRATORS planning to oust Hitler had been thrown into despair by the news of Chamberlain's surprise visit to Berchtesgaden. As the tension began to rise again after the second visit, to Bad Godesberg, their hopes revived. The plans to break into the Reich Chancellery and seize Hitler were confirmed, and the raiding party was put on alert.

A fortnight after his speech at Nuremberg, on the twenty-sixth, Hitler spoke again at the Berlin Sportpalast, in the same manic mood in which he had received Chamberlain's message earlier in the day. Wildly exaggerating the "thousands" of Germans being "butchered" by the Czechs and "hundreds of thousands driven into exile," he demanded Beneš's acceptance of the Bad Godesberg terms:

> My patience is now at an end. . . . The decision now lies in Herr Beneš's hands: peace or war. He will either accept this offer and give us the Germans, or we will go and fetch this freedom for ourselves. Now let Herr Beneš make his choice. [28]

The American journalist William Shirer, who was sitting on the balcony just above Hitler, noted in his diary that, for the first time in all the years he had watched him, he appeared to have completely lost control of himself. When Goebbels shouted, "One thing is sure: 1918 will never be repeated!" Hitler leaped to his feet and, with a great sweep of his hand, which he brought pounding down on the table, yelled at the top of his voice *"Ja!,"* then slumped into his chair exhausted. [29]

Yet Hitler had still not slammed the door. Even at the height of his frenzy in the Sportpalast he had left open the alternative to war he had put forward at Bad Godesberg and, to encourage the peacemakers, had declared that the Sudetenland was his last territorial claim in Europe.

Hitler had given the Czechs until 2 p.m. on the twenty-eighth to accept his terms and on the twenty-seventh sent instructions to Keitel that the shock troops should move up so as to be able to attack by the thirtieth. Von Weizsäcker and others in close contact with the Führer did not think he was bluffing, and this view is supported by Hitler's subsequent behavior. But to conclude from this that Hitler wanted "war" is to confuse different uses of that word. What he wanted was to break up the Czechoslovak state by a military operation in order to "blood" the new German army and psychologically condition the nation to the use of force in the wars that lay ahead.

But a limited war with the isolated and outnumbered Czechs was one thing; a repeat of 1914–18 quite another. Hitler's assumption was that Britain and France would not start a general war over a Czech refusal to grant the Sudeten Germans the right of self-determination. Although he said confidently that he did not care if they did, up to the moment that he gave the order to attack he still retained negotiation—on his terms—as an alternative that could be used to break up the Czech state in two stages.

To keep this alive, as well as to weaken Chamberlain's resolution, on the evening of the twenty-seventh, less than twenty-four hours before the ultimatum to the Czechs expired, he sat down and wrote a reply to the letter from Chamberlain that he had received with such impatience on the twenty-sixth. "I leave it to your judgment," he wrote, "whether you consider you should continue your effort . . . to bring the government in Prague to reason at the very last hour." [30]

Although the Russians informed the French military of the steps they were taking to mobilize their forces, they did so only on September 25, the day after the French had announced their own partial mobilization. This suggests that Stalin was anxious not to find himself left out on a limb as the only one to take action. Once it had become clear that the British and French preferred reaching an agreement with Hitler to organizing resistance, Stalin had an equally strong reason to keep quiet and not compromise his own chances of a deal with Hitler later by drawing attention to the preparations the Red Army had made.

Inevitably the question arises how much difference it would have made—not only to the French and British, but also to Hitler and to the opposition in the German army as well—if they *had* known at the time about Stalin's preparations. If Zakharov's report is correct, and if Russia, France, and Britain had acted together, the balance of forces would have been fifty-one German divisions (only three of which were armored) facing a war, not on two, but on three fronts, against thirty-eight well-equipped Czech divisions, sixty-five French divisions, and ninety Russian, even if the last named were not up to the standard of the others. Was a chance missed that might have changed the course of history?

Even if more evidence comes to light confirming Zakharov's account, the question, like so many other might-have-beens, cannot be more than a subject for speculation. Leaving that aside, however, the *fact* is that, as he came to the moment of decision on the twenty-eighth, Hitler decided against running the risk of a general war and turned to negotiation instead. It may be that he had always intended to do this, after he had pushed his terms for settlement by exploiting the fear of war. It is more likely, however, that he had kept it as an alternative, intending to make up his mind which course to follow only at the last moment.

Several factors appear to have combined to produce Hitler's decision. One was the view of the army leadership that Germany was not strong enough to fight on two fronts—even without taking account of a third. Hitler might brush this aside as defeatism, but it had its effect when reinforced by the warning from the French and British that this was what he would have to face. The two other commanders in chief, Göring and Raeder, supported the army's arguments. A second factor was the reaction of the Berlin crowds which Hitler saw for himself during a demonstration of German military power he had ordered the day after his rousing speech at the Sportpalast. Despite the efforts of press and radio to whip up war fever, an armored division rumbling through the streets of the capital was greeted with almost complete indifference by the crowds, who turned their backs and hurried off in search of their evening trains and buses. A third, which Hitler himself told Göring tipped the balance, was the news that the Royal Navy as well as the French army was mobilizing.

Finally, and perhaps decisive, there was the intervention of Mussolini. On the Italian's suggestion, Ciano and Ribbentrop were to meet on the twenty-ninth to coordinate the two countries' political strategy for war. But when Chamberlain as well as Roosevelt appealed to Mussolini to persuade Hitler to postpone mobilization and agree to a conference, the Duce showed himself as anxious as anyone to avoid a conflict for which Italy was ill prepared. This sudden reversal on Mussolini's part caught Hitler at a moment, midday on the twenty-eighth, when he was under maximum pressure from both diplomatic and military sources not to plunge Europe again into war. Mussolini reported that Chamberlain had a new proposal to make which represented such a "grandiose victory" that it was not worth going to war for more. Chamberlain offered to come to Germany a third time and proposed a four-power conference. Once Hitler concurred, the Czechs would have to accept whatever settlement the four powers agreed on. No attempt was made to include the Russians, who were ignored.

The two dictators met beforehand on the twenty-ninth and Hitler eased his irritation at having agreed by insisting, at length, that there would still have to be a general war with Britain and France while the two of them were alive to lead their nations. Mussolini quieted him with assurances that, if the conference broke down, Italy would support Germany.

Once Chamberlain and Daladier joined them, Hitler left the conference in no doubt about what was required of it:

> He had already declared in his Sportpalast speech that he would in any case march in on October 1. He had received the answer that this action would have the character of an act of violence. Hence the task arose to absolve the action from such a character. Action, however, must be taken at once.[31]

Mussolini played a leading role in the conference, if only because he was the only participant able to speak the others' languages. But he also produced a memorandum that eventually provided the basis for the Munich Agreement. This had been drafted the day before by von Neurath, Göring, and von Weizsäcker in order to forestall Ribbentrop, whom Göring accused of trying to push Germany into war. Attempts by Chamberlain and Daladier to secure representation for the Czechs were met by a categorical refusal from Hitler. Either the problem was one between Germany and Czechoslovakia, which could be settled by force in two weeks, or it was a problem for the great powers, in which case they must take the responsibility and impose their settlement on the Czechs.

The conference had been so hastily arranged that it lacked any organization. No minutes were taken, and there were constant interruptions. But finally, in the early hours of the thirtieth, agreement was reached, and the two dictators left to the British and French the task of communicating to the Czechs the terms for the partition of their country. On October 1, as Hitler had promised and demanded, German troops occupied the Sudetenland.

. . .

THE MUNICH AGREEMENT gave Hitler the substance of what he had demanded at Bad Godesberg. Such modifications as the Western powers tried to add were brushed aside in the meetings of the International Commission charged with its implementation, in which the German members consistently took an aggressive line. No plebiscite was ever held and the new frontiers followed strategic rather than ethnographical lines, including 800,000 Czechs in the districts ceded to the Germans. Together with 11,000 square miles of territory, the Czechs lost their system of frontier fortifications, which greatly impressed the German generals when they inspected them. Beneš went into exile, and the new Czech government showed every anxiety to conciliate the Germans—to no purpose, since the latter continued to make fresh demands on them and Hitler refused to give the guarantee of the truncated state that had been promised at Munich. The Czechs were obliged to cede the Teschen district to Poland and to accept the loss of substantial areas of Slovakia to Hungary. Ribbentrop and Ciano met in Vienna to arbitrate between the Slovaks and Hungarians, producing the first of their two Vienna accords in November 1938.

Relief at a victory without war—the second within six months—raised Hitler's prestige in Germany to new heights—a further triumph for his unconventional methods of political warfare, comparable to the tactics of legality he had followed in his rise to power. It was generally assumed, both in Germany and abroad, that Hitler had been bluffing all the time and had always had a "Munich" in mind, a view that vindicated the superiority of his judgment and silenced those critics, particularly in the army, who had protested that he was failing to take into account the risks of a general war. It was even more disastrous for the conspirators who had planned to seize or kill Hitler, taking the ground away from under their feet. The claim that, if it had not been for the failure of Britain and France to stand up to Hitler in 1938, the army would have overthrown him and the war been averted, cannot be proved. Most historians outside Germany who have examined the evidence have remained skeptical, not of the courage of the conspirators, but of their chances of success, of carrying sufficient support to overthrow the regime, even if Hitler had given the order to march. But there is no doubt that whatever chance they had was destroyed by Chamberlain's and Daladier's offer to secure the cession of the Sudetenland without war.

Hitler savored the sight of the victors of 1918 hurrying across Europe to the city in which he had begun his career as an unknown agitator in order to learn the terms on which he would consent to accept the Czechs' submission. But elation rapidly gave way to anger as he convinced himself that Munich proved that, if he had refused to listen to the generals and the diplomats and had held to his original intention, he could have had his short war and wiped Czechoslovakia off the map, without any real danger of Britain and France intervening to stop him. During the last days of his life, reflecting on the causes of his failure in the Berlin bunker in February 1945, he singled out the mistake he had made in 1938:

> We ought to have gone to war in 1938. Although we were ourselves not fully prepared, we were better prepared than the enemy. September 1938 would have been the most favorable date. And what a chance we had to limit the conflict. [32]

V

FOR A BRIEF MOMENT after Munich, Hitler seems to have considered the possibility of settling finally with the Czechs that autumn. But on second thoughts he decided to wait and postpone it until the spring of 1939. Meanwhile, in November, those in the west who entertained the illusion that, now that Hitler had been granted his "last territorial demand in Europe," the National Socialist regime in Germany would settle down were given as disconcerting a revelation of its true nature as the purges in the Soviet Union had given to the illusions of the left.

If there is one issue with which Hitler and the Nazi regime are indelibly associated it is the persecution of the Jews, culminating in the "Final Solution," the planned extermination of all European Jews.

No other topic in the history of the Third Reich has been more closely examined or more keenly debated. The *fact* that between five and six million Jews were put to death by the Nazis is not in doubt (see Appendix II). Many records were deliberately destroyed, making it impossible to provide an exact estimate of the numbers. As a result, for example, of the opening of the Soviet archives in the 1990s, the number of Jews killed by the Nazis in Russia has now been raised from 900,000 to 1.25 million and may eventually take the total above six million. But the uncertainty about the total numbers should not be allowed to confuse the issue. Despite attempts by anti-Semitic groups and so-called "revisionist historians" to throw doubt on it, no event in the history of the twentieth century has been more firmly established by irrefutable evidence.

The debate has not been about the fact of the Holocaust, but about its explanation—how and why it took place and how the responsibility for it is to be distributed. In the spectrum of historical interpretation on this, as on other controversial issues in the Nazi period, there is a dividing line between those who lean towards what has been described as an "intentionalist" view, and those who favor what can be called a "functional" or "structural" explanation. The first see Hitler's role and his racist ideology as central and stress the continuity between his ideas in the 1920s and the policies followed in the 1940s. They argue that, while there may have been no blueprint or master plan, Hitler knew what he wanted, that this included the annihilation of the Jews, and that, as Karl Dietrich Bracher puts it, the Final Solution was "merely a matter of time and opportunity."

Those who incline toward the second type of explanation have laid stress on the chaotic process of decision making in the Third Reich, and see the Final Solution as the end product of a process of "cumulative radicalization" under the stress of war involving many people and much improvisation rather than as the execution of an ideological program. "On this view Hitler was at most a catalyst, rather than a decision maker."[33]

The view taken here is that it is only by combining elements from both types of explanations that a framework can be constructed which enables the incomplete evidence to be fitted together satisfactorily.

The starting point was in the disordered years following World War I—but it was a starting point, not a fixed plan. Ever since his days in Vienna, "the Jews" had occupied a central place in Hitler's *Weltanschauung* as the destructive element in the struggle of races. After the war, he committed the Nazi party irrevocably from its earliest days to destroying the power of the Jews and driving them out of Germany.

But *how* this was to be put into effect was left vague. Anyone who has read *Mein Kampf* will not find it difficult to believe that among the fantasies in which Hitler indulged privately, in communing with himself, and even in conversation with his intimates, was the evil dream of a final settlement in which every man, woman, and child of Jewish race would be wiped out as a necessary act of purification. But it remained a fantasy; how, when, even whether, it could ever be realized remained uncertain.

For Hitler was a politician as well as a visionary, particularly sensitive about his image and the response to it of public opinion abroad and above all at home. Examination of his early speeches and writings makes clear that, while there is hardly a single utterance between 1920 and 1922 which does not express a venomous hostility toward the Jews, from late 1922 anti-Semitism was replaced by the attack on "Marxism" and "the Weimar system" as the main themes of Hitler's public statements. This represented not a change of mind on Hitler's part but his response to the discovery that anti-Semitism was less of a vote-winner than anti-Marxism. The same is true of his speeches in the electoral campaigns of the early 1930s: "the closer he came to power, the more, for presentational purposes, anti-Semitism had to be subordinated to or subsumed with other components of the Hitler image."[34]

Hitler showed the same care for his image after he came to power. Violence against Jews was at first widespread but was among those radical activities from which he found it politic to distance himself later and which he appeared to have finally repudiated when he suppressed the SA in 1934. The exclusion of the Jews from German society and the insistent propaganda which identified them as "the enemies within" continued unabated. The Nazi view was summed up by Walter Buch, the Senior Party Judge, when he pronounced, "The Jew is not a human being. He is a symptom of putrefaction." The Nuremberg Laws of 1935, however, were as far as Hitler was prepared to go in appeasing the impatience of party members at the lack of "action"—

brutal enough, but aimed at driving Jews to abandon hope of living in Germany and emigrate, at whatever cost, not at inciting murder.

By 1938, the freedom with which the Austrian Nazis had been allowed to beat up the Jews had whetted the appetite of the Nazi rank and file in Germany to enjoy the same opportunity, not only to vent their hatred, but to make the same rich pickings the Austrians had made from the expropriation of Jewish property. The disabilities under which German Jews already suffered had not yet been extended to their systematic exclusion from the economic sphere. The party now pressed to see this introduced in Germany as well.

There was a difference of opinion, however, over how this could best be done. Was "Aryanization" of the economy (the euphemism for spoliation of the Jews) to be carried out in a systematic way by the state, which would corner the profits from it, as Göring wanted, or in the "spontaneous" way in which it had been carried out in Austria by the party, not the state, with great profit to party members as compensation for their long-standing services?

During 1938 three decrees were issued by Göring as Delegate for the Four-Year Plan requiring every Jew to register his assets "in order to ensure that the employment of the property can be brought into harmony with the requirements of the German economy." Once the Czech crisis was over the process was speeded up. At a conference on the Four-Year Plan (October 14), Göring called for the Jewish problem to be tackled "energetically and forthwith: The Jews must be driven out of the economy."

The atmosphere of expectation this created only needed an incident to produce an explosion. This was provided by the assassination of a German diplomat in Paris, vom Rath, on November 7. The shots were fired by a 17-year-old Jew, Herschel Grünspan, in a despairing act of protest at the treatment of his parents and some 50,000 other Polish Jews who were being deported back to Poland, by the Gestapo, without notice. Grünspan's action was at once seized upon by Goebbels to create an atmosphere of crisis and tension. In a directive to all German newspapers, he instructed editors to see that the news of the attack should "completely dominate the front page." Comment must make clear that the attack would have the most serious consequences for the Jewish population.

The ninth of November was the anniversary of the 1923 putsch, and, with the German press full of "the imperative demand to proceed at once against the Jews," the Nazi veterans of the party and SA met for the reunion in Munich which Hitler never failed to attend. In view of the controversy over Hitler's personal responsibility for the Holocaust, his behavior on this earlier occasion is illuminating. On his arrival in the Old Town Hall, Hitler was given the news that vom Rath had died. According to his close companion during the evening[35] he was strongly affected but refused to speak, as he had always done hitherto on this occasion. It was noticed, however, that he had a serious discussion with Goebbels. Shortly afterwards Hitler left, and Goebbels gave the speech in his place. According to Otto Dietrich, Hitler's Press Chief, Hitler had agreed with Goebbels what he should say but then left in order, as head of state, not to be saddled with the responsibility for what followed. As he left he was overheard to say, "The SA must be given their fling."

Goebbels' speech was taken by those who heard it as an inflammatory call to action, but it was cleverly done. He began by referring to anti-Jewish demonstrations that had already taken place, leading to the destruction of Jewish shops and synagogues. The Führer, he continued, had decided that such demonstrations were neither to be prepared nor organized by the party, but insofar as they arose "spontaneously" the party was not to oppose them. In a subsequent report by the party court called on to investigate excesses committed during the rioting that followed, the chairman gave the court's view that:

> The orally transmitted instruction of the Reich propaganda minister was probably understood by all the party leaders to mean that outwardly the party was not to appear as the author of the demonstrations but was in reality to organize and execute them. [36]

As soon as Goebbels finished speaking, the meeting broke up and the assembled Gauleiters and other leaders hurried off to pass on their instructions to the individual districts. The SA needed no incitement: They seized on the opportunity to recapture the heady excitement of 1933–34 when they had been given "the freedom of the streets," before the repudiation of "the second revolution" and their own downgrading in 1934. For one wild night of terror, the SA came into their own again. While the police stood by and refrained from interfering, two hundred synagogues were burned down, 7,500 Jewish shops and businesses were looted and destroyed, and ninety-one Jews murdered. The SS, which was not at first involved, concentrated on arresting 26,000 of the better-off Jews and herding them into concentration camps for more selective treatment.

NEWS OF THE POGROM led to an immediate outcry throughout the Western world at a return to barbarism, which cost Germany much of the residual goodwill it still retained. Even more striking was the degree of disapproval among Germans (on which all reports agree), although this appears to have been more in protest at the disorder, violence, and destruction of property than at the treatment of Jewish people. There was sharp recrimination among the Nazi leaders, Goebbels being attacked by Göring for the cost to the economy of the destruction he had let loose, and by Himmler for making more difficult the SS policy of getting rid of the Jews by forced emigration.

Hitler remained in the background. He agreed to Göring's demand that there should be no repetition of the attacks, but he did not dissociate himself from Goebbels or disown what had happened. He insisted that "the economic solution must be carried through," but put this in Göring's hands as deputy for the Four-Year Plan, singling out Jewish-owned department stores as first candidates for "Aryanization."

Hitler's feelings about the Jews had not altered, but he never lost sight of the difference between the party activists, the core of whom, the *Alte Kämpfer,* had been with him since the 1920s, and the much wider section of the German people whose support he had won by his record of success in the 1930s and could rely on as long as he continued to be successful. The latter were rarely rabid or violent anti-Semites. In a general way they accepted discrimination against the Jews and their expulsion as an alien element hostile to Germany. But the evidence suggests that, during the war as before it, finding "a solution to the Jewish problem" in practice was an issue which most ordinary Germans gave little thought to and deliberately excluded from their minds.[37] It remained important for Hitler, therefore, whatever action he meant to take against the Jews, not to disturb this passive attitude.

The effect of the Kristallnacht* was to shift "the solution of the Jewish problem" from spontaneous ad hoc action by the party on the streets to the systematic, bureaucratic process preferred by Göring and Himmler, and much less likely to attract attention. On November 12 Göring called together the ministers and officials principally concerned and set out his policy of planned expropriation. "Demonstrations" were to cease. The Jews were to be required to surrender all their property to the state in return for compensation—"to be kept as low as possible." A trustee appointed by the government would then dispose of the property to an "Aryan" purchaser at its true value, the state retaining the profit. Göring explicitly rejected what had happened in Austria. The solution of the Jewish problem was not intended as a welfare scheme for party veterans—he knew, he said, of "Gauleiters' chauffeurs who had made half a million marks."

To make good the losses which the state had incurred through the damage done to Jewish businesses on November 9, Goebbels proposed a fine on the Jewish community as compensation for the death of vom Rath. Göring was particularly incensed that German insurance companies should have to pay the Jewish owners compensation. Their representative insisted that, in order not to disturb international confidence in the probity of German insurance, the companies' obligations must be discharged in full. Heydrich, however, found a way out: Pay the insurance in full, then immediately confiscate it. This on top of the fine, fixed at the huge sum of 1 billion marks, satisfied Göring:

> That will do the trick. The pigs won't commit a second murder so quickly. Incidentally I must again say I wouldn't like to be a Jew in Germany.[38]

*This was the ironical euphemism, "Crystal Night," derived from the broken glass littering the streets, by which the events of the night of November 9–10 became known.

In addition to the dissolution of all Jewish-owned enterprises and their transfer to German ownership, Goebbels proposed a further series of decrees excluding Jews from theaters, movie houses, and all other places of entertainment and public meeting. Driving licenses were withdrawn, Jewish children were banned from German schools, and all professions closed to Jews, who were forced to hand over any gold, silver, and precious stones they possessed and were excluded from the law protecting tenancies. The whole code was aimed at making life for Jews in Germany impossible, and the SS-Gestapo supplied the answer: the extension of the program already started in Austria for furthering the emigration of Jews. By a decree published on New Year's Day, 1939, a *Reichszentrale für die Jüdische Auswanderung* (a Central Office for Jewish Emigration) was established in Berlin as well as Vienna, and later in Prague. The whole operation was placed under the control of Himmler's deputy, Reinhard Heydrich.

Deportation was combined with extortion. Wealthy Jews had to contribute foreign currency to provide the minimum sum required for immigration into other countries for poorer Jews as well as themselves. These were the terms on which they were released from the concentration camps. Any assets left over were confiscated.

"The emigration of all Jews living in the Reich" was now described in a circular to all German missions abroad as "the ultimate aim of Germany's Jewish policy." But the German government refused to allow any transfer of assets or foreign exchange abroad. This meant that any Jew emigrating went as a pauper. The reluctance of foreign countries to accept them was counted a success for the Nazi policy of exporting anti-Semitism as well as Jews. Attempts to arrange an orderly emigration, financed by an international loan, came to nothing. In ways which were anything but orderly, 78,000 Jews emigrated or were deported from Germany and Austria during 1939 and 38,000 from Czechoslovakia. The numbers fell sharply with the outbreak of war, but Heydrich announced at the Wannsee Conference in January 1942 (see p. 756 below) that between 1933 and the date the flow stopped (October 1940) the SS had successfully evicted two-thirds of the Jewish population of the Reich in 1933 (roughly 360,000 out of 503,000) and another 177,000 from Austria and Bohemia-Moravia. As a result of negotiations between Heydrich's organization and the Zionists, 70,000 of them made their way to Palestine.

As in the case of the Final Solution, Hitler entrusted the policy to others to carry out. But neither Geobbels on the night of November 9 nor Göring at the conference on the twelvth, any more than Himmler and Heydrich in 1938 or later, would have ventured to make a decision on the treatment of the Jews without the knowledge and authority of Hitler.

Henceforward, the measures to root them out of German life were concealed as far as possible and, until after the outbreak of war in September 1939, stopped short of expulsion. But Hitler was also aware that for the hardline Nazis the pivotal position he gave to "the Jewish problem" in his own *Weltanschauung* was one of the crucial elements in binding them to him. They seized on any reference to it in his speeches as confirmation that he was not wavering in his intention to solve it "once and for all"—whatever he meant by that—and grew impatient at the delays imposed by "tactics." Recognizing this, less than three months after the *Alte Kämpfer* had been disappointed and confused by the reimposition of restraint following Kristallnacht, Hitler gave them a signal that his attitude toward the Jews had not changed in the broadcast speech which he delivered to the Reichstag on January 30, 1939, the sixth anniversary of his becoming Chancellor:

> I have often made prophecies and people have laughed at me. In my struggle for power, the Jews always laughed louder when I prophesied that, one day, I should be the leader of the German state, and that then, among other things, I should find the solution of the Jewish problem. Today I am going to make another prophecy: If the Jewish international financiers succeed in involving the nations in another war, the result will not be world Bolshevism and therefore a victory for Judaism; it will be the destruction [*Vernichtung*] of the Jews in Europe. . . .[39]

What Hitler meant by *Vernichtung* he did not make clear. But in his final reflections in the bunker in 1945 he referred to the warning he had given to the Jews in his 1939 speech and remarked with satisfaction:

> I told them that, if they precipitated another war, they would not be spared and that I would exterminate the vermin throughout Europe, once and for all. . . .
>
> Well, we have lanced the Jewish abscess; and the world of the future will be eternally grateful to us.[40]

THE MEASURES against the Jews led directly to Hitler's plans for expanding rearmament after Munich. Brooding over the setback of Munich, Hitler came to blame everything on the British claim to interfere in a matter that was none of their business. This must be ended once and for all. The purpose of the meeting on October 14 already mentioned was to hear Göring announce the new targets Hitler had set: a twofold increase in the Luftwaffe's front-line strength, increased supplies of heavy artillery and tanks for the army, the development of substitute products, improved communications, the exploitation of the Sudetenland, three-shift work in the factories, and the elimination of all nonessential production. "If necessary," Göring added, "he would be brutal in turning the economy upside down to achieve his aims."[41] This would include taking hold of the Jewish question by every available means and excluding Jews from the economy, an extension of the Aryanization already begun in Austria.

The Jewish contribution figured again when Göring addressed the first meeting of the new Reich Defense Council on November 18, after Kristallnacht. Hitler wanted him "to raise the level of armaments from 100 to 300," he told them, "a gigantic program compared with which previous achievements are insignificant." Göring warned that additional financial resources would be needed and spoke of the critical situation of the Reich Treasury: "Relief will come initially through the fine of one billion marks imposed on Jewry and through the state's profits on the Aryanization of Jewish undertakings."[42] The financial problem was real enough, and Schacht was dismissed as president of the Reichsbank in January 1939 after protesting against the inflationary methods by which Hitler proposed to continue paying for rearmament. Undeterred, the same month Hitler approved the navy's Z Plan. As British historian Donald Watt says, "the yardstick of Hitler's intentions toward Britain was always his policy toward the German Navy."[43] After the weekend crisis in May 1938, he had instructed Admiral Raeder to make a complete revision of the navy's shipbuilding plans: The policy of the Anglo-German Naval Agreement was abandoned, "the Führer must reckon Britain permanently among his enemies."[44] What Hitler wanted was a full-scale battle fleet. In November he ridiculed the modest specifications of the two new 35,000-ton battleships, *Bismarck* and *Tirpitz*, which he was shortly to launch: Guns, speed, and armor were all inadequate. Overruling the naval staff's objections, he insisted that a new plan (the Z Plan) should provide four fast pocket battleships by 1943 and six larger battleships (H class, of 60,000 tons each) by 1944: "If I could build the Third Reich in six years, then surely the navy can build these six ships in six years."[45] So set was he on a fleet capable of taking on the major naval powers, Britain, France, and the U.S.A., that he gave the Z Plan priority over all other rearmament plans including the allocation of raw materials, steel, and armor plating to the two other services.

His plans for the Luftwaffe and the army were equally grandiose. He called for aircraft production of 20,000 to 30,000 planes a year and a strategic bomber force capable of reaching Britain, Russia, and even the U.S.A., which should number 2,000 heavy bombers by 1944. The army's six armored and motorized divisions were to be expanded to twenty by the mid-1940s; by the same date, the mobility of the rest of the army was to be increased by a comprehensive program for the modernization of German railways.

There was more than a touch of megalomania in Hitler's plans. Neither the Z-Plan navy nor the strategic bomber force was ever built. Nor could they have been. What Hitler was demanding far exceeded Germany's resources not only in raw materials—but also in manpower. In February 1939 the army Ordnance Office reported a shortage of one million workers and estimated that to carry out all the various programs Hitler had approved would require an increase in the number of workers of 870 percent.

There was also more than a touch of dilettantism. Bemused by his belief in will, Hitler failed to establish a clear set of priorities, refusing to allow his freedom of action to be restricted in any way. He refused to see, until the middle of the war, that issuing orders for threefold or fourfold increases in armaments made no sense without coordinating the different programs or considering how the economy was to be organized to meet them. And he failed to make and keep to a consistent timetable, transposing or telescoping different stages so that the massive expansion of the navy, which was originally envisaged for the final stage of world hegemony and could not be completed before 1944, was given priority over the program for the army, which first had to conquer the continental empire in the east.

The point on which he appeared to be most consistent—no general war before the period 1943 to 1945, therefore plenty of time for all three services to complete their preparations—proved to be the most misleading of all. War broke out before the end of 1939 and became a general war in 1941 involving Britain, Russia, and by the year's end the U.S.A. as well. By 1943–44, when it was scheduled to start, Germany had already lost it.

O N E   W A Y to increase Germany's resources was by conquest and annexation. Austria again pointed the way, providing much-needed additional manpower, raw materials, foreign currency, and productive capacity. The occupation of Bohemia-Moravia in March 1939 brought further economic gains: By June 1, 40,000 Czech skilled workers had been recruited for work in Germany, and the three German armored divisions leading the campaign against France in 1940 were equipped with tanks, guns, and trucks made in Czech factories.

Economically as well as strategically, the acquisition of Austria and Bohemia-Moravia enabled the Nazi leaders to create a German-dominated *Mitteleuropa* (Middle Europe) extending into the Balkans and up to the Russian frontier. Even before the incorporation of Bohemia and Moravia in March 1939, Czech heavy industry began to supply armaments and raw materials. The vehicle for the integration of their identities into the German economy was the Four-Year Plan and the Hermann Göring Reichswerke, not (with the exception of I. G. Farben) German big business.

In Austria the largest privately owned company, Alpin-Montangesellschaft, was acquired from the Ruhr steel combine, Vereinigte Stahlwerke. This followed a year's harassment by Göring which led Hitler's onetime ally, Fritz Thyssen, to emigrate and allowed Göring to confiscate his industrial holdings as well. Under cover of the Dresdner Bank and the state holding company VIAG, control was secured over thirty-three other major Austrian firms. As an alternative to compulsory purchase, Austrian and Czech banks and shareholders were "invited" to sell their shareholdings on unfavorable terms which few felt able to refuse. Aryanization provided another way into Czech as well as Austrian industry. In the Sudetenland the large industrial holdings of the Petschek family were confiscated and turned into a subsidiary of the Hermann Göring Reichswerke. The Nazis captured Louis Rothschild in Vienna and held him for ransom until his family agreed to hand over their Czech and Austrian holdings in return for his life. When Hitler was bullying the elderly Czech President Emil Hácha into submission on the eve of the German invasion of March 15,* Keitel interrupted to tell him that the largest Czech coal, iron, and steel complex at Vitkovice, in which the Rothschilds were the principal shareholders, was safely in German hands. The German army thought very highly of Czech armaments, and the two most important firms, the famous Skoda works in Prague and the Czech Armament Works, formerly owned by the Czech state, were taken over by the Hermann Göring Reichswerke to work for Germany.

The acquisition of Austria and Czechoslovakia also strengthened Germany's economic relationship with the countries of southeast Europe— Hungary, Yugoslavia, and Rumania. In the course of 1939, Hungary and Yugoslavia moved closer to becoming economically as well as politically dependent on Germany. The collapse of France's position in Eastern Europe had a greater effect on Rumania than any other country besides Czechoslovakia. As soon as the Munich Agreement was signed, the German minister in Bucharest urged a great expansion of German orders for Rumanian wheat and oil and the building up of huge German debts which would tie Rumania permanently to Germany. King Carol visited Germany in November 1938 to improve relations, attempting to show his independence by having Cornelius Codreanu and thirteen other leaders of the pro-Nazi Iron Guard party shot on his return. Rumania, however, still wanted to sell her surplus wheat and Germany to buy Rumanian oil, and negotiations conducted by Göring's special trade assistant Helmuth Wohltat secured an economic treaty—signed on March 23 after the news of the Prague coup and the breakup of Czechoslovakia—the effect of which was to realign the Rumanian economy in Germany's favor, despite the British, French, and Dutch stakes in the Rumanian oil industry.

Every account of German economic penetration of the Balkans always ends by emphasizing that it could not solve Germany's economic problems. In 1938, trade with southeast Europe constituted only 11 percent of German trade and, although this figure was pushed up as the area's economic and political dependence on Germany increased, the statistics for 1940 (the only wartime year for which comprehensive figures are available) show that German imports from Western Europe, and above all from the Soviet Union, increased much more.[46] But what the experience of 1938–39 had already established, even before the war began, was the huge reservoir of food, raw materials, and foreign labor accessible to German expansion— much more so when the expansion became conquest by force, allowing the unrestrained spoliation and exploitation of an occupied Europe extending from the English Channel to the Caucasus. No one has summed up the result better than the American economic historian David Kaiser:

> Having insisted on rearmament for the sake of conquest, Hitler found himself in a situation where conquest was the only means of continuing rearmament. His belief that Germany must conquer a self-sufficient

*See pp. 595–96.

economic empire, rather than rely upon world trade, had become a self-fulfilling prophecy. [47]

VI

HITLER MIGHT SPEAK of the mid-1940s as the date by which German rearmament must reach its peak, but he had no intention of waiting until then to resume an aggressive foreign policy. It was not in his nature or that of the Nazi regime to pause for a period of consolidation; both depended on a continuing dynamism for their survival.

The outcome of the Czech crisis had left him in a mood of increased confidence and frustration, both of which impelled him to raise the stakes, and next time not to weaken in his resolution. He gave expression to his determination in the speech that he made to 400 German newspaper editors in November, and in three speeches that he made to the officer corps in the new year.

To the editors he talked of the need, after the years in which he had spoken of peace, "to reeducate the German people psychologically and make it clear that there are things that *must* be achieved by force." [48] To the officers he declared that it was a duty to seize every opportunity that offered itself: "I have taken it upon myself to solve the German space problem. Take good note of that . . . the moment I believe that I can make a killing, I'll always strike immediately and won't hesitate to go to the brink." [49]

The question was, where to strike next. There was never any doubt in Hitler's mind that he would complete the occupation of Bohemia-Moravia and eliminate the Czech state at some date in the spring. But what else? Europe was full of rumors in the new year, from an invasion of the Netherlands, which the British cabinet felt obliged to take seriously, to the use of the easternmost part of Czechoslovakia, Ruthenia, to establish a base for the creation of an independent Ukrainian state.

Among the variety of prospects pressed on him by different groups in the German leadership, Hitler's preference appears to have been for a challenge to Britain and a settlement with Poland. Brooding over Munich and the triumph out of which he felt he had been cheated, Hitler's resentment focused on Britain's historic claim to intervene in the affairs of the continent. This claim must be ended once and for all, and he sent Ribbentrop to Rome at the end of October with a new proposal for a tripartite military alliance among Germany, Italy, and Japan. With Russia weak for many years, Ribbentrop argued, "all our energies can be directed against the Western democracies." [50]

Hitler does not appear to have had any specific purpose in mind when he proposed the alliance, other than the obvious one of posing a threat to the Mediterranean communications and possessions of Britain and France—both still very much imperial powers in the 1930s—and opening a second front against the French in the event of war. This should be enough to make both powers, whom he regarded as effete and no longer possessing the qualities that had won them their empires, hesitate before intervening in any future moves he might make in Central or Eastern Europe.

Raising the question of German-Polish relations, on the other hand, had very specific purposes: The first was to revise—and eventually no doubt to reverse—the terms of the peace settlement after the World War; the second was to bind Poland more closely to Germany, so as to secure the latter from any threat from the east if it became involved in hostilities in the west and to open up the historic line of attack on Russia when the time came "to solve the German space problem." From Hitler's point of view he was offering Poland a choice between becoming a satellite of Germany and securing a place in the New Europe he planned to create, possibly with compensation at Russian expense for any territory returned to Germany; or the destruction of the Polish state and the enslavement of its people as the first phase of Germany's expansion to the east. From the Polish point of view, the price Poland was being asked to pay was the sacrifice of Polish independence, not an alliance of equals but subservience to German wishes, the end of her alliance with France, and her exposure to the hostility of the Soviet Union. None of this was spelled out initially, but no one in Berlin or Warsaw—or Moscow—had any difficulty in grasping what was at stake.

The proposals that Ribbentrop put to Polish Ambassador Josef Lipski on October 24, 1938, were restrained and designed to win Polish agreement. They did not include any demand for the return of former German territory, other than Danzig, an extraterritorial road and railway across the Polish Corridor, and Poland's adherence to the Anti-Comintern Pact. In return Poland was to receive special rights in Danzig, a German guarantee of her western border with Germany, and an extension of the 1934 Nonaggression Pact. There was no question of an ultimatum; Hitler was prepared to allow time for negotiations, German approval of a common Polish-Hungarian frontier when Czechoslovakia was broken up was also hinted at, and, in order not to alarm the Poles, a German demand for the return of Memel—transferred to the Allies in 1919 and then occupied by Lithuania in 1923—was held over.

The negotiations continued on a friendly basis with Polish Foreign Minister Beck visiting Berlin, and Ribbentrop Warsaw, in January 1939 while attempts were made to find a compromise on Danzig and the Corridor. The sticking point on which Beck was adamant throughout was Poland's refusal—despite her vehement anti-Communism and far from friendly relations with Russia—to join the Anti-Comintern Pact, a gesture that would be seen as giving up Polish independence and accepting a dependent relationship with Germany. After Ribbentrop returned from Warsaw, Hitler appears to have accepted that Warsaw would not negotiate a new settlement except under direct pressure but then continued to hope that this would prove effective in drawing Poland into the German orbit, without the need for war.

EARLY IN February 1939, Hitler decided to complete the elimination of Czechoslovakia. Powerful forces—seven army corps—were assembled to march in, but Hitler was confident that there would be neither resistance nor intervention. The role played by the Sudeten Germans in 1938 was this time allotted to the Slovaks, who had been granted autonomy within the federation of three states (Bohemia-Moravia, Slovakia, Ruthenia) into which Czechoslovakia had been reorganized. The Slovaks, however, preferred to pursue their independence in their own way and showed great reluctance to invite German protection against the Czechs. Monsignor Tiso, a tough, bull-like cleric who had been leader of the Slovak group until pushed out of office by the Czechs, was summoned to Berlin and harangued by Hitler; but he refused either to broadcast a statement of Slovak independence, for which the Germans had prepared a text, or to sign a telegram, again drafted by the Germans, inviting the Führer to "protect" Slovakia. On his return to Bratislava, the Slovak Assembly made its own declaration of independence without the essential appeal for Hitler's protection which was to have served as the pretext for German intervention. German efforts to get Tiso to repair the omission still produced an unsatisfactory result. Hitler's response on the sixteenth bore no relationship to Tiso's message but accepted the Slovak "appeal" and announced the arrival of German troops to guarantee the Slovaks' newly won independence.

A hurriedly launched German press campaign claiming a Czech reign of terror against Germans and Slovaks bore little relation to the facts, but it did prompt the Czech authorities to ask if President Hácha could come to Berlin to see Hitler. Hácha was a nonpolitical figure who had been president of the Czech Supreme Court and had become head of state only out of a sense of duty. Old and sick, he was unable to fly but made a five-hour train journey, to be kept waiting for another four hours before Hitler received him at 1:15 in the morning.

Hácha already knew that German troops had crossed the border and that nothing could stop the occupation of his country; he had no grounds for complaint, he said, over what had happened in Slovakia but he made a last pathetic plea for the Czechs to be allowed to retain their national identity. Hitler's response was that it would be easy for him to grant the Czechs autonomy and an individual existence if there was no resistance. The alternative was a fight in which the Czech army would be destroyed:

> This was the reason he had asked Hácha to come. That invitation was the last good deed he would be able to render to the Czech people. . . . Perhaps Hácha's visit might avert the worst. . . . The hours were passing. At 6 a.m. the troops would march in. He felt almost ashamed to say that for every Czech battalion a German division would come.[51]

When Hácha asked what he could do, Hitler suggested he should telephone Prague. Further talks with Göring and Ribbentrop followed in another room, during which the former said he would be sorry to destroy Prague by bombing, and Hácha fainted. Revived by an injection from Hitler's doctor, Theo Morell, the president finally got through to Prague to urge that there should be no resistance. After more argument Hácha was bullied into accepting a draft communiqué already prepared: The Führer, it announced, had received the president at the latter's request, and the president had "confidently placed the fate of the Czech people in the hands of the Führer." [52]

Hitler could hardly contain himself. He burst into his secretaries' room and invited them to kiss him. "Children," he declared, "this is the greatest day of my life. I shall go down in history as the greatest German of them all." [53] At 8 a.m. he left Berlin to make his entry into Prague with the German troops. When the British and French ambassadors presented their inevitable protests at the German Foreign Office, they were met with the argument that the Führer had acted only at the request of the Czech president. The tactics of "legality" had worked once more—as it happened, for the last time.

Hitler spent the night of March 15 in the Hradčany Castle, the former castle of the kings of Bohemia. With the swastika flag flying from its battlements, he had paid off another of the historic grudges of the Habsburg monarchy: the resentment of the Germans of the empire at the upstart Czechs' claim to equality, a claim that he had first rejected in the working-class quarters of Vienna thirty years before. In his proclamation he declared that "for a millennium the territories of Bohemia and Moravia belonged to the *Lebensraum* of the German people" and had now been restored to "their ancient historic setting." An accompanying clause established a protectorate of Bohemia-Moravia with von Neurath as the first protector.

On the same day, the sixteenth, German troops arrived in Slovakia. By the Treaty of Protection that followed, the Slovaks granted the Germans the right to station garrisons, promised to conduct their foreign policy in agreement with the Germans, and (in a secret protocol) allowed them full rights in the economic exploitation of their country. An attempt by the Ruthenians to follow the Slovak example, declare independence, and secure a German guarantee ended in bloodshed. Hitler had no interest in an independent Ruthenia and invited the Hungarians to march in and take possession of their former territory. Unlike the Poles, the Hungarians had agreed to sign the Anti-Comintern Pact and to leave the League of Nations. Ruthenia was their reward for joining the Axis Powers' camp. The Poles, who refused, were excluded from any part in the second partition of Czechoslovakia.

The whole operation had taken no more than three days, and Hitler was back in Vienna on the eighteenth. His next move followed even more quickly. On March 20 it was the turn of the Lithuanian foreign minister,

Juozas Urbsys, to be summoned to Berlin, where he received the same treatment as Tiso and Hácha. Under threat of an air attack on their capital, the Lithuanians signed an agreement early in the morning of March 23 returning Memel to Germany, and Hitler arrived for a second triumphant entry, marred by a rough journey by sea which made him seasick. Since a Lithuanian coup in 1923, Memel had enjoyed autonomous status guaranteed by international statute. A parallel with Danzig, a free city under the protection of the League, was not lost on the Poles, any more than the fact that, with German garrisons arriving in Slovakia, Poland like Czechoslovakia after the Anschluss was now outflanked to the south as well as the north.

When Ribbentrop, however, repeated the German demands and told the Polish ambassador that Hitler was "increasingly amazed" at his country's attitude, the Polish foreign minister, Colonel Beck, declined an invitation to visit Berlin. While the Polish army called up reservists to strengthen the frontier defenses and Beck made clear that Poland would regard a German coup in Danzig as a *casus belli,* the Polish press, echoing an angry public opinion, warned the Germans not to think the Poles were Czechs.

VII

AFTER MUNICH the Soviet government had shown signs of retreat into isolation. The policy of collective security that it had supported had clearly failed, but neither Stalin nor Litvinov had anything to offer in its place. The Russians were aware from their intelligence sources of the demands Hitler was making on Poland—which Beck was keeping secret. They were ready to accept a Polish suggestion that the two countries should mend their fences and renew the Nonaggression Pact of 1932. The last thing Stalin wanted was to see Russia's western neighbor capitulate and become a German satellite. On the other hand, the Russians were eager to take up a German suggestion for a new trade agreement, signed in December 1938, and were thoroughly put out when the Germans went back on a proposal to accompany this with the grant of a large new credit for the purchase of German guns.

British efforts after Munich to improve Anglo-Soviet relations (in early 1939) were rebuffed, and when Stalin addressed the Eighteenth Party Congress on March 10—five days before the German army occupied Prague—his abuse was directed far more against Britain and France than against Germany. Stalin declared that a new imperialist war had begun, "a redivision of the world, of spheres of influence and colonies, by military action." Two blocs of imperialist powers had been formed: a bloc of three aggressive states united by the Anti-Comintern Pact and a group of nonaggressive states, primarily Britain and France. The failure of this second group to stand up to the aggressors could not be attributed to weakness, since they were unquestionably stronger, both economically and militarily.

Britain and France, however [Stalin continued], have rejected the policy of collective security, of collective resistance, and have taken up a policy of nonintervention, of neutrality. . . . The policy of nonintervention means conniving at aggression, giving free rein to war.

This was a dangerous game that amounted to

having all the belligerents sink into the mire of war . . . to weaken and exhaust one another . . . encouraging the Germans to march east, promising them easy pickings and prompting them: "Just start war on the Bolsheviks and everything will be all right."

At Munich the British and French had given Germany parts of Czechoslovakia "as a price for undertaking to launch war on the Soviet Union, which the Germans now refuse to honor." As other examples of the same game, Stalin pointed to the reports in the Western press that the purges had weakened the morale of the Soviet armed forces and to the hullabaloo they were making over Ruthenia and German plans to invade or subvert the Ukraine. The object of this press campaign seemed to be "to incense the Soviet Union against Germany, to poison the atmosphere, and to provoke a conflict with Germany for which no visible grounds exist." Stalin poured scorn on such maneuvers, assuring the congress that the Soviet Union remained true to its policy of peace combined with strength. Its guiding principle was "to be cautious and not to allow our country to be drawn into conflict by warmongers who are accustomed to have others pull their chestnuts out of the fire for them." [54]

Stalin's speech was later to be hailed by Molotov and Ribbentrop as the signal for the opening of the talks leading to the Nazi-Soviet Pact. [55] If by this is meant that Stalin had already decided in early March in favor of such a policy, it is surely untrue. Stalin had always seen the advantage of restoring good relations with Germany, but the unsuccessful attempts Russia had made to do this—the latest being the trade and credit talks held as recently as the winter of 1938–39—made him cautious as well as skeptical. It was an option he would always be interested in pursuing and, if the Germans interpreted his remark that there were no grounds for conflict between their countries as a hint to reopen talks, so much the better. Germany had always bulked larger on the Bolshevik horizon than any other foreign country and still appeared potentially as Russia's ally. But for the present Stalin was offering no hostages to fortune, expressing his disappointment with the failure of collective security but waiting to see how the international situation would develop before committing himself to the role that the Soviet Union would play.

What is striking about Stalin's report is his endorsement of the deep-seated Soviet suspicion that Britain and France were seeking to foment conflict between Germany and Russia. This reflected the communist conviction that the real enemies of the Soviet Union remained the capitalist powers, Britain and France. In November 1938, for example, replying to a report to this effect from Yakov Suritz, the Soviet ambassador in Paris, Litvinov wrote:

> The fact that Britain and France would like to prod Germany to take action against the East is quite understandable and well known. . . . It is also true that they would like to direct aggression exclusively against us, so that Poland should not be affected. [56]

This suspicion was to play an important role in the diplomacy of 1939, to become an article of faith in the justification of the Nazi-Soviet Pact by later Soviet historians, and to contribute to Stalin's failure to prepare for the German attack in 1941.

STALIN HAD NOT LONG to wait for the international situation to develop. Before the Eighteenth Congress broke up, the news arrived that Hitler had occupied Bohemia-Moravia, an event that led to as dramatic a diplomatic revolution as any in modern European history.

It was the British who precipitated it. The fact that Hitler for the first time, without provocation or negotiations, had seized territory inhabited not by a German minority but overwhelmingly by Czechs, made a profound impression in Britain where it was seen as destroying Hitler's appeal to the principle of self-determination, and with it the case for appeasement. What puzzled foreign observers was the speed with which the same British government that had promoted the Munich settlement now swung around not to a policy of neutrality but to actively organizing resistance to any further act of aggression by Germany. Secret discussions reaching this conclusion, however, had already taken place in February in relation to a possible attack on Holland or Switzerland. The issue, as the British told the Belgians on February 16, was not which country was the next to be threatened but "the attempt of Germany to dominate Europe by force." The change of course, therefore, was less sudden than it appeared, and the change of mood that produced it was shared by all sections of opinion as well as by many in France. Chamberlain, who was slow to respond to it, realized that his political future was at stake and hurriedly made amends in a speech at Birmingham on March 17 which, he told the cabinet, he regarded as "a challenge to Germany on the issue of whether or not Germany intended to dominate Europe by force."

This was the same language the British had used privately in speaking to the Belgians about a threat to Holland a month before. This time, Chamberlain said (basing himself on reports that again proved to be unreliable) the threat was to Rumania. But he now made no attempt, as the British had for so long, to treat Western Europe as the sole area with whose security Britain was concerned. Wherever the threat of a German invasion appeared, similar to that which had just taken place in Czechoslovakia, whether in Western or Eastern Europe, Holland or Rumania, the issue was the same, and the British had no alternative but to make clear in advance that they would take up the challenge. "Our next course," Chamberlain told the cabinet, "is to ascertain what friends we have who will join with us in resisting aggression."[57]

The problems the British and French faced were, first, *how* they were going to organize resistance to Hitler, and, second, how they were going to overcome the distrust that had been built up among the other powers by their record of appeasement since 1935. In the course of the next few days, the British and French governments approached six countries—Russia, Poland, Yugoslavia, Turkey, Greece, and Rumania—to ask if they would support a public announcement of the British and French intention to resist any new act of German aggression in southeast Europe, a warning that they believed might well act as a deterrent. At the same time both the British and French abruptly broke off trade talks with the Germans.

This sudden conversion of the sponsors of the Munich settlement to collective security took all the governments addressed by surprise. All wanted to know what the British and French intended to do. Both King Carol of Rumania and Colonel Beck of Poland decided independently to reject any proposal that threatened to provoke Germany or meant accepting support from the Soviet Union. The Russians proved the most suspicious of all, Litvinov asking if Britain was planning to commit the Soviet Union while leaving her own hands free. Instead, in order to test British intentions—as Maisky, the Soviet ambassador in London, explained—Litvinov proposed an immediate conference in Bucharest of delegates from Poland and Rumania, as well as Britain, France, and the USSR, to discuss common action.

To Litvinov's chagrin, Chamberlain dismissed his suggestion of a conference as "premature" and returned to his own idea of a declaration to be signed by Britain, France, the Soviet Union, and Poland, committing them, if the independence of any European state was threatened, to consult together on the steps necessary to offer joint resistance. After a day's reflection, the Russians agreed to sign if the French and the Poles would; this was precisely what the Poles would not do. They rejected any suggestion of association with the Soviet Union, particularly in action that was bound to provoke Germany. For three days, while Maisky waited for an answer, a divided British cabinet debated the relative merits of Polish and Soviet support, with Chamberlain showing deep distrust of Russia's reliability, arguing that the key was not Russia, which had no common frontier with Germany, but Poland, which had common frontiers with both Germany and Rumania.

The decision was in favor of building a coalition around Poland; it was thought to be impossible to build one around the Soviet Union. It was overtaken, however, by reports that once again proved to be inaccurate, this time of an imminent German attack on Poland. In light of these, Chamberlain and Halifax believed they could not delay before acting, and on March 31 Chamberlain rose in a crowded House of Commons to announce that, while consultations were going on with other governments, if any action threatened Polish independence and the Poles felt it vital to resist, Britain and France would come to their aid. The House cheered a declaration that could be taken to place the decision of war or peace in Polish hands. The announcement was followed by a visit of Colonel Beck to London, the preparation of an Anglo-Polish treaty of alliance, and the issue of British guarantees for Rumania, Greece, and Turkey.

THE BRITISH GUARANTEE surprised and angered Hitler. What it did not do was to act as a deterrent. The day after Chamberlain announced the guarantee, Hitler spoke in Wilhelmshaven at the launching of the new battleship *Tirpitz*:

> When folk in other countries say that they are now arming and will continuously increase their armaments, then I have only one thing to say: "Me you will never tire." I am determined to continue to move on this path. . . . If anyone should really wish to pit his strength against ours with violence, then the German people is in the position to accept the challenge at any time: it is ready and resolved. [58]

In case Poland should change its policy and adopt "a threatening attitude," Hitler ordered preparations to be begun for an attack, not later than September 1, which would destroy Poland's military strength. The political aim would be to isolate Poland and if possible limit a war to Poland only. Whether there was a war, and whether it could be limited, would depend on the attitude of the Western powers, but Hitler put his finger on the factor that was to prove decisive when September 1 came: "The isolation of Poland will be all the more easily maintained, even after the outbreak of hostilities, if we succeed in starting the war with sudden, heavy blows and in gaining rapid successes." [59]

Besides isolating an enemy, Hitler always laid stress on previously demoralizing him. One way of doing this was by magnifying the impression of Germany's military strength. Hitler's fiftieth-birthday celebrations, attended by all the military attachés, provided the occasion for a display that appeared on every newsreel in the world's movie theaters. For hour after hour on April 20 six army divisions—40,000 men with 600 tanks—paraded before him down the new east-west axis boulevard in the center of Berlin, which he had opened the previous night. Another way of increasing tension was by a tour of the western fortifications which Hitler made at the end of May and which was again given maximum publicity by the Nazi propaganda machine.

Throughout the summer, the Germans kept up a "nerve war," through continual reports of the remilitarization of Danzig with arms smuggled across the frontiers, and a series of incidents, any one of which might represent the beginning of an armed coup, designed both to alarm and provoke the Poles. In mid-June, Goebbels appeared in Danzig and made three violent speeches, reaffirming the German claim to its return. German propaganda warned the Poles that they should not trust their new friends, the British, who would sell them down the river as they had sold the Czechs at Munich. At the same time, for the benefit of the British and French, radio and press hammered away on the theme "Is Danzig worth a war?"

One lesson that Hitler had learned from 1938 was not to let himself be trapped again into settling for a set of ostensible demands. The obvious way to avoid that was to drop the proposals he had made to the Poles and instruct German diplomats that they were to avoid any form of negotiation. These precautions taken, for most of the summer Hitler appeared in public as little as possible and went to the Berghof. "The chief impression I had of Hitler," wrote the British ambassador, "was that of a master chess-player studying the board and waiting for his opponent to make some false move which could be turned to his advantage." [60]

Ribbentrop still hoped to bring off his masterpiece, a triple alliance of Germany, Japan, and Italy directed against the Western powers as well as the Soviet Union. All his efforts, however, could not overcome the division in Tokyo that finally defeated him—the conflict between the Japanese army, in favor of such an alliance, and the Japanese navy, determined not to be pushed into a confrontation with the British and Americans. He had better luck with the Italians. Mussolini had been incensed at the German occupation of Bohemia-Moravia, of which he had been informed only the day before. The arrival of Prince Philip of Hesse with another message of thanks for Italy's unshakable support hardly mollified the Duce. "The Italians will laugh at me," he declared. "Every time Hitler occupies a country he sends me a message." However, personal reassurances from Hitler that the Mediterranean and the Adriatic were Italy's sphere of expansion in which Germany would not meddle, accompanied by orders to the SS to start the transfer of the whole population of German speakers out of the South Tyrol, revived Mussolini's calculation that it was best to be on the winning side. "We cannot change our policy now," he told Ciano. "After all, we are not political whores." [61]

Desperate to show that he too was a man of destiny, Mussolini had already decided on the invasion of Albania, resolving in his turn not to tell Hitler until it was already taking place (April 7). Hitler, however, was quick to see that, far from asserting Italian independence, Mussolini's action would bind him more closely to the Axis, underlining, as the attack on Ethiopia and intervention in Spain had, the common interests of the two "aggressor nations" versus the defenders of the status quo, Britain and France.

The Germans now began to press for the signature of the military alliance Mussolini had so far evaded. The Duce, anxious about German intentions toward Poland, agreed to Ciano's meeting Ribbentrop in Milan but gave him a brief that laid great stress on Italy's need for peace for not less than three years. Ribbentrop could not have been more reassuring. According to

Ciano's minutes, he declared: "Germany too is convinced of the necessity for a period of peace, which should be not less than four or five years."[62]

When Ciano telephoned to report that the talks were going well, the impressionable Mussolini ordered him to announce that Italy and Germany had agreed on an alliance. Ribbentrop would have preferred to wait for Japan, but Hitler was eager to seize the chance offered by Mussolini's sudden change of mind, and Ribbentrop dutifully agreed. In drawing up the terms of the alliance, Hitler bound each country to come to the other's aid immediately, with all her power, if either was involved in war, and to conclude an armistice only in full agreement with the other.[63] He was convinced that the effect of the treaty (the "Pact of Steel," signed in Berlin on May 22) would be to isolate Poland by weakening the British and French resolve to come to her aid.

THE BRITISH GUARANTEE to Poland aroused as much anger in Moscow as in Berlin. Although the British were engaged in negotiations with the Russians about means to check aggression in Eastern Europe, they had kept them almost completely in the dark about their sudden change of plan and the decision to make a unilateral declaration. Litvinov may well have felt that the news made his own position more precarious; he brushed aside the attempts of the British ambassador to explain, declaring that all his efforts for Anglo-Soviet cooperation had been "summarily dropped," that the Soviet government had "had enough and would henceforth stand apart, free from any commitments."[64] Leaving aside, however, the blow to Litvinov's standing with the Politburo, the British commitment to come to Poland's aid was not only to bring the Russians back into the diplomatic game, from which they so much resented being excluded, but to put them for the first time at an advantage in relation to both sides. In the summer of 1939 the focus of European diplomatic activity became, not Berlin, London, or Paris, but Moscow, with the British and French competing with the Germans for Stalin's favor.

For five months, from April to August, the British and French pursued their efforts for an agreement with the Soviet Union. They did so, in the face of many doubts, for three reasons. The first was because it soon became clear that if Poland were attacked it would be impossible, without Russian cooperation, for either of them to make the guarantee to Poland effective and give the Poles more than token support. The second was because public opinion, in Britain in particular, saw an agreement with Russia as the key to checking Hitler and the test of the Chamberlain government's repudiation of appeasement. The third was because it was the best way of preventing an agreement between Russia and Germany. The same reasoning led Hitler to see a pact with Stalin as the best way to isolate Poland and defeat the British and French attempt to organize resistance to his plans. From Russia's being a power that could be largely disregarded in the calculations of the other European powers, as had been the case for most of the time since 1933, Stalin found himself promoted to be the arbiter between them.

Stalin was helped in reading the hands of the other powers in the negotiations by well-placed moles—among them, Richard Sorge, the Tokyo correspondent of the *Frankfurter Zeitung,* who was a close friend of the German ambassador, General Eugen Ott, and of a trusted associate of the Japanese prime minister; and John Herbert King, in the communications department of the British Foreign Office. King not only gave the Russians access to the British hand but enabled the NKVD to pass on to the German embassy in London items selected from secret British material to play on German fears.*

The Anglo-Soviet negotiations, which had begun in March, took on a different tone in May when the hard-line Molotov replaced Litvinov and the British and French were soon confronted with a Russian insistence on a full-blown political and military alliance, which went further than the British were prepared to go, and which included guarantees the British believed would alarm and be rejected by the states of Eastern Europe, from the Baltic to the Black Sea, which they purported to protect. After three months' argument in which British reluctance and Soviet suspicion were equally matched, sufficient agreement was reached on a revised text of an alliance for Molotov to declare himself satisfied, and for William Strang of the British Foreign Office to write later that "nothing so comprehensive had been negotiated with the Soviet Union before." [65] Molotov at once called for military discussions to follow in Moscow. By the time they began, however, the alternative of a Soviet agreement with Germany had begun to take shape.

HITLER'S WAITING GAME had so far produced mixed results. The Pact of Steel had been celebrated as a triumph but was offset by Ribbentrop's failure to turn it into a tripartite alliance with the Japanese as well. Economic diplomacy had guaranteed the essential supplies of iron ore from Sweden, oil and wheat from Rumania, chrome from Turkey, copper from Yugoslavia. Politically none of the countries of Eastern Europe, with the exception of Bulgaria, had proved willing to align themselves with the Axis camp as closely as Hitler hoped—the Hungarians, traditional friends of the Poles, were again a disappointment—but none except possibly Turkey was likely to join the other camp. In the Baltic area, Lithuania had ceded Memel under pressure but had declined an offer of the old Lithuanian capital of Vilna in return for joining in an attack on Poland. Latvia and Estonia, which (along with Finland) had rejected guarantees from the Soviet Union, accepted nonaggression pacts with Germany, moves that were followed by a visit from General Halder to inspect fortifications on the Finnish frontier

---

*British historian Donald Watt, who investigated the activities of King, reports that sometimes as little as five hours elapsed between the receipt of a telegram by the Foreign Office and the dispatch of another from the German embassy in London to Berlin summarizing its contents.

with Russia as well as to the Baltic states, increasing Stalin's anxiety about a possible attack on Leningrad. In the west a mixture of reassurances and threats had secured Belgian neutrality, but, despite a flood of rumors, British and French resolve had not weakened. There was no offer from Chamberlain to fly to the Berghof this time; the Poles had not lost their nerve, and the Anglo-French-Soviet talks in Moscow continued.

There was, however, one direction in which Hitler still hesitated to move. He needed no prompting to see that if there was one part of the chess board on which a knight's move could produce a decisive result it was in some sort of deal with Stalin. Without the support of Russia, the one power geographically able to act in Eastern Europe, the Anglo-French guarantees must lose their value. France and Britain could still attack Germany in the west, but this would not prevent the German army from overrunning Poland and presenting the Western powers with a fait accompli which would make continuation of the war appear futile. Could Germany do anything to hinder the progress of the Moscow talks? Better still, was there a possibility of substituting for a Russian agreement with Britain and France a Russo-German agreement that would guarantee Soviet neutrality in the event of war, and do more than anything else to isolate Poland and shake the Western powers' resolution?

The basis for a deal was obvious. As long as Hitler persisted in looking to the east for *Lebensraum,* war with Russia was inevitable; but in the short run the last thing he wanted was to become involved with Russia before he had dealt with Poland and removed the threat of British and French intervention.

On his side, Stalin's priority was to avoid or at least postpone any clash with Germany, certainly as long as he was threatened with a war on two fronts by the Japanese. In default of an alternative, Stalin had supported various schemes for collective security, but he had an inveterate distrust of the Western powers, whom he suspected of trying to embroil the Soviet Union with Germany as a way of weakening both regimes. The hesitations that the British in particular had shown during the recent negotiations had done nothing to remove his doubts. While Chamberlain had been willing to make three visits to Germany in 1938, no British minister had offered to take part in the Moscow talks, although the Russians had specifically asked for the foreign minister, Lord Halifax.

The irritation and distrust that the British attitude provoked in the Kremlin were expressed at the end of June in an article written by Zhdanov and published by *Pravda* under the headline:

THE BRITISH AND FRENCH GOVERNMENTS DO NOT WANT AN EQUAL AGREEMENT WITH THE USSR

What they want is a treaty in which the USSR would play the part of a hired laborer bearing the brunt of the obligations on his shoulders. No self-respecting country will accept such a treaty unless it wants to be a plaything in the hands of people who are used to having others pull the chestnuts out of the fire for them.[66]

Zhdanov's article could be taken either way (and no doubt was meant to be) as pressure on London and Paris, or as an invitation to Berlin. Shortly afterwards, the Anglo-French-Soviet talks were resumed, but this could be because there was no alternative on the table. If such an alternative were to offer the Russians not membership of a coalition in which, if it came to war, they would inevitably have to bear a major share of the fighting, but the opportunity to avoid war and watch Germany and the Western powers weaken each other, would this not be more attractive? Sorge's reports from Tokyo had already made clear to Stalin that the reason for the refusal of the Japanese to join a military alliance with the Germans was the realization that Hitler and Ribbentrop were much more interested in securing their support in a war with Britain and France than with the Soviet Union. If the Soviet Union could also remain neutral in such a war between Germany and the Western powers, this would at least enable Stalin to buy time and possibly secure territorial and strategic advantages in Eastern Europe as part of his price. These could be used to strengthen the Soviet Union against the day when Hitler might feel free to put his designs against Russia into operation, a justification of the pact Stalin was still prepared to use in his broadcast of July 3, 1941, after the German attack had begun.

The obstacles in the way were the same for both parties: the extreme distrust with which each regarded the other and the public commitment that each had undertaken against the other. Hitler had made anti-Bolshevism the leading item in his propaganda stock-in-trade for twenty years; next to anti-Semitism, with which it was identified, it was the most consistent theme in his career, linked with his objective of *Lebensraum* in the east at the expense of Russia. The counterpart in Stalin's case was the anti-Fascist crusade and the role of the Soviet Union and the Comintern in leading the fight against Fascism, the platform on which Stalin had successfully appealed to progressive opinion throughout the world. Both men had to weigh how much a deal of any sort, and the open repudiation of their principles it would involve, would damage their reputations, and how much such an agreement would count against the practical benefits to be gained. Once they had recovered their breath, would not most people be far more impressed by each man's astuteness in getting the other to sign rather than be troubled about any inconsistency? The Russian people would surely be grateful to Stalin for his avoidance of war, and the Comintern would understand the need for tactical moves in the defense of the Workers' Fatherland, no more compromising in the eyes of a committed Communist than the earlier attack on the socialists as "social Fascists." The Germans would surely be impressed by Hitler's skill in removing the danger of a coalition against them, undercutting the Western powers' guarantee and isolating Poland—a tactical move in Hitler's case, too, no more compromising in the eyes of a Nazi *Alte Kämpfer* than "the language of Geneva" with which he had deceived an anxious Europe in the mid-1930s.

VIII

THERE IS LITTLE PROFIT in debating whether the Russians or the Germans made the first approach. There were hints and probes by both parties in the spring of 1939. Molotov's replacement of Litvinov,* who had been identified with the policy of collective security and Geneva, was taken by Hitler as a signal, and on May 20 the German ambassador in Moscow was instructed to suggest reopening the economic talks broken off by Germany at the beginning of 1939. Stalin's response, conveyed by Molotov, was both suspicious and cautious: The Soviet Union would be interested in trade negotiations only if the necessary "political basis" had been established first. When asked to elucidate, Molotov would say only that the nature of the "political basis" was something both governments would have to think about.

Hitler, however, was also cautious and, instead of following up, drew back; he suspected that Stalin might use any approach from Germany as a means of bringing the Anglo-Soviet talks to a successful conclusion, leaving him exposed to a humiliating rebuff, which as von Weizsäcker put it "might even call forth a peal of Tatar laughter." Further attempts in June to start the talks up again made no progress. A new approach by the Russians, however, on July 18 evoked a response. The Russians made it known that, if a few points could be clarified, the prospects for an economic agreement already tabled were acceptable and a treaty could be signed. On July 21, the resumption of trade talks was announced in Moscow and the next day von Weizsäcker cabled the German ambassador in Moscow: "As far as the purely political aspect of our conversations with the Russians is concerned, we regard the period of waiting [imposed by Hitler on June 30] as having expired." Hitler now wanted an agreement as soon as possible; the ambassador was "to pick up the threads again."[67]

Time was beginning to press for the Germans. The military regarded August 25 as the last safe date for an attack on Poland before the mid-September rains would make it difficult to launch a Blitzkrieg. This was just over a month away. Hitler still maintained that Britain and France would not intervene, but much would turn on whether they had Soviet support. If he wanted to make sure by offering Stalin a more attractive alternative than the British and French could, so securing Russian neutrality, he had to act quickly, before the draft treaty that was agreed between them in Moscow on July 23 was turned into a military pact.

On July 26, Karl Schnurre, the chief economic negotiator on the German

---

*Molotov was foreign minister from 1939 to 1949; this was in addition to the office of Soviet premier (chairman of the Council of People's Commissars), which he held from 1930 to May 1941, when he became deputy premier to Stalin.

side, took Georgi Astakhov, the Russian chargé d'affaires, and Eugene Barbarin, the head of the Russian trade mission, out to dinner in a Berlin restaurant. Briefed by Ribbentrop, he did not beat about the bush but asked his two guests:

> What could England offer Russia? At best participation in a European war and the hostility of Germany. What could we offer on the other hand? Neutrality and staying out of a possible European conflict, and, if Moscow wished, a German-Russian understanding on mutual interests which would work out to the advantage of both countries.
>
> There was no problem between these two countries from the Baltic to the Black Sea or in the Far East that could not be solved. . . . [68]

When Astakhov remarked that, although a rapprochement might be in the interest of both countries, it would take time to bring it about, Schnurre had his answer ready: The possibility would be lost the moment the Soviet Union signed an agreement with Britain. German policy, he insisted, was directed against Britain, not Russia, adding that, despite the ideological differences, Germany and the Soviet Union had one thing in common: opposition to the capitalist democracies.

Astakhov promised to report what had been said to Moscow, asking only one further question: "If a high-ranking Soviet personage discussed these questions with a high-ranking German personage, would the German put forward similar views?" Schnurre replied confidently: "Oh yes. Certainly." [69]

It now became the great object of German diplomacy to bring about such a meeting. After long hesitation Hitler was in a hurry: He told Ribbentrop he wanted a pact signed with Stalin; and signed within fourteen days. The German ambassador, von der Schulenburg was instructed to see Molotov as quickly as possible. In the meantime, as a buildup to hostilities, the press campaign against Poland was renewed and a quarrel was started with the Poles over the activities of their customs officers in Danzig.

The Russians, however, were in no hurry. To brief himself, Stalin ordered Dvinsky, Proskrebyshev's assistant, to find the materials available on Hitler and the Nazi movement. In addition to Konrad Heiden's *History of National Socialism,* translated into Russian in 1935, Dorothy Woodman's *Germany Arms,* and Soviet intelligence reports on the size of the German armed forces, Stalin looked through *Mein Kampf,* underlining the passages in which Hitler spoke of his long-term aim to secure Germany's future by acquiring *Lebensraum* in the east at the expense of Russia. [70] The question was, how long was Hitler's long-term aim? When Schulenburg saw Molotov, the Russian showed interest but insisted that talks could only be undertaken by degrees. Not until August 12, more than two weeks after the dinner in Berlin, did Molotov agree to start the discussions. Ribbentrop replied that, as normal diplomatic channels were too slow, he was prepared to come to Moscow himself; the only condition was that he should see Stalin in order to convey Hitler's view to him personally.

Molotov, still not to be hurried, remarked to von der Schulenburg that such a visit "required adequate preparation in order that the exchange of opinions might lead to results." Were the Germans, for instance, prepared to exercise pressure on the Japanese to persuade them to adopt a different attitude toward Russia? Did they wish to conclude a nonaggression pact? Would they agree to a joint guarantee of the Baltic states? All such matters must be discussed in concrete terms.[71]

Hitler, who had realized from the beginning that there would have to be a deal—at the Poles' and others' expense—accepted Molotov's conditions without reserve, and Ribbentrop added that he was ready to fly to Moscow at once, before the weekend, with full powers to conclude a treaty. Once von der Schulenburg finally succeeded in seeing Molotov—after further delays—the latter began by emphasizing that Stalin was following the conversations with great interest and was in full agreement with them. He then read out a lengthy statement reproving the Germans for their hostile statements and actions in the past, particularly the Anti-Comintern Pact. It was entirely the Germans' fault that the Soviet Union had been forced to try to organize a defensive front in the face of Germany's threatened aggression.

However, if the German government was really changing its policy and wanted to be friends, the Soviet government was prepared to do the same. They must proceed "by serious and practical steps." First, they must conclude the trade agreement, which had been hanging fire for several months; then they could turn to a nonaggression pact. But this in turn must be accompanied by "a special protocol defining the interests of the contracting parties in this or that question of foreign policy." When von der Schulenburg asked about Ribbentrop's proposed visit, Molotov said that the Soviet government was gratified by the suggestion; it proved the Germans were serious and made a striking contrast to the British, who had sent only an official of second-class rank. But the Soviets did not like all the publicity such a visit would attract: They preferred "to do practical work, without much fuss." If the Germans wanted to make a start, they could draft a pact together with the protocol he had mentioned.[72]

Molotov's tactics reduced Ribbentrop to frenzy. He demanded that von der Schulenburg seek a further meeting at once, tell him that German foreign policy had reached a historic turning point, and press for a reply. It was not only Ribbentrop but also Hitler on whom the tension and uncertainty were beginning to tell. His entourage began to fear the effect on his health. He relieved his feelings by issuing orders (Saturday, August 19) for twenty-one U-boats and the two pocket battleships, *Deutschland* and *Graf Spee,* to take up their war stations in the Atlantic ready to attack British shipping, but it was only a distraction from the question that absorbed him: Could the Russians be brought to the point of signing in time?

Von der Schulenburg's first meeting with Molotov on the nineteenth gave little ground for hope. Ribbentrop had provided the ambassador with a draft text for a pact. But Molotov had been unimpressed: This was not the Soviet way of doing things. It would be better for the Germans to take one of the pacts the Soviets had signed with other countries—Poland or the Baltic states—and use this as a model. And what about the secret protocol? The Soviet Union expected the Germans to say specifically what was to go into it. The ambassador had spent an hour trying to persuade Molotov to name a date for Ribbentrop's visit—to no avail. The economic agreement had not yet been signed; after this was done, they could move on to the pact and protocol.

Von der Schulenburg, however, had hardly returned to the embassy when he was summoned to the Kremlin to see Molotov again in an hour's time. He found the Soviet premier as affable as he had been cold and formal before. He told the ambassador that he had reported to the "Soviet government" and had been instructed to hand over the Soviet draft of a pact, which he then did. He added that if the economic treaty could be signed the next day (Sunday the twentieth) Ribbentrop could arrive in Moscow on the twenty-sixth or twenty-seventh. [73]

Dr. Friedrich Gaus, the German Foreign Office's treaties expert, described at the Nuremberg Trials how he was summoned to Hitler's study in the Berghof and found him and Ribbentrop bent low over the teleprinter as it tapped out von der Schulenburg's message. Hitler, Gaus recalled, threw his hands in the air in triumph and started to laugh. He spent the rest of the night restlessly wandering round the Berghof waiting for the ambassador's full report. During the early hours, he learned that the head of the Soviet trade mission, on orders from Moscow, had called on Schnurre later on the Saturday evening and had insisted on signing the trade treaty at once—at two o'clock on the morning of the twentieth. But the earliest date for Ribbentrop's visit to Moscow and the signing of the pact still remained the twenty-seventh, a date that (as Stalin must have known) was too late for Hitler's timetable, the day after the German army was due to launch its attack on Poland.

The ambassador's report did not arrive until after Hitler had gone to bed, exhausted, at 7 a.m. The only reason von der Schulenburg could give for the sudden change on the Soviets' part was Stalin's personal intervention, but he could not explain it. It was during the afternoon of the twentieth that Hitler had a moment of inspiration and, acting on it at once, sat down to write a personal letter to Stalin ("M. Stalin, Moscow") accepting the Soviet draft of the pact.

> I am convinced that the substance of the supplementary protocol desired by the Soviet Union can be cleared in the shortest possible time if a responsible German statesman can come to Moscow himself to negotiate.

. . . I therefore propose once again that you receive my foreign minister on August 22 or at the latest on the twenty-third. He will have the fullest powers to draw up and sign the pact as well as the protocol. . . . I should be glad to receive your early answer.

Adolf Hitler[74]

Hitler's letter turned the trick, cutting through the pretense that it was necessary to deal with Molotov as head of the Soviet government and going directly to the real source of authority. The fact that Hitler was prepared to lay his prestige on the line, without first making sure that Stalin would respond, convinced the general secretary that he meant business. On Monday morning von der Schulenburg telegraphed Stalin's reply:

To the chancellor of the German Reich, Herr A. Hitler.

I thank you for your letter. I hope that the German-Soviet Nonaggression Pact will mark a decisive turn for the better in the political relations between our two countries. . . .

The Soviet government has authorized me to inform you that it agrees to Herr v. Ribbentrop's arrival in Moscow on August 23.

J. Stalin[75]

Hitler had already accepted the Russian draft of the pact. But the Russians added a postscript making it valid only if a special protocol were signed simultaneously, covering the points in which they were interested. It was to complete the process of horse-trading that Ribbentrop was to fly to Moscow. Hitler made no difficulty about signing the paper giving him plenipotentiary powers: Like other agreements, it could always be repudiated later when it had served its purpose. What mattered to him was Stalin's signature on the pact, which meant the neutrality of Russia, an end to any threat of an Anglo-French-Russian coalition to block German designs on Eastern Europe, and the isolation of Poland.

Hitler did not immediately tell his entourage, waiting to receive the text of Stalin's message. Speer, who was present, recalls that when he had read it,

Hitler stared into space for a moment, flushed deeply, then banged on the table so that the glasses rattled and exclaimed in a voice breaking with excitement, "I have them! I have them!" Seconds later he had regained control of himself. No one dared ask any questions, and the meal continued.[76]

So far the documentation for the Russian side of the negotiations is much less full than that for the German. But enough is known to establish the tactics Stalin was following. Once Ribbentrop had offered to come to Moscow, Stalin moved into the position he wanted: He would have the rival bids from the two sides before him when he decided which to accept. After Russia's exclusion from the Munich settlement, this was a remarkable reversal. By delaying Ribbentrop's arrival and the final signature of the pact until the protocol was agreed upon, he could exploit Hitler's anxiety about the timetable to extract the maximum concessions and to make sure that there would be no last-minute Munich to deprive them of their value.

The Soviet negotiations with the British and French had been going on since March. During all that time, despite a specific Russian invitation to the foreign secretary, the British cabinet had never thought it worthwhile to send a minister to Moscow. Nor did they or the French include their chief of staff or leading commanders in the military mission sent to continue the discussions, now that agreement had been reached on a political formula. They took nearly two weeks to put together a team, then sent it not by plane or fast naval vessel, but by a slow passenger boat which took five days to reach Leningrad on August 10, too late to catch the night train to Moscow.

Once started, the military talks only showed up the gap between the two sides. The Russians, led by Kliment Voroshilov, wanted to know the strength of the British and French forces and what plans they had made to fight the Germans: The British and French were still thinking in terms of deterrence not of operations, how to avoid war not how to win it. As a test of their seriousness, Voroshilov asked: Would Poland accept the entry of Soviet troops on her territory in order to confront the Germans? Despite the strongest pressure by the French, nothing would persuade the Poles to agree. "Are we then to be obliged," Voroshilov asked, "to beg for the right to fight the common enemy?" The delegations met for the last time on August 21, without result. Ribbentrop's arrival was announced the following day.

The failure of the British and French governments to make a more determined effort to secure a Russian alliance was sharply criticized at the time and has been since by everyone writing about the origins of the war—with justice. The lack of any sense of urgency throughout the negotiations only confirmed Stalin's suspicion that their real objective was a deal with Germany, another Munich, which the *threat* of agreement with Russia could help to secure. Despite the confusion caused by unofficial attempts behind the scenes to bring about discussions with Hitler, there is no evidence that this was ever the British government's intention—or Hitler's—and plenty of evidence that, if it had been, British public opinion would have rejected it. But neither the British nor the French governments had yet accepted the inevitability of war; they still hoped to deter Hitler and had not grappled seriously with the question of what they would do if deterrence failed. If the Russians continued the negotiations despite the Western powers' evident lack of enthusiasm and Stalin's own suspicions, it was to elicit a rival bid from the Germans and to provide a reinsurance if none was forthcoming.

The decisive element that led Stalin to prefer the German proposal was something the British and French could never have matched, whomever they had sent to Moscow and however promptly they had arrived—a share not in the defense of an ungrateful Eastern Europe's independence, but in its partition, and this in return for Russia standing aside, for agreeing *not* to enter any war that might break out. As soon as it was clear that this was what Hitler was prepared to offer, Stalin himself appeared and took over the negotiations.

The meeting in the Kremlin took place within an hour of Ribbentrop's arrival. The only part of the pact to attract Stalin's attention was the high-flown language about Soviet-German friendship which Ribbentrop had added as a preamble. This was too much for Stalin. After six years of pouring buckets of filth over each other's heads, he said, they could not expect their peoples to believe that all was forgotten and forgiven. Public opinion in Russia, and no doubt in Germany, too, would have to be prepared slowly for the change.

What interested Stalin most was the secret protocol. In the event of a territorial and political transformation of Eastern Europe, the Germans proposed to divide Poland into a Soviet and a German "sphere of interest" divided by the rivers Narev, Vistula, and San. The question whether the interests of both parties made the maintenance of an independent Polish state desirable, and if so how its frontiers should be drawn, was left for later determination. As far as the Baltic states were concerned, the Germans proposed to leave Finland and Estonia in the Soviet sphere of interest, claim Lithuania enlarged by the inclusion of Vilna for themselves, and partition Latvia along the Dvina river. Stalin, however, wanted all of Latvia. Ribbentrop telegraphed to Hitler, who, after looking at an atlas, agreed. In southeastern Europe the Soviet side expressed its interest in Bessarabia, and the Germans declared a complete lack of interest in the whole area.

In this fashion, over the table, the fourth partition of Poland was agreed—before a shot had been fired. Stalin's share was the reversion of those parts of Byelorussia and the Ukraine annexed by Poland in 1920, with a sizeable portion of ethnic Poland, plus three of the four Baltic states lost in 1917, so removing the threat to Leningrad that caused him so much anxiety, and Bessarabia, lost to Rumania in 1918.[77]*

While the texts were being prepared for signing, Stalin encouraged Ribbentrop to talk at length about foreign affairs. Both were scathing in their references to Britain, and Ribbentrop assured Stalin that the Anti-Comintern Pact was really directed against the Western democracies, not Russia, venturing to report the Berlin joke "Stalin will yet join the Anti-Comintern Pact." When champagne was brought, Stalin proposed a toast to Hitler: "I know how much the German nation loves its Führer; I should therefore like to drink to his health."

---

*The existence of the secret protocol, long known in the West from captured German documents, was only admitted by the Soviet Union fifty years later, in 1989.

Ribbentrop returned to Berlin in a state of elation. He believed that he brought with him an agreement that would allow Hitler to deal the Poles a blow from which they would never recover. To get it he had been prepared to make nonsense of the Anti-Comintern Pact, of which he was the architect, to risk alienating both the Japanese and the Italians, and to grant sweeping concessions to the Soviet Union in Eastern Europe. But, immediately, this appeared a small price to pay for so dramatic a coup, which at a blow wrote off the Franco-Soviet Pact of 1935, the Anglo-French negotiations in Moscow and—as Ribbentrop was quite convinced—the British and French guarantees to Poland.

Hitler greeted him on his return as "a second Bismarck." The foreign minister could not speak highly enough of the warmth of the welcome they had received in Moscow; he had been made to feel completely at home, "just as if I were among old party comrades." Hitler was particularly interested in the photographs of the historic occasion. He had insisted that his personal photographer, Hoffmann, should accompany Ribbentrop and before leaving had instructed him to be sure to obtain a close-up of Stalin's earlobes. He believed these would show whether Stalin had Jewish blood— whether the earlobes were "ingrown and Jewish, or separate and Aryan." He was relieved to see that Stalin passed the "test" and was not a Jew.

Although more restrained in expressing it, Stalin was equally satisfied with the result. If all went well, he could look forward to seeing both the "imperialist camps" he had spoken of in his March speech—Germany and Italy, and the Western democracies—involved in war, while Russia stood aside and reaped large territorial gains without risk and without cost.

His satisfaction was greatly increased by the news from the Far East. None of the powers was as deeply angered and humiliated by the Nazi-Soviet Pact as Japan. By the Japanese code of behavior they had been betrayed and dishonored by their partner in the Anti-Comintern Pact, and the Japanese government resigned in protest. Their diplomatic humiliation by the Germans coincided with a military humiliation at the hands of the Russians. Following the Japanese reversal in July on the Khalkin-Gol (the disputed zone on the Soviet-Manchurian border) the Russians had launched a new offensive in August, this time under a new commander, General Georgi Zhukhov, who had escaped the purges thanks to the protection of Marshal Timoshenko and made his success on this occasion the foundation of a brilliant career. At the end of August, Zhukhov provided Stalin with a decisive victory over the Kwangtung army, which had been the heart of the Japanese faction campaigning for a military alliance with Germany. The double defeat the Japanese suffered ended the fighting in the Far East. On September 15 they reached a formal agreement with the Soviet Union. Taken together with the Nazi-Soviet Pact, this removed the danger of war from both Russia's exposed fronts, in the east as well as in the west.

IX

ON AUGUST 23, even before Ribbentrop and Stalin had signed the pact, Hitler had directed that the attack on Poland should begin, as planned, early on the twenty-sixth. The day before, on the twenty-second, he had met some fifty of the leading commanders of the army, navy, air force, and SS who had been summoned to the Berghof to hear his plans. He began by explaining that he had wanted to attack the West first, but that it had become clear that, if he did, Poland would attack Germany from the rear. A conflict with Poland had to come sooner or later; it was better now.

> First of all, two personal factors: my own personality and that of Mussolini. All depends on me, on my existence, because of my political talent. Probably no one will ever again have the confidence of the whole German people as I have. There will probably never again be a man with more authority than I have. My existence is therefore a factor of great value.

Much the same applied to Mussolini: Without him Italy's loyalty as an ally could not be counted on.

"IT'S QUEER HOW YOU REMIND ME OF SOMEONE, JOSEF . . ."

For us it is easy to make decisions. We have nothing to lose, everything to gain. Our economic situation is such that we cannot hold out for more than a few years. Göring can confirm this. We have no other choice: We must act. Our opponents will be risking a great deal and can gain only a little. Britain's stake in a war is inconceivably great. Our enemies have leaders who are below average. No masters, no men of action. No one knows how long I shall live. I am now fifty and at the height of my powers. It is better war should come now rather than in five years' time when Mussolini and I will be older.

Hitler repeated his view that the chances of British and French intervention were slight and that it was necessary to accept the risk.

The enemy had another hope, that Russia would become our enemy after the conquest of Poland. The enemy did not reckon with my great strength of purpose. . . .

Today's announcement of the Nonaggression Pact with Russia came as a bombshell. . . . The day after tomorrow Ribbentrop will conclude the treaty. The consequences cannot be foreseen. . . .

We need not be afraid of a blockade. The East will supply us with grain, cattle, coal, lead, and zinc. It is a mighty aim which demands great efforts. I am only afraid that at the last moment some swine or other will yet submit to me a plan for mediation.

The political objective goes further. A start has been made on the destruction of England's hegemony. Now that I have made the political preparations, the way is open for the soldiers. [78]

After lunch, the commanders presented their operational plans. Hitler's concluding address was designed to raise their fighting spirit. There must be no shrinking back from anything.

An inflexible, unflinching bearing, above all on the part of superiors. . . . A long period of peace would not do us any good. . . .

The destruction of Poland has priority, even if war breaks out in the West. . . . I shall give a propaganda reason for starting the war, whether it is plausible or not. The victor will not be asked whether he told the truth. When starting and waging a war it is not right that matters, but victory.

Close your hearts to pity. Act brutally. Eighty million people must obtain what is their right. Their existence must be made secure. The greatest harshness. . . . Any failures will be due solely to leaders having lost their nerve.

The wholesale destruction of Poland is the objective. Speed is the chief thing. Pursuit until complete annihilation. [79]

It is doubtful if Hitler succeeded in convincing many of his audience that Britain and France would not intervene, but the fact that the attack was directed against Poland, the traditional enemy of Prussia, Hitler's emphasis on a Blitzkrieg, and above all the pact with Russia carried the majority with him. The older generation of generals was pleased that Hitler had reverted to the collaboration with Russia which had been the doctrine of von Seeckt as the first chief of the new army after 1918; the younger generals were delighted that they would get the chance to show what they could do against an enemy they were confident of defeating.

ONCE HITLER LEARNED that the pact had been signed he gave the preliminary order for Operation White to begin at 4:30 a.m. on Saturday the twenty-sixth. He also authorized the appointment by the Danzig Senate of Gauleiter Forster as head of state in the Free City, a direct challenge to the Poles and the League. He was convinced that, once the British and French had digested the news from Moscow, they would abandon any idea of intervention. This conviction was not affected by the issue of a statement in London saying that, whatever might be the nature of the German-Soviet pact, the British government was determined to fulfill its obligations to Poland. When British Ambassador Henderson presented this in a personal letter from Chamberlain, Hitler worked himself into a rage, then, when Henderson had gone, burst out laughing: "Chamberlain won't survive that conversation! His cabinet will fall this evening." [80]

Hitler accepted that the Moscow pact would cost him the support of Japan, but he was anxious not to lose that of Mussolini. The day after Ribbentrop's return, he wrote a personal letter to the Duce, as he had after all his other coups, to explain why it had not been possible to consult his ally in advance and to persuade him that through the deal with Russia a completely new situation had been produced "which must be regarded as the greatest possible gain for the Axis." Without actually saying that war was imminent, he added that, in view of the "intolerable provocations" of the Poles, "No one can say what the next hour may bring. . . . I can assure you, Duce, that in a similar situation I would have complete understanding for Italy, and that in any such case you can be sure of my attitude." [81]

The same morning (August 25) that he made this belated bid for Mussolini's support, Hitler learned that the British cabinet had not fallen but that Chamberlain had reiterated in Parliament the British commitment to Poland. Although the latest hour for the code word to send German troops into action on the following morning at 4:30 a.m. was 2 p.m., he secured a postponement of an hour in order to make a further effort to confuse and divide the British. He summoned the British ambassador for 1:30 p.m. and when Henderson arrived told him he had been impressed by Chamberlain's speech and deeply regretted the general war to which the British government's attitude must now lead: "After turning things over in his mind once more, he desired to make a move as regards England which should be as decisive as the step taken in regard to Russia, the result of which had been the recent pact."

Germany was determined to abolish the "Macedonian conditions" on her eastern frontier, but it was not in the interests of either power for Germany and England to enter into a war that would be bloodier than that of 1914–18. Once the Polish problem was solved, he continued,

> I am prepared to approach England once more with a large and comprehensive offer. . . . I am a man of great decisions and in this case also I shall be capable of a great action. I accept the British Empire and I am ready to pledge myself personally to its continued existence and to commit the power of the German Reich to this.

He would approach the British government with concrete proposals immediately after the solution of the Polish question. If they rejected his ideas,
there would be war.[82] As if to underline the parallel with the deal that had
secured Russian neutrality, Hitler put at Henderson's disposal the same
plane that had taken Ribbentrop to Moscow to carry his message to London.

After the ambassador left, Hitler sent for Keitel and at three o'clock gave
the order for the five German armies on the Polish frontiers to attack the
next morning. Four hours later, however, Hitler telephoned Keitel and
asked if the order to attack could be called off. When von Brauchitsch
agreed that it could, urgent orders to this effect were sent out, and by a feat
of organization the advance was halted in time. Two messages had upset
Hitler's calculations: One, from London, reported that the British and Poles
had signed a treaty of mutual assistance; the other, from Mussolini, brought
the news that Italy was not yet prepared to take part in a war with Britain
and France.

During the summer Mussolini had grown increasingly uneasy about
Hitler and what he might do. Between August 10 and 12, Ciano visited
Ribbentrop and Hitler in Bavaria in the hope of finding out. He returned
convinced that they were bent on crushing Poland, and that at all costs Italy
must avoid being dragged in. It took two weeks to convince Mussolini, who
oscillated painfully between fear of what the world would say if he dishonored the Axis alliance after all his braggadocio about the Pact of Steel, and
fear of the consequences of honoring it.

The news of the pact with Russia made a great impression—it was
exactly the sort of coup Mussolini would have loved to bring off himself—
but it did not solve his own dilemma. His message to Hitler on the
twenty-fifth represented what he hoped would appear as a compromise. If
the war was limited to Germany and Poland, Italy would give all the aid
asked of her; if it was not, Italy would take "no initiative of a warlike
character." The Duce defended his decision by saying that, in all his
discussions with Hitler, war had been envisaged only after 1942, by which
time Italy would have been ready. The action Italy could eventually take
would depend on the delivery of large quantities of armaments and raw
materials.[83]

Keitel said later that he had never seen Hitler thrown into such confusion. The combined effect of the messages was to put in question two of the
major assumptions in Hitler's calculation. He had expected that Britain
would not fight and now it appeared she would; he had expected that
Mussolini would fight and now he clearly would not. Mussolini's desertion
struck him particularly hard. Only three days before he had praised Mussolini's steadfastness to his generals as one of the crucial factors in favor of
war in 1939 rather than later. Now, as he immediately remarked, "the
Italians are behaving just as they did in 1914." Moreover, if the Duce had
brought himself finally to admit that Italy could not face a war, it was

because he must be convinced that Hitler was wrong, that a war could not be limited, and that Britain and France were certain to intervene.

It took time for Hitler to recover from the shock, and all accounts agree about the signs of strain that he showed in the remaining days of August. He was unable to sleep, liable to abrupt changes in mood and to bouts of wild talk which at times bordered on hysteria. This was the same sort of erratic behavior that marked other crises. He was under pressure not only from other governments but also from some of his own associates—Göring, for example, and now Mussolini—not to risk war with Britain and France and to settle for another Munich. In the state of tension this produced, an unexpected setback like the two messages he received could throw him off balance, leading to long spells of silence and self-questioning broken by wild accusations of treachery and threats. But as he struggled with the doubts such news revived, he also—consciously or unconsciously—exploited his temperament to draw on his resources of willpower and restore his confidence by a process of self-intoxication. It was the same process that he had developed to establish his mastery of a mass audience.

Characteristic of both was the catalogue of "provocations" and atrocities, for which the Czechs had been responsible the year before, this time the Poles, all of them exaggerated (for example, the accounts of castration) or invented, recited in a voice rising to a scream. Equally characteristic, when talking to an individual, was the sudden return to a normal conversational voice and manner.

The postponement of the attack on the Poles did not mean that Hitler had abandoned it; but he had decided he must take more time—the six days that he had in hand before his original deadline of September 1—to make sure of Poland's isolation. To do that, he needed to find some way of dissuading the Western powers from honoring their promise of assistance. As a first move, he sought to limit the danger that could be caused by Italy's open defection. He reassured Mussolini that he understood the reasons for his decision but discouraged any idea the Duce might have of saving face by offering to act as a mediator: Germany was not interested in a negotiated settlement. The important thing was that the world should have no idea of the attitude Italy meant to adopt. This would help Germany by forcing the British and French to keep substantial forces in the Mediterranean. [84] In fact, the Italians became so alarmed that the Western powers might strike at them while the Germans struck at Poland that late on August 31 Ciano, by a calculated indiscretion, let it be known that Italy would stay neutral.

Hitler, however, was convinced that London was the key, that the French would follow the British lead, and that, left to themselves, the French would not fight. So far no reply had been received from London to his offer of a guarantee of the British Empire, but a new and unexpected possibility offered itself through the unofficial contact that Göring had made with the British through an old friend, Birger Dahlerus, a Swedish businessman.

A suggestion that the Reich marshal might make a secret personal visit to Chequers, the British prime minister's country residence, on August 23 had been vetoed by Hitler, but he had agreed on the twenty-fifth to Göring's sending Birger Dahlerus in his place. Dahlerus was briefed by Göring to ask if Britain would advise Poland to enter into direct negotiations with Germany. He returned to Germany late on the twenty-sixth bearing a letter from Lord Halifax which, in very general terms, confirmed Britain's desire for a peaceful settlement of the dispute between Germany and Poland. Although Halifax described its contents as "platitudinous," Göring claimed that the message was of sufficient importance for him to take Dahlerus to Berlin, rouse the Chancellery, which was by then in darkness, and get Hitler out of bed to hear what Dahlerus had to report.

Ignoring the letter Dahlerus had brought, Hitler took a long time to get to the point, spending half an hour questioning Dahlerus about the years he had spent in England. Only then did he finally turn to the current situation, working himself into a rage, declaring that he had sent his last offer to Britain and boasting of the armed power he had created, unique in German history.

When Dahlerus was finally able to talk about his visit to London, he spoke quietly "to avoid irritating him unnecessarily, since his mental equilibrium was patently unstable":

> Hitler listened without interrupting me . . . but then suddenly got up and, becoming very excited and nervous, walked up and down, saying as though to himself that Germany was irresistible. . . . Suddenly he stopped and stood in the middle of the room staring. His voice was blurred and his behavior that of a completely abnormal person. He spoke in staccato phrases: "If there should be war, then I shall build U-boats, build U-boats, U-boats, U-boats." His voice became more indistinct and finally one could not follow him at all. Then he pulled himself together, raised his voice as though addressing a large audience and shrieked: "I shall build airplanes, build airplanes, airplanes, airplanes, and I shall annihilate my enemies." He seemed more like a phantom from a story book than a real person. I stared at him in amazement and turned to see how Göring was reacting, but he did not turn a hair.[85]

Hitler, however, had not lost his powers of political calculation. Sitting down with Göring and Dahlerus, he produced a new six-point proposal which the latter was not allowed to write down but which he agreed to take to London at once. It comprised a German-British pact; Britain to help Germany obtain Danzig; Poland to get a free port in Danzig and a corridor to Gdynia, the Polish port from which the Poles might be otherwise cut off by the German annexation of Danzig; a German guarantee of Poland's frontiers; guarantees for the German minority in Poland; the return of Germany's colonies; and the German guarantee of the British Empire.

When Dahlerus delivered his message (Sunday, August 27) Chamberlain and Halifax received it with skepticism, but they could not ignore the advance on the earlier message brought by Henderson, suggesting that Hitler was now prepared to negotiate with Poland through the British and accept a peaceful settlement. Their response, which Dahlerus took back to Berlin, was that the British were willing in principle to come to an agreement with Germany, but stood by their guarantee to Poland. They recommended direct negotiations between Germany and Poland on frontiers and minorities, stipulating that the results would have to be guaranteed by all the European powers, not just Germany. They rejected the return of colonies under threat of war, but not indefinitely, and they emphatically declined the offer to guarantee the British Empire.

To Dahlerus' surprise—and Göring's—Hitler accepted the British terms. Göring, sounding very pleased, told the Swede that, provided the official British reply to be delivered by Henderson corresponded with his report, there was no reason why an agreement could not be reached. In the account telephoned to London (early morning, August 28) Dahlerus made it clear that Hitler was suspicious that the Poles would try to avoid negotiations. Halifax acted on this, secured the Polish government's agreement to start negotiations with Germany at once, and included this in the official British reply which Henderson delivered to Hitler on the evening of the twenty-eighth. The next step, the British concluded, was for the German and Polish governments to start discussions. The Poles had agreed; would the Germans? Hitler promised a reply the following day, the twenty-ninth.

The British note and Hitler's reception of it spread hope throughout the other capitals that war might after all be avoided. This was not at all Hitler's intention. His confidence restored, he was now riding high again. The game he was playing is made clear by the telephone call General von Brauchitsch made to Halder, the army chief of the General Staff, after talking to Hitler on the afternoon of the twenty-eighth before he saw Henderson. Halder's note of the call reads:

Attack starts September 1.
Führer will let us know at once if further postponement is necessary.
It is intended to force Poland into an impossible position for negotiations and so achieve the maximum solution.
Führer very calm and clear. . . .
Rumor has it that England is disposed to consider comprehensive proposal.
Plan: we demand Danzig, corridor through corridor and plebiscite. England will perhaps accept. Poland probably not. *Wedge between them!* [86]

The note Henderson presented fitted very well into this pattern. Hitler was surprised but delighted that the Poles were ready to enter into discussions. He was now in the same position he had been at Bad Godesberg the year before, when Chamberlain arrived to say the Czechs had accepted Hitler's demands, and Hitler told him this was no longer sufficient. The danger

Hitler now had to guard against was letting himself be trapped into accepting another Munich settlement. He believed he had the answer.

"Tonight," he told his chief lieutenants after Henderson had left, "I'm going to hatch something diabolical for the Poles, something they'll choke on." Even the idea of an international guarantee attracted him:

> I like it. From now on I shall only do things on an international basis. International troops shall go in—including Russians! The Poles would never agree to that.
>
> We now have to aim a document at the British or the Poles that is little less than a masterpiece of diplomacy. I want to spend the night thinking it over, because I always get my best ideas in the small hours between 5 and 6 o'clock.

When Göring urged caution, "We should stop playing *va banque*," Hitler replied: "I have played *va banque* all my life."[87]*

HALDER'S ENTRY in his diary for the twenty-ninth gives an insight into the tactics Hitler devised overnight:

> Führer has hopes of driving wedge between British and French and Poles.
>
> Today Poles directed by English to go to Berlin as required by Germans. Führer wants them to come tomorrow (August 30).
>
> Basic principles: raise a barrage of demographic and democratic demands . . .
>
> 8/30 Poles in Berlin.
> 8/31 Blow up.
> 9/1 Use of force.[88]

When Henderson returned for the German reply on the evening of the twenty-ninth, he found Hitler in a very different mood from the day before, raging against the Poles for "barbaric acts of maltreatment against the German minority" which were intolerable for a Great Power. The British might still believe these grave differences could be resolved by direct negotiations, the German government unfortunately could not.

Nevertheless, Hitler said, though skeptical of a successful outcome, they would accept the British proposal and enter into direct negotiations as "a proof of the sincerity of Germany's intentions to enter into a lasting friendship with Great Britain." First, however, he added two new provisos: If there was to be a territorial rearrangement of Poland, the German government could no longer enter into guarantees without the Soviet Union being associated with them. Second, they would accept the British offer to secure the dispatch to Berlin of a Polish emissary "with full powers," provided he arrived on August 30, the next day.

Henderson described this as nothing less than an ultimatum, which

---

Va banque: a gambling term meaning "Go for the bank, nothing less."

Hitler denied with the same indignation as at Bad Godesberg the year before, and the interview ended in a shouting match. This time the British did not fall into the trap, refusing to put pressure on the Poles to send a plenipotentiary to Berlin within twenty-four hours.

Hitler had still one more card to play. He had promised that the Germans would list their proposals for a Polish settlement and let the British have them. The German Foreign Office spent the thirtieth drawing these up under sixteen heads, so moderate in their demands that von Weizsäcker described them in his diary as "the first constructive idea for months," adding, "but only for show?" [89] Hitler later confirmed this in the presence of his interpreter, Paul-Otto Schmidt: "I needed an alibi, especially with the German people, to show them that I had done everything to maintain peace. That explains my generous offer about the settlement of Danzig and the Corridor." [90]

It was confirmed again by Ribbentrop's behavior when Henderson arrived at midnight to deliver yet another British note, explaining that it was unreasonable to expect a Polish plenipotentiary to appear within so short a time limit and asking why the proposals could not be given to the Polish ambassador in Berlin in the usual way. Hitler had already seen the text of the British reply, which had been sent in advance, and left Ribbentrop to receive the British ambassador. The interview has earned a place in history for the angry exchanges that brought the two men to their feet shouting at each other and looking as if they might come to blows. When Henderson asked for the German proposals, Ribbentrop read them out in German too fast for the ambassador to follow them. When he asked for a copy, Ribbentrop refused. The time limit for the appearance of a Polish negotiator had elapsed; no Pole had appeared, and the proposals were now past history; the Führer had forbidden him to hand them over.

Further agitated calls were made between the capitals, including Rome, throughout the next day, the thirty-first, and even after the attack on Poland had begun, but these did not alter the situation. Hitler was no longer interested. He had used the limited time available to create the alibi that he wanted. To spend more time on it would be running too great a risk with his freedom to order the attack which had remained his objective throughout. He still had good hopes that the British and French would not intervene, or if they did would do no more than make a token demonstration—as proved to be the case. He would not draw back, he told von Brauchitsch, even if it meant a two-front war.

At 12:40 p.m. he issued his "Directive No. 1 for the Conduct of the War," beginning:

> Now that every political possibility has been exhausted for ending by peaceful means the intolerable situation on Germany's eastern frontier I have determined on a solution by force.
>
> In the West, it is important that the responsibility for the opening of hostilities should be made to rest squarely on Britain and France. [91]

If they attacked, then the West must be held but the Wehrmacht must limit itself to defensive operations.

The German army had used the extra days to complete the mobilization of two million men. The necessary "incident" was provided by the SS, who staged a faked Polish attack on a German radio station at the border town of Gleiwitz, complete with twelve or thirteen criminals who were dressed in Polish uniforms, shot, and left dead on the ground for the press to photograph. All night long, division after division of German troops moved up to the Polish frontier, and, at dawn on September 1, the original date Hitler had fixed in his directive at the beginning of April, the attack began.

In Berlin there were none of the scenes of enthusiasm that Hitler remembered from the declaration of war twenty-five years earlier. The streets were emptier than usual when he drove to the Reichstag to make his speech to the German people. It was not one of his best. He threw the whole blame for the failure to reach a peaceful settlement on the Poles—"for two whole days I sat with my government to see whether it was convenient for the Polish government to send a plenipotentiary." It was the Poles who had started the war by launching an attack which compelled the Germans to counterattack. He disclaimed any quarrel with Britain or France, insisting on his desire for a peaceful settlement of Germany's differences with both. Dahlerus, meeting him afterwards, found him nervous and upset, once again working himself up into a hysterical outburst:

> "If England wants to fight for a year, I shall fight for a year; if England wants to fight for two years, I shall fight for two years. . . ."
> When he finally bellowed, "And if necessary I will fight for ten years," he brandished his fist and bent down so that it nearly touched the floor.[92]

In fact Hitler was still not convinced that the British or the French would intervene, and the two days' delay in their declaration of war—during which Mussolini made one last effort to stage another Munich conference—lent support for his belief.

When Henderson arrived to deliver the British ultimatum on September 3, Ribbentrop was "not available" but sent the interpreter, Schmidt, to receive it. When Schmidt brought the message across to the Chancellery and translated it, there was complete silence.

> Hitler sat immobile, gazing before him. He was not at a loss nor did he rage. He sat completely silent and unmoving. After what seemed an age, he turned to Ribbentrop. . . . "What now?" he asked with a savage look, as though implying that his foreign minister had misled him about England's probable reaction.[93]

Ribbentrop's answer was that they could now expect a French ultimatum. The only comment was Göring's: "If we lose this war, God help us."

FIFTEEN

Hitler's War

I

FOR BOTH HITLER AND STALIN 1934 to 1939 marks a clearly defined period in their careers. It began with the suppression of a challenge which each regarded as a threat to his position. For Hitler, the murder of Röhm removed the danger of being pushed prematurely into a second, more radical revolution which could have cost him the support of the army and the other traditional elites. The murder of Kirov removed the man whom Stalin saw as the potential leader of a move aimed at calling a halt to further radicalization and winning the support of the new Soviet elite with the promise of greater security. Hitler openly proclaimed Röhm's murder and the suppression of the SA as acts of state in which he had acted as "the supreme judge of the German people." Stalin, as always concealing his role, ordered a state funeral for Kirov at which he appeared as one of the chief mourners. He then went on to use the investigation of a murder at which he had connived, if he had not contrived it, as an excuse for starting a witch-hunt that purged everyone in the party, the army, and the other Soviet elites whom he suspected of the same independent thoughts as Kirov.

By the end of the period, each had achieved a unique position that admitted no rivals and no opposition. The paths by which they reached this position, however, were very different.

By the Eighteenth Party Congress, held in March 1939, Stalin could feel that the revolution he had imposed on Russia between the end of his fiftieth year and his sixtieth year had been accomplished. Its central feature was the equation of "building socialism" with the building of an all-powerful state. This was a reversion to an earlier period of Russian history and the image of a "dual Russia" constantly referred to by writers in the nineteenth century like Alexander Herzen. It was an image that opposed the centralized, autocratic power of the tsarist state, official Russia, on the one hand, and the society or people, unofficial Russia, on the other. The Russian historian, V. O. Klyuchevsky, drew the same contrast when he summed up the policy of the tsars between the sixteenth and nineteenth centuries in the striking sentence: "Exhausting the resources of the country, they only bolstered the power of the state without elevating the self-confidence of the people. . . . The state swelled up; the people grew lean."[1]

Where Lenin had seen the original revolution of 1917 as a violent break with Russia's past, Stalin (who was eventually to ban the word Bolshevik) came to see his revolution as a continuation of the historic tradition of tsarist Russia. At the same time he himself moved from being *primus inter pares* in a collective leadership to as autocratic a position as any tsarist predecessor. But, in laying claim to the succession to the tsars, he refused to abandon that to the revolutionary succession as well. It was the combination of these two traditions, the Marxist-Leninist-ideological, with the Russian historical, both refracted through the medium of Stalin's personality, that characterized the Stalinist state.

Herzen traced the separation between the "two Russias" back to Peter the Great and the revolutionary changes he had enforced upon the Russian people, treating them as if they were the inhabitants of a conquered country. Stalin came to feel a strong affinity with Peter and is reported to have repeated with relish Pushkin's famous line in *The Bronze Horseman,* "He raised Russia on its hind legs with his iron curb." Stalin's interest in Peter went back to the late 1920s. When a play about Peter by Alexis Tolstoy was savaged by "progressive" critics Stalin intervened to save it and gave the author "the right historical approach to the Petrine epoch" for rewriting it. Tolstoy later recalled:

> Josif Vissarionovich [Stalin] went over our plans, approved them, and gave directions on which we based our work. . . . The epoch of Peter I was one of the greatest pages in the history of the Russian people. It was necessary to carry through a decisive revolution in the entire life of the country, to lift Russia to the level of the cultured countries of Europe. And Peter did this.
>
> Peter's epoch and ours speak to one another through a kind of burst of force, through explosions of human energy and with power directed to liberation from foreign dependence.

Encouraged by Stalin, Tolstoy went on to produce a large-scale historical novel, *Peter I,* developing the same theme: "The start of my work on the novel coincided with the beginning of the fulfillment of the Five-Year Plan. For me this work on Peter was above all an entry into contemporaneity, grasped in a Marxist way."[2] Or as Tolstoy put it in a more unguarded moment: " 'The father of the people' revised the history of Russia. Peter the Great became, without my knowing it, 'the proletarian tsar' and the prototype of our Josif!"[3]

"We are all servants of the state," Malenkov told the 1941 Party Conference. For this too there was a precedent in earlier Russian history. Another of Russia's earlier rulers whom Stalin promoted to a heroic role in his vision of Russian history was the first to confer on himself the title of tsar, the sixteenth-century Ivan IV (known as Ivan the Terrible). Brushing aside the cruelty of the tortures Ivan inflicted on his opponents, Stalin described his liquidation of the hereditary nobles, the boyars, who sought to limit his autocratic power, as "progressive." The effect of Ivan's reforms was to reduce the Russian nobility from the status of a ruling to that of a serving class, whose rank was made dependent on compulsory service to the state. Peter the Great reinforced this by creating a table of fourteen military and corresponding civil ranks, making nobility a function of rank, and rank of service. In the late 1930s and 1940s Stalin followed suit by establishing a similar table of ranks, complete with uniforms and insignia.

There is a second way of looking at Stalin's attempt to identify with Russia's historical traditions, by focusing on the appeal that this allowed him to make to Russian nationalism. Such an appeal came naturally to Stalin, the Georgian who had voluntarily adopted a Russian identity and whose display of "Great Russian chauvinism" in his dealings with his homeland had first opened Lenin's eyes to his unsuitability for the office of general secretary. The slogan of "Socialism in one country" that he adopted expressed his pride, and that of many of the new generation of party members, in Russia's destiny which, he claimed, had been fulfilled under his leadership.

Sentiment and calculation coincided. To combine the Marxist vision with the deep-seated nationalist and patriotic feelings of the Russian people was to give it a wider and stronger emotional appeal than ideology by itself could generate. As early as June 1934 *Pravda* had sounded the new note, "For the Fatherland,"

> which alone kindles the flame of heroism, the flame of creative initiative in all fields, in all the realms of our rich, our many-sided life. . . . The defense of the Fatherland is the supreme law. . . . For the Fatherland, for its honor, glory, might, and prosperity![4]

The purpose of Stalin's summons to Kirov to spend the summer in 1934 at Sochi was to join him and Zhdanov in laying down guidelines for the rewriting of history textbooks. Published in 1936, *Remarks Concerning the Conspectus of a Textbook on the History of the USSR* produced an abrupt reversal in Soviet historiography, establishing the Soviet regime as the custodian of national interests and traditions. The new history celebrated the great men of Russia's tsarist past—such as Peter the Great, and the two generals of the Revolutionary and Napoleonic periods, Alexandr Suvorov and Mikhail Kutuzov—whose state building, military victories, and territorial conquests had created modern Russia. It was the autocratic tradition, its despotic measures justified by including heroic achievements—such as the repulsing of the French in 1812 and other invaders, not the liberal reforms of the period after 1860—that was highlighted, so establishing a natural link between the new patriotism and the cult of Stalin.

Only when one is confronted with the overwhelming evidence in the form of poems, newspaper articles, telegrams of congratulation, photographs of statues, carvings, and paintings; endless dedications, the naming of towns, kolkhozes, schools, factories, power stations, the highest peak in the Caucasus, Mount Stalin, to honor the man whose universal genius, courage, foresight, dedication, and wisdom exhausted the capacity of the Russian or any other language to express—only when one sees the evidence, is it possible to grasp the scale on which the cult of Stalin was celebrated, and the lengths—and depths—to which adulation could go. The only parallel is the cult of Mao in China, which was modelled on the cult of Stalin just as the Great Leap Forward was modelled on Stalin's crash program of collectivization and industrialization in the 1930s.

That the cult was as contrived as the deification of the Roman emperors is obvious; but that does not alter the fact that Stalin was genuinely popular and revered among the masses of the Russian people who believed him—as many in the west did—when he declared that under his "wise guidance" Russia had become an industrialized power and opened up a better future for them. Both for Stalin himself and for ordinary Russian men and women the cult established a link between the benevolent figure in the Kremlin and the tsars who had ruled there before him as the fathers of the people. It was an identification which revived the ancient myth that, "if only the Little Father knew . . ." he would intervene to prevent the shortages and evils under which his people suffered, as he had in ending the excesses for which not he, but Yezhov and the hated NKVD, had been responsible.

THE STALINIST SYSTEM of government as it emerged at the end of the 1930s, and as it was renewed after 1945, represented the consolidation of the methods by which Stalin had succeeded in carrying through his "revolution from above." Its characteristic features were the concentration of all initiative and authority in the state, identified with a greatly increased and increasingly hierarchical bureaucracy; the continued expansion of the coercive powers of the secret police and of the forced-labor camps that they controlled; the elimination of any potential opposition; the isolation of the population from the rest of the world by an early version of the "Iron Curtain" and the monopoly of agitation and propaganda; and the isolation of individuals from one another by fear and "a system of institutionalized mutual suspicion."[5]

In this system the Communist party was no longer the directing and driving force it had been in the 1920s and in the first part of Stalin's revolution. Its pretensions reduced, it still had a part to play, especially in the field of "agitprop," the counterpart of the NKVD's role of control and repression. But the successor to the former ruling party had become only one—if nominally and by tradition, the most important one—among the large-scale organizations that acted as the "transmission belts" of autocratic government. Paradoxically, it was the local party bosses, away from the center of power in Moscow, who still enjoyed a measure of real authority, always provided they kept in with the local head of the NKVD, the organization Stalin had employed to cut the party down to size—before purging the NKVD itself.

The Central Committee and the Politburo retained their prestige, but were no longer the bodies they had once been when genuine debates had taken place on real issues. Before Lenin's death, the Old Bolshevik T. V. Sapronov (liquidated in 1937) put the question to him: "Who will appoint the Central Committee? Perhaps things will not reach that stage, but if they did, the revolution will have been gambled away." [6] The committee became a formal gathering of the ruling groups, to which it was important for the rising *apparatchik* to secure appointment. Far more important than the committee was its Secretariat, which formed the executive agency of Stalin's high command, controlled as it had been since 1922 by its general secretary and responsible for the *Nomenklatura,* the list of official positions appointed from above, by which Soviet Russia was governed until the 1990s. The "Special Sector" of the Secretariat continued to act as Stalin's personal chancellery under the self-effacing Poskrebyshev.

Now that Stalin had removed all the members of the Politburo who had shown the least sign of independence, he allowed those who remained to enjoy greater security of tenure. The eleven full members of the Politburo who were his closest collaborators in the early 1950s included seven who had been Stalin's men for twenty-five to thirty years (Molotov, Voroshilov, Kaganovich, Andreyev, Malenkov, Mikoyan, and N. M. Shvernik); three more since the early 1930s (Beria, Khrushchev, and Bulganin); only one (Kosygin) from no earlier than the Second World War. The Politburo, however, no longer functioned as a collegial body but was a collection of Stalin's chief lieutenants, each with his own power base and following of clients in the Central Committee. Molotov, for example, was chairman of the Council of People's Commissars, to which the all-union ministries and Gosplan, the State Planning Commission, answered. Voroshilov was commissar of defense and responsible for the armed forces, Beria, head of the NKVD. All, however, knew that they must never meet each other without Stalin's permission and that each of them depended on retaining his favor and doing his bidding to survive. As Khrushchev recalls Bulganin confiding to him: "It has happened sometimes that a man goes to Stalin on his invitation as a friend. And when he sits with Stalin, he does not know where he will be sent next, home or to jail." [7]

If Stalin left them where they were, it was not out of sentiment but "out of the sort of rational political calculation a mafia boss might make." Having instilled fear like any other gangster boss by displaying his power to kill, he had the sense to see that the men he depended on for information and carrying out his orders needed a reasonable expectation of continued favor or they might decide that "the dangers of betraying him were less than the dangers of continued loyal service." [8] One must not push the analogy too far. Shortly before his death, Stalin was preparing another purge which in all probability would have included Molotov, Mikoyan, and Poskrebyshev, who had already fallen out of favor. Still, the surprising thing is that the majority survived.

THE CONSOLIDATION of the revolution and the exaltation of the state at the expense of society made permanent the reversion from the experimentalism of the 1920s to the conservatism of the 1930s. This can be clearly seen in education and the law. Child-centered progressive schools had been replaced by the restoration of discipline, reinforcement of the teacher's authority, and concentration on teaching the basic skills required by an industrial society. These were accompanied by a renewed emphasis on order and obedience, the encouragement of authoritarian family relationships, and the discouragement of divorce.

The legal philosophy of the 1920s had taught that law was a product of a class-dominated social system which would disappear with socialism. As Soviet society moved toward Communism, crime would tend to disappear and the place of law would be taken by a system of administration, based on social not juridical principles. In the 1930s such views were repudiated as heresy, and Vyshinsky formulated a new theory of law to replace them. All law, he explained, must be the expression of the will of the ruling class, backed by force. In the socialist state, it expressed that of the proletariat and, far from withering away, became an expression of the will of the whole people through the power of the state. [9]

Vyshinsky's recognition of the permanence of a legal system and of the state was in keeping with Stalin's insistence, as early as 1930, that Marxian dialectic required "the highest development of governmental power for the purpose of preparing the conditions for the withering away of governmental power." Stalin returned to the question at the Eighteenth Party Congress in 1939. It is sometimes asked, he noted, "Why do we not help our socialist state to wither away?" Stalin's answer was that Engels's original proposition, that this would take place naturally when there were no longer any antagonistic classes, required modification. For even in the present stage when socialism had been achieved in the Soviet Union and class hostility as well as exploitation had been abolished, the state would have to continue to exist—even when the USSR had progressed from socialism to Communism—*as long as it was confronted with capitalist encirclement*. This new condition legitimized the postponement of any reduction in the power of the state until the revolution had triumphed throughout the world.

Such questions of ideology—together with those of history, philosophy, and social questions—Stalin settled, once and for all so long as he was alive, for both the Russian people and the Communist faithful abroad, by the publication in 1938 of the *Short Course*. The one chapter in it that was recognized at the time as having been written by Stalin himself was chapter four, "Dialectical and Historical Materialism." In a resolution passed when the *Short Course* was published, the Central Committee stressed that, besides providing an authoritative history of the party, it was intended to put an end to "the dangerous cleavage . . . between Marxism and Leninism that has appeared in recent years," as a result of which Leninism had been taught as something different from Marxism.

By 1938 Leninism meant Stalinism, even if no one dared to say so. Stalin's purpose was to present a version in which the differences were glossed over and the ideological identity of Marxism and Stalin's version of Leninism was reasserted: socialism in one country; the class struggle becoming fiercer the nearer the approach to socialism; the indefinite postponement of the withering away of the state.

Following the successful model of the *Problems of Leninism,* chapter four took the form of a short and simplified Marxist catechism which was numbered and easily assimilated. It became the authoritative basis of Soviet teaching and thought at all levels, beginning with the upper forms of secondary schools. An entirely new system of party schools was set up, in which the *Short Course* was the main, if not the only, text studied by the next generation of party members, replacing all other accounts of the Soviet Union's ideology as well as its history. Communist ideology became "what Stalin said that Marx and Lenin had said." As Leonard Schapiro wrote:

> No one understood better than Stalin that the true object of propaganda is neither to convince nor even to persuade, but to produce a uniform pattern of public utterance in which the first trace of unorthodox thought immediately reveals itself as a jarring dissonance. [10]

Ideology even when reshaped by Stalin still left a wide gap between his claim that the Soviet Union represented the realization of Marxist socialism and daily life in Russia between 1938 and 1941 as the Russian people experienced it. But the regime's concern was not with what people believed but with what they said. Leszek Kolakowski, once a Marxist philosopher himself, drew on his experience of living under Communist rule when he wrote:

> Half-starved people, lacking the bare necessities of life, attended meetings at which they repeated the government's lies about how well off they were, and in a bizarre way they half believed what they were saying. . . . Truth, they knew, was a party matter, and therefore lies became true even if they contradicted the plain facts of experience. The condition of their living in two separate worlds at once was one of the most remarkable achievements of the Soviet system. [11]

II

DURING THE SAME PERIOD of 1934 through 1939 Hitler's priorities were the reverse of Stalin's: foreign policy and rearmament, not domestic issues. If Stalin had to pay increasing attention to foreign policy and defense in 1938 and 1939, it was not because of expansionist ambitions of his own or a desire to spread revolution but because Hitler's success threatened the security of Stalin's achievement within the Soviet Union. The threat was made explicit and extended to Russia's eastern frontiers by the Anti-Comintern Pact.

It has been argued that the program for foreign policy that Hitler set out in *Mein Kampf* and the *Second Book* cannot be taken seriously as a guide to a policy that culminated in a pact with Soviet Russia, the power he had committed himself to destroy, and a war with Britain, the power he had sought to make an ally. But this is to ignore the difference between Hitler's ultimate objective, the racist empire in the east, and the tactics by which this was to be achieved. The first never varied, but it was the combination of consistency of aim, even when he signed the Nazi-Soviet Pact, with a remarkable flexibility in tactics, that accounted for Hitler's success. Shortly before Ribbentrop flew to Moscow, Hitler told Carl Burckhardt, the League commissioner in Danzig, on August 11, 1939:

> Everything I undertake is directed against the Russians. If the West is too stupid and blind to grasp this, then I shall be compelled to come to an agreement with the Russians, beat the West, and then after their defeat turn against the Soviet Union with all my forces. I need the Ukraine so that they can't starve us out, as happened in the last war.[12]

Hitler's first gamble, the withdrawal from the Disarmament Conference and the League, was the first of many, after each of which success and the absence of resistance encouraged him to reach out further, take bigger risks, and shorten the intervals between his coups. The curve mounted steadily, from the announcement of conscription in the Rhineland, to Austria, Munich, Prague, and Poland.

Although Hitler was exaggerating when he told senior officers of the Wehrmacht in February 1939 that all the decisions in foreign policy since 1933 "represent the implementation of a previously existing plan," he had some justification for his claim that "all our actions during 1938 represent only the logical extension of the decisions that began to be realized in 1933." Looking back from 1939 it is possible to see that the different stages of his foreign policy followed a logical line of development, although their timing and their order were dependent on circumstances.

It is perfectly true that Hitler profited from the weakness and the mistakes of the other powers. But it was Hitler who grasped them and saw how to exploit them, while from the time of the Rhineland onward the experts, whether in the German Foreign Office or the army leadership—even Göring in 1938 and 1939—counseled caution and could not believe that Hitler was right when he predicted that France and Britain would never intervene, or that if they did they would prove to lack the will and the leadership to do so effectively. The only mistake Hitler admitted was Munich, where he listened to those who urged him to compromise—and bitterly regretted it.

Hitler's intuitive understanding of the vulnerability of the Western powers is shown by his exploitation of their peoples' revulsion at the prospect of another war and their uneasiness, especially in Britain, about the treatment of Germany after 1918. Every move against the Versailles settlement was accompanied by a moving assertion of his desire for peace and justified by an appeal to the principles of the settlement itself—the refusal of the right of self-determination to the Austrian Germans and the German minorities in Czechoslovakia and Poland, and the injustice of imposing restrictions on Germany's right of self-defense while the other powers showed no signs of disarming.

Some of the ground gained—for example, the recovery of military sovereignty and a measure of rearmament—could well have been achieved by any German government in the 1930s, as the end of reparations had been before Hitler came to power. But as the stakes were raised from the beginning of 1938, it seems increasingly doubtful whether any alternative leadership available—Brüning, von Schleicher, Göring, Strasser, Schacht, Hugenberg—would have had the nerve and the skill to carry through the Anschluss, to annex the Sudetenland and Bohemia-Moravia, to recover the territory lost to Poland, and to enable the army to carry out a rearmament program on the scale that he did.

From the end of 1937, Hitler showed a mounting impatience. His confidence and contempt for his opponents grew at the same time; he recognized that the head start Germany had gained in rearmament could not last once the other powers followed suit, and he became convinced that, unless he made a breakthrough while he was still at the height of his powers, no one who came after him would have the same combination of will and genius to do it.

This points to a second contrast with Stalin. By 1939 the Russian leader, who was ten years older, had completed his revolution; but Hitler's Second Revolution, postponed in 1934, still had to be launched. The years between 1934 and 1939 had laid the foundation; 1938–39 had seen a quickening of the pace; now in August 1939 he was determined to make the breakthrough.

Hitler had never doubted that the racist empire in the east which was to consummate his revolution—the equivalent of Stalin's collectivization and industrialization—would have to be won by force. But he was also aware that he still had to overcome a widespread reluctance among the German people to become involved in another war which, as the precedent of 1918 showed, could lead to defeat. The successes he had achieved in foreign policy, without war, added to this reluctance. The German people had come to expect that he would continue to secure bloodless victories as he had in Austria and Czechoslovakia.

That helps to explain Hitler's resistance to the suggestion of another Munich as a solution to the dispute with Poland: If the Poles would not accept his demands, this time the settlement must be imposed by war. The task that he set before the Nazi propagandists in November 1938 was: "To depict to the German people diplomatic events in such a light that the inner voice of the nation itself begins to call for the use of force. . . . The fighting spirit of the German people has to be rekindled, the poison of pacificism eliminated."[13]

Nothing would achieve this so effectively as the actual experience of war. Hitler never tired of repeating that his years at the front from 1914 to 1918 had been the greatest experience of his life, had hardened his will and made a man of him. Once he could convince the German people, from experience, that war under his leadership would lead to victory, and that with an army and air force trained to fight not the trench wars of the First World War but "lightning wars" in which conflict would be intense but brief and success guaranteed, he would be able to match the material rearmament of Germany with a mental/spiritual (geistig) rearmament as well. There could not be a more propitious opportunity for such a demonstration than a war on Poland, where the odds in favor of a German victory were high. To exploit such an opportunity, Hitler was prepared to take the risk of a British and French declaration of war—he did not believe it would amount to more than that. September 1939 was the decisive threshold between peace and war to which—without being able to predict the date—he had looked forward when he told the cabinet on February 8, 1933, just over a week after coming to power: "The next five years have to be devoted to making the German people again capable of bearing arms [Wiederwehrhaftmachung]. This has to be the dominant thought, always and everywhere."

THERE WAS ALSO a great difference in style between the two dictators. Partly this was due to differences of temperament. Stalin was the more reserved, Hitler more flamboyant and changeable in mood; Stalin operated in the shadows, Hitler performed best in the limelight. Stalin was more the calculator, Hitler the gambler. The Georgian was un homme de gouvernement, the experienced administrator, disciplining himself to regular work; the Austrian still the artist-politician, hating routine, avoiding any except the most important decisions. The difference was also due to circumstances. Hitler no more trusted any man than Stalin, but he was less suspicious and (with his worst crimes still in the future) felt more secure in 1939 than Stalin could ever feel after liquidating the 40,000—many well known to him— whose death warrants he had signed as well as the hundreds of thousands more who were shot or sent to the camps. The atmosphere in the Kremlin was heavy with fear and suspicion, of revenge in Stalin's case, of his future crimes in everyone else's.

The style was different but the nature of the power they exercised was the same, personal power inherent in the man not the office. The mistake often made is to suppose this means that Hitler and Stalin decided everything—and then argue that this is impossible in a large modern state. There is no disagreement about that. What personal rule meant was that both men were able to decide, not everything—this was clearly impossible—but anything that they chose to; that they were free to reach decisions without consulting anyone else, without seeking the agreement of, or account to, anyone else; that there were no rival centers of power, no effective opposition; that they were not bound by the law and were unlikely to be affected by appeals to conscience, sentiment, or pity.

Finally, each had—in the NKVD and the SS-Gestapo—instruments specially created to carry out such arbitrary decisions, responsible solely to them personally, and licensed to use any degree of force necessary, including torture and death, without regard to the law or the courts.

This is a formidable list. But in most cases it was enough that it was known they possessed these powers, and that their use of them was unpredictable and arbitrary, for them not to be needed. Most of the time those who received orders were eager to carry them out.

One further point needs to be made. The effectiveness of autocratic rule, which suffers from the lack of criticism, depends on the efficiency and reliability of the intelligence services at a ruler's disposal. This was the other indispensable function of the NKVD and the SS, supplemented by access to such other sources as Göring's Forschungsamt and the armed forces' intelligence services.

In 1938 and 1939 Hitler had two advantages. He enjoyed greater security than Stalin, who was only just emerging from the period of the major purges; and as the acknowledged Führer he had no need to disguise his position. Although the "cult of personality" increasingly projected Stalin as a leader of more than human stature, it was part of the fiction necessary, if he was to continue to lay claim to the Marxist-Leninist as well as the tsarist succession, that this should be presented as the spontaneous tribute of the Russian people, embarrassing to a man sprung from the people himself, who asked no more than to serve the masses and the party as its general secretary. Stalin's achievements were legendary, celebrated in every conceivable form of propaganda and the arts, but his power was concealed—"the highest Soviet authorities"—a secret all the more powerful because known to everyone in any kind of office but not to be mentioned in public.

Hitler's power still had to be tested and proved on the same scale as Stalin's, and this had to wait until the war. But already in the summer of 1939 the Nazi-Soviet Pact made clear the same pattern of autocratic power, an example all the more striking because it shows both men making use of their power for the only time in a joint action.

Each of them could make a convincing case for the advantages of such a pact. In Hitler's case it was the ability to attack Poland and, if necessary, the Western powers as well without any fear of Soviet intervention. In Stalin's, it was freedom from the fear of being drawn into a war with Germany for which Russia was ill prepared, with the secret promise of half Poland, and Germany's recognition that the Baltic states and Finland lay within the Soviet sphere of influence.

Still, so undisguised a justification by *raison d'état* (especially when the secret protocol could not be mentioned) presented difficulties for two regimes, each of which was committed to ideological principle and had denounced the other as the embodiment of everything to which it was opposed. For them now to disavow the anti-Bolshevik crusade in defense of Europe, on the one side, and the alliance of all progressive forces in favor of collective security against Fascism, on the other—and then go on to sign a pact of nonaggression, which in effect gave Germany a free hand for aggression against Poland—was bound to come as a shock to many who had taken these professions seriously.

So abrupt a *volte face* could only be made by two men accountable to no one but themselves, who did not have to submit the proposal to debate or fear opposition within their parties and who could dictate how their action was to be presented to their own people and to the world. No doubt both men discussed the pact and the protocol with two or three of their associates, but it was only when Hitler addressed a personal letter to Stalin that the obstacles were removed, and it was a personal reply from Stalin that clinched the deal. Even clearer is the way in which the partition of Poland was decided. When Stalin proposed a different frontier between the zones of occupation, Ribbentrop had to break off and secure Hitler's agreement over the telephone. This was the way in which they settled the fate of a country with which both parties were still at peace.

III

ON THE EVENING of September 3 Hitler left Berlin for Pomerania in his special train, which had been completed in August. Surprisingly named *Amerika,* it consisted of an engine and fifteen carriages and served as a mobile headquarters from which he was able to set out by car each morning to drive to the front line. Wherever he appeared, he was followed by his entourage, which behaved like a court, jostling one another to get closer to the Führer and be photographed with him. The former corporal, who had described himself in his Reichstag speech as "the first soldier of the German Reich," had once more put on the familiar field-gray uniform, declaring that he would not take it off again "until victory is secured, or I will not survive the outcome."

The sights and sounds of the battlefield lifted his spirits. At last he had achieved the war that had been in his mind since he came to power. In front of his eyes, he could see the new German army that he now commanded recapturing the former German lands of Posen and Silesia, the last territories lost in the peace settlement to be restored to the Fatherland. As the army pressed on into the heart of Poland, he already began to plan with Himmler the first stage of his empire in the east.

Hitler had taken the gamble of leaving the western front without tanks or planes and with only three days' ammunition, in order to concentrate the full force of this first Blitzkrieg against the Poles. The Polish army, although it fought with the same bravery as the Polish pilots were later to show in the Battle of Britain, was overwhelmed by the violence of the German attack. The result was settled within a week; the whole campaign was over within three. Hitler made his triumphal entry into Danzig on September 19, and Warsaw was bombed into submission on the twenty-sixth. The Polish government had already fled abroad.

As Hitler had foretold, the French and British, on whose guarantees the Poles had built such hopes, made no move to come to their aid. He had succeeded in his gamble of leaving thirty-three German divisions in the west (twenty-five of them second grade or less) to confront a French force of seventy divisions with 3,000 tanks and command of the air. The French made no attempt to engage, and the British confined the RAF to dropping leaflets on German towns. The world was astonished by the success of a style of warfare that cost the Germans no more than 11,000 dead and 30,000 wounded to overrun half Poland, in contrast to the huge casualties suffered in the stalemate of trench warfare between 1914 and 1918.

Nowhere did it make a greater impression than in Moscow, where nothing like so swift an outcome had been expected. As early as September 8, Ribbentrop sent a message urging the Russians to occupy the part of Poland agreed to in the secret protocol. In order to prepare the Russian people, Stalin hurriedly launched a propaganda campaign, which—with the substitution of White Russians and Ukrainians for *Volksdeutsche* (ethnic Germans)—repeated the earlier German accusations of Polish ill-treatment of minorities, border violations, and provocations. On September 17 the Red Army moved across the Polish frontier and within less than a week occupied the eastern half of Poland at a cost of 737 dead and fewer than 2,000 wounded.

The fourth partition of Poland allowed the Russians to recover the former Russian territories annexed by the Poles in 1920. In justification of what might appear unjustified aggression against a defeated nation, the Moscow communiqué announced: "The Soviet government cannot be in-different to the fact that its kindred Ukrainian and Byelorussian people, who live on Polish territory, have been left defenseless at the mercy of fate." So well had the secret of the protocol been kept—and so little did Hitler trust his generals—that even the heads of his own military staff, the OKW, were taken by surprise. When General Jodl heard the news of the Red Army advance he asked in astonishment, "Against whom?" In places German troops were already 125 miles beyond the agreed demarcation line, of which the Army High Command had never been informed, and had hastily to be withdrawn.

It was now a matter of urgency for the two occupying powers to reach agreement in precise terms on how they would divide Poland. Hitler, still enjoying his triumph, was prepared to leave this to Ribbentrop, but Stalin was determined to use the opportunity to renegotiate the August partition to Russia's advantage and invited the German foreign minister to Moscow for that purpose. When Ribbentrop arrived there on September 27, it was not Molotov but Stalin himself with whom he had to deal. Stalin was very clear about what he wanted—Lithuania, which the Germans regarded as falling within their sphere of influence. Ribbentrop had already promised the Lithuanians to return Vilna to them, their ancient capital seized by the Poles in 1919, only to learn that Soviet troops had already occupied it. To Stalin, control of Lithuania would allow the Russians to close the Baltic corridor leading to Leningrad to which he attached so much importance.

If he had asked for Lithuania in August, Stalin believed Hitler would almost certainly have refused to agree: Instead he had made sure that the provisional division of Poland gave him a large part of central Poland in addition to Byelorussia and the western Ukraine. This part, occupied by ethnic Poles, he was now prepared to cede to Germany as a quid pro quo for Lithuania, moving the dividing line between the two occupation zones eastward from the Vistula to the River Bug. When Ribbentrop tried to secure the oil-producing districts of Drohobycz and Boryslav as well, Stalin had his answer ready: This was part of the Ukraine, the Ukrainian people claimed it as theirs, and he could not disappoint them. He offered instead the entire annual output of the oil wells, 300,000 tons (in exchange for the equivalent in coal and steel tubes), plus another territorial concession, the area between East Prussia and Lithuania, known as the Suwalki triangle.

Ribbentrop's counterarguments made no impression on Stalin, and the unhappy foreign minister was reduced to saying he must consult Hitler. While he waited for a reply, Stalin appealed to his vanity by offering him a gala dinner in his honor in the Kremlin which recalled the splendors of tsarist hospitality. After the dinner, while the German party was whisked away to see the Bolshoi Ballet perform *Swan Lake,* Molotov received Karl Selter, the Estonian foreign minister, who had been summoned to Moscow to give the answer to a Russian proposal for a military alliance. Molotov had added that, if the Estonians did not acquiesce in the proposal, "the Soviet Union will safeguard its security in another way, without Estonia's consent." When Selter learned that the strength of the Soviet garrison to be stationed in the country would be 35,000, he protested that they would outnumber the entire Estonian army. The argument was still going on when Stalin walked into the room and asked what the problem was. When told it was the size of the garrison, Stalin reproved his foreign minister: "Come, come, Molotov, you are being rather harsh on our friends." [14] Stalin suggested a restriction to no more than 25,000, impressing the Estonians present so much with his understanding that the treaty was signed before Ribbentrop and his party returned from the theater.

When they did and resumed their talks with the Russians, the long-awaited call from Hitler about Lithuania was taken by Ribbentrop at Molotov's desk. It was evident that Hitler had misgivings but finally agreed to the proposed exchange, Ribbentrop reported, because "I want to establish quite firm and close relations." Stalin's laconic comment was, "Hitler knows his business."

THE WEEKS FOLLOWING the German victory in Poland saw the beginning of three developments that were to dominate the 1940s: the expansion of a single campaign into a general war; the first stages of Hitler's New Order in Europe; and a preview of Stalin's.

As soon as it became clear that the Poles were defeated, Hitler had to decide what to do next. On September 28 a joint communiqué was published in Moscow after the revised agreement on the partition of Poland had been signed. In it Ribbentrop and Molotov declared that:

> After the definite settlement of the problems arising from the collapse of the Polish state . . . it would serve the true interest of all peoples to put an end to the state of war existing between Germany on the one side and England and France on the other. [15]

The same view was repeated by the German press and radio, and found ready acceptance among the German people and among the army leaders, who had always been in favor of avoiding a war with the Western powers. Mussolini, too, was eager for peace, if only to save his face.

Hitler gave expression to these hopes in the speech he made to the Reichstag on October 6. After exulting in the triumph he had won—"In all history there has scarcely been a comparable military achievement"—and pouring scorn on the Poles and their leaders, he acclaimed the recovery of the territory lost in the east as the culmination of his policy of ridding Germany of the fetters fastened on her by the Treaty of Versailles. This final revision, too, could have been brought about peacefully if it had not been for the warmongers abroad. The last thing he had ever wanted was to quarrel with the French and British:

> Germany has no further claims against France, and no such claim shall ever be put forward. . . . I have devoted no less effort to the achievement of Anglo-German friendship. . . . Why should this war in the West be fought? For the restoration of Poland? The Poland of the Versailles Treaty will never rise again. This is guaranteed by two of the largest states in the world.

Hitler laid great emphasis on Germany's new relationship with Russia—a turning point in German foreign policy. He repudiated as "fantastic" suggestions of seeking to establish German domination in the Ukraine or elsewhere in the east. Germany and Russia had clearly defined their spheres of interest and—where the League of Nations had failed—had removed at least part of the problems that might have led to a European conflict. He made it clear that the reorganization of Central Europe was a subject on which he would not permit "any attempt to criticize, judge, or reject my actions from the rostrum of international presumption." But the future security and peace of Europe would have to be settled one day by an international conference.

> If these problems must be solved sooner or later, then it would be more sensible to tackle the solution before millions of men are sent needlessly to their death. . . . Continuation of the present state of affairs in the West is unthinkable. Each day will soon demand increasing sacrifices. . . . One day there will again be a frontier between Germany and France, but instead of flourishing towns there will be ruins and endless graveyards. . . . If, however, the opinions of Messrs. Churchill and his followers should prevail, this statement will have been my last. Then we shall fight, and there will never be another November 1918 in German history.[16]

The German press at once broke into headlines:

HITLER'S PEACE OFFER. NO WAR AIMS AGAINST FRANCE AND BRITAIN. RESTRICTION OF ARMAMENTS. PROPOSAL OF A CONFERENCE.

As propaganda it was masterly, but as a serious offer of peace Hitler's speech left all the questions unanswered. It contained not a single concrete proposal other than, by implication, the recognition of Germany's conquests as the basis for any discussion. The Anglo-French reply left no doubt that they were not prepared to consider peace on terms that, as Chamberlain put it in the House of Commons, began with the absolution of the aggressor. The day afterwards, October 13, an official German statement announced that Chamberlain had rejected the offer of peace and chosen war. Once again Hitler had established his alibi.

Hitler had already made clear to Keitel and his commanders in chief (September 27) that he planned to launch an offensive in the west as soon as it became clear there was no chance of reaching a settlement with the Western powers. Ciano, who visited him on October 1, in another attempt on Mussolini's part to find out what Hitler was up to, noted the difference from the last time he had come on the same errand, in early August. "At Salzburg," he wrote in his diary "the inner struggle of this man, decided upon action, but not yet sure of his means and of his calculations, was apparent. Now, he seems absolutely sure of himself. The ordeal he has met has given him confidence for further ordeals."[17] Ciano believed that if Hitler could "offer his people a solid peace after a great victory," this might still tempt him. "But if to reach it he had to sacrifice, even to the smallest degree, what seem to him the legitimate fruits of his victory, he would then a thousand times prefer battle."[18]

One of the signs of Hitler's increased confidence was the way he reached his decision to continue the war. He consulted no one, neither the OKW nor the OKH. The first he had never intended to act as a unified High Command of all the armed forces, as its name implied, but treated it as his military bureau. The much larger general staff of the OKH he confined to the role of an executive organ. Neither von Brauchitsch, the Commander in Chief of the Army, nor Halder, its Chief of Staff, were taken into Hitler's confidence. Never sure what was in his mind, they frequently had to rely on picking up indirectly what was going on.

Walter Warlimont, who was a member of the OKW staff, concluded that Hitler's behavior was one more example of "his unerring instinct for the division of authority," for retaining the freedom to make arbitrary decisions. But it was also a recognition on Hitler's part that the army leadership had no confidence in his leadership and did not believe that Germany would win a war against France and Britain or (as he put it) was infected with the spirit of defeatism.

This time, in an effort to convince the army's leaders while waiting for a response to his "peace offer," on October 9 Hitler dictated a lengthy memorandum, entirely his own work (like the 1936 paper on the Four-Year Plan), in which he set out his case for an immediate offensive in the west.

Sooner or later, he argued, the German people would have to face a struggle with the Western powers, who were once more bent on preventing the consolidation of the German position in Europe. There was no time as favorable as the present. The success of the Polish campaign and the agreement with Russia meant that Germany could take on the West with all her forces except for a few troops left to cover the East: The fear of a war on two fronts was removed. But there was no treaty that could guarantee that it would last, that Russia would remain neutral.

The same was true of German superiority in armaments; he now recognized that, with every month that passed, this was being reduced. The longer the Germans waited, the greater was the danger that the British and French would take the offensive, occupy the Low Countries and threaten the Ruhr, the heart of the German war economy. The Germans must beat them to it. Psychologically, the victory in Poland had given them the advantage. The impetus must not be lost. Improvisation "to the utmost" was the key. If necessary, the army must be prepared to go on fighting right into the depths of winter—and they could do this, if they used their armored and mechanized forces to keep the fighting open. "They are not to be lost among the endless rows of houses in Belgian towns," but must sweep across Holland, Belgium, and Luxembourg and destroy the opposing forces before they could form a coherent defensive front. As for the timing of the attack "the start cannot take place too early." [19]

Hitler's arguments did not convince the generals, nor was the opposition confined to OKH. All three of the army group commanders in the west, von Rundstedt, von Bock, and von Leeb, who would be responsible for directing the attack, spoke out against it, maintaining that the German forces were inadequate and would risk defeat. The only result was to harden Hitler's determination, and on October 19 the first directive was issued for Operation Yellow, an attack on the West with seventy-five divisions.

The open disagreement between the military leaders and Hitler aroused the hopes of the opposition group that had come together before Munich that the military might be persuaded to carry out a coup d'état. Beck, Goerdeler, and von Hassell, with Oster and Hans von Dohnanyi of the OKW Abwehr, were again active in urging the generals to use their authority and the forces that they alone controlled to overthrow the regime. The 1938 plans for storming the Chancellery and capturing the leading Nazis were revived. Zossen, the army's GHQ outside Berlin, became the center of the conspiracy, and von Brauchitsch and Halder, who were aware of it, promised a final decision on November 5, after they had returned from a tour of the western front. When von Brauchitsch saw Hitler on the fifth, however, and once more repeated the army's objections, Hitler worked himself into a rage, refused to listen to another word, and peremptorily issued an order for the preparations to continue and the attack to be launched a week later, at dawn on November 12. Von Brauchitsch crumpled before Hitler's fury, and the latter's reference to the "spirit of Zossen" led Halder to believe that he suspected a plot. The army chief of staff ordered all evidence of it to be destroyed, and whatever chance there was of success was lost.

Ironically, while the soldiers hesitated, a skilled German craftsman, Georg Elser, acting entirely on his own, came nearer to killing Hitler than anyone before July 20, 1944. He succeeded in spending between thirty and thirty-five nights unobserved in the beer hall in Munich where Hitler regularly celebrated the anniversary of the November putsch of 1923. After hollowing out one of the stone pillars, he inserted a powerful explosive device and connected it to a clockwork mechanism soundproofed in cork. Hitler normally began his speech at 8:30 and went on until 10 o'clock. At 9:20 the bomb went off, bringing down part of the roof, killing eight and injuring sixty. Only the fact that it was a foggy night and Hitler had decided to leave earlier than usual, at 9:10, saved him.

Elser was arrested the same evening, but attempts to link him to any network or foreign secret service ended in failure: He had concluded that ever since autumn 1938 Hitler had been leading Germany into war and ought to be stopped. He acted accordingly. After endless interrogations, he was not put to death until the final days of the war.

Hitler heard the news of his escape when his train stopped at Nuremberg. In great excitement, he declared: "Now I am content. The fact that I left earlier than usual shows that Providence intends to allow me to reach my goal!"[20]

The date of the offensive was postponed more than once in November, because of unsuitable weather, but Hitler refused to let the army off the hook. On November 23 he summoned the hundred senior officers of the three services to the Chancellery to hear a two-hour address in which he repeated the arguments that he had used in his earlier memorandum. Looking back on his career since 1919 he remarked how few people had ever believed he would succeed—"but Providence has had the last word."

Among the factors leading him to believe that there would be no better moment than the present, Hitler pointed to the fact that for the first time since Bismarck founded the German Empire, Germany did not need to fear a war on two fronts:

> As the last factor I must in all modesty name my own person: irreplaceable. Neither a military nor a civil person could replace me. Assassination attempts may be repeated. I am convinced of my powers of intellect and decision. . . . Now there is a relationship of forces which can never be more propitious. . . .

Declaring that his decision to attack France and England at the earliest possible moment was unchangeable, he brushed aside concern over the neutrality of the Low Countries as meaningless. "No one will question that when we have won."

Hitler was always acting a part, and he had designed the occasion in order to leave on his commanders the impression of an inspired leadership. After urging his audience to pass on an example of "fanatical unity—there would be no failures if leaders always had the courage a rifleman must have"—he ended on a note of exultation:

> I shall shrink from nothing and shall destroy everyone who is opposed to me. . . . Only he who struggles with Destiny can have a good intuition. In the last years I have experienced many examples of intuition. Even in the present development I see the work of Providence.
>
> If we come through this struggle victoriously—and we shall—our time will enter into the history of our people. I shall stand or fall in this struggle. I shall never survive the defeat of my people. No capitulation to the forces without; no revolution from within. [21]

The years that followed were to show that this was not empty rhetoric; as so often with Hitler, one is surprised by the literal meaning he gave to the most exaggerated statements. In the meantime, he remained committed to the offensive in the west. After Hitler's speech on the twenty-third, von Brauchitsch submitted his resignation, but Hitler refused to accept it. The commander in chief must do his duty like every other soldier. He added that he was not oblivious to the "spirit of Zossen" that prevailed in the army and would stamp it out. After repeated postponements in an unusually harsh winter—the last order in the file names January 20 as D-Day—Hitler put off Operation Yellow until May. By then he had provided another convincing demonstration of his ability to stake everything on a gamble, to panic when it threatened to go wrong, and still emerge the winner.

IV

THE TREATMENT of occupied Poland from 1939 through 1941 illustrates the convergence in practice of two regimes which claimed to be ideologically at opposite poles to one another.

Hitler had originally thought of leaving a rump Polish state, hoping that Britain and France might be persuaded to accept this as a form of peace settlement and so not continue the war. This idea was dropped after the rejection of his "peace offer" in favor of a different solution.

In the east of Poland, Russia took over an area of 77,500 square miles, with a population of thirteen million, roughly one-third of which was Ukrainian, one-third Polish, and one-third more or less evenly divided between Jews, Byelorussians, and a number of smaller groups.

In the northwest of Poland, Germany recovered the former Prussian lands of Danzig, Posen, West Prussia, and a substantial part of Silesia. But the territory Hitler annexed, 36,000 square miles in all, was more than double that which Germany had lost as a result of the Versailles settlement, with ten million inhabitants, the majority of whom were Poles.

This left in the center, a third area, 39,000 square miles in extent and containing the cities of Warsaw, Lublin, and Cracow, which was occupied by the Germans, but not annexed to the Reich. Instead it formed an "adjunct territory" with a population of eleven million, the great majority Poles, with a large minority of Jews. It became known as the Government-General, and Hans Frank, Hitler's legal adviser and a Reich minister, was appointed as its governor.

Stalin's and Hitler's objectives were very different. The Germans were aiming at the destruction of a defeated nation, leaving only a residuary mass of slave labor; the Russians (so they claimed) at the liberation of the oppressed masses, in fact an assimilation to the condition of the Soviet population. But both programs had the same immediate purpose, to destroy the social order which had existed in Poland before 1939; both made use of similar agencies, the SS and the NKVD as well as Nazi and Communist party officials brought in from outside; and both employed the same methods.

The imperfections of prewar Poland were undeniable, but it had represented an ordered society. Defeat and occupation had gone a long way to shake its foundations. Instead of allowing it to recover, the activities of both the occupying powers were directed to replacing it with disorder, insecurity, and disorientation, turning upside down the normal world in which the population had existed. A vacuum was deliberately created in which everything familiar disintegrated, and millions of people found themselves at risk, naked, without protection from the law or authority, many separated from their families, deprived of their place in society, unsure any longer of their identity. In such a situation, some rose. In the German zone, it was the former German minority; in the Soviet zone, it was the ambitious, those ready to collaborate with the new masters, particularly if they enjoyed the advantage of having been disadvantaged by reason of their minority status (Ukrainians, Jews), their class, or imprisonment. But the majority in both zones was bewildered and lived in fear of violence, eviction, arrest, or deportation. This was the necessary preliminary to the New Order which each power proposed to create.

Just as the eastern half of Poland was the first foreign country on which Stalin imposed the social and political revolution on the Stalinist model which he was later to export to Eastern and Central Europe, so the western half was the first area in which Hitler could try out the racist principles which he saw forming the basis of the empire he dreamed of conquering as far east as the Urals. No one had a better claim to carry out Hitler's ideas than Himmler, and he was quick to seize the opportunity by presenting a plan which Hitler approved before the fighting in Poland had ended.

A Führer decree published on October 7, 1939 appointed Himmler as *Reichskommissar für die Festigung der deutschen Volkstums* (Reich Commissar for the Strengthening of Germanism) and set out his long-term instructions—without territorial limitation. Well wrapped up in bureaucratic phrases, they gave little indication of the human suffering to which they were to lead:

> It will be the duty of the Reichsführer SS under my instructions
> (i) to repatriate persons of German race and nationality now resident abroad, who are considered suitable for permanent return to the Reich;
> (ii) to eliminate the injurious influences of those sections of the population of foreign origins constituting a danger to the Reich and German community;
> (iii) to form new German settlement areas by transfer of populations, in particular by giving land entitlement to persons of German race and nationality from abroad. [22]

In plain language, the "Germanization" of Eastern Europe meant driving out the native Slav population and resettling it with Germans and families of German stock. Hitler had hoped to start this process when the German army occupied Bohemia-Moravia in March 1939. At that time he talked of deporting six million Czechs, and Himmler suggested the Germans of the South Tyrol as the first settlers. However, Hitler was persuaded that the contribution of Czech industry was so important to the German war economy that the program of Germanization should be postponed.

Poland now offered an alternative, and the settlers Himmler hoped to attract with the offer of a new life and a generous endowment were extended to include *Volksdeutsche,* the German ethnic minorities from the Baltic states, Soviet-occupied Eastern Poland, Rumania, Yugoslavia, and Slovakia. Many of these and their ancestors had been settled in their homes for centuries, but whether they liked it or not were to be uprooted and moved to add to the "racially pure" strength of the Reich population which Hitler regarded as the fundamental source of German power.

Heinrich Himmler, the chief of police and creator of the SS, to whom Hitler now entrusted the organization and execution of his racist policy, is

the best example of the lasting impression Hannah Arendt took away from
the Eichmann trial after the war—"the banality of evil." Far from being a
monster in human shape, Heinrich Himmler was the epitome of the commonplace, described by all who met him as a colorless, insecure personality
with pince-nez and receding chin, captured in Speer's phrase, "half school-
master, half crank."

Himmler was naturally attracted to unorthodox beliefs of many kinds,
from natural healing and herbalism (every concentration camp had to have
its herb garden) to runic inscriptions and the measurement of skulls in the
search for a "pure Aryan" type. Amongst his other enthusiasms was a
campaign to abolish hunting—"every animal has a right to live." At an early
stage in his career he had fallen completely under the spell of Hitler, whom
he regarded as a prophet of genius comparable with the great religious
teachers, and whose pseudoscientific theories of race he accepted as a
revelation of literal truth. Deficient in emotion, he combined his dependence on Hitler, which relieved him of any moral conflict, with ability as an
administrator, ambition, and an overzealous devotion to duty. There is no
sign that the enormity of organizing the deportation, and later the planned
extermination, of millions of human beings disturbed him or even entered
his mind. Carl Burckhardt, the League Commissioner for Danzig, found
him more sinister than Hitler himself, "through the degree of concentrated
subservience, through a certain narrow-minded conscientiousness, an inhuman methodicality about which there was something of the automaton."

In Poland Himmler saw the opportunity for the SS to play the role which
he had long envisaged for it. For he was as much attracted to pseudomysti-
cism as to pseudoscience, and thought of the SS as more than the German
equivalent of the NKVD, as an order of dedicated comrades sworn to
defend the Holy Grail of pure German blood. Its code of honor, buttressed
by initiation rites, ordeals, and rituals, required unquestioning obedience in
the service of an ideal, the ideal of harshness, "to be harsh toward ourselves
and others, to give death and take it." The pride of the SS was in their
capacity to suppress all human feeling, whatever they were called upon to
do, from massacring women and children to carrying out suicidal attacks in
battle.

To coordinate the ethnic German resettlement, the newly appointed
Reichskommissar set up a new commissariat, the RKFVD. Other branches
of the SS, such as the *Rasse und Siedlungshauptamt* (Race and Settlement
Main Office) were also involved, and the handling of the deportation of
non-German populations was given to the SS *Reichssicherheitshauptamt*
(Reich Security Main Office). The RSHA was a new combination of the
Security Police (*Sicherheitspolizei* or SIPO) and the Security Service (*Sicherheitsdienst* or SD). The first, including the political or secret police, the
Gestapo, as well as the criminal police, had originally been under the control
of the state; the second had been a party organization, including its intelligence service. From October 1 they were placed under a single SS com-

mand, the RSHA, with Reinhard Heydrich as chief of both the security police and the SD, responsible through Himmler to Hitler alone.

Cold, clever, and ambitious, Heydrich was skeptical about everything except the obsessive pursuit of power. Seen by some Nazis as a possible successor to Hitler, he was described by Hitler himself as "the man with an iron heart," a figure straight out of the Italian Quattrocento, who provided a necessary complement to Himmler's petit-bourgeois romanticism. Heydrich organized five SS *Einsatzgruppen* (task forces), which moved into the occupied territories immediately behind the army with orders to identify, arrest, and "eliminate" the Polish leadership, local as well as national. In private, Hitler declared:

> Whatever we can find in the shape of an upper class in Poland is to be liquidated; should anything take its place, it will be placed under guard and done away with at an appropriate time. [23]

"Upper classes" in practice meant officers, officials, judges, landowners, businessmen, teachers, intellectuals, priests—anyone with the capacity for leadership. Once arrested they were herded into camps where thousands were executed. On October 17 Hitler repeated:

> The increased severity of the racial struggle permits of no legal restriction; the methods used . . . will ensure that the Polish intelligentsia cannot throw up a new leader class. [24]

A counterpart to wiping out the Polish educated class was the SS program for "the recovery of German blood," which could all too easily be diluted by mixed marriages with inferior races. Himmler believed, however, that something could be done "to recover it for the German *Volk*," even if it flowed in Polish veins. The SS, including Himmler personally, spent a lot of time selecting children whom they claimed to recognize, on the basis of distinctive racial characteristics, to be "racially first class." He involved the SS Lebensborn ("Spring of Life"), which he had set up in 1936 to care for German illegitimate children "of good race," especially children born to those Göring described as "SS stallions." He now used its homes for the reception of thousands of Polish children who were taken away from their parents in order to be brought up as Germans and "restored to the nation."

Himmler's colonization schemes envisaged the mass of the Polish population in the territories annexed to Germany—eight million in all—being deported to the east beginning with the first million (including 550,000 Jews) to be moved into the Government-General by the end of February 1940. Their places were to be taken by the *Volksdeutsch* (ethnic Germans) from the Baltic states and Volhynia (incorporated into the Soviet Union) as well as Germans from the Government-General. Over 80,000 Poles were moved with great brutality by December 1939, but Himmler's plans had to be scaled down and postponed in face of the practical difficulties and of determined opposition from rival Nazi agencies: the Gauleiters of West and

THE PARTITION OF
EASTERN EUROPE 1939–40

Soviet occupied territory

German occupied territory

East Prussia (Forster and Koch) who were determined to defend their fiefdoms against SS incursions; Göring, bent upon retaining the Four-Year Plan's control of industrial and urban property in Poland; Darré, eager to manage requisitioned Polish estates; and Hans Frank, who protested that the mass of Polish and Jewish refugees being crowded into the Government-General created an impossible food situation. As a result, by mid-1941 the total number of German repatriations settled by the SS Race and Resettlement Office was limited to 200,000, who had taken over 10 percent (2.3 million acres) of Polish farmlands and 20 percent of the 60,000 confiscated Polish businesses.

Himmler, however, was not discouraged. In May 1940 he drafted "Some Thoughts on the Treatment of Alien Populations in the East." This time, Himmler proposed that the inhabitants of the Government-General and those to be moved from the German territory incorporated into Germany—more than twenty million human beings whom Himmler described as "ethnic mush," Poles, Ukrainians, White Russians, Jews—should be broken up "into the largest possible number of parts and fragments . . . The racially valuable elements should be extracted from the hodgepodge," and the residue left to wither away. Within ten years the populations of the Government-General "will be reduced to a remnant of substandard beings . . . a leaderless labor force capable of furnishing Germany with casual laborers annually, together with the manpower required for special projects."

Himmler's memorandum is interesting for three reasons. The first is because of the way in which he proposed to deal with the large Jewish population of Poland:

I hope completely to erase the concept of Jews through the possibility of a great emigration of all Jews to a colony in Africa or elsewhere.

That Himmler should say this in a secret memorandum which Hitler approved fits together with other evidence (see pp.756 below) to suggest that in May 1940 they were thinking about "the solving of the Jewish problem" along a different line from that adopted in 1941. A second sentence supports this view. Writing of the de-nationalization of the peoples of eastern Europe, Himmler concluded:

However cruel and tragic each individual case may be, this method is still the mildest and best, if one rejects the Bolshevik method of physical extermination of a people out of inner conviction as un-German and impossible. [25]

The third reason is pointed out by Christopher Browning, again looking forward to the controversy over the absence of any *Führerbefehl* (Führer Order) for the Final Solution. Hitler had read through Himmler's memorandum and authorized him to tell Göring and the Gauleiters in the east that he "had recognized and confirmed" it as containing authoritative guidelines. "This is the only first-hand account of just how a Hitler decision was reached and a *Führerbefehl* was given in the shaping of Nazi racial policy during this period."[26] Himmler did not present Hitler with a precise plan, but knowing Hitler's mind, put onto paper a statement of intent which he had good reason to believe Hitler would accept. Hitler left the details of implementation to Himmler and gave no specific orders to Göring, Frank, and the Gauleiters who would be involved, simply allowing Himmler to make known what he wanted and approved.

The evidence makes clear that, between 1939 and 1941, finding "a solution to the Jewish problem" in practice had to compete with the urgent need to clear the much larger Polish population and make room for resettling the *Volksdeutsche*. It was the Poles who occupied the land which Himmler wanted for his ethnic Germans, not the Jews, and the treatment of the latter was an improvised solution, leaving a permanent one such as Himmler's forced "emigration of all Jews to a colony in Africa or elsewhere" to be found later. In the meantime as many as possible of Poland's 3.3 million Jews were pushed into urban centers such as Lodz and Warsaw, where the local German authorities created ghettoes which were sooner or later sealed off from the outside world. Those who were caught trying to escape were shot, but it was the appalling living conditions in the ghettoes—overcrowding, starvation, and illness due to lack of food, medicine, and fuel, epidemics such as typhus and spotted fever—rather than the deliberate policy of extermination adopted later, which are estimated to have caused the death of over half a million Polish Jews before the ghettoes were suppressed in 1942.[27]

IN EASTERN POLAND, the Russians, on the model of the Soviet Union, abolished private property, nationalized industry and commerce, started to collectivize the farms, and established a single party. After elections had been held for a single list dictated by the occupying authorities, the packed assemblies petitioned "amid great jubilation and political fervor" to be admitted to the Ukrainian Soviet Socialist Republic and the Byelorussian SSR. This petition was granted.

Political officers accompanying the Red Army urged the Ukrainians and the poorer peasants to attack Polish landlords, kulaks, and policemen, revenging themselves for the wrongs they had suffered and the grudges they had accumulated during twenty years of Polish rule. One leaflet read: "*Poliakam, panam, sobakam—sobachaia smert*" ("For Poles, masters, and dogs—a dog's death"). *Pan* is the Polish word for "mister" or "master"; *polskia pany*, Polish Pans, was a phrase in use from the Soviet-Polish war of 1920, uniting the appeal of class emancipation and national liberation.[28]

The Ukrainians and Byelorussians were not slow to respond, forming groups which killed Polish landlords and peasants—often torturing them first—and frequently receiving recognition from the Russians as local militias. Others launched pogroms against Jews. Appeals to the Red Army to restrain these excesses were ignored or dismissed as the inevitable accompaniment of the "revolution" they had come to support.

While eastern Poland was generally regarded as one of the most backward and impoverished parts of Eastern Europe, to the Russians it appeared a land of abundance. First the Red Army, and then the thousands of Soviet officials and their families who moved in, proceeded to plunder the farms and clear the shops of everything. Every house and apartment in towns as well as the countryside was subjected to search, accompanied by robbery on a massive scale. Materially, eastern Poland was rapidly assimilated to the low-level economy of the Soviet Union.

Apart from Jews, the SS and NKVD agreed on the same priority targets for "elimination." Variously described in official documents as the Polish intelligentsia, the Polish elite, the former ruling class, it was the political leadership of the nation, local as well as national, which they both set out to destroy. "Beheading the community" was the phrase used by General Wladyslaw Anders, the Polish officer who was plucked from a Siberian prison camp after the German attack on Russia in 1941 and called on to organize a Polish army from the survivors.

The NKVD, drawing on the recent experience of the Soviet purges, followed the same stock procedures in Poland: arrest, interrogation, torture, prison, execution. Denunciation was not only encouraged but demanded. Those arrested—in the middle of the night—were frequently called on to confess to crimes they had not committed and provide information they did not have. When they "refused to cooperate," they were beaten and tortured. There are no statistics for the numbers arrested, but it is known that there were seven mass arrests, that the prisons were overcrowded, and that conditions were hardly bearable. A Russian saying which became current in Poland divided the whole population into three categories: "Those who were in prison; those who are in prison; and those who will be in prison."

The NKVD did not easily let any of their prisoners go. When the German army invaded Russia in June 1941, with very few exceptions, all prisoners in the western Ukraine and western Byelorussia were moved east, or killed, or both. No fewer than twenty-five prisons have been identified where the inmates were summarily executed before the Germans arrived.

Many of those who were deported did not survive because of the distances to the camps in Siberia. Packed into overcrowded and unheated cattle trucks, many, like the earlier victims of dekulakization, faced journeys which might take three, four, even more, weeks. General Anders, who collected the survivors in 1941 for his Polish army, calculated that of the 1.5 million Poles deported, almost half had died.

The most famous case of all concerned 15,000 Polish officers, most of them reserve officers, who belonged to one or another of the professions and who were sent to three separate camps in western Russia in September 1939. Until May 1940 they were able to communicate with their families, but after that date only one of them was ever seen alive again. In April 1943 the Germans disinterred over 4,000 corpses at one of the camps, Katyn, on the banks of the Dnieper near Smolensk. Most had their hands tied behind their backs and each had been shot in the back of the head. The Nazis claimed they had been killed by the Russians; the Russians that they had been killed by the Nazis. Only in 1989 did the Soviet authorities finally admit that Russians had been responsible for executing all 15,000.

Polish fears of what was in store for them from the Soviet-German partition of their country were to prove more than justified. No country suffered greater misery, destruction, and loss of life in the Second World War than Poland. The figures for the last are confusing because the 2.9 million Jews of Polish nationality estimated to have lost their lives can be counted in two different categories, either in the total of six million Polish nationals killed during the war or in the total of six million Jews put to death in the Holocaust of European Jewry. If they are counted as Poles, then Poland emerges as the nation which lost a higher percentage of its population, 17.2 percent, than any other during the Second World War. Something like a third of that total met their deaths during the twenty-one months when the country was partitioned between a Nazi and a Soviet occupation.

V

STALIN'S AIM in claiming and occupying eastern Poland was to make it the centerpiece of a broad defensive belt of territory against invasion from the west extending all the way from Finland to the Black Sea. At the same time that the Red Army moved into Poland, he forced treaties on the three Baltic states allowing the Soviet Union to garrison bases on their territory. Then he ran into resistance. Three weeks of argument with Molotov in Moscow failed to persuade the Turkish foreign minister to agree to a treaty closing the Black Sea to warships of other powers. Molotov had met his match for obstinacy; instead the Turks signed a mutual-assistance pact with Britain and France, not the USSR.

More serious in its consequences was the breakdown of negotiations with the Finns. Annexed to the Russian crown as the Grand Duchy of Finland in 1809, the Finns proclaimed their independence in December 1917 and secured recognition of it by Stalin in person, as representative of the Bolshevik government. In the Russian civil war Finnish Communists, with Bolshevik support, overran much of southern Finland but were driven out by the Whites, with German support. At a low point in their fortunes the Bolsheviks had to accept the peace terms agreed at Tartu (Dorpat). The Finns drove a hard bargain. They secured Petsamo with valuable nickel deposits and the ice-free port of Pechenga in the north, a number of islands in the Gulf of Finland commanding the approach to Petrograd and the Russian naval base at Kronstadt. The Russo-Finnish border was moved to give Finland the greater part of the Karelian isthmus and bring the frontier within eighteen miles of Russia's second city, soon to be renamed Leningrad. The Soviet delegation, which included Stalin, protested bitterly at the loss of Karelia but had no option other than to sign.

In April 1938, anxious about a German attack on Russia and concerned, as always, about the vulnerability of Leningrad, Stalin reopened the question. After appealing in vain to Hitler, who had recognized Finland as well as the Baltic states to be in the Soviet zone of interest, the Finns agreed to send a representative. They chose the sixty-nine-year-old Finnish minister in Stockholm, Juho Paasikivi, the man who had led their delegation in the negotiations at Tartu in 1920.

The proposal that Stalin put to the Finns on October 12 was to move the existing Soviet-Finnish border on the Karelian isthmus twenty-five miles farther away from Leningrad; and, for better protection of the city from attack by sea, for the Soviet Union to take over all the islands in the Gulf of Finland and lease the port of Hanko for use as a naval base. In the north, he asked for the cession of the Rybachi Peninsula, which commanded the approaches to Murmansk, the Soviet Union's only ice-free port on its western side. In return the Russians offered twice as much territory adjoining the center of Finland, where the narrow "waist" between the Russian frontier and the Gulf of Bothnia exposed the Finns to the danger of an invader cutting the country in two.

In the negotiations, which continued until November 8, Stalin showed himself willing to moderate his demands but not to withdraw them. Both Marshal Carl Gustaf Mannerheim, the hero of the earlier Finnish-Soviet war, and Paasikivi were in favor of coming to terms with the Russians. [29] But the Finnish government, fully supported by public opinion, refused; once the Russians got their foot in, they believed they would break the door down.

Stalin was surprised at the Finnish intransigence; he appears to have hesitated before accepting the view of the hard-liners led by Zhdanov, the party boss of Leningrad, that they should not waste any more time but take what they needed by force. He finally agreed, subject to the proviso that only troops from the Leningrad Military District were to be involved.

The Winter War began on November 30. On December 1 a People's Government of Finland was formed under the veteran Finnish Communist Otto Kuusinen, living in exile in Moscow, and was instantly recognized by the USSR. Voroshilov, the commissar for defense, assured Stalin Soviet tanks would be in Helsinki in six days.

The Finnish army, however, was far better equipped to deal with the bitter cold than the Russians. Better armed and well dug in behind the Mannerheim Line, it not only drove off but also inflicted heavy losses on Meretskov's Seventh Army. A large force sent into central Finland was surrounded by Finns, camouflaged in white and expert on skis, who swooped on it out of the forests and cut it to pieces. A Soviet general summed up the Russian failure in one sentence: "We have conquered just enough Finnish territory to allow us to bury our dead."

On Hitler's orders, arms sales to the Finns were banned and supplies promised to the Soviet submarines blockading Finnish ports. But the British and French, who had done nothing to help Poland, were enthusiastic in their support for a small nation defending itself with such success. Money was raised to send volunteers and both the British and French governments discussed plans for help, the British hoping to use the opportunity to cut off German supplies of iron ore from Sweden at the same time. The Russian loss of face and the unpopularity of the war with the Russian people, especially when the losses became known, forced Stalin to intervene. As commander of the Soviet forces in Finland he appointed Timoshenko, another graduate of the same First Cavalry Army at Tsaritsyn that had produced Voroshilov and Budenny, but an officer who had passed through the higher-command training and reached the rank of general before the purges. The full resources of the Red Army were now mobilized. On January 15, 1940, Soviet artillery began a massive bombardment of the Mannerheim Line which lasted sixteen days. Nearly a thousand tanks and 140,000 troops were poured into the attack on a narrow front. Even then the Finns stood firm for more than two weeks. Not until February 17 did the Russians achieve a breakthrough; the Finnish army had no more men left to provide relief for exhausted troops. On the twenty-second Mannerheim had to withdraw his forces to new positions.

Reports that the British and French were planning to intervene added to Stalin's growing anxiety that what had begun as a local conflict might become part of a general war, which still hung fire. The Soviet breakthrough was not decisive, but it was sufficient to enable Stalin to reopen negotiations without losing face. On the same day as the Finnish withdrawal Stalin sent details of his demands for a peace settlement to Helsinki. The Finns did not reply at once, hoping that the Swedes and Norwegians would allow the passage of British and French troops. Not until March 6 did they agree to send a delegation to Moscow. Three days later Britain and France sent a message that they were prepared to send troops and planes to fight the Soviets, if the Finns asked for them. But by then the Finns had gone too far to turn back.

There was no question of renewing the offer the Finns had turned down in October. The new terms required the cession of the whole of the Karelian isthmus including their second-largest city, Viipuri, as well as the northeastern shore of Lake Ladoga. The Baltic port of Hanko and the Rybachi Peninsula in the north were to be handed over, with additional territory in the waist of the country—in all, a loss of 22,000 square miles. There was no room for negotiation: The Finns either accepted the terms as they stood or the war continued. Shortly after midnight on March 11, they signed and the Winter War came to an end the next day.

Finnish losses were 25,000 dead, 55,000 wounded out of a population of fewer than five million. The Soviet losses were never published: They were certainly far greater than the Finns'. Mannerheim's estimate was 200,000 dead. Loss of men did not worry Stalin either then or later: It never has worried the Russians. The real damage, as Stalin must have been aware, was the blow to the credibility of the Red Army as a military force. The German General Staff made a careful study of the Russian tactics in the Winter War and concluded its report with the verdict: "The Soviet 'mass' is no match for an army and superior leadership." For once, Hitler was prepared to accept the views of the General Staff: It coincided with his belief that no Slav fighting force could stand up to the racially superior Germans. Nothing did more to convince him in 1941 that he was justified in gambling on defeating the Russians in a single campaign than their performance against the Finns.

STALIN MAY HAVE HAD illusions about the length of time the Nazi-Soviet Pact might last, but not about Hitler's ultimate intention to attack the Soviet Union. For the short term, however, it was very much in both parties' interest to see that the promise of cooperation was kept. The pact had enabled Hitler to complete the defeat of Poland and begin the construction of his New Order, with Soviet neutrality guaranteed; it was to allow him to carry out two more campaigns, the occupation of Norway and Denmark, and the crucial offensive in the west, without the threat of a two-front war. It had enabled Stalin to keep the Soviet Union out of war, at least to postpone the threat of attack by Germany, giving him additional time to build up Russia's defenses and economy; and it was to allow him to create a Soviet security zone in Eastern Europe, beginning with eastern Poland and within a year extending to a belt of territory from Finland to the Black Sea, an area of no less than 286,000 square miles—more than a quarter larger than the whole of France.

Both countries continued to provide further examples of the benefits of cooperation, besides German neutrality during the Finnish war. In October 1939 the Russians agreed to allow the German navy to use the ice-free port of Teriberka, east of Murmansk, as a repair and supply base for ships and U-boats operating in the North Atlantic. As a gesture of cooperation between the NKVD and the SS-Gestapo, the former selected some 500 German Communists or ex-Communists serving sentences in Soviet labor camps as "socially dangerous elements" and—after giving them several weeks of special food and medical attention, as well as providing new clothes—handed them over to the Gestapo. All were transferred to Nazi prisons or concentration camps. Among them was Margarete Buber-Neumann, a former Communist herself, as well as the widow of a former confidant of Stalin's, Heinz Neumann, who fell victim to the purges in 1937. After six months in a Gestapo prison, she was transferred to the women's concentration camp at Ravensbrück, emerging in 1945 as one of the very few survivors of both Stalin's and Hitler's camps. [30]

But by far the most important area of Nazi-Soviet cooperation was in the economic field, enabling Hitler to beat the British blockade by importing food and raw materials from—and through—the Soviet Union and allowing Stalin to acquire machinery, arms, and equipment from Germany in return. The pact itself had been preceded by a trade and credit treaty signed in Berlin and flanked by letters of agreement on increasing trade. The initiative in taking these up came from the German side, and Karl Schnurre, who had negotiated both, produced a list of German requirements which he expanded from the original total of 70 million to 1.4 billion marks. Before agreement could be reached, the Russians insisted on sending a Soviet delegation of sixty specialists to Germany, where they demanded to see everything, especially the latest German military developments, and spent November 1939 poking around factories, experimental stations, and bases.

The Germans were exasperated by what they regarded as licensed espionage, and even more taken aback when they saw what the Soviets asked for. The original agreement had envisaged the Germans supplying industrial goods and equipment in return for raw materials. The Soviet list consisted almost entirely of military items and included not only the latest aircraft, artillery, and ships in service but also those still in development; the total value was over a billion marks. Finally, the Russians demanded delivery of everything by the end of 1940, a timetable incompatible with any plan for a German campaign that year.[31]

The Germans protested, maintaining that unless the Soviet government (the code expression by which both sides referred to Stalin) was willing to modify its demands, the whole deal would collapse. Mikoyan's reply on December 19 was: "The Soviet government considers delivery of the entire list the only satisfactory equivalent for the deliveries of raw materials which, under present conditions, are not otherwise obtainable for Germany on the world market."[32] Germany was at war and, as Stalin well knew, was faced either with a war of attrition and a blockade, for which she was ill prepared, or with a bid for a quick victory, to be launched in 1940, before she began to lose the advantage of her earlier rearmament. In either case Hitler was not in a strong bargaining position compared with Stalin, who could afford to wait.

Arguments and appeals by the Germans during December and January produced no effect until Ribbentrop, in desperation, wrote a personal letter to Stalin, on February 3, lifting the argument from the economic to the political plane—"namely, the promise that the Soviet government was willing to support Germany economically during the war which had been forced upon her"—and at the same time reminding Stalin that as "a not inconsiderable advance payment" the Soviet Union had regained its former Polish and Baltic territories, thanks to the efforts of the Wehrmacht. After three days' silence, Stalin summoned the German negotiators to the Kremlin at 1 a.m. on the seventh and told them Ribbentrop's letter had changed everything, and the Germans could have a new treaty.

When it was finally signed on February 11, the list of war material to be delivered by the Germans still filled forty-two closely typed pages and included, for example, prototypes of all the latest German aircraft, warships, and complete installations for still-secret chemical and metallurgical processes, as well as coal. In return the Soviet Union undertook to supply a million tons of feed grains, 900,000 tons of petroleum, half a million tons of phosphate, and half a million of iron ore, 100,000 tons of chromium ores, and many other raw materials. Hardly less important was the guaranteed right to purchase other raw materials from Rumania, Iran, Afghanistan, and the Far East, and to transport these overland to Germany through Russia, so breaking the blockade, and (as Schnurre put it) creating "a wide-open door to the east for us."[33]

Then, as suddenly as the Soviet attitude had thawed, it froze over again. During March 1940, the Russians stopped making deliveries of grain and oil, claiming that the Germans had defaulted on deliveries of coal, and that none of the aircraft they had been promised had been made available. In an effort to restore confidence, Hitler signed a decree giving priority to arms deliveries to the USSR, even when these were at the expense of the Wehrmacht.

On April 9 Molotov was unexpectedly as forthcoming as Mikoyan had been difficult: The suspension of grain and oil deliveries, he explained, had been due to the "excessive zeal of subordinate agencies." Von der Schulenburg believed Stalin was well informed of the British preparations to occupy Norway and was evidently reducing cooperation with Germany to a minimum in order not to give the Western Allies an excuse for attacking Russia. At dawn on April 9, however, the day Molotov summoned von der Schulenburg to see him, German forces landed in Norway, forestalling the Allies, and removing the threat that Stalin had feared. The more Hitler became involved in hostilities with Britain and France and was too occupied in Scandinavia and the west to turn his eyes to the east, the better Stalin was pleased and the more prepared to give Germany the economic support to continue the war.

VI

THE FINNISH WAR had attracted the attention of both Winston Churchill (then first lord of the Admiralty) and Admiral Raeder (commander in chief of the German navy) to the possibility of a British occupation of Norway. If the British could seize and hold the Norwegian ports of Narvik and Bergen, that would allow the Royal Navy to cut the only ice-free route for the transport of Germany's vital Swedish iron-ore supplies, to deny the use of Norway's thousand-mile-long coastal waters to German U-boats and surface raiders, and possibly open a way to send help to Finland. While Churchill was still searching for a plausible reason to breach Norwegian neutrality, and Raeder for a way to forestall him, the *Altmark* incident highlighted the possibilities. The *Altmark* was a German supply ship that had taken on board 300 British prisoners from the nine ships sunk by the German pocket battleship *Graf Spee* in the South Atlantic. In February 1940, with her prisoners safely concealed below decks, the *Altmark* sought the protection of Norway's neutral territorial waters and made for home. Arguing that the Norwegians had failed to prevent a breach of their neutrality, a light British naval force, led by the destroyer *Cossack,* boarded the German vessel and rescued the captives.

Two months before, Raeder had sufficiently impressed Hitler with the importance of Norway for the latter to set the OKW staff to study the form a German intervention might take. Whatever doubts Hitler may have had were removed by the interception of the *Altmark,* and he now demanded the immediate appointment of a commander.

The way in which Hitler chose to organize the planning and direction of the expedition sheds light on his disorderly methods of working—and the element of calculation as well as temperament that they expressed. He was determined to have the deciding voice in war as much as in politics, and he refused to be bound by established procedures, deliberately cutting across them in order to exercise his flair for the unexpected which had served him so well in politics. His battles with the army leadership over the decision to attack Poland, followed by their continuing resistance in taking the offensive in the west, convinced him that, if he allowed bureaucracy, this time in the form of the thousand-strong Army General Staff, to dictate how the Norwegian campaign was to be conducted, their critical approach and natural desire to reinsure against disaster would eliminate the factor of surprise on which he believed success depended.

It was an operation to tax the most experienced commander, requiring that most difficult of all feats, the coordination of all three services. There were no previous studies by the General Staff to go on, and even maps were difficult to obtain. Undeterred, Hitler ignored the army High Command, the OKH, from the beginning. He ordered Keitel, Jodl, and his own small OKW staff to make the necessary arrangements, and to go over the heads of the army commander in chief and chief of staff (who only learned of the decision to open a new theater of operations secondhand) and select the divisions best suited for the task.

General von Falkenhorst, the officer chosen to command (again without consultation with OKH), was currently the commander, not of an army group, but only of a corps. Within eight days, however, he produced a bold plan that called for the occupation of Denmark as well as the invasion of Norway. Hitler approved both on March 1.

Thanks to better intelligence, the Germans knew that the British were also preparing to occupy Norway, while the British did not realize that the Germans were preparing to beat them out of the starting gate and arrive in Norway first. Even less did they anticipate that, instead of moving by land, as they expected, the Germans would challenge Britain's naval superiority and seize the principal Norwegian ports from the sea, including Narvik itself, so far to the north that, when the first reports came in, they seemed so incredible that they were believed to be referring to Larvik, near Oslo. In fact, for a whole week before the attack was launched on April 9, German warships and transports laden with troops and their equipment, including artillery, as well as stores, were steaming up the Norwegian coast strung out over several hundred miles, undetected by the Royal Navy. The final touch to the complete surprise that the Germans achieved was the seizure of Norwegian airfields with airborne troops, despite gales and snowstorms—the first time such an operation had ever been attempted.

On the night of April 6–7 virtually the entire German fleet put to sea, loaded down with thousands more troops. It was a gamble to try the strongest nerves: If only one of the many ships involved were sunk, and the Norwegians and British alerted, the whole enterprise could founder. In fact one was sunk, and troops wearing the unmistakable field-gray uniforms were rescued from the sea; but neither Norwegians nor the British—engaged in mining Norwegian waters—read the signs correctly. The luck that Hitler believed would always respond to a bold enough bid did not desert him. At dawn on the ninth, as planned, German forces seized the ports of Narvik, Trondheim, and Bergen; and by early evening von Falkenhorst reported that Norway—including Oslo, the capital—and Denmark had been occupied "as instructed."

THE COST of the Norwegian campaign to the German navy was heavy: In a naval battle in Narvik Fjord, nine destroyers were sunk (half of Raeder's total destroyer force), and several cruisers were lost or disabled as well. This was followed by a nervous collapse on Hitler's part which was the other side of his boldness as a gambler. Allied landings in Norway in mid-April badly shook him. He was convinced that the British would now occupy Narvik as well and that the German force there, under the command of General Eduard Dietl, would have to surrender.

Hitler seems to have reached a pitch of nervous exhaustion, in which he swiveled between agitated outbursts and periods of brooding silence, sitting hunched in a corner and staring in front of him. Jodl's diary entry for April 14 reads: "The hysteria is frightful." On the seventeenth he noted: "Every unfavorable piece of news makes the Führer fear the worst." At one point, rapping his knuckles on the table, Jodl was driven to reprove Hitler: "*Mein Führer,* in every war there are times when the supreme commander must keep his nerve!"

Only in the last week of April did Hitler recover his nerve and recognize—without admitting it—that Jodl had been right, that Narvik could be held and that the British were in much greater difficulties than the Germans. Finally, on the thirtieth, Jodl was able to tell him that communications had been established between Oslo and Trondheim: "The Führer is beside himself with joy. I had to sit next to him at lunch."[34]

The British never recovered from the advantage that the tactic of surprise had given the Germans. French and Polish as well as British troops were landed at three points, but all had to be withdrawn during May. The last British force occupied Narvik on May 28 but was pushed out on June 9, taking the Norwegian king and losing the aircraft carrier *Glorious* in the retreat. When the Norwegian campaign ended in June, Hitler was left in control of the whole country for the rest of the war with an occupation regime in which Vikdun Quisling served as a puppet minister-president under the direction of the Reichskommissar, Josef Terboven, a former bank official who had become the Nazi Gauleiter of Essen. The future transport of Swedish iron ore was guaranteed and the German navy provided with Norwegian bases from which to operate against the vital North Atlantic traffic as well as, later, against British convoys bound for the Soviet port of Murmansk. But by June 1940 the Norwegian campaign was already forgotten, overshadowed by a far greater victory, over the French and British forces in the west.

IT WAS FORTUNATE for Hitler that his original idea of launching an offensive in the west in the autumn came to nothing. The plan drawn up by OKH, at his insistence, in October 1939 envisaged the main thrust of the attack being delivered by Army Group B (General Fedor von Bock) on the right wing, sweeping through Liège and Namur towards the Channel coast; while Army Group A (General Gerd von Rundstedt) held the center of the line opposite the Ardennes, and Army Group C (General Wilhelm von Leeb) the left wing facing the Maginot Line. As Hitler pointed out, this was a repetition of the Schlieffen Plan of 1914, and "you cannot get away with an operation like that twice." It was precisely the plan that the French High Command expected the Germans to follow and that they set out to meet head-on, in May 1940, by advancing into Belgium from the south. Even if the Germans succeeded in forcing them back they would only be driving the Allies closer to their fortified positions and supply bases.

Hitler argued, from his experience of fighting in Flanders as a young man, that the terrain into which von Bock's Army Group B would be heading was broken by innumerable canals and small streams and that these would hold up the armored forces on which a breakthrough depended. He was attracted instead by the idea of delivering the main attack from farther south, heading northwest along the Somme, so taking the advancing Allied forces in the rear as they moved into Belgium and rolling them up against the Channel coast. He did not press it further, however, in view of his desire to open the offensive as soon as possible.

At the end of January 1940, after Hitler had postponed the attack until the spring, his military adjutant, Colonel Rudolf Schmundt, brought back the news from a tour of the western front that General Erich von Manstein, the chief of staff of von Rundstedt's Army Group A, had had the same idea as Hitler. Working with General Heinz Guderian, the leading expert in tank warfare, von Manstein had satisfied himself that the wooded hills of the Ardennes were not—as they were generally believed to be—impassable for tanks, provided a sufficiently strong force was employed. Von Manstein's plan, if adopted, would mean abandoning the work already done by the General Staff; this assured it a hostile reception, and its author was transferred to the command of an infantry corps in the rear.

Although he was to play only a minor part in carrying it out, however, von Manstein succeeded in putting his proposal to Hitler in a talk on February 17, providing the latter with exactly what he had been reaching for, the element of surprise missing from the OKH plan. For the general belief, shared by orthodox opinion in the French as much as in the German High Command, was that the Ardennes were unsuitable for tank operations. As a result this sector was likely to be weakly defended. If the German panzers could once get through the hills, they would be out into the rolling country of northern France, which was well suited to a rapid advance. That would enable the Germans to sever the lines of communication on which the Allied forces pushing into Belgium would depend and drive them into a trap with their backs to the Belgian coast. Hitler needed no further convincing. The next day he sent for von Brauchitsch and Halder and told them to substitute von Manstein's for their own plan: It was issued as the new directive for the attack in the west on February 24. [35]

Early in May 1940 all British forces were withdrawn from Norway, apart from 12,000 troops still holding Narvik in the far north. Anger at the defeat suffered by the British, despite their boasted command of the sea, led to the fall of Chamberlain's government and on May 10 Winston Churchill replaced him as prime minister. The same day, the German army and air force launched Hitler's long-delayed offensive in the west.

Thanks to the pact with Stalin, the fifty to sixty divisions that would otherwise have had to be retained in the east were reduced to eight, and the Germans were able to deploy 141 divisions in the west against total Allied forces of 144, of which 104 were French, 10 British, and the rest Belgian and Dutch. The Allies had more tanks, the Germans more aircraft. In numbers, therefore, the two sides were roughly equal. Where the Germans had a marked superiority was, first, in their unified command; second, in the skill with which they handled their ten armored divisions (three equipped with Czech tanks); third, in the command of the air which they won and their novel use of airborne troops; and finally, in the qualities of leadership and the high morale displayed at all levels.

Everything went according to the revised German plan, and von Bock's Army Group B in the north secured the surrender of the Dutch within five days. The Dutch and Belgian defense system was overrun by using highly trained parachute and glider troops which secured the vital bridges over the Meuse and the Albert Canal before they could be blown up. Hitler himself had designed the operation that led to the capture of the famous Belgian fortress of Eben Emael by landing on the roof a force of fewer than a hundred German engineers equipped with a powerful new explosive which German propaganda made the most of as an example of Hitler's secret weapons.

But the main thrust, which took the Allies completely by surprise, was through the Ardennes. A force of forty-four divisions, with the bulk of the armor, had been concentrated in Army Group A under von Rundstedt's command. By May 12, the armored columns were through the hills and across the French frontier; by the thirteenth they had crossed the Meuse; by the fourteenth they had opened a gap fifty miles wide between the two main French armies, and within the first week had advanced 200 miles. A major factor in their success was the highly effective support they received from the air. The French air force was overwhelmed; the RAF lost half the 200 bombers it was operating in France—the highest rate of loss it ever suffered—and a million refugees clogging the roads offered the easiest of targets to the dreaded dive-bombers, fitted with special screaming devices to add to the terror they inspired.

By May 20 a German line was established from the German frontier to the Channel coast, cutting off the British and French forces to the north and separating them from their bases in France.

The speed of the advance had taken the German generals by surprise, and there were divided views on how they should proceed. They could hardly believe that the famous French army, with its great military tradition, had been defeated so easily, and they were anxious about the large French forces on the southern flank of their line. So was Hitler, who had already shown signs of being frightened by his own success and accused the High Command of ruining the whole campaign by advancing too fast. [36] For once it was von Brauchitsch and Halder, not Hitler, who favored boldness, arguing the case for allowing the panzer troops to push ahead without delay and round up the Allied forces to the north, while plans were being worked out for the advance to the south. Von Rundstedt, the Army Group A commander, had already halted the tanks on the twenty-third to give them a respite and allow them to regroup. Hitler supported him, overruling von Brauchitsch and Halder, and allowing Göring the opportunity for which he pressed to show that the Luftwaffe could wipe out the encircled Allied troops without assistance from the army.

After the war there was much controversy over who was responsible for this decision, with the generals laying the whole of the blame on Hitler. The important fact, however, appears to be that it was not until the twenty-sixth that it was realized the British were planning to use Dunkirk, the one remaining harbor available to them, to evacuate their expeditionary force by sea. Hitler then released the halted tanks, but the delay gave the British time to dig in and hold the port and beaches sufficiently long (until June 4) to allow 340,000 troops (including 139,000 French) to be taken off by a swarm of boats of every description in a remarkable improvised operation.

The significance of the Dunkirk evacuation only became clear later when Hitler realized that the British were going to continue the war. At the time, the British army was written off as defeated, and the Germans' attention was focused on the approaching battle for France.

This began on June 5, with Hitler and the army High Command again divided on how to conduct it. Halder held to the classic doctrine of concentrating on the destruction of the enemy forces; Hitler wanted first to secure the Lorraine iron-ore basin so as to deprive France of her armaments industry. The truth was that it did not much matter which course they followed, for despite continued resistance by individual French units, the French government and High Command were on the verge of collapse. The Germans reached the Seine within three days and entered Paris, which the government had already left, on the fourteenth. After that the German armies fanned out, the mechanized divisions racing for the Rhône Valley, the Mediterranean, and the Spanish frontier. On the sixteenth the eighty-five-year-old Marshal Philippe Pétain replaced Paul Reynaud as prime minister and the next day asked for an armistice. Efforts to continue the war from overseas came to nothing, and on the twenty-second the armistice was signed and the campaign in the west was over. What the Kaiser's armies had failed to achieve after more than four years of exhausting war with the loss of over 1.8 million German lives, Hitler's armies had accomplished in six weeks at the cost of 27,000.

VII

AS SOON AS HITLER heard that the French were asking for an armistice, he left for a meeting with Mussolini in Munich on June 18 and 19. The much-publicized Pact of Steel, unpopular in both countries, had so far proved a cardboard contrivance. On November 20, 1939, Ciano noted in his diary: "For Mussolini, the idea of Hitler's waging war and, worse still, winning it, is altogether unbearable." [37]

The Duce was particularly put out by Hitler's agreement with Stalin and the subsequent partition of Poland. Early in the New Year of 1940 he committed his grievances to paper in a letter to Hitler which marked the high-water mark of his independence toward his ally. In it he expressed his "profound conviction" that, even with the aid of Italy, Hitler would not succeed in defeating France and Britain; the U.S.A. would never permit that to happen. Mussolini urged his fellow dictator to seek a compromise based on the creation of a Polish state. Opposed to an extension of the war in the west, for his own reasons, he called on Hitler to turn back and seek Germany's *Lebensraum* in the east. "The fact is," he wrote,

> that in Poland and the Baltic it is Russia that has been the great benefi-
> ciary of the war—without firing a shot. I, who was born a revolutionary
> and have never changed, I say to you that you cannot sacrifice the

permanent principles of your revolution to the tactical needs of a passing phase of policy. I am sure that you cannot abandon the anti-Bolshevik and anti-Semitic banner you have brandished for twenty years.[38]

Hitler took two months before he sent a reply. When it came, delivered by Ribbentrop on March 10, it appealed skillfully to Mussolini's desire to play a historic role: "Sooner or later, I believe, Duce, that Fate will force us after all to fight side by side." Mussolini was flattered, and although he complained when the date of a meeting with Hitler on the Brenner was brought forward—"These Germans don't give one time to breathe or think things over"—he went all the same. Ciano wrote in his diary that Mussolini still hoped to persuade Hitler to give up the idea of an offensive in the west, but he added gloomily: "The Duce is fascinated by Hitler, a fascination that involves something deeply rooted in his makeup. The Führer will get more out of the Duce than Ribbentrop could."[39]

The result of the meeting (March 18) was exactly as Ciano had foreseen. Mussolini could hardly get a word in as Hitler overwhelmed him with a flood of talk, and he used the few minutes that were left to reaffirm his intention of coming into the war on Germany's side. On the way back to Rome he grumbled that Hitler had monopolized the conversation, but face-to-face with him he could not conceal an anxious deference, or his fear of being left out of the division of the spoils.

Hitler said nothing to Mussolini of his intention to invade Norway, nor did he give him advance notice of the attack in the west. He found time, however, once the campaign was launched, to write a series of letters to the Duce in which he poured scorn on the feebleness of the French and British, baiting the hook with such success that Mussolini finally screwed up his courage to declare war—but not before June 10, by which time it was virtually over. When Hitler heard that the Italians had waited until the next day to bomb Malta, he exclaimed: "I would have done everything the other way around. This must be the last declaration of war in history. I never thought the Duce was so primitive. Never in my life will I sign a declaration of war. I will always strike first."[40]

After a week's campaign in which the Italian army did not distinguish itself or contribute anything to the defeat of France, Mussolini showed himself grasping when it came to the armistice terms. He demanded the cession of Corsica, Nice, and the French empire in North Africa, as well as Malta, Egypt, and the Sudan from the British. It was to curb his appetite that Hitler made the journey to see him.

Characteristically, Hitler had not asked the OKW or OKH to provide him with advice on the terms of the armistice. He made up his own mind and took a line that surprised both the Italians and the German military. Although Hitler went to great pains to reproduce the setting of November 11, 1918, bringing the old wooden dining car in which Foch had dictated the French terms to the same spot in the forest of Compiègne and inviting the world's press to witness the scene, the demands he made on France were very different from those imposed on Germany in 1918. Nothing was included that might tempt the French to continue the war from North Africa or encourage the powerful French fleet, which was beyond German reach, to join the British. The British themselves, Hitler hoped, would be so impressed by his moderation as to consider seriously a German offer of peace.

The occupation of France was restricted to the north and a coastal strip in the west, leaving two-fifths of the country to preserve a limited independence under Pétain's government in Vichy. The French were allowed to retain their colonial empire, and Mussolini was persuaded to postpone any territorial claims until the peace treaty. To the Duce's great disappointment, all claims to the French fleet were renounced: The French were to be allowed to keep part of it to protect their colonies, the rest was to be put out of commission.

The day after he had reversed the humiliation of 1918 and received the French acceptance of his terms, Hitler fulfilled a longtime dream to visit Paris and see its monuments. No one before him had combined the roles of conqueror and tourist. Arriving at six in the morning, he went up the Eiffel Tower, stood bareheaded and silent before Napoleon's tomb in Les Invalides and delighted in showing off his knowledge of the dimensions of the Opéra. By nine o'clock he was away and that evening ordered Speer (who had accompanied him) to draft a decree for the rebuilding of Berlin. The Reich's capital must outshine all other cities, including Paris, and the work must be completed by 1950.

THE FALL OF FRANCE marks the peak of Hitler's career. At each move he had made between 1933 and 1939, the argument for caution had always been the same: The French might intervene. Every one of the senior officers in the German army had served in the First World War and, under the impression of Germany's defeat, the Treaty of Versailles which France had imposed on Germany, and the alliance system she had built up afterwards, they continued to believe that she was the leading military power in Europe, with a military tradition that no other nation could equal. Over and over again, Hitler declared that the French were no longer the force they had been, that they lacked leaders and had lost the will to fight. The generals did not believe him. Even after the French failed to react to the remilitarization of the Rhineland; after they did no more than protest at the Anschluss (which they had vetoed in 1931) and abandoned their strongest allies, the Czechs, the German General Staff remained convinced that, if Germany attacked Poland, the French army would break through the western fortifications and reoccupy the Ruhr as they had done in 1923.

Not only had Hitler proved them wrong, he had also insisted, again contrary to the professionals' advice, that Germany should take the initiative and attack France. And then within six weeks he had inflicted on France a more complete defeat than any in her long military history.

It is hard to convey the impression the fall of France made at the time and it is hardly surprising that so great a triumph went to Hitler's head. Henceforward he was convinced that he was not only a political but a military genius, the equal not only of Bismarck, but of von Moltke and Frederick the Great—the latter the figure with whom Hitler most frequently identified himself, as Stalin did with Peter the Great. Hitler was not without military talents. If he was an amateur who lacked the training of the professional soldier, the same could be said of Stalin and Churchill. A lifetime's interest had led him to read widely in the history and science of war, and he had developed a remarkable memory for detail. Von Manstein, who was highly critical of Hitler as a strategist, wrote after the war that his "memory and knowledge were astounding in technical questions and in all problems of armaments," adding, "He was particularly fond of making use of this ability when he wanted to change the subject from some topic that was not congenial to him."[41]

Jodl, in notes that he dictated while awaiting trial at Nuremberg, cited as examples of Hitler's personal initiative in armaments the substitution for the 37mm and 50mm antitank guns of the much more powerful 75mm, and his insistence that the short guns mounted on German tanks should be replaced by the long-barreled 75 and 88mm guns. He added that it was again on Hitler's initiative that the Panther, Tiger, and Tiger II tanks were developed. These were all interventions that made a major contribution to the success of the German armored forces. Apart from such important practical contributions, Hitler's grasp of the technological revolution in warfare opened his mind to the independent use of armored forces which was the key to the Blitzkrieg. His support for this major strategic innovation was decisive to the success of the German armies from 1939 to 1941 and put him way ahead of any other national leader, including Stalin, and of professional opinion as well in other armies.

As a commander, Hitler suffered from the fact that he had never commanded even a company. His insistence on willpower as the decisive factor in war as in politics blinded him to the organization and the time that was needed to move large bodies of troops, and to the allowances that had to be made for all sorts of unforeseeable difficulties that might arise. General Warlimont, who observed him closely in 1939 and 1940, believed that it was his lack of experience of command that made him vulnerable to panic when there was no news of how an operation was going or when things went wrong. In his conduct of operations, he showed himself as nervous and hesitant as he was bold in designing them.

As a strategist Hitler was never lacking in imagination, either in politics or in war, as his constant search for ways of taking the enemy by surprise shows. Von Manstein was prepared to admit that Hitler had "an eye for

operational possibilities" and this is borne out by his insistence on extending the attack on Norway to Narvik in the far north and the concentration
of the attack in the west on the center of the front which he and von
Manstein had spotted independently as the unexpected move that could
achieve a breakthrough. Temperamentally, however, the self-taught Hitler
always rejected working with others or accepting advice from experts.
When he debated the different courses open to him, it was always with
himself; his decisions were intuitive, not open to modification in discussions; he distrusted criticism, analysis, and objectivity for their inhibiting
effect on the will.

Jodl, the chief of the OKW Operations Staff, the general officer who
came nearest to establishing a working relationship with Hitler, wrote in his
Nuremberg notes that Hitler's attitude was determined by the experience
he had gained during his rise to power:

> He thought that if he had ever learned to think in the terms of a general
> staff officer, at every single step he would have had to stop and calculate
> the impossibility of reaching the next. Consequently, he would never
> even have tried to come to power, since on the basis of objective calcula-
> tions he had no prospect of success in the first place . . . The Führer
> regarded it as proper in his military leadership, as he had in his political
> activity, to establish goals that were so far-reaching that the objective pro-
> fessionals would declare them impossible. But he did this deliberately,
> convinced that the actual course of events would leave these more modest
> calculations behind.

Hitler was willing to have a working staff that translated his decisions into
orders but not to allow it the role that the German General Staff had always
fulfilled hitherto, that of offering strategic advice. Attempts to put forward
other points of view led only to outbreaks of rage. Jodl went on to say that
it was Hitler's initial success in the campaigns of 1939 and 1940 that
convinced him that it was he and not the General Staff "who was the realist
and who had foreseen actual developments more clearly, precisely because
he had taken into account the incalculable."

From that time on, Jodl concluded, Hitler became convinced of the
infallibility of his judgment in war as in politics and required nothing more
of his staff than the technical support necessary to implement his decisions
and the smooth functioning of the military organization to carry them out.
As long as the war continued to go well, this caused tension and frustration
among his staff, but it worked. When Hitler lost his winning streak, however, and the war started to go badly, his refusal to listen to advice—for
example, at Stalingrad and over the need to organize a strategic retreat on
the Eastern Front—led to disaster. [42]

HITLER'S INITIAL SUCCESS had produced a similar distorting
effect on his judgment in regard to rearmament and the war economy.

Germany's rearmament was due to be completed by 1943 or 1944, and was based on the assumption that a general war involving such major powers as Britain and France—as distinct from limited operations such as that against Czechoslovakia and that planned against Poland—would not break out until the mid-1940s. When, contrary to Hitler's expectations, Britain and France persisted in declaring war in September 1939, the German economy was caught halfway through preparations for a longer war.

One of the first to grasp what this meant was the commander in chief of the German navy, Admiral Raeder. In a note that he made on September 3, 1939, he recalled Hitler's assurance that the war with Britain and France, which actually began that day, was not to be expected before about 1944. By that time Germany would have had a good prospect of destroying the British fleet and so finding "the final solution to the English question" which the navy's High Command had been seeking since Admiral Alfred von Tirpitz and the naval armaments race of the 1900s. This target date of the mid-1940s had been the explicit assumption on which Hitler had given an absolute priority to the navy's Z-Plan over all other parts of the German rearmament program as recently as January 1939, only to cancel it on September 1. Now, Raeder concluded, the German navy was so much weaker than the British "that it can only demonstrate that it knows how to go down with dignity."[43] The Norwegian campaign was to show that Raeder's pessimism was premature, but the German navy's inability to provide cover for the invasion of Britain or to make the blockade of the British Isles effective confirmed his judgment.

A similar assumption by Göring lay behind the heavy-bomber (Heinkel 177) program, which had been drawn up in 1937, with the date of 1941 for its first entry into service and of early 1943 before it would provide the Luftwaffe with the long-range heavy-bomber fleet that would be needed if Germany were to keep up a successful air offensive against British or Russian industry.

It was their knowledge of this timetable that made those concerned with rearmament (including Göring) anxious about the possibility of becoming involved at an earlier date in a war with major powers such as France and Britain, for which Germany was not adequately prepared. When this happened, and when both countries rejected Hitler's peace offer after the Polish campaign, there was an obvious case for a searching review of the unexpected situation in which Germany now found herself and the implications for her rearmament program. To take one example, in November 1939 two of the Ruhr's leading industrialists, Albert Vögler and Hellmuth Poensgen, pointed out to General Thomas, the head of the OKW War Economy and Armaments Office, the folly of continuing to build up the steel capacity of the Reichswerke Hermann Göring in Salzgitter since it would take more steel to construct its blast furnaces than it could actually produce before 1943.[44]

Thomas, the persistent advocate of armament in depth, needed no convincing, but his efforts to persuade Keitel, the chief of OKW—and, through Keitel, Hitler—of the need to mobilize the whole economy for war, now that hostilities had begun, made no impression. Hitler spoke of "converting the whole economy to a war basis," but stipulated that the civilian economy should be spared as far as possible. Although the navy's Z-Plan was now dropped, the priorities Hitler was persuaded to establish were far too wide and in 1940 were subject to repeated changes that made nonsense of long-term production runs. Until the winter of 1941–42, the picture already drawn of the failure to produce a long-term overall plan for mobilizing the country's economic resources remained substantially true.

Hitler responded to immediate needs, such as the crisis over the storage of munitions following the Polish campaign—hence the frequent switches in priorities as he took up and dropped different schemes for what to do next in the second half of 1940. But in economics as in politics and strategy, he showed the same congenital resistance to systematic planning or control, anything that might fetter his ability to make intuitive, off-the-cuff interventions or conflict with his view that it was will stimulated by competition that produced results. Putting Göring in charge of the Four-Year Plan was not inconsistent with this, since he could be sure that Göring would never allow any proposal or report to go forward if he sensed that it would irritate or disturb Hitler. But even more important was the effect of Germany's initial military successes. It was easy enough for him to convince himself that there was nothing fundamentally wrong with an economy capable of producing the armaments and munitions with which German armies had inflicted a defeat on France eclipsing anything achieved between 1914 and 1918—and with which they were to go on in 1941 to overrun Greece and Yugoslavia and drive the Soviet armies back to within twenty-five miles of Leningrad and Moscow. The margin of reserve stocks might be below what the General Staff considered necessary—just as the margin of risk in his Blitzkrieg concept of war was higher—but the results were what counted, and the results were staggering.

It was only when the drive into the Soviet Union was halted in December 1941, when the devastating effect of the Russian winter was experienced by an army and air force unprepared for it, and the hope of defeating Russia in a single campaign had to be abandoned, that Hitler agreed to the radical changes in the organization of the economy for which Todt had been pressing. Todt had already begun to introduce them piecemeal during the latter part of his period of office as armaments minister (March 1940–January 1942), but how much remained to be done is shown by the situation Speer found when he took over in February 1942 after Todt's death.

Two and a half years into the war Speer found five "Supreme Reich Authorities" with independent and often conflicting powers over German war production: the Four-Year Plan (Göring), the OKW's War Economy and Armaments Office (General Thomas), the Ministry of Economics

(Funk), the Ministry of Labor (Robert Ley, also head of the party's Labor Front), and Speer's own ministry (hitherto under Todt). At the next lower level, still largely going their own way, were the ordnance offices of the army, the navy, and the air force, and five plenipotentiaries of the Four-Year Plan (iron and steel, construction, chemical industry, machinery, power, and water). At the middle and lower levels of administration, all the five Supreme Reich Authorities commanded their own regional and local networks. At these lower levels they came up against the resistance to economic mobilization of the party Gauleiters, many of whom had been appointed Reich defense commissioners, and of other party organizations such as the Labor Front, with direct lines to the Führer through Bormann and the party Chancellery. Finally, Himmler had for some time been building his own SS economic empire, which ran its own business enterprises, free of all outside control.

The test of a war economy is, after all, not its design but its effectiveness, and so long as Hitler could keep to the Blitzkrieg formula—one enemy at a time and a sufficient margin of superiority to defeat them in a single campaign—even these cumbersome arrangements could produce the arms needed to keep up the run of victories, especially when supplemented by the additional resources drawn from the occupied territories and employed with the skill and élan that no other army appeared able to match. But when Hitler's leadership involved Germany in a full-scale war with the British Commonwealth and Empire, the Soviet Union, and the United States, the lesson of Germany's defeat in the First World War, her inability to match the economic strength of her opponents, could no longer be ignored. The reforms that Todt, Milch, and Speer introduced led to a remarkable increase in the productivity of the German economy, but they could never make up for the two years lost by Hitler's and Göring's failure to match the German army's victories with the all-out mobilization of the German economy for war from the beginning.

VIII

No one was more taken aback by the German victory in the west than Stalin. He had counted on the sort of stalemate that had developed in 1914—or at least on a campaign that would last a year or two, seriously weaken the Germans, even if they won, and leave him time to strengthen Russia's defenses. His response was to move as quickly as possible to make sure of the gains promised by the Nazi-Soviet Pact.

The secret protocol recognized the Russians' interest (and the Germans' complete disinterest) in their recovery of the Rumanian province of Bessarabia. During the latter part of May, Soviet troops started to move up to the Bessarabian frontier, and Rumania began to mobilize for its defense. The Germans might be disinterested themselves in Bessarabia, but they were very much interested in preventing a war that might threaten the large supplies of food, timber, and above all the 1.2 million tons of oil per annum that they were drawing from Rumania. This was considerably more than they were getting from the USSR and well over half their total imports, made all the more attractive since it was paid for, not in hard currency, but with arms captured in Poland. The Rumanians appealed to Germany for protection. Ribbentrop, however, anxious not to have trouble with Stalin, replied (on June 1) by asking how far they were prepared to go in meeting the Russians' claim to Bessarabia. Taking the hint, the Rumanians agreed to open talks with the Soviets.

In the Baltic states, where Russian garrisons were already stationed, Stalin acted with less concern for appearances. On May 25 Molotov called in the Lithuanian minister and complained sharply of "provocative acts" toward Soviet soldiers. A press campaign was whipped up and further incidents staged on the borders of all three Baltic states. On June 15 these erupted into an unopposed invasion of Lithuania. The Russians' instructions were that if the workers of the Baltic states were to express a wish that these should be called "Soviet" and "Socialist" governments, "Comrade Stalin has said he will have no objections to such demands." Lists of the new ministers to be appointed were thoughtfully provided. The new governments were duly formed and held elections for the "List of the Working Class." On July 21 the newly elected deputies in all three countries proclaimed themselves to be Soviet Socialist Republics and asked to be incorporated into the Soviet Union. The Supreme Soviet, meeting in Moscow, granted their requests on August 3. The Red Army had already started to move in on the first and the occupation of the Baltic states was complete by the sixth.

All businesses were nationalized as was all land except smallholdings. The first wave of deportations to Siberia began before the elections and continued until the German invasion in June 1941: A week before that, in the single night of June 14–15, 60,000 Estonians, 34,000 Latvians, and 38,000 Lithuanians were taken as far away as possible from their former homes. As in occupied Poland, the aim was to get rid of all potential opposition leaders—politicians, trade unionists, intellectuals, teachers. Their places were occupied by Russians—who took over their homes and jobs, just as *Volksdeutsche,* including many thousands from the Baltic states, had done in the four Polish provinces annexed by Germany.

Hitler took no action to protect traditional German interests in the Baltic states, beyond seeing that the remaining *Volksdeutsche* were evacuated. Like the rest of the territory acquired by the Soviet Union under the Nazi-Soviet Pact, he regarded their present occupation by the Russians as a temporary affair which would soon be put right.

The nearest the Germans came to open protest was in Rumania, where the Russians proposed to occupy not only Bessarabia but the neighboring province of Bukovina as well. Molotov made no concession: Bukovina, he told von der Schulenburg, was "the last remnant missing from a unified

Ukraine" and must be dealt with at the same time as Bessarabia. But the following day, as a gesture in response to Hitler's request, Stalin agreed to limit the Soviet occupation to northern Bukovina. Behind the scenes Germany put the strongest pressure on King Carol and the Rumanians not to resist the loss of a third of their territory, and on Hungary and Bulgaria not to seize the opportunity to pursue their own territorial claims against Rumania at the same time. On June 28 the Red Army moved in, and Stalin completed his gains under the secret protocol—a total of 286,000 square miles and over twenty million inhabitants, secured with the loss of hardly a Russian life.

Amidst his anxieties about the war, August 1940 brought Stalin one of the most gratifying moments of his life, the news of Trotsky's assassination. Trotsky's invective had retained its power to get under his skin. Having greeted Stalin's signature of the Nazi-Soviet Pact with the headline, "Stalin, Hitler's Quartermaster," Trotsky predicted catastrophe for the Soviet Union under his leadership and called on Soviet workers to overthrow him in the name of the October Revolution he had betrayed.

Stalin's response was to send for Beria and demand that the NKVD should redouble its efforts to silence Trotsky. His assassination was planned in the Lubyanka; the operator on the spot in Mexico was the NKVD agent Naum Eitingon. The first attempt, in May 1940, was an attack on Trotsky's fortified house by a group disguised as policemen who sprayed it with gunfire. Trotsky escaped unhurt. The second attempt was carried out by a former lieutenant in the Spanish Republican Army, Ramón Mercader, who had been recruited to the NKVD and succeeded in winning Trotsky's confidence. Entering his room while he was working on the manuscript of a life of Stalin, Mercader struck him hard on the head with an icepick, inflicting injuries from which Trotsky died twenty-four hours later. Sentenced to twenty years imprisonment, Mercader steadily maintained his denial of any Soviet involvement. Only after his release did he appear in Moscow in the 1960s and collect the Order of Lenin he had been awarded, with the caution not to wear it in public. Beria's success helped his promotion to Commissar-General of State Security seven months after Trotsky's death. Stalin was well satisfied. The last and most dangerous of the old enemies had been eliminated; of the original group around Lenin only he now remained.

ALL REPORTS on public opinion in Germany in the summer of 1939— those of the different Nazi agencies and of the émigré Sopade*—agreed that there was anxiety about war and that the acid test of Hitler's popularity would be whether, once again, he could avoid one. Yet ten months later, after not one but three campaigns, the same sources agreed that belief and trust in the Führer had reached an unprecedented level. This was not true

---

*The Social Democrats' office abroad had to move hurriedly from Prague to Paris.

of the party, the generally low standing of which had been depressed still further by the contrast between the soldiers serving at the front in their field-gray uniforms, which Hitler, too, now wore as "the first soldier of the Reich," and the brown-shirted Nazi functionaries, who were seen as shirkers staying at home. But for Hitler himself and the image of the Führer that he projected, popular enthusiasm and support reached its peak in the summer of 1940.[45]

Three elements combined in the national mood: patriotic exultation at the triumph of German arms; relief that the fear of a long war had been removed; and anger with the British, who alone stood in the way of final victory and peace. Hitler's own mood was more complicated, as the hesitations and frustration of the next six months were to show. He, too, wanted an end of the war in the west and could see no reason why Britain should continue it.

What use he would make of peace was another matter, on which he spoke with more than one voice. But he did not share the wish of many Germans to see Britain destroyed, repeating to Keitel, von Weizsäcker, and many others that it was not in Germany's interests to defeat the British and break up their empire, thereby providing the Russians, the Japanese, and the Americans with an easy inheritance. Hitler had become involved in war with the Western powers, not because of any demands he had to make on them, but because of their refusal to agree to Germany having a free hand in Central and Eastern Europe. This had been the issue of 1938 and 1939, over Czechoslovakia and Poland, and it remained the issue still, in 1940. He had always been attracted by the idea of working with the British. With their last ally on the continent gone and their army driven into the sea, surely they must see that it was impossible for them to prevent a German hegemony in Europe and come to terms. England would have to recognize Germany's dominant position in Europe and return the German colonies, but that was all. Hitler was prepared not only to make peace with her, but also to conclude the alliance he had always hoped for and to guarantee the continued existence of the British Empire.

So convinced was he that the way was now open to a settlement that on June 14 he gave an order to disband thirty-nine divisions, followed by the assurance that half a million men would be released for the armaments industry. But the news for which he was waiting, a sign from London that the British were willing to consider negotiations, did not come. Tentative soundings through neutral contacts produced no response. On June 18 Churchill, speaking in the House of Commons, declared his government's determination to fight on, whatever the odds, "so that if the British Empire and Commonwealth last for a thousand years, one will still say, 'This was their finest hour.' " On July 3 the British government made clear that this was more than rhetoric when it ordered the Royal Navy to open fire on and disable the French warships at Oran in North Africa. Hitler delayed the speech he intended to make in the Reichstag in order to give the British more time, but there was still no sign that they were prepared to make a move.

Finally, he summoned the Reichstag for the postponed victory celebrations on July 19. It was a great occasion, another scene of triumph, marked by the promotion to field marshal of twelve of the generals (including Keitel and von Brauchitsch) and the creation of a new rank, Reich marshal, for Göring, whose vanity was thereby appeased and who appeared in a sky-blue uniform that he had designed himself. Hitler was at the top of his form as a speaker, full of confidence and scornful of the British leaders. Nonetheless, he ended with a direct appeal to the British people:

> Mr. Churchill ought perhaps, for once, to believe me when I prophesy that a great empire will be destroyed—an empire that it was never my intention to destroy or even to harm. . . .
>
> In this hour, I feel it to be my duty before my conscience to appeal once more to reason and common sense in Great Britain. I consider myself in a position to make this appeal since I am not the vanquished begging favors but the victor speaking in the name of reason. I can see no reason why this war must go on.[46]

If the British would not accept his offer, Hitler had three options. One was to invade the United Kingdom, defeat the British, and dictate terms as he had in France. A second was an indirect approach to the same end: to attack the British position in the Mediterranean and the Middle East, with the help of Italy, Spain, and Vichy France; to threaten the British position in the Far East with the help of Japan; possibly to divert Russia southward to the Persian Gulf and India, and to intensify the U-boat and Luftwaffe campaigns against British shipping. The third was to ignore the British and turn east to win a decisive victory over Russia, providing Germany with the security and the access to raw materials that would enable her to go on and defeat Britain—and if necessary the United States as well.

The last was the original program that had been scheduled for the mid-1940s, when the long-term plans for the German navy and the Luftwaffe would have borne fruit. The timetable for this, however, had been thrown out of order by Britain's intervention in what had been intended as a purely local campaign against Poland. Stalin had been persuaded, with the heavy bribe offered in the protocol, to remain neutral. But the British had refused to accept Hitler's offer to guarantee the British Empire in an equivalent of the Nazi-Soviet Pact, and now were once again frustrating his strategy of dealing with one opponent at a time and seeking to involve him in a long-term general war for which Germany was not equipped and which he wanted to avoid, or at least postpone until she was.

UNTIL THE SUMMER of 1940 Hitler had never seriously considered how an invasion of Britain could be carried out. The first plan produced called for a landing, covered by the German navy and the Luftwaffe, along a front from Ramsgate to west of the Isle of Wight, and Hitler ordered preparations for Operation Sea Lion to be completed by mid-August.

The German army was enthusiastic. But Hitler was as impressed as Admiral Raeder by the difficulties of the operation. The weakness of the German navy was now apparent. Raeder could supply transport for only thirteen out of the forty divisions the army wanted to land, and the cost of the Norwegian campaign—three cruisers and nine destroyers sunk, two cruisers and a destroyer still under repair—made it out of the question for him to provide the protection they would need against the Royal Navy.

In August Hitler accepted the navy's arguments against attempting a landing on the scale originally planned and turned to the Luftwaffe instead to eliminate the RAF and secure the mastery of the air that would allow an invasion to take place on a smaller scale. The reputation that the Luftwaffe had established during the Spanish Civil War, the Polish campaign, and the Battle for France suggested that this was well within their capacity, and on August 13 1,500 German aircraft took part in the opening attack of Operation Eagle.

For the first time, however, the Luftwaffe came up against an air force that could meet it on equal terms, and had the advantage not only of some of the best single-engined fighter planes in the world—the eight-gun Hurricanes and Spitfires—but also of the revolutionary early-warning system, radar, supplemented by a network of a thousand posts manned by the Observer Corps. The RAF's Fighter Command was stretched to the limit. At one point, its No. 11 Group covering London and the southeast had six of its seven main airfields and five of its forward stations put out of action. But except on one day German losses of aircraft of all types exceeded British and by the end of the first phase were approaching a figure of 1,000 machines compared with British losses of 550. This was opposition of a kind that the Luftwaffe had never met before.

The German bombers continued their night attacks on London and other cities into the winter, but by daylight the RAF had denied the Luftwaffe the mastery of the skies over Britain which was the precondition of the invasion. On September 17 Hitler recognized this and called off the invasion by postponing it indefinitely.

The significance of the British victory in the Battle of Britain was only to become clear later in the war. Hitherto, Hitler had always regarded any move against Russia as dependent upon first securing Germany against intervention from the west. Any danger from France had already been removed. Now, exasperated by the refusal of the British to recognize that they too had lost the war, and by his inability to force them to, he decided to act *as if* the British had been defeated and ignore them, fortifying himself with the argument that it must be because they were counting on Russia that they continued to hold out. Hitler gambled that he could defeat the Soviet Union in a single campaign, and then turn to deal with Britain. But when the gamble failed to come off and the war on the eastern front dragged on into a second, a third, and even a fourth year, the price of leaving the British business unfinished became the two-front war which Hitler had always sworn he would avoid.

THE POSSIBILITY THAT Operation Sea Lion might never be launched had been recognized even in July and provisional planning begun by OKH for a campaign against Russia. On July 31, at a meeting with the chiefs of the armed forces, of which Halder has left a record in his diary, Hitler declared:

> Britain's hope lies in Russia and the United States. If the hopes pinned on Russia are disappointed, then America too will fall by the wayside, because elimination of Russia would tremendously increase Japan's power in the Far East. . . .
>
> Russia is the factor on which Britain is relying the most. Something must have happened in London! The British were completely down; now they have perked up again. . . . *With Russia smashed, Britain's last hope would be shattered.* Germany will then be master of Europe and the Balkans.
>
> *Decision: Russia's destruction must therefore be made a part of this struggle. Spring '41. The sooner Russia is crushed the better. Attack achieves its purpose only if Russian state can be shattered to its roots with one blow.* Holding any part of the country will not do. . . . If we start in May '41, we would have five months to finish the job in. Tackling it this year would still have been the best, but unified action would be impossible at this time. [47]*

Hitler's timetable allowed time for him to see if an invasion of the United Kingdom was practicable before the onset of autumn 1940, or if the British would give way before the threat of one. But from July both the OKW and OKH were engaged in preparing plans for an attack on the Soviet Union. At the end of August, Field Marshal von Bock was ordered to move his Army Group B HQ to Poland and prepare to take command of several army corps which were to be transferred there, without being given any indication of what his operational task would be.

The final postponement of the invasion of Britain on October 12 did not affect these preparations for the summer of 1941, but it left Hitler with the problem of what to do during the intervening period besides bombing British cities.

To do nothing meant losing impetus and wasting part of the limited time during which Germany still enjoyed the advantage of her early rearmament. An obvious direction in which to look was the Mediterranean, where Britain was vulnerable to an attack aimed at cutting her communications with her oil reserves in the Middle East and with India, Australia, New Zealand, and the Far East, and where Hitler had potential allies in Spain and Vichy France as well as his Axis partner, Italy.

*Italics in the original.

A Mediterranean strategy was particularly attractive to Raeder. For him and for the German navy, Britain not Russia remained the principal enemy, and on September 6 he urged Hitler to consider the capture of Gibraltar and the Suez Canal, the two keys to Britain's lifeline through the Mediterranean, as an alternative to the risks of attempting invasion of the United Kingdom. When the invasion was postponed, he renewed his advocacy in another meeting on September 26, pointing out that the Mediterranean sea route and control of the Middle East were the vital links in Britain's world position.

In Raeder's mind a Mediterranean strategy—focusing on the Middle East at one end, northwest Africa at the other—was nothing less than an alternative pattern for the war, concentrating on Britain, not Russia, as the chief enemy. At the time, Raeder believed that he had more than half convinced Hitler himself, who promised to discuss his proposals with Mussolini and did in fact devote considerable time to plans for operations in the Mediterranean during the last four months of 1940. Only later did it become clear, as Raeder admitted, that Hitler's mind was already made up on the invasion of Russia and that his interest in the southern theater of war sprang from assumptions very different from those of the German naval staff.

Granted the priority of the east, however, it still made sense, as limited objectives in the meantime, to add to the pressure on Britain from the bombing of her cities and the U-boat war by closing the Mediterranean to her shipping; and to safeguard northwest Africa and the Atlantic islands against occupation by the British and the Free French. He looked to Franco and the Spanish, however, to bear the main burden of any action in the western Mediterranean, just as he expected Mussolini and the Italians to take the lead in North Africa and the eastern Mediterranean, and less hopefully to Pétain and Vichy France to defend their interests in northwest Africa. The German commitment would be limited to a supporting role—specialist troops and dive-bombers for the capture of Gibraltar and a division or two to stiffen the Italian and Spanish armies.

The same idea of creating a coalition against the British revived Ribbentrop's dream of drawing in Japan as well as Italy. For their part, the Japanese, who had reacted sharply against the Nazi-Soviet Pact, now saw the opportunity of taking over the French and Dutch colonies in the Far East and were as eager as Mussolini to join in a division of the spoils. Ribbentrop's Tripartite Pact was finally signed on September 27, 1940, no longer directed like the Anti-Comintern Pact against Soviet Russia, but recognizing the leadership of Germany and Italy in establishing a New Order in Europe, and of Japan in establishing a New Order in Greater East Asia. [48]

The following month Hitler set off on a personal visit to Spain and France to see if he could remove the difficulties and persuade their governments to fall in with his plans.

The memory of his meeting with Franco, which took place at the frontier town of Hendaye on October 23, never ceased to vex Hitler. Instead of succumbing, as he was expected to, to Hitler's confident assertions of Germany's victory and Britain's defeat, Franco asked awkward questions and evaded any commitment to Hitler's offer of a treaty that would bring Spain into the war in January 1941 and provide her with German help in capturing Gibraltar. Hitler had to accept the failure of his effort after nine hours of talks, "rather than go through which again," he told Mussolini, "he would prefer to have three or four teeth taken out."

To all appearances, Hitler's visit to the eighty-five-year-old Pétain at Montoire went very well. The French marshal was ready to accept the principle of collaboration and agreed that France had a common interest with the Axis powers in seeing Britain defeated as soon as possible. In return, Hitler undertook that France should receive compensation from British possessions for any territorial losses she might suffer in Africa. All the details, however, remained to be worked out, and Marshal Pétain's comment to a friend has often been quoted: "It will take six months to discuss this program, and another six to forget it."

IX

WHATEVER SATISFACTION Hitler may have felt at obtaining a promise of French support against England was soon overshadowed by the unexpected news that he found on his return to Berlin that Mussolini was about to launch an attack on Greece. Before setting out for Spain, Hitler had met the Duce at the Brenner Pass, where he found his ally thoroughly irritated by German interest in securing French collaboration and by the prospect of seeing his own anticipated reward of the major share of the French colonial empire being sacrificed to it. On his return to Rome, Mussolini wrote reproachfully to Hitler that "the French thought because they had not fought, they had not been beaten." It was another unannounced German coup, however, this time in the Balkans, that forced him into retaliation.

After the Soviet occupation of Bessarabia, Hitler had become very anxious lest Rumania might disintegrate, and the security of the oil fields on which Germany depended might be threatened. The most immediate danger was the claims of Rumania's neighbors stimulated by the Russian example. Bulgaria demanded the southern Dobrudja at the mouth of the Danube, and Hungary the cession of Transylvania. The first was quickly settled, but Rumanian national pride was aroused over the second, and war between two of Germany's client states appeared possible. To prevent this—and the opportunity it might afford for the Russians to occupy the oil fields—Ribbentrop summoned both parties to Vienna and with Ciano's support dictated a second Vienna Accord dividing Transylvania between them (August 30).

In return for the loss of territory, Hitler offered Rumania a guarantee of her new frontier and secretly ordered a force of twelve divisions to be prepared for open intervention if necessary. The abdication of King Carol in protest over the accord opened the way for General Ion Antonescu (an admirer of the Führer) to set up a dictatorship, adhere to the Axis Pact (September 23), and "request" the dispatch of German troops to guarantee Rumania's independence. A secret order issued from Hitler's headquarters on September 20 instructed the German army and air force to send military missions to Rumania to organize and train her forces. The real task, "which must not become apparent either to the Rumanians or our own troops," was to protect the oil fields and to prepare for the deployment from Rumanian bases of German and Rumanian forces, "in case a war with Soviet Russia is forced upon us." The military missions were followed by German troops (including the Thirteenth Panzer Division), and Rumania was turned into a satellite state over which Hitler's hold was not shaken until the end of the war.

Hitler was well aware that Mussolini had ambitions to make the Balkans an Italian sphere of influence and that he regarded any German move in this direction with anxious jealousy. He had taken care to associate Italy with Germany in the Vienna Accord and had recognized the Italian interest in Yugoslavia and Greece, at the same time urging Ciano to delay any Italian action in either country in order to avoid further Balkan complications.

Hitler, however, had said nothing about the steps he was taking to secure control of Rumania, and when Mussolini learned the next week that German troops were moving in, he burst out to Ciano: "Hitler always faces me with a fait accompli. This time I am going to pay him back in his own coin. He will find out from the newspapers that I have occupied Greece."[49] This was a repetition of Mussolini's occupation of Albania as a tit-for-tat after Hitler occupied Prague. But this time the consequences were more serious. As part of the agreed Axis strategy, the plan had been for the Italians to drive the British out of Egypt. The Italian army had been slow to begin its advance across the Egyptian frontier and Marshal Pietro Badoglio, the Italian chief of staff, was strongly opposed to any extension of Italian commitments. Mussolini refused to listen, insisting on a bold coup to salve his bruised vanity and restore Italian prestige.

Hitler did not receive the letter informing him of Mussolini's intention until he got back from Montoire late on October 24. Whether the Duce succeeded in occupying Greece or not, his action was bound to set the whole Balkan peninsula in turmoil again just as Hitler had succeeded in bringing the Rumanian crisis under control. Quite apart from Bulgaria and Yugoslavia, both with long-standing claims on Greece, Russia would be provided with a further pretext for intervention, while the British would seize the opportunity to land in Greece and acquire bases on the European shores of the Mediterranean. Hitler decided that he must rejoin his special train and head for Florence in the hope that a personal appeal to Mussolini would persuade him to change his mind.

In fact, two hours before he reached Florence, on October 28, Hitler learned that the Italian attack had already begun, and the Duce could not wait to leave the station before telling the Führer of his first successes.

However angry Hitler felt, he allowed no trace of it to appear. Instead, he promised Mussolini full support and placed German parachute troops at his disposal if he required them for the occupation of Crete. He then reported at length on his negotiations with Franco and Pétain, and gave a belated but reassuring account of his relations with Rumania. Ciano recorded with relief that "perfect agreement" had been reached between the two Axis partners on all points. Appearances had been preserved but Paul Schmidt, Hitler's interpreter, wrote in his memoirs:

> Hitler went north that afternoon with bitterness in his heart. He had been frustrated three times—at Hendaye, Montoire, and now in Italy. In the lengthy winter evenings of the next four years, these long, exacting journeys were a constantly recurring theme of bitter reproach against ungrateful and unreliable friends, Axis partners and "deceiving" Frenchmen. [50]

FOUR MONTHS after the victories in the west had apparently left Hitler master of Europe, nothing had gone right for him. On November 4 he told the Wehrmacht commanders that everything must be done to get ready for "a major settling of scores with Russia," but when asked by the army High Command to clarify his priorities for the intervening period, his answer in his directive of November 12 (No. 18) was to list all the options, without any indication of which he meant to pursue. [51] He still hoped for French participation in the war against Britain and the defense of their African colonies; he still believed the Spaniards could be persuaded to capture Gibraltar and close the western Mediterranean to the British. An armored division and air forces were to be held in readiness in case the Italians needed support in North Africa; the army and the Luftwaffe must make preparations to occupy the Greek mainland, if the Italian attempt to do so failed; plans for the invasion of England might be revived in the spring of 1941, and the three services must try in every way to improve these.

The new factor was the importance Hitler now attached to Finland and the Balkans, and particularly Rumania, in view of his plans for attacking Russia. As a result there had been a marked deterioration in German-Russian relations in the late summer and autumn of 1940. After being careful not to become involved in the Russo-Finnish war, Hitler had resumed arms supplies to Finland at the end of July, and in September he had signed an agreement granting Germany the right to send troops to Norway via Finland and to station troops to protect the route. The Russians took these moves to be aimed at them and to be in breach of the Nazi-Soviet Pact. They felt this even more strongly after Hitler's intervention in Rumania in response to their own annexation of Bessarabia. The second Vienna Accord, giving Hungary half of Transylvania, and Bulgaria the southern Dobrudja at Rumania's expense, had been made without consulting Russia and had been followed—again without consultation—by the German guarantee of Rumania's remaining territory (which could only be a guarantee against Russia) and the arrival of German troops.

Ribbentrop's Tripartite Pact signed by Germany, Italy, and Japan on September 27 was bound to appear to the suspicious Stalin, who had not been informed of it until the last moment, as even more plainly directed against the Soviet Union and a revival of the defunct Anti-Comintern Pact. In fact Ribbentrop himself still saw the Nazi-Soviet Pact as his diplomatic masterpiece, and Britain, which had rebuffed him, as Germany's real enemy. If it was possible, he was eager to extend the Tripartite Pact to include the Soviet Union as well, so establishing a worldwide coalition committed to the defeat of Britain and the partition of her empire. There is no evidence that Hitler was prepared to consider such a reversal of policy seriously, but he agreed to invite Molotov to Berlin for discussions.

In a long letter that he dictated for Ribbentrop to sign, Hitler blamed everything that had happened during the past year, including German actions in Finland and Rumania, on the British, who were bent on causing trouble between Germany and the Soviet Union. Describing the Tripartite Pact as both anti-British and anti-American, he invited Stalin to join the other three powers in an alliance to carve up the world.

Stalin's dry reply was in noticeable contrast to Hitler's windy rhetoric:

> My dear Herr Ribbentrop,
>
> I have received your letter. I thank you sincerely for your confidence, as well as for the instructive analysis of recent events. . . . M. Molotov acknowledges that he is under obligation to pay you a return visit in Berlin. He hereby accepts your invitation. . . .
>
> As to joint deliberation on some issues with Japanese and Italian participation, I am of the opinion (without being opposed to this idea in principle) that this question would have to be submitted to a previous examination.
>
> Yours, etc.
> J. Stalin[52]

Whatever Ribbentrop may have hoped for, Hitler had not changed his mind about attacking Russia in 1941. The evidence points to his agreeing to invite Molotov with the purpose of sounding out the Russians' current attitude, and misleading them about his own plans, rather than to exploring the advantages of combining with Russia to eliminate Britain first. The Directive No. 18 issued on the day Molotov arrived in Berlin (November 12, 1940) spoke of political discussions to "clarify Russia's attitude for the coming period" but added that, "regardless of what results these discussions have," all preparations for the east were to be continued and further directives would follow as soon as the plan of operations had been submitted and approved.

When the discussions with Molotov began, Hitler sought to put the discussion of German-Russian relations on the loftiest plane, "beyond all petty momentary considerations." To lay down the course of these over a long period was only possible, "when two nations such as the Germans and Russians had at their helm men who possessed sufficient authority to commit their countries to a development in a definite direction."[33] Looking ahead, Hitler saw the need to forestall the development of American power, which had a more solid foundation than that of the other Anglo-Saxon power, England. The European continental powers had to act jointly against the Anglo-Saxon and set up a kind of Monroe Doctrine for the whole of Europe and Africa, dividing up the colonial territories they each needed and establishing their respective spheres of interest.

Molotov ignored Hitler's attempt to beguile him with world-historical projections and, instead, raised a series of down-to-earth questions about German-Russian relations in the present. What were the Germans doing in Finland, which had been allotted to the Russian sphere of influence? What was the significance of the Tripartite Pact? How far was Germany prepared to respect Russia's interests in Bulgaria, Rumania, and Turkey? What was the meaning of the New Order Hitler spoke of in Europe and Asia and what role would the USSR be given in it?

Hitler assured him there was no question of confronting Russia with a fait accompli. The real difficulty had been establishing collaboration among Germany, France, and Italy. Only now that a settlement between these countries had been accepted in outline had he thought it possible to approach Russia about "the first concrete steps toward comprehensive collaboration," not only in regard to the problems of Western Europe, which were to be settled by Germany, Italy, and France, but also in regard to the Asian issues that were the concern of Russia and Japan, and in which Germany was ready to act as a mediator. "The U.S.A. had no business in Europe, Africa, or Asia."

The following day, Hitler attempted to forestall Molotov's complaints by admitting that the necessities of war—the need to safeguard supplies of raw materials—had obliged Germany to intervene in areas where she had no permanent interests, such as Finland (where Germany needed to secure nickel and lumber) and Rumania (where she was concerned about her oil supplies). "Much greater successes can be achieved in the future, provided that Russia did not now seek successes in territories in which Germany was interested for the future." Molotov was not prepared to let these issues, "which spoiled the atmosphere of German-Russian relations," be brushed aside, and a sharp exchange followed over Finland. Hitler asked if Russia wanted to go to war against Finland again; a war in the Baltic would put a heavy strain on their relations. What more did Russia want in Finland? "A settlement on the same scale as in Bessarabia," was Molotov's reply.

In an effort to bring the discussion back to "more important questions,"

Hitler repeated that both sides agreed in principle that Finland belonged to the Russian sphere of influence, and continued:

> After the conquest of England the British Empire would be apportioned as a gigantic worldwide estate in bankruptcy of [40m. square km.]. In this bankrupt estate there would be access for Russia to the ice-free and really open ocean. Thus far, a minority of 45 million Englishmen had ruled the 600 million inhabitants of the British Empire. He was about to crush this minority. . . .
>
> In these circumstances there arose worldwide perspectives. . . . Russia's participation in the solution of these problems would have to be arranged. All the countries that could possibly be interested in the bankrupt estate would have to stop all controversies and concern themselves exclusively with apportioning the British Empire. This applied to Germany, France, Italy, Russia, and Japan.

Molotov replied that he had followed the Führer's argument with interest and agreed with everything that he had understood. But the decisive thing was first to be clear about German-Russian collaboration. Italy and Japan could be included later. After sitting impassively through a further visionary flight by Hitler, Molotov resumed where he had left off: His next question was the Balkans and the German guarantee to Rumania. If Germany was not prepared to revoke that, what would she say to a Russian guarantee to Bulgaria? Hitler at once retorted that he had not heard of any such guarantee being requested by the Bulgarians. When Molotov pressed him on the Black Sea and the Dardanelles, he added that "if Germany were looking for sources of friction with Russia, she would not need the straits."

Schmidt, who acted as interpreter, wrote that he had not been present at such sharp exchanges since the conversations with Chamberlain during the Sudeten crisis. Franco had only angered Hitler by evasion; Molotov answered back and argued with him. This was a liberty that Hitler did not forgive and he took no further part in the talks, unexpectedly failing to appear at the banquet that Molotov gave in the Russian embassy the same evening.

Halfway through the dinner, a British air raid drove the host and guests to take shelter below ground. Ribbentrop with characteristic maladroitness chose the occasion to confront Molotov with the draft of an agreement that would bring the Soviet Union into the Tripartite Pact, with two additional secret protocols, on the model of the Nazi-Soviet Pact, defining the four powers' spheres of interest. Apart from territorial revisions in Europe at the conclusion of peace, Germany's aspirations were said to be centered in Central Africa; Italy's in North and East Africa; Japan's in Southeast Asia. It was proposed that the USSR's be defined as lying to the south of her national territory in the direction of the Indian Ocean.

This was a bold but transparent proposal aimed at diverting Russia from her traditional areas of expansion—in Eastern Europe, the Balkans, and the

Mediterranean, where she would clash with Germany and Italy—to the Persian Gulf and the Indian Ocean, where she would become embroiled with the British. To make it more attractive, the second protocol promised German and Italian cooperation in detaching Turkey from her commitments to the West and replacing the Montreux Convention with a new agreement for the Straits. As an additional attraction, Ribbentrop held out tantalizing but vague hopes of securing for Russia a nonaggression pact with Japan and Japanese recognition of Outer Mongolia and Sinkiang as lying within the Soviet sphere of influence.

Molotov, as dour as ever, responded with a list of European questions in which Russia was not prepared to disinterest herself: the future of Rumania and Hungary as well as Turkey and Bulgaria; what the Axis proposed for Yugoslavia and Greece; Poland and the Baltic. As Hitler had done, Ribbentrop made one last effort to pull the conversation back to the "decisive question": Was the Soviet Union prepared to cooperate in the liquidation of the British Empire? When Ribbentrop went on insisting that Britain was finished, Molotov made his famous reply: "If this is so, why are we in this shelter, and whose are these bombs that are falling?" His final word was that "all these great issues of tomorrow" could not be separated from those of today and the fulfillment of existing agreements.

MOLOTOV HAD HAD his hands tied and was unable to respond to the proposals with which the Germans attempted to dazzle him. Stalin, however, once he had time to study them, saw advantage in joining Ribbentrop's Four-Power Pact. Russia had done exceptionally well out of the original Nazi-Soviet Pact, and Stalin was prepared to accept a sphere of influence with its center redefined as the area south of Baku and Batum in the general direction of the Persian Gulf. A Soviet reply was sent on November 25, less than two weeks after Molotov's return, accepting Ribbentrop's proposal, provided that Hitler in his turn was prepared to accept certain conditions. These were the immediate withdrawal of all German troops from Finland and a Russo-Bulgarian treaty which, together with a base on the Bosporus to be granted by Turkey, would give the Russians control of passage to and from the Black Sea. [54]

Despite repeated inquiries from Moscow, however, no German reply was ever sent to the Russian note. Hitler's offer had been designed to divert Russia from Europe. Once it became clear that Stalin still insisted on regarding Finland and the Balkans as within his sphere of influence, Hitler lost such interest as he had had in further negotiations. Under the impression produced by Molotov's stubborn questioning and insistence on Soviet rights, Hitler had told Göring, before the Russians left Berlin, that he was confirmed in his decision to attack the Soviet Union in the spring. Göring tried to dissuade him, arguing as Raeder had that they should concentrate on driving the British out of the Mediterranean before turning against Russia, an operation that he had always thought best deferred to 1943 or

1944. Hitler was not to be persuaded; he was convinced that Britain was powerless to damage Germany and could be dealt with after Russia had been defeated. Whatever doubts remained were removed by the Soviet reply and Stalin's attempt to set conditions. On December 5 Hitler ordered the army High Command to accelerate the preparations for an attack in the spring: "The decision about European hegemony will be made in the struggle against Russia."[55]

Hitler was still left with the problem of how to deal with the other issues that had to be resolved in the Mediterranean and the Balkans. The most pressing were the consequences of Mussolini's ill-prepared attack on Greece. By December 7 the Italians had been driven back by the Greeks into Albania and were in danger of a complete rout, unless Germany came immediately to their aid. When Hitler asked for a meeting with the Duce, Mussolini declined to face him. His armies were no more successful in North Africa than in Greece. The battle of Sidi Barrani, which began on December 9, led to the collapse of the Italian threat to Egypt and the headlong flight of Marshal Rodolfo Graziani's Italian troops across Libya pursued by the British. At the other end of the Mediterranean, Franco's final refusal to take part forced Hitler to drop the idea of a joint attack on Gibraltar.

Faced with a crisis, Hitler recovered the power of acting decisively which had eluded him in the past five months. On December 10 he ordered Luftwaffe formations to move to the south of Italy and attack Alexandria, the Suez Canal, and the straits between Sicily and Africa; preparations for an armored division to move to Libya in support of the Italians were to be accelerated.

On December 13 he issued Directive No. 20 for Operation Maritsa, the invasion of Greece. A German task force was to be formed in Rumania, with a maximum of twenty-four divisions, ready to move across Bulgaria and into Greece as soon as the weather permitted, so denying the British the use of bases from which they could bomb Italy and Rumania.

Finally, on December 18, he signed the most fateful of all his directives, No. 21, for Operation Barbarossa:

> The German armed forces must be prepared *to crush Soviet Russia in a quick campaign* even before the conclusion of the war against England. . . .
> Preparations requiring more time are to be started now, if this has not yet been done, and are to be completed by May 15, 1941. . . .
> The mass of the Russian Army in Western Russia is to be destroyed by driving forward deep armored wedges; and the retreat of units capable of combat into the vastness of Russian territory is to be prevented. . . .
> The ultimate objective is to establish a defense line against Asiatic Russia from a line running from the Volga River to Archangel. Then, the last industrial area left to Russia in the Urals can be destroyed by the Luftwaffe.[56]

Hitler gambled that whatever operations might be needed to resolve the Balkan crisis and rescue the Italians in North Africa could be carried out in time for the preparations for Barbarossa to be completed by May 15. His decision remained a secret—only nine copies of the directive were distributed—but for the next five months everything was to be subordinated to this overriding purpose.

SIXTEEN

Hitler's New Order

I

FOR BOTH HITLER AND STALIN, the German-Russian war was the supreme test of their careers. They approached it, however, in very different ways.

Although Hitler, in an expansive mood, would talk of world power, a war between continents challenging the Anglo-Saxon world hegemony, the most consistent objective in his thinking about foreign policy was the conquest of *Lebensraum* in the east as the answer to Germany's economic and social problems. "And when we speak of new territory in Europe," he wrote in *Mein Kampf*, "we must think principally of Russia and the border states subject to her. Destiny itself seems to wish to point out the way for us here."[1] In 1936 he repeated publicly: "If we had at our disposal the Urals, with their incalculable wealth of raw materials and the forests of Siberia, and if the unending wheatfields of the Ukraine lay within Germany, our country would swim in plenty."[2]

Russia would provide not only the raw materials but the manpower needs of Germany as well. "The Slavs," Hitler declared, "are a mass of born slaves who feel the need of a master."[3] This racist version—the opposite of "the civilizing mission" of the Germans in the East—was Hitler's special contribution to the traditional theme of the *Drang nach Osten* (Germany's Drive to the East). Incapable of establishing a state themselves—so Hitler argued—the Slavs owed the creation and maintenance of the Russian state to "the Germanic nucleus of its governing classes."[4] The Bolshevik revolution had destroyed these. Their place had been taken by the Jews with whom Hitler identified the Bolshevik leadership, and "the Jew" could no more hold the Russian state together than the Russians could get rid of the Jews. "The colossal empire in the East is ripe for dissolution. And the end of Jewish domination in Russia will also be the end of Russia as a state."[5]

The decision to attack Russia brought Hitler back to his roots in the National Socialist movement of the 1920s. The diplomatic maneuvers in which he had become involved by the need to secure Russian neutrality while he destroyed Poland, and then by the need to eliminate the threat of Western intervention before he could turn east, were now replaced by the clear-cut decision to go directly for his primary objective by the only means in which he had any faith, by the use of force. In the inevitable letter which he addressed to Mussolini on the day before the attack began, Hitler wrote:

> Let me say one more thing, Duce. Since I struggled through to this decision, I again feel spiritually free. The partnership with the Soviet Union . . . seemed to me to be a break with my whole origin, my concepts and my former obligations. I am happy now to be relieved of these mental agonies.[6]

What had held Hitler back from taking this step earlier had been the need to secure first the conditions he had laid down in *Mein Kampf* as essential to success: the elimination of France as a military power and the conclusion of alliances with Italy and Britain. The first and second had been achieved; it was the third which baffled and eluded him. For alliance he had substituted British neutrality in return for a guarantee of the British Empire. When this too was rejected, he ordered the elimination of Britain by invasion, and when that in turn had to be abandoned, he sought to break the British will to resist by the night bombing of their cities.

The significance of the German defeat in the Battle of Britain now becomes clear. It confronted Hitler with a choice between two very different strategies. The first was to concentrate all his forces on Britain as the main enemy. This was the naval-Mediterranean strategy proposed by Raeder and favored by Göring; it meant postponing any idea of attacking Russia until the British had been knocked out. The second was to put Britain "on hold," and concentrate everything on the conquest of Russia in a single campaign. This would not only eliminate the Soviet Union as an enemy but provide the Germans with such resources as to destroy any British hope of challenging their domination of the continent. Apart from the strategic difficulty of finding a clear-cut way of defeating Britain comparable with the knockout blow which he planned against Russia, Hitler constantly repeated that the destruction of the British Empire—unlike that of the Russian State—had never been part of his program and that, if he undertook it, other powers, not Germany, would be the principal beneficiaries.

In the closing months of the war, in February 1945, when he was faced with the inevitability of defeat as the Red Army closed in on Berlin, Hitler referring to 1941, claimed that he had had no choice:

> I had no more difficult decision to take than the attack on Russia. I had always said we must avoid a two-front war at all costs, and no one will doubt that I more than anyone had reflected on Napoleon's Russian experience. Then why this war against Russia? And why at the time I chose?

His answer was that the only way to bring the British to make peace and so end the prospect of a long, drawn-out war—with increasing participation by the Americans—was to destroy their hopes of Russia's intervention. "For us it was an inescapable compulsion to remove the Russian piece from the European chess board." The very existence of Russia, Hitler repeated, was a threat which could prove fatal to Germany. If the Germans had not struck first before Russian rearmament was complete, they and the rest of Europe would have been overrun by a Russian attack with superior forces:

> Our only chance of defeating Russia lay in anticipating her. . . . Time was working against us. . . . In the course of the final weeks I was obsessed with the fear that Stalin might forestall me.

As proof Hitler claimed that Stalin was steadily reducing the supply of raw materials on which Germany was dependent: "If they were not prepared to give us of their own free will the supplies we had to have, we had no alternative but to go and take them by force."[7] The German as well as the Russian evidence points to exactly the opposite conclusion. Far from reducing, Stalin increased supplies to Germany at a time when Russia could ill afford to do so, for example, in oil and grain. After some sharp bargaining by the Germans, a complete set of six German-Soviet treaties was signed in Moscow on January 10, 1941. The centerpiece was an economic agreement by which Russia agreed to deliver a long list of commodities in the period up to August 1942 to the value of 620 to 640 million Reichsmarks. At the last moment Stalin personally intervened ("a decision of the highest authority") to increase the deliveries of crucial raw materials in short supply: 6,000 tons of copper, 1,500 tons of nickel, and 500 tons each of tin, tungsten, and molybdenum.[8]

Schnurre, who had conducted the economic negotiations throughout, reported that his opposite number, Mikoyan, could not have been more helpful. A jubilant Foreign Office circular sent out to German embassies instructing officials how to present this described the deal as "the biggest economic treaty that has ever been concluded between two states . . . settling also all other questions pending between Germany and the Soviet Union." The Foreign Office circular concluded:

> The Soviet Union has delivered everything she promised. In many fields she has delivered even more than had originally been agreed upon. In the organization of the huge shipments, the Soviet Union has performed in a really admirable manner. Now the trade and transportation channels are operating smoothly.[9]

As before the Polish campaign, Hitler convinced himself that Germany had been forced to act first in self-defense. But the documentary evidence establishes that the detailed planning for Operation Barbarossa made no provision for having to meet a Russian attack, and that both the OKW and the OKH treated the transfer of Soviet troops closer to the border as purely defensive moves. Confidence in the German camp was high because all reports showed that the Russians were ill-prepared to defend themselves, let alone launch an offensive. This is supported, as we shall see, by the evidence from the Russian side and by the actual course of events when the fighting began. The best comment on later attempts to represent Barbarossa as a preventive war is an OKW directive put out on June 21, the day the German attack was due to start. Unperturbed by reports of the Red Army massing forces in the areas around Lvov and Bialystok, the OKW welcomed the news for two reasons: it would facilitate the German plan to encircle Russian troops and enable German propaganda "to convey the impression that the Russians were ready to pounce and that the German attack was a military imperative."

The basis of German confidence was the belief, confirmed by the Red Army's performance in the Finnish war, that the Soviet leadership had been so weakened by the purges that it could not withstand a concentrated German attack, and that organized resistance would collapse. That this was a fatal miscalculation was already clear by the time the German Sixth Army surrendered at Stalingrad in February 1943, and to many today appears so obvious as to be difficult to explain. But in 1940–41 this was far from being Hitler's view alone.

For, whatever reservations the German generals might later claim to have felt, they made no objections comparable to those which they had raised against the offensive in the west. From the summer of 1940, Hitler, the OKW, and the OKH were agreed in reckoning on completing the defeat of Russia in a single campaigning season, originally five months, June–October 1941. The estimates made in London and Washington were even shorter. The Joint Intelligence Committee in London allowed Germany four to six weeks to occupy the Ukraine and reach Moscow, and on June 23, Frank Knox, the U.S. secretary of the navy, wrote to Roosevelt: "The best opinion I can get is that it will take anywhere from six weeks to two months for Hitler to clean up on Russia." [10]

Unlike Hitler, who felt reinvigorated at the prospect of freeing himself from the Nazi-Soviet Pact, Stalin did all he could to preserve it, stubbornly refusing to accept the evidence that the Germans were preparing to launch an attack on Russia. While Hitler's self-confidence reached a peak in 1941, Stalin showed himself more unsure and more in danger of losing his grip as a leader than at any other time in his career. Throughout the first six months of 1941 he followed a policy of appeasement toward Hitler, and right up to the actual German attack on June 22, forbade the Soviet commanders to take any step which might give the Germans the opportunity to claim provocation.

Before we turn, however, to the evidence substantiating such a view of Stalin's attitude, and the reasons for it, it is logical to look first at the preparations made on the German side between December 1940 and June 1941, to which developments in the Soviet Union provided so inadequate a response.

·   ·   ·

DURING THESE six months, the German General Staff gradually assembled on the Soviet frontiers an army of almost 3.2 million men. The Balkan campaigns of the spring of 1941 complicated and delayed the buildup, but considering the inadequate rail and road communications in Eastern Europe and the problems of supplying so huge a number of men and machines, it was a tour de force of German organization.

Everything, however, was based on the premise that the enemy could be defeated in a single campaign, before the onset of the Russian winter brought movement to a halt. Although the distances were far greater—1,000 kilometers from the frontier to Moscow, 1,400 to Rostov, and 2,000 to the oil of the Caucasus, with much poorer roads—it was still as much a blitzkrieg that was planned as the western offensive of May 1940. If the gamble did not come off, then the German army, at the end of long, difficult lines of communication, would be in trouble. Even if it proved possible to maintain supply lines over several hundred miles, General Thomas calculated that there was sufficient fuel oil for only two months of fighting. Hence the urgency of reaching the oil fields in the Caucasus. The German forces were provided with neither winter clothing nor anti-freeze to face a winter in which temperatures regularly fell to −20° or −25 °C.* And behind the army stood an economy which, despite the supplies drawn from the occupied countries, was still not organized to meet the demands of the "total war" Hitler proclaimed.

The appointment in March 1940 of Fritz Todt as minister for weapons and munitions was eventually to lay the foundations for the full-scale mobilization, two years later, of Germany's economic resources. But until the autumn of 1941 it added only one more to the competing agencies whose conflicts prevented the emergence of a long-term overall plan. An example is the production of ammunition for the army. In the second and third quarters of 1940 following Todt's appointment, this rose to 60 to 90 percent above the 1939 level, accompanied by an even sharper increase in the production of aircraft and tanks; but the quantity of munitions produced in the final quarter of 1940 showed a fall which continued in the first six months of 1941, and in the last quarter of that year it was down to, or even below, the level of 1939. This was despite an order issued by Hitler on September 28, 1940 which switched priority from landing craft and bombers to munitions and the other needs of the army for its attack on Russia. Even more striking was the drop in aircraft production, despite the high priority it enjoyed.

How little Hitler foresaw the rate of losses in the Russian campaign is shown by his order on the very day before the invasion began, June 21, 1941, reversing the decision of the previous September and now giving priority to the production of aircraft, tanks, and U-boats over the army's

*In August 1941 Goebbels' suggestion of a national collection of warm clothing was actually turned down by the army leadership.

needs for weapons and munitions. Two months later, on August 16, "in view of the impending victory over Russia," he ordered the size of the armed forces to be reduced and, following the principles of the blitzkrieg, gave instructions that the productive capacity, supply of raw materials, and labor strength of the armaments industry should not be increased further. No provision was made, either in the economic or military preparations, for the possibility of falling short either in the timetable or objectives of the largest military operation ever mounted up to that time.

Whatever shortfall there might be was to be made good from the ruthless exploitation of the territories occupied—grain from the Ukraine and oil from the Caucasus. The planners expected the armies in the east to live off the land and counted on additional deliveries of seven million tons of grain a year to feed the population of the Reich. In a report of the *Wirtschaftstab Ost* (Economic Staff East) dated May 23, 1941, the consequences of such a policy were accepted without any attempt to disguise them. The Ukraine in the future, instead of feeding the rest of the Soviet Union, must turn its face to Europe.

> The population of the [more northerly] regions, especially the urban, will have to look forward to the severest famine. They will die or have to migrate to Siberia. . . .
>
> Efforts to save the population from starving to death by bringing surplus food from the black soil region can be made only at the expense of feeding Europe. They would undermine Germany's ability to hold out in the war and to withstand the blockade. There must be absolute clarity on this point. From this . . . there follows the extinction of industry as well as of a large percentage of the human beings in the hitherto deficit areas of Russia.

The report added that the views expressed "had received the approval of the highest authorities since it is also in unison with the political aim of pushing back the Great Russians." [11]

BEYOND SATISFYING the immediate needs of Germany during the war, there remained to be decided the long-term future of an area which, assuming the objective of a line from Archangel to Astrakhan was achieved, contained over a hundred million people. Hitler had never thought of the invasion of Russia ending with a conventional peace treaty; it was to be war of conquest, the purpose of which was not only to overthrow the Bolshevik regime but to prevent the emergence of any successor Russian state. But what was to replace it?

An unusual insight into Hitler's mind in 1941–42 is provided by his table talk, records of the monologues to which his guests and entourage were subjected after meals at Hitler's headquarters, either the permanent installation in East Prussia which Hitler called *Wolfsschanze* (Fort Wolf), or his temporary Russian headquarters at Vinnitsa in the Ukraine which he called

Werwolf. Hitler would not allow a tape recorder to be used, but he agreed to Bormann's suggestion that a party official might be admitted to his meals who would sit in a corner and take notes unobtrusively. These were later corrected and approved by Bormann, as a record of the Führer's thoughts.

The months from March to the end of October 1941 were a period in which Hitler felt more convinced than ever of his genius, the highpoint of his fantastic career in which he saw himself as the peer of Napoleon, Bismarck, and Frederick the Great—characters to whom he referred in familiar terms—pursuing "the Cyclopean task which the building of an empire means for a single man." [12]

The character of that empire was a subject which fired his imagination and constantly recurred in his talk. After the evening meal on July 27, he defined its limits as a line 200 to 300 kilometers *east* of the Urals; the Germans must hold this line in perpetuity and never allow any other military power to establish itself to the *west* of it.

> It should be possible for us to control this region to the East, with 250,000 men plus a cadre of good administrators. Let's learn from the English, who, with 250,000 men in all, including 50,000 soldiers, govern 400 million Indians. This space in Russia must always be dominated by Germans. . . .
>
> Nothing would be a worse mistake on our part than to seek to educate the masses there. . . .
>
> We'll take the southern part of the Ukraine, especially the Crimea, and make it an exclusively German colony. There'll be no harm in pushing out the population that's there now. The German colonist will be the soldier-peasant, and for that I'll take professional soldiers. . . . For those of them who are sons of peasants, the Reich will provide a completely equipped farm. The soil costs us nothing, we have only the farm to build . . . These soldier-peasants will be given arms, so that at the slightest danger they can be at their posts when we summon them. [13]

Hitler returned to the subject on the evening of October 17, when Todt and Gauleiter Sauckel (who was responsible for conscripting foreign workers) provided an appreciative audience:

> This Russian desert, we shall populate it. . . . We'll take away its character of an Asiatic steppe, we'll Europeanize it. With this object we have undertaken the construction of roads that will lead to the southernmost part of the Crimea and to the Caucasus. These roads will be studded along their whole length with German towns and around these towns our colonists will settle.
>
> As for the two or three million men whom we need to accomplish this task, we'll find them quicker than we think. They'll come from Germany, Scandinavia, the Western countries, and America. I shall no longer be here to see all that, but in twenty years, the Ukraine will already be a home for twenty million inhabitants, besides the natives. . . .
>
> We shan't settle in the Russian towns and we'll let them go to pieces

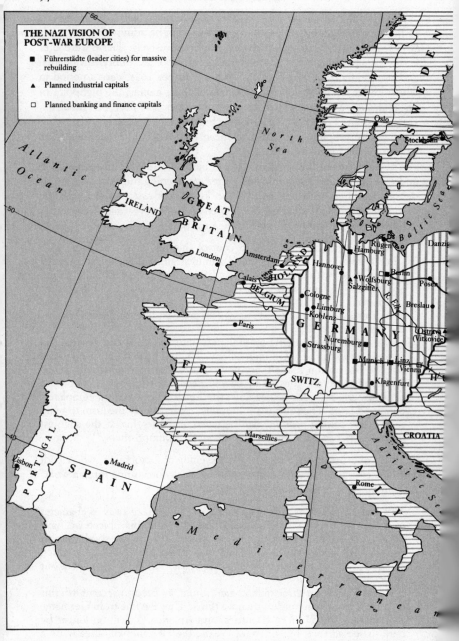

THE NAZI VISION OF POST-WAR EUROPE

- ■ Führerstädte (leader cities) for massive rebuilding
- ▲ Planned industrial capitals
- □ Planned banking and finance capitals

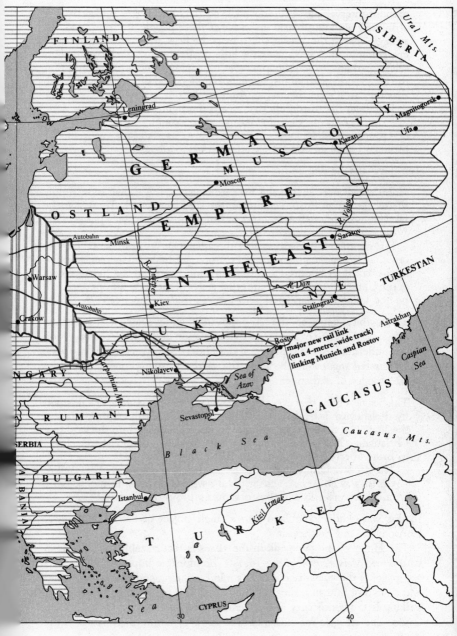

FINLAND

Leningrad

SIBERIA

Ural Mts.

Magnitogorsk

Ufa

Kazan

G E R M A N

M U S C O V Y

O S T L A N D

E M P I R E

Moscow

R. Volga

Saratov

Autobahn

Minsk

I N T H E E A S T

R. Dnieper

Warsaw

R. Don

TURKESTAN

U

Kiev

Stalingrad

Autobahn

Crakow

K R A I N E

Rostov

Astrakhan

major new rail link
(on a 4-metre-wide track)
linking Munich and Rostov

NGARY

Nikolayev

Carpathian Mts.

Sea of
Azov

Caspian
Sea

RUMANIA

CAUCASUS

Sevastopol

Caucasus Mts.

SERBIA

B l a c k   S e a

BULGARIA

Istanbul

Kizil Irmak

ALBANIA

T   U   R   K   E   Y

30

40

S e a

CYPRUS

without intervening. And above all, no remorse on this subject! We're absolutely without obligations as far as these people are concerned. To struggle against the hovels, chase away the fleas, provide German teachers, bring out newspapers—very little of that for us! We'll confine ourselves, perhaps, to setting up a radio transmitter, under our control. For the rest, let them know just enough to understand our highway signs, so that they won't get themselves run over by our vehicles.

For them the word "liberty" means the right to wash on feast days. . . . There's only one duty: to Germanize this country by the immigration of Germans and to look upon the natives as Redskins. . . . In this business I shall go straight ahead, cold-bloodedly. [14]

Ten days later he declared:

Nobody will ever snatch the East from us! . . . We shall soon supply the wheat for all Europe, the coal, the steel, the wood. To exploit the Ukraine properly—that new Indian Empire—we need only peace in the West. . . .

For me the object is to exploit the advantages of continental hegemony. . . . When we are masters of Europe, we have a dominant position in the world. A hundred and thirty million people in the Reich, ninety in the Ukraine. Add to these the other states of the New Europe and we'll be 400 million as compared with the 130 million Americans. [15]

The mythical figure of "the Jew" appears in Hitler's table talk, as in *Mein Kampf,* as the source of the racial contamination and social decomposition which undermine Aryan supremacy. But Hitler also projects onto "the Jew" the frustrated anger which he felt in 1941 with Christian protests against the racist practice of euthanasia.*

The heaviest blow that ever struck humanity was the coming of Christianity. Bolshevism is Christianity's illegitimate child. Both are inventions of the Jew. The deliberate lie in religion was introduced into the world by Christianity. Bolshevism practices a lie of the same nature, when it claims to bring liberty to men, only to enslave them. [16]

The decisive falsification of Jesus' doctrine was the word of St. Paul. [17]

Christ was an Aryan, and St. Paul used his doctrine to mobilize the criminal underworld and thus organize a proto-Bolshevism. [18]

In this way, Hitler combined into a single object of hatred "the Jew," Christianity, and Bolshevism.

The Hitler of the table talk in the 1940s is recognizably the same man who wrote *Mein Kampf* in the 1920s. The indelible impression left by its 700 pages is the vulgarity of Hitler's mind, cunning and brutal, intolerant, and devoid of human feeling, as unabashed as it was ignorant. But no less striking is the consistency and systematic character of his views, however crude. The struggle for existence was a law of nature; hardness was the

*See below, pp. 735–36.

supreme virtue; the key to history lay in race; power was the prerogative of a racial elite; the masses were capable only of carrying out orders; the individual existed only for the *Volk*; force was the only means by which anything lasting was accomplished; "world-historical figures" acting as the agents of Providence could not be bound or judged by the standards of ordinary morality.

Hitler not only believed what he said; he acted on it. Substitute "class" for "race," the Communist party exercising dictatorship in the name of the proletariat for a racial elite; "the individual exists only for the state" instead of "only for the *Volk*"; "agents of history" for "agents of Providence"—and Stalin would have found little to disagree with. Together they represent the twentieth century's most formidable examples of those *simplificateurs terribles* whom the nineteenth century historian Jakob Burckhardt foresaw as characteristic of the century to follow.

HITLER WAS INCAPABLE, however, of translating his vision of the future into concrete plans. A year later, in November 1942, when the decisive battle for Stalingrad was already joined, he was still insisting: "The goal of *Ostpolitik* in the long run is to open up an area of settlement for a hundred million Germans in the east." [19] But he was no nearer to explaining how this was to be achieved. The crucial questions remained unanswered, and the confusion of purpose at the top was compounded by the rivalry of different agencies characteristic of the "authoritarian anarchy" of the Third Reich.

Hitler got as far as laying down that, as the German army advanced, the newly occupied areas should be turned over from military to civilian administration under Reich Commissars answerable to himself. He then assigned the job of working out plans for the three "protectorates" he envisaged, in the Baltic States, Byelorussia, and the Ukraine, to Alfred Rosenberg, appointing him in the summer of 1941 to head a ministry for occupied territories in the east which soon became known as the *Ostministerium*.

Rosenberg was the son of a German shoemaker, born in Reval (Tallinn) Estonia, which at that time—as again in 1941—was part of the Russian Empire. While feeling himself a German, he was steeped in Russian culture, a double inheritance which was to shape his attitude toward his new responsibilities. After the Russian Revolution, he landed in Munich and was an early recruit to the Nazi party, becoming editor of the party newspaper, *Völkischer Beobachter,* in 1921. After the 1923 putsch, Hitler entrusted him with "leading the party" while he was himself in prison—an appointment widely regarded as intended to make sure that Hitler would have no rival and that the party would welcome his return with relief. Since then, while loyal to Hitler and rewarded with a number of offices, Rosenberg had failed to make a success of any of them. A party ideologue and author of the pretentious *Myth of the Twentieth Century,* he was the butt of Goebbels's malicious wit; as foreign policy expert he was ostracized by the Foreign Office; as party politician he picked the wrong side in the quarrel between the SA and the SS and ended up with Himmler as a dangerous enemy.

Now nearing fifty, Rosenberg saw himself about to achieve his life's ambition and enjoy the authority he craved as the party's leading expert on Russia, head of the key ministry for which he set about recruiting a large field staff. In fact it was to prove the culmination of a lifetime of failure, in which, while vainly protesting that all orders for the east must come from his office, he was ignored, brushed aside, undermined, even forgotten. It is difficult not to believe that Hitler saw in Rosenberg, as he had in 1923–24, a minister who could never present a challenge to his authority.*

One of the rivals for whom Rosenberg was to prove no match, Göring, had originally sought to dissuade Hitler from attacking Russia, but once the decision was taken, insisted that it was he who must be given the control of the economic exploitation of the occupied territories as part of his responsibilities for the Four-Year Plan. To strengthen his position, Göring joined with General Thomas and the OKW's Economic Armaments Office (WiRüAmt) in setting up a new agency, *Wirtschaftsstab Ost* (Economic Staff for the East), with responsibility for economic policy in the east and its execution.

Himmler had already staked his claim before Rosenberg was appointed. Its basis was the police and security functions of the SS, but, according to Keitel's OKW directive of March 13, 1941, it also included,

> By direction of the Führer, special tasks in preparation for political administration which result from the final encounter between two opposite political systems.
> Within the framework of these tasks the Reichsführer SS acts independently and on his own responsibility. [20]

As in Poland, the SS was to set up "task forces" *(Einsatzgruppen)* which were to move in behind the army and systematically exterminate, without any pretense of trials, the ideological and racial enemies of the Third Reich, communists, Jews, Gypsies, and other "anti-social elements."

Of the other Nazi bosses who sought to have a hand in shaping Germany's *Ostpolitik,* the most influential was Martin Bormann, the last to establish his own power base through the control of the Nazi party machine. He had built this up as Hess's chief of staff before replacing him as the Führer's deputy for party affairs. Bormann combined this with an increasing influence on Hitler as the secretary who was always at his side, emerging as a major player in the wartime intrigues at the top of the Nazi hierarchy. Unlike Rosenberg and Himmler, Bormann's absorbing interest

---

*In the early 1930s, Hermann Rauschning reports, Hitler said: "Have you not noticed that Germans who have lived a long time in Russia can never again be Germans? The huge spaces have fascinated them. After all, Rosenberg is rabid against the Russians only because they would not allow him to be a Russian." Rauschning, *Hitler Speaks* (London: 1939), p. 135.

was not in the East as such, but in maximizing his own power and blocking an increase in anyone else's. He had strongly supported the choice of Rosenberg for the *Ostministerium* because he preferred a weak to a strong minister in that position; he was equally determined to prevent his most dangerous rival, Himmler, from becoming the decisive policymaker for the East and to press the claims of the party against those of the SS.

One way of doing this, and also of reducing Rosenberg's effectiveness, was by securing the appointment of leading party Gauleiters to take over the civil government of the new "protectorates," as the army advanced. The argument with which he convinced Hitler was that the Nazi party, as "the carrier of the political will" of the German people, should have the decisive voice in the future administration of the East. The fact that this would checkmate the claims of Himmler and the SS was sufficient to win the assent of Rosenberg. Only later did the unwitting minister for the East discover that the appointment of Bormann's nominees, in particular that of the Gauleiter of East Prussia, Erich Koch, as Reichskommissar of the Ukraine, was equally effective in frustrating his own attempts to get his ministry's directives translated into practice.

I I

THE NEWLY ADOPTED POLICY of *glasnost* (openness) opened up a bitter debate in the Soviet Union during the late 1980s over the responsibility for the failure to foresee the German attack and make more adequate preparations to meet it. The debate was extended to the steps taken by Stalin and his successors to suppress the evidence, falsify history, and prevent discussion of it for more than forty years.

The danger of war had been recognized and steps taken to strengthen the country's defenses in the mid-1930s. They included the priority given to the buildup of Russia's military-industrial capacity in the revision of the second Five-Year Plan; the increased defense budget; the reorganization of the Red Army and the recasting of military doctrine associated with the names of Tukhachevsky, Yegorov, Blyukher, Yakir, and Uborevich. This process, however, was abruptly interrupted by the purges, in which the men responsible, from Ordzhonikidze and Pyatakov among the industrial bosses to Tukhachevsky and almost the entire General Staff and higher command of the Red Army and Red Navy, were swept away, and the impetus lost. Although progress was resumed in the period 1939–41, by the time of the attack the Soviet economy and armed forces had not recovered from the shock and disorganization. The losses had not been made good; the ability and experience of the leadership Stalin had destroyed had not been replaced.

Apart from those shot, the large number in concentration and labor camps included many highly qualified managers and technologists as well as officers. Not surprisingly, therefore, such progress as was made in the third

Five-Year Plan was uneven. In the three years from 1938 to 1940 the output of the machinery and engineering industries (including the arms industries) was said to have reached 59 percent of the total planned for five years. On the other hand, the steel industry had only achieved 5.8 percent of its planned five-year increase; rolled metal (due to the shortage of iron ore and coke) only 1.4 percent, and cement 3.6, while the output of oil, a crucial strategic raw material, had expanded so slowly that there was a fuel crisis. [21]

The regime's response, as always, was to increase compulsion, both in the agricultural and industrial sectors. The Central Committee ordered the reduction of private plots on the collective farms, and a total of 2.5 million hectares was recovered. Equally unpopular was the reduction in the number of the peasants' own cattle and pigs, which they were put under pressure to sell either to the kolkhoz or for meat. Stricter discipline was called for, with each peasant required to give a fixed minimum of workdays to the kolkhoz, while the quotas for compulsory delivery of crops to the state were increased and extended to include potatoes and other vegetables. Articles in *Pravda* in the summer of 1940 made it clear that these, and other similar measures, such as an increase in the payments made to the Machine Tractor Stations, marked a return to the policy of increasing supplies by coercion and rooting out "the instinct of petty private property."

The peasants had learned that resistance was futile, but their sense of injustice was kept alive by the resentment they felt when the state, having robbed them of their right to the land, continued to cheat them by the manipulation of prices and quotas. They received the lowest possible return for their labor and were charged the highest possible prices for the consumer goods they had to buy, higher than the same kerosene, soap, cloth, or shoes could be bought for in the towns. Not surprisingly they saw the collective farm as another version of serfdom, binding them to the soil, and grudging them even the minimum they needed to keep alive.

The result was to put at risk (except in cotton) the modest recovery in agricultural productivity made between 1933 and 1938. It was Stalin's good luck that Hitler should not only fail, but scorn, to appeal to the stored-up resentment against the regime. Instead, their brutal treatment at the Germans' hands united the Russian people, as Stalin himself could never have done, in resistance to the invaders.

The Soviet regime's deliberate attack on their standards of living, as the peasants saw it, was matched by a tightening up of labor controls in industry and on construction sites—officially described as made on the recommendation of the trade unions. Labor books were issued to all employed men and women, making it impossible to change jobs without permission. The working day was lengthened from seven hours to eight, the working week from five out of six days to six out of seven, without additional pay. Social insurance benefits were trimmed and absenteeism made a criminal offense. Specialists of many kinds were directed to particular jobs, a million young school leavers were called up for training in labor reserve schools, and fees introduced for the upper forms of secondary schools and higher education. How far such measures succeeded in raising industrial any more than agricultural productivity is uncertain. What is clear is that such improvements as there had been in the standard of living up to 1938 came to an end. This might have been justified as a necessary sacrifice to prepare the country for war, but in the era of the Nazi-Soviet Pact, this was an argument only occasionally heard.

Stalin was obviously aware of the possibility of a war with Germany, but failed to understand the ideological—one could as easily write, the mythological—importance it had for Hitler, which lifted it out of the range of rational calculation. Once he had signed the Nazi-Soviet Pact, Stalin convinced himself that Hitler would be so preoccupied in the rest of Europe that he must see as clearly as he himself did the advantage to both sides of maintaining the pact.

When Churchill sent a message to Stalin at the end of June 1940, warning him of the danger of a German hegemony in Europe, Molotov told the German ambassador (for transmission to Hitler) that Stalin had replied:

> He did not see any danger of the hegemony of any one country in Europe and still less that Europe might be engulfed by Germany. . . . Stalin was not of the opinion that German military successes menaced the Soviet Union's friendly relations with Germany. These relations were not based on transient circumstances, but on the basic national interests of both countries. [22]

No doubt Stalin was encouraged in his belief by the fact that, after a decade of frontier fighting in the Far East, he succeeded in reaching a settlement in 1940 with the Japanese, the other power which posed a threat to the USSR. This was successfully converted into a Neutrality Pact (April 1941), which lasted until Stalin himself declared war on Japan in 1945. His conclusion was that if Russia could not escape an eventual war with Germany, it would not occur until 1942 or 1943, leaving him two to three years longer to prepare for it.

This miscalculation was responsible, more than anything else, for the disasters of 1941, and was made all the more serious by the stubbornness with which Stalin persisted in it in face of the increasing evidence to the contrary in the first six months of that year.

There were serious mistakes of judgment as well as timing on Stalin's part. The only qualification of Marshal Voroshilov, the head of the military establishment as commissar for defense since 1926, was that he had been Stalin's creature since the civil war. His ignorance was proverbial, and he had done more than anyone to put an end to the experiments with mechanized formations which Tukhachevsky and his group had started in the early 1920s. Even Stalin could not ignore Voroshilov's responsibility for the Finnish debacle, and in May 1940 he was replaced by Timoshenko.

Timoshenko, along with Shaposhnikov, the experienced chief of staff who had drawn up the operational plans for the later stages of the Finnish war, were both made marshals. One of their first tasks was to secure the release of some 4,000 Soviet officers from imprisonment or disgrace to fill the gaps left by the purges. A thousand promotions to senior commands followed, including many who were to win prominence between 1941 and 1945 but who as yet lacked the experience of the officers whose places they were taking. Of 225 regimental commanders sampled by the inspector-general in autumn 1940, not one had attended a full course at a military academy and only twenty-five had finished a military school. The Red Army at all levels had to be retrained, but by the summer of 1941, around 75 percent of its officers and 70 percent of its political commissars had been in their posts less than a year.

Timoshenko and Shaposhnikov, however, had not survived the purges without learning that Stalin meant to retain a personal grip on military affairs which left no room for independent views. The men whose advice he was most prepared to listen to were those who owed their advancement not to their abilities but entirely to Stalin's favor. Of the three best known, two had been political commissars associated with Stalin in his Tsaritsyn days, Lev Mekhlis and the former tailor E. A. Shchadenko, both of whom went on to become members of his Secretariat. In 1937 they had played a major role in purging the officer corps and reconstructing the Red Army Political Administration, Mekhlis emerging as the senior political commissar and a deputy commissar of defense. The only qualification of the third, G. I. Kulik, was that Stalin had known him too in Tsaritsyn in 1918 and plucked him from nowhere to become head of the Main Artillery Administration in 1937, another deputy defense commissar, and in 1940 one of the five marshals of the Soviet Union. Between them these three men had more influence with Stalin in military affairs than anyone else, and were put in charge of the key area of procurement, i.e., the choice and production of equipment for the Red Army and its air arm. They have a place of their own in the history of the Red Army for their ignorance of military affairs, the number of wrong decisions they made, and the bad advice for which they were responsible in the early 1940s.

Of course considerable preparations were made. For over a decade priority had been given to heavy industry and the Soviet armed forces had first call on it. The Red Army was enlarged by two and a half times between 1939 and 1941 and had a clear superiority over the Germans in numbers, as well as the largest air force in the world. War production had been increased, troops and supplies transferred to the west, and a hundred thousand men put to work on the fortifications. But virtually none of the preparations were complete, and the country (as Zhukov, the Red Army chief of staff wrote later) was caught in the stage of reorganizing, reequipping, and retraining the armed forces, building up the necessary stores and reserves.

The purges had put a stop to individual initiative, and the sense of urgency which only Stalin could have created was lacking. The result showed in the fact that up-to-date weapons already designed and tested were not put into mass production, and that few soldiers and airmen had been trained in their use when the war began. Examples, all of which proved later to be a match for the Germans' equipment, were the KV-1 and T-34 tanks, the Yak-1 fighter (only 64 machines produced in 1940); the MiG-3 and LaGG-3 fighters; the Yak "Stormovik" fighter bomber, and the Per-2 light bomber. Similarly with the new industrial areas in the Urals, Siberia, and Kazakhstan, which were to be the key to the Russian war effort: These had already been established, but the extraordinary rate of development which was later achieved had to wait until the fighting began and the central industrial areas, in which the major investment in heavy industry and arms production was still being made in 1940, were overrun by the enemy. In 1940, the Donbass produced 94 million tons of coal, the Urals 12 million, the Karaganda fields 6 million. Investment in the central areas in 1940 was nearly three times greater than that in the Urals, and more than seven times greater than that in Siberia. [23]

During the 1930s an elaborate and carefully sited line of fortifications—the Stalin Line—had been built along the Soviet Union's western frontier. Stalin, however, overriding the views of the General Staff, decided that the frontier to be defended must be the one created by the acquisition of new territories in 1939 and 1940—an undulating line running from Finland to Rumania and including a number of dangerous salients. This meant giving up an established system of defense for a new, hastily constructed one which could not be completed in 1941, despite the employment of 100,000 workers. In addition to gaps of anything between 5 and 50 miles when the Germans attacked, the old fortifications had been stripped of their guns, against the advice of Timoshenko and Zhukov. Only 1,000 out of 2,500 concrete emplacements in the new line were furnished with artillery; the rest had no more than machine guns.

Soviet airfields were in the same unfinished state. A plan to build 190 new fields in the western regions was approved in February 1941; the NKVD began this and work on enlarging the old ones all at the same time. As a result, most of the Red Army's planes had to be moved to civilian airports which were near the border and poorly defended.

The new defense system was equally ill furnished with mine fields, thanks to a decision of Marshal Kulik, who regarded mines as the weapon of "the weak." Kulik was also responsible for the failure to grasp the value of the "Katyusha" multiple rocket-launcher, which did not go into mass production until June 1941. Behind the fortifications the entire Soviet military system suffered from the primitive state of its signals and communications network, and from a chronic lack of motor transport.

IT IS ILLUMINATING to compare what Hitler and Stalin were each saying behind closed doors at the time the economic treaties between their countries were concluded. Hitler held a conference with his top military leaders and Ribbentrop on January 9, 1941. After reviewing the general situation, he concentrated on Russia:

> Stalin, Russia's master, is a clever fellow. He will not take an open stand against Germany, but it must be expected that he will increasingly create difficulties . . . for Germany. He wishes to enter upon the inheritance of impoverished Europe, is in need of successes, and is inspired by the *Drang nach Westen*.
>
> The possibility of Russian intervention sustains the British. . . . If they could hold out, activate forty to fifty divisions, and if the U.S.A. and Russia would aid them, then a very difficult situation would arise for Germany. This must not happen.*

Far from seeing Germany threatened by a Russian invasion, Hitler continued:

> Even though the Russian armed forces are a headless colossus of clay, their future development cannot be predicted. Since Russia has to be beaten in any case, it is better to do it now, when the Russian armed forces have no leaders and are poorly equipped, and the Russians have to overcome great difficulties in their armaments industry. . . .
>
> The annihilation of the Russian Army, the seizure of the most important industrial areas, and the destruction of the remainder will be the objective of the operation—and the area of Baku must also be occupied.

With Russia "smashed," either the British would give in or Germany would continue the war with the resources of the whole continent to draw on. At the same time, with Russia knocked out, Japan would be able to turn against the U.S.A. with all her power and prevent the Americans from entering the war. Then, with Russia's "immeasurable riches" at her disposal, "Germany will have the means for waging war even against continents at some future date. Nobody will then be able to defeat her any more. If this operation is carried out, Europe will hold its breath." [24]

IN THE LAST ten days of the month before, December 1940, the senior military commanders of the Red Army assembled in Moscow for a special session of the Main Military Soviet devoted to the lessons of the Finnish war and those to be learned from the startling success of the German blitzkrieg. A report from a special commission which the Central Committee of the party had set up left no doubt of the unsatisfactory state of affairs in the Defense Commissariat:

> There are no agreed opinions on the utilization of tanks, aviation, and parachute troops. . . . The development of tanks and mechanized forces lags behind contemporary requirements. . . . The ratio of mechanized forces is low and the quality of Red Army tanks unsatisfactory. [25]

*It turned out to be an accurate prediction of the situation which Hitler himself created by his invasion of Russia and his declaration of war on the U.S.A.

Stalin and the Politburo took a close interest, and Zhdanov was present as Stalin's representative throughout the military discussions. At the end Timoshenko presided over a war game in which the leading Soviet generals, using large-scale maps, played out two attack-defense operations on the western frontier. In the first, in which Zhukov commanded the "Western" forces, he succeeded in wiping out most of the concentrations of the "Red" forces and driving deep into Russia; in the second, in which Zhukov took the "Red" side, the result was not so clear-cut. On January 13, Stalin unexpectedly summoned the participants to the Kremlin, along with the Politburo and other members of the government, and conducted a cross-examination, demanding to know which side had won, the Western attackers or the Soviet defenders.

General K. A. Meretskov, the newly appointed chief of staff, was caught unprepared and made a mess of his answer, telling Stalin what he thought he wanted to hear, that the Reds had won, even though the ratio of forces was not in their favor. When it came to the second game, Stalin sarcastically asked, "Well, who finally won? Was it the Reds again?" In a panic, Meretskov tried to avoid giving a reply, at which Stalin shouted: "The members of the Politburo want to know which of the opponents turned out to be the winner"—still without getting an answer. Shortly afterwards Meretskov was replaced by Zhukov.

The issue that provoked most discussion in the Kremlin meeting was the use of independent tank forces on the German model. Marshal Kulik started a major row by taking the familiar Voroshilov line and declaring that mechanization was unnecessary. He had fought in the Spanish Civil War and was convinced that infantry with horse-drawn transport would prove as adequate to fight Hitler as they had to fight Franco. Kulik's views were rejected by other speakers, leading Stalin to tell Timoshenko that as long as there was such confusion in the army, "You will never get mechanization or motorization at all." Timoshenko insisted that there was no confusion in the army, only in Marshal Kulik's mind.

Although Kulik was one of Stalin's protégés, on this occasion he got the rough edge of his master's tongue:

> Kulik has spoken against mechanization, he is against the motor which the government is bringing to the army. This is just about the same as if he had spoken against the tractor and the combined harvester, defending the wooden plough and the economic independence of the village. [26]

In his final speech, Stalin declared that the next war would be a war of engines and movements, without saying when he thought it was likely to break out. But many of those present remembered that a year before, in November 1939, Stalin had agreed to the disbandment of all the tank army groups as rapidly as possible, and that it was he who had picked out Kulik and still left him in control of the Red Army's artillery arm. In fact, the re-formation of the Red Army's mechanized corps began in March, and in the first six months of 1941 over 1,000 of the outstanding T-34 tanks were produced. But instead of a systematic plan for making these the basis of self-sufficient armored formations, as the Germans had done, they were dribbled into existing units and mixed up with the older obsolescent machines which urgently needed refitting. Few tank drivers had more than an average of an hour's practice with their machines, new or old, and the armored units were increasingly manned with new recruits and junior commanders brought in from the infantry and cavalry, without any of the experience of the battle-hardened panzer troops they would have to face. [27]

The war game of December 1940 was fought on the assumption that the main German attack with three of their four tank armies would be launched on the western front and aimed at Smolensk and Moscow.

In his report on the exercise, Zhukov claimed that the tactics which his forces had followed with such success had been dictated by the line of the frontiers and the nature of the terrain. He argued that the Germans would make the same calculations (as they did six months later) and, when Stalin was still puzzled why he had been given such strong forces, Zhukov replied that these corresponded to those the Germans could be expected to concentrate for their first strike.

Stalin was sufficiently impressed by the confidence with which Zhukov argued his case to appoint him chief of staff in February 1941, the third man to hold the post in six months. This was one of the best appointments Stalin ever made, but he did not listen to Zhukov's advice. The defense plan which finally emerged between April and May 1941 conformed with Stalin's insistence that the main German attack was to be expected on the southwestern, not the western, front, aimed at the grain of the Ukraine and the coal of the Donbass. [28] Later described as designed for the wrong war—for 1914, not 1941—it was based on the assumption that the Red Army would not be taken by surprise; that enemy operations, to begin with, would be conducted with limited forces, and that the Red Army would be given the time to complete its mobilization. Stalin, on the advice of Mekhlis, refused to countenance proposals from the production agencies and the General Staff that the strategic reserves of fuel, food, and raw materials should be dispersed behind the Volga, out of reach of an invader. They were left intact to the west of the river, or actually moved forward into the frontier districts. There was no contingency planning for the possibility that these might be overrun.

Still convinced that the main attack would come on the western front, on May 15 Zhukov sent Stalin a handwritten note urging that, as the Germans were fully organized and able to launch a surprise attack, the Red Army should forestall them and capture the initiative by attacking them first during their deployment. [29] There is no evidence that Stalin took any notice of Zhukov's note; on the contrary, early in June he ordered the movement of a further twenty-five divisions to the southwestern front.

Stalin still refused to admit, even to his chief of staff, that war was imminent. As a result, no operational plans were issued which would go into action in the event of war, no matter which individual units might be put out of action. Kuznetsov, Stalin's commissar of the navy, reporting this in 1965, wrote:

> Stalin had ideas on how to wage war, but, with his usual pathological distrust, kept them secret from those who had to execute them. Mistaken about the probable date of the conflict, he thought there was still enough time. And when the course of history speeded up, the ideas about a future war could not be transformed into clear strategic concepts and concrete plans. Yet such plans—worked out down to the last detail—were absolutely essential from 1939 to 1941.[30]

III

NOTHING SHOWS MORE CLEARLY Hitler's gambler's temperament than his readiness to put Operation Barbarossa, already the biggest gamble of his career, at further risk by the additional chances he took in the Balkans and North Africa while the forces in the East were building up.

The occupation of Greece and the decision to commit an armored corps to the desert war were calculated risks. The first arose from the need to prevent the British from taking advantage of Mussolini's disastrous attack on Greece, where they had landed an army at the Greeks' invitation, in February 1941; the second, from the rout of the Italian forces in North Africa. Between Germany and Greece lay four countries—Hungary, Rumania, Bulgaria, and Yugoslavia—whose compliance had to be secured before German armies could attack Greece. Hungary and Rumania were already German satellites and, during the winter of 1940–41, German troops, moving across Hungary, built up a task force in Rumania with a strength of 680,000 men. In Bulgaria there was a sharp tussle for influence between the Germans and Russians which the Germans won. On March 1 Bulgaria followed Hungary, Rumania, and Slovakia in joining the Tripartite Pact, and German troops moved over the Danube from Rumania and crossed Bulgaria toward the Greek frontier.

A similar diplomatic tussle took place in Yugoslavia, this time between the Germans and the British. The regent, Prince Paul, was pro-British, but he was impressed by the fall of France and by the offer of Salonika, which Hitler made during a secret meeting at Berchtesgaden early in March. Three weeks later, the Yugoslav foreign minister signed the Tripartite Pact in Vienna, thereby greatly simplifying the German problem of occupying Greece. Hitler's satisfaction was turned to fury when, on the night of March 26–27, a group of Yugoslav officers, led by General Dušan Simović, rebelled against the government's adherence to the Axis cause and carried out a coup d'état in the name of the young King Peter. As soon as he received the news, and without pausing to consider the consequences in delaying Operation Barbarossa, Hitler issued orders for immediate preparations to be made "to destroy Yugoslavia as a nation, without waiting for any possible declarations of loyalty from the new government." Simović's hopes of steering a neutral course were brushed aside. The operation was to be carried out with "merciless harshness."

Hitler's diplomatic preparations provided for stirring up the appetite of Yugoslavia's neighbors (including Italy) to share in the partition of her territory, and for disrupting the Yugoslav state from within by appealing to the Croats, whose grievances against the Belgrade government had long been fostered by the Germans. But it was force Hitler relied on to show that he was not to be trifled with.

On April 6 German troops attacked both Yugoslavia and Greece. There was a difference between them: Greece was to be occupied, Yugoslavia destroyed. To show that Hitler meant the latter threat to be taken literally, no fewer than seven panzer divisions and 1,000 aircraft were employed. After destroying the Yugoslav air force on the ground in a surprise attack, the German bomber pilots then set out to destroy the capital, Belgrade. In three days, flying at roof height without fear of intervention, they carried out more than 500 sorties and killed over 17,000 people in an operation to which Hitler gave the code name "Punishment." The city was occupied on April 13, and the Yugoslav army was driven to capitulate on the seventeenth. Three days later the Greeks, after their six months' heroic resistance to the Italians, were forced to follow suit. On April 22, the 50,000 British, Australian, and New Zealand troops, who had landed on the Greek mainland only two months earlier, began their evacuation. On the twenty-seventh the German tanks rolled into Athens and the swastika flag was hoisted over the Acropolis.

Hitler had only decided on the Yugoslav part of the operation on the afternoon of March 27, demanding that the OKW and the OKH should work through the night to produce a plan the following morning. Ten days later, the forces had been assembled, including hundreds of tanks and aircraft, and the attack was launched. The whole campaign, the occupation of Greece as well as Yugoslavia, despite the difficulties of the terrain, was completed within three weeks.

Hitler owed this, as he owed his success in carrying out his other plans, to the German army and its officer corps, which he never tired of criticizing. Even for them it was a remarkable feat, and without their professional skill it could never have been achieved. But the world gave the credit to Hitler as the leader who saw the possibilities and had the nerve to give the orders. For Hitler himself, on the eve of the Russian campaign, it was confirmation of his military genius, further proof that he was invincible and that anyone who attempted to resist him would be destroyed.

The only incident which for a moment threw him off balance and produced another outburst of fury was the astonishing news that on May 10 Rudolf Hess had flown to Scotland. Paul Schmidt wrote later that when the news was received it produced an effect "as if a bomb had struck the

Berghof." Hitler raged around the house, denouncing Hess as a traitor and demanding to know who else was involved. For some years, and especially since the outbreak of war, Hess had dropped into the background. Although Hitler's deputy for party affairs with the rank of Reich minister, he held no actual ministerial appointment. The transaction of party affairs no longer interested Hitler, whom Hess saw less and less frequently, and his position had been undermined by his former assistant, Martin Bormann, now Hitler's secretary. Resentful and frustrated, Hess cast around for some spectacular act of devotion which would recapture the favor of the leader whom he still regarded with doglike devotion.

Aware of Hitler's reluctance to destroy the British Empire, Hess formed the idea, as early as the summer of 1940, of flying to Britain and returning with the negotiated peace which had so far eluded the Führer. Hitler did not take Hess's "mission" seriously for a moment, any more than the British did. What caused him anxiety was how much Hess knew and might tell of his plan to attack Russia, and what damage British propaganda might do to his own prestige by making capital out of the fact that the deputy leader of the party and one of Hitler's earliest and most devoted followers had flown to the enemy's country. In fact, when interrogated, Hess denied the rumors about Hitler and Russia, and the British, as embarrassed as Hitler by Hess's arrival and the implication that secret negotiations for a compromise peace might be going on, limited themselves to the brief official statement that he had been made a prisoner of war, and made no attempt to exploit the incident for political purposes.

Hitler declared Hess to be mentally deranged, stripped him of his offices, and appointed Bormann to manage party affairs in his place, giving orders that he was to be shot if he ever returned to Germany. According to Churchill, who discussed the matter with him, Stalin persisted in believing that Hess had been invited over by the British secret service and that there had been some deep negotiation or plot, which had miscarried, for Germany and Britain to act together in the invasion of Russia. Investigations made it clear that Hess had acted on his own, and that there was no conspiracy. A nine-day wonder, with no sequel, the affair was soon overtaken by the news of the dramatic airborne landing launched on May 20 which led to the capture of Crete, another painful humiliation for the British in face of their naval superiority, and another spectacular success for Hitler, despite the heavy losses suffered by the Germans. The only person on whom Hess's flight left a lasting impression was Stalin. [31]

It has been argued that the Balkan campaign cost Hitler the chance to capture Moscow, by forcing him to postpone Barbarossa from May 15 to June 22. Some postponement, however, would have been necessary in any case, since the thaw in Russia came late in 1941 and the mud ruled out a start earlier than the first week in June, that is, a delay of three weeks. The actual operations in Yugoslavia and Greece, with the exception of the attack on Crete improvised late in April, were completed within that period and so did not add further to the delay. But the aftereffects, in the damage to tanks and motor vehicles inflicted by bad roads through the mountains, especially on the long journey to Greece and back, meant that Army Group South, to take the most serious case, launched its initial advance into the Ukraine on the revised date, but without a third of its tank strength. Similarly, the losses in the attack on Crete discouraged Hitler from making use of airborne troops on any large-scale operations in Russia. Hitler's decision therefore to take the risk of a separate Balkan campaign during the build-up to Barbarossa certainly added to the odds against a successful blitzkrieg in the East, but can hardly be said, by itself, to have been the cause of his failure.

What was clear beyond doubt was that the Balkan war which Mussolini had begun in an attempt to assert his independence had ended in a German triumph which highlighted the Italian failure. The real relationship between Berlin and Rome was revealed by the partition of Yugoslavia. True to his word, Hitler wiped the Yugoslav state off the map and settled the division of the country in a directive of April 12. Not until the twenty-first was Ciano summoned to Vienna to learn what Italy's share of the spoils was to be, after Hitler had created an independent Croat state.

Italian dependence on Germany was made even clearer in North Africa. The British conquest of the whole of Cyrenaica, following the rout of the Italians, was reversed by General Rommel, who brought a German armored corps with him and took command of all mechanized and motorized forces in the desert. Requested to submit his plans by April 20, he launched a counterattack on March 31 and by April 12 had recaptured all the ground lost and driven the British back to the Egyptian frontier.

To the British defeats in Greece, North Africa, and Crete was added a revolt led by Rashid Ali against the British garrison in Iraq. On May 30 Raeder renewed his argument for a decisive Egypt-Suez offensive in the autumn of 1941 which could deal a fatal blow to British control of the Middle East. Hitler was not to be moved. He was ready enough with promises, including an attack on Egypt from Libya, an advance into Asia Minor from Bulgaria, and the invasion of Iran from positions to be won in Transcaucasia—but only after the Soviet Union had been defeated. The same day, May 30, he confirmed the revised date of June 22 for the invasion of Russia to start.

THE SPEED with which the Germans overran the Balkans took Stalin as much by surprise as their victory in the West had done. When German troops moved into Bulgaria at the beginning of March, Molotov protested that this was an infringement of the Soviet security zone. But the protest was not supported by action, nor was there any attempt to interrupt the flow of supplies under the new economic agreement. On the contrary, after a slow start in Soviet deliveries, March saw a sudden acceleration, despite the fact that Germany had fallen far behind with her part of the bargain. An appeal by the new Yugoslav regime for support produced Soviet recognition and a Soviet-Yugoslav friendship and nonaggression pact, but when the Germans attacked Yugoslavia, Stalin made no move or protest.

While the news was still coming in of the German success, the Japanese foreign minister, Yosuke Matsuoka, arrived in Moscow from Berlin intent on persuading Stalin and Molotov to sign a nonaggression pact which would leave Japan free to fight Britain and the U.S.A. After a week of frustration in which the Russians set impossible conditions, he was about to leave for home when Stalin summoned him to the Kremlin on the evening of the twelfth. Pretending that he had been forced to abandon his stand by Matsuoka's tough bargaining—"You are choking me," he declared, putting his hands round his throat—he withdrew the Soviet demands and suggested that they should sign a full-scale pact of neutrality. When the Japanese minister asked how this would affect the Tripartite Pact, Stalin reassured him that "he was a convinced adherent of the Axis and an opponent of England and America."

The pact was signed the next day and Matsuoka left to return home by the Trans-Siberian Railway. The diplomatic corps and the press were waiting at the station to see him off, when Stalin and Molotov suddenly appeared on the platform—an unheard of event in the case of Stalin, who embraced Matsuoka and wished him a good journey. "The European problem," Stalin declared for all to hear, "can be solved in a natural way if Japan and the Soviets cooperate." Stalin then looked round for the German ambassador, Schulenburg, walked over, and put his arm round his shoulders and again proclaimed: "We must remain friends, and you must now do everything to that end." Not content with this, when he saw the acting German military attaché, Colonel Hans Krebs, he took his right hand between both of his own and said in a loud voice: "We will stay friends with you whatever happens."[32]

As Stalin had intended, this charade was duly reported by the diplomats to their respective governments. The one place where it made no impression was in Berlin. Convinced that Stalin was anxious at all costs to avoid war with Germany, Schulenburg, with the help of other members of the embassy in Moscow, drew up a memorandum for Hitler setting out the reasons why they did not believe Russia had any intention of attacking Germany. Shortly afterwards Schulenburg was in Berlin and sought an interview with the Führer. Although the memorandum was on his desk, Hitler gave no indication that he had even glanced at it, and Schulenburg was no more successful in making an impression on Hitler by what he said. Throughout Hitler affected to show the greatest distrust of Russia: "He had been forewarned by events in Serbia. What had happened there was an example of the political unreliability of a state." After half an hour, Hitler ended the interview, then as Schulenburg reached the door, called after him: "Oh, one more thing: I do not intend a war against Russia."[33] Back in Moscow, the ambassador told his staff that the die had been cast and there would be war with Russia, adding that Hitler had deliberately lied to him.

On May 5 Stalin spoke at a banquet for graduates of the military academies and high-ranking officers. There were very different accounts of what he said, but the gist repeated throughout Moscow was that there was imminent danger of a war with Germany. There followed an announcement the next day that, after all the years he had been content to wield power as general secretary, Stalin was taking Molotov's place as head of the government (chairman of the Council of People's Commissars). Since Molotov continued as deputy chairman and foreign minister, the explanation was taken to be that the international situation had become so dangerous that Stalin himself must publicly assume responsibility for Soviet policy. But, reporting this "event of extraordinary importance" to Berlin, Schulenburg expressed his firm belief that Stalin had taken such a step with the object of preserving the Soviet Union from a conflict with Germany. [34]

There is little doubt that Schulenburg was right. In the course of the next seven weeks there was a steadily increasing flow of reports to the Kremlin giving details of German troop concentrations along Russia's western frontiers and of the German plan to attack the Soviet Union at various dates in May and June. These reports came from a variety of sources. The earliest from a foreign government appears to have been in March from Sumner Welles, the U.S. under secretary of state, passing on information originally picked up by the Americans in Berlin. Churchill sent another message in April, and Eden, the British foreign secretary, saw the Soviet ambassador in London, Maisky, five times between mid-April and mid-June.

The outstanding Soviet spy, the German-born journalist Richard Sorge, recruited by Soviet intelligence in 1929 and active in Japan since 1933, sent his first report of the imminence of the German attack on March 5, 1941. During May he gave a date around June 20 for its start, and on the fifteenth of that month correctly pinpointed it as the twenty-second. In his memoirs Zhukov quotes from a Soviet intelligence report of February 1941, presented to Stalin on March 20, which correctly identified the objectives of the three German army groups and their commanders, with tentative dates of May 20 or mid-June for the attack.

There was of course a screen of false reports put out by the Germans presenting the buildup of German forces in the east as a major deception exercise designed to divert attention from Hitler's real plan, an invasion of England. More effective than the false trails laid by the Germans, however, was the processing of all the reports by the head of the Russian army's Intelligence Division (GRU), General F. I. Golikov. These were sent on to Stalin under two classifications, from "reliable sources" and from "doubtful sources." On March 20 Golikov circulated a note to GRU agents with the instruction: "All documents claiming war is imminent must be regarded as forgeries from British or even German sources." [35] While Golikov did not suppress reports, he was well aware that Stalin seized on anything which confirmed his belief that Hitler had no serious intention of attacking the Soviet Union in the summer of 1941. As a reinsurance for his own position, Golikov classified such reports as reliable, and those—such as the information supplied by Sorge—as doubtful.*

Gnedich, the man responsible for delivering the reports to Stalin, testified in 1966 that Stalin did not fail to read those which did not fit in with his picture of Hitler's intentions, but deliberately chose to ignore them: "Stalin took over the government not to prepare for the country's defense, but to reach agreement with Hitler."[36]

Like Hitler, Stalin soon found arguments to justify his views, convincing himself that Hitler was not such a fool as to think that Russia could be defeated by a blitzkrieg. Surely no one in his right mind would think of attempting to conquer the huge spaces of Russia without many more months of preparation and many more deliveries of strategic war materials. The German buildup must be intended as a way of applying pressure to extort more supplies. (This was also the view of the British Joint Intelligence Committee—though not of Churchill—until late May.) Alternatively, Stalin saw the British and Americans attempting to involve Germany and Russia in a war: hence the warnings which they attempted to "plant" in Moscow in the hope that Russia would take defensive measures and that these would provoke Hitler to attack. At all costs, the Russian forces must be careful to avoid provocation.

Similar suspicions convinced Stalin that Hess had gone on a mission to conclude peace with Britain and secure her alliance for an attack on Russia or at least her neutrality. When Khrushchev voiced this suspicion to Stalin as the view of the whole Politburo, he got the answer: "Yes, that's it. You understand correctly."[37]

Golikov reported direct to Stalin and was not allowed to show any of the intelligence data he collected on German plans to either Zhukov, the chief of the General Staff, or Timoshenko, the commissar for defense. Even without such access, there was plenty of other evidence from commanders in the field of intense German activity close to the frontier. The Luftwaffe carried out frequent flights into Soviet territory to gather intelligence, sending reconnaissance planes to locate and photograph every Soviet air base. From January to June more than 200 such flights were made deep into Soviet territory. The Russian army and air force were strictly forbidden by Stalin to interfere with these flights or open fire on them. As a result a high percentage of the Soviet air force was destroyed on the ground in the opening days of the war.

Similar orders were given to the commanders of ground forces. To bring these up to full strength and put them on a war footing would amount to mobilization, with the danger of provoking the war with Germany which

---

*In reporting this practice, which is well authenticated, Anthony Read and David Fisher describe it as "an example of the Russian three U's syndrome: *ugadat, ugodit, utselet,* best translated as 'sniff,' 'suck up,' 'survive.' "

Stalin wanted to avoid at all costs. When units in the important Kiev military district were moved into the forward zone in mid-June, Zhukov, acting under orders, sent the commander a furious telegram:

"Such actions can immediately provoke the Germans to armed conflict. Cancel the order immediately and report who issued it."[38]

The one response to their anxieties even the most senior commanders could get was "Don't panic. 'The Boss' knows all about it."

HITLER INFORMED neither Mussolini (whom he met at the Brenner Pass on June 2) nor his Japanese allies of his intention to invade Russia. The only countries he would allow to take part in the attack were Finland and Rumania. Both had accounts of their own to settle with the Soviet Union, and the invitation was gladly accepted. In both cases Hitler maintained the fiction of a preventive war to forestall the threat of aggression from Russian forces concentrated on the frontier. Some idea of the scale of the German preparations is given by the figure for the special trains needed to move troops and equipment to the east: up to mid-March, 2,500; in the next ten weeks, another 17,000.

So large a concentration of forces could hardly continue to be passed off as a deception exercise, and the German code traffic which the British were able to decipher left no doubt that this was the real thing, not a bluff. In a final effort to convince Stalin, the head of the British Foreign Office, Sir Alexander Cadogan, asked Maisky to see him on June 10 and dictated a detailed account—dates, numbers, and names—of the German troops deployed along the Soviet frontier. Maisky passed this on to Moscow, but the only response the British received was a Tass statement, which Stalin was believed to have written personally, broadcast by Moscow Radio on June 13 and published the next day.

After referring to rumors in the foreign press of an impending war between Russia and Germany, "responsible circles in Moscow" had authorized the Soviet news agency, Tass, to state that these were "a clumsy propaganda maneuver of the forces arrayed against the Soviet Union and Germany which are interested in a spread and intensification of the war." Germany had addressed no demands to the Soviet Union, and both countries were fulfilling the terms of the Nazi-Soviet Pact to the letter. Soviet circles regarded rumors of a German intention to attack the Soviet Union as without foundation; those of Russian preparations for an attack on Germany were "false and provocative." The call-up of Red Army reservists was a routine operation which took place every year; to interpret this as an action hostile to Germany was nonsensical. Molotov called in the German ambassador specially to give him a copy of the statement.[39]

The day the Tass communiqué was published Hitler held a final briefing of his principal commanders, each of whom reported to him separately. The same day Timoshenko and Zhukov went to see Stalin and urged him to let them put the troops on alert. Stalin would not listen: "You propose carrying out mobilization. That means war! Do you understand that or not?" Kuznetsov, the naval commander, tried to impress him with the latest reports of German ship movements, but found him uninterested. "Is that all?" Stalin asked. When Kuznetsov tried again with Molotov, showing that German ships were leaving Soviet ports with their loading not completed, and that all would be gone by June 21, Molotov dismissed the evidence. "Only a fool would attack us." [40]

In the few remaining days both Hitler and Stalin showed signs of strain. Hitler could not sleep and kept his court circle up to three or four o'clock in the morning. But his nervousness was due to impatience and excitement; his only anxiety was that something might happen to upset his plans. These were now completed down to the final details. The last Russian goods train carrying supplies for Germany would be allowed to cross the German frontier at midnight on June 21–22.

Stalin was obviously under great pressure, showing more and more irritation when anyone came to see him with yet more reports of German preparation. Khrushchev believed he had lost all confidence in the Russian army, that he had no plan at all and was just desperately hoping that, if he avoided any appearance of provocation, the threat of war would go away. On June 19, Zhdanov, whom many regarded as Stalin's successor, was reported to have left for his summer vacation on the Black Sea, another reassuring move in keeping with the fine weather and the atmosphere in Moscow, where none of the Soviet papers gave a hint of the worldwide speculation on the likelihood of war.

As before all his other acts of aggresion, Hitler prepared a proclamation putting all the blame on the aggressive designs of the Soviet Union, "which has broken its treaties with Germany and is about to fall on Germany's back while Germany is in a struggle for her life." On the final evening, June 21, he took a short drive through Berlin, then went through the text of the proclamation with Goebbels, who noted in his diary: "The Führer seems to lose his fear as the decisive moment approaches. It is always the same. He relaxes visibly. All the exhaustion seems to drop away." [41]

Another part of Hitler's ritual before a new campaign was to choose a victory fanfare for the radio announcement of major victories. Speer, with whom he had earlier been discussing plans to build a great new naval base and a city for a quarter of a million people near Trondheim, was called in to listen to a few bars from Liszt's *Les Préludes*: " 'You will hear that often in the future,' Hitler declared. 'How do you like it? . . . We'll be getting our granite and marble from Russia in any quantities we want.' " When he left for bed at 2:30 a.m. he told his entourage: "Before three months have passed, we shall witness a collapse in Russia, the like of which has never been seen in history." [42]

MANY MILES AWAY to the east, in the Kremlin earlier the same evening, Molotov asked the German ambassador to see him. To Schulenburg's relief the foreign minister appeared to be unaware of how close they were to the deadline. Molotov handed over a note protesting at continuing infringements of Soviet air space. With any other nation, he said, this would have led to an ultimatum; but he was sure the Germans would put a stop to the flights. He then mentioned the rumors of war and asked Schulenburg why the Germans appeared to be dissatisfied with the Soviet government. Why had there been no response to the Tass statement of June 13? He would be grateful if the ambassador could tell him what had brought about the present situation in German-Russian relations. The latter could only reply that he had no information.

While Molotov was seeing Schulenburg, Timoshenko and Zhukov went to see Stalin and pressed him to issue a border alert. Zhukov describes what followed in his memoirs.[43] They had information from deserters that the attack would begin early the next morning. While they debated the question, members of the Politburo arrived for a meeting. Stalin asked them, "What are we to do?" No one replied. Timoshenko, however, was sure they must alert all the troops in the frontier districts. Zhukov had a draft in his pocket, and Stalin told him to read it out. When he heard it, Stalin objected: "It's too soon to give such a directive. Perhaps the questions can still be settled peacefully. The troops must not be incited by any provocation." It was only after Zhukov had watered his draft down, and after still further amendment by Stalin, that the latter agreed to its dispatch. By the time it was transmitted, German sabotage units had cut the cables and few of the operational units ever received warning.

Stalin had already left the Kremlin and been driven to his dacha at Kuntsevo when Admiral Kuznetsov tried to report German air attacks on Sevastopol harbor and failed to reach him. At 3:30 a.m. Timoshenko and Zhukov received news of bombing raids from Minsk in the west, from Kiev in the southwest, and from the Baltic states. Unlike Kuznetsov, Zhukov had Stalin's private number. After a long time the general on duty answered: "Comrade Stalin is asleep." Zhukov was not to be put off and, after further delay, spoke to Stalin, reported the attacks, and requested permission to order the troops to fight.

Stalin remained silent. The only thing Zhukov could hear was his heavy breathing. "Did you understand me?" Zhukov asked. Silence again. At last, Stalin told him to go to the Kremlin with Timoshenko and get Poskrebyshev to summon all the members of the Politburo.

At 4:30 a.m. the two generals returned to Stalin's office. "All the Politburo members were assembled. Stalin, his face white, was sitting at the table cradling a tobacco-filled pipe in his hand." Still unwilling or unable to grasp the situation, he argued that if it was war, there would surely have been a formal declaration, negotiations, meetings of foreign ministers. He ordered someone to phone the German embassy to find out what was happening. The reply was that the ambassador was himself asking for a meeting with Molotov.

When Molotov received him, Schulenburg read out a version of Hitler's proclamation in the form of a diplomatic note. At the end Molotov asked, "Is this a declaration of war?" and then, his anger getting the better of him, shouted that the German attack was a breach of faith unprecedented in history. It was nonsense to speak of Soviet troop concentrations threatening Germany. If the German government was offended by them, all they had to do was to tell the Soviet government and they would be withdrawn. "Surely, we have not deserved this." [44]

Stalin had been sure that Schulenburg would convey a list of political, economic, and possibly territorial concessions which Hitler was seeking to secure. When Molotov announced instead that Hitler had declared war on them "Stalin sank back in his chair and fell into deep thought. A long heavy silence ensued." While he now agreed to the generals' demand to order Soviet troops to fight back, they were forbidden to cross the frontier in pursuit, and there was no mention of Germany and Russia being at war. Stalin still found it difficult to take in what was happening. He ordered the Foreign Ministry to remain in contact with Berlin and asked the Japanese government to mediate between Germany and the Soviet Union. Although a full-scale attack by land and air had been taking place across the frontiers from the Baltic to the Ukraine since 3:30 a.m., it was not until afternoon that the Soviet people heard the news from their leaders—and when they did, it was not Stalin, but Molotov who spoke, appealing to them, in Stalin's name, to rally round the Soviet government.

IV

THE MOST SERIOUS CHARGES against Stalin are that he arbitrarily deprived the Soviet Union of almost the whole of its military leadership—between thirty and forty thousand of its ablest and most experienced officers—when it was faced with the danger of war; that he refused to listen to the evidence from a variety of sources that Germany was preparing to attack the Soviet Union, so allowing Hitler the great advantage of surprise; and that he created such an atmosphere of terror that those who realized the extent of the danger were unable either to represent the real situation to him or to take measures themselves to meet it.

Despite the contrast in the summer of 1941 between a Stalin losing his grasp and a supremely confident, militant Hitler, the same criticism can be applied to Hitler too. The German army penetrated deep into Russia and inflicted huge losses on the Red Army, but it failed to win a decisive victory before the winter—the blitzkrieg gamble on which Hitler staked everything. As the consequences of the failure unfolded, compounded by Hitler's stubborn refusal to listen to expert advice—as stubborn as Stalin's in the first half of 1941 and again in 1942—the rashness of such a gamble, and the craziness of his fantasy of exterminating, evicting, or enslaving a hundred million people became more and more apparent. In Hitler's case the power to silence criticism and doubt was fortified more by the spell of success than terror. But, in his case as well as Stalin's, it was the same system, in which all authority was concentrated in one man, with that one man's limitations, which enabled him to commit a whole nation, without protest, to so reckless an enterprise.

The enterprise could not have been launched without the willing, and, in many cases, the enthusiastic cooperation of millions of Germans who share in greater or lesser degree the responsibility for the crimes that were committed. But that still leaves the question whether, if there had been no Hitler, Germany would ever have embarked on an invasion of Russia, aimed not just at the defeat of the Russian army or even the destruction of the Russian state, but at the enslavement of the Russian people. There is nothing to suggest that there was any other member of the Nazi leadership or of the wider circle of German nationalist politicians who combined the imagination to conceive so fantastic an undertaking with the sorcerer's ability to persuade so many others with much greater practical experience of soldiering, business, industry, and administration, to engage in the attempt to carry it out.

The argument still heard in Germany that Hitler had no option because of the threat of a Russian attack does not stand up to examination of the evidence. The Soviet strategic plan, such as it was, was based on the defense of the Ukraine and the Donbass, and Stalin refused to consider any action of a defensive character which might provoke Hitler into an attack. If the answer is that wars are the product of structural, social, and economic tensions, one may ask what tensions and contradictions were there in German society in 1941, as distinct from 1939, which could only be satisfied or diverted by an attack on Russia, when the greater part of the European continent was already under German control and offered virtually unlimited scope to the ambitions, idealism, organizing ability, and greed of Germans of all classes.

THE GERMAN ARMY which invaded Russia numbered nearly 3.2 million men out of a total German field force of 3.8 million. Its striking force consisted of nineteen panzer and twelve motorized divisions, 3,350 tanks, 5,000 aircraft, and 7,000 pieces of artillery. It contained a high proportion of battle-hardened troops and experienced commanders whose confidence had been increased by a recent and unbroken record of success. The German forces were supported by fourteen Rumanian and twenty-one Finnish divisions, joined later by sizeable forces from Italy, Hungary, Spain, and Slovakia.

The war on the eastern front which followed and lasted four years was the longest, most intensive and brutal conflict between two nations in history, costing them in combatants alone twice as many dead as those of all nations killed on all fronts in the First World War,* without counting the millions of civilians, refugees, and deported prisoners caught up and destroyed in the maelstrom.†

The plan (see map on p. 721) which the OKH presented to Hitler on December 5, 1940, placed the main weight of the German attack in the center, where von Bock's Army Group Center had two panzer groups compared with one each allocated to the two other army groups. Their first objective was to encircle the Soviet forces around Minsk; their second, after a pause for recuperation, was to be, in Halder's words, "the ultimate and decisive advance on Moscow." Army Group North under von Leeb was to clear the Baltic states and capture Leningrad; Army Group South under von Rundstedt was to capture Kiev.

Instead of the capture of Moscow, however, Hitler made the primary aim the encirclement of the enemy's forces before they could retreat. For this reason, Army Group Center, once it had completed its own initial encirclement, was to turn one of its two panzer groups north to assist in cutting off the Baltic states and capturing Leningrad, and turn the other south to help in carrying out the major encirclement in the Ukraine. At the time the army leaders made no objection to a change which meant a dispersal of the main drive, concentrated initially on the center, towards the Baltic and the Black Sea. It remains an open question how far they were converted to Hitler's view, how far they accepted it for planning purposes, while intending, or at least hoping, to reopen the matter once the first phase of the attack was completed.

Once battle was joined, the panzer forces raced ahead, covering up to fifty miles a day and breaking up the Russian front into pockets encircled by the German second wave. The Russians had superiority in numbers, but, caught unprepared, this only meant more men to be taken prisoner. The Luftwaffe made roads and railways unusable and, thanks to their previous reconnaissances and the unpreparedness of the Russians, destroyed a large part of their air force on the ground. Russian losses by the end of August are put at over 5,000 planes, close to half their front-line strength.

Denied any advance warning on Stalin's orders, the Soviet commanders were taken by surprise and prevented from concentrating their troops close to the frontier. In many cases, their forces were scattered on exercises and only half-mobilized, needing several days to bring them to full strength. The virtual collapse of the communications system left many commands isolated, without orders, and with no way of finding out what was happening. The confusion in the Kremlin matched that in the field. No high command organization had been created or commander in chief appointed in advance; when the Defense Commissariat prepared a decree naming Stalin as

---

*Combined Russian and German losses in the Second World War were 16,850,000; losses of all nations in the First World War ca. eight million.
†See Appendix I.

commander in chief, he held it back "for discussion with the Politburo."
Experiencing great difficulty in establishing contact with the fronts, those at
the center found it impossible to visualize the extent of the chaos in which
the Soviet forces were floundering, or the scale and force of the attack.

How unreal the picture Moscow had of the situation is shown by Timoshenko's Directive No. 3, issued at 9:15 on the evening of the twenty-
second, ordering all Soviet fronts to take the offensive and hurl the German
army back across the frontiers with a single blow. To front commanders
struggling desperately to hold their forces together at all, this was a message
from a different world. Their efforts to comply, except on the southwestern
front, where Zhukov had been sent to stiffen the front command, proved
uniformly disastrous. On the twenty-third the gap between the northwest-
ern and western fronts was increased to close on eighty miles. The battle on
the frontiers had not been lost; it had never been effectively joined.

General Voronov, the deputy commissar of defense, recalls that in these
first days of the war,

> Stalin was depressed, nervous, and off balance. When he gave assign-
> ments, he demanded that they be completed in an unbelievably short
> time, without considering real possibilities. . . . He misconceived the
> scale of the war, the forces and equipment that could actually stop the
> advancing enemy on a front stretching from sea to sea. He was constantly
> expressing the assumption that the enemy would be defeated in a very
> short time. [45]

In his study of Stalin, General Volkogonov suggests that Stalin put Molotov
up to speak for him, in the belief that within a week the German advance
would be held and he would then be able to speak in person and claim a
victory.

During that first week, however, Stalin suffered some kind of breakdown
following a visit to the Commissariat of Defense on Frunze Street. He was
calm and self-assured when he arrived, but for the first time realized the
magnitude of the danger when he was shown the situation at Minsk, where
two panzer groups were encircling a large Soviet force. Contact had been
lost with them, and nothing could be done to prevent their being cut off.
"Stalin, usually so outwardly calm and deliberate in his speech and motions,
could not restrain himself. He burst out with angry, insulting scolding. Then
without looking at anyone, head down and stooped over, he left the building, got into his car and went home." [46]

The sudden realization of the speed with which the Germans were
advancing, already at Minsk, 100 miles from their starting point, with no
prospect of stopping them, threw him off balance. For two or three days
he was in a state of shock, hiding away in his dacha at Kuntsevo, apparently
in despair that everything would collapse and that he had no idea what to do.

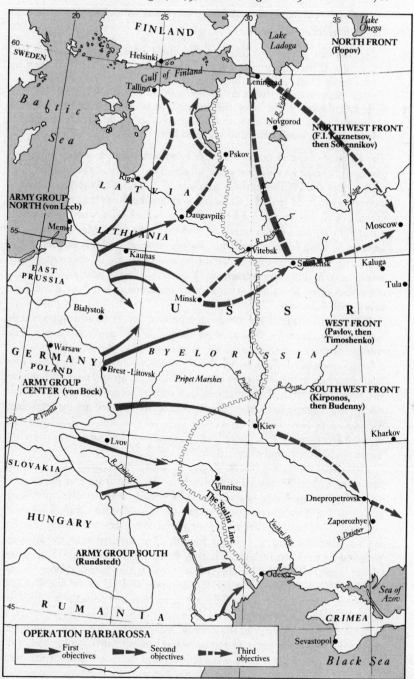

OPERATION BARBAROSSA

First objectives → Second objectives → Third objectives →

Perhaps his daughter, Svetlana, came closest to understanding her father's mind when she wrote:

> He had not guessed or foreseen that the Pact of 1939, which he had considered the outcome of his own great cunning, would be broken by an enemy more cunning than himself. This was the real reason for his deep depression at the start of the war. It was his immense political miscalculation. Even after the war was over he was in the habit of repeating, "Ech, together with the Germans we would have been invincible." But he never admitted his mistakes. [47]

The absence of the all-powerful leader in so centralized a system, where no one dared to take an initiative without him, could not fail to be noticed. The members of the Politburo, the commissar of defense, and the General Staff were overwhelmed with the thousand and one measures that needed to be taken, but all the time they asked: Where is Stalin? Why is he silent at such a time? From remarks he made at a victory dinner on May 24, 1945, he appears to have been seized with the fear—never perhaps far below the surface of his mind—that he would be overthrown: "A different people would have said to the government: 'You have failed to justify our expectations. Go away. We shall install another government which will conclude peace with Germany.' " [48]

When Molotov and the other members of the Politburo appeared at Kuntsevo on June 30, Stalin asked them, "Why have you come?" His strange manner left them with the impression that he thought they had come to arrest him. Mikoyan, who was present, wrote later: "We found him in an armchair in the small dining room. He looked up and said, 'What have you come for?' He had the strangest look on his face and the question itself was pretty strange too. After all, he should have called us in." [49] When Molotov proposed setting up a State Defense Committee (known by its Russian acronym, GOKO) with Stalin as chairman, he looked surprised but made no objection and simply said, "Fine."

From that point on, Stalin began to recover his confidence and to reappear in the Kremlin. Having overcome his own fears and despair, he was able to emerge once again as the indispensable leader, and on July 3 he spoke to the Russian people over the radio using the unusual form of address, "Comrades! Citizens! Fighting men of our army and navy! Brothers and sisters! I turn to you, my friends." For the first time the Russian people were told that Lithuania, Latvia, western Byelorussia, and large parts of the western Ukraine had been lost. Striking the patriotic note, Stalin declared "Our country is in serious danger," and called on the Russian people to destroy everything if forced to retreat, and to wage a relentless struggle against the enemy.

It took longer to sort out the confusion at the top. On June 23, a High Command headquarters (referred to by the Russian word *Stavka*) had been established under Timoshenko as commissar of defense. Stalin at first was only listed as a member of it. Not until July 19 was he named as commissar of defense, and not until August 8 as supreme commander with the *Stavka* as his general headquarters staff.

The formation of an industrial evacuation group was announced on June 24 and then, on the thirtieth, the creation of the State Defense Committee under Stalin's chairmanship. This was given the power to issue overriding directives to all state, party, Soviet, and military organizations. As Stalin was already general secretary of the party and chairman of the Council of Commissars and was shortly to become supreme commander as well, unification of the economic, political, and military direction of the war was complete—in Stalin's hands. As he rarely bothered to make clear in which capacity he was issuing orders, the officials had difficulty in deciding on their distribution.

The experience they had been through had demoralized many units and harsh measures were necessary to restore discipline, but Beria and the reinforced NKVD troops, who were given the task, applied these indiscriminately. Order No. 270 of August 16, 1941 declared that officers and political officials taken prisoner were to be regarded as "malicious deserters" and their families to be subject to arrest. Mekhlis, issuing the instruction "Everyone who has been captured is a traitor to the motherland," without regard to the circumstances, added that they should have committed suicide rather than let themselves be taken alive. This had the effect, and was intended to, of recreating the atmosphere of fear which Stalin regarded as the one reliable means of control. Nor were these empty threats. At the end of the war hundreds of thousands of Russian prisoners who had survived brutal treatment by the Germans were automatically consigned to Soviet camps on their return.

Stalin showed no more confidence in the Russian commanders than he had in their predecessors. Any commander who failed to carry out orders, however unrealistic, was liable to find himself accused of treachery. Political commissars in the army, abolished in 1940, were revived, to watch for signs of defeatism and sabotage. Mekhlis, notorious for the malevolent suspicion with which he regarded the officer corps, was reappointed head of the army's Political Administration. The pressures on Stalin—he worked as much as eighteen out of the twenty-four hours—made him harsher, colder, and more arbitrary than ever. Instead of ordering an investigation of the disasters which had befallen the Soviet forces (which could only have pointed to his own responsibility) he looked for scapegoats and found them in General Pavlov and his commanders on the western front, where the Germans had broken through at Minsk.[50] They were arrested, beaten, and tortured until they "confessed" to having taken part in a military conspiracy against Stalin. When he got the recommendation for their execution, Stalin told Poskrebyshev: "I approve the sentence, but tell Ulrikh to get rid of all that rubbish about 'conspiratorial activity.' No appeal. Then inform the fronts."[51]

At the same time he took steps to wipe out the last remnants of suspected opposition. On September 5 he signed a list of 170 political prisoners for execution, including the survivors of the trials of the 1930s; in October, there were four more generals amongst a second group shot without trial.

There is a report, originating with Beria, that at some date in July, not specified, Stalin discussed with him and Molotov the possibility of approaching Hitler with an offer to hand over the Baltic states, Moldavia, a large part of the Ukraine, and Byelorussia in return for an armistice. Beria was told to get in touch with the Bulgarian ambassador as a possible way of getting the proposal to Hitler, but the ambassador, Ivan Stamenov, told Molotov and Beria (Stalin said nothing throughout) that if they had to retreat to the Urals they would still win in the end, and refused to act as an intermediary. Mikoyan and Khrushchev repeat the report and Stamenov later confirmed it to the Soviet inquiry looking into the case of Beria when he was arrested after Stalin's death. [52]*

Although Stalin did not take the title of supreme commander until August, he was the only possible candidate for the post. Despite his experience as a troubleshooter in the civil war—which bore little relation to the war with which he was now confronted—he had had no more experience of commanding troops than Hitler, and was as willful and difficult to advise. The same gifts which he showed as a politician were of value in military matters: his quickness in grasping a situation, mastery of detail, phenomenal memory, self-confidence (once he had recovered it), and his capacity for sheer hard work. But the same faults offset them, very much as they did in Hitler's case—stubbornness, unwillingness to admit that he might be wrong and others right, and an obsessive suspicion. As with Hitler, political considerations, especially as they affected his power and prestige, overrode arguments based on military grounds, except in crises such as the threatened loss of Leningrad and capture of Moscow, in both of which he swallowed his pride and turned to Zhukov.

In the course of time Stalin established a better working relationship with his staff and chief commanders—Hitler's relations with his got steadily worse—but this was not until the battle of Stalingrad in the winter of 1942–43. During the learning process in 1941 and 1942, the Red Army had to pay a heavy price for his mistakes. Unaware of how much he did not know, like Hitler he became convinced in time that he was a military as well as a political genius. It was only when the Russians began to win victories, however, that the hitherto impersonal communiqués started to bear his signature.

By the end of July the German armies had to pause in order to re-fit. In spite of their success, the Germans had not yet destroyed the Red Army west of the Dnieper-Dvina line, nor had they reached their three principal objectives, Leningrad, Moscow, and the Donets basin. Nor, despite the

*For an alternative version placing this episode in October 1941, see below p. 808.

losses they had inflicted, had they destroyed the Russian army. German intelligence officers were impressed by the fact that, even when cut off, Soviet units frequently continued to fight fiercely and that fresh divisions continued to be put into the battle to attack the German flanks. The dependence of the German forces on long lines of supply already threatened to restrict their mobility. Army Group Center required twenty-five goods trains a day to meet its needs; but on some days in late July and early August only eight arrived and the best actually achieved was no more than fifteen.

The key decision to be made was to fix objectives for von Bock's Army Group Center as soon as its two panzer groups had been re-fitted. It will be remembered that the original OKH plan had been for them to drive on towards Moscow. Now that they had reached Smolensk and successfully completed the first stage of their advance, it was to this that the OKH, von Bock, and the panzer commanders themselves reverted, not (as they insisted) in order to capture the city but, following classical military doctrine, to destroy the main Russian armies where they expected them to be concentrated, in defense of the capital. Hitler, however, from the time he signed the first directive in December 1940, had favored a different course, attaching priority to clearing the Baltic states and capturing Leningrad in the north, and reinforcing the drive southeast toward Kiev and the Dnieper in order to deprive the Russians of the agricultural and industrial resources of the Ukraine and open the way to the Caucasus.

Hitler believed that he had settled the matter, but then fell ill with dysentery only to find, on his recovery, that the generals had taken advantage of his illness to delay action while they reopened the debate in a further memorandum. All the distrust of the professional military mind which Hitler had shown in the western campaign was renewed in full force by this opposition, and he sent a furious reply insisting on having his way and adding the scornful remark that only minds set in the mold of outworn theories could fail to recognize the opportunities in the south. Jodl's private comment was: "The Führer has an instinctive aversion to treading the same path as Napoleon. Moscow gives him a sinister feeling. He fears that there might be a life-and-death struggle with Bolshevism." [53] In the end, a compromise was reached: The drive on Moscow was to be renewed, but only after a breakthrough had been made in the Ukraine.

The initial German onslaught had brought the Russians to the edge of disaster, but had not pushed them over. The German delay in renewing the attack while Hitler and the generals argued about their next objective gave the Soviet High Command a breathing space which it used to regroup, re-fit, and rush up new divisions, however poorly trained and ill-equipped, to fill the gaps. Stalin even began to hope that the front line might be stabilized, telling Harry Hopkins, Roosevelt's envoy, that "the line during the winter would be in front of Moscow, Kiev, and Leningrad, probably not more than one hundred kilometers from where it is now."

The pause ended on August 23. The German attack was then resumed with Guderian's panzer army switched to Army Group South, where it helped to lay the ground for another German victory in the Ukraine. The decision Stalin took in response was as much against the advice of his generals as Hitler's had been. Alarmed at the threat to the Ukraine, Stalin had earlier sent two of his old comrades from the First Cavalry Army, Voroshilov and Budenny, to take charge in the southwest. Both were now marshals of the Soviet Union, but neither proved up to the job. Stalin, however, was still distrustful of the professional soldiers. On July 29 Zhukov, as chief of the General Staff, gave a full report on the whole situation. Stalin would not allow him to begin until he had brought Mekhlis in to listen. Zhukov spoke with a confidence which irritated Stalin, but which proved to be well justified by the events that followed. He pinpointed the junction between the western and the southwestern fronts as the danger point. His proposals were to reinforce the western front covering Moscow; to bring eight divisions from the Far East to strengthen the Moscow axis, and to pull back the southwestern front behind the Dnieper. When Stalin discovered that this meant giving up Kiev, he exploded and told Zhukov not to talk rubbish. Zhukov showed anger in turn and retorted that if the chief of the General Staff was only able to talk nonsense he had better be relieved. "Don't get heated," Stalin told him, "but since you mentioned it, we will get by without you." [54]

After Zhukov had justified his work as chief of the General Staff, Stalin closed the interview. Forty minutes later he called him back and told him he would be replaced by Shaposhnikov, who although aging and unwell, knew better than to argue with "the Boss." Zhukov bridled again over the question of his new appointment. "Calm down, calm down," Stalin repeated, and then told him he would be given command of the Reserve Front. He insisted Zhukov should sit down and drink some tea before going, but the conversation flagged and Stalin's best commander left dispirited.

Zhukov's forecast proved only too well-founded. The junction he had pointed to was where Guderian made his breakthrough at the end of August, opening the way to the encirclement of no less than five Soviet armies on the southwest front. One commander after another—including Budenny—urged Stalin to authorize withdrawal before it was too late. But Stalin was as adamant as Hitler was to be in refusing to give up a square foot of territory. "Kiev was, is, and will be Soviet," was his reply. "I do not permit you to retreat to the Sula River. I order you to hold Kiev and the Dnieper." [55]

On September 18, Kiev was lost and, thanks to Stalin's obstinacy, nearly half a million Soviet troops were taken prisoner, a huge and unnecessary loss which opened the way to the German capture of the Ukraine.

Voroshilov and Zhdanov, whom Stalin had entrusted with the defense of Leningrad, barely escaped a similar disaster. After overrunning the Baltic states, von Leeb's Army Group North broke through the outer defenses of the city and on September 8 cut its last land-link with the rest of the Soviet Union, leaving Lake Ladoga as the only means of communication. With the fall of the country's second city apparently imminent, Stalin sent Zhukov to take command and save it. By the time he arrived on September 13, Hitler had already decided not to storm the city but to starve it into surrender.

By now Hitler's interest in an attack on Moscow had revived. He told his entourage: "In a few weeks we shall be in Moscow. I will raze that damned city and in its place construct an artificial lake with central lighting. The name of Moscow will disappear forever."[56]

To bar a German advance on the capital, the Stavka had concentrated 800,000 men, 770 tanks, and 364 planes, half the Red Army's strength, on the entire Soviet-German front, and one-third of its tanks and planes. The German plan was to launch Operation Typhoon, with three infantry armies, three panzer armies (General Hermann Hoth, Guderian brought back from the south, and Höpner brought back from Leningrad). The plan was to encircle the Russian forces by a pincer operation north and south of the Moscow highway, closing its arms near Vyazma. It was not, however, until October 2 that the advance on Moscow was resumed, not in the summer weather of August—as it might have been if Hitler had not insisted on giving priority to the Ukraine operation—but at the beginning of the autumn, two and a half months after the German army had captured Smolensk on July 16. This was a delay which in the event proved fatal to whatever chances he had of capturing Moscow and to his gamble on winning before the winter a blitzkrieg victory which would lead to the collapse of the Soviet state.

Once again, the German panzers overwhelmed the Russian defenses by the speed and violence of their onslaught. Once again the Russian front disintegrated and another giant encirclement at Vyazma-Bryansk on the scale of that in the Ukraine left the road to Moscow open. Once again, at the eleventh hour, Stalin summoned Zhukov from Leningrad and put him in charge of the capital's defense. From then on Zhukov remained at the heart of the Stavka's war planning until the German surrender. When he assumed command on October 10, the total force at his disposal had been reduced from the 800,000 of the end of September to no more than 90,000, called upon to hold a 150-mile front. The tally of captured Soviet troops was now approaching three million.

Hitler did not wait to declare the enemy beaten and victory achieved. On October 8, Orel was captured, and Jodl reported: "We have finally and without any exaggeration won the war!" The following day Otto Dietrich, Hitler's press chief, announced to war correspondents: "For all military purposes Soviet Russia is done with."

Mid-October was the point at which the Soviet resistance came nearest to cracking. Zhukov recalls Stalin calling him and saying: "You are convinced we shall be able to hold Moscow? I am asking this with pain in my heart. Answer truthfully, as you are a Communist." According to Zhukov, on October 7 there were no Red Army troops between the Germans and Moscow. It was on this date that he claims to have been present when Stalin, declaring himself ready to accept a "new Brest peace," as Lenin had in 1918, ordered Beria to make the approach through the Bulgarian ambassador which others place in July.

The evacuation of the Soviet government to Kuibyshev, 600 miles to the east, began on the fifteenth of October, and this set off a general panic-stricken *sauve qui peut* in the capital. Offices and factories were abandoned, the railway stations besieged, the roads to the east jammed with cars filled with party officials. With no police to protect them, stores were plundered, while on Zhukov's orders demolition squads mined the city's bridges and railway junctions. Stalin himself had planned to leave Moscow, but after hearing Zhukov's assurance that it could be held, decided to stay and lead the hard core who were determined to defend the capital to the end. He put the city under martial law and appointed an NKVD general, P. A. Artemeyev, to enforce it.

One step which Stalin had already taken was to start drawing on the three-quarters of a million experienced and well-equipped Soviet troops in the Far East. Thanks to Richard Sorge in Tokyo, he had received reliable information that, although the Japanese had reinforced their Kwantung army facing the Soviet frontiers, there would be no attack before the spring of 1942. In October and November, when the Germans were convinced the Russians had exhausted their reserves, Stalin was able to move between eight and ten rifle divisions to the west—eventually up to half the divisional strength of the Far Eastern command—together with 1,700 tanks and 1,500 aircraft. No less important was the fact that, however desperate the situation around Moscow, these fresh troops were not dribbled into the battle but held tight in the Supreme Command Reserve which the Stavka was building up.

In mid-October, the German delay in launching their attack began to make its effect felt. Sleet mixed with rain started to fall, turning the ground, with few usable roads at the best of times, into inland lakes of mud. At night the temperature fell and froze it; each morning the thaw returned and movement even for tracked vehicles became a nightmare of slithering and sliding. The mud below was matched by overcast skies above which hindered the activities of the German airforce.

At the end of October the German forces had to halt for reinforcements and regrouping. By then Army Group South, operating in a warmer climate, had taken Kharkov and overrun the "Soviet Ruhr," the Donbass, while Manstein's Eleventh Army took possession of the Crimea except for a heroically defended Sevastopol. Further north, however, Stalin was able to use the pause to build up new reserve armies east of Moscow and send 100,000 men and 300 tanks to reinforce Zhukov's western front, the last line of defense less than fifty miles from the capital.

It is in these last two months of 1941 and the first three of 1942 that the parallel between the roles of Stalin and Hitler becomes most apparent, with the leadership of both men put to the most severe test. On November 6, delegates from the party, the Moscow city administration, and the Red Army crowded into the marble cavern of the Mayakovsky underground station to hear Stalin answer Hitler's "victory speech" of October 3 in the Berlin Sportpalast by hurling defiance at the invader: "If they want a war of extermination, they shall have one."

He followed this up the next day, the anniversary of the revolution, with the bold gesture of taking the salute at the traditional military parade in Red Square, despite the fact that the enemy was at the gates and the capital liable to air attack. In his speech Stalin recalled that in 1918 the Red Army had been in an even worse position, yet still went on to win, and invoked "the great figures of our heroic ancestors—Alexander Nevsky, Dmitri Donskoy, Suvorov, and Kutuzov"—the last-named being the general who had led the Russian army when Napoleon was forced to retreat from Moscow.

Three days later Zhukov took one of his commanders, General P. A. Belov, with him when he went to discuss his plans with Stalin. Passing a bomb crater in the Kremlin, they found him at the end of an underground corridor in a room with a large writing table and a group of telephones. Belov had last seen Stalin in 1933: "He had changed a great deal since that time; before me stood a smallish man with a tired sunken face . . . in eight years he appeared to have aged twenty." What surprised Belov was Zhukov's behavior: "He spoke brusquely, in a very authoritative way. The effect suggested that the senior officer was Zhukov. And Stalin took it all for granted. At no time did any trace of annoyance cross his face."[57] The learning process had begun, but it was Stalin who continued to conduct the war as supreme commander, coordinating the movement of troops and issuing orders by telephone to the northern and southern fronts, as well as approving Zhukov's proposals.

THE FINAL BATTLE for Moscow opened on November 15, with the Russians soon fighting desperately to hold off yet another encirclement. Pressed back against the Moskva-Volga canal, the last major obstacle before the capital, Rokossovsky (who had been brought back after three years in prison camp to command an army corps) received the order from Zhukov:

> Kryukovo is the final point of withdrawal; there can be no further falling back. There is nowhere else to fall back to.[58]

The battlefield was now deep in snow, frozen hard in bitter winds and freezing fog in which the ill-clad Germans and their machines, planes as well as tanks, froze up. In the week which saw November turn into December, both sides fought to the limits of human endurance, while Zhukov pressed for and Stalin still refused a counterblow to relieve his exhausted forces. A few German units actually reached the outer suburbs of the capital and saw the flashes of the antiaircraft guns defending the Kremlin. On December

2, Halder noted in his diary that the Russian defense had reached its climax and had no fresh forces left to throw into the battle. But he deceived himself.

On December 5, in temperatures which had fallen to between −25° to −30°C, the leading German panzer commander, General Guderian, realized that his troops no longer had the strength to carry on the attack and must be withdrawn to a shorter line which he could hope to hold. The same day that the German attack came to a halt, the Soviet counteroffensive was launched with the 700,000 men the Stavka, unknown to the Germans, had been gathering together east of Moscow. Much more used than the Germans to the cold and provided with padded winter clothing, they included substantial forces from the Far East, and for the first time drove the Germans back.

It was at this juncture that Hitler's leadership was put to the same test as Stalin's had been earlier, to show whether he could prevent demoralization from spreading and stop a retreat turning into a rout. The German forces in the east had suffered three-quarters of a million casualties, of whom one in four was dead; the Russian losses had been far greater, and on the western axis in front of Moscow the Germans still had the edge in numbers when the December counterattack began. But in most other ways the invaders were at a serious disadvantage, between 700 and 1,000 miles from their bases, with supplies of everything constantly interrupted by the weather and partisan attacks, suffering heavily from the cold (100,000 cases of frostbite by Christmas), and from the psychological letdown, after so many victories, of falling at the last hurdle. "Only he who saw the endless expanse of Russian snow during this winter of our misery and felt the icy wind that blew across it," Guderian later wrote ". . . can truly judge the events that now occurred." [59] "At the critical moment," says a divisional commander, General von Tippelskirch, "the troops were remembering what they had heard about Napoleon's retreat from Moscow in 1812, and living under the shadow of it. If they had once begun a retreat it might have turned into a panic flight." [60]

Hitler rose to the occasion, as Stalin had. In hour-long telephone conversations with the generals at the front, he categorically refused to permit withdrawal, no matter how urgent their appeals. Field Marshal von Bock was relieved of the command of Army Group Center; when Kluge, his successor, telephoned for permission to straighten his line by withdrawal, Hitler spent from 11:30 at night to 2:30 the next morning arguing with him—interrupted only by half an hour's discussion with Halder, the army chief of staff. Kluge, too, was refused permission and told to hold the line where he stood. When Guderian flew to Hitler's headquarters on December 20 to describe the desperate situation of his troops, Hitler showed no sympathy at all, but asked him, "Do you think that Frederick the Great's grenadiers enjoyed dying for their country either?" When Guderian continued a covert withdrawal, Hitler dismissed him out of hand. Höpner, the other outstanding panzer general, was stripped of his rank and decorations, forbidden to wear his uniform, and deprived of his pension and other rights. Field Marshal von Leeb was retired from Army Group North, and Field Marshal von Rundstedt was replaced after capturing, and then withdrawing from, Rostov.

As a result of Hitler's intervention, the retreat was halted and the front stabilized deep inside Russian territory. Hitler claimed it as proof of what the will could accomplish in face of the experts' doubts. In the short run this was an impressive argument, but it ignored the real measure of the German failure. Every one of the assumptions on which Hitler had based his decision had been proven ill-founded. As a result of the German failure to take account of the size even of European Russia, or of its much greater distances and much poorer communications, the German army had been unable to reproduce in a single campaign the blitzkrieg effect which had proved so effective elsewhere.

Despite the unprecedented size of the forces concentrated for the attack and the remarkable successes they had achieved, they had proved inadequate in relation to the scale of the operation they were required to undertake. The Luftwaffe, for example, called on to operate over a front stretching from Leningrad to the Black Sea, was simply unable, after its initial effort, to match anything like the effect it had had in Poland, France, and Yugoslavia.

Despite the huge losses in men and territory, the Soviet government had not, as Hitler had calculated, collapsed under the impact of the attack, and Soviet resources in manpower, armaments, and industrial potential proved to have been grossly underestimated. It was not the delay imposed by the Balkan campaign, nor the failure to launch the drive on Moscow in time, which was the cause of the German failure, but fundamental flaws in the whole concept of defeating Russia in a single campaign.

Refusing to face this and, like Stalin, ignoring his share of the responsibility for the situation in which the German forces found themselves, Hitler laid the blame on the military leadership for failing to keep him informed of the true state of affairs.

When von Brauchitsch offered his resignation, Hitler at once accepted it and made him a scapegoat. Declaring that he knew of no general capable of instilling the National Socialist spirit in the army, Hitler announced that he would take von Brauchitsch's place himself, becoming commander in chief of the German army as well as supreme commander of the Wehrmacht (Armed Forces). Halder survived for another ten months only because Hitler needed someone of his experience as army chief of staff. As before, the OKW retained control of the other theaters of war—the Balkans, North Africa, and the west—answerable to Hitler as its supreme commander. But the eastern front was henceforward reserved to the OKH, the army's High Command, responsible directly to Hitler, who now took personal control of operations in the east with his headquarters at Rastenburg in East Prussia.

Nothing could have more clearly underlined the importance he attached to victory in the east at all costs.

V

BY THE END OF 1941, the Germans controlled, in one form or another, the greater part of the European continent.* How this Nazi empire was to be organized was still unsettled. As early as May 1940, the campaign in the west had given an impetus to discussions of a European *Grossraumwirtschaft* (an economic sphere of influence). This was in line with Hitler's insistence that the European economy must be reorganized in such a way as to make Germany economically self-sufficient. "We must conquer the things we need but lack," Hitler said to Todt in June 1940, and Göring instructed Funk to set up a special department in his Economics Ministry to prepare plans for a "unified European *Grossraumwirtschaft* under German leadership."

The ultimate boundaries of the *Grossraum* remained fluid, but the heart of it was always seen as the Reich itself expanded by the annexation of Austria, Bohemia-Moravia, Alsace-Lorraine, Luxembourg, parts of Belgium, and the provinces "recovered" from Poland, including Silesia. Most of Europe's heavy industries were to be concentrated in this area, which would play the same role in the European economy as the Ruhr had in the German. The only industrial production allowed outside it would be of consumer goods for Germany. Apart from that, the rest of the conquered territories would produce food for the guaranteed German market. Centralized planning, including the control of credit and labor, would create an international economy tailored to suit the needs of Germany.

In practice Nazi Europe was a patchwork of jurisdictions. Very little was actually annexed to the Reich, apart from the territories "recovered" from 1938 to 1940. Three other large areas, although distinct from the Reich, were completely subordinated to it: the Protectorate of Bohemia-Moravia, the Government-General of Poland, and the two Reich Commissariats of Ostland and the Ukraine. The rest of occupied Europe was either under military occupation (those parts of Russia where operations were still going on, Greece, Serbia, Belgium, and Occupied France) or some form of German civilian control exercised in conjunction with local native administrations (Norway, Denmark, and Holland). The picture was completed by Germany's allies in varying degrees of dependence on the Reich, from the other Axis partner, Italy, which had its own empire, to the puppet states of Slovakia and Croatia. Vichy France fitted into none of the categories, officially enjoying an independent nonbelligerent status, until finally occupied in November 1942.

All the occupied territories were required to pay levies, far above the actual costs of the occupation. These had to be paid, as in all other

*See the map on pp. 734–35.

transactions with the Germans, at an artificially high rate of exchange fixed in favor of the Reichsmark. The gold and foreign currency reserves of occupied countries were taken over, and their banking systems manipulated to give the Germans control over the issue of bank notes and the granting of credits.

As each new area was conquered it was incorporated into the economy of the "New Order" under Göring's direction: one after the other, Poland (1939), Holland, Norway, France (1940), and finally the eastern territories (June 1941).

Göring expressed his economic philosophy succinctly in 1942:

> It seems to me that in earlier times the thing was simple. In earlier times you pillaged. He who had conquered a country disposed of the riches of that country. At present, things are done in a more humane way. As for myself, I still think of pillage, comprehensively. [61]

Pillage, however—grabbing stocks, machinery, raw materials, everything movable, and carrying them off to Germany—had to be balanced against a more effective policy of exploiting local industry and labor on the spot and exporting the finished products to Germany. Industry in the occupied territories was controlled by a system of licenses for raw materials and fuel; agriculture, in western and southeast Europe, through the local ministries of agriculture. These had to meet the quotas for delivery as well as production laid down by the Reich Food Office, which also fixed prices and subsidies. Twenty-five million tons of food were imported from occupied Europe, most of it requisitioned. From 1941 to 1943 these supplies increased the German civilian ration by between a fifth and a quarter, while the population of the occupied territories, especially in the cities, went hungry.

A large percentage, not only of food production, but also of raw materials, had to be delivered to Germany. These were paid for not by equivalent exports from Germany, but by blocked credits to be settled after the war. The overall German debt on this account has been estimated at 42 billion marks by September 1944, and the sum owed to France alone was 8.2 billion marks by the end of July 1944.

In addition to the general control he exercised over the economies of occupied Europe, Göring reached out towards the European economy of the future by setting up integrated structures aimed at controlling production in the aluminium, coal, and oil industries on a European-wide basis, including the neutrals. Plans for other European production controls were drawn up in textiles, iron and steel, and chemicals. This was staking a claim not only for German domination of the European *Grossraumwirtschaft,* but also for the leading role in it of the Four-Year Plan, the economic empire over which Göring presided, against other German rivals.

Although the turn of the tide of war against Germany in 1943 cut short the development of a German-dominated European economy, there is no

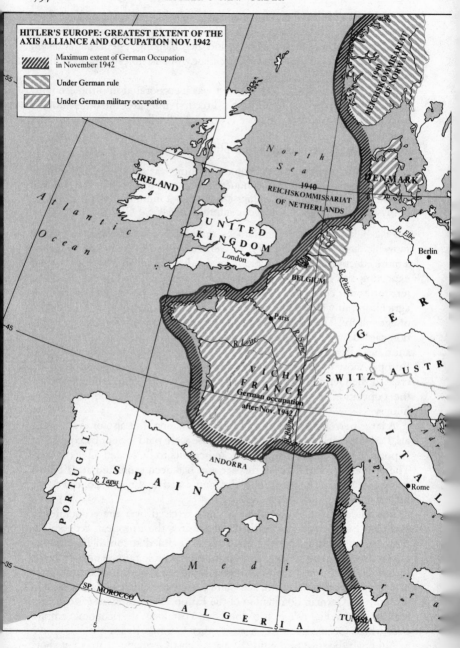

HITLER'S EUROPE: GREATEST EXTENT OF THE
AXIS ALLIANCE AND OCCUPATION NOV. 1942

Maximum extent of German Occupation
in November 1942

Under German rule

Under German military occupation

FINLAND

L. Ladoga

L. Onega

Baltic Sea

Åland Iss.

Leningrad

L. Pskov

Moscow

Riga

1941
REICHSKOMMISSARIAT
OF OSTLAND

U. S. S. R.

Minsk

R. Volga

R. Vistula

R. Don

Stalingrad

Warsaw

1941
REICHSKOMMISSARIAT
OF UKRAINE

Kiev

R. Dnieper

GOVERNMENT-
GENERAL

DON BASS

Vienna

SLOVAKIA

HUNGARY

Sea of Azov

Budapest

R U M A N I A

CROATIA

SERBIA

Bucharest

B l a c k   S e a

MONTE-
NEGRO

ALBANIA
(to Italy)

B U L G A R I A

Adriatic Sea

GREECE

T   U   R   K   E   Y

SYRIA

Cyprus

n   e   a   n

25

35

doubt about the benefits which German war production drew from the occupied territories. When deliveries were at their peak during 1943 and 1944, 30 percent of "Greater German" coal production (98.5 million tons) came from them, above all from Polish Upper Silesia, and around 40 percent of its raw steel production (34.6 million tons). In July 1944 Speer reported that "up to that time, 25 to 30 percent of German war production had been furnished by the occupied western territories and Italy."[62]

Against this can be set a mass of evidence to show how far the exploitation of the occupied countries' economies fell short of the potential, because of the conflict and confusion created by competing German agencies, the endemic Nazi corruption, and the alienation of the population as a result of the failure of the occupying power to establish any common interest with them. An example is the failure to make anything like full use of the French aircraft industry. Its capacity in 1940 was approaching 5,000 aircraft a year. Over the period 1940 to 1944 the Germans secured a total output of no more than 2,517, the bulk of them trainers, around one-tenth of the potential output.[63]

Nothing did more to increase disaffection and resistance than the recruitment of men and women from the occupied countries for work in German factories, mines, farms, and transport. There was already a shortage of labor in Germany before the war, and with the call-up of millions of German workers to the armed forces it became critical. To fill the gap, efforts were made to attract volunteers from other countries; numbers soon fell off as reports of the conditions of work and living spread, and recruitment was replaced by conscription. The numbers rose from 300,000 in 1939 to three million in 1941, six and a half million in 1943, and over seven million in 1944. By that time foreign workers made up 22 percent of those employed in German agriculture and almost 20 percent of the Reich's total work force. A substantial number were prisoners of war (especially French prisoners), but the majority were rounded up and deported. Poorly paid and poorly fed, the conditions under which they lived got steadily worse as the bombing of German towns and communications rose in intensity. This human levy added to the resentment already felt at the increasing shortages of food, fuel, and clothing imposed in order to keep up the Germans' standard of living, however hungry and cold the populations of the occupied countries, and helped to produce the hatred against the Germans and collaborators which burst out in the final stages of the war.

HOWEVER HARD life was in the rest of occupied Europe, it could not be compared with the brutal treatment suffered by the Slav countries of Poland, Yugoslavia, and Russia, the only three countries whose wartime losses exceeded 10 percent of their prewar populations.*

Any war fought on the scale and with the intensity of the Russian

*See Appendix I.

campaign would lead to atrocities being committed by both sides; but even when that is taken into account, there remains an extra dimension of inhumanity on the German side which sprang directly from the racist views to which Hitler had been converted during his Vienna days. In Hitler's view, the Germans were not only superior to the peoples of Eastern Europe, but the gap which separated them from Slavs, and even more widely from Jews, was not based on cultural differences, the product of different historical experiences, but upon inherited biological differences. They were creatures of a different kind, not members of the human race at all— "subhuman" in the case of the Slavs; in the case of the Jews, parasites who preyed upon and destroyed human beings.

Since 1933 these views had been given scientific respectability and taught as part of the curriculum—racial biology—in German schools and universities. Many of the younger men serving on the eastern front had been affected by this process of indoctrination. First put into practice in Poland, Hitler now made his racist ideology an overriding directive for the German conduct of military operations and of the occupation. This time Hitler insisted that the army as well as the SS must accept that "the coming campaign is more than a mere clash of arms; it is also a conflict between two ideologies."[64] He repeated the same message to an assembly of senior officers on March 30. Halder's notes of his address read:

> Clash of two ideologies. . . . Communism is an enormous danger for our future. We must forget the concept of comradeship between soldiers. A Communist is no comrade before or after the battle. This is a war of extermination (*Vernichtungskrieg*). . . . We do not wage war to preserve the enemy.[65]

In the so-called Commissar Order of May 13,[66] Hitler required the army to destroy the Soviet leadership by killing all captured political officials and commissars out of hand, an order which, despite the misgivings of individual officers, was circulated in writing by the army High Command. By another directive of May 6,[67] dealing with the treatment of the civilian population in Russia, the High Command ordered the shooting of all local residents who took part in hostile acts or resisted the German armed forces, if necessary "by collective measures of force against villages from which attacks of any kind have taken place." Two further decrees exempted German soldiers from prosecution for punishable acts on occupied soil and ordered "ruthless and energetic action at the slightest sign of restiveness" on the part of prisoners of war. These completed a comprehensive repudiation of military law and the conventions of war demanded in advance by the supreme commander, Adolf Hitler. As the evidence makes clear, they were implemented by the German armed forces, officers and men, not just the SS, in their conduct of the war in the east.

Rosenberg, whom Hitler had placed nominally in charge of occupation policy in the east, shared Hitler's racist views so far as the Great Russians and the Jews were concerned, but, almost alone among the Nazi leaders, he distinguished between the Russians and the other nationalities of the Soviet Union. Rosenberg saw "Muscovy" as the heart of "Russian-Mongol backwardness" which under tsarist and Soviet regimes alike had suppressed and imposed a forced Russification on the national identities of Ukrainians and Estonians, Georgians, and Tartars. By appearing as liberators from Bolshevik oppression and offering them the opportunity to set up autonomous states of their own under German protection, he believed the Germans could win the cooperation of many millions of the inhabitants of the Soviet Union, break up the Russian state, and build a *cordon sanitaire* against any revival of "Muscovy" and the power of the Great Russians. The details of Rosenberg's plans for partitioning the Soviet Union varied, but common to all of them was the creation of a Ukrainian state and the formation of Baltic and Caucasian federations.

Although Hitler had earlier spoken in similar terms, by the time of the invasion he had turned against any idea of establishing new states in favor of direct German rule. "The road to self-government leads to independence," he declared at one of his lunchtime sessions. "One cannot keep by democratic institutions what one has acquired by force."[68] Force, for Hitler, like fear, for Stalin, was the only thing one could rely on, and by the summer of 1941 success had made him confident enough to believe that he could break up the Soviet state by force alone without any need to appeal to the non-Russian nationalities.

After Hitler's earlier success in exploiting the divisions of Germany's opponents, his refusal to apply the same methods of political warfare in the east was a decision which many Germans came to regret. Already in February 1942 Goebbels had written in his diary: "We were geared altogether too much to a brief campaign and saw victory so close to our eyes that we thought it unnecessary to bother about psychological questions of this sort. What we missed then we must now recoup the hard way."[69]

Once it had become clear that the war in the east was not going to be won in a matter of months, senior officers in the army as well as professional propagandists like Goebbels—in the end even (for tactical reasons) Himmler himself—began to look for a way to develop a political appeal to the Russian as well as the non-Russian peoples. The conclusion of a conference of military government commanders in December 1942 put the argument in two short sentences: "The seriousness of the situation clearly makes imperative the positive cooperation of the population. Russia can be beaten only by the Russians."[70]

But Hitler, fortified by Bormann, remained adamant. While Stalin showed the flexibility to exploit the Soviet population's reaction to German harshness by playing up the nationalist and playing down the Communist appeal, Hitler the master politician was eclipsed by Hitler the master strategist who continued to believe, long after everyone else, that he could still wrest victory from the Fates by force alone.

There are reports that, to begin with, the Germans were welcomed as liberators, certainly in those parts of Poland and the western Ukraine recently occupied by the Russians—in how many other places it is impossible to say. One can do no more than speculate how far the Germans would have succeeded in winning over the Ukrainian population, as Rosenberg urged, if they had appealed to their national traditions repressed by the Russians, and broken up the collective farms, allowing the peasants to reclaim the land again. This was where Stalin's regime was most vulnerable. But Rosenberg was not listened to. Instead, under Hitler's urging, the German armies made war not only on the Bolshevik regime and the Russian state, but on the peoples of Russia as well, Great Russians, Ukrainians, and non-Russians alike. Despite later efforts, the opportunity, once lost, could never be recovered: The impression left by German behavior in those opening weeks of the campaign—the behavior of the army as much as of the SS—was indelible.

The surrender of huge numbers of Russian troops—Soviet figures put the number taken prisoner in the first eighteen months at three million, German figures still higher—points to widespread defeatism and disaffection in the Soviet forces, even if the Germans were impressed by the stubbornness with which other units resisted.

The NKVD was instructed to shoot as deserters any Soviet prisoners who escaped and fell into their hands. But those who remained in German hands were no better treated. The German army, expecting a short war, had made no proper preparations for such overwhelming numbers of prisoners. If the organization was inadequate, the German attitude was also shaped by the Nazis' *Untermensch* propaganda: They were dealing not with human beings like themselves but with a subhuman race.

A further OKW directive of September 8 on the treatment of prisoners of war declared that they had forfeited every claim to be treated as an honorable foe, and that the most ruthless measures were justified in dealing with them. Large numbers were shot out of hand, without any pretext, in order to relieve the army of the burden they represented. Hundreds of thousands were forced to march until they dropped and died from exhaustion or were herded into huge improvised camps and left without food, medical help for the wounded, shelter, or sanitation. According to a German report of February 19, 1942, almost three out of the four million prisoners taken by that date had perished. The Geneva Convention was no help to the Russian prisoners, since the Soviet Union had never ratified it, and this left the Germans free to ignore its provisions. Stalin was no help either, taking the view that any soldier who fell into German hands, including his own son Yakov (whom he disliked and disowned), was ipso facto a traitor and not entitled to protection from his government.

Large areas of Russia remained under military administration throughout the German occupation. Their size made it hard for the army to control them and made the German lines of communications and rear bases vulnerable to guerilla attacks by partisan bands. The brutality with which the Germans treated both prisoners and the civilian population drove many—including stragglers from the Red Army—to take to the forests and join the partisans. By the summer of 1942, the number of these had risen to around 150,000, finally reaching a figure of around half a million. They formed an invisible second front in Byelorussia and the Ukraine, threatening the German rear. The German answer was to take ruthless reprisals. An OKW directive of September 1941 set a figure of 50 to 100 Russians to be shot for the life of every German soldier, adding "the means of execution must increase the deterrent effect still further."[71] Any village suspected of harboring or supplying partisans was liable to be burned down and its inhabitants massacred. The army, as well as the SS, became committed to a war of extermination, which in turn only increased Russian hatred of the invaders and swelled the partisans' numbers.

BEHIND THE AREAS under military administration, occupied Russia was divided into two Reich Commissariats under German civil administration. The more northerly, the Ostland, consisted of the three Baltic states and Byelorussia (known as White Ruthenia) which the Soviet Union had acquired under the Nazi-Soviet Pact and now lost again. The other was the Ukraine, at its greatest extent 75,000 square miles in area (half the size of France), with a population of fifty million.

Rosenberg saw the Ukraine as the key to the failure or success of his policy for Russia. By winning the confidence of the Ukrainians, who had suffered more than any other group from Communist rule, and re-creating a Ukrainian state, he believed that Germany could build a permanent barrier against the revival and expansion of Russian power. To hard-liners such as Göring and Bormann this was nonsense. Once the Ukraine had been conquered, the land and its people were henceforth to serve only one purpose, the satisfaction of German needs during the war and subsequently a prime site for German colonization. By securing Hitler's agreement to the appointment as Reich commissar in the Ukraine of Erich Koch, the Gauleiter of East Prussia, they effectively blocked any chance of Rosenberg's policy being adopted.

Koch could well be taken as the quintessential Nazi *Alte Kämpfer*. Beginning as a petty railway official in the Rhineland, he claimed to have joined the Nazi party in 1921 as its nineteenth member. Gravitating to the radical, anti-capitalist wing of the party, he became a follower of Gregor Strasser and in 1928 was appointed Gauleiter of East Prussia. There he won the reputation of being an energetic party leader, a natural demagogue, hostile to intellectuals and middle-class pretensions, and not troubled by any scruples about the means he used to get things done or to line his own pockets. Always interested in Russia and the east, he had no patience at all with Rosenberg's ideas. Treating the notion of a Ukrainian nation or culture with contempt, he referred to them not only privately, but in speeches, as helots, slaves, niggers, who were best handled with the whip and should be grateful that the Germans allowed them to live at all.

Rosenberg's attempts to curb his nominal subordinate were ineffectual. Koch claimed to be responsible solely to the Führer and was confident that it was he, not Rosenberg, who would have Hitler's and Bormann's support for the hard-line policy of "no concessions," which he maintained consistently until the Ukraine was finally lost in 1944.

Koch was important less for what he did (he was absent much of the time) than for the image of German rule which he created and which agreed well enough with the reality of it as the native population in the Ukraine experienced it. But it was not the Reich commissars—whether Koch in the Ukraine or Lohse in the Ostland—and their minimal staffs who were responsible for imposing German demands and plans in practice, but the various economic agencies and the SS operating in their territories. The Reich minister of finance wrote in exasperation on September 4, 1942: "We ourselves no longer know who constitutes an authority, and who does not, who belongs to an authority, to a semiofficial company, or to the large group of selfish hyenas in the field."[72] But these jurisdictional battles are of marginal interest by comparison with the impact of the operations themselves and the policy they reflected.

Göring laid down, to begin with, that the economic objective must be not to restore the Russian economy but to concentrate on the food and raw materials needed by the German army and the German war economy, without regard to the consequences for the local population, who could be left to starve. Once it became clear, however, that the war was not going to be a short one, economic policy changed. The interests of the Reich were still paramount, but were now seen to require short-term exploitation to give way to long-term plans for economic reconstruction. A new directive of May 1942 called for the restoration of maximum production in the east and the revival of private enterprise. Turning over land to the peasants in Byelorussia produced remarkable results in increased goodwill and production, but in the much more important Ukraine, the attempt to introduce a New Agrarian Order was blocked by Koch and at the local level by the German managers of collective farms, many of whom hoped to retain them as their private estates after the war.

The Russians had transferred or destroyed as much of the Ukraine's heavy industry as they could before their retreat. Göring took over control of the mining and metallurgical industries of Nikopol, Krivoi Rog, the Donbass, and Dniepropetrovsk, and transferred them en bloc to the Hermann Göring Reichswerke. But the capital goods, labor, and management needed to restore these were already in short supply in the Reich itself, and even when the big Ruhr firms were ordered to take a share in getting them back into production, the results still fell far short of German expectations. Before they could achieve full production again, the Germans had to retreat before the Red Army's advance, blowing up the plants for a second time be-

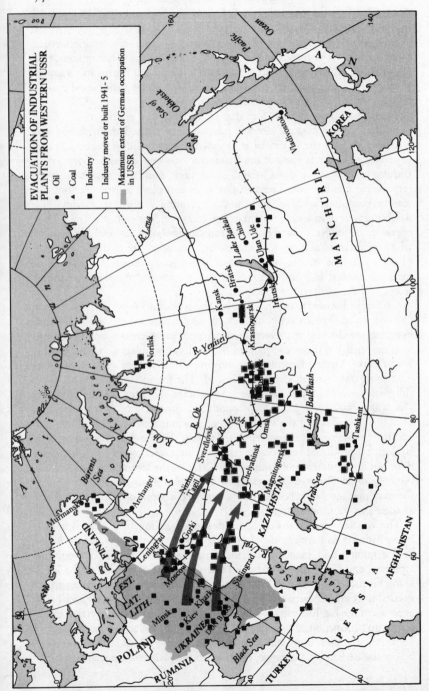

EVACUATION OF INDUSTRIAL
PLANTS FROM WESTERN USSR

● Oil
▲ Coal
■ Industry
□ Industry moved or built 1941-5
▨ Maximum extent of German occupation
in USSR

fore doing so. The German reconstruction had in any case involved heavy investment by the Reich, including, for example, the transport of coal from Upper Silesia to keep the Ukrainian economy operating.

The contradictions in German policy were highlighted by the demand at the same time for the recruitment of the maximum number of agricultural and industrial workers from the east to make good the labor shortage in the Reich itself. Hitler's loss of confidence in Göring as economic supremo had already been signaled by his appointment of Speer, not Göring, to succeed Todt. It was underlined by the appointment of Fritz Sauckel as plenipotentiary-general for labor, an appointment like Speer's, formally subordinate, to Göring—to save the latter's face—but in fact entirely independent. Sauckel was another party appointment (he had been Gauleiter of Thuringia since 1927), further proof of the revival of the party's fortunes under Bormann's leadership. Sauckel had none of Koch's panache—Goebbels called him "the dullest of the dull"—but lack of imagination was an advantage when it came to enforcing a program which, in the east as in the west, drove tens of thousands to join the partisan bands rather than wait to be deported as slaves.

Men and women were liable to be seized without warning in marketplaces and churches, or dragged out of their homes without any chance to say good-bye to their families. Houses, even whole villages, were burned down for failure to meet the demands for manpower. In the final stages of the occupation in the east, even children as young as ten were liable to be taken. Including prisoners of war, nearly half the total of male foreign workers in Germany in autumn 1943 (2.4 million) and 83 percent of the women (1.4 million) came from the Soviet Union and Poland. Their treatment in Germany showed the same pattern of discrimination as that of the prisoners of war: The rations, barracks, medical services of the *Ostarbeiter* were of still lower standards than those for workers from France and other Western countries. Even when working for the Germans, *Untermenschen* could manage with less.

VI

CUTTING ACROSS THE ACTIVITIES of the Reich commissars and the many agencies engaged in exploiting the occupied territories was the claim of the SS to an authority which overrode all others. It was based upon the duty, with which it was charged, to defend the regime against its enemies, both internal and external, a duty for which it was responsible to the Führer alone, not to the constitution or the state, and which in the last resort must take precedence over everything else. The SS was far from being a monolithic structure. There were few activities into which Himmler did not seek to extend his power: during the war, the SS developed an economic empire of its own as well as the alternative armed forces of the Waffen SS. Inevitably Himmler's expansionist ambitions brought the SS into conflict with other Nazi agencies—Göring's Four-Year Plan, for instance—and Bormann and the party Gauleiters determined to defend their territory. No less characteristic were the rivalries which developed between the different parts of the SS competing with each other for Himmler's support.

To try and trace the ramifications of the SS bureaucracy would fill a book.* It is more important to concentrate on what the SS actually did. Heydrich's combined Security Police and Security Service (SD) set out to identify and follow the activities of political opponents of the regime inside Greater Germany. As soon as war broke out in 1939, large numbers of those suspected of opposition—including Catholic and Protestant clergy—were seized and placed under "protective custody" in concentration camps, where a considerable number of them had been held before. The first execution of the war was that of a Communist in the Junkers works at Dachau who refused to do air-raid protection work. After arrest and interrogation, Himmler ordered him to be shot; he was executed in the Sachsenhausen camp.

Hitler made clear that there was no need for such cases to be subject to judicial investigation or trial. The Security Police could decide if anyone was guilty and order his imprisonment or execution without further reference or appeal. Between September 1939 and March 1942, the numbers in the concentration camps rose from 25,000 to just under 100,000. Many of the prisoners were from the occupied countries, amongst them those arrested for resistance activities under Hitler's *Nacht und Nebel* (Night and Fog) decree of December 1941. Instead of being tried locally, they were secretly spirited away under cover of "Night and Fog" and held in isolation in Germany, without anyone hearing of their whereabouts.

All such cases could be matched many times over by the NKVD in Stalin's Russia. The unique character of the SS was its role as the instrument for realizing in practice Hitler's ideological vision of the creation of a Germanic racist empire in the east.

Until the war, Hitler had been guarded in revealing the extent to which his radical and racist *Weltanschauung* went beyond the nationalist program of reversing the defeat of 1918, restoring German military power, and establishing Germany as the leading power in Europe. Breaking the barrier which separated peace from war, the German victory over the "racially inferior" Poles and the occupation of half their country marked the opening of a new stage, giving Hitler greater freedom to try out his ideas in practice while still taking precautions to conceal this first move from a nationalist to a racist policy. Both the greater freedom and the concealment are well illustrated by one of his first initiatives following the defeat of Poland.

Long before he came to power, Hitler's obsession with preserving the

---

*It already has. See the English translation of *Anatomy of the S.S. State* by Helmut Krausnick, Hans Buchheim, Martin Broszat, and Hans-Adolf Jacobsen (London: 1968).

health of the *Volk* from degeneration had attracted him to the idea of eliminating those who were physically or mentally impaired. Less than three months after becoming chancellor (in 1933) he introduced a law for the compulsory sterilization of the "hereditarily sick." Sterilization was also made part of the Nuremberg Laws directed against the Jews on the grounds that "the purity of the German blood is essential to the continued existence of the German people." In the autumn of 1939, Hitler went a step further and authorized euthanasia, the medical killing of "life unworthy of life," for adults as well as children. While staying in the Hotel Casino at Zoppot near Danzig, he signed a Führer Order giving the head of his Führer Chancellery, Philipp Bouhler, and his personal surgeon, Dr. Karl Brandt,

> Full responsibility to enlarge the powers of certain specified doctors in such a way that they can grant those who are by all human standards incurably ill a merciful death after the most critical assessment possible of their medical condition.
>
> (signed) Adolf Hitler[73]

In all subsequent references to his speech of January 30, 1939, with its "prophecy" that a new war would bring "the destruction of the Jewish race in Europe," Hitler consistently misdated it to the day on which war began, September 1, 1939. Whether consciously or unconsciously, he did the same with the euthanasia decree, back-dating it from October to September 1, as if to underline that, when that threshold was passed, many things would become possible which it had not been politic to attempt in peacetime. On the other hand, not only was the order marked "Secret," but the studied hypocrisy of the language was to be repeated again and again to disguise the most brutal methods of murder.

The program, known as T4 from the address of the Führer Chancellery, No. 4 Tiergarten, Berlin, involved most of the German psychiatric profession as well as the SS. Six centers were established in Germany in converted mental hospitals, others in occupied Poland. Killing—of children as well as adults—was at first by injection, later by the method Hitler finally decided on, by carbon-monoxide gas. It was a member of the SS Criminal Police, Christian Wirth, who designed the first Nazi gas chamber, disguised as a shower room into which patients were led naked and gassed within five minutes. The bodies were then removed by SS men and burned in ovens. Faked death certificates were drawn up, signed by doctors, and sent with an urn of ashes and a letter of condolence to the family.

The T4 program was abandoned in Germany in August 1941, but "euthanasia" continued on the individual initiative of institutions and doctors. They used drugs or starved patients to death, "the natural method," particularly for children, with the assurance from the medical bureaucracy that they would be removing burdens on the state and its war effort, "useless eaters" who were taking up beds wanted for war-wounded soldiers.

Apart from the invention of the gas chamber, there were several other features of the T4 program which had a direct bearing on the "Final Solution," the later mass killings at Auschwitz and other extermination camps. The first was the secrecy with which the operation was surrounded and the elaborate deception with which those involved disguised what they were doing. The second was the involvement of doctors and the care taken to follow medical procedures: physical examination, doctors in charge of selection as well as the actual killing (as at Auschwitz), and medical certificates. The doctors themselves professionalized the process, laying stress on its therapeutic value, "healing work," merciful to the individual and in the interests of the community, which was "entirely consistent with medical ethics." The third feature was the treatment of Jewish patients. These did not have to meet any of the ordinary criteria for medical killing—incurable diseases, mental deficiency, schizophrenia, length of hospitalization. From April 1940, all Jews who were inmates of German mental hospitals were put to death simply because they were Jews and, as such, carriers of an infection which had to be eradicated.

Finally, there was the open resistance, led by a number of German church leaders, which the program encountered. Among the names never to be forgotten are those of the Protestant pastors Paul-Gerhard Braune and Fritz von Bodelschwingh, both directors of mental institutions, and the Catholic Bishop of Münster, a former officer, Cardinal August Count von Galen, whose famous sermon of August 1941 invoked the wrath of God on those who were killing the innocent. The protests had their effect: Before the month was up, Hitler had ordered the T4 program to be suspended. By then it had claimed more than 70,000 victims.

The lesson Hitler and the Nazis learned was that they should not take the risk of carrying out illegal mass killing in Germany itself. The other lesson was pointed out by Himmler: "If operation T4 had been entrusted to the SS, things would have happened differently; when the Führer entrusts us with a job, we know how to deal with it correctly, without causing useless uproar."[74]

POLAND WAS ANOTHER WORLD, a shattered society in which normal standards of behavior had been destroyed, a people whom most Germans were ready to believe did not belong to the civilized world. Here the SS could uproot Poles, force Jews into ghettoes, and start on the work of resettlement free from the sort of protests which euthanasia had aroused in Germany.

Nonetheless, the twenty-one months between September 1939 and the invasion of Russia in June 1941 were a period of frustration for the SS. The disappointing results which they achieved in resettling not more than 200,000 ethnic Germans by May 1941 were due to the opposition of other Nazi bosses over the problems created for them by SS activities and to the practical difficulties caused by more immediate claims on resources in the middle of a war. The most serious example of the first was the resistance of Hans Frank to the SS plan to move more than seven million Poles into his already crowded Government-General. Hitler's intervention silenced Frank's opposition and Heydrich secured Hitler's agreement to a crash program to deport a million more refugees into the Government-General, but the execution of his plan came to an abrupt halt in March 1941, by which time no more than 25,000 had been moved, this time because the German army's need of all available transport in the build-up for Barbarossa had to take priority.

A similar frustration affected Nazi policy toward the Jews. Following the outburst of *Kristallnacht* the Nazis had reverted to their systematic exclusion from German life, the "Aryanization" of their assets, and pressure to emigrate. In all, Heydrich claimed, this policy had taken 360,000 Jews out of Germany and another 177,000 from Austria and Bohemia-Moravia. The war, however, effectively put an end to emigration at the same time that occupation of Poland increased the number of Jews in German-controlled territories by more than three million. Emigration still remained Nazi policy and two alternative destinations were considered. The first, proposed by Eichmann but rapidly abandoned, was an area in the Government-General southwest of Lublin, around Nisko on the River San. The other was proposed by Franz Rademacher, the Jewish expert of the German Foreign Office, in June 1940, when the defeat of France appeared to open the way to a redistribution of the French empire. Rademacher's idea was to move six million Jews from Europe to colonize the island of Madagascar. "One could found a state of Israel in Madagascar," Hitler told Mussolini in June, and the idea was taken up with enthusiasm by Eichmann and by Hans Frank, who saw in it a "colossal relief" to the demands made on his Government-General.

Realization of the Madagascar plan, however, required the defeat of Britain as well as France. When it became clear, in September 1940, that this was not likely to follow, interest in Madagascar rapidly faded. By the early months of 1941 Nazi policy toward the Jews had reached an impasse.

THE IMPASSE WAS BROKEN by the invasion of Russia, bringing together into a common focus the ideological with the strategic elements in Hitler's thinking. The destruction of Russian military strength as the strategic key to the hegemony of Europe and the acquisition of the raw materials, food, and slave labor Germany needed to defeat the Anglo-Saxon nations in the final struggle for world power—these were now combined naturally with his racist *Weltanschauung*, with its belief in the superiority of the Aryan Germans over the "subhuman Slavs"; his pursuit of *Lebensraum* to provide for the future of the Germanic *Herrenvolk*; his anti-Marxism and anti-Semitism, coinciding in the crusade to save Europe from the plague of Jewish Bolshevism and destroy its source in Moscow.

With the invasion of Russia, Hitler completed the break from a nationalist program, with limited objectives, to embark on this racist-imperialist adventure with unlimited horizons, not the sort of war the Germans had waged in the west, but (as he constantly insisted) a *Vernichtungskrieg,* an ideological war of destruction in which all rules were to be disregarded.

The logical connection in Hitler's mind between the overthrow of the Soviet state and the "solution of the Jewish problem" was reinforced by the fact that the parts of Russia to be invaded and occupied by the German army contained the largest Jewish population in Europe. Added to the still unresolved problem of what was to be done with the Jewish population of Poland, Germany, Austria, and Czechoslovakia, this meant strong pressure from below on practical grounds for a radical rethinking, a "final" solution of the Jewish problem.

Any hesitation Hitler might still have felt was removed by his extraordinary run of successes between the spring and autumn of 1941. After the uncertainty he had shown in the months following the defeat of France, his belief in his mission guided by Providence, and the confidence this gave him, was carried to fresh heights by the defeat and occupation of Yugoslavia and Greece, by the defeats inflicted on the British in North Africa and Crete, and, above all, by success in the greatest of all his gambles, leading him by mid-October to claim that the war in the east was won.

This was the context in which the "Final Solution," of the Jewish problem, as the Nazis called it, the Holocaust, as it has come to be called— the planned extermination of all European Jews—took shape. It is impossible to point to a particular date when the decision was made, but this is not surprising. Such a decision, for which there was no precedent, and the execution of which had to be kept as secret as possible, was very unlikely to be made in that way. By way of comparison, it has been pointed out that Hitler first mentioned his resolve to attack Russia to his generals on July 31, 1940, and a first operational draft by the General Staff was ready on August 5. The directive for Operation Barbarossa was issued on December 18, 1940, but the date for actually launching it was not fixed until May 1, 1941, and the final order to attack was given only on June 17. In short, the decision took the best part of a year. Yet, by comparison with a decision to exterminate all the Jews in Europe, the decision to launch the invasion of the Soviet Union, although on an unprecedented scale, was straightforward, an exercise which the German General Staff was able to accomplish with a practiced professionalism, very different from one not only without precedent, but presenting formidable logistic and technical as well as moral and political problems.

There were, in fact, two "decisions," if the term can be used to describe a process which, in each case, took several months to complete. The first, which led to the massacre of the Jewish population of Russia, had its origin in Hitler's directive for four SS *Einsatzgruppen* to be employed in the same role as in Poland, disguised for general circulation as "special tasks," described by Hitler himself as "the elimination of all Bolshevik leaders and commissars, the Bolshevik-Jewish intelligentsia." In practice, however, most of the commissars and officials had fled in advance of the German arrival and shooting them represented only a small part of the *Einsatzgruppens'* activities by comparison with the mass killing of Jews, originally adult male Jews, but by the autumn of 1941 Jewish women and children as well. On October 15, for example, *Einsatzgruppe A* reported that it had so far liquidated 125,000 Jews and 5,000 others, mainly Soviet commissars and functionaries.

In final briefing sessions immediately before the invasion, Heydrich made clear to the officers what was expected of them.* The gist of it was summed up by one of them, Dr. Rudolf Lange, in another report of January 1942: "The goal that *Einsatzkommando 2* had in mind was a radical solution to the Jewish problem through the execution of all Jews. [75]

As the SS groups moved further into the vast spaces of Russia it became clear that their numbers—3,000 all told—were inadequate to carry out the task before them. In Byelorussia alone, Artur Nebe, commander of *Einsatzgruppe B,* reported there were one and a half million Jews.

Hitler, however, was not in a mood to be daunted by difficulties. The German army's rapid advance in Russia convinced him that they were on the verge of victory, and when he met Göring and other Nazi leaders on July 16 he was in a mood of exaltation in which anything appeared possible. Germany, he declared, would never leave the territories into which the German army was now thrusting. He welcomed the Russian resort to partisan warfare: "It gives us the opportunity to exterminate anyone who is hostile to us. . . . Naturally the huge area must be pacified as quickly as possible; this will happen best through shooting anyone who even looks askance at us." [76] Himmler was not present at the meeting, but received the minutes and acted accordingly: Within a week of Hitler's remarks he assigned another 11,200 SS troops to reinforce the *Einsatzgruppen.* By the end of 1941, their total strength had been brought up to 30,000; by June 1942 to 165,000; by January 1943 to 300,000. Throughout they were able to count on the help of the German army, which was indispensable.

Proof of Hitler's personal interest is provided by a code message sent by Müller, the head of the Gestapo, dated August 1, 1941: "The Führer is to be kept informed continually about the work of the *Einsatzgruppen* in the east. . . . To this end, visual materials of special interest, such as photographs, are needed." [77]

Russian Jews were quite unprepared for their fate. In keeping with the Nazi-Soviet Pact, the Nazi attitude to the Jews had hardly been reported

---

*The majority of the officers had a professional background and included well-qualified academics, ministerial officials, lawyers, a Protestant priest, and an opera singer.

MAPS OF HELL

PRINCIPAL NAZI EXTERMINATION AND CONCENTRATION CAMPS

—— Border of Grossdeutsches Reich

■ Concentration camps

● Extermination camps

SOVIET GULAG ARCHIPELAGO

A Basin of the Pechora River

B Basin of the Kolyma River

C Railway of death

■ Forced labor camps

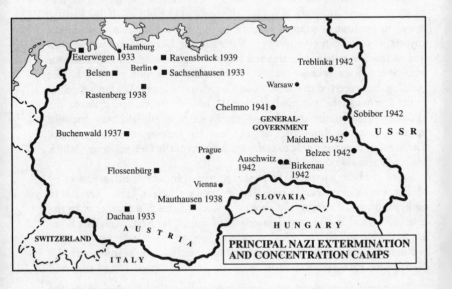

PRINCIPAL NAZI EXTERMINATION
AND CONCENTRATION CAMPS

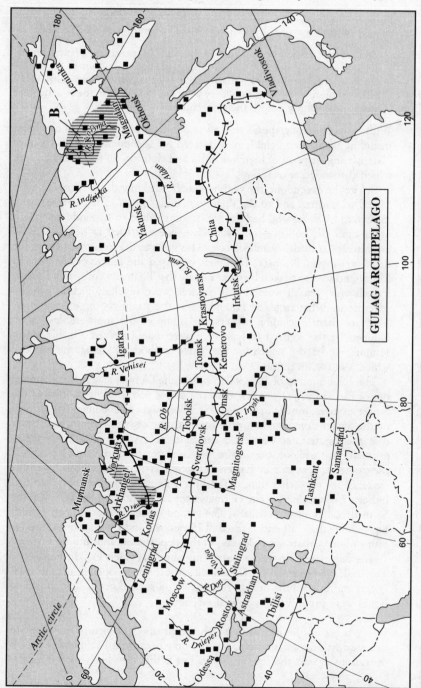

GULAG ARCHIPELAGO

in the Soviet press, and the SD took full advantage of their innocence. This extract is from a report by *Einsatzgruppe C* operating in the Ukraine:

> In Kiev the Jewish population was invited by poster to present themselves for resettlement. Although initially we had only counted on 5,000–6,000 Jews reporting, more than 30,000 Jews appeared; by a remarkably efficient piece of organization, they were led to believe in the resettlement story until shortly before their execution.[78]

With equal efficiency, the SS shot all 30,000. In another town, 34,000 Jews, including women and children, registered for accommodation in a camp. "After being stripped of their valuables and clothing, all were killed, a task which demanded several days."

Before the executions, the victims were herded into the countryside, then forced to undress and to dig their own mass graves. Their corpses were thrown in by those who had not yet been executed or by local laborers; in other cases the bodies—some still alive—were just left in heaps, without any attempt at burial. While on one of his visits to the *Einsatzgruppen* in the field, on August 15, 1941, Himmler witnessed the killing of 200 Jews at Minsk and was so shaken by what he saw that he nearly collapsed. Following his visit, Jewish women and children were regularly included in the executions. What troubled Himmler was the strain on the executioners. Many of them, including officers and some of the most ruthless, were haunted by the scenes in which they were daily involved. On his return Himmler ordered a search for alternative methods of killing, the result of which was the invention of the gas van.

The total number of Jews killed before the Germans were finally driven out of Russia in 1944 was originally put at 900,000. But the opening of the Soviet archives, for example, the two million pages of documents assembled by the Soviet Commission for the Investigation of Nazi Crimes, has shown that this figure is too low and needs to be revised, on a conservative estimate, to 1,250,000, possibly more. The opening of the archives both in the Soviet Union and in Eastern Europe has produced incontrovertible evidence for two other things. The first is the much greater role than had hitherto been realized of the German army and military police as well as the SS in atrocities against civilians. The second is the collaboration on a much bigger scale than hitherto realized of Ukrainians and Lithuanians, as well as Hungarians, Croats, and Slovaks, in the deportation and murder of Jews.

The final operation was to destroy the physical evidence of the massacres. This task was given to SS Commando 1005, which opened up the mass graves and burned the human remains on oil-soaked grids. Any remaining bones were ground up by special machines.

JULY 1941, the month in which the prospect of victory led Hitler to believe anything was possible, was not only decisive for reinforcing the SS operations against the Jews in Russia but is the most likely month for the setting in motion of the second, even more monstrous decision, the Final Solution of the Jewish problem by killing the whole Jewish population of Europe. The first definite evidence is the directive which Göring, as chairman of the Reich Defense Council, issued to Heydrich as chief of the unified Security Forces on the last day of July:

> To supplement the task that was assigned to you on January 24, 1939, which dealt with the solution of the Jewish problem by emigration and evacuation in the most suitable way, I hereby charge you with making all necessary preparations with regard to organizational, technical, and material matters for bringing about a total solution of the Jewish question within the German sphere of influence in Europe. Wherever other governmental agencies are involved, these are to cooperate with you. [79]

Neither Göring nor any other Nazi leader could have issued such a directive without Hitler's authorization, least of all in July 1941, when the vindication of his decision to invade Russia gave him a unique authority.

Himmler was a frequent visitor to Hitler's headquarters in the summer of 1941, and the most likely origin of the directive could well have been one of his discussions *unter vier Augen* ("under four eyes"). At this stage a "decision" is most likely to have taken the form of authority to start planning the deportation and extermination of the rest of the Jewish population of Europe, possibly on the same occasion that Hitler approved Himmler's proposal to send SS reinforcements to expand the program already being carried out in Russia.

The fact that the directive bears Göring's, not Hitler's, signature is entirely in keeping with the care Hitler had long taken to keep his own name from being associated with measures against the Jews. From beginning to end the whole operation was clothed in secrecy. As little as possible was committed to paper, and where that was unavoidable, it was standard procedure to employ such coded euphemisms as "evacuation" or "resettlement" for extermination.* Hitler made clear what he wanted orally, leaving it to others—Himmler, Göring, or in military matters Keitel or Jodl—to convey the necessary orders, using the formula "in accordance with the Führer's wishes."

The Final Solution was intended to take place not in Germany, but in Poland and Russia, the publication of news from which, especially in wartime, was tightly controlled. This could not prevent reports spreading by word of mouth, but when a German industrialist, Eduard Schulte, brought news secretly to Allied representatives in Switzerland at the end of July 1942 of what was being organized and had already begun, the scale of the operation was received with skepticism. It was not until mid-December that any of the Allied governments—at the insistence of Churchill and the

---

*In notes written after the war, Keitel referred to such expressions as "semantic conventions" which the Führer employed in communicating with his aides. (Gerald Fleming, *Hitler and the Final Solution* (London: 1985), p. 19)

British government—felt able to confirm the reports, condemn such an outrage against humanity, and promise punishment of those responsible.[80]

Those who needed to know that the measures to be taken had Hitler's approval were told under seal of secrecy. Eichmann, who had a central role to play, told an Israeli interrogator in 1960 that Heydrich summoned him in the late summer of 1941 and informed him:

> "The Führer has ordered the physical extermination of the Jews." He said this sentence to me and then, quite contrary to his habit, paused for a long time as if he wanted to test the effect of his words on me. At first I could not grasp the implications because he chose his words carefully. But then I understood and said nothing further because there was nothing more I could say.[81]

In an affidavit he made in 1946, Höss, the commandant of Auschwitz, recalled being summoned to Himmler's office in Berlin in the summer of 1941 and told:

> The Führer has ordered the final solution of the Jewish question and we—the SS—have to carry out this order. . . . I have earmarked Auschwitz for this task. . . . It will be onerous and difficult and will require your full personal commitment.
>
> You will maintain the strictest silence concerning this order, even vis à vis your superiors. . . . Every Jew we can lay hands on must be exterminated without exception. If we now fail to destroy the biological basis of Jewry, then one day the Jews will destroy the German people.[82]

IN THE TWENTY-TWO MONTHS which separated the commitment to the Final Solution in July 1941 from the overrunning of Poland in the autumn of 1939, the SS and the Nazi party had become more and more habituated to the indiscriminate killing of large numbers of Jews and Poles. Starting with the "euthanasia" program in Germany and Poland, this had become widespread in occupied Poland and then was extended, on an even larger scale, by the "special tasks" which Hitler assigned to the SS in Russia. As one historian puts it, "Murder was in the air."[83] It was not only the Nazi party and the SS, but the Wehrmacht, too, which was affected by the growing barbarization of warfare in Russia, evident from the beginning in the inhuman treatment of Russian prisoners of war.

These practical problems by themselves did not generate the Final Solution, the initiative for which came from above, not from below, but they prepared the ground for it. A minute which an SS officer in Posen, Höpner, sent to Eichmann on July 16 illustrates the practical problems with which Nazi officials in the field found themselves faced. Reporting a discussion about moving 300,000 Jews to a camp in the Warthegau, he wrote:

> This winter there is a danger that not all the Jews will be able to be fed. Serious consideration must be given as to whether the most humane solution might not be to finish those Jews who are incapable of work with

some quick-acting preparation. This would be more pleasant than letting them starve.

Furthermore it was proposed to sterilize all those Jewesses who are still fertile so that the Jewish problem will be finally solved with the present generation. [84]

A final solution which involved the systematic killing of Jews had become conceivable to hard-pressed officials in the field, like Höpner, not only as an answer to the practical problems with which they were confronted, but as a logical end to a course on which they had already advanced halfway.

But an answer still had to be found to the question of *how* the SS proposed to put to death, under conditions of secrecy, several million Jews brought together from all over Europe. The answer was not ready-made. It was eventually put together by merging four programs with which the SS had already had experience: the concentration camp system, the euthanasia gassings, the *Einsatzgruppen* operations and, for moving large numbers of victims while keeping them in ignorance of their fate, the methods developed with forced resettlement.

One of the first SS officers to respond to Himmler's search for an alternative method of killing was Herbert Lange in Posen who, under the euthanasia program, "evacuated" inmates from hospitals in East and West Prussia, disposing of them by releasing carbon monoxide into an airtight compartment mounted on a motor truck. His most successful operation was to kill 1,558 patients from East Prussian hospitals in this way in May 1940. SS mechanics in Berlin produced an improved model which used carbon monoxide from the exhaust. Lange, moving over from the abandoned euthanasia programs, installed three such vans on an isolated estate near Chelmno close to the Lodz ghetto in Poland, and the first Jewish victims were "processed" there on December 8, 1941. When Eichmann visited Chelmno he was highly critical of Lange's system, which frequently broke down before the victims were dead. Nonetheless, the Chelmno gas vans continued in use, and more than 152,000 Jews were ultimately put to death in them.

A more effective method was provided by another recruit from the euthanasia program, Christian Wirth, who had been out of a job since that closed down and who designed a system of purpose-built gas chambers made to look like bathhouses, again using carbon monoxide. The first of his installations, opened on March 17, 1942, was the Belzec camp built close to the Lublin-Lvov railway, with six gas chambers which could deal with 15,000 victims a day. The first victims of Belzec were an entire ghetto, the Jewish community of Lublin.

This success was greeted with enthusiasm by the Government-General administration after months of experiment and uncertainty: "The Jewish 'resettlement' has proven that such an action even on a large scale can also be carried out for the entire Government-General." [85] Others followed at

Sobibor, Treblinka (with a capacity of 25,000 a day), and finally at Maida-nek. Wirth's claim, however, to be the inventor of the most efficient way of killing large numbers of Jews was challenged by the SS technicians of the largest concentration camp in the German-occupied east, Auschwitz, in Upper Silesia, which Höss was converting into another extermination fac-tory. They discovered a new killing agent, the prussic acid gas, Zyklon B, sold as an antivermin substance. This enabled the Auschwitz complex—the largest of all concentration-extermination camps, with two satellites, Bir-kenau and Monowitz, in addition to the main site—to exceed the "produc-tivity" of all other death factories. The use of such a term is revealing: From the point of view of those who organized the camps, they were engaged in the industrialization of mass murder.

HITLER, HOWEVER, HAD NOT WAITED for the planners and technicians to solve their problems. His decisions on "the Jewish question" were closely linked to his moods, and these in turn to the military situation. In September 1939 victory in Poland had been followed by authorization of the euthanasia program and the mandate to Himmler to embark on the racial reorganization of Eastern Europe. In the summer of 1940, victory in France was accompanied by his approval of Himmler's May memorandum on the break-up of the Polish state and the Madagascar plan. In July 1941 the decision to proceed with the Final Solution followed the news that German troops were only 150 miles from Moscow.

In August, however, he vetoed proposals from Heydrich, then from Goebbels, to start deporting Jews from the Old Reich to the east. This was the month in which Hitler closed down the euthanasia program in the face of public protests. Deportation, he ruled, would have to wait until the war was over.

Then, in mid-September, with his confidence restored by the fall of Kiev and the capture of half a million Soviet troops, he changed his mind and agreed to allow deportation to the territories annexed from Poland as a first step. The first cities to be cleared of Jews should be Berlin, Vienna, and Prague. By October 10, following the news of the double encirclement of Vyazma and Bryansk, Hitler allowed Heydrich to announce in Prague: "The Führer wishes that by the end of the year as many Jews as possible are removed from the German sphere." [86]

On October 15, the day the Soviet troops in the Vyazma pocket surren-dered and panic spread to Moscow, the first deportation train left Vienna for Lodz, followed immediately by another three crowded trains from Prague, Luxembourg, and Berlin and by forty-two more in the period up to the end of February 1942. Although the Jews were stripped of all their property, the move was elaborately disguised as "resettlement" in the east. Among other devices was a home purchase contract: In return for a sub-stantial sum, a place was guaranteed in an old people's home, relieving "the contracting party, for the duration of his life, of the liability to pay for accommodation or welfare, laundry facilities, medical care, drugs, and medicine." A final clause added that the purchase money would not be repaid "even following the death of the contracting party." In fact all were marked for killing. What was done to them was a matter of indifference to Hitler, as long as it took place out of sight and hearing of the German people.

The gas chambers were not yet ready to receive such numbers. To take two examples of what happened in the Ostland (the former Baltic states), five convoys of German Jews from Munich, Berlin, Frankfurt, Vienna, and Breslau that arrived in Kovno were massacred in Fort IX on November 25 and 29. In Riga, another thousand from Berlin who had been kept in a siding all night were pulled out of the train and shot between 8:15 and nine o'clock in the morning. They were followed the same day by 14,000 Jewish inhabitants from Riga itself who were massacred in snow-covered pits in the Rumbuli Forest outside the city.

A participant later described the scene at his trial: "In the pits the Jews had to lie flat, side by side, face down. They were killed with a single bullet in the neck. To make the best of available space, those next in line had to lie on top of those shot immediately before them. They were shot by marksmen who actually stood on the dead."[87] Eight days later another 13,000 were murdered, and the pits filled in. Jeckeln, the SS officer in charge, interrogated after the war, estimated that between 200,000 and 250,000 Jews had been put to death in the Baltic states.

Those Jews who were not shot on arrival were crammed into the already overcrowded ghettoes of Warsaw, Lodz, and other Polish cities, and those who survived the conditions there were gassed during the "cleansing" of the ghettoes in 1942.

Having launched the deportation program precipitately in the autumn of 1941 on Hitler's orders, Heydrich found it necessary to call a conference to discuss the large-scale problems of organization involved in carrying out "a total solution of the Jewish question in Europe." Known as the Wannsee Conference, it met in Berlin on January 20, 1942. On the agenda were questions of selection (How was a Jew to be defined?) and possible exceptions (for example, Jews employed in the war economy, the *Mischlinge,* i.e., half and quarter Jews). The most difficult problems were how to remove hundreds of thousands of terrified people from their homes, to transport them hundreds of miles in the middle of a war, and then to provide for their reception in the occupied territories before they were put to death.

The minutes of the conference were written by Eichmann. Later he testified that the discussions took place "in very blunt terms—the talk was of killing, elimination, and annihilation."[88] But the circulated record is all the more horrifying because of the official, businesslike, and objective way in which it records such points as,

> Around 11 million Jews come into consideration for this final solution of the European Jewish question, who are distributed among the individual

countries as follows. [Among those listed were the 330,000 Jews in England and the 4,000 in Ireland.]

In the process of carrying out the final solution, Europe will be combed through from west to east. [89]

A year later Himmler had a report prepared for Hitler on the progress made with the Final Solution during 1942. The total number of Jews who had received "special treatment"—altered to read "who had passed through camps in the Government-General"—was 1,873,539. Retyped on the special Führer typewriter with large letters for Hitler to read, it was eventually returned to Eichmann with Himmler's instruction: "The Führer has taken note: destroy. HH." [90]

THERE WAS ONLY one man among the Nazi leaders who could have conceived of carrying out literally so grandiose and bizarre a plan. Not the bureaucrats who attended the Wannsee Conference and were concerned with the practical problems it presented. Nor the SS and party bosses in the Government-General, the Warthegau, and the Ostland, who wanted to find ways—and were quite prepared to consider mass killings—to relieve the overcrowding in the ghettoes and camps for which they were responsible. They had no interest at all in bringing large additional numbers of Jews into their territories and seeing these used as killing grounds for the extermination of the whole of European Jewry.

Hitler alone had the imagination—however twisted—to come up with such a plan. How long he may have nursed it, no one can say, but it was entirely in keeping with the importance he had attached to "the Jewish question" since he made his first speech at the end of the First World War, and if there was one year in which he was capable of making the leap from imagining such a "solution" as fantasy to imagining it as fact, it was 1941.

This was the year in which he had shown his terrifying capacity to turn into fact another part of his "world view," the fantasy of *Lebensraum* in the east, by launching the German army against the Soviet Union in an unprovoked act of aggression. As in the case of Operation Barbarossa, Hitler himself had neither the ability nor the interest to organize the execution of his Final Solution himself: That he left to Himmler and Heydrich, to the Eichmanns and Hösses, as he had left organizing the invasion of Russia to the army General Staff. But if there had not been a Hitler to conceive of such projects and to convince others that they could actually take place, neither would have occurred. This was Hitler's unique gift, already demonstrated in bringing the obscure Nazi party to power, in making a defeated Germany again the most powerful state in Europe, in defeating the French. As he said in his "prophecy" speech about the destruction of the Jews, at every stage he had been laughed at and not taken seriously; the Final Solution was to prove one more example of his claim that those who had mocked him as a prophet would end choking on their words.

Hitler's second contribution to the Final Solution was to legitimize it. Those involved in carrying it out knew very well that it was a state secret which could never be admitted in public. They understood why there was no signed Hitler order. Hitler's references to his "prophecy speech"—to which he referred six times in major speeches, each broadcast between January 1942 and March 1943—were enough to convince them when Himmler and Heydrich said they were carrying out the Führer's orders. As Führer, he combined all the principal offices in the state, party, and armed forces, giving him a unique authority with which to reassure them that, however disturbing the job they were called upon to do, they were acting in the interest of the German *Volk*. As Himmler told his SS commanders: "This is a page of glory in our history which has never been written and is never to be written. . . . We had the moral right, we had the duty to destroy this people which wanted to destroy us."[91] Hitler was the guarantee of this.

Hitler's final contribution was to supply the will not only to launch such an operation but to insist that it would continue up to the end of the war, long after everyone knew it was lost. The search for Jews continued all over Europe: in France, Holland, Italy, Greece. The transport was found to move them to Poland at a time when the railways were under constant attack from the air and hard-pressed by the demands of war. As late as July 1944, Eichmann despatched another 50,000 Hungarian Jews to Auschwitz. Once there they were put through the same ghastly routine. White-coated doctors—with a gesture of the hand—selected those fit enough to be *worked* to death. The rest were required to give up all their clothing and possessions and then, in a terrified column of naked men and women, carrying their children or holding their hands and trying to comfort them, were herded into the gas chambers. When the screaming died down and the doors were opened, they were still standing upright, so tightly packed that they could not fall. But where there had been human beings, there were now corpses, which were removed to the ovens for burning. This was the daily spectacle which Hitler took good care never to see and which haunts the imagination of anyone who has studied the evidence.

Hopes of being liberated from the camps as the Red Army advanced were crushed by the SS, who organized death marches to the west, the horrors of which few survived. Those who did were shot in concentration camps in Germany. The last death march of the war, from Mauthausen in Austria to Günskirchen, took place in the first week of May 1945, after Hitler had committed suicide.

Continuity is not a conclusive argument in proving Hitler's responsibility for the Final Solution, but neither can it be ignored. Sitting amid the ruin of his hopes in the Berlin bunker, the man who had first appeared in history twenty-five years before ranting against the Jews found consolation in the thought: "Well, we have lanced the Jewish abscess; and the world of the future will be eternally grateful to us."[92]

VII

WHILE HEYDRICH AND EICHMANN concentrated on the long-term plan for making Europe *Judenrein,* "cleansed of Jews," Hitler's response to two events which occurred in the second week of December 1941 fundamentally changed the odds in the gamble on which he had embarked with the invasion of Russia. The first, already described, was the Soviet counteroffensive on the central front launched on December 5 and 6; the second was the Japanese attack on the U.S. naval base at Pearl Harbor, launched suddenly, with devastating effect, on December 7. Both confronted Hitler with a choice.

Halting the German retreat in face of the Russian counteroffensive and stabilizing a front line was not an answer. The real question was what to do after that: to renew the attack in the spring of 1942 or be content with what had already been captured and make peace.

There is no evidence that Hitler seriously considered the second option. He insisted that, with the spring, the German forces should renew the offensive and secure in a second campaign the victory which had eluded them in the first.

The choice Hitler had to make in the second case was more complicated. Despite the Tripartite Pact, he had been watchful of his Japanese allies, particularly when they engaged in long drawn-out talks with the Americans. If these led to an agreement, it could seriously alter the strategic balance by giving the U.S.A. greater freedom to back up the British and Russians against Germany, and by relieving Britain of anxiety about the defense of her possessions in Southeast Asia and India.

At the same time, Hitler had become more and more irritated by the American government's increasing support of the British and Russian war efforts. The transfer of fifty U.S. destroyers to Britain in 1940 had been followed by the Lend-Lease Act of March 1941, which was soon extended to Russia as well as Britain. The growing number of incidents involving American ships had led to a virtual state of war between the U.S. navy and the U-boats, and to the repeal of the American Neutrality Act in November 1940.

Despite his anger, however, Hitler had hitherto been careful to avoid an open confrontation with the United States. This accounts for his restrained reaction to the occupation of Iceland by American troops in July 1941, and to Roosevelt's order to "shoot on sight," if necessary, to protect American ships threatened by German naval and air patrols. At some stage in the future Hitler considered it inevitable that Germany, in its bid for world power, would have to challenge the United States, but he hoped to defer this until he had defeated the Soviet Union, created an economic base in Europe proof against any blockade, and built up a navy and air force capable of fighting a transoceanic war, he hoped in alliance with Britain.

Japan's attack on Pearl Harbor simplified the situation for Hitler. By committing themselves to fighting America, the Japanese relieved him of any anxiety about their intentions. There was no need, however, for him to do the same. While assuring Japan of his general support, he could have continued with his policy of deferring open conflict with the U.S.A., confident that the war in the Pacific in which the Americans were now embroiled would make it increasingly difficult for them to maintain their aid to Britain and Russia, even more so to interfere in the European war.

There is no evidence, however, that Hitler ever considered the alternative. Less than a week after the Russian counteroffensive, which he was still struggling to contain, only four days after Pearl Harbor, which had been followed by an American declaration of war on Japan but not on Germany, Hitler gratuitously declared war on the United States.

Why did Hitler act so precipitately without counting the consequences? Part of the answer is psychological. He was depressed by the failure to defeat Russia in a single campaign and frustrated by the restraint he felt it necessary to practice toward the United States. The news of the American humiliation at Pearl Harbor gave a great boost to his confidence and restored his faith in Providence. He felt liberated and excited by the prospect of a war between continents. In announcing his decision to a hastily summoned Reichstag, he exulted:

> I can only be grateful to Providence that it entrusted me with the leadership in this historic struggle which, for the next 500 or 1,000 years, will be described as decisive, not only for the history of Germany but for the whole of Europe and indeed for the whole world. . . . A historical revision on a unique scale has been imposed on us by the Creator. [93]

In declaring war on America first, without waiting for the Americans to act, he saw himself recapturing the psychological initiative, pursuing his favorite tactic of surprise, demonstrating to the German people the value of the Japanese alliance (soon to be greatly increased by the defeats inflicted on the British and the loss of Singapore), and so reviving their faith in his leadership.

These psychological factors were combined with a double miscalculation. Always speaking of the United States with contempt as another degenerate democracy, "a society corrupted by Jews and niggers," he failed to take the measure of America's economic strength or of her ability to convert this into military, naval, and air power capable of mounting major campaigns at the same time on both sides of the world, in the Atlantic, North Africa, and Europe as well as in the Pacific. This first miscalculation was made much more dangerous by a second, which brings together Hitler's declaration of war on America with his decision to renew the war against Russia in 1942. He was confident that no American attack could be launched to secure re-entry to Europe before the end of 1942 at the earliest and that *by then he would have defeated the Russians,* so leaving the German Wehrmacht free to concentrate its forces in the west and throw any British and American landing force into the sea. In preparation for that, three days after his speech to the Reichstag on December 14, 1941, he ordered fortifications, the so-called West Wall, to be built along the whole of the western coastline of Europe from the Arctic Ocean to the Pyrenees.

But everything turned upon keeping the timetable. By making the repulse of the Western allies depend upon defeating the Russians first, Hitler was in effect redoubling the odds on a gamble which had already failed in 1941. After committing Germany to war with Russia before defeating Britain, he had now also committed her to war with the U.S.A. before defeating either Britain or Russia.

Both Hitler and Stalin, in fact, drew identical conclusions from the experience of the winter of 1941–42. With his confidence restored after turning back the German attack on Moscow, Stalin was convinced that, by continuing the offensive without pause, the Red Army would "accomplish the total destruction of the Hitlerite forces in 1942" (Stalin's directive of January 10, 1942). With *his* confidence restored by halting the German retreat with an act of will of which he declared Napoleon had been incapable, Hitler committed himself (in his directive of April 5, 1942) to "the final destruction of the Red Army and the elimination of the vital source of Soviet strength" by a breakthrough in the south which would carry the Wehrmacht to the Caucasus and its oil fields.

FROM DECEMBER 1941 Hitler left the other theaters of war—the Balkans, North Africa, the west—to the OKW, of which he remained supreme commander, while reserving the eastern front only for the OKH, of which he made himself head by taking Brauschitsch's position as commander in chief of the German army. This made clear the importance he attached to the war in the east, in which he and Stalin were now pitted against each other in direct personal command of operations. Hitler's remark to Halder, the army chief of staff, was one which Stalin might well have echoed:

Anyone can do the little job of directing operations in war. The task of the C-in-C is to educate the army to be National Socialist [in Stalin's case, read "Communist," with the political commissars to see it was carried out]. I do not know any army general who can do this as I want it done. I have therefore decided to take over the command of the army myself. [94]

The parallel extended further than that. Marshal A. M. Vasilevsky, who was already deputy to Shaposhnikov as chief of the General Staff and was soon to succeed him, writes in his memoirs:

Stalin expressed great dissatisfaction with the work of the General Staff. . . . At that time Stalin's performance suffered from miscalculations, sometimes quite serious ones. He was unjustifiably self-confident, headstrong, unwilling to listen to others. He overestimated his own knowledge and ability to guide the conduct of a war directly. He relied very little on the General Staff and made no adequate use of the skills and experience of its personnel. Often for no reason at all he would make hasty changes in the top military leadership. . . . Stalin quite rightly insisted that the military abandon outdated strategic concepts, but he did not do so himself as quickly as we would have liked.[95]

This paragraph could be used to describe the relations between Hitler and the German General Staff without changing a word.

So could the description of their methods of working. Hitler at least had an advance headquarters built at Vinnitsa in the Ukraine which he used at times, although he never visited the front line. Stalin paid only one short visit to the headquarters of the western and the Kalinin fronts, in August 1943. This was as near as he ever got to the fighting he directed. Neither Stalin nor Hitler had a clear picture in their minds of the terrain and the conditions in which their orders had to be carried out, or of what a modern war was like. Their own experience was of the civil war twenty years before or of Flanders in the First World War. The 1941–1945 war they conducted from maps spread out on tables in the secluded atmosphere of the Kremlin and Hitler's East Prussian headquarters at Rastenburg, where the only disturbing factors were their own temperaments as they berated anyone who showed signs of disagreement or failed to carry out the orders they had been given.

Neither Hitler nor Stalin was content with assuming the strategic direction of the war; they constantly intervened in operations as well. Commanders were summoned from the front to see them—often without consulting the General Staff or their superior officers in the field. Alternatively they would be brought to the phone, often in the middle of a battle, to be cursed by Stalin or Hitler personally for failing to carry out orders, or given new ones. Both were indifferent to the confusion this created, trusting no one but themselves to inspire or strike fear into officers to drive their men to the limits of human endurance, and beyond, in pursuit of their objectives.

In mid-December 1941, while the Soviet press was still celebrating the repulse of the Germans before Moscow, Stalin was already personally planning the counteroffensive which was to hurl them back where they had come from. Far from the confusion of the battlefield, Stalin could see the gaps and the opportunities beckoning on the maps. It was now Stalin's imagination which became fascinated with the image of 1812. As the front commanders in turn were summoned to receive their orders, the scale of the operations he was planning became clear. They extended from Leningrad besieged in the north to Sevastopol besieged in the south. After Leningrad had been relieved, both the German Army Group North and Army Group Center were to be destroyed in massive encirclements, accompanied by the recapture from Army Group South of the Ukraine and the Crimea.

What worried Marshal Shaposhnikov, the experienced chief of staff, was the ability of the Soviet forces to meet the immense demands Stalin was proposing to make on them. To his professional eye, they were still—after the huge losses of 1941—without a decisive superiority, even in numbers, on any front, and badly lacking in weapons and equipment as well as training. General Batov, summoned to the Kremlin from the Crimea and to his bewilderment switched to command an army on the Bryansk front, found Shaposhnikov gloomy and preoccupied. "We still need to assimilate the experience of modern war," he told Batov, adding that although the Germans had been thrown back from Moscow, "neither here, nor today, will the outcome of the war be decided; the crisis is still far off."[96] But Shaposhnikov, who was aging and sick, had learned that there was no point in arguing with Stalin.

On January 5, 1942, Stalin summoned a reinforced Stavka, at which Shaposhnikov, without comment, presented Stalin's plan for a general offensive which would engage and destroy all three German army groups which Hitler had ordered to stand fast at all costs and yield not a foot of territory. Zhukov argued that they should concentrate their forces in an attack on Army Group Center, which had been hardest hit in the December fighting, instead of spreading their resources over every front with the risk of failing to make a breakthrough and suffering unjustifiable losses. He was supported by N. A. Voznesensky, the chairman of Gosplan in charge of the economic war effort, who said flatly that the necessary supplies could not be provided for simultaneous attacks on all fronts. Stalin brushed their objections aside. As Zhukov suspected, Shaposhnikov confirmed that he had been wasting his time: The directives had already been sent to the front commanders.

In the course of January the Red Army engaged in an all-out offensive on a front almost a thousand miles long where the temperature at times fell to −30° or even −40°C, and supplies were so short that many formations were well below strength and could only eat when they overran German dumps. Like Hitler, Stalin would only listen to intelligence reports that told him what he wanted to hear, convinced that it was the will to overcome, not material resources, that would decide the outcome—convinced also, again like Hitler, that the professional training of the officers equipped them only to see difficulties and make objections. To ginger them up, Stalin sent out his personal representatives, Mekhlis, Bulganin, and Malenkov, who waded in without any military experience and did more to undermine confidence and create confusion than to put heart into any commander they visited.

After seventy days' bitter fighting, with Stalin constantly intervening by radio telephone to correct what he saw as the mistakes of the commanders, dismissing, promoting, and switching them and formations from one front to another, the troops and the reserves were exhausted. The Soviet spring offensive slowed down and finally halted at the end of March 1942. Although the German line had been dented and heavy losses inflicted on their forces (at the cost of equally heavy losses on the Russian side), the Germans still held their key positions, Leningrad had not been relieved, nor a single one of Stalin's objectives achieved.

THE MOST IMPORTANT lesson Stalin had failed to learn was the need for time in which the Soviet armed forces and the Soviet war economy could make good the unparalleled losses inflicted on them in the 1941 campaign. In addition to the millions killed, wounded, and taken prisoner, who must now be replaced, a large part of the Russian industrial effort of the 1930s was wiped out by the German occupation. By the end of November 1941 the Soviet Union's overall industrial production had been halved. Included in the losses were 63 percent of the country's coal production, 68 percent of pig iron, 58 percent of steel, and 60 percent of aluminium. Agriculture was equally hard hit: 38 percent of the grain production was lost by the end of 1941, the numbers of cattle halved between the end of 1940 and the end of 1942, and those of horses reduced from twenty-one to eight million.

The eventual Soviet victory depended on two things. The first was the fact that the Red Army survived the disasters of the first six months of the war as an organized fighting force. The second, hardly less important, was the removal of industry from the threatened western areas and the expansion of production in the east which enabled the Soviet Union to survive as an industrial power. The movement of between ten and twelve million workers to the east was an incredible achievement by itself in the confusion of wartime, and on inadequate railways already overburdened by the movement of men and supplies to the west. Nothing like this had ever been attempted before. But this was only half the story, for with them (to quote the report by Voznesensky), "Hundreds of enterprises, tens of thousands of machine tools, rolling mills, presses, hammers, turbines, and motors . . . 1,360 large enterprises—mostly war enterprises—were evacuated to the eastern regions of the USSR."[97]

When Leningrad was cut off, the Soviet Union lost the production from one of its most important industrial areas; but, before the siege was complete, no less than two-thirds of the city's capital equipment (buildings excepted) had been moved away. Two other illustrations give an idea of the haste with which the operation had to be carried out and the human effort that was involved. The first is from Zaporozhe in the Ukraine:

> In only nineteen days, from August 19 to September 5, 1941, there were removed from the Zaporozhstal' steelworks 16,000 wagons of vital machinery, including exceptionally valuable sheet-steel rolling-mill equipment. . . . The generator of the large turbine of the Zuevo power station was dismantled and loaded in eight hours.

The second is the evacuation of an aircraft factory to a site on the Volga:

> The last train carrying the equipment arrived on November 26, 1941, and in two weeks' time, by December 10, the first MiG plane was assembled.

. . . By the end of December the factory had already produced thirty MiG planes and three IL-2 Stormoviks.[98]

There was only time to put up wooden structures to house the machinery, and so short was accommodation that workers frequently slept on the floor between the machines. The hardships, even by Russian standards, were exceptional: Food was scarce and every service, from hospitals to schools, was lacking. Workers in war industry were mobilized and put under military discipline, but the demands of the armed forces for men reduced the total labor force from twenty-eight million to below twenty by 1943. By then half the workers in war industry were women (Stalin, like Bevin in the United Kingdom, did not share Hitler's inhibitions about women doing war work) and in agriculture women made up two-thirds of the labor force.

Inevitably, the disruption led to a sharp drop in production; 300 armament factories were put out of action. Yet, even in 1942, the arms industry managed to produce 25,436 aircraft, 60 percent more than in 1941, and 24,688 tanks, or nearly four times more than in 1941. The next year, Russian production of both passed the German figures.

Control over all resources was highly centralized. Gosplan, under the leadership of Voznesensky, produced an emergency war plan for 1941–42, and thereafter annual military-economic plans. Decisions were centralized in the small but all-powerful State Defense Committee (GOKO), which met almost daily under Stalin's chairmanship and raised the percentage of national income devoted to military purposes from 15 percent in 1940 to 55 percent in 1942, a figure which may be the highest ever achieved anywhere.[99] Nineteen forty-two, and particularly the first six months of 1942, was the crucial period. By the middle of that year overall arms production exceeded its prewar level. Plenty of mistakes were made, as they were in the wartime expansion of all the belligerents' industries, but the achievement of the Russian people on the economic front under the Soviet system and Stalin's leadership was remarkable and in the end more than offset Stalin's dismal record in the same period on the military front.

BY DECEMBER 1941 it was no less clear to the German leadership that the war with Russia would continue into a second year and would therefore demand a massive increase in German war production. Whether the Führer Command "Armament 1942" marked the vital break with the economics of blitzkrieg and the conversion to a total war economy, or was aimed at "improving the performance of an economy already committed to total war,"[100] the objective was not in dispute. The two questions to be settled were how it was to be achieved and (always the crucial question in the politics of the Third Reich) by whom. Sensing a threat to his economic empire, Göring was already planning a preemptive bid to take over Todt's responsibilities as minister of armaments and munitions. This would make the Four-Year Plan the instrument for the rationalization of production which Todt had successfully pioneered and which a Führer Command of December 3 now made mandatory. Göring, however, had powerful enemies who believed that the greatest obstacle to increasing productivity was his inability to discharge the responsibilities he had already amassed in the economic field.

Enough of this and of Göring's intrigues reached Hitler for him to conclude that any addition to the Reich marshal's powers would achieve no more than increase the size of the Four-Year Plan's military-industrial bureaucracy, of which he was already critical. When Todt was unexpectedly killed in an air crash on February 7, 1942 and Göring tried to rush Hitler into making him Todt's successor, so completing his control over the economy, he was met with the answer that Hitler had already appointed Albert Speer—who was still in the room, recovering from his own surprise. Speer was already a member of Hitler's personal entourage as his architect and had established his ability as an organizer while acting as Todt's deputy for construction work. In making him a minister, Hitler seems to have been influenced by the consideration that Speer had no independent position and would be politically dependent on himself. This would allow him to increase his control over armaments, just as he had steadily increased his control over strategy and military affairs by replacing the minister of defense in 1938 and more recently the commander in chief of the army. The day after Speer's appointment was officially announced, he held the first of his Führer Conferences, which continued until the end of the war and at which Speer, or later his deputy, Otto Saur, would discuss questions of policy with Hitler and record his decisions.

In order to avoid a confrontation with Göring, who still retained his control over general economic policy, Speer proposed and Göring ultimately agreed that he should be appointed as plenipotentiary for armament tasks "within the framework of the Four-Year Plan." Göring insisted that air-force armaments (which accounted for 40 percent of armaments by value) should remain his concern, but Speer found a way around this by establishing good relations with Milch, who was effectively in charge of aircraft production. Milch joined Speer on the new three-member Central Planning Board, which had been set up in April to control the allocation of all raw materials except coal, synthetic fuel, and rubber.

Under Speer's chairmanship, the Zentrale Planung extended his control to other sectors of the economy besides armaments. The new committee, he told General Thomas of the WiRüAmt (War Economy and Armaments Office), would plan for the economy as the General Staff planned military operations. The first step in his concentration of authority was the transfer of Thomas's own organization from the OKW to Speer's ministry. The sector of which he failed to secure control was labor. Gauleiter Sauckel, appointed as plenipotentiary general for labor in March 1942, went his own way, responsible (as he claimed) only to Hitler and paying no attention to either Speer or Göring.

Speer had not replaced Göring as economic supremo, but he had created a powerful instrument with which—so long as he continued to enjoy Hitler's support—he was able to carry further the process which Todt had begun of rationalization and closer cooperation with industrialists. He developed the system of production and development committees—Todt's Self-Administration and Responsibility of German Industry—so making it possible to introduce such reforms as mass production, simpler designs, and fixed-price in place of cost-plus contracts.

However the credit is to be divided between Speer and Todt, there is no doubt about the results. Between February and July 1942, the general index of finished armaments production rose by 55 percent. In October 1942 it started to rise again and by May 1943 was up by another 50 percent. The third and final burst was between December 1943 and July 1944, the period when Allied air attacks reached their peak, but German production rose by yet another 45 percent. Over the whole period of two and a half years, there was a threefold increase in the production of weapons, ammunition, and aircraft; almost a sixfold increase in the production of tanks.[101]

Nothing could make good Germany's lack of indigenous raw materials, especially oil, or her inferiority to the combined resources of her enemies, the USSR, the U.S.A., and the British Commonwealth. That this was clearly recognized in Berlin is shown by the fact that, after America entered the war, a Führer Command forbade any discussion of Germany's long-term ability to keep up with the Allies' production. To make the ban effective, no information on Allied war production was to be circulated to government departments, even those with an official interest in receiving it. Nor could Speer make good the two years lost—especially in the production of items such as aircraft and warships with a long lead in their development—before the German economy was effectively converted into a war economy. But with the potential of German industry at last being mobilized, Hitler could make one more bid for victory in 1942, and, even when that eluded him, could continue the war for nearly two and a half years more.

UNLIKE STALIN, Hitler had to provide forces for other theaters of war besides the eastern front. But his preoccupation with the latter compounded the fundamental weakness of his strategy: his failure—for all his talk of a war between continents—to grasp the unity of the war, his neglect until too late of the Mediterranean and the Atlantic, his underestimation of Britain's recuperative power and America's strength.

Before the attack on Russia, Hitler had put Admiral Raeder off by promising to take up his proposals for intensifying the war in the Mediterranean after Russia was defeated. The forces he sent there during 1941 and the winter of 1941–42 were for defensive purposes only, to prevent an Italian collapse. But at the end of the winter Raeder returned to the attack and caught Hitler's interest by dressing up his idea as "the Great Plan," to push through the Middle East, link up with the German drive to the Caucasus, and join the Japanese in a vast encirclement of the British Empire.

As a first stage, Hitler agreed to a twofold operation in the summer of 1942: Operation Aïda was to be a revival of the desert offensive aimed at Egypt, Suez, and beyond to Persia; the capture of Malta was to secure the key to Rommel's supply route. Rommel began well with the capture of Tobruk and the invasion of Egypt. By the end of June, he had reached El Alamein, sixty-five miles from Alexandria. But Hitler found an excuse after this to postpone the other half of the plan, the attack on Malta, so allowing the impetus of Rommel's attack to be lost and the British to build up their forces. Hitler's interest was fitful in any other theater than the Russian, and until he was about to lose North Africa he treated it as a sideshow, never grasping its place in the total pattern of the war, as Churchill did even when Britain's fortunes were at their lowest point, in 1940.

Hitler made another, even greater mistake, in underestimating for too long the importance of seapower and the Battle of the Atlantic. Raeder had continually argued that the one sure way of defeating Britain was by attacking her trade routes and blockading her ports. Not only were Göring's objections allowed to stop a naval air force from being established and to deny Raeder the Luftwaffe's effective cooperation in attacks on British shipping and ports, but Hitler neglected the possibilities of submarine warfare in favor of building warships. Yet it was the U-boats which had come closest to subduing Britain in 1917, and they might well have succeeded in the 1940s where the Luftwaffe had failed. They might also have prevented the Americans from building up in Britain the strength needed to force a reentry into Europe.

At the beginning of the war, Admiral Karl Dönitz, the commander of the U-boats, had only fifty-seven submarines instead of the 300 he believed necessary, and only twenty-three of these were capable of ocean-going operations. By 1941 new construction was sufficiently ahead of losses to allow him to show what his force could do, and in that year losses at sea of ships sailing on British account were over four million gross tons (1,299 vessels). Losses of this order could not be made good, and in 1942 they were nearly doubled, thanks in part to the Germans' adopting a new naval cipher which the British analysts were unable to break.

These results were so striking that Hitler was converted and began to talk of U-boats as the factor that might decide the outcome of the war. In one month, March 1942, they sank 273 ships, totalling 834,164 tons. In May Dönitz was summoned to attend the Führer's conferences for the first time, and Hitler agreed to exempt men engaged on U-boat construction or repair from military service. More than 300 U-boats were in fact completed in 1942 and total British losses for the year were 7.8 million tons (1,664 vessels).

This was the nearest the Germans came to victory anywhere after 1941. Churchill needed no convincing that the Atlantic was the one place where Britain could still lose the war, and the losses inflicted by the U-boats stretched British and Allied shipping resources to the limit until well into 1943. The strain was greatly increased by the opening of the Far Eastern war on the other side of the world. The U.S.A., faced with a war in the Pacific, could no longer continue to give the same degree of help to the British in the Atlantic, and the humiliating succession of British losses— Malaysia, Singapore, Burma—and the Japanese threat to India destroyed Britain's "imperial myth" and appeared to mark the end of the British Empire. The value of British naval power as well was called into question by the Japanese air force sinking two of the Royal Navy's most modern warships, the *Prince of Wales* and the *Repulse.*

The loss six months before (May 1941) of the new and "unsinkable" battleship *Bismarck,* also crippled by air attack, produced a similar disillusionment on Hitler's part. "I was always a champion of big ships before," he told his naval adjutant in December 1941. "But they've had their day. The danger of air attack is too great." [102] On no account could her sister ship *Tirpitz* be exposed to the same risk, and Hitler ordered Raeder to give up any idea of using the remaining German capital ships for commerce raiding in the Atlantic and to withdraw them to Norway. There the German surface fleet could attack the Allied convoys carrying supplies to north Russia and strengthen the coastal defenses against the assault which Hitler convinced himself the British and Americans were planning in order to recapture Norway.

At the same time, in the summer of 1942, his anxiety about an Allied invasion across the English Channel led him to bring up the strength of the German forces in France and Belgium to twenty-nine divisions under von Rundstedt's command. "What is the use of victories in Russia," he said to Halder, "if I lose Western Europe?" To prevent the British—and now the Americans—from regaining a foothold in Europe, he called for the completion by April 1943 of his West Wall, to house half a million troops in 15,000 concrete bunkers, with another 150,000 in reserve.

Hitler never lost sight of the threat of an Anglo-U.S. invasion. This was the "second front" in the west to which Stalin came to attach so much importance, but Hitler did not believe it would be launched before 1943. By then he hoped the war in Russia would have been won, the West Wall finished, and Germany able to concentrate her forces to defend it. A "second front" of a different kind, however, began to take effect in 1942. This was the Allied air offensive aimed at the German homeland itself, the only way Germany's opponents had of bringing the war home to the German people. Although the hope of winning the war by strategic bombing proved illusory and until the summer of 1944 German industry matched increased bombing with increased production, the Luftwaffe's inability to defend German cities against attack was a severe blow to the Nazis', and especially Göring's, prestige. The RAF carried out its first 1,000-bomber raid on Cologne at the end of May 1942, and later in the summer savaged Hamburg with seven heavy attacks in nine days. Incendiary bombs created uncontrollable fires, destroying half the houses and damaging over half the remainder; 50,000 of the population were killed and another million fled the city. Yet morale did not break in either city, any more than it had in London, and in 1943 the German night fighters began to inflict a rate of loss on the bombers which forced both the British and U.S. air commands to rethink their tactics.

VIII

WHILE THE SOVIET winter offensive was still petering out, Stalin and the Stavka began discussion of the plan to be followed in the spring of 1942. The conclusion of the General Staff, presented in mid-March, was that the Red Army ought to stay on the defensive, holding the German attacks and inflicting heavy losses, while building up its own reserves of trained men and supplies for a decisive counteroffensive against a weakened enemy later in the summer. During the defensive period, Shaposhnikov and Vasilevsky recommended that the main attention of the Soviet command should be directed to the central fronts covering Moscow.

Stalin did not contest the General Staff view directly, but he sought to combine the general defensive posture with "partial offensives." At a midnight session in the Kremlin, he argued: "Don't let us sit down in defense, with our hands folded, while the Germans attack first. We must ourselves strike a series of blows to forestall them on a broad front and upset enemy preparations." [103]

Stalin was particularly attracted by Timoshenko's proposal to take the offensive in May against Army Group South and recapture Kharkov. Where it suited him, he made private "deals" with individual commanders, such as Lieutenant General M. S. Khozin, who was put in command of a renewed attempt to break the German grip on Leningrad. Stalin secured agreement to three more "partial offensives" on the north and central fronts as well as a renewal of the Kerch offensive to clear the Crimea, despite the misgivings of the General Staff that these would compromise the chances of building up adequate reserves for the later strategic offensive.

Stalin was convinced that the Allies would open a second front in the west during 1942 and that this would draw off German forces from the east. He was even more dogmatic in refusing to take seriously the possibility that Hitler was intending to attack in the south, not the center, where he now persisted in concentrating Soviet forces. Even when the two best Soviet intelligence sources, "Lucy" and "Werther," produced the German operational orders for Operation Blue aimed at the Caucasus, Stalin insisted this was another German "feint" and heaped abuse on Soviet intelligence for

failing to discover evidence of the "real" German intentions. Heartened by
the extraordinary efforts of the industrial plants in the Urals, which produced over 4,500 tanks, 3,000 aircraft, and nearly 14,000 guns during the
winter, Stalin was determined to allow no repetition of the 1941 bid to
capture Moscow, and with luck hoped to raise the siege of Leningrad,
recover Kharkov, and liberate the Crimea.

German military intelligence had been equally successful in acquiring
evidence of Soviet intentions and forecasting Timoshenko's Kharkov offensive, with which Stalin opened the campaigning season in May. Once again,
Soviet armies found themselves threatened with encirclement, this time
southeast of Kharkov. Vasilevsky, the deputy chief of staff, supported by
Khrushchev, Timoshenko's political commissar, attempted to persuade Stalin that the Kharkov offensive must be halted. But not until May 19 was
Stalin prepared to agree and allow Timoshenko's troops to concentrate on
fighting their way out of the German trap. By then it was too late. Thousands of Russian officers and men lost their lives in desperate but unsuccessful efforts to break through the ring, and more than 237,000 were taken
prisoner. The nine divisions of Vlasov's Second Shock Army suffered the
same fate on the Leningrad front.

Farther south, Stalin had sent Mekhlis to galvanize the Crimean front and
relieve Sevastopol. All Mekhlis succeeded in doing by his meddling was to
throw the local command into such confusion that it was overwhelmed
when von Manstein's Eleventh Army launched a surprise attack on the
Kerch Peninsula in May. Twenty-one divisions of these Soviet armies disintegrated in a disaster that ended in the loss of another 176,000 men and
most of the front's 350 tanks and 3,500 guns. Mekhlis and all the local
commanders involved were demoted or dismissed. After capturing Kerch
there was nothing to stop von Manstein from carrying out in June one of
the most concentrated assaults of the war on the fortress of Sevastopol.
After twenty-seven days of continuous bombardment by heavy artillery and
planes the fortifications were shattered and all but remnants of the garrison
of 106,000 men were destroyed.

VON MANSTEIN'S VICTORIES put the final touch to the failure of
the Russian offensive and heralded the opening of Hitler's second summer
offensive. The fact that Hitler's winter success had been accomplished by
an act of will in defiance of the professional advice of his generals had
strengthened his sense of mission. In the speech he delivered on January
30, 1942, at the height of the winter crisis, he spoke of his "unbounded
confidence, confidence in myself, so that nothing, whatever it may be, can
throw me out of the saddle, so that nothing can shake me." [104] Goebbels
wrote in his diary:

> The meeting [to celebrate the anniversary of Hitler's becoming chancel-
> lor in 1933] was as successful as those in 1930, 1931 and 1932. . . . The

Führer has charged the entire nation as if it were a storage battery. . . . As long as he lives and is among us in good health, as long as he can give us the strength of his spirit, no evil can touch us. [105]

Visiting him at his headquarters in March, however, Goebbels was shocked at the toll the winter campaign had taken of Hitler: "He has already become quite gray and merely talking about the cares of the winter makes him seem to have aged very much." [106] But the crisis was over, and he had mastered it. "I believe I am in the protection of Providence," he told Mussolini, and, with that fatal facility for convincing himself of the truth of whatever he wanted to believe, Hitler shut his mind against any consideration of his own share of responsibility and put the blame wholly on the army's leadership. After the winter of 1941–42, he was less prepared than ever to listen to advice—or even information—that ran contrary to his wishes. This ruled out learning from self-criticism and in the end cut him off from all contact with reality.

The striking force with which Hitler launched his second summer offensive against Russia was less than half the size of that with which the Germans had attacked in 1941: 68 instead of 153 divisions, including 8 instead of 17 panzer divisions, and 7 motorized divisions instead of 13. Hitler hoped to compensate for this by concentrating on one part of the front, the southern. Germany's allies were also called upon to increase their contributions, and between them the Italians, Hungarians, and Rumanians provided 52 divisions, in all a quarter of the forces engaging the Russians. Their value was more uncertain; the German estimate was that they had only 50 percent of the fighting value of their own divisions.

Although plans for the first phase of Hitler's Operation Blue fell into Russian hands, Stalin persisted in believing it was a "plant" and was caught on the wrong foot when the Germans launched their attack, not at Moscow, but aimed at establishing themselves on the River Don, capturing the big communications center of Stalingrad and driving on to the oil fields of the Caucasus. While Stalin and the Stavka made desperate efforts to reorganize their fronts and avoid another huge encirclement of Soviet troops in the bend of the River Don, Hitler in mid-July moved to his forward headquarters at Vinnitsa in the Ukraine, confident that the Russians were "finished." The German plan was for Army Group B to continue its drive down the Don, link up with List's Army Group A in the south, and take Stalingrad. Their leading forces moving eastward across the lower Donets and the Don had actually made contact when Hitler abruptly abandoned the idea of a rapid advance on Stalingrad. Instead he swung Army Group A around to capture Rostov in the south, preparatory to striking eastwards to the Caucasus.

This proved to be a crucial mistake, based on Hitler's belief that the Russian resistance was collapsing as it had in 1941 and that he could afford to carry out at the same time two operations that had originally been seen

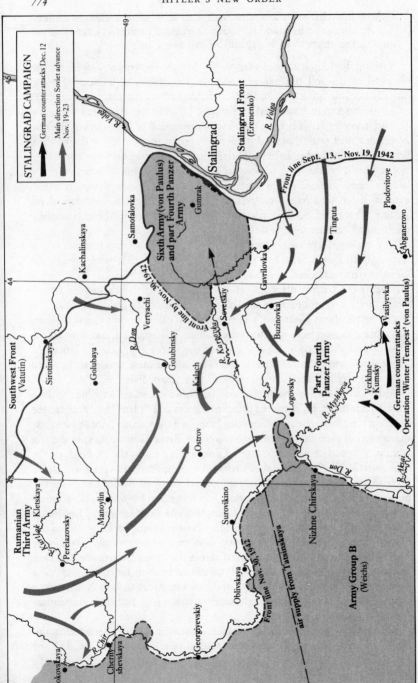

STALINGRAD CAMPAIGN

→ German counterattacks Dec. 12
→ Main direction Soviet advance Nov. 19-23

Stalingrad Front (Eremenko)

Stalingrad

R. Volga

Front line Sept. 13, – Nov. 19, 1942

Plodovitoye

Abganerovo

Tinguta

Gumrak

Samofalovka

Sixth Army (von Paulus) and part Fourth Panzer Army

Kachalinskaya

Front line by Nov. 30, 1942

Vertyachi

R. Don

Gavrilovka

Buzinovka

Vasilyevka

Golubinsky

Sovetskiy

R. Karpovka

Verkhne-Kumsky

Southwest Front (Vatutin)

Sirotinskaya

Golubaya

Kalach

Part Fourth Panzer Army

German counterattacks Operation 'Winter Tempest' (von Paulus)

Logovsky

R. Myshkova

Ostrov

Manoylin

Rumanian Third Army

Kletskaya

R. Tsutskan

Perelazovsky

Surovikino

R. Don

R. Aksai

Oblivskaya

Front line Nov. 30, 1942

air supply from Tatsinskaya

Nizhne Chirskaya

Army Group B (Weichs)

Georgiyevskiy

Bokovskaya

R. Chir

Chernyshevskaya

as sequential—first Stalingrad, and then the Caucasus. Now, without waiting for the capture of Stalingrad, the German forces began to fan out. As soon as Rostov was taken (July 23) List's Army Group A was ordered to advance around the eastern coast of the Black Sea toward Batum, while the First and Fourth Panzer Armies were detached from Army Group B and ordered to strike for the Caucasus oil fields at Maikop, Grozny, and eventually Baku.

This left Army Group B, with its German core reduced to General Friedrich Paulus's Sixth Army, plus three allied armies, Italian, Hungarian, and Rumanian, but minus most of its armor, to capture Stalingrad and cut the vital road and rail communications between the Caucasus and central Russia. The Eleventh Army, whose commander von Manstein would have much preferred to cross the straits of Kerch and join up with the German forces in the south, was switched away north to the Leningrad front.

Since the beginning of 1942, the Russians had suffered one defeat after another; they had lost the industrial region of the Donbass and now saw their major source of fuel in the Caucasus threatened. Learning from earlier mistakes, they had withdrawn most of the troops Hitler had planned to encircle at Rostov. But the Luftwaffe was still supreme in the air, capable of flying 3,000 sorties a day, ten times as many as the larger Russian air force. Changing plans again, Hitler recalled the Fourth Panzer Army from the Caucasus to give Paulus and the Sixth Army the extra strength to defeat the Russian forces in the Don bend, cross the river, and drive the thirty-five miles to reach the Volga in the northerly suburbs of Stalingrad on August 23.

Stalin had defended the city named after him—then Tsaritsyn—against the Whites in the civil war. Khrushchev was now the political commissar, and he and the front commanders as well as Vasilevsky, newly promoted to be chief of the general staff, received the full force of Stalin's anger over the radio telephone, after he learned of the German success. When they raised the question of evacuating civilians and industry across the river in view of the damage already done by the Luftwaffe, Stalin gave them a short answer:

> I refuse to discuss this question at all. It should be understood that if the evacuation of industry and the mining of factories starts, that will be taken as a decision to surrender Stalingrad. For that reason the State Defense Committee forbids any preparations for the demolition of industry or for its evacuation.

As John Erickson, the British authority on the Russo-German War, puts it: "With those words, Stalin had committed himself, the Red Army, and the Russians at large to one of the most terrible battles in the history of war."[107]

Hitler was as determined to capture Stalingrad as Stalin was to prevent him from doing so. But he had missed his opportunity. The Fourth Panzer Army, which he had taken away from Army Group B and diverted to the

Caucasus, could probably have taken the city quite easily in July, but by the time it was brought back Russian resistance was stiffening and, try as they might throughout September and October, the Germans could not break it.

Vinnitsa, a summer camp of wooden huts, was an ill-chosen spot for a second headquarters: The heat was sweltering, the climate humid, and the site swarming with malarial mosquitoes. Hitler complained that he had a constant headache and could not think straight. Seeing a decisive victory for the second time slipping from his grasp, he blamed the army for everything. Halder, the chief of the general staff who had to bear the brunt of his anger, wrote later:

> His decisions ceased to have anything in common with the principles of strategy and operations as they had been recognized for generations past. They were the products of a violent nature following its momentary impulses, a nature that acknowledged no bounds to possibility and that made its wish the father of its need. [108]

The same might have been said of Stalin in the first half of 1942, but Stalin had survived his mistakes—however great the cost—and was beginning to establish more stable relations with a small group of outstanding Soviet officers. The consequences of Hitler's mistakes, however, were only now beginning to catch up with him; in the process, his relations with the army and its General Staff deteriorated beyond repair.

Hitler resisted, as strongly as Stalin had, intelligence reports that called into question the picture he had formed of the Russians being at the end of their resources. Recalling such a scene, Halder writes:

> When a statement was read to him which showed that Stalin would still be able to muster another one to one and a quarter million men in the region north of Stalingrad (besides half a million more in the Caucasus) and which proved that the Russian output of tanks amounted to 1,200 a month, Hitler flew at the man who was reading it with clenched fists and foam in the corners of his mouth, and forbade him to read such idiotic rubbish. [109]

In September, List's Army Group A had come to a halt in the Caucasus in the face of stiffening Russian resistance there as well as at Stalingrad. Hitler, beside himself with impatience, sent General Jodl to investigate. When Jodl, on his return, ventured to defend List, Hitler again flew into a fury. What angered him more than anything was Jodl's quoting from his own earlier directives to show that List had only been carrying out his orders. For the rest of the year he refused to eat anymore with his staff, told Jodl he would replace him with Paulus as soon as the latter had captured Stalingrad, and required Field Marshal List to resign, appointing himself to the command of Army Group A in the Caucasus. To provide himself with an answer, if anyone else should ever again dare to quote him against himself, Hitler ordered Bormann to fly out a team of Reichstag stenographers to East Prussia, and a verbatim record was made of everything said at the military conferences—some 500 pages a day. The conferences themselves were no longer held in Jodl's map room but in Hitler's own quarters in an icy atmosphere.

On September 13 the Germans launched an all-out air and ground assault on Stalingrad. Furious fighting went on in its streets and ruined buildings where the Germans met their match in the Russian Sixty-second Army commanded by General V. I. Chuikov, a fighting general always in the thick of the battle, winning back by night the ground lost during the day. When Halder recommended breaking off the attack, Hitler told him he must go: "Half my nervous exhaustion is due to you. It is not worth it to go on. We need National Socialist ardor now, not professional ability. I cannot expect this of an officer of the old school like you."[110]

Halder's successor, the eleven-years-younger Kurt Zeitzler, repeated the same advice, but Hitler would not hear of abandoning the attack. On October 14, the fighting reached a new intensity even for Stalingrad when Chuikov and the Sixty-second Army were called upon to defend all that they still held of the city—a bridgehead around three big factories, only 4,000 yards deep, with the Volga immediately at their backs—against a German assault force of 90,000 men which outnumbered them by two to one with 2,000 guns and mortars, 300 tanks, and the Fourth Air Fleet of 1,000 aircraft.

In so restricted a space furious fighting, often hand-to-hand, went on from house to house. Its character is well illustrated by the story of "Pavlov's house," which became one of the landmarks of the battle. A four-storyed house that covered the approaches to 9 January Square, it was seized by Sergeant Pavlov of the Thirteenth Guards Division who filled it with sixty men, mortars, heavy machine guns, and antitank weapons. Snipers operating from the third story could pick off any movement on the ground and by mining the square Pavlov held off any tanks. The house came under artillery and mortar fire as well as bombing; but for fifty-eight days Pavlov succeeded in beating off every attack.

Although the Germans split Chuikov's army in two, reduced his bridgehead to under 1,000 yards and reached the Volga bank, after fifteen days and nights of uninterrupted fighting both sides broke off exhausted, leaving the Russians still holding out on the western bank of the Volga.

Russian counterattacks had been launched to give relief to Chuikov but had had little success. Stalin's attention was concentrated on the situation in Stalingrad itself. Since mid-September, however, Vasilevsky and Zhukov (who had become deputy to Stalin as defense commissar) had been planning a much more ambitious move which, if successful, would not only relieve Stalingrad but encircle Paulus's Sixth Army. The strategic counteroffensive called for the two arms of the encirclement to sweep wide from north and south of Stalingrad covering a 200-mile front. The attack would not be launched until a force of over a million men had been assembled and briefed. Once Stalin had accepted the plan, Zhukov and Vasilevsky were given the responsibility of carrying it out. At the last moment, on November 11, when Zhukov was in Moscow reporting to Stalin on the final preparations, Chuikov and the Sixty-second Army had to face a renewed German attack on the bridgehead which they only managed to hold off for a crucial week at the limit of physical endurance, with their ammunition running out and floating ice on the Volga preventing reinforcements from reaching them.

Hitler had refused to take seriously the threat to the Sixth Army's flanks and had thought it sufficient to strengthen them by moving up the Rumanian armies and a number of divisions formed from Luftwaffe personnel with little or no training. These collapsed in the face of the three Russian army groups that swept around behind the Sixth Army and encircled its twenty-two divisions within five days.

No other event has a better claim to be considered the turning point in the war on the eastern front than the combination of holding Stalingrad itself, in the face of all the Germans could hurl against it, with the success in carrying out an encirclement on so large a scale. So far the advantage had remained on Hitler's side. His summer offensive had more than wiped out the winter setback before Moscow. Zhukov and Vasilevsky knew they had checked him at Stalingrad, but they could not foresee that this would prove to be much more than a local success and that the military balance in the east, finely poised at the end of 1942, would, as a result of what was achieved at Stalingrad, swing to the Russian side in 1943 and never swing back again.

38, 39. The similarity of the propaganda
techniques, as well as the supposed
aspirations of the workers, illustrated by
a Hitler campaign poster of the 1930s and
a cover of the Communist International
from *c*. 1920.

40, 41. Hitler's masterful diplomacy: *left,* addressing the crowd in the Burgplatz in Vienna after the Anschluss in March 1938; *above,* feigning concern during Chamberlain's visit at the time of the crisis over the Sudetenland in September 1938.

42. *Above,* the entry of German troops into Prague in March 1939. Note the pure hatred on the faces of the two young men in the front row of the crowd.

43. The Nazi-Soviet Pact: *above,* Hitler hails Ribbentrop on his return from Moscow as "a second Bismarck."

44. *Left,* Molotov signs, while Stalin and Ribbentrop look on.

45. *Above,* a photograph officially captioned "Comrade Germanyuk, member of the Plenipotentiary Commission of the National Assembly of western Byelorussia, thanks Stalin for the liberation of the people from the Polish yoke."

46, 47. *Above,* the attack in the east, June 1941—the beginning of the greatest single war in human history. *Below,* the attack halts in front of Moscow in December 1941 in temperatures of − 40°F.

48, 49. Stalingrad, the turning point: *above,* fighting in the "Red October" factory, 1942; *below,* the German retreat—figures hanging from a balcony, Kharkov, March 1943.

50, 51. The plot of July 1944. *Above*, Hitler shows Mussolini the wreckage: "After my miraculous escape from death today I am more than ever convinced that it is my fate to bring our common enterprise to a successful conclusion." *Below*, a strained Hitler, shortly after the explosion, in conversation with Göring and Mussolini.

52, 53. Hitler inspecting a unit of the Hitler Youth taking part in the battle as the Russians closed around Berlin. These are the last photographs of him to have survived.

54. April 30, 1945: "It was twelve years and three months to the day since Hitler had appeared on the balcony to the cheering crowds as chancellor of the German Reich. That same evening, a Russian soldier planted the Victory Banner on the top of the Reichstag."

55, 56. The victors. *Above,* on Stalin's right, the two outstanding Russian soldiers of the Great Patriotic War, Marshal Vasilevsky and Marshal Zhukov. On his left, Voroshilov and Bulganin, successive ministers of defense, whose primary qualification was their total subservience to Stalin's wishes. They were also made marshals of the Soviet Union. *Below,* "At his feet they threw the banners and standards of Hitler's army, as Kutusov's soldiers had thrown those of Napoleon's army at the feet of the tsar Alexander."

57, 58. *Above,* Teheran, December 1943: Churchill (with his back to the camera) presents the Sword of Stalingrad to Stalin. "Receiving it with the same dignity and emotion, he silently raised the great sword to his lips and kissed the scabbard. For a moment, all were touched by a sense of history." *Below,* The Big Three at Yalta, February 1945. "Yalta was the high point for Stalin in his personal career no less than for the Alliance."

59, 60. Potsdam, July 1945: Stalin triumphant.

61, 62. The aging dictator: *above,* Stalin's seventieth birthday, with, *left to right,* Mao Tse-tung, Walther Ulbricht, and Khrushchev; *left,* Stalin watches Malenkov taking the place he would himself normally occupy to make the main political report at the Nineteenth Party Congress in 1952.

63, 64. "The human capacity for evil": *above,* exhumed victims of the NKVD killing fields at Kuropaty, near Minsk; *below,* the concentration camps as they were overrun by the Allies in 1945.

SEVENTEEN

Stalin's War

STALIN   1943 – 1944   *(Age 63–65)*
HITLER   1943 – 1944   *(Age 53–55)*

I

NINETEEN FORTY-THREE was the decisive year of the war. At the end of it, it was as certain as anything can be in war that Germany could not win it. The gamble of the blitzkrieg and one enemy at a time had failed. The coalition of powers that Hitler had raised against himself had too great a superiority in reserves and (after the Teheran Conference at the end of the year) sufficient agreement on how to deploy them for it to be only a question of time before Germany was defeated.

All this is clear enough now, and was—without its implications—even at the end of 1943, but it was not at all clear at its beginning or during the greater part of the year. Since December 1941 the war had been a world war but in practice continued to be fought as three separate wars: the eastern front, the war against Japan in the Pacific Far East, and the Anglo-U.S. operation in the west, including the Battle of the Atlantic and the bombing offensive against Germany, but not as yet the opening of a second land front in continental Europe. Churchill and Roosevelt were in daily contact but did not succeed in meeting together with Stalin until the Teheran Conference of November 1943. Agreement had been reached with him on not concluding a separate peace, and the flow of war supplies to the Soviet Union had started in the summer of 1941. But there was no agreement on an overall strategy nor had the three powers succeeded in coordinating their divergent interests.

The messages exchanged between the three leaders bring out clearly enough the two objectives that Stalin consistently pursued from the beginning, which were to prove a continuing cause of disagreement. As early as his message to Churchill of July 18, 1941, Stalin had urged that the best way to relieve the Russians was for the British and Americans to make a landing in northern France. None of the alternatives proposed over the next two years, such as the landings in North Africa and Italy, were ever accepted by the Russians as a satisfactory substitute; not until the invasion of Normandy was launched in June 1944 was Stalin prepared to recognize that his allies were making an equal contribution to the defeat of Germany.

His second objective was to secure Western agreement to Russia's recovery of the territorial gains she had made in eastern Europe as a result of the Nazi-Soviet Pact. This was an issue for the peace settlement but as early as December 1941 when Anthony Eden, by then the British foreign secretary, visited Moscow, a Russian attempt to commit the British to recognizing the Baltic states as part of the Soviet Union proved a stumbling block to the signature of an Anglo-Soviet treaty of alliance. Six months later, a way around it was found by omitting any mention of territorial commitments, so opening the way to signing the treaty (May 26, 1942). But this only postponed the issue which, when it resurfaced in 1942–43, focused on the question of Poland's postwar frontiers.

There was no way of postponing the other question: when and where Anglo-American land forces would open up a new front in the European theater. The British and Americans found it difficult to agree on the answer themselves and ended up with a compromise: a landing in French North Africa, which could hardly satisfy Stalin. Even before he learned of the outcome, Stalin had protested to Churchill: "I must state most emphatically that the Soviet government cannot tolerate the postponement of the second front in Europe until 1943."[1] Churchill's reply was to offer to travel to Russia to tell Stalin in person what he and Roosevelt had decided.

His mission was made no easier by a British decision to suspend convoys to Russia by the exposed northern route after no more than eleven out of the thirty-four merchant ships carrying war supplies in the June convoy, PQ 17, had reached Archangel. Churchill wrote later:

> I pondered on my mission to this sullen, sinister Bolshevik state I had once tried so hard to strangle at its birth. . . . It was like carrying a lump of ice to the North Pole. Still I was sure it was my duty to tell them the facts personally and have it all out face-to-face with Stalin.[2]

Arriving on August 12, 1942, Churchill began by giving his hosts the worst news first: There would be no landing in Europe before 1943. When he had finished, "there was an oppressive silence." After that he sought to relieve the tension by announcing a commitment to land in North Africa no later than the coming October with a view to clearing the Mediterranean. At the second meeting, following twenty-four hours for reflection, Stalin claimed that the British and Americans had agreed to launch the invasion of Europe in 1942, and were now going back on their word and at the same time failing to deliver the supplies they had promised. In the memorandum he presented, Stalin declared that the British refusal "inflicts a moral blow to the whole of Soviet public opinion, which calculates on the creation of a second front," adding in the discussion that, if the British army had had as much experience of fighting the Germans as the Russian army had, it would not be so frightened of them.[3] Churchill rebutted the charges with vigor, leading Stalin to remark before his words were translated that he liked the spirit with which he spoke.

Before he left, Churchill had another talk with Stalin alone, except for interpreters, which turned into an improvised dinner and lasted half the night. Stalin showed his guest around his apartment in the Kremlin and introduced him to his daughter, then said as if on the spur of the moment: "Why should we not have Molotov? He is worrying about the communiqué. We could settle it here. There is one thing about Molotov—he can drink." They actually sat at the dinner table, Churchill recalls, from 8:30 p.m. to 2:30 a.m. The atmosphere was relaxed, although at one point, referring to the canceled convoys, Stalin suddenly asked, "Why has the British navy no sense of glory?" Having kept his temper, Churchill in his turn asked if the stresses of war had been as great for Stalin personally as carrying out the collectivization of the peasants' farms. At 1:30 in the morning, Stalin's usual dinner hour, he demolished a suckling pig single-handed, and then went into his office to receive the latest reports from all fronts.[4]

The Soviet record of the meeting concludes that Stalin assured his visitor that:

> He and Churchill had gotten to know and understand each other and if there were differences of opinion between them, that was in the nature of things. . . . The fact that he and Churchill had met and gotten to know each other and had prepared the ground for future agreement had great significance. He was inclined to look at the matter more optimistically.[5]

But the issue between them remained unresolved, and before the year was out Stalin was pointedly asking if Churchill was going back on his "Moscow promise to open a second front in Western Europe in the spring of 1943."[6]

I T   W A S   N O T an Allied landing in the west but Hitler's obstinacy that helped the Russians to win the most famous victory of their Great Patriotic War at the beginning of 1943. Both Hitler and the German General Staff had been taken by surprise by the Russian offensive that cut off Paulus' Sixth Army in November 1942, particularly by its scale. Only ten days before, Hitler had assured the Nazi *Alte Kämpfer* at their annual celebration of the 1923 putsch (with much heavy sarcasm about "Herr Stalin and the town named after him") that the German army had already captured it apart from mopping up a few small pockets. For a long time Hitler continued to insist that Stalin must have exhausted his reserves and would not be able to keep up the pressure; the most he would admit was that the Sixth Army might be in danger of "a temporary encirclement." He resisted Zeitzler's and Paulus' urgent pleas to allow the latter's troops to break out from the trap while there was still time, insisting "We are not budging from the Volga!" Instead, the Luftwaffe would keep the encircled army supplied from the air while von Manstein, hastily summoned back from the Leningrad front, was ordered to create a new army group and break through the Russian ring from the outside.

There was considerable skepticism about the ability of the Luftwaffe to fly in the several hundred tons of fuel, food, and ammunition that Paulus needed daily to supply the quarter of a million troops trapped in the pocket west of Stalingrad. Göring, however, was anxious not to appear backward when there was already so much criticism of the Luftwaffe for its inability to prevent the Allied air attacks on German cities: He at once gave Hitler his "personal assurance" that the Luftwaffe would do whatever was necessary, without even looking into what that would mean. Von Manstein was equally reassuring, forecasting on December 9 that the relief force he was assembling should be able to make contact with Paulus' Sixth Army by the seventeenth. The OKW war diary entry, recording this, concluded: "The Führer is very confident and plans to regain our former position on the Don. The first phase of the Russian winter offensive can be regarded as finished, without having shown any decisive successes." [7] Once the front had been stabilized, Hitler proposed to resume the offensive in at least one sector in the spring of 1943.

These hopes were soon proved illusory. As Wolfram von Richthofen, the commander of the Fourth Air Fleet had foreseen, the Luftwaffe did not have enough transport planes in the east to keep up the delivery of 300 tons daily which was the minimum Paulus needed, and the ice and fog that marked the beginning of the Russian winter frequently grounded those it did have. Von Manstein's relief operation, although it reached halfway to Stalingrad, had to be abandoned when a new Soviet attack broke through the Italian army covering his left flank and forced him to pay attention to the danger of his own forces being cut off. Both Zeitzler and von Manstein again pressed for the Sixth Army to make a last-minute attempt to break out—if it could find the fuel to do so. Hitler refused: "The Sixth Army must stand fast. Even if I cannot lift the siege until the spring." This was the fatal legacy of his success the year before. He was convinced that if he hardened his will, as he had then, and refused to allow withdrawal, whatever the cost in lives, once again he would be able to master the crisis.

Only Zeitzler's persistence got Hitler to agree that the 700,000 men of von Kleist's Army Group A should be withdrawn from the Caucasus before they, too, were cut off and suffered the same fate as the Sixth Army. When Hitler changed his mind and tried to stop the order from being sent, Zeitzler was quick enough to answer that it was too late, it had already gone. As a result Army Group A was able to make good its withdrawal during January with minimal losses of life and equipment. But with it, as Hitler had foreseen, went any hope of securing the oil fields that Germany needed if it was to continue the war.

On January 9 the Russian commander Konstantin Rokossovsky called on Paulus to surrender. When he refused, a Soviet barrage with 7,000 guns and mortars pounded his starving, ragged, and abandoned troops into the ground. Two days later, it was the turn of the Hungarians to be shattered by a Russian attack farther north on the Voronezh front. Hitler's headquarters was in turmoil: the generals blaming the Luftwaffe for its failure to keep the Sixth Army supplied; the Luftwaffe commanders blaming the army for allowing the airlift's air fields to be overrun. But Hitler was adamant. When the Russians again proposed to Paulus that he should end a pointless resistance, Hitler insisted, "Surrender is ruled out." The legend of Stalingrad and the German soldiers who fought to the death rather than surrender would be worth more than the divisions it cost to substantiate it. This was Hitler's reply to the demand for Germany's unconditional surrender which Roosevelt had first made at the Casablanca Conference.* As a gesture of encouragement he promoted Paulus to field marshal.

When Hitler heard that Paulus had given himself up to the Russians along with eleven other German and five Rumanian generals, he was outraged. Without sparing a thought for the many thousands of men condemned to death or captivity by his orders, he could talk only of their commander's ingratitude and disloyalty. The minutes of the noonday conference on February 1 record Hitler's comments verbatim:

> The man should have shot himself just like the old commanders who threw themselves on their swords when they saw their cause was lost. That goes without saying. Even Varus gave his slave the order: "Now kill me!" . . .
>
> You have to imagine, he'll be brought to Moscow. There he will sign anything. He'll make confessions, make proclamations. You'll see: They will now walk down the slope of spiritual bankruptcy to its lowest depths. . . . The individual must die anyway. Beyond the life of the individual is the Nation. But how anyone could be afraid of this moment of death, with which he can free himself from this misery, if his duty doesn't chain him to this Vale of Tears. No!
>
> What hurts me most, personally, is that I promoted him to field marshal. I wanted to give him this final satisfaction. That's the last field marshal I shall appoint in this war. You mustn't count your chickens before they are hatched. I don't understand that at all. So many people have to die, and then a man like that besmirches the heroism of so many others at the last minute. He could have freed himself from all sorrow and ascended into eternity and national immortality, but he prefers to go to Moscow. What kind of choice is that? It just doesn't make sense.[8]

For the Russians Stalingrad was the most important victory of the war. It destroyed the belief that the German army could not be beaten, a belief that after the disasters of 1941 and the setbacks of 1942 was shared by many Russians as well as Germans. The Sixth Army was one of the most formidable in the Wehrmacht. In the initial battle for the city it had enjoyed every advantage over the Russian defenders, both in the air and on the ground. But it met its match in Chuikov's Sixty-second, which at the end of a

*See pp. 791–92.

three-month siege, before any relief came from the counteroffensive, was still holding on to the Volga bank, after what remains one of the most fiercely fought battles of the Second World War. The counteroffensive that followed and took the Germans by surprise showed that they could not only be out-fought but out-generaled as well.

After Stalin's purge of the Red Army and its poor performance in the Finnish war, the War Offices in London, Paris, and Washington as well as Berlin had written Russia off as a serious military power. Stalingrad forced them to revise their judgment. The shock to the German people, who had become accustomed to their army winning every battle and campaign it engaged in, was more than matched by the effect on the Russians. For Russian soldiers in particular, from army commanders to tank drivers, it meant breaking through the psychological equivalent of the sound barrier and shedding the inhibitions that had undermined their confidence.

Nor was it merely a question of confidence. Shaposhnikov's despondent remark after the Germans had been thrown back from Moscow—"We still need to assimilate the experience of modern war"—was no longer true. On October 16, 1942, Stalin issued Order No. 325, a full-length report that officers down to company level were required to study, analyzing the reasons for previous failures and setting out new independent roles for tank and mechanized units. Tank armies were being formed, and one of them at least was used in the Stalingrad counteroffensive, where tanks and mech-anized formations were given the task of breaking through the enemy's defenses and exploiting their success in depth. The lessons they had learned from the Germans were already being applied. The skill with which an operation involving more than a million men was planned, organized, and concealed from the enemy; the handling of mobile units; the coordination between the air force and ground forces; the massing of artillery and the improvement in communications—all showed how much the Red Army had absorbed and incorporated into its own practice.

No one was more affected by this gain in confidence than Stalin himself. His refusal to admit the threat of invasion by Germany; his temporary loss of nerve when it took place; his insistence on standing fast and "attack, attack, attack"; his reliance on old cronies like Voroshilov and Budenny, politicians with no military experience like Zhdanov or placemen like Mekhlis and Kulik to see that his orders were carried out—all these were expressions of his lack of confidence in the effectiveness of a Red Army whose officer cadres he had destroyed. Its unreliability in his eyes was demonstrated by its inability to withstand the German attack and by the huge number of Russian troops who surrendered rather than fight.

The success of the Stalingrad counteroffensive was a product—and acted as a confirmation—of a new relationship between Stalin and the army leadership that had emerged from the searching test of the 1941–42 cam-paign. During that initial period Shaposhnikov, the chief of the General Staff, and Timoshenko were the only two professional soldiers among the survivors who enjoyed sufficient trust from both Stalin and the army to fill the gaps left by the purges—and Timoshenko could hardly be called a successful commander. Shaposhnikov had been a colonel in the tsarist army and was the only military man from whom Stalin was willing to learn; his manner was quiet and he impressed Stalin by the quality of his mind, by the combination of logic and experience with which he presented an argument rather than by strength of personality. According to Zhukov, Stalin showed his respect for Shaposhnikov by always addressing him as Boris Mikhailovich, by never raising his voice when they spoke, even if he disagreed with him, and by allowing him, alone among the members of the Stavka, to smoke in his Kremlin office. The two crucial appointments that were made in the summer of 1942 were those of Zhukov as deputy to Stalin, at first as the defense commissar, then as the supreme commander, and Vasilevsky as chief of the General Staff. A third member of the team was N. N. Voronov, head of the Red Army's prestigious artillery arm. With Vasilevsky and Zhukov spending much of their time away from Moscow at the various fronts, a great deal of the day-to-day strain in relations with Stalin fell on the General Staff's chief of operations. Holders of this key post in 1941–42 had barely lasted two or three months before being fired by Stalin, but in December 1942 Vasilevsky found in A. I. Antonov a staff officer who satisfied Stalin so well that he held the office for the rest of the war.

Stalin kept Antonov in Moscow but more and more made use of the others to travel and coordinate the execution of important operations in the field—as Zhukov and Vasilevsky already had for the Stalingrad counteroffensive. Their employment in this capacity did not mean any slackening of the tight control he himself kept over operations. The Stavka, which they represented, was the personal staff of the supreme commander, with the General Staff as its operational planning group. Stalin was still the supreme commander in fact as well as name. Vasilevsky, for example, was accompanied on his travels by a General Staff signals unit and reported twice a day to Stalin on what was happening: at noon on the previous night's events, between 9 and 10 p.m. on the day's. Urgent news was signaled at once. After discussion with Zhukov and other members of the Stavka in Moscow, Stalin would approve Vasilevsky's proposals or order modifications.

These exchanges, which went on all the time between Stalin and the different front commanders and Stavka representatives, were frequently conducted in great detail. For example Voronov, sent to coordinate the operations of the Voronezh and adjoining southwestern fronts in December 1942, received the following instruction on the twenty-eighth:

> The main shortcoming of the plan you presented lies in the fact that the main and the supporting attacks diverge from each other. In the Stavka's view, your main task must be the splitting up and annihilation of the western group of encircled enemy troops in the Kravtsov-Baburkin-

Marinovka-Karpovka area in order to turn the main attack by our troops south from the Dmitrovka-Baburkin area into the Karpovka railway-station district, and to direct a supporting attack by Fifty-seventh Army from the Kravtsov-Sklyarov area into linking up with the main attack, so that both join at Karpovsk railway station.

In line with this should be organized an attack by Sixty-sixth Army through Orlovka towards *Krasnyi-Oktyabr* and—to meet this—an attack mounted by Sixty-second Army so that both attacks can link up and thus cut off the factory district from the main enemy forces.

To carry out this plan for the inner encirclement at Stalingrad, Stalin agreed to bring the force engaged up to a strength of forty-seven divisions (218,000 men) with 7,000 guns and 300 planes. When Voronov asked for a four- or five-day delay to incorporate the reinforcements, he got a sharp reply, which bore Stalin's unmistakable stamp:

> You'll sit it out so long down there that the Germans will take you and Rokossovsky prisoner. You don't think about what can be done, only about what can't be done. We need to be finished as quickly as possible there and you deliberately hold things up. [9]

Nonetheless Stalin gave Voronov the four days he asked for, and the attack opened on time on January 10, with the concentrated bombardment of the encircled German troops already described.

Stalin also continued to make use of members of the Politburo—Khrush-chev on the southern front, Zhdanov on the northern—and of members of the State Defense Committee (GOKO) such as Malenkov to act as his political representatives. But even before the Stalingrad counteroffensive opened, the army won a much-prized victory that clearly marked the change in Stalin's attitude toward the senior army commanders. Order No. 307, published on October 9, abolished the control functions of the political commissars, the system of "dual command" under the hated Mekhlis's direction, which had been hastily reintroduced in July 1941 to meet the crisis of fronts collapsing before the German attack. "Unitary command" was reinstated and vested in the military commander.

The rehabilitation of the army was completed by three further steps in 1943. The first was the promotion to marshal of those who had been the architects of the Stalingrad victory: Zhukov and Vassilevsky to marshals of the Soviet Union; Voronov to marshal of artillery; and Novikov (who had rescued the Red Air Force from the disasters of 1941) to marshal of aviation. Most significant of all was Stalin's appointment of himself as marshal of the Soviet Union, publicly identifying himself with the new military elite, on the first Red Army Day, January 23, 1943. Promotion was also accorded to the field commanders such as Rokossovsky (although none as yet to the rank of marshal) and a whole range of decorations was created, such as the Order of Suvorov, commemorating one of the great names of

Russia's military prowess in the time of Tsar Alexander I and the defeat of Napoleon.

The second step was even more evocative of the past: the reintroduction of badges of rank and of the shoulder boards, the *pogon,* which the soldiers in revolt in 1917 had torn from the uniforms of officers of the Imperial Russian Army. Stalin hesitated a long time but finally accepted the argument that this was a way of strengthening morale and followed logically on the abolition of "dual command." Six months later, in July 1943, the equivalent ranks from corporal to lieutenant general were formalized and the continuity with the Imperial Officer Corps reestablished by the reintroduction of the word *officer,* which had remained subject to a class taboo after being banned by the revolution.

Never having seen a battle under modern conditions, Stalin was unable to visualize the time it took for operations to be carried out or to grasp the tactical problems that so much preoccupied commanders in the field. The action of military units smaller than armies, Zhukov said, was obscure to him. According to General Volkogonov, who had access to the military archives, he devised a way of dealing with operational planning that preserved his reputation as commander in chief without exposing it to too much risk. The records show that he worked out his ideas on two levels. One was general, such as his declaration at the Stavka meeting in January 1942: "We must not allow the enemy to recover his breath, we must pursue him westward." This expressed a wish but lacked any precise strategic concept. The other level was that of adjustment or refinement of a concrete plan or timetable. He put his remarks in the form of a resumé. The entire plan would have been worked out in detail by the General Staff but Stalin's authoritative summing up created the impression that it was his work.[10]

What shocked the professional soldiers most was Stalin's complete indifference to the cost of an operation in lives—another characteristic that he shared with Hitler. The cost of the war to the Soviet people was an estimated twenty million dead—10 percent of the entire population—and it may yet prove to have been higher. A substantial part of that huge loss—and of another ten million wounded—is attributable to Stalin's refusal to allow adequate preparations before the German attack, and to the ill-judged and extravagantly costly orders that he issued during the first eighteen months. These were not ended by Stalingrad. As Vasilevsky recognized, Stalingrad was a milestone, but it was not until the battle of Kursk that Stalin grasped the new forms and methods of combat.[11]

This is borne out by the plans for the winter offensive in the opening months of 1943. In the euphoria produced by the Stalingrad victory, Stalin insisted on repeating the same maneuver of a simultaneous offensive against all three German army groups which had failed in the winter of early 1942. Confident that the strategic initiative was now in Russian hands, he planned both to destroy the enemy forces in the field and to liberate the Ukraine with the wealth of industrial resources in the Donbas.

The offensive began in the south on January 29 aimed at bringing the Soviet armies to the Dnieper by the time the spring thaw set in. On the way they recaptured Rostov, Belgorod, and (on February 16) the prize of Kharkov, the second city of the Ukraine. It was at this point that it became clear that Stalin had made the same mistake as in the winter of 1942. Once again, he had underestimated the enemy and overestimated the Red Army's capacity to score a decisive success in a single continuous operation following right after the Stalingrad victory.

THE SIX-WEEK-LONG AGONY of the Sixth Army and his inability to rescue them had put a heavy strain on Hitler. However well he disguised it in public, he kept his staff up later and later, exhausting them with his monologues, rather than going to bed and facing the nightmares that haunted him. The crisis was not over when Paulus surrendered. The threat that the Red Army might exploit its advantage and the German front disintegrate was a real one.

Hitler was well aware that the generals were highly critical of his constant intervention in operations. As von Richthofen put it to him: "The army commanders were all right . . . but must be given tactical freedom to act as their own local experience dictated. Leading them by the scruff of the neck as though they were children just did harm." The unorthodox and outspoken von Richthofen, who had protested against the idea of an airlift saving the Sixth Army and then thrown himself into trying to make a success of it, was one of the few men Hitler allowed to speak frankly to him (he decided shortly afterwards to make him a field marshal), but as von Richthofen went on to record: "The Führer replied that if he hadn't led them like that they would have been fighting in Germany by now." [12]

Hitler was more prepared than he had been before to listen to the professionals' advice. He agreed to abandon territory in order to shorten the front line in the east, and he accepted that 1943 would have to be a year of strategic defense on all fronts until Speer, Milch, and Dönitz among them could increase the production of tanks, aircraft, and U-boats. But he would not look at the suggestion—which, in the end, no one dared to make to his face—that he should give up the office of commander in chief of the army, or at least appoint von Manstein as commander in chief in the east.

All the evidence suggests that Stalingrad was the greatest single shock of the war to the German people, "the low point of wartime morale on the home front." [13] Until the final days the certainty of disaster—and its scale— had been concealed. The Russian counteroffensive was not mentioned and, even when the news was given, the "Special Announcement" spoke of officers and men fighting heroically until the last shot and made no mention of Paulus' surrender.

For the first time there was muttered criticism not just of the regime, but of Hitler himself. Goebbels, according to Speer, declared privately, "We are not having a 'leadership crisis' but strictly speaking a 'leader crisis.' " [14] Evidently aware of this, Hitler summoned all the Gauleiters to his headquarters on February 7 and told them, according to one who was present, "What you are witnessing is a catastrophe of unheard-of magnitude," adding, "If the German people fails, then it does not deserve that we fight for its future." [15]

At Munich University, the small "White Rose" group of young students had the courage to distribute copies of a manifesto declaring that at Stalingrad 330,000 Germans had been senselessly led to their death: "Our Führer, we thank you! . . . Fellow students! The German people look to us to destroy the terror of National Socialism, as they did in 1813 to destroy the Napoleonic terror. . . . The dead of Stalingrad adjure us." [16] For this they paid with their lives. But the opinion reports showed that the general mood was "despairing, despondent, and war weary—apathetic rather than rebellious." [17]

It was this mood that Goebbels's "total war" campaign was designed to counter. Hitler accepted Goebbels's argument that they must now do all they could to arouse the equivalent of the "Dunkirk spirit" in the German people by confronting them with the reality of total war—including "unconditional surrender"—and the demands it made on everybody without exception. Goebbels launched his campaign with a successful speech in Berlin on February 18, but Hitler's own speech broadcast on Heroes' Memorial Day a month later was described as leaden and uninspiring, and nobody believed his statement that German losses in the whole war so far amounted to 542,000.

The one thing Hitler would not look at was a political solution in any form. Among proposals he turned down were Ribbentrop's for putting out peace feelers toward Moscow; Goebbels's for a political proclamation to the Russian people "to fight on with us against hated Bolshevism, bloody Stalin, and his Jewish clique"; Rosenberg's rival scheme for promising to restore private property, freedom of religion, and autonomy for Russia's ethnic minorities; and the suggestion of giving support to the Russian Liberation Movement headed by the captured Russian general, Andrei Vlasov, which Zeitzler among others recommended. Hitler ruled out any such move until after the German army had won a major military victory—and when it did, he was certain to reject any such move as unnecessary.

Hitler's hopes were centered on von Manstein's Army Group South, which, after regrouping, was preparing to launch a counteroffensive to regain Kharkov and the eastern Ukraine. Von Manstein's headquarters was at Zaporozh'ye on the Dnieper, where the huge hydroelectric power station had been rebuilt by the German AEG, allowing electricity to be supplied again to the neighboring coal mines and munitions factories. Speer hoped to expand the heavy chemical and explosives industries in the Donbass, but he could do this only if the Soviet drive to clear the Ukraine was halted.

Hitler flew to Zaporozh'ye to give encouragement at the start of von Manstein's attack. As he left, the gunfire of Russian tanks could be heard from the airfield.

Once again the German army showed its skill, with the panzers—now Waffen SS as well as army armored divisions—taking the Russians by surprise, halting their advance and threatening to cut their communications. By the middle of March von Manstein's forces had recaptured Kharkov and Belgorod, putting an end to Russian hopes of regaining the Donbass and reaching the Dnieper. As the spring thaw brought the fighting to an end, the Russians were glad to have ended their retreat and stabilized their front on the Rivers Donets and Mius. Further north, German withdrawals, to which Hitler agreed in order to shorten their line, allowed the Russians to advance fifty miles eastward, but Stalin's hopes of capturing Orel, Bryansk, and Smolensk and of encircling von Kleist's Army Group Center faded in the face of tough German resistance.

Overall the Soviet gains over the previous few months were impressive. The position on the southern wing of the front had been transformed by the Stalingrad victory and the German withdrawal from the Caucasus. In the process the Russians claimed to have put a million men of the German and their allies' forces out of action between November 1942 and March 1943, and left them with a strength of under half a million on the whole *Ostfront*. But the Germans still stood deep inside the frontiers of Russia and, with their morale restored, Hitler in March approved the army's plan for Operation Citadel, a major combined attack by Army Groups South and Center aimed at the Russian positions round Kursk, halfway between Moscow and the Sea of Azov.

If Citadel had been carried out in May 1943, as originally intended, it might have succeeded; but, when May came, Hitler was confronted with a major threat in Italy. Citadel had to be postponed and arrangements made, if necessary, to move eight armored and four infantry divisions from the eastern front to Italy. By the time Citadel was launched, on July 5, the delay had given the Russians time to build up their own forces and prepare to meet the German challenge.

I I

OPERATION TORCH, the landings in French North Africa on November 8 and 9, 1942, brought American land forces into the Mediterranean and very soon into the European theater of war. Hitler had not been far off in saying that it would be a year before the U.S.A. would have any effect on the war in Europe; where he was wrong was in supposing that, when the year was up, the war in Europe would have been won.

French resistance in Morocco and Algeria lasted only three days. But the invasion force failed to secure Tunisia, the key strategic objective if the Allies hoped to clear North Africa and achieve control of the Mediterranean. Although taken by surprise, Hitler reacted at once to the news. Within forty-eight hours, as soon as he got wind of a deal between the Americans and Admiral Jean François Darlan (until recently, deputy prime minister and foreign minister in the Vichy government, who happened to be in Algeria), he ordered the occupation of Vichy France. German troops failed to take over the French fleet at Toulon, which ignored Darlan's orders to sail to North Africa and preferred to scuttle its ships rather than let them fall into German hands. But Hitler showed himself much quicker than the Allies to exploit opportunities in Tunisia. He was already alive to the shakiness of Mussolini's personal position and the possibility that the Italians might seek a way to get out of the war. If he could occupy Tunisia before the Allies, he could hold off any attack on Italy and so secure more room and time for maneuver. To make sure, he poured in men and equipment by sea and air. By December 1942 he had provided General Jürgen von Arnim, commanding the newly established Fifth Panzer Army, with 78,000 German and 27,000 Italian troops to hold the former French colony and prevent Montgomery's Eighth Army in the east from joining up with the Allied invasion forces from the west.

The reasons for the failure to push home the Allied attack were as much political as military. Roosevelt refused to have anything to do with de Gaulle, and the deal with Darlan, the representative of Vichy, aroused a storm of protest in Britain as well as France, from the worst consequences of which the Allies were only rescued by the latter's assassination. To reestablish confidence, Roosevelt suggested to Churchill and Stalin that a meeting of the three leaders should be held in January. Stalin's answer was that, with the Stalingrad battle reaching its climax, he could not be absent for a single day. Churchill and Roosevelt therefore held their meeting at Casablanca without him—for the third time in thirteen months. If this was not the wish of his Western partners it was nonetheless unfortunate in view of the strain on the alliance from the failure to meet Stalin's continuing demand for a second front in Europe. Stalin refused a further invitation to meet in March but left no doubt of his feelings in a message to Roosevelt on December 17, 1942, that he was counting on the promises given by the Western leaders, originally for 1942 and now for 1943, to open a second front with their joint forces in the spring. Roosevelt's declaration that the Allies would enter into no peace negotiations but would demand unconditional surrender from the Germans seems to have been prompted by a desire to allay Stalin's suspicions.

But the other important decision reached at Casablanca—to invade Sicily—only added to the uncertainty surrounding the second front. It was combined with plans to prepare for seizing a bridgehead in the Cotentin Peninsula of Normandy and a return to the continent in August 1943, but when Stalin pressed to be told what this meant in concrete terms, the caveat was entered that shipping and landing craft would be "limiting factors." The operation might be delayed until September and was described as "dependent upon the condition of German defensive possibilities across the Channel at the time." [18]

In a final exchange in March, Stalin claimed that while the Allied advance in North Africa was at a standstill, the Germans had moved thirty-six divisions, including six armored, to the eastern front. He insisted that the Sicilian operation could not replace a second front in France, that further delay would be "a serious danger," and that "the vagueness of your [Roosevelt's] statement about the opening of a second front in France provokes alarm which I cannot suppress." [19]

The real cause for concern, whether Stalin recognized it or not, was the difference, which was papered over, between British and American views of what was to follow the invasion of Sicily. Was it to lead on to the invasion of Italy, and if so, did this mean that a second front in France would be delayed until the summer of 1944?

In March 1943 the Anglo-U.S. forces advancing from the west and Montgomery's Eighth Army advancing from the east had not yet joined up. The weakness in the German position was not lack of troops. The difficulty was in keeping them supplied, especially with fuel, in the face of Allied air and sea attacks on their supply route. In February only 25,000 tons had arrived instead of the 80,000 required, and von Arnim is quoted as saying, "You can work out with pencil and paper when the end will come." [20]

Rommel was pessimistic and urged Hitler to allow withdrawal. Hitler's answer was to order him to attack Montgomery in front of the Mareth Line (which the French had built to keep the Italians out). When he did so and was out-generaled by the British and forced to retreat, Rommel was immediately recalled. Hitler decided that the "Desert Fox" had lost his nerve as a result of the long retreat from Egypt and had better go on sick leave and not return to Africa. His removal from the scene, however, was kept a secret: Rommel's reputation was too valuable an asset to throw away. All von Arnim could do was to hang on for another two months, until the Afrika Korps had exhausted its ammunition and 140,000 of Hitler's best troops were taken prisoner along with a similar number of Italians.

Hitler maintained that the loss was worth the six months he had gained; but it remained to be seen what use he could make of the delay. He was still left with the threat of an Allied landing in Europe and the defection of Italy. The British and Americans had recaptured the initiative. All Hitler could do was to wait another two months—until July—for the threat to materialize, making preparations to move troops from Russia at short notice, delaying Citadel and, as he told his generals on May 15, accepting that it might be necessary to make further withdrawals in the east.

ON THE SAME DAY, May 15, 1943, Stalin unexpectedly announced the dissolution of the Comintern, the organization that for more than twenty years had symbolized the Soviet Union's commitment to world revolution. Its abolition was welcomed in the West as further evidence that Russia's leaders were more concerned with the defense of her traditional national interests than with revolutionary plotting to overthrow capitalist governments and subvert their working classes. Stalin said as much in an interview, expressing the hope that this would put an end to the "slanders" that Communist parties took their orders from outside and worked on behalf of Moscow rather than their own people. His second comment came nearer to the real reason for the decision: It would make it easier for Communists in other countries to join broad national fronts against Hitler.[21] Two months later, the creation of a National Committee for a Free Germany in Moscow showed what Stalin had in mind. It included the future leader of the Communist German Democratic Republic, Walther Ulbricht, and a captured German officer, Graf Heinrich von Einsiedel, Bismarck's great-grandson, and its "national" appeal was underlined by the adoption of the black-white-red colors of Imperial Germany.

Stalin later told the Yugoslav Communist, Djilas, that the Comintern had become a nuisance as well as an anachronism, with its émigré members attempting to promote policies that were out of line with Stalin's: "There was something abnormal, unnatural about the very existence of a general Communist forum at a time when the Communist parties should have been searching for a national language and fighting against the conditions in their own countries."[22] Looking ahead to the postwar situation, Stalin preferred to deal separately (and secretly) with individual Communist parties, without general discussions in the Comintern Executive. This would give him much greater freedom in varying the tactics to be adopted in each country as the Red Army began the advance that would end with the occupation of Eastern and much of Central Europe.

During May Churchill traveled to Washington and in discussions with Roosevelt agreed—again without Stalin—that the invasion of Sicily should go ahead, with the consequence that a cross-Channel invasion of France would have to be postponed until 1944. They braced themselves for a stiff protest from Stalin, who remonstrated at a decision "which may have grave consequences for the further conduct of the war," and with which he refused to associate himself. In further exchanges, Stalin declared it was a question of preserving Soviet confidence in the Alliance, a confidence "being subjected to severe strain." The enormous sacrifices of the Soviet armies, compared to which Anglo-American losses were "insignificant," must be reduced. Invitations to meet, however, and to thrash out the difficulties came to nothing in view of the fact that on July 5 Hitler at last launched Operation Citadel.

There could be no doubt at which sector of the eastern front this third attempt to destroy Russian resistance would be aimed. A hundred and fifty miles north of Kharkov (which was in German hands) the important railway junction at Kursk was at the center of a huge Russian salient (about half the size of England), open to attack by Army Group Center (von Kluge) from Orel in the north and by Army Group South (von Manstein) from Belgorod and Kharkov in the south. At the end of March 1943, the German troops included twenty panzer divisions, among them four SS armored divisions on which Hitler particularly relied to show a true National Socialist fighting spirit. From then to the beginning of July, both sides built up their forces. Soviet war production was now running at levels that the Germans could not equal—2,000 tanks and self-propelled guns a month and 2,500 planes. On April 1, 1943, there were 1,200 Soviet tanks in the salient; two months later this number had been trebled. The Russians used the time not only to build up forces and supplies but also to create a series of fortified lines and to train and exercise their troops. As in the Stalingrad counteroffensive, Zhukov, Vasilevsky, and Voronov were responsible for coordination at the front, reporting back twice a day to Stalin and the Stavka in Moscow.

Hitler, preoccupied with the Italian situation, as well as the Allied air offensive against German cities, left the planning of Citadel to Zeitzler and the two commanders, von Manstein and von Kluge. They had high hopes, fortified by a concentration of Luftwaffe strength—1,800 planes—never before seen on the eastern front, a combined force of a million men and 2,700 tanks and assault guns. When the German attack began on July 5, it rapidly developed into the biggest tank battle in history, of an indescribable fury and horror. At the end of a week, on July 12, Stalin launched his counteroffensive and in the area of Prokhorovka huge concentrations of armor crashed into each other to form a roaring, whirling tangle of over a thousand tanks locked together in combat for over eighteen hours. This was the climax of a battle that became famous for the ferocity of the fighting and was ended only by the exhaustion of both sides. The Waffen SS panzer divisions—SS Death's Head, SS Adolf Hitler, and SS Das Reich—who prided themselves on being harder than any troops in the regular army and were well provided with the new Tiger and Panther tanks, met their match and suffered particularly heavy losses. The result was described by Guderian, recalled to act as inspector-general of the German panzer troops, as a decisive defeat. On both sides the losses of men and machines were appallingly high, but at the end of the day it was the Soviet forces that held the field and advanced, the Germans who retreated.

WHILE THE RESULT of Citadel was still in the balance, Anglo-American forces landed in Sicily. Apart from the threat to the Italian mainland, the capture of Sicilian airfields created the possibility of reopening the passage of the Mediterranean, with an enormous saving of shipping which until that was secured had to make the much longer voyage around the Cape. Hitler was caught off guard, misled by faked evidence into believing the Allies' objective was Sardinia. The Italians offered little serious resistance, and their fleet did not engage; but the 40,000 German troops on the island put up stiff resistance. It was not until August 17 that the Americans reached Messina, to find that the Germans, to their own surprise, had been able to escape to the Italian mainland.

By then, Hitler's worst fears had been realized and Mussolini, his fellow dictator, had been thrown out of office. The Duce proved incapable of making the break with Hitler which was secretly urged on him by Germany's other allies, Rumania and Hungary, as well as by his own Fascist chieftains. The Italians' hearts had never been in the war, and the losses suffered by Italian troops in Russia and Tunisia as well as Allied air attacks united public opinion in the desire to get out of the war at any cost—if not with Mussolini, then without him. On July 24 the Fascist General Council met for the first time since the outbreak of war. After listening to an hour-long attack by Dino Grandi, a leading figure of the Fascist regime, on Mussolini's conduct of the war, the council voted at two o'clock in the morning to restore the king as commander in chief. The following day Victor Emmanuel dismissed the Duce from the office of prime minister to which he had appointed him twenty years before, and a listless Mussolini submitted to arrest without resistance.

Hitler needed no one to point out that, if the Italians could get rid of Mussolini, the Germans might follow suit. In May, crippling German losses of thirty-eight U-boats, compared with fourteen in April, had forced Dönitz to call off the campaign in the North Atlantic—as it turned out, another decisive defeat. U-boat losses could be concealed but not the RAF's bombing of one German city after another, with several hundred planes night after night. The news from the fronts was alarming, but this was the weapon that hit directly at the German people's morale, already depressed in the fourth year of the war.

In the four winter months of 1942–43 Berlin itself suffered sixteen heavy night raids and, to Hitler's fury, small and fast RAF Mosquito bombers, made of wood, proved capable even in daylight of making lone flights all the way to the capital, keeping millions in the air-raid shelters, while the unescorted plane circled overhead before dropping its 4,000-pound load and evading the German defenses all the way back again. Between March and July RAF Bomber Command concentrated forty-three major raids on the Ruhr's industrial cities, culminating in a devastating incendiary raid on Wuppertal-Barmen. This was followed by four fire raids on Hamburg which came close to wiping out the center of the city. Since 1942, the RAF had been joined by American B17s, the Flying Fortresses, which kept up the attack by day. Losses for both were high, over 5 percent rising to 10 percent; and until the end of 1943 Speer was able to keep up the rate of industrial production despite the damage to factories and communications. But most Germans discounted such claims. What they saw with their own eyes was the damage, and what they asked was: Why doesn't the Führer do something to stop it?

This was the question Hitler himself asked. Göring's inability to make

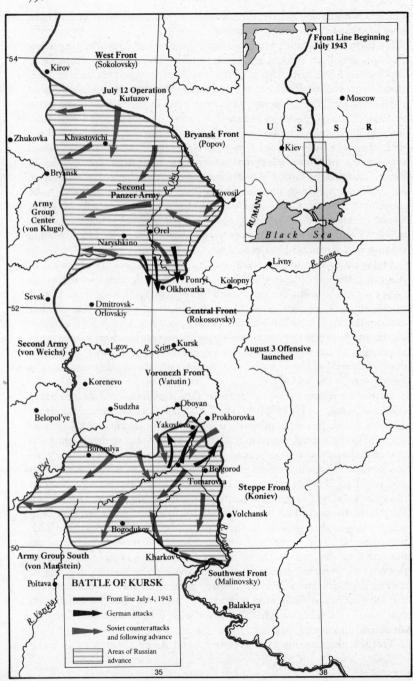

Front Line Beginning July 1943

Moscow

U S S R

Kiev

RUMANIA

Black Sea

54

Kirov

West Front (Sokolovsky)

July 12 Operation Kutuzov

Zhukovka

Khvastovichi

Bryansk Front (Popov)

Bryansk

R. Oka

Novosil

Second Panzer Army

Army Group Center (von Kluge)

Orel

Naryshkino

Livny   *R. Sosna*

Sevsk

Dmitrovsk-Orlovskiy

Ponyri   Kolopny
Olkhovatka

52

Central Front (Rokossovsky)

Second Army (von Weichs)

Lgov   *R. Seim*   Kursk

August 3 Offensive launched

Korenevo

Voronezh Front (Vatutin)

Belopol'ye

Sudzha   Oboyan

Yakovlevo   Prokhorovka

Boromlya

R. Psel

Belgorod

Tomarovka

Steppe Front (Koniev)

Bogodukov

Volchansk

R. Donets

50

Army Group South (von Manstein)

Kharkov

Poltava

Southwest Front (Malinovsky)

Balakleya

R. Vorskla

BATTLE OF KURSK

Front line July 4, 1943

German attacks

Soviet counterattacks and following advance

Areas of Russian advance

35   38

good his promise to supply the Sixth Army at Stalingrad by air had already gone far to destroy his reputation as the Luftwaffe's commander in chief. His air force's failure to prevent the Allied bombers from ranging over Germany or to carry out the retaliatory raids on Britain, which he promised, finally discredited him. General Hans Jeschonnek, the chief of air staff, went so far as to urge Hitler to take over the leadership of the Luftwaffe as he had that of the army in 1942. Hitler was unwilling to destroy openly the reputation of the man he had marked as his successor; this could only damage the regime. But throughout 1943 he made all the major decisions in the air war himself, including the tactical disposal of Luftwaffe units on both the eastern and the Mediterranean fronts. But he failed to get to the bottom of the tangle of incompetence, rivalries, and special interests that prevented the Luftwaffe and the aircraft industry from producing a new generation of machines to match those that the British, Russians, and Americans had brought into service since the beginning of the war. In despair, Jeschonnek committed suicide.

Milch at least succeeded in checking the fall in aircraft production that had taken place between 1940 and 1942, and in 1943 Germany produced 43,000 machines compared with 26,000 in 1942. But the Allies' production figures rose from 100,000 to 151,000.[23] Not only did the Germans fail to produce a long-range heavy bomber to match the RAF's Lancasters and make possible attacks on the British and Russian equivalents of the Ruhr, but there also was no agreement on strategy—whether it should be defensive as Milch urged, with priority given to the production of fighters, or offensive, with priority for bombers and the "special weapons" that increasingly occupied Hitler's imagination.

This accumulation of anxieties and frustrations affected Hitler's health. After Stalingrad he had fallen ill from influenza, complicated by an inflammation of the brain which his doctor Morell attributed to the prolonged period of strain he had been through. The treatment was several weeks of rest, which Hitler could not afford to take. The result was splitting headaches, a tremor in one of his arms (which Morell suspected was of hysterical origin, but may have been the first sign of Parkinson's Disease), and a tendency to drag one of his legs. He suffered from bouts of severe depression which Morell tried to alleviate with hormone injections. Guderian, who had not seen Hitler since December 1941, describes him in February 1943 as a changed man:

> His left hand trembled, his back was bent, his gaze was fixed, his eyes protruded but lacked their former luster, his cheeks were flecked with red. He was more excitable, easily lost his composure, and was prone to angry outbursts and ill-considered decisions as a result.[24]

Goebbels, who saw Hitler shortly afterwards, noted for the first time that he had begun to age.

Having no exercise and continually brooding on the military situation,

Hitler again began to suffer from stomach cramps and to find it difficult to sleep even with sedatives. (He now refused to go to bed until the last British bomber had left German air space.) To reduce his pains he started to take a patent medicine, of which Morell secured large supplies, Dr. Koester's Anti-Gas Tablets—anything from eight to sixteen tablets every day. Not until October 1944 did a visiting doctor have the chance to get past Morell's guard and look at the prescription on the label. It emerged that Hitler had been dosing himself daily with pills the principal constituents of which were two poisons, strychnine and atropine, both of which acted as a powerful stimulant to his nervous system.

The tension from which Hitler was suffering was increased by the long delay between the fall of Mussolini and a denouement that he feared to precipitate by premature intervention. Mussolini had been succeeded as prime minister by Marshal Badoglio, who negotiated secretly with the Allies in Lisbon and Madrid while constantly assuring the Germans of his loyalty. Although Churchill and Roosevelt had agreed to follow up the conquest of Sicily with the elimination of Italy from the war, they had not formed any plans in advance to deal with the very likely event of an Italian attempt to secure this by political negotiations and so avoid a German occupation. This was as much in the Allies' interest as the Italians', but their own slogan of "unconditional surrender" appears to have blinded the two leaders to the obvious danger that the only alternative might well be to fight a long and difficult campaign against the Germans up the length of the Italian peninsula, and so delay still further the second front in France which, alone would satisfy Stalin. In Algeria, a deal had been struck with Darlan in three days; General Eisenhower, the Allied commander, asked for powers to act quickly on July 29, but it was not until three weeks later (August 17) that he received his instructions and not until September 3 that he was able to reach agreement with the Italians.

While Hitler waited impatiently, convinced that the Italians were plotting to defect but hesitating to act until he could see which way the cat would jump, Stalin launched a massive new offensive aimed at recapturing the Donbass and driving the Germans back across the Dnieper. Hitler agreed reluctantly on August 11 to von Manstein's request to withdraw to the East Wall, the building of which had first been ordered after Stalingrad. But resistance on Hitler's part, followed by disagreements about the line it should follow and who should build it, the army or Speer, meant that by the time the troops were driven back to the Dnieper, there was nothing ready for them to take over.

Hitler's reaction to Mussolini's overthrow was to demand immediate action to seize Rome, arrest the Badoglio government, and take the king and crown prince as hostages. But, as it became clear—helped by a transcript of a transatlantic conversation between Churchill and Roosevelt—that the Allies were in no hurry to exploit the situation, he took the opportunity to move German troops into Italy. The Italians were playing the same game, protesting their loyalty to the Axis but doing all they could to hinder the German movement of troops and concentrate a strong force of their own around Rome. Neither side was taken in. On August 30, after the troops in Sicily had completed their evacuation, the German forces were instructed as soon as the code word "Axis" was issued to disarm the Italians and "pacify" the north, while those in the south carried out a fighting retreat to Rome.

A report of the Italian surrender was broadcast by the BBC on September 8, taking the Italians as well as the Germans by surprise. Hitler was at Zaporozh'ye in the Ukraine, where he had been summoned the same morning after the alarming news that the Russians had broken through the junction between von Manstein's and von Kluge's army groups, and were pouring west toward Kiev and the Dnieper. He flew back to East Prussia, almost as soon as he had landed, on a hunch that the denouement in Italy had arrived. The code word was issued and the Germans seized Rome and its airfields before an Allied airborne force with the same objectives could take off. The Italian troops were disarmed, while the Luftwaffe attacked the Italian fleet making for Malta, sank the battleship *Roma,* and damaged her sister ship, *Italia.*

The Germans had expected an Allied landing to be made near Rome and had therefore prepared to withdraw all their forces from south of the capital. This was the plan prepared by Rommel, the commander in the north, who foresaw the loss of southern and central Italy as inevitable. But when the main landing was made at Salerno, south of Naples, Hitler switched to the alternative proposed by Field Marshal Albert Kesselring, the commander in Rome, to form a defensive line along the Volturno south of the capital. This was the key decision, forcing the Allied armies to fight a long and arduous campaign for nine months over mountainous terrain before finally reaching Rome, not in September 1943, but in June 1944. At the same time, a bold and skillfully executed coup by the SS officer Otto Skorzeny rescued Mussolini by air from his mountain prison in the Gran Sasso to preside over a German-sponsored Italian Republic in the north.

III

FOLLOWING MUSSOLINI'S REMOVAL from office, Hitler had appointed Himmler as minister of the interior in place of Frick (August 20, 1943). The SS were the best guarantee that what had happened in Italy would not be repeated in Germany.

Hitler's confidence in Himmler had been greatly increased by the success of the Waffen SS on the eastern front. The regular army had always regarded the growth of a rival with the same hostility it had shown toward Röhm's SA. During the 1930s Himmler looked upon the militarized formations of the SS as a force to be used for internal purposes only, including the suppression of a possible putsch by the army. It was the war and Hitler's order that they should be placed under the command of the commander in chief of the army that turned them into a fighting formation in the field. But the generals were critical of their performance, regarding them as undisciplined and inadequately trained, and did their best to prevent any expansion of their numbers by their control of the draft.

Gottlob Berger, however, who had been put in charge of recruiting in the SS Head Office, found a source outside the control of the Wehrmacht in the young men of the *Volksdeutsche* living in other countries who were excited by the Nazi propaganda for a Greater Germany and even more by the brilliant successes of the Norwegian and French campaigns in which the Waffen SS played a striking part. Berger began with Rumania and with such volunteers raised the Waffen SS numbers to 160,000 by the time of the invasion of Russia. In their performance against the Russians they won Hitler's praise for their "National Socialist qualities." They fought with an unorthodox mixture of fanaticism, élan, and ruthlessness, more akin to the traditions of the Freikorps than those of the Prussian army, but in 1942 and 1943 they proved themselves as elite troops by their ferocity in attack and tenacity in defense, accompanied by losses far higher than those of the regular army.

By 1944 the total numbers of the Waffen SS passed half a million, by 1945, 910,000—more than a third drawn from all parts of Europe, including Balts, Ukrainians, Russians, and Balkan Muslims. By that time, as a result of their losses and the shortage of manpower, the character of the earlier formations had been much diluted, but in 1944 Hitler still looked upon them as his Praetorian Guard.

Himmler had never lost his interest in the Germanization of the east. In May 1942, a General Plan East, produced by his SS planning office and accepted by Hitler, visualized the whole of western Russia, up to a line from Leningrad via the Valdai Hills and Bryansk to the great bend in the Dnieper, being settled by Germans. Fourteen million people of other races were to be deported further east to make room for them. The Government-General and the Baltic states were to be completely repopulated; 85 percent of the twenty million Poles and 65 percent of the West Ukrainians were to be moved to western Siberia to make room for German immigrants.

Himmler was particularly pleased with the proposal that all land in the east should be under his authority as Reichsführer SS, the liege lord of the east, granting "life fiefs" and "hereditary fiefs." "Just imagine what a sublime idea!" Himmler told his Finnish masseur, Felix Kersten:*

It's the greatest piece of colonization the world will ever have seen linked to a most noble and essential task, the protection of the western world against an irruption from Asia.

---

*Kersten was able to use the knowledge he acquired of Himmler's plans to save the lives of the Jews of Finland and then thousands of other Jews who were able to emigrate to Sweden.

To protect the fully Germanized parts of Poland and the Baltic states, three "Marks" were to be established whose population would become 50 percent Germanized during the first twenty-five years. Three "Marks" were envisaged: the area west of Leningrad, to which Himmler gave the name Ingermanland, the Crimea-Kherson area (to be renamed Gotenland), and the Memel-Narev area. Twenty-six settlement strongpoints would be set up, small towns of about 20,000 each, surrounded by a ring of German villages. Their SS peasant-warriors would guard the intersections of German communications. The settlers, however, would be provided by the ethnic German communities overseas, other Germanic countries of northern Europe and natives suitable for Germanization. [25]

Except for the prospective colonists, the hundreds of thousands of *Volksdeutsche* uprooted and left with nowhere to go until they were caught up in the German retreat,* this remained another Hitler-Himmler fantasy, this time, fortunately, not put into effect. But Himmler's ambition to extend his empire to the economic as well as the military field had more substance. The part played by Berger in developing the Waffen SS was played by Oswald Pohl in developing the WVHA (*Wirtschafts und Verwaltungshauptamt,* the SS Economy and Administration Department). Pohl, an ex-navy paymaster, had risen to become financial administrator of the entire SS. From this he expanded his reach to take over the administration and supply of the Waffen SS, to control the twenty concentration camps and 165 labor camps, to direct all SS and police building projects, and all SS economic undertakings. The last had begun in the 1930s and by 1942 included a large number of individual enterprises in a whole range of activities from quarrying and brickmaking to foodstuffs and textiles.

The key to Pohl's success was his control of concentration and labor camps, which enabled him, at a time of growing labor shortage, to employ their inmates—including prisoners of war—in SS enterprises and also to lease them out, at a price, to other factories under state or private management. This rapidly became big business, especially in supplying labor to the firms making armaments.

The effect was to change the purpose of the concentration camps. Shortly after his appointment, Pohl wrote to Himmler on April 30, 1942:

> Custody of prisoners for security or preventive reasons is no longer the primary consideration. Emphasis has now shifted to the economic side . . . mobilization of all prisoner labor, initially for . . . increase of arms production and later for peacetime building.

Pohl called for measures to transform "the concentration camps from their previous purely political form into an organization capable of meeting our economic requirements." [26] That had been the case in the Soviet Gulag labor camps from a much earlier date.

*See pp. 824–25.

Himmler welcomed the new development, seeing it as a way to establish an economic power-base for the SS after the war and in the meantime to create his own armaments industry. It also enabled him to find a solution to another problem. In his efforts to carry out the Final Solution he had continually encountered resistance from the OKW (Armed Forces) Armament Inspectorate and from the two Gauleiters (Lohse and Kube) responsible for the administration of the Ostland on the grounds that, as more and more Poles and Russians were drafted to relieve the shortage of labor in Germany, they must be allowed to keep those Jews who were skilled workers—100,000 in the Government-General—and had become indispensable to the war economy in the occupied territories. Himmler refused to allow this: Economic considerations could not weigh against racial principles. But he was prepared to transfer all Jewish employees and the contracts on which they were working to concentration camps, where they could be employed by the SS for as long as they were fit to work (the average expectation of life in the camps was six months), and then shot, gassed, or, more often, literally worked to death.

The new orientation towards the provision of labor was reflected in the rapid increase in the number of concentration camp inmates. Between September 1939 and March 1942, this rose slowly from around 25,000 to just under 100,000. By August 1944 the total was over half a million, and by January 1945 over 700,000—with 40,000 guards.

The concentration camp at Maidanek, near Lublin, was one used for mass exploitation of Jewish prisoners; over 200,000 of them were worked to death there, gassed, or shot. The largest of all concentration camps, Birkenau, was established as part of the Auschwitz complex and housed 100,000 prisoners. Birkenau served at one and the same time as a center for the industrial exploitation of Jewish labor and as an extermination camp. It was here that the infamous "selection" procedure was developed when the trains arrived from all over Europe, separating those members of families judged fit to work from those directed immediately to the gas chamber. The gas program at Auschwitz-Birkenau did not stop until November 2, 1944, by which time it had accounted for more than a million victims, mainly Jews, but also Poles, gypsies, and Russian prisoners of war. The inhuman conditions in which they perished have earned Auschwitz the name *anus mundi*, the arse-hole of the world.

Auschwitz-Birkenau was close to the industry of Upper Silesia, for which it provided labor. The same consideration, the availability of cheap labor, led Germany's leading chemical firm, I. G. Farben, to build a synthetic rubber factory adjoining Auschwitz and to add a labor camp of its own at Monowitz as part of the Auschwitz complex.

Many other German firms made use of camp prisoners, and during the last years of the war larger and larger groups of foreign workers from the east were held in concentration camps and organized by the SS. By then the camps contained only a minority of German prisoners—only 5 to 10 percent in 1945. Every other nationality in occupied Europe was represented—from Russian prisoners of war to French and Dutch imprisoned under the *Nacht und Nebel* decree.* Productivity, as in the Soviet labor camps, remained low, and for the same reason: These forced-laborers were treated so badly, worked for such long hours, were fed so poorly, and housed in such primitive conditions that many of them died, quite apart from those who were executed.

THE DEPORTATION of Jews from the Old Reich and Bohemia-Moravia to the east for "resettlement" had begun in the autumn of 1941. The Wannsee Conference in January 1942 accepted that priority must now be given to the "cleansing" of the Polish Government-General. Goebbels wrote in his diary on March 27, 1942:

> Starting with Lublin, the deportation of the Jews from the Government-General to the East has been set in motion. It is a pretty barbarous business—one would not wish to go into details—and there are not many Jews left. I should think one could assume that about 60 percent of them have been liquidated and about 40 percent taken for forced labor. The former Gauleiter of Vienna [Globocnik, now in the SS] is carrying it out with a good deal of circumspection. . . . One simply cannot be sentimental about these things. . . . The Führer is the moving spirit of this radical solution both in word and deed. [27]

Himmler demanded that Operation Reinhard, the cleansing of the Government-General to which Goebbels referred, should be completed by the end of 1942. Reinhard Heydrich, after whom it was named, had not lived to see the plans drawn up at his Wannsee Conference put into effect. Appointed protector of Bohemia-Moravia, he had been killed by two parachutists, a Czech and a Slovak, dropped from a British plane. In reprisal more than 1,500 Czechs were summarily shot, 3,000 Jews were sent to be killed in Poland, and the village of Lidice, selected at random, was burned to the ground after the whole of its male population had been shot and all its women deported to concentration camps.

Himmler required the members of each SS team selected for "special duties" in the Polish Government-General to swear personally an oath of silence, telling them: "I have to expect of you superhuman acts of inhumanity. But it is the Führer's will." [28] The first part of the operation consisted of concentrating all Jews in ghettoes. In Warsaw, 150,000 additional Jews had been crowded into an area already occupied by 280,000, and a wall was built round it to isolate them from the rest of the world. Other ghettoes were situated in Lodz and around Lublin. The second part consisted in deporting their inhabitants to the extermination camps as these became available under the plan for the Final Solution. When the deportation (always disguised as resettlement) had reduced the numbers in the

*For the "Night and Fog" decree of December 1941, see p. 744.

Warsaw ghetto to 70,000, those who remained banded together to resist. Two thousand Waffen SS troops, equipped with tanks, flame-throwers, and dynamite were sent in to burn down and blow up the ghetto. To the astonishment of SS General Jürgen Stroop, their commanding officer (who later had a special photograph album prepared to celebrate his "victory"), the Jews, women as well as men, fought with such determination that it took four weeks (April–May 1943) for the much better-armed Germans, advancing block by block, to wipe them out. Of the 56,000 finally rounded up, 7,000 were shot, 22,000 were sent to death camps, the remainder to labor camps.

In the course of 1942 all the main extermination camps had come into operation, all situated in occupied Poland. The estimated number of Jews put to death in the five most important besides Auschwitz is: Chelmno, 152,000; Belzec, 600,000; Treblinka, 700,000–800,000; Sobibor, 250,000; Maidanek, 200,000. With more than a million killed in Auschwitz and Birkenau, the total is around three million. Another two to three million Jews were killed in Russia, elsewhere in Poland, and in other European countries. At the height of its operations several trains each day would arrive at Auschwitz and the average "output" of its four gas chambers and ovens rose to 20,000 bodies a day. This level of "productivity" could be maintained only by the careful timing appropriate to an industrial operation.

That this was the SS view is supported by the equal care they took in costing their operations. Pohl's WVHA, which was responsible for organizing the labor of those who were assigned to work themselves to death rather than to the gas chambers, made an estimate of their operating costs:

> The hiring of concentration-camp inmates to industrial enterprises yields an average return of 6 to 8 RM [Reichsmarks], from which 70 pfenning must be deducted for food and clothing. Assuming an inmate's life expectancy to be nine months, we must multiply this sum by 270. The total is 1,431 RM. This profit can be increased by rational utilization of the corpse, i.e., by means of gold teeth fillings, hair, clothing, valuables, etc., but on the other hand every corpse represents a loss of 2 RM, which is the cost of cremation. [29]

Those who were immediately condemned to death were allowed eight to ten minutes to undress and walk into the gas chambers. The women were allowed fifteen minutes because they had to have their heads shaved first. The hair was then sold for the manufacture of mattresses. It is this "routinization" of extermination (the precise time-tabling of the trains is another example) that adds a unique touch of horror to the already sickening record of cruelty and dehumanization that became "normal" behavior throughout the camps.

Of the total of eighteen million victims of Nazi brutality in the whole of

Europe (including Russia), eleven million met their deaths in occupied territories that had belonged to the former Polish Republic.

Others besides Jews included in the total of eleven million were non-Jewish Poles, Russian prisoners of war, and Gypsies, the last named a group whose extermination the SS pursued with almost the same determination as that of the Jews.

It is important to place these figures on record. But because they can have the effect of numbing the imagination, which cannot conceive of human suffering on such a scale, it is equally important to underline that every single figure in these millions represents acts of cruelty, terror, and degradation inflicted on an individual human being like ourselves—a man, a woman, a child, or even a baby.

IN JUNE 1943 Himmler saw Hitler at the Berghof and reported that the clearing of the Government-General was on the way to being accomplished. He noted: "The Führer said that the deportation of the Jews must go on regardless of any unrest it might cause during the next three to four months, and that it must be carried out in an all-embracing way." [30]

It took until October 1943 before Operation Reinhard was completed. In the same month Himmler spoke to a number of SS leaders at Posen about "a very grave matter":

> We can talk about it quite frankly among ourselves and yet we will never speak of it publicly. It appalled everyone, and yet everyone was certain that he would do it next time if such orders should be issued. . . . I am referring to the Jewish evacuation program, the extermination of the Jews. . . . Most of you will know what it means when a hundred corpses are lying side by side, or five hundred or a thousand are lying there. To have stuck it out and to have remained decent, that is what has made us tough. This is a glorious page in our history that has never been and can never be written. [31]

Two days later, on October 6, 1943, Himmler spoke to the party leaders:

> By the end of the year, the Jewish question will have been settled in all the occupied countries. Only a few individual Jews who have managed to slip through the net will be left. . . .
> You must listen to what I have to say and let it go no further. All of us have asked ourselves: What about the women and children? I have decided that this, too, requires a clear answer. I did not consider that I would be justified in getting rid of the men—in having them put to death—only to allow their children to grow up to avenge themselves on our sons and grandsons. We have to make up our minds, hard though it may be, that this race must be wiped off the face of the earth. [32]

It was not only Jews from Germany and Poland who were murdered in the camps. Eichmann's program for the Final Solution, organized from

Berlin, extended to the whole of occupied Europe—and many of the victims from these countries were deported to Poland.

One of the most thorough operations was in Holland, where 110,000 of the 140,000 Dutch Jews were deported, of whom only 6,000 survived. On February 3, 1944, the sixty-seventh train left Paris for Auschwitz carrying 1,214 Jews. Of these, fourteen were over eighty; more than a hundred under sixteen years old. Only twenty-six survived the war. Another train, a week later, had 1,229 on board. [33]

There were some countries where the Jews received help and protection: Italy and Italian-occupied France, where the Italian army intervened; Denmark, where (thanks to the intervention of the Danish royal family and the connivance of the Reich plenipotentiary, Werner Best) only 500 out of 7,200 Jews were deported—the rest were shipped to safety in Sweden; Finland, where all but 11 out of 4,000 Jews were saved; Slovakia and Bulgaria. But the SS arm was a long one: It reached out and took the 260 Jews of Canea in Crete; the 1,800 Jews of Corfu; 43,000 out of the 56,000 Jews of Salonika, where they had lived since the time of St. Paul. It was not only cities that were combed. Small towns and villages, where no more than a handful of Jews lived, were searched—four examples at random were 2 Jews from Colibasi in Bessarabia on the River Prut; 9 from Duja Poljana in Serbia; 3 from the Greek island of Samothrace, 8 from the Estonian town of Johvi on the Gulf of Finland. [34]

Eichmann's last great coup was the extermination of the Hungarian Jews. When the Hungarian regent, Admiral Nikolaus Horthy, assented to the German occupation of his country in March 1944, he accepted Hitler's demand that its 8,000 Jews should be handed over to the SS "for relocation in the eastern territories," as the German foreign office phrased it. Eichmann moved to Budapest. More than 40,000 out of 50,000 Hungarian Jews serving in labor battalions on the eastern front had already been killed. The first stage now, as in Poland, was to concentrate the rest in ghetto areas, telling them they would be moved to the east to help with the harvest and work in brick and timber yards. In mid-May the first deportations began, from Ruthenia and Transylvania. In all, 437,000 Hungarian Jews were deported to Auschwitz in the summer of 1944, before international protests led the Hungarian government in July to stop any further trainloads setting out. [35]

This time it was Hitler himself who acted as apologist to the army commanders summoned to the Berghof. Asked if the expulsion of the Jews "from their privileged positions" could not have been done more humanely, he replied: "My dear generals, we are fighting a battle of life and death. If our enemies are victorious in this struggle, the German people will be extirpated." Blaming the Jews for the war—"this entire bestiality has been organized by them"—he continued:

> Kindness here as indeed anywhere else would be just about the greatest cruelty to our own people. If the Jews are going to hate me, then at least I want to take advantage of that hatred. . . .

Look at the other countries . . . Hungary! The entire country sub-
verted and rotten, Jews everywhere. . . . Here, too, I intervened and this
problem is now being solved too. . . . The Jews had as their program the
extirpation of the German people. I announced in the Reichstag, if any
man believes he can extirpate the German nation in a world war, he is
wrong; if Jewry really tries that, then the one that will be extirpated is
Jewry itself.[36]

Who, listening to the anti-Semitic diatribe of a street-corner agitator in
Munich in the early 1920s would ever have believed what it would lead to?

I V

CONSIDERING THE COURSE OF EVENTS in the Mediterranean
since El Alamein and the landings in North Africa, Hitler could congratulate
himself in the autumn of 1943 on the effective way in which by energy,
determination, and luck he had retrieved a disastrous situation. The greater
part of Italy was under German occupation, and the Allies were held well
south of Rome. The Germans had moved to take over the Italian zones of
occupation in Croatia, Albania, and Greece, where Hitler had for some time
been apprehensive of a British landing. The rescue of Mussolini and the
creation of the Italian Social Republic with the Duce as its head, however
empty a gesture it proved in reality, could be presented as a triumphant
ending to a crisis that had threatened in the summer to leave the southern
frontiers of the Greater German Reich directly exposed to Allied attack.

But it was hardly a victory. Taken with the defeats the Germans had
suffered at Stalingrad and Kursk, 1943 marked the loss of the diplomatic
and military initiative that Hitler had held for ten years, since the Germans'
walkout at Geneva in October 1933.

In the follow-up to the victory at Kursk, the Russians had captured Orel
and Kharkov in August and further south in the Ukraine had launched an
overlapping series of attacks in which more than two and a half million men
were involved against German forces half that strength, although more equal
in the number of tanks and planes. The Donbass was cleared and the Dnieper
reached before the end of September. The German withdrawal was carried
out with skill along a 400-mile front, and once across the river von Manstein's
forces stubbornly contested every bridgehead. Kiev, however, was captured
by the Russians on November 6 and held despite a German attempt to retake
it. When the early-winter rains and mud closed down the fighting, the
German Army Group South still maintained a coherent front, but the Soviet
forces had established themselves firmly on the west bank of the Dnieper,
while north of the Pripet Marshes others had begun to attack the huge
German salient protecting Byelorussia and its capital Minsk. At the close of
the first week of December, the Stavka completed its final plans for a winter
offensive, designed to begin at the year's end, unroll without pause, and drive
the invader back over the Soviet frontiers.

With the Red Army advancing westward, with the Axis destroyed and Italy now a "cobelligerent" of the United States and Britain, Germany's other allies—Rumania and Hungary, which had suffered heavy losses on the eastern front, Slovakia, Bulgaria, and Finland—read the handwriting on the wall and redoubled their efforts to find ways of following the Italians and changing sides. German intelligence and intercepts of Allied communications kept Hitler well informed of their maneuverings. As in the case of Italy, however, he judged it better to hold back from taking action for the time being rather than provoking the collapse of his satellite system.

Hitler was adamant that Germany herself should not seek a way out of her difficulties by negotiation. He told Ribbentrop to drop the contacts he was pursuing in Stockholm, with the comment: "You know, Ribbentrop, if I settled with Russia today, I would only come to grips with her again tomorrow—I just can't help it." [37] When Goebbels, too, argued that they must come to an arrangement with one side or the other and get out of a two-front war, Hitler's reply was that negotiations with Churchill would lead to no result, as he was "guided by hatred, not by reason," and that while he would prefer negotiations with Stalin, "he did not believe these could be successful either," because (as Goebbels noted in his diary), "Stalin cannot cede what Hitler demands in the East." [38]

When the party Old Guard met in Munich to celebrate the twentieth anniversary of the 1923 putsch, Hitler impressed them all by the vigor and confidence with which he spoke. This was the "old Führer" again, not at all what they had expected from reports of his health. If only from relief, they cheered him at the top of their lungs, particularly when he promised retaliation against the British for their bombing raids.

Hitler was a consummate actor. But how was he able to persuade himself sufficiently to convince others, even the generals,* that there was still a chance of victory? Part of the answer, of course, lay in his basic belief in the power of the will. This was the testing time, and he repeated over and over again that it was he whose nerve held out the longest who would win. The primary concern that governed his behavior in the remaining year and a half of his life was to protect his strength of will by rejecting and avoiding anything that might undermine it.

An example of the first was his angry refusal to accept the figures for the size of the Soviet forces and the scale of their war production. Stalin, he insisted, was at the end of his resources; his troops were too exhausted to continue the offensive; it was nonsense, impossible (so he told von Manstein) that the Russians had fifty-seven new divisions. Those who believed such figures were defeatists. This was the constant burden of his criticism of the staff officers, who (he claimed) lied and deliberately exaggerated

---

*Rommel wrote to his wife after the speech: "What power he radiates! What faith and confidence he inspires in his people!" Quoted by David Irving, *Hitler's War* (London: 1977), p. 581.

reports of the enemy's strength in order to justify their own lack of courage and faith.

An example of the second—of avoidance—was his refusal to visit the front or the bombed cities to see for himself the suffering and the damage inflicted by the bombing. On one occasion when an ambulance train pulled up alongside his own and he could see the wounded lying in their bunks, he hastily demanded that the blinds be pulled down and the sight excluded. Another example was his refusal to appear in public, despite Goebbels's constant pleas. He was instinctively fearful, with his sensitivity to an audience's mood, that he might not be able to master the feelings of doubt and hopelessness with which he was likely to be confronted. His reluctance to go to Berlin, shutting himself away in the Berghof or in his headquarters, eventually in an underground bunker, was all part of the same intense effort to shut out the harsh reality that threatened his power to hold on.

The counterpart to rejection and avoidance of negative factors was his snatching at anything that could bolster his belief that, if he did not give way, his luck would return and the sense of mission to which he clung would be justified. There are examples of this in the talks with Goebbels already quoted: his juggling with figures to prove that he would be able to create a central operational reserve of thirty-four divisions; his prophecy that within four months the U-boats would return to the Atlantic with a deadly new magnetic torpedo; and his assurance that "the great reprisal campaign with rockets" would be launched early in 1944. "If submarine warfare develops as we hope," Goebbels wrote in his diary, "and if in January or February our retaliation weapon swings into action, both these German successes will hit the English hard at a time when they are tired of the war. Possibly a fundamental change can be effected in the British attitude toward the war." Even about the eastern front, Hitler declared himself much more optimistic than the General Staff:

> Our present retreat [he told Goebbels] merely means that we are retiring to a line behind the Dnieper. . . . The Führer expects to hold the line along the Dnieper throughout the winter. By this operation we would save about 350 kilometers. That would make available the divisions we need for the new central operational reserve . . . the alpha and omega of our present strategy. [39]

Hitler returned again and again to his old hope, despite the bombing, that the British would eventually realize that their true interests lay in joining Germany in his crusade against Bolshevism. Its logic was so obvious that it had to happen. Here was another reason for holding out, for winning time for the disagreements and distrust between Russia and the West to break up the Alliance.

HITLER TOLD GOEBBELS that seventeen German divisions were held in the west to prevent a cross-Channel invasion. The Allied landings in Sicily and Italy had also aroused the hopes of resistance movements in every occupied country. In Norway, the threat of an armed uprising by the Norwegian resistance movement in cooperation with an Allied landing led him to keep yet another thirteen army divisions, 90,000 naval personnel, 6,000 SS men, and 12,000 paramilitary troops to control a population of three million. Resistance had a moral and, with an eye to the postwar situation, a political value; but in Western Europe its practical contribution to the defeat of Germany until the Allies landed was largely limited to forcing the Germans to dissipate their power in this way. Before the Allied landings in 1944, attempts to challenge the occupying forces directly were doomed to failure and the severity of German reprisals—fifty or a hundred hostages executed for one German life lost—far exceeded the damage inflicted in all but a handful of cases.

The Balkans provided more favorable opportunities for resistance movements, partly because of the mountainous nature of much of the country and its poor communications, partly because of the long coastline and the proximity to Allied naval and air bases in the Mediterranean. Hitler told Goebbels that another seventeen German divisions were stationed in the Balkans and that they had their hands full keeping even a semblance of order.

Fearing a landing in Greece, Hitler made sure that control of its cordon of islands, which had been held by the Italians, would not fall into British hands. The defense of Crete was strengthened, and throughout October and November of 1943 German troops captured and occupied the Dodecanese. The Greek National Liberation Front (EAM) controlled most of the country outside Athens and Salonika but was as much preoccupied with maneuvering for power after liberation and forestalling the return of the monarchy as with operations against the Germans.

By far the most formidable opponents, unique among resistance movements, were the Yugoslav partisans. Field Marshal Maximilian von Weichs, Hitler's commander in chief in the Balkans, wrote in his diary:

> Not that you can speak of "partisans" anymore—under Tito a powerful Bolshevik army has arisen, moving from strength to strength and growing more deadly every day. It has strong British support.
> The impotence of the Croatian government [under Pavelić] is an increasing menace. Should the enemy invade Dalmatia and Albania, we can expect general Communist uprisings to break out there. [40]

Tito has the unique distinction of having successfully defied both Hitler and Stalin; and he held Churchill, Roosevelt, and Truman at arm's length, while maintaining the independence of his country under a native Communist regime. With a nucleus of 300 Communist veterans from the Spanish Civil War, he began to organize resistance as soon as the Germans invaded the Soviet Union. Between 1941 and 1943 the Germans launched no fewer than four offensives against the partisans, forcing them to take refuge in the mountains. But despite the heavy losses they suffered and the brutal reprisals the Germans inflicted on their villages,* they refused to give up the struggle. The Italian collapse transformed the partisans' situation. They seized large quantities of arms, which enabled them to recruit and equip an army of 200,000 and to survive yet a fifth campaign that the German army launched against them. With substantial support from the British and Americans they were able to extend their control to much of Croatia and Dalmatia and eventually to achieve the liberation of their own country as well as the establishment of a Communist-dominated government before the arrival of the Red Army.

THE AUTUMN of 1943 and the spring of 1944 brought another example of Hitler's convulsive clutching at anything that might produce quick returns and another bizarre twist in the history of the Luftwaffe's decline.

During 1943 Speer had continued to expand his war-production empire, taking over responsibility for Dönitz's U-boat building program, for major sectors of the civilian economy from Funk's Ministry of Economics, and for a large part of Göring's Four-Year Plan. Thanks to the dispersal of industry and the mobile teams built up for the repair and reconstruction of bombed factories, Speer's ministry was still able to maintain the extraordinary increase in arms production that had been achieved from the beginning of the year. But the most costly, complicated, and, in 1943, vital branch of armaments, aircraft production, remained outside Speer's control—all the more jealously guarded by Göring as his power and influence declined.

Because the decisions that would have maintained the Luftwaffe's initial superiority had not been made in 1940 and 1941, it was more and more at a disadvantage by comparison with the RAF (the British Royal Air Force) and the USAAF (the U.S. Army Air Force). Milch had succeeded in reversing the actual decline in aircraft production by concentrating his efforts on providing fighters for the defense of the Reich, a policy that enabled the Luftwaffe to raise the British and American rate of loss to levels—over 10 percent—which no bomber fleet could sustain for long.

Hitler, however, was opposed to such a policy, stubbornly insisting that the antiaircraft ground defenses should be able to drive off the bombers, and that the key to halting the RAF and American attacks was retaliation on British cities. In the autumn of 1943, he demanded a revival of the bombing offensive against Britain. Göring, desperate to restore his reputation, undertook to provide him with "a new Luftwaffe." Plans were made for a renewed blitz on London as well as for the strategic bombing of Soviet industrial targets. But the Luftwaffe bomber force had suffered heavy losses

---

*Yugoslavia suffered heavier losses in the Second World War as a percentage (10.9) of total population than any other country except Poland (with the inclusion of Poland's Jewish population). In *The Embattled Mountain* (Oxford, 1971), Bill (now Sir William) Deakin provides an unequaled account of the experiences of the partisans' war, which he shared with them, after being sent by Churchill in 1943 to report on their activities.

during 1943 and was down to fewer than 600 serviceable aircraft in the late summer. Hitler ordered the new campaign to begin on December 1 with an attack on London, but it was not until January 22 that the Luftwaffe could collect a force of 462 planes for a raid, which proved a fiasco. In disgust, Hitler described the Heinkel as "the worst junk ever manufactured." After a few more ineffectual raids, the new initiative petered out; no attacks on Soviet industry were even attempted.

In his frustration, Hitler turned to the "secret weapons." There was one secret weapon, a German nuclear bomb, which could have fulfilled his hopes of altering the course of the war if it had been dropped on London. But it was not taken seriously enough in Germany to generate the effort needed to make such a project practicable. Why this should have been so is not easily explained. Nuclear fission had been originally discovered in Germany; nuclear physicists remaining in Germany continued their work with encouragement from the state; they followed much the same lines of research as the American and British scientists. The crucial difference appears to have been the conclusion of the German Army Ordnance in early 1942, after discussions with the scientists whom they had been supporting in nuclear fission research, that it would not be possible to produce a nuclear bomb before the end of the war—the opposite of the conclusion reached by the Americans and British, who assumed that the war would last longer. The German research continued with the longer term objective of harnessing nuclear power to postwar uses, but the German army handed over control of it to the civilian Reich Research Council, deciding that rocket research offered the promise of quicker results than nuclear fission. Neither German soldiers nor German scientists saw nuclear weapons—whether German or American—playing a role in the Second World War. Ironically, it was the Americans' conclusion not only that they were feasible, but that the Germans were likely to come to the same conclusion, which led them and the British to make an all-out effort to develop such weapons first.

Considering Hitler's interest in military technology, it is a remarkable piece of good fortune that, absorbed in the winter war in the east, he appears to have heard little if anything of the decision or to have been informed of the potential destructiveness of nuclear weapons. When the German physicist C. F. von Weizsäcker, asked Erich Schumann, the most powerful figure in the Army Ordnance, if it would not be good to raise the issue at a higher level, he got the reply:

> Please don't. If Hitler hears that nuclear weapons are possible, he will say: Half a year and then they must have them. You know that this is not feasible, and for you and me it would be a very bad position. Please keep away from such ideas. [41]

There is no doubt about the resources that Hitler mobilized to produce the secret weapons in which his interest *had* been aroused. Where he allowed himself—and was only too willing—to be misled was over the time they would take to come into operation. Over a hundred of the Mark XXI all-electric high-speed U-boats were being built, but it was not until January 1945 that Dönitz was able to assure Hitler that the first would begin operations in March, and by then the Battle of the Atlantic was already lost. Jet aircraft, flying bombs (V-1s), and long-range rockets (V-2s) were all produced and brought into use, but again too late to affect the outcome of the war. The same was true of the underground armaments factories on which Hitler fastened as another answer to the Allied bombing attacks. Speer and the private industrialists refused to cooperate, believing that the dispersal plan worked out by Speer and Milch would be more effective. But Hitler was persistent and made it a test of party loyalty which Göring and Himmler were glad to take up and use to undermine Speer's position. By the time the factories were built, however, and came into production, they could not prevent or offset the collapse of the German economy which began in the autumn of 1944.

V

THERE WERE ENOUGH DIFFICULTIES between the Western powers and Russia in 1943 to keep alive Hitler's hopes that, if he held out, their divergent interests would lead to a breakdown of the Alliance. The German discovery in April 1943 of the bodies of 4,000 Polish officers buried in Katyn Forest gave him the opportunity to add to the difficulties. The Poles rightly concluded that they were among the 15,000 Polish officers deported to Russia whom they had been unable to locate, but the Russians indignantly denied the German accusations and most people in the West believed the Germans themselves to be the guilty party. When the Polish government in London asked for an independent investigation by the Swiss Red Cross, Stalin at once denounced them as reactionaries, whose hatred of Russia led them to lend themselves to the purposes of German propaganda. A Union of Polish Patriots had already been established in Moscow as rivals to the group in London, and Stalin now seized the opportunity to break off relations with the Polish government in exile. Churchill could offer the Poles no support: The need to beat the Germans had to take priority over everything else, and with it the need to maintain good relations with the Kremlin.

Katyn marks the beginning of yet another chapter in the tragic history of the postwar settlement imposed on the Polish people by the Russians with the reluctant acquiescence of the British and Americans. Stalin's action throws light on the tactics he was to follow in securing it. Instead of defending or disowning the massacre committed at Katyn, the truth about which he must have known, he took the high ground of moral indignation with his accusation that those who spoke for the victims of Russian ruthlessness and of his cooperation with the Nazis in destroying their country in 1939 were playing the German game.

The Allies' failure to open a second front in France—Stalin dismissed Italy as a substitute—and the suspension of the Arctic convoys were the subject of further Russian complaints. To these was added a protest from Stalin that he had been excluded from the Anglo-U.S. peace negotiations with the Italians, despite the fact that Italian troops had fought on the eastern front: It was "impossible to tolerate such a situation any longer," and Stalin proposed a three-power commission to discuss negotiations with other governments breaking away from Germany.

Even between Roosevelt and Churchill there was still no sure agreement about Operation Overlord, the invasion of France, thanks to the latter's persistent efforts, much distrusted by the Americans, to keep open the option of a Balkan campaign. When the president insisted in October 1943 that no diversion should prejudice Overlord, Churchill's reply was a long list of doubts about its planning: "My dear friend," he ended his letter, "this is much the greatest thing we have ever attempted. . . . I desire an early conference." [42] He had his wish at Teheran at the end of November, the first occasion on which all three of the Alliance's leaders sat down together, and the first of the two occasions on which Roosevelt met Stalin. On the eve of it Stalin revived the issue of the second front by informing his allies that, far from the Anglo-U.S. efforts relieving the Red Army, German divisions from Italy, the Balkans, and France were now moving to the eastern front.

THE TEHERAN CONFERENCE lasted from November 28 to December 1. Besides the crucial military decisions they reached, for the first time the three leaders exchanged thoughts about the postwar settlement and, perhaps most important of all, formed impressions of one another in private meetings between Stalin and Roosevelt, and Stalin and Churchill, as well as around the conference table and at lunch and dinner.

The fact that it was nearly two and a half years after the German invasion before the three leaders met gave Stalin a double advantage. That which he derived from the military situation was compounded by the lack of agreement between Churchill and Roosevelt on strategy, and by the priority that Roosevelt gave to establishing a special relationship with the Russian leader, which must, to some extent, be at the expense of the unique relationship that he and Churchill had enjoyed. As long ago as March 1942, long before they met, Roosevelt had convinced himself—and told Churchill—that he could handle Stalin better than any of the British could: "He hates the guts of all your top people. He thinks he likes me better, and I hope he will continue to do so." Roosevelt has been criticized for the naïveté of his belief that he could "manage" Stalin as he had so many American politicians. But he can hardly be criticized for his early recognition of the fact that the success of any postwar settlement would depend on cooperation between the U.S.A. and the USSR, and this in turn on creating relations of trust between them before the war ended.

On his side Stalin showed an unexpected flexibility in the way he adapted to a situation where he could not in any case exercise power arbitrarily, where he was under no threat to his own position, and where he was clearly accepted as the equal of the other two leaders. "What Stalingrad was to Stalin militarily, Teheran was diplomatically."[43] But there was this difference, that while the first was a cooperative achievement in which the greater part of the credit belonged to the Red Army, its commanders, and General Staff, the credit for the second—the diplomatic exploitation of those victories—was Stalin's alone. Whatever Stalin needed to learn about the conduct of war, the man who had negotiated the Nazi-Soviet Pact with such advantage to Russia needed no instruction in the art of diplomacy. As far as the Baltic states, Poland, and Bessarabia were concerned, he was traversing the same ground, and he achieved the same result.

Stalin's diplomatic successes at Teheran, Yalta, and Potsdam were as great as Hitler's in the 1930s, but they were achieved by very different methods. Like Hitler he was quick to read the hands of those across the table and to exploit their weaknesses, while concealing his own and keeping his cards to his chest. But there was none of Hitler's exploitation of his temperament. The paranoid and despotic side of Stalin's character was kept out of sight and the political gifts that had brought him to the top in Russia given full play. Instead of pacing up and down the room as was his habit during discussions in the Kremlin, he sat impassively, listening intently, avoiding the expansive confidences in which Churchill and Roosevelt indulged when talking with him privately. His questioning could be sharp and his comments blunt, but his tone was reasonable, his judgments sensible, and his arguments cogent, as when he demolished Churchill's case for operations in the Balkans or eastern Mediterranean which might delay the invasion of France.

General Brooke, the British chief of staff, who had much experience of working with Churchill and whom Stalin baited at dinner for being anti-Russian, was impressed by his performance. Although the Soviet leader was unaccompanied by expert advisers, Brooke noted: "Never once in any of his statements did Stalin make any strategic error, nor did he ever fail to appreciate all the implications of a situation with a quick and unerring eye."[44]

Stalin's attitude showed that he clearly distinguished between Roosevelt and Churchill, the former the representative of the rising power of the U.S.A., the latter of the declining power of the British Empire. He met Roosevelt's wish for closer contact by offering the American delegation more secure accommodations in the compound of the Soviet legation—no doubt wired for the occasion. In the first of three private talks that the president sought, he expressed agreement with Roosevelt's views that the day of colonial empires was over, and with the American president's disparaging remarks about Churchill's resistance to independence for British colonies and his anachronistic view of India. The arguments during the conferences were all between Stalin and Churchill—whether in plenary session or private talks—not between Stalin and Roosevelt. At an early stage Stalin confirmed the promise, of special significance for the Americans, to join the war against Japan as soon as Germany was defeated, and after initial skepticism he came around to accepting the scheme for an international organization, the origin of the United Nations, to which Roosevelt attached so much importance.

Roosevelt opened the plenary sessions[45] by confirming the date of May 1, 1944, for the launch of the invasion across the Channel (Overlord) and asked Stalin how best the Allied forces in the Mediterranean could be used to bring relief to the Soviet armies. He mentioned as possible areas for operations Italy and the Adriatic and a junction with Tito's partisans; the Aegean and Greece, and Turkey, some of which might involve a delay of two or three months for Overlord. The question brought a sharp disagreement between Stalin and Churchill. Stalin maintained that the one thing that mattered was to attack the Germans in France, and not waste time and forces in the Mediterranean; Churchill persisted in arguing that, without abandoning Overlord, they should look at the possibilities of the eastern Mediterranean–Balkans area. Roosevelt sought to end the dispute by ruling that nothing should be done to delay Overlord and that instead of the eastern Mediterranean they should look at the possibility of landing a force in southern France. At the second plenary Stalin brushed aside all the other suggestions except the president's, which he said would contribute directly to the success of the main invasion across the Channel. He called for the appointment of a supreme commander for Overlord and a firm date so that the Red Army could launch a simultaneous offensive from the east. When Churchill tried to keep open the eastern option, Stalin asked him point-blank: Did the British really believe in Overlord or merely talk about it to keep the Russians quiet? The only result of Churchill's persistence was to underline his isolation in the face of Soviet-American agreement, which was ratified by the third session.

At one point, the proceedings were interrupted for a ceremony. "By the king's command," Churchill presented the Sword of Honor, which had been specially designed and wrought as a British tribute to the Russian defenders of Stalingrad. Few could match Churchill's ability to create an atmosphere and convey emotion on such an occasion. But Stalin? Although he was one of the shortest men in the hall, which was filled with Russian officers and soldiers, he achieved as great an impression as Churchill. Receiving the gift with the same touch of dignity and emotion, he silently raised the great sword to his lips and kissed the scabbard. For a brief moment all were touched by a sense of history, and the sword was solemnly carried from the room escorted by a Russian guard of honor—but not, as Churchill noted, before Voroshilov had managed to drop it.

In the general discussion of the postwar settlement, Stalin drew a gloomy picture of the revival of German power fifteen to twenty years after her defeat and insisted that arrangements for the control and disarmament of Germany must be rigorous. Without going into details, he appeared to favor the dismemberment of Germany and the establishment of Poland's western frontier on the Oder, although he subsequently added that nothing could exclude the possibility of Germany reuniting.

Stalin formed the impression that on Germany, too, Churchill was out of step and in favor of greater leniency. At dinner in the Soviet embassy, according to the American interpreter Chip Bohlen, "He lost no opportunity to get a dig in at Churchill, and apparently desired to put and keep him on the defensive." It was on this occasion that Stalin proposed the liquidation of the 50,000 German officers, who were the heart of Germany's military power, as the only way to destroy it—evidently aiming his remarks at Churchill. The latter rose from the table, saying that neither he nor the British people would have anything to do with mass executions. When Stalin persisted, repeating, "Fifty thousand must be shot," and Elliott Roosevelt, FDR's son, made a speech expressing enthusiasm, Churchill walked out of the room in disgust. He was quickly followed by Stalin, who put both hands on his shoulders, assured him that he had not been talking seriously, and persuaded him to return. In his memoirs, Churchill remarks: "Stalin has a very captivating manner when he chooses to use it, and I never saw him do so to such an extent as at this moment, although I was not then, and am not now, convinced that all was chaff, and there was no serious intention behind it." [46] What Churchill does not say is whether he reflected that it was by such means that Stalin had come close to destroying the strength of the Red Army.

Following Stalin's earlier reference to the Poles' western frontier with Germany being advanced to the Oder—without saying anything about their eastern frontier with Russia—both Churchill and Roosevelt separately and gratuitously proposed that Poland as a whole should move westward. The territory the Poles gained from Germany in the west would then compensate them for that which they ceded to Russia in the east. Churchill suggested that they should agree on a frontier. "Stalin asked whether it would be without Polish participation. I said 'Yes' and when this was all informally agreed between ourselves we could go to the Poles later." [47]

Stalin was noncommittal. But the next day Roosevelt, apparently also in an attempt to propitiate Stalin, told him without being asked that he would like to see the frontiers of Poland moved to the west, although domestic politics (six or seven million Polish Americans) would prevent his saying so in an electoral year. At the same time he put in a muted appeal for the peoples of the Baltic states, only to add jokingly that he did not propose to go to war with the Soviet Union if its armies reoccupied their territories.

At the final session Roosevelt asked if the Soviet government would resume relations with the Polish government-in-exile so that they could accept any decision arrived at on frontiers. Stalin's refusal was vehement. "The Polish government and their friends in Poland were in touch with the

Germans. They killed the Polish partisans." But he was now ready to discuss frontiers with a map, making clear that Russia would adhere to those established in 1939, which gave the Soviet Union the western Ukraine and Byelorussia. When Eden asked if he meant the Ribbentrop-Molotov Line, Stalin replied indifferently: "Call it whatever you like." Eden's attempt to get the Russians to accept the Curzon Line* started an argument as to whether this had left Lvov on the Russian or the Polish side. Stalin insisted that the correct version of the Curzon Line gave it to Russia. According to Churchill: "I said that the Poles would be wise to take our advice. I was not prepared to make a great squawk about Lvov." [48]

The two Western leaders had more success in persuading Stalin to be magnanimous to the Finns, provided they broke with the Germans. They also reached agreement on the fullest possible support for Tito and the Yugoslav partisans. A Roosevelt plan for the dismemberment of Germany, which Stalin liked but Churchill had doubts about, was referred to a tripartite European Advisory Commission set up by the three foreign ministers. But Churchill still wanted to get a formula for the future frontiers of Poland that he could put to the Poles. Stalin then said that if Russia was given the northern part of East Prussia, including Königsberg, he could accept the Curzon Line as the frontier between the Soviet Union and Poland. "He said the acquisition of that part of Eastern Prussia would not only provide the Soviet Union with an ice-free port but would also give to Russia a small piece of German territory which he felt was deserved." [49]

It was the occupation of Poland by the Red Army that settled the Poles' postwar frontiers. But the fact that Churchill and Roosevelt, their allies, should have suggested a move westward, without consultation, and promised Stalin their support, appeared an act of treachery to the Poles, just as their subsequent attempts to qualify that agreement by further intervention on the Poles' behalf appeared to Stalin as an attempt to go back on their word.

Of the three participants in the Teheran Conference, Stalin had the most cause to congratulate himself, and the enthusiasm of the Soviet press reflected his satisfaction with the result. He had finally pinned the Allies down to opening a second front in France, and the concurrent attacks from west and east that followed in the summer of 1944 put the seal on Germany's defeat. At the same time he had averted the danger, represented by Churchill's proposals, of a rival Anglo-American intervention challenging his prospective sphere of influence in the Balkans. Nor had he met any opposition to his claim to keep the Soviet gains of the Nazi-Soviet Pact or to his plan to provide Poland with compensation at Germany's expense.

The one who had least cause for satisfaction was Churchill, who left with growing uneasiness about the future and the diminished power of Britain

---

*The Curzon Line was the eastern frontier of the new state of Poland proposed by British Foreign Secretary Lord Curzon in 1919.

to influence it. This was a bitter conclusion for him to accept. Whatever might be said about the appeasement of Hitler at the time of Munich, Britain was the only one of the three powers that had declared war on Hitler without waiting to be attacked. It was her resistance alone during the period of nearly two years in which Stalin under the Nazi-Soviet Pact had continued to pour supplies into Germany that had prevented Hitler from making peace after the defeat of France. While Britain lacked the population to field land forces on the scale of Russia or America, her people—including British women—were more fully mobilized than the Germans, and in addition to the leading part she was playing in the Mediterranean, in the air war and in the crucial Battle of the Atlantic, she was providing the indispensable base, and a substantial part of the forces, without which the Anglo-American invasion of Europe and the second front Stalin so much wanted could never be launched. After all that it was hard for Churchill to have to recognize—for the first time at Teheran—that British views would count for less in the final stages of the war and in the making of the postwar settlement than those of the other two powers.

Roosevelt, on the other hand, was well satisfied. He returned to Washington with the date for Overlord finally settled and the firm promise of a Soviet offensive to coincide with it. No less important for the future was Stalin's undertaking to join in the war against Japan and his acceptance of Roosevelt's proposal for an international organization. This went a long way toward confirming the president's conviction that he had established a personal relationship with Stalin that would outlast the war and make possible the U.S.-Soviet cooperation on which he believed a durable peace settlement would depend.

VI

ON HIS RETURN to Moscow from Teheran, Stalin found waiting for his final approval the plans for a major winter campaign in the early months of 1944. The Red Army now had in the field a force of five and a half million men. The lesson of independent mobile formations had been well learned, and the Soviet High Command now had at their disposal six tank armies with more than 5,000 tanks of modern design. It had also carried much further the concentration of artillery which had been begun by General Voronov and had done more than anything else to save the Red Army from total defeat in 1941. Its artillery arm, still under Voronov (now a marshal), controlled its own artillery regiments, divisions, and corps, and was once again to play a decisive role in the battles of 1944 and 1945.

According to Russian figures, the U.S.A. and Britain supplied, in all, 18,700 planes, 9,600 guns, and 10,800 tanks. There is no doubt, however, that the greater part of the Red Army's equipment, its artillery, machine guns, and tanks, was designed and produced in the Soviet Union. The most valuable Western contribution was the planes and, particularly appreciated by the Russians, the transport: huge numbers of trucks, jeeps, tractors, and half-tracks, including those which towed the guns, thanks to U.S. Lend-Lease.

Thanks to a drastic draft, which could not be repeated, the German army was still able to put into the field a force that, despite the claims of Italy, the Balkans, and the potential western front, was not much inferior in numbers. Its 236 divisions were estimated by the Russians to contain nearly five million men (only 700,000 Axis troops, the rest German) with roughly the same number of tanks as the Red Army, although fewer aircraft. Their quality and the skill with which they were handled were never shown to greater advantage than during this later period of the war when, fighting on the defensive, and increasingly outnumbered, they conducted a retreat all the way from the Ukraine to the Oder without ever losing their cohesion or their power to strike back fiercely on occasion.

The main weight of the Russian attack was directed to the southwest, aimed at recovering the whole of the Ukraine with its agricultural, mineral, and industrial resources, then pressing on to the Soviet-Rumanian border. (See map, p. 821.) On Christmas Eve, Vatutin's First Ukrainian Front opened the attack and by the end of the year recaptured Zhitomir. In mid-January 1944 the Leningrad and Volkhov fronts opened up and by January 26 had cleared the Moscow-Leningrad railway, ending the siege which had lasted 900 days. Neither during the siege nor later did Stalin visit the city.

Determined defense by the Germans holding the Korsun salient on the Dnieper held up the advance in the south until the middle of February, but once this had been eliminated, the Stavka committed all six Soviet tank armies to exploit the breakthrough. The strategic Lvov-Odessa railway was cut, and during March Koniev's forces crossed the Dniester and reached the Rumanian frontier on the River Prut. The following month Koniev drove on into Bessarabia, Bukhovina, and Moldavia, while Malinovsky captured Odessa and cleared the Black Sea coast.

From the Dnieper to the Prut is 250 miles, from Kiev to Odessa the same, distances that give some idea of the size of the area that the Russian armies had recaptured. By mid-April they had destroyed, captured, or driven out the whole of von Manstein's Army Group South, and in May they completed the destruction of von Kleist's Army Group A, cut off in the Crimea.

With the loss of the Ukraine (Byelorussia was to follow in the summer) Hitler's dream of founding a new German empire in the east was finally shattered. He might try to convince himself that, once he had defeated the Anglo-American attempt to land in the west, he would return and reconquer the lost territories in the east, but he convinced few others, least of all those who had encountered the Russian armies in battle.

But it was Hitler who had defeated himself and frustrated his own ambitions by the racist character he gave to his conquest of *Lebensraum*. Any invader of the Soviet Union should have been able to exploit the

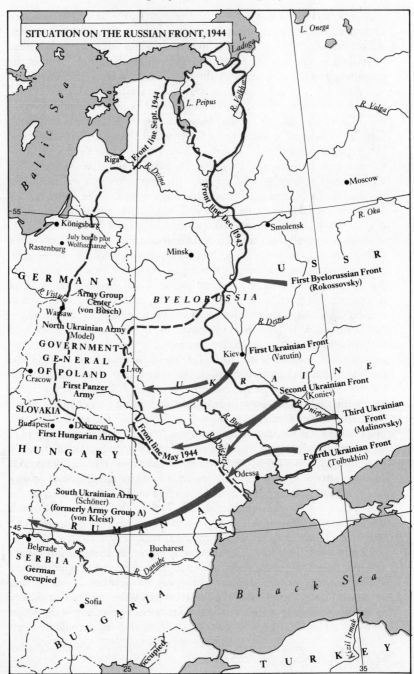

SITUATION ON THE RUSSIAN FRONT, 1944

L. Ladoga

L. Onega

L. Peipus

R. Volkhov

Baltic Sea

Front line Sept. 1944

Riga

R. Dvina

Front line Dec. 1943

R. Volga

Moscow

55

Königsberg

R. Oka

July bomb plot
Wolfsschanze

Rastenburg

Smolensk

U   S   S   R

Minsk

First Byelorussian Front
(Rokossovsky)

GERMANY

R. Vistula

Army Group
Center
(von Busch)

BYELORUSSIA

Warsaw

R. Desna

North Ukrainian Army
(Model)

GOVERNMENT-

GE-NERAL

Kiev

First Ukrainian Front
(Vatutin)

OF POLAND

Lvov

U   K   R

A   I   N   E

Cracow

First Panzer
Army

Second Ukrainian Front
(Koniev)

R. Bug

R. Dnieper

Third Ukrainian
Front
(Malinovsky)

SLOVAKIA

Budapest

Debrecen

Front line May 1944

R. Dniester

First Hungarian Army

Fourth Ukrainian Front
(Tolbukhin)

HUNGARY

Odessa

South Ukrainian Army
(Schöner)
(formerly Army Group A)
(von Kleist)

45

R   U   M   A   N   I   A

Belgrade

Bucharest

SERBIA

German
occupied

Black   Sea

R. Danube

Sofia

BULGARIA

Kizil Irmak

occupied

25

T   U   R   K   E   Y

35

economic, social, and nationalist discontents left by the brutal methods used
to impose revolutionary changes on its peoples from above. Hitler had
deliberately turned his back upon the opportunities this presented. Instead
of seeking to win over the peasantry, for example, by the abolition of the
collectives and a return to the traditional pattern of family farming, Koch
and those who spoke his language went out of their way, with Hitler's full
approval, to alienate them, brandishing the whip and constantly rejecting
any idea of allowing these Slav *Untermenschen* to collaborate with their
German masters. The Nazi methods of exploitation were not only brutal
but stupid. Instead of mobilizing the peasantry to work for them, they drove
them to join the partisans. By giving the invasion the character not of an
attack aimed at overthrowing the Stalinist regime, but of a war to enslave
not only the Russian but the Ukrainian people as well, it was Hitler and the
Nazis who rallied them to the regime and inspired them with the determination to throw back an enemy whom they had quickly learned to hate.

By 1942 a number of officers in the German army, and of officials in the
Ostministerium, as well as Goebbels's Propaganda Ministry, were beginning to realize the mistake that was being made and to ask if it was not
possible to pursue a more intelligent policy. The German army, short of
manpower and purely as a practical measure, recruited large numbers of
helpers (*Hilfswillige,* abbreviated to *Hiwis*) for manual, noncombat tasks—
half a million, it is estimated, by spring 1943. For the same reason and
without official sanction, a smaller number of former Red Army men were
organized in combat units (often for intelligence work or to fight the
partisans) under German command. But only two groups of military collaborators were formally sanctioned: the Cossacks, because Hitler admired
their earlier rebellion against Russian rule, and the non-Slav nationalities of
the Caucasus and Central Asia, as well as Tatars and Kalmyks. Klaus von
Stauffenberg, the German officer who was later to carry out the July 1944
attempt to kill Hitler and was head of the Organization Section of the army
General Staff, was a key figure in this development of volunteer indigenous
auxiliary forces, organized as "legions" and recruited from Russian prisoners, which he foresaw forming 10–15 percent of the German army in the
east. Estimates put the number of such Turkic, Caucasian, and Cossack
soldiers on the German side at 153,000 in spring 1943[*] as compared with
some 80,000 in Russian ethnically mixed battalions.[50]

Henning von Tresckow, the operations officer of Army Group Center
and also, like von Stauffenberg, active in the underground opposition to
Hitler, was another who argued that the way for Germany to win the war
in the east was to turn the native population into allies. He saw that the key
to this lay in better treatment of Russian prisoners, recognition of the Soviet
peoples' aspirations, and the formation of more Russian military units

[*]Among the nationalities represented were Volga Tatars, Georgians, Armenians, Azerbai-
janis, North Caucasian Muslims, Turkestanis.

(Osttruppen) to fight alongside the Germans as comrades in arms. By February 1943 this point of view was sufficiently widespread among the officer corps serving in the east for the two army group commanders, Field Marshal Ewald von Kleist and Field Marshal von Manstein, to issue directives the burden of which was: "The population of the occupied Eastern territories . . . is to be treated as allies."[51]

The logical conclusion to such a change of policy was to create a Russian National Committee and a Russian Army of Liberation. A focus for such a development was provided by the capture in July 1942 of Lieutenant General A. A. Vlasov, a well-known Soviet general of peasant background who turned against the Soviet regime as a result of what he saw as the wanton sacrifice of the army he commanded on the Volkhov front. Vlasov's aim was to form a Russian countergovernment and army which, in alliance with the Germans, would overthrow the Stalinist regime and create a new Russia, neither tsarist nor Communist. The Vlasov movement received support from the German army and attracted several thousand recruits from among Russian prisoners. But it also aroused strong opposition from Koch, Bormann, and Himmler, who appealed to Hitler to stop a movement that could only compromise the original aims of the attack on Russia.

Hitler's decision, given at a conference with Zeitzler and Keitel on June 8, 1943, restricted Vlasov's activities to putting his name to German propaganda appeals to Russian troops on the other side of the front line to desert—the equivalent of those broadcast from Moscow in the name of the National Committee for a Free Germany and the Union of German Officers which had been formed from those captured at Stalingrad and elsewhere on the eastern front. Vlasov was not to appear in the occupied territories nor to recruit volunteers:

> No German agency must take seriously the bait contained in the Vlasov program.[52]

> We must avoid the least encouragement of the opinion on our side that in this way [by boosting Vlasov] we might really find a compromise solution—something like the so-called free or national China [of the puppet ruler Wang Ching-wei, set up by the Japanese] in East Asia.[53]

Hitler's ruling settled the matter. Vlasov and the fiction of a Russian National Committee were to be used for propaganda only. No real cooperation between the aims of the Third Reich and a non-Stalinist Russia was possible. When there was a growing number of defections to the partisans from the *Osttruppen* serving with the German armies, the decision was made to transfer all the "reliable" units to France, the Netherlands, Italy, and the Balkans where they could be used against local resistance movements; and to dissolve the "unreliable" units on the spot.

Parallel with the abortive move to recruit Russian troops in the fight against the Stalinist regime, there had been increased efforts by Rosenberg's

Ostministerium to win the cooperation of the Russian peasants by offering them permanent ownership of the land they cultivated. Supported by the economic agencies as well as by the army, this initiative got as far as receiving Hitler's support in May 1943 and was turned into Rosenberg's Declaration on the Introduction of Peasant Landed Property, the so-called *Agrar-Erlass*. For once Koch's opposition found little support in view of the pressing need to secure greater productivity and more food. But the victory for the anti-Koch forces was an empty one. As the *Wirtschaftsstab Ost* (Economic Staff East) recognized, the time had passed and the military situation by the autumn of 1943 had so far deteriorated that Rosenberg's declaration was a fiasco.

As the armies fell back, the German economic agencies were ordered to salvage cattle, grain, equipment, and peasants by moving them westward, and to destroy everything that could not be taken away, leaving behind a desert in which nothing moved or grew.

Insofar as economic exploitation had been the immediate purpose of the occupation, 80 percent of all the grain collected by the Germans,* nearly 90 percent of all the cattle and meat, and 90 percent of all the butter was not sent to Germany but consumed by the German army, German officials, and their collaborators on the spot. The German occupation extended to roughly 400,000 square miles with a predominantly rural population of sixty-five million and some of the richest surplus grain areas in the Soviet Union. Even if one accepts that only half that area could be systematically exploited, either because it was occupied for too short a time or was too devastated, the results were unimpressive. The German people would have done better by continuing to receive deliveries under the Nazi-Soviet Pact without the huge loss of life and waste of resources for so little return.

Insofar as resettlement by the German *Herrenvolk* had been the objective, even less had been achieved. Between 1939 and 1945 the SS resettled 400,000 ethnic Germans in the annexed territories of Poland, such as the Warthegau, but the half million others forcibly transferred from their homes in Hungary, Slovakia, Rumania, and Yugoslavia remained refugees, moved from one camp to another. Those who got as far as the Ukraine and Byelorussia had to start moving back westward in 1943–44, as the German army retreated—first to camps in the Government-General and the territories annexed from Poland, then joining the great tide of refugees pouring into the Old Reich and its heavily bombed cities from all over Eastern Europe. With them went another 350,000 ethnic Germans who had long been settled in Russia along the Black Sea coast. These *Russlanddeutsche* had been "liberated" by the German army and now had to escape while there was time before the Red Army arrived.

It is of course true that the German colonization of the empire in the east had been seen as a postwar development. The resettlement began in war-

*Around 10 million tons from July 1941 to March 1944.

time only because of Hitler's and Himmler's impatience to make a start with their great dream. The sole project actually started in the Ukraine was at Hegewald, where seven villages were cleared of their Ukrainian inhabitants by force and a group of ethnic Germans brought in from the neighboring province of Volhynia—also by force. None of those moved during the war were Reich Germans; all were *Volksdeutsche* (ethnic Germans) settled outside the Reich, often for centuries, who had to be wrenched from their homes in order to satisfy Himmler's demand for colonists. As the supply dwindled, the criteria of racial selection had to be lowered—as they were for the Waffen SS.

During the war, the only Reich Germans who moved were the half million who settled in the territories annexed from Poland, not the sturdy farmer-soldiers of Darré's and Himmler's imaginations, filling Hitler's *Lebensraum* and holding the frontier on the Urals against the Asiatic hordes—they were far too busy fighting—but almost all city dwellers, officials, and businesspeople in search of economic pickings, loot, and protected jobs. They too were to pack their bags and leave hurriedly during the summer as the Red Army moved across the frontiers and into Poland and Central Europe.

THROUGHOUT THE FIRST five months of 1944 Hitler was waiting for the British and Americans to carry out their landing in the west. The slow progress that the Allies made in Italy, fighting their way laboriously up the peninsula and failing to use their naval and air superiority to leapfrog northward was a great encouragement to him. The Anglo-U.S. landing at Anzio in January was still thirty miles south of Rome, which Hitler knew they had hoped to capture by the end of that month. They had obtained their footholds in Africa and Italy, he reasoned, only because of treachery by the French and the Italians. There would be no one to let them in when they attacked across the Channel. Hitler now relied increasingly on Rommel, despite his nominal subordination to von Rundstedt as commander in chief west. Rommel (unlike von Rundstedt, but like Hitler) believed that the enemy had to be defeated on the beaches and flung himself into strengthening the coastal fortifications, laying millions of mines along the Channel shore and constructing submerged barriers to rip open the hulls of landing craft.

On the eastern front, the big Russian breakthrough in the south did not take place until mid-March 1944. Until then the Germans, although retreating, had fought tenaciously. When the Russians broke loose, Hitler put into effect an already prepared plan to take over Hungary and so secure the defense of her Carpathian frontier. He had good reason to believe that Regent Horthy was planning an Italian-style move to take his country out of the war. Horthy was invited to meet Hitler at Klessheim, and while they were talking Hitler informed him that four German battle groups had invaded Hungary and a new pro-German government had been installed.

By the time the regent got back to Budapest the coup was complete. It was the last of Hitler's coups and one of the most successful. No blood had been shed; Hungarian industry was taken over at the same time; the Hungarian forces on the eastern front were doubled; and the southern route to Central Europe was barred to the Red Army.

But this did not halt the Russian advance toward Rumania and its oil wells. At the end of March, both the field marshals, von Manstein (Army Group South) and von Kleist (Army Group A, which had fought its way back from the Caucasus), flew to see Hitler and asked to be allowed to carry out a withdrawal. Hitler's answer was to replace both men with commanders whom he believed would enforce his order to stand and fight: Walter Model, who had stopped the German rout in the north after the relief of Leningrad, and Ferdinand Schörner, who was close to the party and had been recommended by Himmler.

He followed the same course a few days later when, on April 8, the Russians launched their all-out attack to recapture the Crimea. Hitler had thought of the Crimea with its wonderful climate as the first area to be settled by German colonists; he thought of it now as the staging post to the Caucasus and its oil when the Germans returned after knocking out the invasion in the west. To give it up hurt more than any other setback in the spring of 1944, and when Zeitzler urged him to bring out the 180,000 German troops while there was still time, he categorically refused.

It was not Hitler, however, but the Russians who decided the issue: Reversing von Manstein's victory of two years before, they stormed Sevastopol within five days. Hitler was furious that his orders had not been carried out. He demanded the court-martial of General Erwin Jaenecke, the commander of the Seventeenth Army, who had ordered the evacuation of his troops when there was still time to get them out—only to have his order canceled by Hitler.

After Sevastopol there was a pause on the eastern front, which Hitler at once interpreted as proof that the Russians had exhausted their strength. When von Richthofen came up from Italy to report that the Allies had started an offensive against Monte Cassino and the Americans had broken out from the Anzio bridgehead, he found Hitler looking older but calm. After their talk, he wrote in his diary: "Again and again one can't help feeling this is a man blindly following his summons, walking unhesitatingly along the path prescribed to him without the slightest doubt as to its rightness and the final outcome." [54] This was the image Hitler summoned up all his power to present not only to his commanders, but above all to himself. Hitler assured von Richthofen that time was on their side, if only they held out until the new weapons could be brought into play and the Alliance began to disintegrate. He told his staff that he would never let it be said of him that he lost his faith in final victory just when it was within his grasp—as had happened (so he said) in November 1918.

VII

IN FEBRUARY 1944 Hitler left his headquarters in East Prussia and moved to the Berghof. The house was covered with camouflage netting, which shut out the famous view and allowed only twilight even at midday. By night the RAF flew overhead to attack targets in Austria and Hungary, forcing the Führer and his staff to go down to the air-raid shelters tunneled into the mountainside. When Munich was bombed, the red glow of fires could be seen reflected in the night sky. By daylight the sun picked out American bombers, which were now able to operate from bases in Italy, flying high overhead to attack targets in southern Germany.

Speer and Milch had overcome the problem of who was to be responsible for aircraft production by merging their staffs in a joint Fighter Staff under the direction of Karl Saur, Speer's ambitious deputy, so boosting the production of fighters for Germany's air defenses. Hitler was persuaded to agree to this plan in March, and by a combination of measures—flying squads to get bombed plants back into production quickly, a cutback in bomber production, dispersal of factories, longer hours of work in return for more food and more clothing—the numbers produced were raised from 1,300 a month at the beginning of 1944 to over 3,000 in July. As a result, in June Speer and Milch were able to secure Hitler's agreement at last to moving responsibility for all aircraft production from Göring's Air Ministry to Speer's Ministry of War Production—ironically at a time when Speer's own standing with Hitler was in decline. But the rise in production came too late to alter the balance of advantage in the air war, coinciding as it did with improvements on the Allied side, such as heavier bomb loads and the introduction of longer-range fighters (the Mustang, in particular) to act as escorts. These enabled the British and Americans to keep ahead and move to round-the-clock bombing of Germany. Their most effective attacks were those directed at communications and the plants producing synthetic fuel—not only aviation fuel, but carburetor and diesel fuel as well, which threatened the army and the U-boats as well as the Luftwaffe. In May, production of aviation fuel fell below air-force consumption, and in June Speer warned Hitler that, if attacks continued at the same level, by September the armed forces' needs of fuel could no longer be met.

But Hitler was more interested in attack than defense. In March, Milch delighted him with the news that the V-1 flying bomb was in mass production. In April Dönitz's first two Mark XXI U-boats were launched; and on Hitler's birthday Saur organized a demonstration of two tanks—a 38-tonner and one that combined speed with a long 75mm gun. These were the weapons, Hitler declared, with which he would win the Battle of the Atlantic and roll back the eastern front. In May he learned of the cutback in bomber production to allow more fighters to be built. He rejected this out of hand, demanding a fleet of 2,600 bombers in addition to 7,000 fighters. Hitler was particularly counting on a jet bomber, the Messer-schmitt 262, fast enough to break through the Allies' fighter screen and attack the invasion troops as they disembarked on the French beaches. Only on May 23 did he discover to his fury that the Me 262 was being produced solely as a jet fighter and that his orders had been disregarded. He insisted that it must be redesigned as a fighter bomber, even when told that it would take five months to do this.

News of the V-2 rocket was equally disappointing: It would not be ready for use before September. Nor would the projectiles needed for the massive underground gun battery equipped with Krupp's "Gustav" guns for shelling London. Hitler's original idea had been to launch a combined attack on London with his flying bomb, V-2 rocket, long-range guns, and new bomber force, to coincide with the anticipated invasion. Of these only the first was available; but he decided to go ahead and use it on its own in mid-June, in the belief that the V-1s would have such an effect that Churchill would be forced to launch a premature invasion. He told Slovakia's prime minister, Josef Tiso, who visited him at the Berghof, that if the British put out peace feelers he would refuse to listen until after the invasion. Once that had been defeated, as he was confident it would be, he would resume the conquest of Russia.

STUBBORN DEFENSE by the Germans held the Allied troops in Italy south of Rome until the middle of May 1944. Hitler declared Rome an open city, which saved it from being destroyed, but did not prevent the Allies from occupying it on June 4. Militarily it was a hollow victory. The Germans had withdrawn in good order at the end of May to another defensive line based on Lake Trasimene and a stronger one beyond, the Gothic Line in Tuscany.

Any hopes that Italy would open a way for the Allies to break into Central Europe or the Balkans had to be abandoned. By then Italy had become a secondary theater, and Allied divisions were removed for an advance up the Rhône Valley, leaving the German commander, Kesselring, with a superiority in land forces, although not in the air. In Italy at least Hitler's energetic reaction in September 1943 had defeated the Allies' plans. All they could do was to resume the same laborious advance, capturing Florence and Rimini in the autumn of 1944 but failing to take Bologna or break into the Po Valley before the winter brought them to a halt. It was not in fact until late April 1945, just as the war in Europe ended, that the Allied forces spread out over the north of the peninsula.

It was no longer in Italy but in France, as Hitler had long foreseen, that the decisive battle in the west would be fought. When the invasion came, however, on June 6, two days after the Allied entry into Rome, it took Hitler and Rommel by surprise and found the Germans of two minds. The scale of the Anglo-U.S. operation can be judged from the fact that 4,000 barges, tugs, and landing craft were assembled to move the initial landing force and its gear, and 1,200 naval vessels, including seven battleships, to escort them, sweep mines, and bombard the coastal defenses. General Eisenhower had 7,500 aircraft available for direct support and could call at will on 3,500 bombers, which also continued the bombing of Germany. While the Germans had become more or less convinced that the main attack would be delivered at Normandy, a successful British deception operation, including radio activity simulating the presence of large Allied forces in southeast England, led Hitler to fear a second attack—which might be the more important or a diversion—by the short sea route aimed at the Pas de Calais where the strongest German defenses had been built. There was no such danger, but German inferiority in the air prevented the Luftwaffe from carrying out the air reconnaissance that would have revealed this and have allowed the Germans to concentrate their forces in Normandy. As it was, they were dispersed. Of the sixty divisions available, only eighteen were in Normandy, no fewer than nineteen in Belgium and northern France, five in Holland, and seventeen south of the Loire.*

Rommel believed that the invading force had to be defeated on the beaches and not allowed to consolidate a beachhead. By June 17, when Hitler held a conference with him and von Rundstedt near Soissons, it was clear the Germans had failed to do this: Over 600,000 Allied troops were ashore, a million by the end of the first week in July. The Allied air forces had established so complete a superiority that the Luftwaffe was swept from the skies and the movement of German troops by day became impossible.

The meeting was held in a headquarters prepared for the invasion of Britain in 1940. An eyewitness, General Hans Speidel, described Hitler as "looking worn and sleepless, playing nervously with his spectacles and an array of colored pencils, which he held between his fingers. He was the only one who sat, hunched upon a stool, while the field marshals stood."[55] Hitler was bitterly critical of the defense and refused to let the two generals convince him of the seriousness of the situation. He talked of "masses of jet fighters" that would shatter the Allies' air superiority, described the military situation in the east as stabilized, and lost himself in a cloud of words prophesying Britain's imminent collapse under the V-bombs. When Rommel tried to persuade him to end the war in view of Germany's desperate situation, he retorted: "Don't you worry about the future course of the war. Look to your own invasion front." He left without going near the front line.

Even when the scale of the landings in Normandy became clear, Hitler refused (as late as June 29) to let the Fifteenth Army be moved from the Pas de Calais to provide reinforcements for the hard-pressed troops trying to stop the Allies from breaking out of their bridgehead. Hitler eased his frustration by replacing von Rundstedt as commander in chief west with Field Marshal Günther-Hans von Kluge. The Germans rallied to deny General Sir Bernard Montgomery possession of Caen until late in July and

*The total of sixty was completed by the division stationed on the Channel Islands.

prevent the armored forces from making a dash for Paris until mid-August. By then it had become clear that the V-1s had failed to achieve the knockout blow Hitler had hoped for, and on June 22 the Red Army had resumed its offensive in the east. Three years to the day after he had dismissed the risk of a war on two fronts and had attacked the Soviet Union while Britain was still undefeated, Hitler was confronted with the reality. The day before, 2,500 U.S. bombers raided Berlin in broad daylight.

In the east as in the west, Hitler failed to foresee the direction of his opponents' attack. A month before, Stalin had summoned a conference of commanders to discuss with the General Staff the proposed elimination of the Byelorussia salient by encircling and destroying the German Army Group Center east of Minsk. The meeting was notable for Rokossovsky's insistence, in the face of Stalin's objections, that his First Byelorussian Front should be allowed to make a double attack on Bobruisk along both banks of the Beresina, instead of the single concentrated blow Stalin preferred. Stalin twice sent him out of the room to "think it over." The second time he was followed by Molotov and Malenkov, who asked him, "Do you know who you are arguing with?" But Rokossovsky, who had already spent three years in a camp, stood fast and declared he would ask to be relieved of his command if the Stavka insisted on a single attack. After he had presented his case a third time, Stalin agreed, declaring that he liked generals who knew their job and their own mind.[56]

Farther south, on the First Ukrainian Front, I. S. Koniev pressed for a similar double attack to encircle and destroy the German Army Group North-Ukraine and capture Lvov. To this too Stalin first objected, then agreed, telling Koniev over the telephone: "You are a very stubborn fellow. Well, go ahead with your plan and put it into operation on your own responsibility."[57]

The Russian plan involved an elaborate strategic deception, aimed at persuading the Germans that the main attack would be made south, not north, of the Pripet Marshes. This led Hitler and the General Staff to believe all five Soviet tank armies were on the southern sector of the front, and in consequence twenty-four of their own thirty panzer and mechanized divisions were kept south of the marshes. The campaigning season, in fact, opened with a powerful Soviet assault on the Finns, following the breakdown of secret peace talks. When the main attack opened, aimed at Byelorussia, it was launched on four fronts with great force, with over a million and a quarter men, 4,000 tanks and self-propelled guns, 24,000 pieces of artillery, and 6,000 planes. The whole operation was coordinated by Zhukov and Vasilevsky at the front.

As soon as Hitler realized what the German troops were faced with, he ordered four strongpoints to be held at all costs; all four were captured in the first week. As in the west, he replaced Busch as commander of Army Group Center with Model: But the change could not hold up the Soviet advance. Attempts to carry out Hitler's orders and not withdraw only led to more German troops being killed or encircled. By July 3, Minsk had fallen to the Red Army, which had torn a gap of 250 miles in the German front, marking their greatest single success on the eastern front with the encirclement and destruction of Army Group Center and the obliteration of twenty-five to twenty-eight German divisions, 350,000 men in all. On July 17, a column of 57,000 German prisoners led by their generals was marched through the streets of the Russian capital, lined by silent crowds: Hitler's troops had reached Moscow at last.

The way was now open into Poland and Lithuania. Vilnius was taken on July 13, Lublin, Brest-Litovsk, and Bialystok before the end of the month. Liberating the first of the death camps, Maidanek, on the way, Rokossovsky's troops raced on to the Vistula, finally pulling up on July 31 in front of Praga, the heavily defended suburb of Warsaw on the eastern bank of the river.

Further south, on the First Ukrainian Front, Marshal Koniev captured Lvov and broke the German Army Group North-Ukraine in two halves, one falling back to the Vistula, the other to the Carpathians. Farther north the Russian armies overran Estonia and Latvia, reaching the Gulf of Riga, threatening to cut off Army Group North from the rest of the German army in the east and from East Prussia. In Finland, President Risto Ryti resigned on August 1 to allow Marshal Mannerheim to take his place, break away from the Germans, and seek an armistice with Moscow. In these and the battles on the Byelorussian fronts, more than six million men were drawn into the fighting.

The Red Army, as well as the Germans, had suffered heavy losses, but with an advance of more than 300 miles in six weeks, they had cleared the whole of Russian territory of the invader and were now within 400 miles of Berlin. By the time Montgomery took Amiens on the last day of August, the Western Allies were little more than 500 miles away. The question the Germans now began anxiously to ask was, Who would reach Berlin first? In the midst of all these troubles, Hitler was faced with something Stalin had always feared, but as far as we know had escaped: an attempt at assassination.

VIII

FOR A MOMENT in the autumn of 1938 it had seemed possible that army officers might lead a revolt against Hitler to avoid war, but with Chamberlain's intervention leading to the Munich settlement the conspiracy came to nothing. As long as Hitler continued his run of successes, there had been little prospect of mounting another serious attempt to overthrow him.

Among those who continued to meet and discuss the chances of action against the regime were the two older men generally regarded as the leaders of the conspiracy—General Ludwig Beck, the former chief of staff of the army, and Dr. Karl Goerdeler, a former Oberbürgermeister of Leipzig—

together with the ex-ambassador to Rome, Ulrich von Hassell. A key figure since 1938 had been Hans Oster, the chief assistant of the enigmatic Admiral Canaris in the Abwehr, the Armed Forces Intelligence. The Abwehr provided admirable cover for keeping contact, and Oster—"a man such as God intended men to be"[58]—gathered a small group of devoted friends around him, among them Hans von Dohnanyi, Claus Bonhoeffer, and the latter's brother Dietrich, a young Protestant pastor and theologian who had once been minister of the Lutheran Church in London.[59]

One of the uses to which the conspirators put the facilities of the Abwehr was to try to make contact with the British and Americans in the hope of securing some assurances as to the kind of peace the Allies would be willing to make if Hitler's government were overthrown. In May 1942 Dietrich Bonhoeffer traveled to Stockholm to meet Bishop George Bell of Chichester, using forged papers prepared by the Abwehr. Bishop Bell passed on all that he learned of the conspirators' plans to the British government, and other contacts were made through Allen Dulles, the head of the American Office of Strategic Services (OSS)* in Switzerland. None of these approaches, however, elicited any positive response. The Allies remained skeptical about any German opposition, and (particularly after the demand for an "unconditional surrender" expressed at the Casablanca Conference in January 1943) the conspirators had to face the need to act on their own without any encouragement from outside.

The conspirators devoted much time and energy to discussing how Germany and Europe should be organized and governed after the overthrow of Hitler.[60] Discussion of such questions was the purpose of the group that Graf Helmuth von Moltke, thirty-eight years old, a former Rhodes Scholar at Oxford and bearer of one of the most famous names in German military history, brought together on his estate at Kreisau in Silesia. The Kreisau Circle was drawn from a cross-section of German society. Among its members were two Jesuit priests, two Lutheran pastors; conservatives, liberals, and socialists; landowners and former trade unionists. The discussions at Kreisau were concerned, not with planning the overthrow of Hitler, but with the economic, social, and spiritual foundations of the new society that would come into existence afterwards.

The downturn in Hitler's fortunes in 1942–43 revived the hopes of those who thought in terms of action. Their problem remained, however, to secure the support of some institution, without which any opposition appeared to be condemned to remain in the hopeless position of individuals pitting their strength against the organized power of the state.

There were two institutions in Germany that still retained some independence. The first was the churches. Among the most courageous demonstrations of opposition during the war were the sermons preached by the Catholic bishop of Münster, Graf von Galen, and the Protestant pastor, Dr.

*The forerunner of the CIA.

Martin Niemöller. Nazi zealots like Bormann regarded the churches with a venomous hostility, while Catholic priests as well as Protestant pastors were active in the anti-Nazi opposition. Neither the Catholic Church nor the Evangelical Church, however, as institutions, felt it possible to take up an attitude of open opposition to the regime.

It was natural, therefore, that those few Germans who ventured to think of taking action against Hitler should continue to look to the army, the only other institution in Germany that still possessed a measure of independent authority, if its leaders could be persuaded to assert it, and the only institution that commanded the armed force needed to overthrow the regime.

Hitler's relations with the army continued to deteriorate in 1943–44. Again and again he reversed the decisions of his senior commanders, ignored their advice, upbraided them as cowards, forced them to carry out orders they believed to be impossible to execute, and dismissed them when they failed. Hitler's criticism of the German officer corps was directed against its conservatism and its "negative" attitude toward the National Socialist revolution. In practice, the revolutionary spirit meant willingness to carry out Hitler's orders without hesitation and without regard for the cost. Those who won favor were rough-and-ready soldiers, like the two who replaced von Manstein and von Kleist, Model and Schörner, who went up to the front, drove their men to the limit, and did not worry their heads too much about the strategic situation. Nonetheless, so far the generals had continued to obey his orders, to fight his battles for him despite his continual interference, and to accept the titles, decorations, and gifts he bestowed on them.*

THERE WERE a small number of German officers, however, below the level of army commanders, who were committed to ridding Germany of her Nazi masters. Outstanding among them was Henning von Tresckow, the senior operations officer (GSO-I) of Army Group Center on the eastern front, who used his position to gather together a group of like-minded officers in the same way that Oster had in the Abwehr. A Pomeranian gentleman-farmer of an old Prussian military family, von Tresckow, like other officers who joined the opposition, had at first been enthusiastic about the new regime which he saw liberating Germany from the abuses of the Weimar system and the humiliation of Versailles. But when he became aware of the true character of the Nazi regime in practice, he turned into a determined opponent, telling Fabian von Schlabrendorff, who became his aide-de-camp, in the summer of 1939: "Both duty and honor demand from us that we should do our best to bring about the downfall of Hitler and National Socialism in order to save Germany and Europe from barba-

---

*As late as March 1944 von Manstein was given a large estate when he was replaced by Model. Field Marshal von Kluge was presented with a gift of 250,000 marks by Hitler in October 1942.

rism."[61] His subsequent behavior showed that these were not empty words.

After Stalingrad, von Tresckow believed that a coup could be organized, if Hitler could be assassinated first, and that the army would accept this. General Friedrich Olbricht had recently been recruited by the opposition and he agreed to use his position as deputy to the commander in chief of the *Ersatzheer,* the Replacement Army,* to organize the follow-up operation after Hitler had been killed. Von Tresckow made himself responsible for the assassination.

The attempt was made on March 13, 1943, when Hitler paid a visit to von Kluge's headquarters at Smolensk. Von Tresckow and von Schlabrendorff succeeded in placing a time bomb on the plane that carried him back to East Prussia. The bomb failed to explode. With remarkable coolness, von Schlabrendorff flew at once to the Führer's headquarters and recovered the bomb before it was discovered—it had been hidden in a package of two bottles of brandy to be delivered to a friend—and took it to pieces on the train to Berlin.

As many as six more attempts on Hitler's life were planned during the later months of 1943, but all for one reason or another came to nothing. In the meantime Himmler's agents, although singularly inefficient in tracking down the conspiracy, were beginning to get uncomfortably close. In April 1943 they arrested Dietrich Bonhoeffer and Hans von Dohnanyi. Too many threads led back to the Abwehr, which the rival SS Intelligence Service was eager to put out of business, and in December 1943 General Oster, the key figure in the Abwehr, was forced to resign.

Fortunately, just as the Abwehr circle was being broken up, the conspiracy was strengthened by a new recruit who promised to bring to it qualities of decision and personality that the older leaders lacked. Claus Schenk, Graf von Stauffenberg, born in 1907, came of an old and aristocratic Catholic family from south Germany. He was a tall, striking figure, with a love of horses and outdoor sports. At the same time he was widely read and responsive not only to music but to the romantic mysticism of the poet Stefan George, of whose circle he became a member and whose poem "Anti-Christ"[62] he used to recite with passion.

Originally, like von Tresckow, attracted by the idea of reconciling nationalism and socialism in a *völkisch* community, von Stauffenberg had been alienated by Nazi methods. But he was a soldier and continued to do his duty even after he had become convinced of the need to remove Hitler, serving with distinction as a staff officer in Poland, France, and Russia. It was while in Russia that his doubts about Hitler hardened into a conviction of the need to act. His new purpose was not altered by the severe wounds that he suffered in the Tunisian campaign, which cost him his left eye, his

---

*This was not an active command but an organization for mobilizing and training recruits who were sent in drafts to the different fronts.

right hand, and two fingers of the other hand. As soon as he had recovered, he secured appointment to Olbricht's staff in Berlin and threw himself into preparations for a renewed attempt at a coup d'état.

Besides filling the gaps in the field army, the Replacement Army provided the organization by which all recruiting and training units, and all soldiers on special courses, could be mobilized quickly to deal with emergencies, including a possible uprising by the millions of foreign workers in Germany. The orders for Operation Valkyrie, as this was called, provided for all twenty-one army commands in the enlarged Reich and in Paris to form combat groups within six hours. This was the machinery von Stauffenberg proposed to use, revising the standing orders in detail and making contact with officers sympathetic to the opposition in as many commands as possible to make sure the orders were put into operation quickly. With the help of men on whom he could rely at the Führer's headquarters, in Berlin and in the German army in the west, von Stauffenberg hoped to push the reluctant army leaders into action once Hitler had been killed.

There is a danger in talking of the "German opposition" of giving altogether too sharp a picture of what was essentially a number of small, loosely connected groups, fluctuating in membership, with no common organization and no common purpose other than their hostility to the existing regime. Their motives for such hostility varied widely: In some it sprang from a deeply felt moral aversion to the whole regime, in others from patriotism and the conviction that, unless he were halted, Hitler would destroy Germany. To diversity of motives and temperamental differences, increased by the strain under which all were placed by the need to live double lives, must be added considerable divergence of views about the steps to be taken in opposing Hitler as well as the future organization of Germany and Europe. In the summer of 1944, however, agreement was reached on including in the government to replace the Nazis representatives of the former Social Democrats (Julius Leber, as minister of the interior) and of the trade unions (Wilhelm Leuschner, as vice-chancellor) as well as conservatives like Goerdeler.

Von Stauffenberg's energy had put new life into the conspiracy, but the leading role he was playing also roused jealousies. So did his views. Von Stauffenberg was by temperament a radical, highly critical of Goerdeler's old-fashioned conservatism and much closer to the socialist wing of the conspiracy around Leber and Leuschner. These differences were heightened by the knowledge that they were now working against time. Further arrests were made early in 1944, including that of von Moltke. In February, the greater part of the Abwehr functions were transferred to a unified Intelligence Service under Himmler's control, and Himmler told Admiral Canaris, now deprived of his office as head of Military Intelligence, that he knew very well a revolt was being planned in army circles and that he would strike when the time came.

At this moment came the news that the Allies had landed in Normandy.

Von Stauffenberg had not expected the invasion so soon and he, Beck, and Goerdeler were at first so taken aback that they hesitated about whether to go on. With the Anglo-American armies as well as the Russians pressing the Germans back, was there any longer a chance of securing a compromise peace, even if Hitler were removed? Would they not simply incur the odium of a second "Stab in the Back" without being able to alter the course of events? It was von Tresckow who spoke out firmly and steadied von Stauffenberg's and the others' purpose.

> The assassination [he replied to a message from von Stauffenberg] must be attempted at all costs. Even should it fail, the attempt to seize power in the capital must be undertaken. We must prove to the world and to future generations that the men of the German Resistance dared to take the decisive step and to hazard their lives upon it. Compared with this object, nothing else matters. [63]

Von Tresckow's advice was heeded, and by good luck von Stauffenberg was now placed in a position from which he could put his plans into operation more easily: At the end of June he was promoted to full colonel and appointed chief of staff to the commander in chief of the Replacement Army, General Friedrich Fromm. This not only allowed him to send out orders in the name of his commander, but also gave him frequent access to Hitler, who was particularly interested in finding replacements for his losses in Russia. He had now decided that to make sure that the essential preliminary, the assassination of Hitler, was properly carried out, he should undertake it himself, despite the handicap of his injuries.

Time, however, was now more pressing than ever. On July 4–5 Leber was arrested following an attempt to get in touch with an underground German Communist group. On July 17 a warrant was issued for the arrest of Goerdeler. The plot was now in danger of being wrecked by further arrests within a matter of days, if not hours. Von Stauffenberg had already prepared two attempts to carry out the assassination of Hitler, both of which had come to nothing. On July 20, he flew to Hitler's headquarters in East Prussia determined that his third attempt would be decisive.

Mussolini was due to visit Hitler there on the twentieth, and for that reason the daily conference had been moved to 12:30 p.m. Von Stauffenberg was expected to report on the creation of new formations. He brought his papers with him in a briefcase in which he had concealed a bomb fitted with a device for exploding it ten minutes after the mechanism had been started. The conference was already proceeding when von Stauffenberg joined the group of officers around a large, heavy oak table on which were spread out a number of maps. Neither Himmler nor Göring was present. The Führer himself was standing toward the middle of one of the long sides of the table, constantly leaning over the table to look at the maps. Von Stauffenberg placed his briefcase under the table, having started the fuse before he came in, and then left the room unobtrusively on the excuse of a telephone call to Berlin. He had been gone only a minute or two when a loud explosion shattered the room, blowing out the walls and the roof, and setting fire to the debris that crashed down on those inside.

In the smoke and confusion, with guards rushing up and the injured men inside crying for help, Hitler staggered out of the door covered with dust. His hair was scorched, his right arm hung stiff and useless, one of his legs had been burned, a falling beam had bruised his back, and both eardrums were found to be damaged by the explosion. But he was alive. Those who had been at the end of the table where von Stauffenberg placed the briefcase were either dead or badly wounded. Hitler had been protected, partly by the tabletop over which he was leaning at the time, and partly by the heavy wooden support on which the table rested and against which von Stauffenberg's briefcase had been pushed before the bomb exploded.

Although badly shaken Hitler was curiously calm, and in the early afternoon he appeared on the station platform to receive Mussolini. Apart from a stiff right arm, he bore no traces of his experience and the account that he gave to Mussolini was marked by its restraint.

As soon as they reached his headquarters Hitler took Mussolini to look at the wrecked conference room. Then, as he began to reenact the scene, his voice became more excited. "After my miraculous escape from death today I am more than ever convinced that it is my fate to bring our common enterprise to a successful conclusion." Nodding his head, Mussolini could only agree: "After what I have seen here, I am absolutely of your opinion. This was a sign from heaven."[64]

In this exalted mood Hitler went with Mussolini to his own quarters, where an excited group had gathered for tea. Göring, Ribbentrop, and Dönitz had joined Keitel and Jodl, and sharp recriminations began to be exchanged over the responsibility for the war. Hitler sat quietly with Mussolini in the middle of this scene until someone mentioned the Röhn "plot" of 1934. Suddenly leaping to his feet in a fury, Hitler began to scream that he would be revenged on them all, that he had been chosen by Providence to make history and those who thwarted him would be destroyed. This went on for half an hour. When he had exhausted his rage Hitler in his turn relapsed into silence, sucking an occasional piece of candy, and letting the protestations of loyalty and a new quarrel that had begun between Göring and Ribbentrop pass over his head.*

In the confusion after the bomb exploded von Stauffenberg succeeded in bluffing his way through the triple ring of guard posts and took a plane back to Berlin. Some time passed before anyone at the Führer's headquar-

---

*An eyewitness account of the scene was given by Eugen Dollmann, the SS leader accompanying Mussolini. Göring, who tried to divert attention from the failures of the air force to the bankruptcy of Ribbentrop's foreign policy, threatened to smack the foreign minister with his marshal's baton. "You dirty little champagne salesman," Göring roared at him. "Shut your damned mouth." "I am still foreign minister," Ribbentrop shouted back, "and my name is *von* Ribbentrop." Trevor-Roper, *The Last Days of Hitler,* (2d ed., London: 1950), pp. 36–37.

ters realized what had happened—at first it was thought the bomb had been dropped from an airplane—and it was longer still before it was known that the attempted assassination had been followed by an attempted putsch in Berlin.

There, in the capital, a little group of the conspirators had gathered in General Olbricht's office at the General Staff Building in the Bendlerstrasse. Their plan was to announce that Hitler was dead and that an anti-Nazi government had been formed in Berlin. Orders were to be issued in its name declaring a state of emergency and transferring all power to the army in order to prevent the SS from seizing control. The entire state administration, the SS itself, the police, and the party were to be subordinated to the army commanders in Germany, in the occupied countries and in the different theaters of operations. All senior party, SS, and police officials were to be placed under arrest. In Berlin plans had been concerted to bring in troops from barracks outside the city in order to surround the government quarter, secure the Gestapo headquarters and the radio station, and disarm the SS. Whether these orders would be obeyed was a gamble, but it was hoped that—once Hitler himself had been removed—those officers who had hitherto refused to join the conspiracy, whether out of fear or scruples about the oath of allegiance, would support the new government.

Everything depended upon two conditions: the successful assassination of Hitler and prompt, determined action in Berlin. The first of these conditions had already been invalidated but this was not known to von Stauffenberg, who left the Führer's headquarters convinced that no one could have survived the explosion in the conference room. The first reports of the explosion to reach the Bendlerstrasse, however, not long after 1 p.m., made it clear that Hitler was not dead, and Olbricht therefore decided not to issue the order for Valkyrie. Thus the second condition failed, too. It was not until von Stauffenberg reached Rangsdorf airfield after a three-hour flight from East Prussia that he was able to get through by telephone to Olbricht and—believing, as he still did, that Hitler had been killed—to persuade him to start sending out orders for action. This was at 3:45 p.m., and it took von Stauffenberg another three-quarters of an hour to get to the center of Berlin and at last supply the drive that had been lacking.

Even von Stauffenberg's energy and determination, however, could not make good the three to four hours that had been lost. Everything still remained to be done. It was not until after four o'clock that General Paul von Hase, the Berlin commandant, was told to bring in troops to occupy the government quarter. Von Hase called in the Guard Battalion Grossdeutschland, under Major Otto Remer, from Döberitz. Remer (who was not in on the plot) acted promptly, but the suspicions of a National Socialist guidance officer, Dr. Hans Hagen, a self-important young man from the Propaganda Ministry who was lecturing to the battalion, were aroused. Hagen got in touch with Goebbels, who called in Remer to speak on the telephone to Hitler's headquarters in East Prussia. The unmistakable voice over the wire convinced Remer that the Führer was not dead, as he had been told: The major was promptly promoted to colonel on the spot and personally ordered by Hitler to use his troops to suppress the putsch.

After von Stauffenberg's return, orders had been hurriedly sent out to the chief army commands to carry out Operation Valkyrie, and action was already in motion in Paris and Vienna when shortly after 6:30 p.m. the German radio broadcast an announcement, telephoned by Goebbels, that an attempt had been made to kill Hitler but had failed. Once this became known, fear of Hitler's revenge and eagerness to reassure became the dominant motives in the minds of the large number of officers who had hitherto sat on the fence and waited to see if the putsch was successful before committing themselves.

The broadcast from Berlin in the early evening had already warned the wary. Soon after 8 p.m. a message was sent by teleprinter to all commands countermanding the instructions issued from Berlin. Hitler had appointed Himmler to replace General Fromm as commander in chief of the Replacement Army and placed him in charge of the security of the Reich. An hour later the radio put out an announcement that Hitler would broadcast to the German people before midnight.

The situation of the little band of conspirators in the General Staff office in the Bendlerstrasse was now hopeless. In the course of the evening a group of officers loyal to Hitler, who had been placed under arrest earlier in the day, broke out of custody, released General Fromm, and disarmed the conspirators. Fromm's own behavior had been equivocal and he was now only too anxious to display his zealous devotion by getting rid of those who might incriminate him. When troops arrived to arrest the conspirators, Fromm ordered von Stauffenberg, Olbricht, and two other officers to be shot in the courtyard, where the executions were carried out by the light from the headlights of an armored car. Beck was allowed the choice of suicide. Fromm was prevented from executing the rest only by the arrival of Ernst Kaltenbrunner, Himmler's chief lieutenant, who was far more interested in discovering what could be learned from the survivors than in shooting them out of hand, now that the putsch had failed. Himmler, reaching Berlin from East Prussia in the course of the evening, set up his headquarters at Goebbels' house, and the first examinations were carried out that night. The manhunt had begun.

In one place only were the conspirators successful—in Paris. There they had been able to count on a number of staunch supporters, headed by General Heinrich von Stülpnagel, the military governor of France. As soon as he received the code word from Berlin, von Stülpnagel carried out the orders to arrest the 1,200 SS men in Paris, and the army was rapidly in complete command of the situation. But here, too, the conspirators were dogged by the same ill luck that had pursued them throughout the day.

In the early months of 1944, Field Marshal Rommel, then recently appointed to his command in the west, had been brought into contact with the group around Beck and Goerdeler, and it was hoped he could be persuaded to take action when the moment came. On July 17, however, while returning from the front, Rommel's car was attacked by British fighters and the field marshal severely injured. Thus, on July 20, Rommel was lying unconscious in the hospital, and the command of his Army Group B, as well as the command in chief in the west, was in the hands of Field Marshal von Kluge, a horse of another color.

Von Kluge knew very well what was being planned. But as soon as it became clear that the attempt on Hitler's life had failed, he refused to consider making an independent move in the west. Without the support of the commander in the field, von Stülpnagel could do nothing: He had created an opportunity with no one to exploit it. So, by dawn on the twenty-first, the putsch had collapsed in Paris as well as in Berlin, and von Stülpnagel was summoned home to report. Now it was Hitler's turn to act, and his revenge was unsparing.

Half an hour after midnight on the night of July 20–21 all German radio stations relayed the shaken but still recognizable voice of the Führer speaking from East Prussia.

> If I speak to you today [he began] it is in order that you should hear my voice and should know that I am unhurt and well, and secondly that you should know of a crime unparalleled in German history. A very small clique of ambitious, irresponsible, and at the same time senseless and stupid officers had formed a plot to eliminate me and the High Command of the Armed Forces. . . .
>
> I am convinced that with the uncovering of this tiny clique of traitors and saboteurs there has at long last been created in the rear that atmosphere which the fighting front needs. . . .
>
> This time we shall get even with them in the way to which we National Socialists are accustomed.[65]

Hitler's threats were rarely idle. The Gestapo's investigations and executions went on without interruption until the last days of the war, and the sittings of the People's Court under the notorious Nazi judge Roland Freisler continued for months. The first trial, held on August 7, resulted in the immediate condemnation of Field Marshal Erwin von Witzleben, Generals Hoepner, von Hase, and Stieff, together with four other officers, and they were put to death with great cruelty on August 8, by slow hanging with a noose of piano wire from a meat hook. The executions as well as the trial are said to have been filmed from beginning to end for Hitler to see the same evening in the Reich Chancellery.*

With a handful of exceptions, saved largely by luck, all those who were

---

*The film of the executions appears to have been destroyed, but the film of the trial was captured intact and gives a vivid impression of the indignities inflicted on the defendants and of their courage.

at all active in the plot, on the civilian as well as the military side, some 200 in all, were arrested, subjected to torture, and executed. Another 5,000, including the entire families of the principal conspirators, such as Goerdeler, von Stauffenberg, von Tresckow, Oster, as well as leading figures not directly connected with the plot, but associated with the past or suspected of independence of mind were arrested and sent to concentration camps—among them Schacht, Halder, and Konrad Adenauer.

No doubt there were some among those executed who joined the conspiracy—and many more who would have, if Hitler had been killed—because they realized that Hitler was leading Germany to a disastrous defeat. But the core of the opposition consisted of men and women who had recognized the true nature of the Nazi regime and committed themselves to its overthrow while Hitler was still winning victories, in not a few cases before the war.

One such was Henning von Tresckow. Only the fact that he had been appointed to an active command in the field prevented him from playing a central role in the events of July 20. As soon as he heard that Hitler had broadcast in person and so provided proof that the plot had failed he immediately made up his mind to take his own life rather than wait to have all he knew about the opposition—including names—extracted from him by torture.

His friend von Schlabrendorff could not dissuade him and the next morning von Tresckow drove into no-man's land and after firing two pistols, to give the impression that he had been killed in action, set off a rifle grenade which blew off his head. After they had parted, on the morning of July 21, von Schlabrendorff wrote down von Tresckow's last words:

> Now they will all fall upon us and cover us with abuse. But I am convinced, now as much as ever, that we have done the right thing. I believe Hitler to be the arch-enemy, not only of Germany, but of the entire world. . . .
>
> Just as God once promised Abraham that He would spare Sodom if only ten just men could be found in the city, I have reason to hope that, for our sake, he will not destroy Germany. No one among us can complain about his death, for whoever joined our ranks put on the poisoned shirt of Nessus. A man's moral worth is established only at the point where he is prepared to give his life for his convictions.[66]

These words can stand as an epitaph for all who joined Henning von Tresckow in the attempt to rid Germany and the world of Hitler and the Nazi regime.

EIGHTEEN

Hitler's Defeat

HITLER   1944-45   *(Age 55-56)*
STALIN   1944-45   *(Age 64-65)*

I

Although the injuries Hitler suffered added to the deterioration of his health, he drew fresh energy from his escape. In his broadcast the same evening, July 20, he declared: "I regard this as a fresh confirmation of the mission given me by Providence to continue toward my goal."[1] He found something else besides the assurance of providential intervention—an explanation of the defeats that he had suffered. Once he convinced himself that he had been betrayed by the officer corps, everything fell into place—the otherwise inexplicable surrenders; the frequent withdrawals in the face of orders to stand firm; the League of German Officers which Generals Walter Seydlitz and Martin Lattmann had set up in Moscow calling on German troops to desert and help to overthrow the Nazi regime;* the number of officers, especially from traditional military families, involved in the plot to kill their supreme commander. They accepted the opportunities he had created for them—the greatest military successes in history, the promotions and decorations, the gifts and estates he showered on them—but they had never accepted him. They had been disloyal from the beginning, defeatist when things began to go badly—and now traitors as well.

Speer describes a meeting with Hitler on July 22 at which Hitler said he now realized that in eliminating Tukhachevsky, Stalin had taken a decisive step toward the successful conduct of the war. By liquidating his General Staff, Stalin had made room for fresh, vigorous men who did not date back to tsarist days. Hitler was no longer so sure that the charges in the 1937 Moscow trials had been trumped up; he could no longer exclude the possibility of treasonable collaboration between the Russian and the German General Staffs. Working himself up to an outburst in which, Speer says, "spite and fury were mingled with a sense of being vindicated," he declared: "Now I know why all my great plans in Russia had to fail in recent

---

*Field Marshal Paulus finally joined the League after July 20.

years. It was all treason! But for those traitors we would have won long ago. Here is my justification before history." [2]

Had Hitler been free to give full rein to his anger, he would have made a clean sweep and imprisoned or shot every general within sight. But in the middle of a grave military crisis this was more than he could afford to do. However reluctant he was to concede it, he still needed the officer corps to wage the war for him. Nor would his own prestige allow him to admit that the army no longer had complete faith in his leadership. In public, therefore, elaborate measures were taken to conceal the split between the army and its commander in chief. In his broadcast on the night of July 20 Hitler insisted that only a small clique of officers was involved, and Goebbels described the plot as a stab in the back aimed at the fighting front and crushed by the army itself.

The order of the day issued by the new chief of staff of the army, General Guderian, on July 23, followed the same line. Pledging the loyalty of the officer corps and army to the Führer, Guderian spoke of "a few officers, some of them on the retired list, who had lost courage, and out of cowardice and weakness preferred the road of disgrace to the only road open to an honest soldier, the road of duty and honor."

The humiliation of the army, however, was complete. The generals who in 1934 had insisted on the elimination of Röhm and the SA leadership now had to accept the Waffen SS as an equal partner with the army, navy, and air force, with Himmler appointed to succeed Fromm as commander in chief of the Replacement Army and soon as the active commander in the field of an army group. The Nazi salute was made compulsory "as a sign of the army's unshakable allegiance to the Führer and of the closest unity between army and party," and a further order insisted that henceforth every General Staff officer must actively cooperate in the indoctrination of the army with National Socialist beliefs. To make quite sure, National Socialist political officers were appointed to all military headquarters, another Russian practice that Hitler admired and now imitated.

FOR THE REMAINING nine months of his life, Hitler excluded anyone on whose total personal loyalty he did not feel he could rely and who showed any reservations about his constantly repeated assertion that, if they only held out, the war could still be won. These qualifications were best met by the *Alte Kämpfer,* those to whom he could appeal by reminding them of the reverses the party had suffered during the *Kampfzeit,* its time of struggle, only to triumph in the end, and whose fortunes were so completely bound up with their Führer's that they had every reason to cling to his belief that he would once again master circumstances.

The change in the balance of power at the top that followed the unsuccessful coup of July 1944 thus marked a double reversal of the settlement that followed the preemptive strike against a second revolution in July 1934—the final dissolution of the alliance with the traditional conservative

German elite, represented by the officer corps and, as its counterpart, the recovery of a leading role by the party, which had been overshadowed between 1934 and 1941. Corresponding with this, in the inner circle around Hitler, was the decline in influence of three men who had each in turn enjoyed Hitler's confidence as his closest collaborator, without ever having been accepted by the *Alte Kämpfer*—Göring, Ribbentrop, and Speer—and the continued rise in influence of Goebbels, Himmler, and Bormann.

Göring was still Hitler's successor. Reichsmarschall, commander in chief of the Air Force, minister for air, plenipotentiary for the Four-Year Plan, and holder of a score of other offices, he had steadily lost authority since the beginning of the war. In 1933–34 he was unquestionably the second man in Germany; by 1942, sloth, vanity, and his love of luxury had undermined not only his political authority but also his native ability. He took his ease at Karinhall, his country estate, hunting and feasting, amassing a fabulous collection of pictures, jewels, and *objets d'art* for which the cities of Europe were laid under tribute, and amusing himself by designing still more fantastic clothes to fit his different offices and changing moods. When he appeared in Rome or at the Führer's headquarters in a new white or sky blue uniform, surrounded by a retinue of aides-de-camp and carrying his bejeweled marshal's baton, he still blustered loudly and claimed a privileged position. But it was a hollow show, with nothing behind to support it. Ciano, meeting him in Rome in 1942, described him as "bloated and overbearing . . . at the station he wore a great sable coat, something between what motorists wore in 1906 and what a high-grade prostitute wears to the opera." [3]

Hitler was tolerant of Göring's weaknesses and still summoned him to important conferences (as on July 20), but he was not blind to what was happening to him. It was the failure of the Air Force to prevent the bombing of Germany or to undertake the reprisals Hitler demanded that finally discredited Göring in his eyes. There were angry scenes between the two men, Hitler accusing the Luftwaffe of cowardice as well as incompetence, and threatening to disband it altogether. Some personal attachment between them remained until the end, but Hitler had no confidence in him, and in the final months of the regime Göring kept out of his way. Only at his trial after the war did he reveal something of the cunning and force he had once possessed.

SPEER HAD RISEN at the expense of Göring's claim to be Germany's economic chief, and his success in doubling German armaments production (the peak overall figure was actually reached in July 1944), despite the bombing, gave him for a time a unique advantage over all other rivals for Hitler's confidence. Speer's weakness was his lack of an independent political base: He was wholly dependent on Hitler's support, and he had powerful rivals as well as enemies in the party and the SS. The aftermath of the plot affected Speer by strengthening the position of the two men from whom he had most to fear, Bormann and Himmler. As an indication of the place they now occupied, both began to appear at the Führer's military conferences.

The party seized the opportunity of the plot to argue that things had gone wrong because the party element had not been given enough scope. The Gauleiters openly regretted the fact that Röhm and the SA had lost out to the Wehrmacht in 1934. If Röhm had succeeded, he would have created an army imbued with the National Socialist spirit, the lack of which had led to the defeats that Germany had suffered. At least the party should take over the civilian sector and see that ministers (like Speer) followed its lead.

In his disillusionment with the army, Hitler was receptive to such talk, which could only work to the advantage of Bormann as the effective head of the party, and to the disadvantage of Speer, who had fought a long-running battle with the Gauleiters—which he now looked set to lose—in his efforts to shut down production for civilian consumption and override their defense of their local economies.

Speer appealed to Hitler and in a letter of September 20, 1944, said that he was the victim of the party's anticapitalist prejudice against his collaboration with leading industrialists, which was now denounced by Goebbels and Bormann as reactionary, alien to National Socialism, and hostile to the party. He demanded a decision as to whether the industrialists and their factory managers were to continue to take responsibility for arms production and be guaranteed against interference, or the Gauleiters and the party were to be allowed to intervene as they saw fit. [4]

Hitler's only answer after looking through the letter Speer handed to him was to say that Goebbels and Bormann would decide what should be done. When Speer was summoned to see them they left him in no doubt that Goebbels would give the orders and he would have to obey them. In future, Bormann warned him, he would not stand for any further attempts by Speer to influence Hitler directly. Speer was not dismissed and retained his position as minister, but henceforward he was excluded from the inner circle.

It was Himmler rather than Bormann or Goebbels who appeared to be the most powerful figure in the Germany of 1944–45. Already head of the SS, the Waffen SS, and the Gestapo, he became minister of the interior as well in 1943. It was Himmler who hunted down those involved in the July 20 plot and took over, with his concentration-camp and prisoner-of-war labor force, an increasing part of the armament and construction program.

Himmler's empire was extensive, but it suffered from the lack of coherence that was the hallmark of the Nazi regime. Like Göring before him, Himmler constantly added to his responsibilities without creating an effective instrument of control. Himmler's SS was no more a monolith than Hitler's "totalitarian" state. Different parts of his empire were in constant rivalry with one another. Lacking Hitler's personal authority and charisma, Himmler found great difficulty in preventing his more aggressive subordinates from behaving as if they were independent authorities.

As the Waffen SS grew to be nearly a million strong, its officers scorned to have anything to do with those from other SS branches, identifying themselves with the army officers alongside whom they fought and using army rather than SS ranks. The ideological instruction that Himmler ordered did not take place, and those who were sent to conduct it were made into laughingstocks.

Bormann saw Himmler as a rival who might threaten his own position with Hitler. Whenever SS leaders thought they could take advantage of Himmler's new authority and invade the preserves of the Gauleiters, Speer testified, "Bormann immediately reported such cases to Hitler and exploited them to fortify his own position. To our surprise it did not take him long to stalemate Himmler as minister of the interior." [5] Himmler's stock was still rising. The Waffen SS won Hitler's praise for its successful actions in Warsaw, Slovakia, and Hungary. As a sign of Hitler's appreciation, on November 8, 1944, he was granted the privilege of taking Hitler's place in Munich and delivering the traditional speech to the party in commemoration of the 1923 putsch. But at this point, when Himmler believed that he had become the obvious person to take Göring's place as heir apparent, Bormann skillfully helped him to destroy his own reputation.

I I

FROM THE TIME the Soviet armies crossed the Russian frontiers into the countries of Eastern Europe, a new chapter in European history began—the making of the postwar settlement. Characteristically, there was no agreement *when* the frontiers were crossed because there was no agreement where they ran. In the case of the Russian-Polish frontier, the Poles took this to follow the prewar line (crossed on January 4, 1944); the Russians, the line established by the Nazi-Soviet Pact of 1939 (crossed on July 19). It was the Russian view that prevailed. Stalin's first objective, as the Germans retreated, was to recover permanently for the Soviet Union the territories that he had secured by his agreement with Hitler, before Hitler had temporarily dispossessed him of them. In Stalin's view, the two Western leaders had already agreed—had indeed suggested—at Teheran that the new Soviet-Polish frontier should follow the line agreed to with Hitler, dressed up for the sake of respectability as the Curzon Line (plus Lvov at Stalin's insistence), with compensation in the west at Germany's expense. This was the first and most difficult part of the postwar settlement to be implemented, in circumstances of unrelieved tragedy.

Unlike the other Eastern European nations from whom Stalin claimed territory, the Poles alone had fought the Germans and had suffered terribly at their hands; had never collaborated with them; had never sent troops to join the Germans in attacking Russia; and in 1941, already fighting as allies of the British and soon of the Americans as well, had signed a Treaty of Friendship and Mutual Assistance with the Soviet Union. None of this carried weight with Stalin. He had already seized the opportunity of the Katyn affair to break off relations with the exiled Polish government in London and refused to recognize the existence of the Polish Home Army (*Armia Krajowa,* AK), which, under the direction of the exiled government, represented a more substantial force than any other European resistance movement except the Yugoslav.

Not only did Stalin refuse to have anything to do with the Polish government, but the Russians also sent in Soviet partisans to flush out and destroy the forces of the London-led AK and established Communist-led Polish guerrillas and regular forces, armed, equipped, and under the control of the Red Army. Once each area was "liberated" by the Russians, the Soviet security forces arrested, frequently on charges of collaboration with the Germans, any who refused to accept the "restored" Soviet authority. On July 22, three days after the Russians had crossed the line they regarded as the Russo-Polish frontier, they set up a hand-picked Polish Committee of National Liberation in Lublin which signed an agreement with the Soviet government at a ceremony in which Stalin, Molotov, and Zhukov took part. To Churchill Stalin explained that it was precisely because "We do not want to, nor shall we, set up our own administration on Polish soil" that they had "gotten in touch" with the Lublin Committee which might form "the core of a provisional Polish government made up of democratic forces."[6]

Stalin no doubt believed himself to be speaking the truth when he said he wanted a strong Poland as a safeguard against a revival of a German threat to Russia and believed the exchange of the smaller but much more valuable territory to her west was a fair compensation for the loss of that in the east. But he was also well aware of the strong anti-Russian feeling among Poles who—after more than a century of tsarist rule and the brutal experience of 1939–41—regarded their eastern neighbors with the same hostility as the Germans. After doing his best to destroy their leading cadres during the 1939–41 occupation, Stalin was determined not to allow a government that he saw as the residual representative of the old leadership to have any part in the new Poland. He meant to replace it by an administration with a Communist core that would be dependent on the Soviet Union—the first model of the satellite state that was to become standard throughout Eastern Europe after the war.

Stalin's move put the Home Army and the Polish government in London in an impossible position. They were being strongly urged by Churchill and Eden to be realistic and come to terms with the Russians, but they believed that, in view of the Russian refusal to recognize them, this was *un*realistic advice. They saw the only options open to them as either to do nothing, allow Poland to fall under Communist control and the Home Army to be suppressed without firing a shot, or to attempt an uprising in the hope of driving the Germans out of Warsaw and establishing themselves in the Polish capital before the Russians could arrive. They left the decision on timing to the leaders on the spot. Acting in the belief that the Russians, already on the Vistula, would in any case reach Warsaw in the opening days of August, the local leaders called on their forces—some 150,000 men, many with little training and with arms for only a quarter of that number—to attack the German occupying troops on August 1, 1944.

Taking the Germans by surprise, the insurgents captured the central suburbs of Warsaw in the first four days but failed to secure the airport, the bridges over the Vistula, or the right-bank suburb of Praga, where they might have made contact with the Russians. After their initial success the Poles were thrown on the defensive. With incredible courage they held out for no less than nine weeks against the most savage attacks. But their tragic gamble failed, first because they had underestimated the reaction of the Germans, who instead of abandoning the city brought up powerful reinforcements to suppress the uprising; second, because they notified neither the Western Allies nor the Russians of their intentions; and third (and in part, as a result of that), because they received virtually no help from outside.

Effective assistance could come only from the Russian army. Both Churchill and Stanislav Mikolajczyk, the prime minister of the Polish government in exile, who, at Churchill's urging, had flown to Moscow, pressed the Russians to give such help. Stalin was skeptical about the uprising, describing it as "unusual" and reports of the fighting as "exaggerated and misleading." He was even more skeptical about its chances of success. He revealed that he had thought that the Polish-born Russian General (later Marshal) Konstantin Rokossovsky's army would capture Warsaw by a *coup de main* by August 6, but added that German counterattacks had proved stronger than expected and had forced the Russians to go on the defensive. He did not, however, at first rule out dropping desperately needed arms and ammunition from the air, and on August 10 told Mikolajczyk: "We shall try to do everything possible to help Warsaw." [7]

After the middle of the month, Stalin's attitude hardened. When Churchill and Roosevelt asked for landing facilities on Soviet airfields for British and American bombers flying from Brindisi and from the west and carrying out arms drops for the insurgents, they were met with a blank refusal. "After a closer study of the problem," Stalin declared, he was convinced that the uprising "was a reckless adventure causing useless victims . . . [and] the Soviet command have decided openly to disclaim any responsibility for the Warsaw adventure." [8]

On August 20, Churchill and Roosevelt sent a joint appeal to Stalin:

We are thinking of world opinion if the anti-Nazis in Warsaw are in effect abandoned. We hope that you will drop immediate supplies and ammunition to the patriot Poles of Warsaw, or will you agree to help our planes in doing it very quickly?" [9]

Stalin made no attempt to answer this appeal but dismissed "the agony of Warsaw," as Churchill called it, out of hand: "Sooner or later the truth about the group of criminals who have embarked on the Warsaw adventure in order to seize power will become known to everybody." [10]

While the Allies argued, the Germans were left free to pen the insurgents in a steadily reduced area of Warsaw and to carry out Hitler's order to raze the city to the ground and deport its population. Control of the operation had been given to the SS general Erich von dem Bach-Zelewski, a specialist in anti-partisan operations. The methods he adopted were exceptional in their cruelty even for the SS. They included drenching wounded insurgents with gasoline and burning them alive; chaining women and children to their tanks as a safeguard against ambushes, and using gas grenades to kill hundreds of Poles who tried to escape through the sewers. Their brutality was directed as much against the civilian population as against the resistance fighters. The withdrawal of the AK from the Wola suburb was followed by a mass execution of 8,000; hospitals were set on fire with nurses and patients in them; the capture of another suburb on August 11 was followed by the massacre of 40,000 people.

Stalin had judged his Western allies correctly: They would protest but not risk breaking up the Grand Alliance for the sake of the Poles. Stalin himself, however, could not risk that either and was aware that he was losing a lot of the goodwill Russia's tremendous contribution to defeating Hitler had won for the Soviet Union in the West. In September 1944 Rokossovsky's armies, regrouped and reinforced, started to move again, and after heavy fighting in which Polish troops attacking alongside the Russians captured Praga, Soviet aircraft belatedly dropped supplies for the insurgents, almost all of which fell into German hands. After a costly attempt by Allied planes to do the same by a round trip from Brindisi, the Russians allowed an American force flying from the west to land on Soviet airfields—because, as Stalin put it, "we can hardly prohibit them." On his own responsibility, General Zygmunt Berling, commanding the First Polish Army as part of Rokossovsky's forces, made a forced crossing of the Vistula in an effort to reach the insurgents but was driven back by the Germans.

None of these last-minute attempts to bring help affected the situation of the resistance fighters, which by now was hopeless. Unless the Soviet archives some day offer new evidence, Churchill's comment carries conviction: "The Russians wished to have the non-Communist Poles destroyed to the full, but also to keep alive the idea that they were going to their rescue." [11]

After two months' merciless struggle, on October 2 General Tadeusz Bór-Komorawski, the commander of the Polish Home Army, capitulated.

Although the AK's own losses did not exceed 20,000, some 225,000 civilians had already been killed; to have continued the fight would have meant raising the latter figure still higher. Ironically the Germans did what Stalin had steadily refused to do and granted the Polish Home Army combatant rights, allowing them to be treated as prisoners of war. More than half a million of Warsaw's inhabitants were deported to concentration camps and another 150,000 sent to forced labor in Germany. German demolition squads blew up such buildings as remained standing. When the Red Army finally entered the ruins in January 1945, they found not a single person still living in a city that had housed over a million and a quarter in 1939.

In the perspective of the war, the suppression of the Warsaw uprising and the denial of the city to the Russians for three more months represented one of the last German successes. In the slightly longer perspective of the Nazi-Soviet Pact, which had divided Poland between Germans and Russians, it represented the final act in their parallel policies of destroying the existing leadership of the Polish nation. In the much longer perspective of the postwar settlement it represented a decisive victory for Stalin.

Stalin can hardly be blamed for the decision to launch the Warsaw uprising. This was a tragic, if understandable, mistake by the AK commanders and the exiled government, deliberately made without consultation with any of the three major Allies. Stalin appears to have been surprised as well as irritated by it. It occurred at a time when the Russian advance in the center had run out of steam and preparations for the next phase of the campaign had not yet begun. This was not in fact launched until mid-January 1945.

Given the unexpected German rally and counterattack on the Vistula front it would have been difficult for Rokossovsky's forces to have broken through to relieve the Warsaw insurgents, even if Stalin had wanted to. But why should he have wanted to? As he soon came to see, the uprising played into his hands. The Germans would save him the trouble of liquidating the Home Army and what remained of an independent Polish leadership, making it much easier to replace it with the Soviet-sponsored Polish Committee of National Liberation. When the Russian army finally occupied the empty shell of the Polish capital, units of the First Polish Army, which had fought side by side with them, marched in a symbolic parade along the line of what had once been the city's main avenue. Two weeks later, the Lublin Committee, transformed into the Communist-led provisional government of the Polish Republic, moved to Warsaw from Lublin and set about the creation of a new Poland intended to have little, if anything, in common with Poland's historic past.

WHILE THE FIGHTING in Warsaw was still going on, late in August, another uprising broke out, this time in Slovakia, directed against the unpopular satellite government of Mgr. Tiso and following the arrival of Russian forces on the other side of the Carpathians. President Beneš had flown from London to Moscow in December 1943 to avoid the situation of the Polish government in exile. He had been rewarded with a treaty of alliance and friendship with the USSR and the promise of Soviet support in reestablishing the Czechoslovak state.

Nonetheless the same problem of the distrust between those who looked to London and those who looked to Moscow reappeared. When the insurrection was started by Soviet-trained and Communist-led partisans, built up and supplied by the Russians, each side blamed the other for failing to establish effective working relations with officers in the Slovak army, in touch with the Beneš government in London, who called for a military revolt. This failure was one of the main reasons for the defeat of the uprising. The other was the inability of the Red Army to break through to its support despite a grueling battle for the Carpathian passes which went on until late November. By that time, a strong German force had moved in and crushed all resistance with the same brutal thoroughness as in Poland.

In Rumania and Bulgaria Stalin's problems were simpler. He relied neither on covert attempts by Rumanian emissaries to get out of the war nor on Rumanian Communists, either in exile or underground, but on Malinovsky's and Tolbukhin's armies. With a million men between them, these destroyed the German forces in Rumania, accepted the capitulation by the Rumanian king after a coup had overthrown Antonescu's dictatorship, and made their entry into Bucharest on the last day of August 1944. This was a major blow to Hitler's hopes of holding the Balkans. Not only had he lost the principal source of Germany's oil supplies, but the way had also been opened for a Russian advance into Central Europe, Hungary, and Yugoslavia as well as Czechoslovakia and Austria. While clearing the Germans out of Rumania cost the Red Army nearly 50,000 dead, Bulgaria was occupied without a shot being fired. Allied to Germany, but resolute in refusing to fight the Russians, with whom Bulgarians had traditional ties of friendship, a "Fatherland Front" carried out a silent coup as soon as Soviet troops crossed the border and greeted them with banners of welcome.

In a paper to Eden written on May 4, 1944, Churchill set out "the brute issues between us [and the Russians]—in Italy, in Rumania, in Bulgaria, in Yugoslavia, and above all in Greece. Broadly speaking the issue is: Are we going to acquiesce in the Communization of the Balkans and perhaps of Italy?"[12] It is surprising that Churchill did not include Poland, but, even if he had, this would still have been to confuse means and ends. Stalin, at this stage at least, was not interested in the form of government or economy in the countries the Red Army was about to occupy, or in building up a "Communist bloc" as such. What he wanted was to stake out his claim to a Soviet sphere of influence in Eastern and possibly Central Europe. Within that, anyone in power would understand clearly that in future their policies would have to be in conformity with Russian wishes, that their resources (especially after the losses the Soviet Union had suffered during the war) would have to be at Russia's disposal and that anybody whom Stalin suspected of anti-Soviet "tendencies" (and he was a very suspicious man) would not be tolerated.

This was what Stalin had sought from Hitler in 1939, with very considerable success. The experience of the war, and the vulnerability of Russia to attack which it had demonstrated, made him more determined than ever to recover the territories he had annexed between 1939 and 1940. In addition he now meant to take advantage of the Red Army's advance westward—welcomed by his allies as essential to the defeat of Nazi Germany—to create the widest possible barrier against a third German attack by extending his control still farther. How far, and whether into Germany itself, remained to be seen.

The tradition of complete subordination of Communist parties everywhere to the interests of the "workers' Fatherland" made local Communists natural instruments for carrying out such a policy. But Stalin was also well aware that too obvious a reliance upon them could be counterproductive, arousing suspicion and opposition on the part of his British and American allies, who now had powerful armies of their own in Europe. He therefore preferred, wherever he could, to work through coalitions in which social democrats, peasant parties, and nationalists took part as well as Communists—"the democratic anti-Fascist front" was the current formula. Well-practiced Communist techniques, such as infiltration, could be used to secure acquiescence, while the multi-party facade was retained to reassure the West. Where Communists, unaccustomed to Stalinist "double-talk," took exception to such compromises on grounds of Marxist principle, they could be expelled or, whenever they refused to accept the Moscow line without question, could be excommunicated, as happened in the case of Tito and the Yugoslav Communist leadership.

STALIN REMARKED to Eden when they first met in 1941 that Hitler's weakness was not knowing when to stop. Stalin did. Compared with Hitler's Utopian dream of a racist empire involving the movement of millions of people and the permanent enslavement of millions more, a modern Sparta on a gigantic scale, Stalin's New Order as it developed in the rest of the 1940s was a perfectly possible and practical scheme. This is proved by the fact that it lasted for thirty-five years after his death in 1953. Unlike Hitler, Stalin recognized there were limits beyond which it would be dangerous to push one's luck. The most striking example of this is his retreat over Berlin in 1949; but there are two other examples in 1944 that are more surprising because they affected areas closer, in one case very much closer, to Russia's borders.

The first was Finland. When the Finns sought peace, the terms they were granted in September made permanent the loss of territory they had suffered in 1940, imposed a substantial indemnity, and required them to lease the naval base at Porkkala to Russia for fifty years. But remembering the international reaction to Russia's earlier attack on them, Stalin allowed Finland to retain a greater degree of independence than any other East European country and acquiesced in the exclusion of the Finnish Communist party from a share in power.

The second example was Greece. Alarmed by the possibility of a Communist government being set up, thereby allowing the Russians to extend their influence into the Mediterranean, Churchill proposed to the Soviet ambassador in May 1944 that Britain agree to accept Rumania as primarily a Russian concern in return for Soviet acceptance of a similar position for the British in respect to Greece. Despite American doubts about spheres of influence, Stalin accepted the proposal to the disgust of the Greek Communists, and kept to it in the civil war that followed the German withdrawal and the British landing later in 1944.

Instead of driving south into Greece, the Russian armies in the Balkans pushed west into Hungary and Yugoslavia. The handwriting on the wall had been clear enough to the Hungarians for a long time. At the end of August the regent, Admiral Horthy, dismissed the prime minister, Sztójay, installed by the Germans after their March coup, and finally brought himself to accept that any armistice would have to be negotiated with the Russians, not the Western powers. An armistice delegation arrived secretly in Moscow on October 1, by which time General Rodion Malinovsky's forces had reached the River Tisza after clearing Transylvania on the way.

Hitler, however, saw clearly enough that to abandon Hungary would mean the loss of the Hungarian-Austrian oil fields on which German forces now depended for four-fifths of their needs and would open the way for the Russians to advance into Germany from the south. A swift action led by Skorzeny, who had rescued Mussolini, forced Horthy to abdicate and restored German control of the government and the capital, while SS reinforcements made sure that it would not be taken without a fight. With a third of Hungary occupied, and within fifty miles of the capital, Malinovsky prepared to launch his attack on Budapest but asked for five days to bring up additional forces before doing so. Stalin, speaking from Moscow on October 28, categorically refused:

> It is absolutely essential that in the shortest possible time you capture Budapest. This has to be done no matter what it costs you. . . .
> The Stavka cannot give you five days. You understand that it is because of political considerations that we have got to take Budapest as quickly as possible.

When Malinovsky argued that his Forty-Sixth Army "for sheer lack of power" could not manage it without reinforcements already on the way, and would inevitably get bogged down in heavy fighting, Stalin told him: "You are arguing all to no purpose. . . . I categorically order you to go over to the offensive for Budapest tomorrow." [13]

Malinovsky obeyed, with the result he had forseen. The Germans mounted a furious counterattack and the capture of Budapest, in street-by-street fighting as savage as anything seen since Stalingrad, was not completed until February 13, 1945, with very heavy losses on both sides. Nor was this the end of the Hungarian campaign. Refusing to recognize that the real danger point was the Vistula-Oder front, Hitler was as obstinate as Stalin had been and insisted on attempting to recover the Hungarian capital, transferring Sepp Dietrich's Sixth SS Panzer Army, withdrawn from the west, in order to do so. Not until the last week in March was the German resistance finally overcome and orders issued by the Stavka for the capture of Vienna.

THE ENTRY of the Red Army into Yugoslavia brought it into the territory of an ally, not of a satellite. This could have been said of its entry into Poland, but the crucial differences were that Tito and the Yugoslav leadership were not only Communist, but were also already in undisputed control of large areas of the country which they had cleared of German troops after heavy fighting. This confronted Stalin with a problem of a different kind which ultimately defeated him and led in 1948 to the first successful challenge to his supremacy in the Communist world.

Milovan Djilas, later to become one of the most trenchant critics of Communism and to suffer years of imprisonment by Tito rather than retract his opinions, was a member of the Yugoslav leadership chosen to go with the Military Mission first sent to Moscow in March 1944. In his reminiscences, Djilas recalls that he approached the Soviet capital and his introduction to Stalin with feelings little short of idolatry. The first Yugoslav leader to meet him, he wrote:

> What could be more exciting for a Communist, one who was coming from war and revolution, than to be received by Stalin? This was the greatest possible recognition of our Partisan fighters. In dungeons and in the holocaust of war, and in the no-less-violent spiritual crises and clashes with the internal and external foes of Communism, Stalin was something more than a leader in battle. He was the incarnation of an idea, transformed in Communist minds into pure idea, and thereby into something infallible and without sin. [14]

Amazed at the impressive setting of the Kremlin, this innocent from the provincial backwoods was a sharp enough observer to give one of the most vivid portraits of Stalin ever written:

> The room was not large, rather long and devoid of any opulence of decor. Above a not-too-large desk hung a photograph of Lenin, and on the wall over the conference table in carved wooden frames were portraits of Suvorov and Kutuzov, looking very much like the lithographs one sees in the provinces.
> But the host was the plainest of all, in a marshal's uniform and soft boots, without any medals except a golden star—the Order of Hero of

the Soviet Union. . . . This was not that majestic Stalin of the photographs or newsreels—with the stiff, deliberate gait and posture. He was not quiet for a moment. He toyed with his pipe, which bore the white dot of the English firm Dunhill, or drew circles with a blue pencil around words indicating the main subjects for discussion, which he then crossed out, and he kept turning his head this way and that while he fidgeted in his seat.

I was also surprised at something else: He was of very small stature and ungainly build. His torso was short and narrow, while his legs and arms were too long. His left arm and shoulder seemed rather stiff. He had quite a large paunch and his hair was sparse. His face was white, with ruddy cheeks, the coloration characteristic of those who sit long in offices, known as the "Kremlin complexion." His teeth were black and irregular, turned inward. Not even his mustache was thick or firm. Still the head was not a bad one; it had something of the common people about it—with those yellow eyes and a mixture of sternness and mischief.

I was also surprised at his accent. One could tell that he was not a Russian. But his Russian vocabulary was rich and his manner of expression vivid and flexible, full of Russian proverbs and sayings. As I realized later, Stalin was well acquainted with Russian literature—though only Russian.

One thing did not surprise me: Stalin had a sense of humor—a rough humor, self-assured, but not entirely without subtlety and depth. His reactions were quick and acute—and conclusive, which did not mean that he did not hear the speaker out, but it was evident that he was no friend of long explanations.[15]

The difficulties that arose between Stalin and the Yugoslav leadership stemmed from the determination of the Yugoslavs not only to fight the Germans but also to establish themselves as an independent government and carry out a revolution of their own. After long hesitation, the three major Allies had agreed at Teheran to accept Tito's National Liberation Army, not General Drazha Mihailović's Royal Yugoslav Army, as the effective resistance movement. But they did not accept the declaration of the Anti-Fascist Council held at Jajce in October 1943 refusing to acknowledge the king or the government-in-exile, and claiming that the National Liberation Committee (NLC) was the only legal government of the Yugoslav people. The Yugoslavs did not expect the Western powers to recognize the NLC as a provisional government, but they were taken aback when they were told that Stalin was "extremely angry" with them. The immediate cause was Stalin's fear that Yugoslav action might be taken by the British and Americans to give substance to their suspicions that the Soviet government was taking advantage of the war to spread revolutionary Communism—precisely the suspicion that the dissolution of the Comintern had been intended to allay.

This came out very clearly in a second conversation that Djilas had with Stalin early in June 1944. Urging the Yugoslavs not to do anything that would alarm the British, Stalin burst out: "What do you want with red stars on your caps? The form is not important but what is gained, and you—Red stars! By God, there's no need for stars!" It was on this occasion that Stalin, not wanting Djilas to think that he had been taken in by the British, made the often-quoted comparison of Churchill and Roosevelt:

> Churchill is the kind of man who will pick your pocket for a kopeck if you don't watch him. Yes, pick your pocket for a kopeck! By God, pick your pocket of a kopeck. Roosevelt is not like that. He dips in his hand only for bigger coins. But Churchill? Churchill—will do it for a kopeck. [16]

But as Tito came to recognize, there were more fundamental reasons for the Russians' displeasure. They regarded it as presumptuous and ridiculous for the leaders of a small peasant country to suppose that they were capable of carrying out a Communist revolution, of which Stalin and the Soviet Union had a monopoly. As leaders of a Great Power they looked with disdain upon the pretensions of these provincial Balkan peasants, without tradition, culture, or knowledge of the world, to set up an independent government of their own, instead of submitting gratefully to the orders of the Red Army and accepting Yugoslavia's role as a satellite in the Soviet sphere of influence. At the beginning of July 1944, in anticipation of the Red Army's arrival in Yugoslavia, Tito asked for the chance to meet Stalin and discuss their cooperation. In September his wish was granted, and he flew to Moscow. Tito described the meeting as very cool. Stalin persisted in addressing his visitor, who had been given the title of marshal of Yugoslavia, as "Walther," the name by which he had been known as an agent of the Comintern at the time of the Spanish Civil War. But Tito held his ground, and the joint communiqué issued after their talks referred to the Soviet "request" to the NLC and the consent of the latter to "the temporary entry of Soviet troops into Yugoslavia" and their withdrawal once their "operational task" was completed. The civil administration in the areas occupied by the Soviet troops was to remain in Yugoslav hands, and the partisans would be under Tito's, not the Russians', command.

Molotov, Zhdanov, and Beria looked aghast at Tito when he bluntly disagreed with Stalin, particularly when "the boss" assured him the Yugoslavs would have to reinstate King Peter.

> The blood rushed to my head [Tito recalled later] that he could advise us to do such a thing. I composed myself and told him it was impossible, that the people would rebel, that in Yugoslavia the king personified treason. . . .
> Stalin was silent and then said briefly:
> "You need not restore him forever. Take him back temporarily and then you can slip a knife into his back at a suitable moment." [17]

Tito, like Djilas, was taken to dinner at Stalin's dacha. He was disgusted by the excessive eating and drinking to which he was unaccustomed and had to leave the room to be sick. Describing these dinners, where everyone helped themselves from heavy silver dishes and sat where they liked, Djilas reports that they lasted from ten at night till four or five in the morning, with conversation ranging from anecdotes to serious political and even philosophical subjects. These occasions were the only relaxation in Stalin's otherwise monotonous life, and a significant part of Soviet policy was shaped at them.

Djilas observed that "Stalin ate food in quantities that would have been enormous even for a much larger man." He drank more moderately than the others, however, mixing red wine and vodka, and he never appeared drunk. Djilas believed that Molotov, the only man whom Stalin addressed with the familiar *ty,* was also the only man who was always present at the dacha dinners—in effect was Stalin's deputy.[18] He was struck by the contrast and the complementarity between the two. He regarded Molotov's mind as "sealed and inscrutable."

> Stalin, however, was of a lively, almost restless temperament. He always questioned—himself and others; and he argued—with himself and others. I will not say that Molotov did not easily get excited, or that Stalin did not know how to restrain himself and dissimulate; later I was to see both in these roles.
>
> Stalin was no less a cold calculator than Molotov. But his was a more passionate and many-sided nature—though all sides were equally strong and so convincing that it seemed he never dissembled but was always expressing each of his roles.[19]

Both Djilas's and Tito's impressions are colored by the later open breach with Stalin. At the time, however, both sides concealed their irritation and distrust. There was certainly nothing halfhearted about the offensive that the Russian armies launched in October side by side with the partisans to drive the Germans out of Yugoslavia. When Belgrade was stormed, the Russians kept their promise to let the Yugoslavs be the first to enter the city. At the victory parade, Tito saluted the "Belgrade Battalion" which had started out from its hometown three and a half years earlier, fought over almost the whole of Yugoslavia, and returned with only two of its original complement left. By the time of the Yalta Conference (February 1945) there were no Soviet troops left in Yugoslavia, where the National Liberation Army mustered 800,000 troops for the final campaign against the Germans, which continued even after the general surrender of May 9.

III

FOR FOUR MONTHS after the attempted assassination, Hitler remained at his headquarters in East Prussia. Shortly after July 20 he moved back into the bunker, which had been rebuilt and strengthened.

> If ever a building can be considered the symbol of a situation [Speer wrote], this was it. From the outside it looked like an ancient Egyptian

tomb. It was actually nothing but a great windowless block of concrete without direct ventilation. It seemed as if the concrete walls, sixteen and a half feet thick, that surrounded Hitler separated him from the outside world in a figurative as well as a literal sense, and locked him up inside his delusions. [20]

While Stalin's horizons were widening all the time—now that he was accepted as a world statesman, sure of victory, and beginning to look ahead to a postwar settlement that would bring Eastern and perhaps Central Europe within the Soviet sphere—Hitler retreated into himself. It was not only separation from people, from the crowds from whom he had formerly received back the validation of his belief in himself and his mission, but also separation from events. He rarely went near the front and never visited the bombed cities. Any tank driver, infantryman, or fighter pilot knew more about what the war was actually like than this recluse shut away in the bunker, poring over maps and ordering armies he never saw into battle or denouncing as traitors those who failed to stand and die rather than retreat.

This deliberate isolation was due not to lack of courage, but to Hitler's belief that his life alone stood between Germany and defeat, that he was the one man who could still turn defeat into victory. He knew instinctively that to do this he must at all costs protect his will from being weakened by contact with reality. To that was added, after the July 20 plot, a universal suspicion of treachery, and of another attempt at assassination. When he held a conference of commanders before the Ardennes offensive in December, all of them were required to surrender their weapons and briefcases. During a long rambling speech that lasted for two hours, armed SS guards stood behind every chair and watched every movement that was made.

The most serious effect of the bomb explosion was the damage to his ears. These gradually healed, but his health showed a marked deterioration in the final stage of his life. This was due to the interaction of three things. The basic cause was the unremitting exertion of his will month after month without any form of relaxation, and with a steadily mounting yet suppressed frustration as one after another of the hopes he clutched at was disappointed. This was made worse by the unhealthy way of life Hitler followed in the damp and depressing climate of East Prussia, immured in his bunker, virtually without exercise or fresh air, without change of scene (he refused to go to the Berghof), of occupation or of company. His insomnia became worse, and he only managed three or four hours in the morning after a heavy dose of sedation. Most men would have broken down under the strain of such a life, but this was where the third factor came into play: Hitler's reliance on drugs administered by his doctor, Morell. These covered up his exhaustion, but only, in the end, at the cumulative cost of ruining the patient's constitution.

Toward the end of September 1944, Hitler suffered a return of his stomach cramps and felt so ill that he stayed in bed. One of his secretaries who visited him came away convinced that he had reached the limit of his strength. Wearing a gray-flannel dressing gown over an army nightshirt, and lying on a camp bed between the bare concrete walls of the bunker, with dull and expressionless eyes he gave the impression that he had lost all desire to go on living.

Hitler recovered sufficiently after two weeks to move about again but in November found his throat hurting, lost his voice, which was reduced to a whisper, and was finally persuaded to move to Berlin for an operation on his vocal cords. The operation, the removal of a tiny polyp, was a success. But, although he resumed his routine, and any fear that he might be suffering from an organic disease was dispelled, all who saw Hitler at the end of 1944 agree in their description of him as prematurely aged—an old man, with a hoarse voice, ashen complexion, shuffling gait, trembling hands, and a dragging leg.

ALTHOUGH MUCH of Hitler's time at the beginning of the autumn was taken up with the fighting in the Balkans and the threat to Hungary, the situation in the west was never far from his mind. In August, a thousand miles away from the battlefield and refusing to recognize the supremacy of the Allies in the air, Hitler issued orders that left the commanders in France with no room for maneuver. Not only the divisions but also the roads and villages through which they were to advance were specified in detail. When this too failed, Hitler's suspicion that none of his generals could be trusted was shown in his remark to Warlimont: "Success only failed to come because Kluge did not want to be successful." As a result of Hitler's refusal to allow a withdrawal behind the Seine, 60,000 Germans were killed or captured after having been trapped in the Falaise pocket.

Field Marshal von Kluge was replaced by Model, but all he could do was prevent the Germans' headlong retreat across the Seine from turning into a rout. On August 25 Paris was liberated intact, despite Hitler's order to destroy it, and Brussels and Antwerp at the beginning of September. A second expeditionary force, which had landed in the south, moved up the Rhône Valley to help liberate the rest of France. On September 11 an American patrol crossed the German frontier; five years after the attack on Poland, the war had reached German soil.

In a conference with three of his generals on the afternoon of August 31, Hitler made it clear that, whatever happened and whatever the cost to Germany, he was determined to maintain the struggle:

> The time hasn't come for a political decision. . . . It is childish and naive to expect that at a moment of grave military defeats the moment for favorable political dealings has come. Such moments come when you are having successes. . . . But the time will come when the tension between the Allies will become so great that the break will occur. All coalitions have disintegrated in history sooner or later. The only thing is to wait for the right moment, no matter how hard it is. . . .

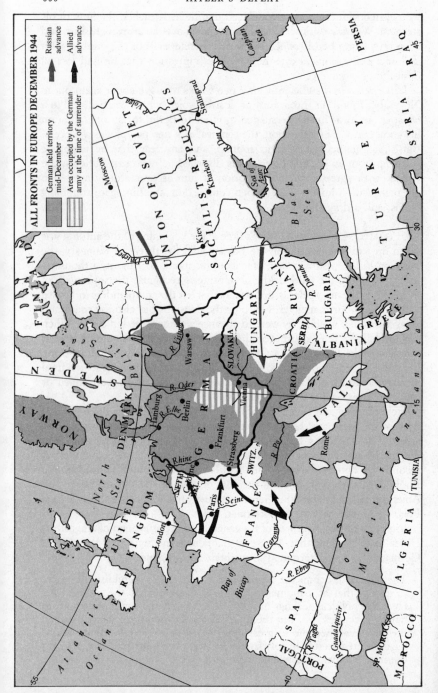

ALL FRONTS IN EUROPE DECEMBER 1944

German held territory mid-December

Area occupied by the German army at the time of surrender

Russian advance

Allied advance

I live only for the purpose of leading this fight, because I know if there is not an iron will behind it this battle cannot be won. I accuse the General Staff of weakening combat officers who join its ranks, instead of exuding this iron will, and of spreading pessimism when General Staff officers go to the front. . . .

If necessary we'll fight on the Rhine. It doesn't make any difference. Under all circumstances we will continue this battle until, as Frederick the Great said, one of our damned enemies gets too tired to fight any more. . . .

If my life had been ended I think I can say that for me personally it would only have been a release from worry, sleepless nights, and great nervous suffering. . . . Just the same, I am grateful to Destiny for letting me live, because I believe. . . .[21]

The Allies' plan was to break into Germany before the winter came and strike at the basis of her war economy in the Ruhr and Rhineland. Bad luck, bad weather, difficulties of supply, and differences of opinion within the Allied High Command combined to defeat their hopes—together with an unexpected recovery by the German army.

At the end of August this had been a broken force on the run; by the end of September it had rallied along the line of the German frontier and succeeded in forming a continuous front again west of the Rhine, a front that the Allies pushed back but failed to break throughout the winter. Behind it the Siegfried Line on Germany's western frontier was hastily restored and manned. The British attempt to breach the river line at Arnhem and turn the German defenses from the north was defeated, while the stubborn rearguard action of the German Fifteenth Army holding the Scheldt Estuary denied the British and Americans the use of the vital port of Antwerp until the end of November, nearly three months after its capture.

Hitler used this respite to build up new forces with which to fill the gaps left by the summer's fighting. Goebbels's proclamation of total mobilization promised a last reserve of manpower. With this Hitler hoped to reform the divisions broken up in the fighting, and—at half strength or less, in order to keep up the illusion that he was still able to find replacements—to create twenty to twenty-five new divisions, 8,000 to 10,000 men strong. These were to be called *Volksgrenadier* divisions in order to distinguish them, as the first formations of a People's Army imbued with the National Socialist spirit, from the old army which Hitler now regarded as having failed and betrayed him. A proclamation of October 18, 1944, called up every able-bodied male between the ages of sixteen and sixty to serve in the new force, organized by Bormann and the party and placed under Himmler's command.

Despite the bombing, German arms production overall in the last four months of 1944 was still above that for the first four months, and much higher than it had been in the time of Germany's successes. The greatest material difficulty was the desperate shortage of oil and gasoline, due to the loss of Rumania and the systematic Allied bombing of synthetic-oil plants, refineries, and communications. Germany made a remarkable recovery in the last three months of 1944, but Hitler was now drawing on the country's last reserves of men, matériel, and morale.

EVERYTHING THEREFORE turned on the use that Hitler decided to make of the forces that had been scraped together. At the beginning of September 1944, apart from the armies on the western and on the main eastern fronts, there were ten divisions in Yugoslavia and seventeen in Scandinavia, thirty cut off in the Baltic states, twenty-four in Italy, and twenty-eight fighting to hold Budapest and what was left of Hungary. But Hitler refused to recall them, because that would mean accepting that the war had failed and that all that remained was to defend the Reich. They were his pledges that the offensive would be renewed when they had gotten through the present critical period.

The same reasoning led him not to think of strengthening the defensive forces on either the eastern or the western front, nor to think in terms of defense at all, but solely of attack. Hitler had always found it natural to think in such terms, especially under the circumstances of September 1944. A defensive campaign could defer a decision, but it would not alter the situation; an offensive would take the Allies by surprise and would enable him to recapture the initiative, so gaining time for the development of new weapons and of the split between Russia and the Western Allies on which he counted to win the war. The idea of staking everything on a gamble nobody expected excited and attracted him; this had been the secret of his successes in the past, and would be again.

If this was to be the character of the operation, there were strong arguments for attempting it in the west rather than the east. Distances were shorter, less fuel would be needed, and strategic objectives of importance were more within the compass of his limited forces than in the more open country of the east, where the fighting was on a different scale. Nor did he believe the Americans and British were as tough opponents as the Russians. The British, he soon convinced himself, were at the end of their resources, while the Americans were liable to lose heart if events ceased to go favorably for them.

After considering various alternatives, Hitler decided on an offensive drive through the Ardennes—the scene of his breakthrough in 1940—aimed at crossing the Meuse and recapturing Antwerp, the Allies' principal supply port. The idea was excellent. The last thing the Allied commanders expected was a German attack, and they were caught completely off guard. The Ardennes sector was in fact the weakest point in their front, held by no more than a handful of divisions, and the loss of Antwerp would have been a major blow to the supply lines of the Anglo-American armies. But the idea bore no relation to the stage of the war that had been reached in the winter of 1944–45. Even if the Germans had taken Antwerp—a feat that every one of the German commanders in the field believed to be beyond their strength—they could not have held it. The utmost Hitler could hope to inflict on the Allied armies was a setback, not a defeat, and in the process he ran the heavy risk of throwing away the last reserves with which the defenses of the Reich could be strengthened.

The attempt of the men in command to argue with Hitler, and to persuade him to accept more limited objectives, proved as unsuccessful as all the other previous attempts. To have admitted that the generals were right would have meant admitting that the war was lost. Hitler's confidence is well illustrated by his rebuke to the chief of the Army General Staff, Guderian, when the latter ventured to argue that he was leaving the eastern front dangerously weak:

> There's no need for you to try to teach me [Hitler shouted back]. I've been commanding the German army in the field for five years, and during that time I've had more practical experience than any "gentleman" of the General Staff could ever hope to have. [22]

Preparations went on in great secrecy during Hitler's illness, and by the beginning of December twenty-eight divisions (including ten panzer divisions) had been collected for the attack, with another six for the thrust into Alsace which was to follow. The final plans, drawn up at Hitler's headquarters, were sent to von Rundstedt with every detail already settled, down to the times of the artillery bombardment, and with the warning in Hitler's own handwriting: "Not to be altered." In order to keep tight control of the battle, Hitler moved from East Prussia (which he was never to see again) first to Berlin, and then on December 10 to Bad Nauheim, in the Taunus, close to the battlefront.

The attack was launched on December 16. It took the British and Americans completely by surprise, and fog kept the Allied air forces out of the battle for the first few days. During that time the German troops made considerable advances which the German press and radio puffed up into one of the great victories of the war. But they did not succeed in crossing the Meuse and were never within sight of reaching Antwerp. By the twenty-fifth it was clear that, if they wanted to avoid heavy losses, they had better call off the battle. Hitler furiously rejected any such suggestion.

Twice Guderian, responsible for the defense of the eastern front, visited Hitler and tried to persuade him to transfer troops, not to Hungary, but to Poland, where there were ominous signs of Russian preparations to resume the offensive across the Vistula. Hitler would not listen to his reports. The Russians were bluffing, he declared: "It's the greatest imposture since Genghis Khan. Who's responsible for producing all this rubbish?" [23] He insisted that Model should make a second attempt to break through the Ardennes and that the attack should be launched in the Vosges. Both failed.

On January 8 Hitler at last agreed to withdrawal after his forces had suffered 100,000 casualties and lost 600 tanks and 1,600 aircraft. By January

16 the front line was back to its original position. The American losses were fewer and could easily be made good; Hitler's men were irreplaceable. The gamble had failed. When Guderian again tried to point out the dangers of the situation in the east, he was met with a hysterical outburst. "He had," Guderian said later, "a special picture of the world, and every fact had to be fitted into that fancied world. As he believed, so the world must be; but, in fact, it was a picture of another world." [24]

GUDERIAN was right. The Russians' plans for the final campaign, which was to carry their armies into the heart of Germany and capture Berlin, had been agreed upon in November and preparations made to open it in the middle of January. It was now the turn of the Russians to operate at a great distance from their supply bases across the scarred desert left by the fighting, in which virtually every building had to be repaired and every railway line relaid. Nonetheless, stocks of fuel, food, and ammunition were built up to supply a huge force of almost six million men deployed on nine fronts along the eastern borders of Germany.

Stalin had no intention of sharing the glory of victory with anyone else. Both Zhukov and Vasilevsky were moved into field commands, and Stalin himself took over, formally at least, the role of Stavka coordinator for all four main fronts. The twin spearheads of the main attack, rivals in the race to reach Berlin first, were the First Byelorussian Front under the command of Zhukov and on his left the First Ukrainian Front under Koniev. Between them they commanded two and a quarter million men and almost 6,500 tanks, giving them a fivefold superiority in manpower and armor over the Germans facing them, and sevenfold in artillery. The first objective of their attack, which Hitler dismissed as a bluff, was to fight their way across the 300 miles separating the Vistula from the Oder: Zhukov by the more northerly route, Lodz-Poznan-Küstrin; Koniev, by the more southerly, Breslau-Glogau. Koniev's route would take him through the rich Silesian industrial basin, which Stalin, with an eye to reparations, was anxious to capture without too much damage. Tracing its outline on the map with his finger, Stalin looked at Koniev and uttered the single word "gold"; the marshal needed no further explanation.

The Germans still had over three million men spread out along the eastern front, and to prevent their being concentrated too heavily in the center, on the shortest route to Berlin where the obvious danger lay, simultaneous Soviet offensives were launched on the wings, against East Prussia in the north, into Budapest and on to Vienna in the south.

The attack was opened by Koniev on January 12, by Zhukov on the fourteenth, in each case preceded by massed artillery bombardments of such violence that they left the German troops dazed and shaken. Warsaw was taken on the seventeenth, Cracow and Lodz on the nineteenth. By January 20 the Russians had achieved a breakthrough reaching from East Prussia to the foothills of the Carpathians, 350 miles apart. By the end of

January both Zhukov and Koniev had put advance forces across the Oder, and Zhukov's bridgehead at Küstrin was only forty-eight miles from Berlin.

I V

THIS WAS THE MILITARY SITUATION when the three Allied leaders met for the second time, at Yalta in the Crimea, from February 4 to 11, 1945.

During the fourteen months since the Teheran Conference ended, the military situation had been transformed. Once the British and Americans had landed in France and the Russians had launched their summer 1944 offensive, the outcome of the war was settled, always supposing the Alliance held together. Hitler was quite right to put his finger on this as the crucial question.

But what would have happened to the Alliance if the July 20 plot had succeeded and Hitler had been killed in 1944? Assuming, for the sake of argument, that the war would then have ended in the summer of 1944, instead of May 1945, many lives would have been saved and the worst of the destruction that was inflicted on Europe between the Seine and the Vistula in the last nine months of the fighting would have been avoided. But would the Alliance have survived? Would there have been a separate peace with the West? Would Stalin have been content to halt the Russian advance short of the German frontier? What would the map of postwar Europe have looked like? Any answers, of course, can only be speculative, but the point of raising such questions is to highlight a question that can be answered: Who gained most from the prolongation of the war for those extra nine months?

There is not much doubt about the answer. Not the Germans, certainly, or the British or the Americans. The advantage accrued almost entirely to Stalin and the Soviet regime. Thanks to the advance of the Russian armies into the heart of Europe and the continued expansion of Soviet power, they were placed in a much stronger position for influencing the postwar European settlement relative to that of either of their two allies. This was already becoming clear at the Yalta Conference in February 1945.

Churchill was more anxious about the postwar settlement than Roosevelt and had borne the brunt of the exchanges with Stalin on Poland leading up to the crisis over the Warsaw uprising. In September 1944 he determined to make a bid to overcome the difficulties that had arisen by offering to go to Russia for further face-to-face talks with Stalin. As soon as Stalin agreed, Churchill was in Moscow within a week (October 9) and stayed for ten days.

The British and American armies were by then operating on German territory and were nearer to Berlin than the Russians. This may have helped to account for Stalin's affability toward Churchill, which was more marked than on any other occasion. The meetings began with Churchill producing—in the absence of the Americans—his scribbled suggestion that Britain and Russia should agree to a division of influence in the Balkans, giving 90 percent to the Russians in Rumania against 90 percent to the British in Greece (where British troops occupied Athens while Churchill was in Moscow); 50-50 in Yugoslavia and Hungary, and 75 percent to Russia in Bulgaria. Stalin said nothing, only ticked the notorious half sheet of paper and passed it back. "It was all settled," Churchill recalled later, "in no more time than it takes to sit down." When Churchill, on second thought, asked if it might not be better to burn the paper, Stalin replied: "No, you keep it." [25] Whether Stalin regarded himself as committed to anything is doubtful, but when civil war broke out in Greece and the Americans were loud in their condemnation of the British, no word of reproach, and no encouragement to the Greek Communists, came from Moscow.

Poland was not so easily disposed of. Churchill at least secured Stalin's agreement to Mikolajczyk, the prime minister, and two other members of the Polish government-in-exile joining them in Moscow. But his efforts to promote agreement made no progress. Stalin insisted on Allied recognition of the Curzon Line (redrawn to include Lvov) as the Russo-Polish frontier and of the provisional government based on the Lublin Committee; Mikolajczyk, despite furious reproaches from Churchill behind the scenes, rejected both.

In the interval between the Moscow meeting in October 1944 and the summit meeting at Yalta (February 4–11, 1945) the Red Army carried the war from Poland into Germany. With the end of the war now in sight, both the Western leaders felt the need for a meeting with Stalin to be so urgent that—despite Roosevelt's increasing physical frailty—they accepted his refusal to leave Russia and made the long journey to the Crimea instead. They brought with them, in twenty-five planes, no fewer than 700 officers and officials.

The three leaders approached the conference with different preoccupations and aims in mind. Before the war in Europe ended, Roosevelt wanted to pin Stalin down on Soviet participation in the war in Asia. His other major goal was to secure accord on the World Organization, the only cause to which he believed he could rally public opinion in the U.S.A. and so avoid a return to isolationism. Averell Harriman, whom he had made his personal emissary first to Churchill, then to Stalin, recalls Roosevelt telling him that "he wanted to have a lot to say about the settlement in the Pacific, but that he considered the European questions were so impossible that he wanted to stay out of them as far as practicable, except for the problems involving Germany." [26] The president's genius for improvisation in finding solutions to problems was not as effective in international relations, where he lacked the intuitive grasp he had of domestic affairs. Both Harriman and Chip Bohlen, who acted as Roosevelt's Russian interpreter, believed that he had no idea of the gulf that separated his American experience of politics from that of Stalin, with whom he persisted in believing that he had more in common than with an Old World figure like Churchill, a belief that Stalin naturally encouraged.

The first of Churchill's two primary objectives was to continue into the postwar world Britain's "special relationship" with the United States, which had been the basis of his wartime policy, and to maintain American involvement in European affairs as a key to his second preoccupation, the re-creation of a balance of power in Europe. To achieve that he was set upon resisting the extension of the Soviet sphere of influence, restoring the status of France as a Great Power, and preventing the defeat of Germany being pressed to the point where it left a political vacuum in the heart of Europe.

Stalin's primary aim can be summed up as security after the traumatic experience of the war—the security of Russian territory and the security of the Stalinist system against any renewed threat from external enemies. The way in which he proposed to achieve this was, first, by extending the frontiers of the Soviet Union to include all the territory that had ever been under Russian rule and, second, by creating beyond her extended borders as large a sphere of influence as possible, both in Europe and in Asia, by securing regimes that could be relied upon to respond to the Kremlin's policies and needs. The extent of this remained undefined but would certainly include those territories occupied by the Red Army at the end of the war, while Russia's needs would require, especially from Germany and those countries that had been involved in the war as German satellites, major contributions to make good the huge losses suffered by the Soviet economy.

The meetings [27] began with a review of the military situation, which Stalin used to give the Russians a tactical advantage by underlining the contrast between the Allied armies, still operating west of the Rhine and making no progress in Italy, and the Red Army, which had achieved a breakthrough carrying them over 300 miles in eighteen days and bringing them to the Oder. Stalin's questioning established not only that operations in the west were on a smaller scale than those in the east, but also that his allies could give no guarantee that they would be able to prevent the continuing transfer of German forces to the east.

The triumvirate then turned to the treatment of Germany after the war had been won. Roosevelt proposed that they should discuss the report of the European Advisory Commission, which they had set up at Teheran on the division of Germany into zones of occupation. But Stalin again took the initiative and substituted his own agenda by insisting that the question they must grapple with was the actual dismemberment of Germany. They had agreed to this in principle at Teheran, he said, but they now had to decide—no longer just to discuss—what they meant by dismemberment in practice. Were they proposing a single German government, or separate ones for each of the three zones? If Hitler accepted unconditional surrender, would they be willing to deal with his government? Should not an "unvarnished" reference to the dismemberment of Germany be included in the terms of surrender?

Roosevelt was inclined to agree with Stalin, but Churchill, now very much concerned with the postwar balance of power in Europe, was opposed. He argued that it was sufficient to agree to dismemberment in principle, but that much more time and study were required before they committed themselves to deciding how to carry it out. Stalin himself does not appear to have had a clear idea at this point of any particular scheme for which he would want to press, and Churchill succeeded in keeping dismemberment out of the final communiqué and confined any reference to it in the protocol of the conference (not published until 1947) to "such steps, including the disarmament, demilitarization, and dismemberment of Germany as they [the Allies] deem requisite for future peace and security." [28] A committee of three, with Eden as the chairman, was appointed to study how dismemberment might be carried out. But it never met. The partition of Germany was not planned but came about as a consequence of East-West disagreement.

At the same time, Churchill succeeded in overcoming the opposition of Stalin and the reluctance of Roosevelt to giving the French a separate zone of occupation and inviting them to join the future Allied Control Council for Germany. His argument was that Britain needed a strong France to share the burden of standing guard against Germany, all the more so after Roosevelt's statement that he did not believe American troops would remain in Europe for more than two years after the war—a statement that Stalin certainly noted but did not comment on.

While agreeing to set up a Reparations Commission to be located in Moscow, Churchill refused to commit himself to the figure of 20 billion dollars suggested by the Russians, of which half would go to the Soviet Union. He based his opposition on the fiasco of reparations after the First World War and was not convinced by the Soviet argument that, by asking for reparations in kind, they would avoid the difficulty created on the earlier occasion by trying to claim financial compensation. He was skeptical about Germany's capacity to meet the scale of reparations mentioned and asked who would profit from reducing the Germans to beggary. At one point Stalin angrily demanded whether the British wanted the Soviet Union to get reparations at all, but Churchill would not give way, and the final protocol recorded Britain's refusal to agree to the Russian figure, which Roosevelt accepted as "a basis for discussion" by the Reparations Commission.

Now that the British and American forces as well as the Russians were on German soil and were preparing to cross the Rhine, Stalin was not in a position to press his views on Germany—insofar as they were yet formed. But Poland was a different case. The Red Army was occupying not only Poland but also a large part of the German territory that Poland was to receive, and there was no prospect of any other power entering this closed preserve. On Poland, Stalin had the last word and was determined not to compromise.

Britain and the U.S.A. had already accepted the new Polish frontiers at Teheran and were on weak ground in reopening the question. There was little argument about the Curzon Line, including Lvov, becoming the eastern frontier of Poland. But Churchill had had second thoughts about the proposal he had made at Teheran and had become alarmed at the extent of the territory that Stalin wanted to assign to Poland in compensation, at Germany's expense. In a phrase no historian has been able to resist quoting, he argued, "I do not wish to stuff the Polish goose until it dies of German indigestion." He therefore fought for and obtained a general reference in the final communiqué recognizing "that Poland must receive substantial accessions of territory in the north and west," but leaving the details to be fought over.

The real issue, however, as all three members of the triumvirate recognized, was not frontiers but the composition and independence of the Polish government. Churchill called it the "touchstone" of the conference. Poland was the largest nation of Eastern Europe and (with the exception of the Czech government-in-exile) the only one that was an ally, guaranteed by the Western powers in 1939, not a German satellite. What was decided in the case of Poland would *a fortiori* be applicable to all the other countries occupied by the Red Army at the end of the war. It is not surprising, therefore, that Poland was discussed at seven out of eight plenary sessions of the Yalta Conference and was the subject of nearly 18,000 words exchanged among the three leaders, in addition to lengthy discussions among their foreign ministers and other subordinates.

It is unnecessary to follow the twists and turns of the argument. The objective of the Western powers was to obtain conditions that would guarantee a genuinely democratic and independent government; that of Soviet diplomacy was to keep as tight a grip on Poland as possible without an open break with the West. Stalin spoke with conviction of Russia's need to be sure that Poland would never again be used as an invasion corridor, as it had been twice in thirty years—and by Napoleon before that. At the same time, he showed his skill as a negotiator by linking the differences about Poland to the issue on which Roosevelt was most eager to secure Russian agreement, the American plan for a world organization.

In an earlier session Stalin had shown much suspicion of the American proposals. His change of attitude shown by his readiness to accept them did not open the way at once for agreement on the composition of the Polish government; but it helped, particularly when it was accompanied by a private discussion between Roosevelt and Stalin in which the president secured a firm commitment on Russian entry into the war against Japan after Germany's defeat. In return, Roosevelt agreed to concessions that Stalin claimed he needed to persuade the Russian people to enter into hostilities with a power with which they had no direct quarrel. These included the Japanese cession of the southern part of Sakhalin and the Kurile Islands together with five other conditions which Roosevelt (without first consulting his ally Chiang Kai-shek) undertook to secure from the Chinese.

It took three more days of argument, revision of drafts, and yet more argument by the foreign ministers and their principals before agreement was reached on a joint statement about the Polish government. At one point, pressed by both Churchill and Roosevelt to say when free elections would be held, Stalin disarmed them by replying that they might be as little as one month away—a conciliatory response that committed him to nothing. At another point, to relieve the tension, Stalin fell into his old habit of walking up and down behind his chair while he expounded upon his argument. The final text called for the government recognized by the Russians to be "reorganized" with the inclusion of "democratic" Polish leaders from inside Poland and from exile, and committed it to hold free elections as soon as possible. It was left to Molotov and the American and British ambassadors in Moscow to carry out the consultations leading to reorganization, and the next few months were to demonstrate Molotov's skill in driving a coach and horses through such loosely phrased instructions.

YALTA WAS the high point of the Alliance, and the conference communiqué with its impressive declaration that the three powers had agreed on the terms of "the unconditional surrender which we shall impose together on Nazi Germany" is a reminder, amid the later disillusionment and recriminations, of how much the Alliance had accomplished. It is all too easy to take it for granted from the beginning that Hitler was bound to be defeated. But even after Yalta Stalin, for one, did not exclude the possibility that Britain and the United States might stand back and allow Hitler to concentrate all his forces on defeating Russia. If that had happened, and Nazi Germany had become the dominant power on the continent, then the fate of Europe would have been very much worse than it has been—for all that it has suffered—in the half century since.

The three leaders were aware—certainly Churchill and Stalin—of how precarious their unity might prove to be once the war was over. But for a brief moment, as the Yalta Conference ended, they felt entitled to congratulate themselves on what they had achieved, and Stalin's tribute to Churchill and Roosevelt was as unstinting as theirs to him. There is no doubt that Churchill and Roosevelt were sincere in what they said about the Alliance and the part that Russia had played as their ally. But what about Stalin? Did he really mean what he said about the indispensable contribution the Alliance had made to the defeat of Hitler, or was this merely pro forma?

De Gaulle had *une certaine idée de la France*. Stalin, no less than Hitler, was sustained by a certain idea of *himself,* a conviction of his place in history comparable with that of the greatest of his tsarist predecessors, which enabled him to resolve the contradictions between the different roles he saw himself called upon to play, the contradictions that others, observing him from the outside, found it impossible to resolve. During this same period at the beginning of 1945, when Hitler was becoming more and more desperate in his efforts to preserve his belief in his mission in the face of defeat, the Yalta Conference represented that moment in Stalin's career when reality came closest to confirming his image of himself.

Not only was the Red Army under his direction about to win the greatest victory in Russian history, eclipsing that over Napoleon, but the two most powerful figures in world politics had accepted his insistence that, if they wanted to discuss the future with him, they would have to abandon the search for a mutually convenient meeting place and come to him, however long and tedious the journey. The symbolism of this was not lost on Stalin's Georgian imagination. If they did not come as suppliants, each was eager to court him, sometimes in Roosevelt's case by disparaging the other. In Russia, among the Old Bolsheviks who remembered Lenin and had watched Stalin's rise, he could not get rid of the feeling that they would never accept him as he saw himself. Even those who met his demand for the most fulsome praise he suspected were flattering him out of fear or the desire to curry favor. But to be accepted as an equal and sought after by the president of the United States and the prime minister of Great Britain and her empire, who came accompanied by hundreds of their chief officials, this was a tribute that satisfied even Stalin's suspicious vanity.

Moreover, Stalin was not only accepted as their equal but proved himself to be such in practice. Hitler detested any sort of committee and lost his temper if anyone argued with him. At the only international conference he attended—the Munich conference of 1938—he was so ill at ease that he had to leave Mussolini to take the lead. Hitler conducted his international negotiations either in front of mass meetings or in private interviews, both of which he could be sure of dominating. Stalin, however—to the surprise of those who knew the impatient manner with which he conducted meetings of the Politburo or the military Stavka, where his authority was unquestioned—adapted himself naturally to the cut-and-thrust of debate in an international conference where he could not expect to control the proceedings.

In the company of two such astute politicians as Churchill and Roosevelt, with their long experience of the turmoil of democratic politics, Stalin impressed all who sat around the table with him, or heard him speak, with his mastery of the business, his remarkable memory—he never made a note or consulted a paper—his skill in debate and the quickness with which he could switch from the "roughness" that Lenin had criticized to the charm that Churchill felt even when he resisted it.

Yalta, therefore, was the high point for Stalin in his personal career no less than for the Alliance. Never before had he and the Soviet Union, which he felt himself to personify, been acclaimed so widely throughout the world—and never would they be again, as it turned out. This was the point at which his ambition was realized, and he took his place with the two other leaders of the victorious Alliance in the history of the twentieth century. There is no reason therefore to doubt the testimony of those who were present at the dinner where he proposed the toast of the Alliance that he was as moved as Churchill and Roosevelt by the occasion, and as sincere when he spoke of the unity of the three Allies as the key to peace after the war and of their duty to see that it was preserved. But the emotion of a historic moment and his future policy were quite separate in Stalin's mind. The test of the future viability of the Alliance would not be sentiment or mutual trust but the extent to which its other members were prepared to accept his claims for the Soviet Union in the postwar settlement.

V

THERE COULD NOT BE a greater contrast than that between Stalin's position as he returned from Yalta and that of Hitler, who had returned to Berlin from the west on January 16, 1945 after the defeat of his last gamble. The capital was under snow, which hid the worst of the damage it had suffered from air raids, and although the Chancellery Speer had built for him had gaping holes in its walls, by some quirk of chance the wing in which Hitler had his own quarters had so far escaped. He was able to hold his conferences in it, and for a time sleep there, with the concrete bunker to retreat to when the Allied bombers arrived.

In the period that followed, it is important not to let the dramatic detail obscure the meaning of what was happening. The background was the climax of the war, with the Allied armies advancing into the heart of Germany, and the Russians drawing closer to Berlin. Within the capital itself, which was frequently bombed and finally became a battlefield, the Chancellery and particularly the underground bunker represented a closed world in which a separate drama took place, increasingly isolated from the tremendous drama of war outside. The link between the two was the daily situation reports and conferences, which in the final weeks bore less and less relationship to what was happening in the real world, until this pressed up to and finally threatened to break into the bunker.

The chief actor—one might well say, the only actor—in this separate psychological drama was Hitler, a man engaged in a desperate struggle to preserve the myth with which he had identified himself, his own belief in his Providential mission as Germany's savior. The struggle took the form of an assertion of Hitler's will to resist the spread of a defeatism which saw the war as already lost.

In January, after he learned that Guderian had told Ribbentrop that the outcome had already been decided and Germany was defeated, Hitler silenced all discussion at the daily war conference by declaring:

> I most emphatically forbid generalizations and conclusions in regard to the whole situation. That remains my affair. In the future anyone who tells anyone else that the war is lost will be treated as a traitor, with all the consequences for him and his family—without regard to rank and prestige. [29]

On another occasion in March, in a very different mood, during his tussle with Speer over a scorched-earth policy he said "in an almost pleading tone":

> If you would believe that the war can still be won, if you could at least have faith in that, all would be well. . . .
> If you could at least hope that we have not lost! You must surely be able to hope . . . that would be enough to satisfy me. [30]

Hitler continued to repeat the ritual references to the secret weapons that would transform the war, including now an atomic bomb, and Speer, visiting western Germany in March, was surprised to find party members, as he had former ministers like Funk and now farmers in Westphalia, who still believed that "The Führer has something in reserve that he'll play at the last moment. Then the turning point will come. It's only a trap, his letting the enemy come so far into our country." [31]

But Hitler himself came to rely more and more on the hope of a political miracle, a repetition of the Miracle of the House of Brandenburg, which had saved Frederick the Great. During the Seven Years War (1756–63) Frederick II, as king of Brandenburg-Prussia, found himself faced with a coalition of Austria, Russia, France, and Sweden. His military successes in the field could not offset the alliance's overwhelming superiority in manpower and other resources. At the end of 1761 he wrote that only the intervention of Providence could save him from disaster and from taking his own life.

Frederick's desperate position was dramatically reversed by the death on January 5, 1762, of Tsaritsa Elizabeth of Russia, who had been the driving force behind the anti-Prussian combination. Her successor was her nephew, Tsar Peter III, who had the greatest admiration for Frederick and who broke up the alliance against him by signing a peace treaty with Prussia, restoring all Russia's territorial gains and placing Russian troops at Frederick's disposal to defeat Austria.

This was the miracle that Hitler hoped to see repeated. All his energies were concentrated on holding out long enough for a similar reversal of fortune to take place.

The lesson of 1918 pointed in the same direction. Germany had not been defeated in 1918, Hitler declared; she had been stabbed in the back by the General Staff. If it had not been for its premature surrender, Germany would have gained an honorable peace and avoided all the postwar troubles. "This time we must not surrender five minutes before midnight." [32]

The accusation of universal betrayal was his final resort in preserving his belief in himself: His destiny had been frustrated not by his own failure but by the failure of others. As General Halder later wrote:

> Except at the height of his power there was for him no Germany, there were no German troops for whom he felt himself responsible. For him there was—at first subconsciously, but in his last years fully consciously—only one greatness, a greatness that dominated his life and to which his evil genius sacrificed everything—his own ego. [33]

A young officer who attended one of the conferences described the impression Hitler made on him in February 1945:

> His head was slightly wobbling. His left arm hung slackly, and his hand trembled a good deal. There was an indescribable flickering glow in his eyes, creating a fearsome and wholly unnatural effect. His face and the parts around his eyes gave the impression of total exhaustion. All his movements were those of a senile man. [34]

Nonetheless, to begin with, Hitler continued to make military dispositions and issue orders as if he were still in control of events. He still talked of the Luftwaffe recovering its supremacy, ordered the jet-fighter program to be given priority, approved Jodl's plan to build up an assault army in the east to check the Soviet offensive, and decided to move Sepp Dietrich's Sixth SS Panzer Army to launch an attack in Hungary.

In December 1944 Bormann had contrived to remove Himmler from the Führer's headquarters by proposing to Hitler that the Reichsführer SS, who could call on the resources of his Replacement Army, should be made commander in chief of a new army group formed to defend the line of the Upper Rhine. This appealed strongly to Himmler's military ambitions, which had been frustrated by the ending of the First World War before he could see service in the field. Although Himmler's efforts to hold a bridgehead across the Rhine were unsuccessful, Hitler—again prompted by Bormann, against Guderian's advice—appointed him to form yet another army group, this time to fill the gap that the Russians had opened between the Vistula and the Oder. Himmler's continued absence from Hitler's side, which Bormann himself never left, and his indifferent performance as a commander were to undermine, as Bormann intended, the position the Reichsführer SS had built up as the second man in the Reich.

Göring kept away to avoid further recriminations about the Luftwaffe's failure to prevent the Allies' bombing of Germany. On one of the occasions when he was present, Hitler suddenly turned to him and asked:

> Do you think that, deep down inside, the English are enthusiastic about the Russian developments?
> *Göring*: They certainly didn't plan that we hold them off while the Russians conquer all of Germany. If this goes on we will get a telegram in a few days. . . . [35]

Instead of a telegram, they received the communiqué at the end of the Yalta Conference announcing that the three Allied leaders had reached agreement on the defeat and occupation of Germany and reaffirming their demand for unconditional surrender.

Hitler found consolation in an illuminated model of the rebuilding of his hometown of Linz which was to outshine Vienna and Budapest as the finest city on the Danube. The architect brought the model to the Chancellery in person on February 9, and Hitler went to look repeatedly at it. It was no longer the early days of the party to which he returned but the fantasies of still earlier days in Linz and Vienna, when he had first formed the belief that he had been singled out for some great destiny—still undefined—which Providence (he believed) would even now rescue him to accomplish by another miracle—also undefined. After viewing the model of the new Linz rising from the ashes of the old, in the company of the head of the Gestapo, another Austrian native of the city, Hitler turned to fix him with his famous hypnotic stare and ask, "My dear Kaltenbrunner, do you imagine I could talk like this about my plans for the future if I did not believe deep down that we really are going to win this war in the end?" [36]

FROM THE PERIOD between September 1942 and the beginning of 1945 there are only a few scattered records of Hitler's table talk. In February 1945, however, Bormann recorded a series of monologues that amount to Hitler's justification and political testament. Hitler still insisted that victory was possible if only one held out, as Frederick the Great had held out. At the end of 1761, he too had been cut off in Berlin, with hostile allied armies advancing on him, and in despair had decided to take his own life. At the last moment Providence had intervened; Providence might yet intervene again:

> Like the great Frederick, we too are fighting a coalition, and a coalition, remember, is not a stable entity; it exists only by the will of a handful of men. If Churchill were suddenly to disappear, everything could change in a flash. [37]

Frederick the Great had long been Hitler's favorite character in German history. The sole decoration in the Führer's suite in the bunker in which he ended his life, one of his few treasured possessions, was Graff's portrait of the Prussian king, and the parallel between Frederick's situation and his own fascinated him. But what if Providence did not intervene? Like Frederick, Hitler had made up his mind that he would wait until the last minute; if there was no miracle, then he would take his life. If so, however, Hitler still wanted the last word and he took care to ensure that he had it by dictating *his* version of events in advance for Bormann to see preserved for posterity.

Unlike the earlier table talk, his final reflections had a single theme: the war and the mistakes that had brought Germany to the position in which she now found herself. Had it been wrong to go to war? No, he had been jockeyed into war: "It was in any case unavoidable; the enemies of German National Socialism forced it upon me as long ago as January 1933."[38] The same was true of the attack on Russia:

> I had always maintained that we ought at all costs to avoid waging war on two fronts, and you may rest assured that I pondered long and anxiously about Napoleon and his experiences in Russia. Why, then, you may ask, this war against Russia, and why at the time I selected?[39]

Hitler gave several answers to this question. It was necessary to deprive Britain of her one hope of continuing the war; Russia was withholding the raw materials essential to Germany; Stalin was trying to blackmail him into concessions in Eastern Europe. But the reason to which he always returned:

> And my own personal nightmare was the fear that Stalin might take the initiative before me. . . . War with Russia had become inevitable, whatever we did, and to postpone it only meant that we would later have to fight it under conditions far less favorable. The disastrous thing about this war is the fact that for Germany it began both too soon and too late.[40]

He needed, Hitler declared, twenty years in which to bring his new elite to maturity. Instead the war came too soon:

> We lacked men molded in the shape of our ideal . . . and the war policy of a revolutionary state like the Third Reich has of necessity been the policy of petit-bourgeois reactionaries. Our generals and diplomats, with a few, rare exceptions, are men of another age, and their methods of waging war and conducting our foreign policy also belong to an age that is passed.[41]

But the war also came too late. From a military point of view, it would have been better to fight in 1938 not 1939. Czechoslovakia was a better issue than Poland; Britain and France would never have intervened, and Germany could have consolidated her position in Eastern Europe before facing world war several years later. "At Munich we lost a unique opportunity of easily and swiftly winning a war that was in any case inevitable." It was all Chamberlain's fault: He had already made up his mind to attack Germany but was playing for time and by giving way all along the line robbed Hitler of the initiative.

But the greatest mistakes, Hitler concluded, had been made by Britain and the United States. Britain ought to have seen that it was in her interests to ally with Germany, the rising continental power, in order to defend the imperial possessions that she was now certain to lose.

> If Fate had granted to an aging and enfeebled Britain a new Pitt instead of this Jew-ridden, half-American drunkard [Churchill], the new Pitt would at once have recognized that Britain's traditional policy of balance

of power would now have to be applied . . . on a worldwide scale. Instead of maintaining . . . European rivalries, Britain ought to do her utmost to bring about a unification of Europe. Allied to a united Europe, she would then still retain the chance of being able to play the part of arbiter in world affairs . . . [But] I had underestimated the power of Jewish domination over Churchill's England. [42]

If Britain ought to have allied with Germany, the United States ought to have realized that she had no quarrel with the Third Reich and preserved her isolation. "This war against America is a tragedy. It is illogical and devoid of any foundation in reality." Once again it was due to the same sinister influence, the Jewish world conspiracy against Nazi Germany.

> Never before has there been a war so typically and so exclusively Jewish. I have at least compelled them to discard their masks. . . . I have opened the eyes of the whole world to the Jewish peril. . . . Well, we have lanced the Jewish abscess; and the world of the future will be eternally grateful to us. [43]

Hitler added a postscript. On April 2, prompted by Bormann, he delivered the last of his monologues, in effect a political testament to the German nation. "I have been Europe's last hope," he had declared in February. If Germany were to suffer defeat after all, it would be utter and complete, and a tragedy for Europe as well as the German people. Then with a last burst of prophetic power he drew his picture of the future:

> With the defeat of the Reich and pending the emergence of the Asiatic, the African, and perhaps the South American nationalisms, there will remain in the world only two Great Powers capable of confronting each other—the United States and Soviet Russia. The laws of both history and geography will compel these two powers to a trial of strength, either military or in the fields of economics and ideology. These same laws make it inevitable that both powers should become enemies of Europe. And it is equally certain that both these powers will sooner or later find it desirable to seek the support of the sole surviving great nation in Europe, the German people. [44]

Hitler's forecast was to prove more accurate than those of the three Allied leaders at Yalta.

IN MARCH, Christa Schroeder, one of his secretaries, was sitting at lunch with Hitler, when he suddenly burst out:

> I am lied to on all sides, I can rely on no one, the whole business makes me sick. . . . If anything happens to me, Germany will be left without a leader. I have no successor. The first, Hess, is mad. The second, Göring, has lost the sympathy of the people; and the third, Himmler, would be rejected by the party—and anyway, is useless since he is so completely inartistic.

After standing lost in thought for several minutes, he turned to go, with the words: "Rack your brains again and tell me who my successor is to be. This is the question that I keep asking myself without ever getting an answer."[45]

Yet orders that Hitler gave in the same month of March made clear that he refused to consider any future for Germany and that the most he saw any successor doing was making the surrender. As the war moved onto German soil, he demanded that the same scorched-earth policy be followed as in Russia and the other occupied countries in the east, destroying everything that the German people might make use of to start rebuilding after the war. Speer, who had concluded before the end of 1944 that the war was lost, was shocked by Hitler's attitude and drew up a memorandum in the hope of changing it.

Within four to eight weeks, Speer wrote, Germany's final collapse was inevitable. A policy of destroying Germany's remaining resources in order to deny them to the enemy could not affect the result of the war. "No one has the right to take the viewpoint that the fate of the German people is tied to his personal fate." The overriding obligation of Germany's rulers, without regard to their own fate, was to ensure that the German people should be left with some possibility of reconstructing their lives in the future. Hitler's response was to tell Speer:

> If the war is lost, the people will be lost also. It is not necessary to worry about what the German people will need for elementary survival. On the contrary, it is best for us to destroy even these things. For the nation has proved to be the weaker, and the future belongs solely to the stronger eastern nation. In any case, only those who are inferior will remain after this struggle, for the good have already been killed.[46]

If Speer was able to prevent the Führer's orders being carried out to flood mines, blow up power plants, and destroy communications in advance of the enemy, it was not because he succeeded in changing Hitler's mind, but because he was able to take advantage of the disintegration of his authority.

V I

ZHUKOV'S AND KONIEV'S ORIGINAL HOPE at the end of January that they might be able to go all out for Berlin had been disappointed. The Russians' rapid advance had led them to outrun their supplies of fuel and ammunition. Losses had been heavy, divisional strengths were down to an average of 4,000 men, and their troops were battle weary. Time was required to bring up reinforcements, to overhaul their equipment—they were operating in winter weather—and to regroup. Stalin was anxious about the possibility of a German flank attack and ordered Zhukov, when he opened his next attack on March 1, to swing northward toward the Baltic to occupy Pomerania, not westward to Berlin. Koniev, too, needed to pause and then to conquer Upper Silesia.

On March 28, Eisenhower sent a message directly to Stalin, informing him that the main Allied thrust in their spring offensive would be directed, not at Berlin (as Montgomery proposed), but in the direction of Erfurt-Leipzig-Dresden, under the command of Montgomery's American rival, General Omar Bradley.

Stalin could hardly believe his luck, but he did his best to make the most of it. In his reply, sent on April 1, he praised Eisenhower's plan, agreed that "Berlin has lost its former strategic importance" (for which reason, he said, only secondary Soviet forces would be committed to its capture), and undertook to effect a junction with the U.S. troops in the Leipzig-Dresden area, toward which Soviet forces would, therefore, launch their main attack in the second half of May. Having sent this message to Eisenhower, who took pride in refusing to let political considerations enter into his operational planning, the politically minded Stalin then proceeded to act in precisely the opposite sense. He had a shrewd appreciation of the value of the capture of Berlin by the Red Army—without Allied participation—as the symbol of the Russians' victory over Germany. An urgent summons brought both Zhukov and Koniev to Moscow where, at a conference with the two marshals on April 1, Stalin confronted them with the question: "Well, now, who is going to take Berlin, we or the Allies?" His remark put both men to the test; they accepted the challenge even though it left them only twelve to fourteen days in which to prepare. Some idea of the scale of the preparations is given by the figure of seven million shells delivered by rail to Zhukov's front alone. The Russians kept to their timetable and opened their attack in the early morning of April 16.

Four years before, in April 1941, Hitler had been preparing Operation Barbarossa, confident that the German army would defeat Russia before the winter and open the way to the foundation of the Nazi empire in the east. There have been few more complete reversals in history. The war, which had swept as far as the outskirts of Moscow in November 1941, was now reaching its climax in the outskirts of Berlin. The German army, with the aging Home Guard (*Volkssturm*) and the young lads of the Hitler Youth serving alongside the Wehrmacht and SS formations, fought with the courage of despair. Millions of refugees fleeing from the east brought news of the revenge that the Red Army was exacting for all that the Russian people had suffered. Crude roadside posters urged the Red Army men "Not to forget—Not to forgive," to be pitiless in meting out retribution. They had not only fought but killed indiscriminately, raped, looted, and burned their way through the cities and countryside of eastern Germany; their thirst for revenge and pillage could be expected to reach its peak when they broke into Berlin, "the lair of the Fascist beast." The whole German people was now paying the price for the war Hitler had started so confidently and the unspeakable crimes the Nazis had committed, in which not all but a great many other Germans, including the German army, had been involved.

· · ·

BY APRIL 1945 Hitler had not only lost control of events but also had the greatest difficulty in finding out what was happening. He no longer showed any grasp of the situation, deciding at the end of March that the Soviet buildup at the approaches to Berlin was only a feint and that the main Russian attack would be in the south, aimed at Czechoslovakia. He insisted on transferring SS panzer divisions from the Oder front to the south, the same mistake he had made earlier in moving the Sixth SS Panzer Army to Hungary. His orders became wilder, his demands more impossible, his decisions more arbitrary.

The final scenes of Hitler's career were played out in the Chancellery bunker, into which he moved, so he said, to get some sleep during the air raids. Speer thought it had a symbolic significance as well.

> This withdrawal into his future tomb . . . put the final seal on Hitler's separation from the tragedy which was going on outside under the open sky. He no longer had any relationship to it. When he talked about the end, he meant his own and not that of the nation. He had reached the last station in his flight from reality, a reality that he had refused to acknowledge since his youth. At the time I had a name for this unreal world of the bunker: I called it the Isle of the Departed. [47]

The level to which the hopes of Hitler and his few remaining intimates had been reduced is illustrated by their reception of the news of Roosevelt's death on April 12. A few days earlier Goebbels had read Hitler the passage in Carlyle's *History of Frederick the Great* in which he describes the Miracle of the House of Brandenburg and the death of the tsaritsa, Elizabeth. Hitler had been deeply moved, and Goebbels had sent for the horoscope of the Führer, which, he claimed, had been astonishingly right about the war and now predicted a great success for Germany in the latter half of April, followed by peace in August. When he heard that Roosevelt had died he phoned Hitler in great excitement: "My Führer! I congratulate you! Roosevelt is dead. It is written in the stars that the second half of April will be the turning point for us." [48] Hitler was equally excited, but the relief did not last long. Unlike the tsaritsa's, the president's death made no difference to the Allied operations. The Americans reached the Elbe and joined up with the Russians, and on April 16 Zhukov and Koniev launched their final attack on Berlin.

Outnumbered and outgunned, the German troops still put up determined resistance. After a barrage laid by 9,000 guns the First Byelorussian Front could not force the German defenses west of the Oder, and Zhukov came in for the rough edge of Stalin's tongue when he failed to achieve a breakthrough until the fourth day of the attack. By April 20, however, both Zhukov's and Koniev's forces were inside the city limits, fighting their way toward the center, street by street.

The twentieth was Hitler's fifty-sixth birthday. In the afternoon he met a group of sixteen-year-olds from the Hitler Youth who were preparing to take part in the battle for the capital, and, at the conference that followed, all the Nazi leaders and the heads of the three services were present for the last time. Their advice was in favor of his moving to Obersalzberg while there was still time. But Hitler, while appointing Admiral Dönitz to command in the north, left open the question whether he would fly to the south and take command there or stay and lead the fight for Berlin.

On the twenty-first, with Russian artillery now firing directly into the capital, he ordered a counterattack by an SS force under General Fritz Steiner to relieve the city, building the most exaggerated hopes on its success. Throughout the twenty-second he kept on demanding news of Steiner's progress. Not until the middle of the afternoon did he learn that no attack had taken place and that the Steiner force was still being organized. This discovery brought the breaking point.

It took the form of a furious outburst which left everyone who witnessed it, or even heard it from outside the room, shaken and exhausted. Hitler denounced his generals, shouting that he was surrounded by traitors and liars. Even the SS now told him lies. No one had ever seen him lose control so completely. The end had come, he declared. The war was lost. There was nothing left but to die. In the middle of his raging, his body was shaken by a violent spasm and he appeared to lose consciousness. When he recovered, he announced that he would meet his end there in Berlin. Those who wished could go to the south; he would never move.

After Eva Braun had told him that she would stay, too, and had been rewarded by a kiss on the lips—a gesture no one had ever seen before—Hitler sent for Goebbels, the only one left besides Bormann whom he trusted. Goebbels told him he, too, would stay and take his life; his wife volunteered to do the same and give poison to their children. In preparation they moved into the bunker, while Hitler sent for his papers and picked out those to be burned.

There followed a final interview with Keitel and Jodl, who still tried to persuade him to leave for the south. Hitler refused to listen. He could not fight, he said, because physically he was a broken man, but he would stay in Berlin until it fell and then at the last moment shoot himself. Neither alive nor dead would he fall into enemy hands. The generals persisted, pointing out that the greater part of the German forces were in the south and that if negotiations were to be started it was now only from outside Berlin that this could be done. If he himself had abandoned hope, he was still the supreme commander, responsible for those still fighting under his orders. "It is simply impossible after you have been directing and leading for so long, that you should suddenly send your staff away and expect them to lead themselves." Hitler insisted that he had no orders to give; if they wished for orders, they should apply to Göring. They protested that there was not a single German soldier who would fight under the Reich marshal. Hitler replied: "There is no question of fighting now; there's nothing left to fight with. If it's a question of negotiating, Göring can do do it better than I can."[49] Jodl at least was still sufficiently true to the Prussian tradition to be outraged by Hitler's behavior: It was an officer's duty—above all, a supreme commander's duty—to give orders and take responsibilities, not to throw in his hand and behave like a hysterical prima donna.

The physical atmosphere of the bunker was oppressive, but this was nothing compared to the pressure of the psychological atmosphere. The incessant air raids, the knowledge that the Russians were now in the city, nervous exhaustion, fear and despair produced a tension bordering on hysteria, which was heightened by propinquity to a man whose changes of mood remained entirely unpredictable.

After the storm of the twenty-second, and now that his decision was made, Hitler became calm and even congenial. He ordered a meal to be served to Keitel before he left for the south and sat with him while he ate, then took care to see that he had sandwiches and half a bottle of brandy for the journey. Speer returned to Berlin the next day, the twenty-third, driven by some inner compulsion that he did not understand to risk death in order to confess to Hitler that he had not carried out his demolition orders but had done his best to block them. Hitler, who now appeared drained of all emotion, heard him out without reacting, and, although "deeply moved" by his account, made no comment.

> I felt [Speer wrote later] as if I had been talking with a man already departed. I have often asked myself since whether he had not always known instinctively that I had been working against him during these past months . . . and whether by letting me act contrary to his orders he had not provided a fresh example of the multiple strata in his mysterious personality. I shall never know.[50]

Before Speer left, he witnessed another example. Göring had been thrown into a state of painful uncertainty when he was told of Hitler's remark that, if it came to negotiating, "the Reich marshal can do better than I can." While his entourage urged him to act to end the war, he was suspicious of a trap, particularly by Bormann. After getting Hans Lammers, the state secretary, to fetch from the safe the decree of June 1941 which named him as the Führer's successor, he decided to radio Hitler for confirmation:

> My Führer,
> In view of your decision to remain at your post in Berlin, do you agree that I take over, at once, the total leadership of the Reich, with full freedom of action at home and abroad, as your deputy, in accordance with your decree of June 29, 1941 . . . ?[51]

Göring, whose message ended with protestations of loyalty, asked for an answer before the end of the day. It did not take long, however, for Bormann, who had been waiting for years to put Göring down, to persuade Hitler that Göring's message was an ultimatum.

Speer reports that Hitler became unusually excited, denouncing Göring as corrupt, a failure, and a drug addict, but adding: "He can negotiate the capitulation all the same. It does not matter anyway who does it."[52]

The addition is revealing. Hitler was clearly angry at Göring's presumption—the habits of tyranny are not easily broken. He agreed to Bormann's suggestion that Göring should be arrested for high treason, and he authorized his dismissal from all his offices, including the succession—yet "it does not matter anyway." As Speer pointed out at his trial at Nuremberg, all Hitler's contempt for the German people was contained in the offhand way in which he made this remark.

To try to make too much sense out of what Hitler said or ordered in those final days would be wholly to misread both the extraordinary circumstances and his state of mind. Those who saw him at this time, and who were not so infected by the atmosphere of the bunker as to share his mood, regarded him as closer than ever to that shadowy line that divides the world of the sane from that of the insane. He spoke entirely on the impulse of the moment, and moods of comparative lucidity, such as that in which Speer had talked to him on the twenty-third, were interspersed with wild accusations, wilder hopes, and half-crazed ramblings.

Hitler found it more difficult than ever to grasp the situation outside the shelter. On the night of the twenty-sixth the Russians began to shell the Chancellery, and the bunker shook as the massive masonry split and crashed to the ground. The Russians were less than a mile away and only a handful of exhausted companies fighting from street to street stood between them and Hitler's shelter. Yet Hitler still went on talking about an army under the command of General Walther Wenck moving up to the relief of Berlin. On the twenty-eighth he radioed Keitel: "I expect the relief of Berlin. What is Heinrici's army doing? Where is Wenck? What is happening to the Ninth Army? When will Wenck and Ninth Army join us?"[53] The answer to Hitler's questions was simple: General Wenck's forces, like the Ninth Army, had been wiped out; General Heinrici's army was in retreat to the west to avoid surrender to the Russians.

On the evening of the twenty-eighth, Hitler was handed a message which precipitated the final crisis. It consisted of a brief Reuter report to the effect that Himmler had held meetings with the Swedish Count Folke Bernadotte for the purpose of negotiating an end to the war.

Himmler's spell as commander in chief of Army Group Vistula had been brief and inglorious. He failed to regain the initiative or counterattack the Russians and took to his bed, spending more and more time in the Hohenlychen clinic of the SS chief medical officer, Karl Gebhardt, claiming to be suffering from influenza and angina. In mid-March Guderian persuaded him to resign "in view of all his other responsibilities." For some months, various members of the SS, with Himmler's knowledge, had been pursuing contacts that they believed might open the way to negotiations with the Western Allies.

The most persistent in urging Himmler to do something to end the war and secure the future of the SS was the young head of the Ausland SD (the SS Foreign Intelligence Service), Walter Schellenberg, who made common cause with Felix Kersten, Himmler's Finnish masseur, in bringing Count Bernadotte, a nephew of the king of Sweden and vice president of the Swedish Red Cross, to meet Himmler at Hohenlychen on February 19, 1945. Bernadotte hoped to secure the release of Scandinavian prisoners held in concentration camps. Himmler, however, was highly nervous and very divided in his mind: "I have sworn loyalty to Hitler," he told Bernadotte, "and both as a soldier and a German I cannot go back on my oath. Because of this I cannot do anything in opposition to the Führer's plans and wishes." [54] Bernadotte visited him a second and a third time during April, and still Himmler could not bring himself to speak out.

But reports of the dramatic scene at the conference on April 22, and Hitler's declaration that the war was lost and that he would seek death in the ruins of Berlin, made much the same impression on Himmler that they had made on Göring. "Everyone is mad in Berlin," he declared. "What am I to do?" Both men concluded that loyalty to Hitler was no longer inconsistent with steps to end the war, but while Göring telegraphed to Hitler for confirmation of his view, Himmler more wisely acted in secret.

On the night of April 23–24, while Hitler was raging at the disloyalty of Göring, Himmler accompanied Schellenberg to Lübeck for another meeting with Count Bernadotte at the Swedish consulate. This time Himmler was prepared to put his cards on the table. Hitler, he told Bernadotte, was quite possibly dead; if not, he certainly would be in the next few days.

> In the situation that has now arisen [Himmler continued] I consider my hands free. I admit that Germany is defeated. In order to save as great a part of Germany as possible from a Russian invasion I am willing to capitulate on the western front in order to enable the Western Allies to advance rapidly toward the East. But I am not prepared to capitulate on the eastern front. [55]

Bernadotte finally agreed to forward such a proposal through the Swedish Foreign Office, while Himmler, now seeing himself as Hitler's successor, proceeded to consider whom he would appoint as ministers in his new government. As Bernadotte had warned Himmler, he returned with the reply that the Western Allies refused to consider a separate peace and insisted on unconditional surrender. But by then reports that Himmler was attempting to negotiate had been published in London and New York.

Hitler was beside himself at the news. "His color rose to a heated red and his face was unrecognizable. . . . After the lengthy outburst, Hitler sank into a stupor, and for a time the entire bunker was silent." [56] Göring had at least asked permission first before beginning negotiations; Himmler, *"der treue Heinrich,"* in whose loyalty he had placed unlimited faith, had said nothing. That Himmler should betray him was the bitterest blow of all, and it served to crystallize the decision to commit suicide, which Hitler had threatened on the twenty-second, but which he had not yet made up his mind when to put into effect.

Hitler's first thought was revenge, and Bormann, who had already made sure that Göring was under arrest, now had the satisfaction of removing Himmler as well from the succession before the Third Reich crumbled into dust. Himmler's representative with the Führer, Hermann Fegelein, had already been arrested after it had been discovered that he had slipped quietly out of the bunker with the apparent intention of making a discreet escape before the end. The fact that he was married to Eva Braun's sister Gretl was no protection. He was now subjected to a close examination on what he knew of Himmler's treasonable negotiations, then taken into the courtyard of the Chancellery and shot.

Himmler was more difficult to reach, but Hitler ordered Ritter von Greim, whom he had summoned to Berlin to appoint commander in chief of the Luftwaffe in place of Göring, to make the attempt to get out again by plane and make sure that Himmler was arrested at all costs. In a trembling voice, Hitler shouted: "A traitor must never succeed me as Führer. You must go out to ensure that he will not." [57] Von Greim got away after midnight on the morning of April 29, and between 1 a.m. and 3 a.m. Hitler gave his reward to one human being at least who had remained true to him by marrying Eva Braun. Afterwards, they drank champagne and talked nostalgically of the old days with the few remaining members of Hitler's staff, Bormann and Goebbels (the two witnesses of the marriage), until Hitler retired with a secretary to dictate his Political Testament and Will.

Unlike Mussolini, who finished his career a broken man, a fugitive no longer recognizable as Il Duce who had once strutted the world stage, Hitler took his own life and ended it defiant without a word of regret or remorse, with his belief in himself as a man of destiny intact. If the end was defeat, the fault was that of others who had failed to play their part. Facing death and the destruction of the regime he had created, he was still recognizably the same Hitler, his mind as tightly closed as twenty years before when he wrote *Mein Kampf,* from which most of what he had to say in his Political Testament could just as well have been taken.

Characteristically, his last message to the German people contained at least one striking lie. Ignoring his abandonment of his responsibility for the men still fighting and for the nation he declared he loved, he spoke of the National Socialist spirit of resistance exemplified by:

the fact that I myself, as founder and creator of the movement, have preferred death to cowardly abdication or even capitulation. . . .

From the sacrifice of our soldiers and from my own unity with them unto death will spring up in Germany the seed of a radiant renaissance of the National Socialist movement. [58]

In the second part of the testament, he announced his arrangements for the succession. Göring and Himmler were expelled from the party and from all offices of state. Admiral Dönitz was his surprise choice for president of the Reich and supreme commander of the armed forces (a final insult to the army)—and Hitler then proceeded to nominate his government for him. Goebbels and Bormann had their reward, the first as the new chancellor, the second as party minister.

The last paragraph returned once more to the earliest of Hitler's obsessions: "Above all I charge the leaders of the nation and those under them to scrupulous observance of the laws of race and to merciless opposition to the universal poisoner of all peoples, international Jewry." [59]

Hitler's will was shorter and more personal. While he had been unable to take the responsibility of marriage during the years of struggle, he declared, he had decided to take as his wife "the woman who after many years of faithful friendship, returned of her own free will to share my fate." Such possessions as he had he left to the party, or if that no longer existed to the state—with the exception of his collection of pictures, which he left to found a gallery in his hometown of Linz. Bormann was named as executor and charged with various bequests to his fellow workers.

While Hitler retired to sleep, Goebbels sat down to compose his own last contribution to the Nazi legend, an "Appendix to the Führer's Political Testament." For days Goebbels had been talking in extravagant terms of winning a place in history. "Gentlemen," he told a conference at the Propaganda Ministry on April 17,

> in a hundred years' time they will be showing a fine color film describing the terrible days we are living through. Don't you want to play a part in that film? Hold out now, so that a hundred years hence the audience does not hoot and whistle when you appear on the screen. [60]

Goebbels's gift as a propagandist did not desert him. Despite Hitler's order, he declined to leave his leader's side and finished his apologia with the promise "to end a life which will have no further value to me if I cannot spend it in the service of the Führer."

Before copies of the documents were sent to Dönitz's headquarters, Hitler added a final message to the armed forces. If it had not been granted to him to lead them to victory, despite their sacrifices, it was because "disloyalty and betrayal have undermined resistance throughout the war." The war had been begun by the Jews—and lost by the General Staff. In neither case was the responsibility Hitler's, and his last word of all was to reaffirm his original purpose: "The aim must still be to win territory in the East for the German people." [61]

During the course of the twenty-ninth, news arrived of Mussolini's end. He too had shared his fate with his mistress, Clara Petacci. Caught by Italian partisans on the shore of Lake Como, they had been shot and their bodies taken to Milan to hang on display in the Piazzale Loreto.

Hitler had no intention of being put on show either alive or dead. On the thirtieth, after saying good-bye to his staff and having a quiet lunch with his secretaries and his cook, he ordered his chauffeur to bring 200 liters of gasoline to the garden above the bunker. Further farewells were said in the company of his wife, Frau Hitler, and the two then retired to the Führer's suite.

Those waiting outside heard a single shot. When they opened the door, they found Hitler lying dead on the sofa: He had shot himself through the temple. His wife lay beside him, also dead: She had taken poison.

Hitler's instructions for the disposal of their bodies were followed to the letter. They were carried upstairs and laid side by side in a shallow depression in the garden. Braving the Russian shells which were bursting on the Chancellery, Hitler's SS adjutant, his valet, and his chauffeur soaked the corpses in gasoline and then set fire to them. As the flames blazed up, the little group of mourners on the porch stood at attention and gave the Hitler salute. Later the charred remains were swept into a piece of canvas and covered over with earth.

It was twelve years and three months to the day since Hitler had appeared on the balcony to the cheering crowds as chancellor of the German Reich. The same evening, a Russian soldier planted the Red Victory Banner on the top of the Reichstag. Appropriately, it was General Chuikov, the heroic defender of Stalingrad, who received the surrender of the city.

ONCE THE SORCERER was dead, the spell that he still exercised to the last over those around him was broken. An attempt was made on the night of May 1–2 at a mass escape from the bunker, and a surprising number succeeded in getting out. Bormann was among them, and for a long time it was believed he had made good his escape. Not until 1972 was a body, believed to be his, found near the bunker and not until 1974 did a comparison between the skull and the dental records establish that it was indeed Bormann's.

Goebbels was not among those who tried to get away. After giving poison to his six children, he and his wife walked up the stairs to the bunker garden, where an SS orderly shot both of them. The bodies were soaked in gasoline and set alight, but they were not destroyed; the Russians found them the next day.

For a long time, however, the Russians insisted that Hitler's remains had never been found; Stalin himself told Harry Hopkins that the story of Hitler's end struck him as dubious and refused to rule out the possibility that he had escaped with Bormann. In fact, on Stalin's orders, an immediate search had found the charred bodies of Hitler and Eva Braun, identified by an autopsy carried out on May 8, 1945 in the Buch Hospital in Berlin by five Soviet doctors. Why Stalin and his successors held back this information for twenty-three years has never been explained. It was not until 1968 that it was published, characteristically not in an official statement, but in a book written by a Soviet journalist, Lev Bezymenski,[62] brought out by a West German publisher, without any explanation of why he had been allowed access to the medical reports and photographs along with other material from the Soviet archives. It then emerged that Hitler's and Eva Braun's identity had been established by comparing their teeth with the dental records found in the ruined Chancellery. The doctors' report also confirmed that Hitler had only one testicle and suffered from the condition known as monorchism.

The doctors' examination left them in no doubt that Hitler, like Eva Braun, had committed suicide by crushing a cyanide ampule in his mouth. After interrogating a number of witnesses who had been present in the bunker and heard a shot, the Russians concluded that this had been fired either by Linge, Hitler's valet, or his adjutant Günsche, acting on Hitler's orders to make sure that he was dead.

Further details were uncovered as a result of interviews with several of the Russians involved which were published in the London *Sunday Express* in 1992.[63] Custody of the bodies was entrusted to a SMERSH* unit reporting directly to Stalin, who was still not satisfied and ordered a second autopsy to be held. This confirmed the findings of the first, and what remained of the bodies was then buried in a garage in Magdeburg and covered with asphalt. Again on Stalin's orders, however, Hitler's organs, which had been placed in jars during the autopsy, were removed to the Kremlin.

The day before the first autopsy was completed, on May 7, 1945, the efforts of Admiral Dönitz to avoid capitulation failed, and General Jodl and Admiral Hans Georg von Friedeburg put their signatures to an unconditional surrender of all the German forces. The Third Reich had outlasted its founder by just one week.

---

*SMERSH (*Smert' shpionam,* Death to Spies) was the name Stalin gave to a secret counterintelligence service, responsible directly to him, which was set up in late 1942.

NINETEEN

Stalin's New Order

I

WITH GERMANY'S DEFEAT and Hitler's death, the Grand Alliance of 1941–45 had achieved its purpose. After all its shortcomings have been acknowledged, to have combined sufficiently to accomplish that much and win a decisive victory in the greatest of all wars was enough to make it one of the most successful in history. For the history of alliances is not an encouraging one; few have accomplished more, most nothing like so much.

Hitler's suicide, however, removed the most important factor holding the Alliance together. How fragile was the mutual confidence among its members, even before the war with Germany had ended, was shown by the accusations Stalin launched and Churchill and Roosevelt vigorously rebutted less than a month after meeting together at Yalta. The consultation between Molotov and the two ambassadors in Moscow over the enlargement of the provisional Polish government turned into a prolonged wrangle over the interpretation of their terms of reference. This was overtaken in the course of March by a much bigger flare-up over the secret contacts between the SS General Wolff and the Allied command in Italy. The Russians had been kept informed of these and Soviet officers invited to take part; but when a German plenipotentiary appeared at Allied headquarters Molotov demanded that the talks in Switzerland be broken off at once and charged that negotiations had been taking place behind the back of the USSR: This was no mere "misunderstanding" and must be construed as "something worse." At the same time, the Allies were informed that Molotov would not attend the San Francisco Conference at which the future world organization, the United Nations, was to be set up, while Stalin—after endorsing Eisenhower's view that Berlin was only of secondary importance—had secretly instructed Zhukov and Koniev at all costs to capture the German capital first.

Charges of bad faith against his allies culminated in Stalin's message of April 3 to Roosevelt:

You insist that there have been no negotiations yet. It may be assumed that you have not yet been fully informed. . . . My military colleagues do not doubt that negotiations have taken place and have ended in an agreement with the Germans on the basis of which the German commander Marshal Kesselring has agreed to open the front and permit Anglo-U.S. troops to advance to the east, and the Anglo-Americans have promised in return to ease the peace terms for the Germans. I think my colleagues are close to the truth. . . .

As a result of this the Germans have stopped fighting against England and America, while they continue the war against Russia, the ally of England and the United States.

Roosevelt's reply, drafted by General Marshall, flatly rejected the accusations and ended with a paragraph that Churchill was sure the president himself had added, which he in turn endorsed: "Frankly, I cannot avoid a feeling of bitter resentment toward your informers, whoever they are, for such vile misrepresentations of my actions or those of my trusted subordinates."[1]

The reports had no substance in them, and the sharpness with which Roosevelt replied evidently made Stalin realize he had gone too far. Without withdrawing the charges, his response disclaimed any intention, in "speaking his mind frankly," of giving offense, and was accepted by Roosevelt on April 12 as closing the matter.

That same day the president died, and there is every indication that Stalin and Molotov were genuinely disturbed by the removal from the scene of a man who had gone out of his way to try to establish relations of trust with the Soviet leadership. As a gesture Stalin agreed that Molotov should attend the San Francisco Conference after all: It would provide an opportunity to size up Roosevelt's unknown successor, his vice president, Harry Truman. In the meantime there was no letup in the Soviet drive to stake out their claims by pushing their troops as far west as possible, regardless of losses. Following the capture of Vienna and the surrender of Berlin, on May 8, Marshal Koniev, on Stalin's express orders, made sure that it was Russian not American troops that liberated Prague.

Seeing the historic capitals of Central Europe fall one after the other, Churchill wrote to Eden (then in the U.S.A.) of the nightmarish prospect of all Europe east of a line from Lübeck to Trieste coming under the domination of Russia—"an event in the history of Europe to which there has been no parallel."[2]

At this stage, to avoid the charge of a Communist takeover, Stalin took care to see that the governments formed, with Soviet approval, were coalitions of radical and peasant parties with Communists holding key ministries, such as the Ministry of the Interior responsible for the police. In the case of Hungary, four non-Communist parties were represented and Communists held only two ministerial offices. In Bulgaria a similar coalition had been formed under the umbrella of the Fatherland Front.

During March 1945 the same pattern was followed in three other countries. At Russian as well as British insistence, Tito included Ivan Šubašić and five other non-Communist ministers in exile in a twenty-seven-strong People's Front government. When they found they were without power and resigned in the course of the summer, Tito accused them of treacherously seeking to provoke foreign intervention. In Rumania, after Communist demonstrations and an ultimatum from Vyshinsky, now the Soviet deputy foreign minister, King Michael was forced to dismiss the Radescu government and install Pétru Groza's National Democratic Front, in which Communists held the Ministry of the Interior and two other ministries. In Czechoslovakia, President Beneš returning from London had to accept a People's Front formed in Moscow with Zolenek Fierlinger (the fellow-traveling Czech ambassador to the USSR) as a figurehead prime minister and representatives of four Czech and two Slovak parties. Communists held the Ministry of the Interior, giving them control of the police and the army, which had been trained in the Soviet Union, as well as three other key ministries—agriculture (land reform), information, and education.

Poland, however, was still the touchstone. The Soviet-imposed regime was encountering more resistance than the Russians had expected, and in March the Russians invited sixteen leaders of the Polish underground to discuss how relations could be improved. Assured of immunity, they presented themselves at Marshal Zhukov's headquarters. After that they were neither seen nor heard from again, and inquiries as to what had happened to them received no reply.

At the end of April Churchill wrote a long and passionate letter to Stalin, declaring that, while Britain would never favor a Polish government hostile to the Soviet Union, the British had gone to war in 1939 on account of Poland.

> They can never feel this war will have ended rightly unless Poland has a fair deal in the sense of sovereignty, independence, and freedom, on the basis of friendship with Russia. It was on this that I thought we agreed at Yalta.

Churchill ended his letter:

> There is not much comfort in looking into a future when you and the countries you dominate, plus the Communist parties in many other states, are all drawn up on one side and those who rally to the English-speaking nations on the other. It is quite obvious that their quarrel would tear the world to pieces. . . . Even embarking on a long period of suspicions, of abuse and counter-abuse and of opposing policies would be a disaster hampering the development of world prosperity for the masses.[3]

Stalin's reply was uncompromising and showed how wide was the gap between them. It was Poland's unique position as a neighbor of the Soviet

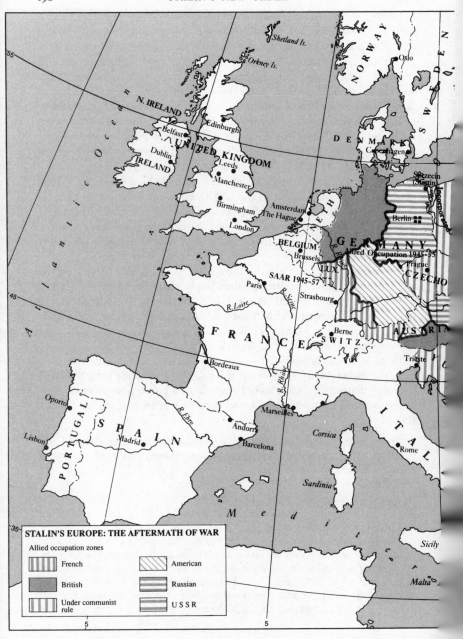

STALIN'S EUROPE: THE AFTERMATH OF WAR

Allied occupation zones

French	American
British	Russian
Under communist rule	USSR

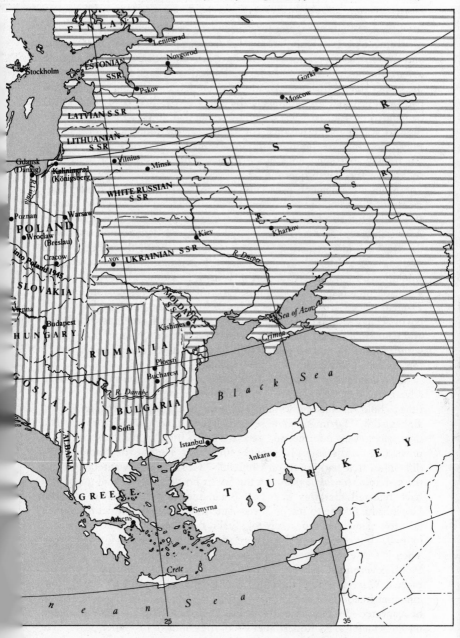

Union and the key to the latter's security that had to be taken into account. It was not enough to suggest for consultation or as members of the Polish government persons who "are not fundamentally anti-Soviet": "We insist and shall insist . . . on persons who have actively shown a friendly attitude toward the Soviet Union and who are honestly prepared to cooperate with the Soviet state." Stalin informed Churchill that the missing sixteen Poles had been arrested for sabotaging the safety of the Red Army and would be handed over for trial. He ended by saying that, in view of the British refusal to accept the provisional government as the foundation of a future Polish government, on the Tito-Šubašić model in Yugoslavia, "I must say frankly that such an attitude excludes the possibility of an agreed solution of the Polish question."[4]

Further disagreements over Tito's attempt to secure Trieste and arrangements for the Allies' joint occupation of Austria added to Churchill's anxiety about the future of Europe and led him to press for the British and American forces that had overstepped the agreed demarcation lines with the Russians in Germany not to be withdrawn, until there had been a meeting and a "showdown" with Stalin. It is doubtful if such a proposal would have found much support in Britain; at a time when the Japanese were still undefeated, it found little favor, if any, in Washington. Instead, Truman placed great hopes on a visit to Moscow by Roosevelt's personal envoy, Harry Hopkins, producing an improvement in relations with Stalin, and Churchill bowed reluctantly to the president's decision in favor of the withdrawal of American and British troops to their agreed zones before the three of them met.

Stalin went out of his way to show every courtesy to his visitor and to take advantage of the absence of Churchill. Beginning in late May, he found time to hold six consecutive meetings in the Kremlin with Hopkins and the ambassador, Harriman, some sessions lasting as long as four hours. The discussions were informal and relaxed, Stalin friendly and reasonable but unyielding on the issues he thought important. He put the blame for the difficulties that had arisen on Churchill: "Great Britain wanted to revive the system of *cordon sanitaire* on the Soviet borders." Churchill might well have retorted that this was what Stalin himself was trying to do; but Hopkins had come to rescue Soviet-American relations, and let the British take the blame. He repeatedly told Stalin that Poland "was not important in itself," but only as a problem in relations between the two Great Powers. Then it was easily solved, Stalin said. He offered four or five places in a Polish government of twenty to be filled by persons not associated with the present Warsaw group (the Yugoslav model again), and he assured Hopkins that freedom of speech and all the other democratic freedoms would be respected—except of course for Fascist parties. Hopkins was not briefed on Polish affairs. As Robert Sherwood, the editor of his papers, says, "He recognized such names as Mikolajczyk or Lange, but as other names came up he had no direct knowledge of their background or reliability." It

sounded all right. When he tried to get Stalin to release the sixteen imprisoned leaders, Stalin shook his head; he could not interfere with judicial
procedures, but hoped their sentences would not be too long.

Leaving Hopkins to report his proposal, Stalin repeated the tactic that
had proved successful at Yalta. The Soviet delegation to the San Francisco
Conference had revived the objections to voting in the Security Council of
the United Nations organization which the Americans had believed settled
at Yalta. On instructions from Washington, Hopkins expressed the American disappointment and asked Stalin to reconsider. Stalin said: "Molotov,
that's nonsense," adding that, if a further look at the documents confirmed
his view, a telegram would be sent that night. The telegram was sent and
the change in the Soviet position—to the great relief of the Americans—
assured the adoption of the UN charter. As Harriman commented: In doing
business with the Soviets, one had to be prepared to buy the same horse
twice.

The Hopkins talks ended inconclusively after ranging over the whole
catalogue of Russian complaints against the Western Allies—the abrupt
ending of Lend-Lease (which had been hastily resumed), China, Japan, and
Germany—the last leading Stalin to remark, "In my opinion, Hitler is not
dead but is hiding somewhere." But the visit had not been in vain: Although not expressed in so many words, there were the makings of a deal.
Stalin overruled Molotov on the Security Council procedure; Truman and
Churchill accepted the Soviet offer on Poland, including a cabinet post as
a vice-premier for Mikolajczyk as the best they could get, and recognized
the Warsaw government. [5] Thus, before the three leaders met in Germany
in July 1945, Stalin's persistence and diplomatic skill had worn down the
opposition and had added to his allies' acceptance of the eastern frontier of
Poland at Yalta the second item on his Polish agenda, their recognition of
the kind of government he had first mentioned at Teheran in 1943. All that
remained was to secure agreement on the third item, Poland's western
frontier.

THE LAST of the summit meetings took place at Potsdam between July
16 and August 2, 1945. Roosevelt had already been replaced by Truman and
his secretary of state, Jimmy Byrnes, and halfway through, as a result of the
British general election, Churchill and Eden were replaced by Clement
Attlee and Ernest Bevin, leaving Stalin as the only survivor of the original
triumvirate. A ruined Berlin could not house the conference and their first
visit to Germany brought home to all the participants the appalling damage
caused by five and a half years' fighting, extending all the way from the
Volga to the French Atlantic ports and London. How destruction on a scale
never even imagined before in human history could ever be overcome was
a question that weighed on everybody's mind—that, together with the
estimated figure of forty million who had died in Europe as a result of the
war, and a number of the same magnitude who had been uprooted from

their homes and turned into refugees. This was the background, never to be lost sight of, to all the arguments and attempts to find settlements during the remaining years of Stalin's life—how to restore the economy and the security of a stricken continent.

It was the great missed opportunity of the postwar period that the condition of Europe, instead of uniting the wartime Allies in a common effort to relieve it, became the issue around which their most bitter quarrels developed. The pattern of charge and countercharge, which became so depressingly familiar in meetings of the Council of Foreign Ministers, and the propaganda war between East and West, already began to take shape at Potsdam. While the British and Americans produced reports of abuse of their power by the Russian occupying forces and local Communist parties in Eastern Europe, the Russians rebutted these and demanded to know why the British were suppressing democracy and supporting "Fascists" in Greece.

In a letter that he wrote just before the Yalta Conference, George Kennan, at that time counselor in the U.S. embassy in Moscow, raised the question whether the best course was not "to divide Europe frankly into spheres of influence—keep ourselves out of the Russian sphere and keep the Russians out of ours." Such a course, as Kennan spelled it out, would have meant writing off Eastern and Southeastern Europe, accepting the complete partition of Germany, and forming a Western European federation to include the western half of Germany.[6] This was not so far from the outcome for which the West finally settled, after years of angry argument with the Russians. No one can say whether, if it had been conceded in 1945, and perhaps supported by the large reconstruction loan for which the Russians tentatively asked, so radical an answer to the problem of East-West relations would have avoided the breakdown that followed. But there can hardly be any doubt that American and British public opinion at the end of the war would never have allowed their governments to consider such a scheme.

It is unlikely that Stalin ever thought there was a chance of the Western powers agreeing to such a solution outright. What he hoped for was to achieve the same result by the power of intervention given by Russian occupation, combined with verbal reassurances to the West, such as the promise to consult "the democratic, anti-Nazi forces" and the Declaration on Liberated Europe,* deprived of any meaning by Molotov's obstructive diplomacy and never implemented in practice. Provided the process was gradual and piecemeal, Stalin calculated that the Western powers would protest but accept it once it was a fait accompli.

The soundness of Stalin's calculation is shown by the answer to one of the two questions that occupied more time than anything else and aroused

*Signed by all three powers at Yalta, this guaranteed "the right of all peoples to choose the form of government under which they live."

the sharpest disagreement at Potsdam—Poland's western frontier. At Yalta the British and Americans had agreed to see Poland given compensation for her territorial losses to Russia in the east by acquiring the greater part of East Prussia and extending her frontier in the west to the River Oder at Germany's expense. No agreement, however, had been reached on the line farther south and whether this was to follow the eastern or the western Neisse. The difference was substantial: Between the two branches of the Neisse lay the city of Breslau and the rich industrial area of Silesia. To their anger the Western powers discovered that the Russians had already settled the matter, without either consulting or informing them, by including Silesia along with the other parts of Germany they transferred to Polish administration. This particular fait accompli brought a sharp clash between Stalin and Churchill, but the fact that the Red Army occupied all the territories concerned proved decisive. Neither the British nor the Americans, now that the war in Europe was over, were going to try to force the Russians and the Poles out.

The other major issue at Potsdam, however, the Soviet claim for reparations from Germany, showed that Stalin's calculation did not apply to areas where the Western powers rather than the Russians were in occupation. The Russians had not waited for the conference to start before taking everything that was movable from their own zone of occupation, but they were not prepared to forgo their claim to reparations from the rest of Germany, particularly from the British-occupied Ruhr, which Stalin tried unsuccessfully to bring under four-power occupation. What they were offered, instead, was a compromise which would combine a "Russian" solution on the issue where the Russians had the obvious advantage, the western Neisse for the Polish-German frontier, with a "Western" solution on reparations, where the Russians were asking for something the Americans and the British had the power to refuse.

In return for abandoning the sum of 10 billion dollars for which they were pressing, the Russians had to accept the principle that each occupying power should meet its claim to reparations from its own zone plus, in the case of the Soviet Union, an additional percentage of the industrial equipment in the western zones not required for the German peacetime economy. In the event, the additional element became a subject of dispute and the Russians got little beyond the reparations they took from the eastern zone.

Mindful of the experience of those who drew up the Treaty of Versailles, their successors at Potsdam agreed not to try to produce a peace settlement too hastily, but to turn over to a new body, the Council of Foreign Ministers, the task of drafting peace treaties first with Italy and the former satellites of Germany. Only when those had been signed—after four or five years—were the foreign ministers to turn to Germany. As a result, although the final communiqué contained no fewer than thirty-seven paragraphs dealing with Germany—demilitarization, de-Nazification, and so on—it said nothing about her political future or frontiers when the occupation came to an end.

The four powers (they had now been joined by France) failed to recognize, however, the political consequences of their reparations deal. While the "Economic Principles" of the conference protocol proclaimed that Germany would continue to be treated as an administrative and economic unit, in practice the arrangements made for reparations worked to keep Germany divided along the lines of the occupation zones. The barrier that the Russians placed in the way of exchange of any sort between their own and the three other zones provided an inexhaustible subject for recrimination between the Occupying Powers.

THE DAY AFTER Truman arrived at Potsdam, he received news of a successful explosion of an atomic bomb at the U.S. test grounds in New Mexico. After lengthy discussion it was agreed with the British to mention to Stalin casually that the Allies had a "new weapon of unusual destructive force," without disclosing its character. Stalin said he was glad to hear of it but showed no special interest, leading Churchill and the others who were watching closely to conclude, with relief, that Stalin knew nothing of the Anglo-U.S. research and the massive American effort to produce an atomic weapon. In this they were mistaken and were to remain in ignorance of the Russians' progress with their own atomic project until, to their astonishment, a Soviet nuclear device was successfully exploded in 1949.

In 1942 G. N. Flerov, a young Soviet physicist serving in the air force on the Voronezh front, wrote to Stalin personally that he was convinced from a study of foreign scientific journals in the Voronezh University library that their silence about nuclear fission meant that an American project was under way. Flerov appealed for a nuclear laboratory to be created for the purpose of "building the uranium bomb." At the end of 1942 the State Defense Committee set up such a laboratory under the direction of Igor Kurchatov, who was Flerov's teacher and has been described as the Soviet equivalent of the American Robert Oppenheimer. The scale of the Soviet operation was small, but by the time the first American bomb was exploded, Kurchatov had begun work on designing an industrial reactor to produce plutonium.

In the meantime Stalin learned of the progress made by the Americans as a result of reports passed secretly to him by the physicist Klaus Fuchs working at Los Alamos and by the British diplomat Donald Maclean, who dealt with atomic matters in the British embassy in Washington. After concealing that he understood the significance of Truman's remark, as soon as Stalin got back to his villa he said to Molotov: "We shall have to have a discussion with Kurchatov about speeding up our work." On his return to Moscow he sent for Kurchatov and told him: "Request all you need. Nothing will be refused." Stalin duly noted not only that the Americans now had a bomb but also that they and the British had never mentioned to him the effort they were making to develop one, or the hopes they had for it. [7]

It was a secret not only from Stalin, but from the British Labour party leaders Attlee and Bevin as well, both members of Churchill's five-man coalition war cabinet, who replaced him halfway through the Potsdam Conference. While awaiting the results of the British general election held in July, Attlee as well as Churchill had been a member of the British delegation; but it never occurred to Stalin that the British electorate would remove Churchill from office at the very moment of victory. The result not only surprised but startled him, confirming his rooted belief that elections where the outcome was not guaranteed were too dangerous to be allowed. Like most people encountering Attlee for the first time, Stalin dismissed him with the remark "he does not look like a greedy man." [8] Attlee was a shrewd observer, however, and in his turn gave an impression of Stalin that for a single-sentence portrait would be hard to better: "reminded me of the Renaissance despots—no principles, any methods but no flowery language—always Yes or No, though you could only count on it if it was No." [9]

It would take years for political leaders to form a realistic judgment of how much and in what way international relations would be affected by the threat of nuclear warfare. But Stalin had a quick foretaste in the Far East of the difference it could make. In his talks with Harry Hopkins he had made clear the importance he attached to the Soviet Union's taking part in the war against Japan. The Japanese continued to try to persuade him to mediate between them and the Western Allies, but to no avail. Stalin was far more interested in the gains he hoped to make and informed the Americans that the Soviet attack would begin on August 8.

Marshal Vasilevsky, who had been given the command in the Far East, had more than a million and a half troops at his disposal to launch an attack aimed at linking up with the Chinese Communists and securing the occupation of Manchuria. The Russians, however, were not informed of the American decision to drop the atomic bomb, first on Hiroshima on August 6, then on Nagasaki. This brought the war in the Far East to an end in less than a week, so leaving (and being intended to leave) the Russians with far less time than they had counted on to secure their objectives. Stalin, however, ignoring the Japanese capitulation, ordered the Russian forces to push on as rapidly as possible regardless of losses. As a result they were able to complete the occupation of central Manchuria, capture Port Arthur, and secure the northern half of Korea, while separate operations, not completed until September 1, brought them the whole of Sakhalin and the Kurile Islands.

Stalin pressed Truman for a Soviet occupation zone in Japan itself, but the Americans regarded Japan in a very different light from Europe and were determined to make it as much an exclusive sphere of influence as the Soviet Union's was in Eastern Europe.

NONETHELESS as the second Great War in thirty years at last came to an end, Stalin had every cause for satisfaction. He had not secured everything he bid for at Yalta—the deal on German reparations, for example, had yet to be put to the test—but he had come remarkably close. If the Russian victory was above all due to the tremendous exertions of the Russian people both in the armed forces and in the industries and communications that kept them supplied, success in turning that victory into the hard currency of political advantage was due to a diplomatic *tour de force* on his part in the final stages of the war that equaled Hitler's before it began.

In their technique and in the circumstances that the two dictators exploited there were obvious differences, but they had at least two things in common that gave them an advantage over democratic opponents—or allies. One was an instinctive grasp of the relationship between diplomacy and force, between war and politics. In Hitler's case this can be seen in his use of the threat of force, exploiting the democracies' fear of war; in Stalin's, in his insistence that military operations must always take account of political objectives, and his recognition that the shape of the peace settlement would be affected, if not determined, by the way the fighting ended. The other was their use of double-talk to disguise political chicanery. In Hitler's case it was the language of the League of Nations, the appeal to national self-determination, the removal of injustice, and equality of rights; in Stalin's, the vocabulary of democratic socialism, popular fronts, anti-Fascism, free elections, universal suffrage, as well as respect for the national sovereignty of the Soviet Union's socialist allies.

In principle all three of the Allied leaders were in favor of keeping the Alliance in place. But in practice, as Stalin had already said at Yalta, difficulties they had not known in wartime would threaten if once they no longer had a common enemy to unite them. Even if the original triumvirate had remained together, the return to peacetime conditions would have made it impossible for Roosevelt and Churchill to continue to commit their countries without going through the normal democratic process of "advise and consent" or without the need to consult other powers. Their successors, Truman, Attlee and Bevin, with none of the shared experience of having had, out of necessity, to make cooperation work during the war, were less prepared to accept Stalin's justification of Soviet policy for the sake of preserving the facade of unity. For his part, Stalin could see advantage in resuming the traditional Soviet stance of the leading socialist country under permanent threat from a hostile capitalist world.

The Cold War did not begin in earnest until 1947–48. The deterioration in relations was slow and uneven. Peace treaties were agreed, and signed with Italy and the other former satellites before the end of 1946, and Bevin and Marshall spent seven weeks in Moscow in the spring of 1947 trying to reach agreement on a German settlement. Not until the end of 1947 did the

London conference of the Council of Foreign Ministers break up with no date fixed for its next meeting. By that time, however, the council had already become a platform for each side to attack the other's good faith, and "the spirit of Yalta" was no longer recognizable in their bitter exchanges.

II

VICTORY IN THE GREATEST of all Russia's wars marked the high point in the relationship between Stalin and the Russian people, just as Yalta marked the high point in his acceptance as Russia's leader in the international community.

The appeal to traditional Russian patriotism had played a great part in rallying the Russian people to support the government against the invaders. Stalin as the national leader, the heir to the tsars, had figured much more prominently in the cult devoted to his name than Stalin as the revolutionary leader, the heir to Lenin. In the defiant speech that he delivered at the Red Square parade on November 7, 1941, with German troops already on the outskirts of Moscow, he addressed his audience as "Brothers and sisters," not "Comrades," and evoked the memory of six victorious Russian military leaders of prerevolutionary times, beginning with Alexander Nevsky, who routed the Teutonic Knights in 1242, and ending with Kutuzov, the conqueror of Napoleon in 1812 and hero of Tolstoy's *War and Peace.*

The war became known in Russia not as the Second World War but as the Great Patriotic War, the Great Fatherland War, and the National War of Liberation, while Stalin underlined his identification with the Red Army—once it was successful—by promoting himself to marshal and thereafter always wearing a marshal's uniform. In 1944 he superintended in person the adoption of a new national anthem in place of the "Internationale," ordering Soviet Russia's two leading composers, Shostakovich and Aram Khachaturian, to collaborate in producing an entry for the competition. His choice, however, was an anthem by Grigori Alexandrov, the director of the Red Army chorus, the words of which included the line "Stalin raised us."*

Of greater significance was the reconciliation with the Russian Orthodox Church, the traditional bastion of Russian nationalism and the tsarist regime, which now became associated with the cult of Stalin and resumed its role as a state church. The invasion and the terrible casualties awakened a strong tide of religious feeling in the country and the Metropolitan Sergius† issued an appeal to all believers, calling on them to defend their country.

---

*Shostakovich gives a hilarious account of his encounter with Stalin, describing how Grigori Alexandrov, "choking with delight and the saliva of a faithful retainer," announced that Stalin had singled out his entry as the successful one.

†Metropolitan was a title conferred upon the bishops of the most important sees or provinces of the Russian Orthodox Church. During the period of repression Metropolitan Sergius was the acting head of the church and was elected its official head, or patriarch, in 1963.

In September 1943—four months after he abolished the Communist International—Stalin received the three metropolitans and concluded what amounted to a concordat with them, allowing them for the first time since the revolution to elect a patriarch of Moscow and all Russia as well as a holy synod, and to open a theological institute. This too had its effect on Western opinion. The first action of the Council of Bishops was to adopt "A Condemnation of Traitors to the Faith and to the Motherland" which threatened with excommunication all who collaborated with the forces of Anti-Christ.

As the Russian armies freed their country of the German invaders, all the powerful emotions of traditional Russian patriotism, magnified by the losses and the suffering, were focused on the heroic figure of Stalin. At the great victory parade to mark the fourth anniversary of Hitler's attack, the Red Army saluted the architect of victory, Stalin, standing on top of the Lenin Mausoleum. At his feet they threw the banners and standards of Hitler's army, as Kutuzov's soldiers had thrown those of Napoleon's army at the feet of Tsar Alexander. The next day it was the turn of Moscow to pay him tribute for the defense of the city in 1941; the day after, he was proclaimed Hero of the Soviet Union and given the unique title of generalissimo.

At a reception in honor of the Red Army commanders the month before, Stalin, for the first and only time admitted:

> Our government made not a few blunders; there were moments of desperation in 1941 and 1942 when our army retreated, abandoned our native villages and cities . . . because it had no choice. Another nation might have said to the government: "You have not justified our expectations, get out; we will set up a new government which will sign a peace with Germany and give us repose." But the Russian people did not take that road because it had faith in the policy of its government. Thank you, great Russian people for your trust. [10]

After that brief moment of candor, the party line that Russia owed victory in the Great Patriotic War to the military genius and heroic leadership of Stalin was set in stone. For forty years no one was allowed to ask who had been responsible for decapitating the Red Army in the prewar purges; who had gained most from the Nazi-Soviet Pact, Russia or Germany; why no notice was taken of the warnings of a German attack and the Russian armed forces were forbidden to prepare for it; why for the first eighteen months of the war Stalin had tried to conduct the war singlehanded and held the professionals at arm's length, preferring to rely on such creatures as Mekhlis, Kulik, Voroshilov, and Budenny, with the encirclement of huge numbers of Russian troops as a consequence; and why Russian military losses (13.6 million including prisoners who died in captivity) were so much greater than German (3.25 million on all fronts) and the civilian loss of life double.

These questions were first discussed openly in 1987–88 and aroused furious controversy. [11] Stalin's critics did not deny that after the disastrous first eighteen months he began to establish a better working relationship with the generals and that then his strong, if arbitrary, political leadership was a great asset. But against this they set, for the first time, the cost of the mistakes made earlier and Stalin's responsibility for them. The anger these revelations aroused, including the anger of many of the older generation who resisted accepting them, showed how effectively "the cult of personality" and what Trotsky called the Stalin school of falsification had worked to blind the Russian people—and for a long time millions outside Russia—to the true character of the regime under which they lived.

But the euphoria of victory and Stalin's gratitude to the Russian people did not last long. Victory had been accompanied by the widespread and passionate hope among the Soviet peoples that things would now be different, that the future would be brighter, that they might enjoy the chance to live normal lives, or at least a breathing space after all the efforts and sacrifices demanded of them. Stalin reacted against this as he had against a similar mood in the party when the Congress of Victors met in January 1934, after the effort and sacrifices demanded by the forced drive for industrialization and collectivization. Stalin's speech of February 9, 1946, immediately attracted attention by the different note it struck. The forms of address he had used during the war—"Brothers and sisters," "My friends, my countrymen"—were discarded in favor of the party greeting "Comrades." And the familiar question-and-answer dialectic was restored. Who had won the war? It was no longer the Russian people: "Our victory means above all that our *social* system has won . . . that our *political* system has won." [12] Stalin reminded his audience—the "electors" to the Supreme Soviet and beyond them the whole nation—of the battles he had had to fight to push through collectivization and rapid industrialization, against the opposition of both the Trotskyites and the right. Were they expecting more consumer goods after the sacrifices of the war? But under Communism heavy industry must continue to have priority. Were they expecting the collective-farm system to be modified, even abolished? No, collectivization remained the cornerstone of the Soviet system. Did they think peace had come to the world? How could there be a lasting peace while capitalism and imperialism were still powerful?

The Soviet people must work harder than ever before in order to carry out the next Five-Year Plan and achieve an annual production of 60 million tons of steel, 60 million of oil, and 500 million of coal. "Only then will our country be guaranteed against all eventualities."

Those who remembered the sort of speech Stalin had delivered in the 1930s must also have recognized the anger with which—even after the defeat of Hitler—he lashed out again at unseen enemies, who had said that the Soviet system was a risky experiment, that it was held together only by the secret police and that one push from the outside would bring the whole Soviet Union tumbling down like a house of cards.

There was nothing on the international scene in February 1946 to account for such a switch from the celebration of victory to a warning of the dangers with which the country was still surrounded. The Grand Alliance had not yet given way to the Cold War. Churchill had not yet delivered his "iron curtain" speech at Fulton, Missouri—and was heavily criticized in Britain and the U.S.A. when he did. There was wrangling between the wartime Allies, but no more than there had been after 1918; their foreign ministers had just met in Moscow and were preparing to hold a peace conference in Paris.

The danger at which Stalin aimed his warning was not from external enemies, but from a relaxation of that combination of threat and effort, a lifting of that permanent state of siege and mobilization, on which the Stalinist system depended not only for success in the task of reconstruction as much as in war, but also for its continued existence. Churchill showed insight when he said: "They fear our friendship more than our enmity." Stalin conceived of the future of the Soviet Union—could only conceive of it—as a revolutionary struggle still to be completed. For psychological as well as political reasons, the search for "enemies of the people" must be resumed, still requiring the demands the state must continue to make on its subjects and still justifying the vigilance of the NKVD and the perpetuation of his own power. His speech of February 1946 served notice on the Soviet peoples that, if the war was over, the emergency was not. As the Russian author Vasily Grossman wrote in his great novel of the 1941–1945 war, *Life and Fate,* "The silent quarrel between the victorious People and the victorious State was continued after the War."[13]

STALIN'S ATTITUDE was made clear in the treatment of the huge number of Soviet citizens who, through no fault of their own, had been brought under German rule or exposed to conditions of life outside the Soviet Union. Over sixty million had lived and suffered under occupation by the Germans. Millions more had been taken prisoner and, where they had not died from maltreatment, had now been liberated by the Red Army. Still more millions had been drafted as forced labor to work in German factories and farms. Hundreds of thousands had fought as partisans against the occupying forces.

Stalin viewed all of these not with sympathy but with suspicion. In his eyes, all were suspect of collaboration, treason, or at the very least contamination with foreign ideas and subversive thoughts. Many no doubt had collaborated with the occupying forces, volunteered for service with German-recruited "legions" and auxiliary formations, or submitted to be drafted for work in the Reich. But many had done so not out of disloyalty but from the instinct to survive when abandoned to their fate by the retreating Soviet armies. The individual circumstances were of no interest to Stalin. Special NKVD units moved into the occupied Soviet territories as they were regained by the Red Army and started to arrest and deport anyone against whom a neighbor could be found to inform—often without even as much evidence as that.

Without waiting for the invading Germans to arrive, the Volga Germans, who had been settled in their homes since the time of Catherine the Great in the eighteenth century and formed the Volga German Autonomous Republic, had been deported en masse to Central Asia and Siberia. After the brief German occupation of the Caucasus was over, in 1943 and 1944 they were followed by the entire population of five of the small highland peoples of the North Caucasus, as well as the Crimean Tatars—more than a million souls—without notice or any opportunity to take their possessions. There were certainly collaborators among these peoples, but most of those had fled with the Germans. The majority of those left were old folk, women, and children; their men were away fighting at the front, where the Chechens and Ingushes alone produced thirty-six Heroes of the Soviet Union. Over 100,000 NKVD troops were employed to uproot these peoples. Similar deportations took place from the Baltic states as they were occupied, and in his famous speech to the Twentieth Party Congress of 1956, Khrushchev brought the house down with his remark that Stalin would have deported the entire Ukrainian nation, all forty million of them, if they had not been so numerous and if he had had any place to deport them to.

Stalin's suspicions were not limited to those in occupied territory but extended to the officers and men of the armies that had borne the brunt of the initial German attack. The huge number of Russian troops taken prisoner in the first eighteen months of the war convinced Stalin that many of them must have been traitors who had deserted at the first opportunity. Any soldier who had been a prisoner was henceforth suspect—even if he subsequently escaped (as many did from encirclements for which Stalin's orders were responsible) and either joined the partisans in occupied Russia or made their way back to the Russian lines. All such, whether generals, officers, or ordinary soldiers, were sent to special concentration camps where the NKVD investigated them. Reporting to Stalin on the work carried out by the NKVD in the rear of the Red Army, Beria gave figures of 582,000 servicemen and 350,000 civilians who had been "checked" in such camps during the year 1943, before the real flow began. In May 1945 Stalin directed the commanders of the six fronts that had carried the war into Germany and Central Europe to set up no fewer than 100 similar camps in their rear zones, each capable of accommodating 10,000 prisoners of war and other Soviet citizens due for repatriation who must first be "processed" by the NKVD.

At the end of the war, there were five and a half million Soviet nationals, prisoners of war, and Soviet civilians deported as foreign workers in those parts of Germany and other countries occupied by the Western Allies. Stalin was determined to get them all back and very largely succeeded. He sent NKVD missions to track them down and where necessary put pressure on them, including the use of force, to return. Of the 5.7 million Soviet prisoners of war captured by the Germans, as many as four million had died in captivity. In searching out the survivors, Stalin had the cooperation of the British and American military authorities, who were anxious to secure the safe return of their own prisoners of war liberated from German camps by the Red Army. Many of the Russians were unwilling to go and protested that, if they did, they would be shot without trial or sent to the camps. Despite their appeals, force was used to send them back to Russia, where all too often their fears proved to be justified. Twenty percent were sentenced to death or twenty-five years in camps; only 15 to 20 percent were allowed to return to their homes. The remainder were condemned to shorter sentences (five to ten years), to exile in Siberia, and forced labor—or were killed or died on the way home. [14]

No one, of course, could deny that there were real difficulties in distinguishing among those, whether prisoners of war, foreign workers, partisans, or simply people living under German occupation, who in some way betrayed their country, and those who were in no way to blame for the situation in which they found themselves. What was characteristic of the Stalinist system was the readiness with which guilt was made the automatic assumption (as it had been in the campaign for collectivization and the purges), even if this meant injustice to hundreds of thousands of innocent people.

Who cared if it did? At a reception in June 1945, during the victory celebrations, Stalin went out of his way to drink a toast for once to "the tens of millions of ordinary people who have few offices and whose status is unenviable but without whom the marshals and commanders could not do anything." If they had ceased to work, he declared, it would have been the end. What impressed Stalin's critics, however, was that even when he was at his most benevolent, in drinking a toast that he never repeated, the word he used to refer to "the tens of millions of simple, ordinary modest people" was *vintiki,* literally "little screws," translated as "cogs in the great state machine," a phrase he repeated: "the *vintiki* who keep our great state machine in motion . . . the people who maintain us as the base maintains the summit." [15]

EVEN THOSE at the summit were vulnerable. Marshal Zhukov, one of the few men Stalin had ever allowed to stand up to him in argument, ended the war as deputy to Stalin as the supreme commander, as commander in chief of the Soviet forces in Germany and Russian member of the Allied Control Council. But his popularity with the Russian people and with the Allies as the Soviet Union's leading military figure aroused Stalin's jealousy as well as suspicion. In 1946 Stalin summoned him to the Kremlin and told him:

Beria has just written me a report on your suspicious contacts with the Americans and the British. He thinks you'll become a spy for them. I don't believe that nonsense. But still it would be better for you to go somewhere away from Moscow for a while. I've proposed that you be appointed commander of the Odessa Military District. [16]

Until after Stalin's death, Zhukov was obliged to stay away from Moscow, at first in Odessa, then in the Urals Military District. The press stopped writing about him and by the third anniversary of the capture of Berlin *Pravda* could describe the battle without even mentioning him—the whole operation had been planned by Stalin, to whom it was now customary to refer to as a "military genius." The names of the other famous wartime commanders also disappeared from the press: among them Rokossovsky, Tolbukhin, Koniev, Voronov, and Malinovsky. Stalin was determined not to share his military glory with any of them.

Unlike their predecessors, however, neither Zhukov nor the other marshals were arrested or executed. This was the difference between the later 1930s and the later 1940s, and extended to the political as well as the military leadership. The membership of the Politburo indeed showed remarkable stability. Of its eleven full members after the war, six (besides Stalin) had been full and two more candidate members in 1939. Eight of the eleven emerged as still members of the Presidium (as the Politburo had been renamed) after the crisis of Stalin's final months; only one (Voznesensky) had been arrested and executed.

Stalin himself was sixty-five at the end of the war, and no man could go through such an experience in his sixties without some loss of vital powers. Although he remained the head of both the government and the party, his authority derived not from any office he might hold, but—as Hitler's had—from his person. It was unquestioned in any matter in which he chose to interest himself, but his interest and his knowledge of what was going on were more restricted than in the 1930s.

During the war Stalin had been absorbed by military and diplomatic matters, assigning much of the responsibility for management of the economy and of war supplies to other members of the State Defense Committee (GOKO). It was through the part they played in this that the newer members of the Politburo, Malenkov and Voznesensky, rose to prominence. Although GOKO was abolished when peace came, they and other members of the Politburo continued to exercise a de facto authority as "overlords" for the same range of activities as they had become responsible for in wartime— Malenkov for industry, Beria for the police, Voznesensky for planning (he was chairman of Gosplan), Molotov for foreign affairs, Mikoyan for foreign trade, Kaganovich for railways and construction. They were able to do this because, in addition to taking part in discussions of policy and politics in the party's Politburo, all of them also exercised the power to get things done through their position at the top of the state hierarchy, as heads of ministries, deputy chairmen of the Council of Ministers (a position held by all those named), and chairmen of the various state committees under the council.

As before, Stalin kept a tight hand on foreign relations. There were no more summits, and first Molotov (until 1949), then Vyshinsky, represented the Soviet Union in the Council of Foreign Ministers. But neither had any freedom to depart from his instructions without first consulting Stalin. If, in domestic affairs, he was content to leave his deputies with more leeway, it was because he knew that in their rivalry with one another and their competition for scarce resources, each was aware that his ability to win and keep the support of "the boss" could be decisive. None of them trusted any of the others; any alliances were temporary and agreement on one issue was compatible with fierce opposition on another. This enabled Stalin to play them off against one another and to change them around—as he did in agriculture, for instance, assigning it to Malenkov, Andreyev, and Khrushchev in turn, none to his satisfaction—while all the time leaving himself free to intervene if he thought fit.

An example of Stalin's personal intervention and of his attention to detail, which only came to light twenty years after his death, was in the sensitive question of currency reform. At five o'clock on a morning in January 1943, when the battle of Stalingrad was nearing its climax, Stalin phoned his minister of finance, A. G. Zverev, and for forty minutes talked to him about currency reform. During the war the persistent imbalance between the supply of money in the hands of individual citizens and the goods and services available had greatly increased. A series of state loan campaigns had failed to mop up this excess purchasing power, which Stalin thought threatened the whole economy. He had therefore hit on the idea of a devaluation which could be presented as a last demand for sacrifice on the part of the people and as a contribution to the reconstruction of Russia at the end of the war. Zverev was told to prepare a plan on these lines in the greatest secrecy. A year later Stalin introduced Zverev's draft to the Politburo and in the autumn of 1945 invited him to his vacation home in the Crimea to discuss the plan further. Awaiting the right moment, he went over every detail of the design of the new currency and the presentation of the scheme to the public. It was not until December 16, 1947, almost five years after he first set Zverev to work, that Stalin was ready to implement it, with immediate effect—at a ratio of one to ten for currency in hand (aimed at speculators but hitting peasants as well, who rarely used banks), though at par for the first thousand rubles, rising to two to one for money held in a bank account. [17]

Stalin was, of course, largely dependent on other members of the Politburo for information, and they in turn on the middle and lower ranks of the bureaucracy, all of whom had long experience in covering up. This was offset by the advantage all saw in informing on one another, a practice Stalin encouraged, as when he sent Kaganovich to "help" Khrushchev in the Ukraine, in practice (as the latter well understood) to send back a stream of adverse reports. A more serious disadvantage was Stalin's resistance to accepting evidence of anything—for example of the famine in the Ukraine in 1945–46, which Khrushchev reported, and of rural conditions in general—which went counter to what he wanted to believe, and the reluctance of those around him to run the risk of falling into disfavor through trying to convince him.

Within the magic circle of the Politburo, reputations and influence rose and fell. How often the full body met is not known. According to Khrushchev, such sessions occurred only occasionally and Stalin had the habit of setting up commissions—known as "quintets" or "sextets"—from which the older members such as Voroshilov and Andreyev, and eventually Molotov and Mikoyan too, were excluded. Decisions were often made informally at the supper parties in Stalin's dacha at Kuntsevo, to which only those members of the Politburo in favor at the time were invited.

A key position was control of the party's Central Secretariat (formerly the Secretariat of the Central Committee), through which Stalin himself had risen to power. He remained its head but no longer so active in its day-to-day direction, which was in the hands of the other secretaries. Zhdanov had already become one of these, along with Stalin, Kirov, and Kaganovich, in 1934. He succeeded Kirov as boss of Leningrad, becoming a full member of the Politburo as well in 1939, and was regarded by many as the coming man. His rival was Malenkov, six years younger, who did not join the Politburo until 1941, but in 1939 on Zhdanov's proposal had been put in charge of the Cadres Directorate of the Secretariat—the function Stalin had turned to such advantage—and during the war made a big reputation as an administrator when he took over responsibility for supervising industry and transportation as well.

In 1943 Malenkov was appointed chairman of the Committee on the Rehabilitation of Liberated Areas, and at the end of 1944 of another major committee, this time to deal with the dismantling of German industry for reparations. The rough-and-ready methods employed, however, and the waste that resulted left him open to criticism, carefully orchestrated by Zhdanov. This in turn led to the appointment of a commission headed by Mikoyan, and the recommendation that dismantling should be replaced by setting up Soviet-owned corporations to manufacture goods for the Soviet Union in Germany. This time Malenkov was on the losing side and paid for it by being dropped from the Secretariat in 1946.

His place had already been taken by Zhdanov. Zhdanov had spent most of the war in Leningrad, where he had more than once come in for sharp criticism from Stalin. Early in 1945, however, with Leningrad now liberated, Stalin called him back to Moscow. The move may have been intended to offset Malenkov's rapid rise—that was certainly the effect it had—but more important is the change of policy it represented: a change that has permanently identified the years 1946–48 with Zhdanov's name as the *Zhdanovshchina,* the suffix intended to point up the association with that other hateful period in Soviet history, the *Yezhovshchina,* the purges of 1936–38.

.   .   .

THE *Yezhovshchina* and the *Zhdanovshchina* had one thing in common: the responsibility for the policies that Yezhov and Zhdanov carried out was not theirs, but Stalin's; the price for being given a free hand to implement them was to take the blame for them. Faced with the huge task of reconstruction, Stalin believed that, far from relaxing, it was necessary to restore discipline; to revive the ideological as well as the patriotic authority of the regime; to insist on the uniqueness of the Soviet Union as a Marxist-Leninist state (in Stalin's version), to reemphasize its superiority and separateness from the West, all contact with which and imitation of whose subversive individualism must be banned under the threat of severe penalties. It was not enough to conduct a witch-hunt among the millions who had been exposed to the West's corrupting influence during the war. The Communist party, which had become demoralized as a result of the purges and overshadowed by the state machine, must be revitalized and resume its role of leadership, launching a propaganda campaign to mobilize the masses, checking and coordinating the work of the state ministries.

Zhdanov, identified throughout his career with the party rather than with the state or the NKVD, was an obvious choice to carry out such a policy. In August 1946 the attack on artistic and intellectual life, which was at the heart of the *Zhdanovshchina*, was opened by the publication of a Central Committee decision denouncing two Leningrad literary journals, *Zvezda* and *Leningrad*. Their offense was to have published "apolitical" and "ideologically harmful" work by such authors as the satirist Mikhail Zoshchenko and the poet Anna Akhmatova. One was "reorganized," the other closed down. Zhdanov followed this up by appearing in person at a meeting of Leningrad writers and elaborating his criticisms. Zoshchenko was denounced for his *Adventures of a Monkey,* which "oozed anti-Soviet poison" and implied that the ape house of a zoo might be a better place to live than Soviet Russia. Akhmatova, whose poetry is among the finest of modern Russian literature, and whom Zhdanov condemned as a mixture of a nun and a whore, was accused of corrupting Soviet youth with her self-obsessed love poems accessible only to an elite and drawing young people away from such "positive" themes as the glory of work and the achievements of the Soviet regime under the leadership of the party. Neither Zoshchenko nor Akhmatova was arrested, but both were at once expelled from the Writers' Union, so losing their livelihood and their chance of being published. Akhmatova suffered even more from the arrest, release, and rearrest of her son, who remained in a camp for years. Out of her experience she made one of the greatest of her poems, *The Requiem:*

> *I have learned how faces fall to bone,*
> *How under the eyelids terror lurks,*
> *How suffering inscribes on cheeks*
> *The hard lines of its cuneiform texts.* [18]

Zhdanov's attack was intended as a signal to the whole of the Soviet literary and artistic world to fall into line and devote itself to promoting the values of "socialist realism," recognizing that they too were servants of the party and the state. As such they were required to contribute to rebuilding the economy, and reinforcing ideological orthodoxy. The degenerate values and alien influence of the West—bourgeois individualism, cosmopolitanism, "formalism"—were to be rooted out in favor of the collectivist ideals of Soviet Russia.

Zhdanov soon extended his campaign to the other arts, such as film and the theater. Among those pilloried were the two leading Soviet filmmakers, Sergei Eisenstein and Vsevolod Pudovkin. In the winter of 1947–48, it was the turn of Soviet musicians—among them Prokofiev and Shostakovich—who were criticized for failing to celebrate the thirtieth anniversary of the revolution. A decree of February 1948 declared them guilty of "formalism," of writing avant-garde compositions for a limited audience, instead of appealing to the masses with tuneful music in celebration of Soviet achievements.

The great difference between the *Zhdanovshchina* and Yezhov's reign of terror was that those whose work was condemned by Zhdanov did not suffer arrest or death. As many as a thousand writers and artists—among them Meyerhold, the theater director, the short-story writer Isaac Babel, and the poet Osip Mandelstam—had perished in the purges of the 1930s. But to be expelled from the Writers' or Composers' Union, to be pilloried, humiliated, and ostracized in a society as regimented as the Soviet Union, was a serious enough form of persecution for a creative artist, several of whom were among the greatest in the twentieth century. Once established, this suppression of freedom of expression persisted long after Stalin's death, as the treatment of Solzhenitsyn shows. The fact that such a policy crippled originality, debased taste, and impoverished Soviet life—even if he recognized it—would have left Stalin unmoved. This and the isolation of Russia from the West were a small price to pay for the insulation of the Stalinist system against ideas dangerous to Russian rulers, which had so often come from the West, as the example of the original Russian Marxists themselves showed and as the Slavophiles had always maintained.

Zhdanov's wider program to revitalize the party and bring it back to the center of Soviet life was, however, far less of a success than the corresponding move in the last period of the Third Reich. In the attempt to assert their power against the ministries and the SS, Bormann and the Gauleiters came off very much better than Zhdanov and the regional secretaries did against the NKVD. The fact that Hitler had never purged the Nazi party on the scale that Stalin had, leaving many of the original leaders in place, was no doubt one of the reasons for this.

No party congress was held between 1939 and 1952 and the Central Committee Plenum met only once between 1945 and 1952. If the party was to resume the supervisory role it had played in the original drive for industrialization, the Central Secretariat had a network of 200,000 party officials to call on. But few of them had the training or experience to challenge the expertise that ministry officials and industrial managers had acquired during the war. The role that party secretaries at all levels had learned to develop was to work with them, a much more congenial relationship and one likely to be more productive of benefits for their regional or local constituencies. [19]

This convergence was strengthened by the fact that, of the six million party members in January 1947, some 900,000, including a large part of its ablest and better-educated members, were employed in ministries or in enterprises under the control of ministries. In any conflict of interests they were much more likely to show loyalty to the organizations that employed them than to the party, which most of them had simply been obliged to join in order to further their careers.

III

WHILE THE REST OF THE WORLD was impressed by the military strength that Russia had mobilized to defeat the Germans, what impressed Stalin was the strain this had imposed on the already inadequate economic base that supported it, when compared with the immense increase mobilization had brought to America's economic strength. The Russians' first priority had to be to make good the huge cost of their victory—losses in terms of men and physical plant on a scale none of their allies had experienced—to rebuild their economy and start on the daunting task of catching up with the United States. This not only remained the overriding objective of whatever domestic policy was adopted, but had major implications for external policy as well.

The need to conceal the extent of the destruction their country had suffered, the time it would take to make it good, and the low standards of living to which this condemned the Soviet peoples in the meantime (a widespread famine in 1945–46, to begin with) provided a powerful additional reason for the isolation from the rest of the world on which Stalin insisted. The length to which this was taken is illustrated by the fact that the few Americans and Britons who had married Russian women during the war found it impossible in almost all cases to get their wives out of the Soviet Union, despite appeals to Stalin by the governments of both countries. The refusal to publish accurate economic information, the severe restrictions on travel for diplomats and correspondents serving in Russia, and the harsh penalties imposed on Soviet citizens who had anything beyond the minimal official relations allowed with Westerners effectively prevented the outside world from realizing how unlikely it was that the Soviet government would face the risk of engaging in war with the United States, especially at a time when the U.S.A. alone had the capacity to employ nuclear weapons. Stalin was determined to break the American monopoly of such weapons, and by a remarkable effort in a devastated country the Russians succeeded, thanks not least to the contribution of scientists and engineers still held in the camps while they carried on with their research. The first Soviet atomic bomb was successfully tested in the summer of 1949, followed in 1953 by its first hydrogen bomb; but it is unlikely that the Russians had developed the capacity to engage in nuclear warfare on equal terms with the U.S.A. until after Stalin's death.

What the world saw, however, was that the Red Army remained in occupation of half of Europe after inflicting a crushing defeat on the strongest military power of modern times. This created sufficient impression by itself to give Soviet diplomacy the backing of military power without being required to spell out explicitly what use would be made of it if the implied threat were put to the test.

For the first year and a half after Potsdam there was in any case little disposition to do this. Roosevelt was dead, the new president, Truman, was still unsure of himself, and Byrnes, the U.S. secretary of state, was inclined to look for deals that would enable the United States to limit and eventually end its commitment in Europe. Churchill had been turned out of office; the Labour government in Britain, with a large majority in Parliament and a great fund of goodwill toward socialist Russia, was far more interested (and experienced) in domestic reform than foreign affairs. Relaxation of effort, which Stalin was determined to prevent in the Soviet Union, affected public opinion in both the Western democracies. In both there was great reluctance to face continuing difficulties in international affairs, now that the war was over, Hitler defeated and dead, and the United Nations set up to take care of the future. The British, it soon appeared, were faced with bankruptcy unless they could secure a loan from the United States and would find it hard, even with a loan, to hold their Commonwealth and empire together and play a leading role in Europe.

This was a promising situation for Soviet diplomacy to exploit. Stalin had already shown himself alive to the difficulty the democracies had in following a consistent long-term policy in foreign affairs, when they had to pay attention to a public opinion that was subject to short-term swings of mood. He continued to distinguish between the Americans and the British, making this a guiding principle in Soviet tactics. At all times he treated the Americans' economic strength and military potential with respect but believed these were combined with an instability of political purpose that would soon lead them to lose interest in European problems and withdraw their troops, as Roosevelt had foreseen, in two years at the most. On the other hand, Stalin was quick to see that the British, while their long experience made them more realistic in their political judgment, no longer had the resources to support a world, or even a leading European, role. In the case of Britain, therefore, pressure and persistence in postponing agreement might well produce favorable results, particularly where the United States had no interests of her own that might lead her to come to Britain's support.

OVER THE NEXT five years relations between the Soviet Union and her wartime allies were conducted in a continuous public debate, punctuated by the exchange of increasingly acrimonious notes between their representatives in the Council of Foreign Ministers, at the Paris Peace Conference, and the United Nations. Stalin himself rarely appeared and the history has to be pieced together from the British and American records, which fortunately are exceptionally full as well as accessible, and from the diplomatic correspondence and public exchanges between the participants. These are inevitably official in character, but no one questions that Stalin's views continued to be as decisive in the conduct of Soviet relations with the Western powers and with the countries of Eastern Europe as they had been at the time of the Nazi-Soviet Pact and during the war.

In the earlier part of the period, up to the spring of 1947, there were two main issues between the Soviet Union and the Western powers. The first was the peace settlement in Eastern Europe and the willingness of the Western powers to acquiesce in their exclusion from the sphere of influence the Soviet Union had established there. By the end of 1946, Stalin could be well content with the results of Soviet persistence. All the East European governments had been recognized, and the territorial settlements agreed by the Peace Conference largely followed those already put into effect by the Russians.

The second issue was of a different kind: Soviet interest in the Northern Tier, the group of states in the Middle East from Greece and Turkey to Iran and the Persian Gulf.

In November 1940, during Molotov's visit to Berlin, Hitler had invited Stalin to join Germany, Italy, and Japan in dividing up the British Empire and taking as the Soviet share the area south of Batum and Baku in the general direction of the Persian Gulf and the Indian Ocean.* Stalin had shown willingness to consider the invitation, but only provided it was extended to include Russia's interest in the Balkans and the Straits,† from which Hitler's offer was intended to divert her. This was enough to make Hitler drop further discussion, but in 1945–46 Stalin was in a position to explore the suggestion and, now that the rest of the Balkans were in the Soviet sphere of influence, to extend it to Turkey, the Straits, and Greece. Soviet pressure was exerted in a number of different ways. Russian and British troops had occupied Iran during the war in order to keep open the

---

*See pp. 682–84.

†Control of the Bosporus and the Dardenelles, the straits connecting the Black Sea and the Mediterranean, had been a controversial issue in international relations during the nineteenth and early twentieth centuries, with the claims of Russia resisted by the Turks with the support of the Axis powers.

main channel of supplies to the Soviet Union. When the war was over the Russians delayed their part in the promised withdrawal while autonomous Azerbaijani and Kurdish People's Republics were set up with Russian encouragement in the north of the country close to the Soviet-Iranian border. In this case an appeal to the UN Security Council with strong backing from the Americans led to a resumption of the Soviet withdrawal (May 1946) and the restoration of Iranian sovereignty.

Turkish familiarity with Russian expansion toward the Mediterranean had a long history of no less than thirteen wars going back to the time of Peter the Great. This time Molotov demanded Soviet bases in the Straits and the cession of the frontier provinces of Kars and Ardahan. British support in the form of arms and subsidies was provided under the Anglo-Turkish Treaty of Mutual Assurance of 1939, and, as long as this continued to be given, the Turks were prepared to sit out the Russian war of nerves.

While Turkey had remained neutral during the war, Greece for a time after the fall of France had been Britain's only ally. A British army landing after the German withdrawal at the end of 1944 frustrated plans for a coup by the Greek Communists. But their leaders had not given up hope that if they could only get the British out they would still be able to seize power. Stalin remained skeptical about their chances and took care not to intervene directly, but he did not need to, since Greece's neighbors, Yugoslavia, Albania, and Bulgaria, all under Communist control, were ready to supply arms and provide a refuge when necessary to the Communist guerrilla forces. The Soviet contribution was to keep up a full-scale propaganda campaign aimed at the West, denouncing the continued presence of British troops in support of a "Fascist" government.

As long as the British could continue to provide backing for both Greece and Turkey, it was unlikely Stalin would go further in either case. But if Britain's economic difficulties forced her to abandon the leading role she had played in the Middle East since the First World War the Greeks might well be absorbed into the Soviet sphere of influence in the Balkans and Turkey be forced to make concessions over control of the Straits.

The crisis point was reached in February 1947, when the economic difficulties Britain had encountered after the war came to a head and forced the British government to admit that it could no longer play the world role to which it had been accustomed since the eighteenth century. Within a matter of days the British government announced a date for final withdrawal from India (soon extended to Ceylon and Burma as well), handed over the problem of Palestine (where it faced a Jewish revolt) to the United Nations, and agreed in secret that British aid to Greece and Turkey could not continue after March 31 and British troops would have to be withdrawn. The British Empire appeared to be in the process of dissolution, and the British themselves to lack either the resources or the will to prevent it.

If this were to happen—the eventuality that Hitler had put to Stalin in November 1940—it seemed unlikely that the Americans would be prepared to fill the gap in a part of the world where, as yet, they had no interests of their own, so leaving the way open for the Soviet Union to achieve its historic ambitions in the Near East.

On February 21 the British themselves put the question to the U.S. State Department: Would the United States be prepared to take over the commitments to Greece and Turkey that Britain would have to give up in five weeks' time? Those who had to make the decision in Washington were aware that much more than aid to Greece and Turkey was at stake. If the British were driven by economic necessity to withdraw the garrisons and economic support they had provided during the period of instability following the war, a vacuum would be created all the way around the perimeter of Asia from the Aegean to Southeast Asia, which the Soviet Union would be better placed to fill than any other power. When added to the territorial gains and enlargement of her sphere of influence, which Russia had already made in Europe and in the Far East,* the question was whether this did not represent an alteration in the world balance of power to which the United States could not remain indifferent.

If that question had been put a year earlier, not in March 1947 but in March 1946, when a warning of Soviet expansion by Churchill in his much-publicized speech at Fulton, Missouri, and his plea for Anglo-U.S. cooperation had aroused more criticism than applause, the answer would have been hesitant at best, quite possibly a rejection. But the experience of the year between, the aggressive attitude adopted by Soviet diplomacy and use of the United Nations as a platform for attacking the Western powers, had produced a change in American opinion and allowed President Truman to give a different answer on March 12.

No mention was made of Russia, and Truman's justification was in terms of ideology rather than the balance of power: "helping free people to maintain their free institutions and national integrity against aggressive movements that seek to impose upon them totalitarian regimes." But the president added a specific request to Congress for authority for financial assistance and "the assignment of personnel" to Greece and Turkey. To most people at the time it was not more than a temporary arrangement to meet a short-term emergency. Only by the end of 1947 did it become clear that it was the beginning of a revolution in American foreign policy, and the end of isolation.

THE NEWS OF what became known as the Truman Doctrine arrived halfway through the meeting of the Council of Foreign Ministers in Moscow, and it was received without comment from the Soviet side. It was at this meeting, after Hitler had been dead for nearly two years, that the four powers at last came to grips with the legacy he had left them by his prolongation of the war: the prospect of a divided Germany in the heart of

*See pp. 935–39.

a divided Europe, an issue that, once raised, dominated international relations for the next three years, until the Korean war.

The Moscow meeting of the Council of Foreign Ministers lasted for no less than six weeks, forty-three sessions in all, from March 10 to April 25, 1947. In the course of the previous two years the priority for the occupying powers had moved from the destruction of the Nazi regime and German military power to reaching agreement on the economic and political future of Germany. It had become clear that this must be the centerpiece of any peace settlement, and that the economic recovery and political stabilization of the rest of Europe would to a large extent depend upon the way in which it was decided.

The Russians' concentration on reparations reflected their preoccupation with restoring their own economy after the damage inflicted on it by the Germans. So did the French claims: coal deliveries from the Ruhr and priority for the restoration of French before German industry. The American and British attitudes, on the other hand, reflected the state of affairs in the zones of Germany for which they were responsible, particularly the British zone, which contained the greater part of German industry, including the Ruhr. Historically dependent on food supplies from those parts of Germany now under Russian and Polish occupation, the heavily bombed cities of the Rhineland and Westphalia, overcrowded with refugees from the east, faced mass unemployment and starvation unless industrial production could be started up again to pay for the food they needed. In the meantime, the British and Americans had to provide subsidies and supplies to keep the population alive.

The British, whose own industry had been brought to a halt by the severe winter just before the conference opened, were in no position to go on finding the funds to provide these. It was for this reason that they pressed for the economic unity of Germany, agreed to at Potsdam, to be implemented, allowing the barriers to interzonal trade to be removed and a joint plan for dealing with the Germans' economic problems to be put into effect by all four of the Occupying Powers. Failing this, of which by now they had little hope, they saw no alternative other than, as in the case of Greece and Turkey, to turn to the Americans for aid, this time through the projected merger of their two zones.

The Moscow conference did little more than highlight the disagreement among the participants. [20] The crucial question underlying the discussions for both the British and the Russians was how far the Americans, who alone had the resources to make a success of any plan they might put forward, still thought of withdrawing from Europe after a limited period of time—which Roosevelt had put at two years after the war ended—or were now willing to remain until the independence and economic recovery of those parts of Germany and Europe outside the Soviet sphere of influence were safeguarded. Following hard on the Truman Doctrine, the American response suggested that they might be willing to accept some such commitment. In

March, George Marshall, the former U.S. army chief of staff, who had succeeded Byrnes as secretary of state, told the conference he was not sure that the conflicts that had emerged between the Occupying Powers could be remedied. The U.S.A. wanted Germany to be treated as a single economic entity, but they were not seeking an agreement for agreement's sake. "The U.S. recognizes," he added, "that its responsibilities in Europe will continue and it is more concerned in building solidly than in building fast."

Marshall delayed his meeting with Stalin as long as possible, in order to see whether there was anything on which the foreign ministers could agree. When they finally met on April 15, he spoke calmly but did not disguise the serious view he took of the situation and of the deterioration in relations between their two nations. Going beyond the immediate issues, the secretary of state repeated the essentials of Truman's declaration of American policy a month before. The U.S.A. did not question the right of any country to live under the kind of political and economic system it chose but was determined to give all the assistance it could to countries threatened with economic collapse and, as a result, with the collapse of any hopes of preserving democracy.

Stalin remained silent and impassive until Marshall finished, puffing at his cigarette and doodling with his pencil. Then, speaking as quietly as the American, he reviewed and defended the main Russian positions at the conference. But, he remarked, it was wrong to give too tragic an interpretation to their present disagreements.

> Differences had occurred in the past on other questions, and as a rule, after people had exhausted themselves in dispute, they then recognized the necessity of compromise. These were only the first skirmishes and brushes of reconnaissance forces. It was possible that no great success would be achieved at this session, but he thought that compromises were possible on all the main questions, including demilitarization, the political structure of Germany, reparations, and economic unity. It was necessary to have patience and not become pessimistic. [21]

As often before, Stalin applied a soothing balm to offset the impact of Molotov's tough tactics at the conference table—without in any way modifying their substance. There is no evidence available on the Soviet side that would make it possible to read what was in Stalin's mind when he made these remarks. But in quoting them in his broadcast report to the American nation, Marshall was at pains to warn Stalin against the most obvious mistake he might be making:

> I sincerely hope [he added] that the generalissimo is correct in the view he expressed. But we cannot ignore the factor of time involved here. The recovery of Europe has been far slower than expected. Disintegrating forces are becoming evident. The patient is sinking while the doctors deliberate. So I believe that action cannot await compromise through exhaustion. Whatever action is possible to meet these pressing problems must be taken without delay. [22]

MARSHALL AND the American team returned from Europe convinced of two things. The first was that the threat of economic breakdown and starvation in the Western zones of Germany was too serious to risk further delay in setting German industry to work again; the second was that any plan to bring about a German recovery had to be put in the wider context of a European economy—including the British—which was equally in need of rehabilitation. It was out of this perception that the idea of the Marshall Plan was born. A Policy Planning Staff with George Kennan in charge was put to work in the State Department to prepare a European recovery plan and by June 5 had made sufficient progress for the secretary of state to put forward his famous proposal in a speech at Harvard.

The Americans made clear from the beginning that any hope of securing the agreement of Congress to voting large sums of money for aid to Europe was dependent on the Europeans themselves getting together first and producing an integrated plan for recovery, agreed among themselves. A piecemeal approach, country by country, would have no chance of being accepted. On the initiative of the British and French a special conference to which all European countries, including the Soviet Union, were invited met in Paris on June 27, 1947. The proposal put before it was for a joint European program of mutual self-help to be prepared by a directing committee composed of France, Britain, and the Soviet Union, with six specialized subcommittees involving other countries. Only when this had been drawn up and agreed upon would it be presented to the Americans, it was hoped by September 1.

There are few issues on which it would be more interesting to see any Soviet record of discussions between Stalin, Molotov, and other members of the Politburo than those concerned with the Russian reply to Marshall's offer and the Anglo-French initiative. Was the possibility of the Soviet Union taking part in such a European recovery plan discussed? Was there even, as some historians have speculated, a change of attitude over the weekend between Molotov's opening speech and his final statement?

From the beginning Molotov took exception to the idea of a *joint* European plan. Instead, he suggested that each country should prepare a list of its own needs, that these lists should then be combined and the U.S.A. asked how far it was prepared to meet them. He also argued for the exclusion of ex-enemy states and insisted that Germany's problems must be reserved for discussion by the Council of Foreign Ministers. As the idea of an overall European plan including Germany was at the heart of the American proposal, the Russian attitude did not augur well for agreement. But, after further discussion, Molotov asked for more time to consult Moscow (for which read Stalin) before giving a definite reply.

Nothing is known, so far, of any further discussion that may have taken place in the Kremlin. At the final meeting, however, on July 2, Molotov's instructions were clear. He accused the British and French of using the Marshall offer (of which, he insisted, nothing was known definitely) to set up an organization that would require other countries to sacrifice their national independence in order to qualify for American aid. The Soviet Union therefore rejected the Anglo-French plan, which not only infringed upon national sovereignty but also ignored the Soviet Union's and other countries' claims to reparations from Germany. Molotov ended by warning the British and French governments of the serious consequences of their action if they persisted in going ahead. [23]

I V

MOLOTOV'S REPLY was consistent with the policy Stalin had followed since Yalta. He had made good use of the Council of Foreign Ministers in continuation of the wartime Alliance, but never lost sight of the fact that his partners in it, the U.S.A. and Britain, were also his principal potential enemies.

If, nonetheless, the Council of Foreign Ministers continued, up to its Moscow meeting in 1947, to reach settlements, this was due to the willingness of the other powers to allow the Soviet representative to interpose a veto, or at least a delay, and only proceed when all were agreed. If that was no longer to be the rule, then in Stalin's eyes the council would have exhausted its usefulness and could prove a trap, leaving Russia in a permanent minority.

The denial of reparations from the Western zones, the recourse to America's vastly greater economic resources, and the requirement that those wishing to take part in the European recovery program should submit their needs to mutual examination, all pressed on the area where the Soviet Union was most vulnerable—its economic weakness after the war—and where its leader was most sensitive. On the other hand, Stalin was also aware of the economic weakness of Western Europe and skeptical about America's political will to carry the Marshall Plan through, particularly if—as Soviet economists opportunely forecast—the United States could be expected to run into an economic depression.

Both sides prepared for a confrontation. Neither government thought of this in terms of going to war. Fear of another war was widespread in Europe, and both the Soviet Union and the West took advantage of this in the hope of strengthening the resolution of their own side and undermining that of the other. But until the Korean war broke out in the summer of 1950, the evidence suggests that the leaders on neither side seriously thought of making use of military forces in actual conflict (as distinct from the threat to do so), or, except for a few weeks when the blockade of Berlin began in 1948, supposed that the other side would. This appears to apply to the use of the atomic bomb as well. The Russian attempt to force the other Occupying Powers out of Berlin by the blockade, as well as the invasion of South Korea by the Communist North and the subsequent intervention of Chinese regular troops—neither of which could have happened without Russian agreement—took place during the period when Stalin was aware that the U.S.A. either had a monopoly or a clear superiority in atomic weapons and the means of delivering them.

But the exclusion of war left a wide range of political, economic, psychological, and subversive action that could be used. The object on the Soviet side was to strengthen their hold on Eastern Europe and to pressure the West into returning to the conference table and resuming the process of bargaining; on the Western side, to "contain" any further expansion of Soviet territory or influence, to deprive the Communists of the power to hold up recovery, to rescue the economy and restore the confidence of Europe outside the Soviet bloc. Each side angrily accused the other of aggression and claimed to be acting defensively itself: the pattern of the Cold War that lasted for more than a generation.

I N 1 9 4 7, however, it was an open question whether the Anglo-American plan to go ahead without the Soviet Union would work, and Stalin was determined to put every obstacle in its way.

The Americans and Europeans involved in trying to bring American economic aid to Europe feared that it might arrive too late. Anyone who traveled in Western Europe that summer encountered a widespread fear— not only among those involved in government but also among the ordinary population—that the economy might break down before the end of the year and the population of the cities, already on short rations, be left without food or fuel. If conditions were worst in Germany, the fear was no less strong in France and Italy. Even in Britain, industry was still on a three-day week and the convertibility of the pound sterling had to be suspended in August. If the committee set up at the Paris Conference* did not succeed in reaching agreement by September 1 and in getting the supplies from America moving, Western Europe would face the winter with only six weeks' supply of grain. Even when agreement was reached, it was not until December, after a hard-fought battle in Congress, that President Truman was able to sign an Interim Aid Bill, and not until April 3, 1948, after further debate, that Congress authorized the main appropriation of 17 billion dollars for a four-year period.

Fear in Europe in 1947–48 extended to more than the prospect of hunger and unemployment—to attempts by the Communists to seize power in France and Italy, to civil war, war, and occupation. To dismiss these fears as exaggerated (as they proved to be) or as Cold War propaganda, is to fail to understand the atmosphere of the time—just as much as it would be to dismiss Soviet fears of the West, particularly of a restored Germany. It was only two years since the end of the war in which more than twenty million other Europeans besides twenty million Russians had lost their lives. In the

---

*This was the origin of the Organization for European Economic Cooperation (OEEC), today's Organization for Economic Cooperation and Development (OECD).

years since the beginning of 1938 all but four of the twenty-nine countries of Europe that were independent then had known in their own homelands war, occupation, and (hardly less costly) liberation. The experiences of the most terrible decade in European history had taught people that the worst—even the unimaginable—could happen.

During the last three years the Communists, with the support of the Soviet Union, had acquired positions of power, which they were soon to turn into monopolies, over a hundred million people in Eastern and Central Europe. In Greece a civil war was raging in which 100,000 Greeks lost their lives: more than during the German occupation. In the light of what men and women had seen take place in their own towns and villages, it was not surprising that they were afraid that the Communists might seek to extend their power to other countries, or that the Russians who had fought their way from the Volga to the Elbe might continue to the Rhine or the Seine.

To turn these fears as well as the economic weakness of Western Europe to Soviet advantage, Stalin could call upon the two most powerful Communist parties outside the Soviet Union. The French Communists, with some 900,000 members, formed by far the strongest party in France, dominated the trade-union movement and at the same time attracted a large following of intellectuals. They might have attempted to seize power during the chaotic and potentially revolutionary situation of the first months after liberation but were discouraged from doing so by Stalin, who was wary of a confrontation with the Anglo-American forces at that stage and preferred to see the Communists become part of a coalition government. In Italy, where as in France they had played a major role in the Resistance, the Communists under Palmiro Togliatti's leadership increased their membership to two million and remained members of the postwar coalition until excluded by Alcide de Gasperi from the new government that he formed in May 1947. The objective of both parties was to make it impossible for governments to continue without them and to force their way back into office.

French Communists made great efforts through their control of the trade unions to foment strikes, demonstrations, and public discord and succeeded in forcing the government of Paul Ramadier to resign on November 19. Its successor, however, formed by Robert Schuman, showed sufficient determination to face them down. With the strikes continuing but failing to produce a decisive result, the Communist leader Thorez paid a flying visit to Stalin and returned with instructions to use anything short of armed force— including flying squads formed from Communist militants—to keep up the pressure. These tactics were to be pursued at whatever cost to the party and preparations were made for its cadres to go underground if banned. They suffered a more decisive defeat, however, in December 1947 in the loss of working-class support, the collapse of the strike wave, and the formation of an independent trade-union group, Force Ouvrière.

The trial of strength in Italy took place in the general election of the following April (1948) and was an open contest between those who looked to the United States and those who looked to the Soviet Union. The Communists' appeal was boosted by a combined list with the Majority Socialists led by Pietro Nenni, but their joint vote of 40 percent in 1946 was reduced to 31 percent, and de Gasperi's Christian Democrats, with over 48 percent, won a clear majority of seats in the Chamber.

The striking fact about both defeats was that they took place before any of the benefits from the Marshall Plan had begun to appear, while material conditions for the working classes in France and Italy were such as to give the Communists a natural advantage, and in the case of Italy, followed a successful Communist coup in Prague, which gave substance to Togliatti's claim that Communism represented the irresistible wave of the future.

Nineteen forty-eight was a crucial year for another reason. An American election was due in November, and all the indications were that Truman would be defeated. Until the result was known, little progress could be made with the still-secret plan for an Atlantic security pact, the origin of NATO, which the British believed was essential to create the confidence needed for Marshall Aid to be effective by underwriting it with an American commitment to the defense of Western Europe as well. If Truman was defeated—the instability in the American system on which Stalin had counted—both Marshall Aid and the security pact might well be thrown into the melting pot. If he were elected, then progress in 1949 could be much more rapid.

IN THE MEANTIME, Stalin responded by tightening Soviet control over Eastern Europe. In the first two years after the war, only Yugoslavia and Albania could be described as single-party Communist states, although even here the name was avoided in favor of the People's Front and Democratic Front. The governments of the other five—Poland, Czechoslovakia, Hungary, Rumania, and Bulgaria—were all coalitions. In two cases at least (Czechoslovakia and Hungary) they were genuine coalitions in which several parties with their own organizations and very different views combined to carry out a short-term radical program with such reforms as the redistribution of land. When elections were held in Czechoslovakia in May 1946 and in Hungary in November 1945 they were generally regarded as fair, producing a Communist success in the first case with 38 percent of the vote, and a Communist defeat in the second, with 57 percent for the Small Farmers' party.

In Poland, on the other hand, there was interference with the other parties from the beginning. Although Mikolajczyk had been made a vice-premier, he was excluded from any real part in government and in summer 1946 went into opposition to organize the Polish People's party, which attracted strong peasant support. Every obstacle was placed in his way—meetings were broken up, delegates arrested, offices raided, and at least two of the party's leaders murdered. When elections were finally held in January 1947, Mikolajczyk claimed that over 100,000 of his party members were in prison and 142 of its candidates had been arrested; in ten out of fifty-two electoral districts, his People's party lists were disqualified. The government bloc secured 394 out of 444 seats, the People's party 28. A coalition facade was maintained by including the Socialist party in the government and making its general secretary, Josef Cyrankiewicz, prime minister. The election was followed by the adoption of a constitution on the Soviet model, and after extensive purges of the Socialist party a fusion congress was held in December 1948 and a single Polish United Workers' party formed, on the model of the Soviet Communist party.

To coordinate their political tactics and propaganda campaigns with those of the Soviet Union, Stalin summoned the leaders of the French and Italian parties, together with those of the East European parties, to a conference in Poland in September 1947 at which the Communist Information Bureau (Cominform) was set up. All Communist parties were called on "to take the lead in resisting the plans of American imperialist expansion and aggression in all spheres." The ideological basis was provided by Zhdanov's thesis of "two camps":

> The imperialist and antidemocratic camp has as its basic aim the establishment of the world domination of American imperialism and the smashing of democracy, while the anti-imperialist and democratic camp has as its basic aim the undermining of imperialism, the consolidation of democracy, and the eradication of the remnants of fascism.

In words recalling the policy that Stalin imposed on the Comintern in the early 1930s, the Cominform directed its attack against European social democracy:

> A special place in the imperialists' arsenal of tactical weapons is occupied by the utilization of the treacherous policy of right-wing Socialists like Blum in France, Attlee and Bevin in England, Schumacher in Germany, who strive to cover up the true rapacity of the imperialists . . . acting as their faithful accomplices, sowing dissension in the ranks of the working class and poisoning its mind. [24]

Zhdanov and Malenkov were present to make clear that these were not just the views of a revived Communist International (Cominform's membership was much more restricted) but had the endorsement of the Soviet government. Zhdanov's keynote speech was printed in full in the first number of the organization's new journal *For a Lasting Peace, for a People's Democracy.** A special task, he declared, fell to the fraternal Communist parties of France, Italy, and Britain to take the lead in resisting the economic and political enslavement of their countries.

---

*According to Djilas, Stalin himself thought up the cumbersome title in order to make the Western press repeat the slogan each time they quoted from it. He also overrode the decision of the delegates that the seat of the Cominform should be in Prague, insisting, when Zhdanov and Malenkov phoned the Kremlin for approval, that (for reasons that will become apparent in the next section) it should be in the Yugoslav capital of Belgrade.

By the time the Council of Foreign Ministers met in London on November 25, the Soviet propaganda line against the Marshall Plan was fully developed. American policy was identified with capitalism, imperialism, Fascism, and war; Soviet resistance to it with social justice, national independence, democracy, and peace. Calling for the immediate creation of a German government for a united Germany, Molotov described the Marshall Plan as aimed at preventing Germany's economic recovery in the interests of her American and British commercial rivals, destroying her as a united state, and converting the Ruhr into a war-industry base for the Anglo-American domination of Europe. Although the conference continued over seventeen sessions until December 15, no serious attempt emerged to break the deadlock. The Russians evidently believed that they could still mobilize sufficient opposition to halt the implementation of Western plans, and Molotov saw no need to offer concessions in order to keep negotiations going.

V

THE EIGHTEEN MONTHS that separated the end of the London meeting of the foreign ministers in December 1947 and their next meeting at the Palais Rose in Paris in May 1949 was the decisive period in the trial of strength between Stalin and his former allies. To Stalin's surprise and that of many people in the West as well, the political will of the Western powers proved sufficiently strong to overcome the differences among them, and to lay the foundations for a recovery of confidence and an extended period of economic growth in non-Communist Europe during the 1950s and early 1960s.

Such evidence as there is does not justify the conclusion that from the end of the war Stalin had a uniform plan or a timetable for replacing coalition governments in Eastern Europe with a Communist monopoly of power behind the facade of a united front. His requirement to begin with was governments that could be relied upon to respond to Soviet wishes. But just as the Western leaders were constrained in their freedom of action by the pressures of their democratic systems at home, so Stalin was constrained by that of the Stalinist system which he had created in the Soviet Union. Suspicion and distrust were not by-products of that system but essential to it, and the fact that Stalin, instead of relaxing the Soviet system at home at the end of the war, found it necessary to reinforce it strongly suggests that its extension to Eastern Europe was only a matter of time.

Marshall's offer, however, had been open to all the countries of Europe, including the Soviet Union and those in the Soviet sphere of influence. This was an alarming prospect from Stalin's point of view. The promise of access to American aid, which the Soviet Union had no chance of matching, could be a far more dangerous solvent of the Soviet hold on the countries of Eastern and Central Europe than Allied diplomacy or the threat of the atom bomb. This must have been a major consideration in his decision to refuse the offer. Even after Molotov's rejection at the Paris meeting, an invitation (sent to twenty-two countries) to take part in the follow-up Conference on European Reconstruction was accepted by the Czech government (on July 7) and might have been accepted by others if Stalin had not imposed an immediate ban.

The foundation of the Cominform, which followed, was designed to mount a joint propaganda offensive against acceptance of the Marshall offer, and to keep up the pressure on the other East European leaders to stay in line. Two developments early in 1948, a Communist coup in Prague and the opening of a breach between the Soviet Union and Yugoslavia, made clear that coordination was not enough for Stalin, that he was determined to root out all vestiges of independence and reduce the role of any other party beside the Communists to that of puppets.

There is no evidence so far to establish that the political crisis in Prague in February 1948 over Communist control of the police was engineered by the Communists on instructions from Moscow. But, when the non-Communist ministers resigned from the government, the decision to set up action committees and seize the opportunity of securing full control cannot have been made without consultation with Stalin. The new government was still in form a coalition, but none of the other parties had any voice in choosing their single "representative" member and the fellow-traveling Fierlinger led the socialists into fusion with the Communists. A new constitution was adopted based on that of the USSR and the result of new elections, with no opposition parties allowed, was announced as 90 percent for the official list in Bohemia-Moravia, 86 percent in Slovakia.

The Czech coup had a profound effect on Western opinion. It was only nine years before that Hitler's strident campaign to break up Czechoslovakia, culminating in his occupation of Prague, had proved to be the prelude to war. This time, even without the Red Army's intervention or the threat of war, the Communists had proved able to capture power from within, and it was easy to draw the conclusion that what had happened in Prague might once again provide a precedent, this time for what could happen in Paris or Rome—or, as actually turned out to be the case before the summer ended, in Berlin.

Both the parallel and the precedent proved to be misleading, but nobody could be sure of that at the time. With local variations, Hungary, Rumania, and Bulgaria conformed to the same pattern by the end of 1948. In December the veteran Comintern leader Dimitrov, now head of the Bulgarian government, speaking to his Party Congress, summed up the transformation of the People's Democracies:

> The Soviet regime and the Popular Democratic Front are forms of the same system of government, both based on the dictatorship of the proletariat.

Soviet experience is the only and the best pattern for the building of socialism in our country as well as in other countries of Popular Democracy. [25]

This was soon extended to East Germany as the German Democratic Republic and for the next forty years, punctuated by the Hungarian revolt of 1956 and the Czech of 1968, Central and Eastern Europe were governed by satellite regimes of the Soviet Union, a Stalinist New Order in place of that earlier imposed on them by Hitler and the Nazis.

THE EXCEPTION was Yugoslavia, where Tito's Communist regime, the product of the civil war that had accompanied the partisans' war against the Germans, had the best claim of any to have come to power by its own efforts, not as a result of the Red Army's occupation. No Communist leadership had been more aggressive toward the West (more than once to Soviet embarrassment), none had been more naive in its idolization of Stalin, none more ready to support Molotov's rejection of Marshall's offer. But this was not enough; Stalin could still detect in their attitude the taint of independence: While agreeing with Soviet policy, they still gave the impression of having made up their minds for themselves.

For once there is sufficient evidence—from the Yugoslav side, admittedly, but supplemented and confirmed by correspondence from the Soviet side as well—to open a window through the blank wall behind which relations between the Kremlin and the other East European states were conducted. Although it later became clear that there had been friction between them for some time—over Yugoslav relations with their neighbors, over the activities of the Soviet intelligence services, and over Soviet handling of their economic relations with Belgrade—recognition of this was suppressed, and it was not until December 1947 that a Yugoslav delegation was summoned to Moscow to discuss Yugoslav policy toward Albania.

Stalin asked especially for Djilas and the day he arrived immediately asked him to dinner without his companions. In the Kremlin beforehand —with Molotov and Zhdanov—Stalin began to bait him: "So, members of the Central Committee in Albania are killing themselves over you! This is very inconvenient." When Djilas tried to explain, Stalin would not let him finish, declaring, "We have no special interest in Albania. We agree to Yugoslavia swallowing Albania."

At this [Djilas continues] he gathered together the fingers of his right hand and bringing them to his mouth, made as if to swallow them. . . .

Djilas was shocked and again tried to explain:

"It is not a matter of swallowing, but of unification."
Molotov: "But that *is* swallowing."
And Stalin added again with that gesture of his: "Yes, yes. Swallowing! But we agree with you: You ought to swallow Albania—the sooner the better."

Later, in Stalin's dacha, the puritan in Djilas was again revolted by the heavy drinking and eating, but he reminded himself that Peter the Great too had held such suppers with his assistants, at which they gorged and drank themselves into a stupor, while ordaining the fate of the Russian people. He thought Stalin had aged in the three years since he had last seen him; he ate like a glutton as if he feared there would not be enough for him, and his mind was no longer so sharp. "In one thing, though, he was still the Stalin of old: stubborn, sharp, suspicious whenever anyone disagreed with him." [26]

During the course of the six hours they spent around the table Djilas sensed that Zhdanov and Beria were sounding him out, while Stalin watched and waited, to see if he might prove the man who could be used to split the Yugoslav leadership. When he refused to be drawn in, the gaps in the conversation became longer and longer; in the end, nothing was said openly.

The Russians' disappointment soon affected the dispatch of business. The promises of quick decisions on Soviet military and economic aid were not kept, and the Yugoslavs were left to cool their heels for nearly a month. Then, at the end of January, *Pravda* printed a sharp attack on Dimitrov for venturing to speak in public about a Balkan federation, to include Bulgaria and Yugoslavia, without any mention of the Soviet Union being a member of it. As the Yugoslavs had just signed treaties of friendship and mutual assistance with Bulgaria, Hungary, and Rumania, they and the Bulgarians were summoned to Moscow to explain themselves. The Russians expected Tito as well as Dimitrov to appear, but Tito, already wary of what might happen, sent another of his close associates, Edvard Kardelj, to join Djilas.

At the meeting in the Kremlin on the evening of February 10, Molotov began with a severe rebuke for concluding a treaty of alliance between the two countries which the Soviet government had first learned of from the newspapers. After that Stalin attacked Dimitrov, who was unwell and aging, for talking about a federation. The Bulgarian's attempt to explain, admitting he had made a mistake, only made Stalin angrier; he continually interrupted him:

> You bandy words like a woman of the streets. You wanted to astonish the world, as if you were still the secretary of the Comintern. Bulgaria and Yugoslavia tell us nothing about what they are doing, and we must learn about it in the streets.

When Kardelj pointed out that the draft of the treaty had been submitted to the Soviet government in advance with no objection raised—which Molotov confirmed—and took this to show that there were no differences between them and Moscow, Stalin shouted: "Yes, there are, and profound differences, too . . . You don't consult at all. That is not your mistake; but your policy—yes, your policy!" When a customs union was suggested, Stalin dismissed it as an impractical idea. Kardelj pointed to Benelux as an example of one that worked well, only to get into an argument with Stalin about its membership. Stalin stubbornly insisted that it consisted only of Belgium and Luxembourg, not Holland, and would not submit to correction, angrily declaring: "When I say 'no' it means 'NO.' "

He then switched his attack on Dimitrov from the proposed Bulgarian federation with Yugoslavia to objecting to one between Bulgaria and Rumania. "Such a federation is inconceivable. You wanted to shine," he shouted at Dimitrov, "you wanted to be original. What historic ties are there between Bulgaria and Rumania? None." To the astonishment of his listeners he now declared himself in favor of a federation between Bulgaria and Yugoslavia, with Albania thrown in:

> "There are historic and other ties. This is the federation that should be created and the sooner the better. Yes, the sooner the better—right away, if possible tomorrow! Yes, tomorrow! Agree on it immediately. First Bulgaria and Yugoslavia ought to unite, and then Albania." [27]

Not surprisingly the Yugoslavs present came to the conclusion that Stalin's demand for an immediate federation was intended to break up the unity of their own country.

The meeting in Moscow was followed by a series of moves to isolate Yugoslavia and the withdrawal of all Soviet advisers and specialists. An acrimonious correspondence was begun by Stalin and Molotov, in which they spoke to Tito and his associates as if they were addressing inferiors. Tito's efforts to give a reasoned response to their criticisms were met with the reply: "We consider your answer untruthful and therefore wholly unsatisfactory."

Specific complaints were soon inflated into ideological heresy, and Tito and his associates were accused of Trotskyism, Bukharinism, and Menshevism. Their refusal to plead guilty, their insistence that, unlike the other states occupied by the Red Army, they had made their own revolution and were capable of creating their own socialist society, only increased their offense.

At the end of June the Cominform was called upon to expel Yugoslavia, condemning Tito and the other leaders for their nationalist deviation and calling upon "healthy elements" in the Yugoslav party to replace them. The other members of the Cominform hastened to break off relations with Yugoslavia. Stalin, according to Khrushchev, was confident that his displeasure would bring Tito down: "I will shake my little finger—and there will be no more Tito. He will fall." [28] Not for nothing, however, had Tito been a member of the Comintern in Moscow at the time of the purges. The "healthy elements" on whom Stalin might be counting, including two members of the Yugoslav ruling group, Sreten Zujović and Andrija Hebrang, were arrested and a Party Congress called which gave Tito a massive vote of support. Soviet statements belittling the wartime struggle of the partisans were quite enough to rouse a fierce nationalist response.

The Yugoslavs prepared to withstand military action, but although the Russians kept up a war of nerves with menacing troop movements and border incidents, Stalin was cautious enough not to risk war. Soviet propaganda until Stalin's death in 1953 continued an unrestrained campaign of vilification, denouncing Tito and "his gang" as counter-revolutionaries, traitors to the cause of socialism and "jackals of American imperialism," but nothing could disguise the fact that for the first time a Communist party had successfully defied Moscow's anathema.

The Communist party of a small impoverished Balkan country hardly represented a danger to the supremacy of Stalin and the Communist party of the Soviet Union, fortified by the defeat of Germany and the occupation of half of Europe. But the fact that, despite all the pressure exerted against them, Tito and his party had not only rebelled and survived but in the face of excommunication had also maintained their claim to represent a genuine alternative model of socialism dealt a blow to the monolithic image of Communist unity, the consequences of which were to continue long after Stalin's death.

IF STALIN'S JUDGMENT was bad in his attempt to put down Tito, he showed a surer touch in his handling of what remained the central issue for both Russia and the West: the future of Germany. Since 1945 the British and Americans had committed themselves to merging their two zones of occupation, originally to help the British out of their financial difficulties. After the failure of the foreign ministers to reach agreement in Moscow, this bi-zone became increasingly seen as the framework for the German economic recovery they were prevented from carrying out in a united Germany, and ultimately as the basis for a West German state. In the course of 1947–48 the U.S.A. and Britain had come to regard the rehabilitation of the German economy, and offering the German people a future in association with the West rather than the Soviet bloc, as essential to their plans for European recovery, and beyond that for European security.

Such a design, pointing inevitably, as it seemed, to the revival of German power in alliance with the West, was bound to raise fears in Moscow, just as surely as Russian actions in Eastern Europe, the obstacles they placed in the way of German recovery and unification, and the disruptive tactics of French and Italian Communists raised fears in the West. Each "camp," to use Zhdanov's term, feared and became convinced of the other's aggressive intentions.

There were serious difficulties, however, for the British and American governments in turning their design into reality. The French, whose cooperation was essential to its success, were very reluctant to accept the central place assigned to Germany and deeply disturbed by the threat of war. The Americans in an election year were by no means sure that public opinion and Congress would continue to support the commitment to Europe that the Truman government was entering into. The British, struggling with their own economic difficulties, were embarrassed by lacking, for the first time, the resources with which to back up their policy.

Here was a situation that a skillful opponent might exploit to frustrate a design that was still a long way from realization. Stalin's choice of Berlin as a place to apply pressure was masterly. All four powers shared in the occupation of the city, but not on equal terms. For Berlin was situated in the middle of the Soviet zone, and the Western powers were dependent on Russian goodwill to allow them access for bringing in the supplies needed to maintain their garrisons and the two and a half million Germans who lived in the three Western sectors of the city. The Russians did not need to mount an open challenge. The first steps to cut Berlin off from the West were taken in March 1948 and were described as temporary interruptions due to the need for repairs. The blockade was not complete until August, and each step in tightening it was followed by a pause to see how the West reacted and to assess the danger of war, which the Russians correctly concluded the West no more wanted than they did.

The Western powers' military assessment was pessimistic. In June 1948 stocks in the Western sectors were sufficient to provide food for no more than thirty-six days and coal for the power stations for no more than forty-five. The calculation on both sides was that, at best, the Western powers could hold their position in Berlin only for a limited period of time, at the end of which they would have to choose among three options: using force to break the blockade, making a humiliating withdrawal, which was bound to have a big effect on German public opinion and its confidence in Western promises, or purchasing the right to stay by accepting the Russian terms. The Russians, on the other hand, ran no risk that they could not at once minimize by relaxing the blockade—with the possibility always of restoring it later. Stalin took care not to define his terms at all precisely. Sometimes the interruption of traffic was blamed on technical difficulties; at other times, Soviet hints suggested that the price for allowing the Western powers to remain in Berlin would be abandonment of their plans for consolidation of the Western zones and a return to the Potsdam agreement, with a built-in Soviet veto on any German settlement.

The crisis came at the end of June 1948, when the three Allied powers decided to introduce a new currency in the three Western zones of Germany, a step that turned out to be the key to releasing German energies and reviving the economy. The Russians retaliated by introducing a new currency of their own in the Eastern zone and claiming that it alone would be valid throughout all the sectors of Berlin. At this point the reaction of the Berliners themselves was crucial.

For weeks, during which they had received no guarantee from the Western powers that they would not withdraw from Berlin, the people of Berlin and their leaders had been subjected to a war of nerves by the Communists. Its main theme was that the West would leave them in the lurch and that, when they left, the whole city would be taken over by the Russians and those who had been active on the other side would be victims of reprisals. On June 23, in the face of Communist intimidation and mob violence, the Berlin City Assembly (meeting in the Soviet sector and denied police protection) nonetheless voted in favor of accepting the Soviet currency as valid only for the Soviet sector of the city, and the Western currency in the other three sectors, thereby preserving the four-power status of the city. This was a courageous decision and it was applauded by a mass meeting of some 80,000 Berliners the next day. But it still left the problem of how to supply a city with 900,000 families, if the Russians took up the challenge and closed off all access to it.

Only one answer had been suggested—an airlift. But few believed that the combined air forces could bring in more than 1,000 of the 4,000 tons that were needed daily (coal as well as food) or maintain even that figure for more than a few weeks. Those who had to make the decision in Washington and London, however, believed they had no option but to stand firm. The lesson of appeasing Hitler in the 1930s had to be learned. They were in Berlin by right, and to back down in the face of Russian pressure would destroy their credibility—that minimal basis of confidence, already at a low level in France and Germany, on which any hope of carrying out their plans depended. If they did, no one would again take the risk the Berliners had, of relying on the Americans and British to support them, only to find themselves left to face the Russians, the secret police, and their informers.

Without any guarantee that they would be able to sustain it, the Anglo-American airlift started on June 26, and as a symbolic backup three groups of American B29 bombers capable of delivering atom bombs were transferred to Europe. At the same time the Western powers continued with the talks designed to produce a Basic Law as the framework for a West German state, and the Russians with a parallel process for an East German state with Berlin as its capital. In August the three Western ambassadors in Moscow had two meetings with Stalin at which he showed himself in a conciliatory and reasonable mood. He dismissed any idea that the Soviets meant to push the West out of Berlin—"We are still allies." The source of the trouble was in the West's plan to set up a German state of its own. He even gave the impression that he might consider lifting the blockade. Any hopes raised by Stalin were dashed when Molotov, performing his familiar act, dourly stated the minimum Soviet demands. If accepted by the West, these could only leave the impression on the Berliners that they were simply being used as a bargaining chip between the Occupying Powers, to be dropped as soon as they reached agreement.

The Russians were in no hurry; the blockade gave them no problems. In the meantime mass demonstrations organized by the Communists, which led to rioting and the occupation of the city hall, forced the majority of the City Assembly and its executive committee, the Magistrat, to take refuge in the British sector. There they called for fresh elections to be held in Berlin in defiance of a Soviet ban.

Everything, however, still turned on the airlift. If that had failed in the face of the winter weather (and on the last day of November 1948 fog reduced the number of aircraft able to land in Berlin to ten) the Berliners' courage in the face of the siege conditions under which they had to live would have been in vain. To the surprise even of those closely involved, the joint effort by the USAF and the RAF, with Berliners working around the clock to unload and turn around the planes, succeeded in supplying food and coal for two and a half million people for eleven months, right through the winter, from June 1948 to May 1949, reaching a figure of 8,000 tons a day.

Two other equally surprising events marked a decisive swing of the balance in favor of the West. In November 1948 President Truman was elected, opening the way for the talks to go ahead on a North Atlantic Treaty of mutual assistance, and on December 5 the people of Berlin, refusing to be intimidated, turned out in force to give a majority of over 83 percent in the city elections to the three democratic parties that had resisted Communist pressure.

Once again there is no evidence to show why or even when Stalin decided to admit his gambit had failed. The Russian retreat was characteristically oblique. In February 1949, in answering questions submitted by an American journalist about Soviet conditions for lifting the blockade, Stalin omitted any mention of the currency issue. When an American diplomat, Philip Jessup, inquired informally of Jacob Malik, the Soviet representative to the UN, whether the omission had any significance, the latter promised to inquire, and a month later, on March 15, reported that it was "not accidental." In the meantime Molotov had been replaced as Soviet foreign minister by Vyshinsky, who let it be known that, if a date could be fixed for the Council of Foreign Ministers to meet, the blockade could be lifted.

Before that took place, the foreign ministers of Britain, France, and the U.S.A. met in Washington to sign the NATO treaty and the detailed agreements creating a framework within which developments toward a West German state could now take place.

Moscow's answer was to launch a massive campaign denouncing NATO as an aggressive treaty aimed at the USSR, in violation of the UN Charter. The principal vehicle for mobilizing opposition was the Partisans of Peace. Based on the "front technique," this had been developed to combine a leading role for eminent non-Communists with Communist control of the organization and its direction exclusively against the "American warmongers" and their European allies. An International Committee of Intellectuals for Peace was set up which attracted the support of many distinguished figures with left-wing sympathies in literature, science, and the arts. Following the World Congress of Partisans of Peace in Paris in April 1949 the

World Peace Movement became a major instrument of Soviet foreign policy, comparable with the Popular Front movement of the 1930s and capable of securing the signatures of many millions, who had no Communist affiliations, for the Stockholm Peace Appeal of 1950, for which Picasso designed a special dove of peace. (The appeal was also signed by the whole of the North Korean army just before it launched its attack on South Korea.) At the same time the Communist leaders in East Germany launched a parallel campaign for Unity and a Just Peace, a National Front to fight for the future of a united not a divided Germany, making a great effort to attract neutralist and nationalist support in West as well as East Germany.

Against this background the Council of Foreign Ministers met in Paris at the end of May 1949. Both the Western powers and the Russians made much of their different versions of a united Germany; but both were more concerned in practice with preventing the progress they had made toward creating two separate Germanys in their own image from being undone.

Djilas records that, fifteen months before, Stalin had twice declared to the Yugoslavs his conviction that Germany would remain divided: "The West will make Western Germany their own, and we shall turn Eastern Germany into our own state." [29] At the end of all the agitation of the intervening year, this was the result. Elections were held in the future Federal Republic in August 1949 and Konrad Adenauer elected as the first chancellor by the Bundestag in September. In October the Russians called in the East German party leaders and told them to go ahead with the creation of a German Democratic Republic, a process completed a year later, in October 1950. Berlin remained occupied by all four powers.

THE CONSOLIDATION of the two Germanys was matched by measures to consolidate the two Europes. The fact that the Soviet defeat in Germany coincided with Tito's successful defiance of Moscow made it inevitable that in the Eastern half this should take the form of a tightening of Russian control. Comecon, a Council for Mutual Economic Assistance, was set up in January 1949 as a counterpart to OEEC and the Marshall Plan, and was followed by a series of purges which continued until Stalin's death in 1953. These repeated the liquidation of all potential centers of opposition, even independence, by the same methods that had convulsed the Soviet Communist party and the Comintern in the 1930s—denunciation, arrest, torture, confession, "trial," including show trials of the leaders, followed by imprisonment or execution. Personal rivalries and local feuds played a large part in deciding who was to be denounced, but the driving force came from the Kremlin, from Stalin and Beria, and extended to the Soviet party itself—including members of the Central Committee.

The first of the trials was held in Hungary in September 1949, when László Rajk, the minister of the interior, was accused of having been an informer and police spy throughout his career, working both for the Americans and for Ranković, the Yugoslav minister of the interior. After confessing to these and other equally improbable charges, he was found guilty and shot. Traicho Kostov, deputy prime minister of Bulgaria, threw himself out of a window of the police headquarters in Sofia because he feared he would not be able to resist further torture to make him denounce his comrades. With both his legs broken he was tried for treason and hanged, after withdrawing his confession in open court. A third deputy prime minister, Koçi Xoxe in Albania, was tried for "Titoism" and duly executed. The big show trial in Czechoslovakia did not take place until November 1951. By that time Stalin had become rabidly anti-Semitic (see pp. 951–53) and had sent Mikoyan to Prague to order the arrest of the most powerful figure in Czechoslovakia, the Stalinist Secretary-General of the Czechoslovak Communist party, Rudolf Slansky, who happened to be a Jew, together with the other Jewish member of the Czechoslovak Politburo, B. Geminder. In the trial which followed, eleven of the fourteen defendants were Jewish. While Tito, the CIA, and the Gestapo still figured in the indictment and the "confessions," under Mikoyan's direction the real emphasis was placed on their links with the Zionist movement, which was alleged to be undertaking espionage and subversion in socialist countries in return for American support of the new state of Israel.

Many others were tried and sentenced to long terms of imprisonment, among them Wladyslav Gomulka in Poland and Ana Pauker in Rumania. Altogether a quarter of the 2.3 million party members are said to have been purged in Czechoslovakia, 300,000 in Poland and East Germany, 200,000 in Hungary. No one could feel safe, any more than in Russia in the 1930s—precisely the effect intended. Tito remains the only Communist to have defied Hitler and Stalin and to have died in his bed in 1980, still president of the republic he had founded more than thirty years earlier.

V I

IT WAS NOT IN EUROPE or the Near East that Communism made further gains in Stalin's final years, but in the Far East. Far from the local Communist forces receiving support from the Soviet Union, however, at least before 1950, their efforts were regarded with skepticism by Stalin and discouraged rather than encouraged. The exception was Korea, which had been annexed by Japan in 1910. The closing days of the Pacific war saw a hasty and costly operation by the Russians that left them in occupation of half the country to the north of the thirty-eighth parallel, with the Americans moving into the southern part. Kim Il-sung's Communist government owed little if anything to local Communist initiative: It had been installed by the Soviet forces which remained until January 1949, and its leaders, some of whom had been trained in Moscow, were chosen by the Russians. Elsewhere—in China, Indochina, and Indonesia for example—Stalin found it difficult, as he did in Yugoslavia, to accept the idea, still less the fact, of indigenous Communist parties obtaining power by their own efforts and showing signs of following an independent policy.

Soviet policy toward China in the 1940s continued to be based, as it had been in the 1920s and 1930s, on the assumption that the Kuomintang and Chiang Kai-shek would remain the key factors in Chinese politics, to which the Chinese Communist party (CCP) must adapt its own role. The agreement that the CCP made with Chiang in 1937, recognizing his authority as the national leader, was a crucial success for Soviet policy in securing Russia's eastern frontiers, to which the interests of the CCP had to be subordinated.

Stalin continued the same policy of cooperation with the Chinese Nationalists after the war. By the treaty of friendship and alliance, which the Soviet Union signed with Chiang Kai-shek on August 14, 1945, Stalin secured Chinese acquiescence in the promises Roosevelt had made to him at Yalta as the price for Russia's entry into the war against Japan. These included recognition of Outer Mongolia's "independence" under Soviet protection, a Soviet share in the Manchurian Railway, port facilities at Dairen, and a naval base at Port Arthur—all of them concessions painful for any Chinese leaders to accept. Communist discipline, however, required that the Chinese Communist party should not question Stalin's decision.

By urging the CCP to renew the wartime cooperation with Chiang and the Nationalists, and discouraging them from ideas of turning China, or part of it, into a Communist state, Stalin hoped to avoid arousing American suspicions and delaying the withdrawal of their troops. With a far better idea of the weakness of the Nationalist regime and of the Americans' increasing disillusionment with its corruption, Mao Tse-tung believed that Stalin exaggerated the American commitment, failed to recognize the strength of the Communists' position, or to take a bold enough view of their chances of winning an outright victory if the civil war were renewed.

There was no question of openly challenging the Moscow line, and Chou En-lai, Mao's chief lieutenant, continued negotiations with Chiang until January 1947; but the talks made no progress. As Stalin told Djilas in February 1948:

> When the war with Japan ended, we invited the Chinese comrades to reach an agreement as to how a *modus vivendi* with Chiang Kai-shek might be found. They agreed with us in word, but in deed they did it in their own way when they got home: They mustered their forces and struck. It has been shown that they were right, not we. [30]

Stalin would hardly have been so complacent about admitting his mistake if he had realized that in the course of 1948 Mao's forces would overrun the whole of Manchuria and northern China, and nine months later would go on to conquer the rest of the Chinese mainland and proclaim from Peking the formation, not of a coalition, but of an avowedly Communist government of a People's Republic of China. He would have been even more surprised to learn that the Americans, who were apparently prepared to risk war over the Berlin blockade and pour billions of dollars into European recovery, would allow such a reversal to take place without any serious attempt to intervene in a part of the world that Stalin regarded as more central to U.S. interests than Europe.

The dramatic story of the extension of Communist rule over the most populous country in the world was deliberately played down by the Soviet press, which gave more space to the activities of the Greek Communists (then on the verge of defeat) and far more to denunciations of Tito and of the "traitors" exposed for Titoist sympathies in other countries of Eastern Europe. Not until the day after the proclamation of the People's Republic in Peking was the news from China allowed for the first time on the front page of *Pravda*—the same day that Chou En-lai informed the Soviet consul general and requested Soviet recognition. This extraordinary lack of preparation can hardly have been accidental; it reflected Stalin's unwillingness to recognize the importance of what was happening in China and his instinctive dislike—in the year that saw a peak of adulation in the celebration of his own seventieth birthday—of having to share the limelight with another Communist movement and its leader.

Earlier in 1949, Mao had appeared to pay more attention to keeping Russian goodwill than to avoiding the risk of a last-minute intervention by the U.S.A. In April the Chinese joined with the European Communist parties in condemning the North Atlantic Treaty and proclaiming their loyalty to their "ally, the Soviet Union." In July Mao declared: "We must lean to one side. . . . Not only in China but throughout the world one must lean either to imperialism or socialism." When the Yugoslavs, seeing a parallel vis-à-vis Russia between their own and the Chinese Communists' situation, enthusiastically reported the CCP's successes, the CCP responded by joining in the violent denunciations of Tito which became routine throughout the Soviet bloc.[31]

Mao later said he believed that Stalin was already contemplating the possibility that he might turn out to be another Tito, and that he had done his best to remove Stalin's suspicions. In common with the leaders of the other Communist parties (with the exception of Tito), Mao made the long journey by train to pay homage to Stalin on his anniversary, declaring that he was "the teacher and friend of the whole world, the teacher and friend of the Chinese people." Stalin reciprocated by telling Mao at a reception given by the Politburo on the day of his arrival: "I never expected you to be so young and so strong. You have won a great victory, and victors are above censure."[32]

Mao, however, had come for more than an exchange of civilities. Despite the urgent business that required his attention in Peking so soon after coming to power, he remained in Moscow for no less than two months.

What he wanted was an alliance and economic aid, in effect a revised version of the treaty signed with Chiang Kai-shek in 1945, and he gave every indication of staying until he got it.

Later Mao was to claim that Stalin had been unwilling to negotiate. No Soviet record of the discussions in the Kremlin has been published, but whatever the arguments that were used, by January 10 Stalin had yielded sufficiently for the Chinese prime minister, Chou En-lai, to assemble a delegation to take to Moscow for negotiations. These began between Chou and Vyshinsky on January 20, and the treaty was signed on February 14. The contrast with the concessions that Chiang had been obliged to make was underlined by the preamble:

> A new People's Government has been formed which has united all China
> . . . and has proved its ability to defend the state independence and
> territorial integrity of China, the national honor and dignity of the Chi-
> nese people. [33]

The treaty promised mutual assistance against aggression by Japan or by "any other state which should unite with Japan, directly or indirectly, in acts of aggression." This provided cover against the Russian fear of indirect aggression by the U.S.A. using Japan as an instrument; but it did not offer the Chinese a guarantee of Soviet aid against an attack launched by Chiang Kai-shek from Formosa (where he had retreated) with U.S. assistance. The most important gain for the Chinese was Soviet agreement to transfer to the Chinese the Manchurian Railway with all its property (which the Japanese had made the basis of their industrial development of the country) either on the conclusion of a Japanese peace treaty or not later than 1952. The same arrangement covered the return of Port Arthur and Dairen (where the USSR might retain landing rights). In addition the Russians agreed to make a loan, a modest credit of 300 million dollars over five years at 1 percent. It must have gone against the grain for Stalin to abandon territory and rights that Russia had first acquired before the revolution, and regained after the defeat of Japan. But whatever reservations he may have felt—and Mao, too—Stalin was realist enough to know that he could not treat the Chinese like the Yugoslavs.

In a conciliatory gesture, Mao asked Stalin to send him a political adviser. Stalin may have taken this with a grain of salt—at least none was sent. Nonetheless, at a time when the Russians were encountering stiffer resistance to their policies in Europe, Mao's successes brought home the fact that the weakening of the colonial powers—Britain, France, and the Neth-erlands—during the war had created a promising situation for the expan-sion of Communist influence which the Soviet leadership had been slow to recognize. Part of the reason for this was the difficulty the Russians had in taking seriously any movements calling themselves Communist and claiming to be inspired by Marxism, which in the absence of an industrial working class were based upon peasant support. They saw them instead as movements for national liberation and agrarian reform and were slow to repeat Lenin's bold reply to the Mensheviks in 1917–18, that what mattered was not the state of a country's economic and social development, but revolutionary potential and revolutionary opportunities.

There was other evidence to back up that of the CCP's successes: the Communist guerrilla war with which the British were confronted in Malaysia, the attempted Communist coup in the former Dutch colony of Indonesia, and Ho Chi-minh's war to drive the French out of Indochina. Taken together they pointed to the conclusion that Western imperialism was proving to be much weaker than orthodox Marxist analysis had predicted, and that for all the talk of American imperialism the United States showed no great disposition to help reestablish or take over the imperial heritage of her allies.

It would be fascinating to learn how far the Kremlin's changing perspective on Communist prospects and the tactics to be followed in Asia were discussed between Stalin and Mao during the latter's prolonged stay in Moscow. It can hardly have been a coincidence that, following Ho Chi-minh's visit to pay homage to Stalin on his seventieth birthday, his government was recognized by the Chinese on January 18 and by the Russians on the thirtieth, while Mao was still in the Soviet capital. In the case of China, Stalin had delayed recognition until there could be no doubt that the CCP had actually won the civil war, the same caution that led him not to give diplomatic recognition to the Greek Communists. According to Krushchev, who was present, Stalin took pleasure in inflicting petty humiliations on Ho Chi-minh, then, with the arbitrariness characteristic of his final years, he unexpectedly agreed to recognition, only to declare subsequently: "We were too hasty; it's too early for recognition," and refused to allow Ho Chi-minh to announce that he had been officially received in Moscow as president of Vietnam. Recognition, however, was not withdrawn and, although Ho Chi-minh's victory did not come until after Stalin's death, the connection was established between events in Asia and the confrontation with the West in Europe. In the case of Indochina, for example, the more deeply the French army became involved in fighting in Southeast Asia, the less it could contribute to NATO, and the more anxious the French became to avoid any risk of war with the Russians over Germany.

A THIRD VISITOR to Moscow for the anniversary celebrations was Kim Il-sung, who took advantage of the occasion to seek Stalin's agreement to an operation designed to touch off a Communist-led uprising in South Korea and the overthrow of the Syngman Rhee government installed there by the Americans. According to Khrushchev, Stalin was cautious, telling Kim to think over the risks of American intervention and work out a plan in detail. At the same time Kim asked Mao Tse-tung for advice. The Korean leader was confident that the whole operation could be carried out so swiftly that American intervention would be avoided, and Mao added his support, arguing that the Americans would regard it as an internal matter which the Koreans should be left to settle for themselves. [34]

If the Americans had not intervened to save Chiang Kai-shek from defeat in the far more important case of the Chinese civil war, why should they do so in South Korea, which the U.S. secretary of state, Dean Acheson, had specifically excluded, as recently as a speech of January 12, 1950, from America's sphere of interest and defense commitments in the Pacific? On this basis, Stalin gave his approval, and on June 25 the North Korean forces, which had been equipped and trained by the Soviet military, launched a successful surprise attack which rapidly captured the South Korean capital of Seoul.

A double miscalculation, however, frustrated Kim Il-sung's plans. The first was the failure of the Communists in the South to launch the uprising on which he had counted; the second was the immediate and vigorous reaction of the Americans. Within forty-eight hours, the United Nations Security Council, on an American motion, condemned the attack as an act of aggression, so opening the way for President Truman, acting on behalf of the UN, to order the U.S. armed forces to come to the aid of the beleaguered Syngman Rhee. The extent of American anxiety is shown by Truman's accompanying his promise of support to South Korea with an order to the U.S. Seventh Fleet to bar any attempt by the Chinese Communists to invade Formosa (Taiwan). At the same time he sent a military mission to Indochina and ordered an increase in U.S. aid to the Philippines, where a Communist guerrilla movement was active.

No other event in the decade after the war gave so sharp a shock to Western opinion as this unexpected outbreak of war in Korea. Coming on top of the Prague coup, the Berlin blockade, and Mao's victory in the Chinese civil war, it appeared to substantiate the belief that the non-Communist world was faced with a deliberate act of aggression which at once recalled Hitler's tactics of "one at a time" in the 1930s. On the one hand, fear of seeing a similar attack launched across the dividing line of a partitioned Germany produced the German reaction summed up in the frequently heard phrase *"ohne mich"* ("count me out"); on the other, the lesson drawn from appeasement in the 1930s mobilized support for immediate action while there was still time to prevent a similar buildup to a third world war. The report in September 1949 that the Soviet Union had successfully developed an atomic bomb added to the urgency of both arguments.

Such evidence as has emerged since, however, suggests that Stalin may have been as surprised by the American reaction as the West was by the event itself. While he remained prepared to probe and test the strength of Western resolution (as in the case of Berlin) and to take advantage of any weakness, it was because he had been convinced by the argument that Kim Il-sung's proposal would not involve the risk of confrontation with the Americans that he had agreed to it.

Even before the attack began, Stalin had insisted on recalling the Soviet advisers who had been responsible for building up the North Korean army. The reason he gave to Khrushchev was the need to avoid any justification for accusing the Russians of being involved in the operation. For the same reason he ordered the Soviet delegation to the UN to boycott the Security Council rather than veto the American motion condemning the North Korean aggression and so place the Soviet Union in open opposition to the large majority of UN members. When the North ran into trouble and Khrushchev suggested sending someone like Marshal Malinovsky to advise Kim Il-sung on how to handle the situation, "Stalin reacted to my remarks with extreme hostility."[35] After the U.S. Army recaptured Seoul and pressed on to the Chinese border along the Yalu river, it was Chinese, not Russian "volunteers" who intervened (November 1950) and drove the Americans back. How this came about is not clear. According to Khrushchev again, Chou En-lai flew to see Stalin at Sochi and the two at first agreed that it was fruitless for China to intervene. Just before Chou was due to return, however, they reopened the question—"either Chou on Mao Tse-tung's instructions or else Stalin himself"—and agreed that China should give active support to the Koreans.[36]

However the decision was reached—whether Stalin persuaded or pressured the Chinese, or agreed to a Chinese initiative—the result was to turn the Korean war into a bitter U.S. confrontation with China, not Russia, in which the Chinese suffered heavy losses of at least three-quarters of a million men. After his initial miscalculation Stalin was able to distance himself from the war, in which no Russian troops were ever involved, to redirect American anger and hostility toward China, and to make the first call for a ceasefire and armistice (June 1951). Although truce negotiations were started in July 1951, they broke down and the war dragged on sporadically for another two years, an armistice only being concluded in July 1953, after Stalin's death.

As in the case of the Berlin blockade, Stalin showed that he knew when to stop. Nor did he ever forget that, unlike the Chinese, he was engaged in two-front diplomacy in which (as during the Second World War) the European would always take priority over the Far Eastern. The long-term result of the Korean war in the Far East brought a serious setback for Soviet diplomacy in the close relationship that it cemented between the U.S.A. and Japan. Instead of the American withdrawal from Japan for which Stalin had hoped, the peace treaty with Japan that the U.S.A. pushed through in September 1951, in the face of Soviet opposition, was followed by an American-Japanese security pact, which gave the U.S.A. the right to maintain bases and armed forces.

In Europe, however, the impact of the Korean war worked to Russia's advantage. As the Americans became more deeply involved in the war, and anti-Communist feeling in the U.S.A. hardened—the early 1950s were the years of Senator Joseph McCarthy's witch-hunt—the earlier support of

America's allies for her stand against aggression gave way to increasing distrust of American leadership and fear that it might plunge the world into a third world war. The millions who signed the Stockholm Peace Appeal to abolish atomic weapons found it easy to see American imperialism rather than Communism as the real aggressor. The Americans on their side became increasingly irritated with allies who had plenty of criticism to offer but little support in a war that they felt they were being left to fight on behalf of the free world and the United Nations.

In the last intervention he made at a party congress, in October 1952, Stalin argued—as he did in his *Economic Problems of Socialism,* published the same year—that the contradictions and conflicts within the "imperialist bloc" remained greater than those between the "two camps" of capitalism and socialism. The area in which Stalin was most eager to exploit these differences was German rearmament. The NATO treaty had been signed in April 1949, but the only troops that the Alliance possessed in 1952 were a few American, British, and French divisions with two or three token brigades from the smaller countries, hardly (as Montgomery and Bradley pointed out at the time of the Berlin blockade) a fighting force with which to confront the powerful Soviet armed forces stationed in Central Europe. Not until 1955 did the Russians think it worth their while to mobilize East European forces in the Warsaw Pact as an answer to West German integration into NATO.

With the French army involved in a war in Indochina, and the American in Korea, the obvious answer already pressed by the Americans was to build up NATO with a strong West German contingent. Without this, the Russians were unlikely to take NATO seriously. By the same token, of all the possible developments the Russians were concerned with preventing after their experiences in the Second World War, a revival of German military power was the one in which they saw the greatest danger, greater than in the American lead in nuclear warfare. The French, who already had to swallow seeing the restoration of German economic power take priority over their own, were as opposed as the Russians to seeing Germany become a fully fledged military partner in NATO, and five years were spent between 1949 and 1954 trying to find a workable formula for a European Defense Community that would enable West Germany to contribute to the Alliance without reestablishing a separate German army.

In 1949 Stalin had matched the creation of the Federal Republic in West Germany by setting up the German Democratic Republic (GDR) in the east. But twice after that he offered to ditch the GDR if this would block the remilitarization of Germany. The first occasion was in November 1950, when a meeting of the foreign ministers of the USSR and her satellites in Prague called for the four occupying powers to forbid the creation of German armed forces and carry out the Potsdam agreement to establish a united and disarmed Germany from which all occupying forces would be withdrawn. The second occasion was in March 1952 when a Soviet diplomatic note again proposed four-power talks leading to a peace treaty and the unification of Germany, with this additional condition: that a unified Germany should be allowed to rearm, provided she bound herself to follow a policy of neutrality.

These later initiatives have left historians as divided as they did contemporaries in assessing how far a real opportunity to negotiate was missed. Were the Russians really prepared to give up a Communist-controlled East Germany for the promise of neutrality by a reunited country? Or was this one more attempt, in a series of such going back to the Council of Foreign Ministers in 1947, to hold up plans for the economic and political restoration of the three Western zones and throw the future of Germany back onto the drawing board. It would be characteristic of Stalin not to have made up his mind how far he was prepared to go until he had tried out the strength and weakness of the other parties' positions around the negotiating table. But the Western powers were not prepared to risk further delays and a revival of uncertainty in order to find out how serious he was.

So the search for an answer to the question of Germany's place in Europe and German-Russian relations which cost so many million lives ended inconclusively. In 1952 Hitler had been dead for seven years, but his presence had been felt at every one of the European meetings since then. For it was Hitler who had first posed the question by his plan, set out in *Mein Kampf* in the mid-1920s, when he was still an insignificant figure on the margin of German politics, to destroy the Soviet state and replace it by a new German empire ruling over Eastern Europe and western Russia and reducing their inhabitants to slavery. It was Hitler who had launched the most powerful army ever assembled in history across the Russian frontier in June 1941 to put his plan into effect. It was Hitler who, when his plan failed, insisted on prolonging the war for more than three years after Stalingrad until in place of a German army on the Volga there was a Russian army on the Elbe. Failing a peace settlement, of which there was no prospect, the effective legacy of the Hitler-Stalin era was to leave half of Europe and half of Germany under one form or another of Soviet rule.

VII

BEHIND THE INVISIBLE WALLS that Stalin erected to shut off the Soviet Union from the rest of the world, a remarkable economic recovery took place in the first five years after the war.

There is no agreement among economists about how much of this was due to reparations. Much transport and industrial equipment, including whole factories such as the Zeiss works at Jena, was removed bodily from eastern Germany, Austria, Hungary, Rumania, and Manchuria. It amounts to a huge total. But there are no comparable statistics on the Soviet side showing how much of what was taken reached Russia, or was successfully put into production when it did. The same is true of the half-shares in joint companies, and the trade treaties negotiated with countries occupied by the Russians or within their sphere of influence. There is every reason to believe that these arrangements worked to the advantage of the Russians at the expense of the other parties. But there are no data to quantify the advantage. At most, reparations, in whatever form they were taken, can hardly have done more than help to offset the looting and destruction to which Russia had been subjected by the Germans and their allies during the war. The postwar reconstruction, like the evacuation of factories and workers and the remarkable increases in productivity during the war, was above all due to the efforts of the Soviet people themselves.

The huge country was still so disorganized in 1945 and 1946 that, despite the fall in arms production, overall industrial production also fell, and the food situation was so bad that there was famine in the Ukraine and other areas. But after 1946 the targets of the fourth Five-Year Plan were exceeded in all the main industries except textiles, footwear—and, of course, agriculture. [37] The Ukraine, which had suffered more heavily than any other part from the destruction of its industries, was able to report by 1950 that its flooded mines were restored and the great Dnieper dam rebuilt, while its output of coal, electricity, and the products of its metallurgical and engineering industries had risen above the levels of 1940, the last full year of peace. Since the productive capacity of the Urals and Siberia had not been interrupted and continued to grow, this meant that the overall figures were well above those for 1940.

This result had been achieved by a concentration of investment (88 percent) in heavy industry and the production of capital goods. Consumer goods, housing, and food (the second in particular) remained in short supply. Between 1947 and 1952 there was a surprising and very welcome improvement in real wages for workers (peasants always excepted)—43 percent over the figure for 1940—but still too little to spend them on, a poor distribution system, and waiting lines a familiar feature of Soviet life.

Stalin must have been informed of the debates and acquiesced in the decisions that lay behind this industrial recovery. There is no evidence, however, that he was actively involved in them, as he had been in the early 1930s, when he was the driving force behind Soviet industrialization. Nor is there evidence to show how far the issues were thrashed out in the Politburo itself, or how far the real battles over policy, investment, and allocations took place at the top level of the state economic ministries, involving for their political support only individual members of the Politburo with supervisory functions in the economic field. Stalin could still make sporadic arbitrary interventions, but he was no longer master of the machine he had created.

Where Stalin's influence was still decisive was in the highly centralized character he had given to the process of bureaucratic decision-making and the overriding importance he had always attached to producing as much as possible, at the expense of quality and cost—a tradition reinforced by the suppression of statistics and the various devices used to inflate the few figures that were published. What mattered—what brought rewards and promotion—was to fulfill, better still to overfulfill, the plan, and the simplest way to do that was to go on using the same designs, even when they had become obsolete.

The effect was to put a premium on conservatism and to discourage innovation, the criticism of the pattern of Russia's postwar industrial recovery subsequently made by Soviet economists. This effect was encouraged by Stalin's insistence on reducing contact with the rest of the world to a minimum and the official line that Russia had nothing to learn from a decadent West. The war had provided a great stimulus to Russian inventiveness, and her designers had learned both from the enemy and from Russia's allies. Once the war was over, the stimulus of competition was lost and the links with the West were severed. Soviet industry fell behind in technological development, for example in the chemical industry and plastics and synthetics; in new nonsolid fuels like natural gas in which Russia was particularly rich; and in computer technology. But the military pressure generated by the Cold War—rearmament and the buildup of Soviet forces was resumed in 1950—soon showed that Russia did not lack the scientific talent to develop nuclear weapons and explore space. The launch of the Sputnik in 1957 gave as great a shock to American complacency as the explosion of the first Soviet atom bomb in 1949. But success in this specialized field only served to show the extent to which the rest of the Soviet industry remained in the smokestack, coal, and steel phase.

Fifteen to twenty years earlier, Stalin himself had been the innovator; now in his seventies he was no longer capable of providing the drive he had supplied then. But age made him more jealous than ever of the unique position he claimed for himself in Soviet history, and those closest to him knew that he would not tolerate a potential successor seeking to renew and extend a revolution that had become ossified.

WHATEVER MAY have been true of industry, there is no doubt of Stalin's influence on the postwar development of Soviet agriculture. After the famine of 1946—the evidence for which he had refused to accept at the time—it was agreed that priority must be given to a major effort to expand agricultural production. There was no lack of plans nor of funds for the necessary investment and, at the Party Congress of 1952, Malenkov (with Stalin sitting on the platform) declared that the grain problem had been solved once and for all. As long as Stalin was alive, this continued to be the official line: The much-publicized measures introduced between 1948 and 1952 under his aegis had transformed the situation. Only in 1953, after Stalin's death, when Khrushchev felt free for the first time to tell the Supreme Soviet the truth about the state of agriculture, was it revealed that, however the results were measured, Soviet farming had not yet recovered (except in the cotton crop) to prewar levels or, in the case of livestock, to those of 1928 or even of 1916.

Subsequent publications by Soviet economists have confirmed the dismal picture Khrushchev drew and suggest two directions in which to look for an explanation of why the efforts failed to change it. The first was Stalin's stubborn refusal to allow any attempt to win the cooperation of the *kolkhoz* workers in raising productivity by offering them material incentives. He continued to see the rural population of Russia, as he had from the beginning, as enemies who could never be trusted but must be compelled to carry out orders from above.

Stalin appeared determined to make the peasants bear a disproportionate share of the burden of the postwar recovery without allowing them to share in the benefits. While additional funds went to the machine-tractor stations and the power stations which produced rural electricity for the state farms (but not for the *kolkhozes*), a series of fresh burdens was laid on the backs of the *kolkhoz* workers. Taxes on the collective farms as well as on the workers' private plots were increased; they were no longer allowed to obtain their seeds from the state but had to build up seed reserves of their own, and the level of the procurements for livestock products as well as crops was increased by 50 percent.

Obstinately refusing to believe those who reported on the impoverishment of the countryside, or to go and see for himself, Stalin told the minister of finance, Zverev, that all a peasant had to do was to sell one chicken more to keep the tax collector happy, brushing aside the reply that some would not be able to pay their taxes if they sold their only cow.[38]

A second reason for failure, reinforcing the first, was Stalin's readiness to listen to "miracle-working" schemes proposed by unorthodox scientific prophets—the best known, but by no means the only one of whom was Trofim Lysenko. The scientific doctrine of "Michurinism," for example, was named after a self-taught breeder of fruit trees who never actually produced any new varieties, but whose claims were hailed as an important Soviet proletarian contribution to science, establishing man's ability to overcome "so-called natural laws" and control his environment.

Lysenko had originally attracted attention by claiming to revolutionize growing grain by "vernalizing" winter-wheat seed—that is, by moistening and chilling it and planting it in the spring. The questionable results of his experiments and the claim that he was applying Marxist principles to genetics led him into conflict with the scientific establishment. But Lysenko's glib promises of what he could achieve, if given a free hand, impressed party officials on the lookout for a breakthrough in crop production. His attack on "bourgeois genetics" as a reactionary science inhibiting socialist attempts to transform the environment fitted in with Stalin's repudiation of Western influences, including Western science, in favor of Russian innovative genius.

In 1948 Lysenko, who had become head of the Lenin Institute for Agricultural Sciences, succeeded in arousing Stalin's interest in a plan to plant three huge belts of trees, totaling more than 5,000 kilometers in length, which, he claimed, would prevent soil erosion and moderate the extremes of cold and heat. Even more important was the backing from Stalin that Lysenko obtained in his long-standing feud with other Soviet biologists and agriculturists in the Academy of Sciences who attacked him as a charlatan.

In April 1948 Lysenko appealed to Stalin in a letter in which he claimed that the academicians were preventing him from achieving exciting developments across the whole field of agricultural science because of their opposition to the "Michurinist" philosophy. This taught that living nature could be changed and recognized the inheritance of acquired characteristics. What impressed Stalin was Lysenko's report that, with the results he had already achieved with a packet of seed Stalin had asked him to test, he could eventually promise a five- or tenfold increase in the wheat harvest. Even if he got only a 50-percent increase, Stalin declared, that would be more than enough.

Stalin then ordered a conference to be held at the Lenin Academy at which Lysenko delivered a report on the "Situation in Biological Science," which he claimed Stalin had helped him to edit, and which overturned the established Weismann-Mendel tradition in genetics in favor of his own "Michurinist" views. Henceforward, Lysenkoism became the new orthodoxy which all Soviet scientists were required to accept, and, thanks to the power that Stalin's patronage gave Lysenko, three thousand biologists were dismissed from their posts. [39]

The practical outcome of Lysenko's triumph was the adoption of his tree-planting scheme as the centerpiece for the "Stalin Plan for the Transformation of Nature," adopted in October 1948. This grandiose project, which the peasants were to carry out largely at the *kolkhozes'* expense, was to take fifteen years to accomplish, beginning in 1950. By the end of 1951, Malenkov claimed, 1.5 million hectares had already been planted. The fact that many of the seedlings died because of the dry climate they were planted to transform was not reported. Unperturbed, Stalin went on to sign four state decrees for a series of "Great Stalinist Constructions" which would improve irrigation and communications by building four new canals and four new dams. At the point where the new Volga-Don Canal was to join the Volga, he ordered a giant statue of himself to be erected, for which thirty-three tons of copper were set aside.

None of these schemes succeeded sufficiently to provide an alternative way of raising the low level of agricultural productivity; all they did was to divert attention, effort, and funds away from the obvious solution which Stalin refused to consider, that of providing a fairer return to the poorest and most exploited class in Russia, the rural workers on the *kolkhozes*—a striking prejudice for a man who claimed to be the leader of the world's first socialist society.

. . .

ZHDANOV DIED at the end of August 1948. Since he was known to be in bad health and suffering from a heart condition, this caused no surprise. It was only Stalin's later denunciation of the Kremlin doctors for having murdered him by medical means that raised doubts. Stalin had done this before in 1938 when Yagoda, after his fall from favor, was charged and "confessed" to arranging the medical murder of Gorki and the assassination of Kirov.

Whatever the truth about Zhdanov's death—and the presumption is still in favor of its being unaided—he was already falling from favor before he died. Stalin may have come to feel that he was becoming too powerful and that the time had come for the balance among his entourage to be changed, or that he had failed and the time had come to make a change in policy—or both. A sure sign was the return of Malenkov, just over a month before Zhdanov's death, to the Central Committee Secretariat (he had remained all the time a member of the Politburo).

After losing his position in the Secretariat, Malenkov had been transferred to a job in Central Asia. He is reported to have owed his return to Moscow to Beria, and the two remained close allies until Stalin's death. In their reminiscences, both Stalin's daughter, Svetlana, and Khrushchev speak of Beria with horror as the evil genius of Stalin's final years. As soon as they could summon up their courage after Stalin's death, the other members of the Politburo had him arrested and shot, in June 1953.* Stalin's relationship with him was highly ambivalent. Beria was a Georgian, who could speak to him in their original language, and who knew all the secrets of Transcaucasia from which both of them came. He first attracted Stalin's attention as a regular visitor to his summer dacha near Sochi, and in November 1932 was appointed first secretary for all Transcaucasia. His meteoric rise was due to the publication in 1935 of a book, *On the History of the Bolshevik Organization in Transcaucasia,* which grossly exaggerated Stalin's role as the leader of the Bolsheviks in Transcaucasia and the hammer of the Mensheviks. Stalin's approval led to the original edition of 100,000 copies being followed by eight more as well as by foreign translations. Three years later in 1938 Beria was nominated to succeed Yezhov as head of the NKVD. Charged with the security of the regime, he had access to Stalin at all times. But Stalin also distrusted him, and toward the end of his life feared him as well, and was taking steps to destroy him.

When the NKVD was broken up (after January 1946) into the MVD

---

*Unable to rely on the secret police to detain Beria, Khrushchev and Malenkov arranged for no less than eleven of the leading marshals and generals, fully armed, to be in the next room, within call, and for them to carry out the arrest. The first to appear was Marshal Zhukov, who commanded Beria to put his hands up. He was then taken, not to the Lubyanka, but to a bunker at the Air Defense Commander's headquarters. The investigation was entrusted to R. A. Rudenko, who had acted as the chief Soviet prosecutor at the Nuremberg Trials of the Nazi leaders.

(Ministry of the Interior) and MGB (the Political Police), Beria was no longer the working head of either. But at the same time he was promoted to full membership in the Politburo—possibly as compensation—and retained an undefined responsibility for security as the man the secret police still looked to. V. S. Abakumov, for example, who was appointed by Stalin as head of the MGB, was one of Beria's men and (according to Khrushchev) always reported first to him before speaking to Stalin.

Besides the political police with their "special sections" in every Soviet institution including the ministries, Beria's fiefdom still extended to the MVD in charge of the camps and the slave labor of the Gulag archipelago also; and to SMERSH, the counterintelligence agency, with its network of informers at home and agents abroad.

In keeping with the custom of all tyrannies since Greek times, the fall of a favorite was followed by the ousting of his retainers. Taking Zhdanov's place as the effective head (under Stalin) of the party's Central Secretariat, Malenkov got rid of the three other secretaries whom Zhdanov had brought in—A. A. Kuznetsov, G. M. Popov, and N. S. Patolichev—and replaced thirty-five out of the fifty-eight first secretaries of the regional parties in the Russian Federated Republic. Some of Zhdanov's policies were continued, for example in the cultural field; but the attempt to revive the leading role of the party was abandoned. Although Malenkov had risen through the Secretariat, his power base was not the party but the Council of Ministers, of which he became first deputy chairman, and the state bureaucracy, employing millions in the network of economic ministries and nationalized industries, in which he had made his reputation as an administrator during the war.

The period that now followed saw a return, on a smaller scale, to the uncertainty and fears of earlier years, reaching a climax in the six months before Stalin's death in March 1953. Forty years later, despite *glasnost,* knowledge of the historical facts is still fragmentary and interpretation of them open to dispute.

In March 1949, it was announced that three senior members of the Politburo and Council of Ministers, Molotov, Mikoyan, and Bulganin, were to relinquish their ministerial posts: Molotov as minister of foreign affairs to Vyshinsky; Mikoyan as minister of foreign trade to Mikhail Menshikov; Bulganin as minister of defense to Marshal Vasilevsky. No reason was given, and all three retained their positions as deputy chairmen of the Council of Ministers. But these titles were honorific, no substitute for the loss of their power bases and patronage. Those practiced in reading the signs took the move as the first step in demotion, a view confirmed by the fact that as soon as Stalin was dead all three immediately repossessed their former offices.

As those who replaced them in 1949 were men of lesser standing, members neither of the Politburo nor of the Council of Ministers, it could be assumed that the move enhanced the position of Malenkov and Beria, and by removing Molotov in particular, hitherto seen by most people as

Stalin's deputy, improved their chances as the youngest of the possible contestants for succeeding Stalin when the time came. This was an unmentionable subject, but with "the boss" in his seventieth year and not in good health, it was increasingly in the minds of those close to him. What part, if any, Malenkov and Beria took in engineering the move against Molotov and Mikoyan is not known; only Stalin could have made it, but he may have been persuaded to do so. The blow must have been a bitter one for Molotov after the part he had played in international relations since 1939. There are other signs, however, that he had lost Stalin's favor, which he was never to recover; among them was the arrest and exile of his wife.*

The same month of March 1949 saw the beginning of the Leningrad Affair, the removal this time of younger men than Malenkov and Beria—Kuznetsov, Voznesensky, Kosygin—who belonged to a generation that owed everything to Stalin and were the natural replacements for the Old Guard—Molotov, Mikoyan, Voroshilov—who had joined the party before the 1917 revolution. The other thing they had in common was association with Leningrad and its former boss, Zhdanov. The specific charges brought against them have not been revealed, and were not known to Khrushchev, although he admitted that he signed the order for execution when it was passed around at a Politburo session. [40]

No one had moved more rapidly to the top or appeared to be more in Stalin's favor than Nikolai Voznesensky. From head of the economic planning office in Leningrad, he had been appointed head of Gosplan (the State Planning Office) in 1938, at the age of thirty-four. In 1941 he was made a deputy chairman of the Council of Ministers and in 1942 a deputy chairman of GOKO, the all-important State Defense Committee, in which he often sat in for Stalin during the discussion of economic matters. Resuming direction of Gosplan after the war he was made a full member of the Politburo in 1947 and the next year, after Stalin himself had read and approved it, was awarded a Stalin Prize for his book *The War Economy of the USSR*.

This brilliant career was cut short and Voznesensky relieved of all his posts at a single blow. No explanation was given, but in 1963 it emerged that he had been charged at a secret trial with allowing important documents to be lost or stolen. Although some of his subordinates had to serve a prison sentence for "lack of vigilance," Voznesensky himself was acquitted. But the frame-up had achieved its organizers' object: Stalin's suspicions had been aroused. No new job was found for him, his book was withdrawn, and his repeated attempts to see Stalin—in whose honesty and goodwill he still believed—were rebuffed. According to Khrushchev, Stalin more than once asked Malenkov and Beria: "Isn't it a waste of time not letting Voznesensky work while we're deciding what to do with him?" Without disagreeing, they did nothing. Stalin brought the matter up again: "Maybe

*See p. 953.

we should put Voznesensky in charge of the State Bank. He's an economist, a financial wizard."[41] Nobody objected, but again nothing happened.

In the meantime the security police under the direction of Abakumov had been busily engaged in fabricating a conspiracy involving scores of party and state officials in Leningrad appointed by Zhdanov. After Stalin's death, Abakumov and several of his assistants were tried at a special session held in Leningrad, where they were found guilty and put to death for falsifying the case on which the 1949–1950 purge was based; in 1962 an official statement named Malenkov as well as Beria as having been responsible for the Leningrad Affair, adding that "from beginning to end it was fiction and provocation."

At the time, however, with Stalin's agreement at least, if not under his direction as Khrushchev reports, the investigation, with the usual crop of "confessions" and denunciations, led to a thousand—other reports say two thousand—arrests. Among those whose lives Khrushchev says hung by a thread were Kosygin, another Leningrader and later chairman of the Council of Ministers in Brezhnev's day, and the first secretary of the Moscow party, G. M. Popov, whom Khrushchev was summoned from the Ukraine to replace. A conspiracy, Stalin told Khrushchev, had been uncovered in Leningrad, and "Moscow too is teeming with anti-party elements."

Voznesensky had been left for six months without any word from the Kremlin, during which, to keep himself sane, he completed an 800-page treatise on the political economy of Communism. In November 1949 the police at last arrested him. After the waiting and the silence it was a relief—a carefully calculated part of the process of breaking down a prisoner and securing his confession. On January 13, 1950, it was announced that, "in answer to popular demand," the death penalty, which had been abolished in 1947, was to be restored for the crime of treason. In order to obtain the essential confession on which Stalin always insisted, Voznesensky, along with others, is reported to have been tortured before finally being condemned and shot in September 1950. All copies of his treatise were ordered to be destroyed. How many others were executed or imprisoned has never been revealed. Kosygin, however, survived.

A QUITE DIFFERENT security operation between 1948 and 1950 marked the beginning of the anti-Semitic campaign that was a feature of Stalin's final years. Anti-Semitism had been endemic in Russia before the revolution (*pogrom* is a Russian word) and did not disappear from Russian life after it. Although not actively anti-Semitic earlier in his career, Stalin appears to have shared this common Russian prejudice but not to have allowed it to influence policy until after the war. During the war, the Jewish Anti-Fascist Committee was set up with his approval to secure international support for the Soviet Union, especially in the United States. In November 1946, however, Mikhail Suslov sent a note to Stalin warning him that the committee was engaged in "harmful activities," a pointer to the cryptic persecution of Jews which was to follow, bursting into full publicity with the "Doctors' Case" at the beginning of 1953.

This was a period when social and cultural factors—the isolation of the Soviet Union from the rest of the world, the heightened mood of Russian chauvinism, the Zhdanov campaign against foreign influences in Soviet culture—were strengthened by political developments, such as the breach with the United States, the arch-imperialist power, with its influential and highly vocal Jewish lobby and its support of Zionism; the emergence of the state of Israel claiming the allegiance of Jews throughout the world, including the Soviet Union; and the revival of the call for vigilance against "enemies of the people" and "traitors within." These combined to create a situation in which Jews were all too easily identified as aliens, "rootless cosmopolitans," Europeanized intellectuals, responsible for the spread of decadent modern art, at the same time "Zionist agents of American imperialism."

Stalin succumbed to the same virus of anti-Semitism as Hitler, substituting the Jewish world-conspiracy of capitalism and Zionism, with its headquarters in Wall Street, for Hitler's Jewish world-conspiracy of Bolshevism, with its headquarters in the Kremlin. To Stalin's anger, his elder son, Yakov, married a Jewess, and his daughter Svetlana's greatest offense was falling in love with an older Jewish man—who spent ten years in the camps for his temerity—then going on to marry another Jew. "That first husband of yours," Stalin shouted at her, "was thrown your way by the Zionists,"[42] and he forbade her ever to bring him home.

The USSR was actually one of the first states to recognize the Israeli government in 1948, apparently with the intention of using Israel to make trouble for the West. But the arrival in Moscow of Golda Meir in October 1948 as the first Israeli ambassador produced a sharp reaction. A spontaneous demonstration in her honor outside a Moscow synagogue by a large and enthusiastic crowd of Russian Jews convinced Stalin that anyone with Zionist sympathies must be a traitor to the Soviet Union. When Svetlana protested at Stalin's suspicions, he pounced on her and declared: "The entire older generation is contaminated with Zionism and now they're teaching the young people, too."[43]

One of the earliest victims of the anti-Semitic campaign was the great Jewish actor and director of the Moscow Yiddish Theater, Solomon Mikhoels. Famous for his portrayal of the aging tyrant King Lear, he had more than once presented Lear and other Shakespearean characters to Stalin in private. Early in 1948 he was reported to have died in a car accident at Minsk; Svetlana overheard her father suggesting this on the telephone as the cover-up story.

The continuing campaign against "rootless cosmopolitan influences" in intellectual and cultural circles was very easily given an anti-Jewish slant. Jewish critics were forbidden to write for Soviet journals; Jewish schools, theaters, and publications were closed down; restrictive quotas were placed on the admission of Jews to universities and scientific institutes and their employment in the diplomatic and legal services.

The Jewish Anti-Fascist Committee now appeared as a crypto-Zionist center, a secret tunnel burrowing under the defenses that Stalin had erected against hostile foreign influence. The MGB soon found the necessary "evidence." The committee was dissolved in November 1948 and its director Solomon Losovsky, a former assistant foreign minister, was arrested and executed in August 1952 together with twelve others, including the Soviet Union's leading Yiddish writers.

Among other members of the committee arrested in 1948 was Molotov's Jewish wife, Pauline, who had engaged Mrs. Meir in an animated conversation. Stalin had long regarded her with suspicion as one of his wife's closest friends and the last person with whom she had talked before committing suicide. Her husband's position as foreign minister did nothing to save her: She was sentenced and imprisoned in a camp in Central Asia and released only when Stalin died. She was not the first nor the last among the wives of Stalin's closest collaborators to suffer such treatment. Yekaterina Kalinin, the wife of Mikhail Kalinin, who was Soviet head of state until his death in 1946, was held in a labor camp after having been beaten unconscious by a woman NKVD officer in the presence of Beria.

VIII

IN KEEPING WITH the revival of the death sentence, the treatment of those who were held in the Gulag camps or had been exiled to Siberia was made harsher. During the war, the numbers in the camps had not been reduced except by death. Those who survived from the earlier purges had their sentences increased by five, eight, ten years, and many were transferred from general to special camps with an "intensified" regime. The camp population was replenished and increased at the end of the war with those returning from the front, those who had been deported to work in Germany, and those who had lived under German occupation—many of whom were sentenced to forced labor on charges of treason. As a result of a chance remark by Stalin in 1947 that "the Russian people had long dreamed of a safe outlet to the Arctic Ocean," scores of thousands of prisoners were drafted in to build a railway, 1,800 kilometers long, across the tundra to Igaska. Known as the Railway of Death because of the appalling conditions in its eighty-odd camps, 850 kilometers of track were actually completed, at enormous cost of life, before the project was abandoned after Stalin's death and the line, its equipment and locomotives left to rust in the snow. [44]

The total number of prisoners in camps in the late 1940s is estimated at between twelve and fourteen million. At the end of the decade, those who were released on completing their sentences were condemned, along with those exiled and deported during the war, to remain in the remote and inhospitable districts of the north "forever," without any hope of returning to their families or hometowns. Unseen, never referred to in public, but never out of mind, the Gulag archipelago remained the somber background to Soviet life.

Little publicity was given to the Leningrad Affair or, to begin with, to the persecution of the Jews. But in the two capitals, Moscow and Leningrad, and throughout the upper echelons of the party and the state bureaucracy, rumor was rife and combined with the official silence to renew the atmosphere of menace. By comparison with 1937–38 only a small number were so far directly affected, but nobody knew how far it would spread, or who might be next.

When the Soviet peoples and the world's Communist parties united in December 1949 to celebrate Stalin's seventieth birthday, it was hard to find fresh words with which to pay tribute to a man who had come to be described as a "universal genius." From the heir of Lenin, through equal partnership with him, the "two chiefs" who had created the Bolshevik party and carried out the October Revolution together, the cult of Stalin had progressed to the point where it eclipsed the cult of Lenin on which it had been originally modeled. Historical accounts were constantly revised to keep in step.

In his secret speech to the Twentieth Party Congress in 1956, Khrushchev quoted a number of passages inserted in the 1948 edition of Stalin's *Short Biography*. Among them was this appreciation of himself as a strategist:

Comrade Stalin elaborated the theory of the permanently operating factors that decide the issue of wars, of active defense, and the laws of counteroffensive and offensive . . . of the role of big tank masses and air forces in modern war. At the various stages of the war Stalin's genius found the correct solution that took account of all the circumstances. . . . His military mastership was displayed both in defense and offense. His genius enabled him to divine the enemy's plans and defeat them.

To which Stalin added:

Although he performed his task of leader of the party and the people with consummate skill and enjoyed the unreserved support of the entire Soviet people, Stalin never allowed his work to be marred by the slightest hint of vanity, conceit, or self-adulation. [45]

No less than seventy-five leading figures, including all the members of the Politburo, Lysenko, and Shostakovich, served on the committee that coordinated the birthday celebrations. The Soviet Academy of Sciences held a special meeting to honor "the greatest genius of mankind" and published a large volume illustrating Stalin's contributions to the different branches of learning. The members of the Politburo each contributed an essay to a collection published in many periodicals. Malenkov led off with a piece, "Comrade Stalin—the Leader of Progressive Mankind," the opening sentence of which read: "Comrade Stalin constantly warns us that not conceit but modesty adorns a Bolshevik."

The celebration culminated in a gala held in the Bolshoi Theater at which Mao Tse-tung, Togliatti, Ulbricht, and other visitors came to pay tribute to the enigmatic figure who sat apart from the rest, smiling but silent throughout the proceedings. All the members of the Politburo were present but none of them spoke, either; the visitors' speeches were interspersed by contributions from minor Soviet figures, underlining the distance that separated Stalin from the leaders of all other Communist parties, including Mao Tse-tung.

The presentation of gifts not only from every part of the Soviet Union but from Communists all over the world conveyed the love and admiration of the masses. Until a permanent museum could be built, a selection was displayed in the Museum of the Revolution. At night batteries of searchlights focused on a giant portrait of the leader suspended over the capital from a balloon—"hung in the sky like a hero of antiquity become a constellation."[46]

Stalin must have been fully aware at the conscious level of his mind of the part that compulsion played in such a demonstration of enthusiasm and admiration. Profoundly skeptical as he was about human nature, this would not have worried him. His answer to the question of whether he would prefer his people to be loyal out of fear or out of conviction has already been quoted: "Fear. Convictions can change but fear remains." But at the same time, even if it had to be organized, at another level he needed the display of spontaneity, if only to still the skepticism that he could never banish from his mind when he was dealing with his own people, and especially with members of the party. As he sat on the stage of the Bolshoi, listening to the tributes, he combined disbelief in their sincerity with the imperious demand that they be paid nonetheless, and an unfailing ear for anything less than total conviction.

KHRUSHCHEV HAD MOVED back to Moscow by the time of Stalin's birthday celebrations. He had survived the period when he fell out of favor with Stalin and Kaganovich had been imposed on him; now he was welcomed back, not only as a reinforcement against the threat of conspiracy but also as a counterbalance to the dominant position of Malenkov and Beria in the inner circle. Working closely again with Stalin, he was struck by the extent to which he had become "even more capricious, irritable, and brutal; in particular his suspicion grew to unbelievable dimensions."[47]

Knowing Stalin's susceptibility to suggestions of treachery, particularly in written form, Beria fed his suspicions with scraps of evidence, which, given any encouragement, the MGB could then work up into one of its "novels" (as they were known to their compilers) and extort the "confessions" with

which to support a case. Beria exploited a characteristic of which Yezhov
had also taken advantage: While Stalin might question oral evidence of
"treachery," he was much more likely to accept evidence on paper at face
value; he found it hard to believe that anyone would try to mislead him in
writing. But Stalin also distrusted and feared Beria. Never far from either
man's mind was the way Stalin had destroyed Beria's predecessors, Yagoda
and Yezhov. Beria was on his guard against a repetition in his case, Stalin
watchful of any attempt by Beria to forestall it by arranging his own death
first.

For this reason Stalin would not always listen to Beria's insinuations:
Among those he refused to let Beria set up were three names that came to
light in 1988. One was Zhukov: Mikoyan recalls Stalin telling Beria, "I won't
give you Zhukov. I know him, he is not a traitor."[48] A second was the
leading Russian physicist, Kapitsa, who refused to work on the atom bomb
under Beria's direction. The third was Marshal Peter Voronov, the wartime
commander of the Red Army's artillery. Admiral Isakov recalls an occasion
when Voronov failed to turn up for a meeting, and Stalin demanded of
Beria:

> "Lavrentii, is he with you?"
> Beria, walking about the room, said over his shoulder, "Yes, he is."
> Stalin looked at him meaningfully, and we saw Beria cower and even
> grow shorter.
> "Can he be back tomorrow?" Stalin asked.
> "Not tomorrow," Beria answered, not knowing where to put his hands
> or himself.
> "The day after tomorrow?" Stalin continued, fixing Beria with a firm
> look.
> "He will be here the day after tomorrow. Definitely."

The meeting was postponed and on the determined day Voronov was in his
place. No one asked him, nor did he volunteer, where he had been.[49]

Once Stalin's suspicions were aroused, however, he was not easily persuaded to let them drop. On Khrushchev's return from the Ukraine Stalin
confronted him with a denunciation of G. M. Popov, his predecessor as
Moscow party boss. Khrushchev claims to have talked Stalin out of acting
on it but was sure that he would not rest until he could trip up Popov. So
a job was found for him as director of a factory in Kuibyshev. Whenever
Stalin referred to the charges against Popov, as he did from time to time,
demanding to know where he was, the reply was "In Kuibyshev"—and this
seemed to calm Stalin down.

Stalin no longer had the power of concentration or the energy to retain
his grip on the machinery of government. He spent much less time in his
office, preferring his dacha at Kuntsevo and extending his annual vacation
on the Black Sea coast from the end of August to late November or early

December. The bureaucracy functioned without him, and eventually he was merely sent lists of the proposed decisions to confirm rather than the draft decisions themselves. Only occasionally did he preside over the Council of Ministers. When he did turn up unexpectedly, it threw everybody off. Khrushchev recalls an occasion on which a difficult debate was expected on the allocation of resources. Without previous notice Stalin suddenly appeared and took the chair. Pointing to a pile of documents in front of him, he said, "Here is the plan. Any objections?" Since none of the ministers liked to be the first to speak, there was silence. In that case, Stalin announced, the meeting was adjourned and they could all go to see a film which he had arranged to be shown that afternoon. On the way out he was heard to remark: "We fooled them good." [50]

Part of the historical image Stalin still sought to cultivate was that of the original thinker as well as the politician. His *Collected Works* were already being published to stand alongside those of Lenin. Following his decisive intervention in support of "progressive tendencies" in the biological field in the summer of 1950, he astonished the Soviet intellectual world by finding time, in the middle of the Korean crisis, to make an equally powerful intervention in the field of linguistics. A group of militant Marxist philologists had taken up the theories of N. Ya. Marr, who had died in 1934 and had argued that language was to be seen as part of the "superstructure" of society, erected on the base of the relations of production and dependent on class. With this ideologically sharpened weapon, the Marrists succeeded in waging a campaign of persecution against their orthodox colleagues, and in June 1949, following Lysenko's triumph, the Soviet Academy of Sciences passed a resolution that Marr's teaching was to be regarded as "the *only* materialist Marxist theory of language."

This time Stalin intervened to put down the progressives. A. S. Chibikova, a philologist whose relations with the Marrist faction were equivocal, was summoned to Stalin's dacha, closely examined about Marr's views, and given the task of writing a discussion article for *Pravda.* Stalin wrote comments on two successive drafts and had Chibikova back to discuss them: "Contrary to the widespread opinion," Chibikova reported, "it was possible to argue with him and sometimes he agreed." When Chibikova's article appeared it was heavily attacked by the Marrists. Their consternation can be imagined when Stalin himself published no fewer than three articles in *Pravda,* in which he defined language as belonging neither to the "superstructure" nor to the "base" in Marxist terms and denounced Marr's views as nonsense. In the same number, no fewer than eight professors of linguistics expressed their unbounded admiration for Stalin's insight, which had opened a new era in linguistics.

Although there was nothing in the least original about Stalin's views, time has not dulled the piquancy of his attack on Marr's followers for setting up an "Arakcheyev regime" comparable to the tyranny exercised by Count

Arakcheyev during the reign of Tsar Alexander I in the first quarter of the nineteenth century:

> No science can develop and prosper without the clash of opinions, without freedom or criticism. This rule has been violated. . . . A closed group of infallible leaders has been created which, while insuring itself against criticism, has begun to act in a willful high-handed manner.[51]

Once past the age of seventy, Stalin became increasingly conscious of, and angered by, his age. The fear grew in him that he might no longer be able physically and mentally to maintain the unquestioned despotism over those around him that he had exercised for so long. He was afraid that those like Molotov and Mikoyan who had known him in his prime would notice his decline, and those like Malenkov and Beria who were twenty years younger would find out that he was no longer the man he had been and conspire behind his back. The inner circle in the Soviet Union during the Stalin period could hardly ever be thought of as a government in any ordinary sense of that word, but rather a mixture of conspiracy, Mafia, and court. Now they were a Mafia with an aging gang leader, boyars whose minds turned to the question of how long the tsar would live and who would then succeed. The irritability, the inflamed suspicions of the final years, the unpredictability, and self-imposed isolation all reflected these fears. Not for nothing was *Boris Godunov* Stalin's favorite opera.

Despite the difference in circumstances—the one the victor, the other the defeated—there are points of resemblance between the final period of Stalin's and Hitler's careers. Neither was interested in who would succeed him; neither had any intention of abdicating or surrendering; both immured themselves in their fantasies, shutting out reality beyond the narrow private world they controlled; both were determined to defend their power to their dying day—and did so.

Like Hitler, Stalin gave up making speeches—only two between 1945 and 1953—nor did he any longer give interviews: Those that were published were based on questions submitted and answered in writing. Neither appeared in public, partly to conceal the ravages of strain in Hitler's case, of age in Stalin's; both felt instinctively that the Führer image and the Stalin icon were more effective if they could not be compared with mortal human beings.

The corps of guards assigned to protect Stalin grew constantly larger. Wherever he spent the night, his residence was ringed by troops and dogs. He never traveled by air. When he went by train to the south for his vacation, all other traffic on the lines was stopped, MVD troops were posted every 100 yards along the route and two or three separate trains would set out, in one of which Stalin would travel, as he decided at the last moment. When in Moscow itself he constantly changed the route by which he traveled to and from his dacha at Kuntsevo.

In this self-imposed isolation, Stalin's principal relaxation continued to be the films shown in his private theater and the inevitable all-night dinner afterwards at his dacha. The half-dozen members of his entourage whom he now tolerated—Molotov, Mikoyan, and Voroshilov were finally excluded altogether—had to be ready to drop anything they were doing and obey the summons to join him. Although everything was cooked in his own kitchen, Stalin would not touch food or drink until others had tasted it first to see if it was poisoned. The same stories were told over and over again but everyone had to laugh or applaud as if they had never heard them before. Stalin took pleasure in plying the others with drink until they became so drunk they made fools of themselves.

> For some reason [Khrushchev writes], he found the humiliation of others amusing. I remember once Stalin made me dance the Gopak. I had to squat down on my haunches, kick out my heels and try to keep a pleasant expression on my face. But as I later told Mikoyan: "When Stalin says dance, a wise man dances."
>
> The main thing was to occupy Stalin's time so he wouldn't suffer from loneliness. He was depressed by loneliness and he feared it. [52]

But it was impossible to feel at ease with him: "If there was anything worse than having dinner with Stalin, it was having to go on vacation with him. . . . It was a terrible physical strain." [53] Stalin's daughter, Svetlana, who made uneasy contact again with him after the war, said the same. Recalling a vacation she spent with him in the south, she wrote: "It took me several days before I felt like myself again. . . . It cost me an enormous amount of nervous energy." [54] In 1951, when she spent another two weeks with him in Georgia, she noticed his anger when a crowd gathered spontaneously and made a tremendous fuss over him. She thought that by this time "he was so desolate and empty inside that he no longer believed people were capable of being genuinely warmhearted and sincere." [55]

In the new wave of arrests at the end of 1948, both Svetlana's aunts had been imprisoned. When she asked why, he replied bitterly:

> "They talked a lot. They knew too much and they talked too much. And it helped our enemies."
>
> He saw enemies everywhere. It had reached the point of being pathological, of persecution mania, it was all a result of being lonely and desolate. [56]

This was a state of affairs that could not continue indefinitely—as Stalin himself appears to have felt. On vacation at Afon in the south, in 1951, he summoned Khrushchev and Mikoyan to keep him company. "One day," Khrushchev relates, "we were taking a walk round the grounds when Stalin came out on the porch. He seemed not to notice Mikoyan and me. 'I'm finished,' he said to no one in particular. 'I trust no one, not even myself.' " [57] Who took the initiative in proposing that a party congress should be called, the first since 1939, is not certain. Khrushchev says it was Stalin;

others have speculated that it may have been his lieutenants, seeing this as the best way to end uncertainty, to bring about a change and restore confidence.

Whoever proposed the congress, it was Stalin who produced the surprises when over a thousand delegates assembled, in October 1952. He no longer felt strong enough to deliver the Report of the Central Committee, the role in which he had first established and then confirmed his domination of the party at every congress from 1924 to 1939. He entrusted the task to Malenkov, but at the same time he appointed Khrushchev to make the second most important speech, with Molotov to open and Voroshilov to close the proceedings.

To make sure that he would still steal the limelight, on the very eve of the congress, which met on October 5, two entire issues of *Pravda,* published on the third and fourth, were devoted to his new and unexpected work, *Economic Problems in the USSR.* This obliged every speaker to improvise laudatory references, following Malenkov's example, to "a new stage in the development of Marxism . . . of world-historic importance." It was very far short of that but Stalin took the opportunity to devote thirty-one pages to "Errors of Comrade Yaroshenko," an economist rash enough to have suggested that he should be commissioned to write a textbook who now found himself accused of following in the footsteps of Bukharin. After Stalin's restatement of orthodoxy, Soviet economists rushed to publish recantations in the same way that linguisticians and geneticists had, following his pronouncements in their fields. Stalin also secured the passage of two resolutions, one dropping the word "Bolshevik" from the title of the party, the other replacing the original term "Politburo" with "Presidium," both changes reducing the links with the party's Leninist past.

Although he attended few of the sessions, toward the end Stalin unexpectedly mounted the tribune for the last time to capture the one standing ovation of the congress with a rousing six-minute call to the Communists of the world to free mankind from imperialism and war. "There," he said to his entourage, "look at that! I can still do it." His most original stroke was to double the size of the Central Committee and more than double its Secretariat—then, when the enlarged committee held its first Plenum, to propose to treble the size of the new Presidium which replaced the old Politburo. Unexpectedly he asked the Plenum to accept his resignation as general secretary, citing his age and the disloyalty of Molotov, Mikoyan, and several others. Whether this was meant to be taken seriously or not, the Plenum refused and begged him to stay. Having agreed, he then produced a paper out of his pocket and read out a list of the new members he proposed for the new Presidium, which was accepted without comment. The list included ten of the eleven members of the existing Politburo, but an even larger number of younger and less well-known figures.

These moves were taken by everybody as preparations for a purge intended to replace the Old Guard with newcomers who knew nothing of the party's earlier history and would endorse Stalin's wishes without question. Confirmation of this was provided by the open attack that Stalin made at the Plenum on Molotov and Mikoyan for cowardice and capitulation while he had been on vacation. They appeared, he declared, to act like agents of certain Western governments. Konstantin Simonov, who was present as a candidate member of the Central Committee, later wrote that the attack was so merciless that their replies sounded like the last words of the accused at a trial. Both were omitted from the membership of the Bureau of the Presidium which (despite the fact that the newly revised party statutes made no provision for such a body) Stalin proceeded to appoint in order to deal with business and make whatever decisions were necessary.

It was characteristic, however, of Stalin's wavering purpose in old age that, having organized this coup, he did not follow through with it. Everything went on as before. The Presidium never met and the Bureau usually meant the same inner circle of himself, Malenkov, Beria, Khrushchev, and Bulganin. The difference was that Molotov and Mikoyan were now absolutely excluded and Kaganovich and Voroshilov rarely invited. The new Presidium members were appointed to some wide-ranging commissions, but these were left without assignments or guidance and proved completely ineffectual.

> The government [Khrushchev sums up] virtually ceased to function. Everyone in the orchestra was playing on his own instrument any time he felt like it, and there was no direction from the conductor.[58]

Stalin's loss of grip reflected his failing health. The unhealthy sedentary life he had lived for so long was catching up with him; he was suffering from high blood pressure, attacks of angina, and the effects of trying to give up his lifelong habit of smoking. After the party congress, for the first time, he did not take his usual vacation in the south.

A sign of Stalin's psychological instability was his sudden turning on the two longest-serving and most faithful of his personal retainers, Vlasik and Poskrebyshev. In both cases the initiative came from Beria, who was bent upon isolating Stalin and played on a suspicion which had now become all consuming. Vlasik had entered Stalin's service as a bodyguard in 1919 and risen to the rank of major general with responsibility for Stalin's protection, for his residences, food, and domestic staff. Summoned for interrogation by Beria, he was beaten up and threatened with death unless he signed a confession, including incriminating evidence against Poskrebyshev. Once he had complied, he was dismissed from Stalin's service but allowed to live in exile.

Poskrebyshev was the longest serving member of Stalin's staff, for many years acting as his principal secretary and head of his Special Section. He was privy to most of his secrets, controlling the flow of information which reached Stalin as well as all his appointments. As ruthless as his master but selfless in his devotion to him, he had already suffered the same humiliation as Molotov of seeing his wife, Bronislava, arrested, imprisoned for three years and then shot despite his pleas to Stalin. Poskrebyshev continued to work for Stalin until, shortly before the latter's death, he too was accused of leaking state secrets, was summarily dismissed, and spent the time until Stalin died sitting at home waiting for the security police to come for him.*

Besides the two men who had served him throughout his career as bodyguard and *homme de confiance,* Stalin turned on his personal doctor as well, Academician A. N. Vinogradov, "the only one he trusted," according to Svetlana. Vinogradov was arrested in November along with several other specialists on the staff of the Kremlin hospital-clinic reserved for the Soviet elite. The arrests were ordered on the basis of accusations by a young radiologist, Lydia Timashuk, who is said to have first attracted Stalin's attention as a medical student in 1939 when she proposed a competition for finding means of prolonging the life of Comrade Stalin, "so precious to the USSR and to all mankind." Now recruited as an informer by the security police, she denounced the doctors for seeking to kill Stalin and other leaders by applying the wrong kind of treatment.

Who inspired Timashuk to write the letter has never been made clear. Stalin is widely believed to have been aware of what was planned, if he did not actually set up the "Doctors' Case," as Khrushchev claims. Her letter is said to have displeased Beria and alarmed MGB officials who feared being accused of insufficient vigilance. Abakumov, the minister of state security, ordered the head of the MGB investigation branch, M. D. Ryumin, not to carry out an investigation and even arrested him. But Stalin intervened to order Ryumin's release, dismiss Abakumov, who was one of Beria's men, and appoint S. D. Ignatiev, from outside the security services, as minister in his place.[59] These moves may have been connected with Stalin's underhanded campaign against Beria.

Stalin took charge of the "Doctors' Case" himself, ordering that Vinogradov should be put in chains and the other doctors beaten. During his secret speech to the 1956 congress, Khrushchev pointed to Ignatiev, who was present, and recalled that Stalin had told him: "If you do not obtain confessions from the doctors, we will shorten you by a head." When they were produced, Stalin distributed them to the members of the Presidium Bureau, telling them: "You are blind like young kittens; what will happen without me? The country will perish because you do not know how to recognize enemies."[60]

The "results" of the investigation were made public on January 13, 1953, and nine doctors in all named, six of them Jewish. They were alleged to have confessed to murdering Zhdanov in 1948 and before that Shcherbakov, former head of the Moscow party and a secretary of the Central Committee. Their confessions recalled Yagoda's "admission" that he had organized the medical murder of Gorki and Kuibyshev, and the persistent rumor that

*In fact, thanks to Stalin's death, Poskrebyshev survived unhurt until his death in 1966.

Stalin himself had organized that of Frunze, the commissar for war, way back in 1925.

Less than a month after Stalin's death all the doctors were released and fully rehabilitated, and Ryumin, the chief investigator, arrested and later shot. But in January 1953 the full resources of Soviet propaganda were employed to blacken the doctors' names. They were divided into two groups. The first allegedly worked for American intelligence through "the international bourgeois Jewish-Zionist organization known as Joint," apparently a reference to a philanthropic body, the American Joint Distribution Committee, founded before 1917 to assist Jews in the Russian Empire, an organization of which the Jewish actor Mikhoels was now named as chairman and so drawn retrospectively into the plot. The other smaller group was alleged to have worked as agents of British intelligence. This scenario enabled the press to elaborate a double theme: vigilance against spies and traitors working for foreign powers, and against Jews as the "enemy within."

In the last of Stalin's propaganda campaigns, all the targets of his suspicions over the years—former Mensheviks and Trotskyites, Soviet national minorities, the Russian intelligentsia from doctors to economists, the writers and artists who went a-whoring after fashionable foreign models, those tainted by contact with foreigners—were held up as scapegoats, and the Soviet people urged to denounce them. After the rewards of such public-spiritedness had been illustrated by the award of the Order of Lenin to Dr. Lydia Timashuk, the self-seekers rushed to follow her example. "Similar scenes," Nadezhda Mandelstam wrote, "were played out all over the place; everyone raved about saboteurs and killer doctors."

The campaign deliberately appealed to the anti-Semitism endemic in Russia, and actions and demonstrations directed against Jews were reported from many parts of the country, including reports of pogroms from the Ukraine. On January 31, *Pravda* claimed to have established links between the doctors and the plotters unmasked in Poland and Czechoslovakia, particularly in the Slansky trial in Prague, where eleven of the party and state officials sentenced for acting as Western agents were Jews "recruited by the Zionists."

But it was not only Jewish citizens who had cause to fear the repeated incitements to "unmask the enemy." Frol Kozlov, second secretary of the Leningrad party, touched on a widely shared anxiety when he wrote an article for the January *Communist* hinting at another mass purge of the party. One of the most ominous of all Stalin's speeches was recalled by the assistant procurator-general, the speech that served as a prelude to the Great Terror and was delivered at the meeting of the Central Committee in February–March 1937.* On that occasion Stalin had given the same warning that was being repeated now—against enemies who did not dare

*See pp. 483–84.

to come out openly against the regime but tried "to lull the vigilance of Soviet people by false assurances of . . . devotion to our cause."[61] No doubt is left by contemporary witnesses of the sense of foreboding created, and intended to be created, by this obviously inspired propaganda. A secret memorandum submitted to Stalin gave a total of twelve million prisoners in the camps in early 1943.[62]

I have suggested earlier that it is unprofitable to try to determine how far Stalin actually believed in the conspiracies that he claimed to detect, how far he made use of them to isolate and destroy those he saw as threats to his position, arguing that he made no such distinction himself—just as it is unprofitable to ask whether Hitler believed or, like an actor, was thinking only of the effect he produced, when he worked himself into a paroxysm over the Jewish world-conspiracy.

This was the period at the very end of his life in which the Soviet psychiatrist quoted earlier placed the final attack of Stalin's paranoia. Did he really intend to launch another purge comparable with those of the 1930s—including this time, as Khrushchev suggests, the Old Guard of the Politburo who had served him so well, and to deal with Beria as he had dealt with his predecessors, Yagoda and Yezhov? Did he believe, a sick man at the age of seventy-three, that he still possessed the strength or the authority to carry it through? Or is the truth that Stalin himself did not know how far he meant to go, and that only the event would have shown—shown him as well as us—how far he could?

BEFORE THE EVENT could provide the answer, Stalin himself was dead. On the evening of February 28, the inner group, Beria, Malenkov, Khrushchev, and Bulganin watched films with him in the Kremlin. Stalin was in high spirits if only because he got drunk. The party did not break up until five or six o'clock on the morning of March 1. At some time between then and 3 a.m. on the second he had a stroke. The guards were afraid to disturb him earlier than 3 a.m., and it was not until twenty-four hours after they had left him that Malenkov, Beria, and company returned with doctors who diagnosed paralysis. Taking turns, two at a time, they kept watch by his bedside for the three and a half days it took Stalin to die. Although he occasionally regained consciousness he was unable to speak.

The thoughts of his lieutenants as they waited were already concentrated on what would happen when he died. Both Khrushchev and Svetlana, who watched with them, agree that the only person who betrayed the conflict of his feelings was Beria.

As soon as Stalin showed signs of consciousness [Khrushchev writes], Beria threw himself on his knees, seized Stalin's hand and started kissing it. When Stalin lost consciousness again and closed his eyes, Beria stood up and spat . . . spewing hatred.[63]

Svetlana herself experienced a painful conflict of emotions. "All those days I couldn't cry and I couldn't eat. Grief and a sort of calm turned me to stone." It is to her we owe the description of Stalin's last hours:

> The death agony was terrible. God grants an easy death only to the just. He literally choked to death as we watched. At what seemed like the very last moment he suddenly opened his eyes and cast a glance over everyone in the room. It was a terrible glance, insane or perhaps angry and full of fear of death. . . . Then something incomprehensible and terrible happened that to this day I can't forget. . . . He suddenly lifted his left hand as though he were pointing to something up above and bringing down a curse on us all. The gesture was incomprehensible and full of menace. . . . The next moment, after a final effort, the spirit wrenched itself free of the flesh.[64]

Like Hitler, Stalin preserved his image of himself intact to the end, without retraction or regret. Both men died defying their enemies. Hitler denied the Allies the satisfaction of capturing him alive and putting him on trial; Stalin denied his lieutenants whatever hope they had of putting him aside and taking his place.

As long as they remained alive—Hitler preparing to commit suicide in the bunker, Stalin lying unconscious in his dacha—their spell held, Hitler was still the Führer, Stalin the *vozhd'*. The moment they were dead, it was broken. Those left in the bunker at once set about making their escape. In the dacha, "We all stood frozen and silent for a few minutes," Svetlana wrote. "It seemed like ages. Then the members of the Politburo, Beria in the forefront, rushed for the door."[65] The shadow of fear was lifted, they had survived and had a future to fight over.

But as the news of Stalin's death spread throughout Russia, the people were stunned and fearful. When he was buried, many wept in the streets. After more than twenty years, they could not imagine a future without him.

TWENTY

Perspective

I

NEITHER HITLER NOR STALIN had a successor. But each left a legacy, one the legacy of defeat, the other the legacy of victory, which combined to weigh heavily on Europe in the succeeding decades. Now that the legacy has disintegrated as a result of the events of 1989–91 it is possible to look at the Hitler-Stalin period in European history in a different historical perspective.

One way of doing so is to place it in a series of attempts to redraw the map of Europe in the twentieth century. The first was made by the Germans in the war of 1914–18, the most concrete evidence of which is the Treaty of Brest-Litovsk of March 1918. The second was the peace settlement following the First World War and the collapse of four dynastic empires: the Habsburg, the Hohenzollern, the Romanov, and the Ottoman. The third was the changes imposed by Hitler between the annexation of Austria in 1938 and the peak of German power in 1942, when it extended over the whole of Eastern Europe and much of western Russia. The fourth was the result of Hitler's insistence on prolonging the war and the failure to conclude a peace settlement after it, leaving Stalin and the Soviet Union in effective control of Eastern Europe and much of Germany.

At each stage it has been that part of Europe lying east of a line from Lübeck to Venice which has been the area most affected by the changes and most often in dispute. This confirms the importance of the German-Russian axis to which I referred in the Introduction as a major theme of this as, in different forms, it has been of so many earlier periods of European history. It is certain to be so again in any fifth attempt which may be made to settle the map of Europe, following the collapse of the Communist regimes and the Soviet sphere of influence in Eastern Europe. The stability of Eastern Europe and above all the ability of Russia, the Ukraine, and the other successor states of the former Soviet Union to avoid a relapse into civil war or a return to dictatorship, are once more questions, rooted in the Hitler-

Stalin period and its legacy, the answers to which will have a great effect on the future not only of Eastern but of Western Europe as well.

A SECOND WAY of looking at the period and its legacy is to focus on its ideological dimension. Not since the French Revolution have there been two such aggressive ideologies as Communism and Nazism. There has been much argument about the relationship between Nazism and Fascism. Is Nazism to be regarded as the German form of Fascism or, by virtue of its emphasis on biological factors, on racism and anti-Semitism, as a separate phenomenon? Once launched on Hitler's and Himmler's racist program in occupied Poland, it is the difference between Nazism and Fascism which becomes more obvious. But during the 1930s it was their affinities: Few of those who took part in Popular Front rallies against Fascism or supported the Republican cause in Spain made any distinction between the two, any more than they questioned the goodwill of their Communist allies. For many of the younger generation between the wars the only choice was between an undifferentiated left and an undifferentiated right, alternative versions of the "wave of the future."

Nazism and Fascism glorified will, authority, power, and war. Their validity depended on success: neither could survive defeats as total as those which overtook Hitler and Mussolini. Those who had been involved in them were only too anxious to disavow any connection and cover their traces.

Communism, on the other hand, gained enormously from Soviet Russia's part in the war. After that, the Communist takeover in Eastern Europe and Mao's spectacular success in China (1949), a new generation of converts and fellow-travelers—in the Third World as well as the West—proclaimed the inevitability of Communism's ultimate triumph. Disillusionment was slow even after the revelations about Stalin in Khrushchev's secret speech began to circulate and the Red Army suppressed the Hungarian revolt by force—both in 1956. It took over thirty years more before the collapse of the Stalinist regimes, first in Eastern Europe, then in the Soviet Union itself, revealed that Communism as well as Nazism and Fascism—the rival ideologies which fought for supremacy in the 1930s and 1940s—was morally as well as politically bankrupt.

THERE IS STILL ARGUMENT whether Stalinism was "a logical and probably inevitable stage in the organic development of the Communist party."[1] Many of the elements which characterized Stalin's system of rule are to be found in Lenin's. Adding the words "of the proletariat" to dictatorship could not disguise the fact that it meant an unrestricted and ruthless exercise of power, including terrorism and the repression of all other parties. But it is argued that there was no "straight line" from Lenin's earlier period of power to Stalin's.[2] Bolshevism itself, so the argument runs, contained within itself a diversity of views, such as those of the Workers' Opposition, which might well have proved to be "seeds" with a future. After the Kronstadt mutiny, Lenin himself made an abrupt change of course, first in adopting the New Economic Policy, then in coming to see NEP not as a tactical retreat but as the basis for a new gradualist approach to the problems with which the party was confronted.

Perhaps the most important point is that made by Boris Souvarine:

> What had existed under Lenin was carried by Stalin to such extremes that its very nature changed. . . . Differences in degree grew into differences of kind. [3]

What distinguished Stalin from the other Bolshevik leaders, and constantly took them by surprise, was how far he was prepared to go. "Excesses were the essence of historical Stalinism."[4] (The same can be said of Hitler.)

Another line of argument makes a distinction between the highly centralized, single party system, which was the outcome of the Bolshevik revolution, and the very different political system produced when this was combined with Stalin's personal rule.[5] Lenin's personality was not despotic, and whatever potential for personal dictatorship the system possessed was not realized in his lifetime, when it was run by an oligarchy of party leaders. It took Stalin a long time to overcome the resistance in the party to his replacement of this with personal rule, and after his death the system returned to its original collective leadership.

On the other hand, even when the element of personal rule was removed, the collective Communist leadership of Stalin's successors in Russia and Eastern Europe, or Mao's successors in China, was no more successful than Lenin in finding an answer to the dilemma he left unresolved: When you have imposed a revolution by force, what alternative is there in practice between a retreat which compromises the changes the revolution has made, and the solution Stalin adopted of consolidating them by force? If there are too many unanswered questions for Stalinism to be described as the inevitable outcome of Lenin's revolution, it was certainly a logical one, and Stalin's career remains the greatest challenge to any who may still put their faith in a Leninist revolution from above "in the name of" the poor and the exploited.

This does not mean the end of ideology. Continuing inequalities and injustices can be expected to keep alive the search for a just and more equitable society and for myths (in the Sorelian sense) to sustain the hope of creating it. In the same way hatred of foreigners, fears of a flood of refugees, and increasing tensions in multiracial societies can be expected to keep alive ethnic antagonisms and the racist fantasies that sustain them. It remains an open question whether these will produce a revival of a neo-Marxist or a neo-Nazi version of millenarianism—or will find expression in such new forms as religious fundamentalism. A similar question mark hangs over the still older ideology of nationalism, which played a major role in fortifying both Nazism and Stalinism. A sense of national identity helped European nations to recover from experiences that could have been expected to destroy them, but the outbreak of civil war in Yugoslavia and the threat of similar conflicts elsewhere in Eastern Europe and in the borderlands of the former Soviet Union show how easily nationalist memories and hatreds can still be appealed to and exploited to set peoples divided by racial, cultural, or historical differences at each others' throats again, despite all the suffering and losses they have experienced in the great wars and since.

I I

A THIRD WAY of looking at the Hitler-Stalin period is in terms of human suffering. Not counting the millions who were wounded or permanently maimed, the estimated number of premature deaths between 1930 and 1953 reached a figure in the order of forty to fifty million men, women, and children. Suffering on such a scale is beyond the imagination's power to comprehend or respond to. Moreover, unlike the Black Death of the fourteenth century, which is believed to have destroyed something like a third of Europe's population, this was a man-made, not a natural disaster.

Millions died as combatants in war: over thirteen and a half million Russians, three and a quarter million Germans; many more as civilians from the consequences of war, such as air raids and famine.* The unique feature of this period, however, was the fact that, in addition to the casualties of war, half or even more of the total of forty to fifty million died as the result of deportation, torture, and brutal treatment in prisons and camps, of murder, massacre, and planned extermination. Nothing has weighed so heavily on the consciousness and conscience of the survivors and succeeding generations in Europe as this, together with the correlative fact that hundreds of thousands of men—and some but not many women—were found willing to inflict such terrible cruelties upon fellow human beings without regard to sex or age. There have been many similar crimes against humanity, but on such a scale these are without precedent in human history.

The map† on which I have sought to represent these facts geographically brings together both the German and the Russian campsites and deliberately presents what took place in these places without differentiation of responsibility as crimes against a shared humanity. In adopting this unusual course I have been influenced by the controversy which developed in Germany during the 1980s and which is known as the *Historikerstreit,* "the historians' fight."

The controversy brought out a conflict of views on several issues, political as much as historical.[6] The central one, however, was the question whether the Jewish Holocaust was to be regarded as a unique event, or whether it could be shown that there were other examples of genocide, or of other inhuman acts comparable with it. Those who raised the question and

*See Appendix I.
†"The Maps of Hell," pp. 750–51.

claimed that other examples could be found were moved by a desire to free Germany from what they saw as an unnecessary and damaging stigma as the only nation to have committed genocide; their critics not only rejected the claims but accused them of seeking to "normalize" the Nazi period and "trivialize" the crimes of the Holocaust.

The crux of the argument was whether the Soviet Union could be regarded as guilty of atrocities comparable with those of the Holocaust. If the figures exclude those killed as a result of the war, the Stalinist repression was responsible for a greater number of deaths, on some calculations up to double the number put to death by the Nazis.[7] So a comparison between the two is valid.

There were, however, important differences. The Stalinist system used terror, including mass murder, as an instrument to secure political and social, not biological, objectives. These ranged from forcing through collectivization and breaking the resistance of the Ukrainian peasants to destroying potential opposition in the party, the armed forces, and the bureaucracy, the threat of which was grossly exaggerated by Stalin's paranoid suspicions. But nowhere was there a counterpart to the Holocaust, the centerpiece of the Nazi repression accounting for three quarters of their total figure, the planned extermination of all European Jews in which mass murder became not an instrument but an end in itself.

The inhumanity and excesses of the Stalinist repression were as "unique," in different ways, as those of the Nazis, but they do not cancel out the uniqueness of the Holocaust. Nothing that happened in Russia affects the fact that, as the German historian Eberhard Jäckel wrote:

> Never before had a state . . . decided that a specific human group, including its aged, its women, its children, and its infants, would be killed as quickly as possible and then carried through this regulation using every possible means of state power.[8]

As many who took part in the controversy pointed out, the issue of "uniqueness" is an unsatisfactory focus. It looks at the experience of terror and extermination in this period too much from the point of view of those who may be held responsible for inflicting it, too little from the point of view of the victims. This is why I have designed the map to bring out the monstrous total of the victims of repression in these years, whichever regime they suffered under, rather than to lose sight of this in arguments about which had the worse record.

OF COURSE the question of responsibility cannot be ignored. Leaving aside the question of collective guilt, which is better suited to discussion by philosophers and theologians than historians, there was a very large number of people involved in these operations, all of whom share that responsibility. They include not only the SS and NKVD troops, the camp and prison guards, the torturers, the murder squads, but also the administrative staffs, the police who made the arrests, the railway officials, the drivers, the technicians, the "helpers" who removed the bodies and collected the possessions, and beyond those again the interrogators, the tribunals, and the shadowy army of informers.

One group which has attracted attention has been the Nazi doctors. They played a leading part in the scientific "justification" of racist views, were involved in the operation of the death camps, and engaged in experiments on prisoners carried out without anesthetics and without regard for their suffering or death. Another group that appears in almost every account of the Soviet camps was the "trusties," given special privileges in return for spying on and lining up the other prisoners; commonly criminals, they delighted in humiliating and bullying the "politicals" and the more educated inmates.

Motives varied from sadism to money and perks. The extent to which ordinary human beings with no particular sadistic impulses could become hardened to brutalities and the suffering of others, their capacity for suppression, rationalization, and routinization has been documented in every study. For those who might still be troubled by suppressed feelings of anxiety or revulsion, complicity was a powerful force, well understood by the system, which established a web of guilt and fear from which there was no escape.

From the operations on the ground, responsibility reached up through the administrative hierarchy to the planners and organizers, of whom Eichmann is the archetype, finally to Yagoda, Yezhov, and Beria to Himmler and Heydrich. Neither Hitler nor Stalin, however, so far as is known, ever witnessed, still less took part in, the terror and repression which were not peripheral but absolutely central to the exercise and preservation of their power.

Stalin was careful to see that other members of the Politburo as well as himself signed the death warrants; responsibility in public was taken by Yagoda and Yezhov, both of whom were made to pay for the "excesses" which Stalin duly condemned. Hitler left no Führer Order, no minute or memorandum which would associate him directly with the Final Solution. Nor is there any reason to doubt that there were "excesses"; that such operations could be improvised "from below" and could also acquire a momentum of their own, going further on occasion than was intended.

Nonetheless, when due allowance has been made for these other factors, I believe that the responsibility Hitler and Stalin bore for conceiving of deportation, imprisonment, torture, and killing on such a scale, for ordering and above all legitimizing them is different in kind from that borne by anyone else.

In *Notes from the House of the Dead,* Dostoevski wrote:

Whoever has experienced the power, the complete ability to humiliate another human being . . . with the most extreme humiliation, willy-nilly

loses power over his own sensations. Tyranny is a habit, it has a capacity
for development, it develops finally into a disease . . . Blood and power
are intoxicating. . . . The human being and the citizen die within the
tyrant for ever; return to humanity, to repentance, to regeneration becomes almost impossible. [9]

Dostoevski's words can be applied to all those who were involved in the
elaborate system of terror in both countries, but to none so aptly as to the
two men who bore the chief responsibility for it.

III

HAVE THE ROLES of Hitler and Stalin been exaggerated?
   In the 1960s and 1970s a younger generation of historians reacted against
the model of the monolithic totalitarian state (which its critics saw as a
product of the "Cold War mentality") and against the popular stereotype
of Hitler as an all-powerful dictator dominating events. This revolt fitted in
with, and drew strength from, the dominant trend in the postwar study of
history, the rise of social and economic history, of history seen "from
below," challenging the traditional concentration on political history, history seen "from above."
   Social and economic historians, like social scientists, find it natural to seek
historical explanations in terms of such impersonal factors as demographic
changes, movements of population, the impact on society of industrialization and technological innovation, and to concern themselves with human
beings collectively as members of groups in which individual characteristics
are submerged in the average. Such an approach is well suited to a period
like the present century in which the growth in population, the scale of
economic and social organization, and the pace of change have all increased
so rapidly as to make it difficult to believe that individuals can have an
impact on the course of history.
   No one can reasonably question this as the norm in countries which
combine some degree of stability with democratic institutions. But a different situation arises when war, revolution, or some other form of violent
upheaval disrupts normality and continuity. Communities then become
destabilized, behavior unpredictable, and more extreme courses conceivable. In such circumstances it is possible for an individual to exert a
powerful, even a decisive, influence on the way events develop and the
policies which are followed—as Lenin did when he returned to Russia in
1917.
   Such occasions are not common. There are many more situations where,
for lack of leadership, a crisis is never resolved and the opportunity for a
decision is missed. The moment more often than not fails to find the man,
as it did in Russia in 1905. Where a leader does emerge, however, as
happened for example with Kemal Pasha in Turkey, or with Mao in China,
he can establish a position which allows his personality, his individual gifts,

and his views to assume an importance out of all proportion with normal experience. And, once established, it is very difficult to dislodge a leader from such a position. I believe this to have been the case with Hitler and Stalin.

In other circumstances than those in Germany in the early 1930s, or in Russia in the 1920s, either Hitler or Stalin might never have been heard of. Even in those circumstances it is perfectly possible to construct alternative scenarios for Germany and the Soviet Union without them. Neither was indispensable. In Germany, it could have taken the form of a right-wing coalition (perhaps with the participation of a National Socialist party under Gregor Strasser) which would have permanently replaced parliamentary by presidential government and at least got rid of the reparations and disarmament clauses of Versailles. In Russia, if Lenin had lived beyond the age of fifty-four, it could have taken the form of a modification of the New Economic Policy along the lines he foresaw in his later writings and for which Bukharin campaigned.

There were plenty of others besides Hitler and Stalin who tried to get control of the situation. Luck and the mistakes of others played an important part, but it was Hitler, not Papen or Hugenberg, and Stalin, not Trotsky or Zinoviev, who saw how to turn them to their advantage.

The fact that they were underestimated by their rivals was a positive advantage to both men. Only later did it become clear how much difference it made who won. But now that it is clear, I find it difficult to imagine under any other German leader the extraordinary successes of a right-wing radical party like the Nazis between 1930 and 1933; the foreign policy and military successes of 1936–41; the attack on Russia, the attempt to found a new slave empire in the East, and the racist massacres to which this led, culminating in the attempt to exterminate the Jewish population of Europe. I find it equally difficult to imagine under any other Soviet leader than Stalin the Great Leap Forward of the forced collectivization of agriculture imposed without regard to the cost in human lives, the destruction of Lenin's original party, the purge of the Red Army, the creation of the Gulag empire, and the combination of Marxism-Leninism with tsarist autocracy in the Stalinist state.

After the pendulum has swung between exaggerating and underestimating their roles, the longer perspective suggests that in both cases neither the historical circumstances nor the individual personality is sufficient explanation by itself without the other.

GERMAN NATIONALISTS were later to argue that the trouble with Hitler was that he had not known when to stop. If only he had been content with what he had achieved by 1938, say with the incorporation of Austria, and not gone to war, or had halted after the defeat of Poland, or at the very latest after the defeat of France and not attacked Russia—then he would have gone down in history as one of the greatest German leaders who had completed Bismarck's work by realizing the nationalist dream of *Gross Deutschland* (Greater Germany) without risking the disasters that followed.

But this was to mistake both the character of Hitler and his program. The invasion of the Soviet Union was not a risky further gamble which Hitler was tempted into making because his original gamble of war had succeeded beyond his hopes and at so little cost. Hitler was by temperament a revolutionary, a right-wing radical who had no intention of restoring the traditional stiff, class-conscious, backward-looking hierarchical society to which many German nationalists looked back with regret. Hitler meant to have his revolution all right, but instead of setting one class against another as the left proposed, meant to unite the nation and turn its energies outwards to the conquest of a very different German empire in the east and the enslavement of its native peoples.

If there was an improvisation, it was the war in the west, which Hitler had hoped to avoid altogether, if possible securing the British as allies, at least persuading them to stay neutral, while he concentrated on the realization of his racist dream of Germany's future where he had always seen it lying—in the east. If Hitler had succeeded, it would have transformed German society as thoroughly as any left-wing revolution based on the slogans of class war, with the advantage that the cost of it would have been borne by other people, not by Germans. Fortunately this did not happen, but paradoxically Hitler's refusal to recognize that he had failed and his prolongation of the war until the whole of Germany was occupied produced a revolutionary effect of its own from which a new Germany was able to emerge after the war.

Defeat cost the German people a terrible price, but at least it spared them—and the world—the perpetuation of the Nazi regime. Victory cost the Russians an even greater price but did not liberate them. It was not enough for Stalin that he could claim to have vanquished the Germans and won the gratitude of the Russian people for his leadership in the Great Patriotic War. It was not enough that Russia had emerged from the war as the only other superpower besides the United States and that he himself, now that Roosevelt was dead and Churchill out of office, enjoyed a unique prestige as a world leader. Instead of relaxing he renewed his demands upon the Russian people; the old suspicion and distrust returned, increased by the prospect of his power being curtailed by age and death.

The numbers in the camps in 1952 were higher than ever before; and in the final years even those who had served the aging tyrant faithfully, such as Molotov and Poshkrebyshev, lost favor and were threatened.

Stalin's death lifted the fear of another purge like those of the 1930s, but it no more liberated the Soviet peoples than victory had done. Although modified by the collective leadership which replaced Stalin, the Stalinist system which he had fastened on them continued to shackle their energies and deny them freedom for more than another thirty-five years, seventy in all since the revolution of 1917. As the final decade of the century opened, the situation of the Russian and German peoples was reversed. By the time the German Federal Republic faced the task of German reunification, it had behind it a record of prosperity and stability no other European state could equal. By the time the Soviet Union collapsed, the Russian peoples emerged economically crippled and politically divided with no clear idea, certainly no agreement, on what was to take the place of the regime under which they lived for three-quarters of a century.

I V

NO ONE CAN YET FORESEE the political and economic future of the several hundred million people who live in the huge area extending from Central Europe to Central Asia and Russia's Far Eastern territories. We have still not grasped the scale of the changes set in motion by the events of 1989–91, but already uncertainty about the future, magnified by the world recession, has turned the euphoria which these events created at the time into disillusionment and anxiety.

An historian is no more able to read the future than anyone else. But he has one advantage: He knows from the past how unexpected the future has, again and again, turned out to be. If I end this book with an open mind about Europe's future it is because there is no other period of which this is more true than the end of the Hitler and Stalin period and its sequel.

To visit Europe after the war was to be brought face-to-face with the effects of loss of life, physical destruction, and the dislocation of whole societies on a scale which had never been seen before. Standing on the hills overlooking the Ruhr valley in July 1945, I watched an apparently endless column of Poles and Russians trudging their way slowly eastward through a district whose mines and factories had been synonymous with German industrial power, but now stood silent and gutted. I wrote in a letter that night that it was impossible to believe that Germany could ever rise again, and as I traveled further in the next few years, to France, Austria, and Czechoslovakia, the impression grew, and was widely shared by others, that it was hard to believe that Europe, not just Germany, could ever recover from the wounds inflicted on it in the years between Hitler's and Stalin's rise to power and the end of the war.

To these were now added their legacy in the partition of Europe, the quarrel between Russia and the West, and the fears this generated: The fear that Europe would not be able to feed itself or provide employment for its people, the fear that the Communist takeover of Eastern Europe might be extended to the West, and the fear of a third world war, this time fought with nuclear weapons.

It is easy enough to say now that these fears were exaggerated, but they were real enough to the men and women who had seen the unbelievable happen and experienced first hand in their own lives what war and occupation means. And their fears were renewed by a succession of crises, from the Communist takeover in Prague in 1948, the Berlin blockade, and the Korean War (a possible foretaste of what might happen in a partitioned Germany) to the Soviet invasion of Hungary, the Berlin Wall, and the Cuban missile crisis of 1962.

What nobody could know then was how much was actually being accomplished in the very years 1947–1962, when the fears were most acute. Nobody could foresee the recuperative power and vitality which the peoples of Western Europe, including the peoples of West Germany and Austria, would discover in the 1950s and 1960s, leading to one of the most prosperous and stable periods in their history. It is true, of course, that in the initial phase of recovery Western Europe, and particularly West Germany, owed a great deal to American aid which will not be forthcoming again. But it is also true that—as experience has shown time and again in other countries—aid by itself will not produce economic recovery unless it is matched by an upsurge of indigenous energy, which in Europe soon replaced it.

After three wars between them since 1870, who would have believed that it would be a postwar partnership between French and Germans which would create the European Community and make another war between them unthinkable? Equally unforeseen was the success of the Spanish people in shaking off the legacy of the Franco regime, without a renewal of their civil war, and going on to establish a democratic state. Finally, even those who came to believe that the Communist regimes and the Soviet sphere of influence in Eastern Europe would not last hardly supposed that they would disappear without violence, except in the single case of Rumania; still less that the Soviet Union itself, as the world had known it since 1917, would cease to exist and the threat of a nuclear war between Russia and the West would be lifted.

Obviously the record so far, remarkable as it is, does not guarantee that it will continue, and that Europe will again be capable of the effort which renewed it after 1945. It may be—tragic loss to Europe as it is to contemplate—that Russia will again turn its back on the West, and the Balkans sink back into the misery of ethnic conflicts. But for Western and Central Europe it is far too early to write off their capacity to adapt to new circumstances, cement the unification of Germany, and absorb at least Poles, Czechs, and Hungarians into an enlarged community. Even five years after 1945 there was little sign of the return of confidence which was to come in the 1950s. If it now takes the rest of the century to carry out this further program, ten years from the revolutions of 1989–91, it would still be a year less than it took to get as far as signing the Treaty of Rome in 1956.

There is another reason, of a different kind, why I do not despair of Europe's future. The years I have recalled in this book showed, as perhaps never before, the depths of evil of which human beings are capable in their treatment of each other. But the historical record also shows that even in the worst circumstances, not only in battle but in overcrowded prisons and camps, under torture, in the Resistance, and in the face of certain death, there was a handful—drawn from every nation—who showed to what heights men and women can rise.

In Jerusalem the Jewish people have created a memorial museum, Yad Vashem, to remind themselves and the rest of the world of the horrors of the Holocaust. It is impossible to go round it and see the evidence they have collected without emerging overwhelmed and crushed. As you come out, however, you enter an avenue of trees known as the Avenue of the Righteous, every tree in which commemorates someone not Jewish who did not stand aside but risked his or her life to help the Jews in their distress.

I have never forgotten the juxtaposition of the Holocaust Museum and those trees. They remain for me the double image of those years, the unbelievable cruelty *and* the courage, the callousness *and* the compassion— the human capacity for evil, but also the reassurance of the possibility of human nobility. More than that, they lay upon those of us who have been fortunate enough to survive an obligation not to forget and not to give up in the face of difficulties.

APPENDICES

APPENDIX ONE

German Political Parties 1919–1933[*]

GERMAN ELECTORAL RESULTS 1919–1933

PARTY	NATIONAL ASSEMBLY JAN. 19, 1919			JUNE 6, 1920			MAY 4, 1924			DEC. 7, 1924			MAY 20, 1928		
	TOTAL VOTES	%	NO. DEPUTIES	TOTAL VOTES	%	NO. DEPUTIES	TOTAL VOTES	%	NO. DEPUTIES	TOTAL VOTES	%	NO. DEPUTIES	TOTAL VOTES	%	NO. DEPUTIES
ELIGIBLE VOTERS	36,766,500	—	423	35,949,800	—	459	38,375,000	—	472	38,987,300	—	493	41,224,700	—	491
VALID VOTES CAST	30,400,300	82.7	—	28,196,300	78.4	—	29,281,800	76.3	—	30,290,100	77.6	—	30,753,300	74.6	—
SPD Majority Socialists	11,509,100	37.9	165	6,104,400	21.6	102	6,008,900	20.5	100	7,881,000	26.0	131	9,153,000	29.8	153
USPD Independent Socialists	2,317,300	7.6	22	5,046,800	17.9	84	—	—	—	—	—	—	—	—	—
KPD Communists	—	—	—	589,500	2.1	4	3,693,300	12.6	62	2,709,100	9.0	45	3,264,800	10.6	54
Center party	5,980,200	19.7	91	3,845,000	13.6	64	3,914,400	13.4	65	4,118,900	13.6	69	3,712,200	12.1	62
BVP Bavarian People's party	—	—	—	1,238,600	4.4	21	946,700	3.2	16	1,134,000	3.7	19	945,600	3.0	16
DDP Democrats	5,641,800	18.6	75	2,333,700	8.3	39	1,655,100	5.7	28	1,919,800	6.3	32	1,505,700	4.9	25
DVP People's party	1,345,600	4.4	19	3,919,400	13.9	65	2,964,400	9.2	45	3,049,100	10.1	51	2,679,700	8.7	45
Wirtschaftspartei Economy party	275,100	0.9	4	218,600	0.8	4	692,600	2.4	10	1,005,400	3.3	17	1,397,100	4.5	23
Nationalists DNVP	3,121,500	10.3	44	4,249,100	14.9	71	5,696,500	19.5	95	6,205,800	20.5	103	4,381,600	14.2	73
NSDAP Nazis	—	—	—	—	—	—	1,918,300	6.5	32	907,300	3.0	14	810,100	2.6	1
Other parties	209,700	0.6	3	651,200	2.5	5	2,059,700	6.9	19	1,389,700	4.4	12	2,903,500	9.2	2

[*]For a description of the principal parties, see Glossary, pp. 1027–1034.

SEPT. 14, 1930			JULY 31, 1932			NOV. 6, 1932			MARCH 5, 1933			NOV. 12, 1933			PARTY
TOTAL VOTES	%	NO. DEPUTIES	TOTAL VOTES	%	NO. DEPUTIES	TOTAL VOTES	%	NO. DEPUTIES	TOTAL VOTES	%	NO. DEPUTIES	TOTAL VOTES	%	NO. DEPUTIES	
42,957,700	--	577	44,226,800	—	608	44,373,700	—	584	44,685,800	—	647	45,141,900	—	661	ELIGIBLE VOTERS
34,970,900	81.4	—		83.3	—	35,471,800	79.9	—	39,343,300	88.0	—	42,988,100[1]	95.2	—	VALID VOTES CAST
8,577,700	24.5	143	7,959,700	21.6	133	7,248,000	20.4	121	7,181,600	18.3	120	—	—	—	SPD Majority Socialists
—	—	—	—	—	—	—	—	—	—	—	—	—	—	—	USPD Independent Socialists
4,592,100	13.1	77	5,282,600	14.6	89	5,980,200	16.9	100	4,848,100	12.3	81	—	—	—	KPD Communists
4,127,900	11.8	68	4,589,300	12.5	75	4,230,600	11.9	70	4,424,100	11.7	74	—	—	—	Center party
1,059,100	3.0	19	1,192,700	3.2	22	1,094,600	3.1	20	1,073,600	2.7	18	—	—	—	BVP Bavarian People's party
1,322,400	3.8	20	371,800	1.0	4	336,500	1.0	2	334,200	0.8	5	—	—	—	DDP Democrats
1,578,200	4.5	30	436,000	1.2	7	661,800	1.9	11	432,300	1.1	2	—	—	—	DVP People's party
1,362,400	3.9	23	146,900	0.4	2	110,300	0.3	1	—	—	—	—	—	—	Wirtschaftspartei Economy party
2,458,300	7.0	41	2,177,400	5.9	37	2,959,000	8.8	52	3,136,800	8.0	52	—	—	—	Nationalists DNVP
6,409,600	18.3	107	13,745,800	37.4	230	11,737,000	33.1	196	17,277,200	43.9	288	39,638,800	92.2	661	NSDAP Nazis
3,724,300	10.5	49	1,119,300	2.8	9	1,526,100	4.4	11	766,146	1.9	7	—	—	—	Other parties

[1]No. of invalid votes: 3,349,363

APPENDIX TWO

Estimated Loss of Life (not including civilian losses) in the First World War

COMBATANTS

UK*	744,702
France*	1,327,000
Italy	460,000
Russia**	1,700,000
USA	115,660
Germany	1,808,545
Austria–Hungary**	1,200,000
Turkey	325,000
Estimated total losses	**ca. 7,800,000**

Notes

*British and French figures do not include losses among troops from the British and French empires.

**Estimated figures not necessarily complete. They do not include losses in the Russian Civil War.

Estimated Loss of Life among the European Nations and the USA in the Second World War

	Total	Percentage of Population	Military (including POWs)	Civilians
USSR (1941–45)	21,300,000	11.0	13,600,000	7,700,000
Germany (1939–45)	6,850,000	9.5	3,250,000	3,600,000
Great Britain (1939–45)	388,000	0.8	326,000	62,000
France	810,000	1.9	340,000	470,000
Poland	6,123,000	17.2	123,000	6,000,000 *(of whom 2.9m. were Jewish)*
Yugoslavia	1,706,000	10.9	300,000	1,400,000
Hungary	420,000	3.0	—	—
Greece	520,000	7.2	—	—
Rumania	460,000	3.4	—	—
Austria	480,000	7.2	—	—
Italy	410,000	0.9	330,000	80,000
Czechoslovakia	400,000	2.7	—	—
All other European nations	425,000		—	—
Total losses of all European nations	**ca. 40,000,000**			
USA 1941–45 *(including Pacific theater)*	295,000	0.4		

Note

If the losses in the Spanish and Russian civil wars are added to those in the two world wars, the total rises to ca. fifty-eight million killed in thirty-one years.

Second World War	ca. 40,000,000
First World War	ca. 7,700,000
Spanish Civil War	ca. 600,000
Russian Civil War	ca. 10,000,000
	ca. 58,300,000

Even that does not take into account the five million deaths in the Russian famine of 1921–22, the losses imposed on the Russian peasantry during the 1930s by Stalin's collectivization campaign, and the numbers of those executed in the purges or dying in the Gulag camps. If these are added it takes the total loss of life in Europe from the effects of violence in the period 1914–53 to ca. seventy-five million.

APPENDIX THREE

The Holocaust

Estimates of the number of Jewish men, women, and children who were put to death between 1939 and 1945, divided according to nationality, not place of death.

COUNTRY	Estimated Number of Jews
Poland (*1939 boundaries*)	2,900,000
USSR (*boundaries prior to 1939*)	1,250,000
Hungary	300,000
Rumania	250,000
Czechoslovakia	245,000
Baltic States	200,000
Germany (*1938 boundaries*)	160,000
Netherlands	104,000
France	64,000
Austria	58,000
Greece	58,000
Yugoslavia	54,000
Italy	8,000
Other European countries	11,000
Total	**ca. 5,672,000**

Note

According to the Nazi estimate given at the Wannsee conference in January 1942, the total Jewish population in Europe, including Russia and the Ukraine, was ca. eleven million.

Abbreviations Used in the Notes and Bibliography

*	English translation
DBFP	*Documents on British Foreign Policy, 1919–1939*
DGFP	*Documents on German Foreign Policy, 1918–1945*
ND	Nuremberg Documents presented at the International Trial of Major War Criminals in Nuremberg
VB	*Völkischer Beobachter,* the Nazi party newspaper
VfZ	*Vierteljahresheft für Zeitgeschichte* (Munich)
FRUS	*Papers Relating to the Foreign Relations of the United States*
PRO	Public Record Office, Kew, London
RIIA	Royal Institute of International Affairs
TMWC	Trial of the Major War Criminals: Proceedings and Evidence

NOTES

INTRODUCTION

1. See Carl J. Friedrich and Z. K. Brzezinski, *Totalitarian Dictatorship and Autocracy*, 2d ed. (New York: 1966); Hannah Arendt, *The Origins of Totalitarianism* (New York: 1968); and Carl J. Friedrich, M. R. Curtis, and B. R. Barber, *Totalitarianism in Perspective: Three Views* (New York: 1969).

2. See Leonard Schapiro, *Totalitarianism* (London: 1972).

ONE: Origins

1. Quoted by Robert C. Tucker, *Stalin as Revolutionary* (New York: 1973), p. 73. Iremashvili's reminiscences were published as early as 1932, after he had emigrated to Germany: Joseph Iremashvili, *Stalin und die Tragödie Georgiens* (Berlin: 1932), pp. 11–12. Most biographers of Stalin have made use of them, with varying doubts about their reliability.

2. Quoted by Tucker, *Stalin as Revolutionary*, p. 80.

3. August Kubizek, *Young Hitler* (London: 1954), ch. 8. See also Bradley F. Smith, *Adolf Hitler: His Family, Childhood and Youth* (Stanford: 1967).

4. *Mein Kampf*, trans. James Murphy (London: 1939), p. 30.

5. Ibid., p. 31.

6. Sigmund Freud, *Collected Papers*, vol. IV (London: 1952). Quoted by Tucker, *Stalin as Revolutionary*, p. 76.

7. See, for example, J. Brosse, *Hitler avant Hitler. Essai d'interpretation psychoanalytique* (Paris: 1972); R. G. L. Waite, *The Psychopathic God: Adolf Hitler* (New York: 1977); and Rudolph Binion, *Hitler among the Germans* (New York: 1977).

8. Erik H. Erikson, *Childhood and Society*, 3d. ed. (New York: 1963), p. 337.

9. See Erich Fromm, *The Anatomy of Human Destructiveness*, pb. ed. (London 1977), pp. 498–515.

10. Ibid., pp. 271–79.

11. Robert C. Tucker, *Stalin in Power: The Revolution from Above, 1928–1941* (New York: 1990), p. 4, and Karen Horney, *Neurosis and Human Growth* (New York: 1950).

12. Alex de Jonge, *Stalin and the Shaping of the Soviet Union* (London: 1986), p. 33. Cf. Adam Ulam, *Stalin: The Man and His Era*, 2d. ed. (London: 1989), p. 24: "Where his training is clearly discernible is in the repeated question and answer form characteristic of his oratory. ('Can it

be said that National Socialists are Nationalists? No!')"

13. Svetlana Alliluyeva, *Only One Year* (*New York: 1969), pp. 313–14. She is wrong in saying Stalin spent ten years in the seminary; it was only five.

14. Tucker, *Stalin as Revolutionary*, p. 120.

15. The name Messame Dassy (Third Group) was adopted to distinguish it from Meori Dassy (Second Group), a progressive liberal organization of the 1880s, and the earlier Pirvali Dassy, which had advocated the abolition of serfdom. For the development of Russian Marxism, see Leopold H. Haimson, *The Russian Marxists and the Origins of Bolshevism* (Cambridge, Mass.: 1955).

16. Iremashvili, *Stalin*, p. 24.

TWO: Experience

1. Bradley F. Smith, *Adolf Hitler: His Family, Childhood and Youth* (Stanford: 1967), p. 145, quoting from the account that Honisch provided for the NSDAP Hauptarchiv in 1938.

2. *Mein Kampf*, trans. James Murphy (London: 1939), pp. 32–33.

3. Ibid., p. 39.

4. Ibid., p. 40.

5. Ibid., p. 47.

6. Ibid., p. 62.

7. Ibid., p. 42.

8. This was first recognized by Hugh Trevor-Roper in an essay, "The Mind of Adolf Hitler," published as the introduction to the English translation of *Hitler's Table Talk, 1941–1944* (London: 1953).

9. *Mein Kampf*, trans. Murphy, pp. 59–60.

10. See A. G. Whiteside, *Austrian National Socialism before 1918* (The Hague: 1962).

11. See the discussion in Alec Nove, *An Economic History of the USSR*, 2d. ed. (London: 1989), ch. 1.

12. Quoted from Alex de Jonge,

who translated it from Arsenidze, *Novyi Zhurnal*. See his *Stalin and the Shaping of the Soviet Union* (London: 1986), pp. 55–56.

13. J. Stalin, *Collected Works*, vol. I (Moscow: 1952–55), pp. 62–73.

14. For the earlier history of the Russian revolutionary tradition, see Franco Venturi, *Roots of Revolution* (*London: 1960) and Tibor Szamuely, *The Russian Tradition* (London: 1974), part II.

15. Quoted by Bertram Wolfe, *Three Who Made a Revolution* (London: 1956), p. 193.

16. Interview with Emil Ludwig quoted by Isaac Deutscher, *Stalin: A Political Biography* (London: 1949), p. 19.

17. Ibid., pp. 25–26.

18. Robert C. Tucker, *Stalin as Revolutionary* (New York: 1973), p. 140.

19. Dates established by Robert H. McNeal, *Stalin: Man and Ruler* (London: 1988), p. 339, nn 36 and 39.

20. Joseph Iremashvili, *Stalin und die Tragödie Georgiens* (Berlin: 1932), pp. 39–40, quoted by Ronald Hingley, *Joseph Stalin: Man and Legend* (London: 1974), p. 32.

21. Quoted by Deutscher, *Stalin*, p. 98.

22. *Khrushchev Remembers*, trans. and ed. Strobe Talbot (London: 1971). See *Khrushchev on Khrushchev* (Barton: 1990) by Sergei Khrushchev (Nikita's son), which documents the history and authenticity of the reminiscences.

23. Quoted by Deutscher, *Stalin*, p. 104.

24. This was the controversy with Bogdanov and Lunacharsky that led Lenin to abandon political work for a time in order to write *Empirio-Criticism and Materialism* in an effort to destroy his opponents. For a brief explanation of dialectical materialism and other

terms that may be unfamiliar, see *The Fontana/Harper Dictionary of Modern Thought,* ed. Alan Bullock and Stephen Trombley, rev. ed. (London: 1988).

25. Quoted by Deutscher, *Stalin,* p. 110.

26. Quoted by Adam Ulam, *Stalin: The Man and His Era,* 2d. ed. (London: 1989), p. 123.

27. Quoted by Hingley, *Stalin,* p. 76.

28. Quoted from unpublished memoirs by Roy Medvedev, *Let History Judge,* *2d. ed. (Oxford: 1989), p. 36.

29. Speech at Hamburg, August 17, 1934. *The Speeches of Adolf Hitler,* trans. and ed. Norman H. Baynes, vol. I (London: 1942), p. 97.

30. *Mein Kampf,* trans. Murphy, p. 117.

31. Ibid., p. 145.

32. A description by one of Hitler's fellow soldiers quoted by Konrad Heiden, *Der Führer* (*reissued London: 1967), p. 74. Heiden closely followed the activities of Hitler and the Nazis from 1920 onward and published his first account of the party (translated as *A History of National Socialism*) in 1932. *Der Führer,* originally published in 1944, is a remarkable study of the movement and its leader up to the Röhm purge of 1934. It still repays reading.

33. Joachim Fest, *Hitler* (*London: 1974), pp. 69–70.

34. *Mein Kampf,* trans. Murphy, p. 146.

THREE: October Revolution, November Putsch

1. Merle Fainsod, *How Russia Is Ruled* (Cambridge, Mass.: 1953), pp. 85–86.

2. Remembered by Raskolnikov and quoted by Robert M. Slusser, *Stalin in October: The Man Who Missed the Revolution* (Baltimore: 1987), p. 49.

3. Lenin's "April theses," presented to the conference on April 4, were printed in *Pravda* under the title "The Tasks of the Proletariat in the Present Revolution." *The Essentials of Leninism,* vol. II (*London: 1947), pp. 17–21.

4. E. Yaroslavsky, *Landmarks in the Life of Stalin* (*Moscow: 1940), p. 94.

5. Lenin's speech on the dissolution of the Constituent Assembly, delivered to a meeting of the Soviets' Central Executive Committee, January 6, 1918: *Essentials of Leninism,* vol. II, p. 250.

6. Quoted in George Leggett, *The Cheka: Lenin's Political Police* (Oxford: 1981), p. 17.

7. Quoted in ibid., p. xxxii.

8. See Appendix, ibid., p. 468, using Robert Conquest's estimates.

9. *The Bolsheviks and the October Revolution: Central Committee Minutes of the RSDLP (Bolsheviks), 1917–18* (*London: 1974), pp. 173–78.

10. Leggett, *Cheka,* p. 111.

11. Quoted by K. D. Bracher, *The German Dictatorship* (*London: 1971), p. 30.

12. K. A. von Müller, *Im Wandel einer Welt: Erinnerungen, 1919–32* (Munich: 1966), quoted by Joachim Fest, *Hitler* (*London: 1974), p. 113.

13. The full text of Hitler's letter was printed by Ernst Deuerlein in *VfZ* (1959), 2, pp. 201ff.

14. Hitler's Political Testament, in *Hitler Reden und Proklamationen, 1932–1945,* vol. II, ed. Max Domarus (Würzburg: 1963), pp. 2236–69.

15. *Mein Kampf,* trans. James Murphy (London: 1939), p. 298.

16. Ibid., p. 48.

17. Quoted by J. P. Stern, *Hitler: The Führer and the People* (London: 1975), p. 35.

18. *Mein Kampf,* trans. Murphy, pp. 394–95.

19. Ibid., pp. 391–92.

20. Ibid., p. 403.

21. For the history of the Protocols see Norman Cohn, *Warrant for Genocide* (London: 1967).

22. Fest, *Hitler*, pp. 128–29.

23. Hermann Rauschning, *Hitler Speaks* (*London: 1939), p. 89.

24. See Martin Broszat, *The Hitler State* (*London: 1981), ch. 2.

25. The two quotations are juxtaposed in Aryeh L. Unger, *The Totalitarian Party: Party and People in Nazi Germany and Soviet Russia* (Cambridge: 1974), pp. 8–9.

26. Maurice Duverger, *Political Parties* (*London: 1954), p. 2.

27. See Michael Kater, *The Nazi Party: A Social Profile of Members and Leaders, 1919–1945* (Oxford: 1983), chs. 1 and 7.

28. Konrad Heiden, *Hitler: A Biography* (*London: 1936), pp. 102–3.

29. Friedelind Wagner, *The Royal Family of Bayreuth* (London: 1948), p. 8.

30. *Hitler's Table Talk, 1941–1944* (*London: 1953), p. 107.

31. Quoted from the transcript of the trial, *Der Hitler-Prozess* (Munich: 1924).

32. See Henry Ashby Turner, Jr., *German Big Business and the Rise of Hitler* (New York: 1985), pp. 47–60, for the period 1919–23.

33. Ibid., p. 60.

34. *Adolf Hitlers Reden* (Munich: 1933), pp. 89–93.

35. See Albrecht Tyrell, *Vom Trommler zum Führer* (Munich: 1975).

FOUR: The General Secretary

1. Quoted by Merle Fainsod, *How Russia Is Ruled* (Cambridge, Mass.: 1953), p. 303.

2. Quoted by Robert C. Tucker, *Stalin as Revolutionary* (New York: 1973), pp. 184–86.

3. Quoted by Ronald Hingley, *Joseph Stalin: Man and Legend* (London: 1974), p. 117; Isaac Deutscher, *Stalin: A Political Biography* (London: 1949), pp. 196–97.

4. Quoted by Tucker, *Stalin as Revolutionary*, pp. 192–93.

5. Quoted by D. A. Volkogonov, *Stalin: Triumph and Tragedy* (*London: 1991), p. 57.

6. Quoted by Tucker, *Stalin as Revolutionary*, p. 201.

7. Quoted by Roy Medvedev, *Let History Judge*, rev. ed. (Oxford: 1989), p. 64, from unpublished notes by Trotsky dated January 4, 1937.

8. In a speech of October 17, 1921, quoted in Leszek Kolakowski, *Main Currents of Marxism*, vol. II: *The Golden Age* (*Oxford: 1978), p. 484.

9. Pp. 122–27 of the English version published in 1921.

10. *The Essentials of Leninism*, vol. I, (*London: 1947), p. 177.

11. Quoted by Deutscher, *Stalin*, p. 221.

12. Quoted by Leonard Schapiro, *The Communist Party of the Soviet Union*, 2d. ed. (London: 1970), p. 221.

13. Quoted by R. V. Daniels, *The Conscience of the Revolution: Communist Opposition in Soviet Russia* (Cambridge, Mass.: 1960), pp. 211–12.

14. Section 3 of the resolution: *Essentials of Leninism*, vol. II, p. 684.

15. Quoted by Schapiro, *Communist Party*, p. 212.

16. Quoted in Aryeh L. Unger, *The Totalitarian Party: Party and People in Nazi Germany and Soviet Russia* (Cambridge: 1974), p. 15.

17. November 13, 1922: *Essentials of Leninism*, vol. II, p. 819.

18. Quoted by Tucker, *Stalin as Revolutionary*, p. 208. Preobrazhensky was one of the two secretaries of the party deprived of office after the Tenth Congress in 1921. He was later shot, without a public trial, because he

refused to confess to the crimes of which he was accused (Schapiro, *Communist Party,* p. 426).

19. L. Trotsky, *Stalin* (*London: 1947), p. 357.

20. Quoted by Alex de Jonge, *Stalin and the Shaping of the Soviet Union* (London: 1986), p. 157.

21. Quoted by Tucker, *Stalin as Revolutionary,* pp. 252–53.

22. Ibid.

23. First published in Russia in 1963, and quoted by Adam Ulam, *Stalin: The Man and His Era,* 2d. ed. (London: 1989), p. 216.

24. Trotsky, *Stalin,* p. 365.

25. Quoted in full in Medvedev, *Let History Judge,* pp. 79–81.

26. Quoted in ibid., p. 81.

27. Ibid., pp. 84–85.

28. Lenin, *Collected Works,* vol. XXXVI (Moscow: 1960–80), pp. 605–10.

29. The three articles are reprinted in *Essentials of Leninism,* vol. II, pp. 840–55.

30. Lenin to Mdivani, March 6, 1923: L. Trotsky, *The Stalin School of Falsification* (*New York: 1937), p. 69.

31. Quoted in full by Khrushchev in his 1956 speech. See *The Anti-Stalin Campaign and International Communism* (New York: 1956), pp. 8–9.

32. Quoted by R. W. Davies in the *Observer,* April 22, 1990.

33. Quoted by Deutscher, *Stalin,* p. 258.

34. The article was published in the periodical *Questions of Soviet Economy and Administration,* January 1924, quoted by Daniels, *Conscience of the Revolution,* p. 167.

35. Trotsky, *My Life* (New York: 1931), p. 481.

36. Report by Stalin to the Fourteenth Party Congress, 1927 (Stenographic Report, Moscow: 1928).

37. Quoted by Daniels, *Conscience of the Revolution,* p. 212.

38. The letter is reprinted in L. Trotsky, *The New Course* (*New York: 1943), pp. 153–56.

39. A translation of the "Declaration of the 46" is in E. H. Carr, *A History of Soviet Russia,* vol. IV: *The Interregnum, 1923–24* (London: 1954), pp. 369–73.

40. Quotations given by Daniels, *Conscience of the Revolution,* pp. 220–21.

41. Trotsky's letter is reprinted in Trotsky, *The New Course,* pp. 89–98.

42. Thirteenth Party Conference: J. Stalin, *Collected Works,* vol. VI, pp. 5–46.

43. Boris Bazhanov worked in Stalin's Secretariat as his secretary for Politburo affairs from August 1923 to the end of 1925, attending all Politburo meetings. Disillusioned with Communism, he escaped from Russia at the beginning of 1928, and published his memoirs *Avec Staline dans le Kremline* (Paris: 1930) (German edition, *Der Rote Diktator* [Berlin: 1931]). A much fuller account was published in Paris in 1979 and in English translation in the U.S.A. in 1990, *Bazhanov and the Damnation of Stalin* (Ohio U.P.) This quotation is taken from a radio interview, published in G.R. Urban, ed., *Stalinism: Its Impact on Russia and the World,* pb. ed. (Aldershot: 1985), p. 26.

44. Nadezhda Mandelstam, *Hope Abandoned,* pb. ed. (*London: 1975), pp. 237–88.

45. Quoted by Walter Duranty, *I Write as I Please* (New York: 1935), pp. 225–26.

46. Ronald Hingley's phrase, *Stalin,* p. 155.

47. Stalin, *Collected Works,* vol. VI, (Moscow: 1952–55), pp. 47–53.

48. This suggestion is elaborated by Robert Tucker in *Stalin as Revolutionary,* pp. 279–88.

FIVE: The Creation of the
Nazi Party

1. All quotations from the transcript of the trial, *Der Hitler-Prozess* (Munich: 1924).

2. Quoted by Joachim Fest, *Hitler* (*London: 1974), p. 195.

3. Hitler speaking in the Bürgerbräukeller on November 8, 1933. Max Domarus, ed., *Hitler. Reden und Proklamationen, 1932–45,* vol. I (Würzburg: 1962), p. 327.

4. Hitler speaking in November 1934, after the prospect of a "second revolution" had been rejected by the action against Röhm and other leaders of the SA. *VB,* November 10, 1934.

5. D. C. Watt's introduction to the English translation of *Mein Kampf* by Ralph Manheim (London: 1969), pp. xiii–xiv.

6. *Mein Kampf,* trans. James Murphy (London: 1939), p. 183.

7. Speech at Chemnitz, April 2, 1938: *Hitler's Words,* Speeches 1922–43, ed. Gordon W. Prange (*Washington, D.C.: 1944), pp. 8–9.

8. *Mein Kampf,* trans. Murphy, p. 242.

9. Ibid., p. 243.

10. Ibid., p. 242.

11. *Mein Kampf,* trans. Manheim, p. 598.

12. *Mein Kampf,* trans. Murphy, p. 330.

13. *Hitler's Secret Book,* English trans. of *Hitlers Zweites Buch* (New York: 1961), p. 24.

14. Ibid., p. 27.

15. H. Preiss, ed. *Adolf Hitler in Franken. Reden aus der Kampfzeit* (Munich: 1939), p. 81.

16. *Hitler's Secret Book,* pp. 212–13.

17. *Mein Kampf,* German ed. (Munich: 1930), p. 225.

18. The interview was published in the Leipzig news magazine, *Der National-Sozialist,* August 17, 1924, and is quoted by Eberhard Jäckel, *Hitler's World View* (*Middletown: 1972), p. 57.

19. *Mein Kampf,* trans. Murphy, p. 392.

20. Ibid., p. 32.

21. Otto Strasser, *Hitler and I* (*London: 1940), pp. 76–77.

22. *Mein Kampf,* trans. Murphy, p. 392.

23. Ibid., pp. 160–61.

24. Ibid., p. 161.

25. Ibid., p. 437.

26. Ibid., p. 438.

27. Kurt G. W. Lüdecke, *I Knew Hitler* (*London: 1938), p. 214.

28. Report in the *VB,* March 7, 1925, quoted by Fest, *Hitler,* p. 227.

29. Quoted by Dietrich Orlow, *The History of the Nazi Party,* vol. I: *1919–33* (Newton Abbot: 1971), p. 70.

30. Ibid., p. 69.

31. Owing to a road accident in which he was injured, Strasser did not take up this position until September 1926; he held it until the end of 1927.

32. Quoted by Fest, *Hitler,* p. 241. See Joseph L. Nyomarkay, "Factionalism in the NSDAP, 1925–1926: The Myth and Reality of the Northern Faction" in *Nazism and the Third Reich,* ed. Henry Ashby Turner, Jr. (New York: 1972), pp. 21–44.

33. Quoted by Henry Ashby Turner, Jr., *German Big Business and the Rise of Hitler* (New York: 1985), p. 65.

34. Quoted by Orlow, *Nazi Party,* vol. I, p. 87, n. 43.

35. See Michael Kater, *The Nazi Party* (Oxford: 1983), pp. 34–38.

36. See Turner, *German Big Business,* pp. 65–68.

37. See ibid., pp. 83–99, based on accounts of Hitler's addresses to four meetings before closed audiences in Essen in 1926–27; his address to the Hamburg National Club in February 1928; and his speech before an invited

audience of businessmen in Heidelberg in March 1928.

38. Untersuchungs-und-Schlichtungs-Ausschuss (Committee for Investigation and Settlement). Its chairman was a retired general, Heinemann, succeeded at the beginning of 1928 by a younger retired officer, Walter Buch, who had been a member of the party since 1921.

39. Orlow, *Nazi Party,* vol. I, p. 80.

40. See Horst Gies, "The NSDAP and Agrarian Organization in the Final Phase of the Weimar Republic," in *Nazism and the Third Reich,* ed. Turner, pp. 45–88.

41. Quoted in ibid.

42. See Turner, *German Big Business,* pp. 111–24. Professor Turner's researches have been generally accepted as conclusive in regard to the contributions of German big business (with the emphasis on "big") before Hitler came to power. But this acceptance does not extend to Professor Turner's argument that his research exculpates big business from an important share of the responsibility for undermining the Weimar Republic, and for showing readiness to come to terms with Hitler as a suitable candidate for the chancellorship.

43. The only account we possess of the discussion is Otto Strasser's, but there is little doubt that it can be accepted as accurate in substance. It was published very shortly afterwards, it was never challenged or repudiated by Hitler—although it must have done him considerable damage in some quarters—and all that Hitler is reported to have said is perfectly consistent with his known opinions. The account that follows is taken from Otto Strasser, *Ministersessel oder Revolution?,* the pamphlet version he published at the time (1930), and

from the briefer English version in his *Hitler and I,* pp. 109–27.

44. Quoted, together with the crack by Tucholsky, in Fest, *Hitler,* p. 277.

SIX: Lenin's Successor

1. Leonard Schapiro, *The Communist Party and the Soviet Union* 2d. ed. (London: 1970), p. 314.

2. From a radio interview in 1979: G. R. Urban, ed., *Stalinism: Its Impact on Russia and the World* (Aldershot: 1982), p. 18. Cf. the account given by B. Bazhanov in *Avec Staline dans le Kremline* (Paris: 1930), pp. 43–45. Roy Medvedev, while describing Bazhanov's portrait of Stalin as having the ring of truth, says that Lenin's Testament was not read to the Plenum (*Let History Judge,* rev. ed., Oxford: 1989, p. 84); Volkogonov, op. cit., p. 92, however, quotes the Central Committee's resolution that "these documents, read out at the Plenum," should be communicated to the congress in the way described.

3. Bazhanov, *Avec Staline,* p. 21, quoted by Isaac Deutscher, *Stalin* (London: 1949), p. 274.

4. Ruth Fischer, *Stalin and German Communism* (*Cambridge, Mass.: 1948), p. 366.

5. Ibid., p. 369.

6. Ibid., p. 368.

7. Bazhanov, *Avec Staline,* p. 21.

8. Quoted by Robert C. Tucker, *Stalin as Revolutionary* (New York: 1973), p. 310.

9. A. I. Mikoyan's memoirs (Moscow: 1970), pp. 136–39, quoted in ibid., p. 298.

10. Quoted by Deutscher, *Stalin,* p. 290.

11. Tucker, *Stalin as Revolutionary,* p. 313.

12. See the discussion in Medvedev, *Let History Judge,* pp. 821–22, and in Tucker, *Stalin as Revolutionary,* pp. 324–29. This Ksenofontov is to be

distinguished from I. K. Ksenofontov, who was a member of Stalin's Secretariat.

13. By the time of Stalin's death, over seventeen million copies of the *Foundations,* continually updated and expanded, had been issued. The quotations in the text have been taken from the English translation in the collection of Stalin's speeches and publications: J. Stalin, ed., *Leninism* (*London: 1940), pp. 1–85.

14. Walter Laqueur, *Stalin: The Glasnost Revelations* (London: 1990), p. 46.

15. Taken from an account of a conversation between Zinoviev and Trotsky at Kamenev's home in 1926 after the three had become reconciled in the United Opposition. The notes of the conversation were published by Trotsky in exile in 1929, *The Stalin School of Falsification* (*New York: 1962), pp. 89–95.

16. Ibid.

17. See note 13 above.

18. Stalin's first published espousal of "socialism in one country" came in "The October Revolution and the Tactics of the Russian Communists," written in December 1924 to serve as the preface to a collection of articles *On the Road to October,* published early in 1925. An English translation is available in Stalin, *Leninism,* pp. 86–117.

19. Quoted by Tucker, *Stalin as Revolutionary,* p. 379.

20. R. V. Daniels, *The Conscience of the Revolution: Communist Opposition in Soviet Russia* (Cambridge, Mass.: 1960), p. 252.

21. J. Stalin, *Collected Works,* vol. VI, (Moscow: 1952–55), p. 246.

22. Fischer, *Stalin,* p. 405. One of the delegates Stalin recruited was Heinz Neumann, who spoke Russian and became a confidant of his. The latter made good use of him not only

in Germany but also in China, until he rebelled against Stalin's policy of toleration toward the Nazis in the early 1930s. He was then dropped, arrested in 1937, and eliminated in the purges. (Ibid., pp. 446–47, n. 9.)

23. April 17, 1925: *Bolshevik,* no. 8 (1925).

24. For the Bukharin-Preobrazhensky debate, see Stephen F. Cohen, *Bukharin and the Bolshevik Revolution, 1888–1938* (New York: 1974), ch. 6, and Daniels, *Conscience of the Revolution,* pp. 288–95.

25. The question is discussed by Medvedev, *Let History Judge,* pp. 155–59. In 1926 the writer Boris Pilnyak published a story in *Novy Mir,* "The Tale of the Unextinguished Moon," which, although under thinly disguised names (Stalin was referred to as Number One), provided a circumstantial account of Frunze's death and implied that Stalin was responsible for it. All copies of the publication were at once confiscated.

26. Quotations from the stenographic record of the Fourteenth Party Congress given by Daniels, *Conscience of the Revolution,* pp. 268–69.

27. J. Stalin, *Problems of Leninism* (Moscow: 1931), pp. 306–10 (another collection of Stalin's speeches and articles).

28. Daniels, *Conscience of the Revolution,* p. 266.

29. Quoted in ibid., p. 278.

30. Quoted by Isaac Deutscher, *The Prophet Unarmed: Trotsky, 1921–1929* (London: 1959), pp. 296–97.

31. The speeches at the Fifteenth Party Congress were reported in *Pravda* between November 5 and 12, 1926.

32. Quoted by Cohen, *Bukharin,* p. 240.

33. Quoted by Daniels, *Conscience of the Revolution,* p. 315.

34. Ibid.

35. *Khrushchev Remembers,* trans. and ed. Strobe Talbot (*London: 1971), pp. 25–26.

36. Quoted in Medvedev, *Let History Judge,* p. 183.

37. Robert C. Tucker, *Stalin in Power: The Revolution from Above, 1928–1941* (New York: 1990), p. 80, quoting two articles published in August 1988 by Vladimir Tikhonov of the Academy of Agricultural Sciences in Moscow.

38. Quoted by Medvedev, *Let History Judge,* 2d. ed., p. 217.

39. Quoted by Tucker, *Stalin as Revolutionary,* p. 407.

40. Stalin, *Collected Works,* vol. XI, p. 5. Stalin's speeches were not reported at the time and were not printed until twenty-five years later, and then in condensed form.

41. Quoted in Moshe Lewin, *Political Undercurrents in Soviet Economic Debate* (Princeton: 1974), p. 74.

42. Quoted in Cohen, *Bukharin,* pp. 190–91.

43. Quoted by Leonard E. Hubbard, *The Economy of Soviet Agriculture* (London: 1939), p. 100. The figures in this paragraph are taken from Tucker, *Stalin in Power,* p. 72. See also Moshe Lewin, "Who Was the Soviet Kulak?" in the volume of his collected essays, *The Making of the Soviet System: Essays in the Social History of Inter-War Russia* (London: 1985).

44. Quoted by Daniels, *Conscience of the Revolution,* p. 326.

45. Stalin's speech of April 1928 in *Collected Works,* vol. XI, pp. 160–206.

46. Kamenev's report is in the Trotsky Archives at Harvard. Quoted by Daniels, *Conscience of the Revolution,* p. 332.

47. Stalin, *Collected Works,* vol. X, p. 57.

48. Published in *Pravda* on September 30, 1928.

49. "The Industrialization of the USSR and the Epigones of Populism," quoted by Daniels, *Conscience of the Revolution,* p. 349.

50. Quoted by Cohen, *Bukharin,* p. 296.

51. Ibid., pp. 305–7.

52. J. Stalin, ed., *Leninism* (Moscow: 1940), pp. 240–93, described as an excerpt.

SEVEN: Hitler Within Sight of Power

1. This summary is based on sampling the large number of articles that have been published and four comprehensive studies by H. A. Winkler, *Mittelstand, Demokratie und Nationalsozialismus* (Cologne: 1972); Richard F. Hamilton, *Who Voted for Hitler?* (Princeton: 1982); Michael Kater, *The Nazi Party: A Social Profile of Members and Leaders, 1919–1945* (Oxford: 1983); Thomas Childers, *The Nazi Voter: The Social Foundations of Fascism in Germany, 1919–33* (Chapel Hill, N.C.: 1984). Although I have learned much from the detailed research of Professor Hamilton, I am not convinced by his general conclusions, which seem to me too much colored by his obsession with disproving the "lower-middle class" thesis. (See the review by Jeremy Noakes of the Childers and Hamilton books in the *Times Literary Supplement,* September 21, 1984.) The three books by Kater, Childers, and Hamilton contain full bibliographical references to the periodical literature and regional studies in German and English.

2. Martin Broszat, *Hitler and the Collapse of Weimar Germany* (*Leamington: 1987), p. 86.

3. Mierendorff's article "Was ist Nationalsozialismus?" was published

in *Neue Blätter für Sozialismus,* vol. II, no. 4, and is quoted in Joachim Fest, *The Face of the Third Reich* (*London: 1970), p. 221.

4. Childers, *Nazi Voter,* p. 178.

5. Hamilton, *Who Voted?,* p. 499.

6. Ibid., pp. 37–38.

7. W. S. Allen, *The Nazi Seizure of Power: The Experience of a Single Town, 1930–35* (Chicago: 1965), p. 133.

8. An important source is the collection made by Theodore Abel of some 600 accounts written in 1934 by members of the Nazi party who had joined it during the Weimar period. This collection is now in the Hoover Institution Archives. See Peter H. Merkl, *Political Violence under the Swastika: 581 Early Nazis* (Princeton: 1975) for a reexamination of the accounts in the Abel collection.

9. I owe the reference to Deuerlein's biography of Hitler to Fred Weinstein, *The Dynamics of Nazism* (New York: 1980), p. 81.

10. The suggestion is made in two essays by Fritz Stern: "Germany 1933: Fifty Years Later" and "National Socialism as Temptation," in *Dreams and Illusions: The Drama of German History* (London: 1988). The quotation is from the first, p. 145.

11. Quoted from Freud's "Thought for the Time of War and Death," by Fritz Stern, ibid., pp. 168–69.

12. Reported in the *Berliner Tageblatt,* September 8, 1932.

13. Gregor Strasser, quoted by Joachim Fest, *Hitler* (*London: 1974), p. 289.

14. Childers, *Nazi Voter,* p. 325, n. 7.

15. Quoted by R. W. M. Kempner, "Blue Print of the Nazi Underground" (*Research Studies of the State College of Washington,* vol. xiii, no. 2, p. 121).

16. The trial was reported in the *Frankfurter Zeitung,* September 26, 1930.

17. Quoted by K. D. Bracher, *The German Dictatorship* (*London: 1971), p. 189.

18. H. Brüning, *Memoiren, 1878–1934* (Stuttgart: 1970), pp. 247ff.

19. Quoted in F. L. Carsten, *The Reichswehr and Politics, 1918–33* (Oxford: 1966), pp. 334–35.

20. F. Meinecke, *Die Deutsche Katastrophe* (Wiesbaden: 1947), p. 74.

21. Goebbels's Diary, January 5, 1932; English trans., *My Part in Germany's Fight* (London: 1935), p. 15.

22. The firm figures for membership are 129,563 in September 1930; 849,009 on January 30, 1933 (Kater, *Nazi Party,* p. 365). Dietrich Orlow, *The History of the Nazi Party,* vol. I: *1919–33* (Newton Abbot: 1971) who gives a lower figure for 1933 (719,446) guessed at 450,000 as a reasonable figure for the beginning of 1932 (p. 239). According to Orlow (p. 236), 53,000 joined in November alone, but there was wastage to offset this.

23. Quoted by Fest, *Hitler,* p. 336.

24. Goebbels's Diary, June 11, 1932, p. 105.

25. 3 August 1932: *Documents on British Foreign Policy, 1919–39,* 2d Series, 1930–37 (London 1949–57), vol. IV, no. 8.

26. Goebbels's Diary, August 8, 1932, p. 133.

27. Speech of September 4: H. Preiss, ed., *Adolf Hitler in Franken: Reden aus der Kampfzeit* (Munich: 1939), p. 194.

28. The row Hitler made secured the commutation of their sentence to imprisonment for life; shortly after Hitler came to power, the men were released and hailed as freedom fighters.

29. Goebbels's Diary, October 4, 1932, Eng. trans., p. 167.

30. Ibid., October 15, 1932, p. 172.

31. Henry Ashby Turner, Jr., *German Big Business and the Rise of Hitler* (New York: 1985), pp. 293–95.

32. Goebbels's Diary, November 5, 1932, p. 184.

33. Ibid., December 9, 1932, p. 209.

34. Ibid., December 23, 1932, p. 215.

35. For a concise, up-to-date account, see Broszat, *Hitler and the Collapse of Weimar Germany*, ch. 4.

36. Quoted by Bracher, *German Dictatorship*, p. 193.

37. *Hitlers Auseinandersetzung mit Brüning* (Munich: 1932), pp. 49–51.

EIGHT: Stalin's Revolution

1. Quoted by Adam Ulam, *Stalin: The Man and His Era,* 2d. ed. (London: 1989), p. 291.

2. See Stephen F. Cohen, *Bukharin and the Bolshevik Revolution, 1888–1938* (New York: 1974), pp. 327–29.

3. Quoted in ibid., p. 328.

4. Ibid., p. 295.

5. Robert Conquest, *The Harvest of Sorrow* (London: 1986), p. 74.

6. E. H. Carr, *A History of Soviet Russia: Socialism in One Country, 1924–26,* vol. I (London: 1958), p. 99.

7. See Robert C. Tucker, *Stalin in Power: The Revolution from Above, 1928–1941* (New York: 1990), p. 131.

8. Stalin's speech at the Central Committee Plenum, July 9, 1928, quoted in ibid., p. 84.

9. *Pravda,* November 7, 1929, reprinted in J. Stalin, ed., *Leninism* (Moscow: 1940), pp. 294–305.

10. Stalin's "Address to the Conference of Marxist Students of the Agrarian Question," in ibid., pp. 306–27.

11. See Tucker, *Stalin in Power,* p. 176.

12. Reprinted in Stalin, ed., *Leninism,* pp. 333–39. See also pp. 339–58, "Reply to Collective Farm Comrades," reprinted from *Pravda,* April 3, 1930.

13. Quoted by Tucker, *Stalin in Power,* p. 147.

14. Quoted by Moshe Lewin in "Society, State and Ideology," in *The Making of the Soviet System* (London: 1985), p. 219.

15. Figures given from Soviet sources by Alec Nove, *An Economic History of the USSR,* 2d. ed. (London: 1989), pp. 230–31.

16. Quoted by Conquest, *Harvest of Sorrow,* p. 184.

17. See R. W. Davies, *Soviet History in the Gorbachev Revolution* (London: 1989), pp. 184 and 217 n. 18.

18. Conquest, *Harvest of Sorrow,* p. 219.

19. Ibid.

20. Petro D. Grigorenko, *Memoirs* (*London: 1983), p. 36, quoted by Conquest, *Harvest of Sorrow,* p. 221.

21. Conquest, *Harvest of Sorrow,* p. 223.

22. English trans. (New York: 1977), quoted in ibid., pp. 232–33.

23. Terekhov's account was printed in *Pravda,* May 26, 1964, and is quoted by Conquest, *Harvest of Sorrow,* pp. 324–25.

24. Quoted by Moshe Lewin, "Taking Grain," in *The Making of the Soviet System,* p. 155.

25. Victor Kravchenko, *I Chose Freedom* (New York: 1946), p. 130.

26. *Pravda,* June 24, 1933, quoted by Conquest, *Harvest of Sorrow,* p. 261.

27. Quoted by Conquest, *Harvest of Sorrow,* p. 260.

28. Ibid., p. 264.

29. Ibid., p. 263.

30. *Testimony: The Memoirs of Shostakovich,* ed. Solomon Volkov (*London: 1979), p. 165.

31. For these two paragraphs, see Conquest, *Harvest of Sorrow,* pp. 266–71.

32. *Khrushchev Remembers,* trans. and ed. Strobe Talbot (*London: 1971), p. 120.

33. Quoted by Tucker, *Stalin in Power,* pp. 180–81.

34. Wolfgang Leonhard, *Child of the Revolution* (London: 1957), p. 136.

35. See Conquest, *Harvest of Sorrow,* ch. 9. Kazakhstan in the late 1920s had a population of four million, two-thirds of whom were seminomadic and relied for a livelihood on animal husbandry rather than the cultivation of grain. The attempts to impose collectivization led to a reduction of Kazakh households from 1,233,000 in 1929 to 565,000 in 1936, and the death of a quarter of the population. There was an even more catastrophic fall in the livestock population from 7.4 million cattle in 1929 to 1.6 million in 1933, and of sheep from 22 million to 1.7 million.

36. Robert Conquest, "Excess Deaths and Camp Numbers: Some Comments," *Soviet Studies,* vol. 43, no. 5 (1991).

37. Ronald Hingley, *Joseph Stalin: Man and Legend* (London: 1974), p. 210.

38. Roy Medvedev, *Let History Judge,* 1st ed. (London: 1972), pp. 101–2.

39. John Scott, *Behind the Urals* (London: 1942), p. 9.

40. The speech is given in full in Stalin, ed., *Leninism,* pp. 359–67.

41. Ulam, *Stalin,* p. 341.

42. Quoted in ibid., p. 312.

43. Among books describing this process are: Lynne Viola, *The Best Sons of the Fatherland: Workers in the Vanguard of Soviet Collectivization* (New York: 1987); Sheila Fitzpatrick, ed., *Cultural Revolution in Russia, 1928–31* (Bloomington: 1978); and Hiroaki Kuromiya, *Stalin's Industrial Revolution: Politics and Workers, 1928–32* (Cambridge: 1988).

44. From an account by K. Vorbei, published in Leningrad in 1961, and quoted in Kuromiya, p. 110.

45. Sheila Fitzpatrick, "Cultural Revolution as Class War," in Fitzpatrick, ed. *Cultural Revolution,* pp. 368–87.

46. Quoted by Medvedev, *Let History Judge,* 1st ed., p. 113.

47. Stalin, ed., *Leninism,* pp. 368–87.

48. Ibid.

49. J. Stalin, *Problems of Leninism* (*Moscow: 1953), p. 530.

50. Made at the Seventeenth Party Congress in January 1934.

51. Winston S. Churchill, *The Second World War,* vol. IV: *The Hinge of Fate* (London: 1951), pp. 447–48.

52. Lewin, *The Making of the Soviet System,* p. 271, quoting Marc Bloch, *La Société feodale* (Paris: 1968), p. 347.

53. Figures taken from Alec Nove, *Stalinism and After,* 2d. ed. (London: 1981), p. 44.

54. For example by Moshe Lewin, *The Making of the Soviet System,* "The Immediate Background of Soviet Collectivisation" (London: 1985) as well as by Stephen Cohen and Roy Medvedev.

55. Leonard Schapiro, *The Communist Party of the Soviet Union,* 2d. ed. (London: 1970), p. 464.

56. Ibid., p. 387.

57. Roy Medvedev, *Let History Judge,* rev. ed. (Oxford: 1989), pp. 253–54.

58. Stephen F. Cohen, *Re-thinking the Soviet Experience: Politics and History since 1917* (Oxford: 1985), ch. 3.

59. Stalin's Report to the Seventeenth Congress: Stalin, ed., *Leninism,* pp. 470–539.

60. *Pravda,* May 27, 1930.

61. Quoted in Cohen, *Bukharin,* p. 348.

62. See Medvedev, *Let History Judge*, p. 142; Robert Conquest, *The Great Terror: A Re-Assessment* (London: 1990), p. 51; and Cohen, *Bukharin*, pp. 342–43, with references.

63. Alexander Barmine, *One Who Survived: The Life Story of a Russian under the Soviets* (New York: 1945), pp. 101–2, quoted by Conquest, *The Great Terror: A Re-Assessment*, p. 60.

64. A resolution of the Central Committee quoted by Conquest, *The Great Terror: A Re-Assessment*, p. 54.

65. Davies, *Soviet History*, pp. 83–85; Medvedev, *Let History Judge*, pp. 296–98.

66. Quoted by Medvedev, *Let History Judge*, p. 329.

67. Schapiro, *Communist Party*, pp. 459–64.

68. Boris Nicolaevsky, *Power and the Soviet Elite: "The Letter of an Old Bolshevik" and Other Essays*, ed. Janet D. Zagoria (*London: 1966), pp. 31–32 and 76.

69. Quoted by Tucker, *Stalin in Power*, p. 248.

70. Stalin's Report to the Seventeenth Congress: Stalin, ed., *Leninism*, pp. 507 and 516.

71. *History of the CPSU*, 2d. rev. ed. (Moscow: 1962), p. 486.

72. Medvedev, *Let History Judge*, p. 331.

73. Published in *Ogonek*, no. 50, 1987.

74. Ulam, *Stalin*, pp. 372–73.

75. Ibid., p. 373, quoting the Congress Report.

76. Ibid., pp. 371–72.

77. Quoted by Tucker, *Stalin in Power*, p. 251.

78. Stalin, ed., *Leninism*, pp. 517–18.

79. See Medvedev, *Let History Judge*, pp. 331–33.

80. Tucker, *Stalin in Power*, p. 265.

81. Quoted in ibid., p. 240.

82. Ibid., p. 212.

83. Ibid., p. 275, quoting an article in *Nedelia* (no. 31, August 1989) by Valentin Berezhkov, later an interpreter for Stalin, whose source was Mikoyan.

NINE: Hitler's Revolution

1. Jeremy Noakes and Geoffrey Pridham, eds., *Nazism, 1919–1945: A Documentary Reader*, vol. I: *The Rise to Power, 1919–1934* (Exeter: 1983), no. 87.

2. Ibid.

3. Ibid., no. 90.

4. The phrase is K. D. Bracher's. See the discussion in his book *The German Dictatorship* (*London: 1971), pp. 191–98.

5. Noakes and Pridham, eds., *Nazism*, vol. I, pp. 150–51.

6. Rudolph Diels, *Lucifer ante Portas* (Stuttgart: 1950), p. 200.

7. The long-held belief, skillfully created by Willi Münzenberg and the Comintern propaganda center in Paris, that the Nazis were themselves responsible for the fire, was first challenged by Fritz Tobias, *The Reichstag Fire* (*London: 1964). Most historians today accept Tobias's and Diels's view as correct. Speculation about who started the fire distracts attention from the use the Nazis made of it.

8. Diels, *Lucifer*, pp. 142–44.

9. Noakes and Pridham, eds., *Nazism*, vol. I, no. 95.

10. These reports, together with those collected by the exiled leadership of the SPD in Prague (Sopade), have been systematically studied by Ian Kershaw in *Popular Opinion and Political Dissent in the Third Reich* (Oxford: 1983), and *The Hitler Myth: Image and Reality in the Third Reich* (Oxford: 1987).

11. *Deutsche Allgemeine Zeitung*, March 5, 1933.

12. Quoted by Martin Broszat, *The Hitler State* (*London: 1981), p. 79.

13. Quoted by Joachim Fest, *Hitler* (*London: 1974), p. 415.

14. March 21, 1933: Max Domarus, ed., *Hitler. Reden und Proklamationen, 1932–45,* vol. I (Würzburg: 1962), p. 228.

15. March 23, 1933: ibid., pp. 229–37.

16. Ibid., pp. 239–46.

17. A quotation from one of the best surveys of the historiographical controversy: John Hiden and John Farquharson, *Explaining Hitler's Germany: Historians and the Third Reich* (London: 1983), p. 59.

18. *Documents on German Foreign Policy,* Series C, vol. I, no. 16.

19. Jeremy Noakes and Geoffrey Pridham, eds., *Nazism, 1919–1945: A Documentary Reader,* vol. II: *State, Economy and Society, 1933–1939* (Exeter: 1984), no. 266.

20. Ibid., no. 282.

21. *Mein Kampf,* trans. James Murphy (London: 1939), p. 506.

22. Fest, *Hitler,* pp. 428–29.

23. An official statement of 1937: Noakes and Pridham, eds., *Nazism,* vol. II, no. 311.

24. Martin Heidegger, *Die Selbstbehauptung der deutschen Universität* (Breslau: 1934), pp. 22ff.

25. Jeremy Noakes and Geoffrey Pridham, eds., *Nazism, 1919–1945: A Documentary Reader,* vol. III: *Foreign Policy, War and Racial Extermination* (Exeter: 1988), no. 485.

26. Ibid., no. 484.

27. Ibid., no. 485.

28. Harold W. James, *The German Slump: Politics and Economics, 1924–1936* (Oxford: 1986), p. 347.

29. Noakes and Pridham, eds., *Nazism,* vol. I, no. 117.

30. *Die Deutsche Volkswirtschaft,* 8, 1933–34, quoted by James, *German Slump,* p. 355.

31. May 20, 1937: Noakes and Pridham, eds., *Nazism,* vol. II, no. 178.

32. Ibid., vol. III, no. 472.

33. Domarus, *Hitler. Reden,* vol. I, pp. 270–78.

34. *Daily Mail,* August 6, 1934.

35. Broszat, *The Hitler State,* p. 234.

36. Bracher, *German Dictatorship,* p. 230.

37. Göring, now Minister-President of Prussia, speaking at the ministerial discussion of guidelines for carrying out the law, April 25, 1933. Noakes and Pridham, eds., *Nazism,* vol. II, no. 152.

38. Hans Kerrl was the fifth, appointed Reich church minister in 1935.

39. Noakes and Pridham, eds., *Nazism,* vol. I, no. 115.

40. Hitler's address to the Reich Governors' Conference, July 6, 1933: ibid., no. 117.

41. This paragraph is based on the study of these reports (confirmed by those of the exiled SPD) by Ian Kershaw in *The Hitler Myth,* chs. 2 and 3.

42. The Nazis gave the trial the fullest possible publicity, but the prosecution failed to prove any connection between the Communist defendants and van der Lubbe, and the Supreme Court at Leipzig ordered the Communists' release.

43. Kershaw, *The Hitler Myth,* p. 85.

44. Diels, *Lucifer,* p. 278.

45. Anthony Eden's account of his visit to Berlin in February 1934 is to be found in his memoirs, *Facing the Dictators* (London: 1962), pp. 69–75.

46. June 7, 1934: Noakes and Pridham, eds., *Nazism,* vol. I, no. 120.

47. Domarus, vol. I, pp. 410–24.

48. Kershaw, *The Hitler Myth,* p. 92, and in general chs. 2 and 3.

49. Quoted in Bracher, *German Dictatorship,* p. 241.

50. ND 1919-PS.

51. Broszat, *The Hitler State,* p. 214.

52. Noakes and Pridham, eds., *Nazism,* vol. II, p. 236.

53. Frick's statement, November 1934: ibid., no. 158.

TEN: Stalin and Hitler Compared

1. G. W. F. Hegel, *Lectures on the Philosophy of History,* trans. J. Sibree (London: 1902), pp. 31–32.

2. Ibid., p. 70.

3. Ibid., p. 34.

4. Dmitri Volkogonov, *Stalin, Triumph and Tragedy* (*London: 1991), p. 101.

5. Quoted in G. R. Urban, ed., *Stalinism: Its Impact on Russia and the World,* pb. ed. (Aldershot: 1985), p. 133.

6. J. P. Stern, *Hitler: The Führer and the People* (London: 1975), p. 43, a book to which I am much indebted.

7. Friedrich Nietzsche, *Zur Genealogie der Moral* (1887), sec. II, para. 17, quoted by J. P. Stern, *Hitler,* p. 45.

8. Mussolini (1) from an interview with Emil Ludwig, (2) from Mussolini's *Collected Works,* vol. XX, p. 93, quoted by J. P. Stern, *Hitler,* p. 45.

9. Quoted by K. D. Bracher, *The German Dictatorship* (*London: 1971), pp. 141–42.

10. Hermann Rauschning, *Hitler Speaks* (London: 1939), p. 257.

11. *Hitler's Table Talk, 1941–1944* (*London: 1953), pp. 76–79 (October 21, 1941).

12. Theodore Abel, *Why Hitler Came to Power* (New York: 1938), p. 244.

13. The controversies and confusion that have grown up around Weber's use of the term are conveniently set out and clarified by Ann Ruth Willner in *The Spellbinders: Charismatic Political Leadership* (New Haven: 1984), esp. chs. 1 and 2 and the appendix. The six examples she selects for discussion are Castro, Gandhi, Hitler, Mussolini, F. D. Roosevelt, and Sukarno. Other twentieth-century candidates are: Atatürk, Khomeini, Lenin, Mao, Nasser, Nkrumah, and Peron.

14. Otto Strasser, *Hitler and I* (London: 1940), pp. 74–77.

15. Friedrich Nietzsche, *Human, All Too Human,* para. 52, quoted by J. P. Stern, p. 35.

16. Albert Speer, *Inside the Third Reich* (*London: 1970), p. 75.

17. *Khrushchev Remembers,* ed. and trans. Strobe Talbot (*London: 1971), pp. 41–42.

18. Harold Lasswell, *Psychopathology and Politics* (New York: 1960), p. 173.

19. Quoted by R. W. Davies, *Soviet History in the Gorbachev Revolution* (London: 1989), p. 61, from *Literaturnaya Gazeta,* August 3, 1988.

20. Robert C. Tucker, *Stalin as Revolutionary* (New York: 1973), ch. 12.

21. Stalin's speech to the Central Committee, October 23, 1927.

22. Svetlana Alliluyeva, *Twenty Letters to a Friend* (*London: 1967), p. 86.

23. Lydia Dan, "Bukharin to Staline," *Novy Zhurnal,* no. 75 (1964), quoted by Tucker, *Stalin as Revolutionary,* pp. 424–25.

24. Hjalmar Schacht, *Account Settled* (*London: 1948), p. 219.

25. Ibid., p. 220.

26. Both quotations from K. Sontheimer, *Anti-demokratisches Denken in der Weimarer Republik,* quoted by Ian Kershaw in his illuminating study, *The Hitler Myth: Image and Reality in the Third Reich* (Oxford: 1987), pp. 19–20.

27. Hitler's speech at Munich, March 14, 1936: Max Domarus, ed.,

Hitler. Reden und Proklamationen,
1932–45, vol. I (Würzburg: 1962),
p. 606.

28. Quoted by Robert H. McNeal,
Stalin: Man and Ruler (London: 1988),
p. 151.

29. Quoted by Kershaw, *The Hitler*
Myth, pp. 26–27, from Albrecht
Tyrrell, *Führer befehl!* (Düsseldorf:
1969).

30. Kershaw, *The Hitler Myth,*
pp. 94–95.

31. Text of Jodl's letter in P. E.
Schramm, *Hitler: The Man and the*
Military Leader (*London: 1972),
appendix II, p. 205.

32. *Khrushchev Remembers: The*
Glasnost Tapes (London: 1990),
pp. 15–16.

33. Roy Medvedev, *Let History*
Judge, rev. ed. (Oxford: 1989), p. 303.

34. Volkogonov, p. 146, quoting
A.N. Shepelin, at one time head of
the KGB.

35. Alliluyeva, *Twenty Letters,* p.
217, and *Only One Year* (*New York:
1969), pp. 381–82.

36. Alliluyeva, *Twenty Letters,*
p. 155.

37. Ibid., p. 164.

38. Speer, *Inside the Third Reich,*
p. 129.

39. Heinrich Hoffmann, *Hitler Was*
My Friend (*London: 1955), p. 162.

40. Speer, *Inside the Third Reich,*
p. 92.

41. Ernst ("Putzi") Hanfstaengl,
Hitler: The Missing Years (*London:
1957), p. 52.

42. Erich Fromm, *The Anatomy of*
Human Destructiveness, pb. ed.
(London: 1977), p. 546.

43. Ignatius Phayre's article in
Current History, July 1936, quoted by
John Toland, *Adolf Hitler* (New York:
1976), p. 394.

44. Speer, *Inside the Third Reich,*
p. 119.

45. Ibid., p. 129.

46. Ibid., ch. 7.

47. Ibid., p. 131.

48. Rauschning, *Hitler Speaks,*
p. 220.

49. *Khrushchev Remembers,* p. 111.

50. D. A. Volkogonov, *Stalin:*
Triumph and Tragedy (*London:
1991), pp. 225–28.

51. See Hildegard Brenner, *Die*
Kunstpolitik der National Sozialismus
(Reinbek: 1963).

52. Speer, *Inside the Third Reich,*
p. 42.

53. Ibid., p. 31.

54. Ibid., p. 55.

55. Ibid., p. 56.

56. See Alexei Tarkhanov and
Sergei Kavtaradze, *Stalinist Architecture*
(London: 1992).

57. Rauschning, *Hitler Speaks,*
p. 62.

58. *Hitler's Table Talk,* p. 51.

59. Ibid., p. 87.

60. Jane Degras, ed. *The Communist*
International, 1919–43: Documents, vol.
II: *1923–1928* (London: 1960), p. 525.

61. Report to the Seventeenth Party
Congress: J. Stalin, ed., *Leninism*
(Moscow: 1940), p. 484.

62. Ibid., p. 486.

63. Speech on Stahlhelm Day,
September 23, 1933: report in
Völkischer Beobachter, September 25,
1936.

64. *Hitler's Table Talk,* p. 497.

65. Fabian von Schlabrendorff,
Offiziere gegen Hitler (Zurich: 1946),
pp. 47–48.

66. Nadezhda Mandelstam, *Hope*
against Hope: A Memoir pb. ed.
(*London: 1975), ch. 9.

67. *Der Kongress zu Nürnberg von*
5–6 Sept. 1934, p. 134.

68. Quoted by Aryeh L. Unger, *The*
Totalitarian Party: Party and People in
Nazi Germany and Soviet Russia
(Cambridge: 1974), p. 170.

69. Note provided by Yevgeny
Frelov, a friend and confidant of Jan

Sten's and printed by Medvedev, *Let History Judge*, pp. 438–39. See also Volkogonov, pp. 230–32, quoting the Central Party Archives.

70. Quoted in Robert C. Tucker, "The Rise of Stalin's Personality Cult," *American Historical Review*, 84 (1979), pp. 347–66.

71. See Bracher, *The German Dictatorship*, pp. 256–59.

72. John Willetts, "Socialist Realism," entry in *The Fontana/Harper Dictionary of Modern Thought*, ed. Alan Bullock and Stephen Trombley, rev. ed. (London and New York: 1988).

73. See Jeffrey Herf, *Reactionary Modernism: Technology, Culture and Politics in Weimar and the Third Reich* (Cambridge: 1984), p. 196, an illuminating and well-documented study.

74. Otto Wagener, *Hitler: Memoirs of a Confidant*, ed. Henry Ashby Turner, Jr. (*New Haven: 1985), p. 213.

75. Rauschning, *Hitler Speaks*, ch. 3.

76. Quoted by Alexander Dallin, *German Rule in Russia*, rev. ed. (London: 1981), p. 9.

77. Arthur Schweitzer, *The Age of Charisma* (Chicago: 1984), pp. 106–7.

78. In an interview with G. R. Urban, in Urban, ed., *Stalinism*, pp. 264–65.

79. Leszek Kolakowski, *Main Currents of Marxism*, vol. III: *The Breakdown* (Oxford: 1978), p. 38.

80. The slogan was invented by Bukharin, but it was Stalin who took it up and developed its nationalist implications. See Stephen F. Cohen, *Bukharin and the Bolshevik Revolution: 1888–1938* (New York: 1974), ch. 6, esp. pp. 186–88.

81. Stalin, "The Right Deviation in the CPSU," Speech to the Central Committee Plenum, April 1929: Stalin, ed., *Leninism*, pp. 257–60.

82. *Mein Kampf*, trans. James Murphy (London: 1939), p. 110.

83. Stalin's Speech to Business Executives, June 23, 1931: Stalin, ed., *Leninism*, p. 372.

84. Quoted by Medvedev, *Let History Judge*, p. 601.

85. Robert C. Tucker, "Stalinism as Revolution from Above," in Robert C. Tucker, ed., *Stalinism: Essays in Historical Interpretation* (New York: 1977), p. 95.

86. Quoted by Merle Fainsod, *How Russia Is Ruled* (Cambridge, Mass.: 1953), p. 111. According to Kolakowski (*Main Currents*, vol. 3, p. 101), this argument, repeated by Stalin at the Central Committee Plenum in January 1933, was not original but had already been formulated by Trotsky during the civil war.

87. Stalin's Report to the Seventeenth Party Congress: Stalin, ed., *Leninism*, pp. 470–539.

ELEVEN: The Führer State

1. Jeremy Noakes and Geoffrey Pridham, eds., *Nazism, 1919–1945: A Documentary Reader*, vol. II: *State, Economy and Society, 1933–1939* (Exeter: 1984), nos 170–73.

2. Both quotations are from an undated letter from Frick to Hitler, reproduced in Martin Broszat, *The Hitler State* (*London: 1971), pp. 257–58. I owe an obvious debt to Professor Broszat's book throughout the first two sections of this chapter.

3. Broszat, *The Hitler State*, pp. 284 and 286.

4. Hans Frank, *Im Angesicht des Galgens* (Neuhaus bei Schliersee: 1955), pp. 122–23, quoted by Noakes and Pridham, eds., *Nazism*, vol. II, no. 140.

5. E. R. Huber, *Verfassungsrecht der Grossdeutschen Reiches* (Hamburg: 1939), p. 142, quoted in H.

Krausnick, H. Buchheim, M. Broszat, and H. A. Jacobsen, *Anatomy of the SS State* (*London: 1968), p. 128.

6. Statistics given in Broszat, *The Hitler State*, pp. 331–32.

7. Max Domarus, ed., *Hitler. Reden und Proklamationen, 1932–45,* vol. I (Würzburg: 1962), pp. 229–37.

8. *Mein Kampf,* trans. James Murphy (London: 1939), p. 330.

9. The facts and figures throughout this and the next section are taken from the review of the evidence in Harold W. James, *The German Slump: Politics and Economics, 1924–1936* (Oxford: 1986). For a full discussion of the question, see his chapter 10. For the facts about farming and the land, I am also indebted to David Schoenbaum, *Hitler's Social Revolution: Class and Status in Nazi Germany* (*London: 1966), ch. 5.

10. Estimates vary. A Reichsnährstand report of early 1938 put the number leaving the land for the towns at 650,000 since 1933. The survey already quoted (Josef Müller, *Deutsches Bauerntum* [Würzburg: 1940], quoted by Schoenbaum, *Hitler's Social Revolution,* ch. 5), puts it at 800,000 by 1940—or a million, when family members are included.

11. 20,748 farms with a total area of 325,611 hectares as against 38,771, with an area of 429,934 hectares.

12. The years from 1933 to 1939, which saw steady growth in the urban population—spectacular in the chemical towns of central Germany like Magdeburg and Halle—saw the rural population fall from just under 21 percent to 18 percent of the total German population, and the proportion of workers in agriculture and forestry from just under 29 percent to 26 percent of the total work force.

13. See R. J. Overy, *The Nazi Economic Recovery* (London: 1982), chs. 1 and 2.

14. James, *German Slump,* pp. 380–84.

15. Both quotations are given in ibid., p. 353.

16. Both quotations from R. J. Overy, *Goering: The "Iron Man"* (London: 1984), pp. 42–43.

17. Report of the cabinet meeting, September 4, 1936: Noakes and Pridham, *Nazism,* vol. II, no. 186.

18. Quoted in Overy, *Goering,* p. 47.

19. References given in ibid., p. 251, n. 19.

20. English translation in Noakes and Pridham, eds., *Nazism,* vol. II, no. 185.

21. See pp. 320–21 above.

22. Overy, *Goering,* p. 60.

23. Hjalmar Schacht, *Account Settled* (*London: 1948), p. 103.

24. Ibid., p. 104.

25. ND 1301-PS.

26. Peter Hayes, *Industry and Ideology: IG Farben in the Nazi Era* (Cambridge: 1987), p. 161. Among them were the heads of three of the seven main divisions of the Plan: Keppler (industrial fats), Köhler (raw-materials distribution), Josef Wagner (price control). Three others who were to rise high in Göring's economic empire were Paul Pleiger (low-grade iron and the Hermann Göring Werke), Hans Kehrl (synthetic fibers), and Paul Körner (second in command of the Plan).

27. John R. Gillingham, *Industry and Politics in the Third Reich: Ruhr Coal, Hitler and Europe* (London: 1985), p. 5.

28. Ruhr coal production in 1929 amounted to 123,603,000 tons out of a German total of 163,441,000. In 1937 it amounted to 127,752,000 out of 184,489,000 tons. The new synthetic-petroleum plants alone

required 6.5 million tons per annum; the Reichswerke Hermann Göring under construction at Salzgitter required another 5.7 million for the exploitation of its low-grade iron-ore deposits.

29. Gillingham, *Industry and Politics,* pp. 58–59.

30. Overy, *Goering,* p. 64.

31. In 1914 Germany still had access to the rich resources of iron ore in Lorraine and Luxembourg as well as to the coal of Silesia and the Saar which she lost by the peace settlement of 1919–21.

32. Overy, *Goering,* p. 64.

33. Ibid., p. 65.

34. Hayes, *Industry and Ideology,* pp. 165–66.

35. The main provisions of the January 20, 1934, law are translated in Noakes and Pridham, eds., *Nazism,* vol. II, no. 227.

36. Ibid., no. 445.

37. Article 3 of the Reich Labor Service Law passed on June 26, 1935: ibid., p. 355.

38. Schoenbaum, *Hitler's Social Revolution,* p. 79. The social revolution that destroyed the structure of German society was the war that Hitler started and lost.

39. See the discussion in Ian Kershaw, *The Hitler Myth: Image and Reality in the Third Reich* (Oxford: 1987), pp. 6–8.

40. Noakes and Pridham, eds., *Nazism,* vol. II, no. 446.

41. Quoted in Bormann's record of Hitler's table talk, *The Testament of Adolf Hitler: The Hitler-Bormann Documents* (*London: 1961).

42. Quoted by Hans Buchheim in Krausnick, Buchheim, Broszat, and Jacobsen, *Anatomy of the SS State,* p. 197.

43. Quoted by Schacht, *Account Settled,* p. 102.

44. Broszat, *The Hitler State,* p. 353.

45. Domarus, ed., *Hitler. Reden,* vol. I, pp. 973–77.

46. Quoted by Joachim Fest, *Hitler* (*London: 1974), p. 536.

47. Speech to a meeting of the Nazi Old Guard at Augsburg, November 21, 1937: Domarus, ed., *Hitler. Reden,* vol. I, pp. 759–60.

TWELVE: The Revolution Devours Its Children

1. Vergniaud was the leading spokesman for the moderate Girondin faction in the French Revolution. His fears were realized before the end of 1793; attacked by the more extreme Jacobins, he and his friends were condemned by the Revolutionary Tribunal and guillotined.

2. See Z. K. Brzezinski, *The Permanent Purge: Politics in Soviet Totalitarianism* (Cambridge, Mass.: 1956).

3. *Khrushchev Remembers,* trans. and ed. Strobe Talbot (*London: 1971).

4. The phrase is Merle Fainsod's in *How Russia Is Ruled* (Cambridge, Mass.: 1953), ch. 13. Fainsod was chairman of the School of Russian Studies at Harvard.

5. For the most recent analysis see Robert Conquest's *Stalin and the Kirov Murder* (London: 1989), to which, as to his *The Great Terror: A Re-Assessment* (London: 1990), I am greatly indebted.

6. *Pravda,* December 5, 1934, quoted by Robert C. Tucker, *Stalin in Power: The Revolution from Above, 1928–1941* (New York: 1990), p. 298.

7. These further details were given by Khrushchev to the Twenty-second Party Congress in 1961.

8. *Khrushchev Remembers,* p. 518. Khrushchev's Secret Speech of 1956 was published in the USSR for the first time in summer 1989, thirty years after it was published abroad.

9. N. S. Khrushchev,

"Vospominaniia," *Ogonek,* no. 28, 1989.

10. Stalin's remark was made to a conference of 300 Stakhanovites in the Kremlin, November 17, 1935: J. Stalin, *Problems of Leninism* (*1940 ed.), p. 670.

11. Bukharin had a series of talks in Paris during the summer of 1936 with Boris Nicolaevsky, an émigré Menshevik historian. These were the basis of Nicolaevsky's *Letter of an Old Bolshevik,* published anonymously in 1936–37, and reprinted by Nicolaevsky in *Power and the Soviet Elite* (New York: 1965). See Stephen F. Cohen, *Bukharin and the Bolshevik Revolution, 1888–1938* (New York: 1974), pp. 471–72 n. 143.

12. November 25, 1936: Stalin, *Problems of Leninism,* p. 571.

13. Ibid., p. 589.

14. The invaluable records of the Smolensk Party provide details for one district *(raion).* As a result of a secret circular of May 13, 1935 calling for further "verification" of party membership, 455 out of 4,100 members examined were expelled—after 700 oral and 200 written denunciations. By August 1, a report from Yezhov and Malenkov noted that 23 percent of the party cards in the area had been withdrawn or withheld pending further investigation.

15. These were the Secret Political Department; the Economic Department, responsible for security in industry and agriculture; the Operative Department, responsible among other duties for guarding Stalin, a major operation, involving 3,000 officers; the Special Department, which ran the secret police networks; the Foreign Department, which dealt with espionage and terror abroad; and the Transport Department, which handled security and sabotage on the railways, the all-important lines of communication in Russia.

16. The account in this chapter follows that in Conquest, *The Great Terror: A Re-Assessment,* ch. 4.

17. *Khrushchev Remembers,* p. 510.

18. G. R. Urban, ed., *Stalinism: Its Impact on Russia and the World,* pb. ed. (Aldershot: 1985), pp. 218–19.

19. Robert C. Tucker, "Stalin, Bukharin and History as Conspiracy," in *The Soviet Political Mind* (New York: 1971), pp. 70–71.

20. *Khrushchev Remembers,* p. 510.

21. Alexander Orlov, *The Secret History of Stalin's Crimes* (London: 1954), pp. 129–30. See Conquest, *Stalin and the Kirov Murder,* ch. 13, for a vigorous defense of Orlov and Nicolaevsky as reliable sources.

22. Orlov, *Secret History,* pp. 131–32.

23. *Pravda,* August 21, 1936, quoted by Conquest, *The Great Terror,* p. 99.

24. *Report of the Court Proceedings: The Case of the Trotskyite-Zinovievite Center* (*Moscow: 1936), p. 119.

25. Ibid., p. 171.

26. Nicolaevsky, *Power and the Soviet Elite,* p. 63.

27. *Pravda,* September 10, 1936.

28. In a conversation with N. Valentinov, quoted in Leonard Schapiro, *The Communist Party of the Soviet Union,* 2d. ed. (London: 1970), pp. 384–35.

29. Orlov, *Secret History,* p. 190.

30. Ibid., p. 207.

31. *Report of the Court Proceedings in the Case of the Anti-Soviet Trotskyite Center* (*Moscow: 1937), pp. 127 and 135.

32. Ibid., pp. 463–516.

33. Ibid., p. 541.

34. Quoted by Robert Conquest, *The Great Terror: Stalin's Purges of the Thirties* (London: 1968), p. 266.

35. Quoted by Conquest, *The Great Terror: A Re-Assessment,* p. 168.

36. Ibid., p. 169, quoting *Izvestia*, November 22, 1963.

37. Ibid., p. 169, quoting the article on him in the *Great Soviet Encyclopaedia*, 2d. ed. (Moscow: 1949–58).

38. *Khrushchev Remembers*, p. 548. To the sources quoted here can now be added the testimony of Ordzhonikidze's younger brother, Konstantin, who was present in the apartment during Stalin's visit and served sixteen years in confinement. See Roy Medvedev, *Let History Judge*, rev. ed. (Oxford: 1989), pp. 590–1.

39. Medvedev, *Let History Judge*, pp. 362–65, quoting the memoirs of Larina, Bukharin's wife.

40. Ibid.

41. Published in ibid., pp. 366–67.

42. Stalin's speech appeared in *Pravda*, March 29, 1937.

43. Quoted in *The Moscow Trial*, ed. W. P. and Z. P. Coates (London: 1937), pp. 275–76.

44. Conquest, *The Great Terror: A Re-Assessment*, ch. 7.

45. *Testimony: The Memoirs of Shostakovich*, ed. Solomon Volkov (*London: 1979), pp. 72–79.

46. See the discussion in Walter Laqueur, op. cit., pp. 85–91.

47. Tucker, *Stalin in Power*, p. 436, quoting transcripts published for the first time in *Izvestia* in 1989.

48. Conquest, *The Great Terror: A Re-Assessment*, p. 450, quoting two issues of *Ogonek*, no. 28, 1987, and no. 25, 1989.

49. Medvedev, *Let History Judge*, p. 424.

50. *Khrushchev Remembers*, pp. 526–27. Khrushchev's account of what Zakovsky said was taken from the evidence Rosenblum gave to an inquiry in 1955.

51. "Ivanovo 1937," reminiscences of Mikhail Schreider, an NKVD agent in Ivanovo at the time, published in *Moscow News*, no. 48 (1988).

52. Conquest, *The Great Terror: A Re-Assessment*, p. 223.

53. Z. T. Serpyuk, speech at the Twenty-second Party Congress, October 30, 1961, quoted in ibid., p. 235.

54. D. A. Volkogonov, *Stalin: Triumph and Tragedy* (*London: 1991), p. 339.

55. Published in *Ogonek*, no. 16, 1988, quoted in R. W. Davies, *Soviet History in the Gorbachev Revolution* (London: 1989), p. 67.

56. *Proceedings in the Case of the Anti-Soviet "Bloc of Rights and Trotskyites"* (*Moscow: 1938), p. 36.

57. Fitzroy Maclean, *Eastern Approaches* (London: 1941), p. 86.

58. *Proceedings*, pp. 49–59.

59. Maclean, *Eastern Approaches*, p. 87.

60. *Proceedings*, pp. 157–58.

61. Fitzroy Maclean, *Escape to Adventure* (London: 1950), pp. 61–83.

62. Cohen, p. 376.

63. *Proceedings*, p. 370.

64. Ibid., p. 413.

65. Ibid., p. 474.

66. In a dispatch from Moscow to the Foreign Office: PRO FO 371.N1291/26/38.

67. *Proceedings*, p. 626.

68. Quoted by Cohen, *Bukharin*, p. 380.

69. *Proceedings*, pp. 777–78.

70. Quoted by Medvedev, *Let History Judge*, p. 375.

71. Ibid., pp. 458–79.

72. Ibid., p. 460.

73. Khrushchev's figures were given in his Secret Speech of 1956: *Khrushchev Remembers*, pp. 516–17. See also Medvedev, *Let History Judge*, p. 396.

74. Stalin, *Problems of Leninism* (1945 ed.), p. 625.

75. Robert Conquest's article in

Soviet Studies, cited in Chapter Eight, Note 36.

76. Alexander Solzhenitsyn, *The Gulag Archipelago,* pb. ed. (*London: 1974), pp. 3–4.

77. Ibid., pp. 12–13.

78. Aristotle, *Politics,* V. ii, trans. Benjamin Jowett (Oxford: 1905), p. 228.

79. Leszek Kolakowski, *Main Currents of Marxism,* vol. III: *The Breakdown* (Oxford: 1978), p. 96.

80. Quoted by Boris Souvarine, *Stalin* (*London: 1930), pp. 362–63.

81. Quoted by Conquest, *The Great Terror: A Re-Assessment,* p. 113.

82. Ibid., p. 112.

83. *Proceedings,* pp. 777–78.

84. Quoted by Conquest, *The Great Terror: A Re-Assessment,* p. 125.

85. Khrushchev's speech to the Twentieth Party Congress in 1956.

86. *Pravda,* April 5, 1988. See Davies, *Soviet History,* esp. chs. 5 and 10.

THIRTEEN: 1918 Revoked

1. Jane Degras, ed., *Soviet Documents on Foreign Policy,* vol. III (London: 1953), pp. 48–61.

2. *Documents on German Foreign Policy* (henceforth *DGFP*), Series C, vol. III, no. 373.

3. Max Domarus, ed., *Hitler. Reden und Proklamationen, 1932–45* (Würzburg: 1962), vol. I, pp. 505–14.

4. Hermann Rauschning, *Hitler Speaks* (*London: 1939), p. 116.

5. Quoted by Geoffrey Roberts, *The Unholy Alliance* (London: 1989), p. 70.

6. Gerhard L. Weinberg, *The Foreign Policy of Hitler's Germany: Diplomatic Revolution in Europe, 1933–36* (Chicago: 1970), p. 245.

7. Quoted by Paul Schmidt, *Statist auf diplomatischer Bühne* (Bonn: 1949), p. 320.

8. *Hitler's Table Talk, 1941–1944*

(*London: 1953), pp. 258–59 (January 27, 1942).

9. 22 March 1936: Domarus, ed., *Hitler. Reden,* vol. I, pp. 609–10.

10. Degras, ed., *Soviet Documents,* vol. III, p. 179.

11. Ibid.

12. Quoted by Hugh Thomas, *The Spanish Civil War,* 3d. ed. (London: 1977), p. 232.

13. The following figures were published in Moscow in *Istoriya SSSR* in January 1988 and are quoted by Roberts, p. 78:

	USSR	Germany	Italy
Aircraft	648	593	656
Tanks	347	250	950
Armored cars	120		
Artillery pieces	1,186	700	1,930
Machine guns	20,486	31,000	3,436
Rifles	497,813	157,306	240,747
Mortars	340	6,174	1,426

14. Raymond Carr, *Spain, 1808–1975,* 2d. ed. (Oxford: 1982), p. 683.

15. Jane Degras, ed. *The Communist International, 1919–1943: Documents,* vol. III: *1929–1943* (London: 1965), p. 398.

16. Ibid., p. 396.

17. Quoted by Thomas, *Spanish Civil War,* p. 363.

18. *DGFP,* Series D, vol. I, no. 19.

19. *Ciano's Diplomatic Papers,* ed. Malcolm Muggeridge (London: 1948), p. 58.

20. Ibid., p. 146.

21. Winston Churchill, *The Second World War,* vol. I: *The Gathering Storm* (London: 1948), p. 174.

22. Weinberg, *Foreign Policy 1933–36,* p. 347.

23. Ribbentrop's "Report on the Anglo-German Relationship and the Way to Deal with the Chamberlain Initiative," December 28, 1937:

Jeremy Noakes and Geoffrey Pridham, eds., *Nazism, 1919–1945: A Documentary Reader*, vol. III: *Foreign Policy, War and Racial Extermination* (Exeter: 1988), no. 507.

24. Quoted by John Erickson, *The Soviet High Command: A Military-Political History, 1918–41* (London: 1962), p. 489.

25. August 16, 1945, quoted by Berenice Carroll, *Design for Total War* (The Hague: 1968), p. 73.

26. See Wilhelm Deist, *The Wehrmacht and German Re-armament* (Oxford: 1981) and the full bibliography given there on pp. 129–43.

27. Figures in R. J. Overy, *Goering: The "Iron Man"* (London: 1984), p. 151.

28. Quoted in ibid., pp. 148–49.

29. *GDFP*, Series C, vol. V, no. 490.

30. Ibid., Series D, vol. I, no. 19.

31. See Deist, *Wehrmacht*, pp. 48–52.

32. *GDFP*, Series D, vol. I, no. 19.

33. Quoted by General Walter Warlimont, *Inside Hitler's Headquarters, 1939–45* (*London: 1964), p. 13.

34. Ibid., p. 14.

35. Ulrich von Hassell, *The Von Hassell Diaries, 1938–44* (*London: 1948), p. 28.

FOURTEEN: The Nazi–Soviet Pact

1. Schuschnigg's account of the visit in *Austrian Requiem* (*London: 1947), pp. 19–32.

2. Transcript by Göring's Forschungsamt of the telephone conversations via Vienna: ND 2949-PS.

3. Grolmann's affidavit, quoted in Jürgen Gehl, *Austria, Germany and the Anschluss, 1931–38* (Oxford: 1963), p. 191.

4. Forschungsamt transcript: ND 2949-PS.

5. Quoted by Peter Gay, *Freud: A Life for Our Time* (London: 1988), p. 620.

6. Quoted in ibid., p. 619.

7. A typical phrase taken from a report on public opinion, in this case in the Berchtesgaden area. See the summary of official and Sopade reports in Ian Kershaw, *The Hitler Myth: Image and Reality in the Third Reich* (Oxford: 1987), pp. 127–30.

8. Max Domarus, ed., *Hitler. Reden und Proklamationen, 1932–45* (Würzburg: 1962), vol. I, p. 849.

9. Quoted by Geoffrey Roberts, *The Unholy Alliance* (London: 1989), p. 85.

10. Jane Degras, ed., *Soviet Documents on Foreign Policy*, vol. III (London: 1953), p. 277.

11. Quoted by Gerhard L. Weinberg, *The Foreign Policy of Hitler's Germany: Starting World War II, 1937–39* (Chicago: 1980), pp. 353–54.

12. *Documents on German Foreign Policy* (henceforth *DGFP*), Series D, vol. II, no. 175.

13. Domarus, ed., *Hitler: Reden*, vol. I, p. 861.

14. *DGFP*, Series D, vol. II, no. 221.

15. Jodl's Diary, August 10, 1938: ND 1780-PS.

16. Quoted from the record made by Keitel's adjutant, Captain Eberhard, by David Irving, *The War Path* pb. ed. (London: 1983), pp. 123–24.

17. Ulrich von Hassell, *The Von Hassell Diaries, 1938–44* (*London: 1948), p. 6.

18. Quoted by Irving, *War Path*, p. 119.

19. General Franz Halder, *Kriegstagebuch, 1939–42*, ed. H. A. Jacobsen (Munich: 1962–66), vol. I, August 2, 1938.

20. Recounted by Spitzy,

Ribbentrop's secretary, who was present, and quoted by Irving, *War Path*, p. 129.

21. Jodl's Diary, September 12–13, 1938: ND 1780-PS.

22. Quoted by Irving, *War Path*, p. 134.

23. German minutes of the Hitler-Chamberlain discussions at Berchtesgaden: *DGFP*, Series D, vol. II, no. 487.

24. *Die Weizsäcker-Papiere, 1938–50*, ed. L. Hill (Frankfurt: 1974).

25. Degras, ed., *Soviet Documents on Foreign Policy*, vol. III, pp. 282–94.

26. I am indebted to Dr G. Jukes of the Australian National University for bringing to my notice both Professor Oleg Rzheshevsky's *Europe 1939: Was War Inevitable?* (*Moscow: 1939) and Marshal M. V. Zakharov's *General'nyy Shtab v Predvoyennyye Gody* (Moscow: 1989). Dr Jukes has published an article in the *Journal of Contemporary History* (April 1991) which he allowed me to see in advance and which discusses the questions raised by these two publications at greater length.

27. Kirkpatrick's notes of the Bad Godesberg meetings: *Documents on British Foreign Policy, 1919–39* (henceforth *DBFP*), 3d Series, 1938–39 (London: 1949–57), vol. II, nos 5, 1033, and 1073; the German record in *DGFP*, Series D, vol. II, no. 583.

28. Kirkpatrick's notes in *DBFP*, 3d Series, vol. II, no. 1118.

29. Domarus, ed., *Hitler: Reden*, vol. I, pp. 923–33.

30. William Shirer, *Berlin Diary* (London: 1941), pp. 118–19.

31. *DGFP*, Series D, vol. II, no. 635.

32. Ibid., no. 670.

33. *The Testament of Adolf Hitler:*

The Hitler-Bormann Documents (*London: 1961), pp. 84–85.

34. A phrase of Christopher Browning's summarizing the debate in *Fateful Months: Essays on the Emergence of the Final Solution* (New York: 1985), pp. 8–14.

35. Ian Kershaw, *The Hitler Myth: Image and Reality in the Third Reich* (Oxford: 1987), p. 235.

36. Freiherr von Eberstein, police president of Munich, who gave evidence at the trial of major war criminals in Nuremberg after the war.

37. ND 3063-PS.

38. ND 1816-PS.

39. Max Domarus, ed., *Hitler. Reden und Proklamationen, 1932–45* (Würzburg: 1963), vol. II, pp. 1057–58.

40. *The Testament of Adolf Hitler*, p. 66.

41. ND 1301-PS.

42. ND 3575-PS.

43. Donald Watt, *How War Came* (London: 1989), p. 40.

44. Quoted in ibid., p. 41.

45. Quoted in J. Dülffer, *Weimar, Hitler und die Marine* (Düsseldorf: 1973), p. 502.

46. See David Kaiser, *Economic Diplomacy and the Origins of the Second World War* (Princeton: 1980), pp. 277–83.

47. Ibid., p. 282.

48. Jeremy Noakes and Geoffrey Pridham, eds., *Nazism, 1919–1945: A Documentary Reader*, vol. III: *Foreign Policy, War and Racial Extermination* (Exeter: 1988), no. 529.

49. Quoted by Irving, *War Path*, p. 175.

50. Quoted by Weinberg, *Foreign Policy 1937–39*, p. 505.

51. *DGFP*, Series D, vol. IV, no. 228.

52. Ibid., no. 229.

53. A. Zoller, *Hitler Privat* (Düsseldorf: 1949), p. 84. This is an edited version of the memoirs of Hitler's secretary, Christa Schroeder.

54. Degras, ed., *Soviet Documents,* vol. III, pp. 315–22.

55. For Molotov, see ibid., pp. 363–71; for Ribbentrop, *GDFP,* Series D, vol. VI, no. 441.

56. *Soviet Peace Efforts on the Eve of World War II,* vol. I (*Moscow: 1976), doc. 54.

57. Cabinet Conclusions 12(39), March 18, 1939: PRO, FO 371/22967-C3632/15/18.

58. Domarus, ed., *Hitler. Reden,* vol. II, p. 1125.

59. Directive for Operation White (attack on Poland), issued on April 11, 1939: *DGFP,* Series D, vol. VI, pp. 224–25.

60. Sir Nevile Henderson, *Failure of a Mission* (London: 1940), p. 228.

61. *The Ciano Diaries, 1939–1943* (London: 1947), p. 44.

62. *Ciano's Diplomatic Papers,* ed. Malcolm Muggeridge (London: 1948), pp. 282–87.

63. Text in RIIA, *Documents on International Affairs, 1939–46* (London: 1958), vol. I, pp. 168–70.

64. *Soviet Peace Efforts on the Eve of World War II,* vol. I, p. 203; *DBFP,* 3d. Series, vol. IV, no. 597.

65. "The Moscow Negotiations, 1939," in David Dilks, ed., *Retreat from Power* (London: 1981).

66. *Pravda,* June 29, 1939; *Soviet Peace Efforts,* no. 269.

67. *DGFP,* Series D, vol. VII, no. 700.

68. Schnurre's report: *DGFP,* Series D, vol. VI, no. 729.

69. Schnurre in an interview with Anthony Read and David Fisher, quoted in their book, *The Deadly Embrace: Hitler, Stalin and the Nazi-Soviet Pact, 1939–41* (London: 1988), p. 126.

70. Volkogonov, p. 352.

71. Von der Schulenburg's report: *DGFP,* Series D, vol. VII, no. 70.

72. Ibid., no. 105.

73. Ibid., no. 132.

74. Ibid., no. 142.

75. Ibid., no. 159.

76. Albert Speer, *Inside the Third Reich* (*London: 1970), p. 161.

77. *DGFP,* Series D, vol. VII, no. 228 (Pact); no. 229 (Protocol).

78. Although it was forbidden to take notes, several officers did so. The version printed in *DGFP,* Series D, vol. VII, nos. 192 and 193, was made by Admiral Canaris. Halder's version is printed in Appendix I of the same volume. The best discussion of the sources is in Weinberg, *Foreign Policy 1937–39,* p. 610n.

79. *DGFP,* Series D, vol. VII, no. 193.

80. Ernst von Weizsäcker, *Memoirs* (*London: 1951), p. 203.

81. *DGFP,* Series D, vol. VII, no. 266.

82. Ibid., no. 265.

83. Ibid., no. 271.

84. Hitler's letters to Mussolini of August 26: ibid., nos. 307 and 341.

85. Birger Dahlerus, *The Last Attempt* (London: 1948), ch. 6.

86. Halder's Diary, August 28, 1939: *DGFP,* Series D, vol. VII, pp. 565–66.

87. *Weizsäcker-Papiere,* diary entry for August 29, 1939.

88. Halder's Diary, August 29, 1939; *DGFP,* Series D, vol. VII, p. 567.

89. *Weizsäcker-Papiere,* diary entry for August 30, 1939.

90. Paul Schmidt, *Statist auf diplomatischer Bühne* (Bonn: 1949), p. 460.

91. *DGFP,* Series D, vol. VII, no. 493.

92. Dahlerus, *Last Attempt,* pp. 119–20.

93. Schmidt, *Statist,* p. 464.

FIFTEEN: Hitler's War

1. Quoted by Robert C. Tucker, *The Soviet Political Mind*, 2d. ed. (New York: 1971), p. 123. V. O. Klyuchevsky (1841–1911) became professor of history at the University of Moscow in 1879. His lectures on the history of Russia attracted enthusiastic audiences but could not be published until the 1900s. The full work was published in five volumes from 1911 to 1931.

2. Quoted by Robert C. Tucker, *Stalin in Power: The Revolution from Above, 1928–1941* (New York: 1990), pp. 115–18, quoting Tolstoy's memoirs.

3. Ibid., p. 117, quoting the memoirs of a Russian expatriate painter, Annenkov, whom Tolstoy visited in Paris in 1917.

4. Quoted by Merle Fainsod, *How Russia Is Ruled* (Cambridge, Mass.: 1953), p. 113.

5. The phrase is Merle Fainsod's. See his discussion of "Terror as a System of Power" in ibid., ch. 6.

6. Quoted by Robert Conquest, *The Great Terror: A Re-Assessment* (London: 1990), p. 7.

7. *Khrushchev Remembers*, trans. and ed. Strobe Talbot (*London: 1971), p. 226.

8. See T. H. Rigby, "Was Stalin a Disloyal Patron?," *Soviet Studies*, vol. XXXVIII, no. 3, July 1986, pp. 311–24.

9. Andrei Vyshinsky in *Soviet Legal Philosophy*, trans. Hugh W. Babb (Cambridge, Mass.: 1951), p. 339.

10. Leonard Schapiro, *The Communist Party of the Soviet Union*, 2d. ed. (London: 1970), p. 477.

11. Leszek Kolakowski, *Main Currents of Marxism*, vol. III: *The Breakdown* (Oxford: 1978), p. 97.

12. Carl Burckhardt, *Meine Danziger Mission, 1937–39* (Munich: 1969), p. 272.

13. Jeremy Noakes and Geoffrey Pridham, eds., *Nazism, 1919–1945: A Documentary Reader*, vol. III: *Foreign Policy, War and Racial Extermination* (Exeter: 1988), no. 529.

14. Charles E. Bohlen, *Witness to History, 1929–1969* (London: 1973), p. 91. Bohlen was serving in the U.S. Embassy in Moscow at the time.

15. *Documents on German Foreign Policy*, Series D, vol. VIII, no. 161.

16. Max Domarus, ed., *Hitler. Reden und Proklamationen, 1932–45* (Würzburg: 1963), vol. II, pp. 1377–93.

17. *The Ciano Diaries, 1939–43* (London: 1947), p. 162.

18. *Ciano's Diplomatic Papers*, ed. Malcolm Muggeridge (London: 1948), pp. 309–16.

19. H. A. Jacobsen, ed., *Dokumente zur Vorgeschichte des Westfeldzuges, 1939–1940* (Göttingen: 1956), pp. 5ff.

20. A. Zoller, ed., *Hitler Privat* (Düsseldorf: 1949), p. 181.

21. Domarus, ed., *Hitler Reden*, vol. II, pp. 1421–27.

22. Decree of October 7, 1939 appointing Himmler as Reichskommissar: Noakes and Pridham, eds., *Nazism*, vol. III, no. 649.

23. Quoted by Helmut Krausnick, "Hitler und die Morde in Polen," in *VfZ*, April 1963, p. 203.

24. Ibid., p. 202. See also Martin Broszat, *Nationalsozialistische Polenpolitik, 1939–1945* (Stuttgart: 1961), p. 22.

25. "Some Thoughts on the Treatment of the Alien Population in the East," May 15, 1940; ibid., no. 651.

26. Christopher Browning, *The Path to Genocide* (Cambridge: 1992), p. 17.

27. Ibid., pp. 28–56 and pp. 145–161.

28. Quoted in Jan T. Gross, *Revolution from Abroad: The Soviet*

Conquest of Poland's Western Ukraine and Western Byelorussia (Princeton: 1988), ch. 1.

29. Paasakivi's recommendation is made the more impressive retrospectively by the fact that, although he had taken a tough line in 1920, from 1944 to 1956 he handled Finnish-Soviet relations in such a way as to spare Finland, alone of all the states in Eastern Europe, from being occupied and brought under Communist rule by the Russians. His view was summed up in his reply to a colleague who expressed outrage that the Soviet Union would not allow Finland to follow an independent foreign policy after the Second World War: "We are a country of five million people living next door to two hundred million. If the situation were reversed, and there were two hundred million Finns and only five million Russians, do you think we would allow them an independent foreign policy?"

30. After her release, Margarete Buber-Neumann, who was born in 1901, lived on until the autumn of 1989. She founded in 1950 a Committee for the Liberation of the Victims of Totalitarian Oppression and won an international reputation for her untiring efforts on their behalf. She published three volumes of autobiography, the third of which bears the title (in German) *Freedom, You Are Mine Again . . . The Strength to Survive.*

31. This account of the Soviet-German negotiations in 1939–40 is based on the German documents in *DGFP,* Series D, vol. VIII. See the Analytical List, ibid., pp. xxiv–xxix.

32. Ibid., no. 474.

33. Schnurre's report, February 26, 1940: ibid., no. 636.

34. Jodl's Diary: ND 1780-PS.

35. Von Manstein's criticism of the OKH plan, and the new directive based on his, are printed in Noakes and Pridham, eds., *Nazism,* vol. III, nos. 559 and 560.

36. General Franz Halder, *Kriegstagebuch: 1939–42,* ed. H. A. Jacobsen (Munich: 1962–66), vol. I, May 17–18, 1940.

37. *Ciano's Diary,* p. 176.

38. Mussolini to Hitler, January 4, 1940: *Hitler e Mussolini: Lettere e documenti* (Milan: 1946), pp. 33–39.

39. *The Ciano Diaries,* pp. 220–21.

40. David Irving, *Hitler's War* (London: 1977), p. 128, quoting accounts by those present.

41. Quoted by P. E. Schramm, *Hitler: The Man and the Military Leader* (*London: 1972), pp. 104–5.

42. Printed in Appendix II to ibid.: Jodl's memoir, "The Influence of Hitler on the Leadership of the War: Brief Reflections on Hitler as a Strategist."

43. "Thoughts of the C-in-C of the Navy on the outbreak of war on September 3, 1939": Noakes and Pridham, eds., *Nazism,* vol. III, no. 555.

44. Cited by R. J. Overy, *Goering: The "Iron Man"* (London: 1984), p. 98.

45. See Ian Kershaw, *The Hitler Myth: Image and Reality in the Third Reich* (Oxford: 1987), pp. 143–57.

46. Domarus, ed., *Hitler: Reden,* vol. II, pp. 1540–59.

47. Halder, *Kriegstagebuch,* vol. II, July 31, 1940, pp. 46ff.

48. Text in *DGFP,* Series D, vol. XI, pp. 204–5.

49. *The Ciano Diaries,* p. 297.

50. Paul Schmidt, *Statist auf diplomatischer Bühne* (Bonn: 1949), p. 506.

51. Text of Führer's Directive No. 18, November 12, 1940 in *DGFP,* Series D, vol. XI, no. 323.

52. Ibid., nos. 176 and 211.

53. The German record of the discussions is printed in ibid., Series D, vol. XI, pp. 533–70.

54. The text of the memorandum that Ribbentrop presented to Molotov during the air raid is given in ibid., series D, vol. XI, no. 329; the Soviet reply, dated November 26, is no. 404.

55. Halder, *Kriegstagebuch,* vol. II, December 5, 1940, p. 186.

56. *Nazi-Soviet Relations, 1939–41* (Washington, D.C.: 1948), pp. 260–62.

SIXTEEN: Hitler's New Order

1. *Mein Kampf,* trans. James Murphy (London: 1939), p. 533.

2. Reported in the *VB,* September 13, 1936.

3. *Hitler's Table Talk, 1941–1944* (London: 1953), p. 33 (September 17–18, 1941).

4. *Mein Kampf,* trans. Murphy, p. 533.

5. Ibid.

6. *Documents on German Foreign Policy* (henceforth *DGFP*), Series D, vol. XII, no. 660.

7. *The Testament of Adolf Hitler: The Hitler-Bormann Documents* (*London: 1961), pp. 63–65.

8. *DGFP,* Series D, vol. XI, no. 612.

9. Ibid., no. 640.

10. Quoted by William L. Langer and S. Everett Gleason, *The Undeclared War* (New York: 1953), p. 538.

11. ND 126-EC.

12. *Hitler's Table Talk,* p. 44 (night of September 25–26, 1941).

13. Ibid., pp. 15–16 (July 27, 1941).

14. Ibid., pp. 68–69 (October 17, 1941).

15. Ibid., pp. 92–93 (October 16–27, 1941).

16. Ibid., p. 7 (July 11–12, 1941).

17. Ibid., p. 76 (October 21, 1941).

18. Ibid., p. 143 (December 13, 1941).

19. Ibid., p. 261 (November 28–29, 1942).

20. ND 447-PS.

21. Figures from Alec Nove, *An Economic History of the USSR,* 2d. ed. (London: 1989), pp. 247–48.

22. Von der Schulenburg's report to Berlin, July 13, 1940: *DGFP,* Series D, vol. X, no. 164.

23. Nove, *Economic History,* pp. 260–61.

24. Max Domarus, ed., *Hitler. Reden und Proklamationen, 1932–45* (Würzburg: 1963), vol. II, pp. 1652–53.

25. Quoted by John Erickson, *The Road to Stalingrad: Stalin's War with Germany* (London: 1975), p. 40.

26. Ibid., p. 52, quoting the 1965 account of General Kazakov, who was present.

27. Based on Erickson, *Road to Stalingrad,* p. 62, quoting Marshal Rokossovsky.

28. D. A. Volkogonov, *Stalin: Triumph and Tragedy* (London: 1991), pp. 397–98; Erickson, op. cit., pp. 80–81.

29. Quoted by Volkogonov, *Stalin: Triumph and Tragedy,* p. 398, from Soviet defense ministry archives.

30. Quoted by Roy Medvedev, *Let History Judge,* rev. ed. (Oxford: 1989), p. 743, from an article in *Oktyabr* (1963), no. 11.

31. Winston S. Churchill, *The Second World War,* vol. III: *The Grand Alliance* (London: 1950), p. 49. For a full account of the Hess episode, see James Douglas Hamilton, *Motive for a Mission: The Story Behind Hess's Flight,* 3d. ed. (Edinburgh: 1993).

32. *DGFP,* Series D, vol. XII, no. 333.

33. Ibid., vol. XII, no. 423.

34. Von der Schulenburg to Berlin, May 7 and 12, 1941: ibid., nos 468 and 505.

35. Anthony Read and David Fisher, *The Deadly Embrace: Hitler, Stalin and the Nazi-Soviet Pact, 1939–41* (London: 1988), p. 618, quoting A. M. Nekrich, *1941, 22 Iyunia* (Moscow: 1965).

36. Read and Fisher, p. 619.

37. *Khrushchev Remembers*, trans. and ed. Strobe Talbot (*London: 1971), p. 148.

38. G. Zhukov, *Reminiscences and Reflections* (*Moscow: 1985), vol. I, p. 236.

39. *DGFP*, Series D, vol. XII, no. 628.

40. Kuznetzov in S. Bialer, ed., *Stalin and His Generals: Soviet Military Memoirs of World War II* (New York: 1966).

41. *The Goebbels Diaries, 1939–41*, ed. Fred Taylor (*London: 1982), June 21, 1941.

42. Albert Speer, *Inside the Third Reich* (*London: 1970), p. 180.

43. Zhukov, *Reminiscences*, vol. I, pp. 281–82.

44. Described by Gustav Hilger, who was present. G. Hilger and A. G. Meyer, *The Incompatible Allies* (New York: 1953), pp. 336–37.

45. Quoted by Medvedev, *Let History Judge*, pp. 756–57, from N. N. Voronov, *Na sluzhbe voennoi* (Moscow: 1963).

46. Medvedev, *Let History Judge*, p. 754, quoting Chakovsky, "Blokada," published in *Znamya* (1968), no. 11, p. 49.

47. Svetlana Alliluyeva, *Only One Year* (*New York: 1969), p. 392.

48. May 24, 1945, quoted by Alex de Jonge, *Stalin and the Shaping of the Soviet Union* (London: 1986), p. 460.

49. Mikoyan's memoirs in *Politicheskoe obrazovanie*, 1988, No. 9, p. 75.

50. It was revealed in 1988 that Pavlov was one of three officers who had sent a petition to Stalin protesting the arrest of Marshals Blyukher, Rokossovsky, and others. Rokossovsky was released and played a leading part in the Second World War. But all three of the petitioners were in due course arrested and executed. Stalin had a long memory. R. W. Davies, *Soviet History in the Gorbachev Revolution* (London: 1989), p. 103.

51. D. A. Volkogonov, *Stalin: Triumph and Tragedy* (*London: 1991), pp. 412–13. Volkogonov got the story from Marshal Moskalenko, for whom he worked in the 1970s and who took part with Procurator General Rudenko in the investigation into Beria's record in the 1950s. It was Moskalenko who also told Volkogonov that the former Bulgarian Ambassador Stamenov had confirmed the report in conversation with Rudenko and himself during the investigation.

52. See ibid., p. 422.

53. Jodl's comment was made to General Heusinger and is quoted by General Walter Warlimont, *Inside Hitler's Headquarters, 1939–45* (*London: 1964), p. 189.

54. Quoted by Erickson, *Road to Stalingrad*, pp. 178–79, from Zhukov's *Reminiscences*.

55. Reported by an intelligence officer, S. M. Yakomenko, and quoted by Medvedev, *Let History Judge*, p. 757.

56. Quoted in A. Zoller, ed., *Hitler Privat* (Düsseldorf: 1949), p. 160.

57. Quoted by Erickson, *Road to Stalingrad*, p. 253, from P. A. Belov, *Za nami Moskva* (Moscow: 1963).

58. Erickson, *Road to Stalingrad*, p. 258.

59. Heinz Guderian, *Panzer Leader* (London: 1953), pp. 254–55.

60. Quoted by B. H. Liddell Hart, *The Other Side of the Hill*, 3d. ed. (London: 1951), p. 289.

61. Quoted by R. J. Overy, *Goering: The "Iron Man"* (London: 1989), p. 120.

62. Jeremy Noakes and Geoffrey Pridham, eds., *Nazism, 1919–1945: A Documentary Reader*, vol. III: *Foreign Policy, War and Racial Extermination* (Exeter: 1988), p. 906.

63. Overy, *Goering*, p. 144.

64. Jodl's memorandum of Hitler's intentions, March 3, 1941, General Walter Warlimont, *Inside Hitler's Headquarters, 1939–45* (London: 1964), pp. 150–51.

65. Halder's Diary, March 30, 1941. See also Warlimont, *Inside Hitler's Headquarters, 1939–45*, pp. 160–62.

66. Doc. 050-C, TMWC, xxxiv, pp. 252–55.

67. Doc. 877-PS, TMWC, xxvi, pp. 403–06.

68. *Hitler's Tischgespräche*, ed. H. Picker (Bonn: 1951), p. 50.

69. Joseph Goebbels, *The Goebbels Diaries, 1942–42*, ed. Louis P. Lochner (*London: 1948), p. 61 (February 24, 1942).

70. Quoted by Alexander Dallin, *German Rule in Russia, 1941–44* (rev. ed., 1981), p. 497.

71. ND 389-PS.

72. ND NG-4900, quoted by Norman Rich, *Hitler's War Aims: The Establishment of the New Order* (New York: 1974), p. 341.

73. The decree was cited in the Nuremburg Trials (ND 630-PS) and is reproduced in R. J. Lifton, *The Nazi Doctors* (London: 1986), p. 63.

74. Quoted by R. J. Lifton, *The Nazi Doctors*, p. 95.

75. Cited by Christopher Browning, *The Path to Genocide* (Cambridge: 1992), p. 103.

76. Noakes and Pridham, eds., *Nazism*, vol. III, no. 630.

77. Quoted from an SS-RSHA document by Gerald Fleming, *Hitler and the Final Solution* (London: 1985), pp. 109–10.

78. R. M. W. Kempner, *SS im Kreuzcerhör* (Munich: 1964), p. 29. This has become known as the massacre of Babi Yar.

79. Noakes and Pridham, eds., *Nazism*, vol. III, no. 825.

80. For the remarkable story of Eduard Schulte and the reception of his message, see Walter Laqueur and Richard Breitman, *Breaking the Silence* (New York: 1986), ch. 6.

81. Noakes and Pridham, eds., *Nazism*, vol. III, no. 826.

82. Ibid., no. 889.

83. Christopher Browning, *The Path to Genocide*, p. 25.

84. Noakes and Pridham, eds., *Nazism*, vol. III, no. 824.

85. Christopher Browning, *The Path to Genocide*, p. 113.

86. Ibid., p. 116.

87. Gerald Fleming, *Hitler and the Final Solution*, p. 79.

88. Noakes and Pridham, eds., *Nazism*, vol. III, no. 850.

89. Wannsee Conference minutes: ibid., no. 849.

90. Gerald Fleming, *Hitler and the Final Solution*, p. 138.

91. At Posen, October 4, 1943: ND 1919-PS.

92. *The Testament of Adolf Hitler*, p. 57.

93. Domarus, ed., *Hitler. Reden*, vol. II, pp. 1794–1811.

94. Quoted by Warlimont, *Inside Hitler's Headquarters*, p. 214.

95. Quoted by Medvedev, *Let History Judge*, pp. 768–69.

96. Batov's memoirs and interview with him, quoted by Erickson, *Road to Stalingrad*, p. 287.

97. Quoted by Peter Calvocoressi,

Guy Wint, and John Pritchard, *Total War*, 2d. ed. (London: 1989), p. 484.

98. Nove, *Economic History*, p. 263, quoting E. Lokshin, *Promyshlennost' SSSR, 1940–63* (Moscow: 1964).

99. Nove, *Economic History*, p. 265.

100. The first view is set out in Alan Milward's *The German Economy at War* (London: 1965), pp. 65–71; the second in Overy, *Goering*, pp. 205–8.

101. Milward, *The German Economy*, p. 100.

102. Quoted by David Irving, *Hitler's War* (London: 1977), p. 367.

103. Vasilevsky, quoted by Erickson, *Road to Stalingrad*, pp. 337–38.

104. Domarus, ed., *Hitler. Reden,* vol. II, pp. 1826–34.

105. *The Goebbels Diaries*, p. 27.

106. Ibid., p. 92.

107. Quotation and comment in Erickson, *Road to Stalingrad*, p. 370.

108. General Franz Halder, *Kriegstagebuch: 1939–42*, ed. H. A. Jacobsen (Munich: 1962–66), vol. III, pp. 55–56.

109. Ibid., p. 57.

110. Ibid., September 24, 1942.

SEVENTEEN: **Stalin's War**

1. *Stalin's Correspondence with Churchill, Attlee, Roosevelt and Truman, 1941–45* (*Moscow: 1957), no. 57, July 23, 1942.

2. Winston S. Churchill, *The Second World War*, vol. IV: *The Hinge of Fate* (London: 1951), p. 428.

3. *Stalin's Correspondence*, no. 65; Churchill, *Second World War*, vol. IV, pp. 440–41.

4. Churchill, *Second World War*, vol. IV, pp. 445–49.

5. Quoted by Robin Edmonds, *The Big Three: Churchill, Roosevelt and Stalin in Peace and War* (New York: 1991), p. 302.

6. *Stalin's Correspondence,* no. 89, November 27, 1942.

7. Quoted by David Irving, *Hitler's War* (London: 1977), p. 459.

8. Felix Gilbert, ed., *Hitler Directs His War* (New York: 1950), pp. 17–22. Varus was the commander of the Roman army on the Rhine in A.D. 9. When his army was ambushed and destroyed, he committed suicide.

9. Quoted by John Erickson, *The Road to Berlin: Stalin's War with Germany,* pb. ed. (London: 1983), pp. 26–27.

10. D. A. Volkogonov, *Stalin: Triumph and Tragedy* (*London: 1991), pp. 455–56. See the whole of ch. 45.

11. A. M. Vasilevsky's memoirs (1974) quoted by Roy Medvedev, *Let History Judge,* rev. ed. (Oxford: 1989), pp. 768–69.

12. Von Richthofen's unpublished diary, quoted by Irving, *Hitler's War,* p. 484.

13. Ian Kershaw, *The Hitler Myth: Image and Reality in the Third Reich* (Oxford: 1987), p. 192.

14. Albert Speer, *Inside the Third Reich* (*London: 1970), p. 258.

15. Irving, *Hitler's War,* pp. 483–84, quoting Herbert Backe.

16. Jeremy Noakes and Geoffrey Pridham, ed., *Documents on Nazism* (London: 1974), pp. 319–20.

17. Kershaw, *The Hitler Myth,* p. 197.

18. Churchill to Stalin, February 9, 1943: Churchill, *Second World War,* vol. IV, pp. 666–67.

19. Stalin, *Correspondence,* no. 129, March 15, 1943.

20. Quoted by Irving, *Hitler's War,* p. 494.

21. Jane Degras, ed., *The Communist International, 1919–1943: Documents,* vol. III, *1929–1943* (London: 1965), pp. 476–77.

22. Milovan Djilas, *Conversations with Stalin* (*London: 1962), p. 77.

23. Figures from R.J. Overy, *The Air War, 1939–45* (London: 1980), p. 150.

24. Heinz Guderian, *Panzer-Leader* (London: 1952), p. 442.

25. The details are taken from the article by Hellmut Heiber, "Der Generalplan Ost," published in *VfZ,* 1958(3), pp. 284ff.

26. Helmut Krausnick, Hans Buchheim, Martin Broszat, and H. A. Jacobsen, *Anatomy of the SS State* (*London: 1968), p. 273.

27. Quoted in ibid., pp. 103–4.

28. Ibid., p. 97.

29. Quoted by Norman Davies, *God's Playground: A History of Poland* (Oxford: 1981), vol. II, p. 463.

30. Quoted by Krausnick et al., *Anatomy of the SS State,* p. 123.

31. Jeremy Noakes and Geoffrey Pridham, eds., *Nazism, 1919–1945: A Documentary Reader,* vol. III: *Foreign Policy, War and Racial Extermination* (Exeter: 1988), no. 908.

32. Quoted in Krausnick et al., *Anatomy of the SS State,* p. 123.

33. Detailed figures taken from Martin Gilbert, *Atlas of the Holocaust* (London: 1982), pp. 178–79.

34. Ibid.

35. Ibid., pp. 196–99.

36. Hitler's speech is recorded in Himmler's files and is quoted by Irving, *Hitler's War,* pp. 631–32.

37. *The Ribbentrop Memoirs* (*London: 1954), pp. 170–11.

38. September 23, 1943: Joseph Goebbels, *The Goebbels Diaries, 1942–43,* ed. Louis P. Lochner (*London: 1948), p. 383.

39. Ibid., p. 377.

40. Quoted by Irving, *Hitler's War,* p. 583.

41. Mark Walker, *German National Socialism and the Quest for Nuclear Power, 1939–49* (Cambridge: 1989), ch. 5. Weizäcker's account of his conversation with Schumann is taken from the transcript of the BBC program "Horizon: Hitler's Bomb," broadcast on February 24, 1992, p. 25.

42. Warren F. Kimball, ed., *Churchill and Roosevelt: The Complete Correspondence* (Princeton: 1984), vol. II, C-471.

43. Adam Ulam, *Stalin: The Man and His Era,* 2d. ed. (London: 1989), p. 587.

44. Alanbrooke's notes quoted by David Fraser, *Alanbrooke,* pb. ed. (London: 1983), p. 385.

45. The account of the Teheran Conference is based on *Foreign Relations of the United States: The Conferences at Cairo and Teheran* (Washington: 1961); *The Teheran, Yalta and Potsdam Conferences: Documents* (*Moscow: 1969); Winston S. Churchill, *The Second World War,* vol. V: *Closing the Ring* (London: 1952), chs. 20–22; Edmonds, *The Big Three.* There is no published British record; the relevant British files in the Public Record Office are CAB 80/77, CAB 120/113, and PREM 3/136/10.

46. Churchill, *The Second World War,* vol. V, p. 330.

47. Ibid., p. 320.

48. Ibid., p. 351.

49. Bohlen's minute in the *FRUS* (see note 44 above); Robin Edmonds, p. 357, for confirmation from the Soviet records.

50. See Alexander Dallin, *German Rule in Russia, 1941–44,* rev. ed. (London: 1981), p. 541, n. 1. Professor Dallin's book is a mine of information on the contradictions and complexities of German occupation policy.

51. Quoted in ibid., p. 550.

52. Ibid., p. 575.

53. Ibid., p. 574.

54. Quoted by Irving, *Hitler's War,* p. 628.

55. Hans Speidel, *We Defended Normandy* (London: 1951), p. 106.

56. Rokossovsky's own account in 1964 quoted by Erickson, *Road to Berlin,* p. 203.

57. Ibid., p. 207.

58. This is the phrase used of him by Fabian von Schlabrendorff, one of the leading conspirators, who survived the plot of July 20 and subsequent arrest. See his account of Oster in *The Secret War against Hitler* (*New York: 1965).

59. See Peter Hoffmann, *The History of the German Resistance, 1933–45* (*London: 1977).

60. See Gerhard Ritter, *Carl Goerdeler und die Deutsche Widerstandbewegung* (Stuttgart: 1955); abridged English trans., *The German Resistance: Carl Goerdeler's Struggle against Tyranny* (London: 1958).

61. Von Schlabrendorff, *Secret War,* p. 121.

62. The poem is quoted, with an English translation by Sir Maurice Bowra, in John Wheeler-Bennett, *The Nemesis of Power: The German Army in Politics, 1918–1945* (London: 1953), p. 582. This provides the best account in English of the events of July 20, 1944.

63. Von Schlabrendorff, *Secret War,* p. 277.

64. Paul Schmidt, *Statist auf diplomatischer Bühne* (Bonn: 1949), p. 582.

65. Max Domarus, ed., *Hitler. Reden und Proklamationen, 1932–45* (Würzburg: 1963), vol. II, pp. 2127–29.

66. Von Schlabrendorff, *Secret War,* pp. 294–95.

EIGHTEEN: Hitler's Defeat

1. Max Domarus, ed., *Hitler. Reden und Proklamationen, 1932–45* (Würzburg: 1963), vol. II, pp. 2127–29.

2. Albert Speer, *Inside the Third Reich* (*London: 1970), pp. 390–91.

3. *The Ciano Diaries, 1939–1943* (London: 1948), p. 430.

4. Speer, *Inside the Third Reich,* pp. 396–98.

5. Quoted by H. R. Trevor-Roper, ed., *The Bormann Letters* (London: 1954), p. 42.

6. Stalin to Churchill, July 23, 1944: *Stalin's Correspondence with Churchill, Attlee, Roosevelt and Truman, 1941–45* (*Moscow: 1957), no. 301.

7. Quoted by John Erickson, *The Road to Berlin: Stalin's War with Germany* (London: 1983), p. 280.

8. Ibid., p. 283.

9. Winston S. Churchill, *The Second World War,* vol. VI: *Triumph and Tragedy* (London: 1954), pp. 119–20.

10. Ibid., p. 120.

11. Ibid., p. 127.

12. Winston S. Churchill, *The Second World War,* vol. V: *Closing the Ring* (London: 1952), p. 623.

13. Malinovsky interview quoted by Erickson, *Road to Berlin,* p. 396.

14. Milovan Djilas, *Conversations with Stalin* (*London: 1962), p. 56.

15. Ibid., pp. 59–60.

16. Ibid., p. 70.

17. Quoted by Vladimir Dedijer, *Tito Speaks* (London: 1953), pp. 232–35.

18. Djilas, *Conversations with Stalin,* pp. 72–73.

19. Ibid., p. 67.

20. Speer, *Inside the Third Reich,* p. 473.

21. The transcript breaks off at this point and is incomplete: Felix Gilbert, ed., *Hitler Directs His War* (records of

Hitler's military conferences; New York: 1950).

22. Heinz Guderian, *Panzer Leader* (London: 1952), p. 378.

23. Ibid., p. 387.

24. Guderian's interrogation by the U.S. army, quoted by Chester Wilmot, *The Struggle for Europe* (London: 1952), p. 622.

25. Churchill, *Second World War,* vol. VI, p. 198.

26. W. Averell Harriman and Elie Abel, *Special Envoy to Churchill and Stalin, 1941–46* (New York: 1975), p. 369.

27. The account of the Yalta Conference is based on *Foreign Relations of the United States: Diplomatic Papers, 1945: The Conferences at Malta and Yalta* (Washington: 1955); *The Teheran, Yalta and Potsdam Conferences: Documents* (*Moscow: 1969); the unpublished British papers are accessible in the Public Record Office, in CAB 120/170 and PREM 4/78/1.

28. British White Paper, Cmd 7088 (1947).

29. Speer, *Inside the Third Reich,* p. 423.

30. Ibid., pp. 452–53.

31. Ibid., p. 446.

32. Hitler's remark after a conference on January 30, 1945, quoted by Guderian, *Panzer Leader,* p. 337.

33. General Franz Halder, *Hitler as Warlord* (*London: 1950), pp. 69–70.

34. Captain Gerhardt Boldt, *In the Shelter with Hitler* (*London: 1948), ch. 1.

35. Gilbert, *Hitler Directs His War,* pp. 117–18.

36. Quoted by David Irving, *Hitler's War* (London: 1977), p. 768.

37. *The Testament of Adolf Hitler: The Hitler-Bormann Documents* (*London: 1961), p. 6.

38. Ibid., p. 41.

39. Ibid., p. 63.

40. Ibid., p. 66.

41. Ibid., pp. 58–59.

42. Ibid., pp. 30–32.

43. Ibid., p. 57.

44. Ibid., p. 107.

45. A. Zoller, ed., *Hitler Privat* (Düsseldorf: 1949), pp. 203–5.

46. ND, Speer Document 026.

47. Speer, *Inside the Third Reich,* p. 473.

48. Quoted by Hugh Trevor-Roper, *The Last Days of Hitler,* 2d. ed. (London: 1950), pp. 112–13.

49. Ibid., pp. 134–35.

50. Speer, *Inside the Third Reich,* p. 480.

51. Trevor-Roper, *Last Days,* p. 145.

52. Speer at the Nuremberg *Trial of Major War Criminals,* Part XVII, p. 57.

53. Keitel's interrogation, *Nazi Conspiracy and Aggression* (Washington 1946–48), Supp. volume B, pp. 1281–82.

54. Count Fulk Bernadotte, *The Curtain Falls* (New York: 1945), p. 22.

55. Ibid., pp. 106–13.

56. Evidence of Hanna Reitsch, who was present in the bunker: ND 3734-PS.

57. Ibid.

58. The Political Testament and the will are contained in ND 3569-PS.

59. Ibid.

60. Rudolf Semmler, *Goebbels: The Man Next to Hitler* (London: 1947), p. 194.

61. Quoted by Trevor-Roper, *Last Days,* p. 214.

62. Lev Bezymenski, *The Death of Adolf Hitler: Unknown Documents from Soviet Archives* (*London: 1968).

63. *Sunday Express,* July 5, 1992; *Daily Express,* July 6, 1992.

NINETEEN: Stalin's New Order

1. Winston S. Churchill, *The Second World War,* vol. VI: *Triumph and Tragedy* (London: 1954), pp. 392–94.

2. Churchill to Eden, May 4, 1945: ibid., p. 438.

3. Churchill to Stalin, April 29, 1945: ibid., pp. 431–34.

4. Stalin to Churchill, May 5, 1945: ibid., pp. 435–37.

5. This account is based on those in W. Averell Harriman and Elie Abel, *Special Envoy to Churchill and Stalin, 1941–46* (New York: 1975), pp. 463–75; Charles E. Bohlen, *Witness to History, 1929–1969* (London: 1973), pp. 218–21; and Robert E. Sherwood, *Roosevelt and Hopkins* (New York: 1950), pp. 890–908.

6. The letter was addressed to Bohlen and was reprinted by him: *Witness to History,* pp. 175–76.

7. Based on Robin Edmonds's account, using Soviet sources, in *Setting the Mould* (Oxford: 1986).

8. Quoted by Alan Bullock, *Ernest Bevin, Foreign Secretary, 1945–51* (London: 1983), p. 25.

9. Quoted by Kenneth Harris, *Attlee* (London: 1982), p. 267.

10. Quoted by Marshal A. M. Vasilevsky, *A Lifelong Cause* (*Moscow: 1981), p. 453.

11. For example, in the articles by the leading military historian A. V. Samsonov. These, together with readers' letters, were published in book form, *Znat i pomnit* (Moscow: 1988).

12. J. Stalin, *Collected Works* (Stanford: 1967), vol. XVI, p. 7.

13. Vasily Grossman, born in a Ukrainian Jewish community in 1905, was a war correspondent who witnessed at firsthand the battle of Stalingrad, the liberation of the Treblinka death camp, and the capture of Berlin. *Life and Fate,* often compared with Tolstoy's *War and Peace* for its picture of Russia during the war of 1941–45, was completed in 1960 but immediately banned; the Russian text was not published (in Lausanne) until 1980, sixteen years after Grossman's death.

14. Nikolai Tolstoy, *Victims of Yalta* (London: 1977), p. 409.

15. R. W. Davies, *Soviet History in the Gorbachev Revolution* (London: 1989), pp. 80–81.

16. Roy Medvedev, *Let History Judge,* rev. ed. (Oxford: 1989), p. 782, quoting N. N. Kuznetsov, *Nakanune* (Moscow: 1966), p. 212.

17. A. G. Zverev, *Zapiski ministra* (Moscow: 1973).

18. *Poems of Akhmatova,* selected and trans. Stanley Kunitz and May Haward (Boston: 1967), p. 99.

19. See Jerry Hough, *The Soviet Prefects: The Local Party Organs in Industrial Decision-Making* (Cambridge, Mass.: 1968).

20. U.S. record of the Moscow meeting in *Foreign Relations of the United States,* 1947, vol. II.

21. Ibid.

22. Text of Marshall's broadcast in B. R. von Oppen, *Documents on Germany under Occupation, 1945–54* (London: 1955), pp. 219–27.

23. The proceedings of the Paris Conference were published by the French at the time: *Documents de la Conférence à Paris 1947* (Paris: 1947).

24. RIIA, *Documents on International Affairs, 1947–48* (London: 1952), pp. 122–46.

25. Quoted by Hugh Seton-Watson, *The East European Revolution* (London: 1950), p. 167.

26. Milovan Djilas, *Conversations with Stalin* (London: 1962), pp. 154–68.

27. Vladimir Dedijer, *Tito Speaks* (London: 1953), ch. 19.

28. Khrushchev's speech to the

Twentieth Party Congress, 1956: *Khrushchev Remembers,* trans. and ed. Strobe Talbot (*London: 1971), p. 544.

29. Djilas, *Conversations with Stalin,* p. 139.

30. Ibid., p. 164.

31. See Adam Ulam, *Expansion and Coexistence* (London: 1968), pp. 489–92.

32. Robert H. McNeal, *Stalin: Man and Ruler* (London: 1988), p. 289, quoting the memoirs of Wu Xiuquan, published in 1983.

33. RIIA, *Documents on International Affairs, 1949–50* (London: 1953), p. 543.

34. *Khrushchev Remembers,* ch. 11.

35. Ibid., p. 335.

36. Ibid., p. 336.

37. Alec Nove, from the second edition of whose book, *An Economic History of the USSR* (London: 1989), these details are taken, reports that while the total output indices for national income and gross industrial production are useless, physical output figures, with the exception of those for grain, "have been regarded as reliable by virtually all scholars" (pp. 280–86).

38. Medvedev, *Let History Judge,* p. 801, quoting Zverev's memoirs.

39. Based on Z. A. Medvedev, *The Rise and Fall of T. D. Lysenko* (New York: 1971) and two articles by V. Soifer quoted in Davies, *Soviet History,* pp. 70–73.

40. *Khrushchev Remembers,* ch. 8.

41. Ibid.

42. Svetlana Alliluyeva, *Twenty Letters to a Friend* (*London: 1967), p. 206.

43. Ibid.

44. Robert Conquest, *Stalin, Breaker of Nations* (London: 1991), p. 294.

45. *Khrushchev Remembers,* p. 550.

46. Alex de Jonge, *Stalin and the*

Shaping of the Soviet Union (London: 1986), p. 486.

47. Khrushchev's speech, 1956: *Khrushchev Remembers,* p. 541.

48. An extract from Mikoyan's diary, published in *Komsomol'skaya Pravda,* February 21, 1986.

49. Quoted by Davies, *Soviet History,* p. 68, quoting Isakov in *Zvezda,* no. 3 (1988).

50. Quoted by Adam Ulam, *Stalin: The Man and His Era,* 2d. ed. (London: 1989), p. 702.

51. Quoted by Ronald Hingley, *Joseph Stalin: Man and Legend* (London: 1974), p. 410.

52. *Khrushchev Remembers,* pp. 267 and 265.

53. Ibid., p. 269.

54. Alliluyeva, *Twenty Letters,* p. 206.

55. Ibid., p. 212.

56. Ibid., pp. 206–7.

57. *Khrushchev Remembers,* pp. 272–73.

58. Ibid., p. 263.

59. Medvedev, *Let History Judge,* p. 805.

60. *Khrushchev Remembers,* p. 545.

61. Quoted by Ulam, *Stalin,* p. 738.

62. Ignatiev's memorandum was first reported by Yulien Semenov, who had access to it, in *Moskovski Komsomo'ts* and quoted in *The Times,* London, February 26, 1988.

63. *Khrushchev Remembers,* p. 284.

64. Alliluyeva, *Twenty Letters,* p. 18.

65. Ibid., pp. 15–16.

TWENTY: Perspective

1. H. T. Willets in *Survey,* April 1965, p. 9. See also Leszek Kolakowski, *Main Currents of Marxism,* vol. III: *The Breakdown* (Oxford: 1978), pp. 1–5.

2. See Stephen F. Cohen, *Re-thinking the Soviet Experience* (Oxford: 1985), chs. 2 and 3, in

which he challenges the "continuity" thesis and argues strongly in favor of discontinuity between Lenin and Stalin.

3. Boris Souvarine, "Stalinism," in M. M. Drachkovich, ed., *Marxism in the Modern World* (Stanford: 1965), p. 102.

4. Cohen, *Re-thinking the Soviet Experience,* pp. 48–49.

5. See the article by the Australian scholar T. H. Rigby, "Stalinism and the Mono-Organizational Society," in Robert C. Tucker, ed., *Stalinism: Essays in Historical Interpretation* (New York: 1977).

6. The best account of the *Historikerstreit,* with a bibliography that includes a full list of articles in journals and newspapers, is by Richard J. Evans, *In Hitler's Shadow* (London: 1989).

7. Charles Maier in *The Unmasterable Past* (Cambridge, Mass.: 1988), a discussion of the *Historikerstreit,* the Holocaust, and German national identity, gives a figure of ca. 20 million for Soviet victims and ca. 7 to 8 million for Nazi victims.

8. Eberhard Jäckel in *Die Zeit,* September 12, 1986, quoted by Maier, pp. 75–76.

9. Quoted by Roy Medvedev, *Let History Judge,* rev. ed. (Oxford: 1989), p. 517.

ABBREVIATIONS AND GLOSSARY

RUSSIAN AND EAST EUROPEAN

Bolsheviks: The radical faction of the Russian Social Democratic Labor party which under the leadership of Lenin became the Russian Communist party in 1918.

Central Committee: The chief policy-making body of the CPSU (q.v.) between Congresses. It met two or three times a year, frequently in a Plenum with the Central Control Commission. Between Plenums policy was made by the Politburo, technically a body elected by the Central Committee.

Cheka: An acronym formed from the initials of the Russian words for Extraordinary Commission, the organization set up by the new Soviet government in December 1917 to combat counterrevolution and sabotage. This was the origin of the Soviet security police, which became the GPU in 1922.

Cominform: The Communist Information Bureau, set up on Soviet initiative in September 1947 and dissolved in 1956. It had a much more restricted membership than the former Comintern, limited to eight European Communist parties besides the CPSU and was confined to propaganda against the Western powers, the Marshall Plan, and NATO.

Comintern: The Third (Communist) International, formed in 1919 from Communist parties under the leadership of the Communist party of the Soviet Union, with its headquarters in Moscow. Closed down by the Russians in 1943.

CPSU: The Communist Party of the Soviet Union, the successor to the Bolshevik party.

EAM: The Greek National Liberation Front, set up to resist the German occupying forces in 1941 with ELAS, the Greek National People's Liberation Army, as its military arm. Although claiming to represent a united front of democratic and progressive forces, EAM was under Communist leadership from the beginning and was the focus of opposition to the Greek government during the civil war that followed the German withdrawal.

GOKO or GKO (Gosudarstvennyi Komitet Oborony): The State Defense Council, set up on June 30, 1941, under Stalin as chairman with overall responsibility for the direction of the economy and of military production during the war. Its members frequently took part in the meetings of the Stavka (q.v.).

Gosplan: The State Planning Commission.

GPU: The initials for State Political Administration, the successor to the Cheka as the Soviet security police in 1922. Renamed the OGPU in 1924 (see below) it was succeeded in turn by the NKVD in 1934.

Gulag: The Main Administration of Corrective Labor Camps, a branch of the State Security Agency (q.v.) under a succession of names. See pp. 284 and 506–7.

KGB: In 1954 the MGB (Ministry of State Security) was reduced in status to a committee responsible directly to the Council of Ministers but still exercising formidable powers.

Kolkhoz: A collective farm, nominally owned collectively by its members like a cooperative but in practice required to deliver each year a quota, fixed by the Soviet government, of agricultural produce at prices also fixed by the government.

Komsomol: The youth organization of the Soviet Communist movement, for ages fourteen to twenty-eight. The only officially permitted political organization for young people in the USSR. From ten to fifteen they were organized in the Pioneers.

Kremlin: A citadel in a Russian town, specifically the citadel in Moscow that housed and was identified with the government of the USSR.

Kulak: Traditionally, a well-to-do peasant. See the discussion on pp. 256, 258.

Mensheviks: The non-Leninist wing of the Russian Social Democratic Workers' party which represented the minority (Mensheviki) as against the majority (Bolsheviki) after the party split at its 1903 Congress. Led by L. Martov, they opposed Lenin's emphasis on the dictatorial role of a highly centralized party and rejected Lenin's seizure of power without waiting for Russia to go through the bourgeois revolution which they regarded as the necessary precursor, according to Marx, of a socialist society. After the Bolshevik Revolution the Mensheviks attempted to form a legal opposition but were suppressed in 1922, when their leaders went into exile.

MGB: The Ministry of State Security, which succeeded the NKGB in 1946, at the same time as the separate NKVD was succeeded by MVD, Ministry of Internal Affairs.

MTS: Machine and Tractor Station. A state-owned depot of agricultural machinery for use by *kolkhozes* which became an instrument for reinforcing government control of the collective farms.

MVD: See under MGB.

NEP: The New Economic Policy introduced by Lenin after the Kronstadt revolt in 1921.

NKVD: The OGPU was reorganized as the People's Commissariat of Internal Affairs (NKVD) in 1934. This was the security organization numbering hundreds of thousands with which Stalin carried out his purges, trials, and repression in the late 1930s. In 1941 a separate People's Commissariat of State Security was established (NKGB), leaving police duties not directly involving state security to the NKVD. The NKGB was succeeded by the MGB in 1946.

Nomenklatura: Literally, a list of official positions in the Soviet system that could be filled only by appointment from above. By extension this came to represent the holders of such positions, especially the most highly placed, who were the chief beneficiaries as well as controllers of the system.

OGPU: Following the adoption of the constitution of the Union of Soviet Socialist Republics (ratified January 31, 1924) the GPU was attached directly to the Soviet Council of People's Commissars (Sovnarkom) as a "unified" commissariat operating both at the USSR level and in the constituent republics. The letter *O* now prefixed to GPU stood for *obedinennoe,* the Russian word for "unified." Succeeded by the NKVD in 1934.

Politburo: The Political Bureau of the Central Committee of the CPSU, its chief policy-making body between Central Committee Plenums. In practice it was the center of power in the Soviet Union, laying down the policies carried out by the government machine. From 1952 to 1966 it was renamed the Presidium.

POUM (Partido de Unificación Marxista): A Spanish Marxist party influenced by Trotskyite ideas which was persecuted by the Spanish Communist party and liquidated on Soviet orders during the Spanish Civil War.

RSFSR: The Russian Soviet Federated Socialist Republic. The largest and most central of the fifteen republics forming the Union of Soviet Socialist Republics. Often referred to as the Russian Republic.

Socialist Revolutionary Party: A revolutionary party founded in Russia in 1902 to work for the nationalization of the land. They attracted strong support from the peasants in 1917 but split when confronted with the Bolshevik seizure of power. The left SRs joined the Bolsheviks in a coalition government but went into opposition rather than accept the terms of the Brest-Litovsk Treaty. After an unsuccessful revolt they were suppressed by force in 1918.

Sovnarkom: Council of People's Commissars, the highest government body in the USSR, equivalent formally to a cabinet in Western governments, but in practice limited to carrying out policies laid down by the party's Politburo.

State Security Agencies: The Soviet security police system under a succession of names and acronyms, as follows:

CHEKA   1917–22
GPU   1922–24
OGPU   1924–34
NKVD   1934–41
NKGB   1941–46
MGB   1946–54
KGB   1954–

Stavka: The general headquarters of the Supreme Command of the Soviet armed forces, over which Stalin presided. It was responsible for the military direction of the war as GOKO was for its economic direction.

Vozhd': A leader with the natural unquestioned authority that Lenin enjoyed in the Bolshevik party and that Stalin hoped to acquire.

NOTE:
There were three changes in Russia between 1914 and 1924 that are liable to cause confusion:

(a)   The change in dating from the Old Style (Julian Calendar) to the New Style (Gregorian Calendar). Carried out in Catholic Europe in the sixteenth century, and in England and her colonies in the eighteenth century, it was not adopted in the Soviet Union until 1918. According to the New Style, the October Revolution of 1917 took place in November and has continued to be celebrated in November, not October.

(b)   St. Petersburg, which Peter the Great had made the new capital of Russia on its foundation at the beginning of the eighteenth century, adopted the Russian form Petrograd at the beginning of the 1914 war and was renamed Leningrad in honor of Lenin after his death in 1924.

(c)   From 1712 to 1918, St Petersburg-Petrograd replaced Moscow as the capital of Russia. The capital was moved back to Moscow in the spring of 1918 out of reach of the German forces, which were within eighty miles of Petrograd.

GERMAN

Abwehr: The intelligence and counterespionage service of the German High Command (OKW). Its head was Admiral Canaris and it provided cover for a number of those active in the German resistance to Hitler.

Allgemeine SS: The general body of the SS as distinct from the militarized Waffen SS.

Barbarossa: Code word for the German attack on the Soviet Union on June 22, 1941.

CSSD (Chef der Sicherheitspolizei und des Sicherheitsdienstes):   Chief of the Security Police and Security Service—a post held by Heydrich until 1942, then by Kaltenbrunner.

DAF (Deutsche Arbeitsfront):   The German Labor Front, the largest of all the Nazi party's affiliated organizations, to which all workers, as well as entrepreneurs and managers, were obliged to belong under the leadership of Robert Ley.

DDP: Deutsche Demokratische Partei (Democrats). A left liberal party founded in 1918 and reorganized in 1930 as the Deutsche Staatspartei (DSP).

DNVP: Deutschnationale Volkspartei (German National People's Party), known as Nationalists or Conservatives, the traditional conservative party.

DVP: Deutsche Volkspartei (German People's Party). A right-wing liberal party which provided the Weimar Republic with its most distinguished political figure, Gustav Stresemann, German foreign minister from 1923 to 1929.

Einsatzgruppen: Task forces of the Sipo and SD (q.v.) for special missions (usually massacres in occupied territory). Each *Gruppe* consisted of up to six *Einsatzkommandos*.

Freikorps: Volunteer military organizations formed by officers and NCOs after the demobilization of the Imperial Army in 1918–19. They were employed by a hard-pressed government to suppress left-wing insurrections and infighting on the disputed frontiers with Poland and the Baltic states. Strongly antirepublican and antidemocratic in their views, their members gravitated naturally to right-wing groups like the Nazi party and the SA.

Frontkämpfer: Literally, front fighters. Veterans of the First World War, particularly those who, like Adolf Hitler, looked back upon life in the trenches as the greatest experience of their lives, the *Fronterlebnis,* the shared experience of the front.

Führerprinzip: Literally, leadership principle, the basic organizational pattern of the Nazi party, subsequently transferred to the state: the Führer who was responsible to no one but himself and his sense of mission. All members of the party, later of the German people, owed him unquestioning obedience and loyalty.

Gau: The main territorial unit of the Nazi party, which divided Germany into forty-two *Gaue.*

Gauleiter: The regional Nazi party boss responsible in each *Gau* for all political and economic activity, as well as for the mobilization of labor and civil defense. The Gauleiters defended their autonomy vigorously against intervention by the central government and party headquarters alike and never hesitated to appeal to Hitler— usually with success—when they considered their position threatened.

Gestapo (GEheime STAats POlizei):   Secret State Police. Originally the Prussian political police, absorbed into the RSHA (q.v.) in 1939.

Gleichschaltung: Literally, coordination. The colorless euphemism that concealed the ruthless takeover of all other parties and organizations by the triumphant Nazis in 1933–34.

Government-general: The Government-General of German-occupied Poland and its administration, headed by Hans Frank.

Hitlerjugend: The Hitler Youth, the Nazi youth organization under the leadership of Baldur von Schirach, built up a monopoly position, recognized in March 1939, when membership of it was made compulsory for all boys and girls between the ages of ten and eighteen.

HSSP (Höherer SS- und Polizeiführer):   Senior SS and police commander. Himmler's personal representative and liaison officer in each *Wehrkreis* (military district) and also in the occupied territories.

Kampfzeit: Literally, the Time of Struggle. The period up to 1933, and particularly before the electoral tide turned in the Nazis' favor in September 1930, when membership of the party called for sacrifice and commitment. Those who joined the party in this period and remained with it were bound to Hitler, and he to them, by stronger ties than the many who joined later.

KPD: Kommunistische Partei Deutschlands (Communists). A founding member of the Third International, in which it was second in importance only to the Russian party.

Kriminalpolizei (Kripo):   The Criminal Police which, together with the Gestapo (q.v.) formed the Security Police (Sipo).

Kultur: See the discussion on p. 168.

Land (pl. Länder): One of the fifteen "states" or territorial divisions into which Weimar Germany was divided, each with its own government and Landtag (elected chamber of deputies). From 1933 the *Länder* were controlled by the central government through the office of Reichsstatthalter (governor, an office frequently held by a Gauleiter).

Lebensraum: Living space. Hitler argued that the German people did not have adequate *Lebensraum* in which to develop their economic and military strength. He saw the key to their future in providing this by the conquest of a racist empire in Eastern Europe and the Soviet Union.

Majority SPD: Sozialdemokratische Partei Deutschlands. The German Socialist party, known as the Majority Socialists from the wartime split in 1915, when the majority continued to support the war effort while a minority broke away to form the USPD (see below). Along with the USPD and the KPD (in fact their bitter rivals), the Majority Socialists were the target of Hitler's attacks on "the Marxists."

MEFO: An acronym for Metallurgische Forschungsgesellschaft, the Metal Research Corporation, an innocuously named institution that issued bills as a concealed way of financing rearmament. See p. 435.

Ministerpräsident: Minister President. The prime minister of a *Land* government under the Weimar Republic.

Mischlinge: Mongrel or half-caste, the offspring of mixed German-Jewish marriages.

Mittelstand: Middle class. See p. 67.

NS: National Socialist.

NSBO (Nationalsozialistische Betriebsorganisation): The NS Works or Factory Cell Organization which Gregor Strasser set up to compete with the trade unions and develop a radical anticapitalist policy for the Nazi party in industrial relations. Its hopes were dashed when the Nazis came to power and Hitler chose to reach agreement instead with industrialists and businessmen as the best way to secure Germany's economic recovery and rearmament.

NSDAP (Nationalsozialistische Deutsche Arbeiter Partei): The National Socialist German Workers' party, the full title of the Nazi party.

Oberkommando des Heeres (OKH): High Command of the Army.

Oberkommando der Wehrmacht (OKW): High Command of the Armed Forces.

Rassenpolitik: Literally, race policy. Stressed the importance of preserving racial purity and avoiding "racial pollution" by mixed marriages with lesser breeds.

Rechtsstaat: A constitutional state in which political activity and power are governed by law, and are not exercised arbitrarily.

Reich: Empire, realm. Frequently used to distinguish between national and regional authorities, e.g., between the national Reichsleiters and the regional Gauleiters of the Nazi party, or (under Weimar) between the national Reichstag and the state Landtags.

Reichsführer SS und Chef der Deutschen Polizei: Reich SS Leader and Chief of the German Police, Himmler's full title from June 1936.

Reichsleiter: One of the Nazi party's national officers in the party's central administration in Munich. Cf. Gauleiter.

Reichsstatthalter: Governor of a *Land* (q.v.), frequently identical with the party Gauleiter.

Reichswehr: The army of 100,000 to which Germany was restricted by the Treaty of Versailles.

RKF (Reichskommissar für die Festigung des Deutschen Volkstums): Reich Commissar for the Strengthening of Germanism. The office created for Himmler in 1939 to direct the repatriation of ethnic Germans and the settlement of German colonies in the eastern occupied territories.

RSHA (Reichssicherheits Hauptamt): Reich Security Head Office. Formed in 1939, it combined the Security Police (Gestapo and Kripo) and the SS Security Service (SD). Its head was Reinhard Heydrich; he was succeeded in 1943 by Ernst Kaltenbrunner.

SA (Sturmabteilung): Literally "Storm Detachment," the original Nazi paramilitary organization, the Brownshirts, founded in 1921.

SD (Sicherheitsdienst): The SS Security Service formed by Heydrich in 1932, and merged with the Sicherheitspolizei in 1939 to form the core of the RSHA.

Sipo (Sicherheitspolizei): The Security Police consisting of the Gestapo and the Kripo, under Heydrich.

Sopade: The exiled SPD leadership (SOzialdemokratsche PArtei DEutschlands) set up in Prague in 1933 after the party had been suppressed in Germany. Moved to Paris and London later. Its reports are an important source for conditions and attitudes in Germany during the Nazi period.

SPD: See above under Majority SPD.

SS (Schutzstaffeln): Literally, "Protection" or "Guard Detachments." The black-shirted elite guard, built up under Himmler as the Führer state's executive arm able to act outside the law.

SS Gruppenführer: Senior SS officer equivalent in rank to a major-general.

SS Obergruppenführer: Equivalent to a lieutenant general.

SS Standartenführer: Equivalent to a colonel.

Staatssekretär: State secretary. The permanent civil service head of a ministry under the political direction of the minister.

Stahlhelm: The nationalist ex-servicemen's organization founded by Franz Seldte in 1918 and compulsorily merged with the SA in 1933.

Standarte: An SS (or SA) formation, equivalent to a regiment.

Totenkopfverbände: Literally "Death's Head Formation," the SS concentration-camp guard units. In 1939 they formed the nucleus of the SS Totenkopf Division, one of the first field formations of the Waffen SS.

Untermenschen: Subhuman, the racist description of inferior races, such as the Slavs, who were believed to be incapable of creating civilizations or states of their own.

USPD: Unabhängige Sozialdemokratische Partei Deutschlands (Independent Socialists). A left wing party which split from the Majority SPD in 1915 over support for the war and briefly became the second largest party in the country in the revolutionary period of 1919–20. By 1924 it had ceased to exist, losing its supporters to the breakaway Communists or the Majority Socialists.

Verfügunstruppe: The militarized formations of the SS, renamed Waffen SS in the winter of 1939–40.

Volk, völkisch, Volksgemeinschaft: See the discussion of their meaning on p. 68.

Volksdeutsche: Racial or ethnic Germans. German-speaking minorities in foreign countries, often long established there.

Waffen SS: Fully militarized SS formations which constituted an alternative army with a peak strength of 910,000 men (including panzer divisions) in the Second World War.

Wehrmacht: The armed forces of the state, of which the army (*Heer*) was a part.

Weltanschauung: Worldview; philosophical and historical conception of the world.

WiRüAmt (Wehrwirtschafts und Rüstungsamt): The War Economy and Armaments Office of the OKW (q.v.). Its head, Colonel (later General) Thomas, was one of the most persistent critics of Hitler's failure to carry out rearmament in depth and mobilize the German economy for a long war. See pp. 668–70.

WVHA (Wirtschafts und Verwaltungs Hauptamt): The SS Economics and Administration Head Office, set up in 1940, which controlled the SS economic enterprises and administered the concentration camps. Its head was Obergruppenführer Oswald Pohl.

Zentrumspartei: The Center Party, based on the affiliation of its members to the Roman Catholic Church, with wide differences in political views. It supported the Weimar Republic in the 1920s but later moved to the right under the leadership of Brüning.

SELECTED BIBLIOGRAPHY

1. PUBLISHED SOURCES

A. Germany

(a) *The Trial of the Major War Criminals before the International Military Tribunal: Proceedings.* Vols I–XXIII. Nuremberg: 1947–49; *Documents in Evidence.* Vols XXIV–XLII. Nuremberg: 1947–49.

A verbatim report of the trial proceedings was published by HM Stationery Office in twenty-two parts, *The Trial of German Major War Criminals.* London: 1946–50.

Translations of many of the documents presented in evidence, affidavits, and interrogations were published by the U.S. Government Printing Office. *Nazi Conspiracy and Aggression.* 8 vols with two supplementary vols A and B. *Washington: 1946–48.

(b) *Trials of War Criminals before the Nuremberg Military Tribunals under Control Commission Law No. 10.* 15 vols. Washington: 1952–53): The Milch Case (vol. 2), The Flick Case (vol. 6), The I.G. Farben Case (vols 7–8), The Krupp Case (vol. 9), The Diplomats' Case (vol. 12), The Ministries' Case (vols 13–14).

(c) A comprehensive selection of captured material from the German Foreign Office and other governmental sources has been published under the auspices of the British, French, and U.S. governments. These volumes are primarily concerned with German foreign policy but contain documents throwing light on other aspects of German policy and on the foreign policy of other powers, for example on Soviet foreign policy during the period of the Nazi-Soviet Pact. The first two series to be published, Series C and D, appeared in English and French as well as German. Series E was published only in German.

After the captured German documents were returned to Germany, on German initiative the international character of the project was retained, with English, French, and American scholars joining German colleagues in the selection and editing of documents for Series A and B.

Series A. *Akten zur Deutschen auswärtgen Politik, 1918–25.* 12 vols.
Series B. *Akten zur Deutschen auswärtgen Politik, 1925–32.* 21 vols.
Series C. *Documents on German Foreign Policy. 1933–36.* 6 vols.
Series D. *Documents on German Foreign Policy. 1936–41.* 13 vols.
Series E. *Akten zur deutschen auswärtigen Politik. 1941–45.* 8 vols.

(d) *Hitler. Reden und Proklamationen, 1932–45.* Edited by Max Domarus. 2 vols. Würzburg: 1962–63.
The Speeches of Adolf Hitler, 1922–1939. Edited by Norman H. Baynes. 2 vols. Oxford: 1942.
Hitler's Words. Edited by Gordon W. Prange. *Washington: 1944. Speeches 1922–43.
My New Order. Edited by Raoul de Roussy. *New York: 1941. Hitler's speeches.
Adolf Hitler in Franken. Reden aus der Kampfzeit. Edited by H. Preiss. Munich: 1939.

(e) *Der Hitler Prozess.* Munich: 1924. Record of the court proceedings in Munich in 1924.
Hitlers Auseinandersetzung mit Brüning. Munich: 1932.
Hitler's Table Talk 1941–4. *London: 1953.
The Testament of Adolf Hitler: The Hitler-Bormann Documents, February-April 1945. *London: 1961.

(f) Adolf Hitler, *Mein Kampf.* 2 vols. Munich: 1925–27: English translation by James Murphy. London: 1939; English translation by Ralph Manheim. London: 1974.
Hitlers Zweites Buch (written in 1928, published in 1961. English translation. *Hitler's Secret Book.* New York: 1961, and the *VfZ* published by the Institut für Zeitsgeschichte in Munich.

(g) *Dokumente der deutschen Politik, 1933–41.* 9 vols. Berlin: 1937–44. A collection of official Nazi documents.
Führer Conferences on the German Navy, 1939–45. 8 vols. *Washington: 1946–47.
Hitler's War Directives, 1939–45. Edited by H. R. Trevor-Roper. London: 1964.
Hitler Directs His War: Secret Records of His Daily Military Conferences. Edited by Felix Gilbert. New York: 1950.
"Hitlers Denkschrift zum Vierjahresplan, 1936." Edited by Wilhelm Treue. *VfZ* 3 (1955): 184–210.

(h) Two British scholars, Jeremy Noakes and Geoffrey Pridham, have put all teachers of European history in their debt by editing *Nazism, 1919–1945: A Documentary Reader.* Exeter: 1983–88. These three volumes contain over 900 documents in English translation with historical commentary, including all the key documents (especially in vol. III) and a substantial number of less well-known extracts which throw light on the character of the Nazi racist empire. Wherever possible I have given references in the text and notes to this collection.

Jeremy Noakes and Geoffrey Pridham, eds., *Nazism, 1919–1945: A Documentary*

Reader. Vol. I, *The Rise to Power, 1919–34*. Exeter: 1983. Vol. II, *State, Economy and Society, 1933–39*. Exeter: 1984. Vol. III: *Foreign Policy, War and Racial Extermination*. Exeter: 1988.

In addition to the published sources, the German, American, and British archives have been opened to independent scholars, leading to a proliferation of scholarly studies, often containing unpublished material, a selection of which is given in Section 3A below.

B. Soviet Union and Eastern Europe

Nothing comparable to the wealth of published sources for the history of Germany or to the freedom of access to unpublished material in the archives of Germany, the U.S.A., and the UK exists yet in the Soviet Union. Except for a number of publications in the area of international relations (see Section 1C below), neither the Soviet government nor the Communist party has published or allowed freedom of access to its records. This situation has hardly been changed by the policy of *glasnost*. Individuals, including a number who have held high office, have enjoyed much greater freedom to speak out and publish their reminiscences of the Stalin period (see Sections 2B and 2C below) and General Volkogonov has had access to parts of the central archives in writing his biography of Stalin. All this has made possible a much more open and frank discussion, but historians of the Stalin years in search of reliable documentary evidence are still at a disadvantage compared to those working on the period 1928 to 1953 in Western countries. Stalin surrounded the operations of government and party in the USSR with a wall of secrecy, and its dismantling has still a long way to go. All the more reason therefore to be grateful to those pioneering scholars who have devoted themselves to laying the foundations of a critical study of an era in European history that is far too important to be left out of account.

(a)   The principal source for the history of the CPSU between 1917 and 1953 remains the Protocols, Resolutions, and Stenographic Reports of the Party Congresses. Although not available in translation they have been widely used and quoted by historians.
R. H. McNeal, ed., *Guide to the Decisions of the CPSU*. Toronto: 1972.
R. H. McNeal, ed., *Resolutions and Decisions of the CPSU*. 5 vols. Toronto: 1974–82. Vol. III covers *The Stalin Years, 1929–1953*.

(b)   Stalin's *Collected Works*, vols. 1–13, were published in Moscow in 1946–52; and vols 14–16 in 1967 by the Hoover Institute in Stanford (ed. R. H. McNeal).
    I have used the English version published in Moscow in 13 vols. (1952–55) and two collections of Stalin's most important speeches, articles, and publications under the misleading titles: J. Stalin, *Leninism* and *Problems of Leninism*. There is a considerable overlap between the two. Both have appeared in several editions; the latest is not always the most satisfactory as there have been changes and deletions in the course of time. The edition of *Leninism* I have used was published in 1940 and those of *Problems of Leninism* in 1931, 1945, and 1953.
    Lenin's *Collected Works* were published in 47 vols. *London: 1960–80. I have used the two-volume selection translated in Moscow, *The Essentials of Leninism*. *London: 1947.

(c) *A History of the CPSU (Bolsheviks): Short Course.* *2d. rev. ed. Moscow: 1962.
J. V. Stalin. *Marxism and Linguistics.* *Moscow: 1951.
J. V. Stalin. *Economic Problems of Socialism in the USSR.* *Moscow: 1952.

(d) The Trotsky Archive, Harvard University Library. See *The Trotsky Papers.* Edited by J. M. Meijer. 2 vols. The Hague: 1965, 1971.
The Smolensk archive, US National Archives, Washington. See Merle Fainsod. *Smolensk under Soviet Rule.* New York: 1958.

(e) Verbatim Report of the Court Proceedings (in English).
The Case of the Trotskyite-Zinovievite Terrorist Center, August 19–24, 1936. Moscow: 1936.
The Case of the Anti-Soviet Trotskyite Center, January 29–30, 1937 (Moscow: 1937).
The Case of the Anti-Soviet Bloc of Rights and Trotskyites. March 2–13, 1938. Moscow: 1938.

(f) Jane Degras, ed., *The Communist International, 1919–43: Documents.* 3 vols. London: 1956–65.
RIIA, *The Soviet-Yugoslav Dispute: Text of the Published Correspondence.* London: 1948.
"The Bukharin-Kamenev Meeting 1928," *Dissent* (Winter 1979): 78–88.

For Soviet publications on foreign policy, see following Section 1C.

C. International Relations

Besides the series of *Documents on German Foreign Policy, 1918–45* (see p. 1036 above) comparable series have been published by the British, French, and U.S. governments.

(a) *Documents on British Foreign Policy, 1919–39.* 1st Series, 1919–29. 2d Series, 1930–37. 3d Series, 1938–39. 9 vols. London: 1949–57.
There is a gap in the British series of published documents for the war years; but the documents (Cabinet, Foreign Office, Ministry of Defense) are available in the Public Record Office at Kew and have been widely quoted by historians.
Publication has been resumed with a new series, *Documents on British Policy Overseas:*

Series I, vol. I: The Conference at Potsdam, 1945
II: Conferences and Conversations, 1945, London, Washington and Moscow
V: Germany and Western Europe, 1945
Series II, vol. I: The Schuman Plan, the Council of Europe and Western European Integration, 1950–52
II: The London Conferences: Anglo-American Relations and Cold War Strategy, 1950
III: German Re-armament, 1950

(b) *Documents diplomatiques français, 1932–39.* 1st Series, 1932–35. 2nd Series, 1938–39 (Paris: in progress).

(c) *Papers Relating to the Foreign Relations of the United States (FRUS).* This is an ongoing series, with several volumes for each year, for example *FRUS, 1938.* 4 vols; *FRUS, 1948.* 9 vols. In addition there are volumes devoted to a particular area, for

example *FRUS: The Soviet Union, 1938–39.* There are also separate volumes for important conferences:
FRUS: The Conferences at Cairo and Teheran. Washington: 1961.
FRUS: The Conferences at Malta and Yalta. Washington: 1955.
FRUS: The Conference of Berlin: The Potsdam Conference. Washington: 1960.

(d) *Churchill and Roosevelt: The Complete Correspondence.* Edited by Warren F. Kimball. 3 vols. Princeton: 1984.
Correspondence between the Chairman of the Council of Ministers of the USSR and the Presidents of the USA and the Prime Ministers of Great Britain during the Great Patriotic War of 1941–45. 2 vols. *Moscow: 1957.

(e) *Documenty vneshnei politiki SSSR.* Twenty-one volumes of documents dealing with Soviet foreign policy between 1917 and 1938 were published between 1957 and 1977 under the chief editorship of A. A. Gromyko.
  The following English versions of Soviet documents have been published:
International Affairs, published in Moscow, devoted four numbers in 1963 to "The Struggle of the USSR for Collective Security in Europe during 1933–35."
Soviet Peace Moves on the Eve of World War II. 2 vols. Moscow: 1973.
The Tehran, Yalta and Potsdam Conferences: Documents. Moscow: 1965.
Soviet Foreign Policy during the Patriotic War: Documents and Materials. Edited by A. Rothstein. London: 1946.
The Soviet Union and the Berlin Question: Documents. Moscow: 1948.
The Soviet Union and the Berlin Question: Documents. 2d series. Moscow: 1949.
The Soviet Union and the Quest of the Unity of Germany and of the Peace Treaty: Documents. Moscow: 1952.

(f) Collections of documents:
Hitler e Mussolini: Lettere e documenti. Milan: 1946.
Ciano's Diplomatic Papers. Malcolm Muggeridge *London: 1948.
RIIA, *Documents on International Affairs.* London: 1929–53. Annual volumes for 1929 to 1953 apart from the war years.
Soviet Documents on Foreign Policy, 1917–41. Edited by Jane Degras. 3 vols. London: 1950–53.
Documents on Germany under Occupation, 1945–51. Edited by B. Ruhm von Oppen. Oxford: 1955.
The Polish White Book: Official Documents concerning Polish-German and Polish-Soviet Relations, 1933–39. *London: 1980.
Documents on Soviet-Polish Relations, 1933–39. *London: 1961.

2. LETTERS, DIARIES AND MEMOIRS

A. Germany

  Bernadotte, Count Fulk. *The Curtain Falls.* New York: 1945.

  Boldt, Gerhard. *In the Shelter with Hitler.* *London: 1948.

  Bonhoeffer, Dietrich. *Letters and Papers from Prison.* *London: 1971.

  Bormann, Martin, and his wife. *The Bormann Letters.* Edited by H. R. Trevor-Roper. London: 1954.

Burckhardt, Carl. *Meine Danziger Mission, 1937–39.* Munich: 1969.

Ciano, Galeazzo. *The Ciano Diaries, 1939–43.* *London: 1948.

Dahlerus, Birger. *The Last Attempt.* London: 1948.

Dietrich, Otto. *Mit Hitler in die Macht.* Munich: 1934.

Dietrich, Otto. *12 Jahre mit Hitler.* Munich: 1955.

François-Poncet, André. *The Fateful Years.* *London: 1949.

Frank, Hans. *Im Angesicht des Galgens: Deutung Hitlers und seiner Zeit.* Munich: 1953.

Gisevius, Hans B. *To the Bitter End.* *London: 1948.

Goebbels, Joseph. *My Part in Germany's Fight, 1932–3.* *London: 1938.

Goebbels, Joseph. *The Goebbels Diaries, 1942–43.* Edited by Louis P. Lochner. *London: 1948.

Goebbels, Joseph. *The Early Goebbels Diaries, 1925–26.* Edited by H. Heiber. *London: 1962.

Goebbels, Joseph. *The Goebbels Diaries, 1939–41.* Edited by Fred Taylor. *London: 1982.

Goebbels, Joseph. *Die Tagebücher von Joseph Goebbels: Samtliche Fragmente.* Edited by Elke Fröhlich, ongoing. Vols 1–4. Munich: 1987–.

Guderian, Heinz, *Panzer-General* *London: 1952.

Halder, General Franz. *Kriegstagebuch, 1939–42.* Edited by H. A. Jacobsen. 3 vols. Munich: 1962–66.

Hanfstaengl, Ernst. *Hitler: The Missing Years.* *London: 1957.

Hassell, Ulrich von. *The Von Hassell Diaries, 1938–44.* *London: 1948.

Hoffmann, Heinrich. *Hitler Was My Friend.* *London: 1955.

Hossbach, Friedrich. *Zwischen Wehrmacht und Hitler, 1934–38.* Wolfenbüttel: 1949.

Keitel, Wilhelm. *Memoirs.* *London: 1965.

Kersten, Felix. *The Kersten Memoirs, 1940–45.* *London: 1956.

Kleist, Peter. *Zwischen Hitler und Stalin, 1939–45. Aufzeichnungen.* Bonn: 1950.

Krebs, Albert. *The Infancy of Nazism: The Memoirs of ex-Gauleiter Albert Krebs, 1923–1933.* Edited by W. S. Allen. *London: 1978.

Kubizek, August. *The Young Hitler: The Story of Our Friendship.* *London: 1954.

Lüdecke, Kurt G. W. *I Knew Hitler.* *London: 1938.

Manstein, Erich von. *Lost Victories.* *Chicago: 1958.

Mend, Hans. *Adolf Hitler im Felde.* Munich: 1931.

Molthe, Helmuth James von, *Letters to Freya: A Witness Against Hitler.* London: 1991.

Schacht, Hjalmar. *Account Settled.* *London: 1948.

Schmidt, Paul. *Hitler's Interpreter.* *London: 1951.

Speer, Albert. *Inside the Third Reich.* *London: 1970.

Strasser, Otto, *Hitler and I.* *London: 1940.

Trott zu Solz, Adam von. *A Noble Combat: The Letters of Sheila Grant-Duff and Adam von Trott zu Solz, 1932–39.* Edited by K. von Klemperer. Oxford: 1988.

Wagener, Otto. *Hitler: Memoirs of a Confidant.* Edited by Henry Ashby Turner, Jr. *New Haven: 1985.

Wagner, Friedelind. *The Royal Family of Bayreuth.* London: 1948.

Warlimont, General Walter. *Inside Hitler's Headquarters, 1939–45.* *London: 1964.

Weizsäcker, Ernst von. *Memoirs.* *London: 1951.

Weizsäcker, Ernst von. *Die Weizsäcker-Papiere, 1933–1950.* Edited by Leonidas Hill Frankfurt am Main: 1974.

Zoller, Albert, ed. *Hitler Privat.* Düsseldorf: 1949. The memoirs of Christa Schroeder, Hitler's secretary.

B. Soviet Union and Eastern Europe

Alliluyeva, Svetlana. *Twenty Letters to a Friend.* *London: 1967.

Alliluyeva, Svetlana. *Only One Year.* *New York: 1969.

Barmine, Alexander. *One Who Survived: The Life Story of a Russian under the Soviets.* New York: 1945.

Bazhanov, B. *Stalin, der Rote Diktator.* Berlin: 1930.

Bazhanov, B. *Bazhanov and the Damnation of Stalin.* *Athens, Ohio: 1990.

Buber, Margarete. *Under Two Dictators.* *London: 1949.

Buber-Neumann, Margarete. *Von Potsdam nach Moskau: Stationen eines Irrweges.* Stuttgart: 1957.

Chuikov, Marshal V. I. *The Beginning of the End.* *New York: 1963.

Chuikov, Marshal V. I. *The End of the Third Reich.* *New York: 1967.

Deakin, F. W. D. *The Embattled Mountain.* London: 1971.

Djilas, Milovan. *Conversations with Stalin.* *London: 1962.

Ehrenburg, Ilya. *Memoirs, 1921–1941.* *New York: 1964.

Ehrenburg, Ilya. *Post-War Years, 1945–1954.* *New York: 1967.

Fischer, Ruth. *Stalin and German Communism.* *Cambridge, Mass.: 1948.

Ginsburg, Eugenia Semyonovna. *Journey into the Whirlwind.* *London: 1967.

Gorbatov, General V. A. *Years Off My Life.* *New York: 1965.

Grigorenko, Petro D. *Memoirs.* London: 1983.

Gromyko, A. A. *Memories.* *London: 1989.

Hilger, Gustav, and Alfred G. Meyer. *The Incompatible Allies: A Memoir-History of German-Soviet Relations, 1918–1941.* New York: 1953.

Hindus, Maurice. *Humanity Uprooted.* London: 1929.

Iremashvili, Joseph. *Stalin und die Tragödie Georgiens.* Berlin: 1932.

Khrushchev Remembers. Translated and edited by Strobe Talbot. *London: 1971. Includes Khrushchev's secret speech of 1956.

Khrushchev Remembers: The Last Testament. Translated and edited by Strobe Talbot. *Boston: 1974.

Khrushchev Remembers: The Glasnost Tapes. New York: 1991.

Khrushchev, Sergei. *Khrushchev on Khrushchev.* *Boston: 1990. Establishes the authenticity of Khrushchev's memoirs.

Kopelev, Lev. *The Education of a True Believer.* *New York: 1977.

Kot, S. *Conversations with the Kremlin and Dispatches from Russia.* London: 1963.

Kravchenko, Victor. *I Chose Freedom.* New York: 1946.

Leonhard, Wolfgang. *Child of the Revolution.* London: 1957.

Lyons, Eugene. *Assignment in Utopia.* New York: 1937.

Maclean, Fitzroy. *Eastern Approaches.* London: 1949.

Mandelstam, Nadezhda. *Hope against Hope: A Memoir.* Translated by Max Hayward, pb. ed. *London: 1975.

Mandelstam, Nadezhda. *Hope Abandoned.* Translated by Max Hayward, pb. ed. *London: 1976.

Mikolajczyk, S. *The Rape of Poland: The Pattern of Soviet Domination.* New York: 1948.

Orlov, Alexander. *The Secret History of Stalin's Aims.* New York: 1953.

Scott, John. *Behind the Urals: An American Worker in Russia's City of Steel.* Cambridge, Mass.: 1942.

Serge, Viktor. *Memoirs of a Revolutionary, 1901–1941.* *London: 1963.

Shostakovich, Dmitri. *Testimony, The Memoirs of Shostakovich.* Related to and edited by S. Volkov. *London: 1979.

Sukhanov, N. N. *The Russian Revolution 1917: A Personal Record.* Translated and edited by Joel Carmichael. London: 1955.

Trotsky, Leon. *My Life.* *New York: 1930.

Vasilevsky, Marshal A. M. *A Lifelong Cause.* *Moscow: 1981.

Zhukov, Marshal Georgi. *Reminiscences and Reflections.* *Moscow: 1985.

Note: The best guides to the literature in English are R. W. Davies, *Soviet History in the Gorbachev Revolution.* London: 1989 and Walter Laqueur, *Stalin, the Glasnost Revelations.* London: 1990.

C. Soviet History in Russian Literature

Akhmatova, Anna. *Selected Poems*. Translated by Richard McKane. London: 1969.

Grossman, Vasily. *Forever Flowing*. London: 1972.

Grossman, Vasily. *Life and Fate*. Translated by Robert Chandler. London: 1985.

Koestler, Arthur. *Darkness at Noon*. Translated by Daphne Hardy. London: 1940.

Mandelstam, Osip. *Selected Poems*. Translated by David McDuff. Cambridge: 1973.

Marsh, Rosalind. *Images of Dictatorship: Stalin in Literature*. London: 1989.

Pasternak, Boris. *Doctor Zhivago*. Translated by Max Hayward and Maryon Harari. London: 1958.

Pilnyak, B. *The Tale of the Unextinguished Moon in Mother Earth and Other Stories*. Translated by Vera Reck and Michael Green. New York: 1968.

Rybakov, Anatoli. *Children of the Arbat*. Translated by Harold Shukman. London: 1988.

Scammell, Michael. *Solzhenitsyn: A Biography*. London: 1985.

Solzhenitsyn, Alexander. *A Day in the Life of Ivan Denisovitch*. Translated by Max Hayward and R. Hingley. London: 1963.

Solzhenitsyn, Alexander. *The First Circle*. Translated by T. P. Whitney. London: 1968.

Solzhenitsyn, Alexander. *Cancer Ward*. Translated by Nicholas Bethell and David Burg. London: 1969.

D. International Relations

Acheson, Dean. *Present at the Creation: My Years at the State Department*. New York: 1969.

Avon, Earl of. *The Eden Memoirs: Facing the Dictators*. London: 1962.

Avon, Earl of. *The Eden Memoirs: The Reckoning*. London: 1965.

Bedell Smith, Walter. *My Three Years in Moscow*. New York: 1958.

Bohlen, Charles E., with Robert H. Phelps. *Witness to History, 1929–1969*. New York: 1973.

Byrnes, James F. *Speaking Frankly*. New York: 1947.

Cadogan, Sir Alexander. *The Diaries of Sir Alexander Cadogan, 1938–1945*. London: 1971.

Churchill, Winston S., *The Second World War*. 6 vols. London: 1948–54.

Clay, Lucius D. *Decision in Germany*. London: 1950.

Coulondre, Robert. *De Staline à Hitler: Entre deux ambassades, 1936–39* (Paris: 1950).

Dönitz, Admiral Karl. *Memoirs.* *London: 1958.

Gromyko, A. A. *Memoirs.* Translated by Harold Shukman. *London: 1989.

Harriman, W. Averell and Elie Abel. *Special Envoy to Churchill and Stalin, 1941–46.* New York: 1975.

Henderson, Sir Nevile. *Failure of a Mission.* London: 1940.

Kennan, George. *Memoirs, 1925–50.* London: 1969.

Maisky, Ivan. *Memoirs of a Soviet Ambassador.* *Moscow: 1966.

Schuschnigg, Kurt von. *Austrian Requiem.* *London: 1947.

Sherwood, Robert, ed., *The White House Papers of Harry Hopkins.* 2 vols. rev. ed., New York: 1952.

3. BOOKS AND ARTICLES

A. Germany

Abraham, David. *The Collapse of the Weimar Republic: Political Economy and Crisis.* Princeton: 1981.

Allen, William Sheridan. *The Nazi Seizure of Power: The Experience of a Single German Town, 1930–35.* Chicago: 1965.

Ayçoberry, P. *The Nazi Question: An Essay on the Interpretation of National Socialism, 1926–75.* *Paris: 1981.

Backes, Uwe, Hans Mommsen, Fritz Tobias et al. *Reichstagsbrand: Aufklärung einer historischen Legende.* Munich: 1986.

Bartov, Omar. *The Eastern Front, 1941–45: German Troops and the Barbarisation of Warfare.* London: 1985.

Bessel, R., *Political Violence and the Rise of Nazism: The Stormtroopers in Eastern Germany, 1925–1934.* London: 1984.

Bessel, R., and E. J. Feuchtwanger, eds. *Social Change and Political Development in Weimar Germany.* London: 1981.

Bezymenski, Lev. *The Death of Adolf Hitler.* London: 1968.

Binion, Rudolph. *Hitler Among the Germans.* New York: 1977.

Boog, Horst, Jürgen Förster et al. *Das Deutsche Reich und der Zweite Weltkrieg,* vol. IV, *Der Angriff auf die Sowjetunion.* Stuttgart: 1983.

Bracher, K. D. *Die Auflösung der Weimarer Republik: Eine Studie zum Problem der Machtresfalls in der Demokratie.* 4th ed. Villinger: 1964.

Bracher, K. D. *Die Auflösung der Weimarer Republik.* Villinger: 1964.

Bracher, K. D., W. Sauer, and G. Schultz. *Die Nationalsozialistische Machtergreifung.* Cologne: 1960.

Bramsted, E. K. *Goebbels and National Socialist Propaganda, 1925–45.* London: 1965.

Brosse, J. *Hitler avant Hitler: Essai d'interpretation psychoanalytique*. Paris: 1972.

Broszat, Martin. *The Hitler State*. Expanded ed. *London: 1981.

Broszat, Martin. *Hitler and the Collapse of Weimar Germany*. *Leamington: 1987.

Browning, Christopher R. *Fateful Months: Essays on the Emergence of the Final Solution*. New York: 1985.

Browning, Christopher R. *Ordinary Men: Reserve Police Battalion 101 & the Final Solution in Poland*. New York: 1992.

Browning, Christopher R. *The Path to Genocide*. Cambridge: 1992.

Bullock, Alan. *Hitler: A Study in Tyranny*. Rev. ed. London: 1964.

Burleigh, Michael. *Germany Turns Eastwards: A Study of Ostforschung in the Third Reich*. Cambridge: 1988.

Carr, William. *Hitler: A Study in Personality and Politics*. London: 1978.

Carroll, Berenice. *Design for Total War: Arms and Economics in the Third Reich*. The Hague: 1968.

Carsten, F. L. *The Reichswehr and Politics, 1918–1933*. Oxford: 1966.

Childers, Thomas. *The Nazi Voter: The Social Foundations of Fascism in Germany, 1919–33*. Chapel Hill, N.C.: 1983.

Clark, A. *Barbarossa*. London: 1964.

Cohn, Norman. *Warrant for Genocide*. London: 1967.

Conway, J. S. *The Nazi Persecution of the Churches, 1933–45*. London: 1968.

Craig, Gordon. *The Politics of the Prussian Army, 1650–1945*. London: 1968.

Dahrendorf, Ralf. *Society and Democracy in Germany*. *London: 1968.

Dallin, Alexander. *German Rule in Russia, 1941–44*. Rev. ed. London: 1981.

Deakin, F. W. D. *The Brutal Friendship: Mussolini, Hitler and the Fall of Italian Fascism*. London: 1962.

Deist, Wilhelm. *The Wehrmacht and German Re-armament*. London: 1981.

Deist, W., M. Messerschmidt, H.-E. Volkman, and W. Wette. *Ursachen und Voraussetzungen der deutschen Kriegspolitik*. Stuttgart: 1979.

Delarue, J. *The History of the Gestapo*. *London: 1964.

Deuerlein, Ernst. *Der Aufstieg der NSDAP 1919–33 in Augenzeugenberichten*. Düsseldorf: 1968.

Deuerlein, Ernst. *Hitler: Eine politische Biographie*. Munich: 1969.

Deutsch, Harry C. *Hitler and His Generals: The Hidden Crisis, January–June 1938*. Minneapolis: 1974.

Diehl, J. M. *Paramilitary Politics in Weimar Germany*. Bloomington: 1977.

Dornberg, John. *The Putsch That Failed: Munich 1923*. London: 1982.

Dorpalen, Andreas. *Hindenburg and the Weimar Republic*. Princeton: 1964.

Douglas-Hamilton, James. *Motive for a Mission: The Story Behind Hess's Flight*. Rev. ed. Edinburgh: 1979.

Dülffer, J. *Weimar, Hitler und die Marine; Reichspolitik und Flottenbau, 1920–1939*. Düsseldorf: 1973.

Eley, Geoffrey. *Reshaping the German Right: Radical Nationalism and Political Change after Bismarck*. New Haven: 1978.

Evans, Richard J. *Re-thinking German History: Nineteenth-Century Germany and the Origins of the Third Reich*. London: 1987.

Evans, Richard J. *In Hitler's Shadow: West German Historians and the Attempt to Escape from the Nazi Past*. London: 1989.

Farquharson, J., *The Plough and the Swastika: the NSDAP and Agriculture in Germany 1928–1945*. London: 1976.

Fest, Joachim, *The Face of the Third Reich*. *London: 1970.

Fest, Joachim. *Hitler*. *London: 1974.

Fischer, Fritz. *Germany's Aims in the First World War*. *London: 1967.

Fischer, Fritz. *War of Illusions: German Policies from 1911 to 1941*. *London: 1975.

Fleming, Gerald. *Hitler and the Final Solution*. London: 1985.

Fraenkel, E. *The Dual State*. London: 1941.

Franz-Willing, Georg. *Die Hitlerbewegung: Der Ursprung, 1919–22*. Hamburg: 1962

Freeman, M. *Atlas of Nazi Germany*. Beckenham: 1987.

Funke, M., ed. *Hitler, Deutschland und die Mächte*. Düsseldorf: 1977.

Gellately, Robert. *The Gestapo & German Society: Enforcing Racial Policy, 1933–1945*. New York: 1990.

Geyer, M. *Aufrüstung oder Sicherheit: die Reichswehr und der Krise der Machtpolitik, 1924–1936*. Wiesbaden: 1988.

Gilbert, Martin. *Atlas of the Holocaust*. London: 1982.

Gilbert, Martin. *The Holocaust: The Jewish Tragedy*. London: 1986.

Gill, Anton, ed. *The Journey Back from Hell: Conversations with Concentration Camp Survivors*. London: 1988.

Gillingham, John R. *Industry and Politics in the Third Reich: Ruhr Coal, Hitler and Europe*. London: 1985.

Gordon, Harold J., Jr. *Hitler and the Beer Hall Putsch*. Princeton: 1972.

Gordon, Sarah. *Hitler, Germans and the "Jewish Question."* Princeton: 1984.

Haffner, Sebastian. *The Meaning of Hitler*. London: 1979.

Halder, General Franz. *Hitler as Warlord*. *New York: 1950.

Hale, Oron J. *The Captive Press in the Third Reich.* Princeton: 1964.

Hamilton, Richard F. *Who Voted for Hitler?* Princeton: 1982.

Hayes, Peter. *Industry and Ideology: IG Farben in the Nazi Era.* Cambridge: 1987.

Heiden, Konrad. *Der Führer.* *Reissued. London: 1967.

Heiden, Konrad. *A History of National Socialism.* *London: 1932.

Heiden, Konrad. *Hitler: A Biography.* *London: 1936.

Herf, Jeffrey. *Reactionary Modernism: Technology, Culture and Politics in Weimar and the Third Reich.* Cambridge: 1984.

Hiden, John, and John Farquharson. *Explaining Hitler's Germany: Historians and the Third Reich.* London: 1983.

Hilberg, Raul. *The Destruction of the European Jews.* 3 vols. Rev. ed. New York: 1985.

Hildebrand, K. *The Third Reich.* *London: 1984.

Hirschfeld, Gerhard, ed. *The Policies of Genocide: Jews and Soviet Prisoners of War in Nazi Germany.* *London: 1986.

Hirschfeld, Gerhard, and Lothar Kelternacker, eds. *"Der Führerstaat": Mythos und Realität. Studien zur Struktur und Politik des Dritten Reiches.* Stuttgart: 1981.

Hoffmann, Peter. *The History of the German Resistance, 1933–45.* *London: 1977.

Höhne, Heinz, *The Order of the Death's Head: The Story of Hitler's SS.* London: 1969.

Holborn, Hajo, ed. *Republic to Reich.* New York: 1972.

Homze, E. L. *Foreign Labor in Nazi Germany.* Princeton: 1967.

Irving, David. *Hitler's War.* London: 1977.

Irving, David. *The War Path: Hitler's Germany, 1933–39.* London: 1978.

Jäckel, Eberhard. *Hitler's Weltanschauung: A Blueprint for Power.* *Middletown: 1972.

Jäckel, Eberhard, *Hitler in History.* *Hanover, N.H.: 1984.

James, Harold, *The German Slump: Politics and Economics, 1924–1936.* Oxford: 1986.

James, Harold. *A German Identity, 1770–1990.* London: 1989.

Jenks, William A. *Vienna and the Young Hitler.* New York: 1960.

Jetzinger, Franz. *Hitler's Youth.* London: 1958.

Kater, Michael. *The Nazi Party: A Social Profile of Members and Leaders, 1919–1945.* Oxford: 1983.

Kele, M. H. *Nazis and Workers: National Socialist Appeals to German Labor, 1919–1939.* Chapel Hill, N.C.: 1972.

Kershaw, Ian. *Popular Opinion and Political Dissent in the Third Reich.* Oxford: 1983.

Kershaw, Ian. *The Nazi Dictatorship: Problems and Perspectives of Interpretation.* London: 1985.

Kershaw, Ian. *The Hitler Myth: Image and Reality in the Third Reich.* Oxford: 1987.

Koch, H. W., ed. *Aspects of the Third Reich.* London: 1985.

Kochl, Robert L. *RKFDV, German Re-Settlement and Population Policy, 1939–45.* Cambridge, Mass.: 1957.

Kogon, E. *The Theory and Practice of Hell: The German Concentration Camps.* New York: 1950.

Krausnick, Helmut, Hans Buchheim, Martin Broszat, and H. A. Jacobsen, *Anatomy of the SS State.* *London: 1968.

Lane, Barbara. *Architecture and Politics in Germany, 1918–45.* Cambridge, Mass.: 1968.

Laqueuer, Walter, ed. *Fascism: A Reader's Guide.* 2d. ed. London: 1979.

Laqueuer, Walter, and Richard Breitman. *Breaking the Silence.* New York: 1986.

Large, David Clay, ed. *Contending with Hitler.* Cambridge: 1992.

Leach, Barry A. *German Strategy against Russia in 1939–1941.* Oxford: 1973.

Maier, Charles S. *The Unmasterable Past: History, Holocaust and German National Identity.* Cambridge, Mass.: 1988.

Marrus, Michael R. *The Holocaust in History.* Hanover, N.H.: 1987.

Maser, Werner. *Die Frühgeschichte der NSDAP.* Frankfurt: 1965.

Mason, T. W. *Arbeiterklasse und Volksgemeinschaft.* Opladen: 1975.

Mason, T. W. *Sozialpolitik im Dritten Reich.* Opladen: 1977.

Mason, T. W. "The Primacy of Politics." In *Nazism and the Third Reich,* edited by Henry Ashby Turner, Jr. New York: 1972, pp. 175–200.

Meinck, G., *Hitler und die deutsche Aufrüstung, 1933–37.* Wiesbaden: 1959.

Merkl, P. H. *Political Violence under the Swastika: 581 Early Nazis.* Princeton: 1975.

Merson, Allan. *Communist Resistance in Nazi Germany.* London: 1985.

Milward, Alan S. *The German Economy at War.* London: 1965.

Milward, Alan S. *The New Order and the French Economy.* Oxford: 1970.

Mitchell, Allan. *Revolution in Bavaria.* Princeton: 1965.

Mommsen, Hans. *Beamtentum im Dritten Reich.* Stuttgart: 1966.

Mosse, G. L. *The Crisis of German Ideology: Intellectual Origins of the Third Reich.* London: 1964.

Mosse, G. L. *Nazi Culture: Intellectual, Cultural and Social Life in the Third Reich.* London: 1966.

Müller, K. J. *Armee und Dritter Reich, 1933–39.* Paderborn: 1987.

Newmann, F. *Behemoth: The Structure and Practice of National Socialism, 1933–34.* Oxford: 1944.

Nicholls, A. J. *Weimar and the Rise of Hitler.* London: 1968.

Nicholls, A. J., and E. Matthias, eds. *German Democracy and the Triumph of Hitler.* London: 1971.

Nicosia, Francis and Lawrence D. Stokes, eds. *Germans against Nazism.* Oxford: 1992.

Noakes, Jeremy. *The Nazi Party in Lower Saxony, 1921–33.* Oxford: 1971.

Nyomorkay, Joseph. *Charisma and Factionalism in the Nazi Party.* Minneapolis: 1967.

O'Neill, Robert. *The German Army and the Nazi Party.* London: 1966.

Orlow, Dietrich. *The History of the Nazi Party.* Vol. I, *1919–33.* Newton Abbot: 1971. Vol. II, *1933–45.* Pittsburgh: 1973.

Overy, R. J. *The Nazi Economic Recovery, 1932–38.* London: 1982.

Overy, R. J. *Goering: The "Iron Man."* London: 1984.

Peterson, Edward. *The Limits of Hitler's Power.* Princeton: 1966.

Petzina, Dieter. *Autarkiepolitik im Denk der Nationalsozialistische Vierjahresplan.* Stuttgart: 1968.

Philips, W. A. P. *The Tragedy of Nazi Germany.* London: 1974.

Pridham, Geoffrey. *Hitler's Rise to Power: The Nazi Movement in Bavaria, 1923–33.* London: 1973.

Rauschning, Hermann. *Germany's Revolution of Destruction.* *London: 1939.

Rich, Norman. *Hitler's War Aims: Ideology, the Nazi State and the Course of Expansion.* New York: 1973.

Rich, Norman. *Hitler's War Aims: The Establishment of the New Order.* New York: 1974.

Ritter, Gerhard. *The German Resistance: Carl Goerdeler's Struggle against Tyranny.* *London: 1958.

Room, G. van. *German Resistance to Hitler: Count von Moltke and the Kreisau Circle.* *London: 1971.

Schlabrendorff, Fabian von. *The Secret War against Hitler.* *New York: 1965.

Schleunes, K. *The Twisted Road to Auschwitz: Nazi Policy towards German Jews, 1933–39.* Urbana, Ill.: 1970.

Schoenbaum, D. *Hitler's Social Revolution: Class and Status in Nazi Germany.* *London: 1966.

Schramm, P. E. *Hitler: The Man and the Military Leader.* *London: 1972.

Schweitzer, Arthur. *Big Business in the Third Reich*. Bloomington: 1964.

Smith, Bradley F. *Adolf Hitler: His Family, Childhood and Youth*. Stanford: 1967.

Stachura, P. D., ed. *The Nazi Machtergreifung*. London: 1983.

Stachura, P. D. *Gregor Strasser and the Rise of Nazism*. London: 1983.

Stein, G. H. *The Waffen SS: Hitler's Elite Guard at War, 1939–45*. Ithaca, New York: 1966.

Stern, J. P. *Hitler: The Führer and the People*. London: 1975.

Tobias, Fritz. *The Reichstag Fire: Legend and Truth*. *London: 1963.

Toland, John. *Adolf Hitler*. New York: 1976.

Trevor-Roper, H. R. *The Last Days of Hitler*. 2d. ed. London: 1950.

Turner, Henry Ashby, Jr., ed. *Nazism and the Third Reich*. New York: 1972.

Turner, Henry Ashby, Jr. *German Big Business and the Rise of Hitler*. Oxford: 1985.

Tyrell, Albrecht. *Vom Trommler zum Führer*. Munich: 1975.

Waite, R. G. L. *Vanguard of Nazism: The Free Corps Movement in Post-War Germany, 1919–23*. Cambridge, Mass.: 1952.

Waite, R. G. L. *The Psychopathic God: Adolf Hitler*. New York: 1977.

Walker, Mark. *German National Socialism and the Quest for Nuclear Power, 1939–49*. Cambridge: 1989.

Weinstein, Fred. *The Dynamics of Nazism*. New York: 1980.

Wheeler Bennett, John. *Munich: Prologue to Tragedy*. London: 1966.

Wheeler Bennett, John. *The Nemesis of Power: The German Army in Politics, 1918–45*. London: 1957.

Whiteside, A. G. *Austrian National Socialism before 1918*. The Hague: 1962.

Winkler, H. A. *Mittelstand, Demokratie und Nationalsozialismus*. Cologne: 1972.

Zeman, Z. A. B. *Nazi Propaganda*. London: 1964.

B. Soviet Union and Eastern Europe

Ali, Tariq, ed. *The Stalinist Legacy: Its Impact on Twentieth-Century World Politics*. London: 1984.

Antonov-Ovseenko, Anton. *The Time of Stalin: Portrait of a Tyranny*. New York: 1981.

Armstrong, John A. *The Politics of Totalitarianism: The Communist Party of the Soviet Union from 1934 to the Present*. New York: 1961.

Avrich, Paul. *Kronstadt 1921*. Princeton: 1970.

Azrael, Jeremy R. *Managerial Power and Soviet Politics*. Cambridge, Mass.: 1966.

Bailes, Kendall. *Technology and Society under Lenin and Stalin*. Princeton: 1978.

Barber, John and Mark Harrison. *The Soviet Home Front, 1941–1945*. New York: 1991.

Beck, F., and W. Godin. *Russian Purge and the Extraction of Confession*. *London: 1951.

Bialer, S., ed. *Stalin and His Generals: Soviet Military Memoirs of World War II*. New York: 1966.

Broszat, Martin. *Nationalsozialistische Polenpolitik*. Rev. ed. Frankfurt-Hamburg: 1965.

Brzezinski, Zbigniew. *The Permanent Purge: Politics in Soviet Totalitarianism*. Cambridge, Mass.: 1956.

Carr, E. H. *A History of Soviet Russia: The Bolshevik Revolution, 1917–23*. 3 vols. London: 1952.

Carr, E. H. *A History of Soviet Russia: The Interregnum, 1923–24*. London: 1954.

Carr, E. H. *A History of Soviet Russia: Socialism in One Country, 1924–26*. 2 vols. London: 1958–64.

Carr, E. H., *The Russian Revolution: From Lenin to Stalin, 1917–29*. London: 1979.

Carr, E. H., and R. W. Davies. *A History of Soviet Russia: The Foundations of a Planned Economy*. 3 vols. London 1969–78.

Carrère d'Encausse, Hélène. *Lenin: Revolution and Power*. *London: 1982.

Carrère d'Encausse, Hélène. *Stalin: Order through Terror*. *London: 1981.

Chamberlin, W. H., *The Russian Revolution*, 2 vols. New York: 1965.

Ciechanowski, Jan. *The Warsaw Rising of 1944*. Cambridge: 1974.

Cohen, Stephen F. *Bukharin and the Bolshevik Revolution, 1888–1938*. New York: 1974.

Cohen, Stephen F. *Re-thinking the Soviet Experience: Politics and History since 1917*. Oxford: 1985.

Colton, Timothy J. *Commissars, Commanders and Civilian Authority: The Structure of Soviet Military Politics*. Cambridge, Mass.: 1979.

Conquest, Robert. *Power and Policy in the USSR*. London: 1961.

Conquest, Robert. *The Great Terror: Stalin's Purges of the Thirties*. London: 1968.

Conquest, Robert. *Kolyma: The Arctic Death Camps*. London: 1978.

Conquest, Robert. *The Nation Killers: The Soviet Deportation of Nationalities*. London: 1980.

Conquest, Robert. *Inside Stalin's Secret Police*. London: 1985.

Conquest, Robert. *The Harvest of Sorrow*. London: 1986.

Conquest, Robert. *Stalin and the Kirov Murder*. London: 1989.

Conquest, Robert. *The Great Terror: A Re-Assessment.* London: 1990.

Dallin, David J., and Boris I. Nicolaevsky. *Forced Labor in Soviet Russia.* London: 1948.

Daniels, Robert V. *The Conscience of the Revolution: Communist Opposition in Soviet Russia.* Cambridge, Mass.: 1960.

Daniels, Robert V., ed. *The Stalin Revolution: Foundations of Soviet Totalitarianism.* Lexington, Mass.: 1972.

Davies, R. W. *The Industrialisation of Soviet Russia.* 2 vols. Vol. I, *The Socialist Offensive: The Collectivisation of Soviet Agriculture, 1929–30.* Vol. II, *The Soviet Collective Farm, 1929–30.* Cambridge, Mass.: 1980.

Davies, R. W. *Soviet History in the Gorbachev Revolution.* London: 1989.

De Jonge, Alex. *Stalin and the Shaping of the Soviet Union.* London: 1986.

Dedijer, Vladimir. *Tito Speaks: His Self-Portrait and Struggle with Stalin.* London: 1953.

Deutscher, Isaac. *Stalin: A Political Biography.* 1st. ed., London: 1949. 2d ed., 1967.

Deutscher, Isaac. *The Prophet Armed: Trotsky, 1879–1921.* London: 1954.

Deutscher, Isaac. *The Prophet Outcast: Trotsky, 1929–40.* London: 1963.

Deutscher, Isaac. *The Prophet Unarmed: Trotsky, 1921–1929.* London: 1959.

Dunmore, Timothy. *Soviet Politics, 1945–53.* London: 1984.

Erickson, John A. *The Soviet High Command: A Military-Political History, 1918–1941.* London: 1962.

Erickson, John. *The Road to Stalingrad: Stalin's War with Germany.* London: 1975.

Erickson, John. *The Road to Berlin: Stalin's War with Germany.* London: 1983.

Erlich, Alexander. *The Soviet Industrialisation Debate, 1924–1928.* Cambridge, Mass.: 1967.

Fainsod, Merle. *Smolensk under Soviet Rule.* New York: 1958.

Fainsod, Merle. *How Russia Is Ruled.* Cambridge, Mass.: 1953.

Fitzpatrick, Sheila, ed. *Cultural Revolution in Russia, 1928–1931.* Bloomington: 1978.

Fitzpatrick, Sheila. *Education and Social Mobility in the Soviet Union, 1921–1934.* Cambridge, Mass.: 1979.

Getty, J. Arch. *Origins of the Great Purge.* New York: 1985.

Gill, Graeme. *The Origins of the Stalinist Political System.* Cambridge: 1990.

Gross, Jan T. *Polish Society under German Occupation, 1934–1944.* Princeton: 1979.

Gross, Jan T. *Revolution from Abroad: The Soviet Conquest of Poland's Western Ukraine and Western Byelorussia.* Princeton: 1988.

Haimson, Leopold H. *The Russian Marxists and the Origins of Bolshevism*. Cambridge, Mass.: 1955.

Harrison, Mark. *Soviet Planning in Peace & War, 1938–1945*. Cambridge: 1985.

Heller, Mikhail, and Aleksandr M. Nekrich. *Utopia in Power: The History of the Soviet Union from 1917 to the Present*. New York: 1986.

Hingley, Ronald. *Joseph Stalin: Man and Legend*. London 1974.

Hough, Jerry. *The Soviet Prefects: The Local Party Organs in Industrial Decision-Making*. Cambridge, Mass.: 1968.

Hough, Jerry, and Merle Fainsod. *How the Soviet Union Is Governed*. Cambridge, Mass.: 1980.

Hubbard, Leonard E. *Soviet Labour and Industry*. London: 1942.

Inkeles, Alex. *Social Change in Soviet Russia*. Cambridge, Mass.: 1968.

Keep, J. L. H. *The Rise of Social Democracy in Russia*. London: 1963.

Keneally, Thomas. *Schindler's Ark*. London: 1982.

Kolakowski, Leszek. *Main Currents of Marxism*. Vol. 2, *The Golden Age*. Vol. 3, *The Breakdown*. Oxford: 1978.

Kuromiya, Hiroaki. *Stalin's Industrial Revolution: Politics and Workers, 1928–32*. Cambridge: 1988.

Laqueur, Walter. *Stalin, The Glasnost Revelations*. London: 1990.

Laue, Theodore H. von. *Why Lenin? Why Stalin? A Reappraisal of the Russian Revolution, 1900–1930*. New York: 1964.

Lebedeva, Nataliya. "The Katyn Tragedy." *International Affairs* (Moscow: June 1990).

Leggett, George. *The Cheka: Lenin's Political Police*. Oxford: 1981.

Lewin, Moshe. *Lenin's Last Struggle*. New York: 1968.

Lewin, Moshe. *Russian Peasants and Soviet Power: A Study of Collectivisation*. London: 1968.

Lewin, Moshe. *Political Undercurrents in Soviet Economic Debate*. Princeton: 1974.

Lewin, Moshe. *The Making of the Soviet System: Essays in the Social History of Inter-War Russia*. London: 1985.

Lewis, Jonathan, and Philip Whitehead. *Stalin: A Time for Judgement*. London: 1990.

Lucas, R. C. *Forgotten Holocaust: The Poles under German Occupation, 1939–44*. Lexington: 1986.

McNeal, Robert H. *Stalin: Man and Ruler*. London: 1988.

Medvedev, Roy A. *Let History Judge*. London: 1972. Rev. ed. Oxford: 1989.

Medvedev, Roy A. *On Stalin and Stalinism*. Oxford: 1979.

Medvedev, Zhores. *The Rise and Fall of T. D. Lysenko.* New York: 1969.

Nicolaevsky, Boris. *Power and the Soviet Elite: "The Letter of an Old Bolshevik" and Other Essays.* Edited by Janet D. Zagoria. *London: 1966.

Nove, Alec. "Was Stalin Really Necessary?" *Encounter* (April 1962).

Nove, Alec. *Stalinism and After.* 2d. ed. London: 1981.

Nove, Alec. *An Economic History of the USSR.* 2d ed. London: 1989.

Nove, Alec, and Janet R. Millar. A Debate on Collectivisation: Was Stalin Really Necessary?" *Problems of Communism* (July–August 1976).

Pipes, Richard. *The Formation of the Soviet Union: Communism and Nationalism, 1917–1923.* Rev. ed. New York: 1968.

Pipes, Richard. *The Russian Revolution, 1899–1919.* London: 1990.

Reiman, Michael. *The Birth of Stalinism: The USSR on the Eve of the "Second Revolution."* *London: 1987.

Rigby, T. H. *Membership in the Communist Party, 1917–1957.* Princeton: 1968.

Rigby, T. H. "The CPSU Elite: Turnover and Rejuvenation from Lenin to Khrushchev." *Australian Journal of Politics and History* 1 (1970).

Rigby, T. H. "Was Stalin a Disloyal Patron?" *Soviet Studies* 3 (July 1986): 311–24.

Rosenfeldt, Niels Erik. *Knowledge and Power: The Role of Stalin's Secret Chancellery in the Soviet System of Government.* Copenhagen: 1978.

Schapiro, Leonard. *The Origin of the Communist Autocracy.* London: 1955.

Schapiro, Leonard. *The Communist Party of the Soviet Union.* 2d. ed. London: 1970.

Seaton, A. *The Russo-German War.* London: 1971.

Seaton, A. *Stalin as Warlord.* London: 1976.

Seton-Watson, Hugh. *The Eastern European Revolution.* 3d. ed. London: 1956.

Slusser, Robert M. *Stalin in October: The Man Who Missed the Revolution.* Baltimore: 1987.

Smith, Edward Ellis. *The Young Stalin: The Early Years of an Elusive Revolutionary.* New York: 1967.

Solzhenitsyn, Alexander. *The Gulag Archipelago.* 3 vols. *London: 1974.

Souvarine, Boris. *Stalin: A Critical Survey of Bolshevism.* *London: 1939.

Swianiewicz, S. *Forced Labour and Economic Development: An Enquiry into the Experience of Soviet Industrialisation.* London: 1965.

Szamuely, Tibor. *The Russian Tradition.* London: 1974.

Trotsky, Leon. *History of the Russian Revolution.* *New York, London: 1934.

Trotsky, Leon. *The Revolution Betrayed.* *New York: 1937.

Trotsky, Leon. *Stalin.* Translated and edited by Charles Malamuth. New York: 1967.

Tucker, Robert C. "The Rise of Stalin's Personality Cult." *American Historical Review* 2 (1979): 347–66.

Tucker, Robert C. *The Soviet Political Mind.* 2d. ed. New York: 1971.

Tucker, Robert C. *Stalin as Revolutionary.* New York: 1973.

Tucker, Robert C., ed. *Stalinism: Essays in Historical Interpretation.* New York: 1977.

Tucker, Robert C. *Stalin in Power: The Revolution from Above, 1928–41.* New York: 1990.

Ulam, Adam B. *Stalin: The Man and His Era.* Expanded ed. London: 1989.

Urban, G. R., ed. *Stalinism: Its Impact on Russia and the World.* London: 1982.

Venturi, Franco. *Roots of Revolution: A History of the Populist and Socialist Movements in Nineteenth Century Russia.* *London: 1960.

Viola, Lynne. *The Best Sons of the Fatherland: Workers in the Vanguard of Soviet Collectivisation.* New York: 1987.

Volkogonov, D. A. *Stalin: Triumph and Tragedy.* Translated by Harold Shukman. London: 1991.

Vyshinsky, Andrei Y., ed. *The Law of the Soviet State.* Translated by Hugh W. Babb. New York: 1948.

Wolfe, Bertram D. *Three Who Made a Revolution.* London: 1956.

Zeman, Z. A. B. *Pursued by a Bear: The Making of Eastern Europe.* London: 1989.

Zhoravsky, David. *The Lysenko Affair.* Cambridge, Mass.: 1970.

C. International Relations

Bethell, Nicholas. *The Last Secret: Forcible Repatriation to Russia, 1944–47.* London: 1974.

Bolloten, Burnett. *The Spanish Revolution: The Left and the Struggle for Power during the Civil War.* Chapel Hill, N.C.: 1979.

Brandt, Conrad. *Stalin's Failure in China.* Cambridge, Mass.: 1958.

Bullock, Alan. *Ernest Bevin: Foreign Secretary, 1945–51.* London: 1983.

Bullock, Alan. "Hitler and the Origins of World War II." *Proceedings British Academy* 53 (Oxford: 1967).

Calvocoressi, Peter, Guy Wint, and John Prichard. *Total War: The Causes and Courses of the Second World War.* 2d ed. London: 1989.

Carr, William. *Arms, Autarky and Aggression.* London: 1972.

Cattell, David D. *Communism and the Spanish Civil War.* Berkeley: 1955.

Cattell, David D. *Soviet Diplomacy and the Spanish Civil War.* Berkeley: 1957.

Cienciala, Anne M. *Poland and the Western Powers, 1938–39: A Study of the Interdependence of Eastern and Western Europe.* London: 1968.

Compton, J. V. *The Eagle and the Swastika: Hitler, the U.S.A. and the Origins of World War II.* Boston: 1967.

Craig, Gordon A., and Felix Gilbert, eds. *The Diplomats.* New York: 1952.

Dallek, Robert. *Franklin D. Roosevelt and American Foreign Policy, 1932–1945.* New York: 1979.

Davison, W. Phillips. *The Berlin Blockade: A Study in Cold War Politics.* Princeton: 1958.

de Porte, A. W. *Europe between the Super-Powers.* New Haven: 1979.

Drachkovich, M. M., and Branko Lazitch, eds. *The Comintern: Historical Highlights.* Stanford: 1966.

Edmonds, Robin. *The Big Three: Churchill, Roosevelt and Stalin in Peace and War.* New York: 1991.

Fischer, Louis. *The Soviets in World Affairs.* Pb. ed. New York: 1960.

Fraser, David. *Alanbrooke.* Pb. ed. London: 1983.

Freund, Gerald. *Unholy Alliance: Russian and German Relations from the Treaty of Brest-Litovsk to the Treaty of Berlin.* London: 1957.

Friedlander, Saul. *Prelude to Downfall: Hitler and the United States, 1939–41.* New York: 1967.

Gilbert, Martin. *Winston S. Churchill.* Vols III–VIII. London: 1966–88.

Haslam, Jonathan. *The Soviet Union and the Search for Collective Security, 1933–39.* New York: 1984.

Heinrichs, Waldo. *Threshold of War: Franklin D. Roosevelt and American Entry into World War II.* Oxford: 1988.

Hildebrand, Klaus. *The Foreign Policy of the Third Reich.* *London: 1973.

Hillgruber, Andreas. *Hitlers Strategie: Politik und Kriegsführung, 1940–1941.* Frankfurt am Main: 1965.

Hinsley, F. H. et al. *British Intelligence in the Second World War.* London: 1979.

Holloway, David. *The Soviet Union and the Arms Race.* New Haven: 1983.

Jacobsen, H. A. *Nationalsozialistische Aussenpolitik.* Frankfurt am Main: 1968.

Kaiser, David. *Economic Diplomacy and the Origins of the Second World War.* Princeton: 1980.

Kennan, George F., "The Sources of Soviet Conduct." *Foreign Affairs* (July 1947) under the pseudonym "X." Reprinted in *American Diplomacy* (Chicago: 1951).

Kennan, George F. *Russia and the West under Lenin and Stalin.* Boston: 1960.

Komjathy, A., and Rebecca Stockwell. *German Minorities and the Third Reich: Ethnic Germans of East Central Europe between the Wars.* New York: 1979.

Korbel, Joseph. *Poland between East and West: Soviet and German Foreign Policy towards Poland, 1919–1939.* Princeton: 1963.

McCullogh, David. *Truman.* New York: 1992.

McLane, Charles B. *Soviet Policy and the Chinese Communists, 1931–1946.* New York: 1979.

Mastny, V. *Russia's Road to the Cold War.* *New York: 1979.

Mee, Charles L., Jr. *Meeting at Potsdam.* London: 1975.

Messer, Robert L. *The End of an Alliance: Byrnes, Roosevelt, Truman and the Origins of the Cold War.* Chapel Hill, N.C.: 1982.

Michalka, W., *Ribbentrop und die deutsche Weltpolitik, 1938–44.* Munich: 1980.

Middlemas, Keith. *Diplomacy of Illusion: The British Government and Germany, 1937–39.* London: 1972.

North, Robert C. *Moscow and the Chinese Communists.* Stanford: 1953.

Polonsky, A. *The Great Powers and the Polish Question, 1941–45: A Documentary Study in Cold War Origins.* London: 1976.

Prazmorska, Anita. *Britain, Poland and the Eastern Front, 1939.* Cambridge: 1987.

Read, Anthony, and David Fisher. *The Deadly Embrace: Hitler, Stalin and the Nazi-Soviet Pact, 1939–1941.* London: 1988.

Roberts, Geoffrey. *The Unholy Alliance: Stalin's Pact with Hitler.* London: 1989.

Seabury, Paul. *The Wilhelmstrasse: A Study of German Diplomats under the Nazi Regime.* Berkeley: 1954.

Shulman, Marshall. *Stalin's Foreign Policy Re-appraised.* Cambridge, Mass.: 1963.

Thomas, Hugh. *The Spanish Civil War.* 3d ed. London: 1977.

Tolstoy, Nikolai. *Victims of Yalta.* Rev. pb. ed. London: 1979.

Tusa, Ann and John. *The Berlin Blockade.* London: 1988.

Ulam, Adam B. *Titoism and the Cominform.* Cambridge, Mass.: 1952.

Ulam, Adam B. *Expansion and Co-existence: Soviet Foreign Policy, 1917–1967.* New York: 1968.

Watt, D. Cameron. *How War Came: The Immediate Origins of the Second World War, 1938–1939.* London: 1989.

Weinberg, Gerhard L. *The Foreign Policy of Hitler's Germany: Diplomatic Revolution in Europe, 1933–36.* Chicago: 1970.

Weinberg, Gerhard L. *The Foreign Policy of Hitler's Germany: Starting World War II, 1937–39.* Chicago: 1980.

Weinberg, Gerhard L. *Germany and the Soviet Union, 1939–1941.* Leiden: 1954.

Yergin, Daniel. *Shattered Peace.* Boston: 1977.

D. General

Arendt, Hannah. *The Origins of Totalitarianism.* Rev. ed. New York: 1966.

Arendt, Hannah. *Eichmann in Jerusalem: A Report on the Banality of Evil.* New York: 1963.

Aron, Raymond. *Democracy and Totalitarianism.* *London: 1968.

Bell, Daniel. *The End of Ideology.* With a new Afterword. Cambridge, Mass.: 1988.

Billington. James H. *The Icon and the Axe: An Interpretive History of Russian Culture.* New York: 1968.

Borkenau, Franz. *European Communism.* London: 1953.

Craig, Gordon. *Germany, 1866–1945.* Oxford: 1978.

Djilas, Milovan. *The New Class.* London: 1957.

Duverger, Maurice. *Political Parties.* *London: 1954.

Erikson, Erik H. *Childhood and Society.* New York: 1963.

Erikson, Erik H. *Identity: Youth and Crisis.* New York: 1968.

The Fontana/Harper Dictionary of Modern Thought. Edited by Alan Bullock and Stephen Trombley. Rev. ed. London and New York: 1988.

Friedrich, Carl J., and Z. K. Brzezinski. *Totalitarian Dictatorship and Autocracy.* 2d ed. New York: 1966.

Friedrich, Carl J., Michael R. Curtis, and B. R. Barber. *Totalitarianism in Perspective: Three Views.* New York: 1969.

Fromm, Erich. *The Anatomy of Human Destructiveness.* Pb. ed. London: 1977.

Gerth, H. C., and C. Wright Mills, eds. *From Max Weber: Essays in Sociology.* London: 1958.

Hegel, G. W. F. *Lectures on the Philosophy of History.* Translated by J. Sibree. London: 1902.

Hook, Sidney. *The Hero in History.* Boston: 1955.

Horney, Karen. *Neurosis and Human Growth.* New York: 1950.

Kennedy, Paul. *The Rise and Fall of the Great Powers: Economic Change and Military Conflict, 1500–2000.* London: 1988.

Laqueuer, Walter. *Russia and Germany: A Century of Conflict.* London: 1965.

Lasky, Melvin J. *Utopia and Revolution.* Chicago: 1976.

Lasswell, Harold. *Psychopathology and Politics.* New York: 1960.

Latey, Maurice. *Tyranny: A Study in the Abuse of Power.* London: 1969.

Levi, Primo. *If This Is a Man and The Truce.* Pb. ed. *London: 1979.

Meinecke, F. *The German Catastrophe: Reflections and Recollections.* Cambridge, Mass.: 1950.

Michels, Robert. *Political Parties.* *New York: 1959.

Milosz, C. *The Captive Mind.* *New York: 1953.

Milosz, C. *Native Realm: A Search for Self-Definition.* *New York: 1968.

Milward, Alan S. *War, Economy and Society, 1939–45.* London: 1977.

Moore, Barrington, Jr. *Social Origins of Dictatorship and Democracy.* London: 1967.

Nolte, Ernst. *Three Faces of Fascism.* *London: 1965.

Plekhanov, G. V. *The Role of Individuals in History.* *New York: 1940.

Rosenhan, David L., and Martin E. P. Seligman. *Abnormal Psychology.* 2d. ed. New York: 1989.

Schapiro, Leonard. *Totalitarianism.* London: 1972.

Steinberg, Jonathan. *All or Nothing: The Axis and the Holocaust, 1941–43.* London: 1990.

Stern, Fritz R. *The Politics of Cultural Despair: A Study in the Rise of the German Ideology.* Berkeley: 1961.

Talman, J. L. *The Myth of the Nation and the Vision of Revolution.* London: 1981.

Talman, J. L. *The Origins of Totalitarian Democracy.* London: 1952.

Talman, J. L. *Political Messianism: The Romantic Phase.* London: 1960.

Unger, Aryeh L. *The Totalitarian Party: Party and People in Nazi Germany and Soviet Russia.* Cambridge: 1974.

Willner, Ann Ruth. *The Spellbinders: Charismatic Political Leadership.* New Haven: 1984.

INDEX

ACKNOWLEDGMENTS

The author and publishers are grateful to the following for permission to reproduce copyright material: the Controller of Her Majesty's Stationery Office for *Documents on German Foreign Policy* and *Documents on British Foreign Policy*; Curtis Brown Ltd and Houghton Mifflin Company (on behalf of the Estate of Sir Winston Churchill) for *The Second World War* by Winston S. Churchill (Cassell, 1948–54) copyright © Winston S. Churchill MP; HarperCollins Publishers and Harcourt Brace Jovanovich Inc. for *Conversations with Stalin* by Milovan Djilas trs. Michael V. Petrovich (Hart-Davis, 1962); Cassell Ltd for *The Testament of Adolf Hitler* ed. François Genoud trs. R. H. Stevens (Cassell, 1961); Weidenfeld and Nicolson Ltd for *Hitler's Table Talk* ed. Francis Genoud, trs. Norman Cameron and R. H. Stevens, with an Introduction by Hugh Trevor-Roper; André Deutsch Ltd and Little, Brown & Company Inc. for *Khrushchev Remembers* trs. & ed. Strobe Talbot copyright © 1970 Little, Brown & Company Inc.; Oxford University Press and Columbia University Press for *Let History Judge* by Roy Medvedev (rev. edn. Columbia University Press with Oxford University Press, 1989) copyright © 1989 Columbia University Press; Exeter University Press and Schocken Books (published in the USA by Pantheon, a division of Random House Inc.) for *Nazism, 1919–1945: A Documentary Reader* vols. 1–3 ed. J. Noakes and G. Pridham (Exeter University Press and Schocken Books, 1983–88) copyright © 1988 Exeter University Press; Allen & Unwin (a division of HarperCollins Publishers) for *Leninism* by J. Stalin (Allen & Unwin, 1940).

The author and publishers are grateful to the following for permission to reproduce the illustrations specified and/or supplying prints:
David King Collection: 1, 3, 4, 11, 12, 17, 18, 19, 20, 21, 22, 23, 26, 27, 29, 30, 38, 39, 45, 47, 48, 49, 54, 57, 60, 62
Zeitgeschichtliches Bildarchiv Heinrich Hoffmann: 2, 5, 9, 13, 16, 24, 33, 34, 35, 36, 42, 44, 46, 51, 52, 53
Archiv für Kunst und Geschichte, Berlin: 6, 15, 25, 31, 32, 40, 41, 50, 56, 59
Ogonjok: 7, 8, 28, 55
Bundesarchiv, Berlin: 37
Ullstein Bildersdienst: 43, 58, 61
Popperfoto: 64

DATE DUE

11/18/09			